LOCATIONS

ACC	Christ's College, Aberdeen
ANL	National Library of Wales, Aberystwyth
AU	Aberdeen University
Arents	New York Public Library, Arents Collection
C	Cambridge University Library
C(Cr)	The Earl of Crawfords collections of briefs, broadsides and proclamations deposited in Cambridge University Library
CP	Pryme Collection, Marshall Library, Cambridge
CT(R)	Lord Rothschild's Library, Trinity College, Cambridge
CUA	Cambridge University Archives
D	Trinity College, Dublin
DA	Royal Irish Academy, Dublin
DG	Gilbert Collection, Municipal Library, Dublin
DM	Marsh's Library, Dublin
DNL	National Library of Ireland, Dublin
DPRO	Public Record Office, Dublin
DS	Royal Dublin Society Library
De Renne	Wymberley Jones De Renne Georgia Library, Wormsloe
E	National Library of Scotland, Edinburgh
ECA	Edinburgh City Archives
EP	Edinburgh Public Library
EPRO	Public Record Office, Edinburgh
ES	Signet Library, Edinburgh
ESA	Edinburgh Society of Accountants
Ga	Gateshead Public Library
GU	Glasgow University Library
HEH	Henry E. Huntington Library, San Marino, California
JCB	John Carter Brown Library, Providence, Rhode Island
K	Cyril Kenney, London
Kress	Kress Library, Harvard University
L	British Museum
LCH	Customs House Library, London
LCRO	City of London Record Office
LF	Society of Friends Library, London

LOCATIONS

LG	Guildhall Library, London
LHL	House of Lords Library
LICA	Institute of Chartered Accountants Library, London
LIHR	Institute of Historical Research, London
LLI	Lincoln's Inn Library
LPRO	Public Record Office, London
LRIBA	Royal Institute of British Architects Library, London
LSC	Sion College Library, London
LStE	Stock Exchange, London
LU	London University Library (almost exclusively Goldsmiths' Library)
LV(F)	Victoria and Albert Museum Library, Forster Collection
M	John Rylands Library, Manchester
M(Cr)	The Earl of Crawford's collection of pamphlets deposited in the John Rylands Library
MC	Chetham's Library, Manchester
MH	Harvard University Library
MP	Manchester Public Library
NP	Newcastle Public Library
NU	Newcastle University Library
NYP	New York Public Library
O	Bodleian Library, Oxford
OAS	All Souls College, Oxford
OC	Christ Church, Oxford
OF	Oxford University Department of Forestry
OH	Hertford College, Oxford
OUP	Oxford University Press
R	Rothamsted Experimental Station, Harpenden
RU	Reading University (Overstone Collection)
SU	Southampton University Library
T	Toronto Public Library
Thomas	C. Stanley Thomas, Neath
WDA	U.S. Department of Agriculture Library, Washington
WLC	Library of Congress, Washington
Y	Yale University Library

CONTEMPORARY PRINTED SOURCES FOR BRITISH AND IRISH ECONOMIC HISTORY 1701-1750

CONTEMPORARY PRINTED SOURCES FOR BRITISH AND IRISH ECONOMIC HISTORY
1701-1750

BY

L. W. HANSON

KEEPER OF PRINTED BOOKS AT THE
BODLEIAN LIBRARY, OXFORD

CAMBRIDGE
AT THE UNIVERSITY PRESS
1963

CAMBRIDGE UNIVERSITY PRESS
Cambridge, New York, Melbourne, Madrid, Cape Town,
Singapore, São Paulo, Delhi, Tokyo, Mexico City

Cambridge University Press
The Edinburgh Building, Cambridge CB2 8RU, UK

Published in the United States of America by Cambridge University Press, New York

www.cambridge.org
Information on this title: www.cambridge.org/9780521189590

First published 1963
First paperback edition 2011

A catalogue record for this publication is available from the British Library

ISBN 978-0-521-05196-5 Hardback
ISBN 978-0-521-18959-0 Paperback

To
my Father
and to the memory of
my Mother

CONTENTS

PREFACE

It is a real pleasure to me to acknowledge the great help I have been given in compiling this book.

In all the libraries in which I have worked I have met with the most generous aid and encouragement. I hope that the Librarians will accept this general acknowledgement of many much-appreciated kindnesses. For answers to subsequent enquiries I am especially grateful to Mr P. Henchy, Keeper of Printed Books at the National Library of Ireland, Dr D. M. Lloyd, Keeper of Printed Books at the National Library of Scotland, Mr Robert Donaldson, then of the Edinburgh University Library, Miss Hilda Lofthouse, Librarian of Chetham's Library, Manchester, Mr Sidney Horrocks of the Manchester Public Library, Mrs Dorothea Reeves, Librarian of the Kress Library and Dr Thomas R. Adams, Librarian of the John Carter Brown Library.

Dr Douglas Simpson, Librarian of Aberdeen University Library, lent me some rare tract volumes from his own University Library and procured for me the loan of other volumes from Christ's College. Mr J. J. Graneek, when Librarian of the Queen's University Library, Belfast, lent me the catalogue of the Foster Collection there. I am indebted to Mr R. O. MacKenna, Librarian of Glasgow University Library, for information about the Darien collection. Mr Jolly, of the same library, after a determined search, found for me the first edition of *The Regulations of the Town's Hospital at Glasgow* (no. 4832) and persuaded Dr Isabel Brown to write an account of it for *The Bibliotheck*.

Miss M. I. Henderson, when Librarian of Southampton University Library, lent me the typescript of the Perkins Agricultural Library Catalogue and Mr A. Anderson, the compiler of the catalogue, subsequently answered my enquiries about various volumes in it. Miss Margery F. Wild, of London University Library, for many years kept me informed of recent accessions to the Goldsmiths' Library. Miss M. B. C. Canney has been similarly helpful in late years. At the Guildhall Library Mr J. Bromley and Mr D. A. Dawe have found for me material which I should not otherwise have been able to discover. The Marquess of Cholmondeley has kindly allowed me to quote from his unpublished Walpole papers now deposited in Cambridge University Library. The Lord Rothschild has permitted me to include material in his own library, as have Mr C. F. Kenney and Mr C. Stanley Thomas.

Much of my work is founded on that of previous writers from Massie onwards, whose bibliographies I have pillaged. Here I can only make a general acknowledgement.

Professor J. R. Moore sent me his list of the canon of Defoe's writings some years ago. Unfortunately this book was already in page proof when his *Checklist* was published and I have only been able to squeeze in one reference to it (no. 2647), and that to a book which Professor Moore had not seen. I hope, however, that all his new attributions are mentioned in the footnotes.

PREFACE

I am grateful to the Curators of the Bodleian Library who gave me two months' leave at a most opportune time. Miss G. M. Briggs of that library kindly read the typescript and saved me from some errors and inconsistencies.

Finally I cannot praise too highly the patience, forbearance, and understanding of the Cambridge University Press.

L. W. H.

OXFORD
January 1963

INTRODUCTION

This book has a long history—far too long. It was planned and almost completed in its first state by the late Henry Higgs, who envisaged a series of volumes, of which the first, the *Bibliography of Economics*, 1751–1775, was published in 1935. Unfortunately Higgs did not live to see the present volume through the press.

I first came upon it towards the end of World War II when the Board of Trade gave the older portion of its library to the British Museum. I was set to catalogue the seventeenth and eighteenth-century books, and in the course of that work I naturally consulted the appropriate bibliographies. One of the most useful of these was *The Kress Library of Business and Economics. Catalogue covering material published through* 1776. In the preface to that volume I learnt that some of the entries were taken from the galley proofs of the forthcoming *Bibliography of Economics*, 1701–1750, 'with the kind consent of the publisher'. I thought that the kindness of the publisher might well extend to the British Museum and so I wrote to Cambridge to beg a set of the proofs. These were promptly forthcoming and I found them most useful. But I also found that the Board of Trade library included quite a few books not included in the *Bibliography;* that there were errors of transcription; and that my dating of the undated pieces frequently differed from that of Higgs. I therefore wrote to the Cambridge University Press suggesting that some revision of the text was necessary before publication could well be envisaged. The Press promptly asked me to act as editor and I rashly consented; rashly because I very greatly underestimated the amount of work to be done and overestimated the amount of time I should command in which to do it.

The aim of the book is to include every new English work on economic affairs published in the period.[1] The boundaries of economic history are, however, indefinite. Many of the great questions of the period, such as the Union with Scotland, had political and religious as well as economic aspects. Here, and on the frontiers, I have been selective. I have included one or two works on piracy to show that this threat to commerce existed. The navy is considered as a protection for foreign trade, and also, with the army, as an occupation subject to violent changes in employment. I have not however included all the printed individual petitions for arrears of pay.[2]

With some classes of material I have also been selective. Public acts are not included, since they are readily accessible in collections. Private enclosure acts are included, for the full text of them is not elsewhere available. I have not, however, included estate acts or bills. Bills of every other kind I have put in.

[1] New editions of some works originally published before 1701 are included exceptionally, more especially when they contain no evidence of previous publication. Translations are omitted.

[2] There are good collections of these in the British Museum at 816.m.7 and 516.m.18.

INTRODUCTION

A great deal of the material included here relates to parliamentary legislation and the bills provide a convenient peg on which to hang the conflicting views about them. The regular printing of public bills by order of the House of Commons began in this period.[1]

I have also been selective with pleadings before the House of Lords and before the Court of Session. These provide information about specific and individual business transactions, whereas most other printed sources are concerned with generalities. There are very good collections of the House of Lords pleadings in the British Museum,[2] and in the House of Lords itself. The collection of Sessions pleadings in the Advocates' Library is voluminous.[3] Some cases produced pleading after pleading. Most of the facts are given in the first pleading and subsequent ones only elaborate finer points of law. It would be difficult however to find a better description of potteries in Scotland and England than that contained in the *State of the mutual Processes betwixt John Bird of London, Potter and Robert Dinwiddie, Merchant in London* (no. 6431).

Newspapers are excluded from this bibliography, and the only periodicals appearing are those which deal exclusively with economic affairs. Every newspaper contains something of economic interest and the texts of proclamations are most easily accessible in *The London Gazette*, but several volumes would be needed adequately to catalogue the newspapers of the period and rigid exclusion seemed to be the only possible course.

The material has been gathered for the most part in Great Britain and Ireland, and in some libraries more thoroughly than others. In specialized collections arranged in chronological order, such as the Goldsmiths' Library at London University and the Haliday Collection in the Royal Irish Academy, a task of this kind is made easy. As a member of the staff I have had exceptional oppor-

[1] The first order to print a bill in the Journals of the House of Commons was that of 27 February 1703 relating to the Bill for preventing occasional conformity. Wing (B2897) records at Columbia University *A bill to prevent the infamous practice of stock-jobbing* [1700]. Columbia has two undated bills of this title, but they are correctly dated 1733 and 1734. The first is a variant of no. 4612; the second a duplicate of no. 4724. Orders to print are not frequent until the reign of George II when the practice became regular. At this time it was usual to print 600 copies both of bills and of Parliamentary reports. Some of the accounts for printing are to be found in the Treasury Money Books. Those of Samuel Richardson are listed by W. M. Sale in his *Samuel Richardson: Master Printer*, 1950, pp. 368–9. One of them is printed by I. G. Philip in *William Blackstone and the Reform of the Oxford University Press*, 1957, pp. 127–8. In 1705 both Houses made orders that all private bills should be printed before their first reading. That this was at the expense of the promoters is shown by the inclusion of 30*s*. for 'Coppys of Bill for Members' in the Remembrancer of London's list of expenses in passing the Act for continuing an Act for settling the Assize of Bread, printed in O. C. Williams, *The Clerical Organization of the House of Commons*, 1954, p. 317.

[2] At 19.h.1–7 and L.3.a.1. A few of the pleadings in the first set are catalogued separately but there is no general entry for this set in the published Museum General Catalogue. None of the pleadings in the second set is catalogued separately.

[3] They can be consulted in the National Library of Scotland and are given the location of that Library. These separate pleadings are not mentioned in the Stair Society's *Introductory Survey of the Sources and Literature of Scots Law*, 1936, presumably because there are adequate digests of the cases.

tunity at the British Museum and subsequently in the Bodleian; but he would be a bold man who claimed that he had tapped all the resources of the Museum. In other large libraries I have concentrated in general on the pamphlet collections and in particular on the books mentioned in bibliographies or monographs. In manuscript repositories I have looked only at a few main classes. In the Public Record Office I have been guided by the printed calendars of the Treasury Papers and of the Papers of the Commissioners of Trade and Plantations. I have looked at the uncalendared papers of the latter office. In the Scottish Record Office I have seen only the Supplementary Parliamentary Papers.

Some American locations are given, but the books cited are mostly either sequels or replies to books found in Great Britain, or are mentioned in standard bibliographies. The British Museum has a copy of James Crokatt's *Further Observations* on the cultivation of indigo in South Carolina (no. 6076). I have included the original *Observations* (no. 5992) which is to be found in New York Public Library. Henry R. Wagner's excellent *Irish Economics* recorded one or two books which I have only been able to trace in his own collection now at Yale. John Scott's *Darien Bibliography* included a number of pieces from his own library which was dispersed at auction after his death. Some of these were bought by the John Carter Brown Library and I have recorded them. Most of the American copies however come from the Kress Library at Harvard. I have to thank the Curator, Mrs Dorothea D. Reeves, for generous permission to include any material in the Kress Library[1] that I had not been able to find elsewhere. I have restricted my choice to dated books and pamphlets, for I could not well include undated material which I had not myself checked. Anyone familiar with the antiquarian book trade is well aware that most of the material coming on the market today is bought by American libraries. The Kress Library is outstanding, but there are many other great collections in the United States. I regret that I have not been able to visit them.

The material that I have gathered is arranged in the first instance chronologically by years of publication. In this book the year begins on 1 January according to the Julian Calendar then in use in England. This year coincides with the official year in Scotland up to the Union. In England, however, the official year began on Lady Day and this is reflected in the dating of all official publications, such as proclamations and parliamentary reports. It was adhered to by lawyers, such as Archibald Hutcheson. One has also to contend with the unofficial publishers' year. 'The rule generally observed among printers', says John Nichols, 'is that when a Book happens not to be ready for publication before November, the date of the ensuing year is used.'[2] In the first half of the eighteenth century the printers' year started in some cases in October. Richard Rawlinson in his copy of *The Speech of Robert Skinner* dated 1744 noted that it was published on 7 October 1743. Thomas Hearne wrote in his *Diary* on 3 June 1710, 'Printers begin the Year from Michaelmas Term.' A book bearing the

[1] The entries are taken from the printed *Catalogue* of 1948 and the *Supplement* to it published in 1956. Mrs Reeves also sent me some more recent accessions.

[2] *Literary Anecdotes*, III (1812), 249. Quoted by W. B. Todd in 'On the Use of Advertisements in Bibliographical Studies', *The Library*, ser. 5 vol. 8, p. 179.

date 1710 may thus have been published at any time between October 1709 and 24 March 1711 according to our modern reckoning. Opportunity for misdating is manifest, and, although I have checked and corrected dates from contemporary trade lists and magazines,[1] I am sure that I have not avoided error.

The publications of each year are sub-divided in accordance with the following scheme:

GENERAL

England, Scotland, Ireland

AGRICULTURE

General works
Enclosures
Drainage of fens
Forestry
Mining
Land tenure
Forfeited estates
Fisheries

MANUFACTURES

General works
Single industries, arranged alphabetically

COMMERCE

General works
Home trade (England, Scotland, Ireland)
  Price regulation, Quality regulation, Weights and measures
Europe (alphabetically by country)
  Smuggling
Levant
Africa
America (North, Central, South)
Far East
Voyages (of economic interest)
Navy
Piracy

COLONIES
(Internal affairs)

Europe
Africa
America
Asia

FINANCE

General works
National Debt
Taxation

[1] For dating books published in the trade I have used the *Term Catalogues*, *The Political State of Great Britain*, the Stationers' Register, *The Monthly Magazine*, *The Monthly Chronicle*, *The Gentleman's Magazine*, *The London Magazine* and *The British Magazine*. Exact dates of publication can be found in the newspapers but I have made no thorough search of these.

FINANCE—*continued.*

Taxation—*continued.*
- New proposals
- Individual taxes, arranged alphabetically

Government spending
- Civil list
- Commission of Accounts

Malversation
Local taxation
Tithe
Currency
Banking
Brokers
Stock jobbing
Pawnbrokers
Private lotteries
Insurance (Fire, Life, Marine)
Book-keeping

TRANSPORT

Coasting trade
- Harbours
- Pilots

Rivers
Roads and bridges
Postal services
Hackney coachmen, carters, carmen

SOCIAL CONDITIONS

The Poor
- Workhouses
- Hospitals
- Dispensaries
- Collections for sufferers by fire, etc.
- Debtors
- Bankrupts
- Prisons

Refugees (Huguenots, Jews, Palatines)
Naturalization
Working and professional classes
- Sickness benefit clubs
- Pension schemes
- Cost of living

Social evils (Drink, robberies, etc.)
Public services (Fire regulations, street lighting, water supply)

These sub-divisions are not watertight. A work advocating the imposition of a high duty on imported foreign silks in order to protect the woollen industry and to encourage sheep farming and thus to prevent unemployment and poverty may be considered under the heads of Finance, Commerce, Manufactures, Agriculture and Social Conditions. I have put such a work under 'Commerce' for the immediate effect of the adoption of this policy will be to reduce imports from abroad; other hoped-for consequences are speculative. Protests against taxes imposed for revenue are, however, put under 'Finance'. I have tried to keep all the works on one controversy together. In doubtful cases I hope that the subject-entries in the General Index will enable readers to find their material.

The separate entries comprise author's name, title, place of publication, date, size and location. The author's name is placed in square brackets if it does not occur in the book. I have tried in footnotes to give authorities for all attributions of anonymous works. The standard book on English anonyma is Halkett and Laing's *Dictionary of Anonymous and Pseudonymous Literature.* I am much indebted to it, but it is, however, a record of attributions made by others, and where I use it I have always quoted the authorities cited. Some of these are not very convincing and often enough the only evidence is a note in an unidentifiable hand on a copy of the book in some library. Historians will however be able to evaluate the evidence. I have drawn very tentatively upon one source which I have not seen used elsewhere. This is the Stationers' Register. If a work is entered in the Register to someone who is not a publisher there is always the possibility that he may be the author. In one case at any rate there is confirmation. *Thoughts on Trade, and a Publick Spirit* (no. 2217) was entered in the Register to Thomas Baston. That he was the author is confirmed by the edition of 1732 which bears his name.

Titles are transcribed fairly fully. The necessary reduction of capitals to capitals and lower case, if one decides to forgo quasi-facsimile transcription, is bound to cause some ambiguity. I have generally followed the lower case practice of the book when in doubt. Title-page layout demands capitals at the beginning of every line. These have been reduced to lower case where it is clear that they would have been so printed if they had come later in the line.

The decision to exclude collation, pagination and imprint had been made in the original planning. The place of publication is given, followed by the date.[1] In a bibliography divided by years it is necessary to place each entry under a particular year. In some few cases it is not possible to estimate the date of publication within ten or more years. The degree of certainty is expressed as follows:

1710 indicates that the date of publication is given and is correct.

1710 [*1711*] indicates that the date of publication is given as 1710 in the book, but that it was actually published in 1711.

[*1710*] indicates that although the date of publication is not given in the book it is certain from internal or other evidence that the book was in fact published in 1710.

[*1710 ?*] indicates that there is some evidence to suggest that 1710 is a possible date of publication but it may be 1709 or 1711 or indeed an earlier or later date when the same subject was under discussion.

[*c. 1710 ?*] indicates that I have found little evidence for date of publication, which may be within a fairly wide range of years on either side of the date given.

The indication of size follows the normal practice, except that *s.sh.F°* is used (as it was in my time in the catalogue of the British Museum) to indicate either an unfolded half-sheet or an unfolded sheet. *F°* is used for a single sheet folded once and for books made up of such sheets.

One location only is given for each book. The original plan did not include

[1] *n.p.* = no place of publication given; *n.d.* = no date of publication given.

any locations, but I soon realized that some of the material was fairly scarce and that it was necessary to indicate the library in which I had seen it. I did not include more locations because in many libraries I only searched particular collections and it would give a false idea of availability to give only partial holdings.

Only first editions are given full entries. Subsequent editions are recorded in the footnote to the entry of the first edition. Statements on the title-pages are taken at their face value. If a work describes itself as 'the second edition' it is so recorded, although, bibliographically speaking, it may only be a reissue. The place of publication, the date, and the size of later editions are only given if they differ from those of the first edition.

I have added at the end a title-index and a general index. The former is intended for those who have a book in front of them and may wish to find its author if it is anonymous, or may wish to date it, if it is undated. The general index includes authors and subjects. I have not read many of the books, so that the subject entries are generally based on the title-pages.

Printing implies a reading public, but we have little information as to who read these books. Much of the material included in this work was undoubtedly aimed at Members of Parliament. The printing of petitions to Parliament goes back at least to the reign of James I. Their number increased as the century went on and after the Revolution of 1688, when the annual meeting of Parliament became essential, these 'cases' became extremely numerous,[1] and the procedure with regard to them became standardized. A manuscript petition would be drawn up and signed by the petitioners and then presented to Parliament by a Member. Some of these petitions were subsequently entered in the journals by the clerks of the House of Commons (without the names of the signatories), and thus are to be found in the printed *Journals*.[2] At the same time the promoters of the petitions had copies of the text printed, and paid the door-keepers of the Houses to distribute them to Members on the day on which the matter to which they referred was debated.[3] These cases are folio in size and are generally single half-sheets or sheets, without imprint. They were folded, and an endorsed title, which can be read when the case is folded, is often printed on the blank verso.[4] They are undated and since they are not published commercially the main external sources

[1] D. Wing in his *Short-title Catalogue*, 1641–1700, records 460 entries under the heading CASE and over 100 under the heading REASONS. Most of these date from the last decade of the century. Many counter-petitions are to be found under the heading ANSWERS. Wing's examination of the British Museum collections was cursory and he missed many items. I include about 1500 cases in this book.

[2] No petitions were entered in the Journals of the House of Lords.

[3] The doorkeepers of the House of Commons were paid 10*s*. by George Legh to distribute a case (probably no. 3771) in favour of the River Weaver Bill. See T. S. Willan, *River Navigation in England*, 1600–1750, 1936, p. 31.

[4] Contemporaries seem to refer to them by the endorsed title (see for example no. 916) but most library catalogues enter them under the title at the head of the text. I have followed the library practice, but endorsed titles differing significantly are mentioned in footnotes and are entered in the title-index.

for dating them are the Journals of both Houses.[1] On some of them however we have more details. The threat to the linen industry in 1719 and 1720 provoked a vigorous reaction in Ireland and Scotland. The Belfast Linen Board ordered 300 copies of its case to be printed (see no. 2631). In Scotland the Convention of the Royal Burghs sent detailed instructions to its London agent, William Hamilton.[2] These included a draft of a petition to be printed and distributed to members. Hamilton was not required to print the draft *verbatim*. The Royal Burghs, says the letter 'do not confine you to the precise words thereof but do allow you to make use of such other expressions as may be thought more expedient and better calculat for their understanding that matter'. Hamilton duly had the case printed (no. 2633). He was also instructed to engage counsel to appear both in the Commons and the Lords on behalf of the Royal Burghs and to wait on Scottish members to solicit their support. In the promotion of bills, as in the opposition to them, the printing of a petition was only one step of many. George Legh's bill[3] for work done in 1726 and 1727 for the promoters of the bill to make navigable the river Weaver amounted to £380 3*s.* 10*d.* This included the drafting the petition for the bill, drafting the bill itself 'very long', drawing up two manuscript petitions as well as printing and distributing 400 copies of the printed case for the bill.

Pamphlets were directed at a wider audience than Parliament, although members might occasionally expect free copies. *A Proposal humbly offer'd to the Consideration of both Houses of Parliament for Encouraging and Improving Trade in General* (no. 2566) was advertised in *The Post Man* of 15 December 1720 'Price Three Pence. N.B. The Members of either House which have not already receiv'd them, may have them of their Respective Door Keepers; there being a sufficient Number left with them for that Purpose'. There are few circulation figures but when important issues were debated the government propaganda machine was set in motion. Records among the Cholmondeley manuscripts now deposited in Cambridge University Library show that 9817 copies of *Some Considerations concerning the Publick Funds* (no. 4813), 10,305 copies of *The Convention Vindicated* (no. 5296), and 10,306 copies of *The Grand Question, Whether War or no War, with Spain impartially consider'd* (no. 5303) were distributed throughout the country. Members of Parliament, the clergy, collectors of customs and excise, and other employees and supporters of the government were all supplied.[4] These were exceptionally high figures, as a comparison with those in the ledger of William Strahan[5], the printer, makes clear. Pleadings in the

[1] The technique is demonstrated in R. A. Rye's *University of London. Catalogue of the Collection of Broadsides in the University Library*, 1930. The indexes are not easy to use and are very defective by modern standards. They were naturally enough mainly concerned with parliamentary procedure.

[2] *Extracts from the Records of the Convention of the Royal Burghs of Scotland*, v (1885), 227–9.

[3] It is summarized by T. S. Willan in *The Navigation of the River Weaver*, 1951, p. 28, and in the same author's *River Navigation in England*, 1936, p. 31. Legh is possibly the member of the Middle Temple, admitted 24 May 1717, *Register of Admissions*, vol. I (1949), p. 279.

[4] Cholmondeley MS. P75, no. 8a, 11–13.

[5] British Museum Add. MS. 48800.

House of Lords were printed, somewhat surprisingly, in editions of from 500 to 900 copies. The many pamphlets about Hudson's Bay (nos. 5710, 5790, 5800, 5906, 5980, 6269–70, 6274–5) were all of 500 copies, as was *A Scheme for Equipping and Maintaining Sixteen Men of War* (no. 6073). *A Letter from a Gentleman in Edinburgh to a Friend at London* (no. 6362) was printed in 300 copies. All these were primarily intended for Members of Parliament. Thomas Osborne ordered 1500 copies of the account of the '45, *A Journey through Part of England and Scotland along with the Army* (no. 6035), but for most books one has no information.

The study of Strahan's ledger and of the monthly lists of trade publications shows that a good deal of ephemeral material has not found its way into the major libraries of this country.[1] Much of the material is doubtless in America, but much may be in local libraries here. I should be glad to hear of it.

[1] To take an extreme example between 1745 and 1748 Strahan printed nine pieces for Stephen Theodore Janssen in from 500 to 4000 copies. I have only found one of them (no. 5975) for certain. No. 6183 is possibly another. See B.M. Add. MS. 48800, f. 56v. Most of them were half-sheets.

ABBREVIATIONS USED IN THE NOTES

Advocates' Library Catalogue Catalogue of the Printed Books in the Library of the Faculty of Advocates. 7 vols. Edinburgh & London, 1863–79.

Arents Tobacco: its history illustrated by the books, manuscripts and engravings in the library of George Arents [now in the New York Public Library]. Vol. 3. 1698–1783. New York, 1941.

B.M. Catalogue British Museum. General Catalogue of Printed Books. [The interleaved copy in the Reading Room.]

C.B.E.L. The Cambridge Bibliography of English Literature. Edited by F. W. Bateson. 5 vols. Cambridge, 1940–57.

C.J. The Journals of the House of Commons. Vols. 13–25. n.p., n.d.

Cal. S.P. Col. Calendar of State Papers, Colonial Series, America and West Indies, 1701 (–1735–6), preserved in the Public Record Office. Vols. [19]–42. London, 1910–53.

Cal. S.P. Dom. Calendar of State Papers, Domestic Series, of the Reign of William III, 1 April, 1700 to 8 March, 1702, preserved in the Public Record Office. Edited by Edward Bateson. London, 1937.

Calendar of State Papers, Domestic Series, of the Reign of Anne. Vol. I., 1702–3. Vol. II, 1703–4. Edited by Robert Pentland Mahaffy. London, 1916, 1924.

Cal. Treas. Papers Calendar of Treasury Papers, 1697–1701–2 (–1742–5), preserved in Her Majesty's Public Record Office. London, 1871–1903.

Cr. Bibliotheca Lindesiana. (Vols. V, VI.) A Bibliography of Royal Proclamations of the Tudor and Stuart Sovereigns . . . 1485–1714. With an historical essay on their origin and use. By Robert Steele. 2 vols. Oxford, 1910.

Crane, V. W. 'The Promotion Literature of Georgia', in Bibliographical Essays. A tribute to Wilberforce Eames, pp. 281–98. Cambridge, Mass., 1924.

D.N.B. The Dictionary of National Biography. 66 vols. London, 1885–1901.

De Renne Catalogue Catalogue of the Wymberley Jones De Renne Georgia Library at Wormsloe. Vol. 1. 1700–1836. Wormsloe, 1931.

Edinburgh University Library Catalogue Catalogue of the Printed Books in the Library of the University of Edinburgh. 3 vols. [Edinburgh] 1918–23.

Egmont Diary Historical Manuscripts Commission. Manuscripts of the Earl of Egmont. Diary of Viscount Percival, afterwards first Earl of Egmont. 3 vols. London, 1920–3.

Gladstone Library Catalogue Gladstone Library. National Liberal Club. Catalogue of Books and Pamphlets. 1908.

H. & L. Dictionary of Anonymous and Pseudonymous Literature. (Samuel Halkett and John Laing.) New and enlarged edition. 9 vols. Edinburgh & London, 1926–62.

Harleian Miscellany The Harleian Miscellany. A collection of scarce, curious, and entertaining pamphlets and tracts . . . selected from the library of Edward Harley, second Earl of Oxford . . . 10 vols. London, 1808–13. 4°.

Kress The Kress Library of Business and Economics. Catalogue, covering material published through 1776 . . . Boston, Mass., 1940.

Kress S. The Kress Library of Business and Economics. Catalogue Supplement, covering material published through 1776 . . . Boston, Mass., 1956.

Lough Fea Library Catalogue Catalogue of the Library at Lough Fea, in illustration of the History and Antiquities of Ireland. [The author's preface signed: Ev. Ph. Shirley.] London, 1872.

ABBREVIATIONS USED IN THE NOTES

N. & Q. Notes and Queries. London, 1850–

New College Catalogue Catalogue of the Printed Books and Manuscripts in the Library of the New College, Edinburgh. Edinburgh, 1878.

Rothschild The Rothschild Library. A catalogue of eighteenth-century printed books and manuscripts formed by Lord Rothschild. 2 vols. Cambridge, 1954.

Sabin Bibliotheca Americana. A dictionary of books relating to America. Begun by Joseph Sabin, continued by Wilberforce Eames and completed by R. W. G. Vail. 29 vols. New York, 1868–1936.

Somers Tracts A collection of Scarce and Valuable Tracts . . . Selected from an infinite number . . . in the Royal, Cotton, Sion, and other public, as well as private, libraries; particularly that of the late Lord Somers. The second edition, revised, augmented, and arranged, by Walter Scott. 13 vols. London, 1809–15. 4°.

Wagner Irish Economics: 1700–83. A bibliography with notes. [The introduction signed: Henry R. Wagner.] London, 1907.

LOCATIONS

ACC	Christ's College, Aberdeen
ANL	National Library of Wales, Aberystwyth
AU	Aberdeen University
Arents	New York Public Library, Arents Collection
C	Cambridge University Library
C(Cr)	The Earl of Crawford's collections of briefs, broadsides and proclamations deposited in Cambridge University Library
CP	Pryme Collection, Marshall Library, Cambridge
CT(R)	Lord Rothschild's Library, Trinity College, Cambridge
CUA	Cambridge University Archives
D	Trinity College, Dublin
DA	Royal Irish Academy, Dublin
DG	Gilbert Collection, Municipal Library, Dublin
DM	Marsh's Library, Dublin
DNL	National Library of Ireland, Dublin
DPRO	Public Record Office, Dublin
DS	Royal Dublin Society Library
De Renne	Wymberley Jones De Renne Georgia Library, Wormsloe
E	National Library of Scotland, Edinburgh
ECA	Edinburgh City Archives
EP	Edinburgh Public Library
EPRO	Public Record Office, Edinburgh
ES	Signet Library, Edinburgh
ESA	Edinburgh Society of Accountants
Ga	Gateshead Public Library
GU	Glasgow University Library
HEH	Henry E. Huntington Library, San Marino, California
JCB	John Carter Brown Library, Providence, Rhode Island
K	Cyril Kenney, London
Kress	Kress Library, Harvard University
L	British Museum
LCH	Customs House Library, London
LCRO	City of London Record Office
LF	Society of Friends Library, London
LG	Guildhall Library, London
LHL	House of Lords Library
LICA	Institute of Chartered Accountants Library, London
LIHR	Institute of Historical Research, London
LLI	Lincoln's Inn Library
LPRO	Public Record Office, London
LRIBA	Royal Institute of British Architects Library, London
LSC	Sion College Library, London
LStE	Stock Exchange, London
LU	London University Library (almost exclusively Goldsmiths' Library)
LV(F)	Victoria and Albert Museum Library, Forster Collection
M	John Rylands Library, Manchester
M(Cr)	The Earl of Crawford's collection of pamphlets deposited in the John Rylands Library
MC	Chetham's Library, Manchester

LOCATIONS

MH	Harvard University Library
MP	Manchester Public Library
NP	Newcastle Public Library
NU	Newcastle University Library
NYP	New York Public Library
O	Bodleian Library, Oxford
OAS	All Souls College, Oxford
OC	Christ Church, Oxford
OF	Oxford University Department of Forestry
OH	Hertford College, Oxford
OUP	Oxford University Press
R	Rothamsted Experimental Station, Harpenden
RU	Reading University (Overstone Collection)
SU	Southampton University Library
T	Toronto Public Library
Thomas	C. Stanley Thomas, Neath
WDA	U.S. Department of Agriculture Library, Washington
WLC	Library of Congress, Washington
Y	Yale University Library

CORRIGENDA

1344	should	follow	1019
1935	,,	,,	2087
2547	,,	,,	96
2950	,,	,,	3080
3223	,,	,,	3229
3279	,,	,,	3280
3965	,,	,,	3163
4516–7	,,	,,	4521
4607	,,	,,	4721
4778	,,	,,	4502
4900	,,	,,	5036
5968	should	be	5948
6277	should	follow	6301

CONTEMPORARY PRINTED SOURCES FOR BRITISH AND IRISH ECONOMIC HISTORY 1701—1750

1701

GENERAL

1 The New Description and State of England, containing the Mapps of the Counties of England and Wales in Fifty Three Copper-Plates....The several Counties described.... *Lond. 1701*, *8°*. L.

The maps are by Robert Morden, who is also the first named of the three publishers. Hence the whole work has been attributed to him. 2nd edn. 1704 (L).

2 HOUGHTON, JOHN. A Collection for Improvement of Husbandry and Trade. Vol. 15, no. 441–vol. 20, no. 583. 3 Jan. 1700 [O.S.]–24 Sept. 1703. *Lond. 1700–03*, *F°*. O.

Begun 30 March 1692. Another edn. of the essays only, edited by Richard Bradley, 4 vols., 1727, 28, 8° (O). In this edn. vol. 4, entitled Husbandry and Trade Improv'd, is a reprint of the essays in Houghton's earlier *Collection* of 1681–3. 2nd edn. of vol. 4, 1728 (L).

3 [BLANCH, JOHN]. A Dialogue between Mr. Smith, Monsieur Ragouse, Menheir Dorveil, and Mr. Manoel Texiera, in a Walk to Newington. *Lond. 1701*, *4°*. L.

For authorship see Blanch's list of his works in his *Swords into Anchors*, 1725. On the woollen industry and commerce in general.

4 [STEPNEY, GEORGE]. An Essay upon the Present Interest of England. To which are added, The Proceedings of the House of Commons in 1677. upon the French King's Progress in Flanders. *Lond. 1701*, *4°*. LU.

Reprinted, with author's name, in *Somers Tracts*, vol. XI (1814), 195.

5 [DAVENANT, CHARLES]. The True Picture of a Modern Whig, set forth in a Dialogue between Mr. Whiglove & Mr. Double, two Under-Spur-Leathers to the late Ministry. *Lond. 1701*, *8°*. L.

2nd edn. 1701 (O). Reprinted in *The Political and Commercial Works of Charles D'Avenant*, 1771.

6 Remarks by way of Answer, Paragraph by Paragraph, to the Character of a Modern Whig, &c. *Lond. 1701*, *4°*. O.

7 POVEY, CHARLES. The Unhappiness of England, as to its Trade by Sea and Land. Truly stated. Also a lively Representation of the Miseries of the Poor....To which is added, an Essay of the Happiness of Man in observing the Rules of Morality. *Lond. 1701*, *8°*. LU.

8 TRYON, THOMAS. The Merchant, Citizen, and Country-man's Instructor: or a Necessary Companion for all People. Containing, I. Directions to Planters of Sugar, and to make it. II. To a Planter touching Cotton, and the Advantage thereof. III. The Art of Distillation, and the Great

Advantage thereof to England. IV. Of Fermentation, and the Invention thereof.... IX. To make Coal-Fires, and the best Grates, with less Fuel, and better than ordinary. X. The best Method of tempering Clay, making Mortar, Tyles, Flooring and Bricks.... *Lond. 1701*, *8°*. LU.

LU copy has 2 additional title-pages, both dated 1700, one reading: *Tryon's Letters upon Several Occasions ...*; the other *Tryon's Letters, Domestic and Foreign ...*.

9 The Lists of the Liveries of the Fifty six Companies, in the City of London.... With an Account who Poll'd, and who did not at the Late Election of Members of Parliament for the said City of London.... *Lonon* [sic], *1701*, *F°*. O.

10 [Bohun, William]. Privilegia Londini: or, the Laws, Customs, and Priviledges of the City of London. Wherein are set forth all the Charters.... All their general and particular Customs.... The nature of By-Laws.... Also of Masters and Apprentices, Variety of Cases, and Pleading thereon.... Necessary for all Merchants, Tradesmen, Citizens, and others.... *Lond. 1702* [*1701*], *8°*. L.

2nd edn. 1716 (LG); 3rd edn., with author's name, 1723 (L).

11 Brand, John. A Brief Description of Orkney, Zetland, Pightland-Firth and Caithness.... *Edin. 1701*, *8°*. L.

Reissued 1703 as *A New Description of Orkney, etc*. Reprinted in J. Pinkerton's *General Collection of ... Voyages*, vol. 3 (1809); another edn. Edin. 1883 (all L).

12 The People of Scotland's Groans and Lamentable Complaints, Pour'd out before the High Court of Parliament. [*Edin. c. 1701?*], *s. sh. F°*. E.

13 [Paterson, William]. Proposals & Reasons for Constituting a Council of Trade. *Edin. 1701*, *8°*. LU.

Another edn. Glasgow, 1751 (LU), erroneously attributing the work to John Law. Reprinted in *The Writings of William Paterson*, edited by S. Bannister, 1858, vol. 1.

AGRICULTURE

14 The State of that part of Yorkshire, adjacent to the Level of Hatfield Chase: Truly and Impartially Represented. By a Lover of his Country. *York*, *1701*, *4°*. L.

15 The Case of the Earl of Stamford, relating to the Wood lately Cut in Enfeild-Chace. To which is annex'd, A Plan of the Chace, and the Intended Ridings Therein. *Lond. 1701*, *F°*. LU.

16 The Case of the Earl of Stamford considered, relating to the Wood lately cut in Enfield Chace. *Lond. 1701*, *F°*. L.

17 The Fourth Abstract of the State of the Mines of Bwlchyr Eskir-hir, in the County of Cardigan: from the 10th Day of December last (inclusive) to this present 5th Day of May, 1701. *Lond. 1701*, *F°*. L.

Published by the Company of the Mine Adventurers. Previous abstracts had been issued in 1700.

18 A List of the Adventurers in the Mine-Adventure. May the First, 1701. *Lond. 1701*, *F°*. L.

19 Draught of an Act Anent Coal and Salt. [*Edin. 1701*], *s. sh. F°*. LU.

Text begins: Our Sovereign Lord.

20 ASGILL, JOHN. An Essay on a Registry, for Titles of Lands. *Dublin, 1701*, *8°*. DA.

1st and 2nd edns. Lond. 1698. 3rd edn. Lond. 1720 (O).

21 An Argument proving that it is More the Interest of the Government and Nation of England, that the Forfeited Estates in Ireland be Purchased by an Incorporated Company, than by Single Purchasers. *Lond. 1701*, *4°*. L.

Signed: J. H.

22 The Case of Several of His Majesties Subjects in Ireland, commonly called Protectees, most humbly Offer'd to the Consideration of Both Houses of Parliament. [*Lond.? 1701?*], *4°*. O.

The only copy seen lacks title-page.

23 Jus Regium: or, The King's Right to Grant Forfeitures, and other Revenues of the Crown, fully set forth and trac'd from the beginning. His Majesty Vindicated as to his Promise Concerning the Disposal of the Forfeited Estates. The manifold Hardships of the Resumption, and the little Advantage we shall Reap by it, With Remarks on the Trustees Proceedings upon the Irish Forfeitures, Plainly Demonstrated. *Lond. 1701*, *4°*. pp. 63. L.

Another edn. 1701, pp. 84 (O). Reprinted in *A Collection of State Tracts, publish'd during the Reign of King William III.*, vol. 2 (1706).

24 [DELAMERE, WALTER]. A Letter to a Member of Parliament relating to the Irish Forfeitures. *Lond. 1701*, *4°*. pp. 27. L.

Another edn. 1701, pp. 15 (L). For authorship see ms. note in DA copy.

25 A List of the Claims, as they are Entred with the Trustees at Chichester-House on College-Green, Dublin, on or before the Tenth of August, 1701. *Dublin, 1701*, *F°*. L.

Both L copies have decisions, etc. in ms.

26 The Second Report of the Trustees appointed by Parliament for the Sale of the Forfeited Estates in Ireland, to the Honourable House of Commons. *Lond. 1701*, *4°*. O.

First Report, 1700.

27 A Short View of Both Reports in relation to the Irish Forfeitures. In a Familiar Dialogue between A. and B. Most Humbly Offered to the Consideration of Both Houses of Parliament. *Lond. 1701*, *4°*. pp. 24. L.

Another edn. Lond. 1701. 4°. pp. 18. (O).

28 [BRODRICK, ST. JOHN]. Short Remarks upon the late Act of Resumption

of the Irish Forfeitures, and upon the Manner of Putting that Act in Execution. *Lond. 1701*, 4°. LU.

'Irish Forfeitures' in title in black letter. Another edn. 1701, 'Irish Forfeitures' in roman (LU). For attribution see note in DA copy. Reprinted in *Somers Tracts*, XI (1814), 228.

29 To the Honourable the Commons of England in Parliament, a Remedy against Taxes: or, the Resumption of Crown-Lands and Forfeitures. *n.p.* [*c. 1701?*], *F°*. D.

30 [Macburney, James]. A Letter to an Honourable Member of the House of Commons. Briefly shewing, the Wealth, Power and Strength, that the Hollanders and other Nations gain, by Fishing on the Coasts and Seas of Great Britain. And how advantagious it would be to our own Nation if that Trade were well-establish'd in England.... *Lond. 1701*, 4°. MP.

For authorship see *Journal of the Commissioners of Trade & Plantations*, 19 March 1713/4.

31 Act for the more effectual Executing of the Laws against slayers of Black Fish, and destroyers of Smolts, and Fry of Salmond in forbidden time. *Edin. 1701*, *s. sh. F°*. EPRO.

A bill.

MANUFACTURES

32 An Account of Rock-Salt from the 25th of Decemb. 1699, to the 25th of Decemb. 1700. *n.p.* [*1701?*], *s. sh. F°*. L.

33 An Answer to the Paper, entituled, The Case of the Proprietors and Refiners of Rock-Salt. *n.p.* [*1701?*], *s. sh. F°*. LU.

34 A Reply to the Paper, Entituled, An Answer to the Case of the Proprietors and Refiners of Rock-Salt. *n.p.* [*1701?*], *s. sh. F°*. L.

Endorsed: A Reply on behalf of Rock-Salt and Refineries.

35 The Case of Rock-Salt, considered, in relation to a Clause now depending, for prohibiting the Refining thereof at any places, but near the Rock-Pits. *n.p.* [*1701?*], *s. sh. F°*. L.

36 Objections against the Rock-Salt Answered. *n.p.* [*1701?*], *s. sh. F°*. L.

37 The Case of the Salt Manufacturers from Brine-Springs and Sea-Brine, Humbly offered to the Honourable House of Commons. *n.p.* [*1701?*], *s. sh. F°*. L.

38 Some further Considerations humbly offered to the Honourable House of Commons. *n.p.* [*1701?*], *s. sh. F°*. L.

Endorsed: Some further Considerations on the Salt Bill.

39 The Interest of England, in Relation to the Woollen Manufacture, Briefly Consider'd: in a Dialogue between Sir Thomas Flourishing, a Merchant, and Timothy Castdown, a Clothier. Wherein the Nations Detriment, by the Mismanagement thereof, is Discover'd, and Means

Propos'd for making that Trade effectually serviceable to the Advantage of the whole Kingdom, Humbly Offer'd by a Hearty Wisher of the Welfare of his Country. *Lond. 1701*, *4°*. L.

40 The Case of several Thousand Poor of the Wooll Manufacture, ruined by the Printing, Staining and Dying of Linnens in England, and other Parts of his Majesty's Dominions (and that chiefly by French-men) for Outside Garments, being highly Injurious to the Labour of the Poor, and Destructive to the Wooll Manufacture of England. Humbly Addressed to the Honourable House of Commons. *n.p.* [*1701?*], *F°*. L.

41 Unto His Grace, His Majesty's High Commissioner, and the Honourable Estates of Parliament- The Petition of the Owners of Gun-Powder and Allum Works. [*Edin. 1701*], *s. sh. F°*. EPRO.

42 To His Grace, His Majesty's high Commissioner, and the Right Honourable the Estates of Parliament. James Gregory, Professor of Mathematicks in the Colledge of Edinburgh. Humbly Sheweth.... [*Edin. 1701*], *s. sh. F°*. EPRO.

For a patent for his water pump for use in coal mines.

43 Representation for the Silk Manufactories. [*Edin. 1701?*], *s. sh. F°*. E.

44 Draught of an Act brought in from the Committee of Trade, prohibiting the Importation of Silk-Stuffs, &c. [*Edin. 1701?*], *F°*. E.

45 Proposals to his Gaace [*sic*] His Majesties high Commissioner, and the right Honourable the Estates of parliament, in favours of the Woolen Manufactories, and particularly that of Glasgow. [*Edin. 1701?*], *s. sh. F°*. EPRO.

COMMERCE

46 London. Gore Mayor. Jovis Decimo tertio die Novembris 1701.... [*Lond.*], *1701*, *s. sh. F°*. LCRO.

Regulations for drovers bringing cattle to Smithfield market.

47 The Victuallers Case, humbly offered to the Consideration of their Excellencies the Lords Justices, and the Rest of the Kings Ministers. *Lond. 1701*, *F°*. O.

Followed by a petition to the Justices of the Peace for Middlesex signed: S.M. To be allowed to follow their trade on Sundays before and after sermon.

48 The Case of Sir Alexander Rigby, William Shepard, and William Plowman: setting forth the Damages they have Suffer'd by the Imprisonment of William Plowman; Seizure of their Effects, and other Proceedings of the Grand Duke of Tuscany. *Lond. 1701*, *F°*. L.

The firm was established at Leghorn in 1690.

49 The Duke of Anjou's Succession Considered, as to its Legality and Consequences.... *Lond. 1701*, *4°*. L.

On trade with Spain. 2nd edn. 1701 (L); 2nd edn. Dublin 1701 (DA); 3rd edn. Lond. 1701 (O); 4th edn. 1701 (LU). Reprinted in *A Collection of State Tracts, publish'd during the Reign of King William III.*, vol. 3 (1707).

50 The Duke of Anjou's Succession Further Consider'd, as to the Danger that may arise from it to Europe in General; but more particularly to England, and the several Branches of our Trade. Part II. By the Author of the First. *Lond. 1701*, *4º*. L.

Reprinted in *A Collection of State Tracts, publish'd during the Reign of King William III.*, vol. 3 (1707).

51 The Mismanagements of the Customs considered, as the only Means promoting Clandestine Trade.... *Lond. 1701*, *4º*. L.

A reissue, with the addition of a preface, of *A Letter to a Member of Parliament concerning Clandestine Trade*, 1700.

52 African-House. At a General Court of the Adventurers of the Royal African Company of England, held the 27th. day of March, 1701. *n.p.* [*1701*], *s. sh. Fº*. L.

Notice of a call of £4 per share.

53 A Letter to a Member of Parliament, on the Regulation of the Plantation Trade. *Lond. 1701*, *4º*. L.

Signed: J.B. Dated: Feb. 24. 1701.

54 James, Elinor. To the Honourable House of Commons. [*Lond. 1701*], *Fº*. C (Cr).

On the East India Company.

55 [Martyn, Henry]. Considerations upon the East-India Trade. *Lond. 1701*, *8º*. L.

Another edn. 1720 (L), entitled: The Advantages of the East-India Trade to England, consider'd. Wherein all the Objections to that Trade ... are fully Answer'd. With a Comparison of the East-India and Fishing Trades. For authorship see P. J. Thomas, *Mercantilism and the East India Trade*, pp. 171–3. The work is attributed to Martyn in *Bibliotheca Antonij Collins*, pt. 1, lot 3130. Reprinted in *A Select Collection of Early English Tracts on Commerce*, ed. by J. R. McCulloch, 1856, p. 541, reissued Cambridge, 1954.

56 England's Danger by Indian Manufactures. *n.p.* [*1701?*], *4º*. O.

Signed: T.S.

57 A Letter to a Member of Parliament. Shewing the Injustice and Pernicious Consequences of the Proposal lately Made by the Old East India Company, to have the Fund of the New Company [and the Separate Traders] with the Whole Trade of the East Indies, Settled on Themselves by Act of Parliament. *Lond. 1701*, *4º*. LU.

Signed: J.L.

58 [Toland, John]. Propositions for uniting the two East-India Companies: in a Letter to a Man of Quality, who desir'd the Opinion of a Gentleman not concern'd in either Company. *Lond. 1701*, *4º*. L.

For authorship see *A Collection of several Pieces of Mr John Toland*, 1726, vol. 1, p. xlvii.

59 By-Laws, Constitutions, Orders and Rules, for the Good Government of the Corporation of the United Company of Merchants of England, Trading to the East-Indies, and for the better carrying on and managing the Trade of the said Company. *n.p.* [*1701?*], *Fº*. L.

60 The Anatomy of a Project for raising Two Millions. *n.p.* [*1701?*], *4°*. O.

Signed: F.S. On the establishment of a new East India Company.

61 By the King, A Proclamation. *Lond. 1700–1*, *F°*. L.

Dated: 6 March 1700–1. For the apprehension of pirates.

62 A Full Account of the Proceedings in relation to Capt. Kidd. In two Letters. Written by a Person of Quality to a Kinsman of the Earl of Bellomont in Ireland. *Lond. 1701*, *4°*. L.

2nd edn. 1701 (L). Another edn. entitled: A Full Account of the Actions of the late famous Pyrate, Capt. Kidd . . ., *Dublin*, 1701 (L).

63 Piracy Destroy'd: or, A short Discourse shewing the Rise, Growth and Causes of Piracy of late; with a sure Method how to put a speedy stop to that growing Evil.....In a Letter from an Officer of an East-India Ship Lately arriv'd in the River, to the Deputy Governour of the East-India-Company, London. *Lond. 1701*, *4°*. L.

64 EDINBURGH. Act against Landlords Setting of Houses, &c. to Strangers without Testificats. *Edin. 1701*, *s. sh. F°*. EU.

Dated: 28 February 1701.

65 EDINBURGH. Act of the Gild Court, anent the Elnwand...Act of the Gild Court, against Unfree Traders and others. [*Edin. 1701*], *s. sh. F°*. EU.

Dated March 19. 1701.

66 Unto his Grace, James Duke of Qneensberry [*sic*] His Majesty's High Commissioner, and the Honourable Estates of Parliament. The Petition of James Earl of Linlithgow, and Calendar and his Tutors. [*Edin. 1701*], *s. sh. F°*. EPRO.

For two fairs at Falkirk and the right to levy toll at Larbert bridge. Another edn., with Queensberry correctly spelt and toll requested for 19 years (EPRO).

67 Uuto [*sic*] His Grace, His Majesties High Commissioner, And the Right Honourable the Estates of Parliament. The Petition of Sir Patrick Ogilvie of Boyn, and James Ogilvie Younger thereof. [*Edin. 1701*], *s. sh. F°*. EPRO.

For free export of their marble from Portsoy.

68 Proclamation Against importing of Irish Victual. *Edin. 1701*, *s. sh. F°*. E.

Dated: 6 January 1701.

69 Draught of an Act from the Committee of Trade, against the Exportation of Wooll. [*Edin. 1701*], *s. sh. F°*. EPRO.

70 Reasons against Continuing the Act allowing the Exportation of Wool. [*Edin. 1701*], *s. sh. F°*. EPRO.

71 A Short Proposal anent the Export of Wool. [*Edin. 1701?*], *s. sh. F°*. E.

72 Proclamation Anent the Staple-Port at Camphire. *Edin. 1701*, *s. sh. F°*. E.

Dated: 26 September 1701.

73 By the Lords Justices General, and General Governors of Ireland. *Dublin, 1700* [*O.S.*], *F*°. C (Cr).

An order fixing the prices of wines. Dated 12 Feb. 1700.

COLONIES

74 An Essay upon the Government of the English Plantations on the Continent of America. Together with some Remarks upon the Discourse on the Plantation Trade, written by the Author of the Essay on Ways and Means, and Published in the Second Part of His Discourses, on Publick Revenues and on the Trade of England. By an American. *Lond. 1701, 8*°. L.

Another edn., ed. by Louis B. Wright, San Marino, Calif., 1945.

75 [HODGES, THOMAS]. Plantation Justice, shewing the Constitution of their Courts, and what sorts of Judges they have in them. By which Merchants may see the occasions of their great Losses and Sufferings in the Plantation Trade: Lawyers may see such a Model of Justice as they could not have thought of; and Others may see how those Parts of the World are governed. *Lond. 1701, 4*°. L.

2nd. edn. 1702 (L). For authorship see *Cal. S.P. Col.* 1701, p. liii.

76 MONTAGUE, JOHN. Arguments Offer'd to the Right Honourable the Lords Commissioners for Trade & Plantation Relating to some Acts of Assembly past at New-York in America. *n.p. 1701, 4*°. MP.

77 Some Considerations humbly offered to both Houses of Parliament, concerning the Sugar Colonies, and chiefly the Island of Barbadoes. *Lond. 1701, 4*°. L.

78 A few brief Reflections upon a Paper, stiled, Some Considerations Offer'd to both Houses of Parliament, Concerning the Sugar-Colonies, and chiefly the Island of Barbadoes. *n.p.* [*1701*], *4*°. L.

79 HAMILTON, JOHN, Baron Belhaven. A Speech in Parliament on the 10th. day of January 1701....On the Affair of the Indian and African Company, and its Colony of Caledonia. *Edin. 1701, 4*°. LU.

80 [HERRIES, WALTER]. A New Darien Artifice Laid Open; in a Notable Instance of Captain Maclean's Name being used (in the Flying Post, February 11. and 13. $17\frac{00}{01}$) to Vouch for the Caledonian Company, after that Gentleman hath been Persecuted by them these Thirteen Months past for Vouching Against Them. Authore Anti Dariensi. *Lond. 1701, 4*°. LU.

Authorship deduced from internal evidence.

81 [HERRIES, WALTER]. An Enquiry into the Caledonian Project, with a Defence of England's Procedure (in point of Equity) in Relation thereunto. In a Friendly Letter from London, to a Member of the

Scots African and Indian Company in Edinburgh, to guard against Passion, *Lond. 1701, 4º.* JCB.

Signed: Timoniculus. Authorship acknowledged in Herries's *A New Darien Artifice Laid Open* (Congress Cat.).

FINANCE

82 A Postscript to a Discourse of Credit, and the Means and Methods of Restoring it. Written by the Author of the Essay of Ways and Means. And Published in the First Part of his Discourses on the Publick Revenues, and of the Trade of England, 169⅞. *n.p. 1701, 4º.* MP.

The Discourse was by Davenant. The postscript is not.

83 [DEFOE, DANIEL]. The Free-Holders Plea against Stock-Jobbing Elections of Parliament-Men. *Lond. 1701, 4º.* LU.

For authorship see *C.B.E.L.* II, 497, where two editions are recorded.

84 An Account of the Debts at Interest on the Exchequer, the 19th of Dec. 1699. And what was then paid per Annum for the same. Likewise what has been paid off from that time to the 20th of Dec. 1700. *n.p. [1701?], s. sh. Fº.* L.

85 The Case of the Malt-Tickets. In the Eighth and Ninth Years of His Majesty's Reign. *n.p. [1701?], s. sh. Fº.* L.

86 A Clause in the Act of Parliament for laying a Duty on Leather and Skins. *n.p. [1701?], Fº.* LU.

The text of the clause is followed by: The Grievous Case Without a Parallel, which is also the endorsed title. Praying that those who lent money on the security of the expired leather duties might be paid out of the proceeds of the Land Tax.

87 The Extraordinary Deplorable Case of several Persons who did Advance and Pay into the Receipt of His Majesty's Exchequer the Sum of 564700 l. upon the Faith and Credit of an Act of Parliament made in the 6th and 7th Years of His Majesty's Reign, for granting to His Majesty certain Rates and Duties on Stone, Glass and Earthen Wares, Coals and Culm.... *n.p. [1701], s. sh. Fº.* L.

88 *Begin.* This Writing indented witnesseth, that whereas in & by one act of Parliament lately made & passed, entitled, An act for making good the deficiency of several funds...& for enlarging the capital stock of the Bank of England.... *n.p. 1701; Fº.* Kress 2326.

Draft of an indenture between the lords of the Treasury and certain subscribers who are to guarantee to find cash for holders of tallies and orders who may not wish to accept exchequer bills.

89 A Collection of all the Statutes now in Force, relating to the Excise, and the Duties upon Salt: with an Abridgment of the said Statutes, and a Table of the Rates upon the several Liquors, &c. shewing by what

Acts they are Imposed. To which is added A Table of Allowances for Common Brewers, &c. *Lond. 1701, 12°.* LU.

90 The Several Proceedings and Resolutions of the House of Commons. In relation to the Bill for Taking, Examining and Stating the Publick Accounts of the Kingdom, together with the Copy of the Bill. *Lond. 1701, F°.* LU.

91 CROSFEILD, ROBERT. Corrupt Ministers the Cause of Publick Calamities; or, the Interest of the King and his People, One. Being a Brief Relation of some Publick Crimes Committed in the Government, during the Late War. Humbly offer'd to the Consideration of the Honourable House of Commons. *Lond. 1701, 4°.* O.

92 PASCHALL, JOHN. Mr. Paschall's Letter to a Friend in the Country, stating the Case of Mr. Parkhurst and Himself, together with the Rest of the Principal Commissioners for Prizes. *Lond., 1701, F°.* LU.

2nd edn. 1701 (O).

93 A Letter, directed to the Honourable Robert Harley, Esq., Speaker to the Honourable House of Commons, relating to the great Abuses of the Nation. *n.p. [1701], 4°.* L.

On excise, customs, etc. Dated: May the 3d. 1701.

94 The Case of the Freeholders and Miners of and within the respective Parishes of Ashover, Matlock, Darley, Bonsall, and Carsington, in the County of Derby, against a Bill now Depending in the Honourable House of Commons, Entituled, An Act for Preventing Multiplicity of Vexatious Suits, and for Settling and Ascertaining the Tythes of Lead-Oar in the said County. *n.p. [1701], s. sh. F°.* L.

95 The Case Relating to the Bill for Preventing Multiplicity of Vexatious Suits, and for Ascertaining a certain ancient Customary Tyth in the County of Derby. *n.p. [1701], s. sh. F°.* O.

96 A List of the Names of all the Proprietors in the Bank of England, March 25. 1701. *n.p. [1701], F°.* LG.

97 [DEFOE, DANIEL]. The Villainy of Stock-Jobbers Detected, and the Causes of the Late Run upon the Bank and Bankers Discovered and Considered. *Lond. 1701, 4°.* LU.

2nd edn. 1701 (LU). For authorship see *C.B.E.L.* II. 497.

98 SNELL, CHARLES. Rules for Book-Keeping, according to the Italian Manner: now in General Use.... *Lond. 1701, F°.* LICA.

99 Memorial to Members of Parliament of the Court Party. *[Edin. 1701], 4°.* LU.

Mainly on taxation in Scotland.

100 Proclamation anent the Old Fourteen-Shilling-Pieces, and their Halfs and the old Fourty-Penny-Pieces. *Edin. 1701, s. sh. F°.* E.

Dated: 18 November 1701.

101 Unto his Grace James Duke of Queensberry His Majesties High Commissioner, and right honourable Estates of Parlianmet [*sic*]. The Representation of the Servants in the Exchequer. [*Edin. 1701*], *s. sh. F°*. EPRO.

Frequent meetings of Parliament lessen their fees.

102 Proclamation Anent the Excise. *Edin. 1701*, *s. sh. F°*. E.

Dated: 5 August 1701.

103 To His Grace His Majesties High Commissioner, and the Right Honourable the Estates of Parliament. The Petition of William Menzies late Baillie of Edinburgh, and Alexander Wood Merchant there, Tacks-Men of the annexed Excise. [*Edin. 1701*], *s. sh. F°*. EPRO.

104 By the Lords Justices and Council a Proclamation. *Dublin, 1701*, *F°*. DPRO.

Dated: 2 June 1701. Fixing the rates of foreign coins.

TRANSPORT

105 An Abstract of the Rules, Orders and Constitutions, of the Company of Water-men and Lighter-men.... *Lond. 1701*, *8°*. L.

The preface signed: E. Knight.

106 Act for a general and voluntar Contribution, for Rebuilding the Port and Harbour of Eymouth. *Edin. 1701*, *s. sh. F°*. ES.

Dated: 4 March 1701.

107 Proclamation For Rouping the Inland Letter-Office. *Edin. 1701*, *s. sh. F°*.

Dated: 23 July 1701. Cr. 3210. Now mislaid.

SOCIAL CONDITIONS

108 Arguments proving that the Poor of England Cannot be Imploy'd on the Wooll Manufacture, but to a National Loss; and the Ruine of the Clothing Trade. And the Vulgar Error of Building Workhouses, Hospitals, and raising Money in all Towns and Corporations for that purpose, plainly Detected and Confuted. And shewing in what the Poor may be profitably Imploy'd for their own and the Publick Good. By Philanglus.... *Lond. 1701*, *4°*. L.

109 A Short State and Representation of the Proceedings of the President and Governors for the Poor of the City of London. *n.p.* [*1701*], *F°*. L.

Title taken from the endorsement. L also has the [1702] report.

110 Reasons Humbly Offer'd against Lynn Poor-Bill. *n.p.* [*1701?*], *s. sh. F°*. MC.

Endorsed: Reasons against Passing the Bill for Lynn-Poor.

111 Reasons for Passing the Bill for Better Employing the Poor of Lynn; In Answer to some Pretended Reasons lately Publish'd against it. *n.p.* [*1701?*], *s. sh. F°*. MC.

112 Several objections against the Lynn poor-bill humbly offer'd, &c. *n.p.* [*1701?*], *s. sh. F°*. Kress 2186.

113 Proposals humbly offered by John Apletre Esq; for the better Maintenance of the Poor of the County of Worcester. *n.p.* [*1701?*], *s. sh. F°*. L.

114 The Present State of Physick & Surgery in London. With an Estimate of the Prizes of all the Medicines now in Use. In a Letter from a Merchant in London, to a Dispensary Physician, with the Physicians Answer. *Lond. 1701*, *4°*. L.

115 Bellum Medicinale, or the Present State of Doctors and Apothecaries in London. Being Remarks upon a Letter from a Merchant-Dispensary Physician to himself, and his Answer. In a Letter from a Chymist in the City to a Country Physician, with the Physician's Answer.... *Lond. 1701*, *4°*. L.

116 An Abstract of the Rents of Great Haseley and Latchford in the County of Oxon, from Michaelmas 1695 to Lady-Day 1701. With Observations thereupon. *n.p.* [*1701*], *s. sh. F°*. L.

Endorsed: Haseley and Latchford, Com. Oxon. Valued. In Relation to the Bill for Regulating the King's-Bench and Fleet Prisons.

117 The Case of John Clements, Gent., Dame Mary Lisle, Katherine Venne, Anne Turner, Elizabeth Lowe, and Susan Lowe, Executors and Divisees of Sir Edward Lowe Executor of George Lowe, Esq; relating to a Bill, Entituled, An Act for the better regulating of the Prisons of the King's Bench and the Fleet. *n.p.* [*1701*], *s. sh. F°*. L.

118 The Case of John Clements, Gent. Dame Mary Lisle, Widow, Katherine Venn, Anne Turner Widow, Eliz. Low and Susan Low [and others].... Relating to the Amendments made by the Right Honourable the House of Peers to the Bill Entituled, A Bill for Regulating the Prisons of the Kings-Bench and Fleet. *n.p.* [*1701*], *s. sh. F°*. L.

119 Reasons humbly offered to the Right Honourable the Lords Spiritual and Temporal in Parliament assembled, for the Passing the Bill for Regulating the Prisons of the King's Bench and Fleet. *n.p.* [*1701*], *s. sh. F°*. L.

120 Some Considerations about the Regulating of the Kings-Bench and Fleet Prisons. *n.p.* [*1701*], *s. sh. F°*. LU.

Endorsed: Relating to the Bill for Dissolving the Kings-Bench and Fleet Prisons. Another edn., with additions and corrections, [1701], endorsed: Considerations about the Regulating the King's-Bench, and Fleet Prisons (LU).

121 Some Considerations humbly offered, relating to the Bill for the Regulating the Prisons of the Kingsbench and Fleet; as the same is amended by the Lords. *n.p.* [*1701*], *s. sh. F°*. LU.

122 Some Considerations relating to the Bill for Regulating the Kings-Bench and Fleet Prisons. *n.p.* [*1701*], *s. sh. F°.* L.

123 Remarks upon Reasons against the Bill for the more easy and speedy Recovery of small Debts within the Town and Borough of Southwark, &c. *n.p.* [*1701?*], *F°.* LLI.

124 The Right and Liberties of Englishmen Asserted. With a Collection of Statutes and Records of Parliament against Foreigners. Shewing that by the Constitution of England, no Outlandish Man, whether Naturaliz'd or not, is capable of any Office in England or Ireland....That no Outlandish Man ought to work or trade, but under the Government of English Men. That no Outlandish Broker ought to be imployed here. With other useful Observations.... *Lond. 1701*, *4°.* L.

Signed: D–f G–d. Attributed to Thomas Wagstaffe by H. & L. without quoting authority. Not included in the list of his father's works sent by the younger Wagstaffe to Rawlinson (Bodleian Rawlinson MS.4° J.1 f.51).

125 Reasons humbly offered against passing the Bill, Entituled, An Act for Naturalization of Adrian Lofland, and others. *n.p.* [*1701*], *s. sh. F°.* L.

126 SUDBURY, JOHN. Proposals, humbly offered to the Honourable House of Commons...to prevent Seamen being cheated of their Pay, by Ticket-Buyers and others; and to Mann the Fleet with more Expedition and less Charge, than has yet been, and that without any farther Charge to the King or Nation. *n.p.* [*1701?*], *s. sh. F°.* L.

127 DONALDSON, JAMES. Certain and Infallible Measures laid down whereby the whole Begging-Poor of the Kingdom may be Alimented at much less Charge then they are at present; and Begging intirely Supprest, &c. *Edin. 1701*, *4°.* E.

128 Edinburgh, The Ninteenth day of December, One thousand seven hundred and one Years. *Edin. 1701*, *s. sh. F°.* ECA.

Regulations for cleansing the streets.

1702

GENERAL

129 CHAMBERLAYNE, EDWARD. Angliæ Notitia: or the Present State of England: with divers Remarks upon the Ancient State thereof....The Twentieth Edition, with Large Additions and Improvements.... *Lond. 1702, 8°.* L.

21st edn. 1704; 22nd 1707; 22nd edn. entitled Magnæ Britanniæ notitia, 1708; 23rd 1710; 24th 1716; 25th 1718; 26th 1723; 27th 1726; 28th 1727; 29th 1728; 30th 1729; 31st 1735; 32nd 1736; 33rd 1737; 34th 1741; 35th 1743; 36th 1745; 37th 1748 (all L).

130 BREWSTER, Sir FRANCIS. New Essays on Trade, wherein the present State of our Trade, it's Great Decay in the Chief Branches of it, and the Fatal Consequences to the Nation (unless timely Remedy'd) is considered, under the most Important heads of Trade and Navigation. *Lond. 1702, 8°.* LU.

131 A Brief History of Trade in England. Containing, the Manner of its Birth, Growth, and Declension; and the several Occasions thereof: With some proper Remedies to Recover it from its present Languishing Condition, to its former Flourishing Estate. By One who hath been an Exporter and Importer above Forty Years, and is now considerably Interested both in Trade and Land. *Lond. 1702, 12°.* L.

132 England's Corruptions and Mismanagements Discover'd. In a Dialogue between Trueman and Legion. Setting forth the Vitious and Corrupt Practices of those, who endeavour to Enslave and Ruine this Nation.... *Lond. 1702, 4°.* LU.

133 Tom Double Return'd out of the Country: or, the True Picture of a Modern Whig, set forth in a Second Dialogue between Mr. Whiglove & Mr. Double, at the Rummer Tavern in Queen-street. *Lond. 1702, 8°.* L.

Another edn. 1702 with 'and' and 'Queen street' in title (O). The attribution to Davenant is recorded and rejected by David Waddell in *The Library*, ser. v, vol. II, p. 212.

134 SNOW, T. pseud. [i.e. Richard Neve.] Apopiroscopy: or, a Compleat and Faithful History of Experiments and Observations: not only Chymical and Curious, but Mechanical; and in several Arts, Sciences and Professions. Being Pleasant, Useful and Profitable. Extracted from the most Authentick Writers, Manuscripts, and the Author's Experience. *Lond. 1702, 8°.* L.

135 [NEVE, RICHARD]. Art's Improvement: or, Choice Experiments and Observations in Building, Husbandry, Gardening, Mechanicks, Chimistry, Painting, Japanning, Varnishing, Guilding, Inlaying, Embossing, Carving, Preserving several Things in their Natural Shape and Colour. And in other Arts and Sciences, Profitable and Pleasant.... By T.S. *Lond. 1703 [1702], 8°.* L.

A reissue of no. 134. 2nd edn., without initials, but 'By the Author of The Builders Dictionary', 1723 (E). In the *Term Catalogues*, III, 374–5, *Art's*

Improvement is said to be by the same author as *The City and Country Purchaser*, of which the later editions bore Neve's name. The L copy of the first edition has a ms. attribution to T. Smith. The second edition is erroneously attributed to William Salmon in the *Advocates' Library Catalogue*.

136 The Traveller's Companion. Containing Variety of Useful yet Pleasant Matters relating to Commerce and Converse; To which is subjoin'd, An Account of Timber-Measure.... *Lond. 1702, 12°.* L.

Preface signed: T.H. Thomas Harbin is the publisher and probable author.

137 A Treasury for Dealers, or The Merchant, Cash keeper, Masters, Owners of Ship, Freighters, Factors, Mariner, and Notary Publick's, best Instructor and Companion, in three parts. Part 1. Containing an account of Merchants, and Merchandize, Exchanges, and Bills of Exchange....Part II. Instruction for young Saylors....Part III. Containing useful Writings, as Bonds, Bills, Wills....By J. C. Notar. Pub. *Lond. 1702, 12°.* LU.

138 [Fairfax, Blackerby]. A Discourse upon the Uniting Scotland with England....With divers Original Papers deliver'd by the Commissioners of Both Nations to One another about an Union in 1667. *Lond. 1702, 8°.* LU.

For authorship see ms. note by James Knapton in LU copy.

139 A Memorial briefly pointing out some Advantages of the Union of the Two Kingdoms, Humbly offered to the Consideration of the Commissioners appointed to that end. *Lond. 1702, 4°.* L.

Pp. 9–16 comprise a 'Memorial Shewing the Advantages the Kingdom of Scotland may have by the Undertaking, and Improvement of Fishings for Export, whether by Societies, or singular Persons, mostly taken from the Pens and Mouths of Men of the greatest Knowledge and Experience in Fishing and Trade. Printed in the Year 1700'. The dedication signed: J.B. The Harvard copy has a ms. attribution to John Buchan.

140 [Mackenzie, George, Earl of Cromarty]. Parainesis Pacifica; or, a Perswasive to the Union of Britain. *Edin. 1702, 4°.* LU.

Another edn. Lond. 1702 (L). For authorship see *D.N.B.*

141 [Morer, Thomas]. A Short Account of Scotland. Being a Description of the Nature of that Kingdom, and what the Constitution of it is in Church and State. Wherein also some notice is taken of their Chief Cities and Royal Boroughs.... *Lond. 1702, 8°.* L.

Another edn., with author's name, Lond. 1715 (L).

AGRICULTURE

142 The Petition and Case of several Landholders, Maltsters, and Brewers, in the Counties of Middlesex, Essex, Surry, and Kent, &c, *n.p.* [*1702?*], *F°.* L.

For the enforcement of the laws to encourage the consumption of malted corn. Title taken from endorsement.

143 Leicester, Francis. The Little Mine Adventure: or, An Essay on the value of the Mine called Pant, nigh Holywell in Flintshire, on

Whitford Rake. Suppos'd to be the Famous Silver Mine spoken of by Camden. By F. L. Gent. the present Leassee. *Lond. 1702*, *8°*. L.

The dedication signed: Francis Leicester.

144 A short account of the proceedings of the select committee of the Mine-Adventurers, in pursuance of a general meeting made the twentieth day of December last, for lengthening their term and enlarging their boundaries. With the reasons and advantages thereof. *Lond. 1702*, *F°*. Kress S. 1089.

145 [BINNING, JOHN]. A Letter to a Member of Parliament. *n.p.* [*c. 1702?*], *4°*. E.

On the development of mining in Scotland. Author's name given in ms. in E copy.

146 The Several Addresses of some Irish Folkes To the King And The House of Commons. *n.p.* [*1702*], *4°*. L.

On the forfeited estates.

147 Some Remarks, upon a late Scandalous Pamphlet; entituled, An Address, of some Irish-Folks to the House of Commons. *n.p. 1702*, *4°*. D.

Another issue, entitled A Letter from a Soldier, being some Remarks upon a late Scandalous Pamphlet...n.p. 1702, 4° (D). Another edn., entitled Remarks upon a late scurrilous Pamphlet, intituled, An Address of some Irish-folks to the House of Commons. Lond. 1702, 4° (L).

148 A Letter from a Souldier to the Commons of England, occasioned by an Address now carrying on by the Protestants in Ireland, in order to take away the Fund appropriated for the Payment of the Arrears of the Army. *Lond. 1702*, *4°*. LU.

149 [BRODRICK, ST. JOHN]. Some Few Remarks upon a Pamphlet entitul'd, A Letter from a Soldier to the Commons of England, &c printed for E. Mallet. *n.p.* [*1702*], *4°*. DA.

For the authorship see ms. note in DA copy.

150 The Secret History of the Trust: with some Reflections upon the Letter from a Soldier. In a Familiar Discourse between J. Truncheon Esq; and Mr. Inquisitive. *Lond. 1702*, *4°*. L.

On the Irish forfeitures. Largely a satire on John Trenchard. The DA copy has a ms. note: By Capt. Stafford and Others.

151 A True Narrative of the Proceedings before the Honourable Trustees in Ireland, on the Claims of John Wade Esq; and Mr Francis Nangle, for 248 Acres in Harbert's Town....In a Familiar Dialogue between A. and B. Humbly offer'd to the Honourable House of Commons. *Lond. 1702*, *8°*. L.

MANUFACTURES

152 Some Observations upon the Bill for Preventing the making unwholesome and unmerchantable Brandy's from Corn, and for preventing the Clandestine Importation of French Brandy's: In Respect of the Distil-

lers not Free of the Distillers Company, (tho' many of them free of other Companies of London) with Relation to the Clause for giving a Power of Inspection to the Master, Wardens and Assistants of that Company alone. *n.p.* [*1702*], *s. sh. F°.* L.

Endorsed: Some Considerations upon the Distillers Bill.

153 Reasons humbly offered by the Master, Wardens, and Assistants of the Distillers Company, in relation to a Clause brought in to impower unexperienc'd Persons not bred Distillers to inspect with them the goodness of Brandy and Strong-Waters; in Answer to a Printed Paper, Intituled, Some Observations upon the Distillers Bill. *n.p.* [*1702*], *s. sh. F°.* L.

154 HALE, CHARLES. An Advertisement to all that are concerned in the Use of Sheet-Lead, demonstrating First, That Cast-Lead for Covering of Churches, Houses, &c. is worse, and at least 50 per Cent. dearer than Mill'd Lead, in supposing their Price to be equal....Secondly, That it is above 30 per Cent. dearer at the different Rates they are commonly Sold.... *Lond. 1702, F°.* L.

155 Reasons humbly offered for the passing a Bill for the Encouraging an Invention of Damasking, Striking and fixing Colours into all sorts of Cloths, Stuffs, &c. And raising and Embossing various Flowers and Shades on the same; in Answer to several Objections which have been made against it. *n.p.* [*1702*], *s. sh. F°.* L.

The petition for the bill was presented to the House of Commons by Thomas Ferrers and others on 23 Feb. 1702. *C.J.* XIII, 756.

156 SAVERY, THOMAS. The Miners Friend; or, an Engine to raise Water by Fire, described. And of the manner of Fixing it in Mines. With an Account of the several other Uses it is applicable to; and an Answer to the Objections made against it. *Lond. 1702, 8°.* L.

Another edn. 1827. Also reprinted as part of Sir E. Durning-Lawrence's *Steam in Relation to Cornwall*, 1904.

157 WALCOT, HUMPHREY. Sea-Water made Fresh and Wholsome. Objections against the Use thereof Removed, and the Advantages Prov'd to be very Great. *Lond. 1702, 4°.* L.

Advocating the method patented by his uncle William Walcot.

COMMERCE

158 Whiston's Merchants Weekly Rembrancer, of the Present-Money-Prices of their Goods Ashoar in London, On Monday, November 16th. 1702. *Lond. 1702, F°.* LU (film).

159 Her Majesties most Gracious Declaration, Concerning Ships Stopt before the Declaration of War. *Lond. 1702, F°.* L.

Dated: 1 June 1702. Cr. 4326. Two other edns. in 1702 (LPC. Cr. 4327); LPRO. Cr. 4328).

160 Reasons Humbly offered for the Bill brought in, upon the Petition of the Weavers of London, Norwich and Canterbury, &c. For the Importation of Fine Italian Thrown Silk. *n.p.* [*1702*], *s. sh. F°.* L.

161 SYMONDS, WILLIAM. England's Golden Fleece Preserv'd, in Proposals Humbly laid before a Committee of the Honourable House of Commons now Assembled in Parliament. *n.p.* [*1702*], *4°.* L.

A scheme to prevent the export of wool.

162 SYMONDS, WILLIAM. A New-Years-Gift to the Parliament, or, England's Golden Fleece Preserv'd, in Proposals humbly laid before this Present Parliament. *Lond. 1702*, *4°.* LU.

An expanded version of the preceding.

163 The Deplorable Case of the Chief and other Agents or Officers that have been deputed and concerned in the Preventing the Carrying away and the Exportation of the Wool of this Kingdom, &c. *n.p.* [*1702?*], *s. sh. F°.* LPRO.

Endorsed: The Case of the Wool-Agents or Officers, &c.

164 A short Survey of the Loss which is computed to be sustained in England by the Exportation of our Clothing-Wool, one Pack whereof, Weighing 240 Pounds, to be Wrought into fine Broad-Cloth, being sufficient for the Employing of Sixty Three People at hard Labour for a Week; and double such Number if Wrought into Hose. *n.p.* [*1702?*], *s. sh. F°.* LPRO.

165 The Case of Nathaniel Senior, Relating to Clandestine Trade with France, during the time of, and since the late War with France aforesaid. *n.p.* [*1702?*], *s. sh. F°.* LLI.

166 At a General Court of the Adventurers of the Royal African-Company of England, held...the 15th day of December, 1702. *n.p.* [*1702*], *s. sh. F°.* L.

Notice of a call of £6 per share.

167 SMITH, THOMAS. An Affidavit taken and Sworn at York, before Tho: Mosley, Mark Gill, Rog: Shakcleton, Esq; Three of his Majesties Justices of the Peace, there the 14th. day of Feb: 1701. Setting forth and Containing the hardships of the Case of several Merchants in the said City Trading to his Majesties Dominions in America and the Plantations thereunto belonging. *n.p.* [*1702*], *s. sh. F°.* LPRO.

On the seizure of his ship by the Customs authorities in Pennsylvania.

168 VEITIA LINAJE, JOSE DE. The Spanish Rule of Trade to the West-Indies. ...Made English by Capt. John Stevens. To which are added, Two Compleat Lists: One of the Goods Transported out of Europe to the Spanish West-Indies; the other of Commodities brought from those Parts into Europe. *Lond. 1702*, *8°.* L.

Another edn. entitled: The Rule Establish'd in Spain, for the Trade in the West Indies, Lond. [1711 ?] (Sabin 98781); 2nd edn., with original title, 1720 (Sabin 98782). The lists are not in the original which was published in 1672.

169 This Indenture Tripartite, Made the Two and twentieth Day of July, in the Year of Our Lord One thousand seven hundred and two, and in the First Year of the Reign of our Sovereign Lady Anne...Between our said Sovereign Lady the Queen's most Excellent Majesty of the First Part, The Governor and Campany [*sic*] of Merchants of London Trading into the East-Indies of the Second Part, and the English Company Trading to the East-Indies of the Third Part.... *n.p.* [*1702*], *F°.* LU.

170 Quinque Partite, Indenture of Conveyance of the Dead Stock of the Two East-India Companies. Dated the 22nd of July, 1702. *n.p.* [*1702*], *F°.* LPRO.

171 A list of names of all the members of the English company trading to the East-Indies, who are also members of the General society, April 4, 1702. Together with part of the 20th and 25th by-laws concerning elections.... [*Lond. 1702*], *40.5 cm.* Kress S. 1090.

172 A Journal or Account of William Daniel, his late Expedition or Undertaking to go from London to Surrat in India.... *Lond. 1702*, *8°.* L.

Daniel was a messenger sent overland by the East India Company.

173 DENNIS, JOHN. An Essay on the Navy, or England's Advantage and Safety, prov'd Dependent on a Formidable and well-Disciplined Navy; and the Encrease and Encouragement of Seamen....By the Author of the Seamen's Case. *Lond. 1702*, *4°.* L.

Dedication signed: John Dennis. Last page blank. A later issue has a poem and errata on last page (L).

174 The Present Condition of the English Navy set forth in a Dialogue betwixt Young Fudg of the Admiralty, and Capt. Steerwell, an Oliverian Commander. *Lond. 1702*, *4°.* L.

175 The Sailors Groans; or a Short, but Faithful Relation of many of the Horrid Abuses and Oppressions our English Seamen lay under during the late War....With some Proposals for increasing their Pay, and incouraging of them; that our Fleet may be always well Man'd and in a Readiness, and our Seamen well Used....By a Saylor. *Lond. 1702*, *8°.* LU.

176 Her Majesties most Gracious Declaration, For the Incouragement of Her Ships of War and Privateers. *Lond. 1702*, *F°.* L.

Dated: 1 June 1702. (Cr. 4329.) On the distribution of prize-money. Another edition, 1702 (C. Cr. 4330).

177 By the Principal Commissioners for Prizes. Instructions for the Agents in the several Ports. *n.p.* [*1702*], *F°.* L.

178 By the Principal Commissioners for Prizes. Instructions for the Sub-Commissioners in the several Ports. *n.p.* [*1702*], *F°.* L.

179 By the Principal Commissioners for Prizes. Instructions for the Agents in the Foreign Ports. *n.p.* [*1702*], *F°.* L.

180 A Third List of Recalls. *Lond. 1702, s. sh. F°.* MC.

List of ships with dates of wages due and paid. The two previous lists were published in 1699 and 1700.

181 EDINBURGH. Act anent the Importing and Lodging of Gun-powder within the Good-Town of Edinburgh, &c. *Edin. 1702, s. sh. F°.* E.

Dated: 14 August 1702.

COLONIES

182 Proposals for carrying on an Effectual War in America, against the French and Spaniards. *Lond. 1702, 4°.* L.

Reprinted in *Harleian Miscellany*, I (1808), 389.

183 New Providence. An Account of the Illegal Tax and Imposition of Brazaletta Wood laid on the sundry Inhabitants of this Government hereafter mentioned, by Elias Haskett late Governor of this Island. (More Exactions and Exortions of the said Elias Haskett from sundry other Persons, both in Mony and other Things of value, as followeth.) *n.p.* [*1702?*], *F°.* L.

184 Articles, Depositions, &c. of the People of New Providence, in an Assembly held at Nassau, October the 5th, 1701. against Elias Haskett, Governor. Humbly Offered to the Consideration of the Lords Proprietors, and the Right Honourable the Commissioners of Trade. And also Capt. Michael Cole's Narrative taken on Oath before a Master in Chancery. *Lond. 1702, F°.* L.

185 The Memorial of Elias Haskett, Esq; Governour of Providence, &c. And also an Answer to a Libel, entitled, Articles, and Depositions, of the People of Providence, against the said Governour.... *Lond. 1702, F°.* LPRO.

186 The Case of William Freeman Esq; and others, the Proprietors of Lands in the Charibbee Islands in America, under the Government of Coll. Codrington, the present Chief Governour there. *n.p.* [*1702*], *s. sh. F°.* O.

187 A Copy of the Articles exhibited by Mr. Freeman to the House of Commons against Col. Codrington: and Some Observations and Remarks in Answer to the same. *n.p. 1702, 4°.* L.

188 A Copy of the Petition of William Freeman, Esq; in behalf of Himself and Others, against Col. Christopher Codrington Governour of the Leeward Islands. Presented to the House of Commons the 19th. of February, 1701. With some Remarks thereon. *n.p. 1702, 4°.* L.

189 A Brief Representation of My Lord Dupplin's Title and Right to the Payment of One Thousand Pound per Annum, and of what is due unto him by way of Arrears, out of the Four and a Half per Cent. charged on all Commodities Exported from Barbadoes: Humbly laid before, and submitted to the Wisdom and Justice of the Honourable the House of Commons. *n.p.* [*1702*], *F°.* L.

190 BYRES, JAMES. A Letter to a Friend at Edinburgh from Roterdam; Giving an account of Scots affairs in Darien. *n.p. 1702, 8°.* GU.

191 London the 27th of April 1702. Saturday last, the following Address of the Council-General of the Scots Indian and African Company, was presented to Her Majesty, by the Right Honourable, the Earl Marischal of Scotland, introduced by the Duke of Hamilton. *n.p.* [*1702*], *s. sh. F°.* E.

192 Her Majesties Most Gracious Letter to the Parliament, in Answer to the Address from the Parliament, in Relation to the Company Trading to Affrica and the Indies, and concerning the Union with England. *Edin. 1702, s. sh. F°.* E.

FINANCE

193 The Case of the Clothiers of the Army. *n.p.* [*1702?*], *s. sh. F°.* LLI.

For payment.

194 The Case of the Clothiers of the Army, humbly Offer'd to the Honourable the Commons in Parliament Assembled. *n.p.* [*1702?*], *s. sh. F°.* LLI.

195 The Case of the Officers upon Half-Pay. *n.p.* [*1702*], *s. sh. F°.* L.

For payment.

196 The Deplorable Case of the Poor Creditors of the Navy of a National Debt, upon an Establishment always put upon the Front of the Debt of the Navy, and laid before several Parliaments since the Revolution. *n.p.* [*1702?*], *s. sh. F°.* L.

197 The Case of the Malt-Tickets in the Eight and Ninth Years of His Majesty's Reign. *n.p.* [*1702?*], *s. sh. F°.* L.

Some copies have 'Eighth'. A clause from the Act for Granting to his Majesty certain Duties upon Malt, with resolutions of the House of Commons.

198 The Case of the Malt-Tickets in the Eighth and Ninth Years of His Majesty's Reign. *n.p.* [*1702?*], *s. sh. F°.* L.

Clauses from two acts of Parliament, with resolutions of the House of Commons.

199 [DRAKE, JAMES]. An Essay concerning the Necessity of Equal Taxes; and the Dangerous Consequences of the Encouragement given to Usury among us of late years. With some Proposals to promote the Former, and give a Check to the Latter. By the Author of the History of the Last Parliament. To which is added, Some Considerations on the present posture of Affairs at Home and Abroad....By the same hand. *Lond. 1702, 4°.* LU.

O copy has ms. attribution of authorship. See *D.N.B.* for Drake's authorship of *The History of the Last Parliament*.

200 The Case of the Commissioners of Her Majesty's Customs, with Referrence to an Accompt delivered into the Honourable House of Commons, on the 21th day of February 1701. *n.p.* [*1702*], *s. sh. F°.* LLI.

201 [CARKESSE, CHARLES]. The Act of Tonnage & Poundage, and Rates of Merchandize, with The Further Subsidy; The Old Impost; The Additional Impost; And all other Duties relating to Her Majesties Customs, now Payable upon any sort of Merchandize Imported or Exported. Digested into an Easier Method....As also the Duties of Excise on Imported Commodities.... *Lond. 1702, 8°.* LU.

For authorship see the ms. notes in the L & LU copies which are presentation copies from the author. Another edn. 1726, F° (L); Supplement, 1737, F° (L).

202 By the Queen, A Proclamation For the better Observance of the Act for Laying Duties upon Malt, Mum, Cyder and Perry. *Lond. 1701 [O.S.], F°.* L.

Dated: 8 March 1701.

203 The Case of the Fruiterers, and other Retailers of Cyder, in Relation to their Ordinary and Damaged Cyder. *n.p. [1702], s. sh. F°.* L.

For a drawback of the duty.

204 Some Considerations Humbly Offer'd to the House of Commons, concerning the Bill entitled, A Bill for Regulating the Frauds and Abuses in the Salt Duties. *n.p. [1702?], s. sh. F°.* L.

205 A Collection of all the statutes now in force, relating to the duties upon salt, with so much of the laws of excise, as are particularly referr'd to, in the said statutes. To which is added, An abridgement of the whole, alphabetically digested under proper heads and titles. *Lond. 1702. 15½ cm.* Kress 2342.

206 JAMES, ELINOR. March 7. 1702. To the Honourable House of Commons. *[Lond. 1702], F°.* C (Cr).

Thanks the House for having flung out the Wine-Bill. Entreats that no further duty be laid on paper.

207 The Case of the Hundred of Hemlingford, in the County of Warwick. *n.p. [1702], s. sh. F°.* L.

Assessment for land tax.

208 The Case of the Commissioners of the Land Tax for the Hundred of Hemlingford, in the County of Warwick, in Answer, to the Petition of John Chetwind, Esq; and some other Inhabitants of part of the Hundred of Hemlingford. *n.p. [1702], s. sh. F°.* L.

209 The Case of Arthur Shallett of London, Merchant. *n.p. [1702], s. sh. F°.* L.

Has been arrested for debts due at the Customs-House and Excise Office for duties on wine and salt imported. Would not have become indebted if he had been paid promptly for his ships in the Transport Service.

210 An Account of the Civil List Expences between November 5, 1688, and Lady Day, 1702. *n.p. [1702], obl. s. sh. F°.* LU.

211 [PATERSON, WILLIAM]. England's Great Concern. In the perpetual Settlement of a Commission of Accounts: with Clauses and Powers fixing National Benefit thereby in the several Branches following.....

With a Discovery of some notable Frauds committed in Collecting the Supplies. *Lond. 1702, 4°.* LU.

Reprinted by S. Bannister in *The Writings of William Paterson*, 1858, vol. 1.

212 The Proceedings of the Right Honourable the House of Lords, in relation to the Bill for Taking, Examining, and Stating the Publick Accounts of the Kingdom together with the Amendments to the said Bill, which were rejected by the House of Commons the last Session of Parliament, Made Publick in order to vindicate John Parkhurst, and John Paschal, Esquires: With some Remarks in Justification of Mr. Whitaker's Fidelity, in his Place of being Solicitor to the Admiralty, from the Reflections of a late Author in his Book, Entituled, the True Picture of a Modern Whig. In a letter to a Person of Quality. *Lond. 1702. F°.* LU.

213 Some Remarks on the Bill for Taking, Examining and Stating the Publick Accounts of the Kingdom: and on the Proceedings thereon in both Houses, the last Session. *Lond. 1702. 4°.* LU.

Reprinted in *A Collection of State Tracts, publish'd during the Reign of King William III.*, vol. 3 (1707).

214 The Tryal, Sentence, and Condemnation of Fidelity, as it was lately Acted on the Publick Stage. With a Dialogue between Corruption and Fidelity: Wherein is Discovered the Vitious and Corrupt Practices of those who publickly Exclaim against the Members, and Proceedings of True English Parliaments.... *Lond. 1702. 4°.* O.

Mostly on corruption in naval administration.

215 [Everett, George]. An Answer to Mr. Paschal's Letter to his Friend in the Countrey, stating the Case of Mr. Parkhurst and Himself, &c. Being a Vindication of the Proceedings of the House of Commons against those Gentlemen Commissioners for Prizes.... *Lond. 1702, 4°.* L.

Signed: Trueman, Authorship deduced from internal evidence. On p. 7 the author refers to his *A Word in Season* which was published under his name.

216 The Case of Mr. Edward Whitaker, late Solicitor to the Admiralty and Navy. *n.p.* [*1702*], *F°.* L.

On the clause requiring him to account again in the Bill for taking, examining and stating the public accounts.

217 Some Remarks and Observations on the Report of the Five Commissioners to the Honourable House of Commons, Dated the 25th of November, 1702. relating to Mr. Whitaker's Accounts. *n.p.* [*1702?*], *F°.* LU.

218 Some Reflections upon the Present State of our Coin and Bullion. *n.p.* [*1702?*], *s. sh. F°.* L.

219 Assurance for Widows and Orphans. The Articles of Settlement, Agreed to, and Subscribed by the several Members of the Second Society of Assurance for Widows and Orphans.... *n.p.* [*1702*], *F°.* L.

No. 320 is a later edition of this.

220 [Armour, James]. A Premonitor Warning or Advice, by a true Lover of his Country, unto All whose Hands This may come. *n.p. 1702, 4°.* LU.

Signed: J.A. On James Armour's project for a land bank, presumably by Armour himself.

221 A Proclamation anent the Pole-money, Imposed in the Year 1698. *Edin. 1702, s. sh. F°.* E.

Dated: 8 August 1702.

222 A Proclamation Discharging Forraign Copper or Brass-Coyn. *Edin. 1702, s. sh. F°.* E.

Dated: 21 May 1702.

223 Young, Charles. A Collection of Several Acts and Statutes relating to Her Majesty's Revenue of Ireland; Together with the Rates of Customs and Excise, Fees of Officers, and Description of the Ports and Lawful Places for Shping [sic] and Landing of Goods and Merchandize.... Whereunto is Added by way of Appendix, An Epitome of the Art of Gaging....Ordered to be Published by the Chief Commissioners and Governours of Her Majesty's Revenue of Ireland. *Dublin, 1702, 8°.* LU.

The author's name is given in the dedication.

TRANSPORT

224 Reasons against the Hoy-Mens Bill for Kent and Essex. *n.p. [1702], s. sh. F°.* L.

The bill exempted from various Customs bonds those engaged in the provision trade from Kent and Essex to London.

225 The Case of the Owners of the Upper-Levels: relating to a Bill Depending in Parliament, about the Harbour of Rye. *n.p. [1702?], s. sh. F°.* L.

226 The Case of the Town and Port of Whitby, in the North Riding of the County of York. *n.p. [1702], s. sh. F°.* L.

227 Act for a Contribution to the Burgh of Elgine, Anent the Building a Harbour at Lossemouth. *Edin. 1702, s. sh. F°.* ES.

Dated: 15 January 1702.

228 Proclamation anent the Post-office in favours of the Post-master-general and his Deputs. *Edin. 1702, s. sh. F°.* E.

Dated: 4 August 1702.

SOCIAL CONDITIONS

229 A new project to make England a flourishing kingdom. Proposed as worthy the consideration of the ensuing Parliament. *Lond. 1702, 4°.* Kress 2358.

Felons to be slaves for life in the docks and yards.

230 COOKE, THOMAS. Work-houses the best Charity: A Sermon, Preacht at the Cathedral Church of Worcester, February 2d 1702.... *Lond.* [*1702*], *4°*. L.

231 A Short Account of the Work-House belonging to the President and Governors for the Poor, in Bishopsgate-street, London. December the 24th, 1702. *n.p.* [*1702*], *F°*. L.

232 PITT, ROBERT. The Craft and Frauds of Physick Expos'd. The very low Prices of the best Medicines Discover'd. The Costly Preparations now in great Esteem, Condemn'd. And the too frequent Use of Physick prov'd Destructive to Health. With Instructions to Prevent being Cheated and Destroy'd by the prevailing Practice. *Lond. 1702, 8°*. L.

2nd edn. 1703; 3rd edn. 1703 (both L).

233 A farther Account of the Dispensaries at the College of Physicians, and in St Martins Lane, Westminster, and others to be Erected in and about London, for the Service of the Publick. *n.p.* [*1702?*], *F°*. L.

234 A further Account of the Dispensary, at the College of Physicians, and St. Martin's-Lane, Westminster, and others to be erected in London for the service of the Publick. *n.p.* [*1702?*], *F°*. L.

Different from the preceding.

235 The Necessity and Usefulness of the Dispensaries lately set up by the College of Physicians in London, for the Use of the Sick Poor. Together with an Answer to all the Objections rais'd against them by the Apothecaries, or Others. *Lond. 1702, 4°*. L.

236 The Necessity of the Dispensary asserted by the College of Physicians. [*Lond.*], *1702, s. sh. F°*. L.

237 A Pill to Purge the Dispensary Doctors: or, a Cure for the present State of Physick. *Lond. 1702, 4°*. L.

238 [MOYLE, JOHN]. The Present ill State of the Practice of Physick in this Nation Truly Represented: and Some Remedies thereof Humbly Proposed to the Two Houses of Parliament. By a Member of the College of Physicians. *n.p. 1702, 4°*. L.

For authorship see H. & L. quoting H. B. Wheatley as authority.

239 The Case of Margaret Mortimer, Widow, and Seventeen more Sufferers by a dreadful Fire, which happened in Derby Court, Westminster, the 6th of April, 1697. *n.p.* [*1702?*], *s. sh. F°*. L.

240 A Postscript: explaining Some of the Frauds of the three Country Collectors mentioned in the Case of the Sufferers by Derby Court Fire, as plainly appears by Mrs. Mortimers Perusal of the Briefs, to lay them fit for the Master's Inspection, and is Confirmed to be true by the Master's Report, which is as followeth. *n.p.* [*1702?*], *s. sh. F°*. L.

241 The Case of the Traders and Dealers of England, set forth in a Dialogue between Mr. Trader and Mr. Cheator. Most Humbly Offered to the

Consideration of the Honourable the Commons of England, in Parliament Assembled. *Lond.* *1702*, 4°. O.

On imprisonment for debt.

242 Remarks, Upon the Bill for preventing Escapes out of the Queens-Bench and Fleet-Prisons. *n.p.* [*1702*], *s. sh. F°.* L.

243 The Case of the Inhabitants, for the Establishment of Courts of Concience, within the Bills of Mortality. *n.p.* [*1702?*], *s. sh. F°.* L.

244 Reasons for Erecting Courts of Conscience in the City of Westminster, Borough of Southwark, Finsbury-Division, and the Tower-Hamlets. *n.p.* [*1702?*], *s. sh. F°.* L.

245 Reasons for passing a Bill in Parliament to Erect three Courts of Conscience, in the three several Divisions hereafter Named, being within the Bills of Mortality, and without the City of London, and the Liberties thereof; for Relief of poor Debtors and Creditors, under the Value of Forty Shillings, to prevent vexatious and chargeable Arrests and Suits at Law. *n.p.* [*1702?*], *s. sh. F°.* L.

246 The Case of several Register'd Seamen, and their Widows and Children. *n.p.* [*1702*], *s. sh. F°.* MC.

For arrears of bounty money.

247 The Constitution Articles of the Amicable Society of Coach & Coach-Harness-makers. Containing Rules, Orders, and Directions, for the better and more easie managing a Monthly Contribution.... 1. Towards the Relief and Support of Poor Masters and Journey Men.... 2. Towards the maintenance of Poor Widows of deceased members.... 3. Towards the defraying the necessary Funeral Charges of the deceased Members of their Society.... *Lond.* *1702*, *12°.* O.

L has another edn. dated on the titlepage 1704 but in which occur documents dated 1706.

248 [Breck, Thomas]. The Reasonableness of the Augmentation of Poor Vicarages; with the Proposals thereunto. *Cambridge*, *1702*, 4°. M.

For authorship see ms. note in M copy.

249 Act For a General Collection to the Distressed Inhabitants in the Town of Leith. *Edin.* *1702*, *s. sh. F°.* ES.

To repair damage caused by an explosion of gunpowder.

250 Entry cancelled.

251 The Rules and Constitutions for Governing and Manageing the —— Maiden-Hospital. With an List of the Subscrivers and Donators, or Contributors thereto, preceeding the 1st. of July, 1702. *Edin.* *1702*, 8°. EU.

The editor's preface signed: G.M. Other edns. 1707, 1708, 1731, 1734 (all EU).

1703

GENERAL

252 GANDER, JOSEPH. The Glory of Her Sacred Majesty Queen Anne, in the Royal Navy, and Her Absolute Sovereignty as Empress of the Sea, Asserted and Vindicated. Also a Treatise of Navigation and Commerce; With some Remarks on the Royal Hospital at Greenwich; And Improving the Woollen Manufactury. *Lond. 1703, 4°.* LU.

The dedication signed: Joseph Gander.

253 A Dialogue between a Member of Parliament, a Divine, a Lawyer, a Freeholder, a Shopkeeper, and a Country Farmer; or, Remarks on the Badness of the Market, on our Happiness that England is not made the Seat of War...upon the Publick Accounts and Mismanagements; on the Commons Address; on Exchequer Bills....With a Question upon the whole Matter, Whether England is to be Undone for the Sake of Three Men. *n.p. 1703, 8°.* L.

Possibly by Charles Davenant. See David Waddell. 'The Writings of Charles Davenant' in *The Library*, ser. v, vol. II (1956), pp. 211–12.

254 A Letter from Mr. Hodges at London. To a Member of the Parliament of Scotland. *Edin. 1703, 4°.* E.

A general survey.

255 The Tradesman's Lawyer and Countrey-man's Friend. 1. Directing them in Contracts, Bargains and Agreements....2. Concerning borrowing, lending and restoring, and of Goods pledged and pawned. 3. Setting forth several adjudged Cases relating to Tradesmen, &c. 4. Cases relating to Farmers, and concerning stoppage of Ways, Water-courses, Lights, Commons, and several other Nusances...8. Certain Statute Laws, concerning Labourers, Tradesmen, Artificers, Apprentices, Servants, Petty Chapmen, &c.... *Lond. 1703, 8°.* L.

256 [BROWN, ANDREW]. Some Very Weighty and Seasonable Considerations tending to Dispose, Excite and Qualify the Nation, for the more effectual Treating with England in Relation to an Union of Confederacy as the nearest and most proper Expedient to put the Nation in a way of Prosperitie and Thriveing. [*Edin.*], *1703, 4°.* LU.

For authorship see Advocates' Library Catalogue.

257 [HODGES, JAMES]. The Rights and Interests of the Two British Monarchies, Inquir'd into, and Clear'd; With a special respect to An United or Separate State. Treatise I (III). 2 pt. *Lond. 1703,06, 4°.* L.

Another edn. of Treatise I, Edin. 1703 (L). For authorship see Advocates' Library Catalogue.

258 [MAXWELL, HENRY]. An Essay towards an Union of Ireland with England. Most Humbly offer'd to the Consideration of the Queen's

Most Excellent Majesty, and Both Houses of Parliament. *Lond. 1703*, 4°. LU.

Another edn. Dublin, 1704, entitled An Essay upon an Union... (LU). On the cattle and woollen trades. For authorship see ms. note in LU copy of the 1704 edn. and the preface to his *Proposals to render the Possession of Minorca, and Gibraltar, more useful to the Commerce of Britain*, 1723.

259 The Case of Scots-Men residing in England and in the English Plantations. Containing an Account...of the Difficulties they labour under, by a new Construction of some late Acts of Parliament: With Instances upon that Head.... *Edin. 1703*, 4°. E.

260 Several Grievances given by a Countrey Man, anent decay of Trade within the Kingdom of Scotland. *n.p.* [*1703*], *s. sh. F°*. E.

261 [Sinclair, Sir Archibald]. Some Thoughts on the Present State of Affairs. Humbly offered to the High Court of Parliament by a Lover of his Queen and Countrey. [*Edin.*], *1703*, 4°. E.

On the state of Scotland. For authorship see Advocates' Library Catalogue.

262 A Memorial concerning the Disorders of the Highlands, especially the Northern Parts thereof, and the Isles of Scotland. With an Account of some Means, by which the same may be Redressed and Prevented, and how Religion and Vertue may be promoted in these Parts. *Edin. 1703*, 4°. L.

Advocates religious instruction.

263 Martin, Martin. A Description of the Western Islands of Scotland. Containing A Full Account of their Situation, Extent, Soils, Product, Harbours, Bays, Tides, Anchoring Places, and Fisheries....A Brief Hint of Methods to Improve Trade in that Country, both by Sea and Land. With a New Map of the Whole....To which is added a Brief Description of the Isles of Orkney, and Schetland. *Lond. 1703*, 8°. L.

2nd edn. 1716 (L); another edn., ed. D. J. Macleod, Stirling, 1934.

AGRICULTURE

264 Young, John. The Improvement of the Marsh, and of the Country near about it: Being an Account of some Proposals for furnishing the Marsh with Fresh-water, with Reasons for the same, Reflections thereon, and Objections answered. To which is subjoyned a farther Proposal for mending the Sea-walls about Dimchurch. *n.p.* [*1703?*], 4°. O.

265 An Abstract of the Register Bill, for the West-Riding of the County of York. *n.p.* [*1703?*], *s. sh. F°*. L.

The preamble states that the object of the bill is to enable cloth manufacturers to borrow money more easily.

266 The Clerk of Inrolments in Chancery, their Case, humbly offered to the Honourable the House of Commons, against the Passing of the Registry Bill for the West-Riding of the County of York. *n.p.* [*1703*], *s. sh. F°*. L.

267 [FITZGERALD,]. The Exorbitant Grants of William the III. Examin'd and Question'd. Shewing the Nature of Grants in Successive and Elective Monarchies; and proving...that Crown-Lands are Inalienable, That Resumptions were common all the world over.... *Lond.* *1703*, *4°*. LU.

Signed: B.B. 2nd edn. 1703 (L). Reprinted in *Somers Tracts*, XII (1814), 416. For authorship see *Cal. S.P. Dom.* 1703/4, p. 39.

268 [FITZGERALD,]. The Exorbitant Grants of William the III. Examin'd and Question'd....With Reflections on each Paragraph. *Lond.* *1703*, *4°*. O.

The text of the preceding with criticism interpolated in it.

269 Animadversions upon a Seditious Libel, intituled, The Exorbitant Grants of William III. Examin'd and Question'd, &c..... *Lond.* *1703*, *4°*. L.

270 A Book of Postings and Sale of the forfeited & other estates and interests in Ireland.... [*Dublin*, *1703*], *F°*. L.

Printed lists of the estates to be sold with the buyers' names, prices and other details added in ms. The title-page is in ms.

271 The Case of the Governor and Company for making Hollow-Sword-Blades in England. *n.p.* [*1703*], *s. sh. F°*. LLI.

On their title to forfeited estates in Ireland.

272 The Case of the Petitioning-Receivers, under the Trustees appointed for Sale of the Forfeited, and other Estates and Interests in Ireland. *n.p.* [*1703?*], *s. sh. F°*. L.

For adequate payment.

MANUFACTURES

273 [NEVE, RICHARD]. The City and Countrey Purchaser, and Builder's Dictionary: or the Compleat Builder's Guide. Shewing the Qualities, Quantities, Proportions, and Rates or Value of all Materials relating to Building....By T. N. Philomath. *Lond.* *1703*, *8°*. LU.

2nd edn., with author's name, 1726 [1725] (LU); 3rd edn. 1736 (L).

274 DEANE, MOSES. A Wheel within a Wheel, or a Mystery with a Trade Discovered, to the Detriment and Damage of the Woollen Manufactory and Dying-Trade of England, in Markets both at Home and Abroad. *Bristol*, *1703*, *4°*. MP.

On dyeing.

275 Memorial concerning the State of the Manufactures before and since the Year 1700, at which time the Laws concerning Trade and Manufactures were Revived and Increased: As also, some Remarks upon the Arts used for Eluding these Laws, humbly offered to His Grace, and the Honourable Estates of Parliament. [*Edin.* *1703?*], *F°*. E.

276 Memorial to His Grace Her Majesty's High Commissioner, and Estates of Parliament, from the Hat-makers of Edinburgh. [*Edin.* *1703?*], *s. sh. F°*. EPRO.

Ends: 'now to be included'.

277 Unto his Grace Her Majesties high Commissioner, and honourable Court of Parliament, The Petition of Robert Douglas elder and younger Soap boylers in Leith. [*Edin. 1703*], *s. sh. F°*. EPRO.

Against the granting of sole privileges to William Montgomery and George Lind to establish pottery works.

278 Overture of an Act of Parliament For Measuring and Sealing of Linning and Woollen Cloath, &c. [*Edin. 1703*], *F°*. EPRO.

COMMERCE

279 London. An Act of Common-Council for Preventing the Seacoal and Corn-Meters Alienation of their Offices. [*Lond.*] *1703*, *F°*. LG.

280 Proposals Made by the several Coal and Corn-meeters of this City of London, on behalf of themselves, and other the Officers of the same City. *n.p.* [*1703*], *s. sh. F°*. L.

Dated: Septemb. the 1st, 1703.

281 Alingham, William. A Short Account of the Nature and Use of Maps. ...To which is subjoined A Catalogue of the Factories and Places now in Possession of the English, French, Dutch, Spanish, Portugueze and Danes, both in the East and West Indies.... *Lond. 1703*, *8°*. L.

282 [Dennis, John]. A Proposal for putting a Speedy End to the War, by Ruining the Commerce of the French and Spaniards, and Securing our Own, without any additional Expence to the Nation. *Lond. 1703*, *4°*. LU.

Reprinted in *The Select Works of Mr. John Dennis*, 1718.

283 Reasons Humbly Offer'd to the Honourable House of Commons, for Granting an Act for the Importation of Salt-Petre from Holland. *n.p.* [*1703*], *s. sh. F°* L.

Endorsed: Proposals for the Importing Salt-Petre from Holland to England.

284 The Case of Miles Fleetwood, Merchant. *n.p.* [*c. 1703?*], *s. sh. F°*. L.

Complaining of wrongful dismissal from his post as Consul for the Turkey Company in Cairo.

285 A List of the Names of the Governour, Deputy, and Twenty-four Committees of the Honourable the East-India-Company, Elected for the Year 1703. *n.p.* [*1703*], *s. sh. 4°*. O.

286 *Begin.* London, 11th February, 170 2/3. Whereas Her Majesty, for the Encouragement of Trade and Commerce, hath thought fit to appoint Boats to convey Letters and Pacquets between England and the Islands of Barbadoes, Antegoa, Montserat, Nevis, St. Christophers, and Jamaica in America.... *n.p.* [*1703*], *s. sh. F°*. L.

Notice of the monthly mail from the General Post Office, with fees. This is the service operated by Edward Dummer.

287 Sudbury, John. An Answer to an Objection Made to the Proposal, Entituled, The Grievance of the Seamen. *n.p.* [*1703?*], *s. sh. F°*. L.

288 An Historical and Political Treatise of the Navy: with Some Thoughts how to Retrieve the Antient Glory of the Navy of England. Humbly Offer'd to the Consideration of Both Houses of Parliament. *Lond.* *1703*, *4°*. L.

289 Tack About; or, A New Model of a Marine Establishment, for Raising Seamen for the Continual Service of Her Majesty's Fleet.... To which is added upon the same Ground of Establishment, A Probable Method to Supply continual Convoys to Support Our New-Castle Trade, without the Charges of Wages to maintain, or Raise such Convoy-Seamen to the Government. And keep Coals at a Moderate Price. *Lond.* *1703*, *F°*. LU.

The dedication signed: C.W. All seamen to be registered.

290 [Rowe, Peter]. A True Method, I. For Raising of Soldiers, II. For bringing those Seamen that are in the Land, into the Navy, III. For the Increase of Seamen. IV. For Employing of Seamen in time of Peace. V. For the Improvement of Seamen. VI. For the Incouragement of Seamen. VII. For the Improvement and Encouragement of the Officers. VIII. For the Security of the Royal Navy in Harbour. IX. For the Encouragement and Interest of Privateers. *Lond.* *1703*, *4°*. L.

For authorship see ms. note in L copy.

291 Her Majesties most Gracious Declaration, For the further Encouragement of Her Ships of War and Privateers. *Lond.* *1703*. *F°*. L.

Dated: 17 May 1703. Cr. 4357. Duties on fish oils and plantation produce taken in prizes to be reduced. Another edn. 1703 (LPRO. Cr. 4358).

292 Two Speeches; The One Relating to Trade. (Spoken in the Present Parliament of Scotland.) The other Relating to the Limitations of the Crown thereof. *Edin.* *1703*, *4°*. DA.

293 Overture For an Act. [*Edin.* *1703*], *s. sh. F°*. EPRO.

Confirming the privileges of the Royal Burghs. On the verso is the 1698 Act Regulating the Trade betwixt Burghs Royal and Burghs of Regality, Barrony and others.

294 Overture of an Act for a Free Communication of Trade. *n.p.* [*1703*], *s. sh. F°*. E.

Dated: August 30, 1703.

295 Overture for An Act to make this Kingdom A Free-Port. [*Edin.* *1703*], *s. sh. F°*. EPRO.

296 Unto His Grace James Duke of Queensberry, &c. Her Majesties High Commissioner, and the Right Honourable the Estates of Parliament, the Petition of the Merchands Retailers in Edinburgh. *n.p.* [*1703?*], *F°*. LU.

Enclosing 'Memorial concerning the State of the Kingdom, and of the Merchands in particular, with relation to the late Laws upon Trade'.

297 To his Grace Her Majesties high Commissioner, and the right Honourable the Estates of Parliament, The Petition of The Magistrats and

Town-Council of Edinburgh for themselves, and in name of the Good Town. [*Edin. 1703*], *s. sh. F°*. EPRO.

For the inclusion of Edinburgh among the ports from which the export of sheep and lamb skins is permitted.

298 Proposals Anent the Irish Victual. [*Edin. 1703*], *s. sh. F°*. E.

299 Act Discharging the Importation of Irish Victual. [*Edin. 1703*], *s. sh. F°*. EPRO.

Dated: August 25th 1703. A bill.

300 Answers to The Memorial given in for the Export of Skins. [*Edin. 1703*], *F°*. EPRO.

Followed by: Answers for The Skinners, Shoe-Makers, &c.

301 Unto his Grace, James Duke of Queensberry, Her Majesty's High Commissioner: And the Right Honourable, the Estates of Parliament. The Petition of Mr. William Cochran of Ocheltrie, and other Delegates from the Wool and Silk Manufactories in Edinburgh, Glasgow, and Aberdeen, for themselves and the saids Manufactories. [*Edin. 1703*], *s. sh. F°*. EPRO.

On frauds in exporting wool. Signed in ms.: Wm. Black.

302 Overture of an Act of Parliament, Continuing the Prohibition of Exporting English or Irish Wooll till the next Session of Parliament Inclusive. [*Edin. 1703*], *s. sh. F°*. E.

COLONIES

303 The Case of William Atwood, Esq; by the late King William...constituted Chief Justice of the Province of New York in America.... With a True Account of the Government and People of that Province; particularly of Bayard's Faction.... *Lond. 1703*, *F°*. L.

304 [Bugg, Francis]. News from Pensylvania: or a brief Narrative of several Remarkable Passages in the Government of the Quakers in that Province. Touching their Proceedings in their Pretended Courts of Justice; their Way of Trade and Commerce; with Remarks and Observations upon the whole. Published by the Author of The Pilgrim's Progress, &c. *Lond. 1703*, *8°*. L.

For authorship see Joseph Smith, *A Descriptive Catalogue of Friends' Books*, 1867, I. 343.

FINANCE

305 Bailey, Zachary. A Project to Raise 50000 l. per Ann. Humbly Offered to the Consideration of the Honourable House of Commons. *n.p.* [*1703?*], *s. sh. F°*. MC.

For a tax on alehouses.

306 A Proposal to raise 2062400 l. by way of Loan, or Subscription, to the great Ease of the Land-Tax, and Advantages of the Government, and all Lenders, and Subscribers. *n.p.* [*1703?*], *s. sh. F°*. L.

307 Instructions for Officers for Gauging and Ascertaining the Duties on Malt. *Lond. 1703, 8º.* L.

308 The Case of Daniel Le Febvre, of the Island of Guernsey, Gent. *n.p.* [*1703?*], *s. sh. Fº.* MC.

Against paying duty on salt imported into England from Guernsey.

309 An Abstract of the Several Acts for Licensing Hawkers and Pedlars, for a further Provision of Interest for the Transport Debts. That is, so much thereof as Relates to the Impositions upon Hawkers, &c. *Lond. 1703, s. sh. Fº.* LPRO.

310 The Proceedings of the Right Honourable the Lords Spiritual & Temporal in Parliament Assembled, upon the Observations of the Commissioners for Taking, Examining and Stating the Publick Accounts of the Kingdom: delivered into the House of Peers. *Lond. 1702* [*O.S.*], *Fº.* L.

Another edn. Lond. 1702, s. sh. Fº (DA). Another ed. Edin. 1703, 4º entitled The Report of the Proceedings of the House of Peers upon the Observations... (LU).

311 An Account of the Proceedings of the House of Peers, upon the Observations of the Commissioners for Taking, Examining and Stating the Publick Accounts of the Kingdom: with their Address to Her Majesty; and Her Majesties Most Gracious Answer thereunto: Together with the Papers Referred to in these Proceedings. *Lond. 1702* [*O.S.*], *Fº.* pp. 82. LU.

Another edn. pp. 86 (LU).

312 The Report of the Conferences and Free Conference, Relating to the Message from the Lords the 4th of February, 1702. [O.S.], Touching the Commissioners of Accounts, and the Proceedings thereupon. Published by Order of the House of Commons. *Lond. 1703, Fº.* LU.

313 The Reasons which the House of Commons Deliver'd at a Conference with the Lords, why they could not agree to the Amendments made by their Lordships to the Bill, Entituled, An Act for the Taking, Examining and Stating the Publick Accounts of the Kingdom. *n.p.* [*1703*], *Fº.* L.

Followed by: The Reasons which the Lords deliver'd at a Conference with the Commons why they insisted on their Amendments to the said Bill.

314 An Apology of Mr: Jacob vander Esch, late Paymaster of his late Majesty's Dutch and other forces, in a letter to his friend. *n.p. 1703, 4º.* O.

Defending himself from charges made against him by the Commissioners of Public Accounts.

315 Crosfeild, Robert. The Government Unhing'd: or, an Account of many great Encroachments made upon the Liberties and Properties of the People of England. Shewing, the Notorious Breach of Trust of some Publick Ministers and Officers. Humbly Offered to the Consideration of the Honourable House of Commons. *Lond. 1703, 4º.* O.

316 [Hore, Charles]. A True and Exact Account of many Great Abuses committed in the Victualling Her Majesties Navy, from February 3, 170⅔. to July 1703. As appears by the Informations and Depositions of several Witnesses, with the Proceedings thereupon, both at the Admiralty Office, Hicks's-Hall, and Elsewhere.... *Lond. 1703, F°.* LU.

Authorship obvious from internal evidence.

317 The Mystery of Tithe-stealing Display'd and Abdicated. Or the Penitent Countrymen's Confession in Lent. A Dialogue between Farmer K——and some of his Neighbours met at Banbury Market in Oxfordshire, on Thursday the 18th of February, 170⅔. Published for the Benefit of all Counties, and Tithing-Men, by Farmer K——. *Lond. 1703, 4°.* O.

318 Forbes, William. A Methodical Treatise, concerning Bills of Exchange. Wherein is an account of the Rise and Progress of Exchange; the nature and kinds of it explained...and all curious and useful Cases, Questions and Controversies touching Bills fairly stated and discuss'd, according to the Analogy of the Scots Law. *Edin. 1703, 8°.* L.

2nd edn. 1718 (L).

319 An Abridgment of the most Material Things in the Articles of Settlement, Agreed to, and Subscrib'd by the several Members of the First Society of Assurance for Widows and Orphans. *n.p.* [*1703?*], *s. sh. 4°.* L.

320 Assurance for Widows and Orphans. The Articles of Settlement, Agreed to, and Subscrib'd by the several Members of the Second Society of Assurance for Widows and Orphans.... *n.p.* [*1703*], *F°.* L.

For an earlier edition see no. 219.

321 Overture for an Act, for Revising the Publick Accompts. [*Edin. 1703*], *s. sh. F°.* E.

322 Act Appointing Commissioners to Examine, State, and take the publick Accompts of the Kingdom. [*Edin. 1703*], *s. sh. F°.* EPRO.

A bill.

323 Act in favours of the Burgh of Elgine. [*Edin. 1703*], *s. sh. F°.* EPRO.

A bill. For the right to levy a tax on ale.

TRANSPORT

324 The Present State of the Coal Trade: Humbly Presented to the Consideration of the Honourable House of Commons. *n.p.* [*1703*], *s. sh. F°.* MC.

Endorsed: The State of the Coal Trade.

325 The Case of the River Derwent, in respect of Navigation, and of the Bill now in Parliament concerning the same. *n.p.* [*1703?*], *s. sh. F°.* L.

326 An Answer to the new Objections against making the River Derwent Navigable. *n. p.* [*1703?*], *s. sh. F°.* O.

327 Act of Her Majesties Privie Council, For a Voluntarie Contribution, for building a Bridge over the Water of Dee. *n.p.* [*1703*], *s. sh. F°.* ES.
Dated: 20 September 1703.

SOCIAL CONDITIONS

328 London Work-House. Easter, 1703. A True Report of the great Number of Poor Vagrant, and other Children, as also of the other Grown and Able Poor, Beggars, Vagabonds, and other Idle and Disorderly Persons, Educated, Maintained, and Imployed by the President and Governors for the Poor of the City of London; at their Work-House in Bishopsgate-street in the Year last past. *n.p.* [*1703*], *s. sh. F°.* LG.
Endorsed: A True Report of the Poor, Maintained and Imployed in the Work-House. Easter 1703. Published annually. L has the reports for 1703/4 and 1704/5; Kress the one for 1706/7 (S. 1187); LG the one for 1726/7.

329 BROWNE, JOSEPH. The Modern Practice of Physick Vindicated, and the Apothecaries clear'd from the Groundless Imputations of Dr. Pitt.... *Lond. 1703, 8°.* L.
2nd edn. 1704 (L).

330 The Dispensaries and Dispensary Physicians Vindicated, &c. *n.p.* [*c. 1703?*], *s. sh. F°.* L.

331 To the Lords Spiritual and Temporal, and Commons of England in Parliament Assembled, The Humble Petition of Margaret Mortimer Widow, who with several others were great Sufferers by the dreadful Fire which happen'd in Derby-Court, Westminster, the 16th of April 1697. *n.p.* [*1703?*], *s. sh. F°.* L.
Endorsed: Petition of Mrs. Mortimer, in relation to the Collection upon Briefs for Fire.

332 Begin: Anne, by the Grace of God.... *Lond. 1703, s. sh. F°.* O.
Letters patent authorising collections for the sufferers and bereaved in the storm of 26 & 27 November 1703. Dated: 23 December [1703].

333 Mr. William Fuller's Trip to Bridewell, with a true Account of his barbarous Usage in the Pillory. The Characters of the several People, who came to see him beat Hemp, and discours'd with him....Together with his Reception in the Queen's Bench. Written by his own Hand. *Lond. 1703, 8°.* L.

334 Trick upon Trick, being an Account of all the Cheats of both Prisons, the Queen's Bench, and Fleet, to their Creditors, during their Confinement, and in the Liberty of the Rules. Written by one that was a Prisoner in both Places. *Lond. 1703, 4°.* L.

335 Liste des Protestans Francois refugiez en Angleterre, qui étant dans le besoin, ont part a l'Assistance Charitable de Quinze mille Livres

Sterlings qui leur sont accordees tous les Ans dans ce Puissant & Heureux Royaume. Laquelle Liste est imprimee par Ordre des Seigneurs nommez par la Reine pour avoir Inspection sur la Distribution desdits quinze mille Livres Sterlings. *Londres*, [*1703*], *F°*. O.

336 A Historical and Law Treatise against the Jews and Judaism: shewing that by the Antient Establish'd Laws of the Land, no Jew hath any Right to Live in England, nor to appear without Yellow Badges upon his or her upper Garment...Together with a Computation of the two Arguments us'd by some for the Re-Admission of the Jews. *Lond. 1703*, *4°*, L.

The dedicatory epistle signed: B.B. Later editions are without this epistle. Another edn. 1720, entitled 'An Historical Treatise concerning Jews and Judaism, in England'; another ed., with original title, 1721; 2nd edn. 1753 (all L).

337 The Recorder's Letter of Advice to the Lord Mayor of London, January 14. 1702. [*Lond. 1703*], *F°*. LCRO.

On the lease of the London Bridge Waterworks. Signed: S. Lovell.

338 Edinburgh. Act Appointing a Company for quenching of Fire, and Rules to be observed by the Inhabitants thereanent. *Edin. 1703*, *s. sh. F°*. E.

Dated: 21 April 1703.

339 The Case of Michael Cole, Gent. Concerning the Lights of the City of Dublin. *n.p.* [*1703?*], *F°*. DA.

1704

GENERAL

340 DAVENANT, CHARLES. Essays upon Peace at Home, and War Abroad, In two parts. Part I. *Lond. 1704, 8°.* LU.

No more published.

341 Tom Double against Dr. D-v-n-t; or; the learned author of the Essays on Peace at Home and War Abroad, Consider'd, so far as his Past Actions Run Counter to his Present.... *Lond. 1704, 8°.* L.

2nd edn. 1704 (DA).

342 HARRIS, JOHN. Lexicon Technicum: or, an Universal English Dictionary of Arts and Sciences explaining not only the Terms of Art, but the Arts themselves. *Lond. 1704, 10, F°. 2 vols.* L.

2nd edn. of vol. 1, 1708 (L); 3rd, 1711 (K); 4th, 1725 (O); 2nd edn. of vol. 2, 1723 (L); 5th edn of both vols., 1736 (L); Supplement, 1744 (L).

343 PAXTON, PETER. A Discourse concerning the Nature, Advantage and Improvement of Trade: with Some Considerations why the Charges of the Poor do and will Increase. *Lond. 1704, 8°.* LU.

344 WHISTON, JAMES. England's State-Distempers, Trac'd from their Originals: With Proper Remedies and Means to make Her Vertuous and Prosperous....The Mismanagements in Trade Discovered, and adapt Methods to Preserve and Improve it....With an Appendix shewing the Decrease of Protestants in Europe. 2 pt. *Lond. 1704, 4°.* LU.

345 Dictionarium Rusticum & Urbanicum; or, a Dictionary of all Sorts of Country Affairs, Handicraft, Trading, and Merchandizing.... *Lond. 1704, 8°.* L.

2nd edn. 1717; 3rd 1726 (both L). Ascribed to Nathan Bailey and to John Worlidge, but I have not found any authority for either attribution, both of which are improbable.

346 An Essay concerning Inland and Foreign, Publick and Private Trade; together with some Overtures, shewing how a Company or National Trade, may be constituted in Scotland, with the Advantages which will result therefrom. *n.p.* [*1704*], *4°.* LU.

Signed: T.W., Philiopatris. Reprinted in *The Writings of William Paterson*, ed. by S. Bannister, 1858, II, liii–lix, where it is attributed to Paterson.

347 [SINCLAIR, Sir ARCHIBALD]. The State of the Nation enquir'd into, Shewing, The Necessity of Laying hold of the Present Opportunity, to Secure Our Laws and Liberty, from English Influence; and Procure a Free Trade with that Nation. [*Edin. 1704?*], *4°.* E.

Attribution of authorship in the Advocates' Library Catalogue.

AGRICULTURE

348 SMITH, J. Profit and pleasure united; or, The husbandman's magazine. Being a most exact treatise of bulls, oxen, cows....Together with

easie plain rules and methods for improving arable and pasture-lands....To which is added, the art of hawking, angling, and the noble recreation of ringing.... *Lond. 1704*, *15×3½ cm.* Kress 2441.

349 At a Court of Directors of the Governour and Company of the Mine-Adventurers of England, Held...on Thursday the 15th day of June, 1704. [*Lond. 1704*], *F°.* L.

Contains 'A Proposal for Advancing the Interest of the Company...by William Shiers, Secretary'.

350 [WALLER, WILLIAM]. A Description of the Mines in Cardiganshire. *n.p.* [*1704*], *8°.* L.

With maps. Another issue (L) has a preface signed by Waller in place of the title. It begins: Honour'd Sirs, It is not from the vanity of appearing in print.

351 A list of the names of the governour and company of the mine-adventurers of England. November the twenty-third, 1704. *Lond.* [*1704*], *35½ cm.* Kress 2430.

352 A Letter from a Gentleman in the City, to his Friend in the Country. [*Edin. 1704?*], *4°.* E.

Signed: Philergo's. On wool.

353 Act Anent Draining of Lochs, Marishes, &c. [*Edin. 1704*], *s. sh. F°.* EPRO.

354 Act for Repairing the Banks of Rivers, Waters and Burns, where they are in hazard of running out of their ordinary Channel. [*Edin. 1704*], *s. sh. F°.* EPRO.

355 A New Overture to Her Majesty's High Commissioner, and the Right Honourable Estates of Parliament, for passing the following Act, that Coals may be more plentiful and at easier Prices then they are at present in this Kingdom. [*Edin. 1704*], *s. sh. F°.* EPRO.

356 Draught of an Act Anent Coal and Salt. [*Edin. 1704*], *s. sh. F°.* EPRO.

Text begins: Our Sovereign Lady.

357 The Report of the Trustees for the Forfeited Estates of Ireland. That was delivered to the Queen and Parliament of England. Containing a Short Account of their Proceedings, from the beginning of their Commission, to the End thereof. *Dublin, 1704, 4°.* C.

358 A Letter from a Gentleman to the Trustees of the Irish Forfeitures. Which perhaps may be Worth the Perusal of some other Persons. *Lond. 1704, 4°.* L.

359 Proposals for Raising a Million of Money out of the Forfeited Estates in Ireland: Together, with the Answer of the Irish to the same, and a Reply thereto. *Dublin, reptd., 1704, 4°.* DA.

MANUFACTURES

360 The Case of the Berry and Bean Button-Makers, and Traders in Berry and Bean-Buttons, in and about the City of London. *n.p.* [*1704*], *s. sh. F°.* LLI.

361 The Case of the Horn-Button Makers in Sheffield, and within the Liberties of the Corporation of Handicrafts-men there. *n.p.* [*1704*], *s. sh. F°.* LG.

362 The Case of the Poor Button-Makers, Humbly Offer'd to the Honourable House of Commons. *n.p.* [*1704?*], *s. sh. F°.* LLI.

363 The Horn-Button Makers Reply, to the Answer to their Petition. *n.p.* [*1704?*], *s. sh. Fo.* L.

364 The Case of the Free Workmen-Printers, relating to the Bill for Preventing the Licentiousness of the Press. Humbly Offer'd to the Consideration of the Honourable House of Commons. *n.p.* [*1704*], *s. sh. F°.* L.

365 Reasons for an Act Intituled, An Act for the further Encouragement of the New Art, or Invention, of Working and Applying of Precious and more common Stones for the greater Perfection of Watches, Clocks, and other Engines. *n.p.* [*1704*], *F°.* L.

366 Reasons of the English Watch and Clockmakers against the Bill to confirm the Pretended New Invention of using Precious and Common Stones about Watches, Clocks, and other Engines. *n.p.* [*1704*], *F°.* L.

Endorsed: The English Clock and Watchmakers Reasons against the Frenchmens Bill.

367 Further Considerations for Encouraging the Woollen Manufactures of this Kingdom, Humbly Offer'd to the Lords and Commons in Parliament Assembled. *n.p.* [*1704?*], *s. sh. F°.* L.

368 Reasons Humbly Offered against Restraining the Using and Wearing of Printed Calicoes in England, Ireland, and the Plantations. *n.p.* [*1704?*], *s. sh. F°.* LLI.

Endorsed: The Case of the Callico Printers.

369 An Answer to the Reasons offered against Restraining the Use and Wearing of Printed Callicoes in England, Ireland, and the Plantations. *n.p.* [*1704?*], *s. sh. F°.* L.

370 The Case of the Wooll-Combers of London, and Parts Adjacent. Most Humbly Offer'd to the Honourable House of Commons. *n.p.* [*1704?*], *s. sh. F°.* L.

371 The Stuff Weaver's Case against Printing Callicoes Examined. *n.p.* [*1704*], *s. sh. F°.* L.

Endorsed: An Examination of the Weavers Case.

372 The Case of the Master Taylors, duly qualified in the Taylors Trade, within the Cities of London and Westminster, and the Burrough of Southwark, and Weekly Bills of Mortality; and within divers other Cities, Towns and Places within the Realm of England. *n.p.* [*1704?*], *s. sh. F°.* L.

For powers to prevent unqualified persons practising their trade.

373 Unto his Grace Her Majesties high Commissioner, and the honourable

Estates of Parliament. The Petition of the Manufactories of this Kingdom. [*Edin. 1704*], *s. sh. F°*. EPRO.

The ms. original in the Scottish Record Office is signed: Wm. Black.

374 Memorial to His Grace Her Majesties High Commissioner, and Estates of Parliament, from the Hat-makers of Edinburgh. [*Edin. 1704?*], *s. sh. F°*. EPRO.

Ends: 'during the space above-written'. For an act to prohibit the exportation of hare and rabbit skins and wool.

375 Information for James Watson, and other Printers in Edinburgh: against Agnes Campbel Relict of Andrew Anderson. *n.p.* [*1704?*], *F°*. O.

Followed by 'Errata of the New Testament Printed by Mrs. Anderson 1703, and presently sold in her shop'. An attack on the Bible monopoly.

376 Unto his Grace, John Marquess of Tweddale, &c. Her Majesty's High Commissioner, and Honourable Estates of Parliament. The Representation of the Merchants of Edinburgh. *n.p.* [*1704*], *s. sh. F°*. E.

For a total prohibition of the wearing of silk.

377 Answers humbly offered unto His Grace John Marquess of Tweeddale, &c. Her Majesty's High Commissioner, and Honourable Estates of Parliament, by the Masters of Silk Manufactories: To a Representation from the Retailing Merchants in Edinburgh. [*Edin. 1704*], *s. sh. F°*. E.

378 Unto his Grace John Marquess of Tweeddale, Her Majesty's high Commissioner, and to the Right Honourable the Estates of Parliament. The Petition of James Lyel of Gardin. [*Edin. 1704*], *s. sh. F°*. EPRO.

That his woollen manufactory may be declared a free manufactory.

379 CARY, JOHN. Some Considerations relating to the carrying on the Linnen Manufacture in the Kingdom of Ireland, by a Joint-Stock. *n.p.* [*1704*], *8°* pp. 14. L.

Another edn. [1704 ?], pp. 8 (L).

COMMERCE

380 The Case of the Booksellers and Printers, relating to the Patentees for the sole Printing all Books of the Common-Law. *n.p.* [*1704*], *s. sh. F°*. L.

381 Reasons humbly offered to the Honourable the House of Commons by the Traders in Books for the Better Securing of their Properties therein. *n.p.* [*1704?*], *s. sh. F°*. L.

382 The Wine Merchants Proposals, for preventing Sophisticating and Vitiating Wines, &c. Humbly Offer'd to the Honourable House of Commons. *n.p.* [*1704?*], *s. sh. F°*. L.

383 LONDON. Comune Concil' ten't' in Camera Guihald' [*Lond.*] *1703*, *s. sh. F°*. L.

An order fixing the hours of business at the Royal Exchange, dated 16 March 1703 [O.S.].

384 EDINBURGH. Act anent Landlords Setting of Shops and Cellars, &c. *Edin. 1704, s. sh. F°.* EU.

Dated: 22 March 1704.

385 The Case of Prohibitions and Correspondence with our Enemies, Truly Represented. Distinguishing in what Instances they may be Profitable, and in what Injurious to the Nation; and proving that they ought never to be rigorously observ'd. In a Letter to a Member of the Honourable House of Commons. *n.p. [1704?], F°.* LLI.

386 Reasons for Leave to Import Tarr, otherwise than from the Places of the Growth. *n.p. [1704?], s. sh. F°.* L.

387 The Case of Sir Alexander Rigby, and William Shepard, Complainants, as to Their Particular Damages by the Great Duke of Tuscany's Proceedings, in the Seizure of William Plowman, and of their Effects. *Lond. 1704, F°.* O.

For an earlier statement see no. 47.

388 The Case of the Owners of the John-Galley, and her Prize. Being an Article comprehended in the Account of Damages suffer'd by the Proceedings of the Great Duke of Tuscany, Complain'd of by Sir Alexander Rigby, William Shepard, and William Plowman. *Lond. 1704, F°.* O.

389 The Case of the Ship Charles. Being an Article comprehended in the Account of Damages suffer'd by the Proceedings of the Great Duke of Tuscany, Complained of by Sir Alexander Rigby, William Shepard, and William Plowman. *Lond. 1704, F°.* O.

390 The Answer of the Merchants-Petitioners, and Trustees for the Factory at Legorn, to the Account of Damages, laid to the Charge of the Great Duke of Toscany, by Sir Alexander Rigby, Mr. Will. Shepard, and Mr. Will. Plowman: Together with their Reply, and the Merchants-Petitioners Second Answer thereto. As also Divers Original Papers and Proofs; Deliver'd in Writing to Sir John Cooke, Judge Advocate, and John Pollexfen, Esq;...With several other Matters and Papers since come to Hand from Legorn. *Lond. 1704, F°.* LU.

391 An humble apology to the Queen on behalf of the merchants-petitioners and trustees for the factory at Leghorn, for printing their cases. *Lond. 1704, 32 cm.* Kress S. 1116.

392 At a General Court of the Adventurers of the Royal African Company of England, held...the 1st Day of June, 1704. *n.p. [1704], s. sh. F°.* L.

Notice of a call of £7 per share.

393 The Royal African Company of England, Appellants. William Dockwra, and Roger Langdon and Phillis his Wife, Administratix of Richard Dickenson, Respondents. The Case of the Appellants, etc. *n.p. [1704], s. sh. F°.* L.

Signed: J. D'arnal.

394 A List of the Names of the Directors for the English Company Trading to the East-Indies, Elected the 11th of April, 1704. for the Year ensuing. *n.p.* [*1704*], *s. sh.* *4°*. O.

395 Remarks on the Accounts relating to the East-India Trade. *n.p.* [*1704*], *s. sh.* *F°*. L.

Title from endorsement. The accounts were those laid before the House of Commons on 13 January 1704.

396 A Speech without Doors, which would be spoken within Doors, if the Author had the Honour to be a Member of this House of Commons, and therein to Offer his Sense of the Bill for the more Effectual Encouragement of the Manufactures of England, and Setting the Poor at Work. *n.p.* [*1704*], *F°*. L.

Endorsed: A Speech concerning the Manufactury-Bill, &c. Defends the two East India Companies.

397 The Case of the Separate Traders to the East-Indies, which are not in the Joint-Stock. *n.p.* [*1704*], *s. sh.* F°. L.

Against the bill to restrain the exportation of gold and silver.

398 Churchill, Awnsham and Churchill, John. A Collection of Voyages and Travels, some now first Printed from Original Manuscripts. Others Translated out of Foreign Languages, and now first Publish'd in English....In Four Volumes. With a General Preface, giving an Account of the Progress of Navigation, from its first Beginning to the Perfection it is now in, &c..... *Lond.* *1704*, *F°*. L.

Published by J. & A. Churchill, who are clearly the editors. Another edn. 1732, when 2 further volumes were added (L). 3rd edn. 1744–6 (L). In 1747 the 2 volumes of *A Collection of Voyages and Travels... Compiled from the... library of the late Earl of Oxford* were reissued as vol. 7, 8 of this collection. Another edn. 1752 (L).

399 The Humble Representations, or Addresses, of the Right Honourable the Lords Spiritual and Temporal in Parliament Assembled, presented to Her Majesty on Friday the Thirty first Day of March, 1704. And Her Majesties most gracious Answer thereunto. *Lond.* *1704*, *F°*. L.

On abuses in victualling the Navy, West India convoys, etc. Another edn. Dublin, 1704, 4° (DNL).

400 A Proposal to Encourage and Encrease the Number of Seamen, Humbly Offered as an Expedient, I. To Save the Lives of many of them. II. To Secure the Profit of their Voyage from the great Discouragement they labour under by the Remiss Account of Sea-Damages Extraordinary. III. To Encourage Landmen to betake themselves to the Sea-Service.... *n.p.* [*c.* *1704?*], *s. sh.* *F°*. L.

Title from endorsement. To ensure seaworthiness by the compulsory keeping of logs open to inspection.

401 Answers humbly offered to His Grace, Her Majesty's High Commissioner, and the Honourable Estates of Parliament. To the Memorial given in by the Merchant Retailers in Edinburgh, with relation to the Laws anent Trade. [*Edin.* *1704*], *F°*. EPRO.

402 Scotland's Interest: or, The Great Benefit and Necessity of a Communication of Trade with England. Being a Brief Account of the Chief Motives, that ought to engage us to insist on it, at this Juncture: And of the Danger of Neglecting so to do. Humbly offered to the Consideration of the High Court of Parliament. *n.p. 1704, 4°.* LU.

The attribution to Andrew Fletcher recorded in the Catalogue of the Advocates' Library, is rejected by R. A. Scott Macfie in his *Bibliography of Andrew Fletcher of Saltoun*, 1901, p. 139 (*Publications of the Edinburgh Bibliographical Society*, vol. 4).

403 Additional Reasons against the Exportation of Wooll. [*Edin. 1704?*], *F°.* E.

404 A Letter to a Member of Parliament, concerning Manufacture and Trade. *n.p. 1704, 4°.* LU.

A Scottish tract, proposing an export duty on wool.

405 A Speech Without Doors concerning Exportation of Wool. [*Edin.*] *1704, 4°.* LU.

406 [Mackenzie, George, Earl of Cromarty]. A Speech in Parliament, concerning Exportation of Wool. By E. C. 22d. August, 1704. [*Edin.*] *1704, 4°.* E.

For authorship see Advocates' Library Catalogue.

407 Act Against Molosses. [*Edin. 1704*], *F°.* E.

408 Act for providing Arms for the Fencible Men. [*Edin. 1704*], *s. sh. F°.* EPRO.

Importation from Holland.

409 To His Grace John Marquess of Tweeddale, Her Majesty's High Commissioner, and the Right Honourable Estates of Parliament. The Petition of the Court of Directors of the Company of Scotland, Trading to Africa and the Indies. *n.p.* [*1704*], *F°.* E.

Followed by 'The Case of the Company of Scotland Trading to Africa and the Indies, with Relation to their two Ships, The Speedwell and The Annandale, with their Respective Cargo's'.

410 The Case of the Ship Annandale, Belonging to the Company of Scotland, Trading to Affrica and the Indies. *n.p.* [*1704*], *s. sh. F°.* O.

411 An Abstract of the Acts of Parliaments of the Kingdoms of England and Scotland, for Establishing the East-India Companies of each respective Kingdom; and Observations thereupon, in relation to the Case of the Ships Annandale and Speedwell. *n.p.* [*1704?*], *s. sh. F°.* MC.

COLONIES

412 By the Queen A Proclamation, For Settling and Ascertaining the Current Rates of Foreign Coins in Her Majesties Colonies and Plantations in America. *Lond. 1704, F°.* L.

Dated: 18 June 1704.

FINANCE

413 The Case of Francis Robinson, Esq; Provost-Martial General of Her Majesty's Forces. *n.p.* [*1704*], *s. sh. F°.* L.

The endorsement adds 'As to 522 1. 9d. Due to him for Subsisting the French Prisoners in the Years 1695. 1696, and 1697.'

414 The Case of the Officers, Victuallers and Clothiers of the Four Companies of New-York. *n.p.* [*1704*], *s. sh. F°.* L.

For payment.

415 The Deplorable Case of the Officers, Soldiers, and Clothiers, Proprietors of the Army and Transport Debentures. *n.p.* [*1704*], *s. sh. F°.* L.

416 Reasons offered to the Consideration of the Honourable House of Commons, relating to the Bill now depending for Laying an Additional Duty on all Commodities imported, as far as it relates to the Trade of Virginia and Maryland. *n.p.* [*1704?*], *s. sh. F°.* L.

417 Some Reasons Humbly Offer'd to the Honourable House of Commons, against Laying a farther Duty upon Wines in the Retailers Hands. *n.p.* [*1704?*], *s. sh. F°.* L.

418 To the Honourable House of Commons. The Case of the Gentlemen, Freeholders, and Inhabitants in the Parts of Holland in the County of Lincoln. *n.p.* [*1704*], *s. sh. F°.* LLI.

Against paying any of the county's deficiency in the land-tax.

419 Sir Michael Biddulph's Case. *n.p.* [*1704*], *s. sh. F°.* LLI.

As surety for Morgan Whitley, the defaulting Receiver of Taxes for Chester and North Wales.

420 The Report of the Lords Committees appointed to take into Consideration the Report of the Commissioners appointed by Act of Parliament, Anno 1. Annae Reginae, For Taking, Examining, and Stating the Publick Accompts of the Kingdom; so far as relates to the Accompts of the Right Honourable Edward Earl of Orford, late Treasurer of the Navy. *Lond. 1704*, *F°.* L.

421 The Answers of the Earl of Orford (late Treasurer of the Navy) to the Observations made by the Honourable Commissioners of Accompts upon his Accompts of the Navy; exclusive of the Victualling. Delivered at the Bar of the House of Peers, February 10. 1703. With the Reply of the Commissioners of Accompts. *Lond. 1704*, *F°.* LU.

422 To the Lords and Commons, in Parliament Assembled, is Humbly Offered an Account of some Few of the Many Sufferings of the People call'd Quakers, by the several Methods of Sequestrations, Excommunications, &c. *Lond. 1704*, *4°.* L.

Reissued in 1705, with a slightly different title-page reading: To the Lords... an Account of some Few of the Many Severe Sufferings of the People call'd Quakers, for Tythes (L).

423 LONDON. Commune Concil' tent' in Camera Guihald'....An Act to prevent the further declining State of the City of London. [*Lond.*], *1703*. *F°*. LG.

Suppressing sinecures.

424 A Timely Caveat of the Inferiour Clergy of Ireland, against a Bill Entituled, An Act for Purchasing Glebes, &c. *Lond. 1704*, *4°*. DA.

425 Reasons, humbly offered, for Encreasing the Number of Brokers. *n.p.* [*1704*], *s. sh. F°*. LLI.

426 Reasons, humbly offered, for Passing the Bill to Encrease the Number of Brokers. *n.p.* [*1704*], *s. sh. F°*. LLI.

427 Reasons Humbly Offered against continuing an Act for limiting the Number of Brokers in the City of London. *n.p.* [*1704?*], *s. sh. F°*. MC.

Endorsed: Reasons Against Limiting the Number of Brokers.

428 [RICARD, SAMUEL]. A General Treatise of the Reduction of Exchanges, Money and Real Species of most Places in Europe, in Two Exact Tables...Newly Published at Amsterdam...and now made English. By a Well-Wisher to Trade. *Lond. 1704*, *8°*. LU.

The translator's introduction signed: A.J., i.e. Alexander Justice. For authorship see Justice's preface to his *General Treatise of Monies and Exchanges*, 1707.

429 HAWKINS, JOHN. Clavis Commercii: or, the Key of Commerce: shewing, the True Method of keeping Merchants Books, after the Italian Manner of Debtor and Creditor. By J.H. of London, Merchant. The Second Edition. Corrected and Amended by John Rayner. *Lond. 1704*, *4°*. LICA.

First published in 1689.

430 A Speech Without Doors anent the giving a Subsidy before the passing an Act of Security, &c. [*Edin.*], *1704*, *4°*. E.

431 Proclamation Anent the Excise. *Edin. 1704*, *s. sh. F°*. E.

Dated: 28 April 1704.

432 Unto his Grace John Marquess of Tweeddale, Her Majesties High Commissioner, and the Honourable Estates of Parliament, The Report of the Commissioners Appointed for Stating and Examining the Publick Accompts. *Edin. 1704*, *F°*. M (Cr).

Exami-/ning in title. Another edn., with Examining/ Edin. 1704, F° (M (Cr)). Drawn up by Sir John Clerk. See his *Memoirs*, 1892, p. 53.

433 Overture for an Act Anent Misapplying the Funds. [*Edin. 1704*], *s. sh. F°*. EPRO.

434 Representation From a Friend in the Countrey, to the honourable Members of Parliament, anent the several Abuses, and exorbitant Exactions made upon Her Majesties Subjects, by the Deputs and Servants in Publick Offices.... [*Edin. 1704*], *s. sh. F°*. E.

435 A Letter from a Countrey Gentleman to his Writer in Edinburgh, anent the exorbitant Exactions of Dues within the Publick Offices within

this Kingdom; Omitted in the former Representation relating thereto and hereto subjoyned. *n.p.* [*1704*], *4°*. E.

436 *Begin.* Our Sovereign Lady, and Estates of Parliament. [*Edin. 1704*], *s. sh. F°*. EPRO.

Overture of an act to give Musselburgh the right to levy 2d a pint on ale to pay for building a harbour.

437 Proclamation Discharging the Export of Money. *Edin. 1704, s. sh. F°*. E.

Dated: 3 May 1704.

438 A Letter to a Member of Parliament, from a wel-wisher of his Country, in relation to Coin. [*Edin. 1704*], *4°*. L.

439 A List of the Names of the Adventurers in the Bank of Scotland, February 4. 1704. *Edin. 1704, s. sh. F°*. LU.

440 Memorial and Intimation from the Governour and Company of the Bank of Scotland, concerning the present State thereof. *n.p.* [*1704*], *s. sh. F°*. E.

Reprinted in C. W. Boase, *A Century of Banking in Dundee*, 1867.

441 [Armour, James]. Overture for Establishing a Land Bank Office, whereby the Nation may be Rendered Rich and Happie....By an true-Hearted Scots-Man, and lover of his Country. [*Edin. 1704*], *s. sh. F°*. EPRO.

Authorship deduced from internal evidence.

TRANSPORT

442 Robinson, Arthur. Reasons for making a Mould or Harbour in Tor-bay. Humbly Submitted to the Consideration of both Houses of Parliament. *n.p.* [*1704?*], *s. sh. Fo.* L.

443 Act in favours of William Baird of Auchmedden. *Edin. 1704, s. sh. F°*. ES.

Dated: 20 September 1703. Granting him a voluntary collection for building a harbour at Pennan.

444 Reasons Humbly offer'd by the Fellowship of Carrmen, to the Right Honourable the Lord Mayor, Aldermen and Commons of the City of London, for Turn-keeping at the several Wharfs and Keys of the said City. *n.p.* [*1704?*]. *s. sh. F°*. LG.

Endorsed: Fellowship of Carrmen Their Reasons for Turn-keeping.

SOCIAL CONDITIONS

445 A Bill for the Better Relief, Employment, and Settlement of the Poor, as the same was Reported from the Committee to the Honourable House of Commons; in order that (by Reason of the great Importance and Universal Concern of the said Bill) the same be farther Consider'd against the next Session of Parliament. *Lond. 1704, F°*. L.

'Printed by the Directions of Sir Humphrey Mackworth.'

446 [DEFOE, DANIEL]. Giving Alms no Charity, and Employing the Poor a Grievance to the Nation, Being an Essay upon this Great Question, Whether Work-houses, Corporations and Houses of Correction for Employing the Poor as now practis'd in England; or Parish-Stocks, as propos'd in a late Pamphlet, Entituled, A Bill for the better Relief, Imployment and Settlement of the Poor, &c. Are not mischievous to the Nation, tending to the Destruction of our Trade, and to Encrease the Number and Misery of the Poor.... *Lond. 1704, 4º.* LU.

Reprinted in *A Select Collection of Scarce and Valuable Economical Tracts,* ed. by J. R. McCulloch 1859, p. 27. For authorship see *C.B.E.L.* II, 498.

447 A True Account of the Foundation, State, and Design of the Work-House for the Poor of the City of London. Christmas, 1704. Now Published for the Promoting of Charitable Gifts and Legacies thereto. *Lond. 1704, Fº.* LG.

448 Her Majesty's Commission for Greenwich Hospital, for Seamen. April 8. 1704. *n.p. [1704], 4º.* L.

449 PITT, ROBERT. The Antidote: or, the Preservative of Health and Life, and the Restorative of Physick to its Sincerity and Perfection.... *Lond. 1704, 8º.* L.

450 The Censor Censur'd; or the Antidote Examin'd. Wherein the Designs of Dr. Pitt, and the Dispensary Physicians are Detected. *Lond. 1704, 8º.* L.

451 The Case of the College of Physicians London, wherein they are Defendants, in a Writ of Error returnable in Parliament, brought by one William Rose an Apothecary in London, on a Judgment obtained against him by the College in Her Majesty's Court of Queen's Bench, for practising Physick within Seven Miles of London without Licence. *n.p. [1704], Fº.* L.

452 Observations upon the Case of William Rose, an Apothecary, as represented by him to the Most Honourable the House of Lords, upon his bringing the Case before the said House by a Writ of Error, in order to have the Judgment obtain'd against him by the College of Physicians, in the Queen's-Bench, Reversed. *Lond. 1704, 4º.* L.

Another edn. 1704, 8º (O), entitled: William Rose the Apothecary's Case consider'd....

453 Reasons why the Apothecary may be suppos'd to Understand the Administration of Medicines in the Cure of Diseases, as well as the Physician. In a Letter from an Apothecary to a Physician. *Lond. 1704, 8º.* L.

454 Tentamen Medicinale: or, an Enquiry into the Differences between the Dispensarians and Apothecarys. Wherein the latter are prov'd capable of a Skilful Composition of Medicines, and a Rational Practice of Physick. To which are added, Some Proposals to prevent their Future Increase. By an Apothecary. *Lond. 1704, 8º.* L.

455 The Case of the Poor Distressed Widdows, and Orphan Children, whose Husbands, and Fathers, belonged to Her Majesties late Ship the Colchester. *n.p.* [*1704*], *s. sh. F°.* LLI.

456 Reasons Humbly offered to the Parliament Assembled, For the further Relief of Poor Prisoners, who lie confined for Debt and Damages. *n.p.* [*c. 1704?*], *s. sh. F°.* L.

Endorsed: Reasons for the Relief of Debtors. And to Raise Soldiers to Serve Her Majesty.

457 Reasons Humbly Offered, for Passing the Bill for discharging of Insolvent Debtors, upon Listing themselves, or finding others for Soldiers or Seamen in Her Majesties Service. *n.p.* [*1704?*], *s. sh. F°.* O.

458 Several Queries relating to an Act of Parliament made in the Second and Third Years of Her most Sacred Majesty's Reign, entituled, An Act for the Discharge out of Prison such Insolvent Debtors as shall Serve, or procure a Person to Serve in Her Majesty's Fleet or Army. Sent in a Letter, by a Gentleman in the Country to his Friend, a Counsellor at Law in London. With his Answer thereto, and Opinion thereon. *Lond. 1704, 4°.* L.

The letter signed: C.C.; the answer signed: E.G.

459 A Glimpse of Hell: or a short Description, of the Common Side of Newgate. *Lond. 1705* [*1704*], *4°.* O.

Signed: T.H. The corrected date is taken from Luttrell's ms. note.

460 Kennett, White. The Case of Impropriations, and of the Augmentation of Vicarages and other Insufficient Cures, stated by History and Law, from the First Usurpation of Popes and Monks, to Her Majesty's Royal Bounty lately extended to the poorer Clergy of the Church of England. With an Appendix of Records and Memorials relating to that Subject. *Lond. 1704, 8°.* O.

461 By the Queen, A Proclamation, For the Careful Custody and well Ordering of the New River brought from Chadwell and Amwell to the North Part of the City of London. *Lond. 1703* [*O.S.*], *F°.* L.

Dated: 15 February 1703.

462 Unto His Grace John Marquess of Tweedale her Majesty's High Commissioner, and the Right Honourable the Lords and Remanent Members of the High Court of Parliament. The Humble Petition of the Gentlemen, and others concerned in the Invaleid Fond. [*Edin. 1704*], *s. sh. F°.* EPRO.

463 Act for a Voluntar Contribution, In Favours of John Thomson younger, under Slavery in Algier. *Edin. 1704. s. sh. F°.* ES.

Dated: 28 December 1703.

1705

GENERAL

464 POVEY, CHARLES. The General Remark on Trade. *Lond. 1705–8, F°.* L.
The L file is a broken one. O has no. 430, 1 Dec. 1708.

465 PAXTON, PETER. A Scheme of Union between England and Scotland, with Advantages to both Kingdoms. *Lond. 1705, 8°.* LU.
Signed: P. Paxton. Another edn. Edin. 1705, 8° (LU).

466 [SPREULL, JOHN]. An Accompt Current betwixt Scotland and England Ballanced. *n.p. [1705], 4°.* LU.
Signed: By a True Well-wisher to Our Protestant Queen, Country, and Trade. Dated: July 25. 1705. A revised edn., with author's name, follows this entry.

467 SPREULL, JOHN. An Accompt Current betwixt Scotland & England ballanced: togeter with An Essay of a Scheme of the Product of Scotland, and a few Remarks on each. As also a View of the several Products of the Ports or Nations we Trade to, by Comparing and holding forth how our Products and Manufactures may Ballance theirs, with Returns. By J. S. A Lover of our protestant Queen, Countrey, and Trade. *Edin. 1705, 4°.* L.
The dedication signed: John Spruel. A revised edition of the preceding. Reprinted in *Miscellaneous Writing of John Spreull*, Glasgow, 1882.

468 A Dialogue between a Country-Man, and a Landwart School-Master, concerning the Proceedings of the Parliament of England, in Relation to Scots Affairs, &c. *Edin. 1705, 4°.* E.
[continued as:]
Observator or a Dialogue between a Country-Man, & a Landwart School-Master, no. 2–9. 6 April–23 July 1705. *Edin. 1705, 4°.* E.

469 Great Britain's Union, and the Security of the Hanover Succession, consider'd. In a Letter from Windsor of the 30th of December, 1704. to a Member of Parliament in London. By a Person of Quality. *Lond. 1705, 4°.* pp. 20. LU.
Another edn., 1705, pp. 22 (LU).

470 The Occasion of Scotland's Decay in Trade, with a proper Expedient for Recovery thereof, and the Increase of our Wealth. *n.p. 1705, 4°.* LU.
Reprinted in *The Writing of William Paterson*, ed. by S. Bannister, 1858, II, xlvii–lii, where it is attributed to Paterson.

471 [RIDPATH, GEORGE]. The Reducing of Scotland by Arms, And Annexing it to England as a Province, considered. With an Historical Account of the Grievances the Scots complain they have suffer'd in their Religion, Liberty, and Trade, since the Union of the Crowns.... *Lond. 1705, 4°.* LU.
Another edn. Edin. 1705 (E). For authorship see W. Atwood, *The Scotch Patriot Unmask'd*, 1705.

472 ATWOOD, WILLIAM. The Scotch Patriot Unmask'd, in Animadversions upon a Seditious Pamphlet, intituled, The Reducing Scotland by Arms, and Annexing it to England as a Province, considered. *Lond. 1705*, 4°. L.

473 A Speech intended to have been spoken in Parliament by a Member who was necessarily absent. [*Edin. 1705*], 4°. LU.

Urges a Commission for a Treaty of Union with England pursuant to the Queen's Letter to Parliament.

474 Representation of the present Condition and State of the City of Glasgow, and of the Hardship done them by the late Augmentation of their Quota of the Taxt-roll of the Royal Burrows. *n.p.* [*1705?*], *s. sh. F°*. E.

AGRICULTURE

475 KILLIGREW, WILLIAM. The Property of all English-Men Asserted, in the History of Lindsey Levell.... *Lond. 1705*, *F°*. L.

476 The Game Law: or, A Collection of the Laws and Statutes made for the Preservation of the Game of this Kingdom.... *Lond. 1705*, *12°*. LU.

2nd edn. 1707 (L); 4th edn. 1711 (Kress 2720); 5th edn. 1714 (O). The Game Law. Part II. Being an Explanation of the Acts of Parliament, recited in the First Part.... In the Savoy, 1712, 12° (O); 2nd edn. 1718 (L).

477 The Case of Sir Humphry Mackworth, and of the Mine-Adventurers, with respect to the Irregular Proceedings of several Justices of the Peace for the County of Glamorgan, and of their Agents and Dependents. *Lond. 1705*, 4°. pp. 15. LU.

Another edn., slightly enlarged, 1705, 4° pp. 16 (O).

478 Affidavits, Certificates, and Presentments; proving the Facts mentioned in the Case of Sir Humphry Mackworth, and the Mine-Adventurers with respect to the Irregular Proceedings of several Justices of the Peace for the County of Glamorgan.... *Lond. 1705*, 4°. L.

479 HORNE, THOMAS. An Account of the Clear Profits of Extracting Silver out of Lead: by the Governour and Company of the Mine-Adventurers of England, taken from the Original Accounts by which their Officers charge themselves. By Tho. Horne, Accomptant to the Company. *Lond. 1705*, *F°*. L.

480 SHIERS, WILLIAM. A Familiar Discourse or Dialogue concerning the Mine-Adventure. *Lond. 1705*, 8°. L.

A different work from those of the same title published in 1700 and 1709.

481 Overture for an Act for Preserving the Game. [*Edin. 1705*], *s. sh. F°*. E.

482 Act Dissolving Royal Mines from the Crown. [*Edin. 1705*], *s. sh. F°*. LU.

An overture.

483 Overture of an Act anent Herring and White-fishing. [*Edin. 1705*], *s. sh. F°*. E.

484 Act for Advancing and Establishing the Fishing Trade in and about this Kingdom. [*Edin. 1705*], *s. sh. F°.* EPRO.
An overture.

485 A list of names of the members of the corporation for making hollow sword-blades in England, concerned in the joint-stock, for purchasing forfeited estates in Ireland, &c. The twenty seventh day of September, 1705.... *n.p.* [*1705*], *37 cm.* Kress S. 1135.

486 An estimate of the value of the present stock of the Governor and company for making hollow-sword-blades in England, the capital whereof is...l. 403400.... *n.p.* [*1705*], *37 cm.* Kress S. 1134.

MANUFACTURES

487 Lammas, John and Everard, Edmond. To the Queen and Parliament. A Seasonable Remedy to prevent for ever the several Frauds that have been lately discovered, relating to the Fleet-Beer, and other Provisions, by the Proposal of a wholesomer, cheaper, stronger, unchangeable Beer, brewed after a more succint and less cumbersome Way, and drawn from a clear Malt-Extract. *n.p.* [*c. 1705?*], *F°.* L.

488 The Whole Art of Dying. In Two Parts. The First being an Experimental Discovery of all the most useful Secrets in Dying Silk, Wool, Linnen and the Manufactures thereof....Written Originally in the German Language. The Second Part is a General Instruction for the Dying of Wools and Woollen Manufactures of all Colours....Published by the especial Command of the French King in that Language, and Illustrated with several Philosophical and Practical Annotations by the German Translator. Both which are Faithfully rendred into English from their Respective Originals. *Lond. 1705*, *8°.* LU.

489 An Abstract of the Charter, granted by their late Majesties, King William and Queen Mary, in the Fifth Year of their Reign, to the Governor and Company for making Iron with Pit Coal. *n.p.* [*c. 1705?*], *s. sh. F°.* L.

490 The Case of the Manufacturers of English Pantiles. *n.p.* [*c. 1705?*], *s. sh. F°.* L.

491 Reasons for the Bill for the better Breeding of Experienced, Able Shipwrights, and for more Firm and Well Building of Ships and Vessels. *n.p.* [*1705?*], *F°.* L.

492 To his Grace, Her Majesties high Commissioner, and the right honourable, the Estates of Parliament, The Representation of John Hay, Evan Mackgrigor, and Partners in the Card Manufacturie; In Answer to a Nameless Memorial Addressed to his Grace, and the said Estates, Against the said Manufacturie. [*Edin. 1705*], *s. sh. F°.* EPRO.

493 Act of the Council of Trade, Anent the Right Making and Measuring of

Linen Cloath, and Discharging the Exportation of Lint and Linen Yarn, &c. *Edin. 1706*, *F°*. L.

Dated: 28 December 1705.

494 Reasons for passing in Parliament the Act already past in the Committee of Trade, in favours of the Skinners. [*Edin. 1705*], *s. sh. F°*. EPRO.

495 Representation unto his Grace Her Majesties high Commissioner, and Honourable Members of Parliament, For the Tanners of Edinburgh, for themselves, and in name and behalf of the whole Tanners in Scotland. [*Edin. 1705*], *s. sh. F°*. E.

For the prohibition of the import of leather.

496 To his Grace Her Majesties High Commissioner, and the Right Honourable the states of Parliament, The Petition of Sir Robert Adair of Kilhilt. [*Edin. 1705*], *s. sh. F°*. EPRO.

For privileges for his invention of an engine for raising water and distributing it.

497 CROMMELIN, LOUIS. An Essay Towards the Improving of the Hempen and Flaxen Manufactures in the Kingdom of Ireland. *Dublin, 1705*, *4°*. LU.

Another edn. Dublin, 1734 (DA).

COMMERCE

498 Proctor's Price-Courant. no. 588. 7 Jan. 1705. *n.p. 1705*, *F°*. LU (photostat).

499 JUSTICE, ALEXANDER. A General Treatise of the Dominion and Laws of the Sea. Containing what is most Valuable upon that Subject, in Ancient and Modern Authors....Together with Several Discourses about the Jurisdiction and Manner of Proceeding in the Admiralty of England....In all which are explain'd at Large the Laws and Customs of Merchants, and of the Courts in Cases of Bottomry, Insurances, Charter-Parties, Bills of Lading, and of Piracy, and Letters of Marque and Reprisal. To which is subjoyn'd; An Appendix concerning the Present State and Regulations of the Admiralty and Navy, and Means for improving it, and a Proposal for the more easy and expeditious Manning of the Fleet without Pressing.... *Lond. 1705*, *4°*. LU.

The dedication signed: Alexander Justice. 2nd edn., anonymous, [1708 or 1709] (O); 3rd edn., anonymous, [c. 1720 ?] (L); another 3rd edn., anonymous, 1724 (WLC).

500 [DEFOE, DANIEL ?]. A Hint to the Blackwell-Hall Factors: being the True State of the Case between Mr. Samuel Wetherhead, Blackwell-Hall Factor, and Mr. John Hellier, Merchant. *Lond. 1705*, *4°*. O.

Attribution by Professor J. R. Moore. On a dispute about payment for cloth.

501 LONDON. Buckingham Mayor, Martis, Vicesimo tertio die Octobis, 1705. [*Lond.*], *1705*, *s. sh. F°*. LG.

An order that coal-meters, corn-meters, salt-meters, & fruit-meters in London are not to measure or allow to be carried away any goods without warrant from the Lord Mayor or his deputy.

502 The Case of Capt. Tho. Green, Commander of the Ship Worcester, and his Crew, Tried and Condemned for Pyracy and Murther, in the High Court of Admiralty of Scotland. *Lond. 1705*, 4°. L.

503 The English Ointment for the Scotch Mange: or, A Short Memorandum of the Scots Cruelty to Captain Thomas Green, &c. *Lond.* [*1705*], *s. sh. F°.* L.

504 Information for Captain Thomas Green Commander of the Worcester, Captain John Madder his chief Mate, and others, against Mr. Alexander Higgins Advocat, Procurator-Fiscal of the High Court of Admiralty. *n.p.* [*1705*], *F°.* E.

505 Information for Mr. Alexander Higgins Procurator-Fiscal for the High Court of Admiralty, against Captain Thomas Green Commander of the Worcester, and his Crew and Complices. *n.p.* [*1705*], *F°.* E.

506 The Innocency of Capt. Green, and his Crew, Vindicated, from the Murther of Capt. Drummond. Published by Order of the Owners of the Ship Worcester. *Lond. 1705, s. sh. F°* L.

507 The Last Speeches and Dying Words of Captain Thomas Green, Commander of the Ship the Worcester, and of Captain John Madder, Chief Mate of the said Ship.... *Edin. 1705*, 4°. E.

Another edn., Re-Printed at London, [1705], s.sh. F° (L); another edn. entitled The Last Speech and Dying Words.... [Lond. 1705], s. sh. F° (L).

508 Some Cursory Remarks on a Late Printed Paper, called, The last Speeches and Dying-Words of Captain Thomas Green, Commander of the Ship Worcester; and of Captain John Madder, chief Mate of the said Ship, &c.... *Edin. 1705, F°.* L.

509 [Defoe, Daniel ?]. A Letter from Scotland, to a Friend in London: containing a particular Narrative of the Whole Proceedings against the Worcester and her Crew, from her first Arrival in Leith-Road to the 20th of April 1705.... *Lond. 1705*, 4°. L.

Tentative attribution by Professor J. R. Moore.

510 [Menzies, John]. Observations on the Tryal of Capt. Green, and the Speech at his Death, *Lond. 1705, s. sh. F°.* L.

Another edn., entitled: Observations made in England, on the Trial of Captain Green, and the Speech at his Death, Edin. 1705, 4° (L). For authorship see Advocates' Library Catalogue.

511 The Petition of the Scots East-India and African Company, for Reprisal of the Ship Worcester (Tho. Green commander) from East-India, now seized in Scotland, by said Company, for Reprisal of the Ship Annandale, seized in England, by the English East-India Company. *Lond. 1705, F°.* L.

512 Remarks upon the Tryal of Capt. Thomas Green and his Crew.... *Lond. 1705, F°.* L.

513 The Tryal of Captain Thomas Green and his Crew, Pursued before the

Judge of the High Court of Admiralty of Scotland; and the Assessors appointed by the Lords of Privy Council...for Piracy, Robbery, & Murder....Published by Authority. *Edin. 1705. F°.* E.

Another edn. Lond. 1705 (L).

514 A True and Impartial Account of the Proceedings against Capt Green and his Crew, together with the Confessions of severals of them under Sentence of Death. *n.p.* [*1705*], *s. sh. F°.* E.

515 A Vindication of the false Aspersions laid against the Judges of Admiralty in Scotland by Green's Associats in England. *Edin. 1705, s. sh. F°.* E.

516 The Case of several Merchants Trading to Ireland, as well as the Poor Linnen-Weavers in the said Kingdom. *n.p.* [*c. 1705?*], *s. sh. F°.* MC.

517 The Case of Tho. Cary and George Hatley of London, Merchants. *n.p.* [*1705*]. *s. sh. F°.* L.

Endorsed: The Case of Tho. Cary & Geo. Hatley, relating to Their French Wine at Copenhagen.

518 Reponce donnée par l'Envoyé Extraordinaire, & le Commissaire du Commerce, de Sa Majesté Imperiale, sur le Papier qui leur a été Communique par Mons. Harley, Secretaire d'Etat, de la part du Conseil du Commerce de Sa Majesté Britannique, sur le Projet de donner passage au Commerce, que les Sujets de Sa Majeste Britannique font avec le Levant, par la Commodité des Rivieres d'Allemagne & Hongrie. *n.p.* [*1705*], *F°.* O.

Dated: Londres, ce 4/15 Nov. 1705. French and English in parallel columns, the English title beginning: The Answers of the Envoy Extraordinary, and the Commissioner for Trade of his Imperial Majesty.

519 The Case of the Levant-Company, relating to the Importation of Turky Goods from the Neutral Ports in Italy. *n.p.* [*1705?*], *s. sh. F°.* L.

520 Bosman, Willem. A New and Accurate Description of the Coast of Guinea, Divided into the Gold, the Slave, and the Ivory Coasts. Containing a Geographical, Political and Natural History of the Kingdoms and Countries: With a Particular Account of the Rise, Progress and Present Condition of all the European Settlements upon that Coast; and the Just Measures for Improving the several Branches of the Guinea Trade....Written Originally in Dutch...And now faithfully done into English. To which is prefix'd, An Exact Map of the whole Coast of Guinea.... *Lond. 1705, 8°.* LU.

2nd edn. 1721 (L). Reprinted in *A General Collection of Voyages*, ed. by J. Pinkerton, vol. 16 (1814).

521 The Case of Thomas Byfield and Company, Owners of the Ship Dove, Richard Cock Master, Relating to the Bill for Importing Naval Stores from the Plantations. *n.p.* [*1705*], *s. sh. F°.* LPRO.

522 The Clamours of the Weavers and their Abettors against the East-India Company, examin'd. With Remarks upon the Act for the more

Effectual Employing the Poor, by Encouraging the Manufactures of this Kingdom, &c. *n.p.* *1705*, *4°*. L.

The only copy seen is imperfect.

523 Advertisement. These are to give notice that the Packet Boats for the West-Indies are settled, and the Correspondence between England and the Islands of Barbadoes, Antego, Monserat, Nevis, St. Christophers and Jamaica, will be constantly carried on by the said Boats.... [*Lond.* *1705*], *s. sh.* *F°*. LPRO.

524 [DUMMER, EDWARD]. The Proposition which was first laid down & presented, to evince a Probability of maintaining a Monthly Correspondence with all the English-Island Plantations in America. [Followed by:] An Abstract of the Course and Success of the West-India Packets, put in practice upon the Principles of the Scheme on the other side, shewing how nearly the same hath answer'd, & w[t] Accidents have Happen'd therein, since the going out of the first Vessel in Oct[r] 1702. *n.p.* *1705*, *F°*. LPRO.

'Published, 1 Oct. 1705 by E.D.', but dated in ms. 15 Oct. 1705. Another edn., dated in ms. 13 Dec. 1705, has an endorsed title reading: The West India Correspondence How Propounded and How Perform'd by E. Dummer (LPRO). Another issue, dated in ms. 19 Dec. 1705 (LG); another edn., dated in ms. 25 June 1706 (LPRO); another edn., ending "Discontinued 7 August 1711', with a covering ms. letter from Dummer dated 14 July 1712 (LPRO).

525 The Humble Address of the Right Honourable the Lords Spiritual & Temporal in Parliament Assembled, presented to Her Majesty on Munday the Fifth Day of February, 1704 [O.S.]. And Her Majesties most gracious Answer thereunto. *Lond.* *1704*, *F°*. LU.

On the Navy. With monthly accounts of cruisers and home convoys from Jan. to Nov. 1703.

526 Instructions from His Royal Highness Prince George of Denmark, &c. Lord High Admiral of Great-Britain and Ireland, &c. for the Captains of Her Majesties Ships, and Masters of Merchant Ships or Vessels: For the better Security of the latter, when they shall from time to time proceed under the Convoy of the former. *n.p.* [*1705?*], *F°*. C.

527 [CLARKE, GEORGE]. Matters of Fact, relating to the Navy, Truely Stated. *Lond.* *1705*, *F°*. M (Cr).

For authorship see ms. note in M copy.

528 Proper Encouragements for Refiting out our English Privateers, which are now laid Up. *n.p.* [*c.* *1705?*], *s. sh.* *F°*. MC.

For permitting the export of wines, the principal prize goods.

529 Reasons Humbly Offer'd to the Honourable House of Commons, for passing a Clause to Encourage the Seamen, &c. *n.p.* [*c.* *1705?*], *s. sh.* *F°*. L.

530 The Three Establishments concerning the Pay of the Sea-Officers. To which is Prefix'd An Introduction for the better understanding by what Occasions they came to be produc'd. *Lond.* *1705*, *8°*. L.

The preface signed: P.C. 2nd edn. 1714 (LU).

531 Elton, Richard. To the Right Honourable the Knights, Citizens, and Burgesses, assembled in Parliament. A Proposal for Encouragement of Seamen, and Advancing the Credit of the Navy. *n.p.* [*1705?*], *F°*. L.

532 [Stephens, Edward]. The Case of the poor Grecian Seamen. *n.p.* [*c. 1705?*], *4°*. O.

Against impressing them. O copy is in a volume of pamphlets all of which are by Stephens.

533 Harris, John. Navigantium atque Itinerantium Bibliotheca: or, a Compleat Collection of Voyages and Travels.... *Lond. 1705*, *F°*. 2 vols. L.

Another edn. 1744–8 [1744–9] (L); another edn. 1764 (L).

534 Overture of an Act for ease of the Leidges as to the Prices of Fleshes in Edinburgh, Cannongate and Leith. *n.p.* [*1705*], *s. sh. F°*. E.

Followed by 'Reasons for passing the foresaid Overture into an Act'.

535 To his Grace Her Majesties High Commissioner, and the right Honourable the Estates of Parliament, The Petition of the Merchants of Edinburgh, for themselves and in name and behalf of the other Merchants and Traders within this Kingdom. [*Edin. c. 1705?*], *s. sh. F°*. EPRO.

On the seizure by the English of ships going to Portugal, especially the *Adventure* of Leith.

536 Act Prohibiting and Discharging the Importation of all Merchandise, and other Commodities, from England. [*Edin. 1705*], *s. sh. F°*. EPRO.

An overture. On the verso is: Draught of an Act for a Triennial Parliament.

537 Act Anent Destroying Prohibite Goods. *Edin. 1705*, *s. sh. F°*. E.

Dated: 20 February 1705.

538 Overture of an Act Discharging the Importation of Brandy, and all Forreign Spirits. [*Edin. 1705*], *s. sh. F°*. E.

539 Overture of an Act Discharging the Importation and Wearing of Muslen, Calico, and other Forraign Linnen. [*Edin. 1705*], *s. sh. F°*. E.

540 Act discharging the wearing of Silk-stuffs and Velvet, and Stamped Caligo. [*Edin. 1705*], *s. sh. F°*. LU.

On the verso is: Act anent the Coynage of Copper.

541 Act discharging the Importation of Starch and Powder made of Starch. [*Edin. 1705*], *F°*. LU.

An overture. Followed by: Draught of an Act anent Coal and Salt.

542 Act Discharging the Importation of Tobacco. [*Edin. 1705*]. *s. sh. F°*. E.

An overture. On the verso is 'Act Discharging the Victualing of Ships of this Nation outward-bound with Irish and Forreign Beef, or providing themselves with Forreign Small-Beer'.

543 Draught of an Act anent the Exportation of Wooll and Skins. [*Edin. 1705?*], *s. sh. F°*. E.

544 Proclamation Explaining some Clauses in the Commission for Hindering the Importation of Irish Victual, &c. *Edin. 1705*, *s. sh. F°*. E.

Dated: 11 December 1705.

COLONIES

545 [Beverley, Robert]. The History and Present State of Virginia, in Four Parts. I. The History of the First Settlement of Virginia, and the Government thereof, to the present Time. II. The Natural Productions and Conveniences of the Country, suited to Trade and Improvement. III. The Native Indians, their Religion, Laws, and Customs, in War and Peace. IV. The present State of the Country, as to the Polity of the Government, and the Improvements of the Land. By a Native and Inhabitant of the Peace. *Lond. 1705*, *8°*. L.

The engraved titlepage says 'By R. B. Gent'. 2nd edn. 1722 (L). Another edn., with author's name, Richmond, Va. 1855. Another edn., edited by Louis B. Wright, Chapel Hill, 1947.

FINANCE

546 [Broughton, John]. A Letter to a Member of the present honourable House of Commons, relating to the Credit of our Government, and of the Nation in General. *Lond. 1705*, *4°*. L.

Reprinted in *The Vindication and Advancement of our National Constitution and Credit*, 1710.

547 The Case of the Proprietors of the Benefit Malt-Tickets. *n.p.* [*1705*], *s. sh. F°*. LU.

Endorsed: The Hard Case of the Proprietors of the Benefit Malt-Tickets.

548 The Case of the Soldiers, Clothiers, Masters, and Owners of Ships, and others concern'd in the Army and Transport Debentures. *n.p.* [*1705?*], *s. sh. F°*. L.

549 Reasons to Support the Proposal for granting divers Sorts of Annuities, such as the Purses of the Common People may be able to compass. *Lond. 1705*, *s. sh. F°*. L.

Another edn., revised, 1706 (L).

550 A Proposal for Advancing the Revenue of Excise, &c. Humbly Offered to the Honourable the House of Commons in Parliament Assembled. *Lond. 1705*, *F°*. LU.

Put forward by Nehemiah Scott and Partners.

551 Reasons Humbly Offer'd to the Honourable the Knights, Citizens, and Burgesses in Parliament Assembled, For the better Ascertaining the Gauging and Charging of Malt, and Preventing the Queen's being Defrauded of Her Duty and the Subject from being Overcharged. *n.p.* [*c. 1705?*], *s. sh. F°*. MC.

Endorsed: Reasons for the better Ascertaining the Gauging and Charging of Malt.

552 KINGSLEY, M. A Proposal Humbly Offered to the Honourable the House of Commons in Parliament Assembled, for Raising a considerable Sum of Money, without Oppressing the Subject. *n.p.* [*c. 1705?*], *s. sh. F°.* L.

Schoolmasters to pay 6*d.* a scholar a quarter. Endorsed: A Proposal for Raising Her Majesty a Considerable Aid for Carrying on the War.

553 POLHAMPTON, WILLIAM. A Proposal for raising the Annual Sum of 20000 l. and upwards, without Prejudice to the Subjects...humbly offered to the Honourable the House of Commons. *n.p.* [*c. 1705?*], *s. sh. F°.* MC.

For a tax on waggons and carts.

554 An Expedient, which with an Easier Burden to the Subject may raise an Equivalent to the Salt-Duty, if that be laid aside. *n.p.* [*c. 1705?*], *s. sh. F°.* L.

Endorsed: An Expedient how to Remedy the Inconveniences of the Salt-Duty, and how to raise 500000 l. per An. from Candles. A poll tax of 4*d.* per head is also proposed.

555 A Collection of All the Statutes now in Force, relating to the Excise: with an Abridgment of the said Statutes, and a Table of the Rates upon the several Liquors, &c. showing by what Acts they are Imposed. To which is added, A Table of Allowances for Common-Brewers, &c. *Lond. 1705, 12°.* LU.

556 An Act for Impowering the Lord-High-Treasurer of England, or Commissioners of Her Majesty's Treasury for the Time being (or any Two or more of them) to Compound with John Mason, Gent. late Receiver of His Late Majesty's Taxes in the County, University and Town of Cambridge, and Isle of Ely; And with John Pickering, Silkman, One of the said Receiver's Securities. *n.p.* [*1705*], *F°.* L.

557 A Bill to Enable the Lord High Treasurer or Commissioners of the Treasury for the time being, to Compound with Michael Wicks, Esquire, late Receiver General of the Plantation Duties, in the Port of London. *n.p.* [*1705*], *s. sh. F°.* LG.

558 The Case of Mrs. Catherine Spencer, Executrix of William Hunt, Deceas'd, in Relation to the Bill, to enable the Lord High Treasurer to Compound with Michael Wykes, Esq; late Receiver of the Plantation Duties in the Port of London. *n.p. 1704* [*O.S.*], *s. sh. F°.* LLI.

559 HOLBECH, WILLIAM. A Case setting forth, how wilfully a Prosecution in the Exchequer has been neglected; against some Receivers of the Taxes, for Frauds they had committed on the said Taxes. *n.p.* [*1705*], *s. sh. F°.* LLI.

Dated: January 20th, 170$\frac{4}{5}$.

560 A Letter from a Commoner of England to a Member of the Honourable H—— of C——. *Lond. 1704, 4°.* LU.

Signed: W. L., and dated: Braintre, Feb. 19. 1705. On the financial mismanagement of the Navy.

561 FORBES, WILLIAM. A Treatise of Church-lands & Tithes: In two Parts. Containing an Historical Account of Ecclesiastical Revenues...with a particular History of Tithes.... *Edin.* *1705*, *8°*. L.

562 The Case of the People called Quakers, Humbly Offer'd to the Parliament, in Relation to the Perpetuating the Bill for the more easie Recovery of Small Tythes. *n.p.* [*1705*], *F°*. L.

563 The Proceedings of the Barons of the Exchequer at Westminster, in their Court of Equity, for Tythes and Oblations, and other Ecclesiastical Duties, Considered and Examined. By a Counsellor Learned in the Law. *Lond.* *1705*, *4°*. O.

564 The Case of the Provost and Corporation of Moneyers. *n.p.* [*1705*], *F°*. L.

Endorsed: The Case of the Corporation of Moneyers of Her Majesty's Mint.

565 [BROUGHTON, JOHN]. Remarks upon the Bank of England; with regard more especially to our Trade and Government. Occasion'd by the present Discourse concerning the Intended Prolongation of the Bank. Humbly Address'd to the Honourable House of Commons. By a Merchant of London, and a true Lover of our Constitution. *Lond.* *1705*, *8°*. LU.

2nd edn. corrected, 1706 (LU); another edn. 1707 (LU). Reprinted in Broughton's *The Vindication and Advancement of our National Constitution and Credit*, 1710.

566 Considerations against Repealing that part of an Act of Parliament, which restrains the Number of Exchange-Brokers to One Hundred. *n.p.* [*1705?*], *s. sh. F°*. LLI.

Endorsed: Considerations Humbly offered against Altering the Brokers-Act.

567 Reasons Humbly Offered Against Altering the Act for Restraining the Number of Brokers. *n.p.* [*1705*], *s. sh. F°*. MC.

568 Assurance for Widows and Orphans. The Articles of Settlement, Agreed to, and Subscribed by the Several Members of the Society of Assurance for Widows and Orphans, at the Office at St. Austin's-Gate, near the East-end of St. Pauls, London. *n.p.* [*1705*], *F°*. LG.

569 *Begin.* Sir, Thursday the 10th. of May, 1705. is Appointed for Chusing Trustees for the First Society of Assurance for Widows and Orphans.... *n.p.* [*1705*], *F°*. LG.

The notice is followed by a List of the Subscribers from whom the Trustees are to be chosen.

570 Advertisement. From the New Assurance Office, upon the Lives of Men, Women and Children. Lately Established at the Bell and Dragon in Portugal-Street, at Lincolns-Inn Back Gate. *n.p.* [*1705*], *s. sh. F°*. L.

571 Insurance from Loss by Fire. By the Amicable Contributors, at Tom's Coffee-House in St. Martin's-Lane, near Charing Cross, where Attendance is Daily given. *n.p.* [*c. 1705?*], *s. sh. F°*. L.

Last line begins: Dearer.... Another edn., n.d. Last line begins: Times Dearer.... (L).

572 The Friendly Society. A Proposal for Insuring Houses by the Friendly Society. *n.p.* [*c. 1705?*], *s. sh. F°.* L.

This edn. mentions only the address in Palsgrave Court. Another edn. [*c.* 1710?] (L) mentions also Bridge's Coffee House, which was from 1707 the address for entries of houses to be insured.

573 Phenix Office. Houses are Insured at the Phoenix Office for a Sum certain, without any Contribution or Contingency whatsoever. And also by Mutual Contribution. *n.p.* [*c. 1705?*], *s. sh. F°.* L.

Reprinted in F. B. Relton, *An Account of the Fire Insurance Companies*, 1893, p. 48.

574 Phenix Office. The Rates of Insuring Houses, and other Buildings from Fire, for 1, 2, 3, 4 or 7 Years, for a Sum certain (without being liable to any Contribution, or Contingency whatsoever;) At the Fire Office, kept against the Royal Exchange in Cornhill, and at the Rainbow Coffee-House, by the Inner-Temple-Gate, in Fleet-street. *Lond. 1705, s. sh. F°.* L.

On the verso are: The Rates of Insuring Houses, from 1 Year to 7 by Mutual Contribution.

575 Act for returning the Excise from the Liquor to the Malt. [*Edin. 1705?*], *s. sh. F°.* EPRO.

576 Overture of an Act of Additional Excise for Payment of the Arrears of Officers. [*Edin. 1705*], *s. sh. F°.* LU.

577 Unto His Grace, John Duke of Argyle, Her Majesties High Commissioner, and to the Right Honourable Estates of Parliament. The Petition of the Sub-Tacksmen of the Excise, of the Shires of Inverness, Ross, Cromarty, Fife, Kinross, Perth, Angus, Merns, Town of Dundee, Stirling, Linlithgow, Elgine, Bamff, Nairn, Haddingtoun, Berwick, Roxburgh, Forrest, and Peebles. [*Edin. 1705*], *s. sh. F°.* EPRO.

578 Memorial to His Grace her Majesties high Commissioner and the high and honourable Estates of Parliament. In behalf of the Brewars in and about the Town of Edinburgh, for themselves and in name of the hail other brewars within this Kingdom. [*Edin. 1705?*], *s. sh. F°.* EPRO.

Against the present method of levying excise.

579 Entry cancelled.

580 Reasons for Passing the Act in favours of the Town of Glasgow. [*Edin. 1705*], *s. sh. F°.* EPRO.

For the right to tax ale.

581 Memorial for the Brewers living within the City of Edinburgh, and Liberties thereof, containing an account of the Grievances they suffer by the Impost of two pennies upon the Pynt of Ale, Gifted to the Town of Edinburgh. [*Edin. 1705*], *s. sh. F°.* EPRO.

582 Unto his Grace, Her Majesties High Commissioner, and Honourable Estates of Parliament, the Petition of the Brewers within the City of Edinburgh, and Liberties thereof. [*Edin. 1705*], *s. sh. Fo*. EPRO.

Against the tax on ale.

583 Information for the Heritors, and Commissioners of Supply of the Shire of Ross, and Hector Monro, Brother-German to the Deceast Sir John Monro of Fowlis, Collector of the Cess within the said Shire, from Lambmass 1695, till Whitsunday 1704, Inclusive. [*Edin. 1705*], *s. sh. Fo*. EPRO.

584 Unto his Grace John Duke of Argyll, Her Majesties high Commissioner and the Honourable Estates of Parliament, The Report of the Commission of Parliament, Appointed for Stating and Examining the Publick Accompts. *n.p.* [*1705*], *Fo*. LU.

Drawn up by Sir John Clerk. See his *Memoirs*, 1892, p. 54.

585 Proposal by Doctor Hugh Chamberlen, For a Land Credit, presented to the Parliament, By the Committee, to whom it was referred to be Considered. [*Edin. 1705?*], *s. sh. Fo*. E.

586 Proposal by Doctor Hugh Chamberlen, and James Armour, for a Land Credit; Presented to the Parliament, by the Committee, to whom it was referred to be Considered, and Ordered by the Parliament to be Printed. *n.p.* [*1705?*], *Fo*. E.

587 HODGES, JAMES. Considerations and Proposals, for Supplying the present Scarcity of Money, and advancing Trade. *Edin. 1705*, *4o*. LU.

588 The Circumstances of Scotland consider'd, with Respect to the present Scarcity of Money: Together with some Proposals for supplying the Defect thereof, and rectifying the Ballance of Trade. *Edin. 1705*, *4o*. LU.

E copy has a ms. attribution to Sir John Clerk, but the pamphlet is not mentioned in Clerk's *Memoirs*.

589 An Essay for Promoting of Trade, and Increasing the Coin of the Nation. In a Letter from a Gentleman in the Country to his Friend at Edinburgh, a Member of Parliament. [*Edin. 1705?*], *4o*. LU.

590 [BROWN, ANDREW]. An Essay on the New Project for a Land-Mint, proposing a proper and practicable Scheme and Expedient and how to put the same under due and regular Management, in this Conjucture; not only for the speedy supplying the present scarcity of Money; but also for the advancing of Trade and other Navigational Improvements. By the Author of The Character of the true Publick Spirit. *Edin. 1705*, *8o*. LU.

For authorship see Advocates' Library Catalogue. Reissued in *Three Essays*, 1706 (no. 720).

591 [BROWN, ANDREW]. A Second Essay concerning the Land Mint, shewing, that the present necessity, and want of Gold and Silver Money, absolutely requires this, or the like remedy, and that speedily. As also

holding forth the Equivalency of the Land-Mint Money, to Gold or Silver Money, and the sufficiency thereof.... With an Introduction, Clearing how the Establishment of this Land-Mint will prove the most proper way to carry on all national Improvements and Trade.... By the Author of the Character of the true publick Spirit. *Edin. 1705, 8°.* L.

For authorship see Advocates' Library Catalogue. Reissued in *Three Essays*, 1706 (no. 720).

592 [LAW, JOHN]. Money and Trade considered, with a Proposal for supplying the Nation with Money. *Edin. 1705, 4°.* LU.

Another edn. Lond. 1720 (LU); 2nd edn., with author's name, Lond. 1720 (L); other edns. Glasgow, 1750 & 1760 (both LU). Reprinted in *Somers Tracts*, XIII (1815), 775.

593 [LAW, JOHN]. Proposal for Supplying the Nation with Money. [*Edin. 1705*], *s. sh. F°.* LU.

Extracted from *Money and Trade considered.*

594 [CHAMBERLEN, HUGH]. Some Animadversions upon a few small circumstantial Differences, betwixt the Proposal for a Land-Credit, reported to be Mr. Law's, and Dr. Chamberlens, both of them plainly agreeing in the Foundation, as they are contained in the 6 and 7 Chap. of a Book, Intituled, Money and Trade considered, &c. *n.p.* [*1705*], *s. sh. F°.* LU.

Internal evidence suggests Chamberlen's authorship.

595 [DONALDSON, JAMES]. Money Encreas'd and Credit Rais'd: a Proposal for Multiplying the Tale of Money, by Coining a certain quantity of Lye-Money out of a third part of the Plate of the Kingdom; whereupon a National Bank may be Erected to the great Encrease of Money and Credit. Humbly Submitted to the High Court of Parliament. *Edin. 1705, 4°.* E.

For authorship see ms. note in E copy.

596 An Overture for Supplying the present scarcity of Money. [*Edin.? 1705*], *s. sh. F°.* L.

597 [CHAMBERLEN, HUGH]. A Present Remedie for the want of Money: or, Some Remarks, upon a Paper, entituled an Overture for supplying the present scarcity of Money; with a defence of a former, which seems very much preferable to it, and is now by order of Parliament under the consideration of the Right Honourable the Committee for examination of Accompts. [*Edin. 1705*], *4°.* LU.

Authorship deduced from internal evidence.

598 Two Overtures humbly offered to his Grace John Duke of Argyll, Her Majesties High Commissioner, and the right Honourable the Estates of Parliament. The 1. For supplying the present Scarcity of Coyn, and Improving Trade. The 2. For clearing the Debts due by the Government to the Army and Civil List. *n.p.* [*1705*], *4°.* LU.

Reprinted in *The Writings of William Paterson*, ed. by S. Bannister, II, xliii–xlvii, where it is attributed to John Law.

599 A Proposal anent Usury and procuring of Money. [*Edin. 1705*], *s. sh. F°.* LU.

Attributed to William Thomson in a long ms. note in E copy.

600 [SETON, WILLIAM]. Some Thoughts on Ways and Means for making this Nation a Gainer in Foreign Commerce; and for Supplying its present Scarcity of Money. *Edin. 1705, 8°.* LU.

For authorship see Advocates' Library Catalogue.

601 Act Anent the Coynage of Copper. [*Edin. 1705*], *s. sh. F°.* EPRO.

602 COLLIS, JOHN. A National Credit, for a National Use. Written by J. C. Merchant in Dublin. Being a means for the supplying of Ireland, in every Individual County, City and Borough, with what may be sufficient for the Trade, Traffick, and all other necesitous demands, Publick or Private of those Places.... *n.p.* [*1705*], *8°.* L.

Signed: John Collis.

TRANSPORT

603 The Case of the Wharfingers, Proprietors and Farmers of the Free Keys of the Port of London. *n.p.* [*1705?*], *s. sh. F°.* LU.

604 The Case of the Traders of London as it now stands since the Copartnership of the Wharfingers. *Lond. 1705, 8°.* L.

605 The Reasons of Henry Jones Esquire, for Building a Mould or Peer in Whitsand Bay at the Lands End. *n.p.* [*1705?*], *s. sh. F°.* L.

Endorsed: Reasons for making a Harbor in Whitsand Bay at the Lands End. Another edn., entitled: Reasons humbly offered by Henry Jones, Esq; for Building a Mould or Harbour in Whitsand Bay at the Lands-End, in Cornwall. n.p. [1714 ?], s. sh. F° (L). With a map.

606 Several Objections against Whitesand-Bay's being made a Harbour, Answered. *n.p.* [*1705?*], *s. sh. F°.* L.

607 The present Case of about Six Hundred Poor Aged and Maimed Watermen, their Widows and Children. Most humbly submitted to Her Most Excellent Majesty, and the Right Honourable the Lords of Her Majesties most Honourable Privy Council. *n.p.* [*1705*], *F°.* LLI.

608 Proposals for Subscriptions to set up an Office for the cheap and speedy sending all Parcels of Goods and Things of six Pounds Weight and under, any where within the Weekly Bills of Mortality; for the Benefit of Poor Orphans. *London, 1705, F°.* DM.

609 The Case of Robert Kaines, Charles Lloy'd, and Francis Corrale on the behalf of themselves, and the rest of the Hackney-Coach-men, who Hire Hackney-Coach-Licenses, being about 400 in Number. *n.p.* [*1705*], *s. sh. F°.* LLI.

610 The Case of several Hackney-Coachmen that Hire Licenses, which is in Number about 400. Humbly Offer'd to the Knights, Citizens, and Burgesses, in Parliament, Assembled. *n.p.* [*1705?*], *s. sh. F°.* LLI.

Signed by William Coller, Richard Nickell and nine others.

SOCIAL CONDITIONS

611 The Laws Concerning the Poor. Wherein is treated of Overseers, and their Office. Of Rates and Contributions. Of Settlements. Of Families, Vagrants, Children, Servants, &c.... Of Vagrants, Vagabonds.... Of Workhouses, House of Correction, &c.... To which are added Several Forms of Orders of Sessions, Warrants, Mittimus, &c. *Lond. 1705, 12°*. LU.

612 The Bill, Intituled, An Act for the Relief, Imployment and Settlement of the Poor, which came from the House of Commons; and also The Bill, Intituled, An Act for the further and better Relief, Imployment and Maintenance of the Poor: and the Scheme of an Act for the Relief of the Poor, delivered into the House of Peers, from the Commissioners of Trade and Plantations, as Drawn by Them. *Lond. 1705, F°*. LU.

613 The Case of the Poor Sailors of the English-Navy, in Respect to their Hospital at Greenwich; humble [*sic*] Offered to the Consideration of the Honourable House of Commons. *n.p.* [*c. 1705?*], *s. sh. F°*. L.

614 PITT, ROBERT. The Frauds and Villanies of the Common Practice of Physick, from the Excesses of the Apothecaries Ignorance of Diseases. ... Demonstrated to be curable by the College-Dispensary. *Lond. 1705, 8°*. L.

615 A Short Answer to a Late Book, entituled, Tentamen Medicinale. With which are Reprinted several Papers formerly published, touching the Rise, Growth, and Usefulness of the Dispensaries, Erected by the College of Physicians, for the benefit of the Sick Poor in and near London. *Lond. 1705, 8°*. L.

616 Loss by Fire in Morgans-Lane, Southwark, Upwards of 2706l. Anne, By the Grace of God.... *Lond. 1705, F°*. L.

The sufferers in the fire in Morgans-Lane, Southwark, to be allowed to collect alms.

617 The Miserable and Deplorable Case of several Thousands of Poor Insolvent Debtors. Humbly Presented to the Consideration of the Honourable House of Commons in Parliament Assembled. *n.p.* [*1705?*], *s. sh. F°*. LLI.

618 The most Indigent poor Prisoners Letter to a Worthy Member of Parliament; with Reasons Humbly Offer'd for a Bill to free the Subjects from Taxes for their Maintenance, by making every Creditor Maintain his own Debtor. *n.p.* [*c. 1705?*], *s. sh. F°*. L.

619 Proposals made to the Queen and Parliament by Charles Nowes of the Middle Temple, Esq; To Raise Twenty Five Thousand Men before the next Campaign. *n.p.* [*c. 1705?*], *s. sh. F°*. L.

A scheme for enlisting insolvent debtors.

620 The Intolerable Grievances of the Poor French Gentry Among the

Refugees, groaning under the Oppression and Arbitrariness of the French Committee in their Distributing the Publick Charities granted for the Relief of the said Refugees. *n.p.* [*c. 1705?*], *s. sh. F°*. MC.

621 The Intolerable Grievances of the Poor French Refugees Groaning under the Arbitrariness, Oppression and Mal-Administration of the French Committee, in their Distributing the Publick and Private Bounties and Charities granted for the Relief of the said Refugees. *n.p.* [*c. 1705?*], *s. sh. F°*. MC.

Slightly different from the preceding.

622 LONDON. Commune Concilium tent' in Camera Guihald'...An Act for Regulating the Night-Watches within the City of London, and Liberties thereof. [*Lond.*], *1705*, *F°*. LG.

Dated: 16 June 1705. Another edn. 1728; another 1736 (both LG).

623 Work-House Dublin. The Report of the Lord Mayor, and the Seven Assistants of their Proceedings for the Year ending this Fourth Day of June, 1705. *Dublin*, *1705*, *s. sh. F°*. DNL.

1706

GENERAL

624 *Begin.* Anna Dei Gratia, Magnæ Britaniæ, Franciæ & Hyberniæ Regina.... [*Edin. 1706*], *4º*. L.

The proceedings of the Commissioners for the Union. Another edn., entitled: The Journal of the Proceedings of the Lds Commissioners of both Nations, in the Treaty of Union, which began on the 16th of April 1706. and was concluded on the 22nd of July following. With the Articles then Agreed on. Lond. [1706], 4º (O).

625 The Minutes of the Proceedings of the Lords Commissioners for the Union of the Kingdoms of England and Scotland; the Treaty for which Began on the Sixteenth Day of April, 1706. and was Concluded the Twenty second Day of July following. *Lond. 1706*, *Fº*. O.

626 Articles of Union agreed on the Twenty second day of July, in the fifth Year of the Reign of Her Most Excellent Majesty, Anne...by the Commissioners nominated on behalf of the Kingdom of Scotland... And the Commissioners Nominated on behalf of the Kingdom of England. *n.p.* [*1706*], *4º*. E.

627 [Abercromby, Patrick]. The Advantages of the Act of Security, compar'd with These of the Intended Union: Founded on the Revolution-Principles publish'd by Mr. Daniel De Foe. Or, The Present Happy Condition of Scotland...Demonstrated. Wherein is shew'd, That both the Projected Union, and a Nomination of a Successor to the Crown...cannot fail to Compleat the Miseries of This Kingdom.... *n.p. 1706*, *4º*. E.

For authorship see Advocates' Library Catalogue.

628 [Defoe, Daniel]. The Advantages of Scotland, by an Incorporate Union with England, compar'd with these [*sic*] of a Coalition with the Dutch, or League with France. In answer to a pamphlet, call'd, The Advantages of the Act of Security, &c. To which is added, A Postscript in answer to The Letter concerning the Consequence of an Incorporating Union. *n.p. 1706*, *4º*. LU.

For authorship see *C.B.E.L.* II, 500.

629 The Anatomy of an Equivalent, By the Marquess of Halifax, Adapted to the Equivalent in the present Articles, 1706. [*Edin. 1706*,], *4º*. E.

630 A Copy of a Letter from a Country Farmer to his Laird, a Member of Parliament. *n.p.* [*1706*], *4º*. L.

Reprinted in *The Scottish Antiquary*, XII, 99-101.

631 The Cry of the North: Fair Trade, Fair Seizure, Fair Trial. *Edin.* [*1706*], *4º*. E.

632 [Defoe, Daniel]. An Enquiry into the Disposal of the Equivalent. [*Edin. 1706*], *4º*. LU.

For authorship see ms. attribution in E copy and *C.B.E.L.* II, 500.

633 [DEFOE, DANIEL]. An Essay at Removing National Prejudices against a Union with Scotland. To be continued during the Treaty here. Part I. *Lond. 1706*, 4°. L.

Pts. I & II were published together at Edinburgh, 1706 (E). For authorship see *C.B.E.L.* II, 499.

634 [DEFOE, DANIEL]. An Essay at removing National Prejudices against a Union with Scotland. To be continued during the Treaty here. Part II. *Lond. 1706*, 4°. O.

For authorship see *C.B.E.L.* II, 499.

635 [DEFOE, DANIEL]. An Essay, at removing National Prejudices, against a Union with England. Part III. By the Author of the two first. [*Edin.*], *1706*, 4°. L.

For authorship see *C.B.E.L.* II, 499.

636 [DEFOE, DANIEL]. A Fourth Essay, at removing National Prejudices; with some Reply to Mr. H——dges and some other Authors, who have printed their Objections against an Union with England. [*Edin.*], *1706*, 4°. L.

For authorship see *C.B.E.L.* II, 499.

637 [BLACK, DAVID]. Essay upon Industry and Trade, showing the Necessity of the One, the Conveniency and Usefulness of the Other, and the Advantage of Both. *Edin. 1706*, 4°. LU.

For authorship see ms. note in EU copy.

638 An Essay upon the Equivalent. In a Letter to a Friend. [*Edin.*], *1706*, 4°. LU.

639 [CLERK, Sir JOHN]. An Essay upon the XV. Article of the Treaty of Union, wherein the Difficulties that arise upon the Equivalents, are fully Cleared and Explained. *n.p. 1706*, 4°. LU.

For authorship see *Memoirs of the Life of Sir John Clerk*, ed. J. M. Gray, Edin. 1892, p. 66.

640 [HODGES, JAMES]. Essay upon the Union. Shewing, that the Subjects of Both Nations have been, by the Union of the Two Crowns, justly Intitled to all manner of Privileges, which the ensuing Treaty can give them....And the best Security against Incroachments on both sides, is, to have separate Parliaments, with an express Proviso, that no Laws about Trade, or the other common Concerns of the United Nations, shall be of Force, unless agreed to by both Parliaments. *Lond. 1706*, 4°. L.

Another edn. Edin. 1706 (E). For authorship see Advocates' Library Catalogue.

641 The Equivalent Explain'd. *n.p.* [*1706*], 4°. LU.

642 [HODGES, JAMES]. Faithful Advice from England. By an Honest Scotsman. *Edin. 1706*, 4°. E.

Extracts from *The Rights and Interests of the Two British Monarchies... Treatise III*, with a preface by ——Bannantyne (ms. note in E copy).

643 [MACKENZIE, RODERICK]. A Full and Exact Account of the Proceedings

of the Court of Directors and Council-General of the Company of Scotland Trading to Africa and the Indies, with relation to the Treaty of Union, now under the Parliament's Consideration.... [*Edin.*] *1706*, *4°*. L.

Signed: R.M.K. The author's name is given in full on p. 7.

644 [PATERSON, WILLIAM]. An Enquiry into the Reasonableness and Consequences of an Union with Scotland. Containing A Brief Deduction of what hath been done, designed, or proposed, in the matter of the Union, during the last Age. A Scheme of an Union, as accommodated to the present Circumstances, of the two Nations. Also States, of the respective Revenues, Debts, Weights, Measures, Taxes and Impositions, and other Facts of moment. With Observations thereupon.... *Lond. 1706. 8°*. LU.

The preface signed: Lewis Medway, a pseudonym of Paterson's. Reprinted in *The Writings of William Paterson*, ed. by S. Bannister, 1858, vol. 1.

645 A Letter concerning the Consequence of an Incorporating Uniou [*sic*], in relation to Trade. [*Edin.*], *1706*, *4°*. LU.

Dated: October 30. 1706.

646 [DEFOE, DANIEL]. A Letter concerning Trade, from several Scots-Gentlemen that are Merchants in England, to their Country-Men that are Merchants in Scotland. *n.p.* [*1706*], *4°*. L.

Dated: 23 Nov. 1706. Another edn., Dublin, 1706, F°, entitled: A Letter concerning the Union, with relation to Trade, from several Scots Gentlemen, Merchants in England, to their Country-Men, Merchants in Scotland (DA). Another edn., with this title, Lond. 1707, 8° (L). For authorship see C. E. Burch in *N. & Q.* vol. 193 (1948), pp. 101–3.

647 Answer to a Letter concerning Trade, sent from several Scots Gentlemen, that are Merchants in England, to their Countrymen that are Merchants in Scotland. *Edin. 1706*, *4°*. LU.

Internal evidence suggests William Black as the author.

648 [DEFOE, DANIEL ?]. A Letter from Mr. Reason to the High and Mighty Prince the Mob. *n.p.* [*1706*], *4°*. LU.

For authorship see *C.B.E.L.* II, 500. Attributed to James Donaldson in Advocates' Library Catalogue.

649 [CLERK, Sir JOHN]. A Letter to a Friend, giving an Account how the Treaty of Union has been Received here. And wherein are contained, Answers to the most material Objections against it, with some Remarks upon what has been written by Mr H[odges] and Mr R[idpath]. *Edin. 1706*, *4°*. L.

For authorship see *Memoirs of the Life of Sir John Clerk*, ed. by J. M. Gray, Edin. 1892, p. 244.

650 [DEFOE, DANIEL ?]. A Letter to a Member of Parliament, anent the Application of the 309885 Lib: 10 Shil: Sterl: Equivalent; With Consideration of Reducing the Coin to the Value and Standard of England. *n.p. 1706*, *4°*. LU.

For authorship see ms. note in E copy and *C.B.E.L.* II, 500. Rejected by J. R. Moore.

651 [DEFOE, DANIEL]. Observations on the Fifth Article of the Treaty of Union, humbly offered to the Consideration of the Parliament, relating to Foreign Ships. [*Edin. 1706*], *4º*. L.

For authorship see *C.B.E.L.* II, 499.

652 The Queen an Empress, and Her Three Kingdoms one Empire: or, Brief Remarks upon the Present; and a Prospect of the Future State of England, Scotland, and Ireland, in a happy Union. In a Letter to a Noble Peer. *Lond. 1706*, *4º*. O.

653 [BROWN, ANDREW]. A Scheme, proposing a True Touch-stone for the due Trial of a Proper Union betwixt Scotland & England; especially as to its fitness for Scotland....By the Author of The Character of the true publick Spirit. *Edin. 1706*, *12º*. E.

Reissued in *Three Essays*, 1706 (no. 720).

654 [SETON, WILLIAM]. Scotland's Great Advantages by an Union with England: Showen in a Letter from the Country, to a Member of Parliament. *n.p. 1706*, *4º*. LU.

Reprinted in *Somers Tracts*, XII (1814), 519. Attribution of authorship in Advocates' Library Catalogue.

655 [ARBUTHNOT, JOHN]. A Sermon Preach'd to the People, at the Mercat Cross of Edinburgh; On the Subject of the Union. [*Edin.*], *1706*, *4º*. pp. 20. L.

Another edn. Lond. 1707 [1706], 8º pp. 16 (L); another edn. Dublin, 1707, 8º (C); another edn. [Edin ? 1707], 8º, pp. 8 (L.). Reprinted in G.A. Aitken, *The Life and Works of John Arbuthnot*, 1892.

656 [BLACK, WILLIAM]. A Short View of our present Trade and Taxes, compared with what these Taxes may amount to after the Union, even tho our Trade should not augment one Sixpence. With some Reasons, why (if we enter in an Union,) our Trade should be under our own Regulations. *n.p.* [*1706*], *4º*. L.

For authorship see ms. note in E copy.

657 [BLACK, WILLIAM]. Some Considerations in relation to Trade, humbly offered to His Grace Her Majesty's High Commissioner and the Estates of Parliament. *n.p. 1706*, *4º*. L.

For authorship see B.M. Catalogue.

658 [DONALDSON, JAMES ?]. Considerations in relation to Trade Considered, and a Short View of our present Trade and Taxes, compared with what these Taxes may amount to after the Union, &c. Reviewed. [*Edin.*], *1706*, *4º*. LU.

For authorship see ms. note in E copy. William Black was the author of the two pamphlets criticized. Attributed to Defoe by C. E. Burch in *N. & Q.* vol. 193 (1948), p. 73.

659 [BLACK, WILLIAM]. Remarks upon a Pamphlet, Intitled, The Considerations in relaton to Trade Considered, and a Short View of our present Trade and Taxes Reviewed. *n.p. 1706*, *4º*. EU.

For attribution see ms. note in EU copy.

660 [BLACK, WILLIAM]. A Letter Concerning the Remarks upon the considerations of Trade, by the Author of the 4th Essay, at removing National Prejudices. *n.p.* [*1706*], *4º*. LU.

The Fourth Essay was by Defoe. For authorship see ms. note in E copy.

661 [BALLANTYNE, JOHN]. Some Queries Proposed to Consideration, Relative to the Union now intended. *n.p.* [*1706*], *4º*. LU.

For authorship see Advocates' Library Catalogue.

662 An Answer to Some Queries, &c. relative to the Union: in a Conference betwixt a Coffee-Master, and a Countrey-Farmer. [*Edin.*] *1706*, *4º*. M.

663 [DEFOE, DANIEL]. The State of the Excise after the Union, compared with what it is Now. *n.p. 1706*, *4º*. LU.

For authorship see *C.B.E.L.* II, 500.

664 [BLACK, WILLIAM]. Some Few Remarks upon The State of Excise after the Union, compar'd with what it now is. *n.p.* [*1706*], *4º*. LU.

Authorship deduced from internal evidence.

665 [DEFOE, DANIEL]. The State of the Excise &c. Vindicated, from the Remarks of the Author of the Short View &c. Wherein some other Escapes of that Author, are likewise taken notice of. *n.p.* [*1706*], *4º*. E.

For authorship see *C.B.E.L.* II, 500.

666 To His Grace Her Majesties High Commissioner and the Honourable Estates of Parliament. The Heemble Petition of the peer Shank Workers and Fingren Spinners of Aberdeen, and Places thereabout. *n.p.* [*1706?*], *4º*, L.

Reprinted in *The Scottish Antiquary*, XII, 101–5.

667 To His Grace, Her Majesty's High Commissioner, and the Right Honourable the Estates of Parliament, The Address of the Commissioners to the General Convention of the Royal Burrows of this Ancient Kingdom, Conveened the 29th of October last, upon the Great Concern of the Union, Proposed between Scotland and England, for Concerting such Measures, as should be esteemed Proper for Them to take, with Relation to Their Trade, and other Concerns. [*Edin. 1706*], *s. sh. Fº*. L.

668 Ta Hir Grace, Her Majesties high Commissioner, an te Honorable Estates of Parlment: Te Address far te Fishers on te Highland Coasts, an all uthers Inhapiting te Highlands, wha it ma concern, Humbly Representing tat it will pe Exceedingly disadvantageous to Her nane sel, tat te Articles of te Union Concerning Salt, and Excise pe agreed to, without an Mendment in Case the Union is concluded. [*Edin? 1706?*], *4º*. E.

Reprinted in *The Scottish Antiquary*, XII, 105–8.

669 The Freemen of London's Necessary and Useful Companion: or, the Citizens Birth-right, with the Foreigners and Aliens best Instructor.... *Lond. 1706*, *12º*. L.

Reissued in 1707 (L).

AGRICULTURE

670 An Abstract of Letters concerning the Mines [of the Company of Mine Adventurers]. Received since the General-Court, held in November last. *Lond. 1706, F°.* L.

671 Rules, Orders, and By-Laws for the Good Government of the Corporation of the Governour and Company of the Mine-Adventurers of England. *Lond. 1706, 4°.* L.

672 The Case of John Morgan, and several other Persons. Complain'd of by Sir Humphrey Mackworth, for Breaches of Privilege. *n.p. [1706?], s. sh. F°.* LLI.

Relating to his mines at Neath.

673 Criminal-Libel, Captain William Taverner and others, Against Sir James Sinclair. *n.p. [1706?], F°.* M (Cr).

A dispute about fishing from Dumbeath.

MANUFACTURES

674 Haynes, John. A View of the Present State of the Clothing Trade in England, with Remarks on the Causes and pernicious Consequences of its Decay: And a Scheme of proper Remedies for the Recovery of it.... *Lond. 1706, 8°.* LU.

Another edn. 1707 (LU).

675 The Case and Representation of the Merchants, Manufacturers, and other Traders, in respect to Foreign Mournings. *n.p. [1706?], F°.* LLI.

676 The Grievances of those concern'd in the Silk Trade, &c. occasion'd by Frequent and Long Publick Mournings: with an Account how those Mournings affect the whole Trade of the Kingdom. *n.p. [1706?], s. sh. F°.* MC.

Endorsed: The Case of the Silk Manufacturers, &c. relating to Publick Mournings.

677 Reasons Humbly Offer'd for the Bill, for Ascertaining and Limiting the Time of Future Publick Mournings. *n.p. [1706], s. sh. F°.* MC.

678 Some Reasons Humbly Offered to the Consideration of the Honourable House of Commons, for Regulating the Publick and Frequent Mournings for Foreign Princes. *n.p. [1706], s. sh. F°.* MC.

COMMERCE

679 Further Reasons for suppressing all Pedlars and Hawkers, humbly offered to the Consideration of Parliament. In behalf of the Shopkeepers of the Cities, Corporations and Towns in England. *n.p. [1706?], s. sh. F°* L.

680 Case of the Owners and Freighters of the Ship Worcester and Cargoe, Seized and Condemned in Scotland. *n.p. [1706], s. sh. F°.* LLI.

681 At a General Court of the Adventurers of the Royal African Company of England, held the 18th Day of September, 1706. *n.p.* [*1706*], *s. sh. F°.* L.

Notice of 'a General Subscription of the Adventurers for Circulating their Spetia Bonds'.

682 African House. At a General Court of the Adventurers of the Royal African Company of England, held the 26th. Day of June, 1706. *n.p.* [*1706*], *s. sh. F°.* L.

Notice of a call of £4 per share.

683 LE WRIGHT, John. Two Proposals becoming England at this Juncture to Undertake. One, for Securing a Collony in the West-Indies, as Her Majesty's Propriety now to be enter'd upon, or for ever lost. And the other, for advancing Merchandize, and the Crown-Revenue to at least 40000 l. p. An. *n.p. 1706, 4°.* L.

The only copy seen is imperfect.

684 A Copy of Captain le Wright's Warrant for Incorporating a South-West-India Company. Pursuant to former Acts of Parliament, made provisionally for the Improvement of Her Majesties Demain's in America, Darien, and Nicaragua, excepted. *n.p. 1706, 4°.* L.

685 To His Grace, Her Majesty's High Commissioner, and the Right Honourable Estates of Parliament. The Humble Representation and Petition of the Court of Directors of the Indian and African Company. *n.p.* [*1706?*], *s. sh. F°.* O.

Protesting against the prosecution by the East India Company of the English merchants who were partners with the Darien Company in the Annandale. Dated: 28 December 1706.

686 To His Grace, Her Majesty's High Commissioner, and the Right Honourable Estates of Parliament. The Humble Representation of the Council-General of the Company of Scotland Trading to Africa and the Indies. *n.p. 1706, F°.* O.

Endorsed: Representation to the Parliament, By The Indian & African Company 1706. Protesting against their dissolution.

687 Overture for an Act concerning the Payment of the Sums out of the Equivalent to the African Company. *n.p.* [*1706*], *s. sh. F°.* JCB.

688 [OSBORNE, PEREGRINE, Duke of Leeds]. A Copy of the Marquiss of Carmarthen's Method for the Speedy Manning Her Majesty's Royal Navy; and for Encouraging Seamen, Feb. 12. 1705. *Lond. 1706, 8°.* L.

689 The Humble Address of the Right Honourable the Lords Spiritual and Temporal in Parliament Assembled: presented to Her Majesty on Tuesday the Nineteenth Day of March, 1705 [O.S.]. With Her Majesties most gracious Answer. *Lond. 1705, F°.* O.

Suggesting the appointment of a commission to consider the most effectual means of manning the Fleet.

COLONIES

690 The Humble Address of the Right Honourable the Lords Spiritual and Temporal, in Parliament Assembled, presented to Her Majesty on Wednesday the Thirteenth Day of March, 1705. relating to the Province of Carolina, and the Petition therein mentioned. With Her Majesties most gracious Answer thereunto. *Lond. 1705* [*O.S.*], *F°*. L.

The petition, signed by Joseph Boone and others, states that religious persecution will ruin the trade of the colony.

691 GRAVES, JOHN. A Memorial: Or, a Short Account of the Bahama-Islands; Of their Situation, Product, Conveniency of Trading with the Spaniards: The Benefit that ariseth by the great Quantities of Salt that is made by the Sun; and the Safety all Ships that are in Distress near those Parts do find, by having so good a Harbour as Providence to bear away to for Succour.... *n.p.* [*1706*], *4°*. L.

Another edn. Lond. 1708 (LU).

FINANCE

692 [BROUGHTON, JOHN]. An Essay upon the National Credit of England; introductory to a Proposal prepar'd for establishing the Public Credit; in such manner as to render the same highly beneficial to the Government, Trade and People of this Kingdom.... *Lond.* [*1706*], *8°*. L.

Reprinted in *The Vindication and Advancement of our National Constitution and Credit*, 1710.

693 CHAMBERLEN, PAUL. Some Proposals humbly offer'd to the Honourable the Knights, Citizens, and Burgesses in Parliament. *n.p.* [*1706?*], *s. sh. F°*. L.

Endorsed: Proposals for paying off the Debts of the Nation.

694 To the Honourable the Knights, Citizens, Burgesses, and Commishoners, in Parliament Assembled. The Humble Petition of Paul Chamberlen, Doctor of Physick. *n.p.* [*1706?*], *s. sh. F°*. LG.

Ready to communicate a proposal to raise money, when asked.

695 A Proposal for granting divers sorts of Annuities, such as the Purses of the Common People may be able to compass. Humbly offer'd to the Consideration of the Honourable the House of Commons. *Lond. 1706*, *F°*. L.

696 The Case of the Officers that were upon Half-Pay. *n.p.* [*1706?*], *s. sh. F°*. L.

697 To the Honourable the House of Commons the Proposal of Nehemiah Scott, Brewer, and Partners. Humbly Offers, The Advancing of Her Majesty's Revenue of Excise, by Way of Farm and Management.... *n.p.* [*1706?*], *s. sh. F°*. L.

Endorsed: An Abstract of the Proposal for Advancing Her Majesty's Revenue of Excise on Beer and Ale, &c.

698 A Proposal to raise a very great Sum of Ready Monies, by an easie, equal and speedy Way; which neither oppresses the Poor, nor will be heavy upon the Rich, and easily manag'd at a moderate Charge. *n.p.* [*c. 1706?*], *s. sh. F°*. MC.

For a tax of 12*d.* a cart load on coal. Endorsed: A Proposal for Raising a very great Sum of Ready Monies....

699 Instructions for Supervisors, relating to the Duties on Malt. *Lond. 1706, 8°*. LU.

Another edn. Edin. 1713 (LU).

700 Remarks on the Horrible Oppressions, Insolencies, and Unjustifiable Partialities, of the Commissioners of the Excise. With Some Historical Collections of Matter of Fact. *Lond. 1706, 4°*. LU.

Another edn. Lond. 1706, entitled: An Impartial Account of some Late Transactions in the Office of Excise. With an Historical Collection of Matters of Fact (O).

701 Mr. Halford's Case. *n.p.* [*1706?*], *s. sh. F°*. LU.

The duty on coal is stopping its carriage on the river Welland from Deeping to Stamford and the toll duties are decreasing.

702 Dr. Davenant's Opinion anent the Salt and Malt-Taxes in England. [*Edin.*], *1706, 4°*. L.

Extracted from *An Essay upon the probable Methods of making a People Gainers in the Ballance of Trade*, 1700.

703 A Bill to Impower the Lord High-Treasurer of England, or Commissioners of the Treasury for the Time being, to Compound with Francis Clies, as Surety for William Pennecke, late of Exon, Merchant, in Six several Bonds, for Duties on Tobacco, which the said William Pennecke had at the Port of Falmouth, in December, 1701. *n.p.* [*1706*], *s. sh. F°*. L.

704 The Case of Thomas Tomkins, Citizen and late Merchant in London. *n.p.* [*1706*], *s. sh. F°*. LG.

For permission to compound with the Treasury for a debt due for custom duties.

705 A Bill to Impower the Lord-High-Treasurer of England, or Commissioners of the Treasury for the Time being, to Compound with Thomas Tomkins, Cittizen and late Merchant of London, and his Securities, for the Debt by him owing to her Majesty. *n.p.* [*1706*], *s. sh. F°*. L.

706 An Act to Impower the Lord-Treasurer of England, or Commissioners of the Treasury for the Time being, to Compound with Morgan Whitley, Esq; late Receiver-General for the County of Chester, and North-Wales. *n.p.* [*1706*], *F°*. L.

A bill.

707 EDINBURGH. Act anent Tradesmen's Accompts. *Edin. 1706. s. sh. F°*. EU.

Accounts of work done for the city to be more detailed. Dated: 18 December 1706.

708 A Brief Account of Some Severe Prosecutions in the Court of Exchequer, against Several of the People called Quakers, for Non-Payment of Tythes: notwithstanding that Provision is made for the more easie Recovery thereof, by Two Late Acts. Humbly Presented to the Queen and Parliament. *Lond. 1706, 4º*. L.

709 A Discourse on a Land-Bank: or, Ways and Means to increase the Coin of this Kingdom. In two parts. The First containing the Proposals for a Bank, with some Observations on 'em. The Second shewing the Nature and Use of Coin, and the Advantages which will accrue to the Nation by the propos'd Bank. To which is added, A Postscript, with a Proposal to Advance Two hundred thousand Pounds to the Government by way of Gratuity. *Lond. 1706, 4º*. LU.

710 A List of the Names of all the Subscribers to the Loan of 250000 l. to the Emperor of Germany, for Support of the Army, under his Highness Prince Eugene of Savoy, in Italy, and Payable to his Order. Begun the 7th, and Ended the 12th of March, 1705 [O.S.]. *n.p.* [*1706*], *Fº*. MC.

711 POVEY, CHARLES. Proposals for raising a Fund of Two Thousand Pounds per Annum by an Amicable Contribution of Four Thousand Persons, each paying 2*s*. 6*d*. per Quarter, for insuring to the Heirs, or Executors of all or every one of the Subscribers after their Decease...a fair Prospect of gaining Three, Four, or Five Hundred Pounds, or more; but a certain Assurance of having a considerable Sum of Money, and Intitling a certain Number of the said Society, who shall happen to fall to Decay thro' adverse Fortune in five Years time after their Subscribing, to an Annuity of 10 Pounds a Year during their Natural Lives, and a Room to Live in Rent-free. *Lond. 1706, Fº*. LU.

712 An Account of the Amicable Society, for a Perpetual Assurance Office, as now Established and Incorporated by Her Majesty's Letters Patent under the Great Seal of England. *Lond. 1706, Fº*. L.

713 A Letter from a Member of the Amicable Society for a Perpetual Assurance; giving his Friend an Account of That Society, as it now stands Incorporated by Her Majesty's Letters Patent. *Lond. 1706, 4º*. L.

714 Reflections upon a second letter from a member of the Amicable society for a perpetual assurance: in a letter to a friend.... [*London, J. Leake, 1706*], *4 pp. 25 × 20 cm.* Kress S. 1162.

Signed E. S.

715 Unto His Grace, the Duke of Argile, Her Majesty's High Commissioner, and the Right Honourable the Estates of Parliament. The Petition of the Magistrates, Council, and Community of the Burgh of Aberdeen. [*Edin. 1706*], *s. sh. Fº*. EPRO.

For the right to tax ale.

716 Unto his Grace Her Majesties High Commissioner and honourable Estates of Parliament. The Answer for the Brewers of Dundee To the Petition Presented by the Magistrats of that Burgh. [*Edin. 1706?*], *F°*. EPRO.

Against the levy on ale.

717 Information For the Brewers of Dundee Against the Magistrats of that Burgh. [*Edin. 1706?*], *s. sh. F°*. EPRO.

718 Act in Favours of the Burgh of Dysart. [*Edin. 1706*], *s. sh. F°*. EPRO.

For levying 2*d*. a pint on ale.

719 Unto his Grace Her Majesties High Commissioner and the Right Honourable the Estates of Parliament: The Petition of the Brewers in and about Edinburgh. [*Edin. 1706*], *s. sh. F°*. EPRO.

On the hardship of the tax on ale.

720 [Brown, Andrew]. Three Essays. 1. Essay on the New Project for a Land Mint, &c. 2. A Second Essay Concerning the Land Mint. 3. A Scheme proposing a true Touch-stone, for the due Trial of a proper Union betwixt Scotland and England, &c. By the Author of the Character of the True Publick Spirit. *Edin. 1706, 8°*. EU.

All three essays had previously been issued separately; the first two in 1705; the third in 1706. For authorship see Advocates' Library Catalogue.

TRANSPORT

721 A Bill for the Encouraging the Pier and Harbour at Parton, in the County of Cumberland. *n.p.* [*1706*], *F°*. L.

In L copy 'Encouraging' has been altered to 'Enlarging' in ms.

722 The Case of the Harbour of Parton, in the County of Cumberland. *n.p.* [*1706*], *s. sh. F°*. L.

723 The Case of Sir John Lowther, Bar. and of the Inhabitants of the Town and Port of Whitehaven, in the County of Cumberland: with Reasons against a Bill for laying a Duty on Coals, to make an Harbour at Parton, a small Creek, within a Mile of the said Town. *n.p.* [*1706*], *F°*. LLI.

724 The Watermens Bill Considered as amended by the Honourable Committee. With some farther Amendments humbly propos'd. *n.p.* [*1706*], *s. sh. F°*. L.

725 The Watermens Bill Considered as amended by the Honourable Committee. *n.p.* [*1706*], *s. sh. F°*. L.

The first paragraph is identical with that of the preceding, of which this is an expanded version.

726 The Watermen and Lightermen's Case, in relation to the Bill for the better Governing Watermen and Lightermen. Humbly Submitted to the Consideration of the Lords Spiritual and Temporal in Parliament Assembled. *n.p.* [*1706*], *F°*. L.

SOCIAL CONDITIONS

727 Proposals for Establishing a Charitable Fund in the City of London, by Voluntary Gifts and Loans of Mony, to Relieve Necessitous Persons from the Oppressions and Evil Practices of ill Men; providing poor People...with Coals and other Necessaries at a cheap Rate in the Winter and Time of War, maintaining those that are not able to get their Livelihood, setting others to Work, or Employ them to Sweep and Clean the Streets...clear them from Beggars, make convenient Walks, and Repair the High-ways...with Reasons for the same, &c. shewing the Benefits that will arise thereby to the Publick. *Lond. 1706, 80°.* L.

2nd edn. 1706 (L).

728 London. Commun' Concil' tent' in Camera Guihald'....An Act for Raising a Supply towards the further Employing the Poor of the City of London, and Liberties thereof. [*Lond.*], *1704* [sic], *F°.* LG.

Dated: 11 July 1706.

729 A Bill for the better Regulating the Practice of Surgery in and about the City of London and Westminster, and the better Providing Her Majesties Fleet and Army with Skilful and Able Surgeons. *Lond. 1705* [*O.S.*], *F°.* L.

730 The Wisdom of the Nation is Foolishness. I. Taking the Apothecaries from their Shops, from Making and Mizing the Medicines. II. Paying their Advice and Attendance by the Numbers taken of the little dear Doses. III. Requesting them to Sort and Corrupt the Physicians for their own Purposes. Or, The Necessity of Dissolving the Apothecaries Company Demonstrated by the College Discourses.... *Lond. 1706, 8°.* L.

731 Considerations upon the Bill, to prevent Frauds frequently committed by Bankrupts, humbly submitted to the High Court of Parliament; together with Reasons for some Clause or Provision therein to be made, for the Incouragement of Debtors to discover and deliver up their Estates, for the Equal Benefit of their Creditors. *n.p.* [*1706?*], *s. sh. F°.* L.

732 The deplorable Case of such unfortunate Debtors as have been declared Bankrupts. *n.p.* [*1706?*], *s. sh. F°.* LG.

733 Reasons Humbly Offered for Passing the bill, now depending in Parliament, relating to Bankrupts. *n.p.* [*1706*], *s. sh. F°.* LG.

734 [Defoe, Daniel]. Remarks on the Bill to Prevent Frauds committed by Bankrupts, with Observations on the Effect it may have upon Trade. *Lond. 1706, 4°.* L.

For authorship see *C.B.E.L.* II, 499.

735 Observations on the Bankrupts Bill: occasion'd by the Many False Representations, and Unjust Reflections, of Mr. Daniel De Foe, in his

several Discourses on that Head. Humbly offered to the Consideration of all fair Traders. By a Well-wisher to Trade and Credit. *Lond. 1706*, *4°*. O.

The only copy seen is imperfect.

736 Portrait au Naturel du Committé François, ou l'on voit le Dessein que les Commissaires dudit Committé eurent en priant les Eglises Françoises de nommer & de se choisir des Personnes d'entre leurs Anciens, pour être Distributeurs aux Bureaux établis pour faire aux Commun Peuple la Distribution de la Beneficence Royale.... *n.p. 1706*, *8°*. O.

Alleging malversation.

737 Unto His Grace Her Majesty's High Commissioner and the Right Honourable Estates of Parliament. The Petition of the Begging and wanting Poor in the Nation. [*Edin. 1706*], *F°*. E.

738 To His Grace, the Duke of Queensberry, Her Majesty's High Commissioner, and the Right Honourable the Estates of Parliament. The Petition of George Drummond Keeper of the Tolbooth of Edinburgh. [*Edin. 1706*], *s. sh. F°*. O.

1707

GENERAL

739 The Generous Advertiser, or Weekly Information of Trade and Business. To be published every Tuesday and Friday, and 4000 of them always carefully distributed and given away gratis each day in and about the City's of London and Westminster. No. 14, 17, 18, 21. March 18, 28; April 1, 11, 1707. *Lond. 1707*, *F°*. L.

740 BLACK, WILLIAM. The Privileges of the Royal Burrows as contained in their particular Rights, and the Ancient Laws and Records of Parliament, and their General Convention; wherein is considered the Privileges of Merchants, Privileges of Burghs, the Privileges of the Guild...and how far it is the Interest of the Royal Burrows now to observe and maintain their Privileges, by making such Regulations as may tend to the Advantage of all their Trading Society. With an Appendix containing the Privileges and Jurisdictions of the Cities of Edinburgh and Aberdeen. By W. B. Advocat. *Edin. 1707*, *8°*. LU.

The dedication signed: Wil. Black.

741 The Articles of the Treaty for an Union between England and Scotland, Agreed on by the Commissioners of both Kingdoms, on the Twenty Second of July, 1706. And the Act of Parliament pass'd in the Parliament of Scotland for Ratifying the said Articles with Amendments. Together with the Act of Parliament also pass'd there, for Securing the Protestant Religion and Presbyterian Church Government in that Kingdom. *Lond. 1707*, *F°*. O.

742 The Case of Joseph, Thomas and George Musgrave, Sons of Sir Christopher Musgrave, by Dame Elizabeth his second Wife, both deceased, upon the taking off the Duties on Scotch Cattle by the Articles of the Union ratify'd by the Parliament of Scotland. *n.p.* [*1707*], *s. sh. F°*. LLI.

For compensation for the abolition of their tolls.

743 A Discourse between a Mureland Man, and a Stablers Wife, concerning the Burying in Woolen. [*Edin. 1707*], *s. sh. F°*. L.

On the economic consequences of the Union.

744 [DEFOE, DANIEL]. A Fifth Essay, at Removing National Prejudices; with a Reply to Some Authors, who have Printed their Objections against an Union with England. [*Edin.*], *MDCVII* [*1707*], *4°*. LU.

For authorship see *C.B.E.L.* II, 500.

745 The Preface to the Fifth Essay, at Removing National Prejudices, &c. considered, In a Letter to the Author of the Consideration upon Trade. [*Edin. 1707*], *4°*. E.

746 [GRANT, Sir FRANCIS, Lord Cullen]. The Patriot Resolved, in a Letter

to an Addresser, from his Friend; of the same Sentiments with himself; concerning the Union. *n.p.* *1707*, 4°. L.

For authorship see *D.N.B.*

747 [CAMPBELL, DUGALD]. A Reply to the Authors of the Advantages of Scotland by an Incorporate Union; and of The Fifth Essay, at Removing National Prejudices. Or, A Vindication of the Author of the Advantages of the Act of Security, in Opposition to the Incorporating Union. *n.p.* *1707*, 4°. LU.

For authorship see Advocates' Library Catalogue.

748 [BLACK, WILLIAM]. Some Overtures and Cautions in Relation to Trade and Taxes, Humbly Offered to the Parliament. By a Well-wisher to his Country. *n.p.* *1707*, 4°. LU.

For authorship see ms. note in E copy.

749 Remarks for the Salt-Masters, Fishers of Salmond, Herrings and White-Fish, and others who make use of Scots Salt, Humbly Offered upon the Eighth Article of the Treaty of Union. *n.p.* [*1707?*], *s. sh.* *F°*. L.

750 A Scheme for Uniting the two Kingdoms of England and Scotland, different from any that has been hitherto laid down. *n.p.* [*1707?*], 4°. E.

AGRICULTURE

751 [MORTIMER, JOHN]. The Whole Art of Husbandry, or, the Way of Managing and Improving of Land. Being a full Collection of what hath been Writ, either by ancient or modern Authors: With many Additions of new Experiments and Improvements, not treated of by any others.... By J. M. Esq; F.R.S. *Lond.* *1707*, 8°. L.

2nd edn., with author's name, 1708 (L); 3rd edn. 1712 (R). Part II, 1712 (L). 4th edn., both parts, 1716 (LU); 5th edn. 1721 (L); another 5th edn. Dublin, 1721 (R); 6th edn. Lond. 1761 (L).

752 Reasons humbly offered to the Right Honorable The Lords Spiritual and Temporal, in Parliament Assembled, Against Passing a Bill, now before their Lordships, For Better Preservation of the Game, in the Manner 'tis now Fram'd. *n.p.* [*1707*], *s. sh.* *F°*. L.

On behalf of the Poulterers of London and Westminster.

753 The Case of Sir Humphrey Mackworth, and the Mine Adventurers, with Respect to the Extraordinary Proceedings of the Agents, Servants and Dependents, of the Right Honourable Sir Thomas Mansell, Bar. *Lond.* *1707*, 4°. LU.

754 [HETON, THOMAS]. Some Account of Mines, and the Advantages of them to this Kingdom. With an Appendix relating to the Mine-Adventure in Wales. *Lond.* *1707*, 8°. LU.

A later issue of the same year has the author's name on the title-page (L). Reissued 1721 (LU).

755 IMBER, MATTHEW. The Case, or an Abstract of the Customs of the Mannor of Merdon, in the Parish of Hursely in the County of Southampton, which are to be Observed and Performed by the Lord and Customary Tenants of the said Mannor, their Heirs and Successors for Ever.... *Lond.* *1707*, *12°*. L.

756 An Answer to the Objections against the Bill for Inrollment of Deeds and Registring Judgments, &c. in the West-Riding of Yorkshire, and some Reasons Humbly Offered for the said Bill. *n.p.* [*1707*], *s. sh.* *F°*. L.

Title taken from endorsement.

757 The Humble Representation of the Commons of Ireland, against the Proceedings of the late Trustees for the Forfeited Estates in that Kingdom. *Lond.* *1707*. *s. sh.* *F°*. L.

Another edn. Dublin, 1707, s. sh. F° (D).

MANUFACTURES

758 [BLANCH, JOHN]. The Interest of Great Britain consider'd; in an Essay upon Wool, Tin and Leather: proving by Instances of Fact, that the Misfortune, which has attended this Kingdom for above four hundred Years last past, has been chiefly Occasion'd by the Neglect of our Commerce; and that the Ballance of Power in Christendom, is by the Ballance of Trade. With some Remarks upon the Conceptions of Sir Josiah Child. Written by J. B. *Lond.* *1707*, *8°*. L.

A revised edn., with a new preface, of *The Interest of England considered*, published without initials in 1694. For authorship see Blanch's list of his works in his *Swords into Anchors*, 1725.

759 The Case of Mr. John Gumley and his Partners; Proprietors of a Glass-House over against Hungerford-Market: Humbly offered to the Consideration of the Honourable the House of Commons, against the Bill for suppressing of New Glass-Houses, &c. *n.p.* [*1707*], *s. sh.* *F°*. LLI.

760 The Answer of the Proprietors of the Bear-Garden Glass-House to the Case of Mr. John Gumley, and Partners, Proprietors of the Glass-House over against Hungerford-Market. *n.p.* [*1707*], *s. sh.* *F°*. L.

761 The Case of the Company of Gun-Makers. *n.p.* [*1707*], *s. sh.* *F°*. MC.

Endorsed: [The] Gun-Makers Case.

762 The Case of the Royal Lustring Company. *n.p.* [*1707*], *s. sh.* *F°*. L.

763 The Case of the Rope-makers of London, and other Parts of England. Humbly Offered to the Honourable House of Commons. *n.p.* [*1707?*] *s. sh.* *F°*. MC.

764 A Bill for the better Preserving the Ancient Salt-Springs in Droytwych, in the County of Worcester, and the Rights of the Proprietors thereof; And Increasing the Duty of Salt to be made out of those Springs. *n.p.* [*1707?*], *F°*. L.

765 The Case of the Master, Wardens, Assistants, and Commonalty of the Company of Tin-Plate-Workers of London. *n.p.* [*1707*], *s. sh. F°*. LG.

Endorsed: The Case of the Company of Tin-Plate-Workers. Praying relief from the additional duty on tin-plate.

766 The Case of the Upholsters of England, Humbly offered to the Consideration of the Honourable the Knights, Citizens, and Burgesses, Assembled in Parliament. *n.p.* [*1707*], *s. sh. F°*. LLI.

767 [Knox, Thomas]. A Brief Account of the Woollen Manufactury of England, with relation to the Prejudice it Receives by the Clandestine Exportation of Wooll from Ireland into France. *Lond. 1707*, *4°*. C.

2nd edn., with appendix, 1708 (L). The author's letters in the appendix are signed: T.K. For authorship see *Journal of the Commissioners of Trade and Plantations*, 15 Dec. 1707.

768 The Grievances of the Brewers in and about Edinburgh, In a Letter to a Member of Parliament. [*Edin.*, *1707?*], *4°*. M (Cr).

Signed: Philo-Zythepsus.

769 Reasons for passing into an Act, an Overture in Parliament, for making Salt of a new Fashion. *n.p.* [*1707?*], *s. sh. F°*. GU.

For the benefit of shareholders in the Darien Company.

COMMERCE

770 Whiston's Merchant's Weekly Remembrancer of the Prices of their Goods Ashoar in London. 7 July 1707. [*Lond. 1707*], *F°*. LU (photostat).

771 The Case of the Butchers of the Cities of London and Westminster, and Suburbs thereof, and other Freemen of London, against a Grant that is Passing, of a Market, to Mr. Charles and Mr. Richard Hore, to be held Tuesday, Thursdays, and Saturdays, in St. John's Street near Hicks's Hall, as was at first Intended; but now in a Place call'd Vinegar-Ground, in the Parish of St. James Clerkenwell, in the County of Middlesex, for the Sale of the Skins of all such Sheep and Lambs, as shall be Killed within the compass of the Bills of Mortality. *n.p.* [*1707?*], *F°*. *L.*

Endorsed: The Butchers Casė.

772 London. Bedingfield Mayor. Die Martis, Duodecimo die Augusti, 1707.... [*Lond. 1707*], *s. sh. F°*. L.

Regulations with regard to Bartholomew Fair.

773 Reasons humbly Offer'd for a Bill for the Encouragement of Learning, and Improvement of Printing. *n.p.* [*1707?*], *s. sh. F°*. LLI.

For a copyright act.

774 Reasons humbly offered to the Consideration of the Honourable House of Commons, relating to the Bill, for Securing Property in Books, &c. *n.p.* [*1707?*], *s. sh. F°*. LLI.

775 Reasons Humbly Offered against a Clause in a Bill, for taking off the Prohibition on Flanders Lace; by which Clause the Country Lace-Buyers and Lace-Makers are confined to sell their Lace only at such Places as the Lord Mayor and Aldermen of London have or shall License. *n.p.* [*1707*], *s. sh. F°.* L.

776 The Detection of Dangerous and Daily Practices in Selling great Quantities of Unwholsome or Stolen Flesh, of all sorts, within the Bills of Mortality of the City of London, and the proper Means to Prevent the same. Humbly Submitted to the Consideration of the Honourable House of Commons. *n.p.* [*1707*], *s. sh. F°.* LLI.

Endorsed: The Case of the Grasiers of England.

777 Mors in Olla: Or, the common and destructive Practice of Selling Measled Pork, and Diseased and Corrupt Flesh Prevented. Humbly offer'd to the Consideration of the Honourable House of Commons. *n.p.* [*1707*], *s. sh. F°.* MC.

778 Reasons humbly offer'd by the Powder-Makers against the Bill for preventing the Dangers which may arise from bringing great Quantities of Gunpowder into London and the Liberties thereof. *n.p.* [*1707*], *s. sh. F°.* MC.

779 Reasons humbly offer'd to the Lords Spiritual and Temporal, for Passing the Bill, to Prevent the Dangers which may Arise from bringing great Quantitys of Gun-Powder into London, and the Liberties thereof. *n.p.* [*1707*], *s. sh. F°.* MC.

Endorsed: Reasons for Passing the Gun-Powder Bill.

780 The Case of Tho. Bowrey, Tho. Hammond, John Starke, and divers others the Owners and Freighters of the Ship Worcester; Capt. Tho. Green late Commander, Seiz'd and Condemn'd in Scotland. *n.p.* [*1707*], *s. sh. F°.* LLI.

Endorsed: Case of the Owners of the Ship Worcester and Cargoe seized in Scotland.

781 The Clause proposed in the English Parliament to Prevent the French Goods being Imported thro' Scotland; With a short Remark on the same. *Edin.* *1707*, *s. sh. F°.* E.

782 The Humble Address of the Scots Merchants at London, to the Right Honourable the Lords Spiritual and Temporal Assembled in Parliament, against passing the Bill, for laying Duties upon Goods which may be brought by Her Majesty's Subjects, from Scotland to England after the commencement of the Union. *n.p.* [*1707*], *s. sh. F°.* E.

783 A Letter from a Scots Factor at London to a Merchant in Edinburgh, concerning the Proceeding of the House of Commons; to prevent the Importation of Wines and other Goods from Scotland. [*Edin.* *1707*], *s. sh. F°.* L.

Dated: London, 17 April 1707.

784 Reasons against passing the Bill to prevent carrying Forreign Goods from Scotland to England, after the Union, contained in a second Letter from a Scots Factor at London, to a Merchant in Edinburgh. [*Edin. 1707*], *s. sh. F°*. L.

Dated: London, April, 22 1707.

785 [DEFOE, DANIEL]. The Trade of Britain stated; being the Substance of two Papers published in London on Occasion of the Importation of Wine and Brandy from North-Britain. *Edin.* [*1707*], *4°*. L.

For authorship see *C.B.E.L.* II, 500.

786 Votes of the House of Commons concerning Subsidies to be Raised over the Whole Island and for making good the Damage to the Owners of Capt. Greens Ship Condemned in Scotland. *n.p.* [*1707*], *s. sh. F°*. E.

787 The Russia Merchants Complaints against Admiral Whetston's Conduct. With what was said in his Vindication. In a Letter to a Noble Lord. *n.p.* [*1707?*], *F°*. L.

788 The State of the Trade to Africa, between 1680 and 1707, as well under the Management of an Exclusive Company, as under that of Separate Traders, Impartially considered, with Regard to Matter of Fact and Demonstration; whereby it appears the Separate Adventurers have Improv'd that Trade to the Benefit of Great-Britain at least One Million a Year. *n.p.* [*1707*], *F°*. LU.

Endorsed: The Trade to Africa Considered, and Demonstrated to be Improved to the Nation's Benefit near a Million a Year by Separate Traders. Third line of title ends: Re-|; another edn. [1708], F°, with third line of title ending: with | (L).

789 Arthur Zouch his Case, in relation to the Royal African Company's Proceedings against him, as a Criminal, with their Servant Henry Bishop. *n.p.* [*1707*], *s. sh. F°*. L.

790 Henry Bishop's Case, in Relation to the Royal African Company's Proceedings against him. *n.p.* [*1707*], *s. sh. F°*. LLI.

791 An Account of what will do; or; an Equivalent for Thoulon: in a Proposal for an Amicable Subscription for Improving Trade in the South-West Part of America, and Increasing Bullion to about Three Millions Per Annum, both for the East-India Trade, and the Revenue of the Crown, which by Consequence will be Produced if this be Encouraged. *Lond. 1707*, *8°*. L.

792 *Begin.* In the Name of God, Amen. Whereas the Coasts of Chiley, Peru, and Mexico, bordering on the South-Seas, between the Streights of Magellan and California, abound with vast Wealth and Treasure. And whereas the Traffick to these Countries is chiefly driven with the Products and Manufactures of Great-Britain; for which Returns are

made in Gold and Silver, rich Dying-Stuffs, &c..... *n.p.* [*1707*], *12°*. O.

A proposal to form a joint-stock company to be called The Merchant-Adventurers of Great-Britain. The internal evidence indicates James Puckle as the author and a reprint of his *England's Path to Wealth and Honour* follows these proposals.

793 A Letter to a Member of Parliament concerning Trade; and particularly the Trade of the Spanish West-Indies. *Lond. 1707, 4°*, L.

794 A Letter to Sir William Robinson, in Relation to a Proposal for a Trade to the Spanish West-Indies. *Lond. 1707, 4°*. L.

795 The Old and True way of Manning the Fleet: Or how to Retrieve the Glory of the English Arms by Sea, as it is done by Land; and to have Seamen always in readiness, without Pressing. In a Letter from an Old Parliament Sea-Commander, to a Member of the present House of Commons, desiring his Advice on that Subject. *Lond. 1707, 4°*. L.

Another edn. entitled: An Inquiry into the Causes of our Naval Miscarriages: with Some Thoughts on the Interest of this Nation as to a Naval War, and of the only true Way of Manning the Fleet. The Second Edition... Lond. 1707. 4° (L). Reprinted in *Harleian Miscellany*, I (1808), 562.

796 Reasons for Reducing the Pyrates at Madagascar: and Proposals humbly offered to the Honourable House of Commons for, effecting the same. *n.p.* [*1707*], *F°*. O.

797 FUNNELL, WILLIAM. A Voyage round the World. Containing an Account of Captain Dampier's Expedition into the South-Seas in the Ship St George, in the Years 1703 and 1704....Together with the Author's Voyage from Amapalla on the West-Coast of Mexico, to East-India....His Arrival at Amboyna: with a large Description of that and other Spice Islands.... *Lond. 1707, 8°*. L.

798 *Begin.* Edinburgh 3d. February 1707. Sir, The Parliament.... *n.p.* [*1707*], *s. sh. F°*. JCB.

Notice of a meeting of the Council-General of the Darien Company to nominate a committee to settle as to the payment of the Equivalent.

799 To the Right Honourable, The Lords of Her Majestie's Privy Council, The Directors of the late Company of Scotland, Trading to Africa and the Indies. For themselves and others concerned with them in the Ships and Adventures afore-mentioned. [*Edin. 1707*], *s. sh. F°*. E.

800 Report of the Committee concerning the Indian and African Company. Edinburgh 21. February, 1707. *n.p.* [*1707*], *s. sh. F°*. E.

801 Overture Concerning the Debts of the African and Indian Company. *n.p.* [*1707*], *s. sh. F°*. E.

802 Some neutral considerations with relation to Two Printed Papers, which are Cry'd about the Streets, viz., The Committee of Parliament's Report concerning the Indian and African Company, and an Overture,

concerning the Debts of the said Company. In a Letter to a Member of Parliament. *n.p.* [*1707*], *s. sh. F*°. E.

Signed: R.S. Tentatively attributed to R. Seton in John Scott's *A Bibliography of Printed Documents and Books relating to the Scottish Company, commonly called the Darien Company*, no. 195 (*Papers of the Edinburgh Bibliographical Society*, vol. VI).

803 Proclamation anent Payment to the Proprietors of the African-Company. *Edin. 1707*, *s. sh. F*°. E.

Dated: 21 August 1707.

804 The Case of the Land-Officers who went in the Service of the Indian and African Company, on their First Expedition to Caledonia. Humbly offered to the Consideration of the Right Honourable Committee of Parliament, to whom it is referred to adjust the said Company's Quota of the Equivalent, &c. *n.p. 1707*, *F*°. E.

805 Act and Order of the Justices of the Peace of the Shire of Midlothian. Anent the Reducing of the Brewers Casks and Trees. *n.p.* [*1707*], *s. sh. F*°. L.

Dated: 1 Oct. 1707.

806 A Discourse between a Tapster Lass and a Brewers Man, concerning the Gaging, and takging down the Ale Trees. [*Edin. 1707?*], *s. sh. F*°. C (Cr).

807 The Ale-Sellers Complaint, upon taking down the Ale-Barrels, Being a Discourse between a Brewer, a Vintner and a Gauger on that Subject. [*Edin.? 1707*], *F*°. L.

COLONIES

808 [MATHER, COTTON]. A Memorial of the Present Deplorable State of New-England, with the many Disadvantages it lyes under, by the Male-Administration of the Present Governor, Joseph Dudley, Esq. and his Son Paul, &c.... Faithfully Digested from the several Original Letters, Papers, and MSS. by Philopolites. *Boston, 1707*, *4*°. L.

For authorship see T. J. Holmes, *Cotton Mather*, p. 668. Another edn. Boston, 1879, *Mass. Hist. Soc. Coll.* ser. 5, vol. 6.

809 [DUDLEY, JOSEPH]. A Modest Enquiry into the Grounds and Occasions of a Late Pamphlet, intituled, a Memorial of the Present Deplorable State of New-England. By a Disinterested Hand. *Lond. 1707*, *4*°. L.

For authorship see E. Kimball, *The Public Life of Joseph Dudley*, p. 188. Another edn. Boston 1879, *Mass. Hist. Soc. Coll. Ser.* 5, vol. 6.

810 ARCHDALE, JOHN. A New Description of that Fertile and Pleasant Province of Carolina: with a brief account of its Discovery, Settling, and the Government thereof to this Time. With several Remarkable Passages of Divine Providence during my Time. *Lond. 1707. 4*°. L.

Included in B.R. Carroll's *Historical Collections of South Carolina*, vol. 2, 1836, and in A. S. Sally's *Narratives of Early Carolina*, 1911.

811 To the Honourable the Knights, Citizens, and Burgesses in Parliament Assembled. The humble Petition of several Proprietors of Plantations in the Islands of Nevis and St. Christophers in America, and Merchants Trading to the same.... *n.p.* [*1707*], *s. sh. F°.* L.

FINANCE

812 The annuity-bill and grand mortgage, consider'd. In a letter from a country-gentleman, to his friend in London. *n.p.* [*1707*], *21½* × *17 cm.* Kress 2537.

Dated: March 19, 1706–7.

813 Reasons against charging Trade with Annuities, in Answer to a Letter from a Merchant in London, to his Friend in the Country. *n.p.* [*1707*], *4°.* LU.

The only copy seen lacks title-page.

814 Easie Methods for Raising of Moneys for Her Majesty, by a Duty to be laid upon Calicoes & Linen Cloth, &c. to be Glazed and Printed. And upon Soap. *n.p.* [*1707*], *fol.* L.

Title from endorsement. The schemes are entitled: 'Proposals Humbly Offered to the Honourable House of Commons, for Raising of One Hundred Sixty Six Thousand Six Hundred Sixty Six Pounds Thirteen Shillings and Four Pence per Annum, by a Tax or Duty to be laid upon Printers and Glazers of Calicoes and Linen Cloth....' Last Sentence: 'Answered by Thomas Leader, and Two other Persons' and 'Proposals Humbly Offered to the Honourable House of Commons, for Raising above 100000 l. per Annum, by laying a Small Duty upon Soap. By Thomas Leader Soapmaker, and Two other Persons.'

815 A Proposal for raising the immediate Sum of One Million of Money or upwards: and also such an Annual Sum for ever, as will be a sufficient Fund for the raising a further Sum of Two Millions by Annuities, or otherwise without affecting Land or Trade....Humbly offer'd to the Honourable the House of Commons. *Lond. 1707*, *F°.* O.

816 A collection of all the statutes now in force, relating to the duties upon salt, with so much of the laws of excise, as are particularly referr'd to in the said statutes, to which is added an abridgement of the whole, alphabetically digested under proper heads and titles. *Lond. 1707*, *15 cm.* Kress 2547.

817 A Bill to Impower the Lord High-Treasurer of England, or Commissioners of the Treasury for the time being, to Compound with Benjamin Niccoll, Citizen and late Merchant of London, and his Securities, for the Debt by him Owing to Her Majesty. *n. p.* [*1707*], *F°.* L.

Money due for customs duties.

818 An Act to Enable the Lord Treasurer, or Commissioners of the Treasury, to Compound with Thomas [sic for John] Cross, Merchant. *Lond. 1707*, *s. sh. F°.* L.

Money owed for customs duties.

819 A Bill to Impower the Lord High-Treasurer of England, or Commissioners of the Treasury, for the Time being, to Compound with Nathaniel Rich Esq; late Receiver General for the County of Essex. *n.p.* [*1707*], *s. sh. F*°. O.

820 HOLBECH, WILLIAM. A Case relating to the Frauds committed by the Receivers-General or their Deputies. *n.p.* [*1707*], *s. sh. F*°. MC.
Dated: 6th of December, 1707.

821 The Report from the Select Committee appointed to take into Consideration the Petition of Thomas Gore and Simon Sherlock, in Behalf of themselves and Sixty other Persons. *Dublin*, *1707*, *F*°. O.
On frauds in clothing the army.

822 PRIDEAUX, HUMPHREY, Dean of Norwich. An Award of King Charles the First, Under His Broad Seal. Settling Two Shillings of the Pound out of the Rents of the Houses in Norwich for the Maintenance of the Parochial Clergy of that City, in lieu of Personal Tithes. With a Treatise vindicating the Legality and Justice of that Award, and showing, That Personal Tithes...are still due by the Law of the Land. *Lond. 1707*, *4*°. L.

823 [FLEETWOOD, WILLIAM, Bishop of Ely]. Chronicon Preciosum: or, an Account of English Money, the Price of Corn, and Other Commodities, for the last 600 Years. In a Letter to a Student in the University of Oxford. *Lond. 1707*, *8*°. LU.
Another edn., with author's name, 1745 (L). Also included in *A Compleat Collection of the Sermons, Tracts and Pieces of all Kinds, that were written by... Dr. William Fleetwood*, 1737.

824 [JUSTICE, ALEXANDER]. A General Treatise of Monies and Exchanges; in which those of all Trading Nations are particularly Describ'd and Consider'd. With an Account of all the Foreign Banks and different Species and Denominations of Monies....Together with an exact Translation of the excellent Ordinances lately publish'd in France, for Exchange and Commerce, and the Regulations of most Trading Places upon that Subject. With an Introductory Discourse on the Nature and Origin of Exchange....As also, Tables of the Reduction of the Monies and Exchanges of the most Considerable Towns in Europe. To which is subjoyn'd, A General Discourse of the Trade and Commodities of most Nations....Together with an Universal Treatise of the Weights and Measures usual in Trade all over the World.... By a Well-wisher to Trade. *Lond. 1707*, *4*°. LU.
The dedication signed: A.J. For authorship see ms. note in O copy.

825 Animadversions on the Bank of England. In a Letter to a Friend. *Lond. 1707*, *s. sh. F*°. Kress 2536.

826 The Reasons of the Decay of Trade and Private Credit. Recommended to the Perusal of all True Englishmen. By a Merchant of London. *Lond. 1707*, *8*°. LU.
Attacks the Bank.

827 Reasons offer'd against the Continuance of the Bank. In a Letter to a Member of Parliament. *Lond. 1707, 8º.* L.

Price 2 Pence. Another edn.: Price One Penny (L).

828 Reasons against the Prolongation of the Bank: in a Letter to a Member of Parliament, Review'd With a Postscript, prefering the Excise before the Bank. *Lond. 1707, 4º.* L.

A revised edition of the preceding. Another edn. 1708, entitled: Arguments against Prolonging the Bank...(L).

829 A Short View of the Apparent Dangers and Mischiefs from the Bank of England. More particularly address'd to the Country Gentlemen. *Lond. 1707, 4º.* LU.

Reissued in 1708 as: The Mischievous and Dangerous Consequences of Further Establishing the Bank of England, consider'd (LU).

830 [TENCH, NATHANIEL]. A Defence of the Bank of England: or, a Reply to a Late Pamphlet entitul'd Remarks upon the Bank of England, &c. set forth before the last Sessions of the present Parliament, and now again Reprinted. And also, Some short Remarks upon Two Late Pamphlets; one Entitul'd A Short View of the Apparent Dangers and Mischiefs from the Bank of England: The other, Reasons offered against the Continuance of the Bank. In a Letter to a Member of Parliament. *Lond. 1707, 4º.* LU.

For authorship see J. Stow, *Survey*, ed. J. Strype, 1720, bk. 3, p. 33.

831 [CLEMENT, SIMON]. A Vindication of the Bank of England from the Misrepresentations, and Groundless Suggestions of a late Pamphlet, entituled, Remarks upon the Bank of England. To which is added, by way of appendix, Essays upon Banks, upon Credit, and upon Plenty and Scarcity of Money. By a Merchant. *Lond. 1707, 8º.* LU.

Authorship acknowledged in Clement's *Faults on both Sides*, 1710.

832 [BEECKMAN, DANIEL]. A method proposed, that will raise a great sum of money to the government, prevent all robberies on the highways, double the income of the Post-Office, and encrease dealings of all kinds; humbly offer'd to the consideration of the Parliament of Great Britain.... [*London, E. Everingham, etc. 1707*], *37 cm.* Kress S.1166.

Indorsed: A benefit ticket for the traders of Great Britain: or Proposals for a general inland exchange. A plan for a system of branch banks.

833 *Begin.* Sir, Thursday the 8th of May, 1707. is Appointed for Chusing Trustees for the First Society of Assurance for Widows and Orphans.... *Lond. 1707, Fº.* LG.

The notice is followed by a List of Subscribers from whom the Trustees are to be chosen.

834 [RICHARDS, THOMAS]. The Gentlemans Auditor: or a New and Easie Method for keeping Accompts of Gentlemens Estates as well in relation to their layings out, as comings in: With the manner of Auditing and Stating the Accompts of their Cashiers, Stewards, Bailiffs, Rent-

Gatherers, and other Servants...And transposing them to a Ledger kept after the Italian manner....By T.R. *Lond.* 1707, 4°. LU.

3rd edn. 1707 (LICA). *The Young Accomptant's Tutor.... By the Author of the Gentleman's Auditor*, 1710, has a dedication signed: Tho. Richards.

835 Act of the Commissioners for the Equivalent. At Edinburgh, the Twenty Third day of June, One Thousand Seven Hundred and Seven Years. *Edin.* 1707, *s. sh. F°.* EP.

836 Act and Ordinance of Privy Council Anent English Exchequer Bills. *Edin.* 1707, *F°.* L

Dated: 21 August 1707.

837 Proclamation of the Commissioners of the Equivalent. *Edin.* 1707, *s. sh. F°.* E.

Dated: 8 August 1707.

838 Proclamation Anent the Customs and Excise. *Edin.* 1707, *F°.* L.

Dated: 29 April 1707.

839 [CROOKSHANKS, JOHN]. Instructions for the Collectors and other Officers Employ'd in Her Majesties Customs, &c. in the North-Part of Great-Britain; with Forms of Dispatches, Schemes for Calculations, and the regular Methods of Accompting. *Edin.* 1707, *F°.* LU.

Authorship given in ms. note in EU copy.

840 Proclamation anent the Rates and Duties of Excise. *Edin.* 1707, *s. sh. F°.* E.

Dated: 4 July 1707.

841 To the Right Honourable the Lords Commissioners of Her Majesty's Treasury and Exchequer, the Whole Brewers within Edinburgh and Liberties thereof for themselves, and Brewers within that Part of Great-Britain called Scotland, Do Humbly Represent.... *n.p.* [1707], *s. sh. F°.* LPRO.

On the excise.

842 Unto his Grace, Her Majesty's High Commissioner, and the Honourable Estates of Parliament. The Brewers of Dundee. [*Edin.* 1707], *s. sh. F°.* EPRO.

843 Proclamation Concerning the Coin. *Edin.* 1707, *s. sh. F°.* E.

Dated: 5 February 1707.

844 Proclamation Concerning English Coyn. *Edin.* 1707, *s. sh. F°.* E.

Dated: 28 March 1707.

845 Act and Intimation anent opening of the Mint and Re-coining the Forreign Money. *Edin.* 1707, *s. sh. F°.* E.

Dated: 22 August 1707.

846 Proclamation for calling in the Forreign Coyn, now current in Scotland. *Edin.* 1707, *s. sh. F°.* E.

Dated: 19 September 1707.

847 The Crying down of the Money Considered. [*Edin.* 1707], *s. sh. F°.* LU.

TRANSPORT

848 The Case of the Counties Norfolk, Suffolk, City of Norwich, and County of the same, against the Corporation of Great Yarmouth. *n.p.* [*1707*], *s. sh. F°.* LLI.

The price of coal is raised intolerably high by the great dues exacted by the Corporation.

849 Reasons humbly offered to the Honourable House of Commons against passing the Depending Bill in relation to Watermen and Lightermen, in its Present Form. *n.p.* [*1707*], *s. sh. F°.* DG.

850 The Case of the Conservators of the River Tone, in the County of Somerset: Humbly Offered to the Consideration of the Commons of Great-Britain in Parliament Assembled. *n.p.* [*1707?*], *s. sh. F°.* L.

851 The Case of the Inhabitants and Traders residing in the several Counties of Somerset and Devon, and Trading at Coal Harbour in the said County of Somerset. *n.p.* [*1707?*], *s. sh. F°.* LLI.

Endorsed: The Case of the Inhabitants and Traders of the Counties of Somersetshire, Devonshire and Dorsetshire, &c. Against the Bill of the Conservators of the River Sone [*sic* for Tone].

852 The Hackney-Coachmen's Case, that Hire Licenses, which is in Number about 400. Humbly presented to the Knights, Citizens, and Burgesses in Parliament Assembled. *n.p.* [*1707?*], *s. sh. F°.* LG.

853 Unto his Grace, John Duke of Argyll Her Majesties High Commissioner, and the Right Honourable the Estates of Parliament. The Petition of James Cuningham.... [*Edin. 1707*], *s. sh. F°.* C (Cr).

The building of the harbour at Saltcoats in Ayrshire has been a vast expense. Requests to be allowed to continue Tacksman of the Excises of Stevenstown and Ardrossan.

SOCIAL CONDITIONS

854 A List of the Names, and Gifts of all the Persons who have Subscrib'd towards the Establishment of a Charitable Fund in the City of London, by voluntary Gifts and Loans of Money, to relieve Poor, necessitous, and oppress'd Persons...as they stand one after another in the Books of Subscription, and are entitled to Votes at the Election of the Governors or Trustees of the said Fund, according to the printed Proposals that have been distributed. *n.p.* [*1707*], *F°.* LU.

855 [Pitt, Robert]. The Calamities of all the English in Sickness; and the Sufferings of the Apothecaries from their Unbounded Increase, with the Sovereign Legal Remedies, presented to the Governors of St. Bartholomew's-Hospital. With some Proposals to improve the Charity and Revenues of all the famous Hospitals in London. *Lond. 1707*, 4°. O.

For authorship see O copy, a presentation one from the author.

856 An Abstract of the Orders of St. Thomas's Hospital in Southwark, 1707. *n.p.* [*1707*], *s. sh. F°*. L.

857 Mortimer, Margaret. Proposals Tender'd for an Addition to the late Act of Parliament for Collecting Charity on Briefs by Letters Patents.... *Lond. 1707*, *4°*. LU.

858 Mortimer, Margaret. Reasons humbly offer'd to the Parliament of Great Britain for some Alterations and Additions to a late Act of Parliament, intitled, An Act for the better Collecting Charity Mony on Briefs by Letters Patents, and preventing Abuses, &c. *n.p.* [*1707?*], *s. sh. F°*. MC.

859 Considerations Most Humbly Offered to the High Court of Parliament, For the further Relief of Creditors, by some New Bill or Clause to be Enacted. *n.p.* [*1707*], *s. sh. F°*. MC.

Endorsed: Considerations for the Relief of Creditors.

860 The honour and advantage of Great Britain in a general act of redemption for insolvent debtors. Humbly offered to the consideration of the first British Parliament.... *Lond. 1707*, *20 × 15½ cm.* Kress 2557.

861 The Case of Bankrupts return'd from beyond the Seas, at the Request of their respective Creditors, Humbly submitted to the Compassionate consideration of the Honourable House of Commons. *n.p.* [*1707?*], *s. sh. F°*. LLI.

862 Reasons Humbly Offer'd to the Honourable House of Commons, to pass an Explanatory Act, to further Confirm all such Certificates of Bankrupts, as has been Allowed and Confirmed by the Lord Chancellor or Two of the Judges. *n.p.* [*1707?*], *s. sh. F°*. LG.

863 Reasons humbly offered for Altering several Clauses in the Bill depending in Parliament, relating to Bankrupts. *n.p.* [*1707?*], *s. sh. F°*. L.

864 Proposals most humbly offer'd to the Parliament, by the Merchants and Traders of London, for an Act for the Encouragement of Trade and Credit, and amending the late Act for preventing Frauds frequently committed by Bankrupts. *n.p.* [*1707?*], *s. sh. F°*. MC.

Endorsed: Proposals for an Act to encourage Trade and Credit.

865 Proposals most humbly offer'd to the Parliament, by the Merchants and Traders of London, for an Act to promote Trade and Credit, and encourage honest Insolvents, and for supplying the Defects of the late Act for preventing Frauds frequently committed by Bankrupts. *n.p.* [*1707?*], *s. sh. F°*. MC.

Endorsed: Proposals for an Act to promote Trade and Credit, and encourage honest Insolvents. A revised edition of the preceding.

866 Remarks on the Late Act of Parliament to prevent Frauds frequently committed by Bankrupts, with Proposals for the Amendment thereof. *Lond. 1707*, *4°*. LU.

867 An Essay on Credit and the Bankrupt Act. With some Reflections on the Escape-Act. *Lond. 1707, 8°.* LU.

868 Jus Imperij & Servitutis: or, The Law concerning Masters, Apprentices, Bayliffs, Receivers, Stewards, Attorneys, Factors, Deputies, Carriers, Covenant-Servants &c..... *Lond. 1707, 8°.* L.

869 Some Queries humbly Offer'd to the Householders of the Suburbs of London and City of Westminster, and all other Places that are not under the absolute Government of the Convex-Lights, in Answer to a Convex alias Crooked Advertisement, which came Yesterday out of a North-East Wind. *n.p.* [*1707*], *s. sh. F°.* O.

870 Act in favours of the Incorporations of Edinburgh, for erecting a Maiden Hospital. [*Edin. 1707*], *s. sh. F°.* EPRO.

871 An Historical Account of the Rights and Privileges of the Royal College of Physicians, and of the Incorporation of Chirurgions in Edinburgh, Wherein the present ill state of the Practice of Physick, with the Causes thereof is consider'd, and some Remedies humbly proposed. To which is added, An Appendix, giving an account of the Overture given in by the said Chirurgions by the Parliament, against the Physicians. *n.p. 1707, 4°.* O.

1708

GENERAL

872 [HATTON, EDWARD]. A New View of London; or, an Ample Account of that City, in Two Volumes.... *Lond. 1708, 8°.* O.

For authorship see R. Gough's *British Topography*, I, 571–2.

873 [KNOX, THOMAS]. Some Thoughts humbly offer'd towards an Union between Great-Britain and Ireland. *Lond. 1708, 4°.* L.

Another edn., Dublin, 1708–9, 4° (L). Authorship deduced from internal evidence and *Cal. of Treasury Papers*, 1702–7.

874 BURRIDGE, EZEKIEL. A Short View of the Present State of Ireland: With Regard particularly to the Difficultys a Chief Governor will meet there in holding of a Parliament. Written in the Year 1700. *n.p. 1708, 4°.* LU.

Proceded by an anonymous letter on the Irish situation.

AGRICULTURE

875 The Compleat Collier: Or, The whole Art of Sinking, Getting, and Working, Coal-Mines, &c. as is now used in the Northern Parts, expecially about Sunderland and New-Castle. By. J.C. *Lond. 1708, 8°.* NU.

Another edn., without initials, entitled *The Compleat Collier; or, Plain Directions*.... By a Miner, Newcastle, [c. 1730?] (O). The original edn. was reprinted by M. A. Richardson in his *Reprints of Rare Tracts*, 1845; and (following Richardson) by E. McAuliffe, Omahia, 1935 (NU).

876 A List of the Names of the Governour and Company of the Mine-Adventurers, of England. November the Twenty-ninth, 1708. *Lond. 1708, F°.* L.

877 A Bill for the better enabling the Governor and Company of the Mine-Adventurers of England to call in Money from their Partners, for Payment and Satisfaction of their Creditors; and for the more effectual carrying on their Undertaking, for Working Mines and Minerals in Wales, and Extracting Silver from Lead. [*Lond. 1708*], *F°.* L.

878 The Case of the Mine-Adventurers. [*Lond. 1708*], *s. sh. F°.* L.

For the projected Parliamentary bill. The text beings: The Scope and Content of the Bill....

879 SAUNDERS, W. An Essay towards the Establishing the Fishery of Great Britain. Proving I. That it lies fairer for Her Majesties Subjects, than for any other Nation. II. That it will be of Great and Certain Advantage to the Publick. III. That it is absolutely Necessary in order to the support of our Navigation by being a constant, and the best Nursery of stout and able Seamen.... *Lond. 1708, 4°.* L.

880 The Case of the Company of Free Fisher-men of the River of Thames.... *n.p.* [*1708?*], *s. sh. F°*. LLI.

881 To the Honourable the Knights, Citizens, and Burgesses in Parliament Assembled. The Humble Petition of Thomas Coutts, Gilbert Stewart, and William Gordon, Merchants, on Behalf of themselves and other North Britains, concerned in the Fishing Trade. *n.p.* [*1708*], *s. sh. F°*. MC.

For the same allowance upon the exportation of fish cured with foreign salt as in England.

882 By the Queen. A Proclamation. *Lond. 1708*, *s. sh. F°*. L.

Dated: 26 June [1708]. For encouraging fishing at Newfoundland.

MANUFACTURES

883 The Case of the Commissioners for Rebuilding St. Paul's Cathedral, in relation to a Clause in a Bill Passed by the House of Commons, which obliges the Covering the Dome of the said Church with British Copper. *n.p.* [*1708*], *s. sh. F°*. L.

884 An Answer to the Objections against Covering the Dome of St. Paul's with English Copper. *n.p.* [*1708*], *s. sh. F°*. L.

Title from endorsement.

885 Mr. George Porter, Master. At a Court of Assistants of the Company of Distillers: Held the Thirteenth Day of April, 1708. It is Order'd by this Court, That the Abstract of this Company's By-Laws and Ordinances now Read, and herewith under Mention'd, be forthwith Printed, which are as followeth. *n.p.* [*1708*], *s. sh. F°*. LG.

886 To the Honourable the Commons of Great Britain, in Parliament Assembled. The humble Petition of Joshua Price, Glass Painter. *n.p.* [*1708*], *s. sh. F°*. LU.

Offering to paint the figure of St. Paul in the east window of St. Paul's Cathedral for £150.

887 The Case of the Rope-Makers of London, and other parts of Great Britain: Humbly Offered to the Honourable House of Commons. *n.p.* [*1708?*], *s. sh. F°*. L

888 The true State of the Case, with Relation to Foreign Cordage imported and exported; with Regard to what the Queen Receives for Customs by the said Importation and Exportation of Cordage made here; besides the Employment of Her own Subjects in Manufacturing the same. *n.p.* [*1708?*], *s. sh. obl. F°*. LLI.

889 A Bill for the better Preserving the Antient Salt-Springs in Droytwych, in the County of Worcester, and the Rights of the Proprietors thereof. *n.p.* [*1708*], *F°*. L.

890 The Case of the Proprietors of the Ancient Salt-Springs and Pits of Wych, alias Droyt-wych, in the County of Worcester. *n.p.* [*1708*], *s. sh. F*°. LLI.

891 The Case and Reasons of the Freeholders and Inhabitants of and in the Borough of Droitwych (in the County of Worcester) and Places adjoining, and of the Proprietors of the New Salt Works there; Petitioners against the Bill for the better Preserving the Antient Salt-Springs in Droitwych, &c. *n.p.* [*1708*], *s. sh. F*°. LLI.

892 Mr. Steynor's Reasons, Humbly offer'd to the Honourable House of Commons, against some Clauses in the Bill for the better Preserving the Ancient Salt-Springs in Droitwych, and the Rights of the Proprietors thereof. *n.p.* [*1708*], *s. sh. F*°. L.

893 [Defoe, Daniel]. Reflections on the Prohibition Act: wherein the Necessity, Usefulness and Value of that Law, are Evinced and Demonstrated. In Answer to a Letter on that Subject, from a Gentleman concern'd in Trade. *Lond. 1708, 8*°. L.

On the benefits to the silk industry gained by the prohibition of East-India silks. For authorship see *C.B.E.L.* II, 500.

COMMERCE

894 [Addison, Joseph]. The Present State of the War, and the Necessity of an Augmentation, consider'd. *Lond. 1708, 4*°. L.

On the threat to British commerce of the union of France and Spain. Reprinted in his *Works*, 1721.

895 Reasons for the Punctual limiting of Bartholomew-Fair in West-smithfield, to those Three Days to which it is determined by the Royal Grant of it to the City of London. Humbly Addressed to the Right Honourable the Lord-Mayor, and to the Worshipful Court of Aldermen, and to the Common Council. *Lond. 1708, 8*°. O.

896 The Case of Charles Hoar, and Richard Hoar, Touching their Services to the Publick, and their Reward for the same. *n.p.* [*c. 1708?*], *F*° LLI.

Discovered abuses in a brew-house and in victualling the navy. Granted the right to hold a market in sheep and lamb skins as reward. Pray relief because the butchers boycott their market.

897 London. Duncombe Mayor. Die Martis, XIV° die Decembris, Anno Domini 1708.... [*Lond.*], *1708, s. sh. F*°. LCRO.

Enforcing the use of the legal weights and measures in London.

898 Reasons Hůmbly Offered to the Honourable House of Commons, why the Wine Measure, now in the Exchequer, should not be altered. *n.p.* [*c. 1708?*], *s. sh. F*°. MC.

899 The Garbling-Act: With short Remarks relating to the East-India Company. *n.p.* [*1708*], *s. sh. F*°. L.

Title from endorsement.

900 The Brief State of the Case of the Turkey-Merchants, the West-India-Merchants, the Drugsters, Salters, Grocers, and the Merchants Importers of Spices into the City of London, relating to the Bill for Repealing the Statute for the Well Garbling of Spices. *n.p.* [*1708*], *s. sh.* 4°. L.

901 The Case of John Ward of Hackney, Merchant. *n.p.* [*1708*], *s. sh. F°.* L.
Endorsed: The Case of John Ward against the Clause of Indemnity in the Bill for Repealing the Garblers Act.

902 The Case of the Act for the well Garbling of Spices. *n.p.* [*1708*], *s. sh. F°.* L.

903 The Case of the Dyers in ralation [*sic*] to the Garbling-Office. *n.p.* [*1708*], *s. sh. F°.* L.

904 Considerations upon the Act for well Garbleing of Spices, against which the East-India Company desires a Clause of Indemnity for manifest Offences by them Committed in Breach of that useful Law. *n.p.* [*1708*], *s. sh. F°.* LG.
Endorsed: Considerations on the Act for Garbleing, or Making Clean of Spices, and other Marchandizes.

905 Reasons Humbly Offered for continuing the Law made in the Reign of King James the First, concerning the Garbling of Spices, Druggs, &c. *n.p.* [*1708*], *s. sh. F°.* MC.
Endorsed: Reasons Humbly Offer'd for continuing the Garbling-Act.

906 EDINBURGH. Proclamation Anent the Importeing of Ale and Beer from the Country. *Edin. 1708*, *s. sh. F°.* ECA.
Dated: 30 June 1708.

907 Reasons Humbly Offer'd for making Two Fly-Boats, (Russia Built) One Called the Thomas and Henry, and the Other, the Richard and Jane, Free Ships. *n.p.* [*1708*], *s. sh. F°.* L.

908 The Case of the Owners and Freighters of the Ship Worcester, seiz'd in Scotland. *n.p.* [*1708*], *s. sh. F°.* L.

909 An Enquiry into the Causes of the Prohibition of Commerce with France, during the present War: And whether, upon a Recapitulation they will appear considerable enough to carry it against a free Importation, either immediately from thence, or from some neighbouring Country, which being in Amity with us, and maintaining an open Correspondence thither, are capable of supplying Us. With an Account of the fraudulent Methods usually taken to cheat her Majesty of her Customs. And Proposals for preventing the same. *Lond. 1708*, 4°. LU.
Signed: R.F.

910 Reasons humbly offer'd for the Importation of Cocheneal from Spain in Spanish or Neutral Ships or Vessels, during the present War. *n.p.* [*1708?*], *s. sh. F°.* L.

911 The British Interest on the Coast of Africa Consider'd, with the Interest of other Europeans, and the Politicks they used for Carrying on that Trade. *n.p.* [*1708*], *s. sh. F°*. L.

912 The Case between the African Company and the People of England, briefly laid open in some Considerations upon the said Company's Petition. *n.p.* [*1708?*], *s. sh. F°*. LLI.

XV numbered paragraphs.

913 The Case between the African Company and the People of England. *n.p.* [*1708?*], *s. sh. F°*. O.

Another edition of the preceding with XVI numbered paragraphs.

914 Considerations upon the Trade to Guinea. *Lond. 1708, 8°*. LU.

915 Some Observations on Extracts taken out of the Report from the Lords Commissioners for Trade and Plantations. *n.p.* [*1708*], *F°*. L.

Endorsed: The Falsities of Private Traders to Africa discover'd, and the Mischiefs they Occasion demonstrated: And an Account of the Settlements on that Coast purchased, built, and now possest, by the Company.

916 The Improvement of the African Trade farther Demonstrated by Separate Traders, in Answer to a Scurrilous Paper, called, the Falsities of Private Traders Discovered. *n.p.* [*1708*], *F°*. L.

917 The Scandalous Political Arithmetick (as they term it) of the Private Traders detected. *n.p.* [*1708*], *s. sh. F°*. MP.

Endorsed: The Political Arithmetick of the Private Traders Detected.

918 Some Considerations on the Late Act of Parliament, for Setling the Trade to Africa. *n.p.* [*1708*], *s. sh. F°*. L.

Endorsed: Considerations on the present Trade to Africa.

919 The African Companies Considerations on the Late Act of Parliament for Settling the Trade to Africa, Answer'd Paragraph by Paragraph. *n.p.* [*1708*], *s. sh. F°*. L.

Endorsed: Considerations on the present Trade to Africa, Answered Paragraph by Paragraph.

920 A View of the State of the Trade to Africa: Wherein is laid down the present Condition of the English Settlements there: their Use, Value, Strength, and to whom the Property belongs....In a Letter to a New Subscriber. *Lond. 1708, 4°*. LU.

921 Reasons humbly offered by the Merchants trading to Virginia and Maryland, for Incouraging the Exportation of Tobacco, and bringing in of French Wine in return. *n.p.* [*1708*], *s. sh. F°*. LPRO.

922 A List of the Names of all the Adventurers in the Stock of the Governour and Company of Merchants of London, Trading into the East-Indies, the 15th of April, 1708.... *n.p.* [*1708*], *F°*. LU.

LU copy has names of 86 new adventurers added in ms.

923 D'Urfey, Thomas. Honor & Opes: or, the British Merchant's Glory. A Poem congratulatory. On the happy decision and conclusion of all

differences between the Old and New Companies, United in Trade to the East-Indies.... *Lond. 1708, F°.* O.

924 The Case of the Persons Concerned in the Separate Trade to the East-Indies, which are not in the Joint-Stock. *n.p.* [*1708*], *s. sh. F°.* LLI.

925 The Case of the Separate Traders to the East-Indies, which are not in the Grand Monopoly. *n.p.* [*1708*], *s. sh. F°* LLI.

Endorsed: A Representation of the Mischief of a Monopoly to the East-Indies: and Benefit to the Nation of a Free or Separate Trade.

926 A Dialogue between Jest, an East-India Stock-Jobber, and Earnest, an Honest Merchant. *Lond. 1708, 12°.* LU.

927 The Case of John Powell, an Incorporated Member of the General Society, Trading to the East-Indies. With a Clause of Redemption in the Act, for advancing Two Millions, and Settling the Trade to the East-Indies. *n.p.* [*1708?*], *s. sh. F°.* MC.

Title from endorsement.

928 *Begin.* John Powell, a Member of The General Society.... *n.p.* [*1708?*], *s. sh. F°.* MC.

A petition for permission to continue as a separate trader to India.

929 A Letter to a Member of Parliament, relating to the East-India Company, and the Bill that is now brought into the House in their Favour. *n.p.* [*1708*], *F°.* MC.

Dated: February 23. 170⅞.

930 Reasons why the East-India Company ought to Pay the Equivolent agreed to be Paid the Scots Company by the Articles of Union: and also some Cautions Offer'd with respect to the Renewal of their Grant. *n.p.* [*1708*], *s. sh. F°.* LG.

Endorsed: Reasons for the East-India Company's Paying the Scots Company's Equivalent....

931 The Separate Traders to India Propose, I. To Advance their Proportion of the 1,200,000 l. at the same Interest the Company doth.... *n.p.* [*1708?*], *s. sh. obl. 4°.* MC.

932 Some Considerations to prevent being Imposed upon in the Grant of the Trade to the East-Indies. *n.p.* [*1708?*], *s. sh. F°.* MC.

933 By the Queen, A Proclamation, Appointing the Distribution of Prizes taken, and the Bounty for Taking Ships of War or Privateers of the Enemies. *Lond. 1708, F°.* L.

Dated: 20 May [1708]. Cr. 4452. Another edn. 1708 (LPRO). Cr. 4453.

934 The Humble Address of the Right Honourable the Lords Spiritual and Temporal in Parliament Assembled, presented to Her Majesty on Saturday the Seventh Day of February, 1707 [O.S.]. With Her Majesties most gracious Answer. *Lond. 1707, F°.* L.

Supporting the charges of Thomas Wood and other Jamaica merchants against Captain William Kerr for misconduct when in charge of convoys.

935 Captain Kerr's Case, in Answer to Mr. Wood's Allegations. *n.p.* [*1708*], *s. sh. F°.* LLI.

On convoys.

936 The Humble Address of the Right Honourable the Lords Spiritual and Temporal, in Parliament Assembled, with the several Papers Contain'd and Refer'd to therein, presented to Her Majesty on Munday the First Day of March, 1707 [O.S.]. With Her Majesties most gracious Answer. *Lond. 1707, F°.* LU.

On the failure of the navy to protect merchant shipping. Another edn. Dublin, 1708 (DA).

937 The Case of John Corso a Genoese Merchant. *n.p.* [*1708*], *s. sh. F°.* LLI.

Corso had been captured by Kidd the pirate. His goods had been escheated to the Crown and had been granted to Greenwich Hospital.

938 The Case of John Corso Genoese Merchant. *n.p.* [*1708*], *s. sh. F°.* O.

Different from the preceding.

939 Reports and Extracts out of the Register Books of the African and Indian Company of Scotland, Relating to Mr. Paterson's Claim on the said Company. *n.p.* [*1708*], *F°.* JCB.

COLONIES

940 OLDMIXON, JOHN. The British Empire in America, containing the History of the Discovery, Settlement, Progress and present State of all the British Colonies on the Continent and Islands of America.... *Lond. 1708, 8°.* 2 vols. L.

2nd edn., anonymous, 1741 (L).

941 [MATHER, COTTON]. The Deplorable State of New-England, by Reason of a Covetous and Treacherous Governour, and Pusillanimous Counsellors.... To which is added, An Account of the Shameful Miscarriage of the Late Expedition against Port-Royal. *Lond. 1708, 8°.* L.

The dedication signed: A.H. L copy has a ms. note ascribing the work to Sir Henry Ashurst on the authority of White Kennet. It is probable, however, that Ashurst only wrote the dedication, and that the bulk of the book is by Cotton Mather. See T. J. Holmes, *Cotton Mather*, pp. 240–63. Another edn. Boston, 1721; another edn. Boston, 1879. *Mass. Hist. Soc. Coll.* ser. 5, vol. 6.

942 The present State of the Tobacco-Plantations in America. *n.p.* [*1708*], *s. sh. F°.* L.

FINANCE

943 CULPEPER, Sir THOMAS. Sir Thomas Colepeper's Tracts concerning Usury Reprinted. Shewing its Biting Quality on the Private and Publick. With Some Animadversions on the Writings of Dr. Lock, on that Subject.... *Lond. 1708, 4°.* LU.

With 'Postscript 1709'.

944 The Case of the Proprietors of the Army and Transport Debentures. *n.p.* [*1708?*], *s. sh. F*°. MC.

Debentures issued 'about 15 Years since'.

945 GOODWIN, JOHN. An Abstract of a Scheme for the Raising of Three Millions of Money in One Year. Humbly presented to the Honourable the House of Commons. *n.p.* [*c. 1708?*], *s. sh. F*°. L.

A tax on woollens and silks.

946 Proposals humbly offered to the Consideration of the Commons of Great Britain, how to Raise Mony to carry on the War. As also, of raising Annually Six Millions Sterling, in a Method advantagious to the Subject, and Easie to the State, with a Present supply of Six Millions, till the Revenues come in. *n.p.* [*c. 1708?*], *s. sh. F*°. MC.

947 An abridgement of those acts, passed anno sexto Annae Reginae; which relate to the equivalent money. And the settling and establishing a Court of exchequer in Scotland. [*Edinburgh?*], *1708, 12 p. 23 cm.* Kress. S.1193.

948 The Case of Mr. William Paterson, in Relation to his Claim on the Equivalent; as the same is stated in a Petition given in by Himself, and a Report made by Mr. Roderick Mackenzie to the Honourable Court of Exchequer in North-Britain. *n.p.* [*1708*], *F*°. L.

949 A State of Mr. Paterson's Claim upon the Equivalent. *n. p.* [*1708?*], *F*°. L.

Last date in margin of p. 3, August 5, 1708.

950 LANGHAM, THOMAS. The Neat Duties (All Discounts and Abatements deducted) of all Merchandize specify'd in the Book of Rates, begun in the 12 of Car. II. With the several variations to this present year 1708. Both in Decimal and Vulgar Arithmetick....The Turky or Levant Company's Duties....Never yet made Publick. An also a small Treatise of Decimals.... *Lond. 1708, 8*°. L.

A reissue, 1710 (LCH); another edn. 1713 (LCH); 3rd edn. 1715 (Kress 2961); 4th edn. 1718 (K); 8th edn. 1758 (L).

951 The Case of Elizabeth Carter, Spinster, with the whole Proceedings thereupon, touching a Discovery of a Considerable quantity of Cocheneale which has been lately conceal'd, whereby the Queen has been defrauded of her Customs, by Mr. Brewer, late Receiver, or Treasurer of the Prize-Office, &c. *n.p.* [*1708?*], *s. sh. F*°. LLI.

952 The Case of the Mine-Adventurers. [*Lond. 1708?*], *s. sh. F*°. L.

Against the note-issue monopoly of the Bank of England. The text begins: That the Mine Adventurers have the Honour...

953 Some Reasons Against the Clause for Restraining all Corporations but the Bank of England, from keeping Cash, or borrowing Money payable at Demand. *n.p.* [*1708?*], *s. sh. fol.* L.

On behalf of the Sword-Blade Company.

954 *Begin.* Whereas there hath been several false and malicious Reports industriously spread abroad reflecting on Sir Richard Hoare, Goldsmith, for occasioning and promoting a Run for Money on the Bank of England.... *n.p.* [*1708*], *s. sh. F*o. L.

955 A Letter from a Merchant in London, to a Member of Parliament. *n.p.* [*1708?*], *F*o. LG.

Signed: M.B. Endorsed: A Letter about the Brokers Act.

956 Reasons for Continuing the Brokers Act, under further Regulations; In Answer to a Letter from a pretended Merchant to a Member of Parliament. *n.p.* [*1708?*], *s. sh. F*o. MC.

Endorsed: An Answer to the pretended Merchant's Letter, relating to the Brokers Act.

957 Advertisement. From The Charitable Corporation for Relief of Industrious Poor, by Assisting them with Small Sums upon Pledges at Legal Interest, at their House in Duke-Street, Westminster. *n.p.* [*1708?*], *s. sh. F*o. L.

958 From the New Lombard-House in Duke's-Street, Westminster, The Method of Securing the Fund of the Charitable Corporation, &c. By which the Subscribers may at any time Recal their Money without Transferring, and consequently will be prevented All Stock-Jobbing. *n.p.* [*1708?*], *s. sh. F*o. LU.

959 The New Lombard Houses: or, A Short Account of The Charitable Corporation lately constituted by the Queens Letters Patents for Relieving Poor People in their Distress. *n.p.* [*1708?*], *s. sh. F*o. LU.

960 Proclamation for Inbringing and Stating of the Publick Debts due on the Civil and Military Lists. *Edin. 1708*, *s. sh. F*o. E.

Dated: 10 June 1708.

961 Proclamation calling in the Scots Crown Old and New, The Fourty, Twenty, and Ten shilling pieces to be Re-coined. *Edin. 1708*, *s. sh. F*o. E.

Dated: 12 January 1708.

962 Proclamation restoring the Scots Species, viz. Scots Crowns Old and New, Fourty shilling, Twenty shilling, and Ten shilling Pieces to their former Currencie. [*Edin. 1708*], *s. sh. F*o. E.

Dated: 16 March 1708.

963 Proclamation for Calling in the several Scots Species of Money following, viz. Crowns Old and New, Fourty Shilling, Twenty Shilling and Ten Shilling Pieces; the Four Merk, Two Merk, One Merk, Half Merk Five Shilling, and Three Shilling Six Penny Pieces to be Recoined. *Edin. 1708*, *s. sh. F*o. E.

Dated: 28 April 1708.

TRANSPORT

964 The Constitutions of the Company of Watermen and Lightermen.... *Lond. 1708. 8°.* L.

With a preface by Laurence Braddon.

965 An Abstract of the Rules, Orders, and Constitutions of the Company of Watermen and Lightermen.... *Lond. 1708, 12°.* L.

With a preface by Laurence Braddon.

966 The Honesty of the Rulers of the Watermens Company set forth; In a Letter to His Royal Highness Prince George of Denmark, Lord High Admiral of Great Britain, &c. *Lond. 1708, s. sh. F°.* LG.

967 The True and Deplorable Case of the Waggoners, Carryers of Goods into and from the City of London. *n.p. [1708?], s. sh. 4°.* LLI.

968 The Case of the Inhabitants for Fifty or Sixty Miles round London: And likewise of the City and Suburbs. *n.p. [1708?], s. sh. F°.* LLI.

Against the petition of the waggoners who wish to use six instead of five horses.

SOCIAL CONDITIONS

969 Advertisement. From the Charitable Fund intended to be establish'd in London, by voluntary Gifts and Loans of Mony, to Relieve and support poor Seamens Families, and other Necessitous Persons, not otherwise provided for, by giving them Mony, or lending it without any Interest or Charges whatsoever, upon Pledges and Employing such as want Work: In Answer to a Printed Advertisement from the Charitable Corporation for Relief of Industrious Poor. *Lond. 1708, F°.* LU.

970 Communication of Property. Or. A Voluntary Contribution for Publick and Charitable Uses to be Distributed by Lot.... *Lond. 1708, 8°.* LU.

Foxwell had seen a copy with a ms. note: 'by Mr. Hodge'.

971 The Dispensarians are the Patriots of Great-Britain, protect the Life of the Royal Family, the Nobility and Gentry, and the Property of the Poor, viz. the Plenty and Cheapness of Medicines by the College Dispensary. Or the College, assisted by Visitors appointed by the Government will cure the Physicians Subjection to the Apothecaries, their Treachery to the Sick, and their Profession, and their Ignorance of all Diseases and Medicines. *Lond. 1708, 8°.* L.

972 Monopoly made a Property: or, The Navy Surgeons Memorial to the Managing Apothecaries in Black-Friers. *n.p. 1708, 8°.* L.

973 To the Right Honourable, the Commissioners for the Orange and Storm Breifs, issued forth in the Year 1703. The Representation of Richard Bromley. *n.p. [1708?], s. sh. F°.* LLI.

974 Her Majesties most Gracious Letters Patent, In Favours of the Sufferers

by the late Fire in the Head of the Canongate. [*Edin. 1708*], *s. sh. F°*. ES.

Allowing a public collection.

975 The Case of the Poor Insolvent Debtors, now under Close Confinement in Her Majesty's Prison of Ludgate. *n.p.* [*1708?*], *s. sh. F°*. O.

976 Reasons humbly offer'd to the Parliament of Great Britain, for Raising of Recruits for Her Majesty's Fleet and Army. *n.p.* [*c. 1708?*], *s. sh. F°*. L.

Prisoners for debt who owe more than £100 to be released if they promise to enlist.

977 The Bankrupt's Directory: or, Suitable Rules and Directions, both for Bankrupt and Creditor, How to manage their Affairs to the best Advantage, for the Ease and Satisfaction of all Parties, conform to the several Statutes made concerning Bankrupts, to this Day. Together, with an Alphabetical List of all those Persons, who have surrender'd themselves to, or have been summon'd to be examin'd by the Commissioners, according to the two last Acts of Parliament; the one entitl'd, An Act to prevent Frauds frequently committed by Bankrupts; the other, An Act to explain and amend the said Act. *Lond. 1708*, *4°*. O.

978 Entry cancelled.

979 A Letter from a North-Britain, to his Friend in London. *n.p.* [*1708*], *s. sh. F°*. MC.

Signed: A.B. Dated: Edinburgh 30th of April, 1708. On the affairs of Thomas Pitkin, a fraudulent bankrupt, whose practices were investigated by Parliament in 1707.

980 To the Right Honourable the Lords and Commons Assembled in Parliament. The Deplorable Case of the Poor Sailors Wives and Widows. *n.p.* [*c. 1708?*], *s. sh. F°*. LLI.

Endorsed: The Case of Poor Sailors Wives and Widows.

981 A Proposal for the Due Regulating Servants, which will be Beneficial for the Kingdom in General, and to Private Families in Particular, and no ways Obstructive to honest Servants, but will furnish a Supply of Men to Recruit the Army. *n.p.* [*c. 1708?*], *s. sh. F°*. L.

982 LONDON. Withers Mayor. Martis, viij° die Junij, Anno Dom. 1708.... [*Lond. 1708*], *s. sh. F°*. LCRO.

Order to print a clause relating to servants from the Act for the better Preventing Mischiefs that may happen by Fire, with the clause.

1709

GENERAL

983 DEFOE, DANIEL. The History of the Union of Great Britain. *Edin. 1709*, *F°*. LU.

Another edn. Lond. 1786 (L).

984 To the Honourable the Knights, Citizens, and Burgesses, in Parliament Assembled. The State of the Case of several Protestand Traders and Handycraft Men in the several Cities and Corporate Towns in this Kingdom. *n.p.* [*1709*], *s. sh. F°*. D.

Endorsed: The Distressed Condition of the Protestant Traders of the City of Dublin.

985 The Groans of the Inhabitants of the Island of Jersey: or, a Compendious Survey of the Publick Grievances of that Place. By a well-wisher to his Country. *Lond. 1709*, *4°*. O.

AGRICULTURE

986 Objections Humbly Offer'd to Both Houses of Parliament, on Behalf of Several Land-Owners near the City of London, and Several Thousands of Poor People in or near the said City, against a Clause in a Bill, Entitled, A Bill for giving the Commissioners, for the City of London the same Powers as the Commissioners for Counties have: And also For Preventing Annoyances to the Common-Sewers, and to the River of Thames; And for Obliging Collectors for the Sewers, by which Sand is prohibited to be strown in Houses within the Bills of Mortality. *n.p.* [*1709*], *s. sh. F°*. C (Cr.).

Endorsed: The Case of the Land-holders and others concern'd in Sand.

987 At a General Court of the Governour and Company of the Mine-Adventurers of England held...on Tuesday the Fifteenth Day of February...1708 [O.S.]. [*Lond. 1709*], *s. sh. F°*. L.

Minutes.

988 At a General Court of the Governour and Company of the Mine-Adventurers of England, held...on Thursday the Tenth Day of March.... 1708 [O.S.]. [*Lond. 1709*], *s. sh. F°*. L.

989 The Report of the Committee Appointed at a General Court [of the Company of the Mine Adventurers] held at the Mine-Office in Angel Court on Snow Hill, the 6th Day of May, 1708. *n.p.* [*1709*], *F°*. L.

Followed by 'An Account of what Principal Money and Shares, the Governour, Deputy-Governour, and Principal Manager of the Mines, originally had... and now have, &c.'

990 At a General Court of the Governour and Company of the Mine-Adventurers of England, held...on Tuesday the Fifth Day of July... 1709. *n.p.* [*1709*], *F°*. L.

991 An Account of the Proceedings and Care of the Directors of the Governour and Company of the Mine-Adventurers of England, with Relation to their Accounts, their Charter, and other the Affairs of this Company.... [*Lond. 1709*], *F°*. L.

992 [Mackworth, Sir Humphrey]. A Familiar Discourse, or Dialogue concerning the Mine-Adventure. Or, A Vindication of the Proceedings of the Governour and Company of the Mine-Adventurers of England. Containing, An Answer to the Objections made to the Undertaking, the Management, or the Mines. And Demonstrating the Reasonableness and Necessity of a Call, and of Complying with the Resolutions of the General Court. By William Shiers, Secretary. By Order of the Court of Directors, for the Satisfaction of the Creditors and Absent Partners. *n.p. 1709*, *8°*. L.

Mackworth's authorship was disclosed in the Report of the Committee of the House of Commons on the Company (no. 1114). A different work from those of the same title published in 1700 and 1705.

993 A List of the several Estates in the County of Kilkenny, belonging to the Governor and Company for Making Hollow-Sword-Blades in England, with the Quantity of Acres, as by the Survey of the late Trustees for Sale of the Forfeitures. *Dublin, 1709, s. sh. F°*. D.

D has similar, undated, lists for 'Antrim'; 'Clare, Waterford, Down, Longford, Wexford, Ardmagh, Donnegal, Londonderry, Mayo, Rosscommon, Sligo and Wicklow'; 'Limerick'; 'Queens County'; 'Kings County'; and 'Cork'.

994 Proposals Relating to the Fishery. *n.p.* [*1709?*], *4°*. LU.

The only copy seen is imperfect.

995 A Letter from a Gentleman in North Britain to the Right Honourable, the Earl of Seafield, concerning the Improvement of the Salmon Fishing of North Britain. *Edin. 1709, s. sh. F°*. L.

Signed: J.H. N, N, B.

996 A Letter from E. C. to E. N. concerning the Advantages of a Fishery. *Edin. 1709, F°*. L.

Signed: E. C. Britannicus. Tentatively attributed by Higgs to George Mackenzie, Earl of Cromarty.

MANUFACTURES

997 The Case of the Silkmen, Throwsters, Dyers, Twisters, and Winders, in and about the City of London, on Behalf of Themselves and a great Number of Poor, Employed in the Manufacturing of Raw Silk and Mohair Yarn. *n.p.* [*1709*], *s. sh. F°*. L.

COMMERCE

998 By the Queen, A Proclamation, For Putting the Laws in Execution against Forestalling, Regrating, and Engrossing of Corn. *Lond. 1709, F°.* LPRO.

Dated: 24 October 1709. Cr. 4472. Another edn. 1709 (LPRO). Cr. 4473.

999 The Queen and Council's New Order for Lowering the Price of Bread; Which was occasioned by the Extravagant and Exorbitant raising of it. *Lond. 1709, s. sh. F°.* MC.

1000 Reasons humbly offer'd to the Honourable House of Commons. Against the Bill for [prohibiting y^{e}] Exporting Beans, Oats and Barley, when they can be shipp'd off at Reasonable Prices.... *[1709?], s. sh. 4°.* O.

The words in [ ] are added in ms.

1001 An Expedient for preventing the Dearth of Victual, Humbly offered to the Consideration of the Honourable Justices of Peace, and Gentlemen Heritors &c, met at the Quarter Session at Edinburgh, May 4th. 1709. *Edin. 1709, s. sh. F°.* E.

1002 Reasons for preventing the Scarcity and Dearth of Victual, that the Poor may not starve: Humbly offered to the Consideration of the Honourable Justices of Peace, and Gentlemen Heritors &c. met at the Quarter Session at Edinburgh, instant 1709. *Edin. 1709, s. sh. F°.* L.

1003 EDINBURGH. Act anent the present Dearth, and Relief of the Poor by the Justices of the City of Edinburgh. *Edin. 1709, s. sh. F°.* E.

Dated: 12 May 1709.

1004 EDINBURGH. Act and Intimation, against Forestallers of Victual, &c. *Edin. 1709, s. sh. F°.* L.

1005 Reasons for Suppressing the Yearly Fair in Brook-Field, Westminster; commonly called May-Fair.... *Lond. 1709, 8°.* O.

1006 By the Queen, A Proclamation. *Lond. 1709, F°.* L.

Dated: 28 April 1709. Prohibiting plays, interludes, gaming, &c. in May Fair. Booths to be used for goods only.

1007 Reasons Humbly Offer'd to the Honourable House of Commons, Against repealing a Clause in an Act made the last Sessions of Parliament, for preventing one Butcher selling Fat Cattle or Sheep to another, to sell again, either Dead or Alive. *n.p. [1709], s. sh. F°.* O.

Endorsed: [Reasons] Humbly Offer'd to the Honble House of Commons, by the Company of Butchers of London and Westminster and the Liberties thereof.

1008 HOW, JOHN. Some Thoughts on the Present State of Printing and Bookselling. *Lond. 1709, 4°.* L.

1009 The Case of the Booksellers Right to their Copies, or Sole Power of Printing their respective Books, represented to the Parliament. *n.p. [1709?], s. sh. F°.* L.

Reprinted in E. A. Bloom, *Samuel Johnson in Grub Street*, 1957.

1010 The Case of Small Twist Roll Tobacco. *n.p.* [*1709?*], *s. sh. F°.* LLI.
For a bounty on export.

1011 The Case of the Exporters of Fish from Scotland. *n.p.* [*1709?*], *s. sh. F°.* LU.

1012 A Dialogue between S[cotland] and E[ngland]. *n.p.* [*1709?*], *s. sh. F°.* LU.
Endorsed: An Answer to the Case of the Exporters of Fish from Scotland.

1013 The Case of the Exporters of Herrings and other Fish, and of Beef and Pork from Scotland, since the 1st of May, 1707. *n.p.* [*1709*], *F°.* LU.

1014 The Case of Walter Stewart and William Murray. *n.p.* [*1709*], *F°.* LU.
On thirty-nine pieces of alamodes and lustrings imported from Scotland and seized by the Customs as prohibited goods.

1015 Observations on the Acts made for the Encouragement of the Lustring-Company, which relate to the Exportation of French Alamodes and Lustrings; humbly offer'd by Walter Stewart and William Murray, Petitioners. *n.p.* [*1709?*], *s. sh. F°.* LU.

1016 The Case of the Owners of the Ships Berkley-Castle and James, of Montross. *n.p.* [*1709*], *s. sh. F°.* L.
For a bill to make them free ships.

1017 Queries relating to the Importation of French Wine. *n.p.* [*1709?*], *s. sh. F°.* O.

1018 Reasons humbly offer'd by the Portugal, Italian, and Spanish Merchants against Importing French Wines, in Returns for Tobacco. *n.p.* [*1709*], *s. sh. F°.* L.

1019 Reasons humbly offer'd by the Portugal, Spanish, and Italian Merchants, against admitting French Wine to be Imported into Great-Britain. *n.p.* [*1709?*], *s. sh. F°.* O.

1020 To the Honourable the Knights, Citizens, and Burgesses of Great Britain; in Parliament Assembled: the Humble Memorial of Joseph Blake, Gent. *n.p.* [*1709*], *s. sh. F°.* L.
Suggesting Spain should let in our woollen manufactures duty free. Dated January 24 1708 [O.S.].

1021 Blaney, Jo. A Letter to the Committee of the Honourable House of Commons, upon the African Trade. *n.p.* [*1709*], *s. sh. F°.* LU.

1022 An Account of the Number of Negroes delivered in to the Islands of Barbadoes, Jamaica and Antego, from the Year 1698 to 1708. since the Trade was Opened, taken from the Accounts sent from the respective Governours of those Islands to the Lords Commissioners of Trade, whereby it appears the African Trade is encreas'd to four times more since its being laid Open, than it was under an Exclusive Company. *n.p.* [*1709*], *s. sh. F°.* LU.

1023 An Act for the better Improvement of the Trade to Africa, by establishing a Regulated Company. *n.p.* [*1709*], *F°.* LU.
A bill.

1024 The African Company's Property to the Forts and Settlements in Guinea, Consider'd; and the Necessity of establishing the Trade in a Regulated Company, Demonstrated. *n.p.* [*1709?*], *F°*. O.

1025 The Case of the Bond Creditors of the Royal African Company. *n.p.* [*1709*], *s. sh. F°*. LU.

1026 The Case of the Royal African Company. *n.p.* [*1709?*], *s. sh. F°*. LU.
Endorsed: The Right and Property of English Subjects.

1027 The Case of the Royal-African Company. *n.p.* [*1709*], *F°*. L.
Endorsed: The Case of the Royal-African Company.

1028 The Case of the Separate Traders to Africa. With Remarks on the African Company's Memorial. *n.p.* [*1709*], *F°* LU.
Title taken from endorsement.

1029 [Davenant, Charles]. A Clear Demonstration, from Points of Fact, That the Recovery, Preservation and Improvement of Britain's share of the Trade to Africa, is wholly owing to the Industry, Care and Application of the Royal African Company. *n.p.* [*1709*], *s. sh. F°*. L.
Endorsed: The Rise, Preservation, and Improvement of the African Trade Demonstrated. Subsequently printed as chap. III of pt. III of *Reflections upon the Constitution and Management of the Trade to Africa*. Another edn. [1711 ?] endorsed: A Clear Demonstration... (L).

1030 Considerations humbly offer'd to the Honourable House of Commons, by the Planters, and Others, trading to our British Plantations, in Relation to the African Company's Petition, now before this Honourable House. *n.p.* [*1709?*], *s. sh. F°*. L.

1031 A few Remarks proper to be regarded in the Establishment of the African Trade. *n.p.* [*1709?*], *s. sh. F°*. LU.

1032 A Letter from a Merchant at Jamaica to a Member of Parliament in London, touching the African Trade. To which is added, a Speech made by a Black of Gardaloupe, at the Funeral of a Fellow-Negro. *Lond. 1709, 8°*. L.

1033 A Letter to a Member of Parliament concerning the African Trade. *n.p.* [*1709*], *F°*. L.

1034 A Letter to a Member of Parliament, setting forth the Trade to Africa. *n.p.* [*1709*], *F°*. O.
Title taken from endorsement.

1035 A Joint-Letter from the most Considerable Proprietors of the Island of Barbadoes, to Colonel Richard Scot, Colonel Robert Stewart, Richard Bate, Patrick Mein, and Thomas Fullerton, Esqs; and other Friends in England, having Estates or Interests in the said Island; touching the Petition which they lately transmitted to be given in to the Honourable House of Commons, for having the Trade to Africa carried on by a

Company of a sufficient Joint-Stock; together with their Reasons subjoin'd. *n.p.* [*1709*], *F*°. L.

Dated: Barbadoes, August 1709. Signed by 77 names. Endorsed: A Letter from the most Considerable Proprietors.... Another edn. [1713], *s. sh. F*°. (O).

1036 A Memorial touching the Nature and present State of the Trade to Africa. *n.p.* [*1709*], *F*°. L.

1037 A Supplement to the Royal-African-Company's Memorial, Touching the Nature and Present-State of the Trade to Africa. *n.p.* [*1709*], *F*°. MP.

1038 Observations on Some of the African Company's late Printed Papers. *n.p.* [*1709*], *s. sh. F*°. LU.

1039 [Davenant, Charles]. A Proposal for settling the Trade to Africa, in either of the Methods after mentioned. Humbly offered to the Consideration of the Honourable House of Commons. *n.p.* [*1709?*], *s. sh. F*°. L.

Endorsed: Proposals for settling the Trade to Africa. Also published in Davenant's *Reflections upon the Constitution and Management of the Trade to Africa*.

1040 Proposals for Raising a New Company for Carrying on the Trades of Africa and the Spanish West-Indies, under the Title of the United Company. Humbly submitted to the Consideration of the Parliament of Great-Britain. *Lond. 1709*, 4°. LU.

1041 Some short Remarks, on two Pamphlets lately Printed; The one Entituled Considerations upon the Trade to Guinea; the other Entituled Proposals for raising a New Company, for carrying on the Trades of Africa and the Spanish-West-Indies, under the Title of the United-Company. *n.p.* [*1709?*], *F*°. LU.

1042 Reasons against the Bill for the better Improvement of the Trade to Africa, by Establishing a Regulated-Company. Humbly offered to the Consideration of the Honourable House of Commons. *n.p.* [*1709*], *s. sh. F*°. LU.

1043 Reasons for Establishing the African Trade under a Regulated Company. *n.p.* [*1709*], *s. sh. F*°. LU.

1044 Reasons for vesting the Settlements on the Coast of Africa in the Crown: and The Dangers of an Exclusive Company demonstrated. *n.p.* [*1709?*], *s. sh. F*°. O.

1045 [Davenant, Charles]. Reflections upon the Constitution and Management of the Trade to Africa, through the whole Course and Progress thereof, from the Beginning of the last Century, to this Time. Wherein the Nature and uncommon Circumstances of that Trade are particularly consider'd; and all the Arguments urg'd alternately by the Two contending Parties here, touching the different Methods now proposed by them, for carrying on the same to a National Advantage, impartially stated and consider'd. By all which, a clear view is given of such a Constitution, as (if establish'd by Act of Parliament) would, in all Probability, render the African Trade a permanent, creditable and advantageous Trade to Britain. *Lond. 1709, F°.* 3pt. L.

Reprinted in *The Political and Commercial Word of Charles D'Avenant*, 1771.

1046 [DAVENANT, CHARLES]. Several Reasons proving, that our Trade to Africa, cannot be preserved and carried on effectually by any other Method, than that of a considerable Joint-Stock, with exclusive Privileges. *n.p.* [*1709?*], *s. sh. F°.* L.

From Davenant's *Reflections upon the Constitution and Management of the Trade to Africa.* Another edn., with an additional paragraph, entitled: Several Arguments proving..., n.d. (L).

1047 Some Remarks on a Pamphlet, call'd, Reflections, on the Constitution and Management of the Trade to Africa. Demonstrating, the Author's abusive Aspersions therein contained, to be ill Grounded, the Matters of Fact wrong Represented, and the late Management of that Trade set in a True Light. With an Account, of the Needful Charge of the British Settlements in Africa; in what manner they may be best Maintain'd, and the Trade carry'd on to the Benefit of this Nation, and our Plantations in America. *n.p. 1709, 8°.* LU.

1048 John Chidley's Vindication of Himself, from the Slander and Calumny cast upon him, in the sixth and seventh pages of a book, entitled, Reflections upon the Constitution and Management of the Trade to Africa, &c. *Lond. 1709, 8°.* L.

1049 Several Informations of the Evil Practices of Mr. Chidley, late Evidence against the R.A.C. [Royal African Company]. *n.p.* [*1709?*], *F°.* MP.

Endorsed: Extracts and Pa[pers] relating to Mr. Chidley, the Comp[any's] late Factor at Gamb[ia.]

1050 Some General Reflections, humbly offered by John Chidley, in Vindication of himself, from the Calumnies which the African Company have endeavoured to throw upon him, in two late Papers, whereof they dispersed several Copies, even in the Lobby of the House of Commons. *n.p.* [*1709*], *s. sh. F°.* O.

Endorsed: John Chidley's Vindication of himself from the Calumnies of the African Company.

1051 A Short Account of the Present State of the Trade to Africa, Humbly Offered to the Consideration of the Parliament. *n.p.* [*1709*], *s. sh. F°.* LLI.

1052 The Specious Insinuations of the Separate Traders to Africa detected. *n.p.* [*1709?*], *s. sh. F°.* LU.

Title from endorsement.

1053 [DAVENANT, CHARLES]. Some Objections against settling the Trade to Africa, in any of the open Methods proposed by the Separate-Traders, and particularly that of a Regular Company, like the present Russia-Company. Humbly offered to the Consideration of the Honourable House of Commons. *n.p.* *170 8/9*, *s. sh. F°*. LU.

Endorsed: Objections against Settling the Trade to Africa, in any open Method whatsoever. Also printed as chap. 5 of pt. 3 of Davenant's *Reflections upon the Constitution and Management of the Trade to Africa.*

1054 The Case of the Petitioner, Richard Budge, late Commander and Part-Owner of the Ship Hope, and Sole-Owner of her Cargo of Logwood. *n.p.* [*1709*], *F°*. O.

Against the illegal seizure and sale of his ship by Lord Cornbury, Governor of New York.

1055 SLUSH, BARNABY. The Navy Royal: or a Sea Cook turn'd Projector.... *Lond.* *1709*, *12°*. L.

COLONIES

1056 A Deduction of the Right and Title of the Crown of Great Britain, and therein of Our Most Gracious Sovereign Lady Queen Anne, to all the Streights, Bays, Seas, Rivers, Lakes, Creeks, Islands, Shores, Lands, Territories and Places whatsoever, within Hudson-Streights and Hudson-Bay, and of the Right and Property of the Hudsons-Bay Company, derived from the Imperial Crown of Great Britain, by Letters Patent of Incorporation, and a free Grant of all the Premisses from King Charles the Second, Anno. 1670. *n.p.* [*1709*], *F°*. LPRO.

Endorsed: The Right of the Crown of Great Britain to Hudsons Bay and Streights, in North-America, Asserted: And some Account of the Violences Committed by the French, upon the English there in time of Peace.

1057 LAWSON, JOHN. A New Voyage to Carolina; containing the Exact Description and Natural History of that Country: together with the Present State thereof. And a Journal of a Thousand Miles, Travel'd thro' several Nations of Indians. Giving a particular Account of their Customs, Manners, &c. *Lond.* *1709*, *4°*. L.

Published in monthly parts as part of *A New Collection of Voyages and Travels*, 1708–1710. Reissued in 1714 as *The History of Carolina* (L); Another reissue 1718 (MH); another edn. Raleigh, N.C. 1860.

1058 To the Honourable the Commons in Parliament Assembled. The Case of the Poor distressed Planters, and other Inhabitants of the Islands of Nevis, and St. Christophers, in America. *n.p.* [*1709?*], *s. sh. F°*. L.

Endorsed: The Case of the distressed Inhabitants of the Islands of Nevis and St. Christophers, in America.

FINANCE

1059 DAVENANT, GEORGE. A Proposal for Annuities for Life, with the Benefit of Survivorship; such as the Purses of the generality of the People may be able to compass. *Lond.* *1709*, *F°*. LPRO.

1060 A Letter to a Member of Parliament, with Proposals for a Game-Act. *n.p.* [*1709*], *s. sh. F°*. O.

Dated: Jan. 1709. For a small tax 'on every Person that shall Hunt, Hawk, Fish, or Fowl'. Title from endorsement.

1061 A Proposition for a Lottery. *n.p.* [*1709*], *s. sh. F°*. MC.

Another issue, Lond. 1709 (LPRO).

1062 Reasons Humbly offered for the Laying on a farther Duty on French Brandies. *n.p.* [*1709?*], *s. sh. F°*. MC.

Endorsed: Reasons for Raising the Customs on French Brandies.

1063 Reasons Humbly Offered to the Consideration of the Honourable House of Commons, for laying a Duty on Melted Tallow, and not on Candles. *n.p.* [*1709?*], *s. sh. F°*. LU.

1064 The Method of Computing the Customs made plain to the Meanest Capacity. *Edin. 1709*, *4°*. K.

1065 A Bill to Explain the Act of the First Year of Her Majesties Reign, entituled, An Act to oblige Edward Whitaker to account for such Summs of Publick Money as hath been received by him. *n.p.* [*1709*], *F°*. L.

Whitaker had been Solicitor to the Admiralty.

1066 The Suffering-Case of Several of the People Commonly Called Quakers, on Suits mostly Commenced for Tythes, in the Court of Exchequer, since the Acts made For the more easie Recovery of Tythes, in the 7th and 8th of King William the Third. Humbly Presented to both Houses of Parliament. *Lond. 1709*, *4°*. L.

1067 A List of the Names of all the Proprietors of the Bank of England, March 25, 1709. *Lond. 1709*, *F°*. L.

On p. 8 is 'A List of the Names of the Governors, Deputy-Governor, and Directors of the Bank of England, for the Year 1708' and 'Part of the By-Law concerning Elections'.

1068 A preamble to the subscription-books, for enlarging the capital-stock of the Bank of England. London, February the 22nd, $170\frac{8}{9}$.... [*London, 1709*], *4 p. 32 cm.* Kress S.1211.

1069 Advertisement. From the Charitable Corporation, for Relief of Industrious Poor, by assisting them with small Sums upon Pledges at Legal Interest; Concerning the Charitable Fund by the said Corporation Proposed; at their House in Duke-St Westminster. *n.p.* [*1709?*], *F°*. LG.

1070 A short Case of the Charitable Corporation. *n.p.* [*1709?*], *s. sh. F°*. LLI.

A prospectus.

1071 Proposals for establishing a Perpetual Assurance-Office by a voluntary Subscription of Two Thousand Persons; who, for certain Annual

Payments into a Joint-Stock during their Lives, may and will secure to themselves, or to any Person or Persons they shall name (at or before their respective Deaths) such advantageous Sum or Sums of Money as are hereafter expressed. *n.p.* [*1709?*], *4°*. L.

1072 The Articles of the Second Society of Assurance, for the Support of Widows and Orphans. Begun at Dublin the 24th of June, 1708. According to the First Settlement by the Subscribers Votes, and the Pursuant Regulations, &c. To which is Prefix'd, the Sworn Directors Names. And subjoin'd, the Design of this Undertaking in General; and the Advantages of this Society in Particular. Objections Answer'd: and Directions to Remote Subscribers. At the End is a List of the Contributors.... *Dublin*, *1709*, *12°*. L.

1073 From the Lombard-House in Duke-street, Westminster. Household-Goods, and Trading-Stock, Insured from Loss by Fire. *n.p.* [*1709?*], *s. sh. F°*. LU.

1074 From the Lombard House in Duke-street, Westminster. Abstract of the Settlement for Insurance of Goods against Loss by Fire, Inrolled in the High Court of Chancery, by The Charitable Corporation for Relief of Industrious Poor, &c. *n.p.* [*1709?*], *s. sh. F°*. LG.

1075 Snell, Charles. A Guide to Book-Keepers, according to the Italian Manner: now in General Use. Directing Young Accomptants to the Books and Accompts where the Usual Occurrences in Trade are to be Enter'd; and in the Stile proper for such Entrances. *Lond.* *1709*, *F°*. O.

TRANSPORT

1076 A Bill for continuing an Act made in the First Year of Her Majesty's Reign, Entituled, An Act for the Rebuilding and Repairing the Piers of the Town and Port of Whitby, in the County of York. *n.p.* [*1709*], *F°*. L.

1077 Reasons Humbly Offer'd for making the River Weaver in the County of Chester Navigable, from Northwich to Frodsham-Bridge. shewing that Design to be a very Considerable National Advantage as well as Beneficial in Particular to that County, and the Parts adjacent. *n.p.* [*1709?*], *F°*. L.

1078 Povey, Charles. Proposals offer'd to the Honourable House of Commons, for making an Act to Establish the Half-Penny Carriage; To the End that Her Majesty's Revenues arising by Posts may be encreased, and the Inhabitants within the main Pile of Buildings of the Cities and Suburbs of London and Westminster, and Burrough of Southwark, may save 14000 l. per Ann. *n.p.* [*1709*], *s. sh. F°*.

Reproduced in facsimile in the *Postal History Society Bulletin*, no. 35, March 1946, whence this entry is taken.

SOCIAL CONDITIONS

1079 Entry cancelled.

1080 Advertisement from the Charitable Fund intended to be establish'd in London...to relieve and support poor Seamens Families, and other necessitous Persons...by giving them Money, or lending it upon Pledges without any Interest or Charges whatsoever.... *Lond. 1709*, *4°*, LU.

Dated: Apr. 28. 1709.

1081 Reasons Humbly Offer'd to the Honourable House of Commons for passing and making the Bill, for the ease of Insolvent Debtors, General. *n.p.* [*1709?*], *s. sh. F°*. O.

1082 The Fees of the Sheriffs-Court, Chamberlain's-Office, Woodstreet and Poultry Compters, and Ludgate. Also the Rates and Fares of Hackney-Coachmen, Carmen, and Watermen; as they are settled by Act of Parliament, and by the Lord-Mayor, Aldermen, and Common Council of the City of London. *Lond. 1709*, *s. sh. F°*. L.

1083 The Case of the City of London, in relation to the Bill For a General Naturalization of all Foreign Protestants, now depending in the Honourable the House of Commons. *n.p.* [*1709*], *F°*. LG.

Endorsed: The City of London's Case in relation to the Bill For a General Naturalization.

1084 Reasons against a General Naturalization. *n. p.* [*1709*], *F°*. O.

1085 BELLERS, JOHN. To the Lords and other Commissioners, appointed by the Queen to take Care of the Poor Palatines. The Case of the Indigent Poor Consider'd, by which their Wants may be fully Supply'd. *n.p.* [*1709*], *4°*. M.

Dated: The 8th Septemb. 1709.

1086 A brief History of the Poor Palatine Refugees, lately arriv'd in England. Containing, I. A full Answer to all Objections made against receiving them; and plain and convincing Proofs, that the Accession of Foreigners is a manifest Advantage to Great Britain, and no Detriment to any of her Majesty's native Subjects.... *Lond. 1709*, *8°*. L.

Another edn. Dublin, 1709, 8° (DNL).

1087 *Begin*: Good Brother, Her Majesty having been graciously pleased not only to take into Her Own Royal Protection the poor distressed Palatines.... *n.p.* [*1709*], *s. sh. F°*. OC.

A circular letter from William Wake, Bishop of Lincoln, to the clergy of his diocese urging them to stir up their parishioners to liberal contributions. Dated Buckden, 25 July 1709.

1088 The Palatines Case Humbly offered to the Tradesmen of England. *Lond. 1709*, *s. sh. F°*. O.

1089 The Piety and Bounty of the Queen of Great Britain: with the Charitable Benevolence of Her Loving Subjects, toward the Support and Settlement of the Distressed Protestant Palatines. *Lond. 1709*, *F°*. LU.

1090 The Case of the Hamlets of Her Majesty's Tower of London. *n.p.* [*1709?*], *s. sh. F°*. O.

For the better payment of seamen's wages.

1091 The happy Consequences of Passing the Bill for a more Regular Paying Seamens Wages. *n.p.* [*1709?*], *s. sh. F°*. O.

1710

GENERAL

1092 [HOADLEY, BENJAMIN]. The Fears and Sentiments of all True Britains; with respect to National Credit, Interest and Religion. *Lond. 1710*, *8°*. L.

Reprinted in *The Works of Benjamin Hoadly*, vol. 1, 1773.

1093 The Gun-Smiths Queries. *n.p. 1710*, *s. sh. F°*. MC.

Another edn., n.p. 1710, 4° (E). Mostly concerned with peculation and bribery.

1094 [DAVENANT, CHARLES]. New Dialogues upon the Present Posture of Affairs, the Species of Mony, National Debts, Publick Revenues, Bank and East-India Company, and the Trade now carried on between France and Holland. Vol. II. By the Author of the Essay on Ways and Means. *Lond. 1710*, *8°*. LU.

The LU copy is a presentation copy from the author.

1095 [DAVENANT, CHARLES]. Sir Thomas Double at Court, and in High Preferments. In Two Dialogues between Sir Thomas Double and Sir Richard Comover, alias Mr. Whiglove: On the 27th of September, 1710. Part 1. *Lond. 1710*, *8°*. LU.

The LU copy is a presentation copy from the author.

AGRICULTURE

1096 The Case of the Distressed Warreners of England, Humbly Presented to this Honourable Parliament. *n.p.* [*c. 1710?*], *s. sh. F°*. LU.

Endorsed: The Warreners Case. Against poachers.

1097 BATESON, PETER. Some Papers relating to the General Draining of Marshland, in the County of Norfolk. With Mr. Berner's Objections and Proposals. As also an Answer to those objections and Proposals, &c. *n.p. 1710*, *4°*. pp. 10.15. L.

Another edn., with a map, 1710, pp. 24 (L).

1098 The Case of John Soper, Esq; Robert Budd, Sen. Nicholas Mayew, Thomas Budd, John Gilbert, James Budd, Robert Budd, Jun. Robert Yalden, Richard Yalden, John Mayew, and several others, who are seiz'd and possessed of several Large and Considerable Freehold, Copyhold, and Leasehold Estates in the Parish of Ropley, in the County of Southampton.... *n.p.* [*1710*], *s. sh. F°*. LLI.

Endorsed: The Case of Those Tenants that are against the Enclosing that Tract of Ground called Ropley-Common....

1099 The Humble Address of the Convocation of Stannators, or Parliament of Tinners, of the County of Cornwall. Assembled at Truro the Twentieth Day of April, in the Ninth Year of Her Majesty's most Happy Reign. With the Lord Warden's Answer to the Convocation. *n.p. 1710*, *F°*. L.

1100 A Bill for the Relief of the Creditors and Proprietors of Principal Money and Annuities of the Governor and Company of the Mine-Adventurers of England. *n.p.* [*1710*], *F*°. L.

1101 The Answer of Sir Humphrey Mackworth to the several Particulars of the Complaint upon the Petition of several Creditors and Proprietors of Principal-Money, Annuities and Shares of the Company of Mine-Adventurers. *n.p.* [*1710*], *4*°. LU.

Endorsed on the last page: The Case of Sir Humphrey Mackworth.

1102 The Case of Sir Humphrey Mackworth. *n.p.* [*1710*], *s. sh. F*°. LLI.

Against the bill to prevent him leaving the kingdom.

1103 An Abstract of the Case of Sir H. Mackworth. *n.p.* [*1710*], *s. sh. F*°. O.

1104 MACKWORTH, Sir HUMPHREY. A Short State of the Case and Proceedings of the Company of Mine-Adventurers; with an Abstract of the Defence of the Deputy Governor and Directors: Justified by Vouchers. *Lond. 1710*, *F*°. LU.

1105 MACKWORTH, Sir HUMPHREY. The Book of Vouchers, to prove the Case and Defence of the Deputy Governour and Directors of the Company of Mine-Adventurers....Part I. *Lond. 1710*, *F*°. L.

Pt. II was published in 1711.

1106 WALLER, WILLIAM. The Mine-Adventure laid Open; being an Answer to a Late Pamphlet, Intitled, A Familiar Discourse, &c. Published by William Shiers...but acknowledged before the Honourable Committee of the House of Commons to be written by Sir Humphrey Mackworth.... *Lond. 1710*, *8*°. L.

1107 WALLER, WILLIAM. The Answer of Mr. Waller, to Mr. Hawkins's Report, given in at the General Court of the Governour and Company of the Mine-Adventurers of England the 15th of December, 1709.... *Lond. 1710*, *8*°. L.

1108 HAWKINS, THOMAS. The Reply of Mr. Hawkins to Mr. Waller's Answer to the said Hawkins's Report. Given in to the General Court of the Governour and Company of the Mine Adventurers of England, the Tenth of January, 1709 [O.S.]. Printed by Order of the Court of Directors for the Satisfaction of the Company. *Lond. 1710*, *8*°. L.

1109 At a General Court of the Governour and Company of the Mine-Adventurers of England, held...on Wednesday the First Day of February...1709 [O.S.]. [*Lond. 1710*], *s. sh. F*°. L.

1110 The Case of Several Creditors and Proprietors of Principal Money, Annuities and Shares in the Mine-Adventure of England, on Behalf of themselves, and several Widows and Orphans, Members and Creditors of the Company of the said Mine-Adventure upon their Petition. *n.p.* [*1710*], *F*°. O.

Endorsed: The Case of the Creditors of the Company of the Mine-Adventurers of England.

1111 An Abstract of the Deed or Instrument for an Union of all Parties concerned in the Mine-Adventure, Giving Powers to Fifteen Persons according to the Proposal of His Grace the Duke of Leeds, which was executed the 29th of June Anno. Dom. 1710. [*Lond. 1710*], *s. sh. F°*. L.

1112 An Abstract of the Terms of Union between the Creditors of the Company of Mine-Adventurers, and the Proprietors of Principal Money, Annuities and Shares, and of the New Constitution of the United Society, Published and Declared at a General Meeting the 16th of November 1710. at Stationer's-Hall, London. *n.p.* [*1710*], *F°*. OUP.

1113 An Alphabetical List of the Subscribers to a Deed, Impowering Fifteen Trustees in the Affairs of the Company of the Mine-Adventurers of England. [*Lond. 1710*], *s. sh. F°*. L.

1114 The Report of the Committee of the House of Commons, to whom it was referred to consider the Humble Petitions of several Creditors and Proprietors of Principal Mony, Annuities and Shares in the Mine-Adventurers of England; with the Resolutions of the House of Commons thereupon. *Lond. 1710*, *F°*. L.

1115 An Act for the Publick Registring of all Deeds, Conveyances, and other Incumbrances that shall be made of, or that may affect any Honours, Mannors, Lands, Tenements, or Hereditaments, within the County of Berks. *n.p.* [*1710*], *F°*. LU.

A bill.

1116 An Act for the Publick Registring of all Deeds, Conveyances, and other Incumbrances that shall be made of, or that may affect any Honours, Mannors, Lands, Tenements, or Hereditaments, within the County of Surrey. *n. p.* [*1710*], *F°*. L.

A bill.

1117 Forms of Memorials, Certificates, &c. on the late Act of Parliament, for the Publick Registring of all Deeds and Conveyances, Judgments, Statutes, and Recognizances. For the County of Middlesex. And Notes Thereupon. *Lond. 1710*, *4°*. LU.

MANUFACTURES

1118 The Case of Multitudes of Tradesmen and Manufacturers, in respect to Publick Mournings. *n.p.* [*1710?*], *s. sh. F°*. LLI.

1119 George Ball, Appellant. John Coggs, William Dockwra, and Mary Chaffin, Respondents. The Appellant's Case. *n.p.* [*1710*], *s. sh. F°*. O.

Concerning the making of brass and brass wire. Signed: T. Parker, Con. Phipps.

1120 The Brewers Farewell, to the Magistrates, Heritors, Merchants and Crafts of Edinburgh. *Edin. 1710*, *F°*. E.

1121 To the Reasons Already Offer'd by the Levant-Company, for the Bill now depending in the Honourable House of Commons, for Regulating Buttons and Button-holes, They humbly Represent the following Particulars. *n.p.* [*1710*], *s. sh. F*°. O.

Endorsed: Further Reasons offer'd by the Levant-Company, for the Bill now Depending in the Honourable House of Commons, for Regulating Buttons and Button-holes.

1122 An Humble Proposal to the Parliament of Great-Britain. *n.p.* [*c. 1710?*], *s. sh. F*°. O.

For an act to secure the profits of inventions to the inventors.

1123 Proposals of Edward Semeins of Rotterdam in Holland; Humbly Presented to the Parliament of Great Britain. *n.p.* [*c. 1710?*]. *s. sh. F*°. L.

Has invented engines for draining and pumping and needs encouragement.

1124 A Proposal humbly offer'd to the Consideration of the Hon[ble] House of Commons, for the Improvement of the Woollen Manufactory of Great Britain, and for the Imployment of great Numbers of the Poor, Men, Women and Children, now wanting Bread. *n.p.* [*c. 1710?*], *s. sh. F*°. O.

Endorsed: A Proposal for Packing in Woollen.

1125 An Abstract of the whole Proceedings of the Honourable House of Commons, relating to the Gun-Smiths Petitions both in the Lord Pembrooke's and Lord Wharton's Governments from the Original Journals of that House. [*Dublin, 1710?*], *s. sh. F*°. DA.

1126 The Tinn-Plate-Workers Complaint of the A[buse] of their Trade. Address'd to their Fellow-Citizens, the Masters, Wardens, &c. of all the Corporations of the City of Dublin. *n.p.* [*c. 1710?*], *s. sh. F*°. D.

Against interlopers. In verse.

COMMERCE

1127 A Bill for Encouragement of Learning, and for Securing the Property of Copies of Books to the Rightful Owners thereof. *n.p.* [*1710*], *F*°. LLI.

1128 The Booksellers Humble Address to the Honourable House of Commons, in Behalf of the Bill for Encouraging Learning, &c. *n.p.* [*1710?*], *s. sh. F*°. O.

1129 A Letter from Holland, concerning the Right which Booksellers have in their Copies, or Sole Power of Printing their respective Books, in that Nation. *n.p.* [*1710*], *s. sh. F*°. LLI.

Dated: Amsterdam, March 11. 1710. N.S.

1130 Reasons Humbly Offer'd for the Bill for Encouragement of Learning, and for Securing the Property of Copies of Books to the Rightful Owners thereof. *n.p.* [*1710*], *s. sh. F*°. LLI.

1131 More Reasons Humbly Offer'd to the Honourable House of Commons, for the Bill for Encouraging Learning, and for Securing Property of Copies of Books to the Rightful Owners thereof. *n.p.* [*1710?*], *s. sh. Fo.* L.

Reprinted in E. A. Bloom, *Samuel Johnson in Grub Street*, 1957.

1132 Reasons humbly offer'd to the Right Honourable, the Lords Spiritual and Temporal, and Commons in Parliament assembled, for Passing the Bill for setting the Assize of Bread, &c. *n.p.* [*1710*], *s. sh. Fo.* LLI.

1133 Reasons humbly offer'd against the passing of the Bill, as it now is, for Setling the Price and Assize of Bread. *n.p.* [*1710?*], *s. sh. Fo.* LG.

1134 Reasons Humbly Offer'd to the Right Honourable, the Lords Spiritual and Temporal, and Commons, in Parliament, Assembled: For Passing a Clause, for Compelling Persons bringing Meal and Flower to the Cities of London and Westminster, and the Places adjacent, to bring the same to Publick Markets. *n.p.* [*1710*], *s. sh. Fo.* O.

Endorsed: Reasons Humbly Offer'd For Passing a Clause to the Bakers Bill, concerning the Publick Markets.

1135 Some Reasons Humbly Offer'd to the Honourable House of Commons, by the Master, Wardens and Commonalty of the Mystery of Bakers of the City of London, and other Bakers within the Suburbs thereof, and iu [*sic*] the City and Liberty of Westminster and Borough of Southwark, against several Clauses in the Bill for Regulating the Price and Assize of Bread. *n.p.* [*1710*]. *Fo.* LG.

1136 LONDON. Garrard Mayor. Martis, ij°, die Maij. 1710. [*Lond. 1710*], *s. sh. Fo.* LCRO.

An order regulating the assize of bread in London.

1137 Middlesex. From Thursday May 11. to Thursday May, 18.... [*Lond.*], *1710*, *s. sh. Fo.* MC.

An order for the assize of bread.

1138 Middlesex. Saturday, May 27. [*Lond.*], *1710. s. sh. 4o.* L.

An order for the assize of bread.

1139 Act for Regulating the Price and Assize of Bread. Edinburgh, 31 May 1710. *Edin. 1710*, *s. sh. Fo.* C (Cr).

1140 The Baker's Declaration, or, Their Reasons for not Baking till further Orders. *Lond. 1710*, *s. sh. Fo.* LSC.

A skit, 'the late Act of Parliament having oblig'd us in a very strict Sense to be Honest against our Natural Inclinations'.

1141 Considerations for Adiusting both Weight and Measure. *n.p.* [*c. 1710?*], *s. sh. Fo.* MC.

For standard casks and barrels for beer, vinegar and soap.

1142 Act and intimation against forestallers of victual, and for mending and repairing of highway and bridges. Lanark, Tuesday April 4th. 1710.... [*Lanark, 1710*], *broadside. 34·5 × 19·5 cm.* Kress S.1265.

Signed: Ja: Carmichael clerk.

1143 By the Queen, A Proclamation, Requiring Quarantain to be Performed by Ships coming from the Baltick Sea. *Lond. 1710, F°.* L.

Dated: 9 November [1710]. Priced. Another London edn., unpriced (LPRO); another edn. Edin. 1710 (E).

1144 A Copy of a Clause, relating to the Exportation of all Goods entitl'd to a Draw-back; being Part of a Bill now depending in the Honourable House of Commons. *n.p. [1710], s. sh. F°.* L.

1145 Queries relating to a Clause in the Annuity Bill, obliging the Exporters of all Goods entituled to Drawbacks, to give Bond at the Custom-house to the full Value of such Goods, with double Security; which Bonds are to remain in force until Certificates are produced that such Goods are landed in Foreign Parts, &c. *n.p. [1710], s. sh. F°.* O.

1146 Reasons humbly offer'd by the Linnen Drapers of the City of London, to the House of Commons, against a Clause in a Bill, now depending before that Honourable House; Entituled a Bill for granting to Her Majesty new Duties of Excise; and upon several Imported Commodities, and for establishing a Yearly Fund thereby; and by other Ways and Means, to raise Ten Hundred Thousand Pounds, by sale of Annuities (and in default thereof) by another Lottery, for the Service of the Year 1710. *n.p. [1710], s. sh. F°.* O.

Against the clause which required a certificate of export before the grant of the drawback.

1147 Reasons Humbly offer'd to the Honourable House of Commons, by the Merchants Trading in Tobacco, against a Clause relating to the Exportation of Goods entitl'd to a Draw-back. *n.p. [1710], s. sh. F°.* L.

1148 An Abstract of the Charter and large Privileges, granted by the States-General of the united Netherlands, to the Dutch-African and West-India-Company; Dated the 26 of September, 1674. Containing also their Reasons, for carrying on that Trade, by an Exclusive Joint-Stock. *n.p.* $170\frac{9}{10}$, *s. sh. F°.* LLI.

With reasons for supporting the Royal African Company. Another edn. 1713 (O).

1149 An Answer to several pretended Arguments, proving, That our Trade to Africa cannot be preserved and carried on effectually by any other Method than that of a considerable Joint-stock, with Exclusive Privileges. *n.p. [1710?], s. sh. F°.* LLI.

Kress has two issues (S. 1254, 1255).

1150 A Brief Narrative of the Royal-African-Company's Proceedings, with their Creditors the last Year; with some Rules and Restrictions, they are willing to submit to, by a Bill in Parliament. *n.p. [1710], s. sh. F°.* L.

1151 The Case of Sir John and Mr. Charles Crisp, grandsons of Sir Nicholas Crisp, in relation to the Forts and Castles of Africa. *n.p. [1710?], s. sh. F°.* L.

1152 The Case of the Royal-African Company. *n.p.* [*1710*], *F°*. L.
Endorsed: The Case of the Royal-African-Company.

1153 A Memorial on behalf of the Royal-African-Company, relating to their Proposal lately given in to the Honourable House of Commons; for the better Establishment of that Trade: together with their said Proposal Subjoin'd. *n.p.* *170$\frac{9}{10}$*, *F°*. L.

1154 Seasonable Animadversions on all the Papers and Pamphlets lately printed on behalf of the Separate Traders to Africa; and delivered by them, at several times, to the Members of the Honourable House of Commons and others; as pretended Arguments against establishing and carrying on the Trade to Africa, upon the foot of an exclusive Joint-Stock. *n.p.* *170$\frac{9}{10}$*, *F°*. L.

1155 A Second Letter to a Member of Parliament, relating to the settling the Trade to Africa. *n.p.* [*1710*], *s. sh. F°*. L.

1156 The Separate Traders Scheme for carrying on the Trade to Africa. *n.p.* [*1710*], *s. sh. F°*. LU.

1157 A True State of the Present Difference between the Royal African Company, and the Separate Traders: Shewing the Irregularities and Impositions of the Joint-Stock Managers; the Uselessness of their Forts... the Advantages and Reasonableness of an Open Trade to Africa; and, lastly, the Danger of an Exclusive Trade, not only to the Traders of South and North Britain, but, to our American Plantations. Written by a True Lover of his Country, and humbly submitted to the Wise Consideration of Both Houses of Parliament. *Lond.* *1710*, *4°*. L.

1158 A Brief State of the East India Trade, as it relates to the other Branches of the British Commerce: In Order to judge, whether, as it is now carry'd on, that Trade be advantageous to the general Interest of the Nation, or not. *n.p.* [*c. 1710?*], *s. sh. F°*. LU.

1159 A New List of all the Ships and Vessels of Her Majesties Royal Navy; When, Where, and by Whom Built, and Rebuilt. With their Burthen and Number of Men and Guns. *Lond.* *1710*, *8°*. EU.

1160 Proposal for a Publick Journal, to find out, the Main Reason, of many Great Losses by Sea-Damage Extraordinary, to Merchant's Dry Goods in Voyages, and of the total Loss, of Merchants Goods, and the Lives of many Marriners, and Passengers, by the Foundring of Ships, and Vessels, in Ordinary Storms, and in Common Seas and Weather: And also to Explain, the Case of some Ships and Vessels, and how they are taken by the Enemy, in time of War. *n.p.* [*c. 1710?*], *F°*. L.

1161 Proposals Humbly Offer'd to the Consideration of the Honourable House of Commons, for Protecting our Trade. *n.p.* [*c. 1710?*], *s. sh. F°*. L.
Advocating a separate force of cruisers, not to be used either for convoy duty or in the line of battle.

COLONIES

1162 [NAIRN, THOMAS?]. A Letter from South Carolina; giving an Account of the Soil, Air, Product, Trade, Governments Laws, Religion, People, Military Strength, &c. of that Province; Together with the Manner and necessary Charges of Settling a Plantation there, and the Annual Profit it will produce. Written by a Swiss Gentleman, to his Friend at Bern. *Lond. 1710, 8°.* L.

2nd edn. 1718 (Sabin 87860); another 2nd edn. 1732 (L). For authorship see ms. note in B.M. copy and Sabin 87859.

1163 The Case of the Poor distressed Planters, and other Inhabitants of the Islands of Nevis, and St. Christophers, in America. *n.p.* [*1710*], *s. sh. F°.* L.

Endorsed: The Case of the distressed Inhabitants of the Islands of Nevis and St. Christophers, in America.

FINANCE

1164 [DEFOE, DANIEL]. An Essay upon Publick Credit: being an Enquiry how the Publick Credit comes to depend upon the Change of the Ministry, or the Dissolutions of Parliaments; and whether it does so or no. With an Argument, proving that the Publick Credit may be upheld and maintain'd in this Nation.... *Lond. 1710, 8°.* LU.

3rd edn. 1710 (O). Another edition, with attribution to Robert Harley, 1797. Reprinted in *Somers Tracts*, XIII (1815), 27, with attribution to Harley, and in *A Select Collection of... Tracts... on the National Debt*, ed. by J. R. Mcculloch, 1857, p.l. For Defoe's authorship see *Letters of Daniel Defoe*, ed. by G. H. Healey, 1955, p. 277.

1165 [DEFOE, DANIEL]. An Essay upon Loans: or, an Argument proving that Substantial Funds settled by Parliament, with the Encouragement of Interests, and the Advances of Prompt Payment usually allow'd, will bring in Loans of Money to the Exchequer, in sight of all the Conspiracies of Parties to the contrary....By the Author of the Essay upon Credit. *Lond. 1710, 8°.* LU.

Reprinted in *Somers Tracts*, XIII (1815), 35, with attribution to Robert Harley. For Defoe's authorship see *Letters of Daniel Defoe*, ed. by G. H. Healey, 1955, p. 277.

1166 [BROUGHTON, JOHN]. The Vindication and Advancement of our National Constitution and Credit: Attempted in Several Tracts. 1. An Introductory Essay....2. Remarks upon the Bank of England, with regard more especially to our Trade, and the Constitution of the Government. 3. An Essay upon the National Credit of Britain. 4. A Letter to a Member of the Honourable House of Commons, relating to the Credit of our Government and the Nation in general. All written by the same Author. *Lond. 1710, 8º.* LU.

No. 2, 3 & 4 had previously been published separately. For authorship see ms. note in LU copy. Reissued as *Essays on the National Constitution, Bank, Credit, and Trade*, Lond. 1717.

1167 [CLEMENT, SIMON]. Faults on both Sides: or, an Essay upon the Original Cause, Progress, and Mischievous Consequences of the Factions in this Nation....By way of Answer to the Thoughts of an Honest Tory [by Benjamin Hoadly]. *Lond. 1710, 8º.* L.

Mainly financial. For authorship see [Oldmixon, J.] *The Life and Posthumous Works of Arthur Maynwaring*, p. 171, and W. Kennett in Brydges, Sir E., *Restituta*. vol. 3, p. 378. Reprinted in *Somers Tracts*, XII (1814), 678, where it is attributed to Richard Harley. Richard is probably a misprint for Robert, who doubtless inspired the work. 2nd edn. 1710 (O); 3rd edn. 1710, 4° (O); 4th edn. Dublin, 1710, 4º (DNL).

1168 An Answer to that part of the Pamphlet entitul'd Faults on Both Sides, which relates to the Deficiency of the English Army in Spain, at the time of the Battle of Almanza. Being the Substance of Her Majesty's Message to the House of Commons concerning it. *Lond. 1710, 8º.* L.

1169 Faults in the Fault-Finder: or, a Specimen of Errors in the pamphlet, entitul'd Faults on Both Sides. *Lond. 1710, 8º.* L.

Second edn. 1710 (O).

1170 [TRAPP, JOSEPH]. Most Faults on One Side: or, the Shallow Politicks, Foolish Arguing, and Villanous Designs of the Author of a late Pamphlet, entitul'd Faults on Both Sides Consider'd and Expos'd. In Answer to that Pamphlet: Shewing that the many Truths in Modern History related by the Author of it, do not make amends for his many Falshoods in Fact, and Fallacies in Reasoning. *Lond. 1710, 8º.* L.

3rd edn. 1711 (L); another edn. 1711 (L). For authorship see *Gentleman's Mag.* LVI, 662.

1171 [CLEMENT, SIMON]. A Vindication of the Faults on both Sides, from the Reflections of the Medley, the Specimen-Maker, and a Pamphlet, Entituled, Most Faults on one Side. With a Dissertation on the Nature and Use of Money and Paper-Credit in Trade, and the true Value of Joint-Stocks, maintaining the Assertion of the Author, in Relation to those Matters. By the Author of the Faults on both Sides. *Lond. 1700, 8º.* L.

Reprinted in *Somers Tracts*, XIII (1815), 3.

1172 Entry cancelled.

1173 BEVAN, CHA. A Proposal for Raising 125000 l. per Annum. *n.p.* [*c. 1710?*], *s. sh. Fº.* MC.

By licensing inns, coffee-houses, etc.

1174 To the Honourable House of Commons: The Humble Proposal of Richard Dennet. *n.p.* [*c. 1710?*], *s. sh. F°*. O.

Endorsed: An Humble Proposal for Raising Money. Offering to disclose, if suitably rewarded, a method of raising £1,000,000 in 3 months.

1175 SOUTHMEAD, WILLIAM. Proposals humbly Offered to the Parliament. *n.p.* [*c. 1710*], *s. sh. F°*. LPRO.

Has schemes for making money and raising money which he will disclose if rewarded.

1176 A Proposal for Raising a Million of Money for the Use of the Publick, and Sinking all the unsatisfied Debentures without any New Fund. *n.p.* [*1710?*], *s. sh. F°*. MC.

1177 A Proposal for Raising one Hundred Thousand Pounds, by laying a Duty upon Hats. *n.p.* [*c. 1710?*], *s. sh. F°*. MC.

1178 A Proposal Humbly Offer'd to Raise a Considerable Sum of Money Yearly, for the Use of the Government. *n.p.* [*c. 1710?*], *s. sh. F°*. LPRO.

Brewers, distillers and retailers of spirits to take out licences.

1179 Proposals Humbly Offered to the Consideration of the Parliament, for the raising Two Millions, for the vigorous carrying on the War against France, at 6 l. per Cent. *n. p.* [*c. 1710?*], *s. sh. F°*. MC.

Endorsed: Proposals for Raising Two Millions by Lottery.

1180 Proposals for raising 400000 l. per Ann. by a Duty on Signs, Signals, &c. Humbly offer'd by E.D. And others } Gent. *n.p.* [*c. 1710?*], *s. sh. F°*. O.

Title from endorsement. Another edn., Humbly offer'd by E.D. and C.W. } Gent. (O).

1181 A Proposal Humbly Offer'd to the Honourable House of Commons, in Parliament Assembled, for Improving the Woollen Manufacture, for raising 3000000 l. on Funds never yet Impos'd in this Reign, towards carrying on the War, and for other Ends and Purposes for the Benefit of the Publick; as Imploying the Poor, Enabling Tenants cheerfully to pay their Rents, by Annually disposing of their Coarse Wool at good Prices, which will beget a greater Price for their Finer sort of Wool, and raise the Prices of the English Draperies abroad, and prevent the Clandestine Exportation of Wool into France; and in some measure to recompence the plunder'd Islands of Nevis and St. Christopher's, and prevent the laying any farther Charge on Land than the present 4s. per Pound. *n.p.* [*c. 1710?*], *s. sh. F°*. LLI.

For a heavy tax on cloth made in America and for duties on imports into the American colonies.

1182 The Cast of the Wax-Chandlers. *n.p.* [*1710*], *s. sh. F°*. LU.

Against the proposed tax of 4*d* a lb.

1183 Reasons Humbly Offered to the Consideration of the Honourable House of Commons against Laying a Duty on Pepper, or on any other Merchandize Imported, in Hand. *n.p.* [*1710*], *s. sh. F°.* O.

1184 Some more Reasons humbly offered to the Consideration of the Honourable Commons of Great Britain in Parliament, against laying on a farther Duty on Raisins. *n.p.* [*1710*], *s. sh. F°.* O.

1185 The Case of the White Lead-Makers. *n. p.* [*1710?*], *s. sh. F°.* O.

Against being subject to the vinegar duty.

1186 The Case of the Attorneys and other Practicers, relating to the Stamp-Duty. *n.p.* [*1710*], *s. sh. F°.* LLI.

1187 The Case of Samuel Shepherd, John Lambert, and John James David, Merchants of London, humbly offered to the Consideration of this Honourable House for Relief. *n.p.* [*1710*], *s. sh. F°.* O.

Endorsed: The Case of several Merchants of London, relating to the Custom of Wines taken by the French.

1188 Report of George Cruikshank General Examiner, and Richard Savage one of the Clerks to the Secretary of the Commissioners of the Customs, anent the Officers Books at Prestounpans. *n.p.* [*1710?*], *F°.* LPRO.

Followed by: The Representation of the Commissioners of the Customs of North-Britain.

1189 To the Right Honourable the Lords Spiritual and Temporal, and to the Commons of Great-Britain, in Parliament Assembled. The Case and humble Petition of Thomas Trott, late a Custom-House Officer at Limington.... *n.p.* [*c. 1710*], *s. sh. F°.* L.

1190 *Begin.* Sir, Whereas George and Joseph Newell, late of Lombard-street, Goldsmiths.... *n.p.* [*1710?*], *s. sh. F°.* L.

A petition for a bill to enable them to compound with the Treasury for money owed as security for George Dixon, Receiver General of Somerset.

1191 The Bill to prevent Mutiny, &c. and for Payment of the Army, &c. Reasons for a Clause, &c. on behalf of Executors, &c. To oblige Agents to Regiments to Accompt with the Executors as well as with the Officers while alive. *n.p.* [*1710?*], *s. sh. F°.* L.

1192 A Letter to a New Member of the Honourable House of Commons; touching the Rise of all the Imbezzlements and Mismanagements of the Kingdom's Treasure, from the Beginning of the Revolution unto this present Parliament....To which is added, A Parallel Account of the National Expences, from November 3. 1640 to November 1659. And from November 5. 1688. to Michaelmas 1700. *Amsterdam, 1710*, 4°. L.

Signed: W. L. Reprinted in *Harleian Miscellany*, VI (1810), 304, and in *Somers Tracts*, XII (1814), 486.

1193 An Address of the B——k of England to Her M——y. *Lond. 1710*, *s. sh. F°.* LG.

A squib. The Bank asks leave to direct what persons shall form the Government. The Queen replies that she will employ those she can confide in.

1194 A Letter to a Person of Quality, relating to the Bank of England, and Credit of the Nation. *n.p. 1710, 4°.* LU.

1195 The Charter of the Corporation of the Amicable Society for a Perpetual Assurance-Office; Together with the By-Laws thereunto belonging.... *Lond. 1710, 8°.* L.

1196 Proposals set forth by the Company of London-Insurers, for Insuring Houses, Moveable Goods, Merchandizes, Furniture and Wares, from Loss and Damage by Fire. *n.p.* [*1710*], *s. sh. F°.* L.

Dated: From the Sun-Fire-Office, April the 10th. 1710. Rates for London.

1197 Proposals set forth by the Company of London-Insurers, for Insuring Houses, Moveable Goods, Merchandizes, Furniture and Wares, from Loss and Damage by Fire, in any Place within Great Britain, out of the Cities of London and Westminster.... *n.p.* [*1710*], *s. sh. F°.* L.

Dated: From the Sun-Fire-Office, August the 30th, 1710.

1198 Proposals for Insuring on Marriages, By the Beneficial Society, at their Office at the Flying Horse in Pennington-street, near Ratcliff High-Way. *n.p.* [*1710*], *s. sh. F°.* L.

1199 Proposals For Insuring on Births, By the Beneficial Society, at their Office at the Flying-Horse in Pennington-street, near Ratcliff High-Way: Being a Monthly Dividend of Two Thousand Pounds when the Society is Compleat. *n.p.* [*1710*], *F°.* L.

Followed by Second and Third Proposals.

1200 Proposals for Insurance on Marriage, by the Second Beneficial Society, at their Office in King's-Head-Court Petticoat-Lane, near Bishop's-gate-street. November the 23rd, 1710. *n.p.* [*1710*], *s. sh. F°.* O.

1201 Insurance on Marriage, By the Fair Society at their Office, at the Bunch of Grapes, a Fan-Shop, and Sadlers, against the Leg Tavern in Fleet-Street. By a Monthly Dividend. *n.p.* [*1710*], *s. sh. F°.* L.

On the verso are further Proposals, dated December the 19th, 1710.

1202 Insurance on Marriage By the Fair Society at their Office, At the Bunch of Grapes, a Fan Shop, and Sadlers, against the Leg Tavern in Fleet-Street. *n.p.* [*1710*], *s. sh. F°.* L.

On the verso is Insurance on Births. Different from the preceding.

1203 At a certain Charge: Or, Proposals for a Weekly Dividend of 1000 l. on Marriages. By the Flower-De-Luce Society, &c. *n.p.* [*1710*], *s. sh. F°.* L.

Dated: December the 12th, 1710. Flower-de-Luce, at the Back-side of St. Clement's, near Lyons Inn.

1204 The Profitable and Equitable Society, Or, Office of Insurance On Births of Children: at a small and certain charge, by a Weekly Devidend, kept at the Flower-de-Luce, near Lyons-Inn, behind St. Clements. *n.p.* [*1710*], *s. sh. F°.* L.

'Begun December the 21st. 1710.'

1205 Proposals for Insurance on Marriages, by the Friendly-Society [in Finch-Lane]. *n.p.* [*1710*], *s. sh. F°.* L.

1206 Proposals for Insurance on Marriages, by the Second Friendly-Society [in Finch-Lane]. *n.p.* [*1710*], *s. sh. F°.* L.

1207 Proposals for Insurance on Marriage: By the Generous Society: At their Office at Templeman's Coffee-House, at Charing-Cross. *n.p.* [*1710*], *s. sh. F°.* L.

1208 First Proposals for Insurance on Marriage: By the Generous Society: At their Office, at Templeman's Coffee-House, Charing-Cross. *n.p.* [*1710*], *s. sh. F°.* L.

On the verso are: Proposals for Insurance on the Births of Children. By the Generous Society. These are dated December the 6th. 1710.

1209 Second Proposals for Insurance on Marriage: By the Generous Society: At their Office at Templeman's Coffee-House, Charing-Cross. December the 7th. 1710. *n.p.* [*1710*], *F°.* L.

Followed by Third Proposals for Insurance on Marriage, and Proposals for Insurance on the Births of Children.

1210 Propoasls [*sic*] for Insurance on Marriage by the Generous and Amicable Societies, at their Office at Widow Pratts Coffee-House, in Cat-Eaten-Street, by St. Lawrence Church nigh Guild-Hall. *n.p.* [*1710*], *s. sh. Fo.* L.

1211 Proposals for Insurance on Marriage; by the Good and Friendly Society, at their Office in Mansel-street, between Haydon-Yard and the Vinegar-House. *n.p.* [*1710*], *s. sh. F°.* L.

1212 Proposals of Insurance on the Baptizing of Infants; and also, for Insurance on Marriage, by the Good and Friendly Society, at their Office in Mansel-street, in Goodman's fields, between Haydon-Yard and the Vinegar-House. *n.p.* [*1710*], *s. sh. F°.* L.

1213 Proposals for a Weekly Dividend of 1000 l. on Marriage. By the Hand and Heart Society. *n. p.* [*1710*], *s. sh. F°.* L.

On the verso similar Proposals on Births of Infants. Dated: Dec. 15th 1710 At the Hand and Heart Society, by New-Street, between Fetter-Lane and Shoe-Lane.

1214 Proposals by the Honourable and Voluntary Societies, for Insurance on Marriage: at their Office at the Golden Harp near the May-Pole, and almost against Somerset-House in the Strand. *n.p.* [*1710*], *s. sh. F°.* L.

On the verso Proposals for Insurance on Births.

1215 The Third Proposals for Insurance on Marriage, at a Certain Charge, by a Weekly Dividend By the Honourable and Voluntary Society. *Lond.* [*1710*], *s. sh. F°.* L.

Dated: Hind's Court, Noble-street, near Goldsmiths-Hall, Dec. 21. A later edn. records the election of Trustees on 19 Jan. 1710/11 (L).

1216 Proposals for Insurance on Marriage, by the Liberal Society. At their Office at Hargrave's Coffee-House without Bishop's-Gate. *n.p.* [*1710*], *F°*. L.

Ms. note in L. copy: 'Remov'd to Paul's Coffee house In St. Paul's Church-yard.'

1217 Proposals by the Liberal Society, for Insuring 500 Pounds to be Paid on the Baptizing, or Births, of Infants. At their Office at St. Paul's Coffee-house in St. Paul's Church-yard. *n.p.* [*1710*], *s. sh. F°*. L.

1218 Proposals at a Certain Charge, for a Weekly Dividen for Three Societies upon Marriages, by the Original Loyal Society; at the Sign of the City of Chichester, over-against the Spur-Inn in the Borough of Southwark. *Lond.* [*1710*], *F°*. L.

Followed by Proposals for Encouragement of Young Beginners, Proposals for Insurance upon the Birth of Children, and further Proposals for Insurance on Marriages.

1219 Proposals for Insurance on the Birth of Children, by the Loyal Society: at their Office, at the Red-Lyon near Goodman's Yard in the Great Minories. *n.p.* [*1710*], *s. sh. F°*. L.

1220 Proposals for Insurance on Marriage, by the Loyal-Societies, at their Office at the Red-Lyon, near Goodman's Yard in the Great Minories. *n.p.* [*1710*], *s. sh. F°*. L.

1221 New Proposals for Insurance on Marriages, by the Loyal United-Society; or, Monthly Dividend of Eight Hundred Pounds. *n.p.* [*1710*], *F°*. L.

Followed by: New Proposals for Insurance on Marriages. By the Second Loyal United Society: or Monthly Dividend of Sixteen Hundred Pounds.

1222 Proposals for Insurance on Marriage, by the Noble and Honest Society, at their Office, at the Sign of the Vine, over against the Royal Bagnio in Newgate-Street. *n.p.* [*1710*], *s. sh. F°*. L.

On the verso: Proposals on Births.

1223 Proposals by the Noble and Honest Society for Insurance on the Service of Clerks, Apprentices, and Servants, at their Office at the Vine over against the Royal Bagnio in Newgate-street. *n.p.* [*1710*], *s. sh. F°*. L.

1224 Proposals for Insurance on Marriages and Births. By the Nuptial Society: At their Office in Jacob-Street, near Dock-Head, Southwark. December the 11th. 1710. *n.p.* [*1710*], *s. sh. F°*. L.

1225 The Insurance Office on Marriages, and Births and Baptisme of Infants. For Three Charitable Societies open'd the Fourth Instant, &c. At their Office at the Angel and Crown Tavern near the White-Chappel-Barrs, without Aldgate. *n.p.* [*1710?*], *s. sh. F°*. O.

1226 The 85th Claim. Thursday, August the 31th, 1710. At a Meeting of the Master and Trustees, of, and belonging to the First Society of Assurance, upon the Lives of Men, Women and Children; Establish'd at the Bell and Dragon at Lincolns-Inn Back-Gate. *n.p.* [*1710*], *s. sh. F°.* O.

1227 Proposals of the Office, erected and kept in Ironmonger-Lane, near Cheap-side, for raising Advantages for Servants that shall continue in one Place or Service, and that shall behave themselves well during such Service. *n.p.* [*1710*], *s. sh. F°.* L.

1228 Proposals for Insurance on Marriage, at the Office in Bangor Court, in Shoe-Lane, near St. Andrews Church; at Mr. Tills's, a Watch-maker: Particularly design'd for Advantage of such as are already Members of other Societies. *n.p.* [*1710*], *s. sh. F°.* L.

1229 November the 27th, 1710. From the Office in Swan-Yard. Proposals for Insurance on Marriage is kept at Mr. Gray's Glasier in Swan-Yard, over against Somerset-House in the Strand. The Beneficial and Amicable Society. *n.p.* [*1710*], *s. sh. F°.* LG.

On the verso are: Proposals by the Original and Beneficial Society for Insuranc [*sic*] on the Births of Children. At their Office in Swan-Yard....

1230 Proposals by the Original and Beneficial Society for Insuranc [*sic*] on the Births of Children. At their Office in Swan-Yard, over-against Somerset-House, in the Strand. *n.p.* [*1710*], *s. sh. F°.* L.

Dated: December the 21st, 1710.

1231 Proposals by the Perpetual Insurance-Office on Marriages. At the Sign of the City of Bristol at Iron-Gate in St. Catherines. *n.p.* [*1710*], *s. sh. F°.* L.

1232 From the Office in Russel-Street, Covent-Garden. Proposals for Insurance on Marriage. By the Profitable-Society. *n.p.* [*1710*], *s. sh. F°.* L.

1233 Proposals for Insurance on Mariage. And also, for a Weekly Dividend on Mariages and Baptizing of Children. By the Profitable-Society [in Russel-Street, Covent-Garden]. *n.p.* [*1710*], *s. sh. F°.* L.

1234 Proposals for Insurance on Marriage by the Profitable and most Equitable Society, at their Office, at the Tin-Shop, over-against Butcher-Hall-Lane, in Newgate-Street, *n.p.* [*1710*], *s. sh. F°.* L.

1235 Proposals for Insurance on Births by the Profitable and most Equitable Society, at their Office, at the Tin-Shop, over-against Butcher-Hall-Lane, in Newgate-Street. *n.p.* [*1710*], *s. sh. F°.* L.

1236 New Proposals by the Prolifical Society, for Promoting a Contribution, towards Raising a Monthly-Dividend of One Thousand Pounds, on the Birth of Infants, to be Born in Wedlock, and Living on the Second Day after their Birth. *n.p.* [*1710*], *s. sh. F°.* L.

Dated: Finch-Lane, November, the 30th 1710.

1237 Proposals of Insurance on Marriage, By the Safe Society, at their Office at the Old Plough over against the Red Cow the Back-side of St. Clements in the Strand. *n.p.* [*1710*], *s. sh. F°.* L.

On the verso: At a Certain Charge. Proposals for a Weekly Dividend of One Thousand Pounds on Marriages and Births of Children, by the Safe Society, dated: December the 14th. 1710.

1238 Proposals for Insurance on Marriage: By the Secure Society, at their Office, at the Hand and Glove, in Great Russel-street, Covent-Garden. *n.p.* [*1710*], *s. sh. F°*. L.

On the verso: Proposals for Two Societies, for Insurance on the Births of Children, by a Weekly Dividend. By the Secure Society.

1239 Proposals from the Several Offices of Insurance, on the Baptizing of Infants; and also, for Insurance on Marriage, herein after Nam'd. *n.p.* [*1710*], *s. sh. F°*. L.

Eight paragraphs on p. 1. Another edn. seven paragraphs on p. 1, last distributor named on p. 2 Mr. Blackmore (L); another issue, last distributor Mr. Schelton (L).

1240 At a Certain Charge. Proposals for Insurance on Marriage, by The Society, without Loss: At their Office in the Little-Piazza, Covent-Garden. *n.p.* [*1710*], *s. sh. F°*. L.

Paragraph III has 6 lines. Another edn. [1710] (L). Paragraph III has 4 lines.

1241 A Second Proposal for Insurance on Marriage, by The Society without Loss: At their Office, in the Little Piazza, Covent-Garden. *n.p.* [*1710*], *s. sh. F°*. L.

1242 Proposals for Insurance on the Birth's of Children by The Society without Loss: At their Office, in the Little Piazza, Covent-Garden. *n.p.* [*1710*], *s. sh. F°*. L.

Another edn., with comma after 'Children' in title (L).

1243 At a Certain Charge. Proposals for Insurance on Service, by The Society without Loss: At their Office in the Little-Piazza, Covent-Garden. *n.p.* [*1710*], *s. sh. F°*. L.

1244 Proposals for Insurance on Marriage; by the Substantial and Profitable Society. At their Office in St. Olave's-Street in the Borough of Southwark. An Upholder's, over-against the Church. *n.p.* [*1710*], *s. sh. F°*. L.

1245 Proposals for Insurance on Marriage, By the True British Societies; At their Office, at the Vine, the lower End of St. Michael Crooked-Lane, London. *n.p.* [*1710*], *s. sh. F°*. L.

1246 Proposals by the Undoubted and Profitable Society, at their Office at the Sign of the Ship a Stationers, near the May-Pole in the Strand. For Promoting a Contribution toward raising One Thousand Pounds, to be paid on the Birth of any Infant Born in Wedlock. *n.p.* [*1710*], *s. sh. F°*. L.

1247 Proposals for the Benefit of Unmarried Persons by an Amicable Contribution, in The Union Society. At the Black Lyon in Drury-Lane, Linnen-Draper. *n.p.* [*1710*], *s. sh. F°*. L.

Dated: November 15. 1710.

1248 Second Proposals for the Benefit of Unmarried Persons by an Amicable Contribution, in The Union Society. At the Black Lyon in Drury-Lane, Linnen-Draper, *n.p.* [*1710*], *s. sh. F°*. L.

Dated: November 20th. 1710.

1249 Proposals for the Encouragement of Young Beginners, by The Union Society. At the Black Lyon in Drury-Lane, a Linnen-Draper's. *n.p.* [*1710*], *s. sh. F°*. L.

Dated: November, 30th. 1710.

1250 Proposals by the Union Society, for Insurance on Births of Children by a Weekly Dividend. At the Black-Lyon in Drury-Lane Linnen-Draper, over against Shorts-Gardens. *n.p.* [*1710*], *s. sh. F°*. L.

1251 Proposals by the Union Society lately Erected at the Corner Of Ruport-street, near the Upper End of the Hay-Market, St. James's, upon Marriages without Loss. *n.p.* [*1710*], *s. sh. F°*. L.

On the verso: Proposals... upon the Baptism of Children without Loss.

1252 The New Union Society, upon Servants, for Providing an Income or Fortune for themselves, by an yearly Servitude without Loss. At their Office at the Corner of Rupert-Street, near the upper end of the Hay-Market, St. James's. *n.p.* [*1710*], *s. sh. F°*. L.

1253 New Proposals for Insurance on the Births of Children, by the United Amicable Society; Being the First and Only yet Extant of this Nature. *n.p.* [*1710*], *s. sh. F°*. L.

Their office is 'at the Pensilvania-Coffee-House in Birchin-Lane, near the Royal-Exchange in Cornhill, London'.

1254 Proposals by the United Company of Insurers on Marriages, Births, and Servitude, at their Office at the Green Lamp in Downing-Street, Westminster. *n.p.* [*1710*], *F°*. L.

1255 First Proposals for Insurance on Apprentices, by the United Generous Societys. At their Office at the London Coffee-House, in Thread-needle-Street, near the Royal-Exchange. *n.p.* [*1710*], *F°*. L.

On p. 3, 'Second Proposals for Insurance on Marriages by the United Generous Societys'.

1256 Proposals for Insurance on Marriage & Childrens Births. By the Unquestionable Society; At their Office, at the White Lyon, in King-street, near Guild-Hall. *n.p.* [*1710*], *s. sh. F°*. L.

1257 At a Certain Charge: or, Proposals for a Weekly Dividend, of One Thousand Pounds on Marriage: By the Unquestionable Society: At their Office, at the White Lyon, in King-street, near Guild-Hall. December the 21st. 1710. *n.p.* [*1710*], *s. sh. F°*. L.

1258 RICHARDS, THOMAS. The Young Accomptant's Tutor: or, Brief Rules for the most exact keeping of Shop-Books....By the Author of the Gentleman's Auditor. *Lond. 1710*, 4°. LICA.

The dedication signed: Tho. Richards.

TRANSPORT

1259 The Case of the Petitioner Thomas Rogers, Gent. Humbly offer'd in relation to an Inquisition taken at Rochester, pursuant to the Act of Parliament for appointing Commissioners to Treat and Agree for such

Lands as shall be judged proper to be purchased, for the better fortifying Portsmouth, Chatham and Harwich, and in relation to the Bill now depending, for vesting the said Lands in the Crown at the Prices, the Jury upon the Inquisition, valued them at. *n.p.* [*1710*], *s. sh. F*o. L.

1260 The Case of the Cheesmongers, Freemen of London, in relation to the Bill for making a Dock at Leverpool. Humbly represented to the Honourable the Commons of Great Britain, in Parliament Assembled. *n.p.* [*1710*], *s. sh. F*o. O.

1261 Answers to the Objections against the Bill for making a Dock or Bason at Leverpoole. *n.p.* [*1710?*], *s. sh. F*o. O.

1262 [The] Case of the Gentlemen Freeholders, and other Owners of Lands and Tenements on, or adjacent to, the River Kennet, in the County of Berks, relating to the Bill now depending for making the said River Navigable. *n.p.* [*1710*], *s. sh. F*o. O.

1263 Hydrographia Hibernica: or, A View of the Considerable Rivers of Ireland. Being an Abstract of a Plain and Easie Method of making them Navigable, with Ease and Advantage to the Publick, and without any Hazard of Injuring Private Persons in their Mills, Wyers, Fisheries or other Improvements. In a Letter from a Gentleman in the Country to a Member of the House of Commons in Dublin. June 30th, 1710. *n.p.* [*1710*], *4*o. L.

1264 A List of the Stage-Coaches and Carriers, and the Place and Times they come in and go out. *Lond.* *1710*, *8*o. L.

1265 Laverick, George. Proposals Humbly Offer'd; To the Knights; Citizens and Burgesses in Parliament Assembled, (by George Laverick Hackney-Coachman,) for preventing the Stops in the Streets. *n.p.* [*1710?*], *s. sh. F*o. LG.

1266 Laverick, George. Proposals humbly Offer'd to the Consideration of the Honourable House of Commons, To Prevent the Stop of Coaches in the Street. *n.p.* [*1710?*], *s. sh. F*o. LG.

SOCIAL CONDITIONS

1267 [Carter, Samuel]. Legal Provisions for the Poor: or, a Treatise of the Common and Statute Laws concerning the Poor, either as to Relief, Settlement, or Punishment. Being a Methodical Guide for Justices of Peace, Churchwardens, and Overseers....By S.C. of the Inner Temple, Esq; *Lond.* *1710*, *12*o. L.

5th edn. 1725 (L). For authorship see H & L quoting Lincoln's Inn Library Catalogue.

1268 The Case between the Intended Charitable Fund, to be establish'd in London...and, The Charitable Corporation.... *n.p.* [*1710*], *F*o. LU.

1269 To the Honourable the Commons of Great-Britain in Parliament Assembled. The Case of the Poor Seamen, and those that have Clothed them, and Supported their Distressed Families. *n.p.* [*c. 1710?*], *s. sh. F°*. LLI.

1270 A Short State of the Case of Joseph Billers, Citizen of London. Shewing the Occasion of his being concern'd in the Prosecution of Burglars, and other Criminals; his Progress therein; and the many Obstructions he hath met with in the Course of it. *n.p.* [*1710?*], *F°*. LLI.

1271 A True Description of the Mint. Giving an Account of its first becoming a Place of Refuge for Debtors; the Extent of its Antient and Modern Limits. The Manners, Ways, and Customs of the Inhabitants: with their Character, Nature and Temper.... *Lond. 1710, 8°*. LU.

1272 The State of the Palatines for Fifty Years past to this Present Time. Containing, I. An Account of the Principality of the Palatinate.... II. The Case of the Palatines, Publish'd by themselves, and Humbly Offered to the Tradesmen of England. With a List of them, and the Trades which the Men are brought up to. III. The Humble Petition of the Justices of Middlesex to Her Majesty on their Behalf, with Her Majesties Order thereupon....IV. A Letter about Settling and Employing them in other Countries. V. A Proclamation of the States-General for Naturalizing all Strangers....VI. Lastly, Their present Encamping at Camberwell and Black-heath.... *Lond. 1710, 8°*. L.

1273 Reasons Humbly Offer'd for preventing great Abuses daily put upon Her Majesty's good Subjects, by reason of the great Uncertainties most Persons are at in hiring Menial Servants.... *n.p.* [*c. 1710?*], *s. sh. F°*. MC.

Endorsed: Reasons Humbly Offer'd for the Better Regulating of Menial Servants.

1274 A Full Account of the Rise, Progress, & Advantages of Dr. Assheton's Proposal (as now Improv'd and Manag'd by the Worshipful Company of Mercers, London for the Benefit of Widows of Clergymen, and Others; by Settling Jointures and Annuities at the Rate of Thirty per Cent.... *Lond. 1710, 12°*. L.

Other edns. 1710, 1711, 1713, 1724 (all L), 1730, 1741 (both O). First published in 1699.

1275 To the Queen's Most Excellent Majesty, The Humble Representation of, The Governours of the Bounty of Queen Anne, for the Augmentation of the Maintenance of the Poor Clergy, &c. *n. p.* [*1710*], *F°*. OC.

Dated: January 10, 17$\frac{09}{10}$.

1276 THORISBY, THO. and WILMER, RICH. An Humble Proposal for advancing the Credit of Seamens Wages, and for preventing their Fraudulent Selling the same; most Humbly Offered to the Consideration of the Honourable the Commons of Great Britain, in Parliament Assembled. *n.p.* [*c. 1710?*], *s. sh. F°*. LU.

1711

GENERAL

1277 The Useful Intelligencer. For Promoting of Trade and Commerce. no. 39. 10 July 1711. *Lond. 1711, F°.* L.

1278 [Defoe, Daniel]. Armageddon: or, the Necessity of carrying on the War, if such a Peace cannot be obtained as may render Europe safe, and Trade secure. *Lond.* [*1711*], *8°.* LU.

For authorship see *C.B.E.L.* II, 501.

1279 [Defoe, Daniel]. Reasons why this Nation ought to put a Speedy End to this Expensive War; with a Brief Essay, at the probable Conditions on which the Peace now Negotiating, may be Founded. Also an Enquiry into the Obligations Britain lies under to the Allies.... [*Lond.*] *1711*, *8°.* L.

2nd edn. Lond. 1711; 3rd edn. Lond. 1711 (both L); another edn. Edin. 1711 (E). For authorship see *C.B.E.L.* II, 501.

1280 A Letter from a Scots Gentlemen residing in London, to his Friend in Edenborough. *n.p. 1711*, *8°.* U.

On the effects of the Union on Scotland.

AGRICULTURE

1281 Directions for the Sowing and Preparing of Flax. Also, Directions for Sowing and Preparing of Hemp. *Dublin, 1711*, *8°.* DNL.

Printed by order of the Trustees appointed pursuant to the Act of 1710 for the Improvement of the Linnen Manufacture.

1282 An Act for Establishing an Agreement made between the Right Honourable Robert late Earl of Lindsey and the Commissioners of Sewers, and for Confirming the Decrees made by the Commissioners of Sewers concerning the Draining of Lindsey Level in the County of Lincoln. *n.p.* [*1711*], *F°.* L.

A bill.

1283 [Stringer, Moses]. Mineralia Adjuvanda, or a Case shewing who, and what the most Ancient and Honourable Societies and Corporations of the City of London, (of and for the Mines, the Mineral, and Battery Works) are, with their Institution and Constitution.... *n.p.* [*1711?*], *4°.* O.

Distinguishing them from 'the upstart Company of Mine Adventurers'. Reprinted in Stringer's *Mineralia Explicata*, 1713.

1284 The Case of the United Society, for the Improvement of Mineral Works, Creditors of the Governour and Company of the Mine-Adventurers of England, and Proprietors of Principal Money, Annuities and Shares in the said Company. *n.p.* [*1711*], *s. sh. F°.* LU.

1285 MACKWORTH, Sir HUMPHREY. The Second Part of the Book of Vouchers, to prove the Case and Defence of the Deputy Governour and Directors of the Company of Mine-Adventurers. *Lond.* *1711*, *F°*. L.

Pt. 1 was published in 1710.

1286 A Bill for the Relief of the Creditors and Proprietors of the Company of the Mine Adventurers, by Establishing a Method for Settling the Differences between the Company and their Creditors, and for Uniting them, in order to an effectual Working of the Mines of the said Company. *n.p.* [*1711*], *F°*. L.

A different bill from that introduced in 1710. Another edn. with 'setling' in title (L).

1287 The Case of the Company of Mine-Adventurers, relating to Mrs. Lucas, who has exhibited a Petition for a saving Clause in the Bill depending in Parliament. *n.p.* [*1711*], *s. sh. F°*. L.

1288 The Case of the Creditors and Proprietors of the Company of Mine Adventurers. Containing Observations on the Bill entiutled [*sic*] A Bill for Relief of the Creditors and Proprietors of the Company of Mine Adventurers.... *n.p.* [*1711*], *F°*. LU.

Endorsed: Observations on the Bill relating to the Mine-Adventurers. Different from no. 1291.

1289 The Case of the Poor Children belonging to the Charity-School of Saint Sepulchres, London, humbly sheweth.... *n.p.* [*1711*], *s. sh. F°*. L.

Praying for special consideration in the bill relating to the Company of Mine Adventurers in which they had invested £150. Another edn., entitled: The Case of the Poor Children belonging to the Charity School of Saint Sepulchres, London, n.p. [1711], s. sh. F° (O).

1290 A Certificate under the Hand of Gregory King...and of Thomas Horne ...late Accountant to the Governor and Company of the Mine Adventurers of England...relating to the Accounts of the said Company, and to the Proceedings of the Deputy-Governor, extracted out of the Books of the said Company. *n.p.* [*1711*], *s. sh. F°*. LU.

1291 Observations on the Bill relating to the Mine-Adventurers. *n.p.* [*1711*], *F°*. L.

1292 Remarks on a Paper, Intitled, Observations on the Bill relating to the Mine-Adventurers. *n.p.* [*1711*], *F°*. L.

1293 Reasons against Passing the Bill Relating to the Mine-Adventurers. *n.p.* [*1711*], *s. sh. F°*. LU.

1294 Reasons for the Passing of the Mine Adventurers Bill, by Authority of Parliament. *n.p.* [*1711*], *s. sh. F°*. LU.

1295 Reasons humbly offered in Relation to Passing the Mine Adventurers Bill in Parliament, with proper Clauses added for saving the two Antient Corporations of the City of London, of, and for the Mines Royal, and the Mineral, and the Battery Works, and their Mineral

Master General's respective Interests, with their Tenant's Leeses, &c. *n.p.* [*1711?*], *s. sh. F°.* LG.

Endorsed: Reasons for having the saving Clause for her Majesty in the Mine Adventurers Bill, to be amended, by saving the Rights and Properties, and Charities of the Corporations of the City of London, of, and for the Mines, Minerals, and Battery Works, and their Mineral Master General, &c.

1296 In Pursuance of an Act of Parliament pass'd the Last Sessions of Parliament: Entituled, An Act for the Relief of the Creditors and Proprietors of the Company of Mine-Adventurers.... [*Lond. 1711*], *s. sh. F°.* L.

A receipt form for the surrender of the old stock of the Company.

1297 In Pursuance of an Act of Parliament pass'd the last Session of Parliament: Entituled, An Act for the Relief of the Creditors and Proprietors of the Company of Mine-Adventurers.... *n.p.* [*1711*], *s. sh. F°.* L.

A form for the registration of claims against the Company.

1298 An Alphabetical List of such Persons who have made their Claims of Sums respectively due to them for the Stock, Bonds, &c. in and upon the Company of the Mine-Adventurers of England, in pursuance of a late Act of Parliament, for relief of the Creditors and Proprietors of the said Company, &c. Sept. 17, 1711. *n.p.* [*1711*], *F°.* L.

1299 A Bill for the better Preservation and Improvement of the Fishery within the River of Thames, and for Regulating and Governing the Company of Fisherman of the said River. *n.p.* [*1711*], *F°.* L.

1300 The Case of the Fishery of the River of Thames. *n. p.* [*1711?*], *s. sh. F°.* L.

Presented by the Company of Fisherman.

1301 Reasons humbly offered, for the Bill for Preservation of the Fishery of the River Thames, and for Regulating the Company of Fishermen. *n.p.* [*1711?*], *s. sh. F°.* L.

1302 Reasons Humbly Offered to the Consideration of the Right Honourable the Lords Spiritual and Temporal of Great Britain, in Parliament Assembled, against the Clause in a Bill, Entituled, A Bill for the better Preservation and Improvement of the Fishery within the River of Thames, &c. which prohibits the Selling of Fish within the said Market, or 150 Yards of Billingsgate-Dock. *n.p.* [*1711*], *s. sh. F°.* L.

1303 The Case of Several Merchants and Others, concerned in the Fishery of North-Britain. *n.p. 1711*, *s. sh. F°.* L.

1304 Copy of the Agreement concerning the Herring Trade made betwixt Her Britanick Majesty and the City of Hamburg. *n.p.* [*1711?*], *s. sh. F°.* E.

MANUFACTURES

1305 Reasons for a New Act of Parliament relating to Building. *n.p.* [*1711*], *F°.* L.

1306 Reasons Humbly offered to the Honourable House of Commons, by the

Master, Wardens, and Company of Wax-Chandlers, London, for the suppressing of all Mould-Candles. *n.p.* [*1711*], *s. sh. F°.* LU.

Endorsed: The Wax-Chandlers Reasons Against Mould-Candles.

1307 The Case of the Copper and Brass Makers, and the Manufacturers of Brass in Great-Britain. *n.p.* [*1711*], *s. sh. F°.* O.

1308 Reasons against Altering the Standard of Wrought Plate. Humbly offered to the Consideration of the Most Honourable the House of Peers. *n.p.* [*1711?*], *s. sh. F°.* L.

1309 The Hard Case of Sir Polycarpus Wharton Baronet. *n.p.* [*1711*]. *s. sh. F°.* L.

On his losses in his gunpowder factory at Chilworth.

1310 The Case of the Company of Gun-Makers of the City of London. *n.p.* [*1711*], *s. sh. F°.* LU.

Endorsed: The Gun-makers Case.

1311 The Case of the Honest Exporters of Great Britain's Manufactured Iron and Steel to Her Majesty's Plantations and Collonies. *n.p.* [*1711?*], *s. sh. F°.* LLI.

For a stop to the drawback on foreign unwrought iron and steel. Another edn., with an additional paragraph, entitled: The Case of Great Britain's Manufacturers of Iron and Steel, for Her Majesty's Plantations and Colonies, &c. [1711 ?], s. sh. F° (O).

1312 The Case of the Manufacturers of Iron and Steel for Exportation. *n.p.* [*1711*], *s. sh. F°.* LU.

1313 The Case of the Pewterers of England, as to the Exportation of Pewter. *n.p.* [*1711?*], *s. sh. F°.* L.

Endorsed: The Pewterers Case. For exportation duty free.

1314 The Case of Salt Exported for Ireland. Humbly offered to the Consideration of the Honourable House of Commons. *n.p.* [*1711?*], *s. sh. F°.* LU.

The lowering of the Irish duty on rock salt will ruin the white salt manufacture.

1315 The Case of Great Numbers of Weavers, Freemen, and Lawful Workmen, now Working to the Royal Lutestring Company. *n.p.* [*1711?*], *s. sh. F°.* MC.

Endorsed: The Case of the Weavers Now Working to the Royal Lutestring Company.

1316 SUTHERLAND, WILLIAM. The Ship-builders Assistant: or, some Essays towards compleating the art of Marine Architecture.... *Lond. 1711*, *4°.* L.

1317 To the Honourable the Commons in Parliament Assembled. Reasons Humbly Offer'd by the Card-Makers and Wier-Drawers, shewing the Necessity of an Act for Prohibiting the Importation of White Iron-Wire, and the putting Old Wire into New Leather; and for preventing the sale of Old Wool-Cards. *n.p.* [*1711*], *s. sh. F°.* MC.

1318 To the Commons of Great Britain, in Parliament Assembled. Reasons Humbly Offer'd by the Card-Makers, and Wier-Drawers of Froome-Selwood in the County of Somerset, and Parts adjacent, shewing the Necessity of an Act for preventing the Sale of Old Wooll-Cards, and for supplying the Defects of the Act made in the 13th and 14th of Car. II. for Prohibiting the Importation of White Iron Wire, and the putting Old Wire into New Leather. *n.p.* [*1711*], *F°*. LU.

1319 To the Commons of Great Britain in Parliament Assembled. The Clothiers Reasons against Passing the Bill for Prohibiting the Importation of Foreign Wooll Cards, and to prevent the Abuses in making the same with Old Wire. *n.p.* [*1711*], *s. sh. F°*. LU.

Endorsed: The Clothiers Reasons against Passing the Bill for Prohibiting the Importation of Foreign Wool-Cards....

1320 Reasons for Prohibiting the Importation of White Iron-Wire, and against putting Old Wire into New Leather. *n.p.* [*1711*], *s. sh. F°*. LU.

Endorsed: The White-Wire Case.

1321 A Dialogue between Dick Brazenface the Card-maker, and Tim. Meanwell the Clothier; being the Dispute between the Card-maker and the Clothier fairly Stated, in order to set the Merits of that Cause in a true Light; which is humbly offer'd to the Consideration of the Commons of Great Britain in Parliament Assembled. *n.p.* [*1711*], *4°*. LU.

1322 Remarks made by the Wier-Drawers, Card-Makers, and English Wool-Clothiers; on a pretended Dialogue, set forth by the Spanish Wool-Clothiers. Humbly offered to the Consideration, of the Honourable House of Commons. *n.p.* [*1711*], *F°*. LU.

1323 The Reply of the Card-Makers and English Wooll-Clothiers, to the Objections of the Spanish Wooll-Clothiers against the Bill in the House to Prohibit the Importation of Foreign Wooll-Cards, and to Prevent the Abuses in Making the same with Old Card-Wier. *n.p.* [*1711*], *s. sh. F°*. LU.

1324 To the Commons of Great Britain in Parliament Assembled, The Clothiers Answer to the Card-makers Reply, in relation to the Bill in this Honourable House, to Prohibit the Importation of Foreign Wooll-Cards. &c. And also to shew other Reasons against the Passing of the said Bill, not mentioned in the Reasons before Printed, and delivered at the Door of this Honourable House. *n.p.* [*1711*], *s. sh. F°*. L.

Endorsed: The Clothiers Answer to the Card-makers Reply.

1325 A Letter from a Gentleman at Edinburgh to his Friend at London, *n.p.* [*1711*], *F°*. E.

On the rights of the Queen's Printer.

1326 SCARLET, JOHN. A Most Humble and most Submissive Memorial to the Right Honourable My Lord Provost, to the Honourable Baillies, and other Magistrates of the Good Town of Edinburgh; in the Name, and on the Behalf, of the Sail-Cloth Manufactory, Established at Leith. *n.p.* [*1711*], *F°*.

Reissued, with a covering letter, 1712 (LU), the only edition seen.

COMMERCE

1327 An Account of the Obligations the States of Holland have to Great-Britain, and the Return they have made both in Europe and the Indies. With Reflections upon the Peace. *Lond. 1711*, *8°*. L.

Another edn. Lond. [Dublin], 1712 (DA). Attributed to Robert Ferguson in *D.N.B.*, but James Ferguson in his *Robert Ferguson the Plotter* does not accept the attribution.

1328 A Caveat to the Treaters; or, the Modern Schemes of Partition examin'd, with relation to the Safety of Europe in general, and of Great-Britain and Ireland in particular. Including an Answer to several late Pamphlets on that Subject; with a more particular account of the Conferences at Gertruydenberg than has yet been publish'd. *Lond. 1711*, *8°*. LU.

1329 A Letter from an Exchange Broker to a Country Gentleman, concerning Peace and South-Sea Stock. *Lond. 1711*, *8°*. L.

1330 A Letter to a Member of the October-Club: shewing, that to yield Spain to the Duke of Anjou by a Peace, wou'd be the Ruin of Great Britain. *Lond. 1711*, *8°*. L.

2nd edn. with additions, 1711 (LU).

1331 [DEFOE, DANIEL]. Worcestershire-Queries about Peace. By Tom Flock-maker, Clothier of Worcester. *Lond. 1711*, *8°*. O.

Attribution by Professor J. R. Moore.

1332 Reasons formerly published for the Punctual Limiting of Bartholomew Fair to those Three Days to which it is determined by the Royal Grant of it to the City of London. Now Reprinted with Additions, to prevent a Design set on Foot to procure an Establishment of the said Fair for Fourteen Days.... *Lond. 1711*, *8°*. O.

First published in 1708.

1333 Reasons humbly offer'd for continuing the Clause against mixing at the Staiths the Coals of different Collieries, in the Act, entitl'd An Act for dissolving the present, and preventing the future Combination of Coal-Owners, &c. *n.p.* [*1711*], *s. sh. F°*. LU.

1334 Supplement to Mercer's Proposals about Coals. [*Dublin, c. 1711?*], *s. sh. F°*. DM.

On the prices he proposes to charge.

1335 To the Right Honourable the Knights, Citizens and Burgesses in Parliament Assembled. A further and more particular Account of several

Publick Grievances committed by John Mercer, and those concern'd under him in the Coal-Trade, &c. in the City of Dublin.... *Dublin*, *1711*, *s. sh. F°*. D.

Endorsed: The 2d Case: or, A Charge of Grievances against John Mercer...

1336 To the Right Honourable the Knights, Citizens and Burgesses in Parliament Assembled. The Humble Petition of John Whalley. *n.p.* [*1711*], *s. sh. F°*. D.

He is being prosecuted by John Mercer for printing the Case accusing him of being a monopolist in coal.

1337 Middlesex. Wednesday, January 17. 1710 [O.S.].... Order for the Assize of Bread. [*Lond.*], *1710*. *s. sh. F°*. MC.

1338 The Case of the Master, Wardens and Commonalty of the Company of Bakers in and about the City of London, in Relation to the Penalties, and several Clauses in the late Act of Parliament, for Regulating the Price and Assize of Bread: Most Humbly Offered to the Consideration of the Honourable House of Commons. *n.p.* [*1711*], *s. sh. F°*. O.

1339 Some Reasons Humbly Offered to the Honourable House of Commons, for some Alterations Humbly Desired to be made in the Act of Parliament, lately made, for Regulating the Price and Assize of Bread. *n.p.* [*1711*], *s. sh. F°*. O.

Endorsed: Reasons Humbly Offered for some Alterations in the Act, for Regulating the Price and Assize of Bread.

1340 The Case of the Isle of Man, with respect to the Trade thereof, &c. *n.p.* [*1711?*], *s. sh. F°*. LU.

1341 Some Observations, upon the French Kings Edict. For Opening a Trade with England. *n.p.* [*1711*], *s. sh. F°*. L.

1342 Reasons for Repealing the Prohibition of French-Wines. *n.p.* [*1711*], *s. sh. F°*. L.

1343 Reasons Humbly Offer'd against opening a Trade with France for Wines. *n.p.* [*1711?*], *s. sh. F°*. L.

1344 Objections against the Importation of French Wine, Answer'd. *n.p.* [*1709?*], *F°*. O.

1345 By the Queen, A Proclamation, Requiring Quarentine to be Performed by Ships coming from the Baltick Sea, and other Places, &c. *Lond.* *1711*, *F°*. L.

Dated: 6 September [1711]. Cr. 4500. Another edn. 1711 (C (Cr)). Cr. 4501; another edn. 1711 (LPRO). Cr. 4502.

1346 By the Lord Lieutenant of Ireland and Council, a Proclamation. Requiring Quarentine to be Performed by Ships coming from the Baltick-Sea, and other Places Infected. *Dublin*, *1711*, *F°*. DPRO.

Dated: 6 October 1711.

1347 By the Lord Lieutenant and Council of Ireland, a Proclamation. Requiring Quarantain to be Performed by Ships coming from any Port or Place, within the Sound or Baltick-Sea. *Dublin, 1711*, *F°*. DPRO.

Dated: 17 August 1711.

1348 The Case of John Praed, Esq; Most humbly Presented to the High Court of Parliament. *n.p.* [*1711?*], *s. sh. F°*. LU.

Praed had been factor at Zante. Endorsed: The Case of John Praed, Esq; Parallel to the Case of the Creditors of Pitkin, and Brerewood lately laid before this Honourable House....

1349 An Address relating to the African Company, to be presented to Her Majesty.... *n.p.* [*1711*], *s. sh. F°*. L.

Endorsed: An Address to Her Majesty, from the Governour, Council and Assembly, of the Island of Jamaica against an Exclusive Trade to Africa.

1350 The African Trade in no Danger of being Lost, otherwise than by the Designs of the Company. *n.p.* [*1711*], *s. sh. F°*. LU.

A list of ships sent to Africa by the separate traders between Michaelmas 1709 and Michaelmas 1710, with 'the Number of Pieces of Woollen Goods loaded therein, and the Number of Negroes intended to be loaded in each Vessel'.

1351 The Argument touching Security necessary to be given for carrying on the African Trade, demonstrated to be Groundless and Ridiculous. With Reasons against Confining any Part of the Trade to a Company Exclusive. *n.p.* [*1711?*], *s. sh. F°*. LU.

1352 The Case of the Royal African-Company and their Creditors, as to the Prosecution by the Queen for Albert's Debt. *n.p.* [*1711?*], *s. sh. F°*. LLI.

1353 [DEFOE, DANIEL]. An Essay upon the Trade to Africa, in order to set the Merits of that Cause in a true Light and bring the Disputes between the African Company and the Separate Traders into a narrower Compass. *n.p. 1711*, *8°*. LU.

For authorship see *C.B.E.L.* II, 501.

1354 Extract of a Letter Received the 16th of this Instant March $17\frac{10}{11}$, by the Royal African-Company, from Sir Dalby Thomas their Chief Agent on the Coast of Africa, dated the 3d of August last. *n.p.* [*1711*], *s. sh. F°*. LU.

1355 A Letter from a Merchant in Bristol, touching the Trade to Africa, as it relates to the Out-ports of Great Britain. *n.p.* [*1711?*], *s. sh. F°*. LU.

1356 A Letter to a Member of Parliament touching the African Trade. *n.p.* [*1711?*], *s. sh. F°*. LU.

1357 A plain Account of the Loss, this Nation has sustain'd, by laying open the Trade to Africa. *n.p.* [*1711*], *s. sh. F°*. LU.

Title taken from endorsement. The text begins: In Answer to the Separate Traders' Feigned Great Trade for Eighty Thousand Negroes in Thirteen Years.

1358 A Proposal agreed unto for the Effectual Support, and Carrying on the Trade to Africa. *n.p.* [*1711?*], *s. sh. F°*. L.

1359 Reasons against Establishing an African Company at London, Exclusive to the Plantations, and all the Out-Ports, and other Subjects of Great-Britain. *n.p.* [*1711*], *s. sh. F°*. LU.

1360 An Answer to the Reasons against an African Company Humbly Submitted to the Consideration of the Patriots of Great-Britain, in this Present Parliament Assembled. *Lond. 1711, 8°*. LU.

1361 Reasons for Settlement of the Trade to Africa, in a Joynt-Stock, with the Arguments of the Separate-Traders against it, Answer'd. *n.p.* [*1711?*], *s. sh. F°*. LU.

Endorsed: An Answer to the Reasons against Establishing an African-Company.

1362 Reasons Humbly Offered, for Confirming the Royal-African-Company's Charter by Parliament, to such Persons who are willing to become Adventurers in that Trade. *n.p.* [*1711?*], *s. sh. F°*. MP.

1363 Reflections on the Separate Traders Proceedings, in Opposition to the Settlement of the African Trade. *n. p.* [*1711*], *s. sh. F°*. L.

1364 The Scheme humbly proposed to the Honourable House of Commons, for the Effectual Support, and Carrying on the Trade to Africa. *n.p.* [*1711?*], *s. sh. F°*. O.

The cropped endorsed title is: A Further [ ] about [ ] to Afr[ ].

1365 A short and true Account of the Importance and Necessity, of settling the African Trade this Present Session of Parliament; Together with a Comparative View of the two Schemes, Proposed to the Honourable House of Commons, viz. That for a General Joynt-Stock; and that for an open Trade. *n.p.* [*1711*], *F°*. LU.

1366 Short Remarks relating to the African Trade. *n.p. 1711, s. sh. F°*. LU.

Dated: May 22d. 1711.

1367 Short Remarks relating to the African Trade. An Answer to a Paper called, Short Remarks on the African Trade. *n.p.* [*1711*], *s. sh. F°*. LU.

The two papers are printed in parallel columns. Endorsed: An Answer to a Paper called Short Remarks on the African Trade.

1368 Some Queries relating to the present Dispute about the Trade to Africa. *n.p.* [*1711?*], *s. sh. F°*. LU.

1369 Some Short and Necessary Observations, Proper to be Considered, in the Settlement of the African Trade. *n.p.* [*1711*], *s. sh. F°*. LU.

1370 A Specimen of the Falsehoods, Absurdities and Contradictions contained in some late Papers, published by the Separate Traders to Africa. *n.p. 1711, s. sh. F°*. LU.

1371 To the Queen's Most Excellent Majesty, The humble Petition of several Planters, and other the Inhabitants of your Majesty's Island of Barbadoes. *n.p.* [*1711?*], *s. sh. F°*. L.

Endorsed: The Barbadoes Petition, relating to the African Trade. Dated: Barbadoes, August 1710. Signed by 86 names.

1372 A True Account of Eight Years Exports of the Royal African Company, and Eight Years Exports of the Separate Traders. *n.p.* [*1711*], *s. sh. F°.* L.

1373 Two Clauses in the Act of Parliament, for Settling the Trade to the East-Indies, &c. Exclusive of all others. *n.p.* [*1711*], *s. sh. F°.* LU.

Title taken from endorsement. No doubt published to influence opinion on the status of the Royal African Company.

1374 Considerations on the Trade to Newfoundland. *n.p.* [*1711*], *F°.* L.

Reprinted in *A Collection of Voyages and Travels*, 1745. The authorship is disputed. Archibald Cumings claims it in a ms. note on the LPRO copy. In the copy in B.M. Add. MS. 13972, f.2, Peter Thompson notes that it was written by his father Thomas Thompson.

1375 Reasons, humbly offer'd for Incouraging the Exportation of Tobacco, Sugar, Fish, other Plantation-Goods or Manufactures of Great Britain not contraband; and Importation of French Wine. *n.p.* [*1711?*], *s. sh. F°.* O.

1376 Reasons for Encouraging the Importation of Timber, Plank, Boards, and other Wood, from Her Majesty's Plantations, by taking off the Custom, or allowing a Bounty-Money thereon. *n.p.* [*1711?*], *s. sh. F°.* LLI.

1377 LOCKYER, CHARLES. An Account of the Trade in India: containing Rules for good Government in Trade, Price Courants, and Tables: With Descriptions of Fort St. George, Acheen, Malacca, Condore, Canton, Anjengo, Muskat, Gombroon, Surat, Goa, Garwar, Telichery, Panola, Calicut, the Cape of Good-Hope, and St. Helena. Their Inhabitants, Customs, Religion, Government, Animals, Fruits, &c. To which is added, An Account of the Management of the Dutch in their Affairs in India. *Lond. 1711, 8°.* LU.

1378 The Case of John Ward of Hackney, Merchant. *n.p.* [*1711?*], *s. sh. F°.* LLI.

Endorsed: The Case of John Ward against the East-India Company. Refers to the seizure of the Annandale.

1379 The Case of the Late Indian and African Company of Scotland, with other Part-Owners of the Ships Speedwell and Annandale Trading to India. *n.p.* [*1711*], *s. sh. F°.* LU.

Another edn. with the reading 'with other part Owners' (O).

1380 Abstract of the Charter of the Governour and Company of Merchants of Great Britain, Trading to the South-Seas, and other Parts of America, and for Encouraging the Fishery. *n.p. 1711, F°.* LU.

Another edn. 1718 (L).

1381 The Advantages of the South-Sea Trade; In a Congratulatory Letter to the Earl of Oxford, Lord High Treasurer of Great Britain. *Lond. 1711, F°.* MC.

1382 The considerable Advantages of a South-Sea Trade to our English Nation. Humbly offer'd, with other particulars, to the Consideration of this present Parliament, partly from the Information of divers

French Officers, lately taken by one of Her Majesty's Ships, and who had Sailed and Traded in those Seas. *Lond.* [*1711?*], *8°*. LU.

1383 [DEFOE, DANIEL]. An Essay on the South-Sea Trade. With an Enquiry into the Grounds and Reasons of the present Dislike and Complaint against the Settlement of a South-Sea Company. By the Author of the Review. *Lond. 1712* [*1711*]. *8°*. LU.

2nd edn. corrected, 1712 (LU). For authorship see *C.B.E.L.* II, 501.

1384 A Letter to a Member of Parliament, on the Settling a Trade to the South-Sea of America. *Lond.* [*1711*], *8°*. LU.

Reprinted in *Somers Tracts*, XIII (1815), 117. Attributed to Defoe in *C.B.E.L.* II, 501.

1385 Some Queries, which being Nicely Answered may tend very much to the Encouragement of the South-Sea Company, and to forwarding that Laudable Undertaking to our greater Satisfaction. *n.p.* [*1711*], *s. sh. F°*. LU.

1386 [DEFOE, DANIEL]. A True Account of the Design, and Advantages of the South-Sea Trade: with Answers to all the Objections rais'd against it. A List of the Commodities proper for that Trade: and the Progress of the Subscription towards the South-Sea Company. *Lond. 1711*, *8°*. LU.

For authorship see *C.B.E.L.* II, 501.

1387 [DEFOE, DANIEL]. The True State of the Case between the Government and the Creditors of the Navy, &c. as it relates to the South-Sea-Trade. And the Justice of the Transactions on either Side Impartially enquired into. *Lond. 1711*, *8°*. LU.

For authorship see *C.B.E.L.* II, 501.

1388 A View of the Coasts, Countries and Islands within the Limits of the South-Sea-Company. Containing an Account of the Discoveries, Settlements, Progress and Present State....To which is added, An Account of Former Projects in England for a Settlement, and the Accomplishment of the Last in the Establishing the New Company.... Illustrated with a General Map.... By Herman Moll. *Lond. 1711*, *8°*. L.

2nd edn., with large additions, besides the proposal of an eminent merchant, towards uniting the African and South-Sea trade, n.d. [1711 ?] (L).

1389 *Begin.* Whereas the Queen has been pleased to direct, that a Monthly Correspondence be Established between this Kingdom, and Her Majesties Dominions on the Continent of America, by Packet-Boats, to pass to, and from Bristol and New-York.... [*Lond. 1711?*], *s. sh. 4°*. L.

Rates of letters and packets in the service to be run by William Warren.

1390 BOURK, WILLIAM. Proposals, for the better Encouragement of Her Majesty's Navy. *n.p.* [*c. 1711?*], *s. sh. F°*. C.

1391 The Case of the Pursers of Her Majesties Navy. *n.p.* [*1711?*], *F°*. L.

1392 Reasons for continuing the Advantages given to the Officers and Seamen in Her Majesties Ships of War, by the Convoy and Cruisers Act, and against Reestablishing a Prize-Office. *n.p.* [*1711?*], *s. sh. F*°. O.

1393 Sailing instructions for the better keeping Company with Her Majesties Ship [Ruby] Captain [Peter Chamberlain] Commander. [Dated aboard the Ruby this 2d of Oct. 1711. To Mr. Wm. Young Command. of ye Wm. & James.] [*1711?*], *s. sh. F*°. C (Cr).

Words in brackets in ms.

FINANCE

1394 HATTON, EDWARD. An Index to Interest: containing, I. The largest Tables of Simple Interest that have yet been made Publick....II. A Table of Discount....III. Two Tables shewing, by Inspection, the present Worth of Annuities, and the Purchase thereof. IV. An easie Table for the valuation of any number of Years Lapsed in a Church or College-Lease of Land, shewing the Fines payable at one View. V. Tables of the Amount and present Worth of any Sum of Money, and of Annuities to 61 Years.... *Lond. 1711, 8*°. L.

2nd edn. 1714 (L).

1395 A Supplement to Faults in the Fault-Finder. In Answer to the Vindication of Faults on Both Sides. *Lond. 1711, 8*°. L.

1396 To the Honourable House of Commons in Parliament Assembled, the Humble Petition and Offer of James Armour. *n.p.* [*1711?*], *s. sh. F*°. LU.

Means to pay off the National Debt.

1397 [WALPOLE, Sir ROBERT, afterwards Earl of Orford]. A Letter to a Friend, concerning the Publick Debts, particularly that of the Navy. *n.p. 1711, F*°. L.

Reprinted in *The Debts of the Nation Stated and Considered*, 1712. For authorship see W. Coxe, *Memoirs of Sir. R. Walpole*, I, 751 n. Attributed to Arthur Maynwaring with Walpole's assistance in J. Oldmixon's *The Life and Posthumous Works of Arthur Maynwaring*, p. 307.

1398 [WALPOLE, Sir ROBERT]. A State of the Five and Thirty Millions mention'd in the Report of a Committee of the House of Commons. *n.p. 1711, F*°. L.

Another edn. 1712, 4° (O). Reprinted in *The Debts of the Nation Stated and Considered*, 1712. For authorship see W. Coxe, *Memoirs of Sir R. Walpole*, I, 751 n. Also reprinted in J. Oldmixon's *The Life and Posthumous Works of Arthur Maynwaring*, 1715, where it is ascribed to Maynwaring with Walpole's assistance.

1399 Entry cancelled.

1400 The Case as stated to the Honourable House of Commons, in a Petition of Sir William Fownes, Kt. Ephraim Dawson, Esq; William Stannus, and John Savage, Gent. in Behalf of themselves, and many other Persons, Creditors of the Army for One Hundred Thousand Pounds Sterling, in the Years 1690, and 1691, in Order to discover in whose Hands the said Debt now remains; having been deducted in the Year 1700 from the Army in England, for the Use of the Petitioners. *n.p.* [*1711?*], *s. sh. F^o^*. L.

Stannus may be a misprint for Hamms. see C.J. XVI, 514.

1401 The Case of the Proprietors of the Army and Transport Debentures. *n.p.* [*1711*], *s. sh. F^o^*. LU.

Debentures issued 'about Eighteen Years since'.

1402 The Case of the Inn-keepers and Clothiers that Quarter'd and Cloth'd the Army raised by Act of Parliament in 1677, and Disbanded by another Act in 1679 *n.p.* [*1711?*] *s. sh. F^o^*. LU.

For payment.

1403 A State of Mr. Paterson's Claim upon the Equivalent. *n.p.* [*1711*], *F^o^*. E.

On p. 3 a Memorandum dated: 27 Feb. 1710-11.

1404 Mr. Paterson's Claim upon the Equivalent consider'd, by Council Learned in the Law. *n.p.* [*1711?*], *F^o^*. L.

The counsel are Samuel Dodd and James Graham. Dated 1708? in J. Scott, *Darien Bibliography*, no. 205. L copy has ms. note R May 14. 1711.

1405 WILLIAMS, JOHN. To the Right Honourable Knights, Citizens and Burgesses of Great Britain, in Parliament Assembled. The Humble Proposal of John Williams, Gent. for Making Exchequer Bills free from Discompt. *n.p.* [*1711?*], *s. sh. F^o^*. LU.

Endorsed: A Proposal to Pay all Parliament Debts, and to Supply all other Occasions, with Exchequer Bills without Discompt.

1406 A Scheme for Circulating 1,600,000 l. in Exchequer Bills by the Members of the Bank: But separate from the Bank in their Politick Capacity. *n.p.* [*1711*], *s. sh. F^o^*. L.

Dated 19 Jan. $17\frac{10}{11}$.

1407 The Taxes not Grievous, and therefore not a Reason for an Unsafe Peace. *Lond. 1711, 8°*. LU.

Another issue 1712 (EU).

1408 BOIT, CHARLES. Proposals for raising a Supply to Her Majesty of 300000 l. per Ann. and for the Greater Encouragement of the Manufactory of Weaving, by a more Effectual Method of preventing the Clandestine Importation of the Goods hereafter named, and thereby secure Her Majesties Customs, as well as incourage the said Trade, both which are extreamly lessen'd by such ill Practices. *n.p.* [*1711?*], *F^o^*. L.

For a duty on silk woven in England.

1409 CARTER, RICHARD. A Scheme of a Second State-Lottery. *n.p.* [*1711?*], *4°*. O.

Signed: Richard Carter.

1410 CARTER, RICHARD. Several Proposals to raise Money, by sundry and different Methods, humbly offered to the Consideration of the Commons of Great Britain. *n.p.* [*1711?*], *F°*. LU.

Endorsed: Proposals for raising of Money, and a Scheme for a Lottery, &c. The first leaf was apparently reissued separately in [1712] (O).

1411 COOPER, RICHARD. The Country-Man's Proposal: or, a Dialogue between a Gentleman and a Farmer. Wherein the Farmer shews how this Nation may raise the Queen 20000 l every Day in the Year, and neither have Malt nor Salt Tax, nor charge any Man's Land above 2*s*. in the Pound, and to maintain this War with France Twenty Years, and the Nation not one Half-penny the worse. The Second Edition Corrected.... *Nottingham*, *1711*, *8°*. L.

A capital levy.

1412 HOSKINS, THOMAS. A Proposal to the Honourable House of Commons, for raising great Sums of Money for the Government; by Securing the Proprietors in the quiet Possession of their Estates, and quieting the Minds of her Majesties Subjects, & giving Incouragement to great Improvements. *n.p.* *1711*, *s. sh.* *F°*. L.

Crown leaseholders to be allowed to purchase reversions, etc.

1413 HOSKINS, THOMAS and OSMAND, GEORGE. A Proposal for a Fund for the Use of the Government. *n.p.* *1711*, *s. sh.* *F°*. LU.

Endorsed: A Proposal to raise great Sums of Money for the Government.

1414 OSMAND, GEORGE. A Proposal to the Honourable the House of Commons, for raising great Sums of Money all over Great Britain, for the use of the Government, to the Benefit and Security of all those, that are any ways concerned. *n.p.* *1711*, *s. sh.* *F°*. L.

For compulsory nationalized fire insurance.

1415 The Proposals, of Thomas Phipps Esq. To the Committee of the Honourable House of Commons, for ways and means, To raise one Million of Pounds yearly, as long as the Government pleaseth. *n.p.* *1711*, *s. sh.* *F°*. L.

Endorsed: Mr. Phipp's Proposal for raising a Million Yearly. No details given.

1416 TAPSCOTT, WILLIAM. Considerations Hmbly [*sic*] Offered to the Honourable House of Commons, for Raising to Her Majesty the Sum of 89730 l. per ann. And thereby to advance the Interest of the Poor 196575 per ann....And no Duty laid on any Manifactury.... *n.p.* [*1711*], *s. sh.* *F°*. L.

Proposing a tax on all weavers and combers. In LU copy the misprint has been corrected.

1417 Census Catholicus: or, A Project of a Tax, which will be as Large and Extensive as a General Excise, yet not so Difficult in Settling nor so Chargeable in the Management; being Exactly Proportion'd to the Abilities of the Rich, and the Necessities of the Poor: but hardly to be perceiv'd by Any-body. With some Brief Remarks on a Book, entitled,

An Essay for a General Tax, or, A Project for a Royal Tythe: written by the Famous Monsieur Vauban. *Lond. 1711, F°.* L.

Proposes a tax on money. Both copies seen are imperfect.

1418 An Essay how to raise above One Million Sterling per Ann. by an equal and easy Tax.... *n.p. [1711?], s. sh. F°.* L.

All hides and skins to be appropriated to the use of the Government.

1419 A Proposal for carrying on the War. In a Letter to a Nobleman. *Lond. 1711, 8°.* LU.

For launching an appeal for voluntary contributions to the Exchequer.

1420 A Proposal to Raise 1,500,000 l. by way of Loan, and Subscription; to the very great and extraordinary Advantage of the Government, and all Lenders, and Subscribers; and Pay it off again in Twelve Years: Which is Twenty Years less time, than the Lottery will be Paid in; and save the Nation 1600000 l. which the Second Lottery (talk'd of) will Cost; (too great a Sum to be slighted, if it may be saved) plainly Demonstrated, and Intelligible, (without Explanation) to the meanest Capacity. *n.p. [1711], s. sh. F°.* L.

1421 [Blunt, John]. A Scheme for Raising 1,500,000 l. upon Talleys and Orders payable in Course out of a Fund of 140,000 l. per ann. to be Settled for Thirty Two Years, with such certain Increase of Principal from 10 l. to 30 l. on each 100 l. and such Premiums are as mention'd in the following Table. *Lond. 1711, s. sh. F°.* L.

A Supplement to the Scheme.... n.p. [1711], F° (L). For authorship see Boyer, *Political State*, I, 259.

1422 [Blunt, John]. A Scheme for Raising Two Millions upon Standing Orders in the Exchequer, payable in Course out of a Fund of 186,670 l. per ann. for Thirty Two Years; with a certain Increase of Principal and Interest, according to several Classes, in the same manner as was propos'd for Raising 1,500,000 l. And in this Scheme there are 857 Premiums or Prizes, which make about one Premium or Prize in every 22 Tickets or Receipts. *n.p. [1711], s. sh. F°.* L.

A modification of the preceding. See Boyer, I, 295.

1423 A Scheme of a Lottery for 1,500,000 l. upon a Fund of 135,000 l. per Ann. for 32 Years. *n.p. [1711], F°.* LU.

Dated: 6 Feb. 1710/11. Endorsed: Scheme of Lottery for 1,500,000 l. Five Blanks to One Benefit. Some copies have 'Price One Penny' at foot of p. 1 of text and in endorsement.

1424 An Abstract of the intended Lottery for 1,500,00 l. with a Calculation of the paying off the Principal Mony. *n.p. [1711], s. sh. F°.* LU.

Endorsed: Abstract of Lottery for 1,500,000 l. Five Blanks to One Benefit 17 Febr. 17^{10}_{11}.

1425 An Exact Scheme of the present Parliamentary Lottery, appointed for Raising 1500000 L. for the Service of the present Year 1711.... *Edin. 1711, s. sh. F°.* MC.

1426 A Table of Discount to be Allow'd on the Present Lottery for £1500,000 Computed for Tuesday, March 13th, 1710. Being 200 Days to the 29th of September, 1711. *Lond.* [*1711*], *s. sh. F°.* L.

1427 Numb. 1. Praemiums or Benefits in the Adventure of Two Millions, with the Numbers of the Tickets, and the Classis to which they belong, drawn before the Managers and Directors of the said Adventure at Guild-Hall, London, on Wednesday, August 1. 1711. being the First Day. *Lond. 1711*, *s. sh. F°.* LSC.

OUP has the Praemiums for 8, 9 and 11 August, being the 7th, 8th and 10th days.

1428 An Exact table or list of all the numbers of the tickets or receipts drawn in the first [–fifth] classis of the two million adventure August 1. 1711. [–August 10, 11, 13, 14, 15, 1711] before the managers and directors thereof: and the numerical order in which the said tickets or receipts were drawn: with the respective principal sums, praemiums and benefits arising against the same. Published by the special order of the said managers and directors. C. Rhodes Secretary. *Lond. 1711*, *20 × 8 cm.* Kress 2715.

1429 The Present Value of each Benefit in this Year's Royal Lottery, according to the Course of Payment. By which any one at sight may know what each Benefit is worth in ready Money for any Time, from 1 to 32 Years. Together with a Scheme of a new Lottery for one Million.... *Lond. 1711*, *F°.* O.

1430 Proposals for Erecting an Office by Amicable Subscriptions and Contributions for advancing the Value of Blank Lottery-Tickets. *n.p.* [*1711?*], *s. sh. F°.* LSC.

1431 The Case of the Towns of Glasgow, Aberdeen, Dumfreis, and others, praying a Redress of the present Manner of Assessing the Royal Boroughs of Scotland. *n.p.* [*1711?*], *F°.* L.

Endorsed: The Case of the Royal Boroughs of Scotland.

1432 Proposals for Laying a Duty on Rough Tallow, instead of the Duty which is on Candles, and which proves Deficient. *n.p.* [*1711?*], *s. sh. F°.* LU.

1433 Some Considerations Humbly Offer'd to the Honourable the House of Commons, by the Tallow-Chandlers in and about the Cities of London and Westminster. [*Lond. 1711?*], *s. sh. F°.* L.

For an equivalent duty on oil if one is laid on candles.

1434 The Case of the Merchants Importing Genoa Paper, the Stationers, Haberdashers of Small Ware, the English Paper-Makers, and Card-Makers, in relation to the Intended Duty on Cards. Humbly submitted to the Honourable House of Commons. *n.p.* [*1711*], *s. sh. F°.* LU.

Endorsed: The many Losses from several Trades, attending the great Imposition on Cards.

1435 Considerations in relation to the Imposition on Cards, humbly submitted to the Honourable House of Commons. *n.p.* [*1711*], *s. sh. F°*. LU.

1436 Reasons Humbly Offer'd by the Card-Makers, against the Tax upon Playing-Cards. *n.p.* [*1711*], *s. sh. F°*. L.

1437 Reasons Humbly Offer'd to the Honourable House of Commons, by the Company of Card-Makers, Against the Tax upon Playing-Cards. *n.p.* [*1711*], *s. sh. F°*. LU.

1438 The Case of the Glass-makers in and about the City of London. *n.p.* [*1711?*], *s. sh. F°*. O.

Endorsed: The Case of the Glass-makers, Relating to the Duties on Coals, and on Glass Exported and Imported.

1439 A Memorial: shewing the Import, Extent, and Limits, of the Last Clause of an Act made in the 2d Session of the 3d Parliament of Her present Majesty, intitl'd, An Act for continuing part of the Duties upon Coal, Culm, and Cynders, and granting New Duties upon Houses, &c. *n.p.* [*1711?*], *s. sh. F°*. L.

The clause exempting from duty coal carried from the Bridge of Stirling to Dunbar needs more precise definition.

1440 A Memorial shewing the Import of the last Clause of an Act made in the 2d Session of the 3d Parliament of Her Present Majesty, intitul'd, An Act for continuing Part of the Duties upon Coal, Culm, and Cynders, and granting new Duties upon Houses, &c. And repeated in the Lottery Bill this Session. *n.p.* [*1711*], *s. sh. F°*. L.

Different from the preceding.

1441 The Case of the Kid-Skin Dressers, humbly offered to the Consideration of the Honourable the Knights, Citizens, and Burgesses of Great Britain, in Parliament Assembled. *n.p.* [*1711*], *s. sh. F°*. LU.

1442 The Case of the Leather-Sellers and Leather-Dressers of London and Westminster, and Places adjacent, humbly offered to the Consideration of the Honourable the Knights, Citizens, and Burgesses in Parliament Assembled. *n.p.* [*1711*], *s. sh. F°*. LU.

Endorsed: The Leather-Sellers Case.

1443 The Case of the Leather-Sellers and Leather-Dressers of the Cities of London and Westminster, and Parts adjacent, humbly offered to the Consideration of the Honourable the Knights, Citizens, and Burgesses in Parliament Assembled. *n.p.* [*1711*], *s. sh. F°*. LU.

Endorsed: The Case of the Leather-Sellers and Leather-Dressers.

1444 The Case of the Leather-Sellers, humbly offered to the Consideration of the Honourable the Knights, Citizens and Burgesses of Great-Britain, in Parliament Assembled. *n.p.* [*1711*], *s. sh. F°*. LU.

Against the duty on stock in hand.

1445 The Case of the Spanish Leather-Dressers, Humbly offered to the Consideration of the Honourable the Knights, Citizens, and Burgesses, in Parliament Assembled. *n.p.* [*1711?*], *s. sh. F°*. MC.

1446 The Case of the Tanners, which use Leaden-Hall-Market, on behalf of themselves and others, most Humbly Offered to the Serious Consideration of the Right Honourable the Knights, Burgesses, and Commons, in Parliament Assembled. *n.p.* [*1711*], *s. sh. F°.* LU.

Against the tax on leather.

1447 An Humble Representation from the Tanners, Skinners, and Dressers of Leather in North-Britain, concerning the intended Duties upon Tann'd Hydes, and Dress'd Leather, that may be Tann'd and Dress'd in North Britain. *n.p.* [*1711*], *s. sh. F°.* LU.

1448 Objections Humbly Offer'd to the Hon[ble] the House of Commons, in Relation to the Duty on Hides and Skins. *n.p.* [*1711?*], *s. sh. F°.* MC.

Endorsed: The Case of the Dressers and Dealers in Leather.

1449 Reasons Humbly Offer'd Against the Merchants Draw-Back of the Duty in the Leather Bill. *n.p.* [*1711*], *s. sh. F°.* LU.

Title taken from endorsement.

1450 Reasons Humbly offer'd by the Tanners, Curriers, Leather-Sellers, and Spanish Leather-Dressers; Complaining of the many Hardships, there [*sic*] several Trades Labour under. *n.p.* [*1711?*], *s. sh. F°.* L.

1451 Reasons Humbly Offered to the Consideration of the Honourable the Knights, Citizens, and Burgesses, of Great Britain in Parliament Assembled, against a Duty on Kid-Skins Drest in Great Britain. *n.p.* [*1711?*], *s. sh. F°.* L.

1452 Reasons humbly offered to the Consideration of the Honourable the Knights, Citizens, and Burgesses of Great Britain in Parliament Assembled, for a Duty on Raw Hides and Raw Skins. *n.p.* [*1711*], *s. sh. F°.* LU.

Endorsed: Reasons Humbly offered to this Honourable House for a Duty on Raw Hides and Raw Skins.

1453 Reasons humbly offered to the High Court of Parliament, against Laying a Duty upon Allum Leather. By the Master, Wardens, and Fellowship of the Glovers Company. *n.p.* [*1711?*], *s. sh. F°.* MC.

1454 Reasons Humbly Offer'd to the High Court of Parliament, By the Company of Cordwainers, London. *n.p.* [*1711?*], *s. sh. F°.* MC.

Endorsed: Reasons Humbly Offer'd against the Merchant's Draw Back of the Duty in the Leather Bill.

1455 Reasons Humbly Offer'd to the Honourable House of Commons, by the Leather-Sellers, and Leather-Dressers: shewing, the great Grievances that will be to the Subject, if a Duty be laid upon Goat, Kid, Buck, Doe, Sheep and Lamb-Skins, Dress'd in Oyl, White-Leather, or otherwise. *n.p.* [*1711?*], *s. sh. F°.* LG.

1456 Reasons humbly offer'd for Passing the Ingrosed Bill now before the Honourable House of Commons, relating to the Duties upon Prize Goods, without any Amendment. *n.p.* [*1711*], *s. sh. F°.* LU.

1457 Reasons Against Laying a farther Duty upon Prize Coco, Imported from America, which hath already Paid a High Duty there. *n.p.* [*1711*], *s. sh. F*°. LU.

1458 The Report from the Commissioners of Her Majestys Customs, Dated the 19th of August 1710. to the Lords Commissioners of Her Majestys Treasury, relating to the high Duties on Prize Goods in America. *n.p.* [*1711*], *s. sh. F*°. L.

Endorsed: The Case of the Island of Jamaica, in Relation to their Privateers,

1459 Reasons Humbly Offer'd Against Laying a further Duty on Yarn Imported from Ireland. *n.p.* [*1711?*], *s. sh. F*°. L.

Last line begins: ragement. Another edn., n.d., last line begins: found Encouragement (L).

1460 The Case of the General Receivers. *n.p.* [*1711?*], *s. sh. F*°. L.

For payment of their expenses in sending the proceeds of taxes to London.

1461 The Case of John Goddard, Gent. With an Abstract of the several parts of Mr. Sansom's Collection, from the Accounts of the Commissioners of the Customs, laid before the Committee of the Honourable House of Commons. *n.p.* [*1711*], *s. sh. F*°. LU.

Title from endorsement.

1462 The Case of Robert Payne. *n.p.* [*1711*], *s. sh. F*°. LU.

For a bill to compound with the Treasury for money owed as surety on excise bonds.

1463 Addenda's to the Case of Robert Payne. *n.p.* [*1711*], *s. sh. F*°. LU.

1464 The Report of the Commissioners for Taking, Examining, and Stating, the Publick Accounts of the Kingdom, with the Depositions at Large of Sir Solomon Medina, Kt., John Montgomery, Esq; and Captain William Preston, mentioned in the said Report. *n.p. 1711*, *8*°. pp. 36. LU.

Another edn. 1711, pp. 10 (LU).

1465 The Report from the Committee appointed to enquire how far the several Imprest Accountants have passed their respective Accounts, and to consider of Methods for the more effectual and speedy Compelling the said Accountants to pass their Accounts, and to obviate all Irregularities and unnecessary Delays in the same. With the Resolutions and Orders of the House of Commons thereupon. *Lond. 1711*, *F*°. LU.

1466 The Report of the Committee appointed to enquire into the Frauds and Abuses committed in the Victualling Her Majesty's Navy: with the Resolutions and Orders of the House of Commons thereupon. *Lond. 1710* [*O.S.*], *F*°. L.

1467 Sir Charles Cox's Case. *n.p.* [*1711*], *s. sh. F*°. LU.

On abuses in the Victualling Office.

1468 The Re-Representation: or, a Modest Search after the great Plunderers of the Nation: being a Brief Enquiry into Two weighty Particulars, necessary at this Time to be known, Viz. I. Who are they that have plundered the Nation. II. Why they are not detected and punished. *Lond. 1711*, 8°. LU.

Attributed to Defoe in *C.B.E.L.* II, 501, but rejected by Professor J. R. Moore.

1469 The Two Grand Questions propos'd to the Last Session of Parliament. I. Which way was Thirty Millions of Money sunk since the Revolution, and the Queen's Accession to the Throne? II. And if it is matter of Fact, Why are not they who had the Nation's Cash going through their Hands, call'd to an Account for this Mismanagement? With an Answer to the Two Questions. *Lond. 1711*, 4°. L.

1470 ECTON, JOHN. Liber Valorum & Decimarum; being an Account of the Valuations and Yearly Tenths of all such Ecclesiastical Benefices in England and Wales, as now stand Chargeable with the Payment of First-Fruits and Tenths. Also the True Yearly Valuations of all Small Ecclesiastical Benefices, as they have been lately Certified into Her Majesty's Court of Exchequer, in Order to their Discharge from the Payment of First-Fruits and Tenths. To which are added, the Tenths formerly charged upon such last mentioned Small Benefices. *Lond. 1711*, 8°. L.

2nd edn. 1723; 3rd 1728; another edn., entitled *Thesaurus Rerum Ecclesiasticarum*, 1742; 2nd edn. of this, 1754 and later editions (all L).

1471 A most Humble and Seasonable Proposal to the Queen, to raise Money without any Tax, sufficient to Rebuild Her Royal Palace of White-Hall...by a Small Farthing invented and made by the Direction of K. William, and approv'd by him, being light and clean as Silver; and cannot be counterfeited without Loss and immediate Discovery. The Certainty and Advantages thereof, together with some Matters relating to Her Majesty's Farm of Tin, are herein set in a True Light, by a Dialogue between a Merchant, a Pewterer, an Engineer, a Shopkeeper, a Market-Woman, and a Beggar. [*Lond. c. 1711?*], 8°. L.

1472 The Thanks of the Bank. At a General Court of the Bank of England, held at Grocer's Hall, on Thursday the 5th Day of April, 1711. *n.p. 1711, s. sh. F°*. O.

A satire.

1473 Reasons for Passing the Bill, for the better Preserving of Publick Credit, by reviving and continuing the Act made in the Eighth and Ninth Years of the late King William III. Entituled, An Act to restrain the Number and Ill Practices of Brokers and Stock-Jobbers, and and [*sic*] to preserve the Equivalent given to the Lord-Mayor and Commonalty, and Citizens of the City of London. *n.p.* [*1711*], *s. sh. F°*. L.

1474 Reasons on Behalf of the Petition of many Eminent Merchants, for continuing the late Brokers Act under farther Regulations, Humbly submitted to the Consideration of the Honourable the Commons of Great Britain in Parliament Assembled. *n.p.* [*1711?*], *s. sh. F°*. LG.

1475 The Case of The Charitable Corporation for Relief of Industrious Poor, by assisting them with small Sums upon Pledges at Legal Interest. *n.p.* [*1711*], *s. sh. F°*. LLI.

Endorsed: The Case of the Charitable Corporation For Relief of Industrious Poor, &c. Text begins: Divers Charitable Clergy-men....

1476 The Original Company of Generous Contributors, for Settling a Fund, for Relief of the Poor, In Denmark-Court, over-against Beaufort-Buildings in the Strand; whereby all Persons that becomes Contributors may make great Improvement of their Money, and be Enabled thereby to helpt the Poor. *Lond.* [*1711*], *s. sh. F°*. E.

Entered to Thomas Sedgwick in the Stationers' Register, 26 Sept. 1711.

1477 The Best Way to Improve Money. Or, Proposals offered to cause Money to Circulate, with great Advantage to all that shall be concerned therein; being a Sale of Roman Numbers, to be Re-bought of the Purchasers. *Lond.* [*1711*], *s. sh. F°*. LSC.

Entered to Robert Stockton in the Stationers' Register.

1478 September the 6th, 1711. The Most Beneficial Sale, composed of Fans, of Four different Sizes, and each Size of a different Value. At our Appartment, at the Rain-Deer, over against Surry-Street in the Strand. Whereby all Persons that becomes Purchasers or Buyers of the same, may make great Improvement of their Money.... *n.p.* [*1711?*], *s. sh. F°*. LSC.

1479 A Sale of Faith, Hope, and Charity. Proposals with Advantage to the Subscribers, by way of Subscription, during the time this Sale shall Continue.... *n.p.* [*1711?*], *s. sh. F°*. LSC.

An alphabetical sale.

1480 An Answer to a Malicious and Lying Libel; Against James Maculla's Beneficial Adventure. *Dublin*, *1711*, *s. sh. F°*. C (Cr).

Maculla was a dealer in hardware and an importer of pewter, which he offered, with cash, as prizes in his lottery.

1481 A Proposal for Improving Trade, Relieving Families, Sick or Lame, and Supporting such as cannot Pay their Debts, or may become Destitute by the Death of Friends. *Lond.* *1711*, 4°. L.

Insurance schemes.

1482 The First Proposals for Insurance on Marriage. By the Amicable and most Beneficial Society, at their Office in Twelve-Bell-Court, Bow-Church-Yard, fronting Cheapside. Begun October 31. 1710. *Lond.* [*1711*], *F°*. L.

Followed by Second and Third Proposals and 'Proposals... for the Encouragement of Servants that shall Continue in One Place or Service'.

1483 Proposals by the Bee hive Society, at their Office at a Haberdasher of Hats, by St. Clements-Church in the Strand. For Insurance on Clerks,

Apprentices and Servants, by a Weekly Dividend for Three Kalendar Months. *n.p.* [*1711*], *s. sh. F°.* L.

Dated: Tuesday the 20th of February 1710–11. On the verso are: Proposals.... For Insurance on Non-Marriages, for Widowers, Widows, Bachelors and Maids. By Dividends.

1484 Proposals for Insurance for Marriage, By the Bee-hive Society, at a Haberdasher of Hats, by St. Clements-Church, in the Strand. *n.p.* [*1711*], *s. sh. F°.* L.

On the verso are: Proposals... on Births of Children, by Claims.

1485 Proposals by the Bee-hive Society, for Insurance on the Births of Children (Born in Wedlock,) by a Weekly Dividend. At their Office, at the Golden Bee-hive by Norfolk-Street, Strand. *n.p.* [*1711*], *s. sh. F°.* L.

On the verso is: The Bee-hive Society, of Insurance of Marriages by Claims.

1486 Proposals for the Second Society on Marriages, to be opened the 8th of February, 1710 [O.S.]. *n.p.* [*1711*], *s. sh. F°.* L.

Followed by Proposals for a Third, Fourth and Fifth Society.

1487 At the Bunch of Grapes in Fleet-Street. December the 19th, 1710. Proposals. *n.p.* [*1711*], *s. sh. F°.* L.

Another edn. of the proposals on the verso of *Insurance on Marriage, by the Fair Society*, 1710. On the verso of this sheet, however, are: At the Bunch of Grapes in Fleet-Street. Proposals, dated: January the 11th.

1488 From the Safest, and most Advantageous Office of Insurance on Marriages, Births and Services, at the Carv'd Porter, over against Jack's Coffee-House in Kingstreet near Guildhall. Proposals, for Insurance on Marriage, at a Certain Charge by a Weekly Dividend. *n.p.* [*1711*], *s. sh. F°.* L.

1489 From the Safest, and most Advantageous Office of Insurance on Marriages, Births and Services, at the Carv'd Porter, over-against Jack's Coffee-House in Kingstreet near Guildhall. Proposals, for Insurance on Servants, at a Certain Charge by a Weekly Dividend. *n.p.* [*1711*], *s. sh. F°.* L.

1490 From the Safest and most Advantageous Office of Insurance on Marriages, Births, and Services, at the Carv'd Porter, over against Jack's Coffee-House in King-street, near Guildhall. Proposals, for Insurance on Births, at a Certain Charge, by a Weekly Dividend. *n.p.* [*1711*], *s. sh. F°.* L.

1491 New Proposals of Insurance on the Births of Children, born in Wedlock, at the Faithful Office, kept at the Widow Pratt's Coffee-house in Cat-Eaten-Street, by St Laurence Church, near Guild-hall. *n.p.* [*1711*], *s. sh. F°.* L.

1492 At the Widdow Pratt's Coffee-House, in Cat-Eaten-street, by St. Laurence Church, near Guild-Hall, is kept a Faithful and Equitable Office of Insurance on Marriages and Births.... *n.p.* [*1711*], *s. sh. F°.* L.

Dated: December 1710. On the verso are: Proposals by the Generous and Amicable Society for Insurance on Marriages, by a Weekly Dividend. At their Office at Widow Pratt's Coffee-House in Cat-Eaten-Street.... These are dated January the 8th, $17\frac{10}{11}$.

1493 Articles, Rules, and Orders, For the Governing and Establishing the Old Office of Insurance on Marriage, at a Certain and Weekly Devidend: at the Flower-de-Luce, near Lion's-Inn, the Backside of St. Clement's. Made by and with the Consent of the Trustees and Directors of the said Office. *n.p.* [*1711?*], *s. sh. F*^o^. L.

1494 The English Company for Insuring Childrens Fortunes. *n.p.* [*c. 1711?*], *s. sh. F*^o^. OUP.

Books opened on 22 June at Widow Ives Coffee House in Bartholomew Lane.

1495 Farther Proposals by the Hampshire-Society, for Insurance on Marriages, on the Service of Clerks, Apprentices, and all other Servants, and on Wedding-Days, both by way of Claim, and Monthly Dividend. *n.p.* [*1711*], *F*^o^. L.

1496 At a Certain Charge: Proposals for Insurance on Marriage by the Honourable Society, at the Three Crowns next Door to Durham Yard in the Strand. *n.p.* [*1711*], *s. sh. F*^o^. L.

1497 At a Certain Charge: Proposals for Insurance on Births by the Honourable Society, at the Three Crowns next Door to Durham Yard in the Strand. *n.p.* [*1711*], *s. sh. F*^o^. L.

1498 Fair and Easie Proposals for Raising & Improving the Fortunes of Servants, by the Just and Amicable Societies at their Office at the Widow Pratt's Coffee-house in Cat-Eaten-street, between St. Laurence Church and the Corner of Aldermanbury. *n.p.* [*1711*], *s. sh. F*^o^. L.

Dated: January the 11th, $17\frac{10}{11}$.

1499 Proposals by the London Charitable Societies for Insuring on Marriages, and Births born in Wedlock. Office kept at the Golden Heart in Ivy-Lane in Pater-noster-Row, near St. Paul's Church; and to be opened the 1st of February. *n.p.* [*1711*], *F*^o^. L.

1500 Proposals by the Newest and Best Society. For Insurance on Marriages, and Births of Children, both by Claims, or a Weekly Dividend, at the Subscribers Choice; at their Office the next Door to the Dean's Head, in Deans-Court in St. Martins-Le-Grand. *n.p.* [*1711*], *s. sh. F*^o^. L.

Dated: February the 17th. 1711.

1501 Proposals for Insurance on Marriage: By the Political Society: At their Office in Bolt-Court, Fleet-street. Begun January the 2d. 1709. *n.p.* [*1711*], *F*^o^. O.

1502 At a Certain Charge or Weekly Dividend. Proposals for Servants, Clerks and Apprentices. By the Profitable Society at their Office the first House on the Left Hand from the Street near Temple-Bar, entring in Palsgrave-Head-Court over against the Office of Insurance of Houses from Fire. *n.p.* [*1711*], *s. sh. F*^o^. L.

1503 At a weekly Dividend and Certin Charge. Proposals for a Single Life.

By the Profitable Society Without Loss, at their Office in Palsgrave-Head Court without Temple-Bar, over against the Office of Insurance of Houses from Fire. *n.p.* [*1711*], *s. sh. F*°. L.

1504 Proposals by the Profitable Society for a Single Life. At Mr. Meares's at the Barber's Pole, near the Red Lyon in King-street, Bloomsbury. Monday January 22th 1711. *n.p.* [*1711*], *s. sh. F*°. L.

Signed: Samuel Meares and Edward Copping Directors.

1505 Proposals, or Articles, for Insuring 300, or 150 l. on Births by Claims, by the Profitable and Equitable Society, at their Office, at the Flower-de-Luce, near Lyon's-Inn, the Backside of St. Clement's in the Strand. *n.p.* [*1711*], *s. sh. F*°. L.

1506 The Second Profitable Society, or, Office of Insurance on Births of Children, at a weekly dividend, and certain charge, kept at the first House on the Left Hand from the Street near Temple-bar, entring in Palsgrave-head Court, over against the Office of Insurance of Houses from Fire. *n.p.* [*1711*], *s. sh. F*°. L.

1507 The Royal British Society, at their Office, next Door to the Fountain Tavern, in the Strand. On Wednesday the 21st of February, was Opened Three new Books on Births of Children, and Marriages, for One and Two Months, by a Weekly Dividend.... *n.p.* [*1711*], *s. sh. F*°. L.

1508 Proposals of Insurance upon Marriage, Design'd particularly for the Conveniency and Advantage of such as are already Members of other Societies. *n.p.* [*1711*], *s. sh. F*°. L.

'This Office is kept at Mr. Janeway's, Printer.'

1509 JANEWAY, RICHARD. Proposals of Insurance on the Birth of Children Born in Lawful Wedlock. *n.p.* [*1711*], *s. sh. F*°. L.

1510 Proposals of Insurance, on Birth-Days, by the Safe Society. *n.p.* [*1711*], *s. sh. F*°. L.

1511 Articles of the Safe Society, of Insurance for Weekly Dividends, on Marriages, Births, and Apprentices, kept at Mr. Cock's a Shoomaker, near the Market, in Leaden-Hall-Street. *n.p.* [*1711*], *s. sh. F*°. L.

Dated: London, February 7th, $17\frac{10}{11}$.

1512 Proposals for Insuring upon Non-Marriages on Widowers, Widows, Batchelors and Maids, by Claims. By the Secure Society at the Ship and Fox next Door but one to the Five Bell Tavern near the Maypole in the Strand. *n.p.* [*1711?*], *s. sh. F*°. L.

On the verso similar Proposals by Dividends.

1513 Proposals of Insurance on Marriage, By the Secure Societies, at their Office at the Ship and Fox near the May-Pole in the Strand, to be Opened on Saturday the 27th of January, 1710 [O.S.]. *n.p.* [*1711*], *s. sh. F*°. L.

On the verso: Proposals for Insuring on Servants.

1514 Proposals by the Secure Society, at the Ship and Fox near the May-pole in the Strand, for Insurance on Servants and Apprentices by Weekly Dividend. *n.p.* [*1711*], *s. sh. F*o. L.

Followed by Proposals for Births, by weekly dividends and by claims. Dated: February 3. 1710 [O.S.].

1515 At a Certain Charge. Proposals for Insurance on Marriages, by the Secure Society, at the Ship and Fox, near the May-pole in the Strand. *n.p.* [*1711*], *s. sh. F*o. L.

Dated: February the 21th, 1710 [O.S.].

1516 Proposals for establishing a Society of Mutual Contributors, for raising and enlarging Provisions for Children, born in lawful Marriage; calculated for the Ease and Support of those who have, or may have large and numerous Families, and for the general Benefit of the Contributors. *n.p.* [*1711*], *F*o. L.

1517 Proposals for Insurance on Servants duly Serving their Times. By the Substantial Society for the Publick Good. At their General Insurance Office in St. Lawrence's Lane (over-against the Three Golden Lyons) near Cheapside. Began the 27th of January, 1710 [O.S.]. *n.p.* [*1711*], *s. sh. F*o. L.

1518 Proposals for Raising a Loan of 260000 l. Yearly for the Use of the Publick, Humbly offered to the Consideration of Both Houses of Parliament, by the Director, Trustees, Managers, and Subscribers of the United Society, on Births, Marriages, and Servants, kept at the White-Lion without Temple-Bar. *n.p.* [*1711?*], *s. sh. F*o. LU.

1519 Proposals for the Publick Service for Raising a Loan of 260000 l. are humbly offered to the Honourable the House of Lords, by Mrs. Dorothy Petty, the Director, Trustees and Managers of the Trading Society of Insurers on Births, Marriages, and Servants, and the Subscribers to the same, kept at the White-Lion without Temple-Bar, humbly praying a Continuance thereof, the Suppressing of which will be of utter Ruin to several of Her Majesties Subjects. *n.p.* [*1711?*], *s. sh. F*o. MC.

1520 The Case of Dorothy Petty, in Relation to the Union-Society, at the White-Lyon by Temple-Bar, whereof she is Director. *n.p.* [*1711*], *s. sh. F*o. L.

Reprinted in C. Walford, *The Insurance Cyclopaedia*, I, 322.

1521 First Proposals for Insurance on Marriages and Births: By the Union Society: At their Office, at the Cheshire Cheese, near Red Lion-street End, White-Chappel. January the 15th 1710 [O.S.]. *n.p.* [*1711*], *F*o. L.

On p. 3: Insurance at a Certain Charge: or, Second Proposals for a Weekly Dividend, on Marriages and Births.

1522 Second Proposals for Insurance upon Marriage: By the Union Society;

Next Door to Pool's Coffee-House, without Bishopsgate. *n.p.* [*1711?*], *s. sh. F*°. L.

1523 Proposals by the Utible Society, for the Insurance on Marriages, By a Weekly Dividend, at the Office, next Door to the Blue Boar, over-against the Half Moon Tavern in Aldersgatestreet. *n.p.* [*1711*], *s. sh. F*°. L.

On the verso: 'Proposals... for Insurance on Domestick Servants'.

1524 The Articles of the Third Society of the Office of Assurance for the Support of Widows and Orphans, by Raising Money on Marriages, and Births, Commencing on the 25th of March 1711.... *Dublin, 1711*, *8*°. DG.

1525 NICHOLAS, ABRAHAM. The Young Accomptant's Debitor and Creditor: or an Introduction to Merchants Accounts after the Italian Manner.... *Lond. 1711*, *8*°. E.

2nd edn. 1713 (ESA).

1526 SNELL, CHARLES. Accompts for Landed-Men: or; a Plain and Easie Form which they may observe, in Keeping Accompts of their estates. *Lond.* [*1711?*], *F*°. LICA.

2nd edn. 1727 (L).

TRANSPORT

1527 A Bill for making the River Kennett Navigable from Reading to Newbury, in the County of Berks. *n. p.* [*1711?*], *F*°. L.

1528 A Description of the most remarkable High-Ways, and whole known Fairs and Mercats in Scotland, with several other Remarkable Things: as also, A Description of the High-Ways from one Notable Town to another, over all England.... *Edin. 1711*, *12*°. E.

1529 A Bill for Repairing the High-Way between Dunstable and Hockley in the County of Bedford. *n.p.* [*1711*], *F*°. L.

Title taken from endorsement.

1530 A Bill for Repairing the High-ways from Sheet-Bridge, in the Parish of Petersfield, to the Town of Portsmouth, in the County of Southampton. *n.p.* [*1711*], *F*°. L.

1531 By the Queen, A Proclamation, For Enforcing the due Execution of the Act, Intituled, An Act for Establishing a General Post-Office for all Her Majesties Dominions, and for Settling a Weekly Sum out of the Revenues thereof, for the Service of the War, and other Her Majesties Occasions. *Lond. 1711*, *F*°. L.

Dated: 23 June 1711. Cr. 4498. Another edn. 1711 (LPRO). Cr. 4499.

1532 The Rates for Hackney-Coaches and Chairs. By the Commissioners authorized and appointed for licensing and regulating Hackney-Coaches and Chairs. *Lond.* [*1711*], *s. sh. F*°. LG.

1533 The Case of John Nicholson, Walter Storey, William Hudson, Richard Hatt, and Samuel Walters, in behalf of themselves, and the First 400 Ancient Hackney-Coachmen, and the Widows of them. *n.p.* [*1711*], *s. sh. F°.* L.

Verso blank, except for endorsed title. Another issue with 11 lines of additional text on verso (LG).

1534 The Case of the Seven Hundred Hackney-Coachmen, and Widows, Interested in the Present Licenses. *n.p.* [*1711?*], *s. sh. F°.* LG.

1535 The Case of the Unlicensed Hackney-Chairmen, usually Imploy'd within the Cities of London and Westminster, and the Suburbs and Liberties thereof. Most humbly submitted to the Consideration of the Honourable the Commons of Great Britain in Parliament Assembled. *n.p.* [*1711*], *s. sh. F°.* L.

1536 The Hackney Coachmens Case. Humbly presented to the Honourable House of Commons; with a Proposal to Raise for Her Majesty 200000 l. per annum. *n.p.* [*1711?*], *s. sh. F°.* LU.

Endorsed: The Case of the Licensed Hackney-Coachmen within the Bills of Mortality.

1537 To this Honourable House, The Case of the Coachmen; of divers Coachmakers, Harnessmakers, Wheelwrights, Tire-Smiths, Cornchandlers and other Traders, depending upon them, in and about the Cities of London and Westminster, in relation to the Bill for encreasing the Number of Hackney Coaches. *n.p.* [*1711?*], *s. sh. F°.* L.

SOCIAL CONDITIONS

1538 Some Considerations offer'd to the Citizens of Bristol, relating to the Corporation for the Poor in the said City. *n.p. 1711, 8°.* L.

1539 An Abstract of the Charter Granted by his late Majesty King Charles II. (of ever-blessed Memory) for Erecting a Corporation for Relief of the Poor Widows and Children of Clergymen, Dated July 1. 1678. *Lond. 1711, F°.* O.

Followed by lists of the Governors, Court of Assistants and Benefactors, with a form of subscription. Another edn., brought up to date, 1726 (LG); another, 1733 (MC).

1540 Reasons Humbly Offer'd for a General Insolvent Bill, in a Letter from a Country Gentleman, in Answer to a Member of Parliament upon that Occasion. *Lond. 1711, 8°.* LU.

1541 Vox Dei & Naturae: shewing the Unreasonableness and Folly, of Imprisoning the Body for Debt.... In a Letter to Sir T—— H——, Knight of the Shire, for the County of ——. *Lond. 1711, 8°.* LU.

1542 The Reception of the Palatinates Vindicated: in a Fifth Letter to a Tory Member. *Lond. 1711, 8°.* L.

1543 A View of the Queen and Kingdom's Enemies in the Case of the Poor Palatines: to which is added A List of the Persons appointed Commissioners and Trustees of that Charity by Her Majesty's Letters Patents: as also of those Members of the Late Parliament that voted for the Naturalization-Bill. In a Letter from a Gentleman in London to his Friend in the Country. *n.p.* [*1711*], *8°*. L.

Another edn. Dublin, 1712 (DA).

1544 Act of Sederunt anent Bankrupts, the Ranking of their Creditors, and Sale of their Estates. [*Edin. 1711*], *s. sh. F°*. E.

1545 By the Lord Lieutenant and Council of Ireland: a Proclamation. *Dublin 1711*, *s. sh. F°*. DPRO.

Dated: 30 Nov. 1711. Against maimers of cattle.

1546 By the Lords Justices and Council of Ireland: a Proclamation. *Dublin*, *1711*, *F°*. DPRO.

Dated: 13 December 1711. Against houghers and maimers of cattle.

1712

GENERAL

1547 The Useful Intelligence for promoting Trade, &c. no. 10. 11 Jan. 1712. *Lond. 1712*, *F°*. L.

1548 Laws concerning Trade, and Tradesmen. In Two Parts. The First, Treats of the Doctrine of By-Laws, made by Corporations and Companies concerning Trade, &c.... The Second Part, is a Collection of the Statute-Law that concerns Merchants, Tradesmen, and Artificers. *In the Savoy*, *1712*, *12°*. E.

1549 The Citizen and Tradesman's Guide. Seting forth the New Act of the Mayor and Common-Council, concerning Foreigners. The Laws and Customs of the Chamberlains Office, with the Fees for Binding or making Free Apprentices. Likewise Orders and Rules to be observ'd within the Jurisdiction of the City: With the particular Rates and Fares of Coach-men, Water-men and Car-men; with Rules and Orders to be observ'd about the same, and how People who are Injur'd by any of these are to proceed, according to the last Act of Parliament made in that Case. *Lond. 1712*, *4°*. O.

1550 MORTON, JOHN. The Natural History of Northamptonshire.... *Lond. 1712*, *F°*. O.

1551 Natural Reflections upon the Present Debates about Peace and War. In two Letters to a Member of Parliament from his Steward in the Country. *Lond. 1712*, *8°*. EU.

Some economic reasons for peace.

1552 The Dutch Barrier Our's: or, The Interest of England and Holland Inseparable.... To which is Added, An Enquiry into the Causes of the Clamour against the Dutch, particularly with Reference to the Fishery. *Lond. 1712*, *8°*. DA.

AGRICULTURE

1553 MORTIMER, JOHN. The Art of Husbandry. Part II. Containing such Additions as are proper tor the Husbandman and Gardiner: placed under their common Heads; according to the Method of the First Part.... *Lond. 1712*, *8°*. L.

The Whole Art of Husbandry was published in 1707.

1554 An Alphabetical List of the Creditors of the Company of Mine-Adventurers of England; By Bonds, Bills, Notes and other Contracts; and of Proprietors of Principal Money, Annuities and Shares, of and in the said Company, claiming the same; The whole of which, is Reduced into Shares, and Parts of Shares, pursuant to an Act of Parliament, For Relief of the Company of Mine-Adventurers, &c. In

London, September the 9th, 1712. Note, That a Share is computed at 58 l. *Lond. 1712*, *4°*. L.

1555 [MACKWORTH, Sir HUMPHREY]. The Mine-Adventurers Case; In order to explain a Proposal for raising a Stock of 20000 l. for carrying on the Undertaking. *n.p.* [*1712*], *8°*. O.

Authorship obvious from internal evidence.

1556 Observations on Mr. Forty the new Accountant's Behaviour, in several Affairs relating to the Company of Mine-Adventurers, and to the late Deputy-Governour and Directors. *n.p.* [*1712?*], *8°*. L.

Internal evidence suggests Sir Humphrey Mackworth as the probable author. Another issue, entitled: The Shortest Way with a Deputy-Governor; or, Observations on Mr. Forty.... n.p. [1712?], 8° (O).

MANUFACTURES

1557 To the Honourable the Commons of Great-Britain, in Parliament Assembled, The Humble Petition of Abraham, Elton, Benjamin Coole, and Edward Loyd, Merchants in Bristol; John Hitchcock, John Shorey, and James Knight, Merchants in London; in Behalf of themselves, and all the several Manufacturers in Copper Oar, Lapis Caliminaris, Wrought Brass, Battrey, &c. within the Kingdom of Great-Britain. *n.p.* [*1712*], *s. sh. F°*. LU.

Endorsed: The Humble Petition of Abraham Elton....

1558 A Brief Essay on the Copper and Brass Manufactures of England, only Relative to the Present Debate in the House of Commons. Humbly submitted to the Consideration of the present Parliament, by a Disinterested Hand. *Lond. 1712*, *4°*. LU.

In their dedication to the Speaker the manufacturers state that they believe the unknown author to be an M.P.

1559 The Case of the Manufacturers, and Workers of Copper and Brass, Wire, and Battrey or Brass Kettles, &c. in England. *n.p.* [*1712*], *s. sh. F°*. LU.

Against the drawback on the re-exportation of foreign wrought brass.

1560 The Case of the Brasiers, and other Artificers working in Wrought Brass, in this Kingdom. *n.p.* [*1712?*], *s. sh. F°*. LLI.

1561 A farther Explanation of the Case of the Brass Manufacturers; being an Answer to the Allegations and Pretences of the Brasiers, &c. given in to the Parliament. *n.p.* [*1712*], *s. sh. F°*. L.

1562 A Farther State of the Case Relating to the Brass Manufacturers: Particularly as it relates to the Numbers of Poor Families Employed by them, and the Improvements made, and to be made, in the said Manufactures, if the Encouragements they Petitition [*sic*] for are obtained. *n.p.* [*1712*], *s. sh. F°*. L.

1563 DONALDSON, JAMES. A Panegyrick upon the Mysterious Art of Malting and Brewing. *Edin. 1712*, *4°*. L.

In verse.

1564 [Hare, Francis]. Frauds and Abuses at St Paul's. In a Letter to a Member of Parliament. *Lond. 1712*, 8º. LG.

For authorship see Jane Lang, *Rebuilding St Paul's*, 1956, pp. 250–1.

1565 Reasons humbly offered to the Consideration of this Honourable House, by the Master, Wardens and Assistants of the Company of Clock-makers, of the City of London, on Behalf of themselves and the rest of the Members of the said Trade; Against the Bill, Entituled, A Bill for securing to Mr. John Hutchinson the Property of a Movement invented by him for the more exact Measuring of Time, both in Motion and at Rest. *n.p.* [*1712*], *s. sh. F*º. LU.

1566 Reasons for the Bill, entituled, A Bill for securing to Mr. John Hutchinson the Property of a Movement Invented by him for the more exact Measuring of Time, both in Motion and at Rest; In answer to those offered by the Clock-makers of London against it. *n.p.* [*1712*], *s. sh. F*º. LU.

1567 The Clockmakers Farther Reasons against Mr. Hutchinson's Bill and Printed Reasons. *n.p.* [*1712*], *s. sh. F*º. LU.

1568 Further Reasons for the Bill, entituled, A Bill for Securing to Mr. John Hutchinson the Property of a Movement Invented by him for the more exact Measuring of Time, both in Motion and at Rest; In Answer to the Clockmakers further Objections. *n.p.* [*1712*], *s. sh. F*º. LU.

1569 The Gun-Smiths Queries Revived: Shewing the Justice and Candour of some Quondam Legislators. *Lond. 1712*, *s. sh. F*º. LG.

Criticism of the buying of arms abroad, followed by general charges of jobbery and peculation.

1570 A Certain and Necessary Method of Regulating the Press, which will hinder and deter the Daily Insolence of False, Malitious, and Seditious Libels, by an Easy Discovery of their Authors, Printers, and Publishers. Design'd for the Service of Her Majesty's late Gratious Message to the Honorable House of Commons, and their Resolutions in their Address, and Votes concerning the Same. *n.p.* [*1712?*], *s. sh. F*º. L.

1571 A Letter from a Gentleman in Edinburgh, to a Member of Parliament. *n.p.* [*1712*], *F*º. E.

On the rights of the Queen's Printer in Scotland.

1572 A Brief Reply to the Letter from Edinburgh relating to the Case of Mrs. Anderson, Her Majesty's Printer in Scotland. *n. p.* [*1712?*], *F*º. L.

1573 Beaumont, Joseph. Mathematical Sleaing-Tables: or, the Great and only Mistery of Weaving Linnen-Cloth Explain'd. By which the most ignorant Weaver is infallibly directed how to adjust the Reed to the Yarn: and the Buyer truly shewn whether the Cloth be wrought to its due Perfection....Published by the Special Order of the Honourable the House of Commons, and by Order of the Honourable Trustees for the Improvement of the Linnen Manufacture in this Kingdom. To which is added, An Abstract of all the Statutes now in Force, relating to the Linnen Manufacture. *Dublin, 1712, 8°.* LU.

1574 DONALDSON, JAMES. A Panegyrick upon the Most Ancient, Curious, Honourable and Profitable Art of Weaving. *Edin. 1712, 4°.* L.

In verse.

1575 The Clothiers Queries to the Drapers, Humbly Offer'd to the Consideration of the Honourable House of Commons. *n.p.* [*1712*], *s. sh. F°.* L.

COMMERCE

1576 ROBINSON, FRANCIS. Robinson's Merchant's Weekly Remembrancer of the Present Monthly Price of their Goods ashore in London. No. 264, 23 March 1712. *Lond. 1712, F°.* OUP.

Probably a continuation of *The Merchant's Remembrancer*, by James Whiston, first published in 1679.

1577 JAMES, ELINOR. The humble Desire of Elinor James to my Lord Mayor, and Court of Aldermen. Decemb. 15th 1712. *n.p.* [*1712*], *s. sh. F°.* C (Cr).

On behalf of the Coal Meters.

1578 A Bill to make Free the Content-Galley, a Running Ship, Taken from the French, and Condemn'd as Prize. *n.p.* [*1712*], *F°.* O.

1579 A Bill to make the Ship Success, a Free Ship. *n.p.* [*1712*], *s. sh. F°.* LU.

Promoted by Thomas Coventry, of London, merchant, the owner.

1580 DAVENANT, CHARLES. A Report to the Honourable the Commissioners for putting in Execution the Act, intitled, An Act for the Taking, Examining, and Stating the Publick Accounts of the Kingdom. *Lond. 1712, 8°.* L.

Followed by A Second Report. Another edn. 1715, entitled: An Account of the Trade between Great-Britain, France, Holland, Spain, Portugal, Italy, Africa, Newfoundland, &c (L); 2nd edn., with this title, 1736 (MP).

1581 Reasons for a further Duty on Italian Thrown Silks Imported from Italy. Which can be no Damage, but an Advantage to the Kingdom, for the following Reasons: *n.p.* [*1712?*], *s. sh. F°.* L.

1582 By the Queen, A Proclamation, Requiring Quarentine to be Performed by Ships coming from the Sound, the Baltick Sea, and other Places, &c. *Lond. 1712, F°.* L.

Dated: 31 August 1712. Cr. 4512. Another edn. 1712 (C (Cr.)). Cr. 4513.

1583 By the Lords Justices and Council of Ireland, a Proclamation. *Dublin, 1712, s. sh. F°.* DPRO.

Taking off the quarentine imposed by the proclamation of 3 October 1711. Dated: 11 July 1712.

1584 By the Lords Justices and Council of Ireland, a Proclamation. *Dublin*, *1712*, *s. sh. F°*. DPRO.

Revoking the proclamation of 11 July last. Dated: 9 August 1712.

1585 By the Lords Justices and Council of Ireland, a Proclamation. Requiring Quarentine to be Performed by Ships coming from the Sound, the Baltick Sea, and other Places, &c. *Dublin*, *1712*, *F°*. DPRO.

Dated: 16 Sept. 1712.

1586 At a General Court of the Levant-Company, on the 24th of July, 1712. *n.p.* [*1712*], *s. sh. F°*. O.

An order requiring all members of the Company about to ship goods to Turkey to swear that they had shipped no woollen goods to Turkey since 26 Oct. 1710.

1587 Proposals Humbly offered to the Honourable House of Commons, for Enlarging and Protecting the Trade to Africa. *n.p.* [*1712?*], *s. sh. F°*. L.

Endorsed: Proposals for Encouraging the Trade to Africa.

1588 The African Company's Account of the Exports for the African Trade prov'd to be wrong stated and erroneous. *n.p.* [*1712?*], *s. sh. F°*. LU.

1589 A Collection of Papers relating to the Trade to Africa. *n.p.* [*1712?*], *4°*. L.

1590 An Explanation of the African-Company's Property in the Sole Trade to Africa, Making their Right equal with any Subject's Right to his Freehold. *Lond. 1712*, *8°*. L.

1591 Phipps, Thomas. Mr Phipps's Speech to a Committee of the Honourable House of Commons, concerning the African Trade, March the 27th, 1712. *Lond. 1712*, *8°*. L.

1592 A Bill, For making Effectual such Agreement, as shall be made between the Royal African-Company of England, and their Creditors. *n.p.* [*1712*], *s. sh. F°*. O.

1593 An Account of the Ballance of the African Company's Books, given into the Lords Commissioners of Trade, by the said Company and by that Board reported to the House of Commons in the Year 1709.... Some Queries relating to the foregoing Account. *n.p.* [*1712*], *s. sh. F°*. L.

Endorsed: Some Queries Relating to the Bill for making effectual such Agreement, as shall be made between the African Company and their Creditors.

1594 The Case of the African-Company's Creditors: Which, in short, appears; I. From their Inducements to lend Money. II. The Value of their Security. *n.p.* [*1712?*], *s. sh. F°*. L.

Endorsed: The Case of Creditors.

1595 The Answer of the Generality of the Creditors of the Royal African Company, to the Observations of the Separate-Traders, on the Bill for making effectual their Agreement with the Company. *n.p.* [*1712*], *s. sh. F°*. L.

1596 A Few Remarks Recommended to the Consideration of the Creditors of the Royal African-Company. *n.p.* [*1712*], *s. sh. F°.* L.

1597 A Bill for Establishing the Trade to Africa, in a Regulated Company. *n.p.* [*1712*], *F°.* O.

1598 Africa. Reasons against the Regulating Bill. *n.p.* [*1712*], *s. sh. F°.* O.

Endorsed: Africa. A True Britain's Observations on the Separate Traders Bill.

1599 Objections to the Bill for Establishing the Trade to Africa, in a Regulated Company. *n.p.* [*1712*], *F°.* LU.

1600 Some further Objections humbly offer'd to the Consideration of the Legislature, against the Bill, for Establishing the Trade to Africa, in a Regulated Company. *n.p.* [*1712*], *F°.* L.

Endorsed: Africa. Some Further Objections to the Separate Traders Bill.

1601 A Full Answer to all the Objections to the Bill for Establishing the Trade to Africa, in a Regulated Company. *n.p.* [*1712*], *s. sh. F°.* LU.

1602 Precedents relating to the establishing of Foreign Trade, and repealing Monopolies. *n.p.* [*1712*], *s. sh. F°.* LU.

Against the Royal African Company.

1603 Remarks upon some Queries Handed about by the Separate Traders to Africa. *n.p.* [*1712?*], *F°.* LU.

1604 The Separate-Traders Queries, or rather Clamours, against the Bill of the Royal African-Company's Creditors, proved to be Malicious, Groundless and False. *n.p.* [*1712?*], *s. sh. F°.* LU.

Endorsed: The Queries of the Royal African-Company's Creditors. Upon the Separate-Traders Queries.

1605 The Royal African-Company, and Separate Traders, agree, That the following Particulars be provided for, in a Parliamentary Establishment of the African Trade, viz.... *n.p.* [*1712?*], *s. sh. F°.* L.

1606 The unavoidable Consequences of a Trade to Africa, in a Regulated Company, as proposed by the Separate Traders, demonstrated. [*Lond. 1712?*], *s. sh. F°.* L.

Endorsed: The Destructive Consequences of a Regulated Trade to Africa, as promoted by the Separate-Traders.

1607 A Letter from a West-India Merchant to a Gentleman at Tunbridg, concerning that Part of the French Proposals, which relates to North-America, and particularly Newfoundland. With some Thoughts on their Offers about our Trade to Spain and the West-Indies: And an Abstract of the Assiento. *Lond. 1712*, *8°.* L.

1608 A Computation of what Cocoa has been Imported and Exported into the Port of London, since the first of June 1711. *n.p.* [*1712*], *s. sh. F°.* L.

Endorsed: A True Account of all the Cocoa, Imported and Exported since the 1st of June 1711.

1609 The Virtues and Excellency of the American Tobacco Plant, for Cure of Diseases, and Preservation of Health: And the noxious Qualities of the Tobacco Growing in Northern Countries. *Lond. 1712, 8°.* L.

1610 ALLEN, ROBERT. An Essay on the Nature and Methods of carrying on a Trade to the South-Sea. *Lond. 1712, 8°.* LU.

Another edn. entitled: The Great Importance of Havanna, 1762 (LU); another edn., entitled: A New Trade Laid Open, and revised by S. Jemmat, 1763 (L).

1611 A Letter from a Merchant in Amsterdam to a Friend in London, about the South Sea Trade. *Lond. 1712, 8°.* L.

1612 A List of the Names of the Corporation of the Governor and Company of the Merchants of Great Britain Trading to the South-Seas, and other Parts of America, and for Encouraging the Fishery; who are Qualified to Vote at the ensuing Election for Governor, Sub-Governor, and Deputy-Governor, to be made on Tuesday the 5th of August next; and of Directors on Thursday the 7th of August next; together with Part of the 7th By-Law concerning Elections.... June 24th, 1712. *Lond. 1712, F°.* LU.

Presumably published annually. I have seen the editions of 1714 (L); 1720 (O); 1723 (L); 1735 (L); 1747 (LU).

1613 By-Laws, Orders and Rules, for the Good Government of the Corporation of The Governor and Company of Merchants of Great Britain, Trading to the South Seas and other Parts of America, and for Encouraging the Fishery, and for the better Carrying on and Managing the Trade of the said Company. *Lond. 1712, F°.* L.

1614 A Bill for Continuing the Trade and Corporation Capacity of the United East-India Company, altho' their Fund should be Redeemed. *n.p.* [*1712*], *F°.* LU.

1615 A short Answer to the United East-India Company's Reasons for now Granting them a longer Term of Years (for Nothing) after Seventeen Years yet to come, Exclusive of all their Fellow-Subjects, under the specious Pretence of Compassion. *n.p.* [*1712?*], *s. sh. F°.* L.

1616 The Case of John Powell, of London, Merchant; who Originally Contributed l. 3,700 towards the Two Millions advanced on the Credit of an Act of Parliament, For Settling the Trade to the East-Indies; and who was thereupon, with all the other Contributors, Nominally Incorporated into a General Society for that Trade, Exclusive of the Joint-Stock Company. *n.p.* [*1712*], *s. sh. F°.* L.

Endorsed: The Case of John Powell of London, Merchant, relating to the Hardships he suffers from the United East-India Company.

1617 The Case of John Powell, of London, Merchant; Who Originally Contributed l. 3,700 towards raising Two Millions for the Service of the Crown of England, And Settling the Trade to the East-Indies, when the Publick Funds were under great Discounts. *n.p.* [*1712*], *s. sh. F°.* L.

Without endorsement. Different from the preceding.

1618 The Case of John Corso, a Genoese Merchant. (The Report made by the Committed appointed to examine the Allegations of the Petition of John Corso, a Genoese Merchant, taken from the Journals of the Honourable House of Commons is as followeth.) *n.p.* [*1712*], *F°*. LLI.

1619 COOKE, EDWARD. A Voyage to the South Sea, and Round the World, perform'd in the Years 1708, 1709, 1710, and 1711.... *Lond. 1712*, *8°*. L.

Vol. II contains an account 'of the commodities the West Indies are furnish'd with, by way of Trade, from the several parts of Europe, and what returns come from thence'.

1620 ROGERS, WOODES. A Cruising Voyage round the World: first to the South-Seas, thence to the East-Indies, and homewards by the Cape of Good Hope. Begun in 1708, and finish'd in 1711. Containing a Journal of all the Remarkable Transactions...and a brief Description of several Countries in our Course noted for Trade, especially in the South-Sea. ...And an Introduction relating to the South-Sea Trade. *Lond. 1712*, *8°*. L.

2nd edn. 1718 (O); another edn., edited by G. E. Manwaring, 1928.

COLONIES

1621 By Order of the Mineral Master General, at the New-England Coffee-House behind the Royal Exchange, London. *n. p.* [*1712*], *s. sh. F°*. LPRO.

Advertisement of the opening of a subscription list for setting up iron and steel works in New England and copper works in Connecticut.

1622 A Scheme for Improving the Mines, the Mineral and the Battery Works, in New England. *n.p.* [*1712*], *4°*. LPRO.

1623 NORRIS, JOHN. Profitable Advice for Rich and Poor. In a Dialogue, or Discourse between James Freeman, a Carolina Planter, and Simon Question, a West-Country Farmer. Containing a Description, or true Relation of South Carolina, an English Plantation, or Colony, in America: with Propositions for the Advantageous Settlement of People, in General, but especially the Laborious Poor, in that Fruitful, Pleasant, and Profitable Country, for its Inhabitants. *Lond. 1712*, *8°*. L.

1624 The Case of William Sharpe, Esq; *Lond. 1712*, *8°*. L.

Sharpe had been suspended by the Governor from the Barbados Council. Includes some details about paper credit.

FINANCE

1625 An Explanation of the Eleven Resolves of the 5th of February last, 1711. In which the Nation may see, at one View, the mighty Loss to E——nd; and the great Advantages and Savings, both in Men and Money, that the A——s and the D——ch have made, by not being on an Equality with the E——sh, and by their Deficiencies in their Quota's according to their Conventions and Agreement made with Her M——y of E——nd. *Lond. 1712*, 4°. L.

1626 The Miserable Case of Poor Old England fairly stated, in a Letter to a Member of the Honourable House of Commons. Or, The most Powerful and Convincing Reasons, why the E——r, the D——h, the rest of the A——s, the Late Ministry, and the Low-Church, are against making a General Peace with France; and all the main Objections in Opposition to it fairly Answered. *n.p. 1712*, 8°. O.

Mainly financial. Reprinted in *Somers Tracts*, XIII (1815), 205.

1627 An Account of the Funds for Payment of which the Duties on East-India Goods are Appropriated. *n.p.* [*1712*], *s. sh. F°*. LU.

1628 Publick Securities: or, the Parliamentary Funds Established for Paying the Annuities, or other Interests granted to Private Persons or Communities for Moneys at several times advanc'd to the Publick Service. Extracted from all the Acts of Parliament relating thereto. *Lond. 1712*, 4°. L.

With an Appendix dated 1717.

1629 A View of the Taxes, and Publick Revenues of England. *Lond. 1712*, 4°. LU.

Engraved tables, with a sheet of explanatory letterpress. Another edn. 1743 (L).

1630 Navy Office, 19th December, 1711. An Estimate of the Debt of Her Majesty's Navy on the Heads hereafter-mention'd, as it stood on the 30th of September last, with what thereof has and will be satisfy'd by the South Sea Stock, pursuant to the late Act of Parliament on that behalf, and what remains of the said Debt on the said 30th of September to be discharg'd. With Observations thereupon [by Sir Robert Walpole?]. *n.p. 1712*, *F°*. L.

Reprinted in *The Debts of the Nation Stated and Consider'd*, 1712, in the footnote to which the authorship is discussed.

1631 The Observations on the Estimate of the Debt of the Navy, consider'd, in a Letter to a Friend. *n.p.* [*1712*], *F°*. L.

1632 [WALPOLE, Sir ROBERT?]. A Brief Account of the Debts provided for by the South-Sea Act, and the Times when they were incur'd: With some Short Observations. *n.p. 1712*, *F°*. LU.

Another edn. n.p. 1712, 4° (DG). Reprinted in *The Debts of the Nation Stated and Consider'd*, 1712, in the footnote to which Walpole's authorship is discussed.

1633 [WALPOLE, Sir ROBERT?]. The Debts of the Nation Stated and Consider'd in four Papers, viz. I. A Letter to a Friend concerning the Publick Debts, particularly that of the Navy. II. A State of the Five and Thirty Millions mention'd in a Report of a Committee of the House of Commons. III. An Estimate of the Debt of Her Majesty's

Navy on the Heads hereafter mention'd, as it stood on the 30th of September last, with what thereof has and will be satisfied by the South-Sea Stock.... With Observations thereupon. IV. A Brief Account of the Debts provided for by the South-Sea Act, and the Times when they were incur'd: With some short Observations. *Lond. 1712*, *8º*. LU.

Attributed to Walpole in *Some Considerations on the National Debts*, 1729. All four pieces had been previously published separately and W. Coxe in his *Memoirs of Walpole*, I, 751 n., thinks only the first two are by Walpole. Reprinted in *Somers Tracts*, XIII (1815), 307.

1634 A State of Mr. Paterson's Claim upon the Equivalent; with Original Papers and Observations relating thereto. *Lond. 1712*, *4º*. LU.

1635 CARTER, RICHARD. A Proposal for settling a Perpetual Assurance on Lives, and for Advancing the Credit of the 10 l. Lottery-Tickets. By R. Carter, and Others. *n.p.* [*1712*], *Fº*. L.

1636 CARTER, RICHARD. A Scheme of a Lottery for raising One Million eight hundred thousand Pounds, on the settled Fund of 168,003 l. per Ann. for Thirty two Years, on Soap, Paper, Silks, Callicoes, Linens printed, painted, stain'd or dy'd, with Materials for Building. *n.p.* [*1712*], *Fº*. LU.

Endorsed: A Scheme for raising 1,800,000 l. for the Service of the Year 1712. by a Lottery.... Second edn. [1712], with remarks on Mr. Blunt's Scheme (O).

1637 CARTER, RICHARD. A Scheme for a Three Million Lottery. *n.p.* [*1712*], *Fº*. LU.

Endorsed: A Scheme for Raising Three Millions for the Service of the Year 1712. by a Lottery, etc. 2nd edn. [1712] (L).

1638 CHRISTOPHER, EDWARD. A Million sav'd to the Government. In a Scheme for the New Lotteries, for raising 1800000 l. upon a Fund of 168003 per Annum, whereby the Government may raise a 1000000 l. more upon the same Fund, for the Service of this present year 1712.... *Lond. 1712*, *s. sh. Fº*. L.

Title taken from endorsement.

1639 COPPING, J. A Scheme of a Second Lottery for Raising 1,200,000 l. for the Service of the Year, 1712. On a Fund of 82,350 l. per Ann. for 32 Years.... *Lond. 1712*, *s. sh. Fº*. LU.

Title taken from endorsement. The head-title is: A Scheme for Raising 1,200,000 l. for the Service of the Year 1712. by way of Lottery....

1640 GOOD, JOHN. Proposals humbly offer'd to the Honourable House of Commons, for Laying a Duty upon such Live Cattle, as are hereafter mention'd. *n.p.* [*1712?*], *s. sh. Fº*. L.

Endorsed: John Good's Proposals....

1641 PARKER, RICHARD, and Partner. Proposals Humbly Offer'd to the Consideration of the Honourable House of Commons, for Raising Forty Thousand Pounds, or upwards, per Annum, by laying Additional

Duties on all Foreign Papers and Pastboards Imported, and on all sorts of Papers, and Pastboards call'd Mill'd-Boards, made in Great-Britain. *n.p.* [*1712?*], *s. sh. F*°. LU.

1642 Thomas Phipps Esq. his Proposal. For Raising of One Million of Pounds Sterling Yearly, that will neither affect the Lands, or Trade of Great Britaine, or be grevious [*sic*] to them that Pay it, on a Fund already Established by Law, which will need no farther Sanction of Parliament, then to Appoint the Quantum and order the Application. It is a Tax on Licences, for Selling Beer, Ale &c. to which might be added Tea, Coffee, Chocolate, Mum, Syder, Perry, and other such Liquors. *Lond. 1712*, *s. sh. F*°. L.

1643 PHIPPS, THOMAS. The Reasonableness of Laying a Tax on Licenses, for Selling Beer Ale &c. in Great Britain, Justified, the Objections against it Answered, and the Sufficiency of the Scheme Proposed by Mr. Phipps, for its raising one Million of Pounds Sterling Yearly, farther Considered. *n.p.* [*1712*], *s. sh. F*°. L.

1644 SMITH, JAMES, Merchant. Proposals for Regulating Publick-Houses and Raising 100000 l. per Annum. *n.p.* [*1712?*], *s. sh. F*°. L.

Title taken from endorsement. All public houses to be licensed.

1645 THORPE, JOHN. A Proposal for Raising the Annual Sum of 28383 l. 6*s.* 8*d.* *n.p.* [*1712*], *s. sh. F*°. LU.

Proposes a duty of 1*d.* per lb. on English-made starch.

1646 The Case of the Starch-makers. *n.p.* [*1712*], *s. sh. F*°. LU.

Against John Thorpe's proposal.

1647 All Gainers, and the Nation Eas'd. Or, a Proposal of several Schemes for raising the sum of 1,500,000 l. or of 2,000,000 l. by way of another Lottery.... *n.p.* [*1712*], *s. sh. F*°. LU.

1648 A Proposal to raise the Sum of 1000000 l. per Annum, by an equal and easy Tax Exclusive of the Poor, Humbly Offer'd to the Consideration of the Honourable House of Commons.... *n.p.* [*1712?*], *s. sh. F*°. O.

A tax on silk and woollen goods.

1649 Proposals for a Lottery of 1800000 l. divided into 72000 Tickets at 25 l. each. *Lond.* [*1712?*], *F*°. LU.

Title taken from endorsement. The head-title is Proposal for a Lottery....

1650 Proposals for a Lottery of L. 3,000,000, and a Fund to pay the same. *n.p.* [*1712*], *F*°. L.

Title taken from endorsement.

1651 Proposals for laying a Duty on Beds, &c. to raise the Annual Sum of 342,872 l. And on Horses, to raise a farther Annual Sum of 123,912 l. In all 466,784 l. *n.p.* [*1712*], *F*°. L.

Endorsed: Proposals for Raising the Annual Sum of 342,772 l. to Answer the Fund 319,228 l. for paying off a Lottery of Three Millions....

1652 Proposals for Raising Three Millions for the Service of the Year 1712. by a Lottery of Annuities for 32 Years, Redeemable by Parliament.... [*Lond.*] *1712*, *F*°. MC.

1653 A Scheme for a Lottery of Halfe a Million, One Million, One Million and a halfe, or three Millions, by Ten Pound Tickets, and every Tenth Ticket to be a Prize; the lowest Prize to be Thirty Pounds. On Credit of a sufficient Fund for 32 Years. [*Lond. 1712?*], *F°*. LU.

1654 A Scheme for Raising 1,800,000 l. for the Service of the Year 1712. by way of Lottery, upon a Fund of 168,003 l. per Annum for Thirty two Years, being Proportionable to the Fund that was Granted for the Classes the last Year. *Lond. 1712*, *s. sh. F°*. O.

Endorsed: A Scheme for Raising 1,800,000 l. by Three Lotteries of 600,000 l. each....

1655 A Scheme for Raising 1,800,000 l. upon standing Orders in the Exchequer, Payable in Course, out of a Fund of 168,003 l. per Annum, for Thirty two Years; with a certain increase of Principal and Interest, according to several Classes....And in this Scheme, there are 1800 Premiums or Prizes.... *Lond. 1712*, *F°*. LU.

1656 An Account of what Monies were receiv'd and paid by Mr. Blunt for the Class Lottery in the year 1711, and at what times he paid the same into the Exchequer, and how much remains in his hands at this time. *n.p.* [*1712*], *F°*. L.

1657 A True Account of the Payments made by Mr. John Blunt into the Exchequer, on his Receipt of 993,000 l. of the Class Lottery, as appears by the Records of the Exchequer, and several Accounts Deliver'd on Oath to the Commissioners of Accounts. *Lond. 1712*, *F°*. L.

1658 An account shewing the numbers of the tickets entituled to benefits in the lottery for 1500000 l. Anno 1711. With the benefits to which the said number'd tickets are respectively entitul'd, and the days on which they were severally drawn, distinguish'd in a numerical order.... Publish'd by the special order of the managers and directors of the said lottery. *Lond. 1712*, *20 cm*. Kress 2767.

1659 An Exact Table or List of the Course of the Payment of every Thousand of the One Hundred and Fifty Thousand Tickets, in the Lottery for 1,500,000 l. Ann. 1711. *Lond.* [*1712?*], *F°*. LSC.

1660 A Table, shewing the Lowest and Highest Number in every Course of Payment in the 1500000 l. Lottery. *London*, [*1712*], *s. sh. F°*. E.

1661 A Bill to Impower the Pay-Master of the Million-Lottery-Tickets, to Pay Sir William Hodges, Bar^t. the Money due upon Fourteen Tickets in the said Lottery. *n.p.* [*1712*], *s. sh. F°*. LU.

1662 The course of payment of the ten pound lottery for the year, 1712. Digested into a numerical order.... [*n.p.*, *1712*], *19 × 10·5 cm*. Kress S. 1328.

1663 The Case of the Brickmakers, Tilemakers, Slaters, Lime-Men, Masons, and Paviours, in or near the Limits of the Weekly Bills of Mortality, humbly offered to the Consideration of the Honourable House of

Commons, in Relation to the Duty intended to be laid on Bricks, Tiles, Slates, Lime, and Stone, within the Limits of the Bills of Mortality. *n.p.* [*1712*], *s. sh. F°*. LU.

1664 A Just and Exact Account taken out of the Books of the several Brickmakers, Lime-burners, Tilemakers, Slaters, Masons, and Paviers, of the Goods made, or brought in by them, within the Weekly Bills of Mortality, or within Ten Miles of the same, in the Year 1711. in Relation to the intended Duties on Bricks, Lime, Tiles, &c. Humbly offer'd to the Consideration of this Honourable House. *n.p.* [*1712*], *s. sh. F°*. LU.

Endorsed: A True Estimate of the Intended Duty to be laid on Bricks, Tiles, Lyme, &c. within the Weekly Bills of Mortality, and Ten Miles Distance thereof.

1665 Reasons for supporting the Resolves of the Committee of the Honourable House of Commons for laying Duties upon Bricks, Tyles, Lime &c. Humbly Offered. *n.p.* [*1712*], *s. sh. F°*. LU.

1666 Reasons humbly offer'd, against the Laying a Duty upon the Stock of Cards in the Workmen and Tradesmens Hands. *n.p.* [*1712*], *s. sh. F°*. O.

1667 The Case of the United East-India Company. *n.p.* [*1712*], *s. sh. F°*. LU.

Against the duties on cotton goods, drugs, tea and coffee voted 17 May 1712.

1668 The Case of the Clothiers and Fullers of the Counties of Glocester, Devon, Oxford, Worcester, York, Dorset and Wiltshire. *n.p.* [*1712?*], *s. sh. F°*. L.

Increased duties on East India goods will prevent the East India Company buying their manufactures.

1669 Reasons humbly offered by the Merchants of London, Trading to Hamborough and Holland, to the Honourable House of Commons, against a Clause in a Bill now depending before that Honourable House (for granting to Her Majesty new Duties of Excise, &c.) relating to Drawbacks. *n.p.* [*1712?*], *s. sh. F°*. L.

1670 Reasons against a Duty on Stock in Hand upon Drugs, Coffee, and Tea. *n.p.* [*1712*], *s. sh. F°*. L.

1671 Reasons against laying a Duty upon Stock in Hand, on Drugs, Coffee and Tea. *n.p.* [*1712*], *s. sh. F°*. MC.

1672 The Case of the Importers of Common Turpentine, from Her Majesty's Plantations, briefly Stated. *n.p.* [*1712?*], *s. sh. F°*. LU.

For exemption from the proposed tax on drugs.

1673 The Case of the Dressers & Dealers in Leather, Humbly offered to the Consideration of the Honourable the Knights, Citizens and Burgesses, in Parliament Assembled. *n.p.* [*1712*], *s. sh. F°*. L.

Against an increase in the duty of hides and skins.

1674 The Leather-Sellers and Leather-Dressers Case, Humbly Offer'd to the Consideration of the Honourable the Knights, Citizens, and Burgesses of Great Brittain in Parliament Assembled. *n.p.* [*1712*], *s. sh. F*o. LU.

Against a further duty on imported skins.

1675 Reasons for Taking off the Draw-back on Tann'd Calves-Skins. *n.p.* [*1712?*], *s. sh. F*o. LU.

1676 Reasons humbly offered by the Leather-Sellers of the Cities of London and Westminster, and Parts adjacent, to the Consideration of the Honourable the Knights, Citizens, and Burgesses, of Great Britain in Parliament Assembled, against a Duty on Leather. *n.p.* [*1712*], *s. sh. F*o. L.

1677 Reasons humbly offered by the Spanish Leather-Dressers of Great Britain, to the Consideration of the Honourable the Knights, Citizens, and Burgesses of Great Britain in Parliament Assembled, against a Duty on Leather. *n.p.* [*1712*], *s. sh. F*o. L.

1678 Reasons Humbly Offer'd for putting Hides and Skins Curried upon the same Foot upon Exportation, as Hides or Skins that are Rough and Undrest. *n.p.* [*1712?*], *s. sh. F*o. L.

Endorsed: Reasons for a Draw-back on Curried Leather.

1679 Reasons Humbly Offer'd to prevent the Making the upper part of Shoes of any thing but Leather, Silk, Satten, or Velvet. *n.p.* [*1712*], *s. sh. F*o. LU.

Endorsed: Reasons Offer'd for increasing the Duty upon Leather.

1680 Reasons Humbly Offer'd to the Consideration of the Hon[ble] the Knights, Citizens, and Burgesses of Great-Brittain in Parliament assembled, against a further Duty on Goats Skins Tann'd with Shumack, after the manner of Spanish Leather. *n.p.* [*1712*], *s. sh. F*o. LU.

1681 Reasons Humbly Offer'd to the Consideration of the Honourable Knights, Citizens, and Burgesses of Great-Britain, in Parliament assembled, against a Further Duty on Kid-Skins. *n.p.* [*1712?*], *s. sh. F*o. LU.

1682 Reasons Humbly Offered to the Honourable House of Commons, Against an Additional Duty of one Penny per Pound Weight, Proposed to be Laid on Tann'd Sheep and Lamb-Skins, called Bazels; and of Three half-pence per Pound Weight, on all Tawed Sheep and Lamb-Skins, Drest in that Part of Great-Britain, called England, which will be Thirty five per Cent. on Tann'd Sheep and Lamb, called Bazels; And Fifty per Cent on Tawed Sheep and Lamb; and is not proportionable to the Value of Oyl-Sheep and Lamb, nor Scotch Lambs Tawed, nor Sheep-Skins made into Parchment. *n.p.* [*1712*], *s. sh. F*o. L.

1683 Reasons most Humbly offered by the Manufactures [*sic*] of the Coarse Woollens of this Kingdom against laying a greater Duty upon Buck and Doe-Skins, Imported to this Kingdom. *n. p.* [*1712?*], *s. sh. F*o. L.

1684 The Case of the Linnen Drapers and other Dealers in Printed Callicoes and Linnens. *n.p.* [*1712*], *s. sh. F°*. L.

For a lower duty on cheaper qualities and for the exemption of stock in hand from duty.

1685 Reasons for Excepting Brittish Linnen to be Printed, Painted, or Stained, from the Duty of 2d. per Yard. *Edin.* [*1712?*], *s. sh. F°*. LU.

Another edn. n.p. [1712 ?] (L).

1686 Reasons Humbly Offer'd to the Honourable House of Commons, by the Callicoe-Printers, against the Duty Intended to be Laid on Printed Callicoes and Linnens. *n.p.* [*1712*], *s. sh. F°*. L.

Endorsed: The Case of the Callicoe-Printers.

1687 Reasons Humbly Offer'd by the Hambrough Merchants, and other Traders and Dealers in the Woollen Manufacture of Great Britain, against the Intended Duties on several Sorts of German Linnen. *n.p.* [*1712*], *s. sh. F°*. LU.

Endorsed: The Hambrough Merchants Reasons against Part of the Duties in the Lottery-Bill.

1688 The Case of Paul Lorrain, Ordinary of Newgate, Most humbly offer'd to the Honourable House of Commons. *n.p.* [*1712*], *s. sh. F°*. LU.

For the exemption from the stamp duty of the confessions of condemned criminals published by him, on the ground that they are works of devotion or piety.

1689 The Case of the Company of Parish-Clerks, relating to the Duties on Pamphlets, &c. Humbly offer'd to the Honourable House of Commons. *n.p.* [*1712*], *s. sh. F°*. LU.

1690 The Case of the Members of the Sun-Fire-Office, London, relating to the Duties on News-Papers. Humbly represented to the Honourable House of Commons. *n.p.* [*1712*], *s. sh. F°*. LU.

For the exemption from tax of their organ *The British Mercury*.

1691 The Printers Case: with their Proposals for Regulating the Press. *n.p.* [*1712*], *F°*. L.

Title from endorsement. Against the newspaper and pamphlet duties.

1692 Reasons Humbly submitted to the Honourable House of Commons, against laying a Duty on News-Papers and Pamphlets. *n.p.* [*1712*], *s. sh. F°*. LU.

1693 The Case of the Book-Binders of Great-Britain. *n.p.* [*1712*], *s. sh. F°*. L.

Hopes the House of Commons will not 'prohibit the making Mill-boards, which will be...no Way Advantageous to the Duty intended to be laid on Paper'.

1694 The Case of the Book-Binders of Great Britain, Humbly offered to the Consideration of the Honourable House of Commons, relating to the Excessive Duty resolved to be laid on Mill-boards. *n.p.* [*1712*], *s. sh. F°*. LU.

1695 The Case of the Manufacturers of Paper, the Stationers Printers, &c. of this Kingdom relating to several Duties on Paper and Printing, now Voted in the House. Humbly represented to the Honourable House of Commons. *n.p.* [*1712*], *s. sh. F*o. LU.

1696 The Case of the Paper-Makers of Great Britain. *n.p.* [*1712*], *s. sh. F*o. LU.

1697 The Case of the Past-Board-Makers, of the City of London. Humbly Submitted to the Consideration of the Honourable the Commons of Great Britain in Parliament Assembled. *n.p.* [*1712*], *s. sh. F*o. L.

1698 The Case of the poor Paper-Makers and Printers, farther stated. *n.p.* [*1712*], *s. sh. F*o. LU.

1699 The Case of the Printers, Painters or Stainers of Papers for Hangings. *n.p.* [*1712*], *s. sh. F*o. LU.

1700 The Case of the Woollen Manufactorers of Great Britain, relating to a further Duty intended to be laid on Paper. *n.p.* [*1712?*], *s. sh. F*o. L.

1701 Considerations relating to the Duties on Paper, intended upon Stock in Hand, humbly Submitted to the Honourable House of Commons. *n.p.* [*1712*], *s. sh. F*o. L.

1702 Considerations relating to the intended Duties on Paper, humbly Submitted to the Honourable House of Commons. *n.p.* [*1712*], *s. sh. F*o. pp. 1 LU.

Another edn., enlarged by the addition of a table, pp. 1. (O); another enlarged edn., pp. 2 (LU).

1703 Reasons for Amending the Clause for a Drawback to be allow'd to the Universities, &c. *n.p.* [*1712*], *s. sh. F*o. LU.

Exemption from the paper duties will allow the Universities to print 20 per cent more cheaply than in London.

1704 To the Honourable the Commons of Great Britain in Parliament Assembled. The Case of the Traders in, and Exporters of the Woollen Manufacture, in relation to the Duty intended to be laid on Pastboards. *n.p.* [*1712*], *s. sh. F*o. LU.

1705 The Case of the Island of Jamaica. In Relation to their Privateers, and the Bonds given by several Inhabitants for them. *n.p.* [*1712?*], *s. sh. F*o. LU.

1706 Entry cancelled.

1707 Reasons Humbly Offer'd for the relief of several Merchants, Importers of Prize Cocoa, against part of an Act, past last Sessions of Parliament; Entituled an Act for the Encouragement of the Trade to America, so far as relates to Prize Cocoa, that hath paid Her Majesties Customs in America, as shall appear by Certificate. *n.p.* [*1712*], *s. sh. F*o. LU.

1708 Further Reasons, Against Laying a Duty upon Prize Cocoa, Imported from America, which hath already Paid a High Duty there. *n.p.* [*1712*], *s. sh. F°.* LLI.

1709 Reasons humbly offer'd for the Relief of several Merchants, Importers of Prize Sugars, Indico and Cotton, from America. *n.p.* [*1712*], *s. sh. F°.* LU.

1710 Reasons why Prize-Goods, should pay the same Duty as the Merchant. *n.p.* [*1712*], *s. sh. F°.* LU.

1711 The Report from the Commissioners of Her Majesty's Customs, to the Lords Commissioners of the Treasury, relating to the high Duties on Prize Goods in Jamaica. *n.p.* [*1712*], *s. sh. F°.* LU.

The report is dated August 10th, 1710. Endorsed: The Commissioners of Her Majesty's Customs Report in relation to the Bonds taken at Jamaica for Prize Goods.

1712 To the Honourable the Commons of Great Britain in Parliament Assembled; The Return of the Commissioners of the Customs to an Order of this Honourable House, dated the 18th Instant, directing the said Commissioners to lay before this House, An Account of the Bonds taken for Prize Goods brought into Jamaica, which were unsatisfied upon the first of June last, according to the Directions of the Act pass'd the 9th Year of Her Majesty's Reign, for the Encouragement of the Trade to America. *n.p.* [*1712*], *s. sh. F°.* LU.

Dated: 22 Febr. 1711 [O.S.]. Endorsed: A Copy of the Return of the Commissioners of the Customs to an Order of the Honourable House of Commons, touching Bonds given at Jamaica, for the Duty on Prize Goods.

1713 To the Queens most Excellent Majesty, The Humble Address of the Governor, Council and Assembly of Jamaica. *n.p.* [*1712*], *s. sh. F°.* L.

Dated 18th, October, 1711. Endorsed: The Address of the Governor, Council and Assembly of Jamaica, Lately Presented to Her Majesty. On the bonds for duties on prize goods.

1714 BOIT, CHARLES. Some Reasons humbly offered, for laying a Duty upon Wrought Silks. *n.p.* [*1712?*], *s. sh. F°.* LU.

1715 Some Reflections on the Project for laying a Duty on English Wrought Silks. *n.p.* [*1712?*], *s. sh. F°.* LU.

1716 [BOIT, CHARLES]. An Answer to a Paper of Reflexions on the Project for laying a Duty on English Wrought Silks. *n.p.* [*1712?*], *s. sh. F°.* L.

Authorship deduced from internal evidence.

1717 Reasons humbly offered against Laying the New Projected Duty on English Wrought Silks, plainly proving, that it will be Injurious to Trade, Vexatious to Her Majesty's Subjects, and Impracticable to be Levied. *n.p.* [*1712?*], *s. sh. F°.* LU.

In reply to C. Boit's proposals.

1718 The Case of the Manufacturers and Retailers of Silk Goods, under the New Projected Duty. *n.p.* [*1712?*], *s. sh. F°.* LU.

1719 The Case of the Poor People Employed in Weaving Gause for Hoods, Scarfs, Neck-Handkerchiefs, and in Weaving Silk-Handkerchiefs. [*Lond.* *1712?*], *s. sh. F*o. L.

1720 Reasons Humbly offer'd to the Honourable House of Commons, against a Duty intended to be laid upon Silks, Manufactured, Printed, or Stained, as far as it concerns Handkerchiefs. *n.p.* [*1712*], *s. sh. F*o. LU.

1721 The Case of Benjamin Wood. *n.p.* [*1712*], *s. sh. F*o. L.

Wood has perfected the art of staining silk handkerchiefs and will be ruined if a duty is imposed on stained silks.

1722 The Case and Humble Petition of the Hard Cake and White Soap Makers. *n.p.* [*1712?*], *s. sh. F*o. LU.

1723 The Case of the Soap-Makers making Green Soap. *n.p.* [*1712?*], *s. sh. F*o. L.

Text begins: There is not one Commodity or Ingredient us'd in the making Green Soap, but what a Duty is already laid upon it.

1724 To the Knights, Citizens, Burgesses, and Commissioners, in Parliament Assembled, the Humble Petition of Thomas Brooke and John Hellier, of London, Merchants. *n.p.* [*1712*], *s. sh. F*o. LU.

Against paying retail duties on the wine they have imported.

1725 The Case of Messieurs Brooke and Hellier. *n.p.* [*1712*], *s. sh. F*o. LU.

A further statement of their case.

1726 A Farther State of the Case relating to the Petition of Brooke and Hellier. *n.p.* [*1712*], *s. sh. F*o. LLI.

1727 Brooke and Hellier. A Satyr. *Lond.* *1712*, *8*o. L.

1728 The Quack-Vintners: or, a Satyr against Bad Wine. With Directions where to have Good. Inscrib'd to B——ks and H——r. *Lond. & Westminster*, *1712*, *8*o. EU.

Brooks and Hellier. Attributed to E. Ward by H. W. Troyer, without decisive evidence.

1729 The Case of the Manufacturers of Gilt and Silver-Wyre, &c. Humbly offer'd to the Consideration of the Honourable House of Commons. *n.p.* [*1712?*], *s. sh. F*o. LLI.

Against the proposed duty.

1730 The Case of the Parish of St Giles Criplegate. *n.p.* [*1712*], *s. sh. F*o. L.

Against the duty on gold and silver wire.

1731 Reasons humbly offer'd to the Honourable House of Commons against Laying a Duty on Gold and Silver Wyer. *n.p.* [*1712*], *s. sh. F*o. LU.

1732 Reasons Most Humbly Offer'd Against Prohibiting Foreign Silks mixt with Gold and Silver. *n.p.* [*1712?*], *s. sh. F*o. LU.

1733 Instructions to be Observed by the Officers Employ'd in the Duties on Printed, Painted, Stain'd, and Dy'd Silks, Callicoes, Linens and Stuffs. *Lond.* *1712*, *8*o. LU.

1734 Instructions to be Observ'd by the Officers Employ'd in the Duty on Soap. *Lond.* *1712*, *8*o. LU.

1735 Instructions for Tide-Waiters, and Coast Officers, in the Kingdom of Ireland. *Dublin*, [*c. 1712?*], *4°*. DA.

1736 LANGHAM, THOMAS. The Neat Duties, and the Draw-back upon Exportation, (All Discounts and Abatements deducted) of All Drugs specified in the Book of Rates, begun in the 12. of Car. 2. with the several Variations and Additions to this Present Year, 1712. Also the Act of the 3. and 4. of Queen Anne, concerning Unrated Drugs, and Dying Goods. What is declared to be Unrated Drugs, and what for Dyers Use is here determined. *Lond. 1712*, *8°*. L.

1737 RICHARDSON, FRANCIS. Compleat Tables for finding out, in a Minute, the several Rates and Duties chargeable by a late Act of Parliament, on Leather, Vellum, Parchment, &c. either made in Great Britain, or imported from other Countries.... *Lond. 1712*, *8°*. L.

1738 The Case of Job Mathew. *n.p.* [*1712*], *s. sh. F°*. L.

For a bill to enable the Treasury to compound with him for money owed 'as surely for John Goodwin and his partner, merchants that trade to Virginia, for the duties on tobacco'.

1739 The Case of Job Mathew. That some Time since He became Bound in several Bonds to Her Majesty, as Surety for John Goodwin and his Partner, Merchants, that Traded to Virginia, for the Duties on Tobacco. *n.p.* [*1712*], *s. sh. F°*. O.

1740 The Report of the Commissioners for Taking, Examining, and Stating the Publick Accounts of the Kingdom. With the Examinations and Depositions relating thereunto; and the Resolutions of the House of Commons thereupon; with Her Majesty's Gracious Answer to the Resolutions laid before Her Majesty. *Lond. 1712*, *F°*. L.

1741 The Second Report of the Commissioners for the Taking, Examining and Stating the Publick Accounts, &c. *Lond. 1712*, *8°*. L.

Another edn. Dublin, 1712 (DA).

1742 The Case of his Grace the D—— of M——. As Design'd to be Represented by him to the Honourable House of Commons, in Vindication of Himself from the Charge of the Commissioners of Accounts; in relation to the Two and Half per Cent. Bread and Bread Waggons. [*Lond.*], *1712*, *8°*. LU.

2nd and 3rd edns. 1712 (both O).

1743 The Depositions of Sir Solomon de Medina, Against his Grace the D. of M——h. *Lond. 1712*, *s. sh. F°*. C (Cr).

On the bread contracts for the army in the Low Countries.

1744 The Information against the Duke of Marlborough. And his Answer. *Lond.* [*1712*], *8°*. L.

Another edn. Dublin, 1712, 4° (DNL).

1745 A Letter from a Curate of Suffolk to a High-Church Member; concerning the D. of M. and Mr W——le. *Lond. 1712*, *8°*. LU.

Signed: J. F. Attacks Marlborough and Walpole for peculation.

1746 A Speech Without Doors, concerning the Two and a Half per Cent. Jovis 24 Die Jan. 1711, Resolved, That the Two and a Half per Cent. deducted from the Foreign Troops in Her Majesty's Pay is Publick Money, and ought to be accounted for. *Lond. & Westminster, 1712, 8°.* LU.

1747 The New Way of Selling Places at Court. In a Letter from a Small Courtier to a Great Stock-Jobber. *Lond. 1712, 8°.* LU.

Another edn. Dublin 1712 (DA).

1748 Plunder and Bribery Further Discovered, in a Memorial humbly offer'd to the British Parliament. *Lond. 1712, 8°.* L.

Attributed to Defoe in *C.B.E.L.* II, 501.

1749 By the Lords Justices and Council of Ireland, a Proclamation. *Dublin, 1712, F°.* DPRO.

Dated 30 July 1712. Fixing the exchange rates of foreign coins.

1750 A Preamble to the Books for taking a Subscription of Twelve Hundred Thousand Pounds, for the Use of the Bank of England $17\frac{11}{12}$. *n.p.* [*1712*], *F°.* L.

1751 Proposals for the Society of the Five Senses. Being a New Method for more largely improving small Sums of Money than any yet propos'd. And for settling a Fund for Relief of the Poor. In New Round Court in the Strand.... *n.p.* [*1712*], *s. sh. F°.* LSC.

Entered to Robert Thompson in the Stationers' Register.

1752 Proposals for the Society of the seven Liberal Sciences. Being a New Method for more largely improving small Sums of Money than any yet propos'd. And for settling a Fund for Relief of the Poor. In Russell Court in Drury Lane.... *n.p.* [*1712*], *s. sh. F°.* LSC.

Entered to Tho. Wilkinson in the Stationers' Register.

1753 Proposals or [*sic*] the Golden Office for the Society of the Seven Liberal Sciences, being a very advantagious Method, for Improving small Summs of Money, at Nixons Coffee-house by Fetter-lane in Fleet-street, up one pair of Stairs. *n.p.* [*1712*], *s. sh. F°.* LSC.

Entered to John Leman in the Stationers' Register.

1754 News from Athens: or a Defence of the Money Improving Offices. For the Benefit of the Subscribers, in Cards, Fans, Muffs, or the Queens Pictures, Letters, or Numbers, the Golden Office or Society of the Seven Liberal Sciences. With some Remarks on a New Erected Office, Entitl'd Sales Office made to Restore ——. *Lond. 1712, 4°.* LU.

1755 An humble Representation of many Hundreds of Subscribers, belonging to the Alphabetical Sale in Whalebone Court, Loathbury, and to one other in Newgate Street, to the Honourable the House of Commons. *n.p.* [*1712*], *s. sh. F°.* L.

Endorsed: The Case of the Sale Offices in Whalebone Court and Newgate Street. Against their suppression.

1756 Reasons humbly offered in behalf of the Hudson-Bay Company, that they may be Exempted in the Clause that will be offer'd for Suppressing the Insurance Offices. *n.p.* [*1712*], *s. sh. F°*. L.

1757 Articles for establishing an Hereditary Company, for the benefit of the present and succeeding Generations. *n.p.* [*1712*], *4°*. L.

1758 A short Account of some approved Methods already settled, to make Provision for Posterity; with an Assay towards Establishing a Company for that purpose, more Advantageous than any before invented. *n.p.* [*1712*], *F°*. L.

Entered to Thomas Brockett in the Stationers' Register.

1759 The Articles of the Third Society, of Her Majesty's Office of Assurance, for the Support of Widows and Orphans: Begun at Dublin the 25th of March, 1711.... *Dublin*, *1711–12*, *8°*. DNL.

Another edn. Dublin, 1712, 4° (DA).

1760 A List of the Honourable the Trustees, the Directors, and the Managers of Her Majesty's Office of Assurance, for the Support of Widows and Orphans, upon Marriages, Births, and Deaths.... *Dublin*, *1712*, *4°*. DA.

1761 Proposals set forth by the Company of the Sun-fire-office...for insuring houses, moveable goods, merchandize, furniture, and wares, from loss and damage by fire, in any part of Great Britain.... [*London*, *H. Meere*, *1712*] [*2*] *p. 35 cm.* Kress S. 1348.

At head of title: From the Sun-fire-office, July 4. 1712.

TRANSPORT

1762 A Bill for Prolonging the Term for Payment of Certain Duties Granted by an Act made in the Twelfth and Thirteenth Years of His Late Majesty King William, Intituled, An Act for Recovering, Securing, and Keeping in Repair, the Harbour of Minehead, for the Benefit and Support of the Navigation and Trade of this Kingdom. *n.p.* [*1712*], *F°*. O.

1763 The Right of the Poor discover'd and preserv'd. Being an Information in the Exchequer, in the Attorney General's Name; at the relation of Mr. William Smith, Capt. Richard Oldner, Mr. George Oldner, Junior, Mr. John Kibble, Mr. Robert Watts, Mr. Joseph Bennett, and Mr. Thomas Williford, Lighter-men, &c. against many Rulers, Auditors, Assistants, and Comptrolers of the Company of Water-men and Lighter-men, since 1703, for embezelling, or corruptly misapplying, Many Hundred Pounds of that very Money, which an Act of Parliament, and the Constitutions of that Company....Appropriated towards the Relief of the poor, aged, decay'd, and maim'd Water-men and Lighter-men, and their Widows....To which is added the Defence of the

Water-men, Trustees, and Mr. Knight, to a Charge for 3000 l. of that Company's Money, which is (pretended to have been receiv'd, and) unaccompted for. *Lond. 1712*, *8°*. LU.

1764 A Bill for making the River Avon, in the Counties of Somerset and Gloucester, Navigable; from the City of Bath to or near Hanhams-Mills. *n.p.* [*1712*], *F°*. O.

1765 A Bill for Repairing the Road from the Town of High-gate, to and beyond the Town of Whetstone, in the County of Middlesex. *n.p.* [*1712*], *F°*. O.

1766 Reasons humbly offer'd to the Consideration of this Honourable House, in behalf of several Carryers, Travelling thro' the Highgate Road, with the product and Manufactures of several Counties: And also Persons concerned in Feeding Oxen, Sheep, Hoggs, &c. in relaton to the Bill for Erecting a Turn-Pike or Bar, near Whetstone in the County of Middlesex. *n.p.* [*1712*], *s. sh. F°*. L.

1767 Reasons humbly offer'd to the Honourable House of Commons, on the Behalf of several Land-Owners and Tenants in the Parish of Fryern-Barnet, and several other Parishes in the Counties of Hertford and Middlesex, against a Bill, entituled, A Bill for the Repairing the Road from the Town of Highgate, to and beyond the Town of Whetstone in the County of Middlesex. *n.p.* [*1712*], *F°*.

1768 A Bill for Repairing the Highway between a certain Place called Five-Mile Stone and the Town of Stanmore Magna, in the County of Middlesex. *n.p.* [*1712*], *s. sh. F°*. O.

1769 A Bill for the better Repairing and Amending the Road leading from Ipswich to Cleydon, and the Road called the Pye-Road, in the County of Suffolk. *n.p.* [*1712?*], *F°*. O.

1770 LONDON. Commun' Concilium tentum in Camera Guihald'....An Act concerning the Tackle-house and the Ticket Porters, and touching the Publick Beams belonging to the City of London. [*Lond.*], *1712*, *F°*. L.

1771 To the Rt. Honourable the Lord Mayor, Aldermen and Commons in Common-Council Assembled. The Humble Petition, Remonstrance and Representation of the Case of the Tackle-House-Porters belonging unto the Primary Companies of this Honourable City, and more especially of those belonging unto the Mercer's Draper's and Goldsmith's Companies respectively; in Answer to the Case of the Ticket-Porters. *n.p.* [*1712*], *F°*. LLI.

Endorsed: The Case of the Tackle House Porters....

SOCIAL CONDITIONS

1772 Midd. ss. Ad General' Quarterial' Session' Pacis, Dom' Reginae tent' pro Comitatu Middlesexiae, apud Hicks-Hall, in St John-street, in Com' praedict' die Mercurii scilicet Nono die Januarii, Anno Regni

Dominae Annae, nunc Reginae Magnae Britanniae, &c. decimo. *n.p.* [*1712*], *s. sh. F°*. O.

An order for expediting the passing of vagrants through the county.

1773 A Bill for Erecting a Work-House in the City and County of the City of Norwich, for the better Employing and Maintaining the Poor there. *n.p.* [*1712*] *F°*. LU.

1774 The Charter of the Governours of the Grey-Coat-Hospital in Tothill-Fields, of the Royal Foundation of Queen Anne. *Lond. 1712*, *F°*.

1775 LONDON. Commun' Concilium tentum in Camera Guihald'....An Act for securing the Payment to St. Bartholomew's Hospital, of the Sum of Three thousand two hundred fourteen Pounds four Shillings and nine Pence, and Coasts of Suit, Decreed in the High Court of Chancery, to be paid to the said Hospital by the Mayor, and Commonalty, and Citizens of the City of London; And of the yearly Sum of One hundred Pounds to the said Hospital for ever, pursuant to the said Decree. [*Lond. 1712*], *F°*. L.

1776 The Case of Stephen Creagh of London, Merchant, Agent for the Major-part of the Officers and Seamen lately Serving on Board the Duke and Duchess, Two Private Men of War. *n.p.* [*1712*], *s. sh. F°*. L.

Endorsed: Mr. Creagh's Case against the General Clause relating to Agencies for Seamen, added to the Bill for Collecting the Duties to Greenwich-Hospital.

1777 Reasons for Supporting the under-written Clause, in the Greenwich-Hospital Bill. *n.p.* [*1712*], *s. sh. F°*. L.

Endorsed: Reasons for Retaining of the Clause in the Greenwich-Hospital Bill, relating to Agencies.

1778 A Bill for the Erecting a Corporation for the Speedy Finishing the Hospital, and Establishing, Perpetuating and Management of the Charity of the Skippers and Keel-men of the Town and County of Newcastle upon Tyne. *n.p.* [*1712*], *F°*. L.

1779 The Case of the Poor Keel-men at Newcastle. *n. p.* [*1712*], *s. sh. F°*. L.

Endorsed: The Case of the Keel-men of Newcastle. On their hospital.

1780 The Case of Charles Atkinson, John Johnson, John Simpson, and great Numbers of the Trading Hoast-men, commonly called Fitters, of the Town and County of New-Castle upon Tyne. *n.p.* [*1712*], *s. sh. F°*. L.

1781 [DEFOE, DANIEL]. The Case of the Poor Skippers and Keel-men of Newcastle. *n.p.* [*1712*], *s. sh. F°*. O.

The attribution is Professor J. R. Moore's. Reprinted in *Extracts from the Records of the Company of Hostmen of Newcastle-upon-Tyne*, ed. by F. W. Dendy, 1901.

1782 The Case of the Poor Skippers and Keel-men of New-Castle, Truly Stated: with Some Remarks on a Printed Paper, call'd and pretended to be their Case. *n.p.* [*1712*], *s. sh. F°*. L.

1783 [DEFOE, DANIEL]. A Farther Case Relating to the Poor Keel-men of Newcastle. *n.p.* [*1712*], *s. sh. F°*. L.

Attribution by Professor J. R. Moore. Reprinted by F. W. Dendy, op. cit. in no. 1781, p. 175.

1784 Reasons humbly offer'd against Repealing the Act made in 21 Jac. Primi, Cap. 19. Describing Bankrupts. *n.p.* [*1712*], *s. sh. F°*. LLI.

Endorsed: The Case of the Creditors of James Boddington, with Relation to the Statute 21 James I. touching Arrests.

1785 A Bill for making more effectual an Act passed in the Eighth Year of Her Majesty's Reign, entituled, An Act for vesting the Estate and Effects of John Coggs and John Dann, Goldsmiths and Co-partners, in Trustees, for the speedier Payment of their Creditors, and for determining Differences thereupon; and for the more effectual vesting the Estates and Effects of Thomas Pitkin and Thomas Brerewood, still standing out, in Trustees, for the Use and Benefit of the Creditors of the said John Coggs and John Dann. *n.p.* [*1712*], *F°*. M (Cr).

1786 The Case of the Poor Prisoner for Debt and Damages. *n.p.* [*1712?*], *s. sh. F°*. LLI.

1787 The Cries of the Oppressed, Humbly Submitted to the Serious Consideration of the Honourable the House of Commons: or The very Hard Case of Insolvent and other Miserable Debtors set forth in their proper Colours; whereby the Nation may see it is every Man's Concern to prevent this Grand Grievance in England. It being a Trip newly taken to the Queens Bench, the Fleet, and to all the Prisons within the Weekly Bills of Mortality, setting forth the Barbarous Villanies of Bumbs, Gaolers, Judges Clarks, Lawyers, &c. *Lond. 1712*, *4°*. O.

1788 The Deplorable Case of the poor People in the Mint, humbly Offer'd to the Charitable Consideration of the Honourable, the Commons of Great Britain in Parliament Assembled. *n.p.* [*1712?*], *s. sh. F°*. O.

1789 The Present State of the Prison of Ludgate. Fully Discovering all its Customs, Priviledges, and Advantages, whereby it exceeds all other Prisons, and particularly shewing what Treatment the Prisoners meet with from their first Entrance to their Discharge.... *Lond.* [*1712?*], *8°*. L.

The dedication signed: Philopolites.

1790 LONDON. Commun' Concil' tent' in Camera Guihald'....An Act concerning Foreigners. [*Lond. 1712*], *F°*. L.

1791 For the Benefit of Trade. A True List of the Names of Persons Protected by Ambassadors, and other Foreign Ministers: Also a True List of Protections granted by the Lords and Commons in Parliament, as Entered in the Sheriff of Middlesex's Office.... *Lond. 1712*, *s. sh. F°*. OUP.

1792 Report of the Committee, to whom it was referr'd to consider of and prepare Heads of a Bill, for a further Redress of whatever shall be found Amiss in the Present Constitution of the Governours of the Queen's Bounty to the Poor Clergy; and in the Collecting and Managing the Revenue of First Fruits and Tenths, &c. *Lond.* [*1712?*] *F°*. O.

1793 An Apology for the Clergy of the City of Bristol. In their Petitioning an Act of Parliament, for their better and more certain Maintenance. In a Letter to a Gentleman of Bristol. *Lond. 1712*, *8°*. O.

1794 A Letter from a Free-Man of Bristol, to Joseph Earl, Esq; Member of Parliament for that City; in relation to the Clergy's Petition, &c. *n.p. 1712*, *8°*. O.

Signed: Philo-Bristolii.

1795 Reasons offer'd to the Inhabitants of Bristol, against a Tax Solicited for by the Clergy thereof, containing Notes on some Animadversions, Subscrib'd by above Four Hundred of the Inhabitants, most of 'em Members of the Church of England, about Sixty Years ago: With the Animadversions themselves on the other side. *n.p. 1712*, *s. sh. F°*. O.

1796 The Petition that was presented by the Sailors Wives to Her Majesty, and the Honourable House of Commons, for their Husbands Pay. Together with her Majesty's Answer thereto. *Lond.* [*1712?*], *s. sh. F°*. L.

1797 Articles agreed upon by the Workmen of the University Printing-House, Oxford, whose Names are hereunto Subscribed the First Day of March, in the Year of our Lord $17\frac{11}{12}$. for the more effectual carrying on the Contribution, begun the First Day of March, in the Year of our Lord $170\frac{7}{8}$ for the Purposes herein after mentioned. *n.p.* [*1712*], *s. sh. F°*. O.

A scheme for widows' and orphans' pensions.

1798 A Bill for the better and more effectual Supplying the Town and Borough of Boston, in the County of Lincoln, with Fresh Water. *n.p.* [*1712*], *F°*. L.

1713

GENERAL

1799 [DEFOE, DANIEL]. A General History of Trade, and Especially Consider'd as it Respects the British Commerce, as well at Home, as to all Parts of the World. With Essays upon the Improvement of Our Trade in Particular. To be Continued Monthly. *Lond. 1713, 8°.* LU.

Published for June, July, Aug. and Sept. For authorship see *C.B.E.L.* II, 502.

1800 Reasons for Dissolving the Treaty of Union betwixt Scotland and England. In a Letter to a Scots Member of Parliament from one of his Electors. *n.p.* [*1713*], *8°.* E.

AGRICULTURE

1801 A Bill for making Inclosures of some Part of the Common-Grounds in the West-Riding of the County of York, for the Endowing Poor Vicarages and Chapelries, for the better Support of their Ministers. *n.p.* [*1713*], *F°.* O.

1802 Reasons Humbly Offered to the Consideration of this Honourable House, for Passing the Bill for Repealing a Clause in an Act of the Thirteenth of King Charles the Second, Entitled, An Act for Confirmation of certain Decrees of Sewers, made by the Commissioners for the Limits of the Level of the River of Ancholme in the County of Lincoln; And that the said Level may be liable to the Laws of Sewers. *n.p.* [*1713*], *s. sh. F°.* O.

1803 [STRINGER, MOSES]. Opera Mineralia Explicata: or, the Mineral Kingdom, within the Dominions of Great Britain, display'd. Being a Compleat History of the Antient Corporations of the City of London, of and for the Mines, the Mineral and the Battery Works. With all the original Grants, Leases, Instruments...as also the Records of the said Mineral Courts, from the Conquest, down to this present Year, 1713. Likewise Proposals for New Settlements and Plentiful Provision for All the Industrious Poor....By M.S. M.D. *Lond.* [*1713*], *8°.* L.

The author's name is given in full in the introduction.

1804 [NORTH, ROGER]. A Discourse of Fish and Fish Ponds...Done by a Person of Honour. *Lond. 1713, 8°.* L.

Another edn. 1714 (Kress 2915); 2nd edn. 1715 (L); another edn. 1773, with author's name (Westwood & Satchell, p. 157). Reprinted in no. 3562.

1805 [CHOLMONDELEY, DANIEL]. A Proposal for Granting Annuities to Raise a Stock for Improving the Fishery of Great-Britain. In a Method as Advantagious, and on a Fund as good, well and secured, as ever was offered in any Age or Country. *Printed for the Author*, *Lond. 1713*, *4°*. MP.

Another edn. Printed for J. Read, 1713 (MP). For authorship see the *Articles of Settlement*, 1714.

1806 CHOLMONDELEY, DANIEL. A Proposal for Improving the Fishery of Great-Britain, and Supplying such as have Jointures and Fortunes too Small for their Occasions; and for Supporting Widows and Orphans, and Indigent and Infirm Persons, by granting Annuities upon the following Articles and Conditions. *Lond. 1713*, *4°*. L.

The author's name is given on p. 3.

MANUFACTURES

1807 [JENNINGS, RICHARD]. Fact against Scandal: or, a Collection of Testimonials, Affidavits, and other Authentick Proofs, in Vindication of Mr. Richard Jenings, Carpenter, Langley Bradley, Clock-Maker, and Richard Phelps Bell-Founder: To be referr'd to in an Answer which will speedily be publish'd to a late false and malicious Libel, Entituled; Frauds and Abuses at St. Paul's. To which is added, An Appendix relating to Mr. Jones, and Mr. Spencer; and the Copy of a certain Agreement between the Minor-Canons, &c. of the said Cathedral. *Lond. 1713*, *8°*. LG.

For authorship see Jane Lang, *Rebuilding St. Paul's*, 1956, p. 251.

1808 [BATEMAN, THOMAS]. An Answer to a Pamphlet entitul'd Frauds and Abuses at St. Paul's. With an Appendix relating to the Revenues and Repairs of that Cathedral. *Lond. 1713*, *8°*. LG.

For authorship see Jane Lang, *Rebuilding St. Paul's*, 1956, p. 251.

1809 An Abstract of an Answer lately published to a Pamphlet intitled Frauds and Abuses at St. Paul's. *Lond. 1713*, *12°*. LG.

1810 [HARE, FRANCIS]. A Continuation of Frauds and Abuses at St. Paul's, wherein is consider'd at large, the Attorney General's Report, in Relation to a Prosecution of Mr. Jenings the Carpenter: in Answer to Fact against Scandal. With some Remarks on the Second Part of the same Work, Entitul'd an Answer to Frauds, &c. In a Postscript. *Lond. 1713*, *8°*. LG.

For authorship see Jane Lang, *Rebuilding St. Paul's*, 1956, p. 251.

1811 [BATEMAN, THOMAS and JENNINGS, RICHARD]. The Second Part of Fact against Scandal; in Answer to a Pamphlet intitled a Continuation of Frauds and Abuses at St. Paul's. *Lond. 1713*, *8°*. LG.

For authorship see Jane Lang, *Rebuilding St. Paul's*, 1956, p. 251.

1812 To the Honble the House of Commons, The Case of the Spanish Leather-Dressers. *n.p.* [*1713?*], *s. sh. F°*. O.

For a bill for 'preventing other than Leather, Silk, Satten, or Velvet, to be made into the upper part of Shoes'.

1813 The Case of the Manufacturers and Traders in Packthread, Twine and Netting. Humbly offer'd to the Consideration of the House of Commons. *n.p.* [*1713*], *s. sh. F°*. O.

For additional duties on foreign packthread.

1814 Reasons Humbly Offered for Encouraging the Manufacture of Pitch and Tar from Roch or Roof-Stone, within the Kingdom of Great-Britain. *n.p.* [*1713*], *F°*. LU.

1815 The Case of the Manufacturers of British Sail-Cloth. *n.p.* [*1713*], *s. sh. F°*. LU.

1816 Reasons for Encouraging the Manufacturing of Sail-Cloth in Great Britain. *n.p.* [*1713*], *s. sh. F°*. LU.

Another edn. [1713] (LU) adds eight new paragraphs to the five of the original edn.

1817 Proposals Humbly Offer'd for the better Employing of the Poor, by Encouraging the Manufactory of Sail-Cloth in Great Britain. *n.p.* [*1713*], *s. sh. F°*. LU.

1818 [La Caille, Jean De]. The History of the Art of Printing, containing an account of it's Invention and Progress in Europe....And a Preface by the Publisher [James Watson] to the Printers in Scotland. *Edin. 1713*, *8°*. O.

The preface has an account of contemporary printing practice in Scotland.

1819 The Humble Representation of the Clothiers of Great Britain, For the Improving and Encouraging our Home Trade and Manufactures, Recommended by Her Majesty's Speech. *n.p.* [*1713*], *s. sh. F°*. LU.

Endorsed: The Case of the Clothiers.

1820 Donaldson, James. A Panegyrick upon the Most Honourable, Ancient and Excellent Art of Wright-Craft. *Edin. 1713*, *4°*. L.

In verse.

COMMERCE

1821 Advice to the Livery-Men of London: shewing that it is for their interest and honour, to chuse Merchants in Trade, for their Representatives in Parliament.... *Lond. 1713*, *8°*. L.

1822 The Naked Truth. *n.p.* [*1713*], *s. sh. F°*. LU.

On the English export trade, with especial reference to woollens.

1823 By the Queen, A Proclamation, For Altering the Stamp for Hydes and Skins to be Imported. *Lond. 1713*, *F°*. L.

Dated: 15 April [1713]. Another edn. relating to Scotland (L).

1824 By the Lords Justices and Council of Ireland, a Proclamation For the better Performance of Quarentine. *Dublin*, *1713*, *F°*. DPRO.

Dated: 15 Sept. 1713.

1825 Tractatus Navigationis et Commerciorum....Treaty of Navigation and Commerce between...Anne...Queen of Great Britain...and...

Lewis the XIVth, the most Christian King, Concluded at Utrecht the $\frac{31}{11}$ Day of $\frac{\text{March}}{\text{April}}$ 1713. *Lond. 1713, 4°.* LU.

1826 A Collection of Petitions presented to the Honourable House of Commons against the Trade with France: viz. I. The Course of Exchange between London and Paris before the Revolution....II. The Case of the Manufacturers of Gilt and Silver Wire. III. Some Reasons Humbly offered to the Consideration of Both Houses of Parliament; shewing, The Necessity for making a Law this present Sessions of Parliament, to oblige all Foreign Plain Black Silks to be imported at the Port of London, &c. IV. An Account of the Woollen Manufacture Made in the Province of Languedoc, and at Abbeville, in Picardy. V. The Case of the Woollen Manufacturers of Great Britain, and of the Poor they Imploy, &c. VI. Particulars wherein the Bill for laying the Trade to Africa Free and Open, takes away and destroys the Property of the African Company and their Creditors.... VII. The Case of the Clothiers, with Reference to their several Petitions. *Lond. 1713, 8°.* L.

A collected edn. of no. 1837, 1831, 1853, 1829, 1834, 1886 and 1830.

1827 [Janssen, Sir Theodore]. General Maxims in Trade, particularly applied to the Commerce between Great Britain and France. *Lond. 1713, 8°.* LU.

Reprinted, with author's name, in *Somers Tracts*, xiii (1815), 287.

1828 The Tarif settled by the French King and Council, September 18, 1664. Shewing the Duties agreed to be paid upon the several Sorts of Merchandizes, Goods, Wares, &c. being the Growth, Product and Manufactures of Great Britain, which should be imported from England into France. *Lond. 1713, 12°.* L.

Another edn. Edin. 1713, 4° (LU); another edn. Glasgow, 1713, 4° (E).

1829 An Account of the Woollen Manufactures made in the Province of Languedoc, and at Abbeville, in Picardy. *n.p.* [*1713*], *s. sh. F°.* LU.

Published in opposition to the free trade clauses of the Treaty of Utrecht.

1830 The Case of the Clothiers, with Reference to their several Petitions. *n.p.* [*1713*], *s. sh. F°.* LU.

Hopes that the treaty with France will not adversely affect the export trade to Portugal.

1831 The Case of the Manufacturers of Gilt and Silver Wire. Humbly offer'd to the Honourable House of Commons. *n.p.* [*1713*], *s. sh. F°.* LU.

Against the reduction of duties on French wire.

1832 The Case of the Parish of St Giles Criplegate, Before the Act for laying a Duty on Gilt and Silver Wire. *n.p.* [*1713*], *s. sh. F°.* LU.

To import foreign wire will ruin the trade, already in a poor state.

1833 The Case of the Silk-Weavers, Humbly Offered to the Consideration of both Houses of Parliament. *n.p.* [*1713*], *s. sh. F°.* LU.

Against the 8th and 9th clauses of the Treaty of Utrecht.

1834 The Case of the Woollen Manufacturers of Great Britain, and of the Poor they employ, in relation to a Trade with France. *n.p.* [*1713*], *s. sh. F°*. LU.

1835 Cautions to those who are to Chuse Members to serve in Parliament. To which is added a List of those that Voted For and Against the Bill or Commerce, as Publish'd in a late Pamphlet intituled, A Letter from a Member of the House of Commons to his Friend in the Country, &c. *Lond. 1713, 8°*. L.

1836 [DEFOE, DANIEL]. Considerations upon the Eighth and Ninth Articles of the Treaty of Commerce and Navigation, now publish'd by Authority. With some Enquiries into the Damages that may accrue to the English Trade from them. *Lond. 1713, 8°*. LU.

For authorship see *C.B.E.L.* II, 502.

1837 The Course of Exchange between London and Paris before the Revolution: or, A Demonstration that our Bullion was then Exported upon the Ballance of our Trade with France. *Lond. 1713, F°*. M (Cr).

1838 [WITHERS, JOHN]. The Dutch Better Friends than the French, to the Monarchy, Church, and Trade of England. In a Letter from a Citizen to a Country Gentleman. *Lond. 1713, 8°*. O.

2nd, 3rd and 4th edns. 1713 (all L). For authorship see ms. note on L copy of the 4th edn.

1839 The Eight and Ninth Articles of the Treaty of Commerce, with Relation to the Trade of Scotland with France, Considered, in a Letter from a Member of Parliament, to a Member of the Royal Burrows, with a Postscript in Answer to a Letter, directed to the Author of the Mercator. *Edin. 1713, F°*. E.

Another edn. Lond. 1713, 8° (E).

1840 [DEFOE, DANIEL]. An Essay on the Treaty of Commerce with France: With necessary Expositions. *Lond. 1713, 8°*. LU.

2nd edn. 1713 (D). For authorship see *C.B.E.L.* II, 502.

1841 [ADDISON, JOSEPH]. The Late Tryal and Conviction of Count Tariff. *Lond. 1713, 8°*. LU.

Another edn., 'Trial' in title, 1713, s. sh. F° (O); another edn., 'Tryal' in title, 1714, 8° (LU). Reprinted in Addison's *Works*, 1721.

1842 A Letter from a Member of Parliament to a Friend in the Country. With a List of those who voted for and against the Bill of Trade and Commerce: Also a Copy of the Bill. *Lond. 1713, 8°*. LU.

1843 [DEFOE, DANIEL]. A Letter from a Member of the House of Commons to his Friend in the Country, relating to the Bill of Commerce. With a True Copy of the Bill, and an Exact List of all those who voted for and against Engrossing it. *Lond. 1713, 8°*. LU.

For authorship see *C.B.E.L.* II, 502.

1844 Remarks on a Scandalous Libel, entitil'd a Letter from a Member of Parliament, &c. relating to the Bill of Commerce. In which the Trade with France is Consider'd, and the Falsities and Absurdities of the Mercator are Expos'd. To which is added, A Caution to the Freeholders of Great Britain in their Approaching Elections. And an exact List of this House of Commons, under several Distinctions. *Lond. 1713, 8°.* LU.

2nd and 3rd edns. 1713 (both L).

1845 A Letter to a West-Country Clothier and Freeholder, concerning the Parliament's Rejecting the French Treaty of Commerce, by way of Advice, in the Ensuing Elections. With a List of those that Voted For the Bill. [*Lond.*], *1713, 8°.* LU.

1846 A Letter to Sir R—— H—— wherein is considered, what Effect the Repeal of those Laws which now regulate our Commerce with France are likely to have on the Trade and Manufactures of England. *Lond. 1713, 8°.* LU.

Sir R—— H—— = Sir Richard Hoare.

1847 A List of the Names of all the Commodities of English Product and Manufacture, that was Exported to France from England during what may be call'd the Interval of Peace from Christmas 1698, to Christmas 1702. [Followed by 'A List of the Names of all the Commodities Re-Exported to France from England...'.] *Lond. 1713, F°.* LU.

Endorsed: A List of Goods sent from England to France.

1848 [Defoe, Daniel]. Memoirs of Count Tariff, &c. *Lond. 1713, 8°.* LU.

For authorship see *C.B.E.L.* II, 502.

1849 [Defoe, Daniel]. Mercator: or, Commerce Retrieved, being Considerations on the State of the British Trade; particularly as it respects Holland, Flanders, and the Dutch Barrier; the Trade to and from France, the Trade to Portugal, Spain, and the West-Indies, and the Fisheries of Newfound-Land, and Nova Scotia: With other Matters and Advantages accruing to Great Britain by the Treaties of Peace and Commerce, lately concluded at Utrecht...no. 1-181 26 May 1713–20 July 1714. *Lond. 1713,14, F°.* LU.

For authorship see *C.B.E.L.* II, 510.

1850 [Defoe, Daniel]. Extracts from several Mercators; being Considerations on the State of the British Trade. *Dublin, 1713, 4°.* L.

1851 The British Merchant; or, Commerce Preserv'd: In Answer to The Mercator, or Commerce Retriev'd. no. 1–103 [for 102] 7 Aug. 1713–30 July 1714. *Lond. 1713,14, F°.* LU.

Edited by Charles King. Another edn. 1721, 8°, with editor's name (L); 2nd edn. 1743 (L); 3rd edn. 1748 (LU).

1852 [Defoe, Daniel?]. Some Further Observations on the Treaty of Navigation and Commerce, between Great-Britain and France; and on the Scheme of the French Trade, from 1668, to 1669. *n.p.* [*1713*], *F°.* LU.

Another edn. Lond. 1713, 8° (LU); 2nd edn. Lond. 1713, 8° (E). Attributed to Defoe in *C.B.E.L.* II, 502. The attribution is rejected by Professor J. R. Moore.

1853 Some Reasons Humbly Offer'd to the Consideration of both Houses of Parliament; Shewing, the Necessity for making a Law this present Sessions of Parliament, to oblige all foreign plain Black Silks to be Imported at the Port of London, to be there Seal'd and Mark'd, after the Duties laid thereon shall be paid; and for obliging all plain Black Silks manufactured here to be Mark'd or Seal'd before expos'd to Sale. *n.p.* [*1713?*], *s. sh. F°*. L.

Endorsed: Reasons for Obtaining a Seal to Mark all plain Black Silks.

1854 [DEFOE, DANIEL]. Some Thoughts upon the Subject of Commerce with France. By the Author of the Review. *Lond. 1713, 8°*. LU.

For authorship see *C.B.E.L.* II, 502.

1855 The State of the Silk and Woollen Manufacture, considered: in Relation to a French Trade. *n.p.* [*1713*], *F°*. O.

1856 The State of the Silk and Woollen Manufacture, considered: in relation to a French Trade. Also the Case of the Silk-Weavers, Humbly Offered to the Consideration of Both Houses of Parliament. Likewise the Case of the Parish of St Giles Criplegate, before the Act for laying a Duty on Gilt and Silver Wire. *Lond. 1713, 8°*. O.

All three had previously been published separately (no. 1855, 1833, 1832).

1857 Torism and Trade Can never Agree. To which is added, An Account and Character of the Mercator and his writings. Particularly his former Discourses against the Land-Interest, and a Trade with France. In a Letter to Sir G—— H——. *Lond.* [*1713*], *8°*. LU.

Charles Davenant is here wrongly taken to be the editor of Mercator.

1858 [DEFOE, DANIEL]. The Trade of Scotland with France, Consider'd; in Two Letters directed to the Author of the Mercator. *Edin. 1713, 4°*. LU.

Attribution by Professor J. R. Moore.

1859 The Trade with France, Italy, Spain and Portugal, considered: With some Observations on the Treaty on Trade between Great Britain and France. *n.p.* [*1713*], *F°*. LU.

Another edn. Lond., 1713, 8°, pp. 23 (LU); 4th edn. 1713, 8° (RU); another edn. Lond. 1713, 8°. pp. 16 (LU). Reprinted in *Somers Tracts*, XII (1815), 293. Attributed to Defoe in *C.B.E.L.* II, 502, but rejected by Professor J. R. Moore.

1860 The Consequences of a Law for Reducing the Dutys upon French Wines, Brandy, Silks and Linen, to those of other Nations. With Remarks on a Paper, entitled, Mercator, or Commerce Retriev'd, No. 3. *n.p.* [*1713*], *F°*. LU.

Another edn. Lond. 1713, 8° (L).

1861 Reasons Humbly Offered by the Merchants Trading to Italy, Spain and Portugal, against Lowering the Duties on French Wines equal to those of Italy, Spain and Portugal. *n.p.* [*1713*], *s. sh. F°*. O.

Another edn., with an additional paragraph and entitled: Reasons Humbly Offer'd by the Merchants Trading to Spain and Portugal against the Bill for suspending the Duty of 25 l. per Tun on French Wines, [1713] (LU).

1862 The Case of the Merchants trading to Italy, and other Parts in the Mediterranean, and the Traders in Raw and Thrown Silks. *n.p.* [*1713*], *s. sh. F*°. LU.

For 'a farther Duty on all Foreign Wrought Silks'.

1863 A Calculation of the Species and Value of the Manufactures and Products of Great-Britain, Newfoundland, and Ireland, Annually Exported to the Port of Leghorn. *n.p.* [*1713*], *s. sh. F*°. LU.

1864 A True List of the several Ships arrived at Leghorne from Great Britain, Ireland, and Newfoundland, in One Year, commencing at Lady-Day, 1712, to Lady-Day, 1713. *n.p.* [*1713*], *s. sh. F*°. O.

1865 Declaratio et Sponsio de Juribus & Privilegiis Mercatorum Britannicorum in Regno Siciliae, facta Ultrajecti Die $\frac{25 \text{ Februarii}}{8 \text{ Martii}}$ Anno $17\frac{12}{13}$. Declaration and Engagement concerning the Rights and Privileges of the British Merchants in the Kingdom of Sicily.... *Lond. 1713*, *4*°. L.

Followed by: Reglement Provisional du Commerce dans les Pay-Bas Espagnols, Fait à Utrecht le $\frac{15}{26}$ Jour de Juillet, 1713.

1866 Carter, Richard and Ellers, Peter. A Scheme for an Effectual Method to prevent the Exportation of Wooll. *n.p.* [*1713*], *4*°. O.

Title taken from endorsement. Another issue Lond. 1713 (L).

1867 By the Queen, A Proclamation, For Putting in Execution the Laws and Statutes of this Realm, For the Preventing the Exportation of Wooll, Wooll-Fells, Woollen-Yarn, Mortlings, Shorlings, Wooll-Flocks, Fullers-Earth, and Fulling-Clay. *Lond. 1713*, *F*°. L.

Dated: 18 October 1713. Another edn. Edin. 1713 (ES).

1868 A Bill for Establishing the Trade to Africa Free and Open to all Her Majesty's Subjects of Great Britain, and the Plantations. *n.p.* [*1713*], *F*°. M (Cr).

1869 An Account of the Ships Employed in the African Trade, from the Ports of London and Bristol, belonging to the Separate Traders to Africa; with the Value of the said Ships and Cargoes, and the Number of Negroes usually carried by the said Ships. *n.p.* [*1713*], *s. sh. F*°. O.

1870 A Detection of the gross Falsities which the Separate Traders to Africa endeavour to impose on the Publick, by a printed Paper, intituled, An Account of the Ships imployed in the African Trade, &c. *n.p.* [*1713*], *s. sh. F*°. O.

1870A [Defoe, Daniel]. A Brief Account of the Present State of the African Trade. *Lond. 1713*, *8*°. L.

1871 The Case of about One Thousand African-Creditors now united with the Company, by virtue of the late Act of Parliament. *n.p.* [*1713*], *s. sh. F*°. LU.

1872 The Case of John Leadstone, a Private Trader residing in Africa. *n.p.* [*1713*], *s. sh. F*°. LU.

On the oppressions of the Royal African Company.

1873 The Case of the African Company's Property to the Trade and Settlements in Africa, justly distinguished. With Some Reasons for the Bill now before this House for Establishing that Trade Free and Open. *n.p.* [*1713*], *s. sh. F°*. LU.

1874 The Case of the City of Bristol, and all the Outports, in respect to Trade, especially to that of Africa. *n.p.* [*1713*], *s. sh. F°*. LLI.

1875 The Case of the Creditors of the African Company, and of the Company United with them. *n.p.* [*1713*], *s. sh. F°*. O.

1876 The Case of the Creditors of the Royal African-Company, now Incorporated with the said Company, humbly represented to the Honourable the House of Commons. *n. p.* [*1713*], *s. sh. 4°*. O.

1877 The Case of the Creditors of the Royal African-Company. *n.p.* [*1713?*], *s. sh. F°*. LU.

1878 The Case of the National Traders to Africa. *n.p.* [*1713*], *s. sh. F°*. LLI.

1879 Some Remarks on a False and Scurrilous Libel, intituled, The Case of the National Traders to Africa. *n.p.* [*1713*], *s. sh. F°*. LLI.

1880 The Case of the Woollen Manufacturers of the Western Counties, particularly Cornwall and Devon: As it relates to the Trade to Africa. *n.p.* [*1713*], *s. sh. F°*. LU.

1881 Copy of the Royal African-Company's Letter to the Mayor, Aldermen and Common-Council of the City of Bristol, dated London, the 26th of February, $17\frac{12}{13}$. *n.p.* [*1713*], *s. sh. F°*. O.

1882 A Defence of the African Company's Creditors. *n.p.* [*1713*], *s. sh. F°*. LU.

1883 Extract of divers Passages relating to Exclusive Joint-Stock Companies, taken from Monsieur De Witt's [or rather P. de la Court's] Treatise of the True Interest and Political Maxims of Holland and West-Friesland...translated into English in the Year 1702. *n.p.* [*1713?*], *F°*. L.

Against the Royal African Company.

1884 Extract out of the Report of the Lords Commissioners of Trade, laid before the House of Commons in $170\frac{8}{9}$. setting forth the Fictitious and Real Accounts of the African Company, for the Ten per Cent. Duty, being Publick Money, and applicable only for maintaining our African Settlements: With their manner of Accounting on Oath for the same before the Cursitor Baron. As also the True Estimate of the Annual Charge of the British Settlements in Africa, as reported to the House. *n.p.* [*1713*], *F°*. LU.

1885 A Few Remarks upon the Royal African Company, in respect to their Trade and Settlements. *n.p.* *1713*, *s. sh. F°*. LU.

Endorsed: Some Remarks upon the Royal African Company, and Interlopers. 1713.

1886 Particulars wherein the Bill for laying the Trade to Africa Free and Open, takes away and destroys the Property of the African-Company and their Creditors, now united by an Act passed in the last Session of Parliament. *n.p.* [*1713*], *s. sh. F°.* LU.

Endorsed: Particulars Against the Bill for an Open Trade to Africa.

1887 An Answer to a Paper call'd Particulars against the Bill for an Open Trade to Africa: With some Presidents touching the laying Open Foreign Trades, by Act of Parliament. *n.p.* [*1713*], *s. sh. F°.* LU.

1888 The Planters Objections to the Bill Intitled, A Bill for Establishing the Trade to Africa, Free and Open to all Her Majesty's Subjects of Great Britain, and the Plantations. *n.p.* [*1713*], *s. sh. F°.* LU.

1889 The Present Case of the African Trade truly Stated, with Reasons for the Bill for Establishing the same now depending. *n.p.* [*1713*], *s. sh. F°.* LU.

1890 The Present State of the Royal African Company. *n.p.* [*1713*], *s. sh. F°.* O.

1891 Property derived under Charters and Grants from the Crown of England, not Inferior to Property derived under Grants from the Subjects of England. *n.p.* [*1713?*], *s. sh. F°.* O.

For the Royal African Company and its creditors.

1892 A Proposal for settling the Trade to Africa, wherein the Ends proposed to be aimed at, both by the Separate Traders, and the Company; and also by the North Britains, Out Ports and Plantations, and likewise by the Manufacturers, are effectually provided for. *n.p.* [*1713*], *s. sh. F°.* LU.

Endorsed: Proposals for settling the Trade to Africa. Another edn. 1714 (O).

1893 Resolutions of a General Court of the Adventurers of the Royal African Company, held on Thursday the 26th of February, $17\frac{12}{13}$. *n.p.* [*1713*], *s. sh. 4°.* O.

The Company will export goods to the value of £100,000 annually if their monopoly is maintained.

1894 Short Remarks on the Bill for a Free Trade to Africa. *n.p.* [*1713?*], *s. sh. F°.* O.

1895 The Case of the Merchants, and Planters, Trading to, and Residing in, Virginia and Maryland. *n.p.* [*1713*], *s. sh. F°.* L.

For lowering the tobacco duties.

1896 The Assiento; or Contract for Allowing to the Subjects of Great Britain the Liberty of Importing Negroes into the Spanish America. Sign'd by the Catholick King at Madrid, the Twenty sixth Day of March 1713. *Lond. 1713, 4°.* LU.

Text in Spanish and English in parallel columns. Reissued in 1726 (L).

1897 Report of the Committee elected to inspect the by-laws, &c. Deliver'd in to the General court of the United company of merchants of England, trading to the East-Indies, the 17th day of June 1713.... [*n.p.*, *1713*], *32·5 cm.* Kress S. 1358.

1898 East-India Company's Case, with Relation to the Separate Traders to the East-Indies. *n.p.* [*1713*], *s. sh. F*o. LU.

Title taken from endorsement.

1899 The Case of John Powell of London, Merchant; who Originally Contributed l. 3,700, towards raising Two Millions for the Service of the Crown of England, and Settling the Trade to the East-Indies, when the Publick Funds were under great Discounts. *n.p.* [*1713?*], *F*o. LU.

Endorsed: The Case of John Powell, of London, Merchant, Concerning the Oppressions he Suffers from the United Power of the East-India Company. And the Quotations of the Acts of Parliament relating thereunto.

1900 Mr. Powell's Proceedings in relation to his Petition in Parliament, last Sessions, against the Oppressions of the East-India Company, viz.... *n.p.* [*1713*], *s. sh. F*o. LLI.

Endorsed: A Brief of Mr. Powell's Proceedings....

COLONIES

1901 To All whom these Presents may Concern. *New-York*, *1713*, *F*o. LPRO.

On taxation.

1902 To the Inhabitants and Free-holders of Westchester County. *n.p.* [*1713*], *F*o. LPRO.

On taxation in New York.

1903 A Letter to a Member of the P——t of G——t-B——n, occasion'd by the Privilege granted by the French King to Mr. Crozat. *Lond.* *1713*, *8*o. L.

On the threat of Louisiana to the English colonies and commerce.

1904 [Cleland, William]. The Present State of the Sugar Plantations Consider'd; But more especially That of the Island of Barbadoes. *Lond.* *1713*, *8*o. LU.

Reissued, with dedication signed with author's name, 1714 (LU).

FINANCE

1905 Munus Thesaurarij; or, a Critical History of the Lord Treasurers of England, from the Reign of King Henry VI. to this Time. With some brief Observations on the usual Conduct and Management of that Employment, and the frequent Success that has attended therein. *Lond.* *1713*, *8*o. LU.

1906 The Case of the Proprietors of the Classis Orders for the Year 1711. *n.p.* [*1713*], *s. sh. F*o. LU.

1907 The Case of Alice Tuson, and many others of the poorest of the Proprietors, of certain Lands and Tenements, at Portsmouth and Chatham, which by a late Act of Parliament are Vested in Trustees for the Use of Her Majesty, for the better Securing the Harbours and Docks at those Places. *n.p.* [*1713*], *s. sh. F°*. O.

For payment.

1908 The Case of the Proprietors of certain Lands and Tenements by Act of Parliament vested in Trustees, for securing the Harbours and Docks at Portsmouth and Chatham. *n.p.* [*1713?*], *s. sh. F°*. L.

For payment.

1909 A State of Mr. Paterson's Claim upon the Equivalent, as founded on his Contract with the African and Indian Company of Scotland, on the 6th of November 1695.... *n.p. 1713*, *s. sh. F°*. GU.

1910 The Report on Mr. Paterson's Petition, July the 10th, 1713. *n.p.* [*1713*], *8°*. L.

Drawn up by a committee of the House of Commons.

1911 A View of Mr. Paterson's Claim upon the Equivalent. *n.p.* [*1713?*], *F°*. O.

1912 Parker, Ephraim. Proposals for a very Easie Tax to raise between Two and Three Millions of Money, per Annum, (if not a greater Sum) in the room of the Land-Tax, to begin to pay the Publick Debts.... Also Proposals for the further Encouraging the Woollen-Manufactures of this Kingdom in foreign Parts. *Lond. 1713*, *4°*. pp. 12. LU.

Advocating duties on silk, woollen, linen and cotton goods made in Great Britain. Another edn. Lond. n.d. pp. 8 (LU).

1913 A Scheme for raising 500,000 l. for the Use of Her Majesty, upon a Fund of 35,000 l. per Annum, for 32 Years, payable out of all the Funds for the Civil List. *Lond. 1713*, *s. sh. F°*. MC.

Endorsed: A Scheme of a Lottery for 500,000 l. at 100 l. per Ticket....

1914 Case of the Royal Boroughs of Scotland. *n.p.* [*1713?*], *F°*. O.

On their rights to apportion taxation.

1915 Lightbody, James. The Merchant's Directory for casting up Custom Duties and Drawbacks....Together with Tables of all Duties on Merchandizes ready cast up....Also Instructions for the better understanding the Book of Rates. Necessary for all Custom-House Officers. *Lond. 1713*, *8°*. L.

1916 Denneston, E. A Scheme for Advancing and Improving the Ancient and Noble Revenue of Excise upon Beer, Ale, and other Branches, to the Great Advantage of Her Majesty, and the general Good of Her Subjects. Discovering also the Frauds, Neglects and Abuses of the Brewers, Inn-keepers, Ale-Tappers, Gaugers, &c. which have occasion'd the scandalous Sinking of that Revenue. To which are added, Two other Schemes, for the better Security of it for the future. *Lond. 1713*, *4°*. LU.

1917 Reasons for Altering the New Duty of Thirty per Cent. ad Valorem upon Books Imported to a Duty of Twelve Shillings per Hundred Weight, Humbly offer'd to the Honourable House of Commons. *n.p.* [*1713*], *s. sh. F°.* LU.

1918 To the Honourable House of Commons. The Humble Representation of the Booksellers of London, and the Two Universities. *n.p.* [*1713*], *s. sh. F°.* O.

Against the additional duty of 30 per cent *ad valorem* imposed on books last session.

1919 A Case humbly offer'd to the Honourable House of Commons, on behalf of the Packers, &c. Concern'd in the Woollen Manufacture, in relation to Buckrams and Barras. *n.p.* [*1713*], *s. sh. F°.* L.

For exemption from the duty levied on linen.

1920 The Case of the Importers of Linnen and Linnen Drapers in London, as to the several Duties demanded on Linnens, Lawns, Neckcloths, Barras, and Buckrams Imported from Hambrough. *n.p.* [*1713*], *s. sh. F°.* LU.

Text begins: That by an Act passed the last Sessions of Parliament.

1921 An Abstract of the Act for laying Duties on Malt, Mum, Cyder and Perry, 1713: That is, so much thereof as relates to the Duties and Penalties appointed by the said Act. [*Edin. 1713*], *s. sh. F°.* L.

1922 A Letter from a Brewer in the City to a Justice of Peace in the Country, concerning the Malt Tax. [*Edin. 1713*], *F°.* E.

1923 [Defoe, Daniel]. Union and No Union. Being an Enquiry into the Grievances of the Scots. And how far they are right or wrong, who alledge that the Union is dissolved. *Lond. 1713, 8°.* L.

On the imposition of the malt tax on Scotland. For authorship see *C.B.E.L.* II, 502.

1924 The Case of the Poor Sailors (Captors of several Prizes) brought into Jamaica, and several other Inhabitants of the Island concern'd therein. *n.p.* [*1713*], *s. sh. F°.* LU.

On the bonds required for payment of the duties on prize goods.

1925 The Humble Address of the Governor, Council, and Assembly of Jamaica to the Queen; and some Instances of the Duties demanded on Prize Goods brought into that Island, by vertue of an Act, Entituled, An Act to Encourage the Trade to America for the future: With an Account and List of Bonds taken in the Collectors Office at Jamaica for the said Duties. *n.p.* [*1713?*], *F°.* LU.

Title taken from endorsement.

1926 Observations on, and Reasons against Vacating the Bonds taken by Her Majesty's Collector at Jamaica. *n.p.* [*1713*], *s. sh. F°.* LU.

1927 An Answer to some False and Malicious Objections given out, to prevent the Duties on Prize Goods being remitted, with some Observations. *n.p.* [*1713*], *s. sh. F°.* LU.

1928 Reasons humbly offfr'd [*sic*] for Allowing the Merchants, &c. of New-England, New-York, and Carolina, Relief upon the Dutys Paid on Prize-Goods, as those who have Bonded the same in other Colonies. *n.p.* [*1713?*], *s. sh. F°.* O.

1929 The Case of Sir John Lambert, Bar. Samuel Shepheard, and John James David, Merchants of London. Humbly offered to the Consideration of this Honourable House, for Relief. *n.p.* [*1713*], *s. sh. F°.* LU.

Endorsed: Sir John Lambert's Br. Mr. Shepheard's and Mr. David's Case relating to the Custom of their Wines taken by the French.

1930 Reasons humbly offered to the Honourable House of Commons, by the Wine-Merchants, against Payment of Interest on their Bonds, at the Custom-House, the Principal being paid. *n.p.* [*1713?*], *s. sh. F°.* LU.

Endorsed: The Wine-Merchants Reasons against Payment of Interest on their Bonds for Customs.

1931 To the Lord High Treasurer of Great Britain, the Case of James Lightbody, Inventor of Colour'd Stamps. Humbly submitted. *n.p.* [*1713*], *s. sh. F°.* L.

The stamps were those used in the duty on almanacks, etc. Lightbody had been dismissed.

1932 Reasons Humbly Offered for to oblige Robert Peter to deliver up his Estate and Effects for the Use of his Creditors, the Crown being first satisfied. *n.p.* [*1713*], *s. sh. F°.* O.

Endorsed: Reasons for obliging Robert Peter to deliver up his Estate for the Use of his Creditors. Peter had contracted large debts in clothing the Army. He was also Receiver General of the Land Tax for Hertfordshire.

1933 A Report from the Commissioners appointed to Take, Examine and State the Publick Accompts of the Kingdom. [Followed by: A Report from the Commissioners appointed to Take, Examine and Determine the Debts due to the Army, &c.] *n.p. 1713, 8°.* LU.

Some copies are wrongly dated 1703.

1934 N° 4. A Preamble to the Books for taking a Subscription of Ten Hundred Thousand Pounds for the Use of the Bank of England. *n.p. 1713, F°.* L.

TRANSPORT

1935 A Bill for making the River Neene alias Nine, running from Northampton to Peterborough, Navigable. *n.p.* [*1714*], *F°.* O.

1936 LONDON. Acts of Common-Council, concerning the Tackle-house and Ticket Porters, and Public Beams. [*Lond.*], *1712. F°.* L.

1713 in colophon.

1937 The Case and Petition of the Licensed Hackney Chair-men, and the Widows of such, in Behalf of themselves, and their Numerous Families, Residing within the Parishes of the Liberties of the City of Westminster. Humbly Offered to the Consideration of the Honourable House of Commons. *n.p.* [*1713*], *s. sh. F°.* L.

SOCIAL CONDITIONS

1938 LONDON. By the Mayor. *n.p.* [*1713*], *s. sh. F°*. LG.

An order for the arrest of rogues, vagabonds and sturdy beggars found in London, dated 16 June 1713.

1939 Bucks ss. Ad General' Quarterial' Session' Pac' Dominae Reginae tent' apud Aylesbury.... *n.p.* [*1713*], *s. sh. F°*. O.

An order of 16 July 1713 to remedy the evil practices and abuses of constables in passing vagrants through the county.

1940 An Account of the Corporation for the Poor of London; shewing the Nature, Usefulness, and Management of the Work-House in Bishops-gate-Street. And that the Relieving, Educating, and Setting Poor Children to Work therein, is one Principal Design of its Institution: and of great Advantage to the Publick. *Lond. 1713, 8°*. L.

Another edn. 1744 (O).

1941 An Abstract of several Acts of Parliament relating to the City of Norwich. I. The Act for the Erecting a Workhouse for maintaining the Poor. II. For Enlightning the Streets. III. For Erecting a Court of Conscience in the said city. Published by Order of the Clerk of the Workhouse. *Norwich, 1713, 8°*. L.

1942 [RITSCHEL, GEORGE]. An Account of Certain Charities: containing a Catalogue of several Benefactors, who have given or left any thing to Pious and Charitable Uses, as the Church, the Poor, or Free-Schools, in Tyndale-Ward, in the County of Northumberland.... *Newcastle upon Tyne, 1713, 8°*. L.

Another edn., Hexham, 1780 (NPL). Authorship inferred from preface.

1943 WILSON, THOMAS. An Account of the Foundation of the Royal Hospital of King Charles II$^{d.}$ near Dublin, for the Relief and Maintenance of the Antient and Infirm Officers, and Soldiers Serving in the Army of Ireland.... *Dublin, 1713, 8°*. L.

The dedication signed: Thomas Wilson. Later edition, 1725 (no. 3530).

1944 Reasons, humbly offered for a more Extensive Act for Discharge of Prisoners. *n.p.* [*1713*], *s. sh. F°*. O.

Endorsed: Miserere turn'd into Te Deum; or; Reasons....

1945 Reasons humbly offered to the Honourable House of Commons, For a more Extensive Act for Discharge of Prisoners. *n.p.* [*1713*], *s. sh. F°*. LU.

1946 Reasons Humbly Offered for Passing a Bill to give Leave for Will. Ellins, late of London, Merchant, and Co-partner with Edmund Farrington, to return to Great-Britain, in order to surrender himself to the Commissioners appointed for executing a Statute of Bankrupt Awarded against them. *n.p.* [*1713*], *s. sh. F°*. O.

1947 The present Lord Keeper, and Attorney General, their Reports to Her Majesty, in 1704. Touching the pretended Forfeiture of the Fleet Prison. *n.p.* [*1713?*], *s. sh. F°*. LG.

1948 The Case of the Chaplains of Her Majesty's Navy, most Humbly submitted to the Honourable House of Commons. *n.p.* [*1713*], *s. sh. F°*. LU.

For some provision in time of peace.

1949 The Case of the Remaining Part of the Masters Lately Employ'd in Her Majesties Royal Navy. Offered to the Honourable House of Commons. *n.p.* [*1713*], *s. sh. F°*. LU.

For some provision in time of peace.

1950 The Case of the Surgeons of Her Majesty's Royal Navy; Most Humbly Submitted to the Honourable House of Commons. *n.p.* [*1713?*], *s. sh. F°*. O.

For some provision in time of peace.

1951 The Case of the Surgeons of Her Majestys Navy, who shall be out of Employment during the Peace. *n.p.* [*1713?*], *s. sh. F°*. LLI.

1952 Ærarium Sacrum: or, a Proposal towards the Maintenance of the Widows of Beneficed Clergymen. Humbly Recommended to the Consideration of the Convocation; and the Corporation of Clergymens Sons. *Lond.* [*1713*], *8°*. L.

1953 At a Sessions of the Commissioners for Sewers, Pavements, &c. London, held at Guild-Hall, on Friday the Eighteenth day of December 1713. [*Lond. 1713*], *s. sh. F°*. LCRO.

Orders for cleaning the streets.

1954 Reasons Humbly Offered against Passing an Act for the better Preventing Mischeifs that might happen by Fire. *Dublin, 1713, s. sh. F°*. C.

1714

GENERAL

1955 An Essay upon Trade, and Publick Credit; shewing the Advantages of the East-India Prohibition, Bankrupts Affidavits, &c. Dedicated to Mr. T.S. an eminent Citizen, and an universal Merchant....The Second Edition Corrected. *Lond. 1714*, *8°*. L.

Signed: R. S——le.

1956 [MACKY, JOHN]. A Journey through England. In Familiar Letters from a Gentleman here, to his Friend Abroad. 2 vols. (A Journey through Scotland....Being the Third Volume, which compleats Great Britain....) *Lond. 1714, 22, 23, 8°*. L.

2nd edn. of vol. 1, 1722 (L); 3rd, 1723 (O); 4th, 1724 (O); 5th, 1732 (O); 2nd end. of vol. 2, 1724 (O); 3rd, 1732 (O); 2nd edn. of vol. 3, 1729 (L). For authorship see R. Gough, *British Topography*, 1780, 1, 39.

AGRICULTURE

1957 LAURENCE, JOHN. The Clergy-Man's Recreation: shewing the Pleasure and Profit of the Art of Gardening. *Lond. 1714, 8°*. L.

2nd edn. 1714; 3rd edn. 1715; 4th edn. 1716; 5th edn. 1717; 6th edn. 1726 (all L).

1958 The Case of the Land-Owners of the Levells of Havering and Dagnam, in the County of Essex. *n.p.* [*1714*], *s. sh. F°*. L.

For help in the repair of broken sea walls.

1959 An Account of Lead Mines producing Callamie, &c. on Durdham-Downe, near Bristol, in the County of Gloucester; with a Proposal for the Disposing of a small part thereof. *n.p.* [*1714*], *4°*. O.

1960 The Case of Mr. William Waller, in Relation to the Complaint of Edward Vaughan, Esq; a Member of this Honourable House. *n.p.* [*1714*], *s. sh. F°*. L.

Regarding mines in Montgomery leased by Vaughan to the Company of Mine Adventurers.

1961 The Articles of Settlement of the Benevolent Society, for granting Annuities to Raise a Stock for improving the Fishery of Great Britain. *Lond. 1714, 4°*. MP.

Daniel Cholmondeley is the promoter.

1962 Reasons humbly offered for the adding the Word Lobsters, to the Exception made to a Bill, Intituled, A Bill to prevent the Sale, within this Kingdom, of Fish, taken by Forreigners in Forreign Vessels. *n.p.* [*1714*], *s. sh. F°*. L.

MANUFACTURES

1963 The Draper's Bill, intitled, A Bill for Explaining and Amending the Act of the 10th Year of Her Majesty's Reign, relating to Medly Broad Cloth, &c. With the Clothiers Objections to the said Bill. *n.p.* [*1714*], *F°*. L.

1964 The Clothiers Proposal, to Satisfy the Woollen-Drapers in the Water-measure of Cloth. With some farther Overtures, for the Benefit and Improvement of the Woollen Manufactury of this Kingdom. Humbly Offered to the Parliament of Great Britain. *n.p.* [*1714*], *s. sh. F°*. O.

1965 The Clothiers Remarks upon the Bill, Intitled, A Bill for amending the Act of 10 Reginae relating to Medley Cloth, &c. Humbly offered to the Consideration of the Commons of Great Britain in Parliament assembled. *n.p.* [*1714*], *s. sh. F°*. L.

Endorsed: The Clothiers Remarks upon the Drapers Bill.

1966 The Clothiers Reasons for Petitioning the Commons of Great Britain in Parliament Assembled, for adding a Clause (effectually to oblige all Buyers of Cloth upon Credit, to give Notes that may carry Interest, from and after Six Months Date) to the Bill now depending, Entituled For Amending the Act of Decimo Reginae, relating to Medley Cloth, &c. *n.p.* [*1714*], *s. sh. F°*. O.

1967 More Queries, Humbly Offer'd to the Consideration of the Honourable House of Commons. *n.p.* [*1714*], *s. sh. F°*. O.

On the bill relating to medley broad-cloth.

1968 Reasons humbly offer'd against the Bill for explaining and amending the Act of the Tenth Year of Her Majesty's Reign, relating to Medly Broad-Cloth, and for making the said Act more effectual by other Means than are contained in that Bill. *n.p.* [*1714*], *s. sh. F°*. L.

1969 Reasons humbly offer'd, for Amending and Explaining an Act, made in the Tenth Year of Her Majesty's Reign, Intitled, An Act for Regulating, Improving and Encouraging the Woollen-Manufacture, of mixt or medly Broad Cloth, &c. *n.p.* [*1714*], *s. sh. F°*. L.

1970 Reasons propos'd to the Drapers by the Clothiers, For Amending and Explaining an Act made in the Tenth Year of Her Majesty's Reign, Entituled An Act for Regulating, Improving, and Encouraging the Woollen Manufacture of Mixt or Medly Broad-Cloth: Humbly Offer'd to the Consideration of the Honourable House of Commons, &c. *n.p.* [*1714*], *s. sh. F°*. O.

1971 To the Honourable the Knights, Citizens and Burgesses in Parliament Assembled. The humble Petition of the Cordwainers Inhabiting the Cities of London and Westminster, and Parts adjacent, in behalf of themselves and others of their Trade in the rest of the Kingdom. *n.p.* [*1714*], *s. sh. F°*. O.

Endorsed: The Humble Petition of the Cordwainers, &c. Against the draw-back on exported leather.

1972 Some Reasons Most Humbly offer'd to the Honourable House of Commons relating to the Shoe-makers Case, &c. *n.p.* [*1714*], *s. sh. F°*. L.

A drawback of 1½*d.* per lb. on exported shoes will not help them.

1973 The Case of the Thread-makers of Great Britain. *n.p.* [*1714*], *s. sh. F°*. L.

For the removal of the duty on imported brown linen yarn.

1974 HILL, AARON. The Dedication of the Beech-Tree to the Most Honourable the Earl of Oxford, Lord High Treasurer of Great Britain. Occasion'd by the late Discovery of making Oil from the Fruit of That Tree. [*Lond.*], *1714*, *F°*. O.

1975 HILL, AARON. An Impartial Account of the Nature, Benefit, and Design, of a New Discovery, and Undertaking, to make a Pure, Sweet, and Wholesome Oil, from the Fruit of the Beech Tree.... *Lond. 1714*, *8°*. L.

Another edn. 1714, entitled *An Account of a New Discovery to make Oil from the Fruit of the Beech Tree* (L).

1976 HILL, AARON. Proposals for Raising a Stock of One Hundred Thousand Pounds; for laying up great Quantities of Beech-Mast for Two Years; at an Interest of Forty-five Pounds per Cent. per Annum, to the Subscribers, and upon a Security whereby they will always have in their Hands, above Ten Times the Value of the Sum they Contribute.... *Lond. 1714*, *8°*. LU.

COMMERCE

1977 [POVEY, CHARLES?]. The Present State of Great Britain with respect to its Trade by Sea and Land, with Proposals for the improvement of both. *Lond. 1714*, *8°*. L.

W. T. Lowndes, in *The Bibliographer's Manual*, IV (1865), p. 1933, records under Povey's name *The Present State of Great Britain*. This may be that work.

1978 A Book of Fairs: or, A New Guide to the West-Country-Travellers: Shewing them all the Fairs in these Thirteen several Counties following, viz. Berk-shire, Cornwal, Dorset-shire, Devon-shire, Gloucester-shire, Glamorgan-shire, Hereford-shire, Hamp-shire, Monmouth-shire, Oxford-shire, Somerset-shire, Wilt-shire, Worcester-shire....The first Impression Reviv'd by Benjamin Seaward, of Somerton.... *Lond.* [*1714*], *8°*. EU.

1979 Reasons for Making Blackwell-Hall an Absolute Market, and Enacting the Clause for that Purpose. Humbly Offer'd to the Consideration of the Honourable House of Commons in Parliament Assembled. *n.p.* [*1714*], *s. sh. F°*. O.

1980 Reasons Humbly Offered for Passing the Bill for the better Preventing the Covering Alien Goods Imported. *n.p.* [*1714*], *s. sh. F°*. L.

1981 Reasons humbly offer'd against the Bill, for the better preventing the Covering of Alien Goods Imported. *n.p.* [*1714*], *s. sh. F°.* L.

1982 LONDON. Humfreys Mayor Martis XVI° die Novembris, 1714.... [*Lond. 1714*], *s. sh. F°.* LG.

An order prohibiting the sale of bad meat.

1983 The Case of the Fifteen Sea Coal-meters of the City of London, in Relation to their Deputies. *n.p.* [*1714?*], *4°.* M.

1984 Remarks upon the Case of the Fifteen Coal-Meeters of the City of London, in relation to their Deputies. Humbly Offered to the Consideration of the Right Honourable Sir Samuel Stanier Kt. Lord Mayor of the said City, and the Honourable the Aldermen of the same. By the Deputy Coal-Meeters of the said City. *Lond. 1714, 4°.* O.

1985 The Complaint & Address of the Under Coal-Meeters of London.... *Lond. 1714, 4°.* L.

1986 The Report and Order thereupon, made concerning the Coal-Meters, and their Deputies or Under-Meters. *Lond. 1714, F°.* L.

1987 The Case of the Merchants Trading in Tobacco, with relation to the Bill now depending in the Honourable House of Commons, for Lessening the Drawback on Tobacco Exported for Ireland. *n.p.* [*1714*], *s. sh. F°.* L.

1988 The Case of the Merchants who Export Tobacco. *n.p.* [*1714*], *s. sh. F°.* LU.

1989 Reasons humbly offer'd to the Honourable House of Commons, by the Merchants and Traders in Tobacco, with Relation to the Bill, now depending, for Lessening the Drawback, on Tobacco Exported to Ireland. *n.p.* [*1714*], *s. sh. F°.* O.

1990 To the Honourable the Knights, Commissioners of Shires, Citizens and Burgesses of Great Britain, in Parliament Assembled: The Humble Petition of John Rotherham. *n. p.* [*1714*], *s. sh. F°.* O.

On the bill for lessening the drawback on tobacco exported to Ireland.

1991 A Letter to the Honourable A[rthur] M[oo]re, Com[missio]ner of Trade and Plantation. *Lond. 1714, 8°.* LU.

With a folding sheet: 'A Scheme of the Trade... between England and France. London, 29 Nov. 1674.'

1992 Rates Payable by the Tariff of 1664. on all Goods and Merchandizes Imported into, or Exported from France: The Drugs and Spices set apart from the other Goods in the Importations, and the Names of both Alphabetically disposed. To which is prefix'd The King's Edict in the Month of September, 1664. Published by Order of the Lords Commissioners for Trade and Plantations. *Lond. 1714, 8°.* LU.

1993 [EGLETON, JOHN]. A Vindication of the late House of Commons, in Rejecting the Bill for Confirming the Eighth and Ninth Articles of the

Treaty of Navigation & Commerce between England and France.... By a Citizen. *Lond. 1714, 8º.* L.

L copy has the attribution in ms.

1994 Tractatus Navigationis et Commerciorum....Treaty of Navigation and Commerce between...Anne...Queen of Great Britain...and... Philip the Vth, the Catholick King of Spain, Concluded at Utrecht the $\frac{28}{9}$ Day of $\frac{\text{November}}{\text{December}}$ 1713. *Lond. 1714, 4º.* LU.

1995 The Humble Representation of the Right Honourable the Lords Spiritual and Temporal in Parliament Assembled, presented to Her Majesty on Wednesday the Seventh Day of July, 1714. With Her Majesties most gracious Answer. *Lond. 1714, Fº.* O.

On trade with Spain.

1996 The Case of the Distillers of London. *n.p.* [*1714*], *s. sh. Fº.* L.

Endorsed: The Distillers Case, In relation to Preventing the Defrauding Her Majesty of Her Duties, by Running of Foreign Brandies.

1997 The Merchants of London's Observations Humbly Offer'd against the Bill for the more Effectual Preventing the Running of Brandys. *n.p.* [*1714*], *s. sh. Fº.* O.

1998 An Answer to the Merchants Observations against Passing the Bill to prevent the Running of Foreign Brandies. *n.p.* [*1714*], *s. sh. Fº.* O.

1999 Reasons humbly offered to the Honourable House of Commons, for Relieving the Fair-Dealer in Pepper. *n.p.* [*1714*], *s. sh. Fº.* LU.

Against smuggling.

2000 CARTER, RICHARD, and ELLERS, PETER. Some Observations, shewing, wherein there are some Deficiencies in the Bill now depending, for Prevention of Running of Wool; humbly offered to the Consideration of the Honourable House of Commons. *n.p.* [*1714*], *s. sh. Fº.* L.

Endorsed: Some Observations concerning the Prevention of the Running of Wool....

2001 HAYNES, JOHN. Proposals humbly offered to the Honourable House of Commons, for the more effectual preventing the Exportation of Wool, &c. from England and Ireland into Foreign Parts. *n.p.* [*1714*], *s. sh. Fº.* O.

2002 PALMER, FRANCIS, THWAITES, THOMAS and WILMOTE, THOMAS. Proposals Humbly Offered to the Honourable House of Commons, For the Effectual Tracing the Wool of this Kingdom and Ireland from the Sheeps Back until the same be Manufactured. *n.p.* [*1714*], *s. sh. Fº.* L.

2003 PARKER, EPHRAIM. Proposals humbly offered to the Consideration of the Honourable House of Commons, for the more effectual preventing the Exportation of Wooll out of Great-Britain and Ireland. *n.p.* [*1714*], *s. sh. Fº.* L.

2004 By the Queen, A Proclamation, For Putting in Execution the Laws and Statutes of this Realm, for the Preventing the Exportation of Wooll, Wooll-Fells, Woollen-Yarn, Mortlings, Shorlings, Wooll-Flocks, Fullers-Earth, and Fulling-Clay. *Lond. 1714, F°.* L.

Dated: 21 June 1714.

2005 A Collection of all the Statutes now in Force, against the Transportation of Wooll, &c. With Notes in the Margin. *Lond. 1714, 12°.* LU.

2006 By the Queen, A Proclamation. *Lond. 1713* [*O.S.*], *F°.* L.

Dated: 17 January 1713. Respecting passes for trade with Algiers. Cr. 4535. Another edn. 1713 (LPC). Cr. 4536.

2007 By the King, A Proclamation, Requiring all Ships and Vessels, Trading from the Plantations in the way of the Algerines, to Furnish themselves with Passes. *Lond. 1714, s. sh. F°.* L.

Dated: 4 October 1714.

2008 Bleau, Robert. A Letter from One of the Royal African-Company's Chief Agents on the African Coasts. *n.p.* [*1714*], *s. sh. F°.* O.

Dated: Cape-Coast Castle. The 8th of December, 1713.

2009 At a General Court of the Adventurers of the Royal African Company of England, held at their House in Leadenhall-street, London, the 18th of February $17\frac{13}{14}$. where were present a great Number of the Adventurers, this following Scheme for an Additional Stock was twice Read, Debated, and unanimously Agreed to. *n.p.* [*1714*], *F°.* O.

Endorsed: A Scheme for an Additional Stock to the Royal African-Company by Subscription....

2010 An Abstract of several Cases relating to the Trade to Africa. *n.p.* [*1714*], *F°.* O.

Endorsed: The Case of the Merchants Trading to Africa. The Increase of the African Trade....

2011 The Case of the Royal African-Company and of the Plantations. *n.p. 1714, F°.* L.

2012 A Copy of the Papers which were prepared by the Court of Directors, and read in a General Court of the South Sea-Company, on Wednesday the 17th Day of February, 1713 [O.S.]. and by the said General Court Ordered to be Printed. *Lond.* [*1714*], *4°.* L.

2013 [Wood, William]. The Assiento Contract Consider'd. As also the Advantages and Decay of the Trade of Jamaica and the Plantations, with the Causes and Consequences thereof. In several Letters to a Member of Parliament. *Lond. 1714, 8°.* L.

Reissued in Wood's *Occasional Papers on the Assiento*, 1716.

2014 The Trade granted to the South-Sea-Company: Considered with Relation to Jamaica. In a Letter to one of the Directors of the South-Sea-Company; By a Gentleman who has resided Several Years in Jamaica. *Lond. 1714, 8°.* L.

2015 The Representation of Dr. Samuel Page to the South-Sea Company, Shewing that the author of a late Pamphlet, entitled, The Trade Granted to the South-Sea Company considered with relation to Jamaica, had advanced nothing material and practical therein, but what has been publicly proposed, and in a much more advantageous manner by the said Dr. Page many months before. *n.p. 1714, 8o*. Kress 2917.

2016 [CLELAND, WILLIAM]. Some Observations, shewing the Danger of Losing the Trade of the Sugar Colonies. Humbly Offer'd to the Consideration of the Parliament. By a Planter. *Lond. 1714, 8o*. LU.

For authorship see William Wood, *The Assiento Contract Consider'd*, 1714, p. 31.

2017 The Case of John Powell of London, Merchant; who Originally Contributed l. 3,700, towards raising Two Millions for the Service of the Crown of England, and Settling the Trade to the East-Indies, when the Publick Funds were under great Discount. *n.p. [1714], s. sh. Fo*. L.

Endorsed: The Case of John Powell, of London Merchant, Concerning the Oppressions he Suffers by the Power of the United East-India Company.

2018 Reasons Humbly Proposed to the Honourable House of Commons, for Laying a Duty upon East-India Silks, &c. Exported into Her Majesties Dominions; and that no Drawback be allow'd upon Callicoes, Muslins, &c. when Exported to America and Ireland. *n.p. [1714?], s. sh. Fo*. L.

COLONIES

2019 A Model for Erecting a Bank of Credit; with a Discourse in Explanation thereof. Adapted to the Use of any Trading Countrey, where there is a Scarcity of Moneys: More Especially for His Majesties Plantations in America. *London: Printed in the Year, 1688. Reprinted at Boston in New-England, in the Year*, 1714, 8o.

Reprinted in *Colonial Currency Reprints*, ed. by A. M. Davis, vol. 1 (1910), whence this entry is transcribed.

2020 DUDLEY, PAUL. Objections to the Bank of Credit Lately Projected at Boston. Being a Letter upon that Occasion, to John Burril, Esq.... *Boston, 1714, 8o*. L.

Reprinted in *Colonial Currency Reprints*, ed. by A. M. Davis, vol. 1 (1910).

2021 A Letter, from One in Boston, to his Friend in the Country. In Answer to a Letter directed to John Burril, Esqr...[*Boston*], *1714, 8o*.

Signed: F——l. B——t. Reprinted in *Colonial Currency Reprints*, ed. by A. M. Davis, vol. 1 (1910), whence this entry is transcribed.

2022 A Vindication of the Bank of Credit Projected in Boston from the Aspersions of Paul Dudley, Esqr. in a Letter by him directed to John Burril Esqr..... *n.p. 1714, 8o*. L.

Signed by Samuel Lynde, E. Lyde, John Colman and 6 others. Reprinted in *Colonial Currency Reprints*, ed. by A. M. Davis, vol. 1 (1910).

2023 A Projection for Erecting a Bank of Credit in Boston, New England. Founded on Land Security. *n.p. 1714, 8°.* L.

Reprinted in *Colonial Currency Reprints*, ed. by A. M. Davis, vol. 1 (1910).

2024 The Groans of Jamaica, express'd in a Letter from a Gentleman residing there, to his Friend in London; containing a clear detection, and most convincing narrative of some of the crying grievances, and fraudulent oppressions... *Lond. 1714, 8°.* L.

2025 The Case of the Sufferers of Nevis and St Christophers. *n.p.* [*1714*], *s. sh. F°.* LLI.

For incorporating their debentures in the South Sea Company's fund. Title in six lines. Another edn., enlarged, [1715]. Title in 2 lines (L).

2026 BORLAND, FRANCIS. Memoirs of Darien, giving a short Description of that Countrey, with an Account of the Attempts of the Company of Scotland, to Settle a Colonie in that Place. With a Relation of some of the many Tragical Disasters, which did attend that Design. With some practical Reflections upon the whole. Written mostly in the year 1700. while the Author was in the American Regions. *Glasgow, 1714, 8°.* GU.

Another edn., entitled *The History of Darien*, Glasgow, 1779.

FINANCE

2027 The Case of the Creditors of the Office of Ordnance. *n.p.* [*1714*], *s. sh. F°.* L.

Last words of text in roman type 'of that their just Debt'.

2028 A Memorial by William Hamill, Gent. Agent and Trustee for the Officers and Soldiers of the two late Garisons of London-Derry and Enniskilling in Ireland, their Relicts and Representatives. Dedicated to his Principals. *Lond. 1714, 8°.* L.

On arrears of payment.

2029 A Bill for the Relief of William Paterson, Esq; *n.p.* [*1714*], *F°.* O.

Queen Anne is mentioned.

2030 Reasons against the Bill for the Relief of William Paterson Esq; *n.p.* [*1714*], *F°.* L.

2031 A Bill for Relieving William Paterson, Esq; out of the Equivalent Money, for what is due to him. *n.p.* [*1714*], *s. sh. F°.* L.

2032 CARTER, RICHARD. Reasons for Raising the 1400,000 l. by a Lottery of 40*s.* a Ticket; and not by a 10 l. Ticket Lottery. On a Setled Fund of 105,000 l. per Annum for 28 Years only. Whereby near 400,000 l. will be saved to the Government; and the Nation Mortgaged for above four Years less, in point of time. Humbly Submitted to the Consideration of the Parliament of Great Britain. *n. p.* [*1714?*], *s. sh. F°.* L.

Title from endorsement.

2033 CARTER, RICHARD. A Scheme for a Lottery, to raise 1,100,000 l. on a Fund of 110,000 l. per Ann. to be Settled for 16 Years, on Soap, Paper, Callicoes, Transfers and Stamps, &c. *n.p.* [*1714*], *s. sh. F°.* O.

2034 JACKSON, SAMUEL. A Scheme for Raising Two Millions of Money, for the Service of the Year 1714. (Payable with Interest,) by way of Lottery, upon the Credit of the Funds already settled for the Payment of the other Lotterys.... *n.p.* [*1714*], *s. sh. F°.* O.

Endorsed: A Proposal humbly offered to the Honourable the House of Commons. For raising Two Millions of Money immediately, by way of Lottery....

2035 A Proposal for Raising Sixty Thousand Pound per Annum, without Charge of Collecting, in a Treble Benefit to the Nation by the Payment. Humbly Offered to the Parliament of Great Britain. *n.p.* [*1714*], *s. sh. F°.* L.

For a tax on cloth exported by aliens.

2036 A Proposal for Raising Three Millions. *n.p.* [*1714?*], *s. sh. F°.* O.

A lottery scheme.

2037 A Proposal to raise 400,000 l. without any New Fund by a Lottery. *Lond.* [*1714*], *s. sh. F°.* O.

Endorsed: A Proposal for Raising 400,000 l. without any New Fund....

2038 A Scheme for raising 1,400,000 l. for the Use of the Publick upon a good and certain Fond of 105,000 l. per Annum for 32 Years from Michaelmas, 1714. *Lond. 1714*, *s. sh. F°.* O.

Endorsed: Published by Authority. The Scheme of the Lottery for raising 1,400,000 l. for Her Majesty's Supply Anno. 1714.

2039 A Scheme for raising Two Millions upon Annuities for Lives, out of a Fund of 120,000 l. per Ann. appropriated to that Use.... *n. p.* [*1714*], *s. sh. F°.* L.

Endorsed: A Scheme for raising Two Millions Upon Annuities on the Lives of Widows...for the Service of the Year 1714.

2040 [WAGSTAFFE, WILLIAM]. The State and Condition of our Taxes, considered; or, a Proposal for a Tax upon Funds: shewing the Justice, Usefulness, and Necessity of such a Tax, in respect to our Trading and Landed Interest, and especially if we engage in a new War. With Some Directions to the Freeholders of Great Britain, concerning the Choice of the next Parliament. By a Freeholder. *Lond. 1714*, *8°.* LU.

2nd edn. London, 1714 (LU); 3rd edn. Lond. 1714 (L); another edn. Dublin, 1714 (DA). Reprinted in *Miscellaneous Works of Dr. William Wagstaffe*, 1726.

2041 The Case of the Royal Boroughs of Scotland. *n.p.* [*1714?*], *s. sh. F°.* O.

On their rights to apportion taxation.

2042 EDGAR, WILLIAM. Vectigalium Systema: or, A Complete View of that Part of the Revenue of Great Britain, commonly called Customs.... By William Edgar, Inspector General of the Ports in North-Britain. *Lond. 1714*, *8°.* LU.

2nd edn. 1718 (DA).

2043 A Catalogue and Abstract of several Acts of Parliament, so far as they relate to the laying on New and Additional Duties on Goods and Merchandizes, Imported and Exported, since the printing the Book of Rates in Auno [*sic*] 1702, to the 1 of August 1714. As also the Ports of North-Britain, with their Division into Members and Creeks. *Edin. 1714. 8°.* LU.

2044 The Duties at this present Time on all Merchandize, Digested in a new and easie Method. *Lond. 1714, 12°.* LU.

2045 An Abstract of the Statutes relating to the Stamp-Duties in that Part of Great Britain called Scotland, and the Penalties. *n.p.* [*1714?*], *F°.* L.

2046 The Case of British Buckrams for Tillets, asserted. Humbly offer'd to the Honourable House of Commons. *n.p.* [*1714?*], *s. sh. F°.* LU.

Against the removal of the duty on foreign buckram.

2047 A Short Answer to the Case of British Buckrams for Tillets, Asserted. *n.p.* [*1714*], *s. sh. F°.* LU.

2048 The Case of the Importers of Linnen, and Linnen-Drapers, and Packers in London, as to the several Duties demanded on Linnens, Lawns, Neck-cloths, Barras, and Buckrams, Imported from Hambrough. *n.p.* [*1714*], *s. sh. F°.* L.

Text begins: That by an Act passed the Second Session of the last Parliament.

2049 The Case of the Packers and Tillet-Painters of London, Exon, Leeds, &c. concerned in the Woollen Manufacture, relating to Buckrams. *n.p.* [*1714*], *s. sh. F°.* O.

2050 The Case of the Packers, &c. concerned in the Woollen Manufactures, in Relation to Buckrams. Humbly Offer'd to the Honourable House of Commons. *n.p.* [*1714*], *s. sh. F°.* L.

2051 The Case of the Traders and Poor People imployed and maintained in the Linnen Manufacture in North Britain, relating to the present and further Duty intended to be laid upon Scots Linnen, &c. Humbly offered to the Honourable House of Commons. *n.p.* [*1714*], *s. sh. F°.* LU.

2052 Reasons humbly offer'd to the Honourable House of Commons, Against a Further Duty intended to be laid on Callicoes and Linnens, Printed, Painted, or Stained. *n.p.* [*1714*], *s. sh. F°.* L.

2053 Reasons Humbly Offer'd to the Honourable House of Commons against laying any farther Duties on Buckrams. *n.p.* [*1714*], *s. sh. F°.* O.

2054 The Case of the Traders in and Exporters of the Woollen-Manufacture, in Relation to the Duty intended to be laid upon Paper and Buckrams, Humbly Represented to the Consideration of the Honourable House of Commons. *n.p.* [*1714*], *s. sh. F°.* LLI.

2055 An Account of what Duties were payable by the Act of Tonnage and Poundage at the settling the Book, of Rates Anno 1660. Upon one

Hundred Reams of the several sorts of Paper hereafter specified, and likewise what is now to be paid upon Entry of the like Quantity, with what wiil [*sic*] be payable for the same if the further Duties proposed on Paper should be Enacted. *n.p.* [*1714?*], *s. sh. F°*. L.

Endorsed: Observations on the intended Duties on Paper. The misprint is corrected in the MC copy.

2056 Considerations Relating to the Intended Duties on Paper, humbly Submitted to the Honourable House of Commons. *n.p.* [*1714*], *s. sh. F°*. O.

Another edn., with 'relating' in title (L).

2057 The Paper-makers Case, humbly offer'd to the Consideration of the Honourable House of Commons. *n.p.* [*1714*], *s. sh. F°*. O.

2058 Reasons humbly offered, against Laying a further Duty upon Stock in Hand of Paper. *n.p.* [*1714*], *s. sh. F°*. L.

2059 The Case of Benjamin Wood is as follows. *n.p.* [*1714*], *s. sh. F°*. O.

Against any additional duty on 'Culgeed Silks'.

2060 The Case of the Soap-Makers making Green-Soap. *n.p.* [*1714*], *s. sh. F°*. O.

Text begins: That Soap is made of Oyl and Potashes. Against the additional duty.

2061 The Case of the Starch-Makers of the Cities of London and Westminster, and Suburbs of the same. *n.p.* [*1714?*], *s. sh. F°*. O.

Against the additional duty.

2062 To the Honourable the House of Commons. Reasons (Humbly Offer'd) Against Laying a Further Duty on Linnens to be Imported in England; And for the Exporting Linnen directly from Ireland to the English Plantations. *n.p.* [*1714?*], *s. sh. F°*. MC.

Endorsed: Reasons Humbly Offered to the Honourable House of Commons, Against Laying a Further Duty on Linnens to be Imported in England....

2063 The Case of Robert Wise, Late of London, Tobacco-Merchant; Humbly represented to the Consideration of the Honourable House of Commons. *n.p.* [*1714*], *s. sh. F°*. L.

For the bill to enable the Lord High Treasurer to compound with him for duties owed.

2064 The Case of the Tobacco-Merchants, who are become Insolvent, and are Bound to Her Majesty for Duties on Tobacco; Humbly Represented to the Consideration of the Honourable House of Commons. *n.p.* [*1714*], *s. sh. F°*. L.

The first two paragraphs are identical with those of the preceding.

2065 Reasons humbly Offer'd to the Honourable House of Commons, by the Tobacco and Wine Merchants, against Payment of Interest for the Time past on their Bonds at the Custom-house, where the Principal is paid. *n.p.* [*1714*], *s. sh. F°*. L.

Endorsed: Reasons humbly Offered by the Tobacco and Wine Merchants....

2066 Reasons humbly offer'd to the Right Honourable the House of Lords for passing the Bill, entituled, A Bill for Relief of Merchants, Importers of Tobacco and Wine, concern'd in Bonds given for part of the Duties on the same. *n.p.* [*1714*], *s. sh. F*o. LG.

Endorsed: The Tobacco and Wine-Merchants Reasons for passing their Bill...

2067 The Case of the Gold and Silver Wire-Drawers, with reference to their Drawbacks at the Out-Ports. *n. p.* [*1714?*], *s. sh. F*o. L.

2068 A Report from the Commissioners appointed to Take, Examine and State, the Publick Accompts of the Kingdom. And to determine the Debts due to the Army, &c. With a State of the Expence of the Late War. *Lond. 1714, 8*o. LU.

Reprinted in *Somers Tracts*, XIII (1815), 349.

2069 Mr. Stanhope's Answer to the Report of the Commissioners sent into Spain, &c. Together with an Extract of so much of the said Report, as concerns him. [*Lond.*], *1714, 8*o. L.

2070 An Account of the True Reasons and Facts, upon which Capt. William Wright was Turn'd out of the Commissioners Place at Plymouth. *n.p. 1714, s. sh. F*o. DA.

Gross misappropriation of naval stores.

2071 The Case of the Non-Commission Officers and Sea-men of or belonging to the late private Ships of War, Duke and Dutchess of Bristol, fitted out thence in the Year 1708, for an Expedition to the South-Seas; Most humbly offer'd to the Consideration of the Right Honourable the Lords Spiritual and Temporal, and the Commons of Great Britain, in Parliament assembled. *n.p.* [*1714*], *F*o. L.

Endorsed: The Case of the Inferior Officers and Sea-men of the Ships Duke and Dutchess of Bristol who took the Aquapulca-Ship, and other rich Prizes in the South-Seas, in the Year 1709. Alleging malversation of prize money.

2072 An Historical Account of the Constitution of the Vestry of the Parish of St. Dunstan's in the West, London. Wherein are discovered, The secret Managements of certain select Parish Officers, and the Abuses of their respective Trusts.... With an Appendix, wherein some Notice is taken of the Mismanagement of the Assessors and Collectors of the Land Tax in the aforesaid Parish, worthy the Observation of the Commissioners, and proper for all Persons who are Assessed for Stock in Trade, Personal or Real Estates. *Lond. 1714, 8*o. LG.

2073 The Art of being Honest for a little Time, or, the Method of making Parish Rates to Chastise the Inhabitants. Demonstrated, in the Assessments made for the Scavengers of St. Dunstans in the West, London, for the Year 1713 and 1712.... *Lond.* [*1714*], *8*o. L.

2074 Lord Chancellor. Mr. Baron Bury. Mr. Baron Price. Jovis 24. Dec. A.D. 1713. Ex parte Will. Savage, & Mountague Wood, Cl. Civit. Lond. Lord Chancellor's Order upon the Barons of the Exchequer's Opinion, for Fixing Arrears of Tithes of Empty Houses, and of Houses and Hereditaments in Possession of former Tenants, a Charge on the Houses, &c. and succeeding Tenants. *n.p.* [*1714?*], *s. sh. F*o. O.

2075 No. 5. A Preamble to the Books for taking a Subscription of Fifteen Hundred Thousand Pounds, for the Use of the Bank of England. March, 17$\frac{13}{14}$. *n.p.* [*1714*], *F*°. L.
Title taken from endorsement.

2076 Rules to be observed by all Persons, that intend to be Subscribers towards furnishing Fifteen Hundred Thousand Pounds to the Bank, on a Subscription to be opened on Tuesday the 23d of March, 1713 [O.S.]. *n.p.* [*1714*], *s. sh. F*°. L.

2077 FREKE, JOHN. The Prices of Stocks, &c. no. 1–105, 26 March 1714—25 March 1715; no. 1–104, 1–26, 26 March 1715—22 June 1716 (Freke's Prices of Stocks, &c. no. 59–281, 15 Jan. 1716 [O.S.]—22 June 1722). [*Lond.*], *1714–22. 8*° *&* *4*°.
No. 1–105 (LU); no. 1–104, 1–26 (NYP); no. 59–281, with gaps, (L). The LU & NYP sets have collective title pages. 'The Prices of the Several Stocks, Annuities, &c.'

2078 An Attempt to show how far the Land and Trade of England are affected by Usury, and might be Improv'd by Reducing the Legal Interest of our Money from 6 to 4 per cent. *n.p.* [*c. 1714?*], *s. sh. F*°. LU.

2079 An Humble Proposal, for advancing both the Landed and the Trading Interests of the Nation; and more fully imploying the Poor thereof, by a more general Circulation of Mony. *n.p.* [*c. 1714?*], *s. sh. F*°. L.
Signed: J.D. Advocating the reduction of the legal rate of interest.

2080 A Proposal for settling Jointures, and granting Annuities, after the Rate of 40 l. per Cent. per Annum. *Lond. 1714, 12*°. L.

2081 A List of the Names of the Members of the Amicable Contributor for Insuring Houses against Loss by Fire, at Angel-Court on Snow-Hill, September 29. 1714. *Lond. 1714, 4*°. O.

2082 An Account of the State and Condition of the Corporation of the Amicable Society of a Perpetual Assurance Office; and of the Joint-Stock of the said Society, as it stands upon the Account thereof, made up by the Auditors, and brought down to Lady-day, 1714. inclusive. *n.p.* [*1714*], *4*°. LG.

2083 A True State of the Amicable Society, at the Corner of Dean-street, Fetter-lane. With Reasons for Altering the Government of, and Establishing that Society on a solid and sure Foundation. Also a Specimen of Articles Propos'd. And a Scheme at large for a New One. *Lond. 1714, 4*°. L.

2084 The Proposal of the Company of London Insurers, on the Lives of Men, Women and Children.... *Lond. 1714, 8*°. L.
William Adams was the promoter of this Company, which is to be distinguished from that of the same title afterwards known as the Sun Fire Office.

2085 [NORTH, ROGER]. The Gentleman Accomptant: or, an Essay to unfold the Mystery of Accompts. By Way of Debtor and Creditor, commonly called Merchants Accompts....IV. of Banks; those of Venice and the Turkey Company. V. Of Stocks, and Stock-Jobbing; the Frauds therein detected....Done by a Person of Honour. *Lond. 1714, 8°.* LU.

2nd edn. 1715 (LU); 3rd, 1721 (L). The original ms. in North's autograph is B.M. Addit. MS. 32528.

TRANSPORT

2086 MICHELL, RALPH. Reasons humbly offered to the Parliament Assembled, for Building a Mould or Harbour, in Whitsand Bay, at the Lands-End in Cornwal, Situate betwixt the North and South Channels: And also, for Erecting a Light-House on the Por-De-Nac Point, near the said Bay. *n.p.* [*1714?*], *s. sh. F°.* L.

2087 A Bill to Explain and make more Effectual an Act made in the Sixteenth and Seventeenth Years of King Charles the Second, Intituled, An Act for making divers Rivers Navigable, or otherwise Passable for Boats, Barges or other Vessels. *n.p.* [*1714*], *F°.* O.

Refers to the Itchin only. Another edn., entitled: The Bill for Explaining and making more Effectual an Act made in the Sixteenth and Seventeenth Years... with the Objections to the same, n.p. [1714], F° (L).

2088 A New Method of Robert Colepepyr, Gent. For speedy and effectual Preservation of the Navigation on the River Thames; and to Repair the Water-Breach in to Havering and Dagenham Levels, in Essex. *n. p.* [*1714*], *F°.* L.

Endorsed: A Method to preserve the Thames-Navigation in few Days....

2089 A Bill for making more Effectual an Act of the Tenth and Eleventh Years of the Reign of King William, Intitled, An Act for makink [*sic*] and keeping the River Trent, in the Counties of Leicester, Derby and Stafford, Navigable. *n.p.* [*1714*], *F°.* O.

2090 Reasons humbly offer'd against the Bill for the more speedy and effectually making Navigable the River Trent, in the Counties of Licester, Derby and Stafford. *n.p.* [*1714?*], *s. sh. F°.* O.

Endorsed: The Case of the River Trent.

2091 A Bill for Repairing the Highways between Shephards-Shord and Horsely-Upright-Gate, leading down Bagdown-Hill, in the County of Wilts, and other Ruinous Parts of Highways thereunto adjacent. *n.p.* [*1714*], *F°.* O.

2092 A Bill for Repairing the High-way, or Road, from the City of Worcester, to the Burrough of Droitwich, in the County of Worcester. *n.p.* [*1714*], *F°.* LU.

2093 A Bill for Upholding and Repairing the Bridges and Highways in the County of Edinburgh. *n.p.* [*1714*], *F°.* O.

2094 To the Honourable the Commons of Great-Britain, in Parliament Assembled, the Case of the Waggon-Carriers. *n.p.* [*1714?*], *s. sh. F°.* LU.

2095 Some Reasons Most Humbly offered. To the Consideration of the Right Honourable the House of Lords, and the Honourable the House of Commons; by all the 700 Hackney Coachmen and their Widows, to Enable them to pay the Great Tax laid upon them. *n.p.* [*1714*], *s. sh. F*º. O.

Text begins: We Pray, that the Lease....

SOCIAL CONDITIONS

2096 BELLERS, JOHN. An Essay towards the Improvement of Physick. In Twelve Proposals. By which the Lives of many Thousands of the Rich, as well as of the Poor; may be Saved Yearly. With an Essay for Imploying the Able Poor; by which the Riches of the Kingdom may be greatly Increased.... *Lond. 1714*, *4*º. LU.

2097 The Case of the Poor within the City of Bristol. *n.p.* [*1714*], *s. sh. F*º. O.

2098 LONDON. Stanier Mayor. Martis xiiº die Octobris, 1714....It is ordered by this Court, That an Abstract of an Act of Parliament made in the Twelfth Year of Her late Majesties Reign, Intituled, An Act for reducing the Laws relating to Rogues, Vagabonds, Sturdy Beggars, and Vagrants into one Act of Parliament...be forthwith Printed, and delivered by the Beadles to the respective Constables, and every House-keeper in the several Wards of this City, that they may be acquainted with the same, and know the Penalties therein contained; which Abstract hereafter follows. [*Lond. 1714*], *4*º. L.

2099 The Original Design, Progress, and Present State of the Scots Corporation at London, of the Foundation of K. Charles II. To which is added, A List of the Masters and Treasurers, as also of the Benefactors. *Lond. 1714*, *4*º. L.

2100 To the Right Honourable, the Knights, Citizens and Burgesses in Parliament Assembled. The Petition of Martha Bayley relating to the several Grand Abuses in Her Majesty's Royal Hospital near Chelsea. *n.p.* [*1714?*], *s. sh. F*º. L.

2101 The Case of Several Hundreds of Her Majesty's Subjects, Insolvent Debtors, Humbly offered to the Consideration of the Parliament of Great Britain. *n.p.* [*1714*], *s. sh. F*º. O.

2102 The Case of the Merchants and Traders in and about the City of London, on behalf of themselves and the Traders of the Kingdom. Humbly Offer'd to the Honourable House of Commons; Relating to the Bill now depending, for Relief of Insolvent Debtors. *n.p.* [*1714*], *s. sh. F*º. L.

2103 The Piercing Cryes of the Poor and Miserable Prisoners for Debt, in all Parts of England. Shewing the Unreasonableness and Folly of Imprisoning the Body for Debt.... *Lond. 1714*, *8*º. LU.

2104 Provisoes and Amendments Humbly Proposed to the Insolvent Debtors Bill. With Reasons for the same. *n.p.* [*1714*], *F°*. O.

2105 Reasons, Humbly Offer'd for a more Extensive Act for the Discharge of Prisoners. *n.p.* [*1714*], *s. sh. F°*. O.

Endorsed: Reasons, humbly offered for a more Extensive Act for the Discharge of Prisoners. Almost identical with no. 1944.

2106 Reasons Humbly Offered for Passing the Bill for Relief of Insolvent Debtors. *n.p.* [*1714*], *s. sh. F°*. O.

2107 Anno 1714. Reasons relating to the Bill now depending, for Discharging Insolvent Debtors. *n.p.* [*1714*], *s. sh. F°*. O.

2108 Reasons for naturalizing the Jews in Great Britain and Ireland, on the same foot with all other nations; containing also a defence of the Jews against vulgar prejudices in all countries.... *Lond. 1714, 21 cm.* Kress 2926.

2109 Draught of a Bill for making Good Imperfect Returns of Small Livings; and for Putting in Execution Her Majesty's Rules for augmenting the same. *n.p.* [*1714?*], *F°*. O.

2110 Rules and Orders for the Augmentation of the Maintenance of the Poor Clergy, &c. Ratify'd and Confirm'd by Her Majesty, under the Great Seal of Great-Britain, the 5th of March $17\frac{13}{14}$. *n.p.* [*1714*], *s. sh. F°*. MC.

2111 The Case of the Chaplains of Her Majesty's Navy, to the number of about Eighty, most humbly submitted to the Honourable House of Commons. *n.p.* [*1714*], *s. sh. F°*. O.

For some provision in time of peace.

1715

GENERAL

2112 A Short State of the War, and the Peace. *n.p.* [*1715?*], *F°*. L.

Gives figures of exports of woollen manufactures, lead and fish and no. of ships cleared, 1710–14. Another edn. Lond. 1715, 8°; 2nd edn. 1715, 8° (both L). Reprinted in *Somers Tracts*, XIII (1815), 301.

2113 A Short State of the War and the Peace, with Additions. *n.p.* [*1715*], *F°*. MC.

Includes 'The Advantages arising to Great Britain since the Peace by the Encrease of the Navigation and Exportation of the Manufactures and Produce of England, which is as follows', endorsed 'Exportation of Woollen-Manufactures, &c.', which may have been issued separately. MC copy has a ms. note: This was drawn up by Mr. Erasmus Lewis under the Earl of Oxford's direction. Attributed to Edward (Auditor) Harley in no. 5718, p. 120 3rd., edn. Lond. 1715, *F°* (L).

AGRICULTURE

2114 CLERKE, GEORGE. The Landed-Man's Assistant: or, the Steward's Vade Mecum. Containing the newest, most plain and perspicuous Method of keeping the Accompts of Gentlemen's Estates yet extant.... *Lond.* *1715*, *12°*. L.

Another edn. Dublin, 1728, 8° (DA).

2115 SWITZER, STEPHEN. The Nobleman, Gentleman, and Gardener's Recreation: or, an Introduction to Gardening, Planting, Agriculture, and the other Business and Pleasures of a Country Life. *Lond.* *1715*, *8°*. L.

Subsequently published as vol. I of the author's *Ichnographia Rustica*, 1718, 1742 [1741].

2116 TURNER, THOMAS. New Methods of Improving Flax and Flax-Seed and Bleaching Cloath. *Dublin*, *1715*, *8°*. LU.

2117 The Case of the Company of Free-Fishermen of the River of Thames, and other Fishermen of this Kingdom, using the Lobster-Trade. *n.p.* [*1715*], *s. sh. F°*. LU.

2118 The Case of the Coasting-Fishermen of the Kingdom of Great Britain, in relation to a Clause concerning the Size of Nets, proposed to be inserted in a Bill now before the Honourable House, for the effectual preventing the Importation of fresh Fish caught by Foreigners. *n.p.* [*1715*], *s. sh. F°*. LU.

2119 An Answer to the Case of the Coasting Fishermen. *n.p.* [*1715*], *s. sh. F°*. LU.

2120 Reasons humbly offer'd for Passing the Bill, for Preventing the Importation of Fresh Fish caught by Foreigners, and the Preservation of the Brood and Fry of Fish. *n.p.* [*1715*], *s. sh. F°*. LU.

2121 An Answer to the Allegations of the Fishmongers, in their Paper, intitled, Reasons humbly Offered for Passing the Bill for preventing the

Importation of Fresh Fish caught by Foreigners. *n.p.* [*1715*], *s. sh. F°*. LU.

2122 Farther Reasons Humbly Offer'd for Passing the Fish Bill. *n.p.* [*1715*], *s. sh. F°*. LU.

2123 Reasons of Several Owners of Fishing-Vessels, humbly offer'd against a Clause, proposed by some Fishmongers, to Repeal the Law, now in Force, prohibiting Lobsters being Imported by Foreigners. *n.p.* [*1715*], *s. sh. F°*. LU.

2124 Remarks humbly offer'd by some of the Fishmongers, in Answer to the other Part of the Fishmongers Reasons for repealing that Part of the Billingsgate Act, which relates to the prohibiting Lobsters being brought by Foreigners. *n.p.* [*1715*], *s. sh. F°*. LU.

2125 Proposals of Certain Persons, who are desirous to forward the British Herring and Island Cod-Fishery. Together with Reasons in Support of their Proposals. *n.p.* [*c. 1715?*], *s. sh. F°*. LU.

Title taken from endorsement.

MANUFACTURES

2126 HILL, AARON. An Account of the Rise and Progress of the Beech-Oil Invention, and all the Steps which have been taken in that Affair, from the First Discovery, to the present Time. As also, what is further design'd in That Undertaking. *Lond. 1715, 8°*. LU.

2127 HAYNES, JOHN. Great Britain's Glory: or, an Account of the Great Number of Poor Employ'd in the Woollen and Silk Manufacturies, to the Increase of Trade, the Enlargement of the Revenues of the Crown, and Augmenting our Navigation. With the Reasons of the Decay of these Trades, and the Pernicious Consequences which must follow their Destruction. Together with a Scheme of Proposals for preventing the Loss of such Valuable Branches of our National Wealth, and restoring them to their former Grandeur. *Lond. 1715, 8°*. L.

2128 HAYNES, JOHN. Provision for the Poor: or, a View of the decay'd State of the Woollen Manufactory....The second edition. *Lond. 1715, 8°*. LU.

A reissue of the preceding.

2129 Reasons humbly offer'd For Amending and Explaining an Act, made in the Tenth Year of Her late Majesty's Reign, Intituled, An Act for Regulating, Improving and Encouraging the Woollen-Manufacture of mixt or medly Broad Cloth, &c. *n.p.* [*1715*], *s. sh. F°*. LU.

2130 A Bill to make the Act of the Tenth Year of Her late Majesty's Reign, Intituled, An Act for Regulating, Improving and Encouraging of the Woollen-Manufacture, of mixt or medly Broad Cloth, and for the better Payment of the Poor Imployed therein, more Effectual, for the Benefit of Trade in General. *n.p.* [*1715*], *F°*. L.

2131 Reasons Humbly Offer'd for Passing the Bill, now before Your Lordships, For Explaining and Amending an Act passed in the Tenth Year of Her late Majesty's Reign, Intitled, An Act for Regulating, Improving, and Encouraging the Woollen-Manufacture of mixt or medly Broad-Cloths, &c. *n.p.* [*1715*], *s. sh. F°.* LU.

2132 An humble Proposal from the Distillers and Sugar Bakers of the City of Dublin in behalf of themselves and the rest of the Distillers and Sugar-Bakers of the Kingdom of Ireland for the farther Encouragement of the Tillage and Manufactures of this Kingdom. *n.p.* [*c. 1715?*], *s. sh. F°.* LU.

Proposing that all spirits shall be allowed on exportation to draw back the excise duty.

COMMERCE

2133 Some Considerations upon Trade, briefly to shew, I. How much it concerns the Government to take all possible Care of our Commerce: II. Wherein the Care hitherto taken of it by the Government, has prov'd Deficient: And, III. How to render it more Effectual for the Future. *n.p.* [*1715*], *4°.* L.

2134 MAHIEU, ETIENNE. Prix Courant de Marchandises A Londres, le 10 Fevrier, $17\frac{14}{15}$. *Lond.* [*1715*], *F°.* LU (film).

2135 Orders made by the Fifteen Sea-Coalmeters for the City of London, to be observed and practised by their Deputies. *n.p.* [*c. 1715?*], *s. sh. F°.* OUP.

2136 The Corporation of Butchers in Edinburgh, Appellants. The Magistrates of Edinburgh, and Corporation of Candle-makers there, Respondents. The Appellant's Case. *n.p.* [*1715*], *F°.* LU.

Signed: Spencer Cowper. Rob. Raymond. Against the claim of the candle-makers that the butchers must sell all their tallow to them.

2137 The Corporation of Butchers in the City of Edinburgh. Appellants. The Mayor, City Council and Corporation of Tallow-Chandler's. Respondents. The Respondents Case. *n.p.* [*1715*], *F°.* LU.

Signed: J. Jekyl, W. Lechmere.

2138 The Case of the Merchants Trading in Tobacco, at Whitehaven, in the County of Cumberland. *n.p.* [*c. 1715?*], *F°.* L.

2139 A Report from the Committee of Secrecy, appointed by order of the House of Commons to examine Several Books and Papers laid before the House, relating to the late Negotiations of Peace and Commerce, &c. Reported on the Ninth of June, 1715. by the Right Honourable Robert Walpole...Together with an Appendix containing Memorials, Letters, and other Papers referred to in the said Report. Publish'd by Order of the House of Commons. *Lond. 1715*, *F°.* L.

Another edn. Lond. 1715, 8° (L); another edn. Dublin, 1715, 4° (DA).

2140 An Index to the Report of the Secret Committee: By which, in a Short View, the Reader is Presented with the Substance of it. In a Letter to a Friend. *Lond. 1715*, *F°*. L.

Reprinted in *Somers Tracts*, XIII (1815), 597.

2141 The Holland Merchant's Companion: or, Remarks on the Trade, Customs and Exchange of Holland with England....By T.B. *Norwich, 1715*, *8°*. O.

Another edn. Rotterdam, 1748 (CP).

2142 Translation of the Treaty of Commerce, made and sign'd at Barcelona, between the Queen of Great Britain, and Charles III. on the 10th Day of July 1707. *Lond. 1715*, *8°*. L.

2143 Reasons humbly offer'd to the Consideration of the Honourable House of Commons, for bringing in a Bill, pursuant to the Resolutions of a Committee to whom it was refer'd to consider the Laws in being, for preventing the Exporting of Wool from Great Britain and Ireland to France; and how far the same may be made more effectual, and for considering of proper methods for the Encouragement of the Woollen Manufacture. *n.p.* [*1715*], *F°*. O.

Endorsed: Reasons for Bringing in a Bill for effectually preventing the Exportation of Wool to France.

2144 Proposals humbly offer'd to the Honourable House of Commons, by the Gloucestershire Clothiers, and other Woollen Manufactories, for the more effectual preventing the Exportation of Wooll, &c. *n.p.* [*1715*], *s. sh. F°*. O.

2145 SYMSON, WILLIAM. A New Voyage to the East-Indies...To which is added, A particular Account of the French Factories in those Parts, and of the general Trade throughout all India.... *Lond. 1715*, *12°*. L.

2nd edn. 1720 (L).

2146 By the King, A Proclamation, For Encouraging Seamen to Enter themselves on Board His Majesties Ships of War. *Lond. 1715*, *s. sh. F°*. L.

Dated: 5 August 1715.

COLONIES

2147 [BANNISTER, THOMAS]. A Letter to the Right Honourable the Lords Commissioners of Trade & Plantations: or, A Short Essay on the Principal Branches of the Trade of New-England, with the Difficulties they labour under; and some Methods of Improvement. *Lond. 1715*, *8°*. L.

The dedication signed: T. B. For authorship cf. *Cal. S.P. Col.* 1714–15, p. 222.

2148 The Case of His Majesty's Colony of Connecticut in New-England, with respect to their Charter, which is intended to be taken away by a Bill, intitled, A Bill for the better Regulation of Charter and Proprietary Governments in America, &c. *n.p.* [*1715*], *s. sh. F°*. O.

2149 The Case of Charles Lord Baltemore, a Minor, with Relation to his Government of Maryland. *n.p.* [*1715*], *s. sh. F*^{o}. O.

2150 The Case of the Province of the Massachusets-Bay in New-England, with Relation to their Charter, and some Observations thereon. *n.p.* [*1715*], *s. sh. F*^{o}. O.

2151 Presumptive Reasons why the Governments of the Provinces of South and North Carolina, and the Bahama or Lucaios Islands being Proprietary Governments in America, should (more Especially) be Reassumed into the Hands of the Crown of Great Britain: Humbly offer'd to the Consideration of the Committee of the Honourable House of Commons; To whom a Bill, for the better Regulating of the Charter and Proprietary Governments in America, and of his Majesties Plantations, is Committed. *n.p.* [*1715*], *s. sh. F*^{o}. LG.

Endorsed: Reasons for Regulating Charter and Proprietary Governments in America. More Especially Carolina, and the Bahama Islands.

FINANCE

2152 Asgill, John. An Abstract of the Publick Funds Granted and Continued to the Crown since 1 Wm. & M. and still existing....With an Essay for the more Speedy Redemption of the Perpetual Funds: an Apology for the same: and an Appendix, for Exchange of a Revenue in Ireland. *Lond. 1715*, *4*^{o}. O.

2nd edn. 1715 (L). Reprinted in *Somers Tracts*, XIII (1815), 730.

2153 Leigh, Edward. An Essay upon Credit, being a Proposal for the Immediate and entire Payment of the Publick Debts, and raising the Credit of the Nation: Contain'd in a Scheme of Management of Exchequer Credit, by the present Funds; Without any New Tax or Imposition. *Lond. 1715*, *8*^{o}. LU.

Another edn. 1719 (LU).

2154 A Method is here humbly Propos'd, that will enable the Government to pay off that Part of the publick Debt, which is redeemable by Parliament, in much less Time than the present Methods will perform.... *n.p.* [*1715*], *4*^{o}. L.

Followed by 'A Method humbly offer'd, by which, in case a War becomes necessary, The Government may raise Four Millions per Ann. as long as the War shall last' and 'Some Farther Thoughts on Publick Credit, for explaining the two foregoing Proposals'.

2155 A Table Calculated to shew the Interest due on Exchequer Bills, and Bank Seal'd Bills (at 2^{d} per Cent. per Diem) by Inspection. *Lond.* [*c. 1715?*], *obl. s. sh. F*^{o}. LSC.

The imprint of the only copy seen is cropped.

2156 Report on Mr. Paterson's Petition; Presented to the Honourable House of Commons, By Sir James Campbell, Die Jovis 14 Aprilis, 1715. *n.p.* [*1715*], *8*^{o}. O.

2157 Upon the Petition of William Paterson, Esq; *n.p.* [*1715*], *8°*. JCB.
The report made to the House of Commons, 23 May 1715.

2158 A Bill for the Relief of William Paterson, Esq; *n.p.* [*1715*], *F°*. L.
King George I is mentioned.

2159 The Case of Francis Beaumont, Undertaker for Forage, delivered to the Forces in Flanders in the Year 17$\frac{11}{12}$. *n.p.* [*1715*], *s. sh. F°*. O.
For payment.

2160 CARTER, RICHARD. An easie Method to raise this present Year, 1715. 5000 l. per Ann. for ever. Whereby 100 l. a year may thereby be given to each of the Ministers that shall Officiate in the 50 New Churches. Without Taxing either Persons or Trade. *n.p.* [*1715*], *s. sh. F°*. LU.
Title taken from endorsement. A lottery scheme.

2161 CARTER, RICHARD. A Proposal, shewing an Easy method to raise 5 or 6000 l. Certain, this present Year 1715, and to Erect with it a Charity School for 50 Boys for ever, and putting Yearly 10 of them out to Apprentice.... *n.p.* [*1715*], *s. sh. F°*. O.
Title taken from endorsement. Proposing a lottery for £100,000.

2162 Stamp-Office at Lincolns-Inn. Instructions by the Commissioners to the Collectors or Sub-Receivers of His Majesties Duty on Money given, paid, or contracted for with Clerks and Apprentices within that Part of Great-Britain call'd Scotland. *n.p.* [*c. 1715?*], *s. sh. F°*. OUP.

2163 An Abstract of the Penal Laws of the Customs, and Excise, for Goods Imported and Exported. *n.p.* [*1715?*], *F°*. LU.

2164 The Case of Thomas Hammond, Merchant. *n.p.* [*1715*], *s. sh. F°*. LU.
For leave to bring in a bill to enable the Treasury to compound with him for money owed for customs.

2165 Cases relating to the Duties of Excise, and to the Jurisdiction of Justices of the Peace, upon Informations laid before them for Offences against the Laws of Excise: and to the Jurisdiction of the Justices at the Quarter-Sessions, relating to Appeals in Cases of the Duty upon Malt. *Lond.* *1715*, *8°*. L.

2166 The Case of the Farmers and Maltsters, upon the Shortness of Time allow'd for the Payment of the Duty on Malt. *n.p.* [*1715*], *s. sh. F°*. O.

2167 Memorial concerning the Difference of the Custom and Duties on Sope imported, and the Duties imposed on that made in Great Britain. *n.p.* [*1715*], *F°*. LU.

2168 The Case of Anne Millner, Thomas Colmore, and William Hunt, of London, Merchants, having a large Quantity of Tobacco Burnt and Destroyed by the late Fire in Thames-Street. *n.p.* [*1715*], *s. sh. F°*. O.
For return of customs duty or liberty to import duty-free a quantity equivalent to the tobacco burnt.

2169 The Case of the Merchants-Sufferers, in the Late Dreadful Fire, by the Burning of Sugar, Ginger, Oil, and Sarsaparilla. *n.p.* [*1715*], *s. sh. F°*. LU.

Ask to be allowed to import duty-free goods to the value of those burnt.

2170 The Case of Some Particular Merchants of White-Haven, Using the Tobacco-Trade; in Relation to Interest Demanded upon Bonds where the Principal is Paid. *n.p.* [*1715?*], *s. sh. F°*. L.

2171 The Case of Sir John Lambert, Bart. Samuel Shepheard, and the Executors of the late John James David, of London, Merchants. Humbly offered to the Consideration of this Honourable House, for Relief. *n.p.* [*1715*], *s. sh. F°*. O.

Endorsed: The Case of Sir John Lambert, Bart. Mr Shepheard, and others, relating to the Custom of their Wines taken by the French.

2172 The Case of the third Auditor, Referr'd by the Treasury, to the Attorney and Sollicitor General, with their Reports thereon. *Lond. 1715*, *F°*. L.

2nd edn. entitled: The Case of the Third Auditor, as stated by Mr. Lownds, and referr'd by the Commissioners of the Treasury to the Attorney and the late Sollicitor General; with their Reports thereupon, 1715; 3rd edn. 1715 (both L).

2173 The Case of Richard Score, late Collector of the Customs and other Duties at Penzance. *n.p.* [*c. 1715?*], *s. sh. F°*. LLI.

For a reward for discovering frauds at the Customs House relating to the import of East India goods.

2174 The Case of Benjamin Withall, Gent. In His Majesty's Victualling-Office, &c. *n.p.* [*1715?*], *s. sh. F°*. O.

For payment of money due to him as storekeeper in St. John's, Newfoundland.

2175 [The] Case of Benj. Withall, Engineer in His Majesty's Office of Ordinance. *n.p.* [*1715*], *s. sh. F°*. O.

Complaining of wrongful dismissal. Endorsed: Case of Benjamin Withall, Engineer in his Majesties Office of Ordinance, Corrected.

2176 WITHALL, BENJAMIN. The Case of Great-Britain, in relation to His Maj^ys^. Office of Ordnance. *n.p.* [*1715*], *s. sh. F°*. L.

Endorsed: The Case of the Nation, in his Majesty's Office of Ordnance. Another edn., corrected, 1715 (MC). Alleging frauds and abuses.

2177 BOURSOT, PETER. A Purge for Church-wardens and Vestry-men, &c. With Relief for House-keepers, and better Provision for the Poor. Being an Abridgment of all the Acts of Parliament concerning the Poors Rates. By which all Persons may be as well inform'd, as if they had purchased the Statute-Book. Also an Account of the Impositions lately practised in some Parishes, and how they may be Remedied. [*Lond. 1715?*], *F°*. LG.

2178 Entry cancelled.

2179 HOLLAND, JOHN. The Directors of the Bank of England, Enemies to the Great Interests of the Kingdom; and also, not Just to the Trust reposed in them by the Adventurers, who Chose them to do their best Endeavours, by all Honest Means, for the Advantage of the Joint Stock. *Lond.* [*1715*], *4°*. LU.

Signed: John Holland.

2180 HOLLAND, JOHN. The Ruine of the Bank of England, and all Publick-Credit, Inevitable: and the Necessity, in a short Time, of Stopping the Payments upon the several Funds to the Bank, South-Sea Company, Lottery, &c. if the Honourable, House of Commons will not themselves be Judges of the Means that may be Offer'd to prevent it. *Lond.* *1715*, *4°*. LU.

Signed: John Holland.

2181 GRANGER, G. Proposals for the Good of the Publick. By small or great Sums of Money, more than double Improv'd by a great deal, upon Bills to Encourage Trade, both in City and Country, kept at the True and Safest Office...in Strutton Ground, near the New Chappel in Westminster. *n.p.* [*1715*], *s. sh. F°*. LU.

2182 Land Security, for establishing a Perpetual Insurance on Lives of Men, Women, and Children, &c. for raising Provision for Widows and Orphans, &c. Equal to an Estate of Inheritance....By the Friendly Society, &c. *Lond.* *1715*, *8°*. L.

2183 Proposals for the better Establishing and Perpetuating the Friendly Society, for Insurance on Lives, and for raising a Joint-Stock, thereby to secure to the Contributors the several Benefits and Advantages herein after mention'd. *n.p.* [*c. 1715?*], *12°*. LSC.

2184 A Specimen of Articles propos'd, in Order to the making Assurances on Lives. *n.p.* [*1715*], *4°*. O.

Presumably by Robert Thompson, who is nominated registrar in the articles.

TRANSPORT

2185 A Bill to make the River Kennet Navigable, from Reading to Newbury, in the County of Berks. *n.p.* [*1715*], *F°*. O.

2186 Reasons humbly offer'd to this Honourable House, for Passing the Bill, For making the River Kennet Navigable. *n.p.* [*1715*], *s. sh. F°*. LLI.

2187 Answers to the (pretended) Reasons, Humbly Offer'd for making the River Kennet a Free River. *n.p.* [*1715*], *s. sh. F°*. O.

2188 A Bill for making the River Weaver Navigable, from Frodsham-Bridge to Northwich, in the County of Chester. *n.p.* [*1715*], *F°*. O.

2189 For Mending the Roads of England: it's proposed.... *n.p.* [*c. 1715?*], *8°*. L.

Signed: J.P.

2190 A Bill for Repairing and Amending the High-ways, between Tyburn and Uxbridge, in the County of Middlesex. *n.p.* [*1715*], *F°*. L.

2191 A Bill for Repairing the High-ways, from Kickes-End, in the Parish of South-Mims, in the County of Middlesex, to Shafford-house, in the Parish of St Michael, in the County of Hertford. *n.p.* [*1715*], *F°*. O.

2192 The merchants and traders necessary companion for the year 1715. Being a new and perfect account of all the stage-coaches, waggoners, and carriers, that comes to London, Westminster, and Southwark, from all parts of England and Wales.... *London, A. Hinds, 1715. 16·5 cm.* Kress S. 1423.

2193 Some Reasons most humbly Offered to the Consideration of the Right Honourable the House of Lords, and the Honourable the House of Commons; by all the 700 Hackney Coachmen and their Widows, to Enable them to pay the Great Tax laid upon them. *n.p.* [*1715*], *s. sh. F°*. O.

Different from the work of 1714 of the same title. The opening words agree very closely with those of *The Case of John Nicholson, &c.* They are 'Whereas by an Act of Parliament'.

SOCIAL CONDITIONS

2194 The Charitable Society: or, a Proposal for the More Easy and Effectual Relief of the Sick and Needy. *Lond. 1715, 8°*. O.

In an unsigned note in the O copy the author states that the Revd. Mr. Bowyer communicated to him a scheme he had seen in a French sermon. They agreed to translate and publish the substance of it. The author further claims that the origins of Westminster Hospital, St George's Hospital and the hospitals at Winchester, Bath and Dublin go back to this scheme. For a sequel see *A Charitable Proposal*, 1716 (no. 2263).

2195 A Bill for Erecting a Court of Judicature to Determine Differences touching Houses and Buildings Burnt down, Demolished or Defaced in and near Thames-Street, in the City of London. *n.p.* [*1715*], *F°*. L.

2196 At the Court of St. James's the Eleventh Day of January, 1714. Present, The Kings most Excellent Majesty in Council. Upon Reading this Day at the Board a Report from the Right Honourable the Lords Committees of Council, and others appointed to Examine and Enquire into the Abuses of Chelsea-College, Dated the Tenth of this instant, in the Words following.... *Lond. 1714* [*O.S.*], *F°*. M (Cr).

2197 His Majesty's Commission for the Royal Hospital for Seamen at Greenwich. *n.p.* [*1715*], *4°*. O.

2198 The Case of a great Number of poor confined Debtors, within the several Prisoners of Ludgate, the Two Compters, and other Prisons in and about the City of London, as well on behalf of themselves, as also of other Insolvent Debtors; humbly Recommended and submitted to the Consideration and Relief of the Honourable the Commons of Great-Britain in Parliament assembled. *n.p.* [*1715?*], *s. sh. F*o. LLI.

2199 The Case of Creditors, who (with their Fortunes and Credit) have, during, and since the late War, assisted, and subsisted, the Persons and Families of Officers, Soldiers and Seamen, &c. *n.p.* [*1715*], *s. sh. F*o. O.

Endorsed: The Case of Creditors, of Officers, Soldiers and Seamen &c.

2200 Entry cancelled.

2201 Reasons Humbly Offer'd, for Passing the Bill, For Relief of Insolvent Officers and Soldiers. *n.p.* [*1715*], *s. sh. F*o. O.

2202 Reasons Humbly Offered against the Bill now depending, For the Relief of Insolvent Officers, Soldiers and Sea-men. *n.p.* [*1715*], *s. sh. F*o. O.

2203 Reasons for adding a Clause to the Bill, For Relief of Insolvent Officers, Soldiers, and Seamen, for Registring all Letters of Attorney, and Bills of Sale, or Assignments of Seamens Wages, or short Allowance-Money, whereby the Credit of their Tickets may be advanced, and for effectually Securing the Money laid out by Persons supplying them. *n.p.* [*1715*], *s. sh. F*o. O.

Endorsed: Proposals for advancing the Credit of Seamens Tickets....

2204 The Case of Several Unfortunate Officers of his Majesty's Army, Humbly offer'd to the Consideration of Both Houses of Parliament. *n.p.* [*1715*], *s. sh. F*o. O.

For inclusion in the bill for relief of debtors.

2205 Reasons humbly offer'd to the Honourable the Commons of Great Britain, in Parliament assembled, for a more extensive Act for the Relief of Disbanded and Reduced Soldiers. *n.p.* [*1715?*], *s. sh. F*o. O.

2206 Reasons for an Act for the Discharge of Insolvent Debtors, humbly offer'd to the Consideration of both Houses of Parliament. *n.p.* [*c. 1715?*], *s. sh. F*o. L.

Endorsed: By the Debtors in His Majesty's Prison, the Fleet.

2207 Observations relating to the Bill for Relief of Insolvent Debtors, humbly offer'd to the Honourable House of Commons. *n.p.* [*1715?*], *s. sh. F*o. LU.

2208 Reasons humbly offer'd to the Parliament of Great-Britain, for passing the Bill now depending for Discharge of poor Insolvent Prisoners for Debt. *n.p.* [*1715*], *s. sh. F*o. LU.

Endorsed: The Case of the Poor Prisoners for Debt.

2209 Reasons Humbly Offered to the Parliament of Great-Britain: In Favour of the Bill now depending for the Discharge of Poor Insolvent Prisoners for Debt. *n.p.* [*1715?*], *s. sh. F*o. LU.

2210 Reasons humbly offer'd for a General and Unlimited Act, for the Discharging of poor Prisoners for Debt, the last Act of Parliament, For Relief of Insolvent Debtors, being restrain'd to the Sum of 50 l. *n.p.* [*1715*], *s. sh. F°*. LU.

2211 A Confutation of the Reasons for Naturalizing the Jews. Containing the Crimes, Frauds and Insolencies, for which they were Convicted and Punished in former Reigns. *Lond. 1715*, *8°*. L.

2212 The Case of the Warrant Officers. *n.p.* [*1715*], *s. sh. F°*. O.
For relief.

2213 By the King, A Proclamation, For the Careful Custody and Well-Ordering of the New River, brought from Chadwell and Amwell to the North-Part of the City of London. *Lond. 1715*, *s. sh. F°*. L.
Dated: 29 March 1715.

2214 An Historical Account of the Highlanders; describing their Country, Division into Clans, Manner of Living and Fighting; their Habits, Arms, and Government under their Lairds, &c..... *Dublin*, *1715*, *8°*. EU.

1716

GENERAL

2215 WATTS, THOMAS. An Essay on the Proper Method for forming the Man of Business. In a Letter, &c. *Lond. 1716, 8°.* LU.

2nd edn. 1716 (L); 4th edn., with additions, 1722 (L). Another edn., ed. by A. H. Cole, Boston, 1946.

2216 [HILL, AARON]. Essays for the Month of December, 1716 [January, 1717]. To be continued Monthly. By a Society of Gentlemen. *Lond. 1716, 17. 4°.* L.

The Essays for December were reissued in 1718 as: Four Essays: viz. I. On Making China Ware in England....II. On a Method for furnishing Coals at a Third Part of the Price they are usually sold at. III. On the Repairing of Dagenham, or other Breaches. IV. On our English Grapes....By a Society of Gentlemen.... For authorship see ms. note in L copy of 1718 edn. The Essays for January are on silk-worms, rice, afforestation, paper-making, dyeing and dairy farming.

2217 [BASTON, THOMAS]. Thoughts on Trade, and a Publick Spirit. Consider'd under the Following Heads, viz. I. Companies in Trade. II. Stock-Jobbers. III. Projectors. IV. Corruption in the Law and Public Offices. V. Of a Public Spirit.... *Lond. 1716, 8°.* LU.

Reissued in 1732 with author's name as: Observations on Trade and a Publick Spirit (LU).

2218 [FREEBAIRN, ROBERT]. The Miserable State of Scotland, since the Union, briefly represented; and the only Way to render it Happy plainly pointed out. In a Letter to a Friend. *Perth, 1716, F°.* O.

For authorship see no. 2571.

AGRICULTURE

2219 LAURENCE, JOHN. The Gentleman's Recreation: or the Second Part of the Art of Gardening Improved. Containing several New Experiments and Curious Observations relating to Fruit-Trees: Particularly, a New Method of building Walls with Horizontal Shelters. Illustrated with Copper Plates.... *Lond. 1716, 8°.* O.

2nd edn. 1717 (O); 3rd edn. 1723 (O). 6th edn. 1726 (O).

2220 STEVENSON, HENRY. The Young Gard'ner's Director. Furnishing him with Instructions for Planting and Sowing, whatsoever Trees or Seeds have been thought worthy of Care, in a Garden or Orchard, either for Profit or Pleasure. Also containing the Culture of them all.... To which is prefix'd some Directions for the Management of Bees.... By H. S. Philokepos.... *Lond. 1716, 12°.* L.

The preface signed: H. Stevenson. 5th edn., entitled: The Gentleman Gardener instructed, 1764; 8th edn. 1769 (both L).

2221 The Young Surveyor's Guide: or, a New Introduction to the Whole Art of Surveying Land....Now first Publish'd from an Original M.S.... By Edward Laurence. *Lond. 1716, 12°.* EU.

2222 [HEPBURN,]. A Discourse concerning Fews and Superiorities, shewing that the Rigid Observance of them is inconsistent with the Nature of the British Constitution. *Edin. 1716, 8°.* E.

For authorship see ms. note in E copy.

2223 Reasonable Explanations and Alterations in the Act for appointing the Commissioners for the Forfeited Estates. *n.p.* [*1716*], *F°.* O.

MANUFACTURES

2224 HILL, AARON. An Impartial State of the Case between the Patentee, Annuitants, and Sharers, in the Beech-Oil Company. Publish'd by the Patentee, as well in Vindication of his own Measures, as for the General Satisfaction of all the concern'd Parties. *Lond. 1716, 8°.* L.

2225 ACRES, JOSEPH, The Linen Manufacture. A Sermon preach'd at Blewbury, September 19. 1715. Being the Day appointed for an Anniversary Sermon, upon the Account of a large Charity given to the Poor of that Village, by William Malthus, late Citizen and Merchant in London. *Lond. 1716, 8°.* DA.

2226 Reasons Humbly Offered by the Fair Traders and Dealers in Snuff against a Clause in a Bill now depending before Your Lordships, entitled, A Bill to prevent the Mischiefs by Manufacturing Leaves, or other Things, to resemble Tobacco; so far as relates to a Clause for preventing the Abuses in Mixing and Colouring of Snuff. *n.p.* [*1716*], *s. sh. F°.* L.

Endorsed: The Case of the Manufacturers and Traders in Snuff.

2227 To the Honourable the Knights, Commissioners of Shires, Citizens, and Burgesses of Great-Britain in Parliament Assembled. The Case of John Rotherham. *n.p. 1716, s. sh. F°.* L.

Endorsed: The Case of John Rotherham, Humbly Presented to the Honourable the House of Commons, relating to the Manufacturing of Corrupt and Damag'd Tobacco.

2228 BLANCH, JOHN. Speculum Commercii; or the History of our Golden Fleece. Written by the Author of the Beaux Merchant. *Lond. 1716, 8°.* MP.

COMMERCE

2229 Great Britain's Weekly Pacquet: containing the Prices of Goods, with their Neat Duties and Draw-Backs; And a Collection of Sundry Goods Imported and Exported Weekly. With an Account of News Foreign and Domestick. [*Lond.*], *1716, F°.*

No. 5, 21 July 1716 (EU); no. 17, 13 Oct. 1716 (O).

2230 Advertisement. Edinburgh, May 10, 1716. *n.p.* [*1716*], *s. sh. obl. 4°.* E.

An act of the Town Council appointing the keeping of a weekly corn market.

2231 By the King, A Proclamation, For Recalling and Prohibiting Seamen from Serving Foreign Princes and States. *Lond. 1716, s. sh. F°.* L.

Dated: 5 June 1716.

2232 An English Merchant's Remarks, upon a Scandalous Jacobite-Paper, publish'd the 19th of July last, in the Post-Boy, under the Name of a Memorial presented to the Chancery of Sweden, by the Resident of Great-Britain. *n.p. 1716, F°.* O.

2233 Some Considerations relating to the Management of the Affairs of the South-Sea Company. *Lond. 1716, 12°.* LU.

COLONIES

2234 Some Considerations upon the several sorts of Banks propos'd as a Medium of Trade: and some Improvements that might be made in this Province, hinted at. *Boston, 1716, 8°.*

Reprinted in *Colonial Currency Reprints*, ed. by A. M. Davis, vol. 1 (1910), whence this entry is transcribed.

2235 [Marsh, Henry]. A Proposal for Raising a Stock not exceeding Forty thousand Pounds Sterling; by Subscriptions for Forming a Settlement, in a Large and Convenient River in Acadia. And to Improve a great Space of Land on each side the said River. *Lond. 1716, F°.* L.

Revised edn., 1720 (L), has author's name. It is entitled: A Proposal for Raising a Stock of Two Millions of Pounds Sterling... (no. 2718).

2236 [Aylmer, Whitgift]. A Brief Narrative of some Occurrences relating to Jamaica. *[1716], F°.* O.

O copy, the only one seen, begins with B1 and has no title-page. Authorship deduced from internal evidence.

2237 Wood, William. A True State of Mr. Aylmer's Brief Narrative. In a Letter to ——. *Lond. 1716, 8°.* MH. Sabin 105081.

2238 The Representation and Memorial of the Council of the Island of Jamaica, to the Right Honourable the Lords Commissioners for Trade and Plantations. Together with the Addresses of the Governour and Council, and Town of Kingston; and Association of the Principal Inhabitants. With a Preface, by Mr. Wood. *Lond. 1716, 8°.* LU.

2239 [Wood, William]. A View of the Proceedings of the Assemblies of Jamaica, for some Years past. With some Considerations on the Present State of the Island.... *Lond. 1716, 8°.* L.

For authorship see Sabin 35668.

2240 Wood, William. Occasional Papers on the Assiento, and the Affairs of Jamaica. *Lond. 1716, 8°.* MH. Sabin 105079.

A reissue in one volume of nos. 2013, 2237–9.

2241 Wagstaff, A., pseudonym. A True Account of the late Pyracies of Jamaica; the Authors, Abettors, and Encouragers thereof. With other

Transactions relating thereto. By One just arrived from that Island. To which is added, A Genuine Letter to a very Eminent Personage concern'd. *Lond. 1716, 8º.* L.

A skit.

FINANCE

2242 Some Proposals humbly offer'd to the Parliament of Great Britain, for Easing the Nation of the Old Navy-Debt (now the South-Sea-Debt) of Ten Million Sterling, Principal Money.... *Lond. 1716, Fº.* LU.

Signed: B.

2243 Further Reasons most humbly offer'd, for Increasing our Money; putting an immediate Stop to it's being Melted Down, and Sent Abroad; For paying off our Publick Debts; Incouraging Trade; Employing the Poor, &c. [*Lond. 1716*], *Fº.* L.

Signed: B.

2244 The Case of the Merchants Trading to New-England, and of Others residing there, with relation to the Bills of Exchange drawn for the Canada Expedition. *n.p.* [*1716*], *s. sh. Fº.* LLI.

Endorsed: The Case of the New-England Merchants, with relation to the Canada Bills.

2245 ELLIS, JOHN. Instructions for Collectors of Excise, in Prosecutions before Justices of the Peace, for Forfeitures incurred, or Offences committed against the Laws relating to the Duties of Excise, and other Duties under the Management of the Commissioners of Excise.... *Lond. 1716, 8º.* L.

Another edn. 1735 (L).

2246 Extracts from several Acts of Parliament, relating to the Assessing and Collecting the Trophy-Tax in London. *n.p.* [*1716*], *Fº.* LG.

With a resolution of the Commissioners of Lieutenancy for London to enforce the collection of the tax, dated 26 January 1715 [O.S.].

2247 The City's Articles to establish a Publick Treasury, to Lend Money upon any Real Security to Wholesale Dealers, Shopkeepers and others, and to Merchants, Four Months without Interest, to pay the King's Customs for Goods imported.... *n.p. 1716, 4º.* L.

2248 *Begin.* The Paper Intituled, The City's Articles, being now the general Talk of the Town. *n.p.* [*1716*], *4º.* L.

Denying a rumour that the scheme is illegal as infringing the Bank's monopoly.

2249 HARTLEY, JOHN. An Abstract of the Proposals for Erecting and Establishing a New Society, for a Perpetual Assurance for insuring Lives, by the Name of Great-Britain's Royal-Society.... *Lond.* [*1716*], *s. sh. Fº.* EU.

2250 An Abstract of the Charter of Incorporation of the Amicable Society for a Perpetual Assurance-Office. Together with the By-Laws. *Lond. 1716, 4º.* OUP.

2251 Union, or Double Hand-in-Hand Fire-Office, for Insuring Goods and Merchandizes by Mutual Contribution, in the way of the Hand-in-Hand Office for Houses. *n.p. 1716, s. sh. 4°.* L.

TRANSPORT

2252 The Case and Proposal of William Boswell, relating to the Stopping the Breach at Dagenham, &c. *n.p.* [*1716?*], *s. sh. F°.* L.

2253 The Case of William Boswell with the Trustees, appointed by Act of Parliament to Treat for the Stopping of the Breach at Dagenham. *n.p.* [*1716?*], *s. sh. F°.* L.

2254 The Case of Dominick Donnelly, Gentleman. Humbly offer'd to the Consideration of the Honourable House of Commons. *n.p. 1716, F°.* LLI.

Endorsed: The Case of Dominick Donnelly, touching his Proposal for stopping the Breach of Dagenham, &c. 12th of June, 1716.

2255 Reasons demonstrating, that the Breach in the Levels of Havering and Dagenham, hath already done very great Damage, to the Navigation of the River of Thames; and will (if not speedily stopp'd) be more and more prejudicial to it. *n.p.* [*1716?*], *s. sh. F°.* L.

2256 Reasons humbly offer'd to the Honourable House of Commons, against Stopping the Breach in the Levels of Havering and Dagenham, by Dove-Tail Piles. *n.p.* [*1716?*], *s. sh. F°.* L.

2257 The Water-Bailiffs and Trinity-Masters Reports, and the Masters of Attendants and Pilots Certificate concerning Dagenham-Breach. *n.p.* [*1716?*], *F°.* L.

Title from endorsement. The water bailiff was William Boteler.

2258 LONDON. Peers Mayor. Martis xxiiij° die Julii, 1716.... [*Lond.*], *1716, s. sh. F°.* LCRO.

Order that wherrymen and watermen rowing between Gravesend and Windsor are not to draw up or trim their boats at the public stairs.

2259 The Case of the Ticket-Porters. *n.p.* [*1716?*], *s. sh. F°.* O.

Endorsed: The Case of the Ticket, against the Tackle-House-Porters.

2260 LONDON. Bateman Mayor....Curia Prima tent' Die Martis vj° die Novembris, 1716.... [*Lond.*], *1716, F°.* LCRO.

Report of the committee appointed to consider the petition of the London ticket-porters. Another edn. [1716], s.sh. F°. LG.

2261 The Case of Thomas Blunt, John Searing, Charles Sewell, Thomas Holland, Thomas Storey, Cornelius Rose, and the rest of the Eight Hundred Licens'd Hackney Coach-men, within the Cities of London and Westminster, and the Bills of Mortality. *n.p.* [*1716*], *s. sh. F°.* L.

2262 To the Honourable the House of Commons, The Humble Petition of Charles Sewell, Thomas Holland, and George Garrett, on behalf of themselves, and the rest of the Eight Hundred Licensed Hackney Coach-men, and their Widows. *n.p.* [*1716?*], *s. sh. F°*. L.

SOCIAL CONDITIONS

2263 A Charitable Proposal for Relieving the Sick & Needy, and other Distressed Persons. *Lond. 1716, 8°*. E.

Other edns. 1719 and 1720 (both O). A development of the proposal made in *The Charitable Society*, 1715. The original minute book of Westminster Hospital opens with a transcript of this pamphlet. The promoters of the scheme which led to the foundation of the hospital were Henry Hoare, William Wogan, Robert Witham and Patrick Cockburn, one of whom, possibly Cockburn, presumably wrote this piece.

2264 The Report of the Committee appointed to inspect the Poors Rates and the Scavengers Rates within the Cities of London and Westminster, and Weekly Bills of Mortality. *Lond. 1715* [*O.S.*], *F°*. LU.

No. 201 of the Votes of the House of Commons. Another edn. [Dublin], 1716, 4° (D). Mostly concerned with St. Martin's in the Fields.

2265 VERNON, JOHN. Remarks on a Paper, Entituled, An Abstract of the State of the Work-House, for Maintaining of the Poor of the City of Dublin.... *Dublin, 1716, F°*. LU.

2266 *Begin.* Reverend Brother: His Majesty having by his Letters Patents... been pleased...to give Licence and Authority to the Inhabitants of Spalding...Sufferers by a sudden and lamentable Fire, which happened in that Town in April 1714, to ask and receive the charitable Contributions.... *n.p.* [*1716*], *F°*. OC.

A circular letter from John Robinson, Bishop of London, urging the clergy of his diocese to promote this charity.

2267 The Case of the Poor Insolvent Prisoners for Debt, in the several Goals of this Kingdom. *n.p.* [*c. 1716?*], *s. sh. F°*. LLI.

1717

GENERAL

2268 CARY, JOHN. An Essay, towards Regulating the Trade, and Employing the Poor of this Kingdom. *Lond. 1717, 8°.* L.

2nd edn. 1719 (L). Another edn., entitled: A Discourse on Trade, 1745 (L).

2269 [PATERSON, WILLIAM]. An Enquiry into the State of the Union of Great Britain, and the Past and Present State of the Trade and Publick Revenues thereof. By the Wednesday's Club in Friday-street. *Lond. 1717, 8°.* LU.

2nd edn. 1717 (LU). Reprinted in *The Writings of William Paterson*, edited by S. Bannister, 1858, vol. 2.

AGRICULTURE

2270 BRADLEY, RICHARD. New Improvements of Planting and Gardening, both Philosophical and Practical. Explaining the Motion of the Sap and Generation of Plants.... *Lond. 1717, 18, 8°.* 3 pt. L.

2nd edn. 1718 (L); 3rd, 1719, 20 (L); 4th Dublin, 1720, 21 (R); 4th, Lond. 1724 (L); 5th, 1726 (L); 6th, 1731 (L); 7th, 1739 (L).

2271 COLLINS, SAMUEL. Paradise Retriev'd: Plainly and Fully Demonstrating the most Beautiful, Durable, and Beneficial Method of Managing and Improving Fruit-Trees against Walls, or in Hedges, contrary to Mr. Lawrence, and Others upon Gardening. Together with a Treatise on Mellons and Cucumbers. *Lond. 1717, 8°.* L.

2272 A Letter from a Gentleman in the Country to his Friend in Town: concerning Two Books lately published by Mr. Bradley, and Mr. Collins, treating of Planting and Gardening. Containing a more particular Account of Mr. Collins's Performance, and his Unfitness to engage on that Subject. With a Seasonable Rebuke to him for his bold and immodest Conclusion. *Lond. 1717, 8°.* L.

Refers to Bradley's *New Improvements* and Collins's *Paradise Retriev'd.*

2273 JACOB, GILES. The Country Gentlemen's Vade Mecum. Containing an Account of the best Methods to improve Lands, plowing and sowing of Corn: Reaping, Mowing, &c. Hedging, Ditching, and all Sorts of Husbandry.... *Lond. 1717, 12°.* L.

2274 The Registry of the Papists Estates within the Division of Bury St. Edmunds. *n.p.* [*1717?*], *F°.* M (Cr).

2275 A Report from the Commissioners appointed to Enquire of the Estates of certain Traitors, &c. in that Part of Great Britain called Scotland. *Lond. 1717, F°.* L.

Another edn. Edin. 1717 (E).

2276 Act of Sederunt for preventing unnecessary Expences and Delays in Processes concerning forfeited Estates, and for the due Management of such Estates during Sequestration. *n.p.* [*1717*], *F*°. E.

2277 The Case of such Persons as have Claims and Demands upon the Forfeited Estates in Ireland. *n.p.* [*1717?*], *s. sh. F*°. O.

MANUFACTURES

2278 HAMOND, JOHN. The Reasons and Remedies of the Surprising Decay of the Royal Navy of Great Britain; Humbly Submitted to the Consideration of the Honourable House of Commons, by a Shipwright, who has many Years (with Grief) observ'd our fatal Mistakes, and has ever been a zealous Friend to our present Happy Constitution. *n.p.* [*1717*], *s. sh. F*°. LU.

Dated: May 20th, 1717.

2279 SUTHERLAND, WILLIAM. Britain's Glory: or, Ship-Building unvail'd. Being a General Director, for Building and Compleating the said Machines. *Lond. 1717*, *F*°. L.

2nd edn. Lond. 1729 (Kress 3041).

2280 WILLIAMSON, R. Mr. Williamson's Memoirs of a few Passages transacted by Mr. Joseph Allen, late Master-Builder at his Majesty's Ship-Yard, Deptford. When Mr. Williamson was employed to Convert the Timber. *Lond. 1717*, *8*°. L.

2281 Two Clauses which the Weavers of London and Canterbury humbly desire may be made Part of some Bill, this Session of Parliament, for the better preserving their Manufactures. With some Reasons for the same. *n.p.* [*c. 1717?*], *s. sh. F*°. O.

Endorsed: Reasons for Two Clauses to preserve our Manufactures of Silk.

2282 POVEY, CHARLES. The Subject's Representation... With an Account of the New Factory and Exchanges that will be open'd in the Month of March next, at the Charge of Gentlemen and Merchants, also the particulars of the Tolsey and Pay-Chamber that are to be Establish'd, without any Expence to the Publick. *Lond. 1717*, *8*°. LU.

For weavers.

COMMERCE

2283 A Collection of Treaties, Alliances, and Conventions, relating to the Security, Commerce, and Navigation of the British Dominions, made since His Majesty's happy Accession to the Crown. *Lond. 1717*, *4*°. L.

2284 A View of some Deficiencies in the Aids of Trade; With Essays towards the Means for their Supply. Most humbly Address'd to the Consider ation of our Legislature....Occasional Courants, N° XVIII to XXX. *Lond. M.DCC.VII* [sic *for 1717*], *8*°. L.

Dated at end: West-Country, 23d. April, 1717.

2285 By the Lords Justices and Council of Ireland, a Proclamation. *Dublin, 1717, F*⁰. DPRO.

Dated: 14 May 1717. All butter casks to have the tare branded on them.

2286 SLIFORD, THOMAS. A Brief Account of what hath been done towards making a Settlement of Trade at Harburg: together with Three Papers concerning that Trade, written this present Year 1717. Humbly submitted. *Lond. 1717, 4*⁰. O.

Signed: Thomas Sliford. Dated: December the 21st 1717.

2287 By the King, A Proclamation, For Prohibiting Commerce with Sueden. *Lond. 1716, s. sh. F*⁰. C (Cr).

Dated: 2 March 1716 [O.S.].

2288 The Case of the Merchants Trading to Russia. *n.p.* [*1717*], *s. sh. F*⁰. L.

For compensation for ships seized by the Swedes.

2289 A Letter from a Merchant, to a Member in Parliament, concerning the Importation of Swedish Iron from Holland. *n.p.* [*1717?*], *s. sh. F*⁰. L.

2290 Observations upon a Pamphlet, called, An English Merchant's Remarks upon a Scandalous Jacobite Paper Published in The Post-Boy, under the Name of A Memorial presented to the Chancery of Sweden, by the Resident of Great Britain. *Lond. 1717, 8*⁰. O.

2291 A Specifick Account of the Losses and Damages which the British Subjects have sustained by the following Ships and Loadings being brought up and confiscated in Sweden; for which the Underwritten British Resident, does in the King His most Gracious Master's Name, by his Memorial of this Date, demand that full and ample Satisfaction may be made. *Lond. 1717, F*⁰. O.

Two memorials by R. Jackson dated 14 Jan. and 14 June 1715 followed by a petition of the Muscovia Company dated Feb. 5. $17\frac{16}{17}$.

2292 Reasons Humbly Offer'd against the Bill now Depending in the Honourable House of Commons, For Exporting Irish Linnens, to the British Plantations, Duty-Free. *n.p.* [*1717*], *s. sh. F*⁰. O.

2293 An Answer to Reasons (so call'd) against the Bill for Exporting Irish Linen to the British Plantations Duty-Free. *n.p.* [*1717*], *s. sh. F*⁰. O.

2294 The Case of the late Separate Traders to India, Humbly Offer'd to the Consideration of the Commons of Great Britain, in Parliament Assembled. *n.p.* [*1717?*], *s. sh. F*⁰. O.

COLONIES

2295 The Case of the Island of Minorca. *n.p.* [*1717?*], *F*⁰. L.

Titles taken from endorsement. Contains 'An Humble Representation of several Grievances and Hardships his Majesty's most faithful Subjects, the Inhabitants of the Island of Minorca, labour under'.

2296 A Memorial of Several Aggrievances and Oppressions of His Majesty's Subjects in the Colony of New-York in America. *n.p.* [*1717*], *F*o. O.

Apparently drawn up by Samuel Mulford. See *Calendar of State Papers, Colonial Series*, 1717–1718, no. 317.

2297 The Case of the Colony of South-Carolina in America: Humbly Offered to the Consideration of Both Houses of Parliament. *n.p.* [*1717*], *s. sh. F*o. LPRO.

Urges that the government be restored to the Crown.

2298 Mountgomery, Sir Robert. A Discourse concerning the design'd Establishment of a New Colony to the South of Carolina, in the most delightful Country of the Universe. *Lond. 1717, 8*o. L.

One of the JCB copies has an additional 'Appendix to a Discourse lately Publish'd, concerning the Establishment of a new Colony in Azilia'.

2299 Articles exhibited against Lord Archibald Hamilton, late Governour of Jamaica. With sundry Depositions and Proofs relating to the same. *Lond. 1717, 8*o. L.

2300 A Representation concerning the French Part of the Island of St. Christopher's: Being partly an Extract of Reasons given in the Year 1711, for the Crown of Great Britain's insisting on the Reservation of the said Lands, on the ensuing Treaty of Peace; and partly some Thoughts and Remarks which occurr'd on the present Views and Designs of Self-interested People touching that Affair; as also the certain Advantages to the Crown,which must arise from a right Disposal of that Acquisition. *n.p.* [*1717?*], *F*o. O.

FINANCE

2301 An Account of some Proposals for Reducing the Publick Debts. *n.p.* [*1717*], *s. sh. F*o. L.

2302 [Hutcheson, Archibald]. Computations relating to the Publick Debts, taken from the Abstract deliver'd into Parliament the 14th of March, 1716. With some Considerations in relation to the same. *Lond. 1717*, *F*o. LU.

Reprinted, with author's name, in 1720 in Hutcheson's *A Collection of Treatises*.

2303 [Defoe, Daniel]. Fair Payment No Spunge: or, Some Considerations on the Unreasonableness of Refusing to Receive back Money Lent on Publick Securities. And the Necessity of Setting the Nation Free from the Insupportable Burthen of Debt and Taxes. With a View of the Great Advantage and Benefit which will arise to Trade and to the Landed Interest, as well as to the Poor, by having those Heavy Grievances taken off. *Lond. 1717, 8*o. LU.

For authorship see *C.B.E.L.* II, 504.

2304 A General Loan by Act of Parliament: or, a Farther Improvement of the Scheme to Pay the Publick Redeemable Debts, without Real New Taxes. *n.p.* [*1717*], *4°*. L.

2305 [SYKES, ARTHUR ASHLEY]. A Letter to a Friend. In which is shewn the Inviolable Nature of Publick Securities. By a Lover of his Country. *Lond. 1717*, *8°*, LU.

Reprinted in *A Select Collection of...Tracts...on the National Debt*, ed. by J. R. McCulloch, 1857, p. 19. For authorship see J. Disney, *Memoirs of A. A. Sykes*, p. 47.

2306 A Letter to a Member of Parliament: shewing the Justice of a more equal and impartial Assessment on Land: The Sacredness of Publick Engagements: The Advantages of lowering the Customs and high Duties on Trade: And the Ease of reducing by degrees the Debts of the Nation. *Lond. 1717*, *8°*. LU.

2nd edn. 1717 (LU).

2307 [HUTCHESON, ARCHIBALD]. Some Considerations relating to the Payment of the Publick Debts, humbly offer'd to the Commons of Great-Britain in Parliament Assembled. By a Member of the House of Commons. *Lond. 1717*, *4°*. LU.

Reprinted, with author's name, in 1720 in Hutcheson's *A Collection of Treatises*.

2308 Some Proposals, Humbly Offer'd, for Easing the Land-Tax of Two Shillings in the Pound, For the Increase and Preservation of our Currant-Coin, particularly Silver, which is now become very scarce, and (if a proper and speedy Remedy be not apply'd) will all be gone in a little Time; For the Payment of the Publick Debts by degrees (lately recommended to the Honourable House of Commons, by His Majesty, from the Throne,) So as to give every one their full Due, And instead of laying on any New Tax to accomplish this great Work, To make the doing it a particular and general Advantage to all concern'd; And for the Encouragement of Trade. *n.p.* [*1717*], *F°*. O.

2309 A State and Estimate of the Publick Debts, to Lady-day 1717, with Proposals for Redeeming and Paying off the same. *n.p.* [*1717?*], *s. sh. F°*. MC.

The only copy seen is without the Proposals.

2310 Two Letters to a Member of Parliament, concerning the Publick Debts. *n.p.* [*1717*], *F°*. O.

Reprinted, with large additions, in 1718, and entered separately (no. 2399).

2311 [BROOME,]. Wednesday Club-Law; or, the Injustice, Dishonour, and Ill Policy of Breaking into Parliamentary Contracts for Publick Debts. *Lond. 1717*, *8°*. LU.

For authorship see James Crossley in *N. & Q.* vol. 7 (1853), 576. A reply to 2269.

2312 [WATKINS, THOMAS]. A Table of Redemption. Shewing at one View in what Time the Principal and Interest of any Debt from Three to Six per Cent. may be discharged, by any Fund producing Yearly from Three and a Half to Twelve per Cent. With Other Estimates and Remarks relating to the Present State of our Publick Debts.... By T.W. F.R.S. *Lond. 1717, Fº.* L.

For authorship see H. & L. quoting H. B. Wheatley as authority.

2313 A Memorial in Behalf of Mr. James Campbell, Merchant in London. *n.p.* [*1717*], *Fº.* E.

Dated: January 21st $17\frac{16}{17}$. Campbell was agent for the public creditors of Scotland on the Equivalent and claimed his 5 per cent commission before the Court of Session.

2314 The Oeconomy of His Majesty's Navy-Office. Containing the several Duties of the Commissioners and Principal Officers thereof.... By an Officer of the Navy. *Lond. 1717, 12º.* LU.

2315 WITHALL, BENJAMIN. A Detection of the Exhorbitant Oppressions, Publick Frauds, and Mismanagements, that for a long time has been Perpetrated, nay and is now Acting... in His Majesty's Victualling and Ordnance Offices. These...being the prime and multiply'd Causes of the heavy Publick Debts the Nation now groans under.... *Lond. 1717, 4º.* LU.

2316 ELDERTON, EDWARD. The Case of the Farmer, a Trage-Comedy, the like never before acted. *Lond. 1717, 8º.* O.

On his unfair assessment for poor-rates in Stratford and Old Ford.

2317 A Bill for the better Collecting and Levying the Revenue of the Tenths of the Clergy. *n.p.* [*1717*], *Fº.* O.

2318 A Letter to a Member in Parliament, from his Friend in the Country, in Relation to the Coinage of Farthings and Half-pence. *n.p.* [*1717?*], *Fº.* LU.

2319 Of Laws against Melting the Coin. *n.p.* [*1717*], *4º.* MP.

Dated: Feb. 1717.

2320 A Short Discourse, shewing the Occasion of our present great Want of Silver, and the Proper Remedies for preventing the Exportation of it for the Future. By a True Englishman. *Lond. 1717, 12º.* E.

2nd edn., corrected, 1718 (L).

2321 [CLAYTON, DAVID]. A Short but thorough Search into what may be the real Cause of the present Scarcity of our Silver Coin. And a Method proposed, which, if taken, will effectually both produce a speedy Supply, and prevent the like Scarcity of it for the future. With the fatal Consequences that will unavoidably follow, either from the advancing our Silver Coin, or lowering the Price of our Gold. By a hearty Well-wisher of the Peace and Prosperity of his Country. *Lond. 1717, 8º.* L.

Another edn. 1718, entitled: Thoughts on our Silver Coin, both as to what may be the Cause of its Present Scarcity, and what will produce a Speedy Supply. By a Lover of his Country (L). For authorship see Clayton's *A Short System of Trade*, 1719.

2322 By the King, A Proclamation, Declaring the Rates at which Gold shall be Current in Payments. *Lond. 1717, s. sh. F°.* C (Cr).

Dated: 22 December 1717. Press-figure 'c'. Another edn. with press-figure '4' (C (Cr)); another edn. with press-figure '6' (L).

2323 BANSON, WILLIAM. The complete exchanger containing tables of exchange [with Holland] and relation of the monies commonly used. *Lond. 1717, 8°.* Kress 3005.

2324 LUCAS, JOHN. Ways and Means discovered, to enlarge Trade and Commerce, the Improvement of Navigation, the Advancement of the King's Revenue, plentifully supplying the Poor, and for the common Good of all Merchants and Traders....Also is Ways Discovered...how they shall Improve their Money so as to make it Ten Pounds per Cent. per annum certain.... *Lond. 1717, 4°.* L.

A scheme to advance money due for customs duties on the security of part of the cargo.

2325 Abstract of a Scheme for an Office, and raising One or Two Millions Sterling by a Voluntary Subscription, for a Fund to Insure Ships and Merchandize at Sea, &c..... *n.p.* [*1717*], *F°.* LU.

The only copy seen is imperfect.

2326 Reasons for Insuring Ships and Merchandize, by a Company or Corporation. Who may have a Large and Visible Stock, that cannot be parted with; But shall be constantly kept up, to make good the Losses of such Merchants and Owners as shall be Insured by them; Tho' not to exclude private Insurers from Insuring as they have always done. *n.p.* [*1717?*], *s. sh. F°.* LU.

2327 KING, THOMAS. An Exact Guide to Book-keeping by way of Debtor and Creditor: done after the Italian Method.... *Lond. 1717, 4°.* LICA.

TRANSPORT

2328 A bill for enlarging the time granted by an act passed in the eighth year of the reign of Her late Majesty Queen Anne, entitul'd, An act for making a convenient dock or bason at Liverpool, for security of all ships trading to and from the said port of Liverpool.... [*n.p., 1717?*], *3·25 cm.* Kress S. 1448.

2329 An Act for Enlarging the Time Granted by an Act passed in the Eighth Year of the Reign of Her late Majesty Queen Anne, Entitul'd, An Act for making a Convenient Dock or Bason at Liverpool, for Security of all Ships Trading to and from the said Port of Liverpool. *n.p.* [*1717*], *F°.* L.

2330 Reasons Humbly offered to the Honourable House of Commons, against laying a Duty on Ships, towards building a Dock at Leverpool, which they cannot make use of. *n.p.* [*1717?*], *s. sh. F°.* O.

2331 An Account of the Proceedings against the Present Patentees of the Ballast-Office for the River of Thames; (since the Month of September, 1715). Relating to the several Abuses Charged on them.... *Lond. 1717*, 8°. LPRO.

2332 An Impartial Account of the Frauds and Abuses at Dagenham Breach; and of the Hardships sustain'd by Mr. William Boswell, late Undertaker of the Works there. In a Letter to a Member of Parliament. *Lond. 1717*, 8°. L.

2333 CONGREVE, THOMAS. A Scheme or, Proposal for making a Navigable Communication between the Rivers of Trent and Severn, in the County of Stafford. *Lond. 1717*, 8°. L.

Another edn. 1753 (L).

2334 An Act for the more effectual Preservation and Improvement of the River Wear, and Port and Haven of Sunderland, in the County of Durham. *n.p.* [*1717*], F°. L.

2335 Objections against an Act, entitled, An Act for Preservation and Improvement of the River Wear and Port and Haven of Sunderland in the County of Durham. *n.p.* [*1717*], F°. LLI.

Endorsed: Objections against the Wear and Sunderland Bill.

2336 An Act for Repairing the High-Ways from several Places therein-mentioned, leading towards Highgate Gate-House, and Hampstead, in the County of Middlesex; And for Electing Trustees, for keeping up a sufficient Number, for the Repairing the High-ways upon the Roads, from Highgate Gate-house, to Barnet Block-house; And also of the High-ways between Kilburn Bridge, and Sparrows Hern, in the County of Hertford. *n.p.* [*1717*], F°. L.

2337 An Act for Explaining and making more Effectual the Acts of the Fourth and Eighth Years of Her late Majesty's Reign, for Amending the Road between Hockley in the County of Bedford, and Stoney-Stratford in the County of Bucks. *n.p.* [*1717*], F°. L.

2338 A Bill for Repairing the High-ways from that Part of Counters-Bridge, which lies in the Parish of Kensington, in the County of Middlesex, to the Powder-Mills in the Road to Staines, and to Cranford-Bridge in the Road to Colnebrooke, in the said County. *n.p.* [*1717*], *s. sh.* F°. L.

2339 An Act for Repairing the High-ways Leading from the Stones-End in Kent-Street, in the Parish of St. George's Southwark...to the Lime-Kilns in East Greenwich, near Black-heath, and to Lewisham Church, being the Tunbridge Road.... *n.p.* [*1717?*], F°. L.

Another edn. [1718?] with the reading 'in Tunbridge Road' (L).

2340 A Bill and Act for Upholding and Repairing Bridges and Highways in the County of Edinburgh. *Edin. 1717*, 8°. EP.

2341 Orders, By-Laws, and Ordinances, for the good Government and Regulating of the Persons Licensed to Keep and Drive Hackney-Coaches, and their Renters and Drivers. Made, Publish'd, and Declar'd, by John Way, Thomas Sutton, More Molyneux, Charles Barnard, and John Idle, Esqs; Commissioners.... *Lond. 1717, s. sh. F°.* L.

2342 LONDON. An Abstract of the By-Laws and Ordinances relating to Hackney Coaches. *Lond. 1717, F°.* LG.

2343 Rules and Instructions Given by the Lord Provost, Baillies, and Conncil [*sic*] of the good Town of Edinburgh, to be Observed by the Post-Masters, Stablers and others who keep Horses for Hireing within the said Burgh and Suburbs thereof in time coming. [*Edin. 1717*], *s. sh. F°.* ECA.

Dated: The Day of August, One Thousand Seven Hundred and Seventeen Years.

2344 Advertisement. That a Horse-Post is to be set up betwixt Edinburgh and Glasgow, upon Tuesday the 26th Day of March 1717.... *n.p.* [*1717*], *s. sh. F°.* E.

Signed: Ja. Anderson.

SOCIAL CONDITIONS

2345 BRADDON, LAURENCE. An Abstract of the Draught of a Bill for Relieving, Reforming, and Employing the Poor...Hereunto is prefix'd, A Brief Account of what was done by both Lords and Commons in 1704, for reducing all Laws, relating to the Poor, into One General Bill—And also herein is set forth, the principal Considerations, upon which this Scheme is grounded, and the Publick Benefit from thence proceeding. *n.p.* [*1717?*], *8°.* LU.

2346 BRADDON, LAURENCE. The Miseries of the Poor are a National Sin, Shame, and Charge; but by making them Happy, we shall remove that Guilt...and pay Old Debts without New Taxes. By the Judicious Employment of the Poor (under One New General Law) and Present Taxes we may...Discharge...All our National Debts.... *Lond. 1717, 8°.* L.

Reissued in 1723 [1722] with the title: To Pay Old-Debts without New-Taxes...(L).

2347 The History of the Press-Yard: or, a brief Account of the Customs and Occurrences that are put in Practice, and to be met with in that Ancient Repository of Living Bodies, called, His Majesty's Goal of Newgate in London.... *Lond. 1717, 8°.* L.

Attributed to Sir James Williams, *C.B.E.L.* II, 155.

2348 An Answer to the Case of the Reduc'd Officers. In a Letter to the Author. *Lond. 1717, 8°.* O.

1718

GENERAL

2349 WOOD, WILLIAM, Secretary to the Customs. A Survey of Trade. In four Parts. I. The great Advantages of Trade in General, and the Particular Influence of it on Great-Britain. II. The Marks of a Beneficial Trade....III. The great Advantages of our Colonies and Plantations to Great-Britain....IV. Some Considerations on the Disadvantages our Trade at present labours under....Together with Considerations on our Money and Bullion.... *Lond. 1718*, 8°. LU.

2nd edn. 1719 (LU); another 2nd edn. 1722 (C).

2350 DRUMMOND, JOHN. The Accomptant's Pocket-Companion, instructing Merchants, Gentlemen of Estates and others to begin their Books, carry on their Business, and make a Ballance; where nothing is omitted which can occur in the Course of Trade. To which is added, The Method of catching and curing Cod-Fish, Ling, Tusk, Seath and White Herrings, with Tables shewing the Charges and Profits on Fishing, and Directions about boyling Oyl. *Edin. 1718*, 4°. LU.

2351 [BLANCH, JOHN]. A Dialogue between Sir Arthur Cleaveland and Sir Gilbert Proteus, at Garraways. *n.p.* [*1718?*], F°. L.

On commercial policy, the national debt and taxation. For authorship see the list of his works in the author's *Sword into Anchors*, 1725.

2352 The Humble Petition of the Mayor, Sheriffs, Justices, Aldermen and Common-Council of the City of Norwich; to his Majesty King George. *n.p.* [*1718?*], *s. sh.* F°. LU.

On the decay of manufactures and commerce, Jacobite in tone.

AGRICULTURE

2353 APLETRE, JOHN. Proposals for an Undertaking to manage and produce Raw-Silk, of the Growth of England; and to Raise a Fund for the carrying on the same, pursuant to a Patent granted to John Apletre, Esq; under the Great Seal of England. Dated the 23rd Day of May, 1718. *n.p.* [*1718*], 4°. L.

2354 BRADLEY, RICHARD. The Gentleman and Gardeners Kalendar, directing what is necessary to be done every Month, in the Kitchen-Garden, Fruit-Garden, Nursery, Management of Forest-Trees, Green-House and Flower-Garden. With Directions for the Making and Ordering Hop-Grounds.... *Lond. 1718*, 8°. L.

3rd edn. 1720 (L).

2355 LAURENCE, JOHN. The Fruit-Garden Kalendar: or, a Summary of the Art of Managing the Fruit-Garden. Teaching in order of Time what is to be done therein every Month in the Year. Containing several new and plain Directions, more particularly relating to the Vine.... *Lond. 1718*, 8º. L.

2356 SWITZER, STEPHEN. Ichnographia Rustica: or, the Nobleman, Gentleman, and Gardener's Recreation. Containing Directions for the general Distribution of a Country Seat, into Rural and Extensive Gardens, Parks, Paddocks, &c. Ane a general System of Agriculture.... *Lond. 1718*, 8º. 3 vols. L.

Vol. 1 is a new edn. of the *The Nobleman, Gentleman, and Gardener's Recreation*, 1715. 2nd edn. 1742 [1741] (L).

2357 The Report to the Honourable House of Commons of such of the Commissioners of Enquiry as have been appointed to execute the several Trusts and Powers in relation to England, and any other Parts whatsoever, except Scotland, contained in a late Act of Parliament, intituled, An Act for Appointing Commissioners to Enquire of the Estates of certain Traitors....Together with an Additional Report from the Commissioners appointed to Enquire of the Estates of certain Traitors, &c. in that Part of Great Britain called Scotland. *Lond. 1717* [*O.S.*], *F*º. L.

2358 [HALDANE, PATRICK]. The Case of the Forfeited Estates in Scotland. Consider'd, in a Letter to a Noble L——d. *Lond. 1718*, 8º. L.

For authorship see H. & L. quoting a ms. note by David Laing.

2359 [DALRYMPLE, Sir DAVID]. The Laws and Judicatures of Scotland, Vindicated from the Calumnies and False Reasonings contain'd in a late Pamphlet, intituled, The Case of the Forfeited Estates in Scotland, Consider'd: In a Letter to a Noble L——d. *Lond. 1718*, 8º. L.

Another edn. Edin. 1718 (E). For authorship see H. & L. quoting David Laing as authority.

2360 [HALDANE, PATRICK]. The Honour and Justice of the Present Parliament, and of their Commissioners of Enquiry, Vindicated, from the Calumnies and Misrepresentations contained in a late Pamphlet, Entituled The Laws and Judicatures of Scotland vindicated, &c. In a Letter to the Author. *Lond. 1718*, 8º. O.

For authorship see H. & L. quoting David Laing's note in C copy.

2361 [DALRYMPLE, Sir DAVID]. Observations on the Bill for Sale of Forfeited Estates, humbly offered to the Consideration of both Houses of Parliament. *n.p.* [*1718*], *F*º. L.

Another edn. Edin. 1718, 8º, containing also 'Some Reasons humbly offered against the Bill for Sale of the Forfeited Estates' and 'Reasons humbly offer'd against the Bill, entituled, An Act for the Sale of the Forfeited Estates" (L). For authorship see H. & L. quoting David Laing's copy.

2362 Reasons for Some Alterations in the Bill, Entituled, An Act for the Sale of the Forfeited Estates. *n.p.* [*1718?*], *s. sh. F*º. O.

2363 The Reasons for Sustaining the Claims of Personal Creditors of forfeiting Persons, tho' the Bonds and other Vouchers of the Debts were not upon Record before committing the Treason: As the same were pled before, and humbly offered to the Honourable Commissioners and Trustees of the forfeited Estates in Scotland, in the Case of the Governour and Company of the Bank of Scotland their Claims upon the Estates of Southesque and Balnamoon, by the Counsel for the said Governour and Company. *n.p. 1718, F°.* O.

Dated: October 15. 1718. Signed: Ja. Graham. Alex. Hay. Wal Steuart. Ch. Areskine. Jo. Elphinston. With additional remarks by Robert Dundas.

2364 STEELE, Sir RICHARD and GILLMORE, JOSEPH. An Account of the Fish-Pool: consisting of a Description of the Vessel so call'd, lately invented and built for the Importation of Fish alive, and in good Health, from Parts however distant.... *Lond. 1718, 8°.* L.

Reprinted in *Tracts and Pamphlets by Richard Steele*, ed. by Rae Blanchard, Baltimore, 1944.

MANUFACTURES

2365 The Case of the Makers and Wholesale Traders in the Manufacture of English Bone-Lace. *n.p.* [*1718*], *s. sh. F°.* O.

2366 The Practical Distiller: Or, a Brief Treatise of Practical Distillation: In which the Doctrine of Fermentation is methodically explain'd in a new method. With the Description of a New Engine-Still....To which is added, by way of Appendix, A Treatise of making Artificial Wines from several Fruits of the British Production, interspers'd with many useful Reflections and Observations. *Lond. 1718, 8°.* LU.

2367 Reasons humbly offer'd to the Legislature of Great-Britain, by the Goldsmiths, Shop-keepers, and Workers in Silver, in and about the City of London, for altering the Standard of Plate, to the Old Standard again. *n.p.* [*1718?*], *s. sh. F°.* L.

2368 John Baskett, Agnes and Elizabeth Hamiltons, Grandchildren to the deceased Andrew Anderson, His Majesties Printer, and Archibald Campbell Husband to the said Agnes, and Patrick Alexander Husband to the said Elizabeth, for their Interests, and Mr. John Campbell His Majesties Printers in Scotland, Appellants. James Watson Respondent. The Appellant's Case. *n.p.* [*1718*], *F°.* L.

Signed: Spencer Cowper. Sam. Mead.

2369 John Baskett, His Majesty's Printer in London, and the Representatives of Andrew Anderson, Printer to King Charles II. in Scotland. Appell[ts]. James Watson, One of His Majesty's Printers in Edinburgh. Respond[t]. The Respondent's Case. *n.p.* [*1718*], *F°.* L.

Signed: Tho. Lutwyche. Rob. Raymond.

2370 Information for James Watson, One of His Majesty's Printers, against the Representatives of Mrs. Anderson. *n.p.* [*1718*], *F°.* E.

Dated: December 8th, 1718. Signed: Dun. Forbes.

2371 Information for the Executors of the deceased Mrs. Anderson, against James Watson. *n.p.* [*1718*], *F°*. E.

Dated: December 8th, 1718. Signed: Ja. Nasmyth.

2372 Reasons Humbly Offered by the Taylors, Button-Sellers, Button-Makers, Throwsters, Twisters, Dyers, Spinners and Winders, &c. for explaining and amending an Act made the Eighth of Her late Majesty, Entituled, An Act for Employing the Manufacturers, by Encouraging the Consumption of Raw-Silk and Mohair-Yarn. *n.p.* [*1718*], *s. sh. F°*. L.

2373 Reasons humbly offer'd by the Woollen-Drapers, Taylors, &c. for the Repealing an Act made in the Eighth Year of the Reign of Her late Majesty Queen Anne, Entitled, An Act for Employing the Manufacturers, by Encouraging the Consumption of Raw Silk and Mohair-Yarn. *n.p.* [*1718?*], *s. sh. F°*. L.

2374 The Tanners Reasons for prohibiting the Exportation of Oak Bark Explained.... *n.p.* [*1718?*], *8°*. L.

2375 By the King, A Proclamation, For Putting in Execution the Laws made against Unlawful Clubs and Combinations, and for preventing Tumults and Riotous Assemblies, and for the more speedy and effectual Punishing Rioters. *Lond. 1717*, *s. sh. F°*. C (Cr).

Dated: 9 February 1717 [O.S.]. Against combinations of woolcombers and weavers.

COMMERCE

2376 Jacob, Giles. Lex Mercatoria: or the Merchant's Companion. Containing all the Laws and Statutes relating to Merchandize. Wherein our Trade with Foreign Nations is illustrated; our Trade in general amongst ourselves explain'd...and all Maritime Affairs, in the Way of Traffick, are concisely treated of.... *Lond. 1718*, *8°*. LU.

2nd edn. 1729 (O).

2377 A Book of Fairs: or, A New Guide to the West-Country Travellers: Shewing them all the Fairs in these Thirteen several Counties following, viz. Gloucester-shire, Wilt-shire, Somerset-shire, Dorset-shire, Devon-shire, Cornwall, Glamorgan-shire, Monmouth-shire, Hereford-shire, Worcester-shire, Oxford-shire, Berk-shire, and Hampshire....The Tenth Impression Collected by J. Bridges. [*Oxford*], *1718*, *8°*. O.

2378 Reasons offer'd for putting on a General and in a manner Voluntary Regulation, lately offer'd to the Publick, to set Trade on its right foot: providing also at the same time, an easy Tax to be apply'd only towards the Payment of our Debts, and not raise the Price of Goods more than the Duty they'll pay. *n.p.* [*1718?*], *s. sh. F°*. L.

All goods to conform to standards of quality which are to be marked on them.

2379 The Case of the Inhabitants of the Cities of London and Westminster, and the Suburbs thereof, as also of the Inhabitants of the Adjacent

Counties; relating to the Oppression they lye under by means of the Forestallers, Engrossers, and Jobbers of Cattle, and Flesh-Provision brought to the several Markets; Humbly Offer'd to the Honourable House of Commons. *n.p.* [*1718?*], *s. sh. F°.* L.

Endorsed: The Case of the Inhabitants of London, Westminster and Middlesex, relating to Jobbers of Cattle, &c.

2380 An Essay to Prove; that Regrators, Engrossers, Forestallers, Hawkers and Jobbers of Corn, Cattle, and other Marketable Goods, Provisions and Merchandizes, are Destructive of Trade, Oppressive to the Poor, and a Common Nusance to the Kingdom in General.... *Lond. 1718, 8°.* L.

2381 The Case of the City of Exon. *n.p.* [*1718?*], *s. sh. F°.* LLI.

For permission to import wool from Ireland through Exeter.

2382 Reasons Humbly Offer'd against making Exeter, or any other Port in the British Chanel, a Staple Port for Importation of Wooll from Ireland. *n.p.* [*1718*], *s. sh. F°.* L.

2383 By the Lords Justices and Council of Ireland, a Proclamation. *Dublin, 1718, F°.* DPRO.

Dated 29 March 1718. Reinforcing the laws about butter casks.

2384 A Letter from a Merchant at Amsterdam, to his Correspondent in London. *n.p.* [*1718*], *s. sh. F°.* L.

On the effects on commerce of war with Spain.

2385 A Second Letter from a Merchant in Amsterdam, to his Correspondent in London. *n.p.* [*1718*], *s. sh. F°.* L.

2386 [WILLIAMS, REEVE]. A Letter from a Merchant to a Member of Parliament, relating to the Danger Great Britain is in of losing her Trade, by the great Increase of the Naval Power of Spain. With a Chart of the Mediterranean Sea Annex'd. *Lond. 1718, 4°.* L.

The second edn. is in English and French, with an additional title-page in French reading: Lettre d'un Negociant à un Membre du Parlemetn [sic], touchant le Danger que la Grande Bretagne court de perdre son Commerce, par l'Accroissement des Forces Navales d'Espagne....Traduite de l'Anglois par Mr. A. Boyer. In the Walpole (C) copy is a petition from Reeve Williams disclosing that 7000 copies of the English edition were given away by the Earl of Macclesfield's orders and a further 2000 of the English and French edition; 3rd edn. 1718 (O); 6th edn. 1718 (L).

2387 To the Honourable the Commons of Great-Britain: The Humble Remonstrance of Josias Thompson, Late Coast Surveyor from Waxford to Youghill. *n.p.* [*1718*], *F°.* O.

Dated January, 21. 1717–18. On the smuggling of wool to France.

2388 An Abstract of the several Acts of Parliament, Commission for taking Subscriptions, Charter, and By-Laws of the Honourable South-Sea Company. [*Lond.*], *1718, 8°.* L.

Another edn. 1732 (Sabin 88167).

2389 BEECKMAN, DANIEL. A Voyage to and from the Island of Borneo, in the East-Indies. With a Description of the said Island: giving an

Account of the Inhabitants, their Manners, Customs, Religion, Product, chief Ports and Trade. Together with the Re-establishment of the English Trade there, An. 1714, after our Factory had been destroyed by the Banjareens some Years before....With some Remarks and Directions touching Trade.... *Lond.* *1718*, *8º*. L.

Reprinted in *A General Collection of...Voyages*, ed. by J. Pinkerton, vol. 11 (1812).

2390 The United Company of Merchants of England Trading to the East-Indies, Appellants. Tho. Ekines, Esq; Resp. The Respondent's Case. *n.p.* [*1718*], *Fº*. L.

Signed: William Thompson. Spenser Cowper. Ship seized at Batavia in 1702.

2391 The East-India Company, Appellants. Thomas Ekines, Respondent. *n.p.* [*1718*], *Fº*. L.

The appellant's case. Signed: Tho. Lutwyche. John Hungerford. Endorsed: The Case of the East-India Company, Appel. and Thomas Ekines. Respondent.

COLONIES

2392 To the Honourable House of Commons. The most Humble Petition of James Alexander de Soulies. *n.p.* [*1718?*], *s. sh. Fº*. L.

For a patent for salt works in Minorca.

2393 To the Honourable House of Commons. The Humble Petition of James Alexander de Soulies. *n.p.* [*1718?*], *s. sh. Fº*. L.

A sequel to the preceding.

2394 Reasons hnmbly [*sic*] offered for the Encouragement of making Iron and Copper, in His Majesty's Plantations of America. *n.p.* [*1718?*], *s. sh. Fº*. L.

2395 Reasons Humbly Offered for the Encouragement of making Iron in His Majesty's Plantations of America. *n.p.* [*1718?*], *s. sh. Fº*. O.

2396 Reasons Humbly Offer'd against Encouraging the Making of Iron in America. *n.p.* [*1718?*], *s. sh. Fº*. L.

2397 Reasons humbly offered against the Encouragement of making Iron in his Majesty's Plantations. *n.p.* [*1718?*], *s. sh. Fº*. L.

Almost identical with the preceding.

2398 Hamilton, Lord Archibald. An Answer to an Anonymous Libel, entitled, Articles exhibited against Lord Archibald Hamilton, late Governour of Jamaica; with sundry Depositions and Proofs relating to the same. *Lond.* *1718*, *8º*. L.

FINANCE

2399 Two Letters to a Member of Parliament, concerning the Publick Debts. As they were Printed and Delivered to the Members of the House of Commons, on Occasion of his Majesty's Speech, concerning the Reduction of the Publick Debts. To which is added, The Present State of the Coin and Credit of the Kingdom, as it was Published and Delivered to the Members of the House of Commons; on Occasion of their Enquiring into the Reasons of the Scarcity of the Coin in the Kingdom. With some short Remarks on the Whole. *Lond. 1718*, *8º*. LU.

The Two Letters has been first published in 1717 (no. 2310).

2400 A Letter to Archibald Hutcheson, Esq;...Shewing the Insufficiency of his Scheme for the Payment of the Publick Debts. To which is added, A Scheme presented to the House of Commons in February 1717.... With a Vindication of the said Sheme [*sic*], and State of the Coin and Credit, as it stood in March last. With proper Remarks on the Whole. *Lond. 1718*, *8º*. L.

A reissue of the preceding, with the letter to Hutcheson prefixed. Another edn. 1721 (LU), entitled: The Rise of the Stocks, the Ruin of the People....

2401 [HUTCHESON, ARCHIBALD]. An Estimate of the Present National Debt; to which is added a Copy of Remarks which were subjoined to some Calculations made in April 1717. relating to the Publick Debts. *Lond. 1718*, *Fº*. L.

The 'Calculations' here mentioned are Hutcheson's *Computations relating to the Publick Debts*, which were reprinted under his name in *A Collection of Treatises*, 1720.

2402 HUTCHESON, ARCHIBALD. Some Calculations and Remarks relating to the Present State of the Publick Debts and Funds. And a Proposal for the Intire Discharge of the National Debt and Incumbrance in Thirty Years time. *Lond. 1718*, *Fº*. LU.

2nd edn. 1718 (MP).

2403 CROOKSHANKS, JOHN. Some Seasonable Remarks on a Book publish'd in the Month of July, 1718. by Archibald Hutcheson, Esq; relating to the Publick Debts and Fonds. With an Explanation of his Encreased Debts since the Peace at Utrecht: demonstrating what Part thereof properly belongs to the Late and Present Reign, and the Advantages of His Majesty's Wise and Frugal Government. *Lond. 1718*, *Fº*. LU.

The author's name is given in the folding table.

2404 [BOYER, ABEL]. Animadversions and Observations upon a Treatise lately publish'd, entituled Some Calculations and Remarks relating to the present State of the publick Debts and Funds; And a Proposal for the entire discharge of the National Debt...in thirty years time by Archibald Hutcheson....To which is added, A New Proposition to raise Money for the Use of the Publick.... *Lond. 1718*, *Fº*. L.

L has another issue with the author's name on the title-page, but the imprint of this copy has been cropped away.

2405 The Case of a great Number of Seamen, belonging to His Majesty's Royal Navy, and of the Wives and poor Families of many of them, who are still in His Majesty's Service.... *n.p.* [*1718*], *s. sh. F°*. L.

On arrears of pay.

2406 HAYES, RICHARD. The Young Merchant's Assistant: or, His Business at the Custom-House made easy. Containing the Method of Computing all Manner of Duties, their Discompts, and Drawbacks, by several Ways practiced by the Merchants and Custom-House Officers. Also Instructions for such People that are design'd for Employments, as Masters of Ships, or Husbanding the same.... *Lond. 1718, 8°*. L.

2407 Instructions for Officers concern'd in Ascertaining the Duties on Candles in the Country. *Lond. 1718, 12°*. LU.

2408 Anno Regni Jacobi Regis...primo.... *Lond. 1718, 12°*. O.

The text of the Act concerning Tanners (I James I, c. 22); of the Acts for Laying Duties upon Hides and Skins passed in the reigns of Anne and George I; with 'A Table to the Acts relating to Tanning, &c. and to the Duties on Hides'.

2409 GOODALE, DONALD, pseud. Scotland's Complaint against the Malt-Tax, &c. In a Letter from a Scots Farmer, to his Master, a Member of Parliament, Residing at London. *n.p. 1718, 4°*. pp. 8. LU.

Another edn., n.p. 1718, pp. 12 (LU).

2410 The Discarded Country Gager: a Poem. By T.L. late one of that Fraternity. Inscribed to the Gagers of Great-Britain. *Lond. 1718, 8°*. O.

2411 The Undue Administration: or, The Usual Managements of the Customs Consider'd; and Compar'd with the late pernicious Practices of Removing and Placing Officers, contrary to all former Precedents. The whole Impartially Represented, by Persons who now suffer under the Injustice and Oppression of a Quondam Minister of State, To the utter Ruin of Themselves and Families. *Lond. 1718, 8°*. LU.

2412 POVEY, CHARLES. English Inquisition: or, Money rais'd by the New Secret Extent Law, without Act of Parliament....In the Treatise is enter'd An Account of Seven Persecutions rais'd by the Whigs... against one subject that has done a piece of Service for this Government, which Five Hundred Thousand Pounds might not have purchased.... *Lond. 1718, 8°*. L.

Mainly against the exactions of the Commissioners of Excise.

2413 [HUTCHESON, ARCHIBALD]. Abstracts of the Number and Yearly Pay of the Land-Forces of Horse, Foot and Dragoons in Great Britain for the Year 1718....And also, of the Accompt of Half-pay for the Year 1718....With Some Remarks relating to the same. By a Member of Parliament. *Lond. 1718, 4°*. LU.

Reprinted in Hutcheson's *A Collection of Treatises relating to the Publick Debts*, 1720.

2414 Proclamation Prescribing the Method of taking out Impost Bills, by the Retailers of Country Ale and Beer. [*Edin.*, *1718*], *s. sh. F°*. EU.

Set forth by Edinburgh Town Council. Dated: 10 September 1718.

2415 [MADOX, THOMAS]. An Account of all the Gold and Silver Coins ever used in England: particularly, of their Value, Fineness, and Allay, and the Standards of Gold and Silver in all the respective Reigns for the last Six hundred Years. Likewise of it's Plenty and Scarcity....With a Method proposed to Redress our present Grievance, in respect to our Want of Silver.... *Lond. 1718, 8°*. LU.

For authorship, see H. & L., where no authority is quoted.

2416 [JOCELYN, J.]. An Essay on Money & Bullion. Wherein are considered, Value Intrinsick and Extrinsick. Money and Bullion compared. Mr. Locke's Considerations concerning Raising the Value of Coin. The Present State of our Coin. And a Scheme for raising the Value of our Coin, as well Gold as Silver. *Lond. 1718, 8°*. LU.

For authorship see H. & L. quoting ms. note in the Signet Library copy.

2417 A Letter to a Friend, Occasion'd from what was Published in the Daily-Courant, on Monday December 30th 1717, by Sir Isaac Newton, Relating to the Coin, &c. Shewing that the value of the Gold Coin, ought not to be lessen'd, but rather the Silver to be Raised. *Lond. 1718, 8°*. L.

Signed: S. Ph.

2418 A Letter to a Member of Parliament relating to the Coin. *Lond. 1718, 4°*. LU.

2419 [JONES, RICHARD]. A Letter from a Livery-Man of the City of London, to a Member of the Honourable House of Commons. *n.p.* [*1718*], *s. sh. F°*. L.

On the copper coinage. For authorship see *Cal. Treas. Papers*, 1714–1719, p. 360.

2420 Mus Rusticus. *n.p.* [*1718?*], *s. sh. F°*. L.

On the exportation of bullion and for a law to compel the wearing of woollens.

2421 Observations on Raising the Value of Money. Wherein the Interest of Ireland is particularly Consider'd. In a Letter to a Friend. *Dublin, 1718, 8°*. L.

2422 A Proposal humbly offered to the Honble. the Commons of Great Britain, in Parliament Assembled. *n.p.* [*c. 1718?*], *s. sh. F°*. LU.

Endorsed: A Proposal for Raising of Fifty Six Thousand Pounds; by Coining of new Farthings and Halfpence.

2423 Reasons humbly offered for Preventing the Melting down the Coin, and for Circulating of Money, and Encouraging a Coinage, and to preserve the Manufacture of wrought Plate. *n.p.* [*1718?*], *s. sh. F°*. O.

Another issue (O) adds 'and also the Inconveniences that may attend us, by giving a Power to Ship off the Money when Coin'd' to the title, and an additional paragraph to the text.

2424 Reasons Humbly Submitted to the Consideration of the Honourable House of Commons, against the further lowering Guineas; And against giving a Liberty to Export our Coin. With some Remarks upon Sir Isaac Newton's Representtion of the 21st of September last, to the Lords of the Treasury. *n.p.* [*1718*], *s. sh. F°*. L.

Dated: 13th January, 1717–8. Signed: B / B.

2425 [Clement, Simon]. Remarks upon a late Ingenious Pamphlet, entituled, A Short but thorough Search into what may be the real Cause of the present Scarcity of our Silver Coin, &c. Wherein Some Mistakes of that Author are endeavoured to be removed; the Vulgar Errors about the Valuation of Money and Bullion Silver are throughly discuss'd and clear'd; the true Occasion of the Scarcity of Silver shewn; and Such a Remedy proposed, as cannot fail to make it become Plenty again. By an Impartial Hand. *Lond. 1718, 8°*. LU.

2nd edn. 1718 (LU). For authorship see A. Boyer, *Pol. State of Great Britain*, xv, 65.

2426 Some Proposals, Humbly Offer'd, for the Increase and Preservation of our Currant-Coin, Particularly Silver, which is now become very scarce, And (if a speedy Remedy be not apply'd) will all be gone in a little time; For the further Payment of the Publick-Debts, So as to give every one their full Due, And instead of laying on any New Tax to accomplish this Work, To make the doing it an Advantage to all concern'd, And an Encouragement to Trade. *n.p.* [*c. 1718?*], *s. sh. F°*. L.

Signed: B. / B.

2427 The State of the Coin and Credit of the Kingdom. *n.p.* [*1718*], *s. sh. F°*. O.

Another edn. Lond. 1718, 8° (MP). Reprinted in *Two Letters to a Member of Parliament, concerning the Publick Debts*, 1718 (No. 2399).

2428 A Table shewing, at all the Variations of Exchange therein express'd, what Profit arises to the Exporter of our Gold Species, by leaving our Gold in Holland, and taking Bills of Exchange for it, on London. *n.p.* [*c. 1718?*], *8°*. L.

2429 Entry cancelled.

2430 Proposals by the Company of the Sun Fire-Office, In Threadneedle-Street, behind the Royal-Exchange, London, For Insuring Houses, moveable Goods, Merchandize, Furniture, and Wares, from Loss and Damage by Fire, in any Part of Great Britain. *Lond.* [*1718*], *s. sh. F°*. OUP.

Dated. Octob. 14, 1718.

2431 Mercers-Hall. A List of the Names of the Subscribers for Raising the Summe of One Million Sterling, as a Fund for Insuring Ships and Merchandize at Sea; Which Subscription was begun the 12th of August 1717. and compleated the 16th of January, 1717–8. *n.p.* [*1718*], *8°*. L.

2432 LUNDIN, ROBERT. The Reason of Accompting by Debitor and Creditor, with General Rules for attaining to that Way of Accompting. *Edin.* *1718*, *4°*. LU.

2nd edn. entitled: The Fundamental Principles, and Reasons of Accompting by Debitor and Creditor.... Edin. 1736, 4°. (EU).

2433 MACGHIE, ALEXANDER. The Principles of Book-Keeping Explain'd, with the Chief Cases thereof Stated and Resolved. To which are annexed, Two Setts of Books of Fictitious Trade, wherein the Whole is reduced to Practice. *Edin.* *1718*, *4°*. LICA.

2434 MALCOLM, ALEXANDER. A New Treatise of Arithmetick and Book-Keeping. *Edin.* *1718*, *4°*. L.

2435 SNELL, CHARLES. The Merchants Counting-House: or, Wast-Book Instances, with Directions for their Stating and Entrance.... *Lond.* *1718*, *F°*. LICA.

In the L copy a slip bearing the date 1720 has been pasted over the original imprint. Narcissus Luttrell's note of acquisition of this copy is dated Decemb. 1719.

TRANSPORT

2436 The Laws concerning Travelling, &c. Viz. 1. Robbery....4. Of Land-Carriage....5. Of Innkeepers....6. Of Water-Carriage....9. Of the Laws for regulating Hackney-Coaches, Chairs, Carrmen, and Watermen in and about London. *Lond.* *1718*, *12°*. L.

2437 The Cheese-Mongers Case, Relating to Dover Peer. *n.p.* [*1718?*], *s. sh. F°*. L.

For a clause exempting them from harbour dues.

2438 Reasons humbly offered against the Bill for Repair of Dover Peer. *n.p.* [*1718?*], *s. sh. F°*. L.

2439 A Bill for the Enlarging the Time Granted by an Act of the Ninth and Tenth Years of King William, for Cleansing, and making Navigable the Channel, from the Hithe at Colchester to Wivenhoe, and for making the said Act more Effectual. *n.p.* [*1718?*], *F°*. L.

2440 GILLMORE, JOSEPH. A Letter to a Member of Parliament, concerning Dagenham-Breach: occasion'd by the late Ruin of the Works there. *Lond.* *1718*, *4°*. O.

2441 An Act for Repairing the Road from Becconsfield, in the County of Bucks, to Stoken Church, in the County of Oxon. *n.p.* [*1718?*], *F°*. O.

2442 An Act for Amending the Roads from the City of London, to the Town of East Grinstead, in the County of Sussex, and to the Towns of Sutton and Kingston, in the County of Surry. *n.p.* [*1718*], *F°*. L.

2443 A Bill for Repairing the Highways from Maidenhead-Bridge to Sunning-Lane End, in the Road to Reading, and from the said Bridge to Henley-Bridge, in the County of Berks. *n.p.* [*1718*], *F*o. L.

L has the Act also.

2444 To the Honourable House of Commons, The Humble Petition of Charles Sewell, Thomas Holland, and George Garrett, on behalf of themselves, and the rest of the Eight Hundred Licensed Hackney Coach-men, and their Widows. *n.p.* [*1718?*], *s. sh. F*o. L.

Another edn. n.p., n.d., entitled: To the Honourable the House of Commons of Great Britain, in Parliament Assembled; The Humble Petition of Charles Sewell...(L).

2445 By-Laws, Rules and Orders, for the Better Regulating of Hackney Coaches, and Chairs, and the Drivers and Carriers thereof, within the City of Dublin, and Liberties of St. Sepulchers, Thomas Court and Donore.... [*Dublin*], *1718*, *8*o. LU.

Another edn. 1729; another edn. 1749 (both L).

SOCIAL CONDITIONS

2446 The Case of the Work-house and Hospital of the City of Bristol, Erected for the better Employing and Maintaining the Poor thereof; now depending in the Honourable House of Commons. *n.p.* [*1718*], *s. sh. F*o. L.

2447 Hitchin, Charles. A True Discovery of the Conduct of Receivers and Thief-Takers in and about the City of London; to the Multiplication and Encouragement of Thieves, House-Breakers, and other loose and Disorderly Persons. *Lond.* *1718*, *4*o. EU.

2448 The Case of the Shelterers in the Mint. *n.p.* [*1718?*], *s. sh. F*o. L.

2449 Some Considerations humbly offered to the High Court of Parliament for the Benefit of Creditors, and Relief of honest Insolvents. *n.p.* [*1718?*], *F*o. L.

2450 An Abstract of the Considerations for the Benefit of Creditors, and Relief of Honest Insolvents. *n.p.* [*1718?*], *s. sh. F*o. L.

2451 An Abstract of an Act proposed for preventing Frauds frequently committed by Bankrupts. *n.p.* [*1718?*], *F*o. L.

2452 Hell in Epitome: or, a Description of the M——sh——sea [Marshalsea]. A Poem. *Lond.* *1718*, *8*o. LG.

2453 An Account of the Establishment of the Commissioners for the Relief of Poor Proselytes; with an Abstract of their Proceedings from the 30th of April, 1717, to the 30th of April, 1718. *Lond.* *1718*, *8*o. L.

[continued as:]

An Abstract of the Proceedings of the Commissioners for the Relief of Poor Proselytes, from the 30th of April, 1718, to the 30th of April, 1719. *Lond.* *1719*, *8*o. O.

[continued as:]

An Account of the Establishment for relieving Poor Proselytes; with an Abstract of the Proceedings of the Commissioners for that Purpose, from the 30th of April, 1719, to the 3d of February, 1719–20. *Lond. 1720*, *8°*. L.

4th edn. [i.e. 4th Report] 1721, covers 3 Feb. 1719/20–25 Dec. 1720 (L). 5th edn. 1722, covers 25 Dec. 1720–25 Dec. 1721 (L).

[continued as:]

A Report for the Year of our Lord 1728, of the Management of the Commission for Distributing the Royal Bounty, and other Charitable Contributions, towards the Relief of Poor Converts from the Church of Rome. *n.p.* [*1729?*], *F°*. L.

2454 Rey, Claudius. An Account of the Cruel Persecutions, rais'd by the French Clergy, since their taking Sanctuary here, against several worthy Ministers, Gentlemen, Gentlewomen, and Tradesmen, Dissenting from their Calvinistical Scheme....And Containing a Detection of the Fraud in the Distribution of the 15000 l. of the Royal Bounty, Yearly given to the Poor French Protestant Refugees; and of many Falshoods in the List, printed by the Distributors thereof. In Answer to some private Letters of Mr. De La Chapelle, Minister of the French Church in Artillery-Lane.... *Lond. 1718*, *8°*. LU.

2455 The French Plot found out against the English Church: or, a Manifesto upon the unequalness of the Distribution of the 15000 l. of the Money of the Royal Beneficence, given every Year to the French Protestants... *Lond. 1718*, *8°*. O.

2456 To the Honourable House of Commons in Parliament assembled, The Case of the Widows, Orphans, and aged Mothers of Sons, who were their only Support, and were unfortunately lost in His Majesty's Ship the Sorlings, on the 17th of December, 1717. *n.p.* [*1718?*], *s. sh. F°*. L.

2457 Forms of Proposals for Augmenting Small Livings, &c. *n.p.* [*1718*], *s. sh. F°*. OUP.

Dated: Whitehall, Jan. 7. 1718.

2458 Middlesex ss. Ad General' Session' Pacis Domini Regis tent' pro Com. Midds. apud Hicks-Hall in St. John-street, in Com' praed', per Adjorn' die Sabbati primo die Martii, Anno Regni Georgii, nunc Regis Magnae Britanniae, &c. Quarto.... *n.p.* [*1718*], *s. sh. F°*. O.

Rules for licensing victuallers selling beer and ale or other liquors.

2459 The Case of the Inhabitants of the Cities of London & Westminster, and of the Parishes and Places within the Bills of Mortality, with respect to the Laws now in Force for preventing Mischiefs that may happen by Fire. Humbly offer'd to the Consideration of the Parliament of Great Britain. *Lond. 1718*, *8°*. LG.

1719

GENERAL

2460 A Computation of the Increase of London, and Parts Adjacent; with some Causes thereof, and Remarks thereon: particularly, with Respect to the Influence such Increase of the Capital may have on the Body of the Nation, its Constitution and Liberties. *Lond. 1719, 8°.* LU.

Based on the increase of coal imports.

AGRICULTURE

2461 LAURENCE, JOHN. Gardening Improv'd: containing I. The Clergymen's Recreation: shewing the Pleasure and Profit of the Art of Gardening.... II. The Gentleman's Recreation: or, the Second Part of the Art of Gardening improved.... III. The Fruit-Garden Kalendar....Written by John Lawrence....IV. The Lady's Recreation: or, the Art of Gardening farther improved....By Charles Evelyn....With an Appendix explaining the Motion of Sap, and Generation of Plants.... By Richard Bradley. *Dublin, 1719, 8°.* DNL.

2462 Reasons Humbly Offered, for Inclosing Gratwood-Heath, in the Parish of Eccleshall, in the County of Stafford. *n.p.* [*1719*], *s. sh. F°.* OC.

2463 Rules for Raising and Making Hemp. *n.p.* [*1719*], *s. sh. F°.* LPRO.

Endorsed: Rules for Raising Hemp.

2464 BARHAM, HENRY. An Essay upon the Silk-Worm: containing Many Improvements upon this Curious Subject; together with large Collections from the most approved Authors. The whole setting forth: I. The Antiquity of the Silk-Worm....VI. The Certainty and Facility of bringing the Silk Manufacture in England to its utmost Perfection, &c. *Lond. 1719, 8°.* LU.

2465 BOOTHE, NATHANIEL. The Right of His Majesty's Forest asserted, in a Charge given...before the Verderers of the Forest of Windsor, the 27th day of Septem. 1717. *Lond. 1719, 8°.* L.

2466 The Value of Church and College Leases consider'd; and the Advantage of the Lessees Made very Apparent. In a Letter to a Friend. *Lond. 1719, 8°.* O.

2nd edn. 1722 (DA); 3rd 1729 (C). Also issued in 1722, 1729, 1731, 1735 and 1742 as the second part of *Tables for the Renewing and Purchasing of the Leases of Cathedral-Churches and Colleges.* In the 1742 edn. the author is said to be 'a late Bishop of Chichester'. The copy of the 2nd edn. in RIA bears a ms. attribution to Thomas Bowers, Bishop of Chichester, 1722–4. The copy of the 3rd edn. in CUL bears a ms. attribution to Francis Hare, Bishop of Chichester, 1731–40, but this piece is not included in the collected edn. of Hare's *Works.* Attributed to Thomas Manningham, Bishop of Chichester, 1709–22, in *D.N.B.*

2467 The Report to the Honourable the House of Commons, of such of the Commissioners and Trustees [for Forfeited Estates] as have been appointed to Execute the several Trusts and Powers in relation to England Ireland, and elsewhere, (except Scotland).... *Lond. 1719, F°.* LU.

2468 To the Honourable the House of Commons, A Further Report, humbly offered by the Commissioners and Trustees [for Forfeited Estates] who acted in Scotland.... *Lond. 1719, F°.* L.

Ordered to be printed 19 Jan. 1718 [O.S.].

2469 Abstract of the Rental of the real Estate of James late Earl of Panmuir. *n.p.* [*1719*], *F°.* E.

Followed by 'Articles of the publick Sale or Roup'. E has 26 other abstracts relating to the sale of forfeited estates, 1719–22.

2470 A Letter from a Gentleman at Edinburgh to his Friend in London. *Lond. 1719, 8°.* L.

On the forfeited estates in Scotland.

2471 Copy of the Instructions by the Lords and Gentlemen concerned in the Grand-Fishery of Great-Britain, to John Dickson of Edinburgh Merchant. And of the Preamble in the Book for taking in Subscriptions for North-Britain. *n.p.* [*1719*], *s. sh. F°.* E.

2472 Reasons for taking off the present Prohibition of curing Fish in Scotland, with British Salt, for Exportation; while the English lie under no such Restraint. *n.p.* $\frac{18}{19}$, *s. sh. F°.* MC.

2473 Some Remarks on the Present State of the British Fishery. Humbly presented to the Consideration of the Honourable House of Commons. *n.p.* [*1719?*], *s. sh. F°.* L.

MANUFACTURES

2474 Reasons for Passing the Bill for preventing the Enticing of Artificers in Iron, Steel, Bath-Metal, Brass, Tinn, Clocks, and Watches, to go out of this Kingdom to settle these Manufactures in foreign Countries out of His Majesty's Dominions. *n.p.* [*1719*], *s. sh. F°.* L.

2475 Reasons humbly offer'd for Passing the Bill for Preventing the Artificers in the Manufactures of Great Britain, from going into Foreign Parts. *n.p.* [*1719*], *s. sh. F°.* LG.

2476 Answers for James Watson, One of His Majesty's Printers, to the Petition presented by the Representatives of the deceast Mrs. Anderson. *n.p.* [*1719*], *F°.* E.

Dated: February 3. 1719. Signed: Dun. Forbes.

2477 Additional-Information for James Watson, One of His Majesty's Printers. *n.p.* [*1719*], *s. sh. F°.* E.

Dated: January 6th, 1719. Signed: Dun. Forbes.

2478 CLAYTON, DAVID. A Short System of Trade: or, an Account of what in Trade must necessarily be Advantageous to the Nation, and what must of Consequence be Detrimental. *Lond. 1719*, *8°*. LU.

On printed calicoes.

2479 GORDIN, JACQUÉ. Arguments substantiels contre le port des Toiles des Indes Ou'est humblement montré le tort qui est fait à tous les Negoces d'Angleterre, & en particulier à la Manufacture des Luines, au commerce de Turquie & à celui de la mer du Sud.... *Londres, 1719*, *8°*. L.

L also has the title-page only of the English version: Substantial Arguments against the Wearing of Calicoes....By James Gordin.

2480 [DEFOE, DANIEL]. A Brief State of the Question, between the Printed and Painted Callicoes and the Woollen and Silk Manufacture, as far as it relates to the Wearing and Using of Printed and Painted Callicoes in Great-Britain. *Lond. 1719*, *8°*. LU.

2nd edn. 1719 (L.). For authorship see *C.B.E.L.* II, 506.

2481 [ASGILL, JOHN]. A Brief Answer to A Brief State of the Question between the Printed and Painted Callicoes, and the Woollen and Silk Manufactures: as far as it relates to the Wearing and Using Printed and Painted Callicoes in Great Britain. *Lond. 1719*, *8°*. LU.

Another issue, with author's name, 1719 (L); 2nd edn. 1720, with 'An Appendix upon The Spinster' [by Sir Richard Steele] (L).

2482 REY, CLAUDIUS. Observations on Mr. Asgill's Brief Answer to a Brief State of the Question between the printed and painted Callicoes, &c. Wherein his Falsities and Sophistry are laid open. *Lond. 1719*, *8°*. LU.

2483 The Case of the Woollen and Silk Manufactures in Great Britain. Humbly offer'd to the Consideration of the Parliament. *n.p.* [*1719*], *s. sh. F°*. LU.

For the prohibition of East India silks, printed calicos and linens.

2484 An Essay on Trade, wherein the present Dispute about Callicoes, &c. is Consider'd. *n.p.* [*1719?*], *8°*. LU.

2485 [DEFOE, DANIEL]. The Just Complaint of the Poor Weavers truly represented, with as much Answer as it deserves, to a Pamphlet lately written against them Entitled The Weavers Pretences examin'd, &c. *Lond. 1719*, *8°*. LU.

For authorship see *C.B.E.L.* II, 506.

2486 [DEFOE, DANIEL]. The Manufacturer: or the British Trade truly Stated. Wherein the Case of the Weavers and the Wearing of Callicoes are consider'd. no. 3, 6 Nov. 1719; no. 10, 2 Dec.; no. 20–22, 6–13 Jan. 1720; no. 24, 20 Jan.; no. 26–29, 29 Jan.–10 Feb.; no. 31, 17 Feb. *Lond. 1719, 20, F°*. O.

For authorship see *C.B.E.L.* II, 510.

2487 The British Merchant: or a Review of the Trade of Great Britain, so far as it is Falsely Stated by the Manufacturer. no. 1–12, Nov. 8, 1719–Feb. 11, 1720. *Lond. 1719, 20, F°.* O.

2488 [STEELE, Sir RICHARD]. The Spinster: in Defence of the Woollen Manufactures, To be continued Occasionally. Numb. 1. *Lond. 1719, 8°.* LU.

No more published. Reprinted in *Tracts and Pamphlets by Richard Steele*, ed. by Rae Blanchard, Baltimore, 1944.

2489 The Weaver. Or the State of our Home Manufacture Considered. no. 6, 28 Dec. 1719; no. 7, 4 Jan. 1719 [O.S.]; no. 8, 11 Jan. 1720. *Lond. 1719, 20, F°.* O.

2490 [REY, CLAUDIUS]. The Weavers True Case; or, the Wearing of Printed Callicoes and Linnen destructive to the Woollen and Silk Manufacturies. Wherein all the material Objections against the Weavers are fairly stated, consider'd, and answer'd....By a Weaver. *Lond. 1719, 8°.* L.

2nd edn., with author's name, 1719 (LU).

2491 The Weavers Pretences Examin'd. Being a Full and Impartial Enquiry into the Complaints of their wanting Work, and the true Causes assign'd. With some Useful Observations on the Silk, Stuff, and Callicoe Trades, in England, Holland, &c. By a Merchant. *Lond. 1719, 8°.* LU.

2492 A Further Examination of the Weavers Pretences. Being a Particular Answer to a late Pamphlet of theirs, Entituled, The Just Complaints, &c. And a Review of Two others lately Written on the same Side. Wherein the most Material of their Allegations are fairly Stated and Answer'd. By the Author of the Weavers Pretences Examined. *Lond. 1719, 8°.* LU.

2493 Memorial for the Proprietors of the Sugar Manufactories in Scotland. *n.p. [1719], F°.* EPRO.

2494 The several Acts for the Improvement of the Hempen and Flaxen Manufactures in this Kingdom. *Dublin, 1719, 8°.* D.

COMMERCE

2495 A Bill for Preventing the Mischiefs which may happen by keeping too great Quantities of Gun-powder in or near the Cities of London and Westminster, or the Suburbs thereof. *n.p. [1719], F°.* L.

2496 The Case of the Inhabitants of the Parishes of Wapping, Stepney, St. John Wapping and Aldgate, in Behalf of themselves and many Thousands Inhabitants in and about the said Parishes. *n.p. [1719], s. sh. F°.* L.

On the danger of the gunpowder warehouses.

2497 The Case of the Owners and Occupiers of Lands in Wapping, and elsewhere; and also of the Warehouses erected thereon, for Keeping of Gun-Powder. *n.p. [1719], s. sh. F°.* L.

2498 Reasons for an Exception, of the Lease of Johnson's Field, in Wapping, and the Four Gun-Powder Warehouses therein, out of the General Clause for avoiding Leases, added in the Lords Committee, to the Gun-Powder-Bill. *n.p.* [*1719*], *s. sh. F°.* LG.

2499 Reasons humbly offer'd for the Bill to prevent the Mischiefs which may happen by keeping too great Quantities of Gunpowder, in or near the Cities of London and Westminster, and the Suburbs thereof. *n.p.* [*1719*], *s. sh. F°.* L.

2500 The Case of the Makers of and Dealers in Cards and Dice. *n.p.* [*1719*], *s. sh. F°.* LU.

For relaxation of the stringent regulations about exports.

2501 The Case of Several Stationers, Haberdashers, Card-makers and Dice-makers of London and Westminster. *n.p.* [*1719*], *s. sh. F°.* O.

For relief after having violated the strict regulations governing the free export of cards and dice.

2502 By the King, A Proclamation. *Lond. 1718* [*O.S.*], *s. sh. F°.* L.

Dated: 19 March 1718. For apprehending straggling seamen and watermen.

2503 His Majesties most Gracious Declaration, For the Encouragement of His Ships of War and Privateers. *Lond. 1718* [*O.S.*], *s. sh. F°.* L.

Dated: 19 March 1718.

2504 By the King, A Proclamation, For Taking off the Prohibition of Commerce with Sweden. *Lond. 1719*, *s. sh. F°.* L.

Dated: 4 April 1719. Last word of l. 2 'Commerce'; another edn., last word l. 2 'with' (L).

2505 [MACKENZIE, alias MACKENZIE-QUIN, GEORGE]. Truth is but Truth, as it is Timed! Or, our Ministry's present Measures against the Muscovite vindicated by Plain and Obvious Reasons; tending to prove, that it is no less the interest of our British trade, than that of our state, that the Czar be not suffer'd to retain a fleet...in the Baltick. The whole extracted from a representation made...by N.N....in August 1715. *Lond. 1719*, *fol.* L.

Authorship deduced from hints given in A. Boyer, *Pol. State of Great Britain*, XVIII, 160.

2506 Reasons Humbly Offer'd against several Clauses in the Bill. *n.p.* [*1719?*], *s. sh. F°.* LG.

Endorsed: Reasons against Several Clauses (in a Bill Entituled) To prevent Clandestine Trading.

2507 The Substance of the Bill against Clandestine Trade which concerns Merchants. *n.p.* [*1719?*], *s. sh. F°.* LG.

2508 Reasons humbly offer'd against a Clause in the Bill against Clandestine Running of Un-customed and Prohibited Goods, and for the more effectual preventing of Frauds relating to the Customs, which relates to the Package of Coffee for Exportation. *n.p.* [*1719?*], *s. sh. F°.* L.

2509 Reasons humbly offered against Divers Clauses in a Bill now depending before Your Lordships, entituled, An Act against the clandestine Running of uncustomed and prohibited Goods, &c. *n.p.* [*1719*], *s. sh. F*°. O.

2510 Act for Preventing the Running of Goods, and Perjuries at the Custom-houses. At Edinburgh, 22nd May 1719. [*Edin. 1719*], *s. sh. F*°. C (Cr).
By the General Assembly of the Church of Scotland.

2511 A Ballance for Merchants and Mariners: Containing an undoubted Account of the Principal Causes of the great Decay of Trade; with proper Directions to set our Trade again on a right Foot. By a sincere Well-wisher to the Trade and Prosperity of the Nation. *Edin. 1719*, *8*°. L.
On smuggling.

2512 An Account of the Number of Woollen Cloths of all Sorts, Exported by the Levant-Company from England to Turky, in Forty-six Years. from Christmass, 1671, to Christmass 1717. *n.p.* [*1719?*], *s. sh. F*°. L,

2513 The Case of several Members of the Levant Company, complaining of the Restraint of their Trade. *n.p.* [*1719*], *F*°. L.

2514 The Case of the Levant-Company. *n.p.* [*1719*], *s. sh. F*°. L.
Dated 29 Jan. 1718 [O.S.].

2515 Remarks on the Case published by the Levant Company. *n.p.* [*1719*], *s. sh. F*°. L.

2516 Paragraphs of some Letters, among many others, from Aleppo, Smyrna, Constantinople, to prove the Reasonableness of the Levant-Company's late Orders to carry on their Trade by General Ships. *n.p.* [*1719*], *F*°. O.

2517 The Opinion of many of the Levant-Company, relating to the Departure of their Ships to Turky. *n.p.* [*1719*], *s. sh. F*°. O.
Title taken from endorsement.

2518 An Historical Account of the Voyages and Adventures of Sir Walter Raleigh. With the Discoveries and Conquests He made for the Crown of England. Also a particular Account of his several Attempts for the Discovery of the Gold Mines in Guiana.... To which is added, An Account how that rich Country might now be with Ease, Possess'd, Planted and Secur'd to the British Nation, and what Immense Wealth and Encrease of Commerce might be rais'd from thence. Humbly Proposed to the South-Sea-Company. *Lond. 1719*, *8*°. LU.
Attributed to Defoe by Dottin, who says it was issued in Jan. 1720.

2519 The East-India Sale, September the First, 1719, *etc. Lond. 1719*, *8*°. L.
A list of the lots with the prices and buyers' names.

2520 Reasons against the Bill for the better Securing the Lawful Trade of His Majesty's Subjects to and from the East-Indies, and for the more effectual preventing all His Majesty's Subjects Trading thither under Foreign Commissions. *n.p.* [*1719?*], *s. sh. F*°. LU.
Text begins: The Legislative Power of Great Britain.

2521 Reasons against the Bill for the better Securing the lawful Trade of His Majesty's Subjects to and from the East-Indies, and for the more effectual preventing all His Majesty's Subjects Trading thither under Foreign Commissions. *n.p.* [*1719?*], *s. sh. F°.* LLI.

Text begins: The Trade which the Nation granted the East-India Company.

COLONIES

2522 Reasons against a General Prohibition of the Iron Manufacture in his Majesty's Plantations, intended by a Clause in the Bill now depending, entituled, A Bill for Encouraging the Importation of Naval Stores from America. *n.p.* [*1719*], *s. sh. F°.* O.

2523 Reasons for Encourageing the Making of Iron in our Plantations, and the Objections Answer'd. *n.p.* [*1719?*], *s. sh. F°.* O.

2524 The present Melancholy Circumstances of the Province Consider'd, and Methods for Redress humbly proposed, in a Letter from one in the Country to one in Boston. *Boston, 1719, 8°.*

Reprinted in *Colonial Currency Reprints*, ed. by A. M. Davis, vol. 1 (1910), whence this entry is taken, and where the authorship is attributed to John Colman, on slight grounds.

2525 An Addition to the Present Melancholy Circumstances of the Province Considered, &c. March 6th. 1718,9. Exhibiting Considerations about Labour, Commerce, Money, Notes, or Bills of Credit. *Boston, 1719, 8°.*

Reprinted in *Colonial Currency Reprints*, ed. by A. M. Davis, vol. 1 (1910), whence this entry is taken.

2526 [GORDON, WILLIAM]. A Representation of the Miserable State of Barbadoes, under the Arbitrary and Corrupt Administration of his Excellency, Robert Lowther, Esq; the present Governor....With a Preface, containing Remarks on an Address, printed in the Postman, and in the Whitehall Evening-Post of May 14. 1719. *Lond.* [*1719*], *8°.* L.

For authorship see *Cal. S.P. Col.*, 1720–21, no. 9.

2527 The Whole Proceedings of Captain Dennis's Expedition to the Governor of the Havanna; being a Memorial, or Journal of What Occurrences happen'd during his Stay there. *Kingston* [*Jamaica*], *1718* [*O.S.*], *F°.* LPRO.

2528 The Case of Such Sufferers who sustained Losses by the Invasion of the French in the Year 1705, on the Islands of Nevis and St Christopher's, who have Settled on one of the said Islands, and have not their Debentures Issued forth, thro' some doubtful Words in the Acts made for their Relief. *n.p.* [*1719*], *s. sh. F°.* O.

FINANCE

2529 BARBIER, STEPHEN. An Expedient to pay the Publick Debts. With a Letter to the King; as it was most humbly Presented to His Majesty, May the 6th 1719. *Lond. 1719, 4°.* L.

2530 CARY, JOHN. A Proposal for Paying off the Publick Debts by Erecting a National Credit.... *Lond. 1719, 8°.* L.

2531 HUTCHESON, ARCHIBALD. Mr. Hutcheson's Answer to Mr Crookshanks's Seasonable Remarks. *Lond. 1719, F°.* LU.

A reissue, 1720 (L).

2532 Several Reports presented to the House of Commons, by the Commissioners for Taking and Stating the Debts due and growing due to Scotland by Way of Equivalent.... *Lond. 1718,* [*O.S.*], *F°.* LU.

A report presented 8 June 1717 and two reports and a memorial presented 21 Feb. 1718 [O.S.].

2533 An abridgement of a Report made and sign'd by Henry Cartwright and John Boteler, esqrs; two of the commissioners appointed for taking and stating the debts due and growing due to Scotland by way of equivalent: with some remarks. As also Some observations on the Report of commissioners for stating these debts, in the year 1717; and on the Report made and sign'd by Stephen Bisse and Samuel Tufnall, esqrs. other two of the present commissioners, in the year 1718/19. *n.p. 1719, 32½ cm.* Kress 3083.

2534 A Second Letter to a Member of Parliament, concerning the Subject Matter of the Equivalent. *n.p.* [*1719*], *4°.* O.

Dated: March 25, 1719.

2535 Numb. 1, The Benefit Tickets in each of the Lotteries, Anno 1719. Drawn before the Managers and Directors thereof, at Guild-hall, London; on Monday the 21st of September, 1719. being the first Day. *Lond.* [*1719*], *s. sh. F°.* LSC.

2536 [DEFOE, DANIEL]. The Gamester. A Benefit-Ticket for all that are concern'd in the Lotteries; or the Best Way how to get the 20000 l. Prize. Together with some necessary and seasonable Remarks on the Schemes of Insurance relating to the present Lotteries. *Lond. 1719, 4°.* MP.

The attribution is Professor J. R. Moore's.

2537 [DEFOE, DANIEL]. The Gamester. N°. II. Demonstrating what was laid down in N°. I. as to the Schemes of Insurance upon Lottery Tickets, &c. With some Observations, how those evil and pernicious Practices, affect the sensible Decay of our Trade.... *n.p.* [*1719*], *4°.* MP.

The attribution is Professor J. R. Moore's.

2538 A Letter to the Gamester. Numb. I. Wherein the Mistakes of that Author's Calculation, and the Unreasonableness of his heavy Censures are plainly demonstrated. With some Advice to the Stock-Jobbers, and others concern'd in the Lottery Tickets, in Relation to the Two different Sets of Proposals for Insuring Tickets at Mercers-Hall. *Lond. 1719*, 4°. MP.

Signed: Arenarius.

2539 Reasons humbly offer'd against Raising Money by a Lottery, for the Service of the Publick. *n.p.* [*1719?*], *s. sh. F°*. L.

2540 Reasons humbly proposed for a further Act or Clause, to prevent Loss in the Stampt-Duties, and other Inconveniences arising from Clandestine Marriages. *n.p.* [*c. 1719?*], *s. sh. F°*. L.

2541 LOGGIN, ROBERT. The Case fully and truly Stated Representing great Frauds, Committed in his most Sacred Majesty's Customs, in relation to the Duty on Pepper and Tobacco, amounting to near 500,000 l. per. Annum.... *n.p.* [*1719?*], *F°*. LU.

2542 LOGGIN, ROBERT [and ROTHERHAM, JOHN]. The Present Management of the Customs. Being a Detection of Grand Frauds in that Branch of his Majesty's Royal Revenue...by the false Entries of Pepper and Tobacco for Exportation....With an Impartial Account of the Proceeding relating thereunto.... *Lond. 1720* [*1719*], 8°. L.

2543 The Case of John Mason, Gent. Late Receiver of the Taxes in the University-Town and County of Cambridge, and Isle of Ely. *n.p.* [*1719?*], *s. sh. F°*. O.

For inclusion in the terms of the Bill for the relief of insolvent debtors. An act to enable the Lord Treasurer to compound with him for his debt to the Crown had been passed in 1705, but he could not raise the money and had spent 14 years in the Fleet Prison.

2544 Instructions for the Collectors and other Officers employed in His Majesty's Customs in Scotland, for their Government in observing the Directions of the Act, Entituled, An Act for recovering the Credit of the British Fishery, &c. *Edin. 1719*, 8°. O.

2545 Reasons against Ascertaining the Tithe of Hops, drawn up in the Year 1711, in Order to have been put into the Hands of the Members of the Honourable House of Commons, if the House had then proceeded upon the Bill, for Ascertaining the Tithe of Hops. By a Member of the Lower House of Convocation. *n.p. 1719*, 4°. E.

2546 Reasons humbly offer'd against the Bill for Ascertaining the Tythe of Hops. *n.p.* [*1719?*], *s. sh. F°*. L.

2547 The Course of the Exchange, and other things. 3 Jan. 1701—28 Dec. 1750. *Lond. 1701–50. F°. slip*. LStE; L.

Published by John Castaing to 30 April 1725; by Castaing and Edward Jackson 4 May 1725–30 Dec. 1729; by Edward Jackson 2 Jan. 1730–15 July 1735; by Richard Shergold and Castaing's widowed sister 18 July 1735–Oct. 1749; by George Shergold and Castaing's widowed sister Oct. 1749—Dec. 1750. LStE has 1701–1720, 1727, 1732, 1734, 1736–9, 1742–50, almost complete. L has an almost complete set from 1720 to 1755.

2548 HAYES, RICHARD. The Negociator's Magazine: or, the Exchanges Anatomiz'd. In Two Parts. Part I. Of the Foreign Banks and Agio's... Part II. Concise and plain Instructions relating to Bills of Exchange.... *Lond. 1719, 8°.* LU.

2nd edn. 1724 (L); another 2nd edn. 1726 (LU); 3rd edn. 1730 (LU); 4th edn. 1739 (LU); 5th edn. 1740 (O); 6th edn. 1740 (LU); 7th edn. 1740 (LU); 8th edn. 1754 (LU).

2549 [DEFOE, DANIEL]. The Anatomy of Exchange-Alley: or, a System of Stock-Jobbing. Proving that Scandalous Trade, as it is now carry'd on, to be Knavish in its Private Practice, and Treason in its Publick.... By a Jobber. *Lond. 1719, 8°.* L.

2nd edn. 1719 (L). For authorship see *C.B.E.L.* II, 506.

2550 Mons Pietatis Londiniensis: A Narrative or Account of the Charitable Corporation, for Relief of Industrious Poor, by Assisting them with Small Sums upon Pledges, at Legal Interest. In a Letter to ××××××× *Lond. 1719, F°.* L.

2551 SNELL, CHARLES. Book-keeping in a Method Proper to be Observ'd by Super-Cargo's and Factors....The Second Edition. *Lond. 1719, F°.* LICA.

The first edition, not seen, was published in 1709.

2552 WEBSTER, WILLIAM. An Essay on Book-Keeping, According to the True Italian Method of Debtor and Creditor, by Double Entry.... *Lond. 1719, 12°.* LICA.

2nd edn. 1721 (LICA); 3rd, 1726 (LICA); another edn. Dublin, 1734 (L); 5th edn. Lond. 1735 (L); 6th edn. 1738 (L); 7th, 1740; 8th, 1744; 9th, 1747; 10th, 1749 (all LICA).

TRANSPORT

2553 A Bill to Make the River Darwent, in the County of Derby, Navigable. *n.p. [1719?], F°.* L.

2554 LONDON. Ward Mayor. Martis, xxvij° die Octobris, 1719. [*Lond. 1719*], *s. sh. F°.* LCRO.

An order enforcing a clause in the Act for better Regulating Hackney Coaches.

SOCIAL CONDITIONS

2555 The Case of the poor confined Debtors within the several Prisons of this Kingdom. Humbly submitted to the Consideration of the Parliament of Great-Britain, for Relief. *n.p. [1719?], s. sh. F°.* L.

2556 A Bill for the Relief of Poor Insolvent Debtors in the several Goals of this Kingdom. *n.p. [1719], F°.* L.

2557 Reasons humbly offer'd for Altering and Amending the Laws concerning Bankrupts, and for preventing the great Losses that are Daily sustained by their Creditors, since the Expiration of the late Acts, of the Fourth and Fifth Years of the Reign of Her late Majesty Queen Anne. *n.p.* [*1719?*], *s. sh. F*o. L.

2558 A Bill to prevent Frauds committed by Bankrupts. *n.p.* [*1719?*], *F*o. L.

2559 Observations and Proposals most humbly Offered to the Parliament by several Creditors, Merchants and Traders of London, relating to the Bill now depending concerning Bankrupts. *n.p.* [*1719?*], *s. sh. F*o. L.

2560 Reasons humbly offer'd for making more certain the Liberty of such Bankrupts who shall Fairly and Justly Surrender Themselves, and Effects, pursuant to the Act now depending, or any other Acts now in being, to prevent Frauds committed by Bankrupts. *n.p.* [*1719?*], *s. sh. F*o. L.

The endorsed title is: The Case of Such Persons who are Subject to the Laws of Bankruptcy.

2561 LONDON. Ward, Mayor. Martis viij die Septemb. 1719....Abstract of the Bankrupts Act. [*Lond. 1719*], *F*o. LCRO.

2562 LONG, JOHN. An Answer to a False and Scandalous Case, Intituled, The Case of the Creditors of Joseph Long, late of London, Merchant. *n.p.* [*1719*], *s. sh. F*o. L.

Long was a bankrupt.

2563 *Begin.* The Commissioners for the Relief of Poor Proselytes finding that some of their Members slacken their Zeal.... *n.p.* [*1719*], *s. sh. F*o. L.

An appeal for funds. L copy is signed in ms. by Henry Newman and dated 14 Feb. 1718.

2564 ECTON, JOHN. A State of the Proceedings of the Corporation of the Governors of the Bounty of Queen Anne, for the Augmentation of the Maintenance of the Poor Clergy, from their First Establishment in the Year 1704, to Christmas 1718.... *Lond. 1719*, 8o. MP.

2nd edn. Lond. 1721 (L); another 2nd edn. Dublin, 1725 (DA).

1720

GENERAL

2565 GERVAISE, ISAAC. The System or Theory of the Trade of the World. Treating Of the different Kinds of Value. Of the Ballances of Trade. Of Exchange. Of Manufactures. Of Companies. And shewing the Pernicious Consequences of Credit, and that it destroys the Purpose of National Trade. *Lond. 1720, 8°.* LU.

2566 A Proposal humbly offer'd to the Consideration of both Houses of Parliament, for Encouraging and Improving Trade in General. *Lond. 1721* [*1720*], *8°.* LU.

The dedication signed: R.S.

2567 [COX, THOMAS]. Magna Britannia et Hibernia, Antiqua & Nova. Or, A New Survey of Great Britain, wherein to the Topographical Account given by Mr. Cambden, and the late Editors of his Britannia, is added a more large History, not only of the Cities, Boroughs, Towns, and Parishes mentioned by them, but also of many other Places of Note, and Antiquities since discovered.... Collected and Composed by an impartial Hand. *Lond. 1720–31, 4°.* 6 vols. L.

For authorship see R. Gough, *British Topography,* I, 33.

2568 Great Britain's Vade Mecum. Containing, I. A Concise Geographical Description of the World.... II. The several Counties of England and Wales particularly Described.... III. A short view of Trade in general.... IV. A Description of the Cities of London and Westminster.... VII. Directions for Taking up and Entring Goods at the Custom-House.... VIII. The best Instructions for Gauging and Measuring.... IX. The Rates of Post Letters.... X. The Rates and Orders of Coachmen, Chairmen, Carmen, Watermen, &c. XI. An Account of the Roads to London from the Principal Cities and Market Towns in England and Wales.... By G. J. Gent. *Lond. 1720, 12°.* L.

2569 The Present State of the British Court: or, An Account of the Civil and Military Establishment of England. Containing New and Exact Lists of all the Officers of His Majesty's Court and Houshold, the Army, and Navy; and also of the several Branches of the Revenue, with the Nature, Duty, and Business of every particular Office and Officer therein; their Attendance, Salaries, Fees, &c.... To be published Annually. *Lond. 1720, 8°.* L.

2570 STOW, JOHN. A Survey of the Cities of London and Westminster.... Corrected, improved, and very much enlarged.... By John Strype, &c. *Lond. 1720, F°.* L.

Another edn. 1734, 35, ed. by Robert Seymour, the pseudonym of John Mottley; another edn. 1753; 6th edn. 1754, 55 (all L).

2571 Some of the Grievances and Complaints of the poor Commonality of Scotland. I. Holden forth by way of Answer to Mr. Freebairns Pamphlet, correcting the Mistakes of such as that say that Taxations and Customs are the true Causes of Scotlands Poverty and Misery. II. Holden forth that the Instrumental Causes of our Poverty, is occasioned by ill Management of Husbandry and Trade. III. that the Poor are oppressed....IV. Together with other thoughts concerning Husbandry and Trade for the better Management thereof for the good of all by way of Overtures. By a Wellwisher to the present Government. *Glasgow, 1720, 8°*. E.

In reply to *The Miserable State of Scotland since the Union*, 1716 (no. 2218).

2572 An Elegy on the Death of Trade. *Lond. 1720, 8°*. O.

AGRICULTURE

2573 An Act for Enclosing the Common commonly called Baltonsbury-Common, in the Parishes of Baltonsbury and Bradley, in the County of Somerset. *n.p.* [*1720*], *F°*. O.

2574 An Act for Enclosing the Heath, or Common, commonly called Gratwood-Heath, in the Parish of Eccleshall, in the County of Stafford. *n.p.* [*1720*], *F°*. L.

A bill.

2575 A Bill to prevent the Inning or Imbanking any more Salt-Marshes, which do lie on either Side the Chanel from Wisbich Seaward. *n.p.* [*1720*], *F°*. L.

2576 The Case of Augustin Woollaston, Esq; and Reasons humbly offered to the Honourable House of Commons; against the Bill to prevent the Inning or Imbanking any more Salt-Marshes, which do lie on either side the Channel from Wisbech Seaward. *n.p.* [*1720*], *F°*. L.

Endorsed: The Case and Reasons of Augustin Woollaston, Esq; against the Bill for preventing the Inning or Imbanking Sutton-Salt-Marshes in Lincolnshire.

2577 An Answer to the Case and Reasons of Augustine Woollaston, Esq; relating to the Bill to prevent the Inning or Imbanking any more Salt-Marshes, which do lie on either Side of the Chanel, from Wisbich Seaward. *n.p.* [*1720*], *F°*. LLI.

2578 Reasons humbly offered to the Honourable House of Commons, against Imbanking the Salt-Marsh, belonging to Sutton in Lincolnshire; shewing that it will be destructive to the Port of Wisbich, within the Isle of Ely. *n.p.* [*1720*], *F°*. L.

2579 Reasons humbly offered to the Honourable House of Commons, against Imbanking the Salt-Marsh belonging to Sutton in the County of Lincoln; shewing that it will obstruct the Draining a great Part of the Great Level of the Fens. *n.p.* [*1720*], *s. sh. F°*. L.

2580 JOYNES, CLEMENT. An Essay on New Experiments. Wherein is demonstrated, I. That Barren, Waste, and Uncultivated Lands, belonging either to Crown or Subject) may be improved from 1l. to 10l. 20l. 30l. 40l. or 50l. an Acre more than the Rent, with the Art of making Potateo-Starch, and the true Copy of the Starch Patent, &c. II. The whole Art of Gardening and Husbandry reduced to Practical Rules.... III. Several Essays of great Advantage to the Silken Manufactory at Chelsea.... *Lond.* [*1720?*], *8o*. L.

L copy, the only one seen, is imperfect.

2581 The British Improvement of Timber and Uncultivated Lands. *n.p.* [*1720*], *Fo*. LU.

Proposals for a joint stock with a subscription of £2,000,000.

2582 A Clear View of the Fundamental Constitutions, Privileges, and Immunities of the Governor and Company of the Mine-Adventurers of England. As the same are, at large, contained in their Charter, and in an Act of Parliament, of the Ninth Year of the late Queen's Reign, &c. Together with an Alphabetical Index to the whole Contents. *Lond.* *1720*, *8o*. O.

2583 An Abstract of the Resolutions and Agreements of the Governor and Company of Mine-Adventurers of England, in a General Court, for making a Call, and Leasing out some of the Company's Mines: And also of the Orders of the Court of Directors pursuant thereto, and to a Proposal of Ways and Means for raising a New and Voluntary Stock... made by John Wallis, Esquire, one of the Directors.... *n.p.* [*1720?*], *Fo*. L.

2584 The Agreement of Several Persons (Members of the Company of Mine-Adventurers) for raising a Stock of Thirty Thousand Pounds, to carry on the Manufactures, herein after mentioned. *n.p.* [*1720*], *s. sh. Fo*. O.

Dated: 9 June 1720.

2585 An Abstract of the Agreement between Several Persons Members of the Company of Mine-Adventurers, and the Chief Workmen, in the Work-houses of Sir Humphry Mackworth, at Neath, in the County of Glamorgan; for Manufacturing Copper, Brass and Lead, and Extracting Silver out of Lead, and for Rolling and Siltting [*sic*] of Iron. *n.p.* [*1720*], *Fo*. O.

Endorsed: The Agreements with the Workmen; and a Computation of the Profits.

2586 Observations on the Agreement and Undertaking of several Persons, Members of the Company of Mine-Adventurers, for making and Manufacturing Copper, Brass and Lead, and for Extracting Silver out of Lead, and for Rolling and Slitting of Iron, in the Work-houses Erected on the Estate of Sir Humphry Mackworth, at Neath, in the County of Glamorgan. *n.p.* [*1720?*], *Fo*. O.

2587 To the Governour and Company of the Mine-Adventurers of England. The Proposal of Sir Humphrey Mackworth, on Behalf of himself, and several other Persons, Members of the said Company. *n.p.* [*1720*], *s. sh. F*o. O.

Signed: H. Mackworth. Dated: June 30th, 1720.

2588 The Advantage of the New Scheme of the Mine-Adventurers to all the several Parties concerned. *n.p.* [*1720?*], *F*o. L.

2589 A Short Account of the Profit and Security which all Persons will enjoy who shall advance Money by Way of Loan, to encrease the Stock and Dividend of the Mine-Adventurers. *n.p.* [*1720?*], *s. sh. F*o. L.

2590 Williams, Thomas, and Hopkins, John. A View of the Advantages arising to the Copartners or Company of the Mineral Manufactures at Neath, by Making and Manufacturing Copper, Brass, Lead, and Iron, in their Work-houses there Presented to the New Partners. By Thomas Williams, Secretary, and John Hopkins, Accomptant. *Lond. 1720*, *8*o. L.

Another edn., 1721 (O). According to a ms. note in the Rawlinson copy in the Bodleian, this is mostly bogus.

2591 The Form of admitting New Partners into The Company of Mineral Manufactures at Neath; with some Observations thereupon. *n.p.* [*1720*], *F*o. O.

Title from endorsement.

2592 Mackenzie, Roderick. A Familiar Letter to a Gentleman at Bath; containing an Account of the Proceedings of the Governor and Company of the Mine-Adventurers of England, at their two last General Courts, held...the 16th and 23rd days of August, 1720....By R.M. a Member of the said Company. *Lond. 1720*, *F*o. L.

Signed: Rod. Mackenzie.

2593 [Mackenzie, Roderick]. A Letter to Sir J—— C—— Baronet, a Member of the Honourable House of Commons. Wherein Particular Notice is taken of the Report, which was made, ex Parte, on the 13th of March 1709–10, by a Committee of the then House of Commons, touching the then State and Management of the Affairs of the Company of the Mine-Adventurers of England. Containing likewise a clear and irrefragable Vindication of Sir Humphrey Mackworth...By a Member of the Company of the Mine-Adventurers of England. *Lond. 1720*, *F*o. LU.

Signed: R.M. A.A. 2nd edn. 1720 (O). For authorship see Mackenzie's *A Familiar Letter*.

2594 A Representation containing a Vindication of Sir Humphrey Mackworth from the Many False and Scandalous Reflections cast upon him in the House of Commons in the Year 1709. Many by a Committee of Seventeen Persons, as well Directors as others, to the Governour and

Company of the Mine-Adventurers of England, at a General Court held...on Saturday the 28th Day of November, 1720...*Lond. 1720*, *F°*. L.

Another edn. 1720 (O), entitled: A Representation made by a Committee of Seventeen Persons, as well Directors as Others, to the Governour and Company of the Mine-Adventurers of England; containing a Vindication of Sir Humphrey Mackworth....

2595 The Present State of Mr. Wood's Partnership. *n.p.* [*1720*], *s. sh. F°*. L.

A mining company prospectus. Possibly cropped. The text begins: 'The Dominions of Great Britain abounds in as great Variety of Minerals, perhaps, as any Country whatever, of the same Extent'. The title quoted above occurs half-way down the sheet.

2596 [JACOB, GILES]. The Land-Purchaser's Companion: and the Laws relating to Tenants and Tenures.... To which are added, The Laws and Statutes relating to Tithes, so far as they concern Tenants.... *In the Savoy*, *1720*, *12°*. LU.

In some copies the dedication is signed: Giles Jacob.

2597 A Further Report presented to the Right Honourable the Lords Spiritual and Temporal in Parliament assembled, from the Commissioners and Trustees [for Forfeited Estates] who acted in Scotland...with an appendix thereto annexed. *Lond. 1720*, *F°*. L.

2598 A Letter from a Gentleman at Edinburgh, to a Member of the House of Commons in London; concerning the Proceedings of the Commissioners and Trustees for the Forfeitures in Scotland. *Lond. 1720*, *8°* E.

2599 A Letter from a Gentleman at Edinburgh, to a Member of the House of Commons at London; concerning the Proceedings of the Commissioners and Trustees for the Forfeitures in Scotland, touching the Sale of the Estate of James (late) Earl of Panmure. *Lond. 1720*, *8°*. L.

2600 Memorial concerning the Proceedings of the Court of Session in Scotland in hearing and determining Exceptions enter'd against the Survey of the Commissioners and Trustees of the forfeited Estates. *n.p.* [*1720*], *F°*. L.

The Commissioners appealed to the House of Lords and L has many of the individual printed cases, which are not included here.

2601 Extract of Two Acts of Parliament, relating to the Governour and Company of Undertakers for Raising the Thames-Water in York-Buildings. *n.p.* [*1720?*], *s. sh. F°*. L.

Justifying the purchase of the forfeited estates in Scotland.

2602 Articles of the Copartnery of the Freeman-Burgesses of the Royal Burrows of Scotland, for carrying on a Fishing Trade. Dated at Edinburgh, 8th, 9th, 10th, 11th, & 12th August. 1720. *Edin. 1720*, *8°*. L.

2603 Britain's Golden Mines discover'd: or, the Fishery Trade considered, under these Three Heads, I. What Benefit Britain may reap by it. II. Which is the most probably Way of recovering it. III. The Three great

Fishing Trades, viz. That upon our own Coasts, That upon the Coasts of Greenland, and That upon the Coasts of Newfoundland, particularly examined. In a letter from Sally Fisher, at Paris, to Mally Loverus, at London. *Lond. 1720*, *8º*. LU.

2604 The Case of the Company of the Royal Fishery of England. *n.p.* [*1720?*], *Fº*. LU.

2605 The Case of the Merchants, who have raised a Joint-Stock for Recovering and effectual Carrying on the Greenland Whale-Fishery with Vigor. *n.p.* [*1720*], *s. sh. Fº*. LU.

2606 The Importance and Management of the British Fishery Consider'd. In a Letter to a Friend. To which are added, by way of Appendix, the Method of Sorting, Packing, Salting, and Curing of Herrings, us'd by the Dutch. As also an Abstract of the Dutch Laws, relating to the Fishery. *Lond. 1720*, *8º*. LU.

2607 Proposals to the Holy Island Fishery and Salt Pans, &c. for Raising a Stock of 2000000 l. Sterling, in Copartnership, for erecting Salt-Pans in Holy Island, in the County of Northumberland, for establishing a Fishery there, and for Fencing and Bounding there, and in three adjoining Places, above 60000 Acres of Land...and lastly, for Cutting and Polishing Marble, with which the said Island abounds.... *n.p.* [*1720*], *s. sh. Fº*. LPRO.

2608 Proposals for Establishing the British Fishery, Commonly Call'd Robin's Fishery. *n.p.* [*1720?*], *s. sh. Fº*. LU.

A bubble.

2609 Reasons humbly offered to the Honourable House of Commons, for Carrying on a National Fishery. *n.p.* [*1720?*], *s. sh. Fº*. L.

Endorsed: Reasons humbly offer'd...for Establishing the National Fishery.

2610 Rasons [*sic*] humbly offer'd to the Honourable House of Commons, for Incorporating the Subscribers for Carrying on a National Fishery. *n.p.* [*1720*], *s. sh. Fº*. LU.

Endorsed: Reasons humbly offer'd for a National Fishery, &c. Much the same as the preceding.

2611 Rasons [*sic*] humbly offer'd to the Honourable House of Commons, for Incorporating the Subscribers for Carrying on a National Fishery; And to Raise for the Publick Service 1,500,000 l. *n.p.* [*1720*], *s. sh. Fº*. O.

Endorsed: Reasons humbly offer'd to the Honourable House of Commons, for Carrying on a National Fishery; and to Raise 1,500,000 l. for the Publick Service. A revised edition of the preceding.

2612 Reasons most humbly offered to the Honourable the House of Commons, for carrying on an American Fishery, upon the Coast of New England and North Carolina, for Whale, Cod, Macrell, and Herring. *n.p.* [*1720?*], *s. sh. Fº*. L.

MANUFACTURES

2613 The Case of Thomas Forrest, the Petitioner for a Patent for a New Invention of Making Malleable-Iron, with Pit-Coal. *n.p.* [*1720?*], *F*o. O.

2614 The Case of Thomas Forrest, Smelter and Refiner; Petitioner for a Patent for making Malleable Iron with Pit Coal. *n.p. 1720*, *F*o. O.

2615 BUSBY, JOHN. Proposals for Drying of Malt with Hot Air; invented, and brought to Perfection by John Busby. *n.p.* [*1720*], *F*o. L.

2616 Reasons for Encouraging the Manufacture of British Sail-Duck, and the Growth of Hemp and Flax in Great-Britain. *n.p.* [*1720?*], *s. sh. F*o. LU.

2617 An Estimate of the Profits from the Meliorating of Oils, by the Authority of a Patent, Granted [to John Marten] by his present Majesty King George, Tested the 7th day of May, 1720. And Enrolled in the High Court of Chancery. *n.p.* [*1720*], *s. sh. F*o. E.

2618 *Begin.* 'His Most Excellent Majesty King George....' *n.p.* [*c. 1720?*], *s. sh. F*o. LU.

A form of company prospectus relating to a method of extracting oil from poppy seeds invented and patented by Thomas Smith.

2619 The Case of the Workers and Dealers in Plate. *n.p.* [*1720?*], *s. sh. F*o. LG.

2620 The Case of the Working Goldsmiths, in Relation to a Bill now depending in the Honourable House of Commons, for reducing the Standard of Wrought Silver Plate, and laying a Duty thereon. *n.p.* [*1720*], *s. sh. F*o. LU.

2621 Reasons Humbly Offer'd against the Intended Duty to be Laid on Plate, and the Alteration of the Standard. In a Letter to a Member of Parliament. By a Working Silver-smith. *Lond. 1720*, *8*o. LU.

2622 The Exceeding Hardships on the Working Silversmith; by the Bill now in the House for the Alteration of the Standard, and Laying a Duty on Wrought Plate. Humbly offer'd in a Second Letter to a Member of Parliament. By a Working Silversmith. *Lond. 1720*, *8*o. D.

2623 [WATSON, JAMES]. A Previous View of the Case between John Baskett Esq; One of His Majesty's Printers, Plaintiff, and Henry Parson, Stationer. *Edin. 1720*, *4*o. O.

On Bible printing. For authorship see H. & L. (quoting no authority) and L catalogue.

2624 The Case, of the Poor Straw-Hat-Makers, in the Counties of Hartford, Bedford, Buckingham, &c. *n.p.* [*1720?*], *s. sh. F*o. L.

Against imports from Holland and Leghorn. Endorsed: The Case of the Straw-Hat-Makers.

2625 Proposals for Subscriptions to a New Invention for Raising Water, and working several useful Machines. *n.p.* [*c. 1720?*], *s. sh. F*o. L.

2626 EAGLESTON, JOHN. The Callico Quaker's Speech to the honourable House of Lords, in opposition to the Norwich Quaker. *Lond. 1720*, *s. sh. F°*. L.

The Norwich Quaker is John Gurney.

2627 PARKER, EPHRAIM. The Substance of a Letter, delivered to the Bailiffs, Wardens and Assistance of the Weavers Company, with some Additions Added thereunto. *n.p.* [*1720?*], *s. sh. F°*. L.

Title taken from endorsement. Defending his scheme 'proposing a Duty of 10 l. per Cent. on the Silk, and Woollen Manufactories of the Kingdom'.

2628 PARKER, EPHRAIM. Proposals for Increasing the Trade of the Silk, Woollen, and Cotten Manufactories of this Nation, both at Home and Abroad, and consequently the whole Trade of the Kingdom; Humbly presented to the Consideration of the Honourable House of Commons. *n.p.* [*1720*], *s. sh. F°*. LU.

2629 The Answer of the Scots Linnen Manufacturers to the Report of the Lords Commissioners of Trade and Plantations; and to a Paper falsly call'd, The Case of the Printing of Linnen in Great-Britain, &c. Humbly submitted to the Consideration of the Honourable House of Commons. *n. p.* [*1720*], *s. sh. F°*. L.

Endorsed: The Scots Linnen Manufacturers Answer to the Report.

2630 Arret of the Council of State in France, for renewing the Prohibition to import into that Kingdom, to deal in or use Indian, Chinese, or eastern stained Callicoes or Silks, even white Callicoes and Muslins, except Muslins and white Callicoes coming out of the Sales made by the Directors of the India Company. *n.p.* [*1720?*], *s. sh. F°*. L.

The arrêt is dated 27 Sept. 1719.

2631 The Case of Many Thousand Protestants of Ireland, concerned in the Linnen Manufacture. *n.p.* [*1720?*], *F°*. LU.

300 copies were ordered to be printed by the Irish Linen Board on 10 Dec. 1719. See *Precedents and Abstracts from the Journals of the Trustees of the Linen and Hempen Manufactures of Ireland*, 1784, pp. 32–3, where this case is reprinted.

2632 The Case of the British Woollen Manufacturies Humbly offered to the Consideration of the Members of the Honourable the House of Commons in Parliament. *n.p.* [*c. 1720?*], *s. sh. F°*. L.

2633 The Case of the Convention of the Royal Boroughs in Scotland, in relation to the Linnen Manufactory of that Country. *n.p.* [*1720*], *s. sh. F°*. LU.

2634 The Case of the Journey-Men Callico Printers, Humbly offer'd to the Consideration of the Right Honourable the Lords Spiritual and Temporal in Parliament Assembl'd. *n.p.* [*1720*], *s. sh. 4°*. LU.

2635 The Case of the Linen-Drapers, and other Dealers in Printed Callicoes and Linens. *n.p.* [*1720?*], *s. sh. F°*. L.

2636 The Case of the Linnen-Drapers, and other Dealers, in Printed Callicoes, upon the Bill now depending before Your Lordships, to Preserve and Encourage the Woollen and Silk Manufactures of this Kingdom, &c. *n.p.* [*1720*], *s. sh. F°.* LU.

2637 The Case of the Linnen-Drapers, and others, Dealers in printed Callicoes and Linnens, relating to a Bill, now depending before your Lordships, for encouraging the Silk and Woollen Manufactures, &c. *n.p.* [*1720*], *s. sh. F°.* L.

2638 The Case of the Printed Linnens of North Britain. *n.p.* [*1720?*], *s. sh. F°.* LU.

2639 The Case of the Printers of Callicoes and Linens. *n.p.* [*1720?*], *s. sh. F°.* LU.

2640 The Case of the Printing of Linnens in Great Britain, as it particnlarly [*sic*] relates to the Printing of Linnens made in Scotland and in Ireland. *n.p.* [*1720?*], *s. sh. F°.* LU.

2641 The Case of the Quilt-Makers. *n.p.* [*1720?*], *s. sh. F°.* LU.

For a clause to permit the use of printed calico carpets.

2642 The Case of the Unhappy Retailers of Printed Callicoes. *n.p.* [*1720?*], *s. sh. F°.* LLI.

Headed 'Pray, my Lords, consider this Case, or We and our Families are utterly Ruin'd'.

2643 The Case of the Weavers of the City of Coventry, humbly Offer'd to the Honourable the House of Commons. *n.p.* [*1720?*], *s. sh. F°.* LU.

For prohibiting the wearing of printed and painted calicoes and linens.

2644 The Case of the Weavers of the City of London and Parts Adjacent, Humbly represented to the Honourable House of Commons. *n.p.* [*1720*], *s. sh. F°.* LU.

2645 The Charter of the Royal Lustring Company: with a Clause out of an Act of Parliament pass'd in the Ninth and Tenth of William the Third, entitled, An Act for the better Encouragement of the Royal Lustring Company, &c. confirming the same. *Lond. 1720*, *F°.* LU.

2646 The Farther Case of the Woollen and Silk Manufacturers. *n.p.* [*1720*], *s. sh. F°.* LU.

2647 The Female Manufacturers Complaint: being the Humble Petition of Dorothy Distaff, Abigail Spinning-Wheel, Eleanor Reel, &c. Spinsters, to the Lady Rebecca Woollpack. With a Respectful Epistle to Sir R—— St——l, concerning some Omissions of the utmost Importance in his Lady's Wardrobe. By Monsieur de Brocade of Paris. *Lond. 1720*, *8°.* LU.

Attributed to Defoe by J. R. Moore (*Checklist*, no. 423) but not seen by him.

2648 *Begin.* Gentlemen, We attended the Lords Commissioners of Trade and Plantations on the 12th of November, 1719. and deliver'd them a

Representation; of which the following is a Copy.... *n.p.* [*1720?*], *s. sh. Fo*. LU.

The Journal of the Commissioners records the attendance on 12 Nov. 1719 of 'Mr William Fead and some other merchants and factors dealing in Scots linnen'.

2649 The Hambrough Merchants Case relating to the Bill now depending in the Honourable House of Commons, which Prohibits as well the Exportation of all German Linnens Printed and Dyed here, as their Use in this Kingdom. *n.p.* [*1720*], *s. sh. Fo*. LU.

2650 The Humble Address of the Right Honourable the Lords Spiritual and Temporal in Parliament Assembled, presented to His Majesty, on Tuesday the Third Day of May, 1720. With His Majesties most gracious Answer. *Lond. 1720*, *Fo*. O.

For the Commissioners of Trade to prepare a scheme for preventing the wearing of calico.

2651 The Interest of England consider'd, with respect to its Manufactures and East-India Callicoes Imported, Printed, Painted, Stained, and Consumed therein. Or, an Essay shewing from whence the Decay of Trade, the Melting of Coin, the Scarcity of Silver, the Increase of Poor do proceed. By a Citizen. *Lond. 1720*, *8o*. LU.

The dedication signed: J.E. 2nd edn. 1720 (LU).

2652 The Interest of the Nation Asserted. Being a Defence of the Woollen and Silk Manufactures, against some Notions in a late Pamphlet, said to be writ by the famous Mr. Laws. *Lond. 1720*, *8o*. LU.

The pamphlet referred to is John Law's *Money and Trade Considered.*

2653 A Letter from a Gloucestershire Gentleman to a Member of Parliament in London, Signifying the heavy Oppression the Kingdom hath labour'd under by the Use of Painted Callicoes, &c. and the great Advantage it would be to encourage the Woollen Manufacture. *n.p.* [*1720?*], *s. sh. Fo*. LU.

2654 The Linen Spinster, in Defence of the Linen Manufactures, &c. To be Continued as Mrs. Rebecca Woollpack gives Occasion. Number I. By Jenny Distaff. *Lond. 1720*, *8o*. LU.

Dated: December 1719, Salop. No more published.

2655 The List of Woollen or Worsted Stuffs mention'd in the Manufacturer, No. 17. and with which the Weavers pretend Printed Callicoes do interfere with.... *n.p.* [*1720*], *s. sh. Fo*. LU.

The second column contains 'A List of Woollen and Worsted Stuffs that are now wore and used, instead of those the Weavers alledge, are totally or very near sunk by Printed Callicoes, as on the other Side.'.

2656 Observations on the Bill for Prohibiting the Use of Printed Callicoes, &c. as sent from the House of Commons to the House of Lords, the 4th of April, 1720. *n.p.* [*1720*], *Fo*. L.

2657 The Produce of India, Italy, and France, raised in England, by the Silk Manufactures. *Lond. 1720, 8º.* L.

Extracts from Barham's *Essay on the Silk Worm* with proposals for producing raw silk in England by John Apletre.

2658 Proposals for Employing the Weavers in their own Trade, which shall or may want Work, and other Poor People in the Consumption of the Manufactures of Great-Britain. *n.p.* [*1720*], *s. sh. F*º. L.

Dated: The First of June, 1720.

2659 Reasons against prohibiting of Callicoes. *n.p.* [*1720*], *s. sh. F*º. O.

2660 Reasons for adding a Clause to the Bill for Preserving and Encouraging the Woollen and Silk Manufactures, &c. to except Callicoe Manufactured in Great Britain, out the intended Prohibition, humbly offer'd to the Hon[ble] House of Commons. *n.p.* [*1720?*], *s. sh. F*º. LU.

2661 The Scots Linnen Manufacturers Answer to two Papers, entituled, The Case of the Woollen and Silk Manufactures of Great-Britain; and the Case of the Printed Linnens in North Great-Britain. Dispersed in Behalf of the Weavers and Woollen Manufacturers. *n.p.* [*1720?*], *s. sh. F*º. LU.

2662 A Second humble Address from the Poor Weavers and Manufacturers to the Ladies. *n.p.* [*1720?*], *s. sh. F*º. L.

2663 Some Considerations relating to the desired Prohibition of Wearing printed Callicoes, by a Person wholly disinterested otherwise, then for the good of his Country. *n.p.* [*1720?*], *s. sh. F*º. LU.

2664 The State of the Case relating to East-India Callicoes. *n.p.* [*1720?*], *F*º. M (Cr).

2665 To the Right Hon[ble] the Lords Commissioners of Trade and Plantations. The Memorial of Jonathan Wrightson, Richard Score, Thomas Ollive, James Warren, Abraham Vanmildert, Richard Coxeter, Oliver Hurst and Joseph Stephenson, on behalf of themselves, many Eminent Merchants, Linnen Drapers and other considerable Traders and Manufacturers of this Kingdom. *n.p.* [*1720*], *F*º. MP.

Endorsed: A Scheme for effectually imploying the Manufacturers by making of Callicoes in Great Britain....

2666 The True Case of the Scots Linnen Manufacture, Humbly Offer'd to the Consideration of the Honorable House of Commons. *n.p.* [*1720*], *s. sh. F*º. LU.

'Commons' in roman. Another edn. with 'Commons' in italic (LU).

2667 A True Representation of the Manufacture of Combing and Spinning of Wooll. Humbly Offered to the Consideration of the British Legislators. *n.p.* [*1720?*], *s. sh. F*º. LU.

2668 A True State of the Question, as it now stands, between the Woollen and Silk Manufactures, and Printed Callicoes; And as the same is further clear'd up in the following Queries. *n.p.* [*1720*], *s. sh. F*º. LU.

2669 Weavers Hall, At a Court of Assistants of the said Company, held the 6th Day of May, 1720. *n.p.* [*1720*], *s. sh. F*o. LG.

In view of the impending prohibition of the weaving of calico asks masters to keep their men in work as far as possible and urge them to be peaceful.

2670 The Weavers Reply to the Linen-Drapers, and other Dealers in Printed Callicoes and Linens. Wherein Their Case is Considered, and Answered Paragraph by Paragraph. Humbly address'd to the Honourable House of Commons. *Lond. 1720, 8*o. LU.

2671 Reasons for Encouraging the Manufactories in North-Britain, &c. *n.p.* [*c. 1720?*], *s. sh. F*o. L.

The prospectus of a company which proposes to engage in distilling, cotton manufacture, agriculture and mining.

2672 [SWIFT, JONATHAN]. A Proposal for the universal Use of Irish Manufacture, in Cloaths and Furniture of Houses, &c. Uterly Rejecting and Renouncing Every Thing wearable that comes from England. *Dublin, 1720, 8*o. D.

Some copies have the spelling 'Utterly'. Another edition, 1734 (DA). Reprinted in *The Prose Works of Jonathan Swift*, ed. by H. Davis, vol. 9 (1948).

2673 An Answer to the Proposal for the Universal Use of Irish Manufactures, and utterly rejecting and renouncing every Thing that is wearable that comes from England. *Dublin, 1720, 8*o. LU.

Another edn. Lond. 1720, entitled: *A Defence of English Commodities. Being an Answer to the Proposal for the Universal Use of Irish Manufactures.... Written by Dean Swift* (O).

COMMERCE

2674 CLARE, MARTIN. Youth's Introduction to Trade and Business: containing, I. Tables of the most usual Clerk-like Contractions of Words. ...II. Acquittances and Promissory Notes diversify'd....III. Variety of Bills of Parcels, and Bills on Book-Debts....IV. Bills of Exchange, with Directions necessary for the right Understanding and Managements of Remittances....Done upon the Plan of the late Col. Ayre's Essay.... *Lond. 1720, obl. 4*o. L.

5th edn. 1740 (L); another 5th edn. 1741 (LU); 7th edn. 1751 (LICA); at least 5 later editions.

2675 An Act for Licensing Hawkers and Pedlars....Anno 9 & 10 Gulielmi III. Regis. And several Clauses relating to Hawkers and Pedlars in subsequent Acts of Parliament. Together with several Cases, and Opinions thereupon, of Her late and His present Majesties Council Learned in the Law. *Lond. 1720, 8*o. O.

Another edn. 1726 (LU).

2676 [DEFOE, DANIEL]. The Case of the Fair Traders, humbly represented to the Honourable the House of Commons: being a clear View and

State of Clandestine Trade, as now carry'd on in Great Britain. *n.p.* [*1720*], *s. sh. F°*. L.

Attribution by Professor J. R. Moore.

2677 Reasons humbly offered by the Merchants Trading in Wine, for Encouraging and the better Carrying on the said Trade. *n.p.* [*1720*], *s. sh. F°*. LU.

2678 By the King, A Proclamation, For Putting in Execution the Laws and Statutes of this Realm, for the Preventing the Exportation of Wooll, Wooll-Fells, Woollen-Yarn, Mortlings, Shorlings, Wooll-Flocks, Fullers-Earth, and Fulling Clay. *Lond. 1720, s. sh. F°*. L.

Dated: 19 May 1720. Last word of l. 2 'any'; another edn., last word of l. 2 'Wooll-' (L).

2679 [Gordon, Thomas]. Considerations offered upon the Approaching Peace, and upon the Importance of Gibraltar to the British Empire, being the Second Part of the Independent Whig. *Lond. 1720, 8°*. O.

2nd, 3rd, 4th and 5th edns. 1720 (all L). For authorship see *D.N.B.*

2680 A Letter to the Independent Whig, occasioned by his Considerations of the Importance of Gibraltar to the British Empire. *Lond. 1720, 8°*. L.

Signed: Britannus. Attributed to Defoe in *C.B.E.L.* II, 507. Professor J. R. Moore rejects the attribution.

2681 [Beaver, John]. A Letter to the Lords Commissioners for Trade and Plantations, concerning the Advantage of Gibraltar to the Trade of Great-Britain. With Some Proposals to render that Place more useful. By a Turkey Merchant. To which is prefix'd, A Chart of the Mediterranean Sea. *Lond. 1720, 4°*. O.

2nd edn. 1720 (LU). For authorship see Ellis & White Catalogue 52, no. 241, where a copy with a ms. note is advertised. See also B.M. Lansdowne Ms. 771, fol. 22, where H. Wanley records in his diary the gift of a presentation copy from Beaver, who was not a Turkey merchant.

2682 By the Lords Justices, W. Cant. Townshend P. Grafton, Bolton, A Proclamation, Requiring Quarentine to be Performed by Ships coming from the Mediterranean. *Lond. 1720, s. sh. F°*. L.

Dated: 25 August [1720].

2683 By the Lords Justices, W. Cant. Parker C. [and others]...A Proclamation, Requiring Quarentine to be performed by Ships coming from Bourdeaux, or any of the Ports or Places on the Coast of France in the Bay of Biscay. *Lond. 1720, s. sh. F°*. L.

Dated: 12 October [1720].

2684 By the Lords Justices, A Proclamation, W. Cant. Parker C. [and others] ...Requiring Quarentine to be performed by Ships coming from the Mediterranean, Bordeaux, or any of the Ports or Places on the Coast of France in the Bay of Biscay, or from the Isles of Guernsey, Jersey, Alderney, Sarke, or Man. *Lond. 1720, s. sh. F°*. L.

Dated: 27 October 1720.

2685 By the Lords Justices and Council of Ireland, a Proclamation. Requiring Quarentine to be performed by Ships coming from the Mediterranean, Bourdeaux, or any of the Ports or Places on the Coast of France, in the Bay of Biscay, or from the Isles of Guensey, Jersey, Alderney, Sarke, or Man. *Dublin*, *1720*, *F°*. DPRO.

Dated: 4 November 1720.

2686 The British Merchant: Dated June 25. 1714. Shewing the Importance of the Manufacture of Turkey Raw-Silk to this Kingdom, viz. That 500 l. Value of Wooll exported to Turkey, pays 5000 l. to the Lands and Labour of the Nation. *n.p.* [*1720*], *F°*. L.

Endorsed title.

2687 [DEFOE, DANIEL]. The Case Fairly Stated between the Turky Company and the Italian Merchants. By a Merchant. *Lond.* *1720*, *8°*. pp. 44. L.

Another edn. 1720, pp. 48 (L). For authorship see *C.B.E.L.* II, 506.

2688 The Case of the Italian Merchants. *n.p.* [*1720*], *s. sh. F°*. LU.

2689 An Answer to the False Suggestions of the Italian Merchants: Proving, that the Turky Raw-Silk Imported from Italy, is the Return of French, and not of English Manufactures. *n.p.* [*1720*], *s. sh. F°*. LU.

2690 The Case of the Italian Merchants, Importing Goods of the Growth of Asia, by Way of Italy. *n.p.* [*1720*], *s. sh. F°*. LU.

2691 The farther Case of the Italian Merchants Importing Goods of the Growth of Asia, by way of Italy. *n.p.* [*1720*], *s. sh. F°*. LU.

2692 Considerations on the Dispute between the Levant Company and the Italian Merchants, relating to the Importation of Raw Silk from Leghorn. *n.p.* [*1720*], *s. sh. F°*. LU.

2693 Extracts of Letters from Livorno, dated the 13th of March, 1715–16, from Mess. How Gould and Gott, Factors there to a Merchant in London, relating to Turkey Raw Silk. *n.p.* [*1720?*], *s. sh. F°*. L.

Endorsed title is: Extracts of Letters and Accounts of Turkey Raw Silk Exported from Marseilles to Leghorn in the Year 1715. Another edn., omitting 'dated...1715–16' (MC).

2694 The Farther Answer of the Turkey Merchants to the Cases of the Italian Merchants. *n.p.* [*1720*], *s. sh. F°*. L.

2695 A Letter to a Member of Parliament, in Relation to the Bill now depending, for the Repeal of a Clause in the Navigation Act. *n.p.* [*1720*], *s. sh. F°*. LU.

Signed: A.B. The clause allowed raw silk to be imported from France and Italy, although the produce of Asia.

2696 A Letter to a Member of Parliament, occasion'd by a Bill now depending in the Honble House of Commons, to repeal part of the Act of Navigation. *n.p.* [*1720*], *s. sh. F°*. LU.

Title taken from endorsement.

2697 *Begin.* Monday, 21st March, 1719 [O.S.]. To Morrow is appointed, in the Committee of the whole House, to take into Consideration, the Bill now depending, to Repeal a Clause in the Act of Navigation, to prevent the Importation of Goods, the Growth of Asia from Leghorn. *n.p.* [*1720*], *s. sh. obl. 8*°. L.

An appeal 'that the Turkey Company may not gain a Monopoly of the Two greatest Branches of the British Trade: The Cloth and Silk Manufactures'.

2698 Observations on the late Management of the Levant-Company, with Extracts of Letters from Constantinople and Smirna. *n.p.* [*1720*], *s. sh. F*°. LU.

2699 Reasons for the Bill now depending in the Honourable House of Commons, to Repeal a Clause in the Act of the 12th Year of King Charles the 2d, Intituled, An Act for the Encouraging and Encreasing of Shipping and Navigation: Also, Answers to the Queries in the Printed Case of the Italian Merchants. *n.p.* [*1720*], *s. sh. F*°. LU.

Title taken from endorsement.

2700 Reasons humbly offered against the Bill for Repealing Part of the Act of Navigation. *n.p.* [*1720*], *s. sh. F*°. LU.

2701 Reasons humbly offer'd to the Right Honourable the House of Peers, for the Bill to Repeal a Clause in an Act of the 12th Year of King Charles the Second, Entituled, An Act for the Encouraging and Encreasing of Shipping and Navigation. *n.p.* [*1720*], *s. sh. F*°. L.

2702 Reasons offer'd by the Merchants Trading to Italy, against the Bill desired by the Levant-Company, for Repealing a Clause in the Act of Navigation. *n.p.* [*1720*], *s. sh. F*°. LU.

Endorsed: The Reasons of the Italian Traders, Against a Bill now depending, For Repealing Part of the Act of the 12th of King Charles II. For Incouraging and Increasing Shipping and Navigation.

2703 The Turkey Merchants and their Trade Vindicated from the Aspersions and unjust Reproaches cast on them, in several Cases and Pamphlets Published in the Names of the Italian Merchants. By a Merchant. *n.p. 1720*, *8*°. LU.

2704 A List of the names of the adventurers of the Royal African-Company of England....9 May 1720. *n.p. 1720*, *F*°. Kress 3250.

2705 Some Matters of Fact relating to the Present State of the African Trade; demonstrating, That there are not wanting any Subscriptions, or New Projects, for its Support. *n.p.* [*1720?*], *F*°. L.

With lists of ships from London, Bristol and Liverpool, 'now in the African Trade; with the Number of Negroes they usually purchase for the Plantations'.

2706 A Letter to a Member of Parliament, concerning the Naval Store-Bill, brought in last Session. With observations on the Plantation-Trade, and Methods proposed for rendring it more beneficial to Great Britain than hitherto it has been, by promoting the Exports of our Manufactures, and inlarging our Navigation. *Lond. 1720, 8o.* LU.

Another edn. 1721 (O).

2707 Reasons for Importing Naval Stores from our own Plantations, and employing our People there. *n.p.* [*1720?*], *s. sh. Fo.* LU.

2708 Reasons humbly offered for Restraining the South-Sea-Company in their Trade. *n.p.* [*1720?*], *s. sh. Fo.* LU.

2709 The Case of the Exportation of Bullion, and Melting down the Coin: Humbly represented to the Most Honourable House of Commons. *n.p.* [*1720?*], *s. sh. Fo.* L.

An attack on the East India Company.

2710 The Grounds of Complaint of several Merchants and other Traders of the City of London, who are humble Petitioners to the Honourable House of Commons, against the present Managers of the East-India-Company. *n.p.* [*c. 1720?*], *s. sh. Fo.* O.

Against the Company's method of selling its goods.

2711 [Defoe, Daniel]. The Trade to India Critically and Calmly consider'd, and prov'd to be destructive to the general Trade of Great Britain, as well as to the Woollen and Silk Manufactures in particular. *Lond. 1720, 8o* O.

For authorship see *C.B.E.L.* II, 506.

2712 Cornwall, Henry. Observations upon Several Voyages to India Out and Home; as also Remarks on the Ports and Places Touched at in that Voyage; with some Account of the Genius of the Natives and Inhabitants, their Customs, Laws, and the Trade of the several Countries. Illustrated with Sixty One curious Copper Plates.... *Lond. 1720, obl. Fo.* L.

Another edn. 1724 (L).

COLONIES

2713 An humble Representation of several Grievances and Hardships his Majesty's most faithful Subjects, the Inhabitants of the Island of Minorca, labour under, from the arbitrary Proceedings of the Chief Commandants, and the Troops garison'd in that Island.... *n.p.* [*1720*], *Fo.* E.

2714 A Vindication of Colonel Kane, Lieutenant-Governor of Minorca, against the late Complaints made against him, by the Inhabitants of that Island. In a Letter to a Member of Parliament. Shewing the Necessity of Annexing Minorca to the Imperial Crown of Great-Britain. *Lond. 1720, 8o.* L.

2715 The Distress'd Condition of Minorca, set forth in Answer to the Vindication of Colonel Kane. By a Member of Parliament. *Lond. 1720, 8o.* L.

2716 A Discovery of a Large, Rich, and Plentiful Country, in the North America; extending above 4000 Leagues. Wherein, by a very short Passage, lately found out, thro' the Mer-Barmejo into the South-Sea; by which a considerable Trade might be carry'd on, as well in the Northern as the Southern Parts of America. *Lond.* [*1720?*], *8°*. O.

An abridgment of L. Hennepin's *A New Discovery*, 1698.

2717 Some Considerations on the Consequences of the French Settling Colonies on the Mississippi, with respect to the Trade and Safety of the English Plantations in America and the West-Indies. From a Gentleman of America, to his Friend in London. *Lond. 1720*, *8°*. L.

Another edn., edited by B. W. Bond, 1928. Internal evidence suggests James Smith as the possible author.

2718 MARSH, HENRY. A Proposal for Raising a Stock of Two Millions of Pounds Sterling; by Subscriptions for Forming a Settlement, on each side of a Large and Convenient River in Acadia on the Continent of North-America. And to Improve a great Space of Land on each side the said River for Growth of Hemp and Flax, and for Importing Mast-yards, Deals, Staves and other Timber, with Pitch, and Tar, &c. in greater Quantities. Likewise for carrying on the Acadia Fishery in those Parts. *Lond. 1720*, *F°*. L.

An expanded version of the 1716 scheme, no. 2235.

2719 NEAL, DANIEL. The History of New-England....To which is added The Present State of New-England. With a New and Accurate Map of the Country..... *Lond. 1720*, *8°*. 2 vols. L.

2nd edn. 1747 (L).

2720 Reasons for Making of Bar, as well as Pig or Sow-Iron in His Majesty's Plantations. *n.p.* [*1720?*], *s. sh. F°*. L.

2721 Reasons for making Pigg-Iron, and against making Barr-Iron in America. *n.p.* [*1720?*], *F°*. L.

Endorsed title.

2722 [COLMAN, JOHN]. The Distressed State of the Town of Boston, &c. Considered. In a Letter from a Gentleman in the Town, to his Friend in the Countrey. *Boston, 1720*, *8°*.

Reprinted in *Colonial Currency Reprints*, ed. by A. M. Davis, vol. 1 (1910), whence this entry is taken, and where the authorship is established.

2723 [WIGGLESWORTH, EDWARD]. A Letter from One in the Country to his Friend in Boston, containing some Remarks upon a late Pamphlet, entituled, The Distressed State of the Town of Boston, &c. *Boston, 1720*, *8°*.

Reprinted in *Colonial Currency Reprints*, ed. by A. M. Davis, vol. 1 (1910), whence this entry is taken.

2724 COLMAN, JOHN. The Distressed State of the Town of Boston once more Considered. And Methods for Redress humbly proposed, with Remarks on the pretended Country-man's Answer to the Book, Entituled,

The Distressed State of the Town of Boston, &c. With a Scheme for a Bank laid down: and Methods for bringing in Silver Money proposed. *Boston*, [*1720*], *8°*.

Reprinted in *Colonial Currency Reprints*, ed. by A. M. Davis, vol. 2 (1911), whence this entry is taken.

2725 [Wigglesworth, Edward]. A Vindication of the Remarks of One in the Country upon The Distressed State of Boston, from some Exceptions made against 'em in a Letter to Mr. Colman. *Boston*, *1720*, *8°*.

Reprinted in *Colonial Currency Reprints*, ed. by A. M. Davis, vol. 2 (1911), whence this entry is taken.

2726 [Noyes, Oliver]. A Letter from a Gentleman, containing some Remarks upon the Several Answers given unto Mr. Colman's, entituled, The Distressed State of the Town of Boston. *Boston*, *1720*, *8°*.

Reprinted in *Colonial Currency Reprints*, ed. by A. M. Davis, vol. 2 (1911), whence this entry is taken.

2727 [Wigglesworth, Edward]. A Project for the Emission of an Hundred Thousand Pounds of Province Bills, in such a Manner as to keep their Credit up Equal to Silver, and to bring an Hundred Thousand Pounds of Silver Money into the Country in a few Years. *Boston*, *1720*, *8°*.

Reprinted in *Colonial Currency Reprints*. ed. by A. M. Davis, vol. 2 (1911), whence this entry is taken.

2728 [Valentine, John]. The Postscript. [*Boston*, *1720?*], *4°*.

On the state of Massachusetts. Reprinted in *Colonial Currency Reprints*, ed. by A. M. Davis, vol. 1 (1910), whence this entry is taken.

2729 Reflections on the Present State of the Province of Massachuset-Bay in general, and Town of Boston in particular; relating to Bills of Credit and the support of Trade by them: as the same has been lately represented in several Pamphlets. *Boston*, *1720*, *8°*.

Reprinted in *Colonial Currency Reprints*, ed. by A. M. Davis, vol. 2 (1911), whence this entry is taken.

2730 Some Proposals to benefit the Province. *Boston*, *1720*, *8°*.

Signed: F. M. Reprinted in *Colonial Currency Reprints*, ed. by A. M. Davis, vol. 2 (1911), whence this entry is taken.

2731 The Case of William Penn, Esq; Proprietary-Governor of Pensilvania, and of Joshua Gee, Henry Gouldney, Silvanus Grove, John Woods, and others, Mortgagees under the said William Penn. *n.p.* [*1720*] *s. sh. F°*. O.

For a bill for the Crown to buy the colony.

2732 A True State of the Case between the Inhabitants of South Carolina, and the Lords Proprietors of that Province; containing an Account of the Grievances under which they labour. *n.p.* [*1720*], *F°*. LPRO.

2733 An Account of the Foundation, and Establishment of a Design, now on Foot, for a Settlement on the Golden Islands, to the South of Port Royal in Carolina. By Authority of a Royal Charter. *Lond.* *1720*, *4°*. O.

2734 A Description of the Golden Islands, with an Account of the Undertaking now on Foot for making a Settlement there: explaining, 1st, The Nature of that Design in general; 2dly, The Measures already taken: And 3dly, Those intended to be taken hereafter. *Lond. 1720, 8°.* L.

Relates to the project of Sir Robert Mountgomery in 1717 (no. 2298).

2735 The Barbadoes Packet; containing several Original Papers: giving an Account of the Most Material Transactions that have lately happened in a certain Part of the West-Indies. In a Letter from a Gentleman of the said Island to his Friend in London. *Lond. 1720, 8°.* L.

FINANCE

2736 AMHURST, NICHOLAS. An Epistle (with a Petition in it) to Sir John Blount, Bart. one of the Directors of the South-Sea Company. *Lond. 1720, 4°.* L.

In verse. Dated: July 15. 1720. 2nd edn. 1720 (L).

2737 BUDGELL, EUSTACE. The Case of Annuitants and Proprietors of redeemable Debts. *Lond. 1720, F°.* Kress 3161.

2738 The Speech made by Eustace Budgell, Esq; at a General Court of the South-Sea Company, in Merchant-Taylors Hall, on the Twentieth of September, 1720. *Lond. 1720, F°.* LPRO.

Another edn. Dublin, 1720, s. sh. F° (DNL); 3rd edn. Lond. 1720, F° (O).

2739 The Second Speech made by Eustace Budgell Esq; at the General Court of the South-Sea Company, in Merchant-Taylors-Hall, on the 30th of Sept. 1720. *Lond. [1720], s. sh. F°.* L.

2740 A Vindication of E[usta]ce B[ud]g[el]l Esq; from the Imputation of his being the Author of a Printed Speech, said to be spoken at a General Court of the South-Sea Company....Sept. 30, 1720. Wherein the Case of the Sellers and Purchasers of the Third and Fourth Subscription is Considered. *Lond. 1720, 8°.* LU.

2741 CROOKSHANKS, JOHN. Some Matters of Fact relating to the Revolution, the Annuities, the Civil List Branches, and National Debts Taken from the most Authentick Records: in Reply to Archibald Hutcheson, Esq. *Lond. 1720, F°.* LU.

2742 HUTCHESON, ARCHIBALD. A Collection of Calculations and Remarks relating to the South Sea Scheme & Stock, which have been already Published. With an Addition of Some Others, which have not been made Publick 'till Now. *Lond. 1720, F°.* LU.

2743 HUTCHESON, ARCHIBALD. A Collection of Treatises relating to the Publick Debts, and the Discharge of the Same. Published at several times for the Service of the Members of the House of Commons. *Lond. 1720, F°.* LU.

2744 [MACKWORTH, Sir HUMPHREY]. A Proposal for Paying off the Publick Debts by the Appropriated Funds, without Raising any Taxes upon Land, Malt, or other Thing for that purpose. And also for enlarging the Capital Trading Stock of Great-Britain, in Order to Employ the Poor, Improve our Manufactures, Export greater Quantities of our Woollen and other Home Commodities, gain the Ballance of Trade, and consequently to Import greater Quantities of Bullion, and Enrich the Nation.... *London, 1720, 8o.* LU.

Another edn., with author's name, and entitled: A Proposal for Payment of the Publick Debts, for Relief of the South Sea Company, and for Easing the Nation of the Land and Malt Taxes.... Lond. 1720 (LU); 2nd, 3rd, 4th and 5th edns. 1720 (all LU).

2745 Sir Humphry Macworth's Proposal: Being a New Scheme offer'd for the Payment of the Publick Debts, for Relief of the South Sea Company, and for easing the Nation of the Land and Malt Tax.... *Lond.* [*1720?*], *12o*. L.

An edition of the preceding without the preface, dedication and introduction.

2746 Sir H. Mackworth's Proposal in Miniature, as it has been put in Practice in New-York, in America. *Lond. 1720, 8o.* LU.

2747 A Dialogue: or, A Familiar Discourse, concerning Sir Humphry Mackworth's Proposal for Payment of the Publick Debts, for Relief of the South-Sea Company, and for Easing the Nation of the Land and Malt Taxes.... *Lond. 1720, 8o.* LU.

The preface signed: M.C.

2748 A Continuation of the Dialogue: or, A Familiar Discourse, concerning Sir Humphry Mackworth's Proposal for Payment of the Publick Debts, for Relief of the South-Sea Company, and for Easing the Nation of the Land and Malt Taxes.... *Lond. 1721* [*1720*], *8o.* LU.

The dedication signed M.C. N. Luttrell's copy in LU is dated Decemb. 1720 in ms.

2749 Observations on the Scheme of Mr. Law, in France, and of Sir Humphry Mackworth, in Great-Britain; and concerning the Establishing Paper-money, and Forcing Credit. *Lond.* [*1720*], *Fo.* LU.

From internal evidence almost certainly by Mackworth himself.

2750 MACKWORTH, Sir HUMPHREY. An Answer to several Queries relating to the Proposal for Payment of the Publick Debts, for Relief of the South-Sea Company, and for Easing the Nation of the Land and Malt-Taxes. *Lond. 1720, 8o.* LU.

2nd edn. 1720 (O).

2751 MERES, Sir JOHN. The Equity of Parliaments, and Publick Faith; Vindicated. In Answer to the Crisis of Property, and Address'd to the Annuitants. *Lond. 1720, 8o.* L.

2nd edn., corrected, 1720 (MP).

2752 MILNER, JAMES. Three Letters relating to the South-Sea Company and the Bank. The First written in March 1719–20. The Second in April 1720. The Third in Septem. 1720. now first publish'd. *Lond. 1720, 8o*. LU.

2753 PHILIPS, ERASMUS. An Appeal to Common Sense: or, Some Considerations offer'd to restore Publick Credit. *Lond. 1720, 8o*. LU.

Part II appeared in 1721 (LU).

2754 POVEY, CHARLES. Brittain's Scheme to make a New Coin of Gold and Silver to give in Exchange for Paper-Money and South Sea Stock. To which is added A Proposal that will enable the Government to take into the Exchequer all Contracts and Mortgages that have Land Security engag'd for Payment, and the Crown to lend out Money to the Subject upon that Security at Four per Cent. Interest. *Lond. 1720, 8o*. LU.

2755 SHEMAJAH, ELIZAPHAN. A Letter to the Patriots of Change-Alley. Offering some Considerations to prove Stockjobbing to be a great Security and Advantage both to Church and State. *Lond. 1720, 8o*. LU.

2756 STEELE, Sir RICHARD. The Crisis of Property: an Argument proving that the Annuitants for ninety-nine Years, as such, are not in the Condition of other Subjects of Great Britain, but by Compact with the Legislature are exempt from any new Direction relating to the said Estates. *Lond. Printed for W. Chetwood... J. Roberts... and Charles Lillie, 1720, 8o*. L.

Another issue, *Printed for W. Chetwood... J. Roberts... J. Brotherton... and Charles Lillie* (L); 2nd edn. 1720 (O). Reprinted in *Tracts and Pamphlets by Richard Steele*, ed. by Rae Blanchard, Baltimore, 1944.

2757 The Crisis of Honesty. Being an Answer to the Crisis of Property. In a Letter to Sir R—— S—— [i.e. Sir Richard Steele]. *Lond. 1720, 8o*. LU.

2758 Scandal no Argument: An Oxford Annuitant's Letter to Sir Richard Steele, in Answer to the Crisis of Honesty.... *Lond. 1720, 8o*. LU.

2759 STEELE, Sir RICHARD. A Nation a Family: being the Sequel of the Crisis of Property: or, a Plan for the Improvement of the South-Sea Proposal. *Lond. 1720, 8o*. LU.

Reprinted in *Tracts and Pamplets by Richard Steele*. ed. by Rae Blanchard, Baltimore, 1944.

2760 [HUTCHESON, ARCHIBALD]. An Abstract shewing the Loss to the New Subscribers to the South-Sea Stock, at the several Prices following; and the Yearly Profits on Trade necessary to make Good the said Loss ... *n.p. [1720], s. sh. Fo*. LU.

Endorsed: An Abstract of some Calculations relating to the Proposals made by the South-Sea Company, and the Bank of England, to the House of Commons. Reprinted in his *A Collection of Calculations and Remarks*, 1720.

2761 An Account of the Publick Debts at the Exchequer, as they now stand.... To which is added, Seasonable Observations on the Annuities, in Answer to Sir Richard Steele's Crisis. *Lond. 1720, Fo*. LU.

2762 [GILDON, CHARLES]. All for the Better: or, The World turn'd up-side down. Being the History of the Head-Longs and the Long-Heads.... Intermingled with various Discourses, and a Candid Examination, and Censure of the Management and Conduct of the Directors of the South-Sea Company.... *Lond. 1720.* 8°. LG.

Dedication signed: Philopatris. In some copies it is signed: Charles Gildon (O).

2763 An Argument proving that the South-Sea Company are able to make a Dividend of 38 per Cent. for 12 Years. Fitted to the meanest Capacities. *Lond. 1720*, 8°. LU.

2764 An Argument to shew the Disadvantage that would Accrue to the Publick, from obliging the South-Sea Company to fix what Capital Stock they will give for the Annuities. *Lond. 1720*, 8°.

2nd edn. 1720 (LU).

2765 [TRENCHARD, JOHN]. A Letter of Thanks from the Author of the Comparison between the Proposals of the Bank and the South-Sea, &c. to the Author of the Argument, Shewing the Disadvantage which will accrue to the Publick, from Obliging the South-Sea to fix what Capital Stock they will give the Annuitants. *Lond.* [*1720*], 8°. LU.

Reprinted in *A Collection of Tracts. By the late John Trenchard...and Thomas Gordon*, 1751.

2766 The Battle of the Bubbles. Shewing their several Constitutions, Alliances, Policies, and Wars; From their first Suddain Rise, to their late Speedy Decay. By a Stander-By. *Lond. 1720*, 8°. LU.

2nd edn. 1720 (O).

2767 The Case of Contracts for South-Sea Stock, in general, since Taking of the Third Subscription, at 1000 per Cent. *Lond. 1720*, F°. LU.

2768 [WAY, J.]. The Case of Contracts for the Third and Fourth Subscriptions to the South-Sea Company, consider'd. In a Letter to a Member of Parliament. *Lond. 1720*, 8°. LU.

For authorship see ms. note in N. Y. Public Library copy cited in Sabin 102179.

2769 The Case of the Annuitants stated, and compar'd with the other Creditors of the Government. With some Remarks on a late Pamphlet, intitled, An Argument to shew the Disadvantage that would accrue to the Publick from obliging the South-Sea Company to fix what Capital Stock they will give the Annuities. *Lond. 1720*, 8°. LU.

2770 [TRENCHARD, JOHN]. A Comparison between the Proposals of the Bank and the South-Sea Company. Wherein is shewn, That the Proposals of First are much more Advantageous to the Publick than those of the Latter; if they do not offer such Terms to the Annuitants as they will accept of. *Lond. 1720*, 8°. LU.

2nd edn. 1720 (L). Reprinted in *A Collection of Tracts. By the late John Trenchard...and Thomas Gordon*, 1751.

2771 Computations, Shewing the Disproportion of South-Sea Stock allowed to the Redeemable Proprietors and the other new Proprietors, and the Gains thereby arising to the old Proprietors, including the Midsummer Dividend of 10 l. per Cent. supposing Stock worth 140 l. per Cent. *n.p.* [*1720*], *s. sh. F°*. L.

2772 Considerations occasioned by the Bill for Enabling the South-Sea Company to increase their Capital Stock, &c. With Observations of Mr. Law.... *Lond. 1720, 8°*. L.

2nd edn. 1720 (LU).

2773 Considerations on the Present State of the Nation, as to Publick Credit, Stocks, the Landed and Trading Interests. With a Proposal for the speedy lessening the Publick Debts, and restoring Credit, in a manner consistent with Parliamentary Engagements. *Lond. 1720, 8°*. LU.

2774 The Snake in the Grass, discover'd; or, Observations on a late Pamphlet, intituled, Considerations on the present State of the Nation, as to Publick Credit, Stocks, the Landed and Trading Interests; with a Proposal for the Speedy Lessening the Publick Debts, and Restoring Credit, in a Manner consistent with Parliamentary Engagements. *Lond. 1720, 8°*. L.

2775 [Defoe, Daniel]. The Director. no. 1–30. 5 Oct. 1720–16 Jan. 1720 [O.S.]. *Lond. 1720*, [*21*], *F°*. O.

For authorship see *C.B.E.L.* II, 510.

2776 An Essay for Discharging the Debts of the Nation, by Equivalents: In a Letter to the Right Honble Charles, Earl of Sunderland. And the South-Sea Scheme Considered; in a Letter to the Right Honble Robert Walpole, Esq;. *Lond. 1720, 8°*. LU.

2777 An Essay for Establishing a New Parliament Money; with Some Thoughts for the Service of the South-Sea Company. *Lond. 1720, 8°*. LU.

2778 An Estimate of the Intrinsick Value of South-Sea Stock. *n.p.* [*1720*], *s. sh. F°*. L.

Title take from endorsement.

2779 [Hutcheson, Archibald]. An Estimate of the Value of South-Sea Stock. With some Remarks relating thereto. By a Member of the House of Commons. *Lond. 1720, F°*. LU.

Reprinted in Hutcheson's *A Collection of Calculations and Remarks*, 1720.

2780 An Examination and Explanation of the South-Sea Company's Scheme, for taking in the Publick Debts. Shewing, That it is not encouraging to those who shall become Proprietors of the engrafted Stock, to join with the present Proprietors of the Company, at an advanced Price. And that it is against the Interest of those Proprietors, who shall remain with their Stock till they are paid off by the Government, that the Company should make annually greater Dividends than their

Profits will warrant. With some National Considerations and useful Observations. *Lond. 1720, 8o.* LU.

2nd edn. 1720 (L); 3rd edn. 1720 (C).

2781 A Farther Examination and Explanation of the South-Sea Company's Scheme. Shewing, that it is not in the Interest of the South-Sea Company to offer the Annuitants such Terms as may induce them to come in; And that the Proposal of the Bank is more likely to be accepted by the Annuitants, and the Publick not disappointed. *Lond. 1720, 8o.* LU.

2nd edn. 1720 (LU).

2782 An Impartial Enquiry into the Value of South-Sea Stock. With Some Thoughts of the Occasion of the Present Decay of Trade and Credit: and some Means proposed for restoring the same. In a Letter to Sir Richard Steele Knt. *Lond. 1720, Fo.* LU.

The covering letter signed: A.B. 2nd edn., with additions, and the covering letter signed: T.P., 1721 (LU).

2783 An Inquiry into the Causes of the Decay of Publick and Private Credit, in Great Britain and Ireland: With Proposals Humbly Offer'd for their Restoration. *n.p.* [*c. 1720?*], *Fo.* LU.

2784 The Last General Court of the South-Sea Company, held the 23rd of December 1720, Equally Legal, as any General Court preceding it. The Resolutions on the subject Matters then and there Debated, Reasonable and Just. Some Arts and Stratagems now on Foot, in Relation to the next General Court, Examined. *Lond. 1720, 8o.* LG.

Dated: December 29. 1720.

2785 A Letter to a Conscientious Man: concerning the Use and Abuse of Riches, and the Right and Wrong Ways of acquiring them: shewing that Stock-Jobbing is an unfair Way of Dealing; and particularly demonstrating the Fallaciousness of the South-Sea Scheme. *Lond. 1720, 8o.* LU.

2nd edn. 1720 (DG).

2786 [Milner, James]. A Letter to a Friend, concerning the Proposals for the Payment of the Nation's Debts. *Lond. 1720, 8o.* LU.

2nd edn. 1720, entitled: A Visit to the South-Sea Company and the Bank. In a Letter to a Friend, concerning the late Proposals for the Payment of the Nation's Debts. The Second Edition. To which is added, A Second Letter, occasion'd by what has past since, in relation to the South-Sea Company's Bargain (LU). Reprinted, with author's name, *Three Letters relating to the South-Sea Company and the Bank*, 1720 (no. 2752).

2787 A Letter to a Member of Parliament, concerning the South-Sea Company: With Proposals for Settling a Certain Annual Dividend. By a Well-wisher of his Country. *Lond. 1720, 4o.* LU.

2788 A Letter to a Member of Parliament, occasion'd by the South-Sea Company's Scheme for Reducing the Publick Debts. *Lond. 1720, 8o.* LU.

Dated: Jan. 27, 1719–20. 2nd edn. 1720 (LU).

2789 [HUTCHESON, ARCHIBALD]. A Letter to the Author of the Calculations in the White-Hall Evening-Post, relating to South-Sea Stock. Shewing the Mistakes in the said Calculations; and These being Rectified, What the Present Value of South-Sea Stock is. Together with an Answer to the Unjust Insinuations against the Estimate of the Value of South-Sea Stock, lately Published, as if that Treatise were intended to prejudice the Unhappy Sufferers, who have dealt in South-Sea Stock, or to hurt the Publick Credit. By a Member of the House of Commons. *Lond. 1720, F°.* L.

Reprinted in *A Collection of Calculations and Remarks*, 1720, which bears the author's name.

2790 A Letter to the Right Honourable the Earl of Sunderland, with an Account of the Causes of the Present Diminution of Publick Credit. As also the Means of Reviving it. *Lond. 1720, F°.* LU.

The dedication signed: Philanthropos.

2791 Matter of Fact; or, the Arraignment and Tryal of the Di——rs of the S—— S—— Company, with the Pleadings of the Counsel on both Sides. Counsel against the Prisoners. Counsellor Crambo, Counsellor Clamour, Counsellor Query, Counsellor Trifle, Mr. Serjeant Rumour. Coun. for the Prisoners. Philopatris. Judges of the Bench. Truth, Justice, Reason.... *Lond. 1720, 8°.* L.

2792 Multum in Parvo; or, Bubbles in a Nut-Shell. *Lond. 1720, s. sh. F°.* LU.

Dated: London, February 23 $17\frac{19}{20}$. A satire. Proposing to form a society to insure bubbles. Thirty-six of them are named.

2793 The Nation Preserved; or, The Plot Discovered. Containing an Impartial Account of the Secret Policy of some of the South-Sea Directors; with Copies of their Letters to each other, and the Substance of their Debates in several of their Private Conferences: Taken before a Notary Publick. Also a Letter from one of their Agents in France. Addressed to Sir J—— B——. *Lond. 1720, 8°.* LU.

A complete forgery according to an advertisement in *The Evening Post*, no. 1782, 30 Dec. 1720.

2794 The Nature of Contracts Consider'd, as they Relate to the Third and Fourth Subscriptions, taken in by the South Sea Company. In a Letter to a Friend. With a Postscript, concerning the Meeting at Salters-Hall, the 10th instant. By a Tradesman of the City, whose Name is not to be found in any of the Subscriptions. *Lond. 1720, 8°.* LU.

Dated: Oct. 18, 1720.

2795 The Present State of the British Credit Consider'd. In a Letter to W——m Sl——r, Esq; Member of Parliament. *Lond. 1720, 8°.* MP.

2796 The Proceedings of the Directors of the South-Sea-Company. *Lond. printed, and re-printed in Dublin, 1720, s. sh. F°.* C (Cr).

A report of a meeting held on 30 Sept. 1720.

2797 Proposal for a Subscription for Thirty-One Millions. *n.p.* [*1720*], *s. sh. F°.* LU.

Title taken from endorsement. The text begins: To open books for Thirty-one Millions, at 200 l. per cent.

2798 Reasons humbly offer'd to the Honourable House of Commons against passing a Law to oblige, the unhappy Sufferers (who are charged to be Borrowers on the South-Sea Company's Loan) to pay to the Company any part of the said Loan. *n.p.* [*1720*], *s. sh. F°.* L.

2799 Reasons humbly offered to the Honourable House of Commons, on the Behalf of the Subscribers to a Joint Stock, for the Undertaking and Furnishing of Funerals to any Part of England. *n.p,* [*1720?*], *s. sh. F°.* LU.

A bubble.

2800 Remarks on the Celebrated Calculations of the Value of South-Sea Stock, in the Flying-Post of the 9th of April, 1720. Paragraph by Paragraph. In order to remove the Aspersions thereby cast of the Present Contract with that Company, to the great Discouragement of the New Subscribers. *Lond. 1720, 8°.* LU.

2801 Remarks upon Several Pamphlets writ in opposition to the South-Sea Scheme. Particularly, An Examination and Explanation of the South-Sea Scheme, &c. and A Father Examination and Explanation, &c. and A Letter of Thanks from the Author of the Comparison Between the Proposals of the Bank and the South-Sea, to the Author of The Arguments shewing the Disadvantage that would accrue to the Publick from obliging the South-Sea Company to fix what Capital Stock they will give for the Annuities. *Lond. 1720, 8°.* LU.

2802 The Rise of the Stocks the Ruin of the People, Plainly Demonstrated, in Three Letters to a Member of Parliament. Wherein is contained a Short Scheme for the Real reducing of the publick Debts, on Occasion of his Majesties Speech for that Purpose; with a Vindication of the said Scheme, and a State of the Coin and Credit. With proper Remarks on the Whole. *Lond. 1721* [*1720*], *8°.* LU.

A new edn. of *Two Letters to a Member of Parliament, concerning the Publick Debts*, 1718 (no. 2399), with a third letter, dated Oct. 18. 1720, added.

2803 The Schemes of the South-Sea Company and the Bank of England, as Propos'd to the Parliament for the Reducing of the National Debts. *Lond. 1720, F°.* LU.

2nd edn. 1720 (LU).

2804 Seasonable Observations on the Annuities. *n.p.* [*1720*], *s. sh. F°.* L.

2805 A Short View of the Two Schemes of the Publick Debts; and some Queres relating to them. *n.p.* [*1720*]. *s. sh. F°.* LU.

2806 [HUTCHESON, ARCHIBALD]. Some Calculations relating to the Proposals made by the South-Sea Company, and the Bank of England, to the House of Commons; shewing, the Loss to the New Subscribers, at the several Rates in the said Computations mentioned; and the Gain which will thereby accrue to the Proprietors of the Old South-Sea Stock. By a Member of the House of Commons. *Lond. 1720*, *F°*. LU.

Reprinted in Hutcheson's *A Collection of Calculations and Remarks*, 1720.

2807 [TRENCHARD, JOHN]. Some Considerations upon the State of our Publick Debts in General, and of the Civil List in Particular. *Lond. 1720*, *8°*. LU.

2nd edn. 1720 (LU). Another edn. [1723?] (LU). Reprinted in *A Collection of Tracts. By the late John Trenchard...and Thomas Gordon*, 1751.

2808 [HUTCHESON, ARCHIBALD]. Some Seasonable Considerations for those who are desirous, by Subscription, or Purchase, to become Proprietors of South-Sea Stock. With Remarks on the Surprizing Method of Valuing South-Sea Stock, publish'd in the Flying-Post of Saturday, April the 9th, 1720. By a Member of the House of Commons. *Lond. 1720*, *F°*.

Dated: April 14, 1720. Another issue dated: April 21, 1720 (LU). Reprinted in Hutcheson's *A Collection of Calculations and Remarks*, 1720.

2809 The South-Sea Company and Bank Proposals, as they were delivered to the Honourable House of Commons, Stated and Compared. *n.p.* [*1720?*], *s. sh. F°*. LU.

2810 [GOODALL, THOMAS]. The South-Sea Scheme, as it Now stands, Consider'd. And some Proposals whereby to raise their Stock to 400 l. per Cent. By a True Lover of his Country, and an Hearty Promoter of Trade at Home, and Commerce Abroad. *Lond. 1720*, *8°*. LU.

Attributed by Coxe to Sir Robert Walpole, but the ms. in the Cholmondeley Papers has a dedication to Walpole signed: Tho. Gooddalle.

2811 [DEFOE, DANIEL]. The South-Sea Scheme Examin'd: and the Reasonableness thereof Demonstrated. By a hearty Well-Wisher to Publick Credit. *Lond. 1720*, *8°*. LU.

2nd and 3rd edns. 1720 (both LU). The attribution is Professor J. R. Moore's.

2812 The South-Sea Scheme Detected; and the Management thereof Enquir'd into: with the Case of the Subscribing Annuitants; and a Remedy offer'd for our present Grievances. In Answer to a Pamphlet, Entitled, The South-Sea Scheme Examin'd, &c. By a Lover of his Country. *Lond. 1720*, *8°*. O.

2nd edn. 1720 (LU).

2813 [DALRYMPLE, Sir DAVID]. Time Bargains tryed by the Rules of Equity and Principles of the Civil Law. *Lond. 1720*, *8°*. L.

Another edn. Edin. n.d. (E). For authorship see Advocates' Library Catalogue.

2814 To the Honourable the Commons of Great Britain in Parliament assembled, is humbly offer'd, a State of South-Sea Stock, and a Means to restore Credit. *n.p.* [*1720?*], *F*o. L.

Endorsed: A State of South-Sea Stock, as publish'd after a General Court, which shews Dividends may be made of 16 per Cent. for 4 Years, and 14 per Cent. 13 Years longer, and pay 7 Millions to the Nation to restore Credit.

2815 To the Members of the East-India Company, at a general Court held upon the 28th Day of December, 1720. A State of the Proposal made them for taking Nine Millions South-Sea Stock, &c. *n.p.* [*1720*], *s. sh. F*o. LU.

Endorsed: The Offer of Nine Millions South-Sea Stock to the East-India Company consider'd.

2816 [Defoe, Daniel]. A True State of the Contracts relating to the Third Money-Subscription taken by the South-Sea Company. *Lond. 1721* [*1720*], *8*o. O.

Published 31 Dec. 1720 (*Post Boy* no. 4907). Attribution by Professor J. R. Moore.

2817 Ways and Means to make South-Sea Stock more intrinsically worth than Ready Money: by Reducing the Interest of Money to 3 l. per Cent. without an Act of Parliament. *Lond. 1720*, *8*o. LU.

2818 Information for Mr. James Campbel Merchant in London, against the Lord Lyon. *n.p. 1720*, *F*o. E.

Dated: Feb. 1st, 1719 [O.S.]. Signed: Dun. Forbes. Claiming his 5 per cent commission for collecting the Equivalent.

2819 [Jacob, Giles]. The Laws of Taxation: being, A concise Treatise of all the Acts of Parliament, now in Force, or that were ever made and pass'd, relating to the Taxes of England, and the other Branches of the Royal Revenue.... To which are prefix'd, Several New Schemes for Establishing of Funds, and Raising some Millions of Money towards satisfying the National Debts.... *Lond. 1720*, *8*o. LU.

The dedication signed: G.J. 2nd edn., without the dedication, 1721 (LU). For authorship see *D.N.B.*

2820 An Account, shewing, in Numerical Order, the Tickets entitled to Benefits in Each of the Lotteries, Anno 1719. With the Benefits to which the said Tickets are severally entitled, and the Days on which they were drawn....Published by the Special Order of the Managers and Directors. *Lond. 1720*, *8*o. O.

2821 Instructions for a Tidesman. *n.p.* [*c. 1720?*], *s. sh. F*o. O.

2822 Instructions to be observed by the Officers employ'd in the Duties on Paper. *Lond. 1720*, *8*o. LG.

2823 Precedents of Informations and Proceedings relating to the Duties on Hides, &c. *Lond. 1720*, *8*o. L.

2824 Regulations of the Prices of the Commissions in all His Majesty's Land-Forces. Made by the Right Honourable the Board of General Officers;

and Approved by His Majesty. The second edition. *Lond. 1720, F°*. LU.

2825 Forms for Proceedings on such Seizures, as by the late Act for Preventing Frauds, &c. in the Publick Revenues, are to be heard and determined by Justices of the Peace. *Lond. 1720, 8°*. L.

2826 EDGAR, WILLIAM. A Collection of several Statutes and Clauses of Acts Made and Passed in this Kingdom, and in Great-Britain, relating to His Majesty's Revenue of Ireland....As also An Epitome of the Art of Gauging....The Whole designed for the Use and Service of the Officers of the Revenue and of all concern'd in Trade. Ordered to be Published by the Chief Commissioners and Governours of His Majesty's Revenue of Ireland. *Dublin, 1720, 8°*. LU.

2827 ASGILL, JOHN. Several Assertions Proved, in order to create another Species of Money, than Gold and Silver....The second edition. *Lond. 1720, 8°*. O.

1st edn. 1696.

2828 A Detection of the artful schemes of the Dutch and other foreign lotteries, now on foot...shewing how they affect the publick, as well as particular persons; & how to judge of the advantage or disadvantage of lotteries, & other projects of the like nature. *Lond. 1720, F°*. Kress 3343.

Signed: T. W.

2829 The Case of great Numbers of His Majesty's injured Subjects, drawn in by the Artifice of Stephen Ram, of London, Goldsmith, and Agents, to become Proprietors of Lottery Tickets, Pretended to be Brunswick. *n.p. [1720?], s. sh. F°*. LU.

2830 The Case of the Proprietors in a Conditional Subscription, taken in by Philip Helbut, Merchant, about the 23d of December, 1719. *n.p. [1720?], s. sh. F°*. O.

Alleging frauds by Stephen Ram in the office of insurance founded by Helbut.

2831 MIDDLETON, JOHN. For the Good of the Publick. A True Method, shewing All Ranks and Degrees of Men, how to purchase an Estate, or make Provision for Posterity, out of idle Expences.... *Edin. [c. 1720?], 4°*. L.

A life insurance scheme.

2832 Reasons humbly offer'd by the Sadlers-Hall-Society for their Establishment to Insure Houses and Goods from Fire throughout England, with the Security of a Deposited Joint Stock. *n.p. [1720?], s. sh. F°*. L.

2833 Reasons humbly offered to the Honourable the Committee of the House of Commons, for approving the Scheme to erect an Annuity-Company. *n.p. [1720], s. sh. F°*. O.

An insurance company which will improve the cod fishery of Nova Scotia.

2834 A Letter to a Member of Parliament, for Incouraging Offices of Insurance for Ships, Merchandice, Houses and Goods, Annuitys for Life, and upon Survivorship, and particularly for Encouraging the British Fishery in America, more especially the Cod Fishing of Nova Scotia. *n.p.* [*1720*], *s. sh. F°.* O.

Title taken from endorsement.

2835 Reasons humbly offer'd by the Societies of the Mines-Royal, &c. who Insure Ships and Merchandize, with the Security of a Deposited Joint-Stock. *n.p.* [*1720*], *F°.* O.

2836 The Office-Keepers Answer to a Scandalous Reflection on them by the Societies of the Mines-Royal, &c. *n.p.* [*1720*], *s. sh. F°.* LU.

2837 The Case of many Merchants and Traders in and about the City of London, on the Behalf of themselves and other Traders of Great Britain. *n.p.* [*1720*], *s. sh. F°.* O.

Endorsed: The Case of the Mutual Assurers, &c.

2838 Reasons humbly offer'd by the Insurers of Ships and Merchandize, at Sea. *n.p.* [*1720*], *s. sh. F°.* L.

2839 A Letter to a Member of Parliament. By a Merchant. *n.p.* [*1720*], *s. sh. F°.* LU.

Signed: T.S. On marine insurance.

2840 A Second Letter to a Member of Parliament, By a Merchant. *n.p.* [*1720*], *s. sh. F°.* LU.

Signed: T.S.

2841 Reasons Humbly Offer'd against giving the Benefit of Lending Money on Bottomree, to the Societies for Insuring Ships and Merchandize. *n.p.* [*1720*], *s. sh. F°.* LU.

2842 Reasons humbly offer'd against the Societies of the Mines Royal, Mineral and Battery Works, who have undertaken to Insure Ships, and Merchandizes, at Sea, without a Charter. *n.p.* [*1720?*], *s. sh. F°.* LU.

2843 A Letter to the Chairman of the Committee. By a Merchant. *n. p.* [*1720*], *s. sh. F°.* L.

Signed: T.B. On marine insurance, with reference to the committee of the House of Commons 'to inquire into several subscriptions lately taken for establishing of Fisheries, Insurances, &c.'

2844 Reasons humbly offered to the Committee of the Honourable House of Commons, by the Persons conditionally subscribing to the Sum of One Million of Pounds Sterling, for erecting an Office to insure Ships and Merchandize at Sea. *n.p.* [*1720*], *s. sh. F°.* O.

2845 The Special Report, from the Committee appointed to Inquire into, and Examine the several Subscriptions for Fisheries, Insurances, Annuities for Lives, and all other Projects carryed on by Subscription, in and about the Cities of London and Westminster; and to Inquire into all Undertakings for purchasing Joint-Stocks, or Obsolete Charters. *Lond. 1720*, *F°.* L.

2846 By the King, A Proclamation, For putting in Execution an Act for the better Securing certain Powers and Privileges intended to be granted by His Majesty by Two Charters for Assurance of Ships and Merchandizes at Sea, and for Lending Money on Bottomry; and for Restraining several Extravagant and Unwarrantable Practices therein mentioned. *Lond. 1720*, *s. sh. F°.* L.

Dated: 11 June 1720.

TRANSPORT

2847 A Bill for making the River Douglas, alias Asland, Navigable, from the River Rible to Wigan, in the County-Palatine of Lancaster. *n.p.* [*1720*], *F°.* L.

2848 An Answer to the Reasons for Making the River Douglas Navigable. *n.p.* [*1720?*], *s. sh. F°.* O.

2849 Reasons Against the Bill for Making the River Douglas Navigable. *n.p.* [*1720*], *s. sh. F°.* L.

2850 A Bill for Preserving and Improving the Navigation of the River Ouse, in the County of Huntingdon. *n.p.* [*1720*], *F°.* E.

2851 A Bill for making the River Weaver Navigable, from Winsford-Bridge, to Frodsham-Bridge, in the County of Chester. *n.p.* [*1720?*], *F°.* L.

2852 The Case of Charles Cholmondeley, Esq; In relation to the Intended Navigation on the River Weever. *n.p.* [*1720*], *F°.* L.

2853 Copies of the several Petitions to the Right Honourable the Lords Spiritual and Temporal, in Parliament assembled, for passing the Bill to make the River Weaver, in the County of Chester, Navigable from Winsford-Bridge to Frodsham-Bridge. *n.p. 1720*, *F°.* M.

2854 Copy of a Letter from A.D. to H. L-H, Esq. about making the River Weaver, in the County of Chester, Navigable. *Lond. 1720*, *F°.* M.

2855 [Lacon,]. Reasons, against making the River Weaver Navigable from Windsford-Bridge in the County of Chester, to Frodsham-Bridge in the said County. *n.p.* [*1720?*], *s. sh. F°.* L.

L copy has a ms. note: Lacon's Reasons. For Lacon see T. S. Willan, *The Navigation of the River Weaver*, 1951, p. 157.

2856 Reasons against the Bill for making the River Weever Navigable in the County of Chester, as it affects Trade in general. *n.p.* [*1720?*], *F°.* L.

2857 Reasons against the Bill for making the River Weaver Navigable. As it affects Trade in General. And in Particular, The Property of several Persons. *n.p.* [*1720?*], *F°.* L.

On the effects on the salt trade.

2858 Remarks upon the Printed Paper, Entitled, Reasons against the Bill for making the River Weaver Navigable. *n.p.* [*1720?*], *F°*. M.

Reprinted in facsimile in A. F. Calvert, *Salt in Cheshire*, 1915.

2859 Further Answers to Objections of the Brine-Salt-Makers in Cheshire, against making the River Weaver Navigable. *n.p.* [*1720*], *s. sh. F°*. M.

Reprinted in facsimile in A. F. Calvert, *Salt in Cheshire*, 1915.

2860 Reasons for Committing the Bill, for making the River Weaver, in the County of Chester, Navigable from Winsford-Bridge to Frodsham-Bridge. *n.p.* [*1720?*], *F°*. M.

2861 Reasons most humbly offer'd to the Right Honourable the Lords Spiritual and Temporal, in Parliament assembled, for passing the Bill for making the River Weaver, in the County of Chester, Navigable from Winsford-Bridge to Frodsham Bridge. *n.p.* [*1720?*], *F°* M.

Reprinted in facsimile in A. F. Calvert, *Salt in Cheshire*, 1915.

2862 Remarks upon the Petitions preferred, and the Cases and Reasons published against the Bill to make the River Weaver Navigable, from Winsford-Bridge, to Frodsham-Bridge. With some further Reasons humbly offered for Committing and Passing the Bill. *n.p.* [*1720*], *s. sh. F°*. L.

2863 The Laws relating to the Highways, Containing I. The several Kinds of Highways; and the Persons bound to Repair them....II. Of Defaults, &c....III. The Statutes made and pass'd for Erecting of Turnpikes.... *Lond.* *1720*, *12°*. L.

2864 The Case of the Carriers and Waggoners, who carry Goods to Hire. *n.p.* [*1720?*], *s. sh. F°*. L.

Endorsed: The Waggoners Case.

2865 An Act for Repairing the Roads from Stevenidge, in the County of Hertford, to Biggleswade, in the County of Bedford. *n.p.* [*1720?*], *F°*. E.

2866 Reasons humbly offered for Repairing and Amending the Highway or Road leading from Westminster-Ferry through the Town and Parish of Cammerwell into the County of Kent, and part of Sussex, or that the Inhabitants, and others, passing and repassing on the said Road, and to and from London, may be excused from paying to Turnpikes, whereby they receive little or no Benefit. *n.p.* [*1720?*], *F°*. L.

With a map.

SOCIAL CONDITIONS

2867 Braddon, Laurence. A Corporation Humbly Propos'd, for Relieving, Reforming, and Employing the Poor. Herein there will be more Private Gain to the Subscribers, and more Publick Good to Great Britain, than by All Unparliamentary Subscriptions already taken. In a Letter to a Justice of Peace of Middlesex. *Lond.* *1720*, *12°*. O.

2868 BRADDON, LAURENCE. An Humble Proposal for Relieving, Reforming and Employing the Poor. And herein by Vertue of One New General Law, instead of near Forty Statutes, relating to the Premises. We may Comfortably Maintain all th'Impotent Poor....And gradually sink, and in time, totally discharge all our Poor-Rates.... *Lond. 1720*, *8°*. LU.

2869 [FRANSHAM, JOHN]. An Exact Account of the Charge for Supporting the Poor of the City of Norwich, contain'd in the following Tables: viz. I. Tables of the Yearly Charge for Maintenance of the Poor in each respective Parish, from the Beginning of this Century, to this present Year. To which is prefix'd...the Charge for the Year 1690. II. A Table of the Discretional Disbursements only, separated from the Weekly Allowances, for the Years 1711, and 1718, in order to shew, That the Discretional Disbursements are abated since the Workhouse Method commenc'd. III. Tables of the Yearly Charge of the Poor, and Number of the Collections, for a compleat 100 Years, viz. from 1620, to 1720, for Fourteen Parishes....Lastly, A Table for these Fourteen Parishes containing the Yearly Charge, Number of Poor, and Weeks throughout the 100 Years. *Lond. 1720*, *8°*. LU.

The introduction signed: J.F. LU copy has ms. additions. For authorship see ms. note in O copy.

2870 Statutes of the Trinity-Hospital of Edinburgh. *Edin. 1720. 12°*. L.

2871 The Case of the Poor Insolvent Debtors and Prisoners, throughout England, humbly and impartially Stated in a Letter to a Member of Parliament. *Lond. 1720*, *8°*. LSC.

2872 POCOCK, THOMAS. The Relief of Captives, especially of our own Countreymen. Humbly offer'd to the Consideration of the Directors of the South-Sea Company, and to those who have been directed by them. *Lond. 1720*, *8°*. O.

An appeal for funds to redeem slaves in N. Africa.

2873 Rules, of the Society for the Relief of the Widows and Children of Subscribing Clergymen of the Diocese of Dublin. *Dublin*, [*1720?*], *8°*. DA.

2874 LAMBE, AARON. Reasons humbly offer'd for the Entering or Registering all Letters of Attorney, Bills of Sale, or Assignments of Seamens Wages, &c. (employed in the King's Service,) for Preventing the Frauds and Abuses frequently committed for Want thereof. *n.p.* [*1720*], *s. sh. F°*. L.

Dated: April 11. 1720.

2875 ORLEBAR, JOHN. A Scheme whereby His Majesty would never want a Choice of Able Seamen on any Occasion, and at the same time save the great Charge and Trouble of Impressing, &c. *n.p.* [*1720?*], *s. sh. F°*. L.

Endorsed: A Scheme for the better Paying and Encouraging Seamen, by Mr. Orlebar.

2876 A discovery of some gross abuses and disorders in the retail of strong waters.... *Lond. 1720, 16°.* Kress 3198.

2877 A Vade Mecum for Malt-Worms: or, a Guide to Good-Fellows: being a Description of the Manners and Customs of the most Eminent Publick Houses, in and about the Cities of London and Westminster. With a Hint on the Props (or Principal Customers) of each House.... *Lond.* [*1720*], *8°*. O.

2878 A Bill for Incorporating several Undertakers, for the better Accommodating the Inhabitants in and about the Cities of London and Westminster, and the Parts adjacent, with Water. *n.p.* [*1720*], *F°*. L.

2879 Reasons for Passing the Water Bill; which is, For Incorporating several Undertakers, for the better Accommodating the Inhabitants in and about the Cities of London and Westminster, and the Parts adjacent, with Water. *n.p.* [*1720*], *F°*. L.

2880 A Letter, from a Gentleman in the Country, to a Member of the House of Commons, upon a Projection of Serving the City with Water, from the Rivers Colne, Gade, &c. in the County of Hertford: The Bill for which is now depending before the Honourable House of Commons. *n.p.* [*1720?*], *F°*. L.

1721

GENERAL

2881 [DEFOE, DANIEL]. Brief Observations on Trade and Manufactures; And particularly of our Mines and Metals, and the Hard-Ware Works, of which the said Mines and Metals are the Foundation. *Lond. 1721*, *8°*. LU.

For authorship see *C.B.E.L.* II, 507.

2882 [BERKELEY, GEORGE, Bishop of Cloyne]. An Essay towards preventing the Ruine of Great Britain. *Lond. 1721*, *8°*. LU.

Reprinted, with author's name, in *A Miscellany*, 1752.

2883 The Freeholders Journal. Numb. 1–76. Jan 31, 1721–May 18, 1723. *Lond. 1721–23*, *F°*. L.

Includes many contributions by Archibald Hutcheson.

2884 The Present Miserable State of Ireland. In a Letter from a Gentleman in Dublin to his Friend in London. *London Printed: And Reprinted in Dublin by Sarah Harding, 1721, s. sh. F°*. C (Cr).

Signed: J.S. Originally printed in Mist's *Weekly Journal*, 30 Sept. 1721, where it is signed: S.T. See Wagner 9, who dates this sheet 1726–7, on the basis of the imprint, the evidence of which is not conclusive. Another edn. entitled; The Case of the Kingdom of Ireland. Taken into Consideration; in a Letter to a Member of Parliament, in the Behalf of Trade, Dublin, n.d. 8° (LSC); another edn., with original title, Dublin, n.d. 8° (DG); another edn. Dublin, 1735, 8° (CT Rothschild 2244). Reprinted in *The Prose Works of Jonathan Swift*. ed. by Temple Scott, vol. 7 (1905). The attribution to Swift made by Sir Walter Scott is rejected half-heartedly by Wagner and wholly by Professor Herbert Davis.

AGRICULTURE

2885 BRADLEY, RICHARD. A General Treatise of Husbandry and Gardening.... Containing Such Observations and Experiments as are New and Useful for the Improvement of Land.... *Lond.* [*1721*]–*24*[*23*], *8°*. L.

Published monthly from April 1721 to March 1722. Then continued with two numbers for April/May and June/July 1722 entitled: The Monthly Register of Experiments and Observations in Husbandry and Gardening; and concluded with: A General Treatise of Husbandry and Gardening....For the months of August and September, and the remaining part of the second year. This last part is dated 1724 but was advertised in 1723. Collective title-pages dated 1724 were issued when the work was completed. Another edn. 1726 (LU); another edn. 1757 (L).

2886 BRADLEY, RICHARD. A Philosophical Account of the Works of Nature.... To which is added, An Account of the State of Gardening, as it now is in Great Britain, and other Parts of Europe: Together with several new Experiments relating to the Improvement of Barren Ground, and the Propagating of Timber-Trees, Fruit-Trees, &c. With many Curious Cutts. *Lond. 1721*, 4°. L.

2nd edn. 1739 (R).

2887 The Hop-Garden: or, Directions for Planting and Managing Hops. *Lond. 1721*, 8°. L.

The dedication signed: J.A. and dated: Maidstone, May 1. 1721.

2888 An Act for Inclosing the Heath or Common called Broad-Heath, in the Parishes of Ellenhall, Seighford and Ronton, in the County of Stafford. *n.p.* [*1721*], F°. O.

2889 A Bill for Dividing and Enclosing a certain Moor, or Fell, commonly called Lanchester Fell, in the Parish of Lanchester, in the County of Durham. *n.p.* [*1721*], F°. L.

2890 An Act to Inclose the Common-Field of Lighthorne, and a Common call'd Lighthorne Musters, in the County of Warwick. *n.p.* [*1721*], F°. O.

A bill.

2891 Cawood, Francis. An Essay: or, Scheme: towards Establishing and Improving the Fishery, and other Manufactures of Great-Britain. Humbly offered and dedicated to the North-Sea Company....What Goods and Merchandize are proper for Maritime Traffick, whence they are to be had, and what Gain and Profit they will produce to the said Company....By Francis Cawood, of London Merchant, subscribed to in the Years, 1713, 1716, and 1720 now full and still Subsisting. *Lond. 1721*, 8°. L.

2892 The Charter of the Mine Adventurers of England. *n.p.* [*1720?*], F°. O.

Granted 26 April 1704.

2893 Proceedings of the General Court of the Governour and Company of The Mine-Adventurers of England, held at Stationers-Hall, London, on Friday the 24th of February, 172$\frac{0}{1}$. *n.p.* [*1721*], F°. O.

Title taken from endorsement.

2894 A Scheme for advancing the Trading Stock of the Company of Mine-Adventurers of England, and for employing the same to great Profit. Demonstrated by the following Tables. *n.p.* [*1721?*], 4°. L.

2895 [Willison, John]. A Letter to an English Member of Parliament, from a Gentleman in Scotland, concerning the Slavish Dependencies, which a great Part of that Nation is still kept under, by Superiorities, Wards, Reliefs, and other Remains of the Feudal Law, and by Clanships and Tithes. *Edin. 1721*, 8°. E.

Another edn. Lond. 1746 (E); another edn. 1747 (EU). For authorship see *D.N.B.*

2896 The Cry of the Creditors upon Bankrupt Estates in Scotland renewed; Containing a Project for retrieving Credit, and advancing Trade, by preventing tedious Law-Suits.... *Edin. 1721*, 8°. E.

MANUFACTURES

2897 Articles of Partnership for establishing the Company of Mineral Manufactures at Neath. *Lond.* [*1721?*], *F*°. Thomas.

The articles are dated 1713.

2898 The Case of the Copartners, or Company of the Mineral Manufactures at Neath. *n.p.* [*1721?*], *F*°. Thomas.

2899 A Copy of several Affidavits and other Proofs relating to the Undertaking, for Making and Manufacturing Copper, Brass, Lead and Iron, by the Company of the Mineral Manufactures at Neath. Printed at the Request of diverse Partners, and Members of the said Company. *n.p.* [*1721?*], *F*°. O.

2900 [Wood, William]. The State of the Copper and Brass Manufactures in Great Britain; humbly offered to the Consideration of Parliament. *Lond.* *1721*, 4°. L.

For authorship see D. Macpherson, *Annals of Commerce*, III, 116.

2901 The Report and Proceedings of the Inspectors of the Temple-Mills Brass-Works. *Lond.* *1721*, *F*°. O.

2902 Reasons humbly offer'd for the making (by a new Bill) several Acts of Parliament more effectual, for the Incouraging of making Needle-wrought Buttons and Button-holes. *n.p.* [*1721?*], *s. sh. F*°. L.

2903 Short Reasons Humbly offer'd to the Right Honourable The House of Lords, for Encouraging the Making of Needle-wrought Buttons and Button-holes. *n.p.* [*1721*], *s. sh. F*°. LG.

2904 The Hat-Makers Case. *n.p.* [*1721*], *s. sh. F*°. LPRO.

Endorsed: The Hat-Makers Case, shewing, That the present high Duties on Beaver-Skins imported, and the great Drawback allowed to Foreigners on the Exportation thereof, hath been and is the only Encouragement to Foreigners to make Beaver-Hats, and a very great Discouragement to the English Hat-Makers.

2905 Information for John Baskett His Majesty's Printer and others, Against James Watson. *n.p.* [*1721*], *s. sh. F*°. E.

Dated: June 27th 1721. Signed: James Graham.

2906 Information for James Watson One of His Majesty's Printers, against Mr. John Baskett His Majesty's Printer in England. *n.p.* [*1721*], *F*°. E.

Dated: July 17. 1721. Signed: Dun. Forbes.

2907 The Case of the Master Taylors residing within the Cities of London and Westminster, in relation to the Great Abuses committed by their Journeymen. Humbly Offer'd to the Consideration of Parliament. *n.p.* [*1721*], *s. sh. F*°. L.

2908 The Case of the Journeymen-Taylors residing in the Cities of London and Westminster, most humbly offered to the Consideration of both Houses of Parliament. *n.p.* [*1721*], *s. sh. F*°. L.

2909 An Abstract of the Master-Taylors Bill before the Honourable House of Commons; with the Journeymens Observation on each Clause of the said Bill. *n.p.* [*1721*], *s. sh. F*º. L.

2910 FOWNES, Sir WILLIAM. A Proposal for the Universal Encouragement of the Trade and Manufactury of the Poor Weavers, and other Trades Men of the Kingdom of Ireland. With Rules laid down for carrying on the same. *Dublin*, *1720–21*, *s. sh. F*º. D.

2911 KENDRICK, ROGER. A Letter to the Revered Dr. Swift Dean of St. Patrick's Dublin; Relating to the present State of the Manufactures of Ireland. *Dublin*, *1721*, *8*º. DA.

2912 Joshua Minnit, Merchant, Appellant. John Whinery, Stone-Cutter, Respondent. The Appellant's Case. *n.p.* [*1721*], *F*º. L.

Signed: Tho. Lutwych. Con. Phipps. Affairs of a Dublin sugar-boiling firm.

2913 Joshua Minitt, Merchant, Appellant. John Whinery, Merchant, Respondent. The Respondent's Case. *n.p.* [*1721*], *F*º. L.

Signed: Rob. Raymond. Samuel Mead.

COMMERCE

2914 [BLANCH, JOHN]. Great Britain Arraigned as of Felo de se, and Found Guilty, In a brief Chronology of Commerce from its Original.... *Lond.* *1721*, *8*º. LU.

For authorship see the list of his works included in Blanch's *Swords into Anchors*, 1725.

2915 By the King, A Proclamation, For Altering the Stamp for Hides and Skins to be Imported. *Lond.* *1721*, *s. sh. F*º. L.

Dated: 11 November 1721.

2916 LONDON. Fryer Mayor. Die Martis, xº die Januarii, Anno Domini 1720 [O.S.].... [*Lond.*], *1720*, *s. sh. F*º. LCRO.

Enforcing the use of the legal weights and measures.

2917 Calculations relating to the Coal Trade, being An Account of what Coals stand in per Ton, delivered at the Keys of Dublin, by the Whitehaven Ships. Computed according to the known Rules of Merchandizing. Taken from the Books of the Friendship, Seaflower, Sceptre and Love, upon Voyages Considered At a Medium of their Deliveries and Charges; humbly offered to the Consideration of all Masters and Owners of Ships. *n.p.* *1721*, *8*º. LU.

Signed: Clem. Nicholson, John Gale, John Gilpin, James Milham, Isaac Langton.

2918 By the King, A Proclamation, Requiring Quarentine to be performed by Ships coming from the Mediterranean, Bourdeaux, or any of the Ports or Places on the Coast of France in the Bay of Biscay, or from the Isles of Guernsey, Jersey, Alderney, Sark, or Man. *Lond. 1720* [*O.S.*], *s. sh. F°.* L.

Dated: 5 February 1720.

2919 By the Lords Justices and Council of Ireland, a Proclamation. Requiring Quarentine to be Performed by Ships coming from the Mediterranean, Bourdeaux, or any of the Ports or Places on the Coast of France in the Bay of Biscay, or from the Isles of Guernsey, Jersey, Alderney, Sarke or Man. *Dublin, 1721, F°.* DPRO.

Dated: 18 February 1720 [O.S.].

2920 A Letter to a Friend from a Merchant who has Resided many Years at Leghorn: giving an Account of the Methods taken by that State to prevent Infection. Together with the Author's Thoughts what we ought to do at this Conjuncture, in order to preserve our Health and Trade. *Lond. 1721, 8°.* OUP.

2921 The Case of the Inhabitants of the Liberty of Westminster, against the Clauses, proposed by the Justices of the Peace, to a Bill now Passing, to require Quarentine. *n.p.* [*1721?*], *s. sh. F°.* L.

2922 The Case of the Levant Company, in relation to the Bill now depending before this Honourable House, for performing Quarentine. *n.p.* [*1721*], *s. sh. F°.* L.

2923 Observations upon several Laws now in being, relating to the Power of Custom and Excise Officers. With Some Reasons humbly offered against the Bill To prevent bringing in the Infection by the Clandestine Running of Goods. *n.p.* [*1721*], *F°.* L.

2924 Reasons humbly offer'd by the Grocers of the City of London, against Part of the Bill now depending in the Honourable House of Commons, Entituled, A Bill to prevent the bringing in the Infection, by the clandestine running of Goods. *n.p.* [*1721*], *s. sh. F°.* L.

2925 [Wilson, Richard]. A Letter to a Member of Parliament to prevent the Clandestine Running of Wool in England, and the great Frauds in the Revenue. *n.p.* [*1721*], *F°.* LPRO.

Dated: Waterford, June 21st 1721. Signed in ms. by the author.

2926 At the Court at Kensington, the Second Day of October, 1721. Present, the King's most Excellent Majesty in Council. *n.p.* [*1721*], *F°.* L.

Upon petitions from the East India Company complaining of illegal trading between Madagascar and the American colonies the Privy Council orders the strict enforcement of the Navigation Acts in the colonies.

2927 Reasons humbly offer'd for passing the Bill into a Law, for making more effectual the Act made Anno 11° & 12° Gulielmi Tertii Regis, for the more effectual employing the Poor by encouraging the Manufactures of this Kingdom. *n.p.* [*1721*], *s. sh. F°.* LLI.

The bill tightened the penalties for wearing East India goods.

2928 The Case of the Mercers, and other Fair Traders in the Silk and Worsted Manufactures; humbly offer'd to the Consideration of the Parliament of Great Britain. *n.p.* [*1721*], *s. sh. F°.* O.

Endorsed: The Case of the Traders in the Silk and Worsted Manufactures. Against the smuggling of East India goods.

COLONIES

2929 DUMMER, JEREMIAH. A Defence of the New-England Charters. *Lond. 1721*, *8°.* L.

Another edn. Boston, 1745 (WLC); another edn. Boston, 1765 (WLC). Another edn. Lond. [1765] (L).

2930 [PAINE, THOMAS]. A Discourse, shewing, that the real first Cause of the Straits and Difficulties of this Province of the Massachussetts Bay, is it's Extravagancy, & not Paper Money: and also what is a safe Foundation to raise a Bank of Credit, on, and what not, (with some Remarks on Amicus Patriae,) & a Projection for Emitting of more Bills of Credit on the Province. By Way of Dialogue, between a Representative in said Province, and a certain Gentleman, concerned for the Good of his native Country. By Philopatria. *Boston*, *1721*, *8°.*

Reprinted in *Colonial Currency Reprints*, ed. by A. M. Davis, vol. 2 (1911), whence this entry is taken.

2931 A Letter to an Eminent Clergy-Man in the Massachusetts-Bay. Containing some Just Remarks, and necessary Cautions, relating to Publick Affairs in that Province. [*Boston*], *1720* [*O.S.*], *8°.*

Reprinted in *Colonial Currency Reprints*, ed. by A. M. Davis, vol. 2 (1911), whence this entry is taken.

2932 The Second Part of South-Sea Stock. Being an Inquiry into the Original of Province Bills or Bills of Credit, Now in Use in His Majesty's Plantations, more especially in New-England; With Some Thoughts Relating to the Advantage, or Hurt done by Emitting the said Bills. *Boston*, *1721*, *8°.*

Reprinted in *Colonial Currency Reprints*, ed. by A. M. Davis, vol. 2 (1911), whence this entry is taken.

2933 [WISE, JOHN]. A Word of Comfort to a Melancholy Country. Or the Bank of Credit erected in the Massachusetts-Bay, Fairly Defended by a Discovery of the Great Benefit, accruing by it to the Whole Province; With a Remedy for Recovering a Civil State when Sinking under Desperation by a Defeat on their Bank of Credit. By Amicus Patriae. *Boston*, *1721*, *8°.*

Reprinted in *Colonial Currency Reprints*, ed. by A. M. Davis, vol. 2 (1911), whence this entry is taken.

2934 The Case of the Present Possessors of the French Lands in the Island of St. Christophers. Humbly Offered to the Consideration of His Majesty, and both Houses of Parliament. Occasioned by a Petition resolved upon at the last General Court of the South Sea Company, to be presented to His Majesty, that he would be pleased to grant the Company that Part of the Island of St. Christophers which formerly belong'd to the French, in Order to the better carrying on their Trade. *Lond. 1721*, *8°*. LU.

2935 The Humble Address and Representation of the Assembly of Jamaica to His Majesty, with His Excellency's Answer, and some Messages in Relation thereto. *Jamaica*, *1721*, *F°*. O.
On the finances of the island.

FINANCE

2936 Aislabie, John. The Speech of the Right Honourable John Aislabie, Esq; upon his Defence made in the House of Lords, against the Bill for Raising Money upon the Estates of the South-Sea Directors, on Wednesday the 19th of July 1721. *Lond. 1721*, *4°*. L.
2nd and 3rd edns. 1721 (both L). Another edn. Dublin, 1721, 8° (DA).

2937 [Defoe, Daniel]. A Vindication of the Honour and Justice of Parliament againt a most Scandalous Libel, Entituled, The Speech of John A[islabie] Esq; *Lond.* [*1721*], *8°*. LU.
For authorship see *C.B.E.L.* II, 507.

2938 Aislabie, John. Mr Aislabie's Second Speech on his Defence in the House of Lords, on Thursday, July 20. 1721. *Lond. 1721*, *4°*. LU.

2939 Mr Aislabie's Two Speeches Considered; with his Tryal at large in both Houses of Parliament. Wherein the Learned Speeches for and against Him in the several Debates, are faithfully inserted. To which are Added, Remarks upon a Scandalous Libel, called, A Vindication of the Honour and Justice of Parliament. By W—— S—— Esq; *Lond. 1721*, *4°*. OH.

2940 Asgill, John. The Computation of Advantages saved to the Publick by the South-Sea Scheme, as Published in the Moderator of Wednesday the 26th of April, 1721. Detected to be Fallacious. With a Post-script. *Lond. 1721*, *8°*. L.

2941 Baden, Lewis. To His Majesty, the Lords and Commons of Great Britain, is humbly presented, A Proposal for Paying the Debts of the Nation, Principal and Interest, to Support Publick Credit, and Encourage Trade, by an Improvement in the Management of Paper-Credit. *Lond. 1721*, *F°*. LU.

2942 Budgell, Eustace. A Letter to a Friend in the Country, occasion'd by a Report that there is a Design still forming by the late Directors of the South-Sea Company, their Agents and Associates, to issue the Receipts of the Third and Fourth Subscriptions at 1000 l. per Cent. and to extort about Ten Millions more from the miserable People of

Great Britain. With some Observations on the Present State of Affairs at Home and Abroad. *Lond. 1721*, 8°. LU.

2943 GODEFROY, ALEXANDER. A Scheme for Restoring Publick Credit, by New-modelling the South-Sea Company; Humbly offer'd to the Consideration of His Majesty and both Houses of Parliament. *n.p.* [*1721?*], *s. sh. F°*. LU.

2944 HUTCHESON, ARCHIBALD. A Collection of Treatises relating to the National Debts & Funds. The First of them dated April the 11th, 1717. and the Last, April 4. 1721. [another added dated May 13 1721]. *Lond. 1721*, *F°*. LU.

The words in [ ] are supplied in ms. in the LU copy.

2945 HUTCHESON, ARCHIBALD. A Computation of the Value of South-Sea Stock, on the Foot of the Scheme as it now subsists. Made from the Facts as they are Stated by the Directors of the South-Sea Company, in the Accounts and Papers by Them laid before the House of Commons.... With some Remarks relating to these Matters. *Lond. 1720* [*O.S.*], *F°*. LU.

Preface dated: 1720 [O.S.]. February 6.

2946 HUTCHESON, ARCHIBALD. Some Computations and Remarks relating to the Money Subscribers, and the Proprietors of the Publick Debts. And a Letter relating thereto to the Sub-Governor, Deputy-Governor, and Directors of the South-Sea Company. And some further Remarks on the same Subject. *Lond. 1720*, [*O.S.*], *F°*. LU.

Dated: 1st March 1720 [O.S.].

2947 HUTCHESON, ARCHIBALD. Some Computations relating to the Proposed Transferring of Eighteen Millions of the Fund of the South Sea Company, to the Bank, and East-India Company. Shewing how the same will come out on Two different Suppositions, to the Old Proprietors of Bank and India, and to the New Proprietors of the Ingrafted Stock. *Lond. 1720* [*O.S.*], *F°*. LU.

Preface dated: 1720 [O.S.]. January 7th.

2948 HUTCHESON, ARCHIBALD. Some further Computations relating to South-Sea Stock. With a Proposal made therefrom, to be laid before the House of Commons, at the Meeting of the Parliament. *Lond. 1721*, *F°*. LU.

2949 A Proposal for the Relief of the New Proprietors in the South-Sea Company. And a State of the Value of the Reduced South-Sea Capital, according to the said Proposal. With Remarks relating thereto. Collected from several Papers given by Mr. Hutcheson to the Members of the House of Commons. And also a Table, shewing the value of South-Sea Stock in the several Views it hath appeared in since the Reduction of the Subscriptions from 1000 l. and 800 l. to 400 l. per Cent.

Collected from the Treatises published by Mr. Hutcheson. *Lond. 1721*, *F°*. LU.

Dated: 1721. May 13. Included as a supplement in the LU copy of *A Collection of Treatises* (no. 2944).

2950 IRWIN, JOHN. The Phoenix. Or, A New Scheme for Establishing Credit, upon the most solid and satisfactory Foundation, and intirely free from all Objections made to the former intended Bank. *Dublin, 1721*, *8°*. L.

2951 MACKWORTH, Sir HUMPHREY. To the Honourable the Knights, Citizens, and Burgesses of Great Britain, in Parliament assembled, the Humble Proposal of Sir Humphrey Mackworth, for restoring the National Credit, and fixing it upon a lasting Foundation.... *Lond. 1721*, *F°*. L.

2952 Now or Never: or, A Familiar Discourse concerning the Two Schemes for restoring National Credit, either by the United Interest of the Three Great Companies, or by making the Government-Securities current in all Payments, in a New Parliamentary Species of Money, to be secur'd and redeem'd by a proportionable Part of the Publick Revenue, appropriated as a Sinking Fund for that Purpose. By R.M. Esq. *Lond. 1721*, *8°*. LU.

Supports Sir Humphrey Mackworth's scheme. The initials suggest Roderick Mackenzie as the author.

2953 SNELL, CHARLES. Observations made upon Examining the Books of Sawbridge and Company. *n.p.* [*1721*], *F°*. L.

On dealings in South Sea stock. No marginal note on p. 1. Another issue with note on p. 1. (L).

2954 VAN LEUTE, WILLIAM. A Proposal humbly offer'd to His Majesty and both Houses of Parliament. *n.p.* [*1721*], *F°*. L.

Endorsed title: A Proposal to Pay of Eighteen Millions of the South-Sea Fund. Dated: 10 Jan. 1720–21.

2955 To the Honourable House of Commons. The Humble Petition of William Van Leute. *n.p.* [*1721*], *s. sh. F°*. L.

Endorsed title: To Pay off Eighteen Millions of the South-Sea Stock and Funds....

2956 To the Right Honourable House of Lords. The Humble Petition of Merchants and Traders of Great Britain, and others interested in the Bank, East-India, or South-Sea Company, Sufferers by the Fall of Stock. *n.p.* [*1721*], *F°*. L.

Recommending William Van Leute's scheme.

2957 WALKER, MIDDLETON. A Proposal for Relieving the present Exigencies of the Nation by a Land Credit. Inscrib'd to the Right Honourable the Lord Viscount Townshend. *Lond. 1721*, *8°*. L.

A revival of Dr. Hugh Chamberlen's scheme.

2958 An Abstract of Part of the Bill for raising Money upon the Estates of the late Directors, &c. of the South-Sea Company, with some Remarks thereon. *n.p.* [*1721*], *F°*. M (Cr).

2959 *Begin.* Being lately in Company, where some taking the part of the late Directors, as for a Mulct... *n.p.* [*1721*], *s. sh. F°.* MC.

Calculations to show that the Directors of the South Sea Company had been harshly treated.

2960 An Alarm to the Proprietors of the South-Sea Company, and other Publick Securities: Or, Reasons to prove that the Support of the Question recommended by the Directors, is of the utmost Importance to all Creditors of the Government. *n.p.* [*1721*], *s. sh. F°.* L.

2961 The Alarm proved a False Alarm: or, Reasons to prove that the Support of the Question recommended by the Directors is of the utmost Importance to all Creditors of the Government, prov'd no Reasons. *n.p.* [*1721*], *s. sh. F°.* LG.

2962 A Calculation of the New Scheme for the Disposing of the South-Sea Property. Wherein is shewn what Dividend the South-Sea Company can make on the Old Foot; What Dividend the New Scheme proposes, and what Dividend (if the Scheme takes Effect) the Three Companies can really make by their present Profits and the Interest of the New Ingrafted Stock. Being what was intended to have been publish'd in the White-hall Evening-Post. *Lond.* [*1721*], *F°.* LU.

2963 A Calculation Shewing the Most that the Redeemable Proprietors May Possibly Lose by their taking South-Sea Stock at 400 per Cent. *Lond.* *1721*, *F°.* O.

2964 The Case of the Annuitants, and of the Several Interests of the South-Sea Proprietors, Compared and Examined. *Lond.* *1721*, *8°.* LU.

2965 The Case of the Borrowers on the South-Sea Loans, Stated. *Lond.* *1721*, *8°.* LU.

2nd edn. Lond. 1721 (O); another edn. n.p., n.d. (C).

2966 The Case of the Buyers of Subscription for Time, and Praemiums and the Sellers for Ready Money and Praemiums, impartially Stated. With a Quere to prevent the Ruin of them all, and some Reasons for so doing. *n.p.* [*1721*], *s. sh. F°.* L.

2967 The Case of the Purchasers of the First and Second Subscriptions to the South-Sea Company, at 4 to 500 per Cent. and of the Stock at 7 to 800 per Cent. and upwards in ready Money. *n.p.* [*1721*], *s. sh. F°.* L.

2968 The Case of the Sellers of the Third and Fourth Money-Subscriptions. *n.p.* [*1721*], *s. sh. F°.* L.

2969 The Case of the unhappy Purchasers of South-Sea Stock, from three Hundred to L.900 per Cent and upwards, in ready Money, Humbly offered to the Honourable the House of Commons. *n.p.* [*1721*], *s. sh. F°.* L.

2970 The Case of the Unhappy Sufferers by the South-Sea Company, and of Innocent Persons, under the Bill for Relief of such Unhappy Sufferers, now depending in Parliament. *n.p.* [*1721*], *F°.* L.

2971 *Begin.* Charles Snell in his Examination of the Books of Turner and Company.... *n.p.* [*1721*], *s. sh. F°.* L.

2972 Snell, Charles. A Short Answer to a Paper beginning with Charles Snell, &c. *n.p.* [*1721*], *s. sh. F°.* L.

2973 A Collection of the Several Petitions of the Counties, Boroughs, &c. presented to the House of Commons, Complaining of the Great Miseries the Nation labours under, by the Great Decay of Trade, Manufactuures [*sic*] and Publick Credit, Occasion'd by the Mismanagement of the Late Directors of the South-Sea Company, their Aiders, Abettors, and Confederates, &c. *Lond. 1721, 12°.* LU.

2974 A Detection of the Whole Management of the South-Sea Company. From the First Rise of their Stock to its Present Declension. Containing, I. The Secret History of their Four Subscriptions....II. The Case of the Annuitants truly Stated. III. The Fallacy of their Pretended Dividends justly exposed. In a Letter to John Ward of Hackney, Esq; *Lond. 1721, 8°.* LU.

2975 Die Jovis 26 Januarii, 1720. Resolved by the Lords Spiritual and Temporal in Parliament Assembled...*Lond. 1720* [*O.S.*], *s. sh. F°.* O.

Gift of South Sea stock to Members of Parliament 'was a Notorious and most Dangerous Corruption'.

2976 An Essay towards Restoring of Publick Credit: Humbly offer'd to the Consideration of the Honourable House of Commons. Wherein Certain Propositions are laid down, Advantageous to the Proprietors of the Annuities and Redeemable Debts, the Money-Subscribers and Purchasers of South-Sea Stock at High Prices; and for the Relief of Persons concern'd in Contracts, &c. By a Faithful Subject of the Best of Kings, and a Well-wisher to the happiest Constitution in the World. *Lond. 1721, 8°.* LU.

2977 Every One's Interest in the South-Sea Examined; and by Rules of Justice and Equity Settled, to their reciprocal and mutual Advantage. *Lond. 1721, 8°.* LU.

The dedication to Walpole signed: T.G., possibly Thomas Goodall; no. 2810 is mentioned on p. 30.

2978 A Full Computation of the Subscribers Pretensions to Receipts for the First Payment, made upon the Third and Fourth Subscriptions. Wherein the true Case of the Sellers of those Subscriptions is Examined and Answered. In a Letter to a Noble L——d. *Lond.* [*1721*], *8°.* L.

Dated: Feb. 1, 1720 [O.S.].

2979 The History of the Rise and Fall of South-Sea Stock; with A Method Humbly Proposed for the Relief of the Sufferers of all Sorts, in a Letter to a Friend. *Lond.* [*1721*], *8°.* LU.

2980 An Humble Remonstrance to the Lords and Commons of Great Britain, in this present Parliament assembled. An. 1721. *n.p.* [*1721*], *s. sh. F°.* LU.

To make South Sea time bargains void.

2981 John Ketch, Esq; his Letter to the Directors of the South-Sea. *Dublin, 1721*, 8º. DA.

2982 Laws, Ex post Facto; or, The Annulling of Legal Bargains, inconsistent with the British Constitution, and the Privileges of a Free People. *n.p.* [*1721*], *s. sh. F*º. LU.

2983 A Letter from a Gentleman in the Country to a Member of Parliament in England. *Dublin, 1721*, 4º. L.

On his losses in the South Sea Company.

2984 A Letter to a Friend, in Vindication of the Directors of the South-Sea Company, in Answer to the Speech of E——st——ce B——g——ll Esq; made at a General Court of that Company in Merchant Taylors Hall, the 20th of September, 1720. To which are annexed, Some Remarks on his Second Speech, and Mr W——lk——r's. *Lond. 1721*, 8º. L.

2985 A Letter to a Member of Parliament; wherein the Unreasonableness and Improbability of Binding Down the Redeemables, is fully Demonstrated. *Lond. 1721*, 4º. LU.

2986 A Letter to Mr. Law, upon his Arrival in Great Britain. *Lond. 1721*, 8º. *LU.*

2nd edn. [1721] (L); 3rd, 4th and 5th [1721] (all LU).

2987 A Letter to the Author of the London Journal; containing Objections against the present Scheme, to empower the Three Companies to take in Part of the Publick Debts. With a Just Calculation of the Value of a 100 l. Capital, when divided among the said Companies. To which is added, An equitable Proposal for Restoring of Publick Credit. *Lond. 1721*, *F*º. LU.

2988 A Letter to the Sub-Governor, Deputy-Governor, & Directors of the South-Sea Company. *n.p.* [*1721*], *F*º. LU.

Signed: From a True Lover of his Country.

2989 A Memorial of the Contractants with Mr. Aislabie. In a Letter to Licinius Stolo. *Lond. 1721*, 8º. L.

2990 [Hammond, Anthony]. A Modest Apology, occasion'd by the late Unhappy Turn of Affairs, with relation to Publick Credit. By a Gentleman. *Lond. 1721*, 8º. LU.

Both L and LU copies have the attribution in ms.

2991 [Hammond, Anthony]. The Moderator. no. 1–15. 21 April–24 May 1721. *Lond. 1721*, *F*º. O.

Defending the South Sea directors. Hammond's statement of his authorship is in Bodleian Rawlinson MS. D.360 fol. 163v.

2992 [Coningsby, Thomas, Earl of Coningsby]. The Naked and Undisguis'd Truth, plainly and faithfully told: What was the Unhappy Rise, Which were the Fatal Causes, And who the Wicked Authors, of Great

Britain's and Ireland's present dreadful...Calamities. By a passionate Lover of his Country. *Lond. 1721*, 8º. L.

On the South Sea Bubble. For authorship see *Bibliotheca Antonij Collins*, [1731], pt. 1, lot 1466.

2993 A New-Year's-Gift for the Directors. With some Account of their Plot against the Two Assurances; also a few Heads of a New Scheme, in a Letter to Sir B——n J——n. *Lond. 1721*, 8º. LU.

2994 [Gay, John]. A Panegyrical Epistle to Mr. Thomas Snow, Goldsmith, near Temple-Bar: occasion'd by his Buying and Selling of the Third Subscriptions, taken in by the Directors of the South-Sea Company, at a Thousand per Cent. *Lond. 1721*, Fº. L.

2nd edn. 1721 (MH). For authorship see *Poetical Works of John Gay*, 1926.

2995 The Present Case more fully Stated, as to Time Contracts; and particularly those Illegal-Ones for Putting and Refusing of Stock, &c. Also the Tendency and Consequence of the late Proceedings relating hereunto, consider'd. Humbly Submitted to both Houses of Parliament. *Lond. 1721*, Fº. L.

2996 The Proceedings of the Directors of the South-Sea Company, from the first Proposal of that Company, for taking in the Publick Debts, February 1, 1719. to the Choice of New Directors, February 2, 1720 [O.S.]. Wherein will be contained A Particular Account of the Debates in the General Courts of the said Company, during that Time, as likewise in those of the Bank of England, and East India Company, so far as they relate to the New Scheme for restoring Publick Credit....To these are added the By-Laws of the South-Sea Company. *Lond. 1721*, 8º. L.

2nd edn. [1721], entitled: The Proceedings of the late Directors...(Kress 3419).

2997 Proceedings of the House of Lords in relation to the late Directors of the South-Sea Company, and Others: with the Report of their Lordships on the said Proceedings: to which is added, the Conference with the Commons, relating to Mr. Aislabie and Mr. Craggs, with their Lordship's Proceedings thereupon. *Lond. 1721*, Fº. LU.

2nd edn. 1722 (M (Cr)).

2998 A Proposal for granting Relief to the several Proprietors of the Long and Short Annuities, Redeemable Debts, and Money Subscribers, (commonly call'd, The New, or Additional Capital of the South-Sea Company) by returning them a Proportion of the 13,301,480 l. 10s. 2d.½ remaining now indispos'd of in the said Company.... *n.p.* [*1721*], *s. sh.* Fº. L.

Dated May 9. 1721. O copy has a ms. note: 'By General Wade'.

2999 [Armour, James]. Proposals for Restoring Credit; for Making the Bank of England more Useful and Profitable; for Relieving the Sufferers of the South-Sea Company; for the Benefit of that of the East-India; and for Raising the Value of the Land-Interest of Great Britain. Humbly Offered to the Consideration of Both Houses of Parliament. *Lond. 1721*, 4°. L.

Some copies have an appendix and a postscript added. For authorship see his *Proposals for making the Bank of Scotland More Useful and Profitable* (No. 3179), which has much the same wording as this. Entered to Armour in the Stationers' Register.

3000 Queries, Whether South Sea Contracts for Time, and now depending unperformed, ought to be annulled or not? *n.p.* [*1721*], *s. sh. F°.* L.

Endorsed: Queries about South-Sea Contracts.

3001 Reasons against Ingrafting the South-Sea Fund with the Bank and East-India Company. *n.p.* [*1721*], *s. sh. F°.* L.

3002 Reasons for making void and annulling those Fraudulent and Usurious Contracts, into which Multitudes of unhappy Persons have been drawn to the utter Ruin of themselves and Families, by the late Directors of the South-Sea Company, their Agents and Confederates. Humbly submitted to the Consideration of both Houses of Parliament. *n.p.* [*1721?*], *F°.* L.

3003 An Answer to the Reasons for making void and annulling Fraudulent and Usurious Contracts, &c. *n.p.* [*1721*], *F°.* L.

3004 The Performance of Fair and Legal Contracts, the Surest Method to support Publick and Private Credit. In Answer to Reasons for making Void all Contracts, &c. *n.p.* [*1721*], *s. sh. F°.* L.

3005 Further reasons offer'd and and fresh occasions given for making void and annulling fraudulent and usurious contracts, especially those time-contracts for putting or refusal of stock (formerly declar'd illegal) into which...persons have been drawn...by the directors of the South-sea company. *Lond. 1721*, *F°.* Kress 3380.

3006 Reasons for the Proprietors Agreeing with the Resolution of the Court of Directors. *n.p.* [*1721*], *s. sh. F°.* L.

On questions to be submitted to the General Court of the South Sea Company on 9 March 1721.

3007 Reflections on the Advertisements in the Post-Boy, and Mist's Journal of the 13th of May, concerning the Loans, Redeemables, and Money Subscribers. *n.p.* [*1721*], *F°.* L.

3008 [BRADDON, LAURENCE]. The Regular-Government, and Judicious-Employment of the Poor, the most Probable Means of Raising and Securing Publick-Credit, because the Rich will be thereby made, both able and willing, to give Credit to the Publick. In the Second Part will be humbly propos'd, a Parliamentary-Fund for Ten Millions, Sterling, or more, in Exchequer-Bills....And hereby South-Sea-Sufferers may be reliev'd, and thereby Parliamentary-Credit, very much advanc'd *Lond. 1721*, 8°. LU.

Authorship deduced by Foxwell from internal evidence.

3009 Restitution: A Law of the Land, in Relation to the third and fourth Money Subscriptions into the South-Sea Company. *n.p.* [*1721*], *F*o. L.

3010 A Second Letter to Mr. Law. Occasion'd by his Arrival in England, and its being Reported He is to be made a Director of the South Sea Company and a Member of Parliament. *Lond. 1721*, *8*o. LU.

3011 A Short, but True Account, &c. *n.p.* [*1721*], *s. sh. F*o. LU.

For annulling all South Sea contracts made 'by way of Put, or Refusal'.

3012 The Skreen Removed; in a List of all the Names mention'd in the Report of the Committee of Secrecy. With the Sums wherewith they are charged, in Relation to South-Sea Stock, as well on Account of Loans, as otherwise. To which is prefix'd, the Sum total of the late Sub-Governour's, Deputy-Governour's, and every Director's Estate; as also that of the Accomptant, and Deputy-Cashier of the South-Sea-Company, to be confiscated by Act of Parliament for the Use of the Proprietors; With the allowance of Money made for their Support, out of the Sale of their respective Possessions, Real and Personal. *Lond. 1721*, *8*o. LU.

3013 Some Considerations on the late Mismanagement of the South-Sea Stock; On the New Scheme propos'd for Redress; And likewise on Trade. In a Letter to a Friend. *Lond.* [*1721*], *8*o. LU.

3014 Some Considerations submitted to the Proprietors of South-Sea Stock, with Regard to the Question to be determin'd by Ballot, on Thursday the 16th Day of March, 1720 [O.S.]. *n.p.* [*1721*], *F*o. O.

3015 Some Considerations with respect to the Bill for preventing the infamous Practice of Stock-Jobbing; being Remarks upon the Supplement to the Reasons for making void and annulling those Fraudulent and Usurious Contracts, into which, &c. and upon the Reply to a modest Paper, &c. both delivered at the Door of the House of Commons on Friday last. *n. p.* [*1721*], *s. sh. F*o. L.

3016 Some Observations upon the Bill now depending in Parliament, for relief of the unhappy Sufferers in the South-Sea Company. In a Letter from a Gentleman of the Law to a Member of Parliament. *n.p.* [*1721*], *4*o. LU.

3017 Some Queries relating to the Bill of Engraftment, and the present State of the South-Sea-Company. *n.p.* [*1721*], *F*o. L.

3018 Some Reasons for the Question Proposed at the Last General Court, against the Ingraftment; with an Answer to some Reasons given against it. *n.p.* [*1721*], *F*o. L.

3019 A Speech upon the Consolidated Bill. [*Lond.*], *1721*, *4*o. LU.

In defence of Aislabie.

3020 A State of the Case between the South-Sea Company, and the Proprietors of the Redeemable Debts. *n.p.* [*1721*], *F*o. L.

The endorsed title is: The Case of the Annuitants of the Redeemable Debts.

3021 A Stiptick for a Bleeding Nation. Or, a Safe and Speedy Way to Restore Publick Credit, and Pay the National Debts. *Lond. 1721*, 8°. LU.

3022 A Supplement to the London Journal of March 25, 1721; being the State of the Case relating to the Surrender of Mr. Knight, Farther Considered. *Lond. 1721*, 8°. L.

3023 [LAWTON, CHARLWOOD]. Three Letters concerning Civil Comprehension, &c. The last of which is occasion'd by the Present Distresses the Directors of the South-Sea-Company have brought upon these Kingdoms. *Lond. 1721*, 8°. LU.

For authorship see ms. note by William Thomas in LU copy.

3024 [DEFOE, DANIEL]. A True State of Publick Credit: or, a Short View of the Condition of the Nation, with respect to our present Calamities. And Some Considerations how they may be redress'd, and the Landed and Trading Interest advanced. As also Some necessary Observations on the Conduct of the Bank, in this Critical Juncture... *Lond. 1721*, 8°. LU.

For authorship see *C.B.E.L.* II, 507.

3025 The Reports of the Honourable the Committee of Secrecy in Relation to the Late Directors of the South-Sea Company; with the Examination of Sir Theodore Janssen, taken the 20th and 26th of January, 1720, at the South-Sea House, by the Honourable Committee of Secrecy; with their Proceedings thereupon at large being exactly set forth. By A[rchiba]ld H[utche]-son. *Lond.* [*1721*], F°. NYP. (Sabin 88917.)

3026 The Reports of the Committee of Secrecy to the Honourable House of Commons, relating to the late South-Sea Directors, &c. Carefully Corrected. *Lond. 1721*, F°. LU.

3027 The Several Reports of the Committee of Secrecy to the Honourable House of Commons, relating to the late South-Sea Directors, &c. *Lond. 1721*, F°. LU.

3028 A Supplement to the Reports of the Committee of Secrecy: containing, I. A Particular Account of the 574,500 l. South-Sea Stock, commonly call'd the Fictitious Stock....II. A Particular Account of the Exceedings of the Rules, made for regulating the several Loans on South-Sea Stock....II. A Particular Account of the Names of such Persons, to whom Loans have been made on South-Sea Stock. *Lond. 1721*, F°. L.

3029 An Abstract of the Supplement to the Reports of the Committee of Secrecy; which compleats the Abridgment of the said Reports, by a further Addition to the List of all the Names mention'd therein: with the Sums wherewith they are charged, in relation to South-Sea Stock, as well on account of Loans, as otherwise. By way of Appendix to The Skreen Removed.... *Lond. 1721*, 8°. NYP. (Sabin 88168.)

3030 By the King, A Proclamation, For Apprehending and Securing the Person of Robert Knight, Cashire of the South-Sea Company. *Lond. 1720* [*O.S.*], *s. sh. F°*. L.

Dated: 23 January 1720.

3031 The Particulars and Inventories of the Estates of the late Sub-Governor, Deputy-Governor, and Directors of the South-Sea Company: and of Robert Surman late Deputy-Cashier, and of John Grigsby late Accomptant of the said Company. Together with the Abstracts of the same. Volume I. Containing those of Sir John Fellows. Charles Joye, Esq; William Astell, Esq; Sir Lambert Blackwell. Sir John Blunt. Sir Robert Chaplin. Sir William Chapman. Robert Chester, Esq; Stephen Child, Esq; Peter de la Porte, Esq; Francis Eyles, Esq; James Edmundson, Esq; Edward Gibbon, Esq; John Gore, Esq; Sir William Hammond. [Vol. II. Containing those of Francis Hawes, Esq; Richard Horsey, Esq; Richard Houlditch, Esq; Sir Theodore Janssen. Sir Jacob Jacobson. Arthur Ingram, Esq; Sir John Lambert. Sir Harcourt Master. William Morley, Esq; Ambrose Page, Esq; Col. Hugh Raymond. Samuel Reade, Jun. Esq; Thomas Reynolds, Esq; Jacob Sawbridge, Esq; William Tillard, Esq; John Turner, Esq; Mr. Robert Surman. Mr. John Grigsby.] *Lond. 1721*, *F°*. L.

The inventories were also published separately.

3032 The Case of the Right Honble John Aislabie, Esq; [*Lond. 1721*], *4°*. L.

3033 The Case of William Astell, One of the late South-Sea Directors. *n.p.* [*1721*], *s. sh. F°*. L.

3034 The Case of Sir Lambert Blackwell. *n.p.* [*1721*], *s. sh. F°*. L.

A South Sea director.

3035 The Case of Sir John Blunt. *n.p.* [*1721*], *s. sh. F°*. L.

A South Sea director. Addressed to the House of Commons.

3036 The Case of Sir John Blunt, Bar^t.^ His Wife and Family. *n.p.* [*1721*], *s. sh. F°*. L.

Addressed to the House of Lords.

3037 The Case of Sir Robert Chaplin, Bart. one of the late Directors of the South Sea Company. *Lond. 1721*, *8°*. LU.

3038 The Case of Sir William Chapman, Knt. and Bar^t.^ One of the late Directors of the South-Sea Company. *n.p.* [*1721*], *s. sh. F°*. L.

3039 To the Honourable the Commons of Great-Britain, in Parliament assembled. The Humble Petition of Sir William Chapman, Kt. and Bar. *n.p.* [*1721*], *s. sh. F°*. LG.

3040 The Case of Stephen Child. *n.p.* [*1721*], *s. sh. F°*. L.

A South Sea director.

3041 Peter Delaporte's Case. *n.p.* [*1721*], *s. sh. F°*. L.

A South Sea director.

3042 The Case of James Edmundson, One of the late South-Sea Directors. *n.p.* [*1721*], *s. sh. F°*. L.

3043 Mr. Edmundson's Case. *n.p.* [*1721*], *s. sh. F°*. L.

A sequel to the preceding.

3044 A Short State of Mr. Edmundson's Case, one of the late South-Sea Directors, as more at large set forth in his Petition delivered to the Honourable House of Commons. *n.p.* [*1721*], *s. sh. F°*. L.

3045 The Case of Sir John Fellows, Bart. late Sub-Governor of the South-Sea Company; humbly offered to the Consideration of the Lords Spiritual and Temporal in Parliament assembled. *n.p.* [*1721*], *F°*. LLI.

3046 The Case of John Grigsby, Late Accomptant to the South-Sea Company. *n.p.* [*1721*], *s. sh. F°*.

3047 The Case of Francis Hawes, one of the late Directors of the South-Sea Company. *n.p.* [*1721*], *s. sh. F°*. L.

3048 The Case of Richard Horsey, One of the late Directors of the South-Sea-Company. *n.p.* [*1721*], *s. sh. F°*. LLI.

3049 The Case of Richard Houlditch, One of the late Directors of the South Sea Company. *n.p.* [*1721*], *s. sh. F°*. LLI.

3050 The Case of Richard Houlditch, One of the late Directors of the South-Sea Company. *n.p.* [*1721*], *s. sh. F°*. LLI.

To the House of Lords. Slightly different from the preceding.

3051 The Case of Arthur Ingram, One of the late Directors of the South-Sea Company. *n.p.* [*1721*], *s. sh. F°*. LLI.

3052 The Case of Charles Joye. *n.p.* [*1721*], *s. sh. F°*. L.

A South Sea director.

3053 The Case of Sir John Lambert, Bar$^{t.}$ *n.p.* [*1721*], *s. sh. F°*. L.

A South Sea director. Text begins: He has traded.

3054 The Case of Sir John Lambert, Bar$^{t.}$ *n. p.* [*1721*], *s. sh. F°*. L.

Text begins: That he has been.

3055 The Case of Sir John Lambert, Bar$^{t.}$ One of the Late Directors of the South Sea Company. *n.p.* [*1721*], *s. sh. F°*. L.

3056 The Case of Lady Elizabeth Master. *n.p.* [*1721*], *s. sh. F°*. LU.

Her husband, Sir Harcourt Master, was a South Sea director.

3057 The Case of William Morley, Merchant, one of the late Directors of the South-Sea Company. *n.p.* [*1721*], *s. sh. F°*. L.

3058 A Brief Account of what Share Hugh Raymond, one of the late Directors of the South-Sea Company, had in the Conduct of the Scheme for Increasing the Company's Capital. *n.p.* [*1721*], *F°*. L.

Endorsed: The Case of Hugh Raymond, One of the late Directors of the South-Sea Company. Shewing his being out of London during the late Mismanagements of their Affairs.

3059 The Case of Samuel Reade, Jun. One of the late Directors of the South-Sea Company. *n.p.* [*1721*], *s. sh. F°*. L.

3060 Mr. Sawbridge his Case. *n.p.* [*1721*], *s. sh. F*°. L.

A South Sea director.

3061 The Case of Robert Surman. *n.p.* [*1721*], *s. sh. F*°. L.

Clerk to the Cashier of the South Sea Company. Endorsed: The Case of Robert Surman.

3062 The Case of William Tillard, one of the late Directors of the South-Sea-Company. *n.p.* [*1721*], *s. sh. F*°. L.

3063 The Case of the Creditors of the Office of Ordnance. *n.p.* [*1721*], *s. sh. F*°. LPRO.

Last words of text in roman type: 'provided for by the said Act'.

3064 HAMILL, WILLIAM. A View of the Danger and Folly of being Publick-Spirited, and sincerely loving one's country; in the deplorable Case of the Londonderry and Innishkilling Regiments: Being a true and faithful account of their unparalleled Service and Sufferings, at and since the Revolution. To which is added, the particular Case of William Hamill, Gent. their Agent. *Lond. 1721*, *4*°. L.

3065 To the Right Honourable the Lords Spiritual and Temporal in Parliament Assembled, The humble Petition of the Seamen who lately served on Board His Majesty's Fleet in the Mediterranean, under the Command of the Honourable Sir George Byng, now Lord Viscount Torrington, and their distressed Wives, Widows and Children. *n.p.* [*1721?*], *s. sh. F*°. MC.

Endorsed: The humble Petition of the Seamen who lately served on board His Majesty's Fleet in the Mediterranean, &c. For prize money.

3066 The Case of Joseph Billers, Citizen of London. *n.p.* [*1721*], *s. sh. F*°. LPRO.

For a reward for the discovery of various frauds.

3067 BRETT, JASPER. The Sin of With-holding Tribute, by Running of Goods, Concealing Excise, &c. Laid open and Address'd to the Trading Part of the Nation. *Dublin, 1721*, *8*°. LU.

3068 Instructions for the Waiters of Excise at the Port of London. *Lond. 1721*, *8*°. LG.

3069 Two Forms for Informations against Dealers in Brandy. The one for the Twenty Pound Penalty for Non-Entry of a Room us'd for keeping Brandy, &c. The other for Forty Shillings per Gallon, for exposing to Sale Brandy when it was not in any Place enter'd. *Lond. 1721*, *8*°. L.

3070 Instructions for the Officers of the Duties on Silver Plate in London. *Lond. 1721*, *12*°. LG.

3071 Instructions to be observed by the Officers employ'd in charging the Duty on Hops. *Lond. 1721*, *8*°. LG.

3072 A Specimen of the Stock and Minute-Book, to be observ'd by the Officers of Excise, in the Country, who survey Distillers, or Vinegar Makers. *Lond. 1721*, *8*°. LG.

3073 An Abstract of the Statutes relating to the Stamp-Duties in that Part of Great-Britain called Scotland, with the Penalties in the said Acts mentioned. *n.p.* [*c. 1721?*], *F°*. LU.

3074 Considerations on the Duties laid in Ireland on Wooll brought to England, Humbly Submitted to the Parliament. *n.p.* [*1721?*], *F°*. LU.

3075 Copy Bill of Suspension, Preston, &c. against Wightman, &c. [*Edin.*], *1721*, *F°*. ACC.

Dated: November 6th, 1721. Signed: Alex. Stevenson. Alleging malversation in the administration of Edinburgh's finances.

3076 Answers of the Magistrates and Town-council of the City of Edinburgh, to the Bill of Suspension presented in name of George Preston, Charles Hope, Thomas Dundas, Alexander Arbuthnot, Andrew Purdie, Charles Telfer, late Bailies of Edinburgh, &c. [*Edin.*], *1721*, *F°*. ACC.

Dated: November 8th, 1721. Signed: Dun. Forbes.

3077 Memorial for several of the Merchants Burgesses, and of the Corporations of the Crafts of the good Town of Edinburgh, Against the pretended Magistrates of the said City. [*Edin. 1721*], *F°*. ACC.

Dated: November 15th, 1721.

3078 A Vindication of the Conduct of the Magistrates and Town-council of Edinburgh, in answer to a Memorial lately published, Intituled, Memorial for several Merchants, Burgesses, &c. of the good Town of Edinburgh, against the pretended Magistrates of the said City. [*Edin. 1721*], *F°*. ACC.

Dated: November 29. 1721.

3079 Act of the Convention of Royal Burrows. At Edinburgh the 13th December, 1721. [*Edin. 1721*], *F°*, ACC.

Vindicating the magistrates of Edinburgh from the attacks made on them.

3080 EDINBURGH. Rectified Table of the Shore Dues, Merk per Tun, and other Duties payable for all Goods Imported to, and Exported from the Harbour of Leith, or brought into and carried from Leith by Land. [*Edin. 1720*], *s. sh. F°*. ECA.

Dated: Edinburgh, November 7th, 1720.

3081 MAXWELL, HENRY. Reasons Offer'd for Erecting a Bank in Ireland; in a Letter to Hercules Rowley, Esq; *Dublin*, *1721*, *8°*. L.

2nd edn., with additions, 1721 (LU); 3rd 1755 (LU).

3082 ROWLEY, HERCULES. An Answer to a Book, intitl'd, Reasons offer'd for erecting a Bank in Ireland. In a Letter to Henry Maxwell, Esq; *Dublin*, *1721*, *8°*. LU.

2nd edn. Dublin, 1721; another edn. Corke, n.d. (both L).

3083 MAXWELL, HENRY. Mr. Maxwell's Second Letter to Mr. Rowley; wherein the Objections against the Bank are Answer'd. *Dublin*, *1721*, *8°*. LU.

3084 ROWLEY, HERCULES. An Answer to Mr. Maxwell's Second Letter to Mr. Rowley, concerning the Bank. *Dublin*, *1721*, *8°*. L.

3085 A Letter to Henry Maxwell, Esq; Plainly shewing the great Danger that the Kingdom has escaped, and the great Inconveniences, that must of Necessity have happen'd, if a Bank had been establish'd in this Kingdom. *Dublin*, *1721*, *8°*. D.

3086 Remarks on Mr. Maxwell's and Mr. Rowley's Letters: setting forth the Advantages of a Bank and Lumbards in Ireland. In a Letter to a Friend. *Dublin*, *1721*, *8°*. LU.

3087 An Account of the Short Life, sudden Death and Pompous Funeral, of Michy Windybank, only Child of Sir Oliver Windybank. [*Dublin*], *1721*, *8°*. L.

3088 A Dialogue between Mr. Freeport, a Merchant, and Tom Handy, a Trades-man, Concerning the Bank. *n.p.* *1721*, *s. sh. F°*. DM.

3089 The Last Speech and dying Words of the Bank of Ireland. Which was Executed at College-Green on Saturday the 9th inst. *Dublin*. [*1721*], *s. sh. F°*. LU.

3090 The Bank's Ghost appearing to the People of Ireland, or, An Answer to the Last Speech and Dying Words of the Bank. *Dublin*, *1721*, *s. sh. F°*. DNL.

3091 A Letter to a Member of Parliament touching the Late intended Bank. *Dublin*, *1721*, *8°*. LU.

Wagner 17 says 'generally attributed to F. Hutchinson', but this must be a confusion with *A Letter to the Gentlemen of the Landed Interest*.

3092 [HUTCHINSON, FRANCIS, Bishop of Down and Connor]. A Letter to the Gentlemen of the Landed Interest in Ireland, relating to a Bank. *Dublin*, *1721*, *8°*. LU.

For attribution see *The Whole Works of Sir James Ware*, ed. by W. Harris, 1764, I, 216.

3093 [SWIFT, JONATHAN]. A Letter to the K——at Arms. From a Reputed Esquire, one of the Subscribers to the Bank. *Dublin*, [*1721*], *s. sh. F°*. D.

Signed: A.B. Esquire. For authorship see *The Prose Works of Jonathan Swift*, ed. by H. Davis, vol. 9, 1948, p. xx.

3094 Objections against the general Bank in Ireland as it stands now Circumstanciated, whether it Do's or Do's not Receive a Parliamentary Sanction, in Answer to a Letter sent from a Gentleman in the City to his Friend in the Country. *Dublin*, *1721*, *4°*. DNL.

Signed: Patriophilus Misolestes.

3095 Resolutions of the House of Lords in relation to the intended Bank in this Kingdom. *Dublin*, *1721*, *s. sh. F°*. DNL.

3096 A Strange Collection of May-Be's Fully Answered and Cleared Up by a Subscriber and Well-Wisher to the Bank. *Dublin*, *1721*, *s. sh. F°*. D.

3097 [SWIFT, JONATHAN]. Subscribers to the Bank plac'd according to their Order and Quality. With Notes and Queries. *Dublin*, [*1721*], *s. sh. F°*. L.

Reprinted in *The Prose Works of Jonathan Swift*, ed. by H. Davis, vol. 9, 1948.

3098 The Bank of Ireland's Answer to the Author of the Notes and Queries about the Subscribers to the same. By way of Queries upon Queries. *Dublin, 1721, s. sh. F°.* DM.

3099 [SWIFT, JONATHAN]. A Letter from a Lady in Town to her Friend in the Country, Concerning the Bank Or, The List of the Subscribers farther Explain'd. *Dublin,* [*1721*], *s. sh. F°.* DNL.

For authorship see *The Prose Works of Jonathan Swift,* ed. by H. Davis, vol. 9, 1948, p. xx.

3100 *Begin.* Whereas nothing can be a greater Security, that the Bank of Ireland with the Powers granted to it, Shall be Well and Faithfully Managed.... [*Dublin, 1721*], *F°.* LU.

A list of those qualified to be chosen for Governor, Deputy Governor or Director and of those qualified to vote in the election. Wagner, no. 22, where it is reprinted in full.

3101 LONDON. Fryer Mayor. Martis xxxi° die Januarii, 1720 [O.S.].... [*Lond.*] *1720, s. sh. F°.* LCRO.

A resolve to prosecute unlicensed brokers.

3102 The Publick Treasury in Lyme Street, next House but one to Pewterers-Hall is now open'd. To Lend Money upon any Real Security, to Wholesale Dealers, Shop-keepers and others, and to Merchants to Pay the King's Customs for Goods Imported. As also to Buy or Sell Lands, Houses or Goods. *n.p.* [*1721*], *s. sh. F°.* LU.

Dated: February 14th, $17\frac{20}{21}$.

3103 A List of the Members of the Corporation of the Amicable Society for a Perpetual Assurance-Office, who are Contributors on their own Lives, and have a Right to Vote at the Election of Directors. *Lond. 1721, F°.* OUP.

3104 Proposals from the Sun Fire-Office in Threadneedle Street, behind the Royal Exchange, London, for insuring Houses, Moveable Goods, Merchandize, Furniture and Wares, from Loss and Damage by Fire, in any Part of Great Britain, according to the following Articles. *n.p.* [*1721*], *4°.* L.

Dated: July the 28th 1721.

TRANSPORT

3105 PERRY, JOHN. The Description of a Method humbly proposed for the making of a better Depth coming over the Barr of Dublin: as also for the making of a Bason within the Harbour. *n.p.* [*1721*], *4°.* D.

3106 PERRY, JOHN. An Answer to Objections against the making of a Bason, with Reasons for the bettering of the Harbour of Dublin. *Dublin, 1721, 8°.* L.

3107 A Bill to Vest the Ground, Wharf and Key, called Wooll Key, in the Parish of All Saints Barking, in the City of London, with the Buildings and Warehouses thereupon, in Trustees, for His Majesty, His Heirs and Successors, for Ever; subject to Agreements made on His Behalf, with the Wardens and Assistants of the Free School in Sevenoak. *n.p.* [*1721*], *F°*. MC.

3108 A Bill for making navigable the River Daven, alias Dane, from Northwich in the County of Chester, where it joins the River Weever, to the Falling in of Wheelock-Brook, and from thence Wheelock-Brook, up to Wheelock-Bridge.... *n.p.* [*1721?*], *F°*. L.

3109 A Bill for Enlarging the Time Granted for Making the River Kennet Navigable, from Reading to Newbury, in the County of Berks. *n.p.* [*1721*], *F°*. L.

3110 A Bill for making the Rivers Mercy and Irwell Navigable from Liverpool to Manchester, in the County Palatine of Lancaster. *n.p.* [*1721*], *F°*. LU.

3111 [Kinderley, Charles]. The Present State of the Navigation of the Towns of Lyn, Wisbeech, Spalding, and Boston. The Rivers that pass through those Places, and the Countries that border thereupon, truly, faithfully and impartially Represented. And humbly proposed to the Consideration of the Inhabitants of those Places and Countries, and to the Corporation of Adventurers for draining the vast Level of the Fens lying in the six Counties of Norfolk, Suffolk, Cambridge, Huntingdon, Northampton and Lincoln. With a Way laid down how to Remedy all the Inconveniences and Defects which they now labour under. *Bury St Edmunds*, *1721*, *8°*. O.

2nd edn. enlarged, Lond. 1751 (O), entitled: The Ancient and present State of the Navigation of the Towns of Lyn, Wisbeach, Spalding, and Boston.... This edn. has a dedication signed by the author's son Nathaniel Kinderley. The author's Christian name is given by H. C. Darby in *The Draining of the Fens*, 1940.

3112 Perry, John. An Account of the Stopping of Daggenham Breach: with the Accidents that have attended the same from the first Undertaking. Containing also proper Rules for performing any the like Work: and Proposals for rendering the Ports of Dover and Dublin (which the Author has been employ'd to survey) Commodious for Entertaining large Ships. To which is prefix'd, A Plan of the Levels which were over-flow'd by the Breach. *Lond.* *1721*, *8°*. L.

3113 To the Honourable the House of Commons. The Case of the Parishioners, (especially Land-Holders) in the Parish of Mary-bone, Middlesex; with relation to Their Supporting the High Ways against the several Parishes of St. Anne, St. James, St. Paul Covent-Garden, and St. Martin in the Fields, in the Liberty of Westminster; and Paddington, in the County aforesaid. *n.p.* [*1721?*], *s. sh. F°*. LG.

3114 A Bill for Repairing the Road from St. Giles's Pound to Kilbourn-Bridge, in the County of Middlesex. *n.p.* [*1721*], *F*°. L.

3115 A Bill for Repairing the several Roads leading to the Town of Ledbury in the County of Hereford. *n.p.* [*1721*], *F*°. L.

SOCIAL CONDITIONS

3116 BRADDON, LAURENCE. A Proposal for Relieving, Reforming and Employing all the Poor of Great Britain, by Vertue of one desired General Law relating to the Poor, instead of Thirty Statutes, now in Force.... And the most material Objections rais'd, against this Proposal, And a full Answer, to all those Objections, will be shortly publish'd. *Lond. 1721*, *8*°. LU.

French translation, entitled: Plan pour Assister, Corriger, & Emploier tous les Pauvres de la Grande Bretagne.... London, 1721 (MP).

3117 *Begin.* Whereas a Charitable Proposal was publish'd in December 1719. for relieving the sick and needy... *n.p.* [*1721*], *s. sh. F*°. E.

A brief account of the sick poor treated at the Infirmary in Petty-France, Westminster (afterwards Westminster Hospital) in 1720.

3118 Pietas Corcagiensis, Or a View of the Green-Coat Hospital: and other Charitable Foundations, in the Parish of St. Mary Shandon, Corke: shewing the several Steps that have been taken, in Erecting and Supporting those Charities.... *Cork*, *1721*, *4*°. L.

3119 [OWEN, CHARLES]. The Danger of the Church and Kingdom from Foreigners Consider'd; in Several Articles of the Highest Importance. *Lond. 1721*, *8*°. L.

2nd edn. 1722 (L); 3rd edn., with large additions and with author's name, 1750 (O).

3120 The South-Sea Committee of the Poor French Protestans; Or, a curious Apology of the Commissioners, Distributors, of the Royal Beneficence to the Poor of their Nation, with an exact Examination of their Frauds, Crafts and Subtilties.... *Lond. 1721*, *8*°. O.

3121 PARKYNS, Sir THOMAS. A Method proposed for the Hiring and Recording of Servants in Husbandry, Arts, Misteries, &c....Also, A Limitation and Appointment of the Several Rates of Wages of Artificers, Handicraftsmen, Husbandmen, Labourers, Servants and Workmen within the Counties of Nottingham and Leicester. *Bunny*, [*1721?*], *4*°. L.

Another edn. of the first part, Nottingham, 1722, s. sh. F°. (L).

3122 A Bill for the better Suppling [*sic*] the Cities of London and Westminster, and Parts adjacent, with Water. *n.p.* [*1721?*], *F*°. L.
In the O copy the misprint is corrected.

3123 Reasons Humbly offered, in behalf of the Inhabitants of Hemel-Hempsted, and Parts Adjacent, in the County of Hertford, against the Bill, for the better Supplying the Cities of London and Westminster with Water. *n.p.* [*1721?*], *s. sh. F*o. L.

3124 A Proposal for raising Water from the River Thames to serve the City and Suburbs of Westminster. *n.p.* [*1721*], *F*o. LG.

Endorsed: A Proposal for Serving the City of Westminster, and Parts adjacent, with Water from the River Thames.

3125 LONDON. Stewart Mayor. Martis v° die Decembris, 1721.... [*Lond.*], *1721*, *s. sh. F*o. LCRO.

An order to cleanse the public meat markets.

3126 A Bill for the Finishing and Adorning the New Chapel called St. George's Chapel, in Great Yarmouth...and for Inlightning the Streets of the said Town, by a Duty or Imposition on all Coals, Culm, and Cinders to be Landed and Consumed there. *n.p.* [*1721*], *F*o. L.

1722

GENERAL

3127 BURRIDGE, RICHARD. A New Review of London. Being an Exact Survey, lately taken, of every Street....With the Rates of Domestick and Foreign Letters; and a List lately collected, of all the Stage Coaches, Waggons and Carriers, where they Inn at in London, and Days they go out of Town. Peculiarly adapted for Trade and Business.... *Lond. 1722, 8°.* L.

2nd edn. 1722, anon. (OC); 3rd edn. 1733, anon. (L).

3128 Considerations offered to all the Corporations of England, well worth their Observation: containing Seasonable Advice to them in their Future Elections of Burgesses to serve in Parliament; merely in relation to, and so far forth only, as such Elections affect Trade, and are, as will appear hereby, the main Cause of its present great Decay. Written by a Person of Honour. *Lond. 1722, 8°.* LU.

AGRICULTURE

3129 An Act for Inclosing the Commons commonly called Common-Moor, Black-Acre, and South-Moor, alias Alder-Moor, in or near the Parish of Saint John-Baptist, in Glastonbury, in the County of Somerset. *n.p. [1722], F°.* O.

A bill.

3130 [MABBUT, GEORGE]. Tables for Renewing and Purchasing of the Leases of Cathedral-Churches and Colleges, according to several Rates of Interest; with their Construction and Use explain'd. Also Tables for Renewing and Purchasing of Lives....The Second Edition. To which is added, The Value of Church and College Leases Consider'd.... *Lond. 1722, 8°.* L.

First published in 1686; another edn. 1700; 3rd edn. 1729 (O); 4th, 1731; 5th, 1735; 6th, 1742 (all L). The half-titles of the edns. of 1731 and 1735 and the title-page of that of 1742 bear the words 'Sir Isaac Newton's Tables'. The first edn. had a commendation by Newton, but the authorship is established by D. F. McKenzie (*Trans. of the Cambridge Bib. Soc. III*, 165-6). *The Value of Church and College Leases consider'd* was first published in 1719 (no. 2466).

3131 The State of the Roman Catholicks of Ireland: or, Reasons why they may not be allow'd to Purchase, take Mortgages for their Money, Fee-Farm or other Leases. Most humbly offer'd to Both Houses of Parliament. *Dublin, 1722, s. sh. F°.* CT (R).

On verso: An Answer to the State or Case of the Roman Catholicks of Ireland: or Objections against the Reasons there incerted, Viz. That they may not be allow'd to Purchase, take Mortgages, Fee-Farm, or other Leases.

3132 ELKING, HENRY. A View of the Greenland Trade and Whale-Fishery. With the National and Private Advantages thereof. *Lond. 1722, 8°.* L.

2nd edn. 1725 (L). Reprinted in *A Select Collection of Scarce and Valuable Economical Tracts*, ed. by J. R. McCulloch, 1859, p. 61.

MANUFACTURES

3133 Reasons Humbly Offered to shew the High Duties on Brass Imported: whereby upwards of 20,000 l. per Annum is sunk to the Publick, and falls into the Hands of a few Designing Men in and about Bristol, to the great Discouragement of Trade in General. *n.p.* [*1722?*], *F°*. MP.

3134 The Copper and Brass Manufactures of Great-Britain truly stated, in Answer to the Importers Reasons and Queries. *n.p.* [*1722?*], *s. sh. F°*. O.

3135 Reasons for incouraging the Manufacture of Sail-Cloth in Great Britain. *n.p.* [*1722?*], *s. sh. F°*. O.

3136 The Case of the Silk Weavers in and about London, humbly offer'd to the Parliament of Great-Britain. *n.p.* [*1722?*], *s. sh. F°*. L.

3137 The Case of the Inhabitants of Guernsey, Jersey, Alderney, and Sark; and some Reasons humbly offer'd to the Consideration of the Honourable House of Commons, for an Amendment of a small Part of the Bill for Encouragement of the Silk Manufactures of this Kingdom, and for taking off several Duties on Merchandizes exported, and for reducing the Duties upon Beaver Skins, Pepper, Mace, Cloves, and Nutmegs, imported. *n.p.* [*1722*], *s. sh. F°*. L.

3138 The Ostend Trade consider'd; so far as it relates to Prohibited East-India Silks, &c. Humbly Offer'd to the Right Honourable the House of Lords. *n.p.* [*1722?*], *s. sh. F°*. LLI.

3139 The Reasonableness of passing the Bill for Making the Prohibition of all East-India Wrought Silks, &c. more effectual, Humbly Offer'd to the Right Honourable the House of Lords. *n.p.* [*1722*], *s. sh. F°*. LLI.

3140 The several Acts for the Improvement of the Hempen and Flaxen Manufactures in this Kingdom. *Dublin*, *1722*, *8°*. LU.

LU copy has additions down to 1738.

3141 The Defence of the whole Society of [W]ool-Combers of the City and Liberties of the City of Corke, upon their Turn-Out. With their Advice to their Masters the Clothiers of the same. Shewing and Proving that a Mismanagement and Under-Rating the Commodity and not Reduceing an Affair of such Moment to its proper Method and Advantage, is the just Cause of this Reasonable and General Turn-Out. Writ by an Honest Spectator. *Corke*, *1722*, *s. sh. F°*. C.

Signed: E.B.

COMMERCE

3142 London. Stewart Mayor. Martis xx° die Februarij, 1721 [o.s.]... [*Lond.*] *1721*, *s. sh. F°*. LCRO.

An order enforcing the sale of leather at Leadenhall.

3143 Reasons humbly offered against General Certificates for the Conveyance of Tobacco's, &c. *n.p.* [*1722?*], *s. sh. F°.* LLI.

3144 Reasons humbly offered for Regulating the Importation of Tobacco into this Kingdom, for the Preservation of the Revenue, and the better Carrying on of the said Trade. *n.p.* [*1722?*], *F°.* LLI.

3145 The Case of the British Merchants Trading to Portugal. *n.p.* [*1722*], *s. sh. F°.* L.

For power to vary the duties levied to maintain English charities and an English minister at Lisbon.

3146 Account of Ships, (according to the Advices which the East-India Company have received) sent out to the East-Indies under foreign Commissions; with English and Irish Officers, Supra-Cargo's, and Mariners. *n.p.* [*1722?*], *s. sh. F°.* L.

3147 EDINBURGH. Act of Council, anent Fleshes to be brought to the Market. [*Edin. 1722*], *s. sh. F°.* EU.

Dated: 31 October 1722.

3148 By the Lord Lieutenant and Council of Ireland, a Proclamation. Appointing Quigly's Point lying between Red-Castle Road and Cullmore or Rathmullin for the performance of Quarentine instead of Ballymastoker Bay or Red-Castle Road near Londonderry. *Dublin, 1722, F°.* DPRO.

Dated: 11 January 1721.

COLONIES

3149 COXE, DANIEL. A Description of the English Province of Carolana, by the Spaniards call'd Florida, and by the French, La Louisiane, As also of the Great and Famous River Meschacebe or Missisipi, the Five vast Navigable Lakes of Fresh Water, and the Parts adjacent. Together with an Account of the Commodities, of the Growth and Production of the said Province. And a Preface containing some Considerations on the Consequences of the French making Settlements there. *Lond. 1722, 8°.* L.

2nd edn. 1726; another issue 1727; another issue 1741 (all L). On the printing of this book see Robert K. Turner in *Studies in Bibliography*, IX (1957), 252–5.

3150 A General Survey of that Part of the Island of St. Christophers, which formerly belonged to France; and was yielded up to Great Britain for ever, by the late Treaty of Utrecht: together with an Estimate of the Value of those Lands, and a Proposal and Scheme for raising a very considerable Sum of Money, for the Use of the Publick, on the Produce thereof....By Mr R.M. S.B. *Lond. 1722, 8°.* L.

The initials suggest Roderick Mackenzie as author.

FINANCE

3151 HUTCHESON, ARCHIBALD. A Collection of Advertisements, Letters and Papers, and Some Other Facts, relating to the last Elections at Westminster and Hastings. *Lond. 1722*, *8o*. L.

Details of Hutcheson's parliamentary career.

3152 An Account of the Loans of the South-Sea-Company. *n.p. 1722*, *8o*. LU.

3153 An Account of the Subscriptions of the South-Sea Company. *n.p. 1722*, *8o*. L.

3154 The Art of Parliamenteering....To which is added, An Extract from the Reports of the Committee of Secrecy, relating to the Fictitious Stock; and a List of those Members of both Houses who had the said Stock held for them, in order to facilitate the passing the late South-Sea Bill. By the Author of The History of the late Septennial Parliament. *Lond. 1722*, *8o*. LU.

3155 A Compleat History of the Late Septennial Parliament....To which is Prefix'd, Honest Advice to the Freeholders of Great Britain. *Lond. 1722*, *8o*. LU.

Includes a history of the South Sea Bubble. 2nd edn. 1722 (L); 3rd, 1722 (O): 4th, 1722 (L).

3156 Considerations Recommending to the Proprietors of South-Sea Stock, the Proposals for Ingrafting Part of that Company's Funds into the Stock of the Bank, and East-India Companies. *Lond. 1722*, *8o*. LU.

3157 The Hardship of the South-Sea Sufferers Consider'd, and some Proper Remedies for their Relief Propos'd: With an Exact Calculation of their Capital Stock, and what they may be able at present to Divide. To which is added, Some Reflections on the late Proposal for an Ingraftment with the Bank and East-India Company. *Lond. 1722*, *8o*. LU.

3158 Index Rerum & Vocabulorum, for the use of the Freeholders of Counties, and Freemen of Corporations. *Lond. 1722*, *4o*. LU.

Lists of Members of Parliament who subscribed to the South Sea Company. 2nd edn. 1722 (O).

3159 A Letter to Sir John Eyles, Bart. Sub-Governor of the South-Sea Company. *n.p.* [*1722*], *Fo*. L.

Signed: A.B.

3160 A Letter to the Governor of the Bank of England. *Lond. 1722*, *8o*. LU.

3161 The Pangs of Credit: or, an Argument to shew where it is most reasonable to bestow the Two Millions. In a Plain View of the Circumstances of the Redeemable Annuitants under the Two Acts of Parliament commonly called the Scheme-Act, and the Credit-Act. In a Letter to a Member of Parliament. By an Orphan Annuitant. *Lond. 1722*, *8o*. LU.

3162 Proposals for an Agreement between the South-Sea Company and the Bank of England, as Settled by the Courts of Directors of each Company. *n.p.* [*1722*], *s. sh. F*°. LPRO.

3163 To the Honourable the Commons of Great Britain in Parliament assembled. The humble Petition of the Lord Mayor, Aldermen, and Commons of the City of London, in Common Council assembled. *n.p.* [*1722*], *s. sh. F*°. OC.

For further measures to restore trade and public credit after the South Sea disaster.

3164 A Particular of 14 Lots of Hops of the Growth of the Year 1721. on the Estate purchas'd of Morgan Randyll Esq; in Surry, by Richard Houlditch Esq; one of the late Directors of the South Sea Company, which are to be sold by Order of the Trustees for raising Money on the Estates of the late Directors of the said Company.... *n.p.* [*1722*], *s. sh. F*°. MC.

3165 Thoughts of a Project for Draining the Irish Channel. *Dublin*, *1722*, *8*°. L.

A skit on bubbles. Another edn. entitled *Thoughts of a New Project for Draining the Irish Channel*, Dublin, 1722, 8°. (DA).

3166 Information for Mr. James Campbel, Merchant in London, against the Lord Lyon. *n.p.* [*1722*], *F*°. E.

Dated: November 17. 1722. Signed: Dun. Forbes. Claiming his 5 per cent commission for collecting the equivalent money.

3167 [Gordon, Thomas]. The Nature and Weight of the Taxes of the Nation: shewing, that by the Continuance of Heavy Taxes and Impositions, and the Mis-application of Publick Money, Trade is destroy'd, the Poor increas'd, and the Miseries and Misfortune of the Whole Kingdom demand the Consideration of the Freeholders of Great Britain at the Ensuing Election. *Lond.* *1722*, *8*°. L.

Reprinted in *A Collection of Tracts. By the late John Trenchard...and Thomas Gordon*, 1751.

3168 Hayes, Richard. Rules for the Port of London: or, the Water-side Practice. Wherein is shewn, the Method to Compute the Customs by the Book of Rates. Likewise the Manner of making Entries, paying Custom, Free, or by Certificate. Penalties in several Acts of Parliament, relating to Imports and Exports. The Tares and Draughts allowed by the King to the Merchants. With the Fees due to the Officers. And many other things, necessary in Customhouse Dispatches. Composed from the most Authentick Pieces. *Lond.* *1722*, *8*°. L.

3169 A Collection of all the Statutes now in Force, relating to the Excise upon Beer, Ale, and other Liquors....To which is added A Table of Allowances for Common Brewers, &c. *Lond.* *1722*, *12*°. LU.

3170 Instructions for Officers of the Duties on Hides, &c. *Lond.* *1722*, *8*°. LG.

3171 Instructions for the Collectors and Officers for the Duties of Excise upon Imported Liquors. *Lond. 1722, 8º.* LG.

3172 Additional Instructions for Officers who survey Paper-Makers. *Lond. 1722, 8º.* LG.

3173 Instructions to be observed by the Officers employ'd in charging the Duty on Starch. *Lond. 1722, 8º.* LG.

3174 Report to the Right Honourable the Lords Commissioners of His Majesty's Treasury, by Humphry Brent, one of the Commissioners of the Customs in Scotland, of Frauds in the Tobacco Trade. (Answers by the Merchants of Glasgow to the Report of Humphry Brent.) *n.p.* [*1722?*], *Fº.* L.

3175 An Abstract of the Report of Mr. Brent, one of the Commissioners of the Customs in Scotland, to the Lords of the Treasury. *n.p.* [*1722?*], *s. sh. Fº.* L.

3176 An Abstract of the Report of Mr. Brent, one of the Commissioners of the Customs in Scotland, to the Lords of the Treasury. With the Merchants Observations thereupon. *n.p.* [*1722?*], *s. sh. Fº.* MC.

Title taken from endorsement.

3177 Reasons against passing a Bill now depending before the most Honourable the House of Peers, intituled, A Bill for Enlarging the Term granted by an Act...intituled, An Act for continuing the Duty of Two Pennies Scots, or one sixth part of a Penny sterl. on every Pint of Ale and Beer that shall be vended or sold within the City of Edinburgh and Privileges thereof, for the Benefit of the said City, &c. *n.p.* [*1722*], *Fº.* LU.

3178 A List of the Names of the Adventurers in the Bank of Scotland. February 1st, 1722. [*Edin. 1722*], *s. sh. Fº.* E.

3179 Armour, James. Proposals for making the Bank of Scotland More Useful and Profitable: And for raising the Value of the Land-Interest of North-Britain. *Edin. 1722, 4º.* LU.

3180 [Swift, Jonathan]. The Eyes of Ireland Open. Being, A short View of the Project for Establishing the Intended Bank of Ireland: With some Remarks upon its Managers, Promoters and Progress. In a Letter from a Lady at Dublin to her Friend in the Country. To which is added A Description of the Subscription, or, A true and exact Account of the Nobility, Gentry and Traders, who are Subscribers to the Bank, extracted from the List published by Order of the Commissioners appointed to receive Subscriptions, and Interspers'd with Notes and Queries: The second edition.... Printed from the 2d Edition of the Dublin Copies. *Lond. 1722, 8º.* L.

A reprint of *Subscribers to the Bank...*, 1721 (no. 3097) and *A Letter from a Lady in Town to her Friend in the Country...*, 1721 (no. 3099).

3181 A Brief Account of The Charitable Corporation Established for Lending Money to the Industrious and Necessitous upon all Sorts of Goods, &c. *n.p.* [*1722?*], *s. sh. F°.* LU.

3182 An Abstract of the Settlement of the Amicable Contributionship, or Hand-in-Hand Fire-Office, for Insuring Houses, &c. from Loss by Fire. *Lond. 1722*, *F°.* L.

3183 By the Corporation of the London Assurance, establish'd by His Majesty's Royal Charter. Proposals for Assuring Houses, and all other Buildings; all Goods, Wares, and Merchandizes, from Loss and Damage by Fire, in all Parts of the Kingdom of England, Dominion of Wales, and Town of Berwick upon Tweed, the Kingdom of Ireland, and all other Parts of His Majesty's Dominions beyond the Seas. *n.p. 1722*, *s. sh. F°.* MC.

Another edn. 1724 (LG).

3184 [Proposals by the Corporation of the Royal-Exchange Assurance.] *n.p. 1722*, *s. sh. F°.* L.

The heading of the L copy has been cut off. Reprinted in F.B. Relton, *Fire Insurance Companies*, 1893, pp. 160–3.

3185 The Deed of Settlement of the Union Society, for Insuring of Goods and Merchandizes from Loss by Fire; dated Feb. 16. $17\frac{14}{15}$. (Additional Orders, Resolutions, and Agreements...made at several General Meetings of the Union Society.) *Lond. 1722*, *4°.* L.

3186 BRODIE, ALEXANDER. A new and easy method of book-keeping, or, Instructions for a methodical keeping of merchants accompts, by way of debitor and creditor.... *Lond. 1722*, *37 cm.* Kress 3458.

TRANSPORT

3187 [COTESWORTH, WILLIAM]. The Town of New-Castle's Attempt to make a Monopoly of the Coal-Trade in the River Tyne. *n.p.* [*1722*], *s. sh. F°.* GaP.

For authorship see Edward Hughes, *North Country Life*, p. 69. I owe to Professor Hughes the opportunity of seeing this broadside.

3188 Reasons for making the River Dunn in the West-riding of the County of York navigable, and the great Advantages that will accrue to the Nation in general by it. *n.p.* [*1722?*], *s. sh. F°.* L.

Reprinted in *The Methods proposed for making the River Dunn Navigable*, 1723.

3189 PALMER, WILL. A Survey of the River Dunn in order to improve the Navigation from Hull to Doncaster and to continue up to Sheffield. By Will. Palmer & Partners. *n.p. 1722*, *s. sh. obl. F°.* L.

3190 A Bill for Repairing the Highways from the City of Gloucester, to the Top of Birdlip Hill (being the Road to London) and from the Foot of the said Hill, to the Top of Crichley-Hill (being the Road to Oxford. *n.p.* [*1722*], *F°.* O.

3191 A Bill for Repairing and Widening the Road leading from the Black-Bull Inn in Dunstable, in the County of Bedford, to the Way turning out of the said Road up to Shafford-House in the County of Hertford. *n.p.* [*1722*], *F°*. L.

3192 Reasons against the Clause for appointing Commissioners and Trustees in a Bill now depending before your Lordships, intitled, An Act for repairing and widening the Road leading from the Black-Bull Inn in Dunstable, in the County of Bedford, to the way turning out of the said Road up to Shafford-House in the County of Hertford. *n.p.* [*1722*], *s. sh. F°*. LG.

3193 Reasons for Passing the Bill for Repairing the Highways from Brampton-Bridge in the County of Northampton to Welford-Bridge in the said County; as likewise the Great Post-Road between Morter-Pit Hill in the same County, leading into Market-Harborough, in the County of Leicester. *n.p.* [*1722*], *4°*. L.

3194 Reasons why the Bill for amending the High-Ways from Brampton-Bridge, to Welford-Bridge, in the County of Northampton; and also from Mortarpit-Hill in the said County, to Chain-Bridge, leading into Market-Harborough, in the County of Leicester, should not pass into a Law, as it now stands before your Lordships. *n.p.* [*1722*], *s. sh. F°*. L.

3195 A Bill for Building a Bridge cross the River Thames, from a Place called The Prince's Waste, in the Parish of Lambeth, in the County of Surrey, to the Opposite Shore, next Peterborough-House in the Parish of St. Margaret Westminster, in the County of Middlesex. *n.p.* [*1722*], *F°*. L.

3196 Reasons against Building a Bridge from Lambeth to Westminster. Shewing the Inconveniences of the same to the City of London, and Borough of Southwark. *Lond. 1722*, *8°*. LU.

SOCIAL CONDITIONS

3197 [Braddon, Laurence]. The Form of a Petition submitted to the Consideration and Correction of those Noblemen and Gentlemen who desire to Subscribe what Sums shall be necessary for Relieving, Reforming and Employing the Poor: But first to begin only with the Poor of those three Parishes, of St. Martins in the Fields, St. James's, and St. Ann's Westminster.... *Lond. 1722*, *8°*. LU.

For authorship see p. 22 where the author mentions three previous works of his, all of which bear his name.

3198 Braddon Laurence. Particular Answers to the most material Objections made to the Proposal humbly presented to His Majesty for Relieving, Reforming, and Employing all the Poor of Great Britain. *n.p. 1722*, *8°*. L.

3199 [Braddon, Laurence]. Proposed Preventions of all Stock-Jobbing and Bubbling in relation to that desired Commission and Charter for Relieving, Reforming, and Employing the Poor. And, Herewith is Published, That Clause, which, for some time, hath been inserted in All Patents, for Inventions, in order to the Preventing their being Stock-Jobbed, or Bubbled. And Hereunto is Annexed, The Form of that Intended Petition to His Majesty, for a Commission to receive Voluntary Subscriptions for those Charitable and Beneficial Purposes above-mentioned: With some Considerations relating thereunto.... *Lond. 1722*, *8º*. O.

Signed: L.B. On pp. 19, 20, the author gives a list of his works, some of which had been published under his full name.

3200 The Case of the Parish of St. Giles's in the Fields, as to their Poor, and a Work-House designed to be built Employing them. *n.p.* [*1722?*], *Fº*. L.

3201 An Account of the Proceedings of the Charitable Society for relieving the Sick and Needy at the Infirmary in Petty-France, Westminster. *n.p.* [*1722*], *4º*. L.

Apparently the third annual report of what is now Westminster Hospital. From 1733 entitled: The Report of the Trustees of the Publick Infirmary in Westminster, and from 1736: The Report of the Trustees of the Publick Infirmary in James-Street, Westminster. L has the reports for 1722, 1723, 1728–30, 1733–6, 1738 and 1743 (numbered XXV). LSC has 1737 and 1744 (XXVI). O has 1746 (XXVIII).

3202 [Stackhouse, Thomas]. The Miseries and Great Hardships of the Inferiour Clergy in and about London. And a modest Plea for their Rights, and better Usage.... By a Clergyman of the Church of England. *Lond. 1722*, *8º*. L.

2nd edn. 1726; another edn. with author's name 1737; another 2nd edn. [1741] (all L.).

3203 Entry cancelled.

1723

AGRICULTURE

3204 [MOLESWORTH, ROBERT, Viscount Molesworth]. Some Considerations for the Promoting of Agriculture, and Employing the Poor. *Dublin, 1723*, *8°*. LU.

The preface signed: R.L.V.M. Another edn. 1731 (DA). For authorship see S. Peirson, *Farther Considerations*, 1728 (no. 3814), p. 39.

3205 Considerations upon Considerations for the Promoting of Agriculture, and Providing for the Poor. *Dublin*, [*1723*], *8°*. D.

2nd edn., with additions and alterations, 1724 (DNL).

3206 Proposals for the Improvement of Common and Waste-Lands; and also for raising and securing a Supply of Wood and Timber in this Kingdom. Together with some Considerations on the most effectual Methods of maintaining and employing the Poor. *Lond. 1723*, *8°*. MP.

3207 Reasons humbly offered to the Honourable House of Commons, by the Corporation of the Great Level of the Fenns called Bedford Levell. Against the Bill for the better Explaining the Act passed in the 15th Year of King Charles II. intituled, An Act for Settling the Draining of the Great Level of the Fenns called Bedford Level. *n.p.* [*1723*], *F°*. L.

3208 An Answer to Reasons against the Bill for the better explaining the Act for settling the Draining of the great Level of the Fens, called Bedford Level. *n.p.* [*1723*], *F°*. L.

3209 The Case of the Dean and Chapter of Durham, upon the Bill depending in Parliament, for enabling Archibishops, Bishops and others, to grant Leases of Mines not accustomably Letten. *n.p.* [*1723*], *F°*. O.

3210 The Case of the Copyhold and Leasehold Tenants of the Bishoprick of Durham, upon the Bill depending in Parliament, for enabling Bishops and others to grant Leases of Mines, not accustomably letten by them. *n.p.* [*1723*], *F°*. LLI.

3211 Observations on the engrossed Bill depending in the House of Commons Intituled, An Act to Enable Arch-Bishops, Bishops, &c. to make Leases, &c. *n.p.* [*1723*], *s. sh. F°*. O.

3212 A Letter to a Member of the Hon[ble] House of Commons. On Occasion of a Proposal for a Law to be made for setting Church Lands at the present Yearly Rent: How low soever, without any Regard to be had to the Real Value. [*Dublin, 1723*], *s. sh. F°*. DG.

3213 The History of the Popish Clergy: or, the Case of the Laity. With some Queries. *Dublin, 1723*, *8°*. D.

On leases of the lands belonging to the Established Church. The Queries were answered by Swift.

3214 [SWIFT, JONATHAN]. Some Arguments against enlarging the Power of Bishops, in letting of Leases. With Remarks on some Queries lately published. *Dublin, 1723, 8°.* LU.

Reprinted in *The Prose Works of Jonathan Swift*, ed. by H. Davis, vol. 9 (1948).

3215 The Estate of the late Lord Derwentwater is subject to the following Charges and Annuities. *n.p.* [*1723*], *F°.* LU.

Forfeited estate.

3216 A Rental of the Estates late Lord Derwentwater's in the Counties of Northumberland and Cumberland. To be Sold before the Commissioners and Trustees for the Forfeited Estates, on Thursday the 11th Day of July next, 1723. *n.p.* [*1723*], *F°.* LU.

3217 [ELKING, HENRY]. The Interest of Great Britain, Consider'd: or, the Herring Fishery Propos'd, as the most Rational Expedient for paying our National Debts. *Lond. 1723, 8°.* L.

For authorship see B.M. Catalogue.

3218 A Letter from a Gentleman in Town, to a Friend in the Country, concerning the present State of the Fishing-Copartnery in North-Britain. *Edin. 1723, 4°.* LU.

COMMERCE

3219 An Account of Frauds committed in the Exportation of Corn from the Orkneys, discovered by Walter Etherington. *n.p.* [*1723?*], *F°.* O.

3220 MAXWELL, HENRY. Proposals to render the possession of Minorca, and Gibraltar, more useful to the Commerce of Britain, as well as to her Power by Sea, and Land, and to take away the Expence of their Maintenance. With an Essay on Government.... *n.p. 1723, 4°.* LU.

3221 Observations on the following Paragraph, delivered out by the Traders in Tobacco of Glasgow. *n.p.* [*1723*], *s. sh. F°.* MC.

Endorsed: Observations on a Paragraph deliver'd out by the Traders in Tobacco of Glasgow.

3222 Considerations on a Memorial of the Dutch-East-India-Company to the States General. Humbly Offer'd to the Parliament. *n.p.* [*1723*], *F°.* LLI.

On the threat of the Ostend East India Company to our trade.

3223 The Governor and Company of Merchants of Great Britain Trading to the South Seas....Appell[nts.] Eleanor Curzon, Respond[nt.] The Respondent's Case. *n.p.* [*1723*], *F°.* L.

Signed: Tho. Lutwyche. Con. Phipps.

3224 The Governor and Company of Merchants of Great Britain Tradeing to the South-Seas and other Parts of America, and for Encouraging the Fishery, Appellants, Eleanor Curzon, Respondent. The Appellant's Case. *n.p.* [*1723*], *F°.* L.

Signed: Will. Peere Williams. Tho. Bootle.

3225 By the Lords Justices and Council of Ireland, a Proclamation, For a Publick Thanksgiving, and Discharging the Performance of Quarentine in this Kingdom. *Dublin, 1722*, [*O.S.*], *F°*. DPRO.

Dated: 23 March 1722.

FINANCE

3226 HUTCHESON, ARCHIBALD. An Abstract of all the Publick Debts remaining Due at Michaelmas, 1722. And an Estimate of the Annual Sinking Fund towards the Discharge of the same....And also a Computation in what Time the said Publick Debts may be Discharged by the said Sinking Fund. With a Method proposed for the more Clear Stating of the said Publick Debts and Sinking Fund in the Accounts hereafter to be deliver'd to Parliament. And a Proposal for putting an End to all Particular Appropriations, and turning the whole Revenue into One General Fund.... *Lond. 1723, F°*. L.

3227 HUTCHESON, ARCHIBALD. An Abstract of an Account stated by some of the Clerks at the South-Sea House, relating to the Estates of the Late Directors; shewing what will be coming to the Company from those Estates, with and without a Mulct. And Remarks, shewing the Mistakes in that Account.... *Lond. 1723, F°*. L.

3228 HUTCHESON, ARCHIBALD. Some Paragraphs of Mr. Hutcheson's Treatises on the South-Sea Subject; which relate to the Relief of the Unhappy Traders in South-Sea Stock, and to Publick Credit. And the Reason of his Reprinting them at this Time. To which is added, A Near Estimate of the Value of South-Sea Stock, if the Bill now order'd to be brought in, pass into a Law. *Lond. 1723, F°*. LU.

3229 HUTCHESON, ARCHIBALD. The two last Treatises published by Mr. Hutcheson. The first of them published the 17th of January, 1722. The other dated the First of March, and Deliver'd to the House of Commons on Monday the Fourth of March, 1722. And since Published. [To which is added Some farther Calculations and Reasons for a Mulcting Clause relating to the late South Sea Directors. Dated 6th May 1723.]. *Lond. 1723, F°*. LU.

The words in [ ] are added in ms. to the title-page of the LU copy. An edition in one volume of the three preceding works.

3230 Information for the Lord Lyon, against James Campbell of London, Merchant. *n.p.* [*1723*], *F°*. E.

Dated: January 1: 1723. Signed: Ja. Graham. A reply to no. 3166.

3231 Answers for Mr James Campbel of London, Merchant, to the Petition of the Lord Lyon. *n.p.* [*1723*], *F°*. E.

Dated: July 29. 1723. Signed: Ro. Dundas.

3232 Copy of a Letter taken out of the Whitehall Journal. Tuesday, January 1, 1722–23. *n.p.* [*1723*], *F°*. L.

Signed: Tacitus. For a tax on Jews.

3233 A Letter to the Right Honourable William Pulteney, Esq; occasion'd by a Bill depending in the House of Commons, for Raising One Hundred Thousand Pounds upon the Roman-Catholicks. By a Member of the House of Commons. *Lond. 1723*, *F°*. L.

3234 Instructions to be observed by the Officers concerned in surveying Brandy-Retailers in the Country. *Lond. 1723*, *8°*. LG.

3235 [Paul, Robert]. The Business of the Comptroller-General of the Accounts of His Majesty's Customs.... *Lond. 1723*, *8°*. L.

Authorship deduced from errata signed: R.P. and the mention of Robert Paul as assistant to the Comptroller-General.

3236 Hiberniae Notitia: or, a List of the Present Officers in Church and State, and of all Payments to be made for Civil and Military Affairs for the Kingdom of Ireland, upon the Establishment which commenc'd on the 24th day of August, 1717. Including all Pensions on the Civil and Military Lists both to English and Foreigners. With a List of all the Forces on the Irish Establishment. *Lond. 1723*, *8°*. L.

3237 Thomas Bennet, D.D. Vicar of St. Giles's Cripplegate, London, Appell[t]. Michael Trepass, Richard Bocket, and Nichol[s] Whitechell Inhabitants of the said Parish, Respond[ts]. The Appellant's Case. *n.p.* [*1723*], *F°*. L.

Signed: Con. Phipps. Edw. Edlin. The respondents were Quakers who refused to pay tithes.

3238 Thomas Bennet Dr. in Divinity, Vicar of St. Giles's Cripple-Gate London. Appellant. Michael Treppass, Richard Bocket and Nicholas Witchell, Parishioners of the said Parish, Respondents. The Respondents Case. *n.p.* [*1723*], *F°*. L.

Signed: N. Fazakerley. C. Talbot.

3239 Holland, John. Some Letters relating to the Bank of Scotland, written by the late John Holland Esq. Publish'd with Explanatory Remarks, in a Letter to the Proprietors, by Richard Holland M.D. *Lond. 1723*, *8°*. L.

Another ed. Edin. 1723 (LU).

3240 [Maculla, James]. Ireland's Case humbly presented to the Honourable the Knights, Citizens and Burgesses in Parliament assembled, by an Artificer in Metals and a Citizen of Dublin, shewing why Two Hundred Thousand Pounds of light Copper Half-pence should not pass in this Kingdom for the Gold and Silver of the Nation. [*Dublin, 1723*], *F°*. C.

For attribution see *The Drapier's Letters*, ed. by H. Davis, 1935, p. 353.

3241 [Maculla, James]. Ireland's Consternation in the loosing of Two Hundred Thousand Pound of their Gold and Silver for Brass Money. Set forth by an Artificer in Metals, and a Citizen of Dublin, Shewing the fatal Consequence of Coining in another Kingdom Three Hundred Tun Weight of Copper Half-pence, amounting to the Damage of Two Hundred Thousand Pounds Sterl. to this Nation, and the Continuance of the same for Fourteen Years. *n.p.* [*1723*], *F*°. C.

For authorship see Wagner 38 and *The Drapier's Letters*, ed. by H. Davis, 1935, p. 353.

3242 The Pattentee's Computation of Ireland, in a Letter from the Author of the Whitehall Evening-Post concerning the making of Copper-Coin. As also the Case and Address of Both Houses of Parliament. Together with His Majesty's Most Gracious Answer, to the House of Lords Address. *Dublin*, *1723*, *4*°. DA.

3243 A Fyngaull Pakete Jist noo came to Toone. *Dublin*, [*1723*], *s. sh. F*°. C (Cr).

A squib against Wood's halfpence.

3244 The Report of the Committee appointed to examine into the Project, commonly called the Harburg-Lottery. *Lond.* *1723*, *F*°. L.

An unauthorized edn. printed by Henry Parker for Richard Francklin. See C.J. xx, 149.

3245 The Case of the Trustees of the Harburgh-Lottery. *n.p.* [*1723*], *s. sh. F*°. LLI.

Title taken from endorsement.

3246 *Begin*: The Governor and Company for raising Thames-Water in York-Buildings being impowered by Act of Parliament to sell Annuities for Life, by Way of Lottery.... *n.p.* [*1723*], *s. sh. F*°. C (Cr).

Dated at the Edinburgh office of the Company, 4th February 1723.

3247 HEWITT, JOHN. Interest Compleated, in three Parts, viz. 1st. 48 Tables of simple Interest....2d. 4 Tables of Brokerage....3d. A Table of Time.... *Lond.* [*1723*], *4*°. L.

TRANSPORT

3248 A Bill for Reviving and Continuing an Act passed in the Tenth and Eleventh Years of the Reign of His late Majesty King William the Third, For the Clearing, Repairing, Preserving and Maintaining the Haven and Piers of Great Yarmouth. *n.p.* [*1723*], *F*°. O.

3249 The Case of Mr. Wentworth, in relation to the Petition about the River Darwent's being made Navigable from the Ouse to New-Malton. *n.p.* [*1723*], *s. sh. F*°. LLI.

3250 The Methods proposed for making the River Dunn Navigable, and the Objections to it Answered. With an Account of the Petitioner's Behaviour to the Land Owners. To which is annexed, a Mapp of the River, and the Reasons lately Printed for making it Navigable, with the Advantages of it. *Lond.* *1723*, *4*°. L.

3251 A Bill for Enlarging the Term granted by an Act passed in the Eighth Year of the Reign of Her late Majesty Queen Anne, Intituled, An Act for Repairing the Highways between the House commonly called, The Horse-Shoe House, in the Parish of Stoke-Goldington in the County of Bucks, and the Town of Northampton; And for Repairing the Road from the North-Bridge of Newport-Pagnell in the County of Bucks, to the said Horse-Shoe House. *n.p.* [*1723*], *F°*. O.

SOCIAL CONDITIONS

3252 Poor-Laws: or, The Laws and Statutes Relating to the Settling, Maintenance, and Employment of the Poor.... *Lond. 1724* [*1723*], *12°*. LU.

3253 Bellers, John. An Essay for Imploying the Poor to Profit, humbly Dedicated and Presented to the Lords and Commons of Great Britain, in Parliament Assembled. *Lond. 1723*, *4°*. LU.

3254 [Hutchinson, Francis, Bishop of Down and Connor]. A Letter to a Member of Parliament, concerning the Imploying and Providing for the Poor. *Dublin, 1723*, *8°*. L.

For authorship see *The Whole Works of Sir James Ware*, ed. by W. Harris, 1764, I. 216.

3255 Orders and Rules for the Corporation of the Governor and Directors of the Hospital for the Poor French Protestants, and their Descendants, Residing in Great Britain. *Lond. 1723*, *8°*. LU.

3256 Ordres et Reglements pour la Corporation des Gouverneur & Directeurs de l'Hôpital pour les Pauvres François Protestants, & leurs Descendants, résidants dans la Grande Bretagne. *Lond. 1723*, *8°*. O.

Another edn. Lond. 1741, 4°, has the text in French and English and an additional title-page reading: The Statutes and By-Laws of the Corporation of the Governor and Directors of the Hospital for Poor French Protestants, and their Descendants, residing in Great-Britain (O).

3257 The Case of the Insolvent Debtors in Suffolk-Place in the Borough of Southwark stated: And humbly Presented to His Majesty, and Both House of Parliament. *n.p.* [*1723?*], *s. sh. F°*. LLI.

3258 Dutton, Matthew. The Law of Masters and Servants in Ireland.... With all sorts of Precedents, necessary for the Office of a Justice of Peace, touching Masters, Apprentices, Servants, Artificers and Labourers.... *Dublin, 1723*, *8°*. DA.

3259 A Plan of the Design for bringing Water from the Village of Drayton, for the better Supplying the Cities of London & Westminster with Water. *n.p.* [*1723?*], *s. sh. F°*. L.

With 'The Explanation of the above Plan' and 'Reasons for Encouraging the Bringing Water to the Cities of London and Westminster'.

1724

GENERAL

3260 An Essay on Publick Industry: or a Scheme humbly offered for the Increase of our Manufactures, the Suppression of Monopolies, Extending Trade and Commerce, Improvement of Lands, and Providing for the Poor of this Kingdom, without Burthening of Parishes. With an Expedient for Answering the Exigencies of the Government, without Publick Lotteries. And a Proposal for Payment of the National Debts. *Lond. 1724, 8°.* LU.

3261 [JONES, DAVID]. A New Description of England and Wales, with the adjacent Islands....With a Particular Account of the Products, Trade, and Manufactures of the respective Places in every County, and their Improvements or Decays. Together with many uncommon Observations concerning Mines of several sorts....To which is added, a new and correct Set of Maps of each County.... By Herman Moll. *Lond. 1724, F°.* L.

For authorship see L.J. XXII, 350.

3262 [DEFOE, DANIEL]. A Tour thro' the whole Island of Great Britain, divided into Circuits or Journies....By a Gentleman. *Lond. 1724, 25, 27* [*26*], *8°.* 3 vols. L.

Another edn., published in parts, entitled: *Curious and Diverting Journies, thro' the whole Island of Great-Britain*...By A. B. Gent, Lond. 1734, F° (O); 2nd edn., entitled *A Tour*, Lond. 1738, 8°; 3rd, 1742; 4th, 1748; 5th, 1753; 6th, 1762, 61; 7th, with author's name, 1769; 8th, 1778 (all L). Another edn., ed. by G. D. H. Cole, 2 vols. 1927. On the changes in the early 8° editions see Godfrey Davies, 'Daniel Defoe's *A Tour*', *Modern Philology*, XLVIII (1950–1), 21–35.

AGRICULTURE

3263 BRADLEY, RICHARD. New Experiments and Observations, relating to the Generation of Plants: occasion'd by a Letter lately publish'd in the Philosophical Transactions, by Patrick Blair.... *Lond. 1724, 8°.* L.

3264 MILLER, PHILIP. The Gardeners and Florists Dictionary, or a Complete System of Horticulture: containing, I. The Culture of a Kitchen Garden....II. Of a Fruit Garden....III. Of a Flower Garden.... 2 vols. *Lond. 1724, 8°.* L.

3265 SWITZER, STEPHEN. The Practical Fruit-Gardener. Being the best and newest Method of raising, Planting, and Pruning all Sorts of Fruit-Trees, agreeably to the Experience and Practice of the most eminent Gardeners and Nursery-Men....Revised and recommended by the Rev$^{d.}$ Mr. Laurence and Mr. Bradley.... *Lond. 1724, 8°.* L.

2nd edn. 1731 (L); a re-issue, 1752 (L); another 2nd edn. 1763 (R).

3266 An Act for the draining, improving, and inclosing the Common call'd Oxburgh Common in the Parish of Oxburgh in the County of Norfolk. *n.p.* [*1724*], *F*o. L.

A bill.

3267 An Act to Inclose the Common Fields and Commons of Sunningwell cum Bayworth, in the County of Berks. *n.p.* [*1724*], *F*o. L.

A bill.

3268 An Account of the Reasons of some People / in Galloway, their Meetings anent Publick / Grievances through Inclosures. *n.p.* [*1724*], *s. sh. F*o. E.

Another edn. An Account of the Reasons of / some People in Galloway, their / Meetings anent Publick Grie-/ vances through Inclosures. [*1724*], *s. sh. F*o. (E).

3269 News from Galloway; or, The Poor Man's Plea against his Landlord: In a letter to a Friend. *n.p.* [*1724*], *F*o. E.

3270 The Opinion of Sir Thomas More, Lord High Chancellor of England, concerning Inclosures. In Answer to a Letter from Galloway. [*Edin. 1724*], *8*o. E.

Signed: Philadelphus.

3271 [Hope, Thomas]. A Treatise concerning the Manner of Fallowing of Ground, Raising of Grass-Seeds, and Training of Lint and Hemp, for the Increase and Improvement of the Linnen-Manufactories in Scotland. Publish'd for the Benefit of the Farmers in that Kingdom, by the Honourable Society for Improving in the Knowledge of Agriculture. *Edin. 1724*, *8*o. LU.

For authorship see J. A. S. Watson and G. D. Amery, 'Early Scottish Agricultural Writers', *Transactions of the Highland and Agricultural Society of Scotland*, ser. v, vol. 43, p. 64. The work has also been attributed to Robert Maxwell, the secretary of the Society, to Richard Bradley and to William Mackintosh of Borlum.

3272 Slator, Lionel. Instructions for the Cultivating and Raising of Flax and Hemp: In a better Manner, than that generally Practis'd in Ireland. [Followed by: Observations made by Richard Hall...on the Methods used in Holland, in Cultivating or Raising of Hemp and Flax. And likewise, His Remarks on Mr. Slator's Book.] *Dublin, 1724*, *8*o. LU.

The whole edited by the Hon. Thomas Coote. Another edn. Boston, 1735 (Sabin 81701).

3273 [Beale, John]. Herefordshire Orchards, a Pattern for England.... By J.B. To which is added, The newest and best Method for Planting and Managing the Hop-Garden: being a Pattern for Ireland. *Dublin, 1724*, *8*o. DNL.

Beale's work was first published in 1657.

3274 A Further Report from the Commissioners and Trustees for the Forfeited Estates in England, and Ireland, and elsewhere, (except Scotland.)

Presented to the Honourable House of Commons; Friday the 19th day of February, 1719. *Lond. 1724*, *F°*. LU.

3275 A Further Report of the Commissioners and Trustees appointed to Execute the several Trusts and Powers in England and Ireland, and elsewhere, (except Scotland) contained in several Acts of Parliament, for appointing Commissioners to enquire of the Estates of certain Traytors, and of Popish Recusants...Presented to the Honourable House of Commons; Friday the 24th Day of February, 1720.... *Lond. 1724*, *F°*. L.

3276 The Further Report of the Commissioners and Trustees appointed to enquire into the Forfeited Estates in England, and Ireland, and elsewhere, (except Scotland.) Presented to the Honourable House of Commons; Wednesday the 6th day of February, 1722.... *Lond. 1724*, *F°*. L.

3277 The Final Report of the Commissioners and Trustees for the Forfeited Estates in England, and Ireland, and elsewhere (except Scotland.) Presented to the Honourable House of Commons; Wednesday the 15th day of April, 1724.... *Lond. 1724*, *F°*. L.

3278 A Further Report humbly offer'd by the Commissioners and Trustees of the Forfeited Estates in Scotland. Presented to the Honourable House of Commons; Saturday the 6th Day of February, 1719.... *Lond. 1724*, *F°*. L.

3279 The Farther Report of the Commissioners and Trustees appointed to enquire into the Forfeited Estates in Scotland. Presented to the Honourable House of Commons; Thursday the 7th Day of February, 1722.... *Lond. 1724*, *F°*. L.

3280 A Further Report humbly offer'd by the Commissioners and Trustees of the Forfeited Estates, who acted in Scotland. Presented to the Honourable House of Commons; Wednesday the 18th day of January, 1720.... *Lond. 1724*, *F°*. L.

3281 A Further Report from the Commissioners and Trustees of the Forfeited Estates in Scotland. Presented to the Honourable House of Commons; Friday the 20th day of March, 1723.... *Lond. 1724*, *F°*. L.

3282 A list of the adventurers in the Company of the royal fishery of England. ...[*London? 1724*]. *38 × 25 cm.* Kress S. 1599.

3283 A Second Letter from a Gentleman in Town to his Friend in the Country, about the Fishing-Copartnery in North-Britain. *Edin. 1724*, *4°*. E.

A sequel to no. 3218.

MANUFACTURES

3284 Halfpenny, William. Practical Architecture, or a Sure Guide to the true working according to the Rules of that Science: Representing the Five Orders, with their several Doors & Windows. [*Lond. 1724*], 8°. L.

5th edn. Lond. 1730. (LRIBA); another 5th edn. 1736 (L).

3285 Information for William Brown and John Mosman, the Assigns of James Watson deceast, His Majesty's Printers in North Britain, against John Baskett and his Factor. *n.p.* [*1724*], *F°*. E.

Dated: December 30, 1724. Signed: Dun. Forbes.

3286 Information for John Baskett, His Majesty's Printer, and his Factor, against William Brown, and Others, Printers in Edinburgh. *n.p.* [*1724*], *F°*. E.

Dated: Dec. 31. 1724. Signed: Ch. Areskine.

3287 Reasons humbly offered to the Honourable House of Commons, against the Clause now proposed to prevent vexatious Prosecutions, upon the Act of the 11th and 12th of King William III. entituled, An Act for the more effectual employing the Poor, by encouraging the Manufactures of this Kingdom. *n.p.* [*1724*], *s. sh. F°*. L.

Endorsed: The Case of the Manufacturers. The clause indemnified those who had used silks and calicoes in furniture and household stuffs before 25 December 1722.

3288 Pott, John. The Answer of John Pott, to the Manufacturers Case. *n.p.* [*1724*], *s. sh. F°*. L.

3289 Reasons against any Powers that may be given for Encouraging the Wear of Prohibited Silks. *n.p.* [*1724*], *s. sh. F°*. L.

Against the bill to prevent multiplicity of prosecutions under the Act for the more effectual employing the poor, by encouraging the manufactures of this Kingdom.

COMMERCE

3290 A Bill for the better Viewing, Searching and Examining of all Drugs, Medicines, Waters, Oyls, Compositions, used or to be used for Medicines in all Places where the same shall be exposed to Sale, or kept for that Purpose, within the City of London and Suburbs thereof, or within Seven Miles Circuit of the said City: And also, for the Providing a Remedy for the President and College of Physicians in London, to have the Bodies of Persons executed for Felony, or other Offences, within the City of London, and Counties of Middlesex and Surrey, according to the Charters within-mentioned. *n.p.* [*1724*] *F°*. L.

Another edn., revised, entitled An Act for the better Viewing... (LG).

3291 Answer to the Objections of the Physicians against the Apothecaries, at the Bar of the Right Honourable the House of Lords, March 24. 1723 [O.S.]. *n.p.* [*1724*], *s. sh. F°*. L.

3292 The Case of Dr. Robert Eaton, with relation to a Power intended to be granted to the College of Physicians, in a Bill now depending before the Honourable House of Lords. *n.p.* [*1724*], *s. sh. F°*. L.

To secure his property in his 'Balsamick Styptick'.

3293 The Case of the Drugists, Grocers, and other Dealers in Coffee, Tea, &c. in relation to the Bill now depending concerning those Comodities. *n.p.* [*1724*], *s. sh. F°*. L.

Against the duties and the stringent regulations enforcing them.

3294 Instructions for Amendments to the Bill for Viewing Medicines, &c. *n.p.* [*1724*], *s. sh. F°*. L.

Title taken from endorsement.

3295 A Letter to a Noble Lord, occasioned by the Bill for Viewing of Medicines, &c. *n.p.* [*1724*], *s. sh. F°*. L.

Title taken from endorsement.

3296 A Letter to Dr. John Friend, on the Bill now depending, for the Inspection of Drugs and Medicinal Compositions in Apothecaries, Chymists, and Druggists Shops. *Lond. 1724, 8°*. L.

3297 Reasons for the Wardens of the Apothecaries being joined with the Censors of the College in their Viewing, Judging, and Destroying of Defective and Corrupted Drugs and Medicines. *n.p.* [*1724*], *s. sh. F°*. L.

The endorsed title is: Reasons for some Amendments to the Bill for the better Viewing of Medicines, &c.

3298 Reasons humbly offered against Part of the Bill, For the better Viewing, Searching and Examining of all Drugs, Medicines, &c. *n.p.* [*1724*], *s. sh. F°*. L.

3299 Reasons Humbly Offered against part of the Bill For the better Viewing, Searching, and Examining Drugs, Medicines, &c. *n.p.* [*1724*], *s. sh. F°*. L.

Different from the preceding.

3300 *Begin.* Whereas many Disputes have lately happen'd in this City about the Tares of Sugars.... *Bristol*, [*1724*], *s. sh. F°*. L.

An agreement to stand by specified tares signed by 99 names.

3301 Quaeries. *n.p.* [*1724*], *s. sh. 4°*. LU.

An attack on the Russia Company. Dated November 23. 1724.

3302 HOUSTOUN, JAMES. Some New and Accurate Observations Geographical, Natural and Historical. Containing a true and impartial Account of the Situation, Product, and Natural History of the Coast of Guinea, so far as relates to the Improvement of that Trade, for the Advantage of Great Britain in general, and the Royal African Company in particular.... *Lond. 1725* [*1724*], *8°*. LU.

3303 [Defoe, Daniel]. A General History of the Robberies and Murders of the most notorious Pyrates, and also their Policies, Discipline and Government, from their first Rise and Settlement in the Island of Providence, in 1717, to the present year 1724.... By Captain Charles Johnson [pseud]. *Lond. 1724, 8°.* L.

2nd edn. 1724 (L.); 3rd edn. 1725 (L); 4th edn. 1726 (L). Vol. 2, [1728] (L). Another edn., ed. by P. Gosse, 1925, 27; another edn., ed. by A. L. Hayward, 1926. For authorship see *C.B.E.L.* II, 508.

COLONIES

3304 A Vindication of the Governour and Government of His Majesty's Colony of Rhode-Island, &c. From the unjust Aspersions and Calumnies of John Menzies, Judge of His Majesty's Court of Vice-Admiralty in the same: Relating to the Proceedings of the said Government, in the Affair of several Slaves, and other Goods Imported into the said Colony, from a Ship lately lying at Tarpawlin-Cove, &c. *n.p.* [*1724*], *4°.* LPRO.

3305 The Determination of the Case of Mr. Thomas Story, and Mr. James Hoskins, relating to an Affair of the Pennsylvania Company, &c. *Lond. 1724, 4°.* L.

Signed by Benjamin Braine, Josephy Wyeth, Thomas Bradford, Henry Gouldney, Anthony Neat, Andrew Pitt, Samuel Arnold, seven of the twelve arbitrators to whom the case was submitted. The editor's preface signed: Justus, i.e. Elias Bockett. 2nd edn. 1724, 8° (L). First published at Philadelphia in 1724 (Sabin 92322).

3306 Purry, Jean Pierre. A Memorial presented to His Grace the Duke of Newcastle....Concerning the present state of Carolina, and the Means of improving it. *n.p.* [*1724*], *4°.* L.

3307 An Apology or Vindication of Francis Nicholson, Esq; His Majesty's Governor of South-Carolina, from the Unjust Aspersions cast on Him by some of the Members of the Bahama-Company. *Lond. 1724, 8°.* L.

3308 Jones, Hugh. The Present State of Virginia. Giving a particular and short Account of the Indian, English, and Negroe Inhabitants of that Colony. Shewing their Religion, Manners, Government, Trade, Way of Living, &c. With a Description of the Country. From whence is inferred a Short View of Maryland and North Carolina. To which are added, Schemes and Propositions for the better Promotion of Learning, Religion, Inventions, Manufactures, and Trade in Virginia, and the other Plantations. For the Information of the Curious...and for the Use of all Persons concerned in the Virginia Trade and Plantation. *Lond. 1724, 8°.* L.

Another edn. New York, 1865.

3309 [Uring, Nathaniel]. A Relation of the late intended Settlement of the Islands of St. Lucia and St. Vincent, in America; in right of the Duke of Montagu, and under His Grace's Direction and Orders, in the Year 1722. *Lond. 1725 [1724]*, *8º*. L.

Reissued in 1726 in *A History of the Voyages and Travels of Capt. Nathaniel Uring*, 1727 (L); 3rd edn. 1749 (EU); another edn., ed. by A. Dewar, Lond. 1928.

3310 A Description of the Port and Island of Bombay. And an Historical Account of the Transactions between the English and Portugueze concerning it, from the Year 1661, to this Present Time. *Lond. 1724* *8º*. L.

Issued by the East India Company to refute a Portuguese memorial.

FINANCE

3311 [Defoe, Daniel]. Considerations on Publick Credit. In a Letter to a Member of Parliament. *Lond. 1724*, *8º*. LU.

For authorship see *C.B.E.L.* II, 507.

3312 Some Remarks and Observations relating to the Transactions of the Year 1720. *Lond. 1724*, *8º*. L.

A vindication of the directors of the South Sea Company.

3313 The Report from the Trustees of the South Sea Company to the Honourable House of Commons; presented January 25, 1722.... *Lond. 1724*, *Fº*. LU.

3314 The Report from the Trustees for Raising Money on the Estates of the late South Sea Directors and others. Presented March 20, 1723.... *Lond. 1724*, *Fº*. LU.

3315 A Collection of the Reports and Accounts presented to the House of Commons, of the Demands of Foreign Princes and States, for Arrears due to them for Services performed during the Late War against France. And of the Clauses in the several Acts of Parliament for appointing Commissioners to examine and state the Debts of the Army, as far as the same relates to those Demands. Together with an Account of the Sums certified by the Commissioners to be due to the said Foreign Princes and States. With some few Observations upon the Whole. *Lond. 1724*, *Fº*. L.

3316 Information for Mr. James Campbel of London, Merchant, against the Creditors on the Equivalent. *n.p. [1724]*, *Fº*. E.

Dated: February 4. 1724. Signed: Dun. Forbes.

3317 Information for the Creditors of the Equivalent against Mr. James Campbell of London Merchant. *n.p. [1724]*, *Fº*. E.

Dated: February 11th, 1724. Signed Ja: Fergusson.

3318 Information for Mr. James Campbel of London, Merchant, against Some of the Creditors of the Scots Equivalent. *n.p. [1724]*, *Fº*. E.

Dated: July 15. 1724. Signed: Ro. Dundas.

3319 [Stevens, John]. The Royal Treasury of England: or an Historical Account of all Taxes, under what Denomination soever, from the Conquest to this present Year.... *Lond. 1725 [1724], 8o.* LU.

2nd edn., with author's name, 1728 (LU); another 2nd edn., entitled: An Historical Account of all Taxes..., 1733 (L).

3320 Crouch, Henry. A Complete View of the British Customs; containing the Rates of Merchandize....The whole being a continuation and improvement of the late Mr. Edgar's Vectigalium Systema.... *London, 1724, 8o.* L.

Another edn. 1725; 2nd edn. 1731; 3rd 1738; 4th 1745; 5th, 1755. Part 2, (no. 3739) 1728 [1727]; 2nd edn. 1746 (all L).

3321 A Collection of all the Statutes now in Force, relating to the Excise upon Beer, Ale, and other Liquors; and the Duties upon Malt, Brandy, and Hops. With An Abridgment of the said Statutes, and a Table of the Rates upon the several Liquors, &c. shewing by what Acts they are Imposed. *Edin. 1724, 8o.* LU.

3322 A Collection of all the Statutes now in Force, relating to the Duties upon Candles, Leather, Sope, Paper, Silks, Callicoes, &c. and upon Starch, and Gilt and Silver Wire, and Wrought Plate. With An Abridgment of the said Statutes, and a Table of the Rates upon the several Commodities, shewing by what Acts they are Imposed. *Edin. 1724, 8o.* LU.

3323 Instructions for Officers in the London-Brewery. *Lond. 1724, 8o.* LG.

3324 Instructions to be observed by the Officers employ'd in the Duty on Coffee, Tea, and Chocolate, in London. *Lond. 1724, 8o.* LG.

3325 Instructions for Officers in the Country, who take Account of Coffee, Tea, Cocoa Nuts, and Chocolate, and survey Chocolate-Makers. *Lond. 1724, 12o.* LG.

3326 Additional Instructions for Officers who survey Dealers in Coffee, &c. in the Country. *Lond. 1724, 12o.* LG.

3327 A Bill for the Sale of the Estate late of Humphrey Whadcock, deceased, for Discharging a Debt due to the Crown, and for Payment of such other his Debts, as his Personal Estate will not extend to pay; and for settling the Residue of his Lands conformable to his Last Will. *n.p. [1724], Fo.* O.

Whadcock was a collector of excise duties.

3328 A View of all the Publick Services, of the Money thereto appropriated by Parliament, and of the several Supplies granted, from the Year 1715, to 1724, inclusive. Shewing, The Totals of each Service...And the Amount of the Publick Debt, said to be incurred since His Majesty's Accession to the Throne. *Lond. [1724], 4o.* L.

3329 Reasons Humbly Offered, to Prohibit English Broad-Pieces and all

Forreign Gold from passing in Payment, unless they are taken in all the Publick Revenues. *n.p.* [*1724*], *s. sh. F°*. L.

3330 CREAGH, Sir MICHAEL. Remarks upon Mr. Wood's Coyn and Proceedings. *Dublin*, *1724*, *8°*. DA.

3331 An Apology for Mr. Wood, &c. Address'd to all true Lovers of their Country. *Dublin*, *1724*, *s. sh. F°*. LV (F).
Ironical.

3332 Advertisement. Whereas I Thomas Handy of Meath-street, Dublin, did Receive by the last Packet from a Person in London, to whom I am an entire Stranger, Bills of Lading for Eleven Casks of Wood's Half-Pence....[*Dublin*, *1724*], *s. sh. F°*. LV (F).
Statement that he will not accept the casks and has returned the bills of lading. Dated 29th August 1724. Reprinted in *The Drapier's Letters*, ed. by H. Davis, 1935, p. xxxvii.

3333 Advertisement. Whereas several Persons in this Kingdom suspect that John Molyneux of Meath-street, Iron-Monger, and his Brother David Molyneux of Essex-street Iron-Monger, are Interested in the Patent obtain'd by William Wood for Coyning of Halfpence and Farthings for this Kingdom.... [*Dublin*, *1724*], *s. sh. F°*. LV (F).
A denial, dated 22 August 1724, Reprinted in *The Drapier's Letters*, ed. by H. Davis, 1935, p. xxxviii.

3334 Advice to the Roman Catholicks of Ireland. Concerning Woods's Half-pence. *Dublin*, *1724*, *8°*. DA.

3335 The Brewers Declaration. *Dnblin* [sic], [*1724*], *s. sh. F°*. LV (F).
Against Wood's halfpence. Reprinted in *The Drapier's Letters*, ed. by H. Davis, 1935, p. xl.

3336 A Creed for an Irish Commoner. *Dublin*, *1724*, *s. sh. F°*. LV (F).
On Wood's halfpence.

3337 The Declaration of the Corporation of the Butchers. *Dublin*, [*1724*], *s. sh. F°*. LV (F).
Against Wood's halfpence. Reprinted in *The Drapier's Letters*, ed. by H. Davis, 1935, p. xxxviii.

3338 The Declaration of the Corporation of the Guild of St. Loy. *Dublin*, *1724*, *s. sh. F°*. C (Cr).
Against Wood's halfpence.

3339 The Declaration of the Grand Jury, and the Rest of the Inhabitants of the Liberty of the Dean and Chapter of St. Patrick's, Dublin. *Dublin*, [*1724*], *s. sh. F°*. LV (F).
Against Wood's halfpence Reprinted in *The Drapier's Letters*, ed. by H. Davis, 1935, p. xxxiv.

3340 A Defence of the Conduct of the People of Ireland, in their unanimous Refusal of Mr. Wood's Copper-Money. Wherein all the Arguments advanced in Favour of it, are particularly considered. *Dublin*, *1724*, *8°*. pp. 39. LU.

Another edn. 1724, pp. 45 (LU).

3341 The Drapier Demolished And Set out in his own Proper Colours; being a full Confutation of all his Arguments against Mr. Wood's Half-pence. By William Wood, Esq. *Dublin*, [*1724*], *8°*. L.

Ironical, and not, of course, by Wood.

3342 An Excellent New Ballad upon the New Half-Pence. *Dublin*, [*1724*], *s. sh. F°*. D.

3343 An Express from Elisium, to the once-Rev[d.] Dr. M-gee, Couple-Beggar, shewing the only Way for W. Wood, to Gain the Hearts of the unjustly irritated Hibernians, and to make them receive, without Reluctancy: the Brass-Coin. With Advice how to Manage, (and some Observations on) M. B. Drapier. Written by the Late Famous Captain Fleming. *Dublin*, *1724*, *s. sh. F°*. L.

3344 The Fifth and Last Letter to the People of Ireland in Reference to Wood and his Brass. *Dublin*, *1724*, *8°*. DA.

Signed: Hibernicus.

3345 The Flying-Stationers Declaration. *Dublin*, *1724*, *s. sh. F°*. LV (F).

Against Wood's halfpence, Reprinted in *The Drapier's Letters*, ed. by H. Davis, 1935, p. xxxix.

3346 The Funeral of Woods's Halfpence. A Sermon Preach'd against Coining of Base Money. By a Divine of the Church of England. *Dublin*, *1724*, *12°*. C.

A reprint of William Fleetwood's *A Sermon against Clipping*, 1694.

3347 Ireland's Warning, being an excellent New Song, upon Woods's Base Half-pence. *Dublin*, [*1724*], *s. sh. F°*. D.

3348 [Southwell, Edward ?]. A Letter from Dublin, to William Wood, Esquire. *n.p.* *1724*, *8°*. LU.

For authorship see *The Drapier's Letters*, ed. by H. Davis, 1935, pp. 355–6.

3349 [Rooke, George ?]. A Letter from a Quaker-Merch[t]. to Will. Wood Hard-Ware-Man. *Dublin*, *1724*, *8°*. DA.

Signed: Aminadab Firebrass. For authorship see Swift, *Correspondence*, ed. by F. Elrington Ball, III. 220.

3350 A Letter from a Lady of Quality to Mr. Harding the Printer, Occasionally Writ upon the General Out-cry against Wood's Halfpence. *Dublin*, *1723* [sic], *8°*. L.

Signed: Hibernia; and dated: Aug. 22. 1724.

3351 A Letter to the Lord C——t, in Answer to some Arguments lately advanced in Favour of Mr. Wood's Copper Money. By a Member of the Irish Parliament. *Dublin*, *1724*, *8°*. DA.

3352 [SWIFT, JONATHAN]. A Letter to the Shop-Keepers, Tradesmen, Farmers, and Common People of Ireland, concerning the Brass Half-Pence coined by Mr. Woods, with a Design to have them Pass in this Kingdom. By M. B. Drapier. *Dublin, 1723–4, Fo.* LU.

Another edn. n.p. [1724], 4° (CT. Rothschild 2076); another edn., title not within rules, Dublin, [1724], 8° (CT. Rothschild 2077); another issue, with title expanded and within double rules, and with first line of imprint ending '*Molesworth's-*', Dublin, [1724], 8° (L); another edn., as preceding, but with first line of imprint ending 'Harding' and with 'Woods' so spelt in the text, Dublin, [1724], 8° (CT. Rothschild 2079); another edn., same title as preceding, but with the spelling 'Wood' in the text (DNL). The order of editions is discussed by Lord Rothschild in *The Library*, ser. 4, vol. 19 (1939), pp. 107–15, where the description of no. 5 omits two line-endings. Reprinted in *The Drapier's Letters*, ed. by H. Davis, 1935.

3353 [SWIFT, JONATHAN]. A Letter to Mr. Harding the Printer, Upon Occasion of a Paragraph of his News-Paper of Aug. 1st. Relating to Mr. Woods's Half-Pence. By M. B. Drapier. Author of the Letter to the Shop-keepers, &c. *Dublin, Printed by J. Harding in Molesworth's Court, in Fishamble-Street, [1724], 8o.* L.

Dated: Aug. 4. 1724. Another edn. Dublin, [1724], with 'Woods's Half-pence' in title and 'in Fishamble-Street' omitted from imprint (O). Another edn., entitled: An Answer to Mr. Wood's Proposal, Relating to his Copper-Half-Pence....By M. B. Draiper, Limerick, [1724], 8° (CT. Rothschild 2083).

3354 [SWIFT, JONATHAN]. A Letter to the Whole People of Ireland. By M. B. Drapier. Author of the Letter to the Shop-keepers, &c. *Dublin, [1724], 8o.* DA.

Dated: Oct. 13, 1724. 2nd edn. corrected, Dublin [1724] (DA). Reprinted in *The Drapier's Letters*, ed. by H. Davis, 1935.

3355 [SWIFT, JONATHAN]. A Letter to the Right Honourable the Lord Viscount Molesworth. By M. B. Drapier, Author of the Letter to the Shop-keepers, &c. *Dublin, [1724], 8o.* LU.

Dated: Dec. 14. 1724. Reprinted in *The Drapier's Letters*, ed. by H. Davis, 1935.

3356 [ROOKE, GEORGE ?]. A Letter to William Wood, from a Member of that Society of Men, who in Derision are Call'd, Quakers. *Dublin, [1724], s. sh. Fo.* LV (F).

Signed: Abraham Woodhater. For authorship see *The Drapier's Letters*, ed. by H. Davis, 1935, p. 365.

3357 A Letter to William Woods, Esq; from his Only Friend in Ireland. *[Dublin,] 1724, s. sh. Fo.* LV (F).

Signed: Hibernicus.

3358 A New Dialogue between Two Beggars upon the Passing of Wood's Coin. By M. B. *Dublin, 1724, 8o.* DNL.

'Written before Sept. 9, 1723.' See *The Drapier's Letters*, ed. by H. Davis, 1935, p. 373.

3359 The Present State of Ireland Consider'd. In a Letter to the Rev[d]. Dean Swift. By a True Patriot. [*Dublin*], *1724*, *8º*. DNL.

Signed: Hibernicus.

3360 [Swift, Jonathan]. The Presentment of the Grand-Jury of the County of the City of Dublin. *Dublin*, *1724*, *s. sh. Fº*. LU.

Against Wood's halfpence. Reprinted in *The Drapier's Letters*, ed. by H. Davis, 1935, pp. 95–6.

3361 The Report of the Committee of the Lords of his Majesty's most Honourable Privy-Council, in relation to Mr. Wood's Half-Pence and Farthings, &c. *n.p.* [*1724*], *Fº*. D.

3362 [Swift, Jonathan]. Some Observations upon a Paper, call'd, The Report of the Committee of the Most Honourable the Privy-Council in England, relating to Wood's Half-pence. By M. B. Drapier, Author of the Letter to the Shop-Keepers, &c. *Dublin*, *1724*, *8º*. LU.

Dated: Aug. 25, 1724. 2nd edn. Dublin, [1724] (L); 3rd edn. Dublin, [1724] (O); 4th edn. Dublin, [1724] (DA); another 4th edn. (with misprint 'Honourabe') (DA). Reprinted in *The Drapier's Letters*, ed. by H. Davis, 1935.

3363 Another Letter to Mr. Harding the Printer, Upon Occasion of the Report of the Committee of the Lords of His Majesty's most Honourable Privy-Council, In relation to Mr. Wood's Half-Pence and Farthings, &c. lately Publish'd. *Dublin*, *1724*, *s. sh. Fº*. L.

Signed: Misoxulos. Reprinted in *The Drapier's Letters*, ed. by H. Davis, 1935, pp. 247–8.

3364 Owens, Samuel. Remarks upon the Report of the Committee of the Privy Council in Relation to Woods's Half-pence. [*Dublin*], *1724*, *s. sh. Fº*. C.

3365 [Swift, Jonathan]. Seasonable Advice. Since a Bill is preparing for the Grand Jury, to find against the Printer of the Drapier's last Letter, there are several things maturely to be considered by those Gentlemen, before whom this Bill is to come, before they determine upon it. [*Dublin*, *1724*], *s. sh. Fº*. D.

Dated: Novem. 11th 1724. Reprinted in *The Drapier's Letters*, ed. by H. Davis, 1935.

3366 [Swift, Jonathan]. A Serious Poem upon William Wood, Brasier, Tinker, Hard-Ware-Man, Coiner, Counterfeiter, Founder and Esquire. *Dublin*, [*1724*], *s. sh. Fº*. D.

Reprinted in *The Poems of Jonathan Swift*, ed. by H. Williams, 1937, I., 333–8.

3367 A Short Defence of the People of Ireland, occasion'd by the View of a Letter from Mr. Wood, to one of the Managers of his Copper Halfpence in Bristol. *Dublin*, *1724*, *8º*. DG.

3368 The Sixth Letter to the Whole People of Ireland. By an Ancient Patriot. *Dublin*, *1724*, *8º*. DA.

Signed: Well Wisher. On Wood's coinage.

3369 The Soldier's Plea: against Receiving Mr. Wood's Brass-Money. *Dublin, 1724, 8o*. DNL.

3370 [Bindon, David]. Some Considerations on the Attempts made to pass Mr. Wood's Brass-Money in Ireland. By a Lover of his Country. *Dublin, 1724, Fo*. DA.

For authorship see *The Drapier's Letters*, ed. by H. Davis, 1935, p. 364. Reprinted in *Fraud Detected*, 1725 (no. 3483).

3371 [Defoe, Daniel]. Some farther Account of the Original Disputes in Ireland, about Farthings and Halfpence. In a Discourse with a Quaker of Dublin. *n.p. 1724, 8o*. L.

For authorship see *C.B.E.L.* ii, 508.

3372 [Bindon, David]. Some Reasons shewing the Necessity the People of Ireland are under, for continuing to refuse Mr. Wood's Coinage. By the Author of the Considerations. *Dublin, 1724, 8o*. LU.

The dedication signed: D.B. Line 3 of title People of /. Another edn. line 3 of title People of Ire-/ (LU). Reprinted in *Fraud Detected*, 1725 (no. 3483). For authorship see Wagner no. 50.

3373 To the Kings Most Excellent Majesty. The Humble Petition of the Lord-Mayor, Sheriffs, Commons, and Citizens of the City of Dublin, in Common-Council Assembled. *Dublin, 1724, s. sh. Fo*. C.

Against Wood's halfpence. Dated 8. Sept. 1724.

3374 [Hamilton, James, Earl of Abercorn?]. The True State of the Case Between the Kingdom of Ireland of the One Part, and Mr. William Wood of the Other Part. By a Protestant of Ireland. *Dublin, 1724. 8o*. D.

For authorship see Wagner 39 and *The Drapier's Letters*, ed. by H. Davis, 1935, p. 355.

3375 *Begin.* Whereas during the last Session of Parliament...it was Reported, that a Design having been carried on by William Wood.... *Dublin, 1724, s. sh. Fo*. C (Cr).

A declaration of the Guild of St. John Baptist, tailors, that members of it will not receive or pay Wood's coins.

3376 Woods's Confession to the Mobb of the City of Dublin. *Dublin, 1724, s. sh. Fo*. LV (F).

Signed: Will. Wood.

3377 Woods's Plot Discovered by a Member of His Society: with his Apology to his Country-men. *Dublin, 1724, 8o*. L.

3378 A Word of Advice: or a Friendly Caution to the Collectors of Ireland, in Relation of Wood's Brass-Money. *Dublin, 1724, 8o*. DNL.

Signed: Cato Ultonensis.

3379 A Word or Two to the People of Ireland, concerning the Brass Money that is, and shall be Coin'd by Mr. Woods, and which he is endeavouring to Impose upon Us. By a Well-wisher to his Country. *Dublin, [1724], 8o*. DA.

3380 A List of the Names of the Adventurers in the Bank of Scotland. February 6th, 1724. [*Edin. 1724*], *s. sh. F°.* C (Cr).

3381 Clerke, George. The Dealers in Stock's Assistant: or, A Calculation of the Value of any Parcel Of Stocks from 10000 l. to 1 l. at the Rate of $\frac{1}{16}$ of a Pound per Cent. to 200 l. per Cent.... *Lond. 1725* [*1724*]. *12°.* L.

Although dated 1725 the book was advertised in the *Monthly Catalogue* for Nov. 1724 and the L copy has a ms. note of its registration for stamp duty on 16 Nov. 1724.

3382 [Gordon, Thomas]. An Essay on the Practice of Stock-Jobbing, and some Remarks on the right use, and regular improvement of Money. In a Letter to a Gentleman, and a Proprietor of South-Sea Stock. *Lond. 1724, 8°.* L.

Reprinted in *A Collection of Tracts. By the late John Trenchard...and Thomas Gordon*, 1751, vol. 2.

TRANSPORT

3383 A Bill for making more Effectual an Act made in the Ninth Year of His Majesty's Reign (Intituled, An Act for Compleating the Repairs of the Harbour of Dover in the County of Kent, and for Restoring the Harbour of Rye in the County of Sussex, to its Ancient Goodness) so far as the same relates to the said Harbour of Rye. *n.p.* [*1724*], *F°.* L.

3384 An Abstract of the Ancient and Present State of the Navigation of Lynn, Cambridge, &c. and of Draining in the Fens, called Bedford Level, &c. *n.p.* [*1724*], *s. sh. F°.* MP.

3385 The Case of the Navigation of the Port of King's Lynn. *n.p.* [*1724*], *F°.* O.

3386 The Complaints of the Merchants, Mariners and Watermen of Lynn, about Navigation, 1724. *n.p.* [*1724?*], *s. sh. F°.* MC.

3387 Colonel Armstrong's Report, with Proposals for Draining the Fenns and Amending the Harbour of Lynn, 1724. *n.p.* [*1724*], *F°.* O.

Followed by 'A Report touching Lynn Navigation' and 'The Complaints of the Merchants, Mariners and Watermen of Lynn, about Navigation, 1724'.

3388 Bridgeman, Charles. A Report of the Present State of the Great Level of the Fenns called Bedford-Level. And of the Port of Lynn; and of the Rivers Ouse and Nean, the Two great Sewers of that Country. With Considerations on the Scheme propos'd by the Corporation of Lynn, for the Draining the said Fenns, and Reinstating that Harbour. And also a Scheme humbly propos'd for the Effectual Draining those Fenns, and Reinstating that Harbour or Port. From a Survey thereof made in August, 1724. *n.p.* [*1724*], *F°.* O.

3389 An Answer, Paragraph by Paragraph, to A Report of the present State of the Great Level of the Fens, called Bedford-Level, and of the Port of Lynn, and of the River Ouse, &c. And also to a Scheme propos'd by

Mr. Charles Bridgman, for the effectual Draining those Fens, and reinstating that Harbour or Port. Drawn from Authentick Testimonies of the State of that Level, Harbour and River, before and since Denver Dam and Sluices were built, &c. and from a Survey made in the Years 1723, 1724. *n.p.* [*1724*], *F*o. O.

With the text of the Report and of Bridgeman's Scheme.

3390 London. Delme Mayor. Martis Quarto die Februarii, 1723. [*Lond.*] *1723*, *s. sh. F*o. LCRO.

Restricting the parking of country carts in the streets of London.

3391 A List of the Subscribers for Mending the Road from Reading to Caversham; with an Account how the Money has been laid out. *Reading*, *1724*, *4*o. O.

The editor's preface signed: John Watts.

3392 A Bill for Repairing the Road leading from Meriden-Hill in the County of Warwick, to the Town of Northampton. *n.p.* [*1724*], *F*o. O.

3393 A Bill for Enlarging the Term granted by an Act made in the Tenth Year of Her late Majesty Queen Anne; intitled, An Act for Enlarging, Amending and Maintaining the Road betwixt Northfleet, Gravesend, and Rochester, in the County of Kent, and for Explaining the same Act; and for appropriating a Sum of Money arising out of the Toll and Duty, imposed by the said Act, and this present Act, towards Repairing the Road between the Town of Chatham, and Boughton under the Blean in the said County of Kent. *n.p.* [*1724*], *F*o. L.

3394 A Bill for Amending the Roads from the Stones-end in the Borough of Southwark in the County of Surrey, to a place called Highgate, at the Entrance of Ashdown Forest in the Parish of East-Grinsted in the County of Sussex, by Enlarging the Terms granted by Two former Acts; the One of the Fourth, the other of the Sixth Year of His Majesty's Reign. *n.p.* [*1724*], *F*o. L.

3395 A Table shewing the Time when the several Posts Depart from, and Arrive at Edinburgh. *n.p.* *1724*, *s. sh. F*o. E.

SOCIAL CONDITIONS

3396 An Abstract of George Fox's Advice and Warning, to the Magistrates of London, in the Year 1657. concerning the Poor. With Some Observations thereupon, and Recommendations of them...by John Bellers. *Lond.* *1724*, *4*o. LU.

3397 Bellers, John. An Epistle to Friends of the Yearly, Quarterly, and Monthly Meetings; concerning the Prisoners, and Sick, in the Prisons, and Hospitals of Great-Britain. *n.p.* *1724*, *4*o. LU.

3398 [Fownes, Sir William]. Methods Proposed, for Regulating the Poor, Supporting of Some and Employing Others: according to their several Capacities. *Dublin, 1723–4, 8o.* M (Cr).

Another edn. 'By Sir W.F.', Dublin, 1725 (L). For authorship see Wagner 81.

3399 Mr. Crispe's Letter to the Right Honourable Robert Walpole, Esq; *n.p. [1724], Fo.* LLI.

On the affairs of Chelsea Hospital.

3400 The Rules and Statutes of George Watson's Hospital. *Edin. 1724, 12o.* L.

3401 Considerations shewing the Reasonableness of Having an Act for the Discharge of Insolvent Debtors, without Limitation of Sum. *n.p. [1724?], Fo.* L.

3402 A Letter to a Member of Parliament, relating to the relief of Poor Insolvent Prisoners for Debt, occasioned by the several Petitions to the House of Commons. And a Proposal for strengthning the British Plantations in America. *Lond. 1724, 8o.* L.

3403 Reasons humbly offered against passing the Bill to prevent Frivolous and Vexatious Arrests. *n.p. [1724?], s. sh. Fo.* L.

Kress has two issues (S. 1633 & S. 1634).

3404 Reasons humbly offered against the Bill to prevent Frivolous and Vexatious Arrests. *n.p. [1724?], s. sh. Fo.* L.

3405 To the Honourable the Commons of Great-Britain, in Parliament assembled, the Humble Petition of the Prisoners of the King's-Bench Prison. *n.p. [1724], Fo.* L.

3406 An Accurate Description of Newgate, with the Rights, Privileges, Allowances, Fees, Dues and Customs thereof. Together with a Parallel between the Master-Debtors Side of the said Prison, and the several Sponging-Houses in the County of Middlesex.... Written for the Publick Good. By B.L. of Twickenham. *Lond. 1724, 8o.* LG.

3407 Parkyns, Sir Thomas. Queries and Reasons offer'd by Sir Thomas Parkyns...why the County-Hall, Goal, &c. should be built in the County of Nottingham...and not in the Market-Place...of the Town of Nottingham....With the addition of Subordination; or, an Essay on Servants, their Rates of Wages, and the Great Conveniency which will accrue to every County, by Recording with all the Chief Constables, &c. of the same....The Third Edition, with Emendations and large Additions. *Lond. 1724, 4o.* LU.

3408 Parkyns, Sir Thomas. An Appendix to the Queries and Reasons, offer'd by Sir Thomas Parkyns....Why the County-Hall, Goal, &c. should be built in the County of Nottingham....Containing the Statute of XI. and XII. of King William III. to enable Justices of the Peace to Build and Repair Goals in their respective Counties. Reviv'd and continu'd in the 10th of Queen Anne; and made Perpetual the 6th of his present Majesty King George. *Nottingham, 1724, 4o.* L.

3409 [DEFOE, DANIEL]. The Great Law of Subordination Consider'd; or, the Insolence and Unsufferable Behaviour of Servants in England duly enquir'd into.... *Lond. 1724, 8o.* L.

Reissued as: The Behaviour of Servants in England Inquired into.... n.d. (L). For authorship see *C.B.E.L.* II, 507.

3410 [TANCRED, CHRISTOPHER]. A Scheme for an Act of Parliament for the better regulating Servants, and ascertaining their Wages, and lessening the future Growth of the Poor, and Vagrants of the Kingdom. Humbly offer'd to the Consideration of the Parliament of Great Britain. By a Magistrate of the North of England. *Lond. 1724, 4o.* L.

The B.M. cataloguer has seen another copy with a ms. attribution of authorship.

3411 GODFREY, AMBROSE. An Account of the New Method of Extinguishing Fires by Explosion and Suffocation....Wherein a Description is given of the several Machines and their Uses....To which is added, A short Narrative of Mr. Povey's Behaviour in relation to this useful Invention.... *n.p. 1724, 8o.* L.

2nd edn. 1743 (L).

3412 The Design is to bring the Water of the Cowley-Stream into Marybonne-Feilds. *n.p.* [*1724?*], *Fo.* LG.

With a map.

3413 To the Honourable the House of Commons, the humble Petition of Robert Bumpsted, in the behalf of himself and several others. *n.p.* [*1724*], *s. sh. Fo.* L.

For a saving clause on behalf of his pumping engine in the bill to bring water to London from Colebrook.

3414 Heads of a Protestation to be entred before the Right Honourable, the Magistrates and the Honourable the Town-Council of Edinburgh, against a Monopoly intended by the Chirurgeon Apothecaries, to the Prejudice of the Physicians and Burgers residing in the Place. [*Edin.*], *1724, s. sh. Fo.* L.

1725

GENERAL

3415 PHILIPS, ERASMUS. The State of the Nation, in respect to her Commerce, Debts, and Money. *Lond. 1725, 8°.* LU.

2nd edn. 1726: another 2nd edn. 1731 (both LU).

3416 [DEFOE, DANIEL]. A General History of Discoveries and Improvements, in useful Arts, particularly in the great Branches of Commerce, Navigation, and Plantation, in all Parts of the known World....4 pt. Oct. Nov. Dec. [Jan.]. *Lond.* [*1725, 26*], *8°.* L.

Reissued in Dec. 1726 as *The History of the Principal Discoveries and Improvements*...1727 (L). For authorship see *C.B.E.L.* II, 508.

3417 Enquiries into the Principal Causes of the General Poverty of the Common People of Ireland. With Remedies Propos'd for Removing of them. *Dublin, 1725, 8°.* LU.

3418 A Letter from a Clergy-Man in the Country, to H.R. Esq; a Member of Parliament, in the City. *n.p. 1725, F°.* L.

On conditions in Dublin. Signed: Philanthropos.

AGRICULTURE

3419 BRADLEY, RICHARD. A Survey of the ancient Husbandry and Gardening, collected from Cato, Varro, Columella, Virgil, and others the most eminent Writers among the Greeks and Romans: Wherein many of the most difficult Passages in those Authors are explain'd, and the whole render'd familiar to our Climate; with Variety of new Experiments.... *Lond. 1725, 8°.* O.

3420 [PEIRSON, SAMUEL]. The Present State of the Tillage in Ireland Considered, and Some Methods offered for its Improvement. By S.P. *Dublin, 1725, 8°.* LU.

Some copies (e.g. DNL) have an inserted dedication signed: Sam. Peirson.

3421 CROMMELIN, LOUIS. Directions for Propagating and Dressing Lint.... Published for the Improvement of the Linnen Manufactory in Scotland. *Glasgow, 1725, 8°.* E.

Extracted from *An Essay*, 1705 (no. 497).

3422 An Act to Inclose the Common and Tract of Land called Croston Finney in the County of Lancaster. *n.p.* [*1725*], *F°.* L.

A bill.

3423 The Case and Reasons for Inclosing the Common called Croston Finny in the County of Lancaster. *n.p.* [*1725*], *s. sh. F°.* LLI.

3424 The Case of the Greatest Number of Inhabitants of Croston in the County of Lancaster, relating to the Inclosing of a large Town-Field there called Croston-Finney: With Reasons against Passing the Bill now depending for Inclosing thereof. *n.p.* [*1725*], *F°*. LLI.

Endorsed: Reasons against inclosing the Common, called, Croston Finney, in the County of Lancaster.

3425 An Act to inclose divers Parcels of waste Grounds, lying and being in Westhaughton in the County Palatine of Lancaster. *n.p.* [*1725*], *F°*. O.

3426 The Most Advantageous and Necessary Project for England, that Ever yet was Undertaken. Containing I. Very reasonable Proposals for Insuring all the Sea-Walls, or Sea-Banks, and Marsh-Grounds thereunto belonging, within the Kingdom of England...from Loss and Damage by Overflowing Tides and Inundations of the Sea....II. Very Easy Proposals for Gaining all Sorts of Marsh-Lands from the Sea....III. Reasonable Proposals for Insuring Keys and Wharfs, and for Clearing and Enlarging of Docks and Harbours....IV. The Draining of Fens proposed after a New Method....V. Proposals for Preparing, or Forming Mill-Ponds for Rape-Mills, or Corn-Mills, on convenient Creeks of the Sea....Proposals for drawing Canals from Fresh-Water Rivers to Noblemens Seats in the Country, as also for rendering Rivers Navigable. By a Society at London. *Lond. 1725. 8°*. LU.

3427 Articles of Agreement Made, Concluded, and Agreed upon the twentieth Day of July, in the Year of our Lord One thousand, seven hundred and twenty. Between the Governor and Company of Copper-Miners in England, of the First Part. Thomas Chambers, Jun. of the Transfer-Office in the East-India House, London, Gent. of the Second Part. And John Essington of Wandsworth in the County of Surrey, Esq; James Bradley, and Case Billingsley of London, Merchants, of the Third Part. With some short Observations. *Lond. 1725, 4°*. L.

3428 Pearce, Thomas. The Laws and Customs of the Stannaries in the Counties of Cornwall and Devon. Revis'd and Corrected according to the Antient and Modern Practice. In Two Parts.... *Lond. 1725, F°*. LU.

3429 Unto the Right Honourable, The Convention of the Royal Burrows of North-Britain, the Petition of the Burgh of Culross. *n.p.* [*1725*], *s. sh. F°*. E.

Dated: 7th July 1725. For financial help in prospecting for coal.

3430 The State of the Roman Catholicks of Ireland: or, Reasons why they may be allow'd to Purchase, take Mortgages for their Money, Fee-Farm, or other Leases. Most humbly offer'd to Both Houses of Parliament. *Dublin, 1725, s. sh. F°*. L.

Another edn. Dublin, 1733, s. sh. F° (DM).

3431 The Final Report of the Commissioners and Trustees of the Forfeited Estates in Scotland. Presented to the Honourable House of Commons; Saturday the 17th Day of April, 1725.... *Lond. 1725, F°*. L.

3432 Report by the Committee appointed by the general Meeting of the Fishing Copartnery held on Tuesday the 16th of November last. [*Edin. 1725*], *s. sh. F°.* E.

3433 Proposals for Employing the Remaining Stock of the Fishery, so as to be of universal Use and Advantage to the Nation, in a Letter from a Gentleman in the Country, to his Friend at Edinburgh. *Edin. 1725*, *8°.* E.

For founding a hospital.

MANUFACTURES

3434 John Ward, Esquire, Appellant. The Most Noble Edmond Duke of Buckinghamshire and Normanby, an Infant, by the Rt. Hon[ble]. David Earl of Portmore his Guardian, Charles Earl of Orrery, George Lord Willoughby de Brooke, Thomas Lord Trevor, Allen Lord Bathurst,and Patrick Garden, Esq; Respondents. The Appellant's Case. *n.p.* [*1725*], *F°.* L.

Signed: J. Willes, W. Lee. On the lease of alum works in Yorkshire.

3435 John Ward, Esquire, Appellant. The Most Noble Edmund Duke of Buckinghamshire and Normanby [by his Guardian and the Executors of the late Duke]...Respondents. The Respondents Case. *n.p.* [*1725*], *F°.* L.

Signed: C. Wearg. C. Talbot.

3436 The Present Case of the Brewers in and about Edinburgh, Stated, and Offered to Their Consideration. *Edin. 1725*, *4°.* E.

Signed: Love-peace Old-cause.

3437 Unto the Right Honourable, The Lords of Council and Session, The Petition of the several Brewars in and about Edinburgh under subscribing. *n.p.* [*1725*], *4°.* E.

Dated: July 29th, 1725.

3438 Halfpenny, William. The Art of Sound Building, demonstrated in Geometrical Problems: shewing Geometrical Lines for all kinds of Arches, Groins, and Twisted Rails, both Regular and Irregular.... *Lond. 1725*, *F°.* L.

2nd edn. 1725 (LRIBA).

3439 Smith, George. A Compleat Body of Distilling, explaining the Mysteries of that Science, in a most easy and familiar manner; containing an exact and accurate Method of making all the Compound Cordial-Waters now in use...with a computation of the original cost of the several ingredients, and the profits arising in sale... *Lond. 1725*, *8°.* L.

2nd edn. 1730 (not seen); 3rd edn. 1738 (L); another 2nd edn. 1766 (L).

3440 A Description of the Engine for raising Water by Fire. *n.p.* [*1725*], *s. sh. obl. F°.* L.

3441 *Begin.* Richard Newsham, of Cloth-Fair, London, Engineer, Makes the most useful and convenient Engines for quenching Fires.... *n.p.* [*c. 1725?*], *s. sh. F°.* LG.

3442 B., T. Some considerations relating to the several abuses committed in the hempen and flaxen manufacture of this Kingdom.... *Dublin, 1725, 8°.* Kress 3584.

3443 Answers for John Baskett, His Majesty's Printer, to the Petition of William Brown and John Mosman. *n.p.* [*1725*], *F°.* E.

Dated: Jan. 21st, 1725. Signed: Ja. Graham.

3444 Unto the Right Honourable, the Lords of Council and Session, the Petition of John Baskett, His Majesty's Printer. *n.p.* [*1725*], *F°.* E.

Dated: February 12th, 1725. Signed: Ro. Craigie.

3445 Answers for John Baskett, His Majesty's Printer, and John Paton his Factor, to the Petition of Messieurs Brown and Mosman, Printers in Edinburgh. *n.p.* [*1725*], *F°.* E.

Dated: Feb. 26. 1725. Signed: Ro. Craigie.

3446 Answers for John Baskett, His Majesty's Printer, to the Petition of William Brown and John Mosman. *n.p.* [*1725*], *F°.* E.

Dated: July 14. Signed: Hew Dalrymple.

3447 The Case of the Scribblers, alias Dutch-Spinners of the County of Dublin, Presented to the Woollen-Draipers of the said City. *n.p.* [*c. 1725?*], *s. sh. F°.* C (Cr).

3448 A Bill for the better Regulating the Manufacture of Cloth, in the West Riding, in the County of York. *n.p.* [*1725*], *F°.* L.

COMMERCE

3449 [Defoe, Daniel]. The Complete English Tradesman, in Familiar Letters; Directing him in all the several Parts and Progressions of Trade.... *Lond. 1726* [*1725*], *8°.* LU.

Another edn. Dublin, 1726 (O); 2nd edn., with Supplement, also issued separately, Lond. 1727 [1726] (L); Supplement, Dublin, 1727 (DNL); 3rd edn. 1732 (L). Volume II. Lond. 1727 (L); another edn. 1732 (L) 4th edn. of both vols. 1738 (L). For authorship see *C.B.E.L.* II, 508.

3450 A Bill for making more Effectual an Act passed in the Fifth Year of His Majesty's Reign, Intituled, An Act for preventing the Mischiefs which may happen, by keeping too great Quantities of Gunpowder in or near the Cities of London and Westminster, or the Suburbs thereof. *n.p.* [*1725*], *F°.* L.

3451 The whole Tryal between the Rt. Hon. the Lord Mayor and Aldermen of this City, and the Bakers and Meal-men of the same, before a Committee of the Privy-Council held at the Castle of Dublin this 23d of July 1725. *Dublin, 1725, s. sh. F°.* L.

3452 Edinburgh, November 17. Table of the Meal and Corn-market Customs. [*Edin. c. 1725?*], *F°*. EU.

3453 To the Rt. Hble. the Knights, Citizens and Burgesses in Parliament Assembled. The Humble Petition and Case of James Dowan. [*Dublin, 1725*], *s. sh. F°*. L.

The weigh-masters of butter and tallow are promoting a bill to take over his office of weigh-master of green and salt hides.

3454 FORMAN, CHARLES. Mr. Forman's Letter to the Right Honourable William Pulteney, Esq; shewing how Pernicious, the Imperial Company of Commerce and Navigation lately established in the Austrian Netherlands, is likely to prove to Great Britain, as well as to Holland. *Lond. 1725, 8°*. LU.

3455 Gilbraltar a Bulwark of Great Britain. In a Letter to a Member of Parliament. Containing Some Considerations on the Importance of that Place, in respect to our Trade in general; but particularly with regard to Barbary, Spain, France, &c. With Proposals for erecting a Civil Magistracy there, and for lessening the Annual Expence of the Crown in maintaining that Garrison. By a Gentleman of the Navy. *Lond. 1725, 8°*. LU.

Signed: Philalethes. The half-title and running title is: The Importance of Gibralter, Consider'd. 2nd edn. 1725 (O).

3456 Volrath Tham Merchant in Gottenburgh, Appellant. Charles Sheriff and Richard Sheriff Merchants in Prestenpans, Respondents. The Appellant's Case. *n.p.* [*1725*], *F°*. L.

Signed: Dun. Forbes. C. Talbot. Will. Hamilton. Exchange of a cargo of herrings from Scotland for Swedish iron, in 1718.

3457 Volrath Tham, Appellant. Charles Sherriff, and Richard Sherriff, Respondents. The Respondents Case. *n.p.* [*1725*], *F°*. L.

Signed: C. Wearg. C. Areskine.

3458 [WEBB, DANIEL]. The British Woollen Manufacturers Case, or, Cause of the Declining State of their Trade, and High Price on Irish and Low on English Wooll. And Reasons assign'd, that preventing the British and Irish Wooll and Yarn being Run, is of absolute Necessity to preserve the Trade of Great Britain. Humbly Offered to the Consideration of the Members of Parliament. *n.p.* [*c. 1725?*], *s. sh. F°*. LPRO.

For authorship see Webb's letter in LPRO, C.O. 388/94, enclosing this and other pamphlets of his.

3459 A plain and easy Method, shewing how the Publick may be furnish'd with 2,133,300 l. without Interest, or doing the least Hardship to any Person whatsoever. *n.p.* [*c. 1725?*], *F°*. LLI.

An attack on the East India Company suggesting that they should pay for the privilege of their exclusive trade.

COLONIES

3460 [KNIGHT, JAMES?]. The State of the Island of Jamaica. Chiefly in Relation to its Commerce, and the Conduct of the Spaniards in the West-Indies. Address'd to a Member of Parliament. By a Person who resided several Years at Jamaica. *Lond. 1725*, 8°. EU.

Signed: A—— B——. Reissued in 1726 (L). Attributed to Mr. K. by A. Boyer, *Political State*, vol. XXXVI, p. 240.

FINANCE

3461 The Report of the Trustees for Raising Money on the Estates of the late South Sea Directors and others. Presented April 23, 1725.... *Lond. 1725*, *F°*. L.

3462 The Case of Alexander Urquhart, Esq; *n.p.* [*1725*], *F°*. L.

Urquhart was a M.P. involved in South Sea speculations. His creditors petitioned the House of Commons.

3463 Minutes Mr. James Campbel, against the Creditors of the Equivalent. *n.p.* [*1725*], *F°*. E.

Dated: July 7. 1725.

3464 Answers for James Campbel of London, Merchant, to the Petition of the Creditors on the Equivalent. *n.p.* [*1725*], *F°*. E.

Dated: July 19. 1725. Signed: Ro. Dundas.

3465 An Additional Book of Rates of Goods and Merchandizes usually imported, and not particularly Rated in the Book of Rates referred to in the Act of Tonnage and Poundage...With Rules, Orders and Regulations, signed by the Right Honourable Spencer Compton, Esq; Speaker of the Honourable House of Commons. *Lond. 1725*, *F°*. LU.

3466 Instructions to be observed by the Officers employ'd in charging the Duties on Candles and Soap in London. *Lond. 1725*, *12°*. LG.

3467 Instructions for Officers concern'd in ascertaining the Duties on Candles in the Country. *Lond. 1725*, *12°*. LG.

3468 Instructions for the Gagers of the Excise in the Country. *Lond. 1725*. *F°*. LCH.

3469 Instructions given by the Commissioners of his Majesty's Excise, unto Waterman at the Port of . *n.p.* [*c. 1725?*], *F°*. LG.

3470 Instructions to be observed by the Officers for the Duties on Malt, Mum, Cyder, and Perry. *Lond. 1725*, 8°. LG.

Another edn. 1732 (LCH).

3471 Reasons humbly offer'd to the Parliament, in behalf of several Persons concern'd in Paper making, Printing and Publishing the Half penny News-Papers, against the Bill now depending, for laying a Penny Stamp upon every whole Sheet, and a Half penny Stamp upon every half Sheet of all News-Papers. *n.p.* [*1725*], *s. sh. F°*. L.

3472 [FORBES, DUNCAN]. Copy of a Letter from a Gentleman in Edinburgh, to his Friend in the Country, upon the subject of the Malt Tax. *Edin. 1725.* 8°. LU.

Signed: Philo Scotus. For authorship see ms. note in E copy.

3473 Copy of a Letter from a Gentleman in Fife, to his Friend at Edinburgh, upon the Subject of the Malt-Tax. *n.p. 1725*, 8°. LU.

Signed: L.D.L. Coupar, 31 Dec. 1724. 2nd edn. 1725 (E).

3474 A Letter from a Fyfe Gentleman, at present in Edinburgh, to the Chief Magistrate of a Burgh in Fyfe, upon our present Situation, with regard to the Malt-tax: By the Author of a former Letter from Fyfe upon the same Subject, dated 31 December, 1724. *Edin. 1725*, 8°. LU.

Signed: L.D.L. Edinburgh, 3 Aug. 1725.

3475 Some Thoughts concerning the Malt Tax, humbly offered to the Consideration of the landed Interest of Scotland. *n.p.* [*1725?*], 8°. L.

3476 A Letter from a Gentleman at Glasgow to his Friend in London, containing, An Impartial History of the late Tumults at Glasgow, on the Commencement of the Malt-Tax. *Lond. 1725*, 8°. E.

3477 [TONNOCH, W]. A Letter from a Gentleman in Glasgow, to his Friend in the Country, concerning the late Tumults which happened in that City.... *n.p. 1725*, 4°. E.

Ms. attribution of authorship in E copy.

3478 A Letter from the Magistrates of Glasgow, to a Gentleman in Edinburgh, giving an Account of the late Tumult which happened at Glasgow. *n.p.* [*1725*], *s. sh. F°*. E.

Signed: John Stirling, James Johnson.

3479 SCURLOCK, DAVID. The King's Right to his Customs, and the Sin of Defrauding him of them, Consider'd. In Two Sermons lately preach'd at Hackney in Middlesex. *Lond. 1725*, 8°. LU.

3480 To the Right Honourable the Lords Commissioners of His Majesty's Treasury. The humble Petition of Nathaniel Smith, Gent. deceased [erased], late Collector of the Customs at Liverpool, with a true State of his Case annex'd. *n.p.* [*1725?*], 4°. LU.

On his dismissal for exposing frauds.

3481 The Report of the Committee appointed by Order of the House of Commons, to Consider of Proper Methods for the more Easie Passing Sheriffs Accounts. Reported on The Sixth Day of November, 1723. By Thomas Meredyth, Esq; Chair-man of the said Committee.... *Dublin, 1723*, *F°*. DNL.

3482 [SWIFT, JONATHAN]. A Compleat Collection of all the Drapier's-Letters, concerning the Brass-Money... *Dublin, 1725*, 8°. DA.

Original editions, with a collective title-page. The only copy seen is imperfect.

3483 [SWIFT, JONATHAN]. Fraud Detected: or, the Hibernian Patriot. Containing, all the Drapier's Letters to the People of Ireland on Wood's Coinage, &c. Interspers'd with the following Particulars... *Dublin, 1725*, *8°*. L.

Another edn. Lond. 1730 [1729], entitled: The Hibernian Patriot: being a Collection of the Drapier's Letters to the People of Ireland...(LU).

3484 The Case of John Browne, Esq; *Lond. 1725*, *8°*. DA.

A reply to Swift's attacks upon him in the Third Drapier Letter.

3485 The Case of John Browne, Esq; In Answer to a Libel, intitled, Observations upon the Report on the Committee of Council in England, relating to Wood's Half-Pence. By M. B. Draper. *Lond. 1725*, *8°*. O.

3486 A Letter to M. B. Drapier. Author of a Letter to the L[d.] Molesworth, &c. *Dublin, 1724–5*, *8°*. DA.

Signed: Misoxulos.

3487 Seasonable Advice to M, B. Drapier. Occasion'd by his Letter to the Rt. Hon. the Lord Visct. Molesworth. *n.p.* [*1725*], *s. sh. F°*. D.

Signed: M.M.

3488 The Humble Address of the House of Lords against Woods Patent. *Dublin reptd, 1725*, *s. sh. F°*. L.

3489 A Letter ascrib'd to the Rt. Honble the Ld C——f J——st——ce W——. *n.p. 1724–5*, *s. sh. F°*. L.

Chief Justice Whitshed. On Wood's halfpence.

3490 Tom Punsibi's Dream. *Dublin, 1724–5*, *s. sh. F°*. DG.

Reprinted in *The Drapier's Letters*, ed. by H. Davis, 1935. Yale copy has a ms. attribution to—Mollineaux, F. C., of Trinity College.

3491 Woods Reviv'd, or, a short Defence of his Proceedings in Bristol, London, &c. in reference to the Kingdom of Ireland. *n.p. 172–5* [sic], *8°*. L.

3492 DE MOIVRE, ABRAHAM. Annuities upon Lives: or, the Valuation of Annuities upon any Number of Lives; as also, of Reversions. To which is added, An Appendix concerning the Expectations of Life, and Probabilities of Survivorship. *Lond. 1725*, *8°*. L.

2nd edn. corrected, Dublin, 1731 (DNL); another 2nd edn. Lond. 1743 (O); 3rd edn. Lond. 1750 (O); 4th edn. Lond. 1752 (O).

3493 A Letter from a Citizen to J—— B——, Esq; Member of Parliament, relating to the York Buildings Company's Affairs. *n.p.* [*1725?*], *F°*. L.

Signed: D.C. Opposing their financial schemes.

3494 An Abstract of the Settlement of the Westminster Contributionship, for Insuring Houses, &c. from Loss by Fire, including the Additions made by the Members, at their General Meetings. *n.p.* [*1725?*], *F°*. L.

Another edn. *c.* 1730 (MC).

3495 A Proposal for Insuring Houses by the Friendly Society. *n.p.* [*c. 1725?*], *s. sh. F°*. E.

TRANSPORT

3496 BADESLADE, THOMAS. The History of the Ancient and Present State of the Navigation of the Port of King's-Lyn, and of Cambridge, and the rest of the Trading-Towns in those Parts: and of the Navigable Rivers that have their Course through the Great-Level of the Fens, called Bedford Level. Also the History of the Ancient and Present State of Draining in that Level, in the Province of Marshland, and the Hundreds and Parts adjacent. From Authentick Records, and Ancient Manuscripts, and from Observations and Surveys carefully made upon the Spot these Three Years last past. With the Method propos'd for draining the said Fens, and amending the Harbour of Lyn: By Col. John Armstrong. Illustrated with Maps. *Lond. 1725*, *F°*. O.

Another edn. 1766 (O).

3497 PERRY, JOHN. Remarks on the Reasonings and different Opinions laid down in some late Printed Propositions for restoring the Navigation of the Ports of King's-Lynn and Wisbich; and Draining of the great Levels, which have the Outfall of their Waters by the Rivers Ouse and the Nean, thro Mortons-Leam.... *n.p.* [*1725*], *F°*. L.

3498 A Bill to Enable the Pier-Wardens of the Town of Margat in the County of Kent, more effectually to recover the Ancient and Customary Droits, for the Support and Maintenance of the said Pier. *n.p.* [*1725*], *F°*. L.

3499 PERRY, JOHN. A Method propos'd for making a safe and convenient Entrance to the Port of Dublin for Ships of Burthen to come in and go out by Day or Night at Low-water; without those Hazards, Loss of Opportunity of Winds and Difficulties they now are expos'd to in their Voyages. Together with an Estimate of the Charge that will be required for effecting the same, *n.p.* [*1725*], *F°*. LU.

3500 John Perry, Appellant. William Boswell, Respondent. The Appellant's Case. *n.p.* [*1725*], *F°*. L.

Signed: E. Probyn. Phil. Ward. On works at Dagenham Breach.

3501 John Perry, Appellant. William Boswell, Respondent. The Respondent's Case. *n.p.* [*1725*], *F°*. L.

Signed: C. Wearg. Tho. Lutwyche.

3502 A Bill for the better Regulating the Company of Watermen, Wherrymen, and Lightermen of the River of Thames. *n.p.* [*1725*], *F°*. L.

3503 [COSTILLOE, STEPHEN]. Heads of a Scheme for making the Principal Rivers of Ireland Navigable: containing, 1. A Brief View of the Design, Method and Expence of this Service. 2. A List and Description of the several Rivers, with their Course, Extent, Situation and Communication one with another. And, Lastly, A Supplemental Scheme for Executing this Service, with a Saving to all private Properties, and without Expence or Hazard to the Publick, til the Work is Finish't to their Hand. [*Dublin, 1725*], *F*°. Kress 3602.

L has an imperfect copy. Authorship deduced from the following entry.

3504 Heads of a Scheme for Making the Considerable Rivers of Ireland Navigable, Abstracted into a Brief View of the Design, Method, and Expence of that Service. *n.p.* [*1725?*], *s. sh. F*°. C.

Endorsed: The Humble Petition of Stephen Costilloe, in Behalf of Himself and Mortimer Heylen.

3505 A Bill for making more Effectual an Act passed in the Parliament holden in the Twelfth Year of the Reign of Her late Majesty Queen Anne; intitled, An Act for making the River Nine or Nen, running from Northampton to Peterborough, Navigable. *n.p.* [*1725*], *F*°. L.

3506 The Case in relation to a Clause desired to be inserted in the Bill for making more Effectual an Act passed in the Parliament holden in the Twelfth Year of the Reign of Her late Majesty Queen Anne, intituled, An Act for making the River Nine or Nen, running from Northampton to Peterborough, Navigable. *n.p.* [*1725*], *F*°. L.

Endorsed: The Case in relation to a Clause for Preserving Northampton Water-Works.... Addressed to the Lords by William Wykes, the proprietor.

3507 Mr. Wykes's Case in relation to a Saving Clause desired to be inserted in the Bill for making more Effectual an Act passed in the Parliament holden in the Twelfth Year of the Reign of Her late Majesty Queen Anne, intituled, An Act for making the River Nine or Nen, running from Northampton to Peterborough, Navigable. *n.p.* [*1725*], *F*°. LLI.

3508 The Case in relation to a Clause in the Bill for making more Effectual an Act passed in the Parliament holden in the Twelfth Year of the Reign of Her late Majesty Queen Anne, intituled, An Act for making the River Nine or Nen, running from Northampton to Peterborough, Navigable. *n.p.* [*1725*], *F*°. LLI.

Endorsed: The Case in relation to a Clause for Preserving Northampton Water-Works.... Addressed to the Commons by William Wykes, the proprietor.

3509 A letter from a gentleman in White's chocolate-house, to his friend at the Smyrna coffee-house. *Lond. 1725, 19½ cm.* Kress 3606.

Chiefly on a projected canal between Leith and Edinburgh.

3510 A Bill for Repairing and Amending the ancient Road from a Town called Biggleswade, in the County of Bedford, to Bugden, and through Alconberry to the Top of Alconberry-Hill, or Cross-Post, leading into Sautcry-Lane, on the York and Edinburgh Road, in the County of Huntingdon. *n.p.* [*1725*], *F*°. L.

3511 Reasons Humbly Offered Against Changing the Ancient Northern Road from Biggleswade through Bugden, and so on to Alconberry-Hill, by the Way of Waresley, Croxton, Graveley, and Godmanchester, through the Town of Huntingdon. *n.p.* [*1725*], *s. sh. F*°. L.

3512 A Bill for Enlarging the Term granted by an Act passed in the Sixth Year of the Reign of her late Majesty Queen Anne, intituled, An Act for the better Amendment of that Way which leads from Cherrill, through Calne, to Studley-Bridge, in the County of Wilts; and for making the said Act more effectual. *n.p.* [*1726*], *F*o. L.

3513 A Bill for the Repairing Part of the Road from London to Cambridge, beginning at that End of the Parish of Foulmire, in the County of Cambridge, next to Barly, in the County of Hertford, and ending at the the [*sic*] Pavement in Trumpington Street, in the said Town of Cambridge. *n.p.* [*1725*], *F*o. L.

3514 A Bill for Inlarging the Term Granted by an Act made in the Eighth Year of the Reign of her late Majesty Queen Anne; intitled, An Act for Repairing and Amending the Highways, leading from Seven-Oaks, to Woodgate and Tunbridge-Wells, in the County of Kent; and for Explaining and making more Effectual the same Act. *n.p.* [*1725*], *F*o. L.

3515 A Bill for Enlarging the Term granted by an Act passed in the Ninth Year of the Reign of Her Late Majesty Queen Anne, Intituled, An Act for Repairing the Highways from Sheetbridge in the Parish of Petersfield, to the Town of Portsmouth in the County of Southampton; and for making the said Act more effectual. *n.p.* [*1725*], *F*o. L.

3516 A Bill for Enlarging the Term granted by an Act passed in the Fifth Year of the Reign of her late Majesty Queen Anne, Intitled, An Act for Repairing the Highways between Sheppard's Shord, and the Devizes, and between the Top of Ashlington Hill and Rowdford in the County of Wilts: And for Explaining the said Act, and making the same more Effectual and Extensive. *n.p.* [*1725*], *F*o. L.

3517 A Bill for repairing and widening the Road from Sherbrook-Hill, near Buxton and Chappel in the Firth, in the County of Derby, to Manchester, in the County of Lancaster. *n.p.* [*1725*], *F*o. L.

3518 A Bill for Repairing the several Roads leading from the Stones-End in the Parish of St. Martins's in the Fields, to Counter's-Bridge in the Parish of Kensington, and to Fulham-Ferry and North-End; and from the Stones-End in James-Street Westminster, to Chelsea-Ferry, and from thence to Kensington; and from Hyde-Park-Corner to the Road leading from Westminster to Chelsea in the County of Middlesex *n.p.* [*1725*], *F*o. L.

3519 A Bill to Enable to Justices of the Peace for the East Riding of the County of York, to take down the County Bridge, called Stanford-Bridge; and to build a Stone Bridge, at a more convenient Place, over the River Darwent, in the said Riding, instead thereof. *n.p.* [*1725*], *F*o. L.

3520 An exact List of all the Stage Coaches and Carriers. With the Days they set out from London... *Lond.* [*1725?*], *s. sh. F*o. L.

SOCIAL CONDITIONS

3521 THWAITES, THOMAS. A Proposal humbly dedicated to the King, Lords and Commons of Great-Brittain; Setting forth the Manner how we may very profitably Employ our now Idle, Chargeable, Young, Weak, Feeble, and Aged Poor.... *n.p.* [*1725?*], *4°.* L.

For the use of his 'New Invented Spinning Engines'.

3522 An Account of several Work-Houses for Employing and Maintaining the Poor; setting forth the Rules by which they are Governed, their great Usefulness to the Publick, and in particular to the Parishes where they are Erected. As also of several Charity-Schools for Promoting Work, and Labour. *Lond. 1725*, 8°. L.

2nd edn., very much enlarged, 1732 (O).

3523 Rules and Orders to be observed by the Officers and Servants in St. Giles's Work-house, and by the Poor therein. *n.p.* [*1726*], *8°.* L.

3524 The Case of Inhabitants of the Eastward, Southward, Northward, and Westward, within the City of Gloucester, paying Three-Pence per Week in their own Right, to the Relief of the Poor of the said City: Humble Petitioners to the Right Honourable the Lords Spiritual and Temporal, in Parliament assembled, against the Bill now depending before their Lordships, intituled, An Act for the Repealing an Act of Parliament made in the First Year of Her late Majesty Queen Anne, intituled, An Act for the Incorporating certain Persons, for the better providing for, and setting at Work, the Poor of the City of Gloucester.... *n.p.* [*1725*], *F°.* LLI.

Endorsed: The Case of the Petitioners against the Bill relating to the Gloucester Charity.

3525 PARFECT, CALEB. Proposals made in the Year 1720. to the Parishioners of Stroud, near Rochester in Kent, for Building a Work-House there; With an Account of the good Success thereof: And likewise of several Work-Houses in Essex, &c.... By the Minister of Stroud. *Lond. 1725*, *4°.* LU.

The author's name is given p. 11.

3526 PARKYNS, Sir THOMAS. A Sketch and Design of a geeneral [*sic*] Act of Parliament, for the Building, Repairing, Enlarging, and Finishing of Halls, Goals, Prisons, with Work-Houses underneath them, or otherwise, in their respective Counties throughout Great-Britain. *Nottingham, 1725*, *4°.* L.

3527 Orders to be observed by the Pensioners and Servants entertain'd in the Royal Hospital for Seamen at Greenwich. *n.p.* [*c. 1725?*], *s. sh. F°.* C (Cr).

3528 A True Copy of the Last Will and Testament of Thomas Guy, Esq; late of Lombard-street, Bookseller: containing an Account of his Publick and Private Benefactions. *Lond. 1725*, *8°.* O.

3529 An Act for Vesting in Trustees several Lands, Tenements and Hereditaments in the Counties of York and Derby, for the Maintenance of the poor Persons in the Hospital of Gilbert Earl of Shrewsbury, long since deceased, situate at Sheffield, in the said County of York, and for enlarging the Buildings of the said Hospital, and adding more poor Persons to those already established therein. [*Lond. 1725*], *F°*. LHL.

A bill.

3530 An Account of the Foundation of the Royal Hospital of King Charles II. &c. near Dublin, for the Relief and Maintenance of Antient and Maimed Officers and Soldiers of the Army of Ireland.... *Dublin, 1725, 12°*. L.

Dedication signed: Richard Colley. A later edn. of no. 1943.

3531 MANDEVILLE, BERNARD. An Enquiry into the Causes of the Frequent Executions at Tyburn: and a Proposal for some Regulations concerning Felons in Prison.... To which is added, a Discourse on Transportation, and a Method to render that Punishment more Effectual. *Lond. 1725, 8°*. L.

3532 MACKENZIE, RODERICK. Some Necessary Observations on an Act of the last Sessions of Parliament, intituled, An Act for the Relief of Insolvent Debtors, Shewing that (if duly executed, and adverted to by the Creditors themselves, either before or after the Execution thereof) the said Act is Calculated and Enacted, by the Parliament, with equal Regard to the Interest of the Creditors, as to the Relief of those Prisoners for Debt, who are deemed real Objects of Compassion.... With an Appendix, touching a very Extraordinary case, now depending.... *Lond. 1725, F°*. L.

3533 Some Observations upon the Act to prevent Frivolous and Vexatious Arrests. *Lond. 1725, 8°*. LU.

Another edn. 1726 (O).

3534 The Case of divers Poor Distressed Persons, who are under Restraint, although not Actually in Prison. *n.p.* [*c. 1725?*], *s. sh. F°*. LLI.

3535 The Case of the Insolvent Debtors, now in Prison. *n.p.* [*c. 1725?*], *s. sh. F°*. LLI.

3536 A Bill to prevent Violences and Outrages being committed by any Persons, under pretence of sheltering themselves from Debt, or any Process of Law, either within the Hamlet of Wapping-Stepney, &c. *n.p.* [*1725*], *F°*. L.

3537 Reasons humbly offered for Passing the Bill now depending, to prevent Violences and Outrages being committed by any Persons under Pretence of sheltering themselves from Debt, or any Process of Law, either within the Hamlet of Wapping, &c. *n.p.* [*1725?*], *s. sh. F°*. L.

3538 The Case of Prisoners for Debt Considered. *Dublin, 1725, 8°*. DNL.

Another edn. Dublin, 1727 (DNL).

3539 Etats de la Distribution de la Somme de Trente Neuf Mille Livres, accordée par Sa Majesté aux Pauvres Protestants François Laiques Refugiez en Angleterre, pour trois Ans & trois Mois finissant au 25 Decembre 1721. Administrée par le Committée François, sous les Ordres des Seigneurs nommez par Sa Majesté, & par la Direction des Messieurs les Commissaires Anglois. *Londres*, *1725*, *F°*. LSC.

3540 A Preface Prefixed to the Account of the Distribution of the Royal Bounty made by the French Committee, for three Years and a Quarter, ending the 25th of December 1721. Preface du Compte de trois Années & un Quartier de la Beneficence Royale, faite par le Committé François. *n.p.* [*c. 1725?*], *F°*. OC.

English and French in parallel columns.

3541 GRAY, GALFRIDUS. An Effectual Proposal for Manning the Royal Navy. And Prevent the Former Abuse thereof. Also will save many Thousand Pounds per Annum. *n.p.* [*1725*], *F°*. LLI.

3542 [DEFOE, DANIEL]. Every-Body's Business, is No-Body's Business; or, Private Abuses, Publick Grievances: exemplified in the Pride, Insolence, and Exorbitant Wages of our Women-Servants, Footmen, &c. With a Proposal for amendment of the same; as also for clearing the Streets of those Vermin call'd Shoe-Cleaners, and substituting in their stead many Thousands of Industrious Poor, now ready to starve. With divers other Hints, of great Use to the Publick....By Andrew Moreton, Esq; [pseudonym]. *Lond.* *1725*, *8°*. L.

2nd edn. 1725 (L); 3rd, 1725 (L); 4th, 1725 (L); 5th, 1725 (O); another 5th edn., *Dublin*, 1725 (D). For authorship see *C.B.E.L.* II, 508.

3543 Every Man mind his Own Business, or Private Piques no Publick Precedents: being an Answer to a late Scurrilous Pamphlet, intitul'd Every-Body's Business is No-Body's Business.... By Catherine Comb-Brush, Lady's Woman. *Lond.* *1725*, *8°*. E.

3544 SEDGWICK, JAMES. A New Treatise on Liquors, wherein the Use and Abuse of Wine, Malt Drinks, Water, &c. are consider'd. *Lond.* *1725*, *8°*. L.

3545 A Bill for supplying the Cities of London and Westminster, and Places Adjacent, with Water, to be taken from Cowley Stream below Uxbridge, and brought to some Place in or near the Parish of St. Mary la Bonne. *n.p.* [*1725*], *F°*. L.

3546 The Case of the New Project for Bringing Water to London and Westminster, Considered. *n.p.* [*1725*], *s. sh. F°*. LU.

3547 Observations upon the Bill now Depending, for Supplying the Cities of London and Westminster, and Places Adjacent, with Water. *n.p.* [*1725*], *s. sh. F°*. LU.

3548 A Plann of the design for makeing the Rivr. Coln from Watford in Com. Hertford navigable: as also, y[e] cut from y[e] Cowly-Stream, below y[e] town of Uxbridge; for ye better supplying ye cities of Lond^n^. & Westminster wth water wch tis propos'd shall be likewise made navigable to some convenient place in or near, Cavendish Square, in ye parish of Mary le Bone. [*n.p.*, *1725?*], *56 × 53 cm.* Kress S. 1628.

3549 A Plan of the Streams, intended to be made use of, or that can be any ways Affected, by Bringing the water of the Cowley Stream, to Supply the Citys of London and Westminster. *n.p.* [*1725*], *F^o^*, L.

The heading to the letterpress is: The Design is to bring the Water of the Cowley-Stream in to Marybonne-Feilds.

3550 A Short State of the Case in support of the Petition to Parliament for Bringing Water to London, in a Canal to be made navigable from the River Colne below Uxbridge to Marybone, and for making the Petitioners and the Chelsea Company one United Company with a Joint Stock. *n.p.* [*1725?*], *F^o^*. LG.

With a map.

3551 Reasons Against the Navigable-Scheme. *n.p.* [*1725*], *s. sh. F^o^*. L.

3552 An Answer to the Reasons against the Navigable Scheme. *n.p.* [*1725*], *s. sh. F^o^*. L.

3553 To the Honourable the House of Commons the Humble Petition of Robert Bumpstead, in the Behalf of Himself and several others. *n.p.* [*1725?*], *s. sh. F^o^*. L.

For a saving clause on behalf of his pumping engine in the bill to bring water to London from Uxbridge.

3554 To the Right Honourable the House of Lords Spiritual and Temporal, the Humble Petition of Robert Bumpsted, in the Behalf of Himself and several Others. *n.p.* [*1725?*], *s. sh. F^o^*. MC.

See the preceding.

3555 *Begin.* Sir, I Thank you for your candid Answer to my last, and am now sensible of your good Advice in bidding me not to be too supine in believing that the Projector of the Gulchwell Springs Scheme would lay it aside.... *n.p.* [*1725?*], *s. sh. F^o^*. L.

Signed: J. T. D——rs.

3556 For the Benefit of the Publick. An Agreement of the Church-Wardens of the several Parishes in the City and Suburbs of Dublin, at a Meeting on the 19th of November, 1725. *Dublin*, [*1725*], *s. sh. F^o^*. OUP.

On lighting and keeping clean the streets.

3557 A Bill for the better Regulating of Buildings, and to prevent Mischiefs that may happen by Fire. *n.p.* [*1725*]. *F^o^*. L.

1726

GENERAL

3558 [DEFOE, DANIEL ?]. An Essay, on Ways and Means for the Advancement of Trade, and for paying off in a few years, the Debts of the Nation, without laying an additional Burden on Land. *Lond. 1726*, *8°*. LU.

For authorship see *C.B.E.L.* II, 508. Professor J. R. Moore rejects the attribution.

3559 The True State of England. Containing, Lists of the King's Houshold. ...Of the Great Officers of State, and the several other Officers employ'd in the Civil and Military Government of this Kingdom. Together with the particular Duty, Business and Salary of each Officer.... To which is added, A Compleat List of the Knights of the Bath, and their Esquires....Also, An Account of the Government of the City of London, with the Names of the Magistrates, Principal Officers, &c. *Lond. 1726*, *8°*. L.

Another edn., entitled: The True State of England. Containing the particular Duty, Business and Salary of every Officer, civil and military in all the Publick Offices of Great Britain..... 1729 (L); another edn. 1734 (LU).

AGRICULTURE

3560 BRADLEY, RICHARD. The Country Gentleman and Farmer's Monthly Director. Containing Necessary Instructions for the Management and Improvement of a Farm, in every Month of the Year.... *Lond. 1726*, *8°*. L.

Another edn. Dublin, 1727 (DNL); 2nd edn. 1727 (L); 3rd, 1727 (O); 6th, 1732 (L); another 6th edn. 1736 (WDA).

3561 LAURENCE, JOHN. A New System of Agriculture. Being a Complete Body of Husbandry and Gardening in all the parts of them. Viz. Husbandry in the Field, and its several Improvements. Of Forest and Timber Trees....Of the Fruit-Garden. Of the Kitchen-Garden. Of the Flower-Garden.... *Lond. 1726*, *F°*. L.

Another edn. Dublin, 1727, F° (L).

3562 The Gentleman Farmer: or, Certain Observations made by an English Gentleman, upon the Husbandry of Flanders...Also a certain Method of Improving Meadow Grounds from Forty Shillings to Six Pounds an Acre, by Fish-ponds. Written by a Person of Honour in the County of Norfolk. *Lond. 1726*, *12°*. L.

Pt. 1 is a revised and abridged version of Sir Richard Weston's *A Discours of Husbandrie used in Brabant and Flanders*, 1650; pt. 2 is a reprint of Roger North's *A Discourse of Fish and Fish-Ponds*, 1713 (no. 1804).

3563 TOWNSEND, BENJAMIN. The Complete Seedsman: shewing the best and easiest Method for raising and cultivating Every Sort of Seed belonging to a Kitchen and Flower-Garden...Recommended by Richard Bradley. *Lond. 1726*, 8°. O.

The 2nd edn., 1738 (L), entitled: The Compleat Seedsman's Monthly Calendar....By Richard Bradley, has a preface explaining that Townsend's name on the first edition was 'only put to it by the Author to do him a service, by bringing him into business'.

3564 The Grasier's Complaint and Petition for Redress: or, The Necessity of Restraining Irish Wool and Yarn; and of Raising and Supporting the Price of Wool of the Growth of Great-Britain, Consider'd. By a Lincolnshire Grasier. *Lond. 1726*, 8°. L.

3565 A great Number of the Nobility and Gentry having come to a Resolution to encourage the wearing of Home made Linnen Cloth, the Honourable Society for improving in the Knowledge of Agriculture have advised the Publishing of the following Rules for propagating and dressing of Lint and Hemp, and for bleaching and whitning of Linnen Cloth. *n.p.* [*1726*], 8°. E.

3566 An Act for Dischacing and Disfranchising the Chace of Alrewas-Hay in the County of Stafford; and for the Impowering of John Turton, Esq; Owner thereof, to Enclose a Part of such Chace, and for other Purposes in the said Act mentioned. *n.p.* [*1726*], *F°*. LHL.

3567 An Act for Inclosing several Common Fields, in the Parish of Bubnel alias Bobenhull, in the County of Warwick. *n.p.* [*1726*], *F°*. L.

A bill.

3568 An Act for Dividing and Inclosing, or Holding in Severalty, the Common Field within the Parish of Compton-Basset, in the County of Wilts. *n.p.* [*1726*], *F°*. L.

A bill.

3569 An Act for confirming several Awards for Enclosing and Dividing the common Fields and common Grounds, within the Manors of Fangfosse cum Spittle, and Scagglethorpe, in the County of York. *n.p.* [*1726*], *F°*. O.

3570 A Bill for appointing Commissioners to make a Division of certain Common-Field Lands, and Wastes, in the Townships of Scarcliffe and Palterton in the County of Derby, among the Proprietors, in order to enclose the same. *n.p.* [*1726*], *F°*. L.

3571 [Stonyclift, R.]. Proposals and Inducements for a considerable number of People, to join in the Purchas of several thousands Acres, of Drein'd and Derelict Lands, in several Counties of England, which will redound to the vast Advantage of the Purchasors....And most of these Lands proposed, having been under the same circumstances with those of Bedford Level, the History of that Level, is annexed on.... *Lond. 1726*, 8°. L.

Signed: R.S. Authorship inferred from note asking those interested to apply to Mr. Stonyclift at Clifford's Inn.

3572 A Bill for the more effectual Draining and Preservation of the North Division of the Great Level of the Fenns called Bedford Level, by a new Outfall to Sea. *n.p.* [*1726*], *F*o. L.

3573 A Brief Case of the Lincolnshire Petitioners, against the Bedford Level Bill. *n.p.* [*1726?*], *s. sh. F*o. C (Cr).

3574 The Case of the Inhabitants of South-Holland, in the County of Lincoln, in relation to the Bill now depending in the Honourable House of Commons, For the more Effectual Draining and Preserving the North Level, and divers Lands adjoining thereto, in the Manor of Crowland, is thus.... *n.p.* [*1726*], *F*o. L.

3575 Observations on the Reasons for passing the Bill for the more effectual Dreyning and Preservation of the North Division of the Great Level of the Fenns, called Bedford-Level, by a New Outfall to Sea. *n.p.* [*1726*], *F*o. L.

3576 The Laws of Sewers; or the Office and Authority of Commissioners of Sewers. Containing, I. Their Power of Enquiry into Annoyances and Defects of Repair, of Sea-Banks and Walls, publick Streams and Rivers, Ditches and Marsh-Grounds. II. The Authority of the Commissioners in making Laws and Ordinances....III. Of their Power by Law as to Distresses....To which are added, The Laws relating to Rumney-Marsh, and other Marshes and Fens. *Lond. 1726, 8*o. LU.
2nd edn. 1732 (L).

MANUFACTURES

3577 Carter, Edmund. The Artificer's Looking-Glass: containing an exact and diverting Representation of the Lives, Conduct, Characters, and various Humours of the following Professors; as it was taken from their own Mouths, in their several respective Addresses to Mother Art. viz. Limners, Stone-Carvers, Glass Blowers, Frame-work-knitters, Taylors, Hatters, Carpenters, Joyners, Brick-layers, Sawyers, Plaisterers, Glaziers, Weavers, Wine-Coopers, Potters, Dancing-Masters, Pipe-Makers, Watch-Makers, &c. *Lond. 1726, 8*o. L.

3578 Bill to prevent abuses in making of bricks and tiles, and to ascertain the dimensions thereof. [*n.p. 1726?*], *32 cm.* Kress S. 1649.

3579 The Case of the Brick-layers and Builders in and near London, (upon the Discovery of some Brick-makers,) humbly offer'd to the Consideration of the Honourable House of Commons. *n.p.* [*1726?*], *s. sh. F*o. MC.

3580 Langley, Batty. Practical Geometry applied to the useful Arts of Building, Surveying, Gardening, and Mensuration; calculated for the Service of Gentlemen as well as Artisans.... *Lond. 1726, F*o. O.
2nd edn. 1729 (O).

3581 [Defoe, Daniel]. A brief Case of the Distillers, and of the Distilling Trade in England, shewing how far it is the Interest of England to encourage the said Trade, as it is so considerble an Advantage to the Landed Interest, to the Trade and Navigation, to the Publick Revenue, and to the Employment of the Poor.... *Lond. 1726, 8o.* L.

For authorship see *C.B.E.L.* II, 508.

3582 A modest plea for the British distillery. In a letter from a country gentleman, to a member of Parliament.... *London, T. Warner [etc.] 1726, 21·5 cm.* Kress S. 1661.

3583 Notice hereby given to the Publick, of the several useful Inventions, and Engines to raise and force Water: Invented and made by me John Fowke, in Ten-foot-way Nightingale Lane, Wapping, at present an Apprentice to a Plumber; prepared and sold in a fair way of Trade, for the use of my Master, at a moderate Price, without any Pretence to Monopoly, by Patent, or otherwise. *n.p. [1726?], s. sh. Fo.* LG.

3584 Reasons humbly offered to the Legislature of these Nations, by the Workers in Small Silver-Wares in and about the City of London, shewing, Why the Standard Silver of England should be Marked at Goldsmiths-Hall, at a Reasonable Price as in Other Nations. *n.p. [1726?], s. sh. Fo.* L.

3585 Information for the Magistrates and Town Council of Glasgow, against the Proprietors of the Sugar-houses. *n.p. [1726], Fo.* E.

Dated: February 8th, 1726. Signed: James Grahame. With the texts of the acts erecting the sugar houses. The case concerns exemption from tax.

3586 Information for the Easter, Wester, and South Sugar Manufactories in Glasgow, against the Magistrates and Town-council of Glasgow, &c. *n.p. [1726], Fo.* E.

Dated: Feb. 14. 1726. Signed: Cha. Areskine.

3587 An Account of the Journey-men Weavers grateful Congratulation of the Rev. Dr. Swift Dean of St. Patrick's safe Arrival, with his kind Answer, and Bounty to their Corporation, Sep. the 5th 1726. *Dublin, 1726, s. sh. Fo.* C.

COMMERCE

3588 Middx. ss. Ad general' session' pacis Dom' Regis tent' pro com' Middx' apud Hicks-hall in St. John street in com' praed' per adjor' die Jovis scilicet vicesimo tertio die februar' anno Regni Dom' Georgij nunc Regis Magne Britanie, &c. decimo tertio.... *[n.p. 1726], 35·5 × 28 cm.* Kress S. 1647.

Begins: Whereas upon information given unto the Court of the last general quarter sessions of the peace...Refers to dishonesty in inspecting weights and measures on the part of Thomas Robe and John Matthews.

3589 By the Right Honourable the Lord Provost and Magistrates of the City of Edinburgh. The Assize of Bread made of Wheat... to be observed and kept by all Bakers and others, within the City and Liberties thereof, and by the Bakers and others who bring Bread to the Markets of this City for Sale. *n.p.* [*1726*], *s. sh. F*°. E.

3590 The Importance of the Ostend-Company Consider'd. *Lond. 1726, 8*°. LU.

On the threat to our commerce and that of the Dutch.

3591 The Captains Directory, being translated Extracts of the Proclamation of the High & Mighty Lords the States General of the United Netherlands relative to Foreign Ships trading to and from Holland. Also a List of the Customs in Holland inwards & outwards; to which is added, a List of such Goods as are exempt from Premium; Goods subject to Excise; List of Pile Dues, Weights, Measures, Tunnage, & Coins... the Cost of Ballast &c[a]. By T. M. English Ships Broker, at Rotterdam. *Lond.* [*1726?*], *4*°. L.

3592 By-Laws, Orders and Rules, for the Good Government of the Corporation of the Governor and Company of Merchants of Great Britain trading to the South Seas, and other Parts of America, and for Encouraging the Fishery; and for the better Carrying on and Managing the Trade of the said Company. [*Lond.*], *1726, F*°. LU.

3593 A copy of the remonstrance of the merchants and traders, buyers of piece goods, to the Court of the directors of the United East-India company and also of the two representations delivered by the committee of merchants, &c. to the committee appointed by the Court of directors to enquire into the hardships and complaints of the buyers at the Company's sales. Recommended to the serious consideration of the proprietors of East-India stock. *London, 1726, 32 cm.* Kress S. 1644.

3594 SHELVOCKE, GEORGE. A Voyage round the World by the way of the Great South Sea, perform'd in the years 1719, 20, 21, 22, in the Speedwell of London, of 24 Guns and 100 men, (under His Majesty's Commission to cruize on the Spaniards in the late War with the Spanish Crown) till she was cast away on the Island of Juan Fernandes, in May 1720; and afterwards continu'd in the Recovery, the Jesus Maria and Sacra Familia, &c. *Lond. 1726, 8*°. L.

Another edn., edited by W. G. Perrin, 1928; another edn. 1930.

3595 The Four Years Voyages of Capt. George Roberts; being a Series of Uncommon Events, which befell him in a Voyage to the Islands of the Canaries, Cape de Verde, and Barbadoes, from whence he was bound to the Coast of Guiney....With a particular and curious Description and Draught of the Cape de Verd Islands....Written by Himself, and interspers'd with many Pleasant and Profitable Remarks, very instructive for all those who use this Trade.... *Lond. 1726, 8*°. O.

Attributed to Daniel Defoe in *C.B.E.L.* II, 508, and by Professor J. R. Moore. An abridged edn., ed. by A. W. Lawrence, and entitled *A Series of Uncommon Events which befell Capt. George Roberts*, was published in 1930.

3596 A Discourse of the Laws relating to Pirates and Piracies, and the Marine Affairs of Great Britain. *Lond. 1726, 8*°. LU.

COLONIES

3597 PENHALLOW, SAMUEL. The History of the Wars of New-England, with the Eastern Indians. Or, a Narrative of their continued Perfidy and Cruelty, from the 10th of August, 1703. to the Peace renewed 13th of July, 1713. and from the 25th of July, 1722. to their Submission 15th December, 1725. which was Ratified August 5th 1726. *Boston, 1726, 8°.* L.

3598 HOSKINS, JAMES. The Pensilvania Bubble bubbled by the Treasurer, or, An Account of his Admitting Purchasers for Shares, Lodging 8478l. 12s. in the Bank of England, and the Sale of his Lands in Pensilvania to the Company. With an Estimate of how much of the Company's Money he plac'd to his own Account, and of the Loss the Company has sustain'd by him. Together with the Judgment of the Seven Arbitrators in his Favour, and the Reasons of the Five other Arbitrators offer'd in Arrest of Judgment. With Remarks on the Whole. *Lond. 1726, 4°.* L.

3599 [BOCKETT, ELIAS]. The Wit and Honesty of James Hoskins, &c. consider'd in Remarks on their late Pamphlet, call'd the Pennsylvania Bubble. By the Translator of the Pattern of Modesty. *Lond. 1726, 8°.* L.

For authorship see Sabin 6108.

3600 The Interest of the Country in laying Duties: or, a Discourse, shewing how Duties on some Sorts of Merchandize may make the Province of New-York richer than it would be without them. *New-York, [1726], 8°.* L.

3601 The Interest of City and Country to Lay No Duties: or A short Discourse shewing that Duties on Trade, tend to the Impoverishing City and Country.... *New-York, 1726, 8°.* L.

3602 The Two Interests Reconciled: occasioned by two late Pamphlets, called The Interest of the Country and The Interest of City and Country. *New-York, 1726, 8°.* L.

3603 YONGE, FRANCIS. A Narrative of the Proceedings of the People of South-Carolina, in the Year 1719: and of the True Causes and Motives that induced them to Renounce their Obedience to the Lords Proprietors, as their Governors, and to put themselves under the immediate Government of the Crown. *Lond. 1726, 4°.* L.

Reprinted in P. Force, *Tracts and other Papers*, vol. 2 (1838), no. 10.

3604 The Liberty and Property of British Subjects asserted: in a Letter from an Assembly-man in Carolina, to his Friend in London. *Lond. 1726, 8°.* L.

Signed: J—— N——

FINANCE

3605 Advantages which have Accrued to the Publick, and to the South-Sea Company, by the Execution of the South-Sea Scheme. *n.p. 1726*, 8°. L.

Another edn. 1728 (LU).

3606 [GOULD, Sir NATHANIEL]. An Essay on the Publick Debts of this Kingdom. Wherein the Importance of discharging them is considered; the Provisions for that Purpose by the Sinking Fund, and the Progress therein hitherto made, are stated and explained; the Sufficiency of those Provisions are demonstrated...and the Progress of the Sinking Fund described and computed from Midsummer, 1727. To which is subjoined, An Enquiry into the General Convenience of reducing farther the Interest of our Publick Debts below 4 per Cent. per Annum.... *Lond. 1726*, 8°. L.

2nd and 3rd edns. 1726; 4th, 1727 (all L). Reprinted, with author's name, in *A Select Collection of...Tracts...on the National Debt*, ed. by J. R. McCulloch, 1857, p. 47.

3607 Remarks on a late Book, intitled, An Essay on the Publick Debts of this Kingdom, &c. In which the evil Tendency of that Book, and the Design of its Author, are fully detected and exposed.... In a Letter to a Member of the House of Commons. *Lond. 1727* [*1726*], 8°. LU.

2nd edn. 1727 (L).

3608 Justice Vindicated; or, an Explanation of an Act of Parliament, entitl'd, An Act for granting an Aid to his Majesty, by a Land Tax, &c. Wherein is shewn, what Power and Authority Commissioners and Assessors have, and how they ought to demean themselves. What Evidence is legally required to repute a Man a Papist. What Persons are to be assess'd towards raising the Aid singly, and what doubly; and in what Manner it ought to be assess'd, levied, and collected. In a Letter to a Nobleman. By a Person, who, for many Years hath made the Study of the Laws of England, his only Profession. *Lond.* [*1726*], 8°. L.

Signed: L.M.

3609 The Illegality of Banking, in the Hands of an Officer called a Treasurer, Land-Tax Money, collected in the Parish of St. James Westminster. By a Land-Tax Commissioner, Inhabitant of the said Parish. *Lond. 1726*, *F°*. LU.

3610 A Collection of most of the Penal Laws relating to the Customs and Excise: and also to the Inland Duties, thc Duties on Stamps, and Postage of Letters; Together with the Powers granted by Parliament to the East-India and South-Sea Companies. To which are added, Some brief Observations relating to those Laws. *Lond. 1726*, 8°. L.

The dedication to Micajah Perry signed: J.B.

3611 Instructions for the Officers of the Duties on Silver Plate in the Country. *Lond. 1726, 12°.* LG.

3612 The Case of the Greater Number of the Victuallers, inhabiting within London, Westminster, and the Bills of Mortality, humbly Offered to the Consideration of the Honourable the House of Commons, in relation to a Bill now depending in that Honourable House, for granting an Aid to His Majesty, by laying a Duty upon all Victuallers, and Retailers of Beer and Ale, &c. *n.p.* [*1726*], *s. sh. F°.* L.

3613 Memorial concerning the Malt-Tax. *Edin. 1726, 8°.* LU.

3614 The Case of Mr. Richard Collier. *n.p.* [*1726*], *s. sh. F°.* L.

Against a clause in the Malt Bill which indemnifies master against breaches of the laws relating to duties payable on contracts of apprenticeship.

3615 Reasons humbly offered against the Clause in the present Malt-Tax Bill, for Taking away, or Altering the Bounty and Draw-back, upon the Exportation of Malt. *n.p.* [*1726?*], *s. sh. F°.* L.

3616 JOLLEY, JOHN. The Head-Constable's-Assistant: or, a Mize-Book for the County-Palatine of Cheshire. The same being Tables ready Cast up; whereby any Township's just Proportion of any Tax charged by Way of the Mize, may readily and exactly be known. Composed about Twenty Years ago.... *Lond.* [*1726*], *8°.* L.

3617 SOUTHCOMB, LEWIS. Render to All their Dues: or, a Dialogue between Timotheus and Pleonectes, concerning the Converting Tithes and Offerings to Secular Uses. *Exon, 1726, 8°.* DA.

3618 BENNET, THOMAS. *Begin.* You know, I have been near ten Years Vicar of this Parish, and what Forbearance I have all this while us'd towards yourself and others with respect to my Tyths.... *n.p.* [*1726*], *s. sh. F°.* LG.

Announcing his intention to enforce his rights in the parish of St. Giles, Cripplegate.

3619 [LEAKE, STEPHEN MARTIN]. Nummi Britannici Historia: or an Historical Account of English Money, from the Conquest to the uniting of the two Kingdoms by King James I. and of Great-Britain to the Present Time.... *Lond. M.DC.XXVI* [*1726*], *8°.* LU.

2nd edn. 1745 entitled: A Historical Account of English Money, has author's name; 3rd edn. 1793 (both LU).

3620 ROBERTSON, WILLIAM. A Table of the Exchange, between Scotland and Holland.... *Rotterdam, 1726, 8°.* LU.

3621 HAYES, RICHARD. The Money'd Man's Guide: or, The Purchaser's Pocket Companion. Shewing, at sight, what Interest is made by Money laid out in the Companies Stocks, or any other Publick Funds; and also the present Value of any yearly Income. With the Easiest Method to cast up the present Worth of Funds, Houses, Annuities, Fines, repairs, reversions, &c.... *Lond. 1726, 16°.* OH.

3622 Proposals by the Corporation of the Royal-Exchange Assurance, Establish'd by His Majesty's Royal Charter, for Assuring Houses, and other Buildings, Goods, Wares, and Merchandizes, from Loss and Damage by Fire. [*Lond. 1726*], *s. sh.* 4°. OUP.

Dated: December 15, 1726.

3623 Proposals from The Sun Fire-Office, in Threadneedle-Street, behind the Royal-Exchange, London, For Insuring Houses, Buildings, moveable Goods, Merchandize, Furniture, and Wares, from Loss and Damage by Fire, in any Part of Great Britain, according to the following Articles. *Lond.* [*1726*], *s. sh.* 4°. OUP.

Dated: October 14, 1726.

3624 Articles of Agreement to be sign'd by the Friendly Society of the Heritors of Glasgow & Suburbs thereof; For a Mutual Insurance of Tenements and Houses, &c. from Losses by Fire. *n.p.* [*1726?*], *F*o. E.

3625 Ayres, John. Arithmetick Made Easie, for the Use and Benefit of Trades-Men....The Seventeeth Edition. To which is added, A Short and Easie Method; after which Shop-keepers may State, Post, and Balance their Books of Accompts. By Charles Snell....The Whole perused, and many Errors corrected by E. Hatton. *Lond. 1726*, *12*o. L.

16th edition 1723; 18th [c. 1730] (both L).

TRANSPORT

3626 A Bill for Repairing the Roads leading from Birmingham through Warwick to Warmington, and from Birmingham through Stratford to Edghill, in the County of Warwick. *n.p.* [*1726*], *F*o. L.

3627 A Bill for Repairing the Road between a Place called Cory's Mill, in the County of Hertford, and a Place called Lamsford-Mill, in the same County. *n.p.* [*1726*], *F*o. L.

3628 A Bill for Repairing and Widening the Roads from the City of Gloucester to the City of Hereford. *n.p.* [*1726*], *F*o. L.

3629 A Bill to Enlarge the Term granted by an Act passed in the Fifth Year of the Reign of Her late Majesty Queen Anne, for Repairing the Highway between Hockley and Woburne, in the County of Bedford; and for making the said Act more Effectual. *n.p.* [*1726*], *F*o. L.

3630 A Bill for Repairing and Widening the Road from Horsley-Upright-Gate, leading down Bowden-Hill, in the County of Wilts, to the Top of Kingsdown-Hill in the Parish of Box in the said County. *n.p.* [*1726*], *F*o. L.

3631 A Bill for Repairing the Roads from Crackley Bank in the Parish of Idsall alias Shifnall, to the Town of Shrewsbury in the County of Salop. *n.p.* [*1726*], *F*o. L.

3632 A Bill for Repairing the Road from Market-Harborough to Loughborough, in the County of Leicester. *n.p.* [*1726*], *F*o. L.

3633 A Bill for Repairing the Roads leading from the Town of Shenfield to Harwich, in the County of Essex; and the Road leading from Chelmsford, in the said County, to Sudbury in the County of Suffolk; and from Margreting to Malden; and from the Town of Colchester to the Road called the Severalls, in the said County of Essex. *n.p.* [*1726*], *F*o. L.

3634 A Bill for Amending the Highway, therein mentioned, leading from Speenhamland, in the Parish of Speen, in the County of Berks, to Marlborough, in the County of Wilts. *n.p.* [*1726*], *F*o. L.

3635 A Bill for Repairing the several Roads leading from the Town of Tewksbury in the County of Gloucester, to the several Places therein mentioned. *n.p.* [*1726*], *F*o. L.

3636 The Case of the Inhabitants of the Parish of Breedon in the County of Worcester, and above Thirty other Towns and Parishes in the said County. *n.p.* [*1726*], *s. sh. F*o. L.

Against the Tewkesbury turnpike bill.

3637 The Case of the Inhabitants of the Parish of Twyning in the County of Gloucester, and of many other Towns and Parishes adjoyning thereto, in the County of Worcester. *n.p.* [*1726*], *s. sh. F*o. L.

Against the Tewkesbury turnpike bill.

3638 A Bill for Repairing the several Roads leading into the City of Worcester. *n.p.* [*1726*], *F*o. L.

3639 A Bill for Enlarging the Term granted by an Act passed in the Twelfth Year of the Reign of Her late Majesty Queen Anne, Intitled, An Act for Repairing the Highway or Road from the City of Worcester, to the Borough of Droitwich in the County of Worcester, and for making the same more effectual; and for Repairing the Road leading thro' Droitwich to Dyer's Bridge near Bromsgrove in the said County.... *n.p.* [*1726*], *F*o. L.

3640 A Bill for Building a Bridge cross the River of Thames, from the Town of Fulham, in the County of Middlesex, to the Town of Putney, in the County of Surrey. *n.p.* [*1726*], *F*o. L.

3641 PRICE, JOHN. Some Considerations humbly offer'd to the Honourable Commissioners, appointed by Act of Parliament for Building a Bridge over the River Thames, from Fulham to Putney. Together with Proposals relating to a Design drawn for that Purpose, and exhibited to the said Commissioners. In a letter to a Member of the Honourable Corporation. *n.p. 1726*, *8*o. LU.

3642 Mr. Price's Second Letter to one of the Honourable Commissioners appointed by Act of Parliament for Building a Bridge over the Thames from Fulham to Putney. Together with some Proposals for building a Wooden Bridge according to a Draught and Model deliver'd to a Committee of the said Commissioners. *n.p. 1726*, *8*o. LG.

SOCIAL CONDITIONS

3643 ...Proposals for maintaining of the poor, and discouraging of vagabonds, and vagrant and sturdy beggars.... *Edin. 1726. 19 × 15 cm.* Kress 3662.

3644 [Guevarre, Andrea]. Ways and Means for suppressing Beggary, and relieving the Poor, by erecting General Hospitals, and Charitable Corporations...Translated from the Italian [by Abraham Castres]. *Lond. 1726, 4°.* L.

The original was not anonymous.

3645 Whereas several Parishes have erected Work-houses or Houses of Maintenance for the Poor, whereby they are fed, lodged, cloathed, and wholly maintained, and which are found to be very beneficial upon all Accounts; it is not then amiss to acquaint the Publick what Orders are to be observed by the Masters of them in the Regulation of the Poor under their Charge. Orders Agreed upon by the Parishioners and Inhabitants of the Parish of For the better Regulation of the Poor in the Workhouse of the said Parish. *Lond. 1726, s. sh. F°.* MC.

3646 [Marriot, John]. A Representation of Some Mismanagements by Parish-Officers in the Method at present followed for Maintaining the Poor: with a Proposal humbly offered for Rectifying the Same. In a Letter to a Friend. *Lond. 1726. 8°.* L.

For authorship see ms. note on L copy: 'by John Marriot Governor of St. Giles's Work-house'.

3647 At a Meeting of the Vestry at the Work-House, on Tuesday the Fifteenth Day of March 1726, for the better Government and Management of the Work-House, and in Order to the better Observance and Execution of the Orders already made and to be made; it is Agreed and Ordered.... *n.p. [1726], s. sh. F°.* L.

B.M. Catalogue identifies the parish as St. Giles in the Fields.

3648 Regulations Agreed upon and Established this Twelfth Day of July 1726. by the Gentlemen of the Vestry then present, for the better Government and Management of the Work-House belonging to the Parish of St. Giles's in the Fields. *n.p. [1726], 8°.* O.

3649 [Defoe, Daniel]. The Protestant Monastery: or, a Complaint against the Brutality of the present Age. Particularly the Pertness and Insolence of our Youth to aged Persons. With a Caution to People in Years, how they give the Staff out of their own Hands, and leave themselves at the Mercy of others. Concluding with a Proposal for erecting a Protestant Monastery, where Persons of small Fortunes may end their Days in Plenty, Ease, and Credit, without burthening their Relations, or accepting Publick Charities. By Andrew Moreton [pseud.]. *Lond. 1727 [1726], 8°.* DA.

For authorship see *C.B.E.L.* II, 509.

3650 The Articles of the Foundation of King George's College, that is to be open'd upon the Birthday of Her Royal Highness the Most Illustrious Princess of Wales. *Lond. 1726, 8º.* O.

A plan for a hospital and almshouse.

3651 A Letter to a Nobleman, concerning the Bill to Prevent Frivolous and Vexatious Arrests; with the Substance of the said Bill, and Notes thereupon. As also, Reasons publish'd for and against the Bill.... With Observations and Proposals for rendring the Bill more Effectual.... *Lond. 1726, 4º.* L.

The covering letter signed: W.B.

3652 Reasons humbly offered against passing the Bill for preventing frivolous and vexatious Arrests. *n.p.* [*1726*], *s. sh. Fº.* L.

Endorsed: Reasons humbly offered by the Traders concerned in small Credit, against the Bill now depending to prevent frivolous and vexatious Arrests.

3653 Reasons Humbly Offer'd by the Prisoners of the King's-Bench, in behalf of themselves, and many Thousands, for Passing the Bill, for the Insolvent Debtors. *n.p.* [*1726?*], *s. sh. Fº.* L.

Title, taken from endorsement.

3654 To the Honourable the Knights, Citizens, and Burgesses of Great-Britain in Parliament Assembled. Some Considerations humbly Offered, relating to the Relief of such unhappy Gentlemen, who cou'd not receive any Benefit from the last insolvent Act. *n.p.* [*1726?*], *s. sh. Fº.* L.

Another edn. [1727 ?], entitled: To the Honourable the Knights, Citizens, and Burgesses of Great Britain in Parliament assembled, Some Considerations humbly offer'd, relating to the Relief of such Unhappy Gentlemen, who cou'd not receive any Benefit from the last Insolvent Act (L).

3655 The Prisoner's Advocate, or a Caveat against Under Sheriffs, and their Officers; Jayl-Keepers, and their Agents. Shewing, I. The great Abuse all Persons Suffer, both before, and after, they are Committed to Prison. II. The Notorious Imposition, and Fraudulent Practices of Spunging-Houses Detected. III. The Orders of the Court of King's Bench, for Regulating all the Jayls in England, as to the Usage of Prisoners, with relation to their Lodging, Chamber-Rent, &c. IV. An Exact Table of the Fees, belonging to the Fleet and King's-Bench Prisons.... *Lond. 1726, 8º.* LU.

The dedication signed: Philalethes. Entered in the Stationers' Register to Robert Raikes, possibly the author.

3656 The Miseries of the Marshalsea, of White-Chapel and of the other Inferiour Prisons.... [*Lond. 1726?*], *8º.* LG.

A sequel to the preceding. Possibly by Robert Raikes.

3657 Nowell, Charles, and Reyner, William. A Proposal to establish proper Offices to register the Powers or Orders given, and to be given by Sailors in the King's Service, on their Pay...and to supply the necessary Occasions of such Seamen and their Families, at lawful Interest, till their respective Ships are paid.... *n.p.* [*1726?*], *F°*. L.

Endorsed: Scheme for Registering of Seamens Powers...Another edn. n.p., n.d., endorsed: Nowell and Reyner's Scheme for Registering Seamens Powers...(L).

3658 [ROBE, THOMAS]. Ways and Means whereby His Majesty may Man His Navy with Ten Thousand Able Sailors, on Short Notice, with less Expence to the Government than at present, and entirely to the Benefit and Satisfaction of the Merchants. *Lond. 1726, 8°*. LU.

2nd edn., with author's name, has 1726 on title-page but preface dated 1728 (L); 3rd edn. 1740 (L); another edn. 1757 (LU). Also included in the author's *Ways and Means....To which is added A Collection of some Political Essays by Eboranos*, 1734.

3659 LONDON. Forbes Mayor. Commun' Concil' tent' in Camera Guihald'.... [*Lond. 1726*], *s. sh. F°*. L.

Clauses from two acts of Anne relating to servants, reprinted by order dated 24 March 1725 [o.s.].

3660 Articles of Agreement, Made, Concluded, and Agreed upon, by the Loyal Society of Worstead Weavers in the City of Norwich and County of the same; on the 23rd Day of November...1717....Which said Articles were Corrected and Amended on the 12th Day of February 1725–6. consisting of Methods for Raising, Maintaining, and Establishing a Stock or Purse, for the Benefit and Relief of such Members thereunto belonging, which shall by Reasons of any Sickness or Lameness, be render'd incapable of following their Employment. *Norwich, 1726, 8°*. O.

3661 A Generous Exhortation to Undertakers and Journeymen-Weavers, &c. *Dublin, 1726, s. sh. F°*. D.

Urging them to join the Box, a sick-benefit club.

3662 The Tavern Scuffle: or, the Club in an Uproar; Occasion'd by a hot Dispute, between Mr. Swell-Gut, a Brewer, and Mr. Scorch-Gut, a Distiller, concerning Geneva, the Reigning Liquor now in Vogue among the common People. Plainly shewing the ill Effects arising from the Use of that Liquor....The whole Dispute committed to Writing.... By Saynought Slyboots, Secretary. *Lond. 1726, 8°*. DA.

3663 Edinburgh, December Ninth, One Thousand seven hundred and twenty six. *n.p.* [*1726*], *F°*. EU.

Rules and regulations set forth by Edinburgh Town Council for the more effectual extinguishing of accidental fires.

3664 York-Buildings House, Winchester-Street, Nov. 3, 1726. The Governor and Court of Assistants of the York-Buildings Company do hereby give Notice, that they are ready to serve any Person or Persons with clear Thames-Water from their Reservoir near Mary la Bonne.... *n.p.* [*1726*], *s. sh. F°*. MC.

1727

GENERAL

3665 BRADLEY, RICHARD. The Weekly Miscellany for the Improvement of Husbandry, Trade, Arts, and Sciences. no. 1–21. 4 July–21 Nov. 1727. *Lond. 1727*, 4°. L.

3666 CHAMBERS, EPHRAIM. Cyclopædia: or, an Universal Dictionary of Arts and Sciences; containing the Definitions of the Terms, and Accounts of the Things signify'd thereby, in the several Arts, both Liberal and Mechanical, and the several Sciences, human and divine.... *Lond. 1728* [*1727*], F°. 2 vols. O.

2nd edn. 1738 (L); 3rd edn. Dublin, 1740 (NLI); 4th edn. 1741 (L); 5th edn. 1741, 43 (O); another 5th edn. Dublin, 1742 (O); 6th edn. 1750 (O).

3667 Reasons against a War. In a Letter to a Member of Parliament. By an Old Whig. *Lond. 1727*, 8°. LU.

Effects on trade and taxation.

3668 Reasons for Improving the Fisheries, and Linnen Manufacture of Scotland. Wherein are shewn, the Advantages that must accrue to England, by the Increase of the Scots Linnen Manufacture. That the Fishing in Deep Water, is equally an Advantage to all the Subjects of Great Britain.... *Lond. 1727*, 8°. E.

3669 His Majesty's Patent for Improving Fisheries and Manufactures in Scotland. Published by Order of the Trustees. *Edin. 1727*, 8°. L.

3670 Abstract of His Majesty's Patent for Improving Fisheries and Manufactures in Scotland. Published by Order of the Trustees. *Edin. 1727*, 8°. L.

3671 Plan by the Commissioners and Trustees for Improving Fisheries and Manufactures in Scotland, for the Application of their Funds. Published by their Order. *Edin. 1727*, 8°. L.

With addenda, 'Particular Plan for the annual distribution of the L. 700 appropriated for Encouraging and Promoting the Manufacturing of Coarse Wool', [1728], and 'General Plan republished for other Three Years from Christmas 1730', [1731]. Another edn., 1734, to which is added 'Plan by the Commissioners...for the Application of the Funds under their Management for three Years from Christmas last 1733' (L).

3672 [BUCHAN, ALEXANDER]. A Description of St. Kilda, the most remote Western Isle of Scotland. Giving an Account of its Situation, Extent, Soil, Product, Bay, and adjacent Islands or Rocks.... *Edin. 1727*, 8°. E.

Another edn., with author's name, n.p. 1752 (E).

AGRICULTURE

3673 BRADLEY, RICHARD. A Complete Body of Husbandry; collected from the Practice and Experience of the most considerable Farmers in Britain.... *Lond. 1727*, 8°. LU.

Another edn. Dublin, 1727 (R).

3674 BRADLEY, RICHARD. The Country Housewife and Lady's Director, in the Management of a House, and the Delights and Profits of a Farm. Containing Instructions for managing the Brew-House....Directions for the Dairy....Practical Observations concerning Distilling.... *Dublin*, *1727*, *8º*. WDA.

The first edn. (not traced) was published in London in Dec. 1726 (*Monthly Cat.*). 2nd edn. Lond 1727 (L); 3rd edn. 1727 (WDA); another 3rd edn. 1728 (O); 6th edn. 1732 [1731] (L). Pt. 2, Lond. 1732 [1731] (L); another edn. (both parts) 1736 (L); 6th edn. 1762 (O).

3675 BRADLEY, RICHARD. Ten Practical Discourses concerning Earth and Water, Fire and Air, as they relate to the Growth of Plants. With a Collection of New Discoveries for the Improvement of Land, either in the Farm or Garden. *Westminster*, *1727*, *8º*. L.

2nd edn. 1733 (EU); 3rd edn. 1733 (R).

3676 HALES, STEPHEN. Vegetable Staticks: or, An Account of some Statical Experiments on the Sap in Vegetables: being an Essay towards a Natural History of Vegetation.... *Lond. 1727*, *8º*. L.

3677 LAURENCE, EDWARD. The Duty of a Steward to his Lord, represented under several plain and distinct Articles; wherein may be seen the Indirect Practices of several Stewards, tending to Lessen, and the several Methods likely to Improve their Lords Estates. To which is added an Appendix, shewing the Way to Plenty, proposed to the Farmers; wherein are laid down general Rules and Directions for the Management and Improvement of a Farm.... *Lond. 1727*, *4º*. L.

2nd edn. entitled: The Duty and Office of a Land Steward, 1731 [1730] (LU); 3rd edn. Dublin, 1731 (O).

3678 SWITZER, STEPHEN. The Practical Kitchen Gardiner: or, a new and entire System of Directions for his employment in the Melonry, Kitchen-Garden, and Potagery, in the several Seasons of the Year.... *Lond. 1727*, *8º*. L.

3679 The Vineyard: being a Treatise shewing I. The Nature and Method of Planting, Manuring, Cultivating, and Dressing of Vines in Foreign-Parts. II. Proper Directions for Drawing, Pressing, Making, Keeping, Fining, and Curing all Defects in the Wine. III. An Easy and Familiar Method, of Planting and Raising Vines in England....IV. New Experiments in Grafting, Budding, or Inoculating....V. The best Manner of raising several Sorts of compound Fruit, which have yet been attempted in England. Being the Observations made by a Gentleman in his Travels. *Lond. 1727*, *8º*. L.

The dedication signed: S.J.

3680 An Act for Exchanging, Inclosing, and reducing into Severalty, the Lands in the Common Fields, Common Meadows, Mowing Ground, Pasture or Feeding Ground, and all other the Lands lying open in the Parish of Little Rissington in the County of Gloucester. *n.p.* [*1727*], *Fº*. L.

A bill.

3681 An Act for appointing Commissioners to make a Division of certain Common-Field Lands, and Wastes, in the Townships of Scarcliffe and Palterton in the County of Derby, among the Proprietors, in order to inclose the same. *n.p.* [*1727*], *F*o. O.

3682 FURBER, ROBERT. A Catalogue of English and Foreign Trees: which will Thrive in the Natural Ground in England....Collected, Increased, and Sold by Robert Furber, at his Nursery over-against the Park-Gate, at Kensington, near London. *n.p. 1727*, 8o. L.

With this Furber published *A Catalogue of Great Variety of the best and choicest Fruit-Trees*....

3683 A Bill for the effectual Draining and Preservation of Haddenham-Levell, in the Isle of Ely. *n.p.* [*1727*], *F*o. L.

3684 PERRY, JOHN. To the Gentlemen Land-Owners in the Parts of South-Holland, in the County of Lincoln. *n.p.* [*1727*], *F*o. L.

On drainage.

3685 A List of the Names of the Proprietors of the Governor and Company of the Mine-Adventurers of England; who are qualified to vote for the Election of a Governor, Deputy-Governor, and Twelve Directors of the said Company...on Thursday the 9th Day of November, 1727. [*Lond. 1727*], *F*o. L.

3686 Leases for Twenty-One Years, to be granted of an Estate, capable of such Improvements, that the Lessees will be thereby entitled to the Gain of Six-Hundred Pounds for the Payment of One. *n.p. 1727*, 8o. O.

The estate is the manor and parish of Church-Preen in Shropshire, said to be ideal for the erection of iron works.

3687 Information for Sir John Meres Knight. Against the Governour and Company of Undertakers for raising Tames Water, in Yorkbuildings. *n.p.* [*1727*], *F*o. E.

Dated: Decr. 26. 1727. Signed: Ja. Graham. Meres had been governor of the Company.

3688 Information for the Governor and Company of Undertakers, for raising the Thames water in York-Buildings, against Sir John Meres and his Factor. *n.p.* [*1727*], *F*o. E.

Signed: Ro. Dundas. This case produced later statements for the Court of Session in 1728 and 1730, not catalogued here, but to be found in E.

MANUFACTURES

3689 The Case of J—— W——. *n.p.* [*1727?*], 4o. L.

On John Ward's lease of alum works from the Duke of Buckingham.

3690 LANGLEY, BATTY. The Builder's Chest-Book; or a Complete Key to the Five Orders of Columns in Architecture.... *Lond. 1727*, 8o. LRIBA.

Another edn., entitled: The Builder's Vade-Mecum, Dublin, 1729, 12o (DNL).

3691 Reasons humbly offered by the Company of Armourers and Brasiers of the City of London, for Regulating the working up of Goods made up of Copper and Brass, and to prevent the many Frauds used in the said Trade, to deceive the Buyers of the said Goods. *n.p.* [*1727*], *F*°. L.

3692 The Bill to prevent Frauds and Abuses in Working up of Goods, made of Forg'd and Hammer'd Copper and Brass, as the same is desired by the Company of Brasiers to pass into a Law. *n.p.* [*1727*], *F*°. L.

3693 Reasons against Passing the Bill now depending in the Honourable House of Commons, to prevent Frauds and Abuses in the working up of Goods and Wares made of Copper and Brass, within that Part of Great Britain called England: Humbly offered to the Consideration of that Honourable House. *n.p.* [*1727*], *F*°. L.

3694 *Begin.* John Fowke of Nightingale-Lane, Wapping, London, Engineer makes Constant-stream'd Engines for extinguishing Fires.... *n.p.* [*1727?*], *s. sh. F*°. L.

3695 Reasons humbly offered by the Company of Silk-Throwers of the City of London, in Behalf of themselves and others, carrying on the said Trade. *n.p.* [*1727*], *F*°. L.

For a bill to restrain the importation of thrown silks.

3696 A Bill for the effectual Preventing the Importation of Foreign Thrown Silk, which shall be coarser than those known by the Names of Third Bolognia, and Second Orsoy, and all Trams into this Kingdom, from Italy, Naples, and Sicily, for the better Employing the Poor, and Preserving the Silk-Throwing Trade in this Kingdom. *n.p.* [*1727*], *F*°. L.

3697 Reasons humbly offered by the Weavers of London, against a Bill now depending in Parliament, entitled, A Bill for the more effectual Preventing the Importation of Foreign Thrown-Silk, &c. *n.p.* [*1727*], *s. sh. F*°. L.

Endorsed: The Case of the Weavers of London.

3698 Reasons humbly offered in Relation to the Opposition made by the Weavers and Raw-Silk-Men, against Restraining the Importation of Coarse Thrown Silks. *n.p.* [*1727*], *F*°. L.

3699 The Vintner's Mystery display'd: or, the Whole Art of the Wine Trade laid open....A Treatise absolutely necessary for private Families; for by this alone, any Gentleman, or other Person, may Manage, Preserve, or Cure their Wines themselves.... *Lond.* [*1727*], *12*°. L.

3700 [Defoe, Daniel]. A Brief Deduction of the Original, Progress, and Immense Greatness of the British Woollen Manufacture: with an Enquiry whether it be not at present in a very Declining Condition: the Reasons of its Decay; and the Only Means of its Recovery. *Lond.* *1727*, *8*°. LU.

For authorship see *C.B.E.L.* II, 509.

3701 The Devil drove out of the Warping-Bar; or, the Snap-Reel Snap'd. Shewing the Madness of the Weavers, and the Folly and Barbarity of the Clothiers in the West. In a Letter to a Gentleman of Chippenham. And serves as a full Answer to a Pamphlet, lately Published; Entitled, The Devil to do in the West, &c. *Lond. 1727*, *8º*. DA.

3702 Abstract of Regulations contained in the late Act of Parliament, to be observed by the Spinners, Weavers and Stamp-masters, from and after the 1st of November, 1727. *Edin. 1727*, *s. sh. Fº*. L.

COMMERCE

3703 [DEFOE, DANIEL]. The Evident Advantages to Great Britain and its Allies from the Approaching War: Especially in Matters of Trade. To which is added two curious plans, one of the Port and Bay of Havana; the other of Porto-Belo. *Lond. 1727*, *8º*. LU.

For authorship see *C.B.E.L.* II, 508.

3704 [DEFOE, DANIEL]. The Evident Approach of a War; and Something of the Necessity of It, in order to Establish Peace, and Preserve Trade.... To which is Added, An Exact Plan and Description of the Bay and City of Gilbraltar. *Lond. 1727*, *8º*. L.

2nd edn. 1727 (L). For authorship see *C.B.E.L.* II, 509.

3705 Great Britain's Speediest Sinking Fund is a Powerful Maritime War, Rightly Manag'd and especially in the West Indies. *Lond. 1727*, *8º*. LU.

3706 The True Interest of the Hanover Treaty consider'd: and how far France, and the rest of the Allies, may be depended upon. By a Lover of his Country. *Lond. 1727*, *8º*. LU.

Tentatively attributed to Benjamin Good in the LU Catalogue.

3707 PICKMAN, CHARLES. The Tradesman's Guide; or the Chapman's and Traveller's Best Companion. Containing I. Two Alphabetical Lists of all the fix'd and moveable Fairs....II. An Explanation of all the fix'd and moveable Feasts. III. A Description of the Highways and Roads. ...IV. A Table of all the Market-Towns....V. A large Alphabetical List of all the Stage-Coaches and Carriers....VI. The Rates of Carts, Watermen, Hackney-Coaches and Chairs....VII. A List of the Numbers of all the Members each Town and County sends to serve in Parliament. VIII. Tables of Interest.... *Lond. 1727*, *12º*. L.

3708 Stamp Office. A Table of the Prices of Parchment and Paper. *n.p.* [*1727*], *s. sh. obl. Fº*. LPRO.

Another edn. [1730]; another edn. [1738] (both LPRO).

3709 The Case of James Goodwin, Chymist and Apothecary. Upon his Petition to the House of Lords, against continuing the Act for viewing, searching and examining Druggs, Medicines, &c. *n.p. 1727*, *s. sh. Fº*. L.

3710 Reasons humbly offer'd against continuing of the Act for better viewing, searching, and examining of Drugs, Medicines, &c. as the same now stands. *n.p.* [*1727?*], *s. sh. F°*. L.

Another edn., with an additional paragraph, entitled: Reasons humbly offered against continuing of the Act for better viewing, searching, and examining of Druggs, Medicines, &c. as the same now stands, [1731 ?] (L).

3711 Unto the Right Honourable, the Lords of Council and Session, The Petition of Patrick Wallace in Crichan, and others. *n.p.* [*1727*], *s. sh. F°*.

Dated: July 28, 1727. Signed: And. McDouall. Against being deemed unfree traders by the Magistrates of Stranraer.

3712 Answers for the Magistrates of Stranrawer, to the Petition of Patrick Wallace and others. *n.p.* [*1727*], *s. sh. F°*. E.

Dated: December 25. 1727. Signed: Hugh Dalrymple.

3713 Reasons shewing, that Leghorn cannot be deemed a Free Port. *n.p.* [*1727*], *F°*. L.

3714 Reasons why we ought not on any Account to part with Gibraltar, with an exact Plan of the City, Bay, Fortress and the adjacent Places. To which are added curious Remarks on the Importance of that Place to the English Nation, and some Observations on the Spanish Trade, &c. [*Dublin*], *1727*, *s. sh. F°*. D.

3715 [De La Touche, James]. Anglia Restaurata: or, the Advantages that must accrue to the Nation by Effectively putting a Stop to the Detestable and Ruinous Practice of Smuggling Wool, from England and Ireland to France, Ostend, &c.... To which is added A Scheme to put an effectual Stop to the Exportation of our Wool.... By the Cheshire Weaver. *Lond. 1727*, *4°*. L.

The preface of the L copy is signed in ms. with the author's name.

3716 [De La Touche, James]. Excidium Angliae: or, a View of the Fatal Consequences attending the Smuggling of Wool. By the Cheshire Weaver. *Lond. 1727*, *4°*. L.

The preface of the L copy is signed in ms. with the author's name.

3717 Smith, William. Thirty different Draughts of Guinea, by William Smith, Surveyor to ye Royal African Company of England. [*Lond. 1727?*], *obl. F°*. L.

3718 A Bill for Importing Salt, from Europe, into the Province of Pensylvania in America. *n.p.* [*1727*], *F°*. L.

3719 Nicoll, John. The Advantage of Great Britain Consider'd in the Tobacco Trade. With Reasons for Destroying the Tobacco Stalks, Home Consumption; is most Humbly Offered to the Parliament of Great Britain. *Lond. 1727*, *F°*. LU.

3720 Remarks on those Passages of the Letters of the Spanish Ministers, lately publish'd, which relate to the Hostilities committed by the Spanish Guarda-Costas, in the West-Indies, since the Treaty of Utrecht. *Lond. 1727*, *8°*. L.

3721 [KNIGHT, JAMES]. Some Observations on the Assiento Trade, as it has been exercised by the South-Sea Company; proving the Damage which will accrue thereby to the British Commerce and Plantations in America, and particularly to Jamaica. To which is annexed, A sketch of the Advantages of that Island to Great Britain....By a Person who resided several Years at Jamaica. *Lond. 1728* [*1727*], *8°*. LU.

2nd edn. 1728 (LU). Foxwell had seen a copy with a ms. attribution to Knight. Internal evidence supports the ascription.

3722 A Bill to Enable the South-Sea Company, with the Licence and Consent of the East-India Company, to take in Negroes within their Limits of Trade, and to deliver the same at Buenos Ayres. *n.p.* [*1727*], *F°*. L.

Madagascar was to supply the slaves.

3723 A Letter to the Chairman of the East-India Company: in which the Facts contained in the Memorial to the Court of Directors, and the Proceedings of the last General Court, upon the Answer of the Court of Directors to those Memorials, are fully stated and shown. By a Proprietor in the Company's Stock. *Lond. 1727*, *8°*. LU.

3724 HAMILTON, ALEXANDER. A New Account of the East Indies, being the Observations and Remarks of Capt. Alexander Hamilton, who spent his time there from the Year 1688. to 1723. Trading and Travelling, by Sea and Land, to most of the Countries and Islands of Commerce and Navigation, between the Cape of Good-Hope, and the Island of Japon. *Edin. 1727*, *8°*. LU.

Another edn. Lond. 1744 (L). Reprinted in *A General Collection of...Voyages*, ed. by J. Pinkerton, vol. 8 (1811).

3725 John Walker, of London, Merchant, Appellant. Joseph Gascoigne Nightingale, Esq; (Executor of Robert Gascoigne Nightingale Esq; deceased, who was Executor of Sir Robert Nightingale, Bar. deceased) and Francis Chamberlaine, Esq; The Appellant's Case. *n.p.* [*1727*], *F°*. L.

Signed: C. Talbot, T. Lutwych. On the sale of East India goods.

3726 John Walker. Appellant. Joseph Gascoigne Nightingale...Respondent. The Respondent's Case. *n.p.* [*1727*], *F°*. L.

Signed: P. Yorke, N. Fazakerley.

COLONIES

3727 COLDEN, CADWALLADER. The History of the Five Indian nations depending on the Province of New-York in America. *New-York, 1727*, *8°*. L.

Another edn. Lond. 1747; 2nd edn. 1750; 3rd 1755 (all L). Other edns. New York, 1866, 1902, 1904, 1922.

3728 HARTWELL, HENRY, BLAIR, JAMES and CHILTON, EDWARD. The Present State of Virginia and the College....To which is added, The Charter for Erecting the said College, granted by their late Majesties King William and Queen Mary.... *Lond. 1727*, *8º*. L.

Another edn, ed. by H. D. Farish, Williamsburg, 1940.

3729 Some Modern Observations upon Jamaica: as to its Natural History, Improvement in Trade, Manner of Living, &c. By an English Merchant. *Lond. 1727*, L.

Reprinted in *The Poetical Works of Philip late Duke of Wharton*, [1732], whence this entry is taken.

FINANCE

3730 The Case of Dame Susanna Blunt, Wife of Sir John Blunt, Bar[t] one of the late Directors of the South-Sea Company; and of Abraham Crop of London Merchant, and Susanna his Wife, Daughter of the said Dame Susanna Blunt, by her former Husband, John Banner, deceased. *n.p.* [*1727*], *s. sh. Fº*. LLI.

3731 The Case of the Creditors of Robert Knight, Esq; *n.p.* [*1727*], *s. sh. Fº*. L.

Knight was Cashier of the South Sea Company, and his estate was forfeited.

3732 The Case of Messieurs Ralph and Joseph Gulston, and others, in Relation to a Debt of Edward Gibbon, Esq; *n.p.* [*1727*], *Fº*. L.

Gibbon was a South Sea director, whose estate had been forfeited.

3733 An Honest Scheme, for Improving the Trade and Credit of the Nation: for Punishing the Fraudulent, and relieving the unfortunate Bankrupts: for Increasing the Profits of the Bank of England, and for Paying the Publick Debts of the Nation. *Lond. 1727*, *8º*. L.

3734 A Proposal most humbly offered to the Consideration of the Honourable House of Commons, in relation to the publick Taxes and Debts, in order to the more speedy lessening the one, and the more certain just and regular Payment of the other. *Lond. 1727*, *8º*. LU.

3735 [Pulteney, William, Earl of Bath]. Some Considerations on the National Debts, the Sinking Fund, and the State of Publick Credit: In a Letter to a Friend in the Country. *Lond. 1729*, *8º*. LU.

For authorship see ms. note in LU copy.

3736 [Pulteney, William, Earl of Bath]. A State of the National Debt, as it stood December the 24th, 1716. with the Payments made towards the Discharge of it out of the Sinking Fund, &c. compared with the Debt at Michaelmas, 1725. *Lond. 1727*, *4º*. LU.

Reprinted, with attribution of authorship, in *A Select Collection of...Tracts... on the National Debt*, ed. by J. R. McCulloch, 1857, p. 131.

3737 [Gould, Sir Nathaniel]. A Defence of an Essay on the Publick Debts of this Kingdom, &c. In Answer to a Pamphlet, entitled, A State of the National Debt, &c. By the Author of the Essay. *Lond. 1727*, *8º*. LU.

Reprinted, with attribution of authorship, in *A Select Collection of...Tracts... on the National Debt*, ed. by J. R. McCulloch, 1857, p. 201.

3738 FORSTER, SAMUEL. A Digest of all the Laws relating to the Customs, to Trade, and Navigation; with a short Historical Dissertation concerning the Nature, Extent, and Method of Collection of the Ancient Revenue of the Crown. [*Lond.*], *1727*, *8º*. L.

3739 CROUCH, HENRY. A Complete View of the British Customs. Part the Second. Containing ample Instructions for the entering, examining, and delivering of Goods and Merchandizes imported into Great Britain from foreign parts...To which is added, an Appendix, containing the Theory and Practice of Measuring, and Cask-Gauging. *Lond. 1728* [*1727*], *8º*. L.

2nd edn. 1746 (L). Pt. 1 was published in 1724 (no. 3320).

3740 A Compleat Alphabetical Abridgment of the Statutes now in Force relating to the Stamp Duties.... *Lond. 1727*, *4º*. LU.

3741 Instructions for Supervisors of Excise in the Country. *Lond. 1727*, *8º*. LG.

3742 Instructions to be observed by the Collectors of Excise. *Lond. 1727*, *8º*. LG.

3743 Instructions for the Officers of the London Distillery. *Lond. 1727*, *8º*. LG.

3744 Instructions for the Supervisors of the London Distillery. *Lond. 1727*, *8º*. LG.

3745 Instructions for Officers who only Survey Dealers in Brandy, &c. in London. *Lond. 1727*, *8º*. LG.

3746 The Case of John Burton, Commissioner for Licensing Hawkers, Pedlars, &c. *n.p.* [*1727*], *s. sh. Fº*. L.

Denying peculation.

3747 A short State of the Case of John Burton, Late Commissioner for Licensing Hawkers, Pedlars, &c. *n.p.* [*1727?*], *s. sh. Fº*. L.

3748 [SHIPPEN, WILLIAM]. A Speech against Sir R—— W——'s Proposal for increasing the Civil List Revenue: As it was Spoken in the House of Commons, July 3. 1727. By W—— S—— Esq; *Lond.* [*1727*], *8º*. LU.

2nd and 3rd edns. [1727] (both LU). Another edn. Dublin, 1727, s. sh. Fo. (D). Reprinted, with author's name, in *Cobbett's Parliamentary History*, vol. VIII (1811), col. 600–4.

3749 An Epistle to W.S. Esq; containing some political Remarks on his Speech in the House of Commons, against Sir R.W's Proposal for increasing the Civil List Revenue....By a Member of Parliament. *Lond. 1728* [*1727*], *8º*. L.

W.S. = William Shippen; R.W. = Robert Walpole.

3750 [DEFOE, DANIEL]. Parochial Tyranny: or, the House-Keeper's Complaint against the insupportable Exactions, and partial Assessments of Select Vestries, &c. With a Plain Detection of many Abuses committed in the Distribution of Publick Charities: Together with a Practicable

Proposal for Amendment of the same.... By Andrew Moreton, Esq; [pseud]. *Lond.* [*1727*], *8°*. LU.

For authorship see *C.B.E.L.* II, 509.

3751 MACULLA, JAMES. Proposals for a Publick Coinage of Copper Half-pence and Farthings in the Kingdom of Ireland, of the Copper Ore or Mine thereof, for the Common Benefit, both of the Crown and Nation, to the Increase of 254297 Pound Ster. of Gold and Silver Specie. *Dublin, 1727, 8°*. LU.

3752 WATSON, JOHN. Tables of Exchange. In Two Parts. Part First. English Money Exchanged into Irish.... Part Second. Irish Money Exchanged into English.... *Dublin, 1727, 12°*. DG.

2nd edn. 1750 (L).

3753 Copy of a Signature for a New Bank. *n.p.* [*1727*], *4°*. E.

The charter of the Royal Bank of Scotland.

3754 HAYES, RICHARD. A New Method for Valuing of Annuities upon Lives. Shewing at Sight as follows: I. How many Years, Months, &c. Purchase an Annuity upon Life, for any Age, from 30 to 73 Years, is worth, when Money yields 4, 5, 6, 7, or 8 per Cent. Interest. II. How much a Year 100 l. is worth upon Life for any of the abovesaid Ages, &c.... *Lond. 1727, 4°*. O.

2nd edn., corrected, 1746 (L); another edn. Dublin, 1789 (L).

3755 Proposals from the Sun Fire-Office, near the Royal Exchange, for Insuring Houses, and other Buildings, Goods, Wares and Merchandize, from Loss and Damage by Fire. *Lond. 1727, s. sh. 4°*. L.

Dated: July 8, 1727.

3756 An Abstract of the Deed of Settlement of the Union-Society, For Insuring of Goods and Merchandizes, from Loss by Fire, dated Feb. 16, $17\frac{14}{15}$. *Lond. 1726–7, F°*. LU.

TRANSPORT

3757 Joseph Ashton, Esq;... Appellant. Jonathan Smith, Esq; and others the Copartners of the Joint Stock in Question and Peter Delamotte, the Secretary, Respondents. The Appellant's Case. *n.p.* [*1727*], *F°*. L.

Signed: P. Yorke, N. Fazackerley. A dispute between London wharfingers.

3758 Joseph Ashton, Appellant. Jonathan Smith, Esq; and others, Respondents. The Respondents Case. *n.p.* [*1727*], *F°*. L.

Signed: C. Talbot. Tho. Lutwyche.

3759 The Master, Wardens and Assistants of the Corporation of Trinity-House, Appellants. Maltis Ryall, George Noble, & al', Respondents. The Case of the Appellants. *n.p.* [*1727*], *F°*. L.

Signed: P. Yorke. C. Wearg. On rights of lastage and ballastage for ships in the Thames.

3760 The Master, Wardens, and Assistants of the Corporation of Trinity-House, Appellants. Maltis Ryall, George Noble, and others Respondents. The Respondent Maltis Ryall's Case. *n.p.* [*1727*], *F°*. L.

Signed: J. Willes. N. Fazakerley.

3761 A Bill for Cleaning, Deepening, and Widening, a Creek, called Beverley-Beck, Running into the River Hull; and for Repairing the Staithes near the said Beck, and for Amending the Roads leading from the said River to the Town of Beverley..... *n.p.* [*1727*], *F°*. L.

3762 A Bill for making more Effectual the Acts therein mentioned, for making the River Kennett Navigable, from Reading to Newbury, in the County of Berks. *n.p.* [*1727?*], *F°*. L.

3763 A Bill for Improving the Navigation of The River Owze in the County of York. *n.p.* [*1727?*], *F°*. L.

3764 A Bill for Repairing and Amending an Act made in the Sixth and Seventh Years of the Reign of his late Majesty King William the Third, For Preventing Exactions of the Occupiers of Locks and Wears upon the River of Thames, and for Ascertaining the Rates of Water-Carriage, and for settling Towing-Paths, and for other Purposes therein mentioned. *n.p.* [*1727?*], *F°*. L.

3765 A Bill for Repealing an Act passed in the Seventh Year of his present Majesty's Reign, For making the River Weaver navigable from Frodsham Bridge to Winsford Bridge in the County of Chester; and for the more speedy and effectual carrying on and perfecting the Navigation of the said River, from Frodsham Bridge to Northwich, in the said County. *n.p.* [*1727*], *F°*. L.

3766 Proposals humbly offered for making the River Weever Navigable, from Frodsham-Bridge to Northwich in the County of Chester. *n.p.* [*1727?*], *s. sh. F°*. L.

Signed by: Cha. Dukenfield, J. Daniell, W. Blackburne, Thom. Butterworth, John Reddish.

3767 Reasons humbly offered against a Bill passed the Honourable House of Commons,and now Depending before Your Lordships, Entitled, A Bill for Repealing an Act passed in the Seventh Year of His present Majesty's Reign, for making the River Weaver Navigable, from Frodsham Bridge to Winsford Bridge.... *n.p.* [*1727*], *s. sh. F°*. L.

3768 Reasons humbly offered against allowing the County of Chester any Part of the Tonnage Duty for making the River Weaver Navigable; and that the same may be made Navigable on the Easiest Terms. *n.p.* [*1727*], *s. sh. F°*. L.

3769 Reasons humbly offered by John Daniel and William Blackburn, Esquires, for themselves, and on Behalf of Charles Duckenfield, Thomas Butterworth, and John Reddish, Esquires, and others, Gentlemen and Freeholders of the County of Chester, against a Bill for Repealing an

Act made in the Seventh Year of his Majesty's Reign, for making the River Weaver navigable from Frodsham Bridge to Winsford Bridge.... *n.p.* [*1727*], *s. sh. F°.* L.

3770 Reasons humbly offered by the Trustees of Richard Vernon Esq; deceased, against the Bill for Repealing an Act made in the Seventh Year of his Majesty's Reign, for making the River Weaver Navigable from Frodsham Bridge to Winsford Bridge.... *n.p.* [*1727*], *s. sh. F°.* L.

3771 Reasons humbly offered for passing the Bill for making the River Weaver Navigable from Frodsham-Bridge to Northwich, in the County of Chester: With Remarks upon the Proposals from Liverpool. *n.p.* [*1727*], *F°.* L.

3772 A Bill for Explaining and Amending an Act passed in the Seventh and Eighth Years of the Reign of his late Majesty King William III. (intituled, An Act for making Navigable the Rivers Wye and Lugg in the County of Hereford) and for making the same more Effectual. *n.p.* [*1727*], *F°.* L.

3773 A Bill for the more effectual Amending the Highway between Hockliffe and Wooburn in the County of Bedford; and for Repairing the Road leading through Wooburn to Tickford Bridge in Newport Pagnell, in the County of Bucks. *n.p.* [*1727*], *F°.* L.

3774 Anno Regni Annae Reginae.... Nono, *etc.* (An Act for repairing and amending the Highways leading from Royston in the County of Hertford, to Wandesford Bridge in the County of Huntingdon.) *Lond.* *1727*, *8°.* L.

3775 Information for the Magistrates of the Canongate, against the Coach-Men there. *n.p.* [*1727*], *F°.* E.
Dated: Jan. 4th, 1727. Signed: Ch. Areskine.

3776 Information for the Keepers of the Hackney-coaches in and about the Canongate, Against the Magistrates of the Canongate. *n.p.* [*1727*], *F°.* E.
Dated: January 6. 1727. Signed: Ja. Graham.

3777 Unto the Right Honourable the Lords of Council and Session, the Petition of the Magistrates of the Canongate. *n.p.* [*1727*], *F°.* E.
Dated: January 19, 1727. Signed: Ch. Areskine.

3778 Answers for the Keepers of the Hackney Coaches in and about the Canongate, to the Petition of the Magistrates of the Canongate. *n.p.* [*1727*], *F°.* E.
Dated: Feb. 1. 1727. Signed: Ja. Graham.

3779 Petition for the Keepers of the Hackney-Coaches in and about the Canongate. *n.p.* [*1727*], *F°.* E.
Dated: 1st June, 1727. Signed: Ja. Graham.

3780 Answers for the Magistrates of the Canongate; to the Petition of the Keepers of the Hackney-Caches [*sic*] in and about the Canongate. *n.p.* [*1727*], *s. sh. F°.* E.
Dated June 20, 1727. Signed: Cha. Areskine.

SOCIAL CONDITIONS

3781 [GAIRDNER, ANDREW]. A Looking-Glass for Rich People, and People in Prosperity; shewing how they may improve their Riches to the greatest Advantage: or, a Plea for the Poor. *Edin. 1727*, *8*°. L.

Mostly religious exhortation to charity. Authorship acknowledged in Gairdner's *Historical Account of the Old People's Hospital*, 1728 (no. 3890).

3782 Regulations which were Agreed upon and Established the Twelfth Day of July, 1726. by the Gentlemen of the Vestry then present, for the better Government and Management of the Work-House belonging to the Parish of St. Giles's in the Fields. Humbly offered to the Consideration of the House of Commons of Ireland. *Dublin, 1727*, *8*°. O.

Reprinted as a model for the reform of the Dublin workhouse.

3783 A Bill for the more equal Paying and better Collecting, certain small Sums for the Relief of Shipwreck'd Mariners, and Distressed Persons, his Majesty's Subjects, in the Dominions of the Great Duke of Tuscany, and for other Pious and Charitable Purposes, usually contributed to by the Merchants Trading to Leghorn. *n.p.* [*1727*], *F*°. L.

3784 Reasons humbly offered for better Collecting certain small Sums at Leghorn, for Publick and Pious Uses. *n.p.* [*1727*], *F*°. L.

3785 Reasons humbly offered for Supporting a Chaplain, and Supplying the Wants of Ship-wreck'd Mariners and other Distressed Persons at Leghorn. *n.p.* [*1727*], *F*°. L.

3786 His Majesty's Commission for the Royal Hospital, for Seamen at Greenwich. *n.p.* [*1727*], *4*°. O.

3787 A Devonshire Hospital: being a Treatise, shewing, how the Poor of the County of Devon may be maintained and provided for, in their respective Parishes, in a better and more plentiful Manner than now they are, and for half the Charge they now cost in Poor-Rates....By a Philo Devonian.... *Exon, 1727*, *4*°. L.

3788 Reasons against Confining Persons in Prison for Debt, humbly offer'd to the Consideration of Parliament. *n.p.* [*1727?*], *s. sh. F*°. L.

3789 Reasons for Passing an Extensive Act of Insolvency, and making some Law, to redress the Great Grievance, of confining so many Thousand useful Subjects in our Goals for Debt: Humbly Offer'd to the Consideration of the Members of this present Parliament, by the Debtors confin'd in his Majesty's Prison belonging to the Court of King's Bench. *n.p.* [*1727?*], *s. sh. F*°. L.

3790 To the Honourable the Knights, Citizens, and Burgesses of Great-Britain in Parliament Assembled. The most Humble Petition of the several Persons in the Fleet-Prison in Behalf of themselves and several Thousand imprison'd Debtors in the King's Bench, and the several Goals of this Kingdom. *n.p.* [*1727?*], *s. sh. F*°. L.

Endorsed: The Humble Petition of the confined Prisoners in the Fleet-Prison.

3791 Considerations upon Commissions of Bankrupts. [*Lond.*], *1727*, *8°*. LU.

3792 The Debtors Glory; and the Goalers Lamentation, for His Majesties Act, concerning the Imprisonment of Insolvent Debtors. With Orders for Goalers, Turnkeys, Bailiffs, Lawyers, &c. in general, for the better Regulation of all the Goals throughout the Kingdom of England. *Lond.* [*1727?*], *4°*. O.

3793 A Bill to enable the Justices of the Peace for the County of Bucks to finish a Goal and Sessions-Room for the Use of the said County. *n.p.* [*1727*], *F°*. L.

3794 An Act for Vesting several Sums of Money given for Charitable Uses, in the Archbishop of Canterbury, the Bishop of Ely, and the Dean of Canterbury; and to impower them to place the same with the Governors of Queen Anne's Bounty, in order to augment several poor Livings in the Dioceses of Canterbury and Ely. [*Lond.*, *1727*], *F°*. LHL.

3795 LAMBE, AARON. A Proposal for the Encouragement of Seamen; By reviving a Register, and enlarging the Advantages thereof. *n.p.* [*1727*], *s. sh. F°*. L.

Dated: March 13, 1726–7.

3796 A Discovery of the Frauds of the Royal Navy and Means proposed to prevent them, thereby encourage Men to serve His Majesty cheerfully without Impressing. *n.p.* *1727*, *4°*. L.

Title from endorsement. For establishing a record of wages due and how pledged.

3797 A Dissertation upon Drunkenness. Shewing to what an intolerable Pitch that Vice is arriv'd at in this Kingdom. Together with the astonishing Number of Taverns, Coffee-Houses, Alehouses, Brandy-Shops, &c. now extant in London....Also an Account of the Pride, Insolence and Exorbitance of Brewers, Vintners, Victuallers, Coffee-House-Keepers, and Distillers....The Whole proving, that if this Drinking Spirit does not soon abate, all our Arts, Sciences, Trade, and Manufactures will be entirely lost.... *Lond.* [*1727*], *8°*. L.

3798 London, what it Is, Not What it Was: or, The Citizen's Complaint against Publick Nusances. To which is added, A Remonstrance against the great Number of Shops, &c. that sell Geneva and other Drams to the Poor, and the evil Consequences thereof; with some True Causes of the increase of the Poor. *Lond.* [*1727*], *12°*. LU.

1728

GENERAL

3799 A Description of all the Counties in England and Wales, containing I. In what Diocese, Circumference of Miles, Number of Acres and Houses, the Air and Soil, Rivers, Commodities, and chief Seats of the Nobility and Gentlemen of each County. II. Market-Towns, Market-Days, and Distance from London. III. Members of Parliament. IV. Fairs, fix'd and moveable. V. Coaches, Carriers, and Water-bound. VI. Roads from London to the chief Towns, and Cross-Roads.... Likewise the Rates of Coachmen, Carmen, and Watermen, in, and about the Cities of London and Westminster. Faithfully collected by P.W. *Lond. 1728, 12°.* O.

Another edn. entitled: A New Description of all the Counties of England and Wales, without indication of authorship on the title-page but with the preface signed: R.R., 1741 (L); 6th edn. 1752 (O).

3800 [DEFOE, DANIEL]. Augusta Triumphans: or, the Way to make London the most flourishing City in the Universe.... *Lond. 1728, 8°.* O.

2nd edn. 'by Andrew Moreton', 1729 [1728] (L). For authorship see *C.B.E.L.* II, 509.

3801 A Compleat History of the Famous City of Norwich. From the Earliest Account, to this present Year 1728. Shewing the Situation, Manufactures, Churches, and other Publick Buildings; Markets, Fairs.... Likewise, a List of the Posts and Carriers going from this City.... To which is annex'd an Exact Map of the City.... *Norwich, 1728, 8°.* O.

3802 [SWIFT, JONATHAN]. A Short View of the State of Ireland. *Dublin, 1727–8, 8°.* L.

Another edn. Cork, n.d. (C). Reprinted in *The Prose Works of Jonathan Swift*, ed. by H. Davis, vol. 12 (1955).

3803 The Present State of Ireland; being Political Reflections by Mr. Mist, on a Pamphlet lately published at Dublin. *n.p.* [*1728*], *8°.* L.

Largely a reprint of selections from Swift's *A Short View of the State of Ireland.*

3804 [BROWNE, Sir JOHN]. A Letter to the Author of the Short View of the State of Ireland. By the Author of Seasonable Remarks. *Dublin, 1728, 8°.* L.

For authorship see the note to *Seasonable Remarks on Trade* (no. 3808).

3805 [BROWNE, Sir JOHN]. To the R——d Dr. J——n S——t, the Memorial of the Poor Inhabitants, Tradesmen, and Labourers of the Kingdom of Ireland. *Dublin,* [*1728*], *8°.* L.

Urging the importation of corn. Reprinted in *The Prose Works of Jonathan Swift*, ed. by H. Davis, vol. 12 (1955), where the authorship is established.

3806 [SWIFT, JONATHAN]. An Answer to a Paper, called A Memorial of the Poor Inhabitants, Tradesmen and Labourers of the Kingdom of

Ireland. By the Author of the Short View of the State of Ireland. *Dublin, 1728, 8º*. L.

Signed: A.B. Reprinted in *The Prose Works of Jonathan Swift*, ed. by H. Davis, vol. 12 (1955).

3807 [BROWNE, Sir JOHN]. To the R——d D——n S——t. A Reply, to the Answer given to the Memorial of the Poor Inhabitants, Tradesmen, and Labourers, of the Kingdom of Ireland. *Dublin, 1728, 8º*. O.

Presumably by the author of no. 3805.

3808 [BROWNE, Sir JOHN]. Seasonable Remarks on Trade. With Some Reflections on the Advantages that might accrue to Great Britain, by a proper Regulation of the Trade of Ireland. Wrote in London, but now first Publish'd in Dublin, as a Preface to other Essays on the Trade and Manufactures of Ireland. *Dublin, 1728, 8º*. LU.

Another edn. 1729 (LU). Authorship acknowledged in Browne's *The Benefits ...from Navigable Rivers*, 1729.

3809 [BROWNE, Sir JOHN]. An Essay on Trade in General; and, on that of Ireland in Particular. By the Author of Seasonable Remarks. *Dublin 1728, 8º*. LU.

Authorship acknowledged in Browne's *The Benefits...from Navigable Rivers*, 1729.

3810 Considerations on Two Papers lately published. The First, called, Seasonable Remarks, &c. And the other, An Essay on Trade in General, and on That of Ireland, in Particular. *Dublin, Printed in the Year 1728. 8º*. L.

Another issue, Printed by T.P. in the Year 1728 (CT. Rothschild 2239). Attributed to Arthur Dobbs by Wagner (no. 92), but the internal evidence seems to me to be against the attribution.

3811 [BROWNE, Sir JOHN]. A Reply to the Observer on Seasonable Remarks. *Dublin, 1728, 8º*. LU.

In the dedication the author acknowledges the authorship of *Seasonable Remarks* and *An Essay on Trade*. A reply to the preceding.

3812 [BROWNE, Sir JOHN]. An Appeal to the Revd. Dean Swift, by way of Reply to the Observer on Seasonable Remarks. *Dublin, 1728, 8º*. DA.

Another edn. of the preceding, without the dedication.

3813 A Letter in Answer to a Paper, intitled, An Appeal to the Reverend Dean Swift. By the Author of Considerations on Two Papers, &c. *Dublin, 1728, 8º*. DA.

Reprinted in *Reflections Little to the Purpose, on a Paper Less to the Purpose*, 1729, and in *A Collection of Tracts, concerning the Present State of Ireland*, 1729.

AGRICULTURE

3814 PEIRSON, SAMUEL. Farther Considerations for the Improvement of the Tillage in Ireland: with an Account of the Advantages of the Ploughs and Methods recommended in a former Treatise, as since proved on

Tryal. And Some Remarks added for an easy Improvement of the Lands now used in Tillage, and of other Lands in this Kingdom. *Dublin, 1728, 8o.* L.

3815 BRADLEY, RICHARD. The Gentleman and Farmer's Guide, for the Increase and Improvement of Cattle, viz, Lambs, Sheep, Hogs, Calves, Cows, Oxen. Also the best Manner of Breeding, and Breaking Horses, both for Sport and Burden...Also some Observations on the many Benefits of the Woollen Manufactures of Great-Britain, and the great Advantages arising from Hides, Tallow, &c. Illustrated with Copper Plates. *Lond. 1729 [1728], 8o.* L.

3816 LANGLEY, BATTY. Pomona: or the Fruit-Garden Illustrated. Containing sure methods for improving all the Best Kinds of Fruits now extant in England....To which is added, A curious account of the most valuable Cyder-Fruits of Devonshire [by Hugh Stafford]. The whole illustrated with above three hundred drawings.... *Lond. 1729 [1728], Fo.* L.

3817 [SWITZER, STEPHEN]. A Compendious, but more Particular Method, than has ever yet been publish'd, for the Raising Italian Brocoli, Spanish Cardoon, Celeriac, Fenochi, and other foreign Kitchen Vegetables....As also a more authentic Account of the La Lucerne, St. Foyne, Clover, and other Grass Seeds, for the Improvement of Land, than is at present to be found in any Books of Husbandry, or Gardening....To which, is added, the new, but very useful Method of Burning of Clay, for the Improvement of Land....As also, an Appendix, wherein is contain'd a further and full Account of the La Lucerne....By S.S. Author of the Practical Fruit and Kitchen Gardener, &c. *Lond. [1728], 8o.* MP.

2nd edn., with author's name, 1728 (R); 3rd 1729 (L); 4th 1729 (L); another 4th edn. Dublin, 1729 (L); 5th edn. Lond. 1731 [1730] (L); 6th edn. 1735 (R). The only copy seen of the first edition is of the second issue, the first issue being unrecorded. See R. Hagedorn, 'The First Edition of Switzer's *Brocoli*', *The Library*, ser. 5, vol. 7, p. 58.

3818 An Act for appointing Commissioners to make a Division of certain Common-Field-Lands and Wastes, in the Parish of Cherrington in the County of Gloucester, among the Proprietors, in order to inclose the same. *n.p. [1728], Fo.* L.

3819 An Act for Enabling Charles Duke of Grafton, Lord of the Manor of Grafton in the County of Northampton, to Inclose the Common-fields and Waste-grounds within the said Manor, in Pursuance of several Agreements between the said Duke of Grafton and the Rector and Church-wardens of Grafton Regis; and to establish the said Agreements. *[Lond. 1728], 8o.* L.

3820 An Act for Confirming the Inclosure and Division of the Common Fields and Common Grounds within the Manors and Parishes of Overton-Longville, and Butolphsbridge, in the County of Huntingdon. *n.p. 1728, Fo.* L.

3821 An Essay on Draining: more particularly with regard to the North Division of the Great Level of the Fenns, call'd Bedford Level. *Lond. 1729* [*1728*], *8°*. L.

Attributed to Sigismund Trafford in H. & L., without quoting authority.

3822 [Bedford Level. The Account of Edward Partheriche, Esq; Receiver and Expenditor General...pro Anno 1727]. *n.p.* [*1728*], *F°*. O.

O copy lacks all before p. 5. O also has the Account of Gotobed East for 1747 and that of Whetham Robinson for 1750.

3823 LANGLEY, BATTY. A Sure Method of Improving Estates, by Plantations of Oak, Elm, Ash, Beech, and other Timber-Trees, Coppice-Woods, &c..... *Lond. 1728*, *8°*. LU.

Another edn., 1741, entitled: The Landed Gentleman's Useful Companion: or, a Sure and Easy Method of Improving Estates...(L).

3824 A Letter from a Gentleman at Edinburgh, to his Friend at London. *n.p.* [*1728?*], *F°*. L.

On the York Buildings Company's projects in Scotland.

3825 [A] short Abstract of the Hon$^{ble.}$ Samuel Horsey Governour of the York-Buildings Company, his Speeches at their General Court. *n.p.* [*1728?*], *F°*. L.

Followed by 'Remarks on the Governour's Speeches'.

3826 The Governour and Company of Undertakers for raising the Thames Water in York-Buildings, Appellants. Sir John Meres, Respondent. The Appellants Case. *n.p.* [*1728*], *F°*. L.

Signed: Dun. Forbes. C. Talbot. Alex. Garden. Meres was the late Governor of the Company.

3827 The Governour and Company of Undertakers for Raising the Thames Water in York-Buildings, Appellants. Sir John Meres, Knt. Respondent. The Respondent's Case. *n.p.* [*1728*], *F°*. L.

Signed: P. Yorke. Ch. Areskine. Will. Hamilton.

3828 State of the Process, Sir John Meres and his Factor, Pursuers, against the York Buildings Company, Defenders. *n.p.* [*1728*], *F°*. EU.

MANUFACTURES

3829 An Act for the more effectual preventing Abuses in the making of Bricks and Tiles, and for altering the Size of Bricks made for Sale. *n.p.* [*1728*], *F°*. MC.

A bill, apparently.

3830 The Case of the Brickmakers and Bricklayers within the City of London and fifteen Miles thereof, who have conformed to the Act of the 12th of the late King for preventing Abuses in making Bricks, &c. *n.p.* [*1728*], *s. sh. F°*. L.

3831 Reasons Humbly Offered Against the Bill now depending, for explaining an Act made in the 12th Year of his late Majesty King George, to prevent the Abuses in making of Bricks and Tyles. *n.p.* [*1728*], *F°*. MC.

Endorsed: Reasons Humbly Offered Touching the Bill now depending relating to Bricks, &c.

3832 [Halfpenny, William]. The Builder's Pocket-Companion. Shewing an Easy and Practical Method for laying down of Lines, for all Sorts of Arches and Curves used in House-Building, Ship-Building, Gardening, &c.... By Michael Hoare, Carpenter [pseudonym]. *Lond. 1728*, *8°*. K.

2nd edn. 1731 (LRIBA). For authorship see H. M. Colvin, *A Biographical Dictionary of English Architects*, 1954, p. 260.

3833 Information for tne [*sic*] Deacon and Incorporation of the Cordiners in Canongate, Against the Incorporation of Wrights, and the Incorporation of the Hammermen, whereof the Saidlers are a Pendicle. *n.p.* [*1728*], *F°*. E.

Dated: February 13. 1728. Signed: Jo. Graham.

3834 Humphrey Skerrett, Gent. Appellant. John Nesbitt, Esq; William Slack, Joseph Hall, and Christopher Rind, Respondents. The Appellant's Case. *n.p.* [*1728*], *F°*. L.

Signed: Tho. Lutwyche. Will. Hamilton. Iron works at Killyfaddy.

3835 Humphrey Skerret, Gent. Appellant. John Nisbet, Esq; William Slack Administrator of William Slack deceased, Joseph Hall, and Christopher Rynde. Respondents. The Respondent Nisbet's Case. *n.p.* [*1728*], *F°*. L.

Signed: P. Yorke. C. Talbot.

COMMERCE

3836 Atlas Maritimus & Commercialis; or, A General View of the World, so far as relates to Trade and Navigation: describing all the Coasts, Ports, Harbours, and Noted Rivers, according to the Latest Discoveries and most Exact Observations. Together with a Large Account of the Commerce carried on by Sea between the several Countries of the World, as likewise of all Inland Trade by means of Navigable Rivers.... To which are added Sailing Directions for all the Known Coasts and Islands on the Globe; with a Sett of Sea-Charts.... *Lond. 1728*, *F°*. O.

Probably edited by Defoe. See J. R. Moore in *The Library*, ser. 5, vol. XI, 167–9. 'A General Coasting Pilot....By Nathaniel Cutler' forms pt. 2 of the book.

3837 [Defoe, Daniel]. A Plan of the English Commerce. Being a Compleat Prospect of the Trade of this Nation, as well the Home Trade as the Foreign.... *Lond. 1728*, *8°*. L.

2nd edn. 1730 [1731]; reissued 1737, with author's name (both L); 3rd edn. 1749 (O); another edn. Oxford, 1928.

3838 The Wealth and Commerce of Great-Britain consider'd. *n.p. 1728, 8°.* LU.

Another edn. Dublin, 1729, 8° (DA).

3839 The Case of the Coffee-Men of London and Westminster. Or, an Account of the Impositions and Abuses, put upon Them and the whole Town, by the present Set of News-Writers. With the Scheme of the Coffee-Men, for setting up News-Papers of their own; and some Account of their Proceedings thereupon. By a Coffee-Man. *Lond.* [*1728*], *8°*. L.

3840 Reasons humbly offered to the Consideration of the Honourable the House of Commons, against Part of a Bill now depending, intituled, A Bill for Repealing the present Duties payable upon Wine Lees imported, and laying new Duties thereon, and for other Purposes therein mentioned, whereby the Importation of Wine in Bottles is proposed to be prevented. *n.p.* [*1728*], *s. sh. F°*. L.

Endorsed: Reasons humbly offered to the Consideration of the Honourable the House of Commons against prohibiting the Importation of Wine in Bottles, &c.

3841 EDINBURGH. Act of Council regulating the Prices, &c. of Bread within the City of Edinburgh, and Suburbs thereof. [*Edin. 1728*], *s. sh. F°*. ECA.

Dated: 1 May 1728.

3842 By the King, A Proclamation Requiring Quarentine to be performed by all Ships and Vessels coming from the Levant, the Isles of the Archipelago, Zant, Corfu, Veniza, Cephalonia, St. Mauro, or any of the adjacent Islands, or any of the Ports or Places of the Morea, into Great Britain, or the Isles of Guernsey, Jersey, Aldernay, Sark, or Man. *Lond. 1728, s. sh. F°*. L.

Dated: 4 July 1728.

3843 By the Lord Lieutenant and Council of Ireland, a Proclamation, Requiring Quarentine to be Performed by Ships coming from the Islands of Zant, Corfu, Cephalonia, St. Mauro or any Part of the Morea. *Dublin, 1728, F°*. DPRO.

Dated: 13 May 1728.

3844 The Case of the Russia Company. *n.p.* [*1728*], *s. sh. F°*. LLI.

Against admitting Anthony Da Costa, a Jew, into the Company.

3845 The Case of Mr. Anthony Da Costa with the Russia-Company. *n.p.* [*1728*], *s. sh. F°*. L.

3846 [RIGBY, RICHARD]. An Answer to a Calumny: with some Remarks upon an Anonimous Pamphlet, address'd to his Grace the Duke of Newcastle, entitled, Some Observations on the Assiento Trade, as it has been exercised by the South-Sea Company, &c. Whereby the Damage which has, or is likely to accrue thereby to the British Commerce and Plantations, and particularly to Jamaica, is also considered.... By the

Factor to the South-Sea Company, at Whom the Calumny was aimed. *Lond.* *1728*, *8o*. LU.

Authorship deduced from internal evidence. A reply to no. 3721.

3847 [KNIGHT, JAMES]. A Defence of the Observations on the Assiento Trade, as it hath been exercised by the South-Sea Company, &c.... By the Author of the Observations on the Assiento Trade. *Lond.* *1728*, *8o*. L.

3848 Some Considerations on the Nature and Importance of the East-India Trade. *Lond.* *1728*, *8o*. L.

3849 John Morse, Gent. Samuel Clark, Esq; and Thomas Bowdler, Esq; in behalf of themselves and others, the Proprietors and Adventurers of the Old East India Company, at the Time of the Dissolution thereof, Appellants. Charles Dubois, Esq; Arthur Moor, Esq; Edward Gibbons, Esq; and Grantham Andrews, Esq; Executors of Sir Jonathan Andrews, deceased, Respondents. The Appellants Case. *n.p.* [*1728*], *Fo*. L.

Signed: J. Willis [Willes]. N. Fazakerley. On the internal management of the Company.

3850 John Morse, Samuel Clarke, and Thomas Bowdler, Esqrs. on Behalf of themselves and others, Proprietors of the Old East-India Company, Appellants. Charles Dubois, Arthur Moore, Edward Gibbon, and Grantham Andrews, Esqrs. Respondents. The Respondents Case. *n.p.* [*1728*], *Fo*. L.

Signed: P. Yorke. C. Talbot.

3851 Considerations upon the Bill for Encouraging Seamen to enter voluntarily into his Majesty's Service. *n.p.* [*1728*], *Fo*. MC.

3852 The Sailors Advocate. To be continued. 2 nos. *Lond.* [*1728*], *8o*. L.

7th edn. of no. 1. 1777 (L).

3853 [DEFOE, DANIEL]. Some Considerations on the Reasonableness and Necessity of Encreasing and Encouraging the Seamen.... With some proposed Schemes for the effectual performing it, without prejudice either to the Navy, or the Commerce.... *Lond.* *1728*, *8o*. LU.

For authorship see *C.B.E.L.* II, 509.

3854 BETAGH, WILLIAM. A Voyage round the World. Being an account of a Remarkable Enterprize, begun in the Year 1719, chiefly to cruise on the Spaniards in the great South Ocean.... *Lond.* *1728*, *8o*. L.

COLONIES

3855 The Marquis Duquesne Vindicted, in a Letter to a Noble Lord; from the Aspersions cast on his Conduct while Commander of Fort Charles, at Port-Royal in Jamaica, under His Grace the Duke of Portland. Which Aspersions were published in a Letter, said to be wrote by a Gentleman of that Island, and addressed to a Member of Parliament. Dated February, 1725–6. *Lond.* *1728*, *8o*. L.

A reply to *The State of the Island of Jamaica*, 1725 (no. 3460).

FINANCE

3856 Remarks on the Occurrences of the Years 1720 and 1721; relating to the Execution of the South-Sea Scheme. *Lond. 1728*, 8°. LU.

Another edn. 1732 (L).

3857 The Report of the Trustees in whom the Estates of the late South-Sea Directors, and of John Aislabie, Esq; and of James Craggs Sen. Esq; are Vested. Presented the 6th of February 1721.... *Lond. 1728*, F°. L.

3858 The Report of the Trustees for Raising Money on the Estates of the late Directors of the South-Sea Company, and Others. Presented the 25th of April 1726.... *Lond. 1728*, F°. L.

3859 The Report of the Trustees for Raising Money on the Estates of the late late Directors of the South-Sea Company, and Others. Presented the 3d of May, 1728.... *Lond. 1728*, F°. L.

3860 The Case of Robert Surman. *n.p.* [*1728*]. *s. sh.* F°. L.

Endorsed: The Case of Mr. Surman. Surman had been deputy cashier of the South Sea Company.

3861 The Humble Representation of the House of Commons to the King, with His Majesty's most Gracious Answer thereunto. *Lond. 1728*, F°. LU.

On the state of the national debt and the working of the sinking fund. No. 59 of the *Votes* of the House of Commons for this session. Another edn. Dublin, 1728, 8° (DA). Reprinted in *Commons' Journals*, XXI, 120–5, and thence in *A Select Collection of... Tracts... on the National Debt*, by J. R. McCulloch, 1857.

3862 A State of the National Debt, as it stood the 24th of December 1716, with the Addition of such Debts as have been since adjusted and allowed for Services performed before that Time, and an Account of the Sums which have been paid towards the Discharge of the said Sum, to the 24th of December 1727, and the Sums remaining unpaid. *n.p.* [*1728?*], F°. LU.

A table. Followed by a second table, 'A State of the National Debt, as it stood the 24th of December 1727, with an Account of the particular Sums which have in any manner been added to the Debt since the 24th of December 1716'.

3863 MYHILL, SAMUEL. A Proposal for raising the annual Sum of 520000 l, and not touch the prime Cost of wrought Goods above one Farthing in the Shilling. *n.p.* [*1728*], *s. sh.* F°. MC.

For a tax on looms.

3864 HATTON, EDWARD. The Gaugers Guide; or, Excise-Officer Instructed.... To all which is added, A Supplement of the Duties of Excise.... *Lond. 1729* [*1728*], 8°. L.

3865 Instructions to [James Deacon in London] appointed to be a Collector and Receiver of the Rates Duties and Impositions, which by several Acts of Parliament now in Force, are laid on the several Sorts of Coals, Culm, and Cinders, therein particularly mention'd and express'd. *n.p.* [*1728*], F°. LPRO.

The words in [] are supplied in ms., as is the date.

3866 The Case of the Parish of St. Martin in the Fields, with Regard to the Land-Tax. *n.p.* [*1728*], *F°*. L.

3867 The Case of Thomas Hammond, late of London, Merchant. *n.p.* [*1728*], *s. sh. F°*. L.

For a bill to enable him to compound with the Treasury for customs dues owed by him.

3868 The Report of the Commissioners sent into Spain, pursuant to an Address of the House of Commons to her late Majesty Queen Anne, relating to Gibraltar, and some other Places, never Publish'd before. With Authentick Vouchers produc'd by the said Commissioners, to prove that there had been Great Discouragements to Trade, many extravagant and unnecessary Expences, and great Misapplications of the Publick Money in the said Places.... *Lond. 1728*, *4°*. LU.

3869 An Account of the Endowments by a Pound-Rate, of Churches in London, and of such New-Churches within the Bills of Mortality, the Parishes whereof have been taken out of the larger Parishes. *n.p.* [*1728?*], *s. sh. F°*. L.

3870 An Answer to the pretended Reasons against a Pound Rate, in the intended new Parish of Poplar. *n.p.* [*1728*], *s. sh. F°*. L.

3871 MACULLA, JAMES. The Lamentable Cry of the People of Ireland to Parliament. A Coinage, or Mint, Proposed. The Parliament of Ireland's Address, and the King's Answer thereunto, relating to the coining Copper Half-Pence and Farthings for this Nation. With Several Reasons and Observations, shewing the great Necessity there is for such a Coin; and a Scheme laid down.... *Dublin, 1728*, *4°*. L.

3872 To the Lords Spiritual and Temporal, the Right Hon. and Hon. the Knights, Citizens and Burgesses in Parliament Assembled: The Humble Memorial of James Maculla, Metalist, Essay, and Touch-Master, shewing the Nation's Annual loss of 1,200,000 Sterl. and Grievance of 1,360,000. Sterl. drawn off, and proposing to redress the same, and to Manufacture 40 or 50,000 l. Sterl. worth of lawful and valuable Copper Change for Ireland. *n.p.* [*1728?*], *F°*. DA.

Endorsed: The Humble Memorial of James Maculla, Metalist, Essay, and Touch-Master.

3873 An Historical Account of the Establishment, Progress and State of the Bank of Scotland; and of the several Attempts that have been made against it, and the several Interruptions and Inconveniences which the Company has encountered. [*Edin*], *1728*, *4°*. LU.

LU copy has appendices relating to the dispute between the Old Bank and the Royal Bank set up in 1727.

3874 A Letter containing Remarks on the Historical Account of the Old Bank. By a Gentleman concerned in neither Bank. *Edin. 1728*, *4°*. L.

3875 An exact State or Abbreviate of the Affairs of the Bank of Scotland, as they stand ballanced to the 27th March 1728, the Day upon which they were obliged to stop Payments, through Deficiency of Cash: And how the same stands this 18th June the same Year. [*Edin. 1728*], *s. sh. obl. F°*. LU.

3876 Unto the Right Honourable, the Lords of Council and Session, the Petition of the Royal Bank of Scotland. *n.p.* [*1728*], *F°*. LU.
Dated: July 18, 1728. Signed: Dun. Forbes.

3877 Answers for the Bank of Scotland, to the Petition of the Royal Bank. *n.p.* [*1728*], *F°*. LU.
Dated: July 25, 1728. Signed: Ro. Dundas.

3878 BOUVOT, PETER. *Begin.* Introduction. There having been two Memorials printed in the Years 1726 and 1727, about the Second Groningen Lottery, concerning the Irregular Conduct of Messieurs Isaac Barbut, Jaques Fabre, &c. And three other Papers having been since printed this present Year 1728, by some Persons moved thereto by the Egregious Wrong they find done to me (Peter Bouvot) by the Irregular and unjust Behaviour of Isaac Barbut, one of the under Collectors of the Second Groningen Lottery here in London; I thought it proper to print the following Authentick Pieces, with several Accompts relating to the said Lottery, and a short Abstract of the Irregular Conduct of Matthew West, another of the under Collectors of the said Lottery here in London.... *n.p.* [*1728*], *4°*. O.

3879 HAYES, RICHARD. An Estimate of Places for Life: shewing how many Years Purchase a Place for Life is Worth....To which is prefix'd, An Account of the Places which are in the Disposal of the Lord Mayor, Aldermen, and Common Council of the City of London, also of others more immediately belonging to the Crown....Wherein is shewn the Nature and respective Business of the Principal Officers, and in whose Gift most of the said Places are. The whole being interspersed with Directions and Instructions for obtaining Places in General. *Lond. 1728*, *8°*. LU.

3880 Articles and Regulations of the Edinburgh Friendly Insurance against Losses by Fire: and Seal of Cause granted by the Magistrates and Town council of Edinburgh; with the Clause of the Act of Parliament in favours of the said Insurance. *Edin. 1728*, *8°*. O.

TRANSPORT

3881 DOUGLASS, WILLIAM. Some Historical Remarks on the City of St. Andrews in North-Britain. With a particular Account of the Ruinous Condition of the Harbour in that Place; and of what importance the Repairing of it will be, to all concern'd in Trade and Navigation. *Lond. 1728*, *8°*. L.

3882 A Bill for Repairing the Road leading from Chatteris Ferry (which divides the Isle of Ely from the County of Huntingdon) to Somersham Bridge at Somersham Town's-End, in the said County. *n.p.* [*1728*], *F*°. L.

3883 The Case of the Inhabitants of the Town of Parshore in the County of Worcester. *n.p.* [*1728*], *s. sh. F*°. L.

Against the Evesham turnpike bill.

3884 Names of the Commissioners & Trustees for the Bridge between Fulham and Putney. And the Preamble to the Book of Subscriptions for Building the said Bridge. *n.p.* [*1728*], *F*°. L.

SOCIAL CONDITIONS

3885 Some Few Letters Selected, from an Account of Work-Houses and Charity-Schools for Employment of the Poor in England, with a Preface to excite some such Application of our Charity in Ireland. *Dublin*, *1728*, *8*°. LU.

English original 1725 (no. 3522).

3886 An Abridgment of the Statute, made in the first Year of the Reign of King George the IId. For the better Regulating the Work-House of the City of Dublin, and to Regulate and Provide for the Poor thereof: And to prevent Mischiefs which may happen by keeping Gun-Powder within the said City. *Dublin*, *1728*, *8*°. O.

3887 A True Copy of the Remarkable Last Will and Testament of Mr. Francis Bancroft, Citizen and Draper of London.... With a Particular Account of his Donations to the Drapers Company, for the Erecting and Endowing Alms-Houses, &c. *Lond.* *1728*, *8*°. O.

3888 Hawksmoor, Nicholas. Remarks on the Founding and Carrying on the Buildings of the Royal Hospital at Greenwich. *Lond.* *1728*, *4*°. O.

3889 A Memorial, concerning the Erecting in the City of London or the Suburbs thereof, an Orphanotrophy or Hospital for the Reception of Poor Cast-off Children or Foundlings.... *n.p.* [*1728?*], *8*°. LU.

Both L and LU copies have a ms. addition on the title-page: By a Divine of the Church of England in London, Rector of one of the Parish Churches without the City Walls.

3890 Gairdner, Andrew. An Historical Account of the Old Peoples Hospital, commonly called, The Trinity Hospital, in Edinburgh; with Arguments and Motives pleading for Assistance to pay off the present expensive Reparations, and to raise a Fund for maintaining many more People. To which is subjoined, Page 34, Proposals to raise a Fund for the Maintenance of Orphans...under the Title of a Charity-Bank. *Edin.* *1728*, *8*°. LU.

Another edn., 1728, entitled: An Historical Account of the Old Peoples Hospital, commonly called, The Trinity Hospital in Edinburgh; Also Proposals how to raise a Fund... (L); another edn. 1734 (O).

3891 The Case of Insolvent Debtors considered: with Proposals for the Relief both of Them, and their Creditors: Also, Reasons for the Amendment of the Law, and the Lawyers; and for the Restraining the Power and Extortion of Goalers. *Lond.* [*1728?*], *8º*. LU.

3892 The Insolvents Humble Address to Her Majesty. *Lond. 1728*, *4º*. O.

3893 Etats de la Distribution de la Somme de Vint & Quatre Mille Livres, accordée par Sa Majesté le feu Roy, de Glorieuse Memoire, aux Pauvres Protestants François Laïques Refugiez en Angleterre. Administrée par le Committé François, sous les Ordres des Seigneurs nommez par Sa Majesté, & par la Direction de Messieurs les Commissaires Anglois. *Londres*, *1728*, *Fº*. LSC.

3894 Petition and Complaint for Patrick Macduff Merchant Burgess of Edinburgh, and Journeyman Taylor in the Head of rhe [*sic*] Canongate, and Others. *n.p.* [*1728*], *Fº*. E.

Dated: January 12, 1728. Signed: Ja. Graham. About a sickness benefit fund.

3895 Answers for William Clark Deacon of the Taylors in Edinburgh, to the Petition of Patrick McDuff Journeyman Taylor in the Canongate. *n.p.* [*1728*], *Fº*. E.

Dated: January 17, 1728. Signed: Hugh Dalrymple.

3896 [Defoe, Daniel]. Street Robberies, Consider'd: the Reason of their being so Frequent, with Probable Means to Prevent 'em. To which is added, Three Short Treatises; I. A Warning for Travellers....II. Observations on House-breakers....III. A Caveat for Shop-keepers. ...Written by a Converted Thief.... *Lond.* [*1728*], *8º*. L.

For authorship see *C.B.E.L.* II, 509.

3897 A Trip through London: containing Observations on Men and Things.... To which is added, A brief and merry Character of Ireland, by a Berkshire Gentleman lately return'd from that Kingdom. *Lond. 1728*, *8º*. O.

Another edn. revised and abridged 1738 (O), entitled: A Ramble through London....By a True-Born Englishman.

3898 Act of Council. Edinburgh, the Eighteenth Day of March, One thousand seven hundred and twenty eight Years. [*Edin. 1728*], *s. sh. Fº*. EU.

For enforcing the Act of 1705 to prevent fires in the West Bow.

1729

GENERAL

3899 Directions to judge whether a Nation be in a Thriving Condition, and how to advance the Wealth and Power of Great Britain; in which is considered, the Letter in the Daily Journal, Jan. 8, 1728 [O.S.]. *Lond. 1729*, *8°*. L.

3900 [DEFOE, DANIEL]. An Humble Proposal to the People of England, for the Encrease of their Trade, and Encouragement of their Manufactures; whether the present Uncertainty of Affairs issues in Peace or War. By the Author of the Compleat Tradesman. *Lond. 1729*, *8°*. L.

For authorship see *C.B.E.L.* II, 509.

3901 [GEE, JOSHUA]. The Trade and Navigation of Great-Britain considered; shewing that the surest Way for a Nation to increase in Riches, is to prevent the Importation of such Foreign Commodities as may be rais'd at Home.... *Lond. 1729*, *8°*. LU.

Some copies have an additional leaf, containing an address to the reader signed with the author's name. 2nd edn. 1730; another edn. Dublin, 1730; 3rd edn. 1731; 4th edn. 1738; 5th edn. Glasgow, 1750; 6th edn. Glasgow, 1755; another 6th edn. Glasgow, 1760 (all LU); new edn. Lond. 1767 (L); new edn. Glasgow, 1767 (O).

3902 A Collection of Tracts, concerning the Present State of Ireland, with respect to its Riches, Revenue, Trade and Manufactures. Containing I. Seasonable Remarks on Trade.... II. An Essay on Trade in General; and on that of Ireland in Particular. III. Considerations on two Papers lately publish'd. The first call'd Seasonable Remarks, &c. And the other, an Essay on Trade in General.... IV. An Appeal to the Reverend Dean Swift, by way of Reply to the Observer on Seasonable Remarks. V. A Letter in answer to a Paper, intitl'd, An Appeal to the Reverend Dean Swift. *Dublin, 1729*, *8°*. L.

No. I, II and IV by Sir John Browne. All previously published separately in 1728. Another edn. Lond. 1729 (O).

3903 [BROWNE, Sir JOHN]. Reflections Little to the Purpose, on a Paper Less to the Purpose. By the Author of Seasonable Remarks. *Dublin, 1729*, *8°*. L.

A reply to *A Letter in Answer to a Paper, intitled, An Appeal to the Reverend Dean Swift*, which is reprinted at the end of this work. For authorship see *Seasonable Remarks*, 1728 (no. 3808).

3904 DOBBS, ARTHUR. An Essay on the Trade and Improvement of Ireland. *Dublin, 1729, 31*, *8°*. 2pt. LU.

Reprinted in *A Collection of Tracts and Treatises Illustrative of the Natural History, Antiquities, and the Political and Social State of Ireland*, vol. 2, (1861).

3905 A Letter to the People of Ireland. By M. B. Draper. *Dublin, 1729*, *8°*. DNL.

Signed: Publicola.

3906 [PRIOR, THOMAS]. A List of the Absentees of Ireland, and the Yearly Values of their Estates and Incomes spent abroad. With Observations on the Present State and Condition of That Kingdom. *Dublin, 1729,* *8°*. L.

Appendix, Dublin, 1729 (C); 2nd edn. Dublin, 1729 (L); another edn. Lond. 1730 [1729] (L); 2nd edn. corrected, Lond. 1730 [1729] (L); another edn. Dublin, 1730 (L); 3rd edn. corrected, Lond. 1730 (C); another 3rd edn., with additions [and author's name], Dublin, 1745 (L). Many later editions.

3907 The Present State of Ireland Consider'd. *Dublin, 1730* [*1729*], *8°*. L.

Another edn. Lond. 1730 [1729] (O).

AGRICULTURE

3908 BRADLEY, RICHARD. The Gentleman and Farmer's Guide Abridg'd. For the Increase and Improvement of Cattle....Also the best Manner of Breeding and Breaking Horses.... *Dublin, 1729, 12°*. DNL.

3909 BRADLEY, RICHARD. A Philosophical Enquiry into the Late Severe Winter, the Scarcity and Dearness of Provisions, and the Occasion of the Distemper raging in several remote Parts of England.... *Lond. 1729, 8°*. LU.

3910 BRADLEY, RICHARD. The Riches of a Hop-Garden explain'd, from the several Improvements arising by that Beneficial Plant....With the Observations and Remarks of the most celebrated Hop-Planters in Britain. Wherein such Rules are laid down for the Management of the Hop, as may improve the most barren Ground, from one shilling to thirty or forty Pounds an Acre per Annum.... *Lond. 1729, 8°*. L.

2nd edn. [1731 ?] (O); another 2nd edn. Dublin, 1731 (DNL).

3911 [MACKINTOSH, WILLIAM]. An Essay on Ways and Means for Inclosing, Fallowing, Planting, &c. Scotland; and that in Sixteen Years at Farthest. By a Lover of his Country. *Edin., 1729, 8°*. O.

For authorship see *D.N.B.*

3912 Short Rules and Observations for Sowing of Lint-Seed and Hemp-Seed, and for pulling and dressing the Flax and Hemp. *Edin. 1729, 8°*. LU.

3913 An Act for Inclosing Part of a Common called Barnett Common, belonging to the Manor of Chippen Barnett in the County of Hertford, and for Vesting a certain annual Rent-Charge in Trustees for the Benefit of the Poor of the Parish of Chippen Barnett for ever. *n.p.* [*1729*], *F°*. L.

A bill.

3914 An Act for Dividing and Inclosing the Common, called Elsdon Common in the Parish of Elsdon, in the County of Northumberland. *n.p.* [*1729*], *F°*. L.

3915 An Act for Inclosing Aldham and Boyne Commons, belonging to the Parish of Hadleigh, in the County of Suffolk, for the better Maintenance of the Poor of the said Parish. *n.p.* [*1729*], *F°*. L.

3916 An Act for Inclosing and Dividing the Common Fields and Common Grounds in the Parish of Horninghold in the County of Leicester. *n.p. 1729*, *F°*. L.

3917 An Act for confirming the Inclosure and Division of the Common Fields and Common Grounds within the Parish of Thurnscoe, in the County of York. *n.p.* [*1729*], *F°*. L.

3918 A Bill for confirming Exchanges, Allotments, Divisions, and Inclosures of Lands in the Parish of Wick-Risington in the County of Gloucester, and for Establishing the Payment of a Yearly Sum to the Rector and his Successors, in Lieu of Tithes, pursuant to Agreements between Vincent Oakley, Esq; deceased, and the other Proprietors of the said Lands. *n.p.* [*1729*], *F°*. LHL.

3919 An Act for confirming Exchanges, Allotments, Divisions, and Inclosures of Lands in the Parish of Wick-Risington in the County of Gloucester, and for Establishing the Payment of a Yearly Sum to the Rector and his Successors, in Lieu of Tithes, pursuant to Agreements between Vincent Oakley, Esq; deceased, and the other Proprietors of the said Lands. *n.p.* [*1729*], *F°*. L.

3920 BADESLADE, THOMAS. A Scheme for Draining the Great Level of the Fens, called Bedford-Level; and for Improving the Navigation of Lyn-Regis. Founded upon self-evident Principles in experimental Philosophy and practical Mathematicks, and upon Historical Facts. And farther demonstrated by comparing the River Ouse, with the River Thames, &c. and Lyn-Harbour, with the Harbour of Rye. With Reflections upon all the Schemes hitherto proposed for Draining the Fens, shewing wherein they are defective. Also Observations upon Artificial-Scours: Shewing where, and in what Cases they are, or can be of Use: where not. Illustrated with a Map. *Lond. 1729*, *F°*. O.

3921 By the King, A Proclamation, For suppressing Riots and Tumults, committed by Tinners, and others, within the County of Cornwall, and for apprehending the Offenders therein. *Lond. 1729*, *s. sh. F°*. L.

Dated: 26 March [1729].

3922 SPEARMAN, JOHN. An Enquiry into the Ancient and Present State of the County Palatine of Durham. Wherein are shewn the Oppressions which attend the Subjects of this County by the Male-administration of the present Ministers and Officers of the said County Palatine. With some Reasons humbly offered to the Freeholders, Leaseholders and Copyholders of the said County to consider of Ways and Means to remedy the said Abuses.... *n.p. 1729*, *4°*. L.

Pt. I by John Spearman; pts. II and III by Gilbert Spearman. See R. Surtees, *The History and Antiquities of Durham*, vol. I (1816), Introduction p. 7.

3923 [KNIGHTLEY, JOHN]. Reasons humbly offer'd to the Consideration of the Nobility and Gentry of this Kingdom for raising of a Joint Stock Sterl. for the Purposes herein mentioned. *n.p.* [*1729*], *F°*. L.

For developing Irish collieries. Authorship deduced from other letters in the same volume (Add. MS. 21134).

3924 To the Gentlemen and others of the Kingdom of Ireland.... *n.p.* [*1729*], *s. sh. F°*. DM.

An announcement by Benja. Lund and Francis Hawksbee that they possess a patent for working copper and iron mines in Ireland.

3925 A Bill for Publick Registering of all Deeds, Conveyances, and other Incumbrances that shall be made of, or that may affect any Honours, Manors, Lands, Tenements, or Hereditaments within the County of Surrey. *n.p.* [*1729*], *F°*. L.

3926 [HUTCHINSON, FRANCIS, Bishop of Down and Connor]. A Second Letter to a Member of Parliament, recommending the Improvement of the Irish-Fishery. *Dublin*, *1729*, *8°*. LU.

For authorship see *The Whole Works of Sir James Ware*, ed. by W. Harris, 1764, vol. I, p. 216.

MANUFACTURES

3927 Reasons against several clauses in the Bill now depending, Intitled, A Bill to prevent Abuses in making of Bricks and Tiles, and to ascertain the Dimensions thereof. *n.p.* [*1729*], *s. sh. F°*. O.

3928 Reasons Most Humbly Offered for an Amendment to an Act of the twelfth Year of His Late Majesty King George I. intitul'd, An Act for preventing Abuses in making of Bricks and Tiles. *n.d.* [*1729*], *s. sh. F°*. MC.

3929 LANGLEY, BATTY. A Sure Guide to Builders: or, the Principles and Practice of Architecture Geometrically Demonstrated, and made Easy for the Use of Workmen in general....To which is added, An Appendix. Wherein the several Acts of Parliament, now in Force relating to Builders, Building, and Materials, are explain'd for the Service of Surveyors, Master-Builders, Workmen, and Proprietors of Buildings.... *Lond.* *1729*, *4°*. LU.

3930 SMITH, GEORGE, of Kendal. The Nature of Fermentation explain'd; with the Method of opening the Body of any Grain or Vegetable Subject, so as to obtain from it a Spirituous Liquor: exemplified by the Process of preparing Rum, as 'tis manag'd in the West-Indies. With many other useful Reflections and Observations....By way of Appendix to the Compleat Body of Distilling. *Lond.* *1729*, *8°*. L.

3931 MAPLE, WILLIAM. A Method of Tanning without Bark. *Dublin*, *1729*, *8°*. LU.

Another edn., Lond. 1729, entitled: A New and Effectual Method of Tanning without Bark (L).

3932 Information for the Incorporation of Litsters and Bonnet-makers of Edinburgh, against the Wakers and Hatters. *n.p.* [*1729*], 4°. E.

Dated: July 4. 1729. Signed: Jo. Forbes.

3933 Unto the Right Honourable, The Lords of Council and Session, the Petition of the Incorporation of Litsters in Edinburgh. *n.p.* [*1729*], 4°. E.

Dated: December 16, 1729. Signed: Hugh Dalrymple. Claiming a monopoly of dyeing.

3934 Information for the Deacon and other Members of the Incorporation of Taylors of the Burgh of Irvine, against Agnes and Margaret Clarks Manto-makers there. *n.p.* [*1729*], *s. sh. F°.* E.

Dated: January 9, 1729. Signed: And, M'Douall. Against interlopers.

3935 Information for Anna and Margaret Clarks, Mantua-makers in Irvin, Against the Taylors of Irvin. *n.p.* [*1729*], *s. sh. F°.* E.

Dated: January 10, 1729. Signed: Henry Home.

COMMERCE

3936 Observations on the first six of the Morning and Evening Papers, publish'd by the Subscribing Coffee-Men of London and Westminster. Shewing that they contain more Falshoods and Blunders, Impertinent and Trifling Relations, and more Repititions, than the present Sett of News-Papers have done for Twelve Month's past. And that the Complaint, of the Charge of News thrown on the Coffee-Men, is made chiefly by the Keepers of Unaccustom'd Houses, and by Coffee-Men whose Trade won't afford them to take in any News-Papers at all. No. 1. *Lond. 1729*, 4°. L.

3937 The Case between the Proprietors of News-Papers and the Subscribing Coffee-Men, fairly stated. Being Remarks on their Case Lately Publish'd....With a Proposal for Remedying the flagrant, scandalous, and growing Impositions of the Coffee-Men upon the Publick. *Lond. 1729*, 8°. L.

3938 The Case between the Proprietors of News-Papers, and the Coffee-Men of London and Westminster, fairly Stated. Being Remarks on their Case lately publish'd....To which is annex'd, I. Henley the Orator and the Butchers....II. A Whip for the Post-Boy.... *Lond.* [*1729*], 8°. L.

Entirely different from the preceding.

3939 The Case of the Maltsters, Corn-Merchants, and other Dealers in Malt, Barly, &c. trading from the several Coasts and Ports of Great Britain to London: Humbly offer'd to the Honourable the House of Commons. *n.p.* [*1729*], F°. MP.

3940 A Letter to the Rt. Hon. Sir R[ober]t W[alpo]le, with Hints: And a

Letter sent to a Reverend Bishop, and other Chief Magistrates, on the behalf of all Working Men, and all the Poor in general. By Matt. Tell-Truth. *Lond. 1729, s. sh. F°.* C (Cr).

Against the buying up of wheat by such as are not qualified by statute.

3941 EDINBURGH. Act of Council against Unfree Traders, &c. [*Edin. 1729*], *s. sh. F°.* EU.

Dated: Feb. 29 [*sic* for 26]. 1729.

3942 The Case of Many Thousand poor Inhabitants of Dublin: In a Letter to a worthy Member of Parliament, concerning the extravagant Rates and Price, of Coals in this City, with a Recommendation for the importing Kilkenny-Coals here, from Ross and Waterford, and other Ports of this Kingdom. The second Impression with a Postscript, by M.B. *Dublin, 1729, 8°.* DA.

Originally printed in *The Dublin Weekly Journal* of 9 August 1729 (Wagner 108 n.).

3943 To all the House Keepers of the City of Dublin. A Supplement to the Drapier's Letter in the Behalf of many Thousand poor Inhabitants of this City. Or, a Third Letter, in Answer to a worthy Member of Parilament [*sic*]. Concerning the extravagant Rates, and Prices of Coals, with a Recomendation, for the importing Kilkenny-Coals, from Ross, Waterford, and other Ports of this Kingdom. *Dublin,* [*1729*], *8°.* DA.

Signed: C.D.

3944 SEYMOUR, FRANCIS. Remarks on the Scheme for Supplying the City of Dublin with Coals from the County of Tyrone: in a Letter to Thomas Burgh Esq; His Majesty's Engineer and Surveyor-General. *n.p.* [*1729*], *8°.* DA.

Dated: Belfast Septem. 24th 1729.

3945 Animadversions on several Proposals now under Consideration, for Supplying the City of Dublin with Coals from within the Kingdom of Ireland.... *n.p.* [*1729*], *8°.* DA.

3946 A Poem occasion'd by the Lord Mayor's Reducing the Price of Coals, &c. Written by a Fellow-Sufferer in the Hardships of the Times.... *Dublin, 1729, s. sh. F°.* D.

3947 Articles of the Treaty signed at Seville in Spain, between their Catholick and Britannick Majesties. With Remarks on the said Treaty. In a Letter from a Member of Parliament in London to another at Heddon in Yorkshire. To which is prefixed, an Advertisement, inscribed to the English Merchants. *Lond. 1729, 8°.* O.

3948 [DEFOE, DANIEL]. The Advantages of Peace and Commerce; with Some Remarks on the East-India Trade. *Lond. 1729, 8°.* LU.

For authorship see *C.B.E.L.* II, 510.

3949 A Letter to Caleb D'Anvers, Esq; occasioned by the Depredations committed by the Spaniards in the West-Indies. With Observations on the Trade carried on from Jamaica to the Spanish Coast. *Lond. 1729, 8o*. L.

3950 Observations on the Conduct of Great-Britain, with regard to the Negociations and other Transactions abroad. *Lond. 1729, 8o*. LU.

Another edn., Edin., 1729, 8° (L).

3951 The Craftsman Extraordinary. Being Remarks on a late Pamphlet, intitled, Observations on the Conduct of Great Britain, &c. Published by Caleb D'Anvers, Esq; *Printed for R. Francklin, Lond. 1729, 8o*. L.

Signed: W. Raleigh. Another edn. *Printed for B. Franklin*, 1729 (L). Reprinted in *The Craftsman*, vol. 4 (1731), and in *A Collection of Political Tracts*, 1748, the rest of which are by Bolingbroke, who did not, however, use this pseudonym.

3952 One Word with the Craftsman Extraordinary. *Lond. 1729, 8o*. LU.

3953 The Second Craftsman Extraordinary: being Farther Remarks on a Pamphlet lately publish'd, entitled, Observations on the Conduct of Great Britain....Published by Caleb D'Anvers, Esq; *Lond.* [*1729*], *8o*. LU.

Attributed to Henry St. John, Viscount Bolingbroke in H. & L., but the imprint 'Printed for R.F.' suggests that this is spurious (see advt. in *The Craftsman*, 15 Feb. 1729).

3954 Some Farther Remarks on a late Pamphlet, intitled, Observations on the Conduct of Great-Britain; Particularly with Relation to the Spanish Depredations and Letters of Reprisal. In a Letter to the Craftsman. To which is added, a Postscript, in Vindication of the West-India Merchants, against a late Charge of Theft and Pyracy. By Caleb D'Anvers of Gray's-Inn, Esq; [pseud.]. *Lond. 1729, 8o*. L.

3955 Peace and Trade, War and Taxes; or, the Irreparable Damage to our Trade in Case of a War. In a Letter to the Craftsman. By Tho. Merchant, Esq; *Lond. 1729, 8o*. LU.

3956 [Defoe, Daniel]. Reasons for a War, in order to establish the Tranquility and Commerce of Europe. *Lond. 1729, 8o*. LU.

For authorship see *C.B.E.L.* II, 509.

3957 Some Observations on Damages done by the Spaniards: or, a Representation of some of our Sea Damages, in the five Years last past; Collected out of Publick Accounts, by some Trading Men of the City of London.... *Lond.* [*1729*], *8o*. L.

3958 The Case of the Woollen Manufacturers, and particularly those of the City of Worcester, with Relation to the Turkey Trade. *n.p.* [*1729*], *s. sh. Fo*. LLI.

3959 Considerations on the Levant Trade, Relating to the Importation of Silk from Turkey, and Silk Imported from other Parts in Europe. *n.p.* [*1729?*], *s. sh. Fo*. MC.

3960 Observations on the Behalf of the Bill, for the better Employing the Poor, and Encouraging the Manufactures of this Kingdom, by preventing the clandestine Importation of wrought Silks, mix'd with Gold, Silver, or other Materials. *n.p.* [*1729*], *s. sh. F°.* MP.

3961 A Bill for better Preservation of his Majesty's Woods in America, and for the Encouragement of the Importation of Naval Stores from thence, and to Encourage the Importation of Masts, Yards, and Bowsprights, from that part of Great-Britain called Scotland. *n.p.* [*1729*], *F°.* L.

3962 The Case of the Planters of Virginia, and the Merchants Trading thither, humbly represented to the Parliament. *n.p.* [*1729*], *s. sh. F°.* L.

For permission to export tobacco stripped from the stalk.

COLONIES

3963 In the House of Representatives [of Massachusetts], December 20th. 1729. A Bill, Entitled, An Act for Retrieving and Ascertaining the Value of the Bills of Credit on this Province.... *Boston, 1729, F°.* LPRO.

3964 [FRANKLIN, BENJAMIN]. A Modest Enquiry into the Nature and Necessity of a Paper-Currency. *Philadelphia, 1729, 8°.*

Signed: B. B. Reprinted in *Colonial Currency Reprints*, ed. by A. M. Davis, vol. 2 (1911), whence this entry is taken.

FINANCE

3965 [BLUNT, Sir JOHN]. A True State of the South-Sea-Scheme, as it was first form'd, &c. With the Several Alterations made in it, before the Act of Parliament pass'd. And an Examination of the Conduct of the Directors in the Execution of that Act. With an Enquiry into some of the Causes of the Losses which have ensued. As also an Abstract of several Clauses of the Acts of Parliament made against those Directors.... *Lond. 1722, F°.* LU.

Another edn. 1732, 8° (LU). For authorship see A. Boyer, *Political State*, XXXVI, 235.

3966 PLATOE, WILLIAM. An Extraordinary Craftsman: containing, A full and particular Account of a South-Sea Scheme....With some seasonable Advice to a Nation-Plunderer. Revis'd and publish'd by Caleb D'Anvers. *Lond. 1729, 8°.* LU.

3967 The Report of the Trustees for the Estates of the late South-Sea Directors, &c. to the 21st of January 1728 [o.s.]. Presented by Sir John Eyles, the 7th of February 1728.... *Lond. 1728* [*o.s.*], *F°.* L.

3968 Two Letters printed in June and September, 1728. giving an Account of the Rise and Progress of the Sinking Fund. *Lond. 1729, 8°.* LU.

3969 Two Proposals for Raising 1,250,000 l. for the Current Service of the Year 1729. and for Appropriating the Produce of the Sinking Fund. With a Comparison betwixt the Two Proposals; showing the Advantages of the One over the Other to the Publick. With a Letter to —— —— Esq; *Lond. 1729, 8o.* L.

The letter is signed: T—— G——.

3970 A Collection of all the Statutes now in Force, relating to the Duties upon Salt, with so much of the Laws of Excise, as are particularly referr'd to in the said Statutes. *Lond. 1729, 12o.* LU.

LU copy has bound up with this 'A Continuation of the Statutes, relating to the Duties on Salt, from 1729, to 1738'.

3971 The Case of the Victuallers and others, Retailers of Ale and Beer within the Cities of London and Westminster, and Parts adjacent. *n.p. [1729], s. sh. Fo.* L.

Against the duty levied on them.

3972 DOWDALL, W. The Several Statutes made in this Kingdom, and in Great-Britain, relating to His Majesty's Revenue, and the Trade of Ireland, &c. Divided into Clauses, under proper Heads, Alphabetically....To which is added, The Book of Rates.... *Dublin, 1729, 8o.* LU.

3973 The Case of the Merchants, Importers of Wines into the Port of London. *n.p. [1729?], s. sh. Fo.* L.

For equality with the out-ports as regards duties.

3974 SABOURN, REAY. Oppression exposed, or Liberty and Property Maintained: Being an Enquiry into the Mismanagements of Persons concerned in the Revenues of Customs and Excise in Scotland. *Edin. 1729, 8o.* LU.

3975 [PULTENEY, WILLIAM, Earl of Bath]. A Letter from a Member of Parliament to a Friend in the Country, concerning the Sum of 115,000 l. granted for the Service of the Civil List. *Lond. 1729, 8o.* pp. 30. LU.

Another edn. Lond., 1729, pp. 24; another edn. Lond. [1729]; 2nd edn. Lond. [1729] (all LU); 3rd, 4th and 5th edns. Lond. [1729] (all O). For authorship see B.M. Catalogue.

3976 [PULTENEY, WILLIAM, Earl of Bath]. A Second Letter from a Member of Parliament to his Friend in the Country; concerning the Sum of 115,000 l. granted to make good the Civil-List Revenue. Containing, Some Remarks on the Methods generally made use of in the Passing our Money-Bills in the H. of C——. To which are added, Some Considerations on the...Act to prevent Bribery and Corruption in the Election of Members to serve in Parliament....Together with, The Pacifick Fleet; a New Ballad. By the Author of the First Letter. *Lond. 1729, 8o.* L.

For authorship see B.M. Catalogue.

3977 Some Farther Particulars concerning the Sum of 115,000 l. granted on Account of Arrears in his present Majesty's Civil List Revenues; Related in a genuine second Letter from a Member of Parliament to his Friend in the Country. *Lond.* [*1729*], *8°*. LU.

3978 The Case of the Inhabitants of the two New Parishes of Spittlefields and Wapping Stepney. *n.p.* [*1729?*], *s. sh. F°*. LLI.

On parochial taxes.

3979 OLDENBURGH, EDWARD. A Calculation of Foreign Exchanges, as transacted on the Royal Exchange of London: or, Tables, shewing at once, or by a few Additions, any Sum of English Money reduc'd into Foreign Species, and likewise any Sum of Foreign Species reduc'd into English Money, by way of Exchange, at the several Prices, as from Time to Time the Exchange may Rise or Fall. *Lond.* *1729*, *4°*. LU.

2nd edn., with additions, 1735 (L); 3rd edn. 1756 (LU).

3980 BINDON, DAVID. An Essay on the Gold and Silver-Coin currant in Ireland. *Dublin*, *1729*, *8°*. LU.

3981 [MACULLA, JAMES]. A Letteer [*sic*] to the People of Ireland, relating to the Copper Half-pence, Coining in Dublin. Shewing, that this Nation will gain a Hundred Thousand Pounds sterl. Cash by the same. Twenty thousand Pounds thereof is now a Manufacturing. *Dublin*, *1729*, *8°*. LU

Authorship deduced from internal evidence.

3982 MACULLA, JAMES. A new Scheme proposed, to the People of Ireland; for increasing the Cash, of this Kingdom; by making Promissory Notes of Copper, to bear an Intrinsick Value of the British-Halfpence.... *Dublin*, *1728–9*, *8°*. EU.

3983 [PRIOR, THOMAS]. Observations on Coin in General. With some Proposals for Regulating the Value of Coins in Ireland. By the Author of the List of the Absentees of Ireland. *Dublin*, *1729*, *8°*. L.

Another edn. Lond. 1730 (L). Reprinted, with author's name, in *A Select Collection of Scarce and Valuable Tracts on Money*, ed. by J. R. McCulloch, 1856, p. 291.

3984 The Present State of Ireland. Being Sir Isaac Newton's Representation about the Gold and Silver Coins, to the Right Honourable the Lords Commissioners of His Majesty's Treasury. *Dublin*, *1729*, *8°*. L.

A reprint of Newton's Mint report of 21 Sept. 1717 which seems to have been first published in the *Daily Courant* of 30 Dec. 1717.

3985 [BROWNE, Sir JOHN]. A Scheme of the Money-Matters of Ireland. In which the Consequences of raising or lowering the Coin, are impartially consider'd. *Printed by S. Powell and sold by G. Ewing, Dublin*, *1729*, *8°*. LU.

Another issue, with the names of E. Hamilton and T. Watson added in the imprint (D). Authorship acknowledged in Browne's *The Benefits...from Navigable Rivers*, 1729.

3986 A Short Account of the Reasons of the Intended Alteration of the Value of the Coins Currant in this Kingdom. *Dublin*, *1729*, 8°. LU.

Wagner suggests that William Maple is probably the author.

3987 To their Excellencies the Lords Justices, and the Most Hon. the Privy-Council of Ireland. The Humble Address and Representation of the Grand Jury of the County of Dublin, assembled at His Majesty's Chief Bench, this present Easter Term 1729. *Dublin*, *1729*, *s. sh. F°*. DA.

Against devaluing gold.

3988 [MAPLE, WILLIAM]. A Vindication of the Intended Alterations of the Value of the several Coins now currant in this Kingdom from the Objections made against them. *Dublin*, *1729*, 8°. LU.

For authorship see Sir John Browne, *A Short Review of the several Pamphlets that have appeared this Sessions on the Subject of the Coin*, 1729, p. 18, 'generally supposed to be wrote by the ingenious Mr. Maple'.

3989 Warrant of the Charter erecting the Royal Bank of Scotland. *Edin. 1729*, 8°. LU.

3990 The Governor and Company of the Royal Bank of Scotland, and Andrew Cochran Merchant in Glasgow, Appellants, The Governor and Company of the Bank of Scotland, Respondents. The Appellants Case. *n.p.* [*1729*], *F°*. L.

Signed: P. Yorke, Dun. Forbes, C. Talbot, Will. Hamilton.

3991 The Governor and Company of the Royal Bank of Scotland, (called the New Bank) and Andrew Cochran, Merchant, Appellants. The Governor and Company of the Bank of Scotland, (called the Old Bank), Responde ts. The Respondents Case. *n.p.* [*1729*], *F°* L.

Signed: J. Willes, Will. Grant.

3992 BINDON, DAVID. A Scheme for Supplying Industrious Men with Money to carry on their Trades, and for better Providing for the Poor of Ireland. *Dublin*, *1729*, 8°. LU.

2nd edn. 1729 (DA); another edn. 1733 (LU); 3rd edn. 1750 (DA). Advocating the establishment of municipal lombards.

TRANSPORT

3993 The Case of the Owners and Masters of Ships Imploy'd in the Coal-Trade. *n.p.* [*1729*], *s. sh. F°*. L.

3994 A Free and Impartial Enquiry into the Reasons of the present Extravagant Price of Coals; shewing the great Inconveniences which arise from thence, especially to the Manufacturers of the City of London, and adjacent Counties....By Philalethes. *Lond. 1729*, 8°. LU.

3995 BROWNE, Sir JOHN. The Benefits which arise to a Trading People from Navigable Rivers. To which are added, some Considerations on the

Origin of Loughs and Bogs; and a Scheme, for the establishment of a Company, to make the River Shannon navigable.... *Dublin, 1729*, 8°. L.

3996 Considerations on the Act for encouraging In-land Navigation in Ireland. With Some Hints of a Method for Enforcing and Executing that Act. In a letter from a Country Gentleman to his Friend in the House of Commons. *Dublin, 1729*, 8°. LU.

Signed: Patriophilus.

3997 A Bill for making more effectual the Acts passed for repairing the Road, from the Stones-End in Shoreditch, in the County of Middlesex, to the furthermost Part of the Northern Road in the Parish of Enfield in the same County, next to the Parish of Cheshunt in the County of Hertford. *n.p.* [*1729*], *F°*. L.

3998 Unto the Right Honourable, The Lords of Council and Session, The Petition of John Irvine Drover in Dumfries, Against Francis Irvine Tacksman of the Bridge-customs of Dumfries. *n.p.* [*1729*], *F°*. E.

Dated: January 7, 1729. Signed: Ja. Fergusson.

3999 Answers for Francis Irvine Tacksman of the Customs, called, The Bridge Customs of Dumfries, to the Petition of John Irvine Drover in Dumfries. *n.p.* [*1729*], *F°*. E.

Dated: February 13. 1729. Signed: Ro. Dundas.

SOCIAL CONDITIONS

4000 Cases and Resolutions of Cases, adjudg'd in the Court of King's Bench, concerning Settlements and Removals, from the first Year of King George I. to the present Reign.... The Second Edition. *Lond. 1729*, 8°. OAS.

3rd edn. 1732 (L); 4th edn. 1742 (L).

4001 CHAMBRES, CHARLES. A Sermon preach'd at Dartford in Kent, at the Opening of the New Workhouse there, October 5. 1729....To which is added, The Œconomy of this Workhouse.... *Lond. 1729*, 8°. O.

4002 EDINBURGH. Act of Council anent Vagrant Poor. [*Edin. 1729*], *s. sh. F°*. E.

Dated: 6 January 1729.

4003 [MACLAURIN, J.]. The Case of the Poor Consider'd; or, the great Advantages of Erecting a Publick Manufactory, for Maintaining and Employing the Poor. [*Glasgow, 1729*], *F°*. E.

For authorship see ms. note in E copy.

4004 The Case of the Poor of the Kingdom of Ireland, Stated and Considered, upon the common Principles of Christianity. *Dublin, 1729*, *s. sh. F°*. D.

4005 [SWIFT, JONATHAN]. A Modest Proposal for preventing the Children of Poor People from being a Burthen to their Parents, or the Country, and for making them Beneficial to the Publick. *Dublin, 1729, 8°.* O.

Another edn., with author's name, sold by J. Roberts, Lond. 1730 (L); another edn., anonymous, printed for W. Bickerton, Lond. 1730 (L); 2nd edn., as preceding, 1730 (LU); 3rd edn. 1730 (L). Reprinted in *The Prose Works of Jonathan Swift*, ed. by H. Davis, vol. 12 (1955).

4006 An Account of the Money Collected in Pursuance of His Majesty's Letters Patents, and the Manner in which it has been distributed. *Dublin, 1729, s. sh. F°.* C.

For the poor of Dublin.

4007 To His Excellency John Lord Carteret, Lord Lieutenant General and General Governor of Ireland. The Petition of Martha Barret Widdow. *Dublin, 1729, s. sh. F°.* D.

For the grant of a brief to have the charity of Dublin, Kildare and Meath to repair the total loss of her house and possessions by fire. With the grant of the brief.

4008 LACY, JOSEPH. A Letter from Mr. Lacy, late Merchant and Quaker, (who was confin'd Two Years in the Bastile in France by His Excellency the British Ambassador) to his Creditors. *Dunkirk, 1729, 8°.* LU.

On imprisonment for debt.

4009 MACKAY, JOHN. A True State of the Proceedings of the Prisoners in the Fleet-Prison, in order to the Redressing their Grievances, before the Court of Common-Pleas. Impartially Collected, and Publish'd as a Key for the more clear Apprehension of some Part of the late Glorious and Memorable Report in Parliament.... *Westminster, 1729, F°.* L.

4010 The Arbitrary Punishments and Cruel Tortures inflicted on Prisoners for Debt Represented and Describ'd, in several Figures of the Uncommon and Dangerous Instruments used for that Purpose....Also a True State of all the other Miseries and Oppressions of Goals.... To which is added, Copies of all the necessary Forms to be used for the Discharge of Insolvent Debtors....By W.R., a Sufferer in the Fleet and other Goals. *Lond. 1729, 8°.* LU.

4011 The Case of the Unfortunate Truly Stated. The Second Edition, with Additions. By W.M. *Lond. 1729, 8°.* L.

Imprisonment for debt.

4012 An Extract of the Act pass'd 11 Georg. I. intituled, An Act for the Relief of Insolvent Debtors. With Remarks thereon. Written by Mr. Asgill. To which is added, A Postscript concerning Taxes: with a Proposal thereon. *Lond. 1729, 8°.* O.

4013 BYROM, SAMUEL. An Irrefragable Argument Fully Proving, That to Discharge Great Debts is Less Injury, and More Reasonable, than to Discharge Small Debts.... *Lond. 1729, 8°.* L.

4014 A Letter to My Lord S****** concerning the Prisons for Debts. With a Hint or two of a Method for securing the Creditor's Property, without touching the Person of the Debtor. *Lond. 1729, 8o.* LU.

Signed: Philanthropos.

4015 The Miseries of Goals, and the Cruelty of Goalers. Being a Narrative of Several Persons now under Confinement. *Lond. 1729, 8o.* LU.

4016 Seasonable Considerations relating to Insolvent Debtors, drawn from the Practice of Foreign States, addressed to the Right Honourable Arthur Onslow.... *Lond. 1729, 8o.* LU.

4017 [Defoe, Daniel]. Some Objections humbly offered to the Consideration of the Hon. House of Commons, relating to the present intended Relief of Prisoners. *Lond. 1729, 8o.* LU.

For authorship see *C.B.E.L.* II, 510.

4018 Some Thoughts relating to an Extensive Act of Insolvency. *n.p.* [*c. 1729?*], *s. sh. Fo.* LU.

4019 A Speech without Doors, in behalf of an Insolvent Debtor in the Fleet-Prison. With Some Remarks on the Present State of Goal-archy. *Lond.* [*1729*], *8o.* L.

4020 The Unreasonableness and Ill Consequence of Imprisoning the Body for Debt, Prov'd from the Laws of God and Nature, Human Policy and Interest.... *Lond. 1729, 8o.* LU.

Attributed to Defoe in *C.B.E.L.* II, 510, and to Charles Houghton in the Kress Catalogue.

4021 The State of the Case of great Numbers of Gentlemen, Merchants, Tradesmen, Widows, and other unfortunate Persons, confined for Debt in the Marshalsea of the Four-Courts, Dublin; and several other Goals of this Kingdom. Humbly submitted to the Consideration of both Houses of Parliament. *n.p.* [*1729*], *s. sh. Fo.* D.

Endorsed: The State of the Case of the Insolvent Debtors of Ireland.

4022 A Report from the Committee appointed to Enquire into the State of the Goals of this Kingdom: Relating to the Fleet Prison. With the Resolutions and Orders of the House of Commons thereupon. *Lond. 1729, Fo.* LU.

Another edn. Dublin, 1729, 8o. (O).

4023 The Case of Thomas Bambridge, Esq; who was Examin'd by the Committee of the Honourable House of Commons on Friday the 18th Instant. *Dublin, 1729, s. sh. Fo.* D.

4024 Mr. Bambridge's Case against the Bill now depending, to disable him to Hold or Execute the Office of Warden of the Prison of the Fleet; or to have or exercise any Authority relating thereto. *n.p.* [*1729*], *Fo.* pp. 3. L.

Another edn. [1729?], pp. 4 (L).

4025 The Case of Mr. Bygrave, late Clerk to the Papers of the Fleet. *n.p.* [*1729*], *F°*. L.

For compensation if the act depriving Bambridge of the Wardenship grants him an allowance.

4026 A Report from the Committee appointed to Enquire into the State of the Goals of this Kingdom: Relating to the Marshalsea Prison; And farther Relating to the Fleet Prison. With the Resolution of the House of Commons thereupon. *Lond. 1729, F°*. L.

4027 The Committee's Memorial. Being the Goalers and Keepers of Newgate, Marshalsea, King's Bench, Burrough Court, White Chappel, Clink, Westminster Gate-House, and the City Compters, &c. Bloody Calender, with the Examination of the Prisoners therein confin'd; by the Honourable Esq; Oglethorp and Mr. Alderman Parsons, with the rest of the Honourable Committee of the House of Commons.... *Lond.* [*1729*], *4°*. L.

Another edn. n.p. [1729], 4° (L).

4028 Rules and Orders for the better Government of the King's Bench Prison, made and sign'd by the Lord Chief Justice and Judges of his Majesty's Court of King's Bench...this five and twentieth Day of November... 1729. *Lond. 1729, 8°*. LU.

4029 The Case of the Mortgagees of the Fees and Profits of the Office of Marshal of the King's-Bench Prison. *n.p.* [*1729*], *s. sh. F°*. L.

4030 A Report from the Committee appointed to Enquire into the State of the Goals of this Kingdom, relating to Newgate and the Sheriffs Marshalsea. With the Resolutions and Orders of the House of Commons thereupon. *Dublin, 1729, F°*. DNL.

Another edn. Lond. 1729 (O), entitled: A Report from the Committee appointed to Enquire into the State of the Goals of the Kingdom of Ireland....

4031 The Batchelor's Estimate of the Expenses of a Married Life. In a Letter to a Friend. Being an Answer to a Proposal of Marrying a Lady with 2000 l. Fortune. *Lond. 1729, F°*. O.

3rd edn., 1729 (L); 4th, n.d. (MH); L also has two other undated editions, one 12° and one F°. All these include 'The Lady's Answer'. Another edn. 1741, entitled *The Bachelor's Monitor* (not seen). Another edn. Dublin (DA copy has date cropped off). Attributed to Edward Ward by H. E. Troyer in *Ned Ward of Grub street*, p. 232, and to Henry Carey by F. T. Wood in *Notes & Queries*, vol. 165. Although the work was reprinted in Carey's *Cupid and Hymen*, 1748, in neither case is the evidence of authorship conclusive. This pamphlet provoked many replies and rejoinders. Almost all are excluded as having no economic interest.

4032 The Woman's Advocate or the Baudy Batchelor out in his Calculation: being the genuine Answer Paragraph by Paragraph, to the Batchelor's Estimate plainly proving that Marriage is to a Man of Sense and Œconomy, both a Happiner [*sic*] and less Chargeable State, than a Single Life.... *Lond. 1729, F°*. L.

4033 Reasons against the Bill now depending for the better Regulation and Government of Seamen in the Merchant Service. *n.p.* [*1729*], *F°*. L.

4034 The Case of the Master, Wardens and Company of Distillers of London: Humbly offered to the Honourable the House of Commons. *n.p.* [*1729*], *F°*. L.

Against the bill for laying a duty upon compound waters or spirits.

4035 A Proposal most humbly offer'd to the Honourable House of Commons to prevent the Excessive Drinking of Spirituous Liquors...without giving too severe a Wound to the Distilling Manufactury in General. *n.p.* [*1729?*], *s. sh. F°*. MP.

4036 The Distillers Petition to His Majesty. *n.p.* [*1729*], *s. sh. F°*. L.

On the verso is the ballad: The Honest Jury; or, Caleb Triumphant.

4037 The Case of the Company of Distillers of the City of London: With Proposals for Reforming the Abuses practised in the Distilling Trade, Humbly Offered to the Consideration of the Members of the Honourable House of Commons. *n.p.* [*1729?*], *F°*. LLI.

4038 A Letter from a Gentleman in the North of Ireland, to a Person in an eminent Post under His Majesty; concerning the Transportation of great Numbers from that Part of the Kingdom to America. *Dublin*, *1729*, *F°*. D.

1730

GENERAL

4039 Remarks on some Maxims, peculiar to the Ancient, as well as Modern Inhabitants of Ireland. With a Seasonable Hint to G—— B——n about the Woollen-Trade. In a letter from a Gentleman in the County of Kerry, to his Friend in Dublin. *Dublin, 1730, 8o.* L.

Signed: Hibernicus.

4040 A View of the Present State of Affairs in the Kingdom of Ireland, in Three Discourses. viz. I. A List of the Absentees of Ireland [by Thomas Prior]....II. The Present State of Ireland Consider'd.... III. A Modest Proposal for Preventing the Children of Poor People from being a Burthen to their Parents or the Country....By Dr. Sw——ft. *Lond. 1730, 8o.* LU.

All three tracts had been published separately in 1729 (no. 3906, 3907, 4005).

AGRICULTURE

4041 [Rye, George]. Considerations on Agriculture: Treating of the several Methods practised in different Parts of the Kingdom of Ireland, with Remarks thereon. New Improvements on the Manures proper for different Soils, particularly Lime, (with the several Ways of burning it) Sea-Sand, Shells, Clay, and Marle; with what Kinds of them are fittest for Use. Of the Culture of Wheat, and a New Method for preventing a late Harvest, and the evil Consequences thereof. To which is added, Mr. Pierson's two Tracts of the Present State of the Tillage in Ireland, with some Methods offer'd for its Improvements, with a Description of several Kinds of Ploughs, and their Usefulness proved on Tryal. *Dublin, 1730, 8o.* DNL.

For authorship see R. Weston, *Tracts on Practical Agriculture and Gardening*, 1773, p. 58 of the 'Catalogue of English Authors, who have written on Husbandry'.

4042 Cowell, John. The Curious and Profitable Gardener....Containing I. The most useful Experiments for Improving Land by Grain and Seeds. II. Curious Directions for Cultivating the choicest Fruits of the East and West-Indies at a small Expence. III. Extraordinary Remarks concerning the Raising of Flowers from Seed. IV. Particular Observations and Rules for the Management of Dwarf Fruit-Trees, Wall-Trees, Espaliers, and Standards.... *Lond. 1730, 8o.* L.

Reissued as: The Curious Fruit and Flower Gardener.... The Second Edition, 1732 (L).

4043 An Act to inclose divers Parcels of Commons and waste Grounds, lying and being in the Township of Claughton, in the Parish of Garstang, and County Palatin of Lancaster. *n.p.* [*1730*], *Fo.* L.

4044 An Act for confirming several Awards for Inclosing and Dividing the Common Fields and Common Grounds in Dunchurch, Toft, and Thurlaston in the County of Warwick. *n.p.* [*1730*], *F*o. L.

4045 An Act for Inclosing Part of the Waste or Common, called East Wellow Common, belonging to the Manor and Tything of East Wellow in the County of Southampton, and for Vesting a certain Annual Rent-Charge in Trustees for the Benefit of the Poor of the Tything of East Wellow aforesaid for ever. *n.p.* [*1730*], *F*o. L.

4046 A Bill for Dividing and Inclosing the Common Fields and Common Grounds called Flecknoe-Fields in the Parish of Woolfhampcoat, in the County of Warwick. *n.p.* [*1730*], *F*o. L.

4047 An Act for Inclosing several Common Fields, Common Meadows, and other Commonable Lands, in the Parish of Lillington in the County of Warwick. *n.p.* [*1730*], *s. sh. F*o. L.

4048 An Act to confirm an Agreement for Enclosing the Common Fields, Downs, Waste, and Uninclosed Lands, Part of the Manor of Mixbury in the County of Oxon. *n.p.* [*1730*], *F*o. L.

A bill, with blanks. Another edn., with blanks filled in, [1730], Fo (O).

4049 A Bill for Inclosing several Common Fields, Common Meadows, and other Commonable Lands in the Hamlet of Welsbourne Mountfort, in the Parish of Welsbourne Hastings, in the County of Warwick. *n.p.* [*1730*], *F*o. LHL.

4050 Kinderley, Nathaniel. Mr. Humphrey Smith's Scheme for the Draining of the South and Middle Level of the Fens Examined and Compared. *Lond. 1730*, *8*o. O.

4051 A List of the Names of such Proprietors in the Company of the Mine Adventurers of England, as are qualified to Vote for Governor, Deputy-Governor, and Twelve Directors of the said Company; at the Election...on Thursday the 12th Day of November 1730. *n.p.* [*1730*], *F*o. L.

4052 A Method for executing the Powers of a Lease, granted from the Charter of the Mines Royal for Lead-Ore, in the County of Merioneth, in the Principality of Wales. *n.p.* [*c. 1730?*], *fol.* L.

Endorsed: Mines Royal, in the County of Merioneth in Wales.

4053 Laurence, Edward. A Dissertation on Estates upon Lives and Years, whether in Lay or Church-Hands. With an exact Calculation of their real Worth, by proper Tables, and the Reasons for their different Valuations. *Lond. 1730*, 8o. L.

4054 Richards, John. The Gentleman's Steward and Tenants of Manors Instructed. Containing rational, easy and familiar Rules and Tables for finding the Value of Estates of Freehold, Copyhold, or Leasehold....With an Enquiry into the Nature of the annual Disbursements...that Estates in Fields or Houses...are charged with or liable to....*Lond. 1730*, *8*o. L.

4055 Instructions Given by the Commissioners and Trustees for Improving the Fisheries and Manufactures of Scotland to Wreck and Cure-Masters at . *n.p.* [*1730?*], *s. sh. F*°. LU.

About the herring fishery.

MANUFACTURES

4056 The South-Sea Kidnapper. Address'd in a Letter to the Court of Directors of the South-Sea Company, in Answer to the last Paragraph of an Advertisement inserted in the Daily-Post-Boy, the 2nd of August and dated from the South-Sea-House the 30th of July. By an Englishman. *Lond. 1730*, *F*°. L.

Signed: J.B. On the enticement of English craftsmen to Spain by Joseph Belliagos, a Spaniard connected with the South Sea Company.

4057 HOLT, RICHARD. A Short Treatise of Artificial Stone, as 'tis now Made, and Converted into all Manner of Curious Embellishments, and Proper Ornaments, of Architecture.... *Lond. 1730*, *8*°. L.

4058 An Account of Mr. Wood's Iron made with pulveriz'd Oar and Pit Coal. *n.p.* [*1730?*], *4*°. L.

4059 Beware of Bubbles. *n.p.* [*1730?*], *s. sh. F*°. L.

On William Wood's plan to make iron with pit-coal.

4060 A Letter from a Merchant in Whitehaven to his Friend in London. *n.p.* [*1730?*], *s. sh. F*°. L.

On the failure of William Wood's iron foundries at Frizington.

4061 A Letter from a Merchant in Whitehaven, to an Iron-Master in the South of England. *n.p.* [*1730*], *s. sh. F*°. L.

Dated: July 31st, 1730.

4062 Some Considerations on the Present State of the Hair-Trade. *n.p* [*c. 1730?*], *F*°. LU.

4063 Subjects of Enquiry relative to the Barbers Petition. *n.p.* [*c. 1730?*], *s. sh. F*°. LU.

4064 Abstract of the Proof adduced for Matthew Crawford Merchant in Glasgow, Defender, in the Process brought against him, at the Instance of John Walkinshaw of Walkinshaw Purs. *n.p.* [*1730*], *F*°. E.

Concerns a rope manufactory in Glasgow.

4065 Abstract of Regulations contained in the Act of Parliament of 6th Year of King George I. for ascertaining the Breadths, and preventing Frauds and Abuses in manufacturing Searges, Plaidings and Fingrums, and for the Manufacture of Stockings in Scotland. *n.p.* [*c. 1730?*], *s. sh. F*°. LU.

4066 Answers for John Pearson, Walker in Edinburgh to the Petition the Incorporation of Litsters in Edinburgh. *n.p.* [*1730*], *F*°. E.

Dated: January 24th, 1730. Signed: Ja. Fergusson. Denying their right to monopolise dyeing.

4067 Instructions given by the Commissioners and Trustees for Improving the Fisheries and Manufactures of Scotland to Stamp-Master and Lapper in . *n.p.* [*c. 1730?*], *s. sh. F*°. LU.

On the measurement of cloth.

4068 Directions for preparing and using the Colours for stamping of Linnen. *n.p.* [*c. 1730?*], *s. sh. F*°. LU.

Apparently issued by the Commissioners and Trustees for Improving Fisheries and Manufactures in Scotland.

4069 Rules to be Observed at the Competition for the Prizes on Linnen Cloth, to be contended for, at on the Day of 173 . *n.p.* [*c. 1730*], *s. sh. F*°. LU.

Issued by the Commissioners and Trustees for improving Fisheries and Manufactures in Scotland.

4070 Slaying Tables for Weavers of plain Linnen and Diaper. *n.p.* [*c. 1730?*], *s. sh. F*°. LU.

Apparently issued by the Commissioners and Trustees for Improving the Fisheries and Manufactures in Scotland. The first table is 'For plain Linnen'. Another edn. with different tables 'For plain Linen', [c. 1730?], s. sh. F° (LU).

COMMERCE

4071 A Specimen towards a New and Compleat Plan for Regulating and Settling the Military Power of Great Britain, in Concert with Commerce; by Incorporating the Land and Sea-Forces, and Vesting the American Trade in our selves. With a Visionary Epistle to the Right Honourable Sir Robert Walpole; and a Preface to the Freeholders of Great Britain. *Lond. 1730*, *8*°. O.

4072 Richard, James, and Bethel Wellington, Infants, by Bethel Goodwin their Guardian, Appellants. John Poulson, John Darby, Arthur Bettesworth, and Francis Clay, Respondents. The Appellants Case. *n.p.* [*1730*], *F*°. LHL.

Signed: P. Yorke. S. Emlyn. Estate of Richard Wellington, bookseller, d. 1715.

4073 Richard Wellington, James Wellington, and Bethel Wellington, Infants, by Bethel Goodwin, their Guardian, Appellants. John Poulson, John Darby, Arthur Bettesworth, and Francis Clay, Respondents. The Case of the Respondent John Poulson. *n.p.* [*1730*], *F*°. LHL.

Signed: C. Talbott. Tho. Lutwyche.

4074 [Defoe, Daniel]. A Brief State of the Inland or Home Trade, of England; and of the Oppressions it suffers, and the Dangers which threaten it from the Invasion of Hawkers, Pedlars, and Clandestine Traders of all Sorts.... *Lond. 1730*, *8*°. LU.

For authorship see *C.B.E.L.* II, 510.

4075 The Case of the Manufacturers and Shop-keepers in Great-Britain; Humbly Recommended to the Present Parliament. *n.p.* [*1730*], *s. sh. F°*. L.

Against hawkers and pedlars.

4076 The Case of the Shopkeepers, Manufacturers, and Fair Traders of England, against Hawkers, Pedlars, and other Clandestine Traders. *Lond.* [*1730?*], *s. sh. F°*. LU.

Another edn., slightly enlarged, [1730?], with the title reading 'against the Hawkers' (LU).

4077 LONDON. Brocas Mayor. Martis, XXVIII° Die Julij, 1730. [*Lond. 1730*], *s. sh. F°*. L.

A resolve to prosecute users of unmarked and unsealed weights and measures in London.

4078 The Bakers Appeal; or the Ruinous and Deplorable Condition of the Bakers of London, and Parts adjacent, faithfully represented, and humbly address'd to a Member of Parliament. *Lond. 1730*, *8°*. LG.

Against the Assize of Bread.

4079 [WALPOLE, Sir ROBERT]. Observations upon the Treaty between the Crowns of Great Britain, France, and Spain, concluded at Seville on the Ninth of November, 1729, N.S. *Lond. 1729* [*o.s.*], *8°*. LU.

With the text of the treaty. For authorship see J. Ralph, *A Critical History of the Administration of Sir Robert Walpole*, 1740, p. 422 n.

4080 Remarks on the English Woollen Manufactury for Exportation, and Necessity of Preventing the Irish Wool being Run. Humbly Offered to the Consideration of both Houses of Parliament. *Lond. 1730*, *4°*. L.

Another edn. Lond. 1730, 12° (L); another edn. Dublin 1730 (O).

4081 A Proposal by the Manufacturers and Fair Traders for hindering the Running of Prohibited Wrought East India Goods, by more effectually preventing the Use and Wear of the same, and Discovery of the Sellers thereof; most humbly offer'd to the Parliament of Great Britain. *n.p.* [*c. 1730?*], *F°*. L.

Endorsed: A Proposal for the more effectual preventing the Running of Prohibited East India Goods.

4082 Reasons Humbly offer'd to the Consideration of the Legislature, for Discharging the several Persons now in Jail, and for the Relief of those under and liable to Prosecutions, for or in respect of any Duties or Penalties for Run or Prohibited Goods. *n.p.* [*1730*], *s. sh. F°*. L.

Endorsed: Reasons Humbly offer'd for discharging Persons in Jail. Another edn., entitled: Reasons Humbly Offer'd to the Consideration of the Legislature. For Discharging the several Persons now in Jail, and for the Relief of those Under and Liable to Prosecutions, for or in Respect of any Duties or Penalties for Run or Prohibited-Goods, n.p. [1730?], F°, and Endorsed: Reasons humbly offer'd to the Consideration of the Legislature. For the Relief of several Thousands of unhappy Persons now in Jail, and under Prosecution, for importing, and otherwise being concern'd in Run-Goods (O).

4083 The Case of the Royal African Company of England. *Lond. 1730*, 4°. LU.

4084 An Abstract of the Case of the Royal African Company of England. *n.p.* [*1730*], *s. sh. F°*. L.

4085 A Supplement to the Case of the Royal African Company of England. *Lond. 1730*, 4°. L.

4086 Remarks on the Supplement to the African Company's Case. *n.p.* [*1730*], *F°*. L.

4087 The Case of Captain Patrick Wall. *n.p.* [*c. 1730?*], *F°*. L.

On the trade to Brazil and Wall's ill treatment by the Royal African Company.

4088 A Particular of the Royal African Company's Forts and Castles in Africa. As the same was Printed in 1713. *n.p.* [*c. 1730?*], *F°*. LU.

4089 A Particular Valuation of the Company's Forts, Castles, and Factories, in Africa. As the same was made out in the Year 1713. *n.p.* [*c. 1730?*], *F°*. LU.

Endorsed: The Number of the Company's Forts and Factories in Africa. With a Particular of their Quick and Dead Stock, as it was made out 8th May, 1713

4090 The State of the British Trade to the Coast of Africa Considered. *n.p.* [*1730?*], *F°*. L.

4091 Reasons humbly offered for Permitting Rice of the Growth of the British Plantations, to be Transported to Spain, Portugal, and other Places to the Southward of Cape Finisterre, without being first brought to England. *n.p.* [*1730*], *F°*. L.

4092 Reasons humbly offered for Taking off the Enumeration of Rice, made in His Majesty's Plantations in America. *n.p.* [*1730*], *F°*. L.

4093 Unto the Right Honourable, The Lords of Council and Session, the Petition of Andrew Ramsay, John Baird, and many others, Merchants in Glasgow. *n.p.* [*1730*], *F°*. E.

Dated: February 26th 1730. Signed: Pat. Grant. On the tobacco trade and on Richard Graham's claims for acting for them in London in 1723.

4094 Answers for Richard Graham, Merchant in Glasgow, to the Petition of Andrew Ramsay, John Baird, and others Merchants there. *n.p.* [*1730*], *F°*. E.

Dated: July 17. 1730. Signed: Jo. Forbes.

4095 Petition for Andrew Ramsay, John Baird, and many other Merchants in Glasgow, against Richard Graham, Merchant there. *n.p.* [*1730*], *F°*. E.

Dated: 30. July 1730. Signed: Cha. Erskine.

4096 Answers for Richard Graham Merchant in Glasgow, to the Petition of Andrew Ramsay, John Baird, and others Merchants there. *n.p.* [*1730*], *F°*. E.

Dated: December 3. 1730. Signed: Jo. Forbes.

4097 Memorial for the Merchants in Glasgow, against Richard Graham for himself, and as Assigney by Alexander Oswald. *n.p.* [*1730*], *s. sh.* *F°*. E.

Dated: 7th December, 1730.

4098 A Collection of Papers relating to the East India Trade: Wherein are shewn the Disadvantages to a Nation, by confining any Trade to a Corporation with a Joint-Stock. *Lond.* *1730*, *8°*. LU.

4099 A Letter to a Director of the East-India Company. *n.p.* [*1730*], *s. sh.* *F°*. LU.

Signed: A. Dated: March 3, 1729 [O.S.].

4100 A Letter to a Member of Parliament concerning the Proposals of the East-India Company. *n.p.* [*1730*], *s. sh.* *F°*. L.

4101 A Scheme for Raising 3,200,000 l. for the Service of the Government, by Redeeming the Fund and Trade now enjoy'd by the East-India Company, and Reserving to the Publick an Annuity of 96,000 l. for the Disposition of Parliament. *n.p.* [*1730*], *F°*. L.

COLONIES

4102 [Robertson, Robert]. A Letter to the Right Reverend the Lord Bishop of London, from an Inhabitant of His Majesty's Leeward-Caribbee-Islands. Containing some Considerations on His Lordship's Two Letters of May 19, 1727. The first to the Masters and Mistresses of Families in the English Plantations abroad; the second to the Missionaries there. In which is inserted, A Short Essay concerning the Conversion of the Negro-Slaves in Our Sugar-Colonies: Written in the Month of June, 1727, by the same Inhabitant. *Lond.* *1730*, *8°*. L.

For authorship see F. W. Pitman, *The Development of the British West Indies*, 1917, p. 267.

4103 [Gray, Galfridus]. A Letter to a Member of Parliament; setting forth the Value of the Saint Christopher's Lands. *Lond.* *1730*, *8°*. O.

For authorship see *Cal. of Treasury Books & Papers*, 1720–28, p. 427.

FINANCE

4104 A State of the National Debt, Provided or Unprovided for by Parliament, as it stood the 31st of December 1728, and the 31st of December 1729. Together with an Account of the Produce of the Sinking Fund in that Year, and to the Payment of what Debts contracted before the 25th of December 1716, the said Fund hath been applied. Also, an Account shewing how the Money given for the Service of the Year 1729 hath been disposed of.... *Lond.* *1730*, *F°*. LU.

4105 Reasons Humbly offered to the Consideration of the Parliament of Great Britain. For lessening the present heavy National-Debts and Taxes,

Inlarging the Sinking-Fund, Remedying the ill State of the Coin, And thereby reviving Trade and Credit. *n.p.* [*1730*], *F°*. L.

4106 The Remembrancer: or Caleb's Seasonable Exhortation. With the Patriots Collection of Remarks upon Instances of the Usages of former Parliaments in relation to Publick Taxes, and the bringing to Justice Evil and Corrupt Ministers. To which is added, A List of those who Voted for and against the 115,000 l. *Lond. 1730*, *8°*. LU.

Attributed to Nicholas Amhurst in H. & L. quoting the B.M. Catalogue, the new edition of which does not contain the attribution.

4107 The Case of the Officers Employed in the Duties on Salt. *n.p.* [*1730*], *s. sh. F°*. LLI.

4108 Observations on the Duty upon Soap. *n.p.* [*1730*], *s. sh. F°*. LU.

4109 Some Considerations humbly offer'd by the Merchants of the City of Dublin, in behalf of themselves and several other Merchants in the Kingdom of Ireland, to shew that the Reduction of the Duties on Spirits from 2s. 4d. which they now pay to 2s. per Gallon, and the Duties on Tobacco's from Six Pence to Four Pence half-penny per Pound will be the most effectual Means to prevent the future Running of those Commodities, and to increase his Majesty's Revenue on those Heads of Trade. *n.p.* [*c. 1730?*], *F°*. DM.

Endorsed: The Case of the Merchants of the City of Dublin. In relation to the Reduction of the Dutys on Spirits and Tobacco's.

4110 Bohun, William. The Law of Tithes; shewing their Nature, Kinds, Properties and Incidents; by whom, to whom, when, and in what Manner payable; how and in what Courts to be sued for and recovered; what Things, Lands or Persons are charged with, or exempted therefrom.... *In the Savoy*, *1730*, *8°*. D.

2nd edn. 1731 (LSC); 3rd edn. 1744 (L); 4th edn. 1766 (L).

4111 William Kelynack, Richard Richards, Philip Kelynack, and 116 others, Parishioners and Fishermen in the Parish of Paul in the Comnty [*sic*] of Cornwal. Appellants. William Gwavas, Gent. Respondent. The Respondent's Case. *n.p.* [*1730*], *F°*. L.

On tithes of fish caught. Signed: Tho. Reeve. Giles Eyre.

4112 William Kelynack, Richard Richards, Philip Kelynack, and 116 others, Fishermen, Appellants. William Gwavas, Gent. Respondent. The Appellant's Case. *n.p.* [*1730*], *F°*. L.

Signed: J. Sheppard Tho. Bootle.

4113 Observations on the State of Gold and Silver in Great-Britain, both in Coin and Bullion; And the Reason why so little has been Coined at His Majesty's Mint, with a Method of Encouraging the Coinage and keeping it within due Bounds. *n.p.* [*1730?*], *s. sh. F°*. LU.

Dated 2d. March, 1730, possibly O.S.

4114 [Browne, Sir John]. A Short Review of the several Pamphlets that have appeared this Sessions on the Subject of Coin, and in particular of that which is intitled, A Vindication of the intended Alterations, &c. *Dublin*, *1730*, *8°*. L.

The author mentions as his *A Scheme of the Money-Matters of Ireland*, 1729.

4115 LONDON. Brocas Mayor, Cur' Special' tent'....28° die Septembris 1730. [*Lond.*], *1730*, *s. sh. F°*. L.

A resolve to prosecute unlicensed brokers.

4116 By the King, A Proclamation, Prohibiting any Person or Persons to advance or lend any Sum of Money to any Foreign Prince, State, or Potentate, without His Majesty's Licence. *Lond. 1730*, *s. sh. F°*. L.

Dated: 20 April 1730.

4117 The Case of the Charitable Corporation. *n.p.* [*1730?*], *F°*. L.

Endorsed: The Case of the Charitable Corporation.

4118 The Charitable Corporation consider'd, with respect to the National Credit and the Bank of England. *n.p.* [*c. 1730?*], *s. sh. F°*. LU.

4119 London Assurance of Houses and Goods from Fire. Instructions for the Company's Agents in the Country, in their Business of Assurance from Fire. *n.p.* [*c. 1730?*], *F°*. OUP.

4120 Roger Lynch and John Lynch, Appellants. Robert Dalzeel, John Everett, and Henry Cartwright, Trustees for the Sun Fire-Office of Insurance, Respondents. The Appellants Case. *n.p.* [*1730*], *F°*. L.

Signed: P. Yorke. C. Talbot.

4121 Roger Lynch and John Lynch, Appell[ts]. Robert Dalzel, Henry Cartwright, and John Everett, Esqs. Resp[ts]. The Respondents Case. *n.p.* [*1730*], *F°*. L.

Signed: J. Willes. W. Hamilton.

4122 Tho. Ward, Charles Grunsel, and Jasper Stocker, Appell[ts]. William Caloway, and George Minett, Respt[ts]. The Appellants Case. *n.p.* [*1730*], *F°*. L.

The appellants were Trustees for the Sun Fire Office. Signed: P. York, C. Talbot, William Hamilton.

4123 Thomas Ward, Charles Grunsell, and Jasper Stocker, Appellants. William Calloway, Respondent. The Respondent's Case. *n.p.* [*1730*], *F°*. L.

Signed: J. Willes. W. Pere Williams.

4124 A List of the Member of the Corporation of the Amicable-Society, for a Perpetual Assurance-Office, who are Contributors on their own Lives, and have a Right to vote at the Election of Directors. *n.p.* [*1730*], *F°*. L.

TRANSPORT

4125 The Case of the Coal Trade. *n.p.* [*1730*], *s. sh. F°*. LLI.

4126 The Case of many Persons keeping Wharfs, and Others, Dealing in Coals, in the Cities of London and Westminster, and the Parts adjacent. *n.p.* [*1730*], *s. sh. F°*. LU.

4127 The Case of the Lightermen, &c. Employ'd in carrying Coals and other Goods on the River Thames. *n.p.* [*1730?*], *s. sh. F°.* LLI.

4128 The Case of the Owners of Ships Employed in the Coal-Trade. *n.p.* [*1730*], *F°.* LU.

4129 The Case of the Owners of Ships employ'd in the Coal-Trade, being an Answer to a Paper call'd, The Case of the Lightermen; and another stil'd, The Case of the Coal Trade. *n.p.* [*1730*], *s. sh. F°.* L.

4130 The Case of the Watermen and Lightermen working on the River of Thames. *n.p.* [*1730*], *F°.* LU.

On the coal trade and against the Woodmongers.

4131 A Letter to Sir William Strickland, Bart. relating to the Coal Trade. *Lond. 1730, 8°.* O.

4132 Remarks on a Letter to a Member of Parliament relating to the Coal Trade, and on the Case of the Watermen and Lightermen working on the River of Thames. *n.p.* [*1730?*], *F°.* LLI.

4133 LONDON. Brocas Mayor. Martis, XXVIII° die Julij, 1730.... [*Lond. 1730*], *s. sh. F°.* LCRO.

Orders to carry out and enforce the provisions of the Act for the better Regulation of the Coal Trade.

4134 A Bill for making the Acts of the First and Seventh Years of his late Majesty's Reign (for making the River Kennet Navigable from Reading to Newbury...) more effectual. *n.p.* [*1730*], *F°.* L.

4135 Reasons for the Bill for making Navigable the River Stroudwater, in the County of Gloucester. *n.p.* [*1730?*], *s. sh. F°.* LLI.

4136 The Constitution of the Company of Watermen and Lightermen... *Lond. 1730, 8°.* LU.

Another edn. 1790 (O).

4137 The Case of the Barge-Masters and others, Navigating on the River of Isis and Thames, from Oxford to London; shewing the Hardships they labour under, by the exorbitant Sums they pay for passing thro' the several Locks, Wears, Bucks, Gates, and for the Use of Boats belonging to the same, and going over Towing-Paths on the Banks of the said Rivers. *n.p.* [*1730?*], *s. sh. F°.* L.

Endorsed: Reasons humbly offered for Regulating the Abuses committed in the Navigation of the River of Thames, Westward of the City of London.

4138 An Act for Repairing the Road leading from a Gate called Shipston Toll-gate, at Bridgtown in the Parish of Old Stratford in the County of Warwick, through Alderminster and Shipston upon Stower to the Top of Long-Compton Hill in the said County. *n.p.* [*1730*], *F°.* L.

4139 An Act for Repairing and Amending the Road between the Towns of Wisbech and March, in the Isle of Ely; and County of Cambridge. *n.p.* [*1730*], *F°.* O.

A bill.

4140 The Case of the Gentlemen, Merchants, Tradesmen, and other Inhabitants of Wisbech and March, &c. in the Isle of Ely, and County of Cambridge. *n.p.* [*1730*], *s. sh. F*o. LLI.

For the Wisbech to March turnpike bill.

4141 Reasons humbly offer'd to the Honourable House of Commons, against the Bill for Repairing and Amending the Road between Wisbech and March, in the Isle of Ely. *n.p.* [*1730*], *s. sh. F*o. LG.

SOCIAL CONDITIONS

4142 A Method for Suppressing of Beggars, recommended to all Gentlemen, and others, who are House-keepers, or Inhabitants in the Parish of St. Giles's in the Fields. *n.p.* [*c. 1730?*], *s. sh. F*o. L.

4143 The Workhouse Cruelty, Workhouses turn'd Goals, and Goalers Executioners. *Lond.* [*c. 1730?*], *s. sh. F*o. L.

On the treatment of Mary Whistle at the St. Giles in the Fields workhouse.

4144 The Case of the Corporation of the City of Worcester, in Relation to the Work-House. *n.p.* [*1730*], *F*o. L.

4145 Reasons against Passing so much of the Bill relating to the Work-House in the City of Worcester, as impowers the Guardians to Lett or Convert the same to other Purposes than what were originally intended, and which alters the Qualifications of such Guardians and their Electors. *n.p.* [*1730?*], *s. sh. F*o. LG.

4146 [Defoe, Daniel]. The Generous Projector, or a Friendly Proposal to prevent Murder and other enormous Abuses by erecting an Hospital for Foundlings and Bastard-Children....And necessary Hints for redressing divers other publick Grievances, which call aloud for Amendment. *Lond.* *1731* [*1730*], *8*o. LU.

The dedication signed: C. H. An abridgement of *Augusta Triumphans*, 1728. For authorship see *C.B.E.L.* II, 509.

4147 An Account of the Rise and Establishment of the Infirmary, or Hospital for Sick-Poor, erected at Edinburgh. *n.p.* [*1730*], *8*o. LU.

4148 A Report from the Lords Committees appointed to Enquire into a Pernicious Practice carried on in this City, by removing of Foundling Children from One Parish to another, whereby many of the said Children have been Destroyed. *Dublin*, *1729–30*o *F*o. D.

4149 Tancred, Christopher. A Draught of a Bill, for the more Easy and Speedy Recovery of Small Debts.... *Lond.* *1730*, *8*o. LU.

4150 A Bill for the more Easy and Speedy Recovery of Small Debts. *n.p.* [*1730*], *F*o. L.

A later edition entitled: A Bill, intitled, An Act for the more easy and speedy Recovery of small Debts, 1730 (L), was printed by order of the House of Lords.

4151 MALLORY, JOHN. Objections humbly offer'd against passing the Bill, intitled, A Bill for the more Easy and Speedy Recovery of small Debts, into a Law. *Lond. 1730, 8º.* LU.

4152 The Case of the Filacers of his Majesty's Court of Common Places, in regard to the Bill now depending before the Honourable House of Commons, for the more easy and speedy Recovery of Small Debts. *n.p.* [*1730*], *s. sh. Fº.* L.

4153 A Bill for Relief of Poor Insolvent Debtors in the several Goals of this Kingdom. *n.p.* [*c. 1730?*], *Fº.* L.

4154 The Case of Many Unfortunate Bankrupts. *n.p.* [*c. 1730?*], *s. sh. Fº.* LLI.

4155 Observations on the Inconveniences that might have happened to the Publick, if a Bill lately depending, had pass'd into a Law, intituled, An Act for the Relief of Debtors, with Respect to the Imprisonment of their Persons, &c. which were offer'd in behalf of the Petitioners, to the Right Honourable the House of Lords, against the passing of said Bill. *Dublin, 1730, 8º.* DA.

4156 A Report from the Committee appointed to Enquire into the State of the Goals of this Kingdom. Relating to the King's-Bench Prison.... *Lond. 1730, Fº.* L.

4157 Lists of Attornies and Solicitors, admitted in pursuance of the late Acts For the better Regulation of Attornies and Solicitors. Presented to the House of Commons pursuant to their Order of the 26th Day of January 1729. *Lond. 1729* [*o.s.*], *Fº.* O.

4158 Lists, Accounts and Tables of Fees of the Officers and Servants belonging to the Judges of the several Courts in Westminster-Hall, and the Circuits, the Associates and Clerks of Assize: presented to the House of Commons, pursuant to their Order of the 23d Day of March 1729. *Lond. 1730, Fº.* O.

4159 Blunt to Walpole: a Familiar Epistle in behalf of the British Distillery. *Lond. 1730, 8º.* O.

In verse. Signed: A Blunt. On the effects of the Gin Act.

4160 [FORBES, DUNCAN]. Considerations upon the State of the Nation, as it is affected by the Excessive Use of Foreign Spirits.... *Edin. 1730, 4º.* LU.

Another edn. Edin. 1730, 8º (LU). For authorship see H. & L. quoting David Laing, and ms. note in LU copy.

1731

GENERAL

4161 Proctor's London Price-Courant Reviv'd. Giving a Weekly Account of the Prices of all Stocks, South-Sea and East-India Bonds: Also the Prices of Merchandises....no. 182. [1 July 1731.] *Lond.* [*1731*], *s. sh. F°*. L.

4162 SHAW, PETER. Three Essays in Artificial Philosophy, or Universal Chemistry: viz. I. An Essay for the farther Application and Advancement of Chemistry in England. II. An Essay for the Improvement of Distillation, in the Hands of the Malt-Stiller, Rectifier, Compounder, and Apothecary. III. An Essay for Concentrating Wines, and other Fermented Liquors.... *Lond. 1731, 8°*. L.

4163 BROWNE, Sir JOHN. Reflections upon the present unhappy Circumstances of Ireland; in a Letter to His Grace the Lord Arch Bishop of Cashel. With a Proposal for Publick Granaries, as the principal Means whereby to retrieve our Affairs. *Dublin, 1731, 8°*. DA.

4164 WILSON, ROBERT. The Interest and Trade of Ireland Consider'd. *Dublin, 1731, 8°*. L.

The dedication signed: Robert Wilson. Another edn., 'With an Addition and a Letter for relieving the Poor distress'd Inhabitants of this Kingdom', but without author's name, 1732 (DA); another edn. with a further addition, also anonymous, 1733 (Kress 4156).

4165 An Inquiry into Some of the Causes of the Ill Situation of the Affairs of Ireland. *Dublin, 1731, 8°*. L.

Another edn. Lond. 1732 (DA).

AGRICULTURE

4166 [TULL, JETHRO]. The New Horse-Houghing Husbandry: or, an Essay on the Principles of Tillage and Vegetation. Wherein is Shewn, A Method of Introducing a Sort of Vineyard-Culture into the Corn-Fields, In Order to Increase their Product, and Diminish the Common Expence, by the Use of Instruments lately Invented. *Lond. 1731, 4°*. L.

Another edn. Dublin, 1731, 8° (O). The enlarged London edn., 1733 *F°* (L), entitled: The Horse-Hoing Husbandry....By I.T., has the author's full name in the privilege. Another edn. Dublin, 1733, 8° (O). Supplement, Lond. 1736, F° (LU). Addenda, n.p. [1738], F° (LU); Conclusion, n.p. [1739], F° (LU); 2nd edn. of Supplement, including Addenda and Conclusion, 1740 (L). 2nd edn. of the enlarged version of the whole work 1743 (LU); 3rd edn. 1751, 8° (L); 4th edn. 1762 (O); another edn. ed. by W. Cobbett, 1822 (L).

4167 SWITZER, STEPHEN. A Dissertation on the true Cythisus of the Ancients. Proving that the Medicago or Cythisus Maranthæ....is the Plant that was held in so great Esteem among the Romans. Also that it may be successfully made Use of for the Improvement of the most dry, barren, hilly Land, as Lucerne has been for that which is moister and nearer a Level....To which is added, An Account of the Great Profits which arise (if carefully managed) from sowing the Lucerne and Burning of Clay.... *Lond. 1731*, *8°*. L.

2nd edn. 1735 (R).

4168 MILLER, PHILIP. The Gardeners Dictionary: containing the Methods of Cultivating and Improving the Kitchen, Fruit and Flower Garden. As also, the Physick Garden, Wilderness, Conservatory, and Vineyard, according to the practice of the most Experienc'd Gardeners of the Present Age.... *Lond. 1731, 39, F°*. 2 vols. L.

2nd edn. of vol. 1. 1733; 3rd 1737. 6th edn. of the whole work 1752; 7th edn 1759; 8th 1768. Another edn., abridged, in 3 vols., 8° 1735, 40; 2nd edn. 1741; 3rd 1748 (all L).

4169 MILLER, PHILIP. The Gardeners Kalendar, directing what Works are necessary to be done Every Month, in the Kitchen, Fruit, and Pleasure Gardens, and in the Conservatory. *Lond. 1732* [*1731*], *8°*. L.

2nd edn. 1733 (L); 3rd edn. 1734 (L); 2nd edn. Dublin 1735 (L); 4th edn. Lond. 1737 (O); 5th edn. 1739 (O); 6th edn. 1743 (E); 7th edn. 1745 (L); 8th edn. 1748 (O); and at least 7 later edns.

4170 A Bill for Inclosing the Common Fields and Uninclosed Lands, lying within the Manor and Parish of Bishop's Tachbrooke, in the County of Warwick. [*Lond. 1731*], *F°*. LHL.

4171 An Act for Inclosing the Common Fields and Uninclosed Lands, lying within the Manor and Parish of Bishop's Tachbrooke, in the County of Warwick. *n.p. 1730–1*, *F°*. L.

4172 An Act for making Divisions, Inclosures, and Allotments of the open Corn-Fields and Pastures in the Lordship of Catwick in the County of York; and for Settling and Establishing the Payment of a yearly Sum to the Rector of Catwick aforesaid, and his Successors, in Lieu of Tythes, pursuant to Agreement between the present Rector and the Proprietors of the said Lands. *n.p.* [*1731*], *F°*. L.

4173 An Act for Exchanging, Dividing, and Inclosing the Common Fields and Common Grounds in the Parishes of Lower Slaughter and Upper Slaughter, in the County of Gloucester. *n.p.* [*1731*], *F°*. L.

4174 An Act for Exchanging the Parsonage-House and Glebe Lands in Biscathorp in the County of Lincoln, for other Lands belonging to the Lord of the Manor, and for giving a Recompence to the Rector in Lieu of his Tythes, to enable the Lord of the Manor to inclose the Common Fields. *n.p.* [*1731*], *F°*. L.

4175 An Act for Inclosing and Dividing the Common Fields and Common Grounds in the Manor of Nuneaton and Attleborough in the County of Warwick. *n.p. 1731*, *F°*. L.

4176 A Bill for Exchanging, Dividing, and Inclosing the Common Fields, Common Meadows, and Common and Waste Grounds within the Manor of Prestbury in the County of Gloucester. [*Lond. 1731*], *Fo.* LHL.

4177 An Act for Exchanging, Dividing, and Inclosing the Common Fields, Common Meadows, and Common and Waste Grounds within the Manor of Prestbury in the County of Gloucester. *n.p. 1730–1*, *Fo.* L.

4178 An Act for Dividing and Inclosing divers Parcels of Commons and Waste Grounds lying within the Manor of West Broughton in the Parish of Dovebridge in the County of Derby. *n.p.* [*1731*], *Fo.* L.

4179 A Short Enquiry into the Cause of the General Non-Improvement of Land in Scotland; and the best Method to remove it. *Edin. 1731*, *8o.* E.

4180 [BOND, EDWARD ?]. The Countryman's Letter. Containing a few Remarks concerning the Bounty Flax-Seed imported into Ireland: With choice Directions for sowing the same, and preserving its Increase.... Some Methods laid down to prevent sham Proposals and Cheats...and also, two Schemes...the latter of them shewing to a Demonstration; that instead of being at the Expence of Nine or Ten Thousand Pounds, for the Importation of Threee Thousand Hogsheads, we may raise at home Thirty Six Thousand, and have a fine Stock of Twenty Seven Thousand Hogsheads of it by us in the Year 1733, by allowing then in Premiums only Thirteen Thousand Five Hundred Pounds. *Dublin*, *1731*, *8o.* LU.

Signed: William Freeman, a pseudonym if the ms. attribution to Edw. Bond in LU copy is accepted.

4181 KNIGHTLEY, JOHN. Proposals for Establishing a Fund of 30,000 l. to be vested in a Corporation for the purposes therein mentioned.... *Dublin*, *1731*, *8o.* O.

On developing the Ballycastle collieries.

4182 [BURROUGHS, SAMUEL]. An Enquiry into the Customary-Estates and Tenant-Rights of those who hold Lands of Church and other Foundations, by the Tenure of Three Lives and Twenty-One Years. With some Considerations for Restraining Excessive Fines....By Everard Fleetwood, Esq; [pseud.]. *Lond. 1731*, *8o.* LU.

2nd edn. 1732 (O). For authorship see John Nichols, *Literary Anecdotes*, VI, 94.

4183 DERHAM, WILLIAM. A Defence of the Churches Right in Leasehold Estates. In answer to a Book, called, An Enquiry into the customary Estates and Tenant-Rights of those who hold Lands of the Church and other Foundations, &c. and published under the name of Everard Fleetwood, Esq; *Lond. 1731*, *8o.* L.

4184 [GALLY, HENRY]. The Reasonableness of Church and College Fines asserted. And the Rights which Churches and Colleges have in their Estates defended. In Answer to a late book, entituled: An Enquiry into the Customary-Estates and Tenant-Rights of those who hold Lands of the Church.... *Lond. 1731*, *8°*. L.

2nd edn. 1731 (O). For authorship see John Nichols, *Literary Anecdotes*, VI, 94.

4185 [LONG, ROGER]. The Rights of Churches and Colleges defended: in answer to a Pamphlet, call'd An Enquiry into the Customary Estates and Tenant Rights...by Everard Fleetwood Esq. With Remarks upon some other Pieces upon the same Subject. By Dicaiophilus Cantabrigiensis. *Lond. 1731*, *8°*. LU.

For authorship see John Nichols, *Literary Anecdotes*, VI, 94.

4186 A Proposal for Enabling the Clergy to accept Advanc'd Rents, in Lieu of Fines. *Lond. 1731*, *F°*. L.

4187 A True Estimate of the Value of Leasehold Estates, and of Annuities and Reversions for Lives and Years. In Answer to a Pamphlet, intitled, Sir Isaac Newton's Tables for Renewing and Purchasing Leases, &c. and to a Letter added to it, intitled, The Value of Church and College Leases consider'd &c. *Lond. 1731*, *8°*. L.

The Tables are no. 3130.

4188 An Act for ascertaining the Terms, and regulating the Fines, upon Renewal of Leases, for settling the Right, and for the Discovery of, and Improvements in working of Mines in Leasehold and Copyhold Grounds, held under Ecclesiastical Persons; and for the Encouragement of Tillage therein, and planting of Trees thereupon. *n.p.* [*1731?*], *F°*. O.

A bill.

4189 Reasons for Discovering and Opening Mines, &c. *n.p.* [*1731?*], *s. sh. F°*. O.

With reference to the bill for ascertaining the terms, and regulating the fines, upon renewal of leases.

MANUFACTURES

4190 The Case of the Gunpowder-Makers, and of the Merchants, Exporters of Gun-Powder. *n.p.* [*1731*], *s. sh. F°*. LU.

4191 Mr. William Fallowfield's Proposal for making Iron with Peat, at Ten Pounds a Ton, in pursuance of a Patent granted to him by His late Majesty. *n.p.* [*1731?*], *s. sh. F°*. L.

4192 TOMKYNS, THOMAS. A Letter address'd to each Member of the Honourable the House of Commons, by Mr. Tomkyns. *n.p.* [*1731*], *F°*. LLI.

On his method of smelting iron with coal.

4193 This is to give Notice, To all Lovers of Art and Ingenuity, That the most famous Iron Operators who have been practising for above Two Years at Frisington near Whitehaven...are lately come to London.... *n.p.* [*1731*], *s. sh. F°*. L.

An attack on the iron works founded by William Wood.

4194 Information for Matthew Crawford Merchant in Glasgow, against John Walkinshaw of Walkinshaw. *n.p.* [*1731*], *4°*.

Dated: Jan. 1st, 1731. Signed: Dun. Forbes. On a rope manufactory in Glasgow.

4195 Reasons humbly offered for farther Encouraging the Making and Manufacturing of Sail-Cloth in Great-Britain. *n.p.* [*1731?*], *F°*. L.

4196 A Letter from a Citizen of London, to a Member of Parliament, proposing a Method for the Employment of the Vagrant Poor, in the Manufacture of Sail-Cloth. *n.p.* [*1731?*], *s. sh. F°*. L.

4197 To the Gentlemen and Ladies of the Kingdom of Ireland. *n.p.* [*1731*], *s. sh. F°*. DA.

Signed: Smiths and Leathes. Advertising the Irish cambrics made by the firm.

COMMERCE

4198 A Letter from a Hawker and Pedlar in the Country, to a Member of Parliament at London. Shewing, How he was bound Apprentice to a Rich Linnen Draper at London. How he married and set up for himself. How his Master and other Rich Men of the Trade plotted his Ruin, because he sold cheaper than they did....And how he was at last totally undone, and obliged to turn Hawker and Pedlar.... *Lond. 1731*, *8°*. L.

Signed James C——l.

4199 A Second Letter from a Hawker and Pedlar in the Country, to a Member of Parliament at London. In which the true yearly Revenue and Expence of a Nation is fairly Stated. The Encouragement of Frugality is recommended as the best Method to Increase the Nation's Revenue, and Diminish its Expence. All Monopolies proved to be an Encouragement to Idleness and Luxury. Every Restriction upon Trade a Step to Monopoly. The extravagant Profits taken formerly by the Toy-Shops. Our Improvement in that Trade owing to the Hawkers and Pedlars....An Account of the Yearly Expence of a London Shopkeeper. *Lond. 1731*, *8°*. L.

Signed: James C——l. Attributed to Defoe in *C.B.E.L.* II, 510. The Letter is not so attributed although the Second Letter is ostensibly by the same author as the first.

4200 LONDON. Parsons Mayor. Martis 23° die Februarii, 1730.... [*Lond.*], *1730* [*o.s.*], *s. sh. F°*. LCRO.

Billingsgate to be a market for coal-traders only. Coal-heavers are not to intermix with the coal-traders and no one else is to be allowed to sell goods to the interruption of the market.

4201 [GOODWIN, JAMES]. Reasons against the Bill, for Viewing, Searching, and Examining of all Drugs, Medicines, &c. Address'd to the Parliament of Great-Britain: with Proposals Humbly Offer'd for the Regulation of the State of Physick in General, with respect to the Patients Healths and Lives; (which are principally to be regarded) the Physicians Fees, and Apothecaries Medicines, and Bills. To which is added, Mr. Goodwin's Case. By Philanthropos. *Lond. 1731*, *8°*. L.

For authorship see ms. note on L copy and internal evidence.

4202 An Act for the more effectual preventing the the Exportation of Wooll from Great Britain, and of Wooll, and Wooll manufactured from Ireland to Foreign Parts; and for taking off the Duties upon Woollen and Bay Yarn imported from Ireland into England. *n.p.* [*1731*], *F°*. L.

Endorsed: A Bill intitled, An Act....

4203 WARD, BENJAMIN. The State of the Woollen Manufactures Considered: the Reasons of its Present Declension Assigned; and a Method propos'd to Retrieve it. Together with a Discovery of the several Methods used in Smugling Wool from England. *Lond. 1731*, *8°*. LU.

4204 The Interest of England consider'd with respect to the Woollen Manufactures: or, Remarks on a late Pamphlet intitled, Some Thoughts on the Woollen Manufactures of England. In a Letter from a Merchant in the Country, to his Friend in London. *Lond. 1731*, *8°*. LU.

4205 [WEBB, DANIEL]. A Letter from a Spittlefields-Weaver, to one at Norwich, or an Answer to Two at once. *n.p.* [*1731*], *s. sh. F°*. LPRO.

Dated: April 20th 1731. Title from endorsement. The only copy seen is enclosed in a letter from the author.

4206 [BINDON, DAVID]. Observations on the Bill now depending in the House of Lords, with relation to the Woollen Manufacture. By a Clothier. *Lond. 1731*, *8°*. LLI.

For authorship see ms. note in RU (Egmont) copy.

4207 Proposals for preventing the Running of Wool, and encouraging the Woollen Manufacture. *Lond. 1731*, *8°*. LU.

4208 Reasons humbly offered to the consideration of the Honourable Members of the House of Commons, against making any Ports in the South Channel in England, Free, for the Importation of Wooll and Yarn from Ireland. *n.p.* [*1731?*], *F°*. L.

4209 Reasons offered by the Manufacturers of Combing and Spinning in England, against taking the Duty off Irish Yarn imported. *n.p.* [*1731*], *s. sh. F°*. L.

4210 Reasons against taking the Duty off Irish Yarn Imported, Answered. *n.p.* [*1731*], *s. sh. F°*. L.

Title from endorsement.

4211 Some Considerations relating to the Importation of Snap and Bay Yarn from Ireland to Bristoll, &c. Humbly offer'd to the Hon[ble] the House of Commons. By a Person wholly indifferent, and no way Concerned either on one Side or Other. *n.p.* [*1731*], *s. sh. F°*. L.

4212 [PERCEVAL, JOHN, 2nd Earl of Egmont]. Some Observations on the Present State of Ireland, particularly with relation to the Woollen Manufacture. In a Letter to his Excellency the Duke of Dorset. *Printed at Dublin: And Re-Printed at London, 1731, 8°.* L.

For authorship and the priority of this edition see *Egmont Diary*, H.M.C. I, 172. Another edn. London printed, Dublin reprinted, 1731, 12° (L); another edn. Dublin, 1731, 8° (DA); another edn., entitled: A Patriot's Letter to the Duke of Dorset, Dublin, 1749, 8° (L). In the preface to this edition, which is attributed to Burke by A. P. I. Samuels, Sir Richard Cox is hinted at as the author.

4213 [PERCEVAL, JOHN, 2nd Earl of Egmont]. Some Remarks on the Conduct of the Parliament of England, as far as it relates to the Woollen Manufacture: with some Animadversions on the Free Briton's Remarks on a Pamphlet, entitled, Observations on the Present State of Ireland. By the Author of the said Pamphlet. *London, 1731, 8°.* LU.

For authorship see *Some Observations on the Present State of Ireland*, 1731.

4214 [BINDON, DAVID]. Some Thoughts on the Woollen Manufactures of England: in a Letter from a Clothier to a Member of Parliament. *Lond. 1731, 8°.* LU.

2nd edn. Dublin, 1731 (DA). For authorship see ms. note in RU (Egmont) copy.

4215 Some short Reflections on the Situation of Gibraltar, and its importance to the Trade and Maritime Force of this Kingdom; with a Proposal for rendering the late Works of the Spaniards, near that Fortress, ineffectual. *Lond. 1731, 4°.* O.

4216 A Letter to His Majesty King George from...Trudo Audato Povesau Danger Enjo...King of Dauhomay....To which is annexed, Capt. Lambe's Scheme for Trade with the said Emperor. *Lond. 1731, fol.* L.

4217 The Case of the Merchants Trading to and from America. *n.p. [1731], F°.* LLI.

For protection against the Spaniards.

4218 The Cases of some English Ships taken by the Spaniards. Wherein is set forth, the unwarrantable Manner in which they were seized, the illegal Manner of declaring them Prizes; and the barbarous Treatment the Ship's Company met with. Taken from Spanish Documents of unquestionable Authority, done in their own Courts of Judicature. *Lond. 1731, 8°.* L.

4219 A View of the Depredations and Ravages committed by the Spaniards on the British Trade and Navigation. Most humbly offer'd to the Consideration of the Parliament of Great Britain. *Lond. 1731, 8°.* LU.

Another edn. Dublin, 1730 [o.s.?] (DA).

4220 An Act for the better Securing and Encouraging the Trade of His Majesty's Sugar Colonies in America. *n.p. [1731], F°.* L.

Endorsed: A Bill, Intituled, An Act....

4221 Answers to all the Objections made to the Bill for Supporting the Sugar Colonies. *n.p.* [*1731?*], *F°*. LU.

4222 The Case of the British Sugar-Colonies. *n.p.* [*1731*], *F°*. L.

Text begins, 'Our Plantations must always be considered'. Last word on p. 1 'Commerce'. Another edn., without the hyphen and with last word on p. 1 'our selves', [1731 ?] (L); another edn., hyphen restored and last word on p. 1 'ourselves', [1732 ?] (L).

4223 [SHARPE, JOHN]. The Case of the British Northern Colonies. *n.p.* [*1731*], *F°*. L.

For authorship see F. W. Pitman, *The Development of the British West Indies*, 1917, p. 265, and *Cal. S.P. Col.*, *1731*, 1938, no. 265. Last word on p. 1 'Trade'. Another edn., [1731 ?], last word on p. 1 'common' (L); another edn. [1732 ?], last word on p. 1 'Vessels' (L).

4224 Observations on the Case of the Northern Colonies. *Lond.* *1731*, *8°*. LU.

4225 The Case of the Provinces of the Massachusets-Bay, and New-Hampshire, and the Colonies of Rhoad-Island with Providence Plantations, and Connecticut in New England, and the Province of New Jersey, with Respect to the Bill now depending in the Honourable House of Commons, intituled, A Bill for the better securing and encouraging the Trade of His Majesty's Sugar Colonies in America. *n.p.* [*1731*], *F°*. LU.

4226 The Consequences of the Bill now depending in favour of the Sugar Colonies, impartially considered: In a Letter to a Worthy Member of the Honourable House of Commons. *n.p.* [*1731*], *s. sh. F°*. LU.

4227 [HALL, FAYRER]. Considerations on the Bill now depending in Parliament, concerning the British Sugar-Colonies in America. Wherein all the Arguments for the Support of the said Bill are considered. In a Letter to a Member of Parliament. *Lond.* *1731*, *8°*. LU.

For authorship see *Captain Fayrer Hall's Evidence*, 1732.

4228 Considerations on the Dispute now depending before the Honourable House of Commons, between the British, Southern, and Northern Plantations in America. In a Letter to ——. *Lond.* *1731*, *8°*. LU.

Signed: A——r Z——h. Addressed to William Wood, the author of *A Survey of Trade*, 1718.

4229 The Dispute between the Northern Colonies and the Sugar Islands, set in a Clear View. *n.p.* [*1731?*], *s. sh. F°*. LU.

4230 [HALL, FAYRER]. The Importance of the British Plantations in America to this Kingdom; with the State of their Trade, and Methods for Improving it; as also a Description of the several Colonies there. *Lond.* *1731*, *8°*. LU.

In some copies the dedication to Walpole is signed: F. Hall.

4231 The Importance of the Sugar Colonies to Great Britain Stated, and some Objections against the Sugar Colony Bill answer'd. In a Letter to a Member of the House of Commons. *Lond.* *1731*, *8°*. LU.

4232 A Short Answer to an Elaborate Pamphlet, entitled, The Importance of the Sugar Plantations, &c....Shewing, that the Bill now depending for

Prohibiting the Commerce carried on between our Northern Colonies, and the Foreign Sugar Plantations, tends to the impoverishing and ruin of those Colonies; the weakening of the Power of the English Empire in those Parts; and the Damage and Loss of Great Britain; and would put it in the power of our Sugar Plantations to make us pay them what Price they please for their Sugars. In a Letter to a Noble Peer. *n.p. 1731*, *8º*. L.

4233 [HALL, FAYRER]. Observations on the Trade carried on between our Plantations and the foreign Colonies in America: occasioned by a Petition lately presented to the Honourable House of Commons. Printed in the Daily Post-Boy, March the 1st, 1730 [o.s.]. *n.p.* [*1731?*], *Fº*. LLI.

Authorship acknowledged in *Captain Fayrer Hall's Evidence*, 1732. Followed by 'Captain Fayrer Hall's Evidence, before a Committee of the whole House of Commons, in April 1731'.

4234 The Present State of the British Sugar Colonies Consider'd: In a Letter from a Gentleman of Barbadoes to his Friend in London. *Lond. 1731*, *4º*. LU.

4235 [HALL, FAYRER]. Remarks upon a Book, Entituled, The Present State of the Sugar Colonies Consider'd. Wherein some of the Consequences and Effects of Restraining our Trade are examined. *Lond. 1731*, *8º*. LU.

For authorship see *Captain Fayrer Hall's Evidence*, 1732.

4236 [PRIOR, THOMAS] Observations on the Trade between Ireland and the English and Foreign Colonies in America. In a Letter to a Friend. *Lond. 1731*, *8º*. RU.

For authorship see ms. note in RU (Egmont) copy.

COLONIES

4237 Money the Sinews of Trade. The State of the Province of the Massachusetts-Bay Considered, with respect to its Trade for want of a Medium of Exchange wherewith to manage it. Recommended to the serious Consideration of the Trading part in general, more especially to the Merchants and Traders in the Town of Boston. By a Lover of his Country. *Boston, 1731*, *8º*.

Reprinted in *Colonial Currency Reprints*, ed. by A. M. Davis, vol. 2 (1911), whence this entry is taken.

4238 Trade and Commerce Inculcated; in a Discourse, shewing the Necessity of a Well-governed Trade, in order to a Flourishing Common-Wealth. With some Proposals for the bringing Gold & Silver into the Country for a Medium of Trade, as also for the better Supporting the Credit of the Paper Currency. By Amicus Reipublicae. [*Boston*], *1731*, *8º*.

Reprinted in *Colonial Currency Reprints*, ed. by A. M. Davis, vol. 2 (1911), whence this entry is taken.

FINANCE

4239 TRENCHARD, THOMAS. The Inquisitor: or, a Defence of the House of Commons in their Censure on a certain Forage Contract A.D. 1712. In answer to the Free Briton of June 24, 1731....The whole published for the Information of the People; and to be occasionally continued. *Lond. 1731, 8o*. LU.

4240 TRENCHARD, THOMAS. The Inquisitor. Containing a full Answer to the Hyp-Doctor, No. 39. on the Screen and Bank Contract....Together with an Answer at large to the Free-Briton No. 94. published on Thursday, September 16, 1731. Being a clear Refutation of the several Charges urged by that Hireling, Francis Walsingham, against that truly honourable and worthy Patriot, Mr. P. [i.e. William Pulteney].... Number II. to be Occasionally continued. *Lond. 1731, 8o*. L.

4241 To the Proprietors of the South Sea Company. The following Method, except the N.B. at the Conclusion, being inserted in the Daily Post of Thursday last, some Considerations are added to enforce it. *n.p.* [*1731?*], *s. sh. Fo*. OUP.

A scheme for paying off the bonds of the Company.

4242 Some Occasional Letters on National Affairs. *Lond. 1731, 8o*. L.

On the South Sea scheme and the Sinking Fund. O copy has a ms. note 'by Mr. Gibbon'.

4243 A Letter to a Member of Parliament, upon the Deficiency of the Funds and Increase of the Debt, with an humble Proposal to raise a Fund to Pay it. By a Gentleman in the Country. *Dublin, 1731, 8o*. DA.

4244 [HAMMOND, ANTHONY]. The National Debt as it stood at Michaelmas 1730. Stated and Explained. *Lond. 1731, 8o*. L.

For authorship see ms. note in L copy and *D.N.B.*

4245 Reflections on the National Debt; with Reasons for Reducing the Legal Interest; and against a Publick Loan. With Some Advice to the Electors of Members of Parliament. [*Dublin*], *1731, 8o*. L.

4246 The Lords Protest on the Second Rejecting of the Pension-Bill: To which is added, I. A Copy of the said Bill, with the Reasons given against rejecting it last Sessions. II. Copy of the Bill, That all Proceedings in Courts of Justice shall be in the English Langauge. III. Copy of the Bill for naturalizing foreign Protestants, being the Children of natural born Subjects. IV. The State of the National Debt, as it stood on the 31st of Dec. 1730. With an Account shewing how the Money given for the Year 1730 hath been dispos'd of, &c. and the Produce of the Land-Tax for Ten Years last past. *Lond. 1730* [*o.s.*], *Fo*. O.

4247 [PILKINGTON, MATTHEW]. An Infallible Scheme to pay the Publick Debt of this Nation in Six Months. Humbly offered to the Consideration of the present P——t. [*Dublin*], *1731, 8o*. DA.

Another edn. Lond. 1732, 8o, with 'By D——n S——T' on the title-page (O). 2nd edn. London, 1732 (MP). For authorship see Rothschild Cat. no. 1539.

4248 Reasons for Regulating the Coin, and reducing the Interest; With a Scheme for paying part of the National Debt without burthening Ireland. [*Dublin*], *1731*, *8o*. DA.

4249 The Modern Practise of the Court of Exchequer, in Prosecutions relating to His Majesty's Revenue of the Customs....To which is prefix'd, An Account of the Settlements of the Extent and Limits of the several Ports in England and Wales, and of their Several Lawful Keys and Wharfs....By a Gentleman of the Exchequer-Office. *In the Savoy*, *1731*, *8o*. L.

The dedication signed: B.Y.

4250 Unto the Right Honourable, The Lords of Council and Session, the Petition of James Harker Officer of Excise at Hawick. *n.p.* [*1731*], *Fo*. E.

Dated: Dec. 15 1731. Signed: Pet. Wedderburn.

4251 Petition and Answers for Thomas Eliot, Skinner in Hawick; To the Petition of James Harker. *n.p.* [*1731*], *s. sh. Fo*. E.

Dated: December 20. 1731. Signed: James Grant.

4252 The Case of several Gentlemen and Freeholders in the Shire of Angus, and Places adjacent to the Town of Dundee in Scotland, Petitioners against the Bill for continuing the Duty of Two Pennys Scots, or one Sixth part of a Penny Sterling laid upon every Scots Pint of Ale and Beer sold within the Town of Dundee and Privileges thereof.... *n.p.* [*1731?*], *s. sh. Fo*. LLI.

4253 A Bill to prevent Suits for Tythes, where none, nor any Composition for the same, have been paid within a certain Number of Years. *n.p.* [*1731*], *s. sh. Fo*. L.

4254 [Arnall, William]. Animadversions on a Reverend Prelate's Remarks upon the Bill now depending in Parliament: entitled A Bill to prevent Suits for Tythes, where none, nor any Composition for the same, have been paid within a certain Number of Years. By a Member of the House of Commons. To which are prefix'd the Reverend Prelate's Remarks. *Lond.* *1731*, *8o*. LU.

2nd edn., 1731 (L); 3rd edn. 1731 (DA); another issue of this entitled *The Second Part of the Case of Tythes*; *containing Animadversions*, etc. (DA); another 2nd edn. 1734 (O). Reprinted, with author's name, in *The Pillars of Priestcraft and Orthodoxy Shaken*, ed. by R. Barron, 1768, vol. 3, where the *Remarks* are attributed to Thomas Sherlock.

4255 *Begin.* It is a rule in law (as it now stands) that a Layman can't prescribe in non decimando.... *n.p.* [*1731*], *s. sh. Fo*. L.

On the tithe bill.

4256 A Letter to a Member of Parliament, in Relation to the Bill now under the Consideration of the House of Commons, to prevent Suits for Tithes, &c. By a Clergyman. *n.p.* [*1731*], *Fo*. LU.

4257 An Answer to the Remarks upon the Bill now depending in Parliament, concerning Tythes, lately publish'd in the Whitehall Evening-Post.... *Lond. 1731, 8o*. LU.

4258 The Real or Intrinsic Par of Exchange, between London, and the other Cities on which Negotiations in Bills are usually made; Calculated from the Actual Assays made at the Mint, by the Accurate Sir Isaac Newton, of the several Foreign Coins, whereof a Table follows. *Lond. 1731, s. sh. obl. Fo*. LU.

4259 MACULLA, JAMES. King George and his Ancestors Parliamentary Grants to the People of Ireland, Fairly Explained, for the manufacturing Copper Change therein, by Virtue of the Laws, Grants and Statutes of this Kingdom, and by Vertue of the Grants as aforesaid, 40,000 l. of Parliament Halfpence, are speedily to be Manufactured for this Nation. *Dublin, 1731, 8o*. DA.

4260 The Drapier Reviv'd: or Considerations on the Inconveniences which the People of Ireland labour under for the Want of Small Change; with the Reason thereof; and a modest Proposal to remedy the same. By J.B. Esq; *Dublin, 1731, 12o*. DA.

Signed: R. S. Hibernicus.

4261 The Hue and Cry of the Poor of Ireland for Small Change: or, Considerations on the many Inconveniences which our People in general as well as the Trade and Commerce of this Kingdom labours under for Want of Brass or Copper-Coin. As also a proper Regulation in our Silver Specie....By Isaac Broadloom, Clothier [pseud.]. *Dublin, 1731, 8o*. DA.

4262 A Bill for making more Effectual the Act passed in the Sixth Year of the Reign of her late Majesty Queen Anne, for Repealing the Act of the First Year of King James the First, intituled, An Act for the Well-garbling of Spices, and for granting an Equivalent to the City of London, by admitting Brokers. *n.p.* [*1731*], *Fo*. L.

4263 Reasons and Objections against Such Part of the Bill now depending in the House of Commons relating to Brokers, as concerns the Publick Funds and Stocks. *n.p.* [*1731*], *s. sh. Fo*. L.

4264 Some Considerations humbly offer'd to the Honourable House of Commons, why the Bill now pending, concerning Brokers, should not pass into a Law. *n.p.* [*1731*], *Fo*. LU.

4265 *Begin.* At Giles Bacheler's New Lottery-Office.... *n.p.* [*1731*], *s. sh. Fo*. L.

An advertisement for 'the present Hague and Utrecht Lotteries'.

4266 A Bill for Regulating and Restraining the Charitable Corporation... and for Regulating the lending of Money upon Pledges by any other Body Politick and Corporate, or other Persons, and for preventing Usury and Extortion. *n.p.* [*1731*], *Fo*. O.

4267 Asgill, John. An Essay upon Charity. Occasioned by the Calumnies raised against the Charitable Corporation.... *Lond. 1731*, 8°. LU.

4268 Asgill, John. Remarks upon the bill (printed by order of the House of Commons) for regulating and restraining the Charitable Corporation.... *Lond. 1731*, 8°. Kress 3920.

4269 Queries to the Committee and Assistants of the Charitable Corporation. *n.p.* [*1731?*], *s. sh. F°*. C (Cr).

4270 Insurance from Loss by Fire, by the Amicable Contributors, at their Office in Angel-Court on Snow-Hill, London, is upon the following Terms. *Lond. 1731*, *s. sh. F°*. L.

4271 Gio Marino De Ghettoff [and others]...Appellants. And. The Governor and Company of the London-Assurance, Respondents. The Appellant's Case. *n.p.* [*1731*], *F°*. L.

Signed: C. Talbot. W. Melmoth. On the insurance of the *Flandria*, seized by the Dutch on a voyage to China.

4272 Gio Marino De Ghetoff, and others, Appellants. The Governor and Company of the London Assurance, Respondents. The Respondents Case. *n.p.* [*1731*], *F°*. L.

Signed: J. Willes, D. Ryder.

4273 Malcolm, Alexander. A Treatise of Book-Keeping, or Merchants Accounts; in the Italian Method of Debtor and Creditor....To which are added, Instructions for Gentlemen of Land Estates, and their Stewards or Factors: With Directions also for Retailers, and other more private Persons. *Lond. 1731*, 4°. L.

2nd edn. 1743 (L).

TRANSPORT

4274 A Bill for Repairing, and keeping in Repair, the Pier and Harbour of Ilfordcombe, in the County of Devon. *n.p.* [*1731*], *F°*. L.

4275 The Proposals for making the River Chelmer navigable, with the Objections and Answers stated. *n.p.* [*1731*], *F°*. L.

4276 A Bill to Explain and Amend the two Acts of Parliament for making and improving the Navigation of the River Dun, and to Unite the two several Undertakers into one Company. *n.p.* [*1731?*], *F°*. L.

4277 The Case in Relation to the making the River Dun Navigable. *n.p.* [*1731?*], *F°*. LLI.

4278 The Case of the Company of Watermen and Lightermen on the River of Thames. *n.p.* [*1731*], *s. sh. F°*. L.

4279 A Bill for Repairing the Road leading from the Town of Fulham, in the County of Middlesex, through Fulham Fields, to the great Road near the Pound at Hamersmith in the said County. *n.p.* [*1731*], *F°*. O.

SOCIAL CONDITIONS

4280 OLLYFFE, GEORGE. An Essay humbly offer'd for an Act of Parliament to prevent Capital Crimes, and the Loss of many Lives; and to Promote a desirable Improvement and Blessing in the Nation. *Lond. 1731*, *8º*. LU.

4281 DAVIES, JOSEPH. An Humble Proposal for the Increase of our Home Trade, and a Defence to Gibraltar: being a better Security for all our Shipping that Trades in the Straights, and entirely checks and restrains the growth of Highway-men, Foot-pads, House-breakers, Shop-lifters, Horse-stealers Incendiaries and Others, that are guilty of enormous Crimes; rendering them useful, that in case of a War, it will be above a Hundred Thousand a Year in this Kingdoms way. *Lond. 1731*, *8º*. L.

Proposes that criminals be sentenced to man galleys based on Gibraltar and Port Mahon. 4349 is a revised edition of this.

4282 Some Reasons for taking the present Method with Street Beggars. [*Edin. 1731*], *s. sh. Fº*. E.

4283 Rules and Orders for the better Regulation of Hemsted Work-House, agreed upon in Vestry the 29th of May 1731. *n.p.* [*1731*], *s. sh. Fº*. O.

4284 A Case, in relation to an Act of Parliament, humbly desired for the erecting a Work-house, in the Town of Manchester in the County Palatine of Lancaster, for the better employing and maintaining the Poor there. *n.p.* [*1731*], *Fº*. L.

4285 The Case of the Petitioners against bringing in a Bill for Erecting a New Workhouse in the Town of Manchester, and establishing a perpetual Succession of Guardians for ordering the Relief and Employment of the Poor. *n.p.* [*1731*], *Fº*. L.

4286 An Answer to the Case of the Petitioners against bringing in a Bill for erecting a New Work-house, in the Town of Manchester. *n.p.* [*1731*], *s. sh. Fº*. LU.

4287 The Case of the Ministers, Churchwardens, Overseers of the Poor, and principal Inhabitants of the several Parishes within the City of Worcester. *n.p.* [*1731*], *s. sh. Fº*. LLI.

4288 An Account of the Design of Erecting a Charity-School or Work-House in Glasgow; with Proposals thereanent: Concerted by the after mentioned Committee, and now published by Order of the Magistrates, and submitted to the Consideration of the several Societies and Corporations of this City, and of such other well disposed Persons as are inclined to Contribute to this good Design. [*Glasgow, 1731*], *4º*. E.

4289 An Account of the Great Advantages of Erecting a Charitable House for Maintaining and Employing the Poor of this City; with some General Proposals concerning the Plan of the House, and proper Regulations for the due Oversight of it. [*Glasgow, 1731*], *Fº*. E.

4290 Act of the Justices of the Peace of the Shire of Haddington, for Repressing and Punishing of strange and vagrant Beggars, and for Maintenance of the Poor within the said Shire. June 7th, 1731. *n.p.* [*1731*], *s. sh. F°*. E.

4291 PHILIPS, ERASMUS. The Creditor's Advocate and Debtor's Friend. Shewing how the Effects of the Debtor are spent in Law, and other Charges, that may be saved for the Creditor, in like manner as is practiced in Holland.... *Lond. 1731*, *8°*. L.

2nd edn., with Letter on the Bankruptcy Act, 1731 (L).

4292 Reasons for Futher Explanations and Amendments of a late Act of Parliament, entitled, An Act for Relief of Debtors, with respect to the Imprisonment of their Persons.... *Lond. 1731*, *8°*. LU.

4293 A Bill for preventing Frauds committed by Bankrupts, and by the Executors and Administrators of Traders dying Insolvent, and for the Relief of the Creditors of Traders becoming Insolvent. *n.p.* [*1731*], *F°*. L.

4294 [WILLIAMS, JOHN]. An Oration on the Oppression of Jailors: which was spoken in the Fleet Prison, on the 20th of February 173$\frac{0}{1}$ as advertised in the Daily-Post of that Day) and carefully taken in Short-Hand by one of the Audience.... *Lond.* [*1731*], *8°*. LG.

For authorship see *The Daily Post.*

4295 A True State of some Grievances of the Fleet Prisoners, now greatly oppressed. Humbly address'd to the Honourable House of Commons. *n.p.* [*1731*], *s. sh. F°*. LU.

Dated: June 19th, 1731.

4296 LONDON. Parsons Mayor. Martis XIV[to] die Septembris, 1731.... [*Lond. 1731*,] *s. sh. F°*. LCRO.

An order that no negroes or other blacks are to be bound apprentices.

4297 LONDON. Copy of a Clause proposed to be added to the Bill to prevent the Sale of Artificers Places, &c. *n.p.* [*1731*], *F°*. LG.

4298 LONDON. *Begin.* Whereas it hath heretofore been usual to sell and dispose of the several places of the Artificers and Tradesmen belonging to this City and Bridge-house.... *n.p.* [*1731*], *F°*. LG.

Draft of an act of Common Council to prevent this.

4299 LONDON. Common' Council' tent' in Camera Guihald'....An Act to prevent the Sale of the Places of Artificers and Tradesmen of this City and Bridge-house, and the Purveyor at the Bridge-house. *n.p.* [*1731*], *F°*. LCRO.

4300 The Batchelor's Recantation. Or, His Estimate of the Expences of a Married Life Re-consider'd Paragraph by Paragraph, and Retracted. ...By John Single, of Grey's Inn, Esq. *Lond. 1731*, *F°*. O.

4301 Lists of the Officers and their Deputies, belonging to the Several Courts in Westminster-Hall, and elsewhere: with the Lists, Accounts, and

Tables of Fees claimed by them: which were presented to the House of Commons, pursuant to their Order of the 4th Day of March 1730. *Lond. 1731*, *F°*. O.

4302 Additional Lists of Attornies and Solicitors, admitted in pursuance of the late Act, For the better Regulation of Attornies and Solicitors. Presented to the House of Commons, pursuant to their Order of the 22d Day of February 1730. *Lond. 1731*, *F°*. O.

4303 Act of the Town-council of Edinburgh, for the Discouragement of the Sale and Use of Foreign Spirits within this City and its Liberties. [*Edin. 1731*], *s. sh. F°*. EU.

Dated: 24 March 1731.

4304 [Swift, Jonathan]. A Proposal for an Act of Parliament, to pay off the Debts of the Nation, without taxing the Subject, by which the Number of landed Gentry, and substantial Farmers will be considerably encreased, and no one Person will be the poorer, or contribute one Farthing to the Charge. By A—— P——, Esq; *Dublin*, *1732*, *8°*. DA.

The half-title reads: A Proposal for an A—— of P——, &c. to sell the Bishops Lands. Reprinted in *The Prose Works of Jonathan Swift*, ed. by H. Davis, vol. 12 (1955).

1732

GENERAL

4305 FORMAN, CHARLES. A Letter to the Right Honourable Sir Robert Walpole for Re-establishing the Woollen Manufacturies of Great Britain upon their ancient Footing, by encouraging the Linen Manufacturies of Ireland. Also, for Reducing the Pay of the Army, encouraging the Printing Press, renewing the Trade to France upon the Tariff of 1664, and relieving those unfortunate British Merchants that have been ruin'd by the Spanish Guarda de las Costas. With a short Observation upon the Drawback upon Tobaccoes.... *Lond. 1732*, *8°*. LU.

4306 TATE, ROBERT. A Practical Treatise upon several Different and Useful Subjects. In which are contain'd, I. An effectual Method to augment small Livings....II. A Proposal to make the Corporation of Clergymens Sons more useful to its Members. III. A Scheme, for the Relief of the South Sea Sufferers in Distress. Together with Proposals to buy Lands in America....IV. A Rational Way for the Promulgation of the Gospel in America....V. A Method to prevent dangerous Fires.... *Lond. 1732*, *4°*. L.

4307 Britannia Major: the New Scheme, or Essay, for Discharging the Debts, Improving the Lands, and Enlarging the Trade, of the British Dominions in Europe and America. *Lond. 1732*, *8°*. LU.

4308 The Caveat, an Essay upon Incorporate Mercantile Bodies, and the Reduction of Interest by extra-judicial Means. *Lond.* [*1732?*], *8°*. LU.

Very slight.

4309 JACOB, GILES. City-Liberties: or the Rights and Privileges of Freemen. Being a Concise Abridgment of all the Laws, Charters, By-Laws and Customs of London.... *Lond. 1732*, *8°*. L.

4310 New Remarks of London: or, A Survey of the Cities of London and Westminster, of Southwark, and Part of Middlesex and Surrey, within the Circumference of the Bills of Mortality....Collected by the Company of Parish-Clerks.... *Lond. 1732*, *12°*. LU.

4311 [LLOYD, EDWARD]. A Description of the City of Dublin in Ireland. Wherein, besides taking Notice of every Thing remarkable in the City, and the Grandeur of the Court, is represented the happy Situation of Ireland for Commerce....By a Citizen of London, who liv'd twenty Years in Ireland, and made the Collection of News published by Authority.... *Lond. 1732*, *8°*. L.

Another edn., n.d. (DA), has the author's name.

AGRICULTURE

4312 ELLIS, WILLIAM. The Practical Farmer: or, the Hertfordshire Husbandman: containing many New Improvements in Husbandry.... *Lond. 1732*, *8°*. D.

Another edn., Dublin, 1732 (DA); 2nd edn. Lond. 1732 (L); 3rd edn. 1738 (LU); 4th edn. 1742 (R); 5th edn. 1759 (L). Part II. London, 1732 [1735] (O); another edn. Dublin, 1735 (DNL); 2nd edn. Lond. 1741 (R); 3rd edn. Lond. 1752 (LU).

4313 SWITZER, STEPHEN. The Country Gentlemen's Companion: or, Ancient Husbandry Restored; and Modern Husbandry Improved.... *Lond. 1732*, *8°*. L.

A reissue in one vol. of *A Compendious Method for the raising of the Italian Brocoli....The Fifth Edition*, 1731, and *A Dissertation on the True Cythisus of the Ancients*, 1731.

4314 A Bill, intituled, An Act for amending and making more effectual an Act made in the First Year of the Reign of King James the Second (intituled, An additional Act for the Improvement of Tillage.). *n.p.* [*1732*], *F°*. L.

4315 Two New and Curious Essays: I. Concerning the best Methods of Pruning Fruit Trees....Also the Method of Pruning Timber-Trees, &c. II. A Discourse concerning the Improvement of that Excellent Root the Potatoe: Shewing its Manner of Culture and how to make any Soil proper for it....To which is annexed, The Various Ways of Preparing and Dressing Potatoes for the Table. *Lond. 1732*, *8°*. O.

4316 [MACKINTOSH, WILLIAM]. An Essay on the Husbandry of Scotland, with a Proposal for the further Improvement thereof. By a Lover of his Country. *Edin. 1732*, *8°*. E.

For authorship see *D.N.B.*

4317 Abigail Greenfield's Letter to the Honourable Dublin-Society, in behalf of herself, and rest of the Dairy-keepers in Ireland, humbly praying there may be Instructions for good Housewifery, and chiefly for making the best Cheese, such as is imported from Abroad, &c. *n.p.* [*1732*], *s. sh. F°*. DNL.

4318 The Advantages which may arise to the People of Ireland by raising of Flax and Flax-Seed, Considered. Together with Instructions for Sowing and Saving the Seed, and Preparing the Flax for the Market. Drawn up and Published by the Direction of the Dublin Society. *Dublin*, *1732*, *8°*. LU.

An abstract of L. Slator's *Instructions*, 1724, prepared by Thomas Prior (Desmond Clarke, *Thomas Prior*, 1951, p. 29).

4319 An Account of Saffron: the Manner of its Culture and saving for Use, with the Advantages it will be of to this Kingdom. Published by Order of the Dublin Society. *Dublin*, *1732*, *8°*. LU.

'As communicated to the Royal Society in 1729, by Dr. James Douglas, with some Remarks thereon.'

4320 A Compendious Account of the whole Art of Breeding, Nursing, and the right Ordering of the Silk-Worm. Illustrated with Figures engraven on Copper: whereon is curiously exhibited the whole Management of this profitable Insect. *Lond. 1733* [*1732*], *4°*. L.

Dedicated to the Trustees for Establishing the Colony of Georgia by T.B.

4321 Manure for Land. His Majesty has been graciously pleased to grant his Royal Letters Patents to Thomas Liveings, Gent. for the sole Making and Vending an Artificial Compost or Compound Manure.... [*Dublin, 1732*], *s. sh. F°*. DM.

Directions for use.

4322 A Letter to a Member of Parliament. *n.p.* [*1732?*], *s. sh. F°*. LU.

Signed: N. N. Salt, if duty free, might be used as manure.

4323 COWPER, JOHN. An Essay, proving that Inclosing Common-field-Lands, is contrary to the Interest of the Nation: In which some Passages in the New System of Agriculture, by J. Laurence M.A. and in the Duty and Office of a Land-Steward by E. Laurence, Land-Surveyor, are examined.... *Lond. 1732, 8°*. LU.

The dedication signed: John Cowper.

4324 The Great Improvement of Commons that are Enclosed, for the Advantage of the Lords of Manors, the Poor and the Publick.... *Lond. 1732, 8°*. LU.

4325 A Bill for Exchanging, Inclosing, and Reducing into severalty several Common Fields, Common Meadows and Waste Grounds within the Mannor and Township of Little Kineton in the County of Warwick. *n.p.* [*1732*], *F°*. L.

4326 An Act for Enclosing and Dividing a common Pasture Ground called Momes Leaze, in the Parish of Purton in the County of Wilts. *n.p.* [*1732*], *F°*. L.

4327 An Act for Confirming the Exchanges, Inclosure, and Divisions of the Common Fields, Common Meadows, Common Grounds, and Commons, within the Parish of Staunton in the County of Wilts, and for other Purposes therein mentioned. *n.p.* [*1732*], *F°*. L.

4328 COLE, WILLIAM. *Begin.* To the Honourable Edward Harrison, Esq; Surveyor General of the Great Level of the Fenns called Bedford Level. *n.p.* [*1732*], *F°*. O.

The introductory letter is followed by 'The Journal of William Cole, Deputy Surveyor of the South Level, in the Year 1731'.

4329 A Report from the Committee to whom all the Books, Instruments, and Papers relating to the Sale of the Estate of James late Earl of Derwentwater, were referred. Published by Order of the Honourable House of Commons. *Lond. 1732, F°*. L.

Another edn. not published officially, Lond. 1732, F° (M (Cr)).

4330 A Bill for making void the several Contracts for Sale of the Estate of the late Earl of Derwentwater to William Smith, Esq; and also of the Annuity of 200 l. and the Arrears thereof, during the Life of Charles Radcliffe, to Matthew White, Esq; and the several Conveyances made in Pursuance of the same. *n.p.* [*1732*], *F*o. L.

4331 The Case of Sir John Eyles. *n.p.* [*1732*], *F*o. L.

Commissioner for Forfeited Estates censured in the Report on the sale of the estate of the Earl of Derwentwater.

4332 PECK, PHILLIP. Some Observations for Improvement of Trade, by establishing the Fishery of Great Britain; as a proper Means to obtain the Ballance of Trade, employ the Poor, and promote the Interest of the Proprietors of the South-Sea Company.... *Lond. 1732*, *8*o. L.

MANUFACTURES

4333 The Case of the Merchants of London, and Manufacturers of Wheat and Biscuit. *n.p.* [*1732*], *s. sh. F*o. L.

For a bounty on the export of biscuit.

4334 The Hatmakers Case. *n.p.* [*1732*], *s. sh. F*o. L.

Endorsed: The Hatmakers Case. Shewing, That the present Exporting of Beaver Hats of the Manufacture of the Colonies of America, hath been, and is, a very great Discouragement to the English Hatmakers.

4335 A Bill for Preserving and Encouraging a New Invention in England by Sir Thomas Lombe, and granting him a further Term of Years for the Sole Making and Using his Three Italian Engines. *n.p.* [*1732*], *F*o. L.

4336 A Brief State of the Case relating to the Machine erected at Derby for making Italian Organzine Silk, which was discover'd and brought into England, with the utmost Difficulty and Hazard, and at the Sole Expence of Sir Thomas Lombe. *n.p.* [*1732*], *s. sh. F*o. LU.

4337 The Case of the Silk Throwers Company. *n.p.* [*1732*], *s. sh. F*o. LU.

Against the extension of Lombe's patent.

4338 The Case of the Manufacturers of Woollen, Linen, Mohair and Cotton Yarn, in the Towns of Manchester, Stockport, Blackburn, Macclesfield, and Leek, with respect to the Bill now depending in the Honourable House of Commons, entitled, A Bill for preserving and encouraging a New Invention in England, by Sir Thomas Lombe; and granting him a further Term of Years, for the Sole making and using his Three Italian Engines. *n.p.* [*1732*], *s. sh. F*o. LU.

4339 An Act for Explaining, Amending, and Making more effectual an Act made in the Eleventh Year of the Reign of his late Majesty King George the First, intitled, An Act for the better regulating the Manufacture of Cloth in the West Riding of the County of York. *n.p.* [*1732*], *F*o. L.

A bill. Another edn., with the blanks filled in, entitled A Bill, intitled, An Act for explaining.... n.p. [1732], Fo (L).

4340 The Case of the Narrow-Clothiers and other Woollen Manufacturers in the West-Riding of the County of York. *n.p.* [*1732*], *F*o. LU.

4341 The Case of the Writing-Masters in and about the Cities of London and Westminster. *n.p.* [*1732*], *F*o. LU.

Against unskilled teachers of business methods who have not served apprenticeships.

4342 Information for the Magistrates and Town-council of Edinburgh, and their Procurators Fiscal, against Thomas Haddoway and George Arnot, Brewers in Leith. *n.p.* [*1732*], *F*o. E.

Dated: February 14. 1732. Signed Ch. Areskine. Haddoway and Arnot were not burgesses of Edinburgh. This case raised the whole question of the relationship of Leith to Edinburgh and many sessions papers exist on this controversy.

4343 The Poor Man's Case consider'd; or a Pill for Colts and Cure for the Publick: Being the Address of all and singular the Journeymen of the City of Dublin. Humbly inscribed to both Houses of Parliament. *Dublin*, *1732*, *s. sh. F*o. D.

Colts are workmen who have not served an apprenticeship.

COMMERCE

4344 Information for Her Grace the Dutchess of Bucleugh, and the Merchant Free-Traders of the Town of Dalkeith, against the Merchant Unfree-Traders, and other Tradesmen and Inhabitants there. *n.p.* [*1732*], *F*o. E.

Dated: January 14. 1732. Signed: Ro. Dundas.

4345 Information for the Retailers, Mechanicks, Land-labourers, and the Generality of the Inhabitants within the Town of Dalkeith, against Two or three Merchants Traders there, and the Baillie of the Burgh for his Interest. *n.p.* [*1732*], *F*o. E.

Dated: January 26. 1732. Signed: Ja. Graham.

4346 Forman, Charles. A Letter to the Merchants of Great Britain or a proper Reply to the London Journal, of Dec. 12, 1730. By Peregrine English. To which is prefix'd, The scurrilous Letter in the said Journal, and also the Letter to Mr. Fog, which he pretends to answer. *Lond.* *1732*, *8*o. LU.

The preface is signed: Charles Forman. Mostly a comparison between English and Dutch mercantile conditions.

4347 Captain Alexander Hamilton, Appellant. The Lords Directors of the Dutch East-India Company, and Will Drummond their Factor, Respondts. The Appellant's Case. *n.p.* [*1732*], *F*o. L.

Signed: C. Talbot. Ro. Dundas. Will. Hamilton. On the seizure in 1711 of the cargo of the *Satisfaction*.

4348 Capt. Alexander Hamilton Appellant. The Lords Directors of the East-India Company of Holland of the Chamber of Zealand Respondents. The Respondents Case. *n.p.* [*1732*], *F*o. L.

Signed: P. Yorke. Dun. Forbes.

4349 Davies, Joseph. An Humble Proposal most humbly offered to the Consideration of His Majesty and both Houses of Parliament, that may be a better Security for all our Shiping that Trades in the Streights, and a Defence to Gibraltar, and Entirely checks and restrains the growth of Highway-men, Foot-pads, House-breakers, Shop-lifters, Horse-stealers, Incendiaries and Others, that are guilty of enormous Crimes; rendering them useful, that in case of a War, it will be above a Hundred Thousand Pounds a Year in this Kingdom's way. (With a map). *Southwark, 1732, 8o*. pp. 14. (O).

A revised edition of no. 4281. Another edn. 1732, pp. 16 (O). Convicts to man galleys based on Gibraltar and Port Mahon.

4350 [Webb, Daniel]. An Enquiry how far the Declining State of the British Woollen Manufacture for Exportation does affect the English Landed Interest, especially as occasion'd by Running the British and Irish Wool: And some Remarks on the Wool Exported to Jersey & Guernsey, &c. And also on our Woollen Trade in general, and only Means in Great Britain's Power, with Submission, of Restoring, Enlarging, and Securing it. In a Letter from an English Woollen Manufacturer to a Member of Parliament. *n.p.* [*1732?*], *s. sh. Fo*. LPRO.

Endorsed: An Enquiry how far the Running the British and Irish Wool doth affect the Landed Interest in England. The copy seen is enclosed in a letter from the author.

4351 A Letter to a Member of Parliament from a Country Gentleman, concerning the Growth of the Wool, and the Nature of the Woollen Trade in Ireland; wherein such a Method is proposed for preventing the clandestine Exportation of these Commodities, as will be equally beneficial to both Kingdoms. *n.p. 1732, 8o*. D.

Signed: Hiberno-Britannus. Another edn. Lond. 1732 (LU).

4352 [Gray, Jeffery]. A Proposal fully to prevent the Smugling of Wool, which by Methods Entirely New, shows how, and wholly takes of the Former Charge in the old Methods of endeavouring to do it. Also, Adds more than Ten Millions Yearly to the Trade of the British Nation. And is hinted, that the Great National Debt may be Paid in Seven Years and Half, with several other valuable Things.... *Lond. 1732, 8o*. LU.

Signed: Philo-Britannicus. 3rd edn. 1732, signed Philo-Britannicus, alias Jeffery Gray (LU); 4th edn. 1740, entitled: Gray's Proposal... (LU).

4353 Gray, Jeffery. A Proposal, shewing how the Wool-Affair may yet be finished, some Millions to the Nation's Advantage, this Year. *n.p.* [*1732?*], *s. sh. Fo*. LU.

Signed: Philo-Britannicus, alias Jeffery Gray.

4354 A Bill, intituled, An Additional Act for the Encouragement of the Woollen Manufactures of this Kingdom, by the more effectual preventing the unlawful Exportation of the Woollen Manufactures of the Kingdom of Ireland, to Foreign Parts. *n.p.* [*1732*], *Fo*. L.

4355 By the Lord Lieutenant and Council of Ireland, a Proclamation, For preventing the Illegal Exportation of Wool, Worstead, Bay or Woollen Yarn, Woollen Cloath, or other Woollen Manufactures of this Kingdom. *Dublin, 1731, s. sh. F°.* DPRO.

Dated: 13 March 1731.

4356 By the Lords Justices and Council of Ireland, a Proclamation, Offering a Reward for apprehending Murtogh M'Owen Sullivan, John Sullivan, Dennis M'Murtogh Sullivan, Murtogh Sullivan Junior, and Thomas Trinwith, and for discovering and apprehending several other Persons concerned with them in rescuing Eighty Anchors of Brandy seized by the Officers of His Majesty's Revenue, and sinking the Sloop belonging to the said Officers into which the said Brandy was removed, and in traiterously murdering Francis Post one of the Assistants of the said Officers, and dangerously wounding several others of the said Assistants at Beerhaven in the County of Cork. *Dublin, 1732, F°.* DPRO.

Dated: 11 October 1732.

4357 By the Lords Justices and Council of Ireland, a Proclamation, Offering a Reward for discovering and apprehending the Persons who rescued ten Packs of Run Tobacco, and assaulted the Officer of the Revenue and his Assistants in the County of Catherlough, and took from one of the said Assistants one Pound seventeen Shillings Sterling. *Dublin, 1732, s. sh. F°.* DPRO.

Dated: 11 October, 1732.

4358 PULLEN, JOHN. Memoirs of the Maritime Affairs of Great-Britain, especially in relation to our concerns in the West-Indies. To which is prefix'd, The Original Letter of the Author, to...the Earl of Oxford ...in relation to the South-Sea Company, and the Trade they were designed to carry on....To which is added, Capt. Pain's Short View of Spanish America.... *Lond. 1732, 8°.* L.

Another issue, with a different title-page, reading: The Original Plan, Progress, and Present State of the South-Sea-Company, 1732 (O).

4359 An Address to the Proprietors of the South-Sea Capital. Containing, a Discovery of the Illicit Trade, carry'd on in the West-Indies. By a Proprietor of the said Company. *Lond. 1732, F°.* M(Cr).

2nd edn. 1732 (LU).

4360 A Bill, intituled, An Act for the better Securing and Encouraging the Trade of His Majesty's Sugar Colonies in America. *n.p.* [*1732*], *F°.* L.

4361 Captain Fayrer Hall's Evidence, before a Committee of the House of Commons, in April 1731. concerning the Sugar Colony Bill. Remarks on the Examination before the Committee of the Honourable House of Commons. *n.p.* [*1732*], *F°.* LPRO.

The evidence and the remarks also by Hall are in parallel columns. They are followed by A Letter to a Noble Lord concerning the Advantages to the French Sugar-Colonies from the Northern Colony Trade, signed: Fayrer Hall.

4362 [HALL, FAYRER]. *Begin.* My Lord, The Bill upon which I was examined last Year.... *n.p.* [*1732*], *F°*. LPRO.

Correcting his evidence on the Molasses Bill. Authorship deduced from internal evidence.

4363 The British Empire in America, Consider'd. In a Second Letter, from a Gentleman of Barbadoes, to his Friend in London. *Lond. 1732*, *4°*. LU.

4364 A Comparison between the British Sugar Colonies and New England, as they relate to the Interest of Great Britain. With Some Observations on the State of the Case of New England. To which is added A Letter to a Member of Parliament. *Lond. 1732*, *8°*. LU.

4365 The Controversy between the Northern Colonies and the Sugar Islands respectively considered. And some Thoughts humbly offered, to shew how far it may be reasonable to relieve the Sugar Islands, without doing any injury to their Fellow-Subject. *n.p.* [*1732?*], *s. sh. F°*. L.

4366 [ROBERTSON, ROBERT]. A Detection of the State and Situation of the Present Sugar Planters, of Barbadoes and the Leward Islands. With an Answer to this Query, Why does not England, or her Sugar Islands, or both, make and settle more Sugar Colonies in the West-Indies? Written in the Month of December 1731, by an Inhabitant of one of His Majesty's Leward Caribee Islands; and dedicated to the Right Honourable Sir Robert Walpole. *Lond. 1732*, *8°*. LU.

For authorship see F. W. Pitman, *The Development of the British West Indies*, 1917, p. 269.

4367 Hurlo Thrumbo's Lucubrations. Being a Letter from a Gentleman in the Country, to his Friend in Town. Very proper to be bound up with a Pamphlet nonsensically entitled, A true State of the Case between the British Northern Colonies and the Sugar-Islands in America. *Lond. 1732*, *4°*. LU.

4368 Some Considerations humbly offer'd upon the Bill now depending in the House of Lords, relating to the Trade between the Northern Colonies and the Sugar-Islands. In a Letter to a Noble Peer. *n.p. 1732*, *8°*. L.

4369 Some Considerations touching the Sugar Colonies, with Political Observations in respect to Trade. By a Person well acquainted with the Sugar Trade, but at present residing in the Island of Antigua. *Lond. 1732*, *4°*. L.

4370 Some Observations on the Northern Colonie Trade with the French Sugar Colonics with respect to our Acts of Parliament now in force in a Letter to a Noble Lord. *n.p.* [*1732?*], *F°*. L.

4371 A True State of the Case between the British Northern-Colonies, and the Sugar Islands in America, impartially considered, with respect to the Bill now depending in the Right Honourable the House of Lords, relating to the Sugar Trade. *n.p. 1732*, *4°*. L.

COLONIES

4372 Select Tracts relating to Colonies. Consisting of I. An Essay on Plantations. By Sir Francis Bacon....II. Some Passages taken out of the History of Florence, &c. III. A Treatise by John De Witt Pensioner of Holland. IV. The Benefit of Plantations or Colonies. By William Penn. V. A Discourse concerning Plantations. By Sir Josiah Child. *Lond.* [*1732*], 8°. LU.

J. Nichols, *Literary Anecdotes*, II, 17, attributes the editorship of this to Oglethorpe. V. W. Crane considers this attribution somewhat doubtful, but Thomas Coram in a letter in Bodleian Rawlinson MS. D.893, f.130, speaks of 'the stitched books...Wch Mr. Oglethorpe had printed entitled Select Tracts relating to Colonys'.

4373 [Prince, Thomas]. The vade mecum for America: or, A companion for traders and travellers.... *Boston, S. Kneeland and T. Green for D. Henchman & T. Hancock, 1732.* Kress S. 1766.

4374 Lex et Libertas. *n.p.* [*1732*], *F°*. LPRO.

On bills of credit. Dated January 31, 1731, 2. Reprinted in *Colonial Currency Reprints*, ed. by A. M. Davis, vol. 2 (1911). Tentatively attributed to Nathaniel Byfield in *Cal. S.P. Col.*, 1732, p. 74.

4375 The Case of the Tobacco Planters in His Majesty's Colony of Virginia, as to the Bill now depending in the House of Lords, for the more easy Recovery of Debts in His Majesty's Plantations and Colonies Abroad. *n.p.* [*1732*], *F°*. LLI.

4376 [Gooch, William]. A Dialogue between Thomas Sweet-Scented, William Oronoco, Planters, both Men of Good Understanding, and Justice Love-Country, who can speak for himself. Recommended to the Reading of the Planters. By a sincere Lover of Virginia. *Williamsburg, 1732*, *4°*. LPRO.

For authorship see *Cal. S.P. Col.*, 1732, no. 149.

4377 A New and Accurate Account of the Provinces of South-Carolina and Georgia: with many curious and useful Observations on the Trade, Navigation and Plantations of Great-Britain, compared with her most powerful maritime Neighbours in antient and modern Times. *Lond. 1732*, *8°*. L.

Reissued in 1733 (L). Attributed both to James Oglethorpe and, with more probability, to Henry Martyn. See evidence assembled by V. W. Crane cited in Sabin 87900.

4378 [Martyn, Benjamin]. Some Account of the Designs of the Trustees for establishing of the Colony of Georgia in America. *n.p.* [*1732*], *F°*. L.

Lower half of p. 4 blank. Another issue, with a map on lower half of p. 4 (LSC); another edn. Lond. 1732, F° (L). For later reprints see Sabin 86574 For authorship see Egmont Diary I, 289.

FINANCE

4379 TRENCHARD, THOMAS. The Inquisitor. Containing an Answer to the Scurrilous Reflections on the former Numbers by the Free Briton of September 30, and Daily Courant of October 2d. With a List of some Queries in relation to the Forage-Contract, which (unless answered) must fully convince the World of the Iniquity of that Affair....Number III. To be Occasionally continued. *Lond. 1732*, *8o*. O.

The first two nos. were published in 1731.

4380 [DAVIES, JOSEPH]. A Scheme for Payment of the Sum of 49,301,855 l. 6s. 1d.½ being the National Debt of Great-Britain, as it stood the 31st of Dec. 1730, in a few Years, without making any additional Tax on the Subject. Which, if Enacted into a Law, will be of infinite Service to the Merchants Trading to the West-Indies; infallibly secure our Possession of Gibraltar and the Island of Minorca; totally abolish Smuggling; and be of singular Advantage to the Woollen Manufactury.... *Lond. 1732*, *8o*. LU.

Authorship deduced from the fact that part of the scheme is to make all convicts into galley slaves, a favourite nostrum of Davies.

4381 A Letter to a Member of Parliament, concerning the Reduction of Interest. *Lond. 1732*, *Fo*. L.

4382 The Craftsman Extraordinary. Or, a Letter to Caleb D'Anvers, Esq; on the Present State of the Affairs of the South-Sea Company. *Lond. 1732*, *s. sh. Fo*. O.

4383 A Letter to Sr. John Eyles, Bart. Sub-Governour of the South-Sea Company, occasioned by the Debates at the last General Court. *Lond. 1732*, *Fo*. M(Cr).

Dated: 20th Match 1731–2.

4384 A letter to the proprietors of the South-sea stock. Shewing what will be most easy and effectual method to discharge their present bond debt, without prejudice to their capital stock. *London, J. Roberts* [*etc.*], *1732*. *32×20 cm*. Kress S. 1764.

4385 South-Sea House, 20th April, 1732. *n.p.* [*1732*], *Fo*. L.

Notice of a ballot on 'Heads proposed for a Bill in Parliament to divide the present Capital of the South-Sea Company; Part into Annuities, and the Remainder into a Trading Capital'.

4386 Reasons for Appointing a Committee to Examine Accounts; or, A Proper Reply to so much of the last Craftsman as relates to the Court of Directors of the South-Sea Company. *Lond. 1732*, *s. sh. Fo*. C(Cr).

Dated: July 6, 1732.

4387 DOWNES, THOMAS. A Scheme Plainly demonstrating how Several Hundred Thousand Pounds may be raised Yearly to the Government,

Without Officers to collect it, Without Oppression to the Poor, Without hurting Trade, and Without any Person's being oblig'd to pay it, but when he pleases to do so; and by which the Duty on Soap and Candles is proposed to be taken off.... *Lond. 1732*, 8°. 24 pp. LU.

Proposes a tax on bracelets, hats and wigs. Another edn. Lond. 1732. 16 pp. (LU).

4388 The Occasional Monitor: containing a Scheme or Proposal, for Taking off the several Taxes on Land, Soap, Starch, Candles, Leather, Plate, Pot, &c. As also the Duties on the several Commodities us'd in Dying...and Replacing the said Duties by another Way which will bring in more Money in a more Easy and Equal Manner....Part II. *Lond. 1732*, 4°. LU.

For a window tax. Another edn. 1733 8°, entitled: A Scheme or Proposal for Taking off the several Taxes....To which is added, Some Considerations on the several Duties upon Tea, Coffee, Chocolat, and Salt... (LU).

4389 CROUCH, HENRY. A Complete Guide to the Officers of His Majesty's Customs in the Out-Ports. Being Forms, Precedents, and Instructions for the Execution of every Branch of the Business of that Revenue.... *Lond. 1732*, F°. L.

4390 Instructions for the Officers who survey the Large Dealers in Coffee, Tea, and Chocolate, &c. and all Permit-Writers. *Lond. 1732*, 8°. O.

4391 Unto the Right Honourable, The Lords of Council and Session, The Petition of The Commissioners of His Majesty's Excise, for themselves and in Name and Behalf of James Harker Officer of Excise at Hawick. *n.p.* [*1732*], F°. E.

Dated: Jan. 6. 1732. Signed: Cha. Areskine.

4392 Answers for Thomas Elliot, Skinner in Hawick. To the Petition of the Commissioners of his Majesty's Excise, for themselves, and in Name and Behalf of James Harker, Officer of Excise at Hawick. *n.p.* [*1732*], *s. sh.* F°. E.

Dated: January 10, 1732. Signed: William Grant.

4393 Unto the Right Honourable the Lords of Council and Session, the Petition of Thomas Eliot, Skinner in Hawick. *n.p.* [*1732*], F°. E.

Dated: Jan. 19th 1732. Signed: William Grant.

4394 Answers for the Commissioners of Excise, and James Harker, Officer of Excise at Hawick, To the Petition of Thomas Eliot Skinner in Hawick. *n.p.* [*1732*], F°. E.

Dated: January 31. 1732. Signed: Ch. Areskine.

4395 Considerations occasioned by the Craftsman upon Excises. *Lond. 1733* [*1732*], 8°. L.

4396 Short and Plain Reasons against a General Excise. *Lond. 1732*, *s. sh.* F°. O.

4397 The Case of the Salt-Duty and Land-Tax, offered to the Consideration of every Freeholder. *Lond. 1732*, *8o*. LU.

4398 [ARNALL, WILLIAM ?]. A Letter to a Freeholder, on the Late Reduction of the Land Tax to One Shilling in the Pound. By a Member of the House of Commons. *Lond. 1732*, *8o*. LU.

Foxwell had seen a copy with the attribution of authorship in ms.

4399 A Bill, intituled, An Act for Reviving the Duties on Salt for the Term therein mentioned. *n.p.* [*1732*], *Fo*. L.

4400 [PULTENEY, WILLIAM, Earl of Bath]. The Case of the Revival of the Salt Duty, fully Stated and Considered; with some Remarks on the Present State of Affairs. In answer to a late Pamphlet, intitled A Letter to a Freeholder on the late Reduction of the Land-Tax to one Shilling in the Pound. In a Letter from a Member of the House of Commons to a Gentleman in the Country. *Lond. 1732*, *8o*. LU.

For attribution of authorship see B.M. Catalogue.

4401 A letter to a country gentleman on the revival of the salt duty. *Lond. 1732*, *8o*. Kress 4019.

4402 The Case of Thomas Tomkyns, in relation to his Debt due to the Crown, as Cashire to the Hawkers and Pedlars. *n.p.* [*1732*], *s. sh. Fo*. LU.

4403 BOHUN, WILLIAM. A Tithing Table, shewing (by Way of Analysis) of what Things Tithes are or are not Due, either by Common Law, Custom, or Prescription. *Lond. 1732*, *8o*. L.

2nd edn. 1735 (MP).

4404 The Draper's Remarks on the Late Importation of New-Coin'd English Half-Pence, and the Consequences thereof to this Kingdom. With Modest Reasons for the Liberty of a Mint, &c. Humbly offered to the Consideration of those at the Helm. *Dublin, 1732*, *8o*. DNL.

4405 The Tricks of the Town: or, Ways and Means for getting Money. Wherein the various Lures, Wiles, and Artifices, practised by the Designing and Crafty upon the Weak and Unwary, are fully exposed. Recommended to the serious Perusal of all Adventurers and Sharers in Bubble-Undertakings, the Pursuers of Pennyworths, and Bargain-Buyers. Chiefly collected from some Papers of the Ingenious Mr. John Thomson, scattered between Lawrence-Pountney's-Hill and Dover. *Lond., 1732*, *8o*. L.

4406 The Lord Viscount Barrington's Case in relation to the Harburgh Company and the Harburgh Lottery. *Lond. 1732*, *4o*. LU.

4407 AYLIFFE, JOHN. The Law of Pledges, or Pawns, as it was in Use amongst the Romans, and as it is now practiced in most Foreign Nations. Humbly inscribed to a Member of Parliament. *Lond. 1732*, *8o*. LU.

4408 Proposals for a Regulation, or an entire Suppression, of Pawn-brokers. With a Detection of their Fraudulent Practices, and a Recommendation of the Methods used by the States of Holland, for the Relief of the Necessitous, by lending on Pledges. To which are added, Some Considerations on the present Calamities of the Sufferers by the Charitable Corporation.... *Lond. 1732*, 8º. L.

4409 The Report of the Gentlemen appointed by the General Court of the Charitable Corporation held the 19th of October, the 18th of November, and the 21st of December last; to inspect the State of their Affairs, &c. As the same was given into the General Court of January 12, 17$\frac{31}{32}$. by Dr. Mowbray, Chairman. To which is added, A List of the Proprietors of the said Corporation, as they stood October 1, 1731. and the General Account as it stood at Michaelmas last. *Lond. 1732*, Fº. MP.

Another edn. n.p. [1732], Fº (L). 2nd edn. with petitions of the proprietors, 1732, 4º (L).

4410 The Several Reports, with the Appendix, which is to one of them, from the Committee of the House of Commons, to whom the Petition of the Proprietors of the Charitable Corporation for Relief of Industrious Poor by assisting them with small Sums upon Pledges at legal Interest, assembled in the General Court, was referred; and the Proceedings of the said House thereofon.... *Lond. 1732*, Fº. LU.

4411 A Further Report from the Committee to whom the Petition of the Proprietors of the Charitable Corporation for Relief of Industrious Poor...was referred. *Lond. 1732*, Fº. L.

4412 Belloni, Giovanni Angelo. A Letter from John Angelo Belloni, to the Gentlemen of the Committee of the Parliament of England, appointed to inspect the Affairs of the Charitable Corporation. *n.p.* [*1732*], *s. sh.* Fº. L.

In English and French.

4413 Signior John Angelo Belloni's Letter to My Lord ****. *n.p.* [*1732*], 8º. L.

A defence of his previous letter. English and French in parallel columns.

4414 Belloni, Giovanni Angelo. Copy Letter, Seignior John Angelo Belloni, to the Gentlemen of the Committee of the Parliament of England, appointed to inspect the Affairs of the Charitable Corporation. Together with the Resolutions of both Houses of Parliament anent the same, and the Resolution of the Governor and Directors of the said Corporation. As also Belloni's second Letter to my Lord ****. *Lond. 1732*, 8º. LU.

4415 A Bill for the Relief of the Sufferers in the Charitable Corporation. *n.p.* [*1732*], Fº. L.

4416 The Case of the Charitable Corporation. *n.p.* [*1732*], *F°*. L.
Endorsed: The Case of the Charitable Corporation, 1731–2.

4417 The Case of the Charitable Corporation. *n.p.* [*1732?*], *F°*. L.
Endorsed: The Case of the Charitable Corporation and the Relief they Humbly Pray.

4418 The Case of the Borrowers of the Charitable Corporation. *n.p.* [*1732*], *s. sh. F°*. LU.

4419 The Case of the Creditors, by Notes and Bonds, of the Corporation, intitled, The Charitable-Corporation, for Relief of industrious Poor, by assisting them with small Sums upon Pledges, at legal Interest. *n.p.* [*1732?*], *s. sh. F°*. LU.

4420 [Shippen, William]. Four Speeches against Continuing the Army, &c. as they were spoken on several occasions in the House of Commons. As also, a Speech for relieving the Unhappy Sufferers in the Charitable Corporation; as it was spoken in the House of Commons, May 8. 1732. By W—— S——, Esq; *London, 1732, 8°*. E.
The last speech is reprinted, with speaker's full name, in *Cobbett's Parliamentary History*, VIII, 1161–4.

4421 A Letter from a Member of the House of Commons (One of the Committee appointed to enquire into the Affairs of the Charitable Corporation) to his Friends, (some Merchants) at Rome. In which is reveal'd the Secret Means used by some of the Committee-Men, Assistance, and Servants of the said Corporation, for Embezzling the Stock.... *Lond.* [*1732*], *8°*. O.

4422 The Nature of the Charitable Corporation, and its Relation to Trade, Consider'd. In a Letter to a Member of Parliament. *Lond. 1732, 4°*. LU.
Signed: Britannicus.

4423 A Necessary Caution to the Sufferers by the Charitable Corporation; and to all who wish them Relief under their deplorable Circumstances. *Lond.* [*1732*], *s. sh. F°*. LSC.

4424 A Postscript to Asgill's Essay upon Charity. *n.p.* [*1732?*], *s. sh. F°*. L.
Endorsed: Postscript to Asgill's Essay upon the Charitable Corporation.

4425 A short Case of the Present State of the Charitable Corporation. *n.p.* [*1732?*], *s. sh. F°*. LU.

4426 A Short History of the Charitable Corporation. From the Date of their Charter, to their late Petition. In which is contain'd A Succinct History of the Frauds discovered in the Management of their Affairs, which occasion'd the Proprietors Application to Parliament.... *Lond. 1732, 4°*. LU.

4427 Some Thoughts humbly propos'd toward the Relief of the Charitable Corporation. *n.p.* [*1732*], *F°*. LU.

4428 A Bill, intituled, An Act to restrain Sir Robert Sutton...Sir Archibald Grant...Denis Bond, William Burroughs...George Jackson, Benjamin Robinson...Richard Woolley, and Thomas Warren, from going out of this Kingdom...and for discovering their Estates and Effects... and to oblige William Squire to surrender himself.... *n.p.* [*1732*], *F^o^*. L.

All concerned in the Charitable Corporation.

4429 By the King, A Proclamation, For apprehending and securing the Persons of William Burroughs, Esq; and William Squire. *Lond. 1731* [*o.s.*], *s. sh. F^o^*. L.

Dated 17. March 1731. Officers of the Charitable Corporation.

4430 The Case of Sir Archibald Grant. *n.p.* [*1732*], *F^o^*. pp. 4. L.

One of the Committee of the Charitable Corporation.

4431 The Case of Sir Archibald Grant. *n.p.* [*1732*], *F^o^*. pp. 8. L.

Different from the preceding.

4432 The Case of George Jackson. *n.p.* [*1732*], *s. sh. F^o^*. LU.

An Assistant of the Charitable Corporation.

4433 The Case of Mr. Benjamin Robinson, Petitioner against the Bill, now depending in the House of Lords, against Sir Robert Sutton, and others. *n.p.* [*1732*], *s. sh. F^o^*. LG.

4434 The Case of Thomas Warren, in Relation to the Bill to restrain Sir Robert Sutton, and others, &c. *n.p.* [*1732*], *s. sh. F^o^*. LG.

4435 The Particular and Inventory of all and singular the Lands, Tenements, and Hereditments, Goods, Chattels, Debts and Personal Estate whatsoever of the Right Honourable Sir Robert Sutton.... *Lond. 1732*, *F^o^*. L.

Similar inventories were published of the possessions of Sir Archibald Grant, Denis Bond, William Burroughs, Thomas Warren and Richard Woolley, all of whom were implicated in the frauds of the Charitable Corporation (all L).

4436 WHISTON, WILLIAM. An Account of the past and present State of the Amicable Society for a perpetual Assurance-Office; with the Occasions of the low Condition it is now in; and Proposals in Order to recover its former Prosperity. *n.p.* [*1732*], *8°*. O.

4437 RICHARDSON, JOHN. Some Remarks and Considerations on the Original and Supplemental Charters, which incorporate the Amicable Society for a Perpetual Assurance-Office. Occasioned by a View of Mr. Whiston's Account of the Past and Present State thereof. With a Calculation from its Beginning to Lady Day 1732. Shewing, what might have been expected in Six and Twenty Years by fair Management; Compared with the Present State....By a Member and Contributor. *Lond. 1732*, *8°*. MP.

TRANSPORT

4438 A Bill for Enlarging the Term granted by an Act made in the Eleventh Year of the Reign of His late Majesty King George the First, for Rebuilding the Pier and Harbour of Parton in the County of Cumberland. *n.p.* [*1732*], *F*o. L.

4439 A Bill to Enlarge the Pier and Harbour of Scarborough in the County of York. *n.p.* [*1732*], *F*o. L.

4440 A Bill for the better Regulation and Government of Pilots licensed by the Corporation of Trinity House of Deptford Strond in the County of Kent; and to prevent Mischiefs and Annoyances upon the River of Thames below London Bridge. *n.p.* [*1732*], *F*o. O.

4441 The Case of the Corporation of Trinity-House, relating to the Office of Lastage and Ballastage in the River Thames. *n.p.* [*1732*], *F*o. LU.

4442 The Case of the Licensed and Warranted Pilots of the Trinity-House of Deptford-Strond, most humbly offered to the Honourable House of Commons. *n.p.* [*1732*], *s. sh. F*o. LU.

4443 The Case of the Licensed Pilots of the Trinity-House of Deptford-Strond, most humbly offered to the Honourable House of Commons. *n.p.* [*1732*], *s. sh. F*o. L.

4444 The Case of the Merchants, Masters, & Owners of Ships Trading on the River of Thames. *n.p.* [*1732*], *F*o. LU.

4445 The Method taken by the Corporation of Trinity-House of Deptford-Strond, in Weighing or Gauging of their Ballast-Lighters; with their working Tackle on Board, as Masts, Rigging, Sails, &c. *n.p.* [*1732*], *s. sh. 4*o. L.

4446 Reasons Humbly Offered against passing the Act For the better Regulation and Government of Pilots Licensed by the Corporation of Trinity-House of Deptford-Strond in the County of Kent; and to prevent Mischiefs and Annoyances upon the River of Thames below London-bridge. *n.p.* [*1732*], *s. sh. F*o. L.

4447 The Answer of the Corporation of Trinity-House, to the Reasons offered against passing the Act for the better Regulation and Government of Pilots licensed by the said Corporation. *n.p.* [*1732*], *F*o. L.

4448 Some Considerations on the Extraordinary Grants in the Charters to the Trinity House of Deptford Strond, and the Illegal By Laws and Practices of that Corporation. *n.p.* [*1732*], *F*o. LU.

4449 Rules, Orders, and Constitutions made by the Rulers, Auditors, and Assistants of the Watermen and Lightermen of the River of Thames.... *n.p.* [*1732*], *8*o. L.

4450 The Case of the Cheesemongers, in and about the Cities of London and Westminster, relating to the Bill to recover and preserve the Navigation of the River Dee, in the County of Chester. *n.p.* [*1732*], *s. sh. F*o. L.

4451 The Case of the Inhabitants of the County and City of Chester, Petitioners for the Bill to Recover and Preserve the Navigation of the River Dee; In Answer to the Petition of the Cheesemongers in and about the City of London against the said Bill. *n.p.* [*1732*], *F°*. L.

4452 A Bill, intituled, An Act to explain, amend and render more effectual, an Act passed in the First Year of His present Majesty's Reign (intituled, An Act for punishing such Persons as shall wilfully and maliciously pull down or destroy Turnpikes, for repairing Highways, or Locks, or other Works erected by Authority of Parliament, for making Rivers navigable. *n.p.* [*1732*], *F°*. L.

SOCIAL CONDITIONS

4453 LONDON. Barber Mayor. Martis 28. Die Novembris, 1732. [*Lond. 1732*], *s. sh. F°*. LCRO.

An order that constables and beadles finding poor vagrant children sleeping out at night are to lodge them in their watch-houses.

4454 To the Right Worshipful William Falkner, Gentleman and Mayor, of Boston in Lincolnshire; and to William Hart, Esq; one of his Majesty's Justices of the Peace in that County.... *Lond. 1732*, *8°*. O.

Signed: J.H. Followed by 'Proposals to the Right Worshipful the Mayor, the Worshipful the Justices, Aldermen and Common-Council of Boston in Lincolnshire, for maintaining the Poor. To which is added, A Preface to the History of the Ale-Sellers in the said Corporation, which will shortly be Printed and Published, By J.H. of Boston. Printed in the Year, 1721.' Proposing that all retailers of intoxicants should pay heavily for licences.

4455 His Majesty's Commission for establishing a Charity for relief of Poor Widows of Commission and Warrant Officers of the Royal Navy. *n.p.* [*1732?*], *4°*. L.

The commission is dated 6 August 1732.

4456 Establishment for Admitting, Maintaining and Educating of Poor Boys in the Royal Hospital for Seamen at Greenwich, and for Binding them out Apprentices to the Sea-Service. Established at a General Court, held at the Admiralty-Office the 22d of December, 1731. *Lond. 1732*, *4°*. L.

4457 Reasons for a further Contribution, towards Supporting and Enlarging the Charitable Infirmary of the City of Dublin. *n.p.* [*1732?*], *s. sh. F°*. DM.

4458 Proposals by the Dispensary-Society, for supplying the Nobility, Gentry and other reputable Persons or Families, with all Sorts of Medicines required in time of Sickness, at the Rate of Two Shillings by the Quarter to each Subscriber. *n.p. 1732*, *s. sh. F°*. L.

4459 Proposals for Promoting Industry, and Advancing Proper Credit;

advantageous to Creditors in particular and the Nation in general: in a Letter to a Member of Parliament. *Lond. 1732, 8°*. LU.

Signed: Philanthropos. Against imprisonment for debt.

4460 A Bill for preventing Frauds committed by Bankrupts. *n.d.* [*1732*], *F°*. L.

4461 A proposal for rendering bankruptcies less frequent in and about London. *Lond. 1732, 19 cm.* Kress 4033.

4462 Reasons for allowing the Benefits of the Bankrupts-Act to all against whom a Commission shall be issued by the 25th of March next. *n.p.* [*1732?*], *s. sh. F°*. LG.

4463 Reasons humbly offered for Passing the Bill for preventing of Frauds committed by Bankrupts. *n.p.* [*1732*], *s. sh. F°*. L.

4464 A Bill, intituled, An Act to explain, amend, and render more effectual an Act made in the Twelfth Year of the Reign of His late Majesty King George the First [intituled, An Act to prevent frivolous and vexatious Arrests. *n.p.* [*1732*], *F°*. L.

4465 Reasons humbly offered on behalf of the Traders of the City of London, in favour of a Clause proposed to the Consideration of the Right Honourable the House of Lords, to be added to a Bill, Intitled, An Act to explain, amend, and render more effectual....An Act to prevent frivolous and vexatious Arrests. *n.p.* [*1732*], *s. sh. F°*. L.

Endorsed: Reasons for a Clause to restrain the Removal of Causes from the Courts of the City of London, where the Debt or Damages do not amount to Twenty Pounds.

4466 A Serious Call to the City of London, and thro' them to the whole Nation, to the Relief of the persecuted Protestants of Saltzburg. With a Postscript, giving some Account of their Sufferings, and the Numbers that were forc'd out of their Country. *Lond. 1732, 8°*. LG.

4467 LONDON. Child Mayor. Martis XIV° die Martii, 1731.... [*Lond. 1732*], *s. sh. F°*. L.

An order that the Keeper of the Green-Yard is not to receive any beasts as strays without taking the names and addresses of those who drive in the strays.

4468 [SWIFT, JONATHAN]. Considerations upon two Bills sent down from the R—— H—— the H—— of L—— to the H——ble H—— of C—— relating to the Clergy of I********d. *Lond. 1732, 8°*. O.

On their economic condition. Another edn., with Swift's name on the title-page, 'To which is added. A Proposal for an Act of Parliament to pay off the Debt of the Nation, without taxing the Subject.... By A—— P——, Esq.', Lond. 1732, 8° (L). Reprinted in *The Prose Works of Jonathan Swift*, ed. by H. Davis, vol. 12 (1955).

4469 Scheme of the Proportions which the Protestants of Ireland may probably bear to the Papists; humbly offer'd to the Publick. *n.p. 1731–2, 8°*. DA.

4470 An Act for Vesting the Conduits, Springs and Waters in Hyde-Park in Trustees, for the Benefit of His Majesty. *n.p.* [*1732*], *F°*. LU.

A bill.

4471 A Bill for the better and more easy Re-building of the Town of Tiverton, in the County of Devon; and for determining Differences touching Houses and Buildings burnt down, or demolished by reason of the late dreadful Fire there. *n.p.* [*1732*], *F°*. LU.

1733

GENERAL

4472 SLIFORD, WILLIAM. The Court Register, and Statesman's Remembrancer: containing a Series of all the Great Officers, Prime Ministers of State, &c.... From the Restauration of King Charles II. to this present Year. Together with the Commissioners for Managing the several Branches of the Crown-Revenues, from their first Appointment; and also some Account of the Institution, Nature and Business of the several Offices. *Lond. 1733*, *8°*. O.

Dedication signed: William Sliford.

4473 The Landed Interest consider'd: being Serious Advice to Gentlemen, Yeomen, Farmers, and Others, concerned in the Ensuing Election. By a Yeoman of Kent. *Lond. 1733*, *8°*. LU.

Mostly on taxation.

4474 Some Reasons for continuing the Present Parliament. *Lond. 1733*, *8°*. L.

Praising its legislation on debtors, the Fleet Prison, river navigation, and the sugar trade; and suggesting that a new Parliament would mean war.

4475 [LINDESAY, PATRICK]. The Interest of Scotland considered, with regard to Its Police in improving of the Poor, Its Agriculture, Its Trade, Its Manufactures, and Fisheries. *Edin. 1733*, *8°*. E.

Another edn. Lond. 1736 (L). The Rothschild copy of the first edn. is a presentation copy from the author to Pope.

AGRICULTURE

4476 ELLIS, WILLIAM. Chiltern and Vale Farming explained, according to the latest Improvements, by the Author of the Practical Farmer, or the Hertfordshire Husbandman.... *Lond.* [*1733*], *8°*. L.

Another edn., entitled: The Practice of Farming and Husbandry in all Sorts of Soils, Dublin, 1735 (D); Another edn., anonymous, with the original title, Lond. 1745 (O).

4477 MURRAY, Sir ALEXANDER. An Abstract of an Essay on the Improvement of Husbandry and Working of Mines.... *Lond.* [*1733*], *8°*. LU.

4478 The Practical Husbandman and Planter: or, Observations on the Ancient and Modern Husbandry, Planting, Gardening, &c.... To be continued Monthly (till a general System is finished) by a Private Society of Husbandmen, and Planters.... Vol. I. containing April, May, and June. (Vol. II. Containing July, August and September). *Lond. 1733, 4. 8°*. E.

Doubtless edited by Stephen Switzer, who is described in the imprint as the 'principal Assistant to the Society'. Issued in monthly parts and then collected into two volumes. Both the E copy and that in the Royal Agricultural Society Library comprise 6 parts only.

4479 A Philosophical Enquiry concerning the Nature, Use, and Antiquity of Hemp. As it was deliver'd in a Common-Place. In a Famous University. And now publish'd at the Request of the Audience. *Dublin reprinted*, *1733*, *8º*. LU.

4480 An Act for Dividing and Inclosing the Hamlet of Aston Magna in the Parish of Blockley, in the County of Worcester. *n.p.* *1732–3*, *Fº*. L.

4481 An Act for Dividing and Inclosing the Common Fields and Common Meadows in the Parish of Barston, in the County of Warwick. *n.p.* [*1733*], *Fº*. L.

4482 An Act for Inclosing and Dividing the Common Fields, Downs, and Common Grounds in the Tythings of Buckland Newton, Mineterne Parva, and Knowle, in the Parish of Buckland Newton, alias Buckland Abbas, in the County of Dorset. *n.p.* *1733*, *Fº*. L.

4483 An Act for Inclosing and Dividing the Common Fields and Common Grounds, lying in the Manor and Parish of Chipping Warden, in the County of Northampton. *n.p.* *1733*, *Fº*. L.

4484 A Bill for Dividing and Inclosing divers Parcels of Commons and waste Grounds within the Manor of Bisleigh alias Bisley, in the County of Gloucester. *n.p.* [*1733*], *Fº*. L.

4485 The Case of the Petitioners against the Bill for Dividing and Inclosing divers Parcels of Commons and Waste Grounds within the Manor of Bisleigh, alias Bisley, in the County of Gloucester. *n.p.* [*1733*], *s. sh. Fº*. L.

4486 An Act for Inclosing several large Common Fields within the Parishes of Welsbourne Hastings and Newbold Pacy, in the County of Warwick. *n.p.* [*1733*], *Fº*. L.

4487 An Act for Explaining and Amending Part of an Act made in the second Year of the Reign of His Majesty King George the Second, Intituled, An Act for Inclosing Aldham and Boyne Commons, belonging to the Parish of Hadleigh, in the County of Suffolk, for the better Maintenance of the Poor of the said Parish. *n.p.* [*1733*], *Fº*. L.

4488 Advertisement. The Dublin Society has ordered the following Account of the extraordinary Produce of Flax-Seed, to be published, in order to let People see what Increase and Profit they may expect, if they sow their Flax-Seed thin, and manage their Gronnd [*sic*] and Flax in the Proper Manner. *Dublin*, *1733*, *s. sh. Fº*. D.

4489 Advertisement. The great Improvement of Land, which is made by Marle, is so generally known, that it is believ'd most Gentlemen are desirous to have it found on their Estates.... *Dublin*, *1733*, *s. sh. Fº*. DM.

The Dublin Society recommends James Scot as a prospector for marl. The Society also commends James Haffield as skilled in the planting of hops, and praises 'the new Patent English Plow'.

4490 Instructions for Managing Bees. Drawn up and Published by Order of the Dublin Society. *Dublin, 1733*, *8°*. O.

4491 [PRIOR, THOMAS]. Instructions for Planting and Managing Hops, and for Raising Hop-poles. Drawn up and Published by Order of the Dublin Society. *Dubl. 1733*, *8°*. LU.

For authorship see Demond Clarke, *Thomas Prior*, 1951, p. 30.

4492 At a General Court of the Governour and Company of Copper-Miners in England, held the 5th of April 1733. *n.p.* [*1733*], *s. sh. F°*. L.

Resolutions for the payment of a dividend and, on 19 April, for the issue of new shares.

4493 Ballycastle Collieries set in their Proper Light: with Answers to several Objections against the Benefit that may arise to this Kingdom thereby. *Dublin, 1733*, *8°*. DA.

4494 LOGAN, WILLIAM. A View of the Present State of Scotland, in Regard to the Tenures and Slavish Dependencies of the Subjects of that part of North Britain. *Lond. 1733*, *8°*. E.

Edited by Sir Alexander Murray, who reprinted it in his *The True Interest of Great Britain*, 1740 [1741]. Another edn., much edited and anonymous, entitled: Superiorities display'd: or, Scotland's Grievance by reason of the Slavish Dependence of the People upon their Great Men, Edin., 1746, 8° (E).

4495 A Report from the Committee to whom the Petition of the Proprietors of the Stock of the Governor and Company for Raising the Thames Water in York-Buildings, is Referred. *Lond. 1733*, *F°*. LU.

4496 Answer of Samuel Horsey, Esq; Governor of the York Buildings Company, to the Misrepresentations of his Conduct, publish'd in some of the Daily News Papers. *Lond. 1733*, *8°*. L.

4497 The Case of Samuel Horsey, Esq; Governor of the York Buildings Company. *Lond. 1733*, *8°*. L.

4498 The Case of the Proprietors of Stock of the York-Buildings Company. *n.p.* [*1733*], *F°*. LU.

4499 Reasons against the Bill now depending in the House of Lords, for Stating and Determining the Demands of the Corporation of the Governor and Company of Undertakers for raising the Thames Water in York-Buildings. *n.p.* [*1733*], *F°*. LG.

4500 Reasons for Passing the Bill, for stating the Accompts and Demands depending between the York-Buildings Company and their Creditors and Debtors. *n.p.* [*1733?*], *F°*. L.

4501 Reasons humbly offer'd for the farther considering the York Buildings Company's Bill now depending before the Right Honourable the House of Lords. *n.p.* [*1733?*], *s. sh. F°*. LLI.

MANUFACTURES

4502 [Robinson, William]. Proportional Architecture; or, the Five Orders regulated by Equal Parts.... *Lond. 1733, 8°.* L.

2nd edn. 1736, with author's name (L).

4503 Smith, James. The Carpenters Companion: Being an Accurate and Compleat Treatise of Carpenters Works; In which is contained various Sorts of Timber-Floors, Partitions, Bridges, and especially Roofs; with their Manner of Framing, Trussing, &c.... To which is added, The Five Orders of Architecture, in a more easy and concise Method than any yet Published. Exemplified in Forty-One Copper-Plates; With Remarks and Descriptions. *Lond. 1733, 8°.* O.

4504 Brown, J., Distiller. The Interest of the Compound Distiller consider'd. With some Observations on the Distilling Trade. In a Letter to a Member of Parliament. *Lond. 1733, 8°.* O.

4505 The Case of the Master, Wardens, Assistants, and Commonalty of the Company of Distillers; Humbly offered to the Consideration of the Honourable the House of Commons. *n.p.* [*1733?*], *s. sh. F°.* LU.

For a drawback on exported spirits and for leave to make cherry and raspberry brandy.

4506 Peard, Charles. The Woollen Labourer's Advocate. Being a just and compassionate Defence of their tragical Case, against their Masters cruel and detestable Practices of Oppression.... *Lond. 1733, 8°.* LU.

4507 Information for The Incorporation of Baxters in Edinburgh, and John Middlemist, Baxter there, Chargers, against Archibald Punton, Baxter there, Suspender. *n.p.* [*1733*], *F°.* E.

Dated: July 16. 1733, Signed: Hugh Dalrymple.

4508 Information for Archibald Puntoun, Baxter in Edinburgh, Against John Midlemist, Baxter there. *n.p.* [*1733*], *F°.* E.

Dated: July 23, 1733. Signed: Wil. Grant.

4509 The Case of the Bakers of the City of Dublin. *n.p. 1733, F°.* M (Cr).

4510 The Case of the Woolen Manufacturers of the City of Dublin, and Liberties thereunto adjoyning, truly stated.... *Dublin, 1733, F°.* DNL.

4511 The Irish Manufacturer's Plea, in a Letter from a Gentleman of the County, to a Merchant of the City of Corke. *Corke, 1732* [*o.s.*], *8°.* DA.

Dated: Bandon, Feb, 14, 1732–3. and signed: Hibernicus. Another edn., entitled: The Blessings of a Wooll-Trade: or, the Irish Manufacturer's Plea..., with the preface dated: Feb. 4th, 1732–40 [*sic*], signed Hibernicus, Dublin [1733?], 8° (D).

COMMERCE

4512 By the Honourable, The Magistrates of the City of Edinburgh, The Assize of Bread made of Wheat, to be observed during the Month of March 1733, and thereafter until the same is altered by the Magistrates. [*Edin.* *1733*], *s. sh. 4º*. ACC.

Dated: March 14. 1733.

4513 The Case of Henry Eyre, in relation to a Patent granted by his Highness the Bishop and Prince of Liege, &c. the better to prevent the present Notorious Abuse of imposing false and spurious Waters on the Publick, instead of the true Mineral Waters of Spa. *n.p.* [*1733*], *Fº*. M (Cr).

4514 By the Lords Justices and Council of Ireland, a Proclamation Offering a Reward for Discovering and Apprehending the Persons who Assaulted Edward Clarkson, George Boyd, and Oswold Browne, Officers of His Majesty's Revenue and others their Assistants, and Rescued several Anchors of Run Brandy in the County of Dublin. *Dublin*, *1733*, *Fº*. DPRO.

Dated: 31 August 1733.

4515 LACY, J. Observations on the Nature, Use and Trade of Tobacco. *n.p.* [*1733*], *Fº*. L.

Dated: London, March 1st, 1733.

4516 A Bill, intituled, An Act for the better securing and encouraging the Trade of His Majesty's Sugar Colonies in America. *n.p.* [*1733*], *Fº*. L.

4517 The Case of the British Sugar Colonies. *n.p.* [*1733*], *Fº*. LLI.

Text begins: The British Sugar Colonies are of the utmost Consequence.

4518 The Case of the Planters of Tobacco in Virginia, as represented by themselves, signed by the President of the Council and Speaker of the House of Burgesses. *n.p.* [*1733?*], *Fº*. L.

Dated: Williamsburg, June 28, 1732.

4519 Observations on the Case of the Planters of Virginia. In a letter to ——. *n.p.* [*1733*], *Fº*. L.

4520 The Case of the Planters of Tobacco in Virginia, as represented by Themselves; signed by the President of the Council, and Speaker of the House of Burgesses. To which is added, A Vindication of the said Representation. *Lond.* *1733*, *8º*. L.

The Vindication is by Sir John Randolph; see H.M.C. *Egmont Diary*, I, 351.

4521 A Reply to the Vindication of the Representation of the Case of the Planters of Tobacco in Virginia. In a letter to Sir J.R. from the Merchants or Factors of London. *Lond.* *1733*, *8º*. LU.

4522 A Discourse on Trade; more particularly on Sugar and Tobacco: shewing, the True and Natural Means of their Support, and the Unreasonableness of depending upon the Legislature for their Relief. *Lond.* *1733*, *8º*. L.

4523 [ROBERTSON, ROBERT]. An Enquiry into the Methods that are said to be now proposed in England, to retrieve the Sugar Trade. By the Author of The Detection of the State and Situation of the present Sugar Planters of Barbadoes and the Leeward Islands. *Lond. 1733*, *8°*. JCB.

For authorship see *The Detection*, 1732 (no. 4366).

4524 A Letter from a Gentleman in New-York, to his Friend in London. *America* [*New York*], *1733*, *4°*. LPRO.

Signed: P.P. The Governor's services against the Sugar Bill were the reason for the Assembly's voting him £1000.

4525 A Letter to a Noble Peer, relating to the Bill in favour of the Sugar Planters. *n.p. 1733*, *8°*. JCB.

4526 Proposals offered for the Sugar Planters Redress, and for Reviving the British Sugar Commerce. In a further Letter from a Gentleman of Barbadoes, to his Friend in London. *Lond. 1733*, *4°*. L.

The Gentleman wrote a first letter in 1731 and a second in 1732 (nos. 4234 and 4363).

4527 Short Observations on the Bill at present depending in Favour of the Sugar-Islanders. *n.p.* [*1733*] *?*, *s. sh. F°*. L.

Endorsed: Some Observations on the Bill at present depending in Favour of the Sugar-Islanders.

4528 Some further Considerations of the Consequence of the Bill now depending in the House of Lords, relating to the Dispute of the Trade of the British Colonies in America, in a Letter to a Noble Lord, by a Person familliarly acquainted with the English, French, and Dutch Settlements on the Continent, also on the West-India Islands. *n.p.* [*1733*], *F°*. LPRO.

Signed: Philo-Americus. The copy seen is enclosed in a letter by J. Gray.

4529 [ROBERTSON, ROBERT]. A Supplement to the Detection of the State and Situation of the present Sugar Planters of Barbadoes and the Leeward-Islands: shewing, among other new matters, that the surest Way for England to command the Sugar-Market Abroad, is to contract rather than inlarge her Sugar Colonies. In a Letter from an Inhabitant of One of His Majesty's Leeward Caribbee Islands, to a Member of the House of Commons in England....To which is added, A Letter from a Traveller in the Caribbees to his Friend in London. *Lond. 1733*, *8°*. L.

For authorship see F. W. Pitman, *The Development of the British West Indies*, 1917, p. 269, and Sabin, XXIV, 321.

4530 To the Proprietors of the East India Company (February 14. 1732–3). *n.p.* [*1733*], *s. sh. F°*. C (Cr).

On the conduct of Mr. N[ash], whose name is filled in in ms. in the copy seen.

COLONIES

4531 [MARTYN, BENJAMIN]. Reasons for Establishing the Colony of Georgia, with regard to the Trade of Great Britain, the Increase of our People, and the Employment and Support it will afford great Numbers of our own Poor, as well as foreign persecuted Protestants. With some Account of the Country, and the Design of the Trustees. *Lond. 1733*, *4°*. L.

Reissued, with a postscript, 1733 (L). 2nd edn., with author's name, 1733 (L).

4532 The General Account of all Monies and Effects received and expended by the Trustees for establishing the colony of Georgia in America: For the carrying on the good Purposes of their Trust for One whole Year, from the Ninth Day of June in the Year of our Lord 1732....to the Ninth Day of June in the Year of our Lord 1733.... *n.p.* [*1733*], *F°*. L.

L also has the account from 9 June 1733 to 9 June 1734.

4533 SMITH, SAMUEL. A Sermon Preach'd before the Trustees for Establishing the Colony of Georgia in America and before the Associates of the late Rev. Dr. Thomas Bray, for Converting the Negroes in the British Plantations, and for other good Purposes. At their First Yearly-Meeting...on Tuesday February 23, 1730–31....To which is annexed Some Account of the Designs both of the Trustees and Associates [by Benjamin Martyn]. *Lond. 1733*, *4°*. WLC.

Sabin 83978. A list of subsequent sermons is given in Sabin, vol. 20, p. 525.

4534 *Begin:* South-Carolina, George the Second by the Grace of God of Great Britain, France, and Ireland, King.... *n.p.* [*1733*], *s. sh. F°*. LPRO.

A form of grant of crown lands.

FINANCE

4535 A Bill, intituled, An Act for the converting a further Part of the Capital Stock of the South Sea Company into Annuities redeemable by Parliament, and for settling the remaining Part of the said Stock in the said Company. *n.p.* [*1733*], *F°*. L.

4536 The Report of the Committee appointed to Inspect and Examine the several Accounts of the South-Sea Company, laid before the General Court of the said Company the 16th of June, 1732....Made to a General Court held the 9th of May, 1733. *Lond. 1733*, *F°*. LU.

4537 To the Right Honourable the Lords Spiritual and Temporal in Parliament assembled. In Obedience to an Order of this Honourable House of the 3rd Instant [May], the Directors of the South Sea Company did immediately give Orders to the proper Officers of the Company to draw out an Account of what Sums of Money, South Sea Stock, and

South Sea Annuities, have been received from the Trustees for Sale of the Estates of the late Directors....Which they herewith lay before this Honourable House. *n.p.* [*1733*], *F°*. L.

4538 To the Right Honourable the Lords Spiritual and Temporal in Parliament assembled. In obedience to the Order of this Honourable House of the 24th Instant [May], the Directors of the South Sea Company do humbly lay before your Lordships the following Accounts.... *n.p.* [*1733*], *F°*. L.

4539 A Bill for Repealing several Subsidies and an Impost now payable on Tobacco of the British Plantations, and for granting an Inland Duty in lieu thereof. *Lond. 1733*, *8°*. LU.

Another edn., entitled: The Excise Bill.... To which are added, Exact Lists of the Members of Parliament, who Voted for, and against bringing in the said Bill, Lond. [1733] (LU).

4540 BUDGELL, EUSTACE. A Letter to the Merchants and Tradesmen of Great Britain, particularly those of London and Bristol; upon their late Glorious Behaviour and Happy Success, in Opposing the Extension of the Excise-Laws: With a few Seasonable Cautions.... *Lond. 1733*, *8°*. LU.

4541 FORMAN, CHARLES. A Second Letter to the Right Honourable Sir Robert Walpole....To which is added, Farther Reasons against imposing a General Excise upon Britons; Drawn from the Effects of Excises in France and Holland. *Lond. 1733*, *8°*. LU.

4542 HAMILTON, JOHN, Baron Belhaven. The late Lord Beilhaven's Memorable Speeches in the last Parliament of Scotland, holden at Edinburgh, in November 1706. on the Subject-Matter of the then projected Union of Both Kingdoms. Wherein...the slavish Homage and Respect that the People of Scotland should, on the Event of such Union, be in Time oblig'd to pay to every Petty English Exciseman, is expressly predicted. With an Occasional Preface, by the Editor. *Lond. MDCXXXIII* [*1733*], *4°*. LU.

4543 POLHILL, NATHANIEL. Reflections on the present Conduct of the Populace, relating to the Government, particularly the Prime Minister; and the late Motion for a New Excise. *Lond. 1733*, *8°*. L.

4544 SEYMOUR, CLAUDIUS. A Letter of Advice to the Reverend Mr. Scurlock: occasioned by his extraordinary Sermon, preach'd at St. Paul's Cathedral, on Sunday the 7th instant, in vindication of the Excise Scheme. By a Sturdy Beggar, Citizen and Merchant of London.... *Lond. 1733*, *8°*. L.

Signed: Claudius Seymour.

4545 An Answer to the Considerations, occasioned by the Craftsman upon Excise, so far as it relates to the Tobacco Trade. *Lond. 1733*, *8°*. L.

An answer to 4395.

4546 Remarks upon a pamphlet, entituled, Considerations occasioned by the Craftsman upon Excises. *Lond. 1733, 19 cm.* Kress 4129.

4547 An Appeal to the Landholders concerning the Reasonableness and General Benefit of an Excise upon Tobacco and Wine. *Lond. 1733, 8°.* LU.

Another edn. Dublin, 1733 (DA).

4548 [Amhurst, Nicholas]. An Argument against Excises, in several Essays, lately published in the Craftsman, and now collected together. By Caleb D'Anvers of Gray's-Inn, Esq. [pseudonym].... *Lond. 1733, 8°.* LU.

2nd edn. Lond. 1733 (L); another edn. Dublin, 1733 (D). Amhurst was editor of *The Craftsman.* See *D.N.B.* for authorship.

4549 [Amhurst, Nicholas]. The Second Part of an Argument against Excises; in Answer to the Objections of several Writers; especially with Regard to that Part of the Subject, which relates to the Power and Conduct of the Commissioners and Officers of Excise. With Some Remarks on the Present State of Affairs. By Caleb D'anvers of Gray's Inn, Esq; [pseudonym]. *Lond. 1733, 8°.* L.

Reprinted in *The Craftsman*, vol. 10 (1737).

4550 A Collection of Letters from Several Counties, Cities and Boroughs. Containing Instructions to their Representatives in Parliament to Oppose any Extension of the Excise Laws. *Lond. 1733, 8°.* LU.

4551 A Dialogue between Sir Andrew Freeport and Timothy Squat, Esquire, on the Subject of Excises. Being a full Review of the whole Dispute concerning a Change of the Duties on Wine and Tobacco into an Excise. *Lond. 1733, 8°.* LU.

4552 A Discourse on Trade, Liberty and Taxes. Addressed to all Landholders, and Traders in Great Britain.... *Lincoln, 1733, 4°.* LU.

On the excise scheme.

4553 Englishmen's Eyes open'd; or, All made to See, who are not resolv'd to be Blind: Being the Excise Controversy set in a new Light; Completely discuss'd...and brought to a fair and demonstrative Conclusion: between a Landholder, and a Merchant. *Lond. 1733, 8°.* L.

2nd edn. 1734 (L).

4554 An Examination of the Late Conduct of the Ministry, with respect to the Duties on Tobacco and Wine. *Lond. 1733, 8°.* LU.

4555 Excise: being a Collection of Letters, &c. Containing, the Sentiments and Instructions of the Merchants, Traders, Gentry, and Inhabitants of the principal Cities, Counties, Towns, and Boroughs, in England, to their Representatives in Parliament, against a New Excise, or any Extension of Excise Laws, in what Shape soever.... *Lond. 1733, 8°.* L.

4556 Excise Anatomiz'd. Declaring that unequal Imposition of Excise to be the only cause of the Ruin of Trade, the universal Impoverishment, and destructive to the Liberties of the whole Nation. By Z.G. a Well-wisher to the common Good. *Lond. 1733, 8º.* O.

4557 French Excise: or, a Compendious Account of the several Excises in France, and the Oppressive Methods us'd in Collecting them. Published for the Information of the People of Great-Britain. *Lond.* [*1733*], *8º.* LU.

4558 The Genuine Thoughts of a Merchant: shewing, that in all the Libels, Remonstrances, and pretended Letters against A New Method of Levying the Duties on Tobacco and Wine, there is not so much as one Word worth answering. *Lond. 1732–3, 8º.* LU.

An article in *Fog's Journal,* 17 Feb. 1733, quoted in *London Magazine,* 1733, p. 83, ascribes this to Walpole.

4559 The Humble and Loyal Address of the Citizens of London, and Southwark, presented to the Honourable Arthur Onslow, Esq; Speaker of the House of Commons. On Friday, Jan. 12th, 1732. [o.s.]. *Lond.* [*1733*], *s. sh. Fº.* C.

Against the excise.

4560 An Humble Address to the People of England. Being, a Demonstration that a Land-Tax is more prejudicial to Trade and Liberty, than an Inland Duty on Wine and Tobacco. *Lond. 1733, 4º.* LU.

4561 An Impartial Enquiry into the late Conduct of the City of London, relating to the Excise-Bill.... By a Common-Council-Man of the same City. *Lond. 1733, 8º.* LU.

4562 An Impartial Enquiry into the Present Question concerning Excise; In which the Advantages arising to the King and Subject, from raising Duties by Excise, are demonstrated, and the Objections thereto obviated.... *Lond. 1733, 8º.* LU.

4563 A Letter from a Member of Parliament for a Borough in the West, to a Noble Lord in his Neighbourhood there, concerning the Excise-Bill, and the Manner and Causes of losing it. *Lond. 1733, 8º.* LU.

Another edn. Dublin, 1733 (DA).

4564 [Pulteney, William, Earl of Bath ?]. A Letter from a Member of Parliament to his Friend in the Country; giving his Reasons for opposing the farther Extension of the Excise Laws; and shewing, that had the late Attempt succeeded, it had been destructive of Parliament, and fatal to the Constitution. *Lond.* [*1733*], *8º.* LU.

For attribution see H. & L., who do not quote an authority

4565 A Letter from a Member of Parliament to his Friends in the Country, concerning the Duties on Wine and Tobacco. *Lond. 1733, 8º.* LU.

Another edn. Dublin, 1733 (O). Attributed to Walpole in H. & L. without quoting authority.

4566 A Letter from a Member of Parliament to his Friends in the Country, concerning the Duties on Wine and Tobacco....To which is added, The Reply of a Member of Parliament to the Mayor of his Corporation. Together with the Scheme of the Excise itself. *Lond. 1733, 8º.* Arents 678.

4567 [Pulteney, William, Earl of Bath]. The Budget Opened. Or, an Answer to a Pamphlet intitled, A Letter from a Member of Parliament to his Friends in the Country, concerning the Duties on Wine and Tobacco. *Lond. 1733, 8º.* LU.

Reprinted in *The Craftsman*, vol. 10 (1737). For authorship see B.M. Catalogue.

4568 A Candid Answer to a Letter from a Member of Parliament to his Friends in the Country, concerning the Duties on Wine and Tobacco. *Lond. 1733, 8º.* LU.

4569 A Letter from a Merchant of London to a Member of Parliament: In Answer to a Letter from a Member of Parliament to his Friends in the Country, concerning the Duties on Wine and Tobacco. *Lond. 1733, 8º.* LU.

4570 A Short Letter to the Letter-Writer concerning the Duties on Wines and Tobacco. *Lond. 1733, Fº.* O.

4571 A Letter from a Merchant of the City of London, to his Friends the Freeholders in the Country. *Lond. 1733, 8º.* MP.

Mostly on excise.

4572 A Letter from the Mayor of the antient Borough of Guzzle-Down, to Sir Francis Wronghead, their R——ve in P——t. In answer to his Letter of the 19th of Feb. 1732. *Lond. 1733, 8º.* LU.

4573 A Letter to the Free-holders of Great Britain. *Lond. 1733, 8º.* LU.

On the excise scheme.

4574 The List. *n.p.* [*1733*], *Fº.* MC.

Of those voting for and against the Excise Bill.

4575 Some Observations upon a Paper, intituled, The List. That is, of those who Voted for and against the Excise-Bill. *Lond. 1733, 8º.* L.

4576 List of those who Voted For Bringing in the Excise-Bill, (List of those who Voted Against Bringing in the Excise-Bill.—List of the Lords Spiritual and Temporal, who voted For and Against, An Enquiry into the Frauds of the South-Sea Company.) *n.p.* [*1733*], *Fº.* L.

4577 The Lord Mayors Speech and the City Petition about the Excise. *n.p.* [*1733*], *s. sh. Fº.* LG.

4578 The Lords Protests in the late Session of Parliament...To which is added, Britannia Excisa, in two parts. With an Alphabetical List of all the Members who Voted For and Against the Excise-Bill....Also, The Lord Mayor's Speech in Common Council, and the City of London's Petition against the Excise Bill. *Lond. 1733, Fº.* L.

4579 The Most Important Transactions of the Sixth Session of the First Parliament of His Majesty King George II. Anno Domini, MDCCXXXIII. Containing, I. A True Copy of the Excise-Bill.... II. An Exact List of the Members Names who voted for the said Bill; with a very particular Account of what Places of Honour and Profit are possessed by Them, or their Relations. III. An Exact List of the Glorious Two Hundred and Four, who voted against the said Bill.... IV. The Lords Protest, May 30, 1733, on the Sinking Fund, in which are given, some strong Reasons against the Extension of the Excise-Laws. V. The Lords Protest, June 2, 1733, upon the House rejecting the Motion for enquiring into the Affairs of the South-Sea Directors. VI. A True State of the National Debt, provided or unprovided for by Parliament, as it stood, Dec. 31, 1731, and Dec. 31, 1732. Together with the Produce of the Sinking Fund, and to what Debts contracted before Dec. 25, 1732, the same has been apply'd. *Lond.* [*1733*], *4°*. LU.

3rd, 4th and 5th edns. [1733] (LU); 6th edn. [1733] (LSC); another edn. Dublin, 1733 (C).

4580 [PERCEVAL, JOHN, 2nd Earl of Egmont]. The Nature of the Present Excise, and the Consequences of its farther Extension, Examined. In a Letter to a Member of Parliament. *Lond. 1733, 8°*. LU.

2nd edn. 1733 (LU). For authorship see H. & L., IX, 221 & Egmont Diary, II, 51

4581 The Norfolk Scheme: or a Letter to William Pulteney, Esq; on the Present Posture of Affairs, particularly with relation to the Scheme for altering the Method of Collecting the Revenues, by converting Customs into Excises, shewing the dangerous Consequences of such an Innovation.... *Lond. 1733, 8°*. LU.

2nd edn. 1733 (O).

4582 Observations upon the Laws of Excise: shewing, I. That Excises must be destructive of Trade in General. II. That Excises are in consistent with the Liberties of a Free People. *Lond.* [*1733*], *8°*. LU.

4583 Reflections upon a Pamphlet, entitled Observations upon the Laws of Excise. *Lond. 1733, 8°*. LU.

4584 The Origin and Essence of a General Excise. A Sermon preached, on a very Extraordinary Occasion, at a Noted Chapel in Westminster, on Wednesday the 14th of March, 1732 [o.s.]. By Robert Winer, D.D., Rector of the said Chapel. *Lond.* [*1733*], *4°*. LU.

A skit. Winer is, of course, Walpole. 2nd edn. [1733] (O).

4585 The Principal Reasons assign'd for Excising of Wines Considered; in a Letter to a Member of Parliament. *n.p.* [*1733*], *s. sh. F°*. LG.

4586 The Projector's Looking Glass: containing, I. The last dying Words and Confession of Sir Robert Marral, premier Exciseman of Great-Britain. ...II. The Lost Bill, drawn by Robert Bold, of Norfolk....III. A Burlesque Poem on the rejecting a certain Petition.... *Lond.* [*1733*], *4°*. O.

4587 Reasons against subjecting any other Traders of Great Britain to the Laws of Excise, or Excising any other Commodities, either of the Product or Manufacture of this Kingdom or any other Country, than what are already subject to the present Laws. *Lond. 1733, s. sh. F°.* LU.

4588 The Reply of a Member of Parliament to the Mayor of his Corporation. *Lond. 1733, 8°.* LU.

For the Excise Bill.

4589 [WALPOLE, HORATIO, Baron Walpole, and CONCANEN, MATTHEW]. The Rise and Fall of the late Projected Excise, Impartially Consider'd. By a Friend to the English Constitution. *Lond. 1733, 8°.*

Another edn. Dublin, 1733 (L). For authorship see J. Ralph, *A Critical History of the Administration of Sir Robert Walpole*, 1743, p. 274.

4590 A Review of the Excise-Scheme; in answer to a pamphlet, intitled The Rise and Fall of the late projected Excise, impartially considered. With some Proper Hints to the Electors of Great Britain. *Lond. 1733, 8°.* LU.

2nd edn. 1733 (L). Reprinted in *The Craftsman*, vol. II (1737). Tentatively attributed to William Pulteney in H. & L. without quoting authority.

4591 Seasonable Reflections occasioned by the Bills expected in Parliament relating to the Duties on Wines and Tobacco. *Lond. [1733], 8°.* LU.

4592 The Sense of the People of England, particularly the Merchants and Traders of the City of London, in Relation to the present Scheme of an Excise on Tobacco and Wine; and the Reasons of their Opposition consider'd. In a Letter to the Rt. Hon. Sir Robert Walpole. *n.p. [1733], s. sh. F°.* C.

4593 [WALPOLE, Sir ROBERT]. Some General Considerations concerning the Alteration and Improvement of Publick Revenues. *Lond. 1733, 8°.* LU.

For authorship see H. & L. quoting the B.M. Catalogue.

4594 Some Scruples humbly offered by the Company exercising the Trade and Mystery of Apothecaries, arising from the intended Excise, so far as it relates to the Vintners and Brewers of Wine in this Kingdom. *Lond. 1733, F°.* L.

4595 Some Seasonable Animadversions on Excises: Occasion'd by a Pamphlet lately publish'd, entitled, Considerations occasion'd by the Craftsman. *Lond. 1733, 8°.* LU.

4596 Some Thoughts on the Land-Tax, General Excises, and the least burthensome way of raising Taxes; occasion'd by the London Journal on that Subject. *Lond. 1733, 8°.* LU.

4597 The Standard of Equality, in subsidiary Taxes and Payments: or, a Just and Strong Preserver of Publick Liberty. *Lond. 1733, 8°.* MP.

The epistle signed: Philo-Dicaeus.

4598 The Vintner and Tobacconist's Advocate, being Remarks upon, and a Full Answer to those Scandalous Papers published in The Daily Courant, under the Title of the Occasional Financer, and under the Names of Carus and Meanwell. *Lond. 1733*, 8°. LU.

4599 Wednesday, April 11. On Monday last, at a Meeting of the Common-Council of this City, the Right Honourable the Lord Mayor was pleas'd to introduce the Business of the Day in the following Words.... *n.p.* [*1733*], *s. sh. F°*. C (Cr).

Speech and petition against the excise. Another edn., beginning: Wednesday, April 11, 1733 (C (Cr)).

4600 The Whole Proceedings upon the Tryal of Robert Marrall, alias Blue-string alias Bold, of N——lk, Knt. premier Exciseman of Great Britain, on his Arraignment at the Bar of a certain Court, near Westminster-Hall, for divers Male Practices, High Crimes, and Misdemeanours, on Wednesday the 11th, and Friday the 13th of April, 1733.... *Lond. 1733*, 4°. O.

4601 A Word to the Freeholders and Burgesses of Great Britain. Being seasonable and serious Remarks upon the inconsistent Conduct of certain Boroughs, in sending Instructions to their Representatives to oppose the Excise Bill, and yet re-electing them after their being rewarded with Places for voting for the same.... *Lond. 1733*, 8°. LU.

4602 The United Company of Merchants of England Trading to the East-Indies, Appellants. His Majesty's Attorney General, Respondent. The Appellants Case. *n.p.* [*1733*], *F°*. L.

Signed: N. Fazakerley. D. Rider. On the rating of East India goods for duty.

4603 The United Company of Merchants of England Trading to the East Indies, Appellants. Sir Philip Yorke, Kt. his Majesty's Attorney General, on the Behalf of his Majesty, Respondent. The Respondents Case. *n.p.* [*1733*], *F°*. L.

Signed: P. Yorke. C. Talbot.

4604 The Report, with the Appendix, from the Committee of the House of Commons appointed to enquire into the Frauds and Abuses in the Customs, to the Prejudice of Trade, and Diminution of the Revenue. *Lond. 1733*, *F°*. LU.

4605 The Report of the Committee appointed by a General Vestry of the Inhabitants of the Parish of St. Botolph without Aldersgate, London: February 22. 1732. With Some Methods proposed to prevent Abuses for the future. To which is prefixed, Some General Account of the Parish and Church. *Lond. 1733*, 8°. O.

2nd edn. 1733 (O).

4606 Remarks upon a Pamphlet, called The Report of the Committee, &c. of the Parish of St. Botolph's Without Aldersgate: and said to be published by the said Committee. By a Member of that Committee. To which are annexed, Some Errata in the Report of the said Committee. *Lond. 1733*, 8°. O.

4607 [SWIFT, JONATHAN]. Some Reasons against the Bill for settling the Tyth of Hemp, Flax, &c. by a Modus. *Dublin, MDCCXXIV* [*1734*], *8°*. DA.
Reprinted in *The Prose Works of Jonathan Swift*, ed. by H. Davis, vol. 13 (1958).

4608 By the King, A Proclamation, Prohibiting the Currency of Gold Coins, commonly called Broad Pieces. *Lond. 1732*, [*o.s.*] *s. sh. F°*. L.
Dated: 21 February 1732.

4609 A Proposal for the Relief of Ireland, by a Coinage of Monies, of Gold and Silver, and establishing a National Bank. *Lond. 1733*, *8°*. DA.
Another edn. Dublin, 1734 (DA).

4610 A Hue and Cry, or the Citizens Lamentation after the Downfall of B—— and —— Bank: Together with the Lamentations of several honest Men, who got daily Bread by the late A——n P——e, the breaking up of said Bank.... [*Dublin, 1733?*], *s. sh. F°*. C.
The Bank was that of Samuel Burton and Daniel Falkiner. Alderman Page is meant by A——n P——e.

4611 We the Master, Wardens, and Brethern, of the Guild of Merchants, and the several other Merchants, Traders, and Dealers, in the City of Dublin, Hereunto Subscribing, Do Hereby unanimously Declare and Agree to Take and Accept in Payment, the Cash Notes of Hugh Henry Esq; and Company, Mr. James Swift and Company, Mess. Latouche and Kane, Mr Joseph Fade and Company, and Mess. Nuttal and Mc.Gwire. *Dublin* [*1733*], *s. sh. F°*. C.
Dated: Dublin, June 26, 1733.

4612 A Bill to prevent the Infamous Practice of Stock-Jobbing. *n.p.* [*1733*], *F°*. pp. 3. L.
Another edn., with amendments and the blanks filled in, entitled: A Bill, Intitled, An Act to prevent the infamous practice of Stock-jobbing, [1733], F° (L).

4613 [ROBE, THOMAS]. A Proposal Humbly offer'd to the Honourable House of Commons, for the better Regulating Stock-Jobbers, without prejudicing Publick Credit; By the same Hand that inserted it in the Post-Man the 19th of May 1726, from whence it is verbally taken. *n.p.* [*1733?*], *s. sh. F°*. L.
Signed: Eboranos. Reprinted in *Ways and Means, whereby his Majesty may Man his Navy.... To which is added, A Collection of some Political Essays by Eboranos*, 1734.

4614 Some Considerations humbly offered to the Honourable House of Commons, why the present Bill for restraining the Freedom of Buying and Selling the Funds, and publick Securities, should not pass into a Law. *n.p.* [*1733*], *F°*. L.

4615 Some Considerations on Publick Credit. And the Nature of its Circulation in the Funds. Occasioned by a Bill now depending in Parliament, concerning Stock-jobbing. *Lond. 1733*, *8°*. L.

4616 An Answer to a Pamphlet on Publick Credit: Occasioned by the Bill now depending in the House, to prevent the pernicious Practice of

Stockjobbing. Humbly address'd to the various Proprietors of Government Securities. *Lond. 1733, 8°.* LU.

4617 Truth: A Letter to the Gentlemen of Exchange Alley: occasioned by the Bill now depending in the House to prevent the pernicious Practice of Stockjobbing. Dedicated to Mr. Les——m and Mr. All——ft. Occasioned by a Pamphlet entitul'd 'Change Alley Excised. *Lond. 1733, 8°.* LU.

The dedication signed: F.G., F.R.S.

4618 The Report of the Commissioners appointed for Taking, Stating, and Determining the Claims of the Creditors and Proprietors of the Charitable Corporation. Printed by Order of the House of Lords. *Lond. 1732* [*o.s.*], *F°.* L.

Another edn., printed by order of the Commons, 1732 [o.s.], F° (L).

4619 The Report, with the Appendix, from the Committee of the House of Commons, to whom the Petition of the Proprietors of the Charitable Corporation...was referred; and the Proceedings of the said House thereupon. *Lond. 1733, F°.* LU.

Another edn., without the Proceedings of the House, 1733 (O).

4620 [WARBURTON, WILLIAM]. An Apology for Sir Robert Sutton. *Lond. 1733, 8°.* L.

For authorship see A. W. Evans, *Warburton and the Warburtonians*, 1932, p. 28.

4621 A Letter to a Member of the House of Commons. *Lond. 1733, 4°.* O.

On the Charitable Corporation. Internal evidence suggests that William Warburton was the author.

4622 The Present State of the Unhappy Sufferers of the Charitable Corporation, Consider'd. With Reasons humbly offer'd for their Relief. *Lond. 1733, 8°.* LU.

4623 Reasons for Passing the Bill for making effectual such Agreement as shall be made between the Charitable Corporation and their Creditors. *n.p.* [*1733*], *s. sh. F°.* LG.

4624 Reasons humbly offer'd for Relief of the Sufferers in the Charitable Corporation. *n.p.* [*1733*], *s. sh. F°.* LG.

4625 Reasons why the Bill now under your Lordships Consideration, to impower the Charitable Corporation to raise the Sum of 500 000 l. by way of a Lottery, should not pass, Humbly submitted to your Lordships. *n.p.* [*1733*], *s. sh. F°.* LG.

4626 An Abstract of the Original and Supplemental Charters of the Corporation of the Amicable Society for a Perpetual Assurance-Office. *n.p.* [*c. 1733?*], *8°.* L.

Followed by the bye-laws of the Society.

4627 POVEY, CHARLES. The Secret History of the Sun-Fire-Office.... *n.p.* [*1733?*], *8°.* O.

TRANSPORT

4628 Grants of Ballastage to the Corporation of Trinity-House. *Lond. 1733*, *8°*. O.

4629 The Case of the Corporation of Trinity House, relating to their sole and exclusive Right of Ballasting Ships in the River Thames. *n.p.* [*1733?*], *F°*. L.

4630 A Bill for filling up such Part of the Channel of Bridewell-Dock and Fleet-Ditch, as lies between Holborn-Bridge and Fleet-Bridge, and for converting the Ground (when filled up) to the Use of the City of London. *n.p.* [*1733*], *F°*. O.

4631 The Intended Navigation of the River Chelmer, in the County of Essex, Briefly Considered, and humbly submitted to the Perusal of the Members of the Honourable House of Commons; and particularly the Representatives of the said County, and all Gentlemen Freeholders, &c. in the same. *Lond. 1733*, *8°*. O.

4632 A Bill to Recover and Preserve the Navigation of the River Dee, in the County Palatine of Chester. *n.p.* [*1733*], *F°*. L.

4633 The Case of the Citizens of Chester, in answer to Several Petitions from Leverpool, Parkgate, and the Cheesemongers; and also to printed Reasons against the Act to Recover and Preserve the Navigation of the River Dee. *n.p.* [*1733*], *s. sh. F°*. L.

4634 Reasons against a Bill now depending in the House of Lords, to recover and preserve the Navigation of the River Dee, in the County Palatine of Chester. *n.p.* [*1733*], *F°*. LG.

With a map.

4635 A Bill to Explain and Amend Two Acts of Parliament, one made in the Twelfth, and the other in the Thirteenth Year of his late Majesty's Reign, for making Navigable the River Dun in the County of York; and for the better Perfecting and Maintaining the said Navigation, and for Uniting the several Undertakers into one Company. *n.p.* [*1733*], *F°*. O.

4636 A Bill for making more Effectual an Act passed in the Eleventh Year of the Reign of His late Majesty King George the First, for Repairing the Roads therein mentioned, from the Parish of Enfield in the County of Middlesex, to the Town of Hertford, and to the Great Bridge in Ware, in the County of Hertford; and for Amending the Road from the said Great Bridge, to the South-End of the Great Bridge at Wades-Mill; and from the great Road at Chesthunt, to the West-End of Small Lea-Bridge, in the said County of Hertford. *n.p.* [*1733*], *F°*. O.

4637 A Bill for Enlarging the Term granted by an Act passed in the First Year of the Reign of his late Majesty King George the First, intituled, An Act for Repairing the Highways through the several Parishes of Saint

Michael, Saint Alban, Saint Peter, Shenley, Ridge, and South-Mims, in the Counties of Hertford and Middlesex, and for continuing the Powers granted by the said Act. *n.p.* [*1733?*], *F°*. L.

4638 Directions to the Surveyors of the Highways for the County of Westmorland: With some observations on some Laws concerning them. By one of His Majesties Justices of the Peace, for the said County. *Kendal*, *1733*, *4°*. O.

SOCIAL CONDITIONS

4639 The Statutes at Large concerning the Provision for the Poor, being a Compleat Collection of all the Acts of Parliament relating thereto.... *Lond.* *1733*, *8°*. LU.

4640 Rules and Orders for the Government of the Work-House erected for the Use of the Poor of the several Parishes of St. Andrew's, Holborn, above the Bars, and St. George the Martyr, within the same, in the County of Middlesex. *Lond.* *1733*, *4°*. DA.

4641 Heads of a Bill for Relief of Insolvent Debtors and other Persons imprisoned for Debt, with an Abstract of the Laws and Customs of other Nations, with respect to unfortunate Debtors and Bankrupts. Most humbly address'd and submitted to the Consideration of both Houses of Parliament. *Dublin*, *1733*, *8°*. C.

4642 Wood, Simon. Remarks on the Fleet Prison: or, Lumber-House for Men and Women. Written by a Prisoner on the Common-Side, who hath lain a Prisoner near three Years, on the Penalty of a Bond. No Debtor. *Lond.* *1733*, *8°*. L.

4643 [Freeman, William]. A Compleat List, of the Stewards, Presidents, Vice-Presidents, and Treasurers belonging to the Royal Corporation, for the Relief of the Poor Widows, and Children of Clergymen, from the Time their Charter was granted....July 1, 1678....Likewise, An Account of the Present State of the said Corporation.... *Lond.* *1733*, *8°*. L.

For authorship see ms. note in L copy.

4644 [Jackson, William and Carte, Samuel]. An Account of the many and great Loans, Benefactions, and Charities, belonging to the city of Coventry. To which is annexed, a Copy of the Decretal Order of the Court of Chancery relating to the Memorable Charity of Sir Thomas White. *Lond.* *1733*, *8°*. L.

The dedication signed: AB, CD, EF, GH, &c. For authorship see ms. note in L copy.

1734

GENERAL

4645 An Historical Account of the Proceedings of the Last House of Commons. Relating to the Trade, Rights, and Liberties of their Country. Extracted from their Votes; with proper Remarks. Address'd to the New Elected Members. *Lond.* [*1734*], *8°*. L.

4646 A Letter to a Worthy Member of Parliament, on the necessary Support and Encouragement of Trade. With Some Proposals to that End. By True Englishman. *Lond. 1734*, *8°*. E.

4647 Observations on Trade, Customs, Taxes, Excise, Credit, Securities, Publick-Debts, Bankrupts, and Coin....Pointing out a natural and infallible Way to make every British Subject Rich, Safe, and Happy. *Lond. 1734*, *8°*. LU.

Preceding the Observations is 'Abstract of the Committee's Report of Frauds in Tobacco, Wines, Tea, &c.'

4648 [Robe, Thomas]. Ways and Means whereby his Majesty may Man his Navy with Ten Thousand able Sailors, on Short Notice, with less Expence to the Government than at present, and entirely to the Benefit and Satisfaction of the Merchants. To which is added, A Collection of some Political Essays by Eboranos. *Lond. 1734*, *8°*. L.

The essays include: A Proposal...for the better regulating Stock Jobbers, and Reasons for promoting the British Distillery. Reissued in 1735 as: *A Collection of Political Tracts....By Eboranos* (L). *Ways and Means* had been published separately in 1726, without the author's name, which, however, is given in the 1728 edition.

4649 Shaw, Peter. Chemical Lectures, publickly read at London, in the years 1731, and 1732; for the Improvement of Arts, Trades, and Natural Philosophy. *Lond.* [*1734*], *8°*. L.

4650 Switzer, Stephen. The Universal System of Water and Water-Works, Philosophical and Practical. In Four Books. Faithfully Digested, from the Most-approv'd Writers on this Subject.... *Lond. 1734*, *4°*. L.

Much on pumps.

4651 A Journey from London to Scarborough in several Letters from a Gentleman there, to his Friend in London.... *Lond. 1734*, *8°*. O.

4652 Broad Scotch, addressed to all True Scots Men. *Edin. 1734*, *8°*. LU.

Mostly concerned with the excise bill and the malt tax. 2nd edn. 1734 (AU).

4653 An Enquiry into Some Things that concern Scotland, containing Some Remarks upon a certain Book, lately published by a certain Author, who certainly is not a true Friend to his Country. *Edin. 1734*, *8°*. LU.

The book referred to is *Some Reasons for continuing the Present Parliament*, 1733 (no. 4474).

4654 A Letter to the Author of a Pamphlet, intituled, An Enquiry into some Things that concern Scotland; containing Some Remarks upon a certain Book, lately published by a certain Author, who, certainly, is not A true Friend to his Country. *Lond. 1734*, 8°. LU.

Signed: J. Linnendraper, London, Feb. 8th 1734.

4655 Answer to a Letter directed to the Author of a Pamphlet, intitled, An Enquiry into Some Things that concern Scotland, containing Some Remarks upon a certain Book, lately published by a certain Author, who certainly is not a true Friend to his Country. By the Author of the Enquiry. *Edin. 1734*, 8°. AU.

Signed: Katholicus Cheirotechnes.

4656 The Occasional Patriot, written in Plain Scotch, by Way of Notes upon Two Papers, lately publish'd, The One intitul'd, Broad Scotch, &c. The other, An Enquiry into some things that concern Scotland, &c. By an uncertain Person, who is most certainly not an Enemy to his Country.... *Edin. 1734*, 8°. LU.

4657 A List of the Members of the Dublin-Society, for the Improvement of Husbandry and other Useful Arts, for the Year 1733. *Dublin, 1734*, 8°. DA.

4658 Some Useful Cautions to the Publick, in a Letter to his Grace &c. the Arch Bishop of Cashel. *Dublin, 1734*, 8°. DA.

A criticism of Sir John Browne's *Reflections upon the present unhappy Circumstances of Ireland*, 1731 (no. 4163).

AGRICULTURE

4659 The True Interest of the Land-Owners of Great Britain: or, the Husband-men's Essay. Containing a Short View of the Principal Impediments to Inclosing many of our Common Fields; and, shewing the Great Necessity of removing these trivial Difficulties, which obstruct and hinder such vast Improvements. Together with the Best and Only Method of Rend'ring Inclosures more easily accomplish'd.... *Lond. 1734*, 8°. LU.

4660 An Act for Confirming and making Effectual several Articles of Agreement made for inclosing and dividing the Common Fields of Great Cleybrooke and Little Cleybrooke, in the County of Leicester. *n.p. 1734*, F°. L.

4661 An Act for Inclosing the Common or Waste called Lightwood Forest, otherwise Cocknage Banks, and Blurton Common, in the Manor and Parish of Trentham, in the County of Stafford. *n.p. 1734*, F°. L.

4662 An Act for Confirming the Inclosure, Division and Exchanges of several Lands and Grounds lying in the Common Fields of Wollesthorpe, near Belvoir Castle, in the County of Lincoln. *n.p.* [*1734*], F°. L.

4663 GRUNDY, JOHN. Here follow some Propositions, which plainly shew the Necessity of Mathematical and Philosophical Knowledge, in the draining of Lands that lie near to the Sea (or low Fen-Lands;) from whence Corollaries are drawn, which fully prove, it is next to an Impossibility to do any thing with Judgment towards draining those Lands effectually; except such Attempts are grounded upon Philosophical Experiments, and Mathematical Calculations. And likewise some Scholiums, to prove that all the Attempts that have hitherto been made (in the Wapentake of Elloe in the Parts of South-Holland in Lincolnshire) for draining the same, have not been grounded upon any such Principles; and consequently cannot succeed, till some new Method is put in practice wholly depending on the foresaid Knowledge.... *n.p.* [*1734?*], *F°*. O.

4664 STEER, GEORGE. The Compleat Mineral Laws of Derbyshire, taken from the Originals.....And all their Bills of Plaint, Customs, Cross-Bills, Arrests, Plaintiff's Case, or Brief; with all other Forms necessary for all Miners and Maintainers of Mines, within each Manour, Lordship, or Wapentake. *Lond. 1734*, *8°*. L.

4665 Unto the Right Honourable, the Lords of Council and Session, the Petition of Charles Murray, Esq; Son to Sir David Murray of Stanhope, heritable Proprietor of the Lands, Heritages, and Mines lying within the Baronies of Stanhope, Stobo, Ardnamurchan, &c. within the Shires of Peebles and Argyle; for the Publick Good, as well as for his own Interest, and that of his Grace the Duke of Norfolk, and other original Tacksmen, and their Assigns, Co-Partners in the said Mines. *n.p.* [*1734*], *F°*. E.

Dated: July 29. 1734. Signed: Alex Murray. On the incompetent working of the lead and copper mines by the York Buildings Company.

4666 A Bill for Stating and Determining the Demands of the Corporation of the Governor and Company of Undertakers for Raising the Thames Water in York Buildings, and their Creditors. *n.p.* [*1734?*], *F°*. L.

L has another edn., entitled: An Act for Stating and Determining the Accounts and Demands depending between the Corporation...and their Creditors and Debtors respectively. Not passed.

4667 The Case of the York-Buildings Company. *n.p.* [*1734?*], *s. sh. F°*. L.

4668 Plan of an Agreement between the York-Buildings Company and their Creditors. *n.p.* [*1734*], *F°*. MC.

Dated: the 17th of October, 1734.

4669 [GRANT, FRANCIS]. The British Fishery recommended to Parliament. Shewing the great Importance of it to the Trade and Navigation of this Kingdom: What has been formerly done, and what is still wanting for its Encouragement: Why it has hitherto miscarry'd, and how we may succeed in it beyond all other Nations. With an exact Map of the

Coasts of Great-Britain; in which, all the Fishing Stations, and those parts where the Dutch Fleets fish for Herrings, are describ'd. *Lond.* *1734*, *8°*. LU.

Another edn. Edin. 1734 (LU). Internal evidence shows that this work is by the author of *A Letter to a Member of Parliament, concerning the Free British Fisheries*, 1750 [1749], q.v. Both tracts have the same quotation from Thomson on the title-page.

4670 EDINBURGH. Act prohibiting the Dragging of Small or Seedling Oysters. [*Edin. 1734*], *s. sh. F°*. EU.

Dated: 27 February 1734.

MANUFACTURES

4671 SALMON, WILLIAM. Palladio Londiniensis: or, The London Art of Building....To which is annexed, the Builder's Dictionary.... *Lond.* *1734*, *4°*. LRIBA.

3rd edn. 1748 (K); 5th 1755 (L).

4672 The Builder's Dictionary: or, Gentleman and Architect's Companion. Explaining not only the Terms of Art in all the several Parts of Architecture, but also containing the Theory and Practice of the various Branches thereof, requisite to be known by Masons, Carpenters, Joiners, Bricklayers, Plaisterers, Painters, Glaziers, Smiths, Turners, Carvers, Statuaries, Plumbers, &c..... *Lond. 1734*, *8°*. L.

4673 An Advertisement to be inserted in the Second Volume of the Builder's Dictionary. *n.p.* [*1734*], *8°*. L.

Correcting the account of Milled Lead.

4674 The London and Country Brewer. By a Person formerly concern'd in a common Brewhouse at London, but for near twenty Years past has resided in the Country. *Lond.* [*1734*]*–38*. *8°*. 3 pt. L.

Another edn. of pt. 1, Dublin, 1735 (DA); 2nd edn. of pt. 1, Lond. 1736 (LU); 6th edn. 1750 (L); 7th edn. 1759 (L); another edn., entitled: The Compleat City and Country Brewer, Dublin, 1761 (DG).

4675 The Art and Mystery of Vintners and Wine-Coopers. Containing Approved Directions for the Preserving and Curing all Manner and Sorts of Wines. By E.T., a Wine-Cooper of long Experience. *Lond.* *1734*, *8°*. L.

Another edn., without author's initials, 1748 (Kress S. 1938).

4676 Unto the Right Honourable, The Lords of Council and Session. The Petition of John Vert, James Edward, Hugh Paterson, John Gray, James Hay, and John Pierie, all Journeymen Taylors in Edinburgh, for themselves and in the name of the whole Journeymen Taylors of the said Burgh. *n.p.* [*1734*], *F°*. E.

Dated: June 7, 1734. Signed: And. McDouall. For higher wages.

4677 Petition and Answers for the Incorporations of Taylors in Edinburgh and Canongate, Canongate-Head, Potterrow and Westport. *n.p.* [*1734*], *s. sh. F°*. E.

Dated: June 12. 1734. Signed: James Graham.

4678 Information for the Journeymen-Taylors, Suspenders, against the Master-Taylors of Edinburgh and Canongate, Chargers. *n.p.* [*1734*], *F°*. E.

Dated: July 2. 1734. Signed: Ja. Erskine.

4679 Information for the Incorporations of Taylors in Edinburgh and Canongate, &c. against the Journeymen Taylors there. *n.p.* [*1734*], *4°*. E.

Dated: July 16. 1734. Signed: Ch. Areskine.

4680 A Bill to Explain and Amend an Act passed in the Eleventh Year of the Reign of His late Majesty King George the First, Intitled, An Act for the better Regulating the Manufacture of Cloth in the West-Riding of the County of York. *n.p.* [*1734*], *F°*. O.

4681 A Letter from a Weaver at Norwich, to a Member of Parliament concerning the Present State of our Woollen Manufactures. *Lond.* [*1734*], *8°*. LU.

Dated: Norwich, Feb. 10. 1733–4.

4682 ASTON, MILES. An Heroick Poem on the Weaving Trade setting forth 'its Antiquity and Use.... *Dublin*, [*1734?*], *4°*. C.

4683 MELVILL, THOMAS. The True Caledonian, addressed to the People of Scotland, containing an Examination of the Arguments advanced against the Woollen-Manufactures of this Kingdom in a late Book, intituled, The Interest of Scotland considered, &c. Together with a Scheme for promoting our Woollen-Manufactures. *Edin. 1734*, *8°*. LU.

4684 A Letter to the Author of the Interest of Scotland Considered; Containing some Hints about the Linnen Manufactures. *Edin. 1734*, *8°*. LU.

Signed: A.B.

4685 Representation for the Weavers of Glasgow to the Right Honourable the Convention of Burrows. *n.p.* [*1734*], *s. sh. F°*. E.

Dated: July 2d. 1734.

4686 Information for Robert Adam and others, Weavers in Blackfaulds and Calton near Glasgow, and John Orr Master and Proprietor of the said Lands of Blackfaulds and Calton, against the Deacon and Incorporation of Weavers in Glasgow. *n.p.* [*1734*], *4°*. E.

Dated: December 2. 1734. Signed: Ro. Dundas.

4687 Information for the Weavers of Glasgow, against John Orr of Barrowfield, and the Weavers of Calton and Blackfaulds. *n.p.* [*1734*], *4°*. E.

Dated: December 12. 1734. Signed: Dun. Forbes.

COMMERCE

4688 A short State of the publick Encouragement given to Printing and Bookselling in France, Holland, Germany, and at London. With Reasons humbly offered to the Lords Spiritual and Temporal in Parliament assembled, for granting to S. Buckley such Privilege for Thuanus in Latin, as is already granted to every British Subject who is possessed of the Copy of any Book in English. *n.p.* [*1734*], *F*°. L.

4689 A Bill for granting to Samuel Buckley, Citizen and Stationer of London, the sole Liberty of Printing and Reprinting the Histories of Thuanus, with Additions and Improvements, during the Term therein limited. *n.p.* [*1734*], *F*°. LU.

4690 Unto the Right Honourable, the Lords of Council and Session, the Petition of Mr. Alexander Carmichael Bookseller in Glasgow. *n.p.* [*1734*], *F*°. E.

Dated: July 22. 1734. Signed: Ro. Dundas.

4691 Answers for Andrew Stalker Bookseller in Glasgow, to the Petition of Mr. Alexander Carmichael, also Bookseller there. *n.p.* [*1724*], *4*°. E.

Dated: December 12. 1734. Signed: Rob. Craigie.

4692 [Rules and I]nstructions by the Town-[Counci]l of Edinburgh, [to be observed by all] who are permitted to cry Gazettes, and other [Papers, or Sell Roses] and other Flowers, or to carry Links upon the [Streets,] Noblemen and Gentlemens Servants excepted. [*Edin. 1734?*], *s. sh. F*°. AU.

The only copy seen is fragmentary.

4693 Some Remarks upon what is humbly supposed to be a Spurious Paper, intituled, Rules and Instructions by the Town-Council of ——, to be observed by all who are permitted to cry Gazzettes and other Papers, or sell Roses and other Flowers, or to carry Links upon the Streets, Noblemen and Gentlemens Servants excepted. [*Edin.*], *1734*, *8*°. AU.

4694 The Remarker Whip'd: or, An Answer made by the Poor Paper-Cryers, to some Remarks made upon the Rules, &c. printed by that Society. [*Edin. 1734*], *8*°. AU.

4695 By the Lords Justices and Council of Ireland, a Proclamation. For Discharging the Performance of Quarentine in this Kingdom. *Dublin*, *1734*, *F*°. DPRO.

Dated 22 July. 1734.

4696 [Pulteney, William, Earl of Bath ?]. The Politicks on Both Sides, with regard to Foreign Affairs, stated from their own Writings, and examined by the Course of Events. With some Observations on the Present State of Affairs in Great Britain, and the Effects of our Negotiations for several years past. *Lond. 1734*, *8*°. LU.

2nd edn. 1734 (L). Attribution in H. & L. without quoting authority.

4697 A Bill for settling how far Owners of Ships shall be answerable for Goods which have been made away with by the Master or Mariners, without the Privity of the Owners. *n.p.* [*1734*], *F*o. L.

4698 Reasons humbly offered for the Bill, for settling how far Owners of Ships shall be answerable for the Acts of the Master or Mariners. *n.p.* [*1734*], *s. sh. F*o. LLI.

4699 A Proposal from the Woollen Manufacturers. *n.p.* [*1734*], *s. sh. F*o. LPRO.

Title from endorsement. On the smuggling of wool.

4700 Campbell, John. A View of the Dangers to which the Trade of Great-Britain to Turkey and Italy will be exposed, if Naples and Sicily fall into the Hands of the Spaniards. Wherein Enquiry is made, Whether the same Reasons that induced Great-Britain to destroy the Spanish Fleet in 1718, are not still subsisting....With a Chart of the Mediterranean. *Lond. 1734, 4*o. L.

4701 Bluett, Thomas. Some Memoirs of the Life of Job, the Son of Solomon the High Priest of Boonda in Africa; who was a Slave about two Years in Maryland; and afterwards being brought to England, was set free, and sent to his native Land in the Year 1734. *Lond. 1734, 8*o L.

4702 Snelgrave, William. A New Account of some Parts of Guinea, and the Slave-Trade, containing I. The History of the late Conquest of the Kingdom of Whidaw by the King of Dahomè. The Author's Journey to the Conqueror's Camp; where he saw several Captives sacrificed, &c. II. The manner how the Negroes become Slaves. The Numbers of them yearly exported from Guinea to America. The Lawfulness of that Trade. The Mutinies among them on board the Ships where the Author has been, &c. III. A Relation of the Author's being taken by Pirates, and the many Dangers he underwent. *Lond. 1734, 8*o. LU.

Reissued 1754 (L).

4703 Ashley, John. The Sugar Trade, with the Incumbrances thereon, Laid Open. By a Barbadoes Planter. *Lond. 1734, 8*o. LU.

The dedication signed: John Ashley and dated: Barbadoes, Oct 2, 1733.

4704 Bennett, John. A Memorial of the Difficulties, Hardships and Perplexities which Mr. Bennett hath, and doth still labour under; Humbly submitted to the Consideration of the Honourable Court of Directors of the South-Sea Company. *Lond. 1734, 4*o. MP.

COLONIES

4705 Representation of the Board of Trade relating to the Laws made, Manufactures set up, and Trade carried on, in His Majesty's Plantations in America. *n.p.* [*1734*], *F*o. LU.

Title taken from endorsement. Another edn. 1749 [o.s.], entitled: Copy of a Representation of the Board of Trade to the House of Lords relating to the Laws made...(L).

4706 Proposals offered to Consideration, wherein the Good of this Province is aimed at. [*Boston, 1734*].

Dated: March 1st. 1733 [o.s.]. On the currency. Reprinted in *Colonial Currency Reprints*, ed. by A. M. Davis, vol. 3 (1911), whence this entry is taken.

4707 GRADY, . A Description of the famous new Colony of Georgia, in South Carolina, (establish'd by his present Majesty,) of which Colonel David Dunbar is Governor; with an Account of the Inhabitants, Climate, Soil, Birds, Beasts, and other curious Particulars.... *Dublin, 1734, 8º*. De Renne.

'Relates in no way to the Colony of Georgia....The "Georgia" described is said to have been a part of Nova Scotia', De Renne Cat. 1, 50.

4708 RECK, PHILIPP GEORG FRIEDRICH VON. An Extract of the Journals of Mr. Commissary Von Reck, who Conducted the First Transport of Saltzburgers to Georgia: and of the Reverend Mr. Bolzius, one of their Ministers. Giving an Account of their Voyage to, and happy Settlement in that Province. Published by the Direction of the Society for Promoting Christian Knowledge. *Lond. 1734, 8º*. L.

Reprinted in P. Force, *Tracts and other Papers*, vol. 4 (1846), no. 5.

4709 A Letter from one of the Leeward Islands, tending to shew the immediate necessity of a further inspection into the state of the British sugar colonies and trade. [*Lond. 1734*], *19 cm*. Kress 4189.

Dated: Nevis, October 17, 1734.

FINANCE

4710 Percival Lewis, Esq; Appellant. Elias Turner, Jacob Sawbridge, Sir George Caswell, Robinson Knight, and Sir Henry Blunt, Bart. Respondents. The Appellant's Case. *n.p.* [*1734*], *Fº*. LHL.

Signed: The Lutwyche. J. Verney. On South Sea stock dealings in 1720.

4711 Percival Lewis, Appellant. Elias Turner, Sir George Caswell, Knt. Jacob Sawbridge, Robinson Knight, and Sir Henry Blunt, Bart. formerly Henry Blunt. Respondents. The Respondents Case. *n.p.* [*1734*], *Fº*. LHL.

Signed: J. Willes. D. Ryder.

4712 [PULTENEY, WILLIAM, Earl of Bath]. An Enquiry into the Conduct of our Domestick Affairs, from the year 1721, to the present time. In which the Case of our National Debts, the Sinking Fund, and all extraordinary Grants of Money are particularly consider'd. Being a Sequel to Politicks on both Sides. *Lond. 1734, 8º*. L.

2nd edn. 1734 (O); 3rd edn. 1734 (L).; another edn. *Edin.* 1734 (O). For authorship see W. Coxe, *Memoirs of Sir Robert Walpole*, 1, 372.

4713 The Ministry and Government of Great-Britain Vindicated. In Answer to a Book Entituled, An Enquiry into the Conduct of our Domestick Affairs, &c..... *Lond. 1734, 8º*. LU.

4714 [BRUCE, JOHN]. Considerations on the Necessity of Taxing the Annuities granted by Parliament in the Reigns of King William, and Queen Anne; and reducing One Fifth of the Capital Stock of all Persons possess'd of Five Thousand Pounds or more in the South-Sea Company: in order to pay off the National Debt, and Ease Trade, and the Landed Interest. *Lond. 1734*, 8°. LU.

Another edn. 1746 (L). For authorship see *Catalogue of the Books in the Manchester Free Library*, 1864, p. 87.

4715 A bill to explain an act passed in the last session of Parliament, intitled, An Act for the converting a further part of the capital stock of the South-Sea Company into annuities redeemable by Parliament. *n.p.* [*1734*], *s. sh. F°*. Kress 2638.

4716 Instructions to be Observ'd by Supervisors. *Lond. 1734*, 8°. LCH.

Customs service.

4717 Instructions to be Observ'd by Riding-Officer . *London. 1734*, 8°. LCH.

Customs service.

4718 The ever Memorable List of Those who voted for and against the Excise. *Lond. 1734*, *s. sh. F°*. LU.

4719 The Late Excise Scheme Dissected: or, an Exact Copy of the Late Bill, for repealing several Subsidies, and an Impost, now Payable on Tobacco, &c. With all the Blanks filled up, as they probably would have been, if the Bill had passed into a Law; and proper Observations on each Paragraph.... *Lond. 1734*, 8°. LU.

Attributed to William Pulteney in H. & L. without quoting authority.

4720 A Second Review of the late Excise Scheme. To which is added, A Word to the Freeholders of Great Britain, on the approaching Elections. *Lond. 1734*, 8°. LU.

4721 A Vindication of the Conduct of the Ministry, in the Scheme of the Excise on Wine and Tobacco, proposed Last Sessions of Parliament: with a General Examination of the Reasons which determined the said Ministry to it....Also the Motives which engaged the Ministry to lay it Aside.... *Lond. 1734*, 8°. LU.

4722 [BARRINGTON, JOHN SHUTE, Viscount Barrington]. A Speech on the Question, That the Project call'd the Harburgh Lottery, is an Infamous and Fraudulent Undertaking, whereby several unwary Persons have been drawn in to their great Loss: And that the Manner of carrying it on has been a manifest violation of the Laws of the Kingdom. *Lond. 1723*, 4°. L.

Not published until 1734. Authorship deduced from internal evidence

4723 VANDERLINT, JACOB. Money answers all Things: or, an Essay to make Money sufficiently plentiful amongst all Ranks of People, and increase our Foreign and Domestick Trade.... *Lond. 1734*, 8°. LU.

Another edn., ed. by J. H. Hollander, Baltimore, 1914.

4724 A Bill to prevent the Infamous Practice of Stock-Jobbing. *n.p.* [*1734*], *F°.* pp. 7. L.

Another edn. entitled: A Bill, Intituled, An Act to prevent the infamous Practice of Stock-jobbing. [1734] F°. (L).

4725 Some Considerations humbly offered to the Honourable House of Commons, why the Bill now pending concerning Stock-Jobbing, should not pass into a Law. *n.p.* [*1734*], *F°.* L.

4726 Some Observations on the Bill now depending, intitled, An Act to prevent the Infamous Practice of Stock-Jobbing. *n.p.* [*1734?*], *F°.* L

4727 The Report of the Commissioners appointed to Examine, State, and Report, who of the Sufferers in the Charitable Corporation are Objects of Compassion. *Lond.* *1733* [*o.s.*], *F°.* L.

Another edn. 1734 (L).

4728 A Bill to ascertain the Demands of the Charitable Corporation against Persons Debtors, or accountable to them, in a summary Way. *n.p.* [*1734*], *F°.* L.

4729 The Case of the Charitable Corporation, for Relief of Industrious Poor by Assisting them with small Sums upon Pledges at legal Interest. *n.p.* [*1734?*], *F°.* LLI.

Endorsed: The Case of the Charitable Corporation.

4730 Proposals by the Corporation of the London-Assurance, established by His Majesty's Royal Charter, For Assuring Houses and other Buildings, Goods, Wares, and Merchandizes, from Loss or Damage by Fire. *n.p.* *1734*, *s. sh. F°.* L.

4731 Proposals by the Corporation of the Royal Exchange Assurance, Established by His Majesty's Royal Charter, For Assuring Houses and other Buildings, Goods, Wares, and Merchandizes, From Loss or Damage by Fire. *Lond.* [*1734*], *s. sh. F°.* OUP.

Dated: June. 12, 1734.

TRANSPORT

4732 Extracts from the Books of the Mayor and Aldermen of Hertford; together with Copies of Papers in their Custody, relating to the Navigation on the River Lea, between Hertford and Ware. *Lond.* *1734*, *4°.* O.

4733 A Bill to Extend the Navigation of the River Weaver, from Winsford-Bridge to the Town of Namptwich, in the County of Chester. *n.p.* [*1734*], *F°.* O.

4734 A Short Specimen of a New Political Arithmeetic; containing, Some Considerations concerning Public Roads. By a Fellow of the Royal Society. *Lond.* *1734*, *8°.* LU.

4735 ROWE, JACOB. All Sorts of Wheel-Carriage, Improved. Wherein it is plainly made appear, that a much less than the usual Draught of Horses, &c. will be requir'd, in Waggons, Carts, Coaches, and all other Wheel Vehicles....The whole illustrated with Copper Plates. And an Explanation of the Structure of a Coach and Cart, according to this Method. *Lond. 1734, 4°.* L.

4736 Reasons humbly offered to the Consideration of the Right Honourable the House of Lords, against passing the Bill, now depending in Parliament, For continuing, explaining, and making more effectual, two Acts of Parliament, one of the third, and the other of the eighth Year of the Reign of his late Majesty King George the First, for Repairing the Highways, from the several Places in the said Acts mentioned, to Highgate Gatehouse, and Hampstead, in the County of Middlesex; and for amending the Roads, from the South End of the said Town of Hampstead, to the further End of Burrough-Lane, in the Parish of Hendon.... *n.p.* [*1734*], *s. sh. F°.* LG.

4737 Reasons humbly offered to the Consideration of this Honourable House, for the Bill for repairing the Roads leading to Highgate, Hampstead, &c. *n.p.* [*1734*], *s. sh. F°.* LG.

4738 A Bill for making more Effectual an Act passed in the Thirteenth Year of the Reign of his late Majesty King George the First, intituled, 'An Act for the more effectual Amending the Highways leading from Royston in the County of Hertford to Wandsford Bridge in the County of Huntingdon,' so far as the same relates to the Amending that Part of the Road as lies between a Place called the White-Post upon Alconbury Hill and Wandsford Bridge, in the said County of Huntingdon, called The North Division. *n.p.* [*1734*], *F°.* O.

SOCIAL CONDITIONS

4739 SOUTHALL, JOHN. London Made Easy: or, a Scheme for Paying off the Orphans, Work-House, and all other City-Debts; also, for Building General Hospitals, and Work-Houses, for the Poor.... *Lond. 1734, F°.* LG.

4740 A Bill for confirming an Agreement lately entered into between the Mayor, Aldermen, and Citizens of the City of Worcester, and the Guardians of the Poor of the said City, for continuing the Hop-Market of the said City in the Workhouse there, and for vesting the Right of the said Mayor, Aldermen, and Citizens of keeping a Hop-Market in the said City, in the Guardians of the Poor of the said City, and their Successors, for ever. *n.p.* [*1731*], *F°.* O.

4741 An Account of the Occasion and Manner of Erecting the Hospital at Lanesborough House, near Hyde-Park-Corner. Published by Order of the General Board of Governours there, Wednesday, February the 6th, 1733 [o.s.]. *n.p. 1733 [o.s.]*, *F°*. L.

St. George's Hospital.

4742 A Defence of the Majority of the Infirmary at Westminster, against a small Minority of it. A Letter from a Subscriber to the Westminster Infirmary, residing in Westminster, to a Subscriber living in the Country. *n.p.* [*1734*], *F°*. L.

4743 The Trustees of the Publick Infirmary in Westminster, assured that their Conduct is misrepresented by some Gentlemen separated from them, and that a written Case is privately handed about, think it necessary to publish an Account of their Proceedings with regard to the Houses lately in Dispute, which is made in Pretence for the said Separation. *n.p.* [*1734*], *4°*. L.

Endorsed: The Publick Infirmary, January 21, 1733–4.

4744 *Begin.* Whereas Mrs. Mary Mercer, Daughter of the late Thomas Mercer, Doctor of Physick, hath most charitably given a Large Stone-House, at the lower End of Stephen's Street, to the Purpose and Intent of a Hospital.... [*Dublin*], *1734*, *s. sh. F°*. DNL.

A notice telling the poor distressed sick where to apply for relief, and appealing to the wealthy for support.

4745 A Bill for the more Easy and Speedy Recovery of Small-Debts. *n.p.* [*1734*], *F°*. L.

4746 A Bill for the more easy Compelling the Redemption of Mortgages. *n.p.* [*1734*], *F°*. L.

Another edn., with the blanks filled in, entitled A Bill, intituled, An Act for the more easy Redemption and Foreclosure of Mortgages (L).

4747 The Case of Bankrupts and Insolvents Consider'd....Together with a Draught of a Bill for Amending the Law.... *London*, *1734*, *35*. *8°*. 2 pt. LU.

4748 *Begin.* Oxford, April 12. 1734. There is now drawn up, in order to the proposed in Convocation, an Inhibition to the Wine-Cellars lately opened in this Town; the Consequences of which are of such Importance, that they ought to be thoroughly considered by the Members of Convocation, before it be either passed or rejected. *n.p.* [*1734*], *F°*. O.

1735

GENERAL

4749 [Robe, Thomas]. A Collection of Political Tracts. On the following Subjects, viz. I. Ways and Means to Man the Navy upon any Emergency....II. Stock-Jobbing, whether prejudicial to, or the support of the Publick Credit of Great Britain. III. The Advantage of accruing to the Landed Interest of Great Britain, from promoting the British Distillery....IV. Considerations on the more effectual Punishment of Criminals, whereby the Transportation Act will not be eluded. ...V. A Dissertation concerning the Laws of China....By Eboranos. *Lond. 1735*, *8°*. L.

A reissue of: *Ways and Means whereby his Majesty may Man his Navy....To which is added, A Collection of some Political Essays by Eboranos*, 1734 (no. 4648).

4750 A Description of the Diocese of Norwich: or, the Present State of Norfolk and Suffolk. Giving an Account of the Situation, Extent, Trade, and Customs, of the City of Norwich in particular, And of the several Market-Towns in those two Counties....By a Gentleman of the Inner-Temple, and Native of the Diocese of Norwich. *Lond. 1735*, *8°*. L.

4751 Kirby, John. The Suffolk Traveller: or, A Journey through Suffolk. In which is inserted the true Distance in the Roads, from Ipswich to to every Market Town in Suffolk, and the same from Bury St. Edmund's. Likewise the Distance in the Roads from one Village to another; with Notes of Direction for Travellers.... *Ipswich*, *1735*, *8°*.

2nd edn. Lond. 1764 (L).

4752 The Present State of the Island of Jersey. Wherein is set forth the Causes of the Discontents and Troubles among the People, and what has occasioned so many Disorders, greatly Destructive to the Peace and Safety of the Island. *Lond. 1735*, *8°*. E.

4753 [Berkeley, George, Bishop of Cloyne]. The Querist, containing several Queries proposed to the Consideration of the Public. *Dublin*, *MD,CC,XXV* [*1735*], *36*, *37*. *8°*. 3 pt. LU.

Some copies have the date of pt. 1 correctly printed. Another edn. Lond. 1736, 37 (LU); 2nd edn., with author's name, Dublin, 1750 (DA); 4th edn. Dublin, 1750 (DA); 5th edn. Dublin, 1750 (O); another edn. Lond. 1750 (LU); 2nd edn. Lond. 1751 (O); another edn. Glasgow, 1751 (LU); another edn. Dublin, 1752 (DA). Reprinted in *The Works of George Berkeley*, ed. by A. A. Luce and T. E. Jessop, vol. 6 (1953).

4754 Wedd, Daniel. An Enquiry into the Reasons of the Decay of Credit, Trade, and Manufactures in Ireland. *Dublin*, *1735*, *8°*. L.

The dedication signed: Daniel Webb.

4755 [Webb, Daniel]. An Appendix to a Pamphlet, entitled, An Enquiry into the Reasons of the Decay of Credit, Trade, and Manufactures in Ireland. *Dublin*, *1735*, *8°*. DNL.

4756 A Letter to the Author of a Pamphlet, entitled, An Enquiry into the Reasons of the Decay of Credit, Trade, and Manufactures in Ireland. By a Friend to the Author. *Dublin, 1735*, 8°. L.

4757 An Essay, to Induce the Gentlemen of the County of Lymerick, to form a Society for the Improvement of Tillage by English Husbandry, and to Encourage Arts and Manufactures. *Dublin, 1735*, 8°. DG.

AGRICULTURE

4758 A True Method of treating Light Hazely Ground; or, an exact Relation of the Practice of Farmers in Buchan: containing Rules for Infields, Outfields, Haughs, and Laighs. By a small Society of Farmers in Buchan. *Edin. 1735*, 8°. LU.

Another edn., 1811 (SU), in which the editor of the first edn. is shown to have been James Arbuthnot. Also reprinted in David Souter's *General View of the Agriculture of the County of Banff*, 1812 (L).

4759 The Case of the Maltsters, Farmers, and Grasiers in general. *n.p.* [*c. 1735?*], *s. sh. F°*. L.

Urging that distillers should be compelled to distil malted grain only.

4760 [BEVAN,]. A Friendly Proposal to all Gentlemen, Farmers, Gardiners &c. For Preparing Seed, instead of Manuring Land. *Lond.* [*1735?*], *s. sh. F°*. L.

L copy is endorsed in ms. 'Bevans proposal'.

4761 Rules and Conditions upon which the Undertakers for Sowing Lint-Seed or Hemp-Seed shall be entitled to the Præmium of Fifteen Shillings per Acre. *n.p.* [*1735?*], *s. sh. F°*. OUP.

Issued by the Commissioners and Trustees for improving Fisheries and Manufactures in Scotland.

4762 An Old Almanack. Printed in the Year 1710. With a Postscript thereunto. Both Written by the same Author. *Lond. 1734–5*, 8°. L.

The head-title is 'Some Considerations for Improvement of Commons'. The author explains in the preface that he uses the title to remind his readers that the idea of enclosure is not new.

4763 A Bill for Dividing and Inclosing the Common Field, Common Pastures, and Common Grounds in the Manor and Parish of Aldermarston, in the County of Worcester. *n.p.* [*1735*], *F°*. L.

4764 An Act for appointing Commissioners to make a Division of certain Commons and waste Lands, lying within the Mannor and Parish of Chedleton, in the County of Stafford, in order to inclose the same. *n.p.* [*1735*], *F°*. L.

4765 An Act for Inclosing the Common Fields, Common Meadows, and other Commonable Lands, in the Parish of Hunningham, alias Honingham, in the County of Warwick. *n.p. 1735*, *F°*. L.

4766 The Compleat English Copyholder: or, a Guide to Lords of Manors, Justices of the Peace, Tenants, Stewards, Attornies, Bailiffs, Constables, Gamekeepers, Haywards, Reeves, Surveyors of the Highways, &c....By a Gentleman of the Inner Temple. *Lond. 1735*, *8°*. 2 vol. O.

4767 MORRIS, GAEL. Tables for Renewing and Purchasing of Leases. As also for Renewing and Purchasing of Lives. With other Necessary Tables for Computing of Interest, either Simple or Compound. *Lond. 1735*, *12°*. L.

4768 A Bill for the publick Registring of all Deeds, Conveyances, Wills, and other Incumbrances, that shall be made of, or that may affect any Honors, Manors, Lands, Tenements or Hereditaments within the North-Riding of the County of York. *n.p.* [*1735*], *F°*. LU.

4769 September 29, 1735. York-Buildings House, in Winchester-Street. A List of the Members of the Corporation of the Governor and Company of Undertakers, for Raising the Thames-Water in York-Buildings. *n.p.* [*1735*], *F°*. L.

4770 A Report from the Committee to whom the Petition of Esther Crull, Widow, Thomas Moseley...and Others, whose Names are thereunto subscribed, Creditors of the Governor and Company of Undertakers for Raising the Thames Water in York Buildings; as also Proprietors of several Parts and Shares of the Stock of the said Company, on Behalf of Themselves and Others, was Referred. *Lond. 1735*, *F°*. L.

4771 A Further Report from the Committee to whom the Petition of Esther Crull, Widow, Thomas Moseley...and others, whose Names are thereunto subscribed, Creditors of the Governor and Company of Undertakers for raising the Thames Water in York-Buildings, as also Proprietors of several Parts and Shares of the Stock of the said Company, on Behalf of themselves and others was Referred.... *Lond. 1735*, *F°*. L.

4772 A Bill for Appointing Commissioners for Taking, Stating, and Determining all the Claims and Demands of the Creditors of the Corporation of the Governor and Company of Undertakers for raising the Thames Water in York-Buildings, and of all Persons claiming any Share or Interest in the Stock or Fund of the said Corporation. *n.p.* [*1735*], *F°*. L.

4773 The Case of William Jackson, Richard Fowler, and Charles Portales, Three of the Assistants of the York-Buildings Company. *n.p.* [*1735?*], *s. sh. F°*. LLI.

4774 Petition for Sir William Billers and others. *n.p.* [*1735*], *s. sh. F°*. EU.

Signed: J. Graham, and dated: June 22. 1735. On the York Buildings Company.

4775 Memorial for the Duke of Norfolk, General Wade, and other Creditors of the York-building Company. *n.p.* [*1735*], *F°*. EU.

Dated: July 14. 1735.

4776 The Case of the Masters and Owners of Vessels employed in the Fishing Trade of Great Britain. *n.p.* [*1735?*], *s. sh. F*°. LU.

For the prohibition of the importation of lobsters caught by foreigners.

MANUFACTURES

4777 An Account of the Works required to be Performed in the Warehouses intended to be Built, in Fenchurch Street, for the Service of the East-India Company. *n.p.* [*1735?*], *F*°. L.

4778 PRICE, FRANCIS. The British Carpenter: or, a Treatise on Carpentry. Containing the most concise and authentick Rules of that Art, in a more Useful and Extensive Method, than has been made Publick. The Second Edition enlarged with an Addition of Sixteen Copper Plates. *Lond. 1735*, *4*°. L.

3rd edn. 1753 (O); 4th edn. 1759 (LU). The first edition (now O), entitled A Treatise on Carpentry, was published in 1733.

4779 [LINDESAY, PATRICK]. Reasons for encouraging the Linnen Manufacture of Scotland, and other parts of Great-Britain. Humbly submitted to Parliament. By the Author of the Interest of Scotland consider'd, &c. *Lond. 1735*, *8*°. LU.

For authorship see *The Interest of Scotland considered*, 1733 (no. 4475).

4780 Some Considerations on the Improvement of the Linen Manufacture, in Ireland, particularly with Relation to the Raising and Dressing of Flax and Flax-Seed. *Dublin*, *1735*, *8*°. L.

4781 An Argument upon the Woollen Manufacture of Great Britain. Plainly demonstrating, that Ireland must be Speedily Imploy'd therein, as the only Means to Recover its Decay, and to Prevent its Ruin. *Lond. 1735*, *8*°. LU.

2nd edn. [1736], F° (LU); 3rd edn. [1736?], F° (Kress 4254); another edn. Dublin, 1737, 8° (LU); 4th edn. [Dublin, 1737?], 8° (DA).

4782 Unto the Right Honourable, the Lords of Council and Session, The Petition of John Vert, James Edward, Hugh Paterson, John Gray, James Hay, and John Pierie, all Journeymen Taylors in Edinburgh. *n.p.* [*1735*], *4*°. E.

Dated: June 30. 1735. Signed: Will. Grant.

4783 Answers for the Incorporation of Taylors in Edinburgh, Canongate, Canongate-head, Potterraw and West-port; to the Petition of John Vert and others, Journeymen Taylors there. *n.p.* [*1735*], *4*°. E.

Dated: July 24. 1735. Signed: Ro. Dundas.

COMMERCE

4784 LONDON. Bellamy Mayor. An Especial Court held on...Tuesday the 24th. Day of June, 1735.... [*Lond. 1735*], *s. sh. F*°. LCRO.

An order restricting Lady Fair in Southwark to three days.

4785 A Bill for the Encouragement of the Arts of Designing, Engraving, and Etching Historical and other Prints, by Vesting the properties thereof in the Inventors or Engravers, during the Time therein to be maintained. *n.p.* [*1735*], *F°*. LU.

4786 The Case of Designers, Engravers, Etchers, &c. stated. In a Letter to a Member of Parliament. *n.p.* [*1735*], *F°*. LLI.

4787 A Bill for making more Effectual and Act passed in the Eighth Year of the Reign of her late Majesty Queen Anne, intitled, An Act for the Encouragement of Learning, by vesting the Copies of Printed Books in the Authors or Purchasers of such Copies, during the Times therein mentioned. *n.p.* [*1735*], *F°*. LU.

4788 A Bill for the better Encouragement of Learning, and for the more effectual securing the Copies of Printed Books to the Authors or Purchasers of such Copies, during the Times therein mentioned. *n.p.* [*1735*], *F°*. O.

A revised version of the preceding.

4789 Mr. Addison's Representation of the Hardships on Authors as well as Booksellers, for want of a sufficient Act of Parliament to secure the Property of Copies. Tatler. No. 101. *n.p.* [*1735*], *s. sh. F°*. L.

4790 The Case of Authors and Proprietors of Books. *n.p.* [*1735?*], *F°*. L.

4791 An Estimate on the several Papers imported, that are generally made Use of for Printing Books, the Weight per Ream, and the Duty paid thereon; which is also computed by the Hundred Weight; to shew the Loss to the Revenue, by importing printed Books at 6s. 8d. per Hundred Weight. *n.p.* [*1735?*], *s. sh. F°*. O.

4792 A Letter to a Member of Parliament concerning the Bill now depending in the House of Commons, for making more effectual an Act in the 8th Year of the Reign of Queen Anne, entituled, An Act for the Encouragement of Learning, by by [*sic*] Vesting the Copies of Printed Books in the Authors or Purchasers of such Copies, during the Times therein mentioned. *n.p.* [*1735*], *s. sh. F°*. L.

4793 A Letter from an Author to a Member of Parliament. Occasioned by a late Letter concerning the Bill now depending in the House of Commons, For the Encouragement of Learning, &c. *n.p.* [*1735*], *F°*. O.

Dated: April 17, 1735.

4794 A Second Letter from an Author to a Member of Parliament; containing, Some further Remarks on a late Letter concerning the Bill now depending in the House of Commons, For the Encouragement of Learning, &c. *n.p.* [*1735*], *F°*. O.

Dated: April 23, 1735. Another edn., enlarged, dated: April 28, 1735 (O).

4795 Reasons humbly offered to the Consideration of the Honourable House of Commons, in Support of a Bill for making more effectual an Act passed in the Eighth Year of the Reign of her late Majesty Queen Anne,

Intitled, An Act for the Encouragement of Learning, by vesting the Copies of Printed Books in the Authors or Purchasers of such Copies during the Times therein mentioned. *n.p.* [*1735*], *s. sh. F°*. LU.

4796 Farther Reasons humbly offered to the Consideration of the Honourable House of Commons, for making more effectual an Act passed in the Eighth Year of the Reign of her late Majesty Queen Anne, Intitled, An Act for the Encouragement of Learning.... *n.p.* [*1735?*], *F°*. L.

4797 Unto the Right Honourable, The Lords of Council and Session, The Petition of Andrew Stalker Bookseller in Glasgow. *n.p.* [*1735*], *F°*. E.

Dated: January 2. 1735. Signed: Ja. Graham. With the text of the agreement between Stalker and Alexander Carmichael.

4798 The Assize of Bread, as set by the Worshipful John Cotton, Esq; Deputy-Steward of the Court for the City and Liberty of Westminster, October 8. 1735. *n.p.* [*1735*], *s. sh. F°*. L.

4799 The Case of the Mayor and Commonalty, and Citizens of the City of London, Appellants. Thomas Perkins, and others, Respondents. (The Appellants Case). *n.p.* [*1735*], *F°*. L.

Signed: D. Ryder. N. Fazakerly. On the right to levy 8*d.* a ton on cheese brought by ship to London to be sold there.

4800 The Mayor and Commonalty, and Citizens of the City of London, Appellants. Thomas Perkins, Joseph Brown, William Cock, John Jenkins, John Hall, John Chapman, John Neeve, Robert Jones, and Thomas Neville, Respondents. The Respondent's Case. *n.p.* [*1735*], *F°*. L.

Signed: J. Willes. J. Strange.

4801 London. Bellamy Mayor. An Especial Court held on Shrove-Tuesday the 18th day of February 1734.... [*Lond. 1735*], *s. sh. F°*. LCRO.

An order that coal-meters, corn-meters, salt-meters and fruit-meters are not to measure or allow to be carried away any goods without warrant from the Lord Mayor or his deputy.

4802 The Case of Henry Archer of Ross in the County of Wexford, Merchant. *n.p.* [*1735?*], *F°*. M (Cr).

On the seizure of a cargo of tobacco by the Customs.

4803 A Series of Wisdom and Policy, Manifested in a Review of our Foreign Negotiations and Transactions for several Years past. Being a complete Answer to Politicks on both Sides, &c..... *Lond. 1735*, *8°*. LU.

4804 Webber, Samuel. Some Thoughts, worthy the serious attention of the Greatest Men, on the Woollen Manufacturies of England, To prevent their Ruin before too late; setting forth, That by Connivance or Indolence, have brought this most valuable Branch of Trade, on which his Majesty's Wealth and Power depends (under God) to a Universal Decay throughout his Majesty's Dominion. *Lond. 1735*, *8°*. LU.

The author's name is given on p. 5. On the smuggling of wool to the Continent.

4805 ATKINS, JOHN. A Voyage to Guinea, Brasil, and the West-Indies; in His Majesty's Ships, the Swallow and Weymouth....With remarks on the Gold, Ivory, and Slave-Trade.... *Lond. 1735, 8°.* L.

2nd edn. 1737 (L).

4806 ASHLEY, JOHN. Some Observations on a Direct Exportation of Sugar, from the British Islands. With Answers to Mr. Toriano's Objections to it. In a Letter from a Gentleman in Barbados, to his Friend in London. *Lond. 1735, 4°.* LU.

4807 TEMPLEMAN, DANIEL. The Secret History of the late Directors of the South-Sea-Company. Containing a particular Account of their Conduct, with regard to the Assiento Commerce.... *Lond. 1735, 8°.* LU.

Templeman was a clerk in the Company.

4808 [TEMPLEMAN, DANIEL]. An Impartial Enquiry into the Transactions of the late Directors of the South-Sea Company. More especially during the Time that Sir John Eyles was Sub-Governor. Shewing the Necessity of a Parliamentary Inspection. To which is added, The Secret History of the South-Sea Directors. *Lond. 1735, 8°.* LU.

A reprint of the proceeding, with a new preface, but without the author's name.

4809 The Particulars of the Enquiry into Mr. Benjamin Wooley's Conduct; and his being Stationed by the Court of Directors of the South-Sea Company, First Factor at Porto Bello and Panama. Humbly dedicated to Thomas Woodford, Esq;. *Lond. 1735, 8°.* LU.

4810 COCKBURN, JOHN. A Journey over Land, from the Gulf of Honduras to the Great South-Sea. Performed by John Cockburn, and Five other Englishmen.... *Lond. 1735 [1734], 8°.* L.

Reissued in 1740 as: A Faithful Account of the Distresses and Adventures of John Cockburn....The Second Edition...(L). Another edn., [1742?], entitled: The Unfortunate Englishmen; or, a Faithful Narrative of the Distresses and Adventures of John Cockburn, and Five other English Mariners....The fifth edition (L); another edn. 1794 (L); another edn. 1810 (L).

COLONIES

4811 Representation from the Commissioners for Trade and Plantations, to the Right Honourable the Lords Spiritual and Temporal, in Parliament Assembled...relating to the State of the British Islands in America, with regard to their Trade, their Strength, and Fortifications, and to what may be further necessary for the Encouragement of their Trade, and Security of those Islands: As likewise to such Encouragements as may be necessary to engage the Inhabitants of the British Colonies on the Continent in America, to apply their Industry to the Cultivation of Naval Stores of all kinds, and of such other Products as may be proper for the Soil of the said Colonies, and do not interfere with the Trade or Produce of Great Britain. *Lond. 1734 [o.s.], F°.* L.

4812 A New Voyage to Georgia. By a Young Gentleman. Giving an Account of his Travels to South Carolina, and Part of North Carolina. To which is added, A Curious Account of the Indians. By an Honourable Person. And A Poem to James Oglethorpe, Esq; on his Arrival from Georgia. *Lond. 1735*, *8º*. O.

2nd edn. 1737 (L). Reprinted in *Georgia Hist. Soc. Collections*, vol. 2.

FINANCE

4813 [WALPOLE, Sir ROBERT]. Some Considerations concerning the Publick Funds, the Publick Revenues, and the Annual Supplies, granted by Parliament. Occasion'd by a late Pamphlet, intitled, An Enquiry into the Conduct of our Domestick Affairs.... *Lond. 1735*, *8º*. LU.

2nd edn. 1735 (LU). For authorship see W. Coxe, *Memoirs of Sir Robert Walpole*, I, 751. The original ms. in Walpole's hand is among the Cholmondeley MSS. at the University Library, Cambridge.

4814 The Case of the Sinking Fund, and the Right of the Publick Creditors to it considered at large...Being a Defence of an Enquiry into the Conduct of our Domestick Affairs, and a full reply to a late Pamphlet, intitled, Some Considerations concerning the Publick Funds.... *Lond. 1735*, *8º*. pp. 138. LU.

Another edn. pp. 95, Lond. 1735, 8º (LU). Attributed to William Pulteney in J. R. McCulloch, *The Literature of Political Economy*, 1938, p. 322, and to Edmund Waller in the B.M. Catalogue.

4815 Remarks upon a Pamphlet, intituled, Some Considerations concerning the Public Funds, &c. so far as it relates to the Application of the Sinking Fund, the Easing the Civil List of the annual Pensions, the Remission of the Two Millions, the Bank Contract, and the late Votes of Credit and Confidence.... *Lond. 1735*, *8º*. L.

4816 The Case of the Bank Contract. In Answer to the Infamous Scurrilities of several Libels lately printed in the Craftsman. *Lond. 1735*, *8º*. L.

4817 The Case of the Irish Officers Widows. *n.p.* [*1735*], *Fº*. C.

For arrears of pensions.

4818 Unto the Right Honourable, The Lords of Council and Session, the Petition of James M'Ghie, James Robertson, John Yetts, Hugh Campbel and Alexander Hunter, all Merchants in Edinburgh. *n.p.* [*1735*], *Fº*. E.

Dated: December 1. 1735. Signed: Ja. Graham jun. On the tack of the City's impost on wines.

4819 Answers for the Magistrates and Town council of Edinburgh, and the Tacksmen of the Impost upon Wine; to the Petition of James M'Ghie, and others. *n.p.* [*1735*], *Fº*. E.

Dated: Dec. 16. 1735. Signed: Dun. Forbes.

4820 Union Fire-Office, Kept in Gutter-Lane by Cheapside, for Insuring Goods and Merchandizes by Mutual Contribution, on the same easy Terms with the Hand-in-Hand Office for Houses. The Terms and Method whereof are as follow. *Lond. 1735, s. sh. F°.* L.

L also has edns. of 1736, 1738 and 1740. In each of these the list of claims paid is brought up to date.

4821 An Abstract of the Original Charter of the Corporation of the Amicable Society for a Perpetual Assurance-Office, Dated 25 July, 5° Annae Reginae, An. Dom. 1706. *n.p.* [*c. 1735?*], *8°.* C.

The supplemental charter of 1729 and Resolutions made on 29 April 1734 are included.

4822 HAMILTON, WILLIAM. Book-keeping new modelled: or, A treatise of merchants accounts, according to the true Italian method of debitor and creditor....To which are added a specimen of a factor-book, a warehouse book and an invoice book: with directions how to frame a book of charges of merchandize, and a book of personal and household expences.... *Edinburgh, Printed for the author by R. Fleming, 1735, 18 cm.* Kress S. 1792.

TRANSPORT

4823 BADESLADE, THOMAS. Reasons humbly offer'd to the Consideration of the Publick; Shewing how the Works now executing by Virtue of an Act of Parliament to recover and preserve the Navigation of the River Dee, will destroy the Navigation; and occasion the Drowning of all the Low Lands adjacent to the said River. From Observations made on the Spot; and from Instances of the ruinous Effects like Works have had at the Ports of Lyn, Rye, Wisbech and Spalding.... *Chester,* [*1735*], *F°.* L.

2nd edn. [1735] (O).

4824 GRUNDY, JOHN. Philosophical and Mathematical Reasons, humbly offer'd to the Consideration of the Publick, to prove that the Present Works, executing at Chester, to recover and preserve the Navigation of the River Dee, must intirely Destroy the same. With some Remarks on Mr. Badeslade's Reasons, &c. thereon. *Chester,* [*1735?*], *F°.* O.

Another edn. Lond. 1736, 4° (O).

4825 Reasons humbly offered for obtaining an Act of Parliament, for Repairing the Road from Shepherd's Shord to Marlborough, in the County of Wilts. *n.p.* [*1735?*], *s. sh. F°.* O.

4826 A Bill for Repairing the Roads from Saint Peter's Church in Marlborough, to Shepherds-Shord in the Parish of Bishops-Cannings, and other Roads therein mentioned, in the County of Wilts. *n.p.* [*1735*], *F°.* O.

4827 PRICE, JOHN. Some Considerations humbly offered to the Honourable Members of the House of Commons, for Building a Stone-Bridge over the River Thames, from Westminster to Lambeth. Together with some Proposals relating to a Design drawn for that Purpose. In a letter to a Member of that Honourable House. *Lond. 1735, 8°.* LG.

SOCIAL CONDITIONS

4828 [HAY, WILLIAM]. Remarks on the Laws relating to the Poor. With Proposals for their better Relief and Employment. By a Member of Parliament. *Lond.* [*1735*], *8°.* LU.

Another edn. 1751 (LU). Reprinted in the author's *Works*, 1794.

4829 By the Court of Assistants of the Governors of the Work-House of the City of Dublin. Advertisement. *n.p.* [*c. 1735?*], *s. sh. F°.* C (Cr).

All common beggars will be received, but the able-bodied will be kept to the hardest labour.

4830 An Account of the Proceedings of the Governours of the Hospital near Hyde-Park-Corner, from their first Institution, October 19, 1733, to the first of January, 1734 [o.s.]; together with a List of the Governours and Contributors, and an Abstract of some of their By-Laws. Published by Order of the General Board, Friday, February the 7th, 1734 [o.s.]. *n.p. 1734* [*o.s.*], *F°.* L.

Subsequently published annually. From 1736 entitled: An Account of the Proceedings of the Governours of St. George's Hospital. L has the reports published in 1735–41, 44–48.

4831 [GAIRDNER, ANDREW]. A Brief Account of the Rise, Progress, Management and State of the Orphan-School, Hospital and Work-House at Edinburgh, as on 1st January 1735. *Edin. 1735, 8°.* L.

For authorship see H. & L. 1, 233, quoting New College Catalogue.

4832 The Regulations of the Town's Hospital at Glasgow; with an Abstract of the First Year's Expence, from November 1733. to November 1734. Published by Order of the Directors of the Hospital, for the Information and Satisfaction of those who contributed to it. To which is prefix'd a short Narrative of the Erection of that House, and its Success and good Effects for the First Year. *Glasgow, 1735, 8°.* GBI.

2nd edn., Glasgow, 1737, entitled: A Short Account of the Towns Hospital in Glasgow. With the Regulations, and Abstracts of the Expences for the First Three Years....The Second Edition (GU); 3rd end. Edin. 1738; 4th edn. Edin. 1742; 3rd edn., enlarged, with the expenses for the first eight years, Glasgow, 1742 (all GU). Attributed to John McUre by Isabel Brown (*The Bibliotheck*, vol. 1, no. 3, 1958, pp. 37–41), but the evidence is not conclusive.

4833 To the Honourable the Commons of Great-Britain, in Parliament Assembled. The Case of Thomas Bambridge. *n.p.* [*1735*], *s. sh. F°.* L.

On his sufferings since deprived of the Wardenship of the Fleet Prison. Another edn., entitled: The Case of Thomas Bambridge, [1736] (L).

4834 Considerations upon the Mischiefs that may arise from Granting too much Indulgence to Foreigners. Occasioned by the late Election of Broadstreet Ward. With Mr. Addison's Opinion of the French, and their innate Hatred to the English. And an Extract of Sir John Knight's Speech in Parliament against Foreigners. Address'd to the Citizens of London, as a proper Monitor for the next Elections of S—— S—— Directors, Common Council-men, &c. *Lond.* *1735*, *8o*. L.

4835 Order of a Loving Society, held at the House of Mr. Matthew Osman, at the Blackmoor's Head in Gravel-Lane in Houndsditch, London. *Lond.* *1735*, *8o*. C.

A sickness and burial club.

4836 A Common-Council holden in the Chamber of the Guild-hall of the City of London, on Friday the Twenty-sixth Day of September, One thousand seven hundred and thirty five.... *n.p.* [*1735*], *Fo*. L.

The report by the Committee for Letting the City's Lands on street-lighting.

4837 Castle, Richard. An Essay toward Supplying the City of Dublin with Water. *Dublin*, *1735*, *8o*. L.

The advertisement signed: Rich[d] Castle.

4838 Stokes, Gabriel. Observations on a late Essay of Mr. Richard Castle. Collected from some Remarks made in my Travels, on his Latest and Best Works of this Kind now subsisting. Occasioned by his remarkable Advertisement at the Front of his Book.... *Dublin*, *1735*, *12o*. DA.

4839 Stokes, Gabriel. A Scheme for Effectually Supplying every Part of the City of Dublin with Pipe-Water, without any Charge of Water-Engines, or any Water-Forcers, by a close Adherence only to the natural Laws of Gravitation, and the Principles, Rules, and Experiments of Hydrostaticks. *Dublin*, *1735*, *8o*. L.

1736

GENERAL

4840 An Address to the People, occasion'd by some late Acts of Parliament, and the Insult upon them and Publick Justice. *Lond. 1736*, *8º*. L.

On the Gin, Smuggling and Mortmain Acts.

4841 BAILEY, NATHAN. Dictionarium Domesticum, being a New and Compleat Houshold Dictionary. For the Use both of City and Country. Shewing, I. The whole Arts of Brewing, Baking, Cookery, and Pickling....II. The Management of the Kitchin, Pantry, Larder, Dairy, Olitory, and Poultry....III. The Herdsman....IV. The English Vineyard....V. The Apiary....VI. The Family Physician and Herbalist.... *Lond. 1736*, *8º*. O.

4842 [BROWN, JAMES]. The Directory: containing an Alphabetical List of the Names and Places of Abode of the Directors of Companies, Persons in Publick Business, Merchants, and other Eminent Traders in the Cities of London and Westminster, and Borough of Southwark. *Lond. 1736*, *8º*. L.

Subsequently published annually. For authorship and a list of surviving editions see C. W. F. Goss, *The London Directories*, 1932. From 1745 the title was *Kent's Directory*.

4843 McURE alias CAMPBEL, JOHN. A View of the City of Glasgow: or, an Account of its Origin, Rise and Progress, with a more particular Description thereof than has hitherto been known.... *Glasgow, 1736*, *8º*. L.

AGRICULTURE

4844 ELLIS, WILLIAM. New Experiments in Husbandry, for the Month of April.... *Lond. 1736*, *8º*. L.

4845 ALLEN, WILLIAM. Ways and Means to Raise the Value of Land: or, the Landlord's Companion: with Political Discourses on the Land-Tax, War, and other Subjects, occasionally intermixed. *Lond. 1736*, *8º*. LU.

Urges bounties for agricultural products. Another edn. 1742, entitled The Landlord's Companion (L).

4846 An Act for Inclosing and Dividing the Common Field called Alderminster Common Field, Common Pastures, and other Common Grounds in the Parish of Alderminster, in the County of Worcester. *n.p.* [*1736*], *Fº*. L.

4847 A Bill for Inclosing and Dividing the Common and common Field in the Manor of Ixworth, in the Town of Ixworth, in the County of Suffolk. *n.p.* [*1736*], *Fº*. LU.

4848 An Act for Dividing and Inclosing the Common Field and Plots of Commonable Lands, and for Stinting the Common or Heath in the Manor of Ixworth, within the Parish of Ixworth, in the County of Suffolk. *n.p.* [*1736*], *F°*. L.

4849 An Act for Dividing and Enclosing certain Commons and Waste Grounds called Stankham and Soldridge Commons, in the Parish of Old Alresford, in the County of Southampton. *n.p.* [*1736*], *F°*. L.

4850 An Act for inclosing and dividing the Common Fields and Common Grounds in the Parish of West Stafford cum Froom Bellet in the County of Dorset. *n.p.* *1736*, *F°*. L.

4851 Answers for the Annuitants upon the Estates purchased by the York-Building Company in Scotland, and their Trustees, and Mr. John Hamilton Writer to the Signet, their Factor; to the Petition and Additional Petition presented in the Name of the said York-Building Company, and of Mr. Francis Grant, pretended Tacksman of the Coal and Salt-works of Tranent and Cockenzie. *n.p.* [*1736*], *F°*. L.

Dated: November 12, 1736. Signed: Robert Dundas.

4852 The Proposal for enabling the Clergy to accept Advanced Rents in lieu of Fines, Defended and Enforced: and the Justice of the Claim of the Tenants to Renew at usual Times for usual Fines, Asserted. *Lond.* *1736*, *8°*. L.

The *Proposal* was published in 1731 (no. 4186).

4853 A Bill to Restrain the Disposition of Lands, whereby the same become Unalienable. *n.p.* [*1736*], *F°*. L.

4854 Reasons humbly offer'd against the Bill (now depending in Parliament) to Restrain the Disposition of Lands, whereby the same become Unalienable. *n.p.* [*1736*], *s. sh. F°*. LU.

4855 Reasons humbly offered to the Honourable House of Commons, against the Bill now depending for Restraining the Disposition of Lands, whereby the same become Unalienable; as far as relates to the University of Oxford. *n.p.* [*1736*], *F°*. LU.

4856 [Long, Roger]. Reasons humbly offer'd to the Honourable House of Commons, for excepting the University of Cambridge and the several Colleges therein, out of the Bill now depending, for restraining the Dispositions of Lands whereby the same become unalienable *n.p.* [*1736*], *F°*. LU.

For authorship see ms. note in LU copy.

4857 Remarks upon a Bill now depending in Parliament, intituled, An Act to restrain the Dispositions of Lands, whereby the same become Unalienable: shewing, how very different the Spirit and Tendency of it is from two Acts made in the Reigns of King William and Queen Mary, and the fatal Effects it will have upon Charity in general, if it should pass into a Law. *n.p.* [*1736*], *4°*. LU.

4858 Some Plain Reasons humbly offer'd against the Bill, now depending in Parliament, to restrain the Disposition of Lands, by which the same become inalienable. *Lond. 1736, 8°.* L.

4859 A Proposal for Payment of the Creditors of the York-Buildings Company; as agreed to at a Meeting of the Creditors of the said Company, on the 22nd of January, 1735; and at a General Court of the said Company, the 27th of January, 1735. *n.p.* [*1736*], *s. sh. F°.* L.

Title taken from endorsement.

4860 A Proposal to be offered to the Creditors of the York-Buildings Company. *n.p.* [*1736?*], *s. sh. F°.* L.

4861 A Proposal for Satisfying the Debts of the York-Buildings Company. *n.p.* [*1736?*], *s. sh. F°.* EU.

4862 Unto the Right Honourable the Lords of Council and Session the Petition of His Grace the Duke of Norfolk, Sir Robert Sutton and Sir Robert Clifton...Sir Alexander Murray and Sir Archibald Grant ...Lieutenant General George Wade, William Neilson...and Richard Graham and Peter Murdoch.... *n.p.* [*1736*], *F°.* EU.

Signed: Will. Grant. Dated: January 22, 1736. Against the York Buildings Company.

4863 Answers for the Annuitants of the York-building Company; to the Petition of the Duke of Northfolk and others, Creditors of the said Company. *n.p.* [*1736*], *s. sh. F°.* EU.

Dated: Feb. 3, 1736. Signed: Ja. Graham.

4864 Minutes. The Duke of Northfolk; against the York-Buildings Company. *n.p. 1736, s. sh. F°.* EU.

Dated: Feb. 18, 1736.

4865 Unto the Right Honourable, the Lords of Council and Session, the Petition of Edward Duke of Norfolk, Sir Robert Sutton, Sir Robert Clifton, Lieutenant General George Wade, and others, Creditors of the York-Building Company, and Mr. Hugh Crawford Clerk to the Signet, their Factor. *n.p.* [*1736*], *s. sh. F°.* EU.

Signed: Ja. Graham. Dated: Novr. 18, 1736.

MANUFACTURES

4866 Salmon, William. The Builder's Guide, and Gentleman and Trader's Assistant; or a Universal Magazine of Tables.... *Lond. 1736, 8°.* O.

4867 The Case of the Importers of Cotton Wool, and the Manufacturers thereof into Fustian, and of the Traders in that Manufacture. *n.p.* [*1736*], *s. sh. F°.* LU.

4868 The Case of the Worsted and Silk Manufacturers. *n.p.* [*1736*], *F°.* L.

Against the bill 'to encourage the use of any printed or painted stuffs, made of linen-yarn and cotton-wooll'.

4869 A Scheme to Encourage the Printing, Painting and Staining of English Cottons, Irish and Scotch Linnens; and at the same Time to Preserve the Woollen and Silk Manufactures in this Kingdom. *n.p.* [*1736*], *s. sh. F°*. LU.

Submitted to Parliament 'by the Poor Journeymen Weavers of Spittle-Fields'.

4870 Narrative of the Proceedings of the Arbiters in the Submission betwixt Mr. Robert Freebairn, His Majesty's Printer, and Mr. James Blair of Ardblair, and Mr. John Nairn of Greenyards, now aspiring to be King's Printers in Craig's Closs Edinburgh. *Edin. 1736*, *F°*. E.

This dispute, mainly concerned with the legal standing of the King's Printer, occasioned many sessions papers not included here, some of which throw light on printing costs.

4871 Reasons for Encouraging the Manufacture of Sail-Cloth in Great Britain. *n.p.* [*1736?*], *s. sh. F°*. L.

4872 Reasons humbly offered for the Bill now depending in Parliament, for giving a further Encouragement to the Manufacture of British Sail-cloth; and for more effectually securing the Duties now payable on Foreign Sail-cloth imported into this Kingdom. *n.p.* [*1736*], *F°*. LU.

4873 Reasons humbly offered for the Act, intituled, An Act for the further Encouraging and Regulating the Manufacture of British Sail-cloth; And for the more effectual securing the Duties now payable on Foreign Sail-cloth imported into this Kingdom. *n.p.* [*1736*], *F°*. LU.

4874 Reasons humbly offered against the Bill now depending in Parliament, for giving further Encouragement to the Manufacturers of British Sail Cloth, and for more effectually securing the Duties now payable on Foreign Sail Cloth, imported into this Kingdom. *n.p.* [*1736*], *F°*. LU.

4875 DICKINS, JOHN. Proposals for Raising Money for carrying on a Manufacture for making Tin-Plates, and erecting a Town for the Artificers to be employed in the said Manufacture. *Lond. 1736*, *12°*. L.

4876 LLOYD, EDWARD. Thoughts on Trade: intended to have been first publish'd in Ireland, with an Account of the Present State of the Silken Manufacturers, and the Calamitous Circumstances of a Numerous Poor in that Kingdom....To which Thoughts are prefix'd, An humble Application in Favour of the British Distillery.... *Lond. 1736*, *8°*. L.

2nd edn. 1736 (MP).

COMMERCE

4877 BENNETT, JOHN. The National Merchant: or, Discourses on Commerce and Colonies; being an Essay for Regulating and Improving the Trade and Plantations of Great Britain, by Uniting the National and

Mercatorial Interests. To which are added, Some Considerations on providing for, and employing our useless and burdensome People. In several Letters to a Friend. *Lond. 1736, 8°.* LU.

The dedication signed: John Bennet.

4878 Some reasons humbly offered for establishing a yarn-market in the City of Dublin; and a view of certain advantages that would arise to the publick from erecting such a market near the Linnen hall. *Dublin, 1736, 8°.* Kress 4309.

4879 The Case of the Bakers within the Bills of Mortality. *n.p.* [*1736*], *F°.* L.

For amending the laws regulating the price and assize of bread.

4880 A Bill for the better Regulating and Ascertaining the Price and Assize of Bread in the City of London, and Parts adjacent, within the Bills of Mortality. *n.p.* [*1736*], *F°.* L.

4881 EDINBURGH. Act of Council, Regulating the Price of Candle. [*Edin. 1736*], *s. sh. F°.* EU.

Dated: 13 February 1736.

4882 Unto the Right Honourable, The Lord Provost, Magistrates and Town-Council of Edinburgh, The Petition of Patrick Moffat present Deacon of the Candle-makers of Edinburgh, and James Tod present Box-master to the said Incorporation for themselves, and in Name and Behalf of the remanent Members thereof. *n.p.* [*1736*], *4°.* E.

Dated: March 2, 1736. On fixing the price of candles with details of cost of manufacture.

4883 Unto the Right Honourable, The Lords of Council and Session, The Petition of Patrick Moffat present Deacon of the Candle-makers of Edinburgh, and James Tod present Box-master to the said Incorporation, for themselves, and in Name and Behalf of the remanent Members thereof. *n.p.* [*1736*], *F°.* E.

Dated: June 18th, 1736. Signed: William Grant.

4884 Unto the Right Honourable, the Lords of Council and Session, The Petition of Patrick Moffat, present Deacon of the Candle-makers of Edinburgh, and James Tod Box-master for themselves and the said Corporation. *n.p.* [*1736*], *s. sh. F°.* E.

Dated: June 24, 1736. Signed: Will. Grant.

4885 Answers for the Magistrates and Town-Council of Edinburgh; to the Petitions of Patrick Moffat, Deacon, and James Tod, Box-master to the Candle makers of Edinburgh. *n.p.* [*1736*], *F°.* E.

Dated: July 5, 1736. Signed: Dan. Forbes.

4886 EDINBURGH. Act of Council, settling the Measure of Wines and Spirits sold in Bottles. [*Edin. 1736*], *s. sh. F°.* EU.

Dated: 13 February 1736.

4887 A Proposal for preserving the Right and Property in Merchant Shipping, and for preventing the Frauds committed therein. *n.p.* [*1736*], *s. sh. F°.* LU.

4888 Proposals for preserving the Right and Property in Merchant Shipping, and for preventing the Frauds committed therein. *n.p.* [*1736*], *s. sh. F°.* L.

Endorsed: A Proposal for Registring Bills of Sale of Shipping, &c.

4889 BAXTER, SIMON, DAVIS, LEWIS and TAYLOR, THOMAS. Reasons humbly offered to the Honourable House of Commons, for bringing in a Bill, for Registring all Bills of Sale of Ships, and Vessels of Burden, in a General Register Book, with some Objections answered. *n.p.* [*c. 1736?*], *s. sh. F°.* L.

4890 A Bill, for Establishing an Office within the City of London, for the Registring Bills of Sale of Trading Ships, and Parts of such Ships and Vessels, built and hereafter to be built, to prevent the Frauds and Clandestine Sales therein Committed. *n.p.* [*1736*], *F°.* L.

4891 The Privileges of an Englishman in the Kingdom and Dominions of Portugal. Contained in the Treaty of Peace concluded by Oliver Cromwell; and Various Laws, Decrees, &c....made by the Kings of Portugal, in Favour of the English Nation....To which is added, The King of Portugal's New Law, concerning the Diamonds found in the Brasils. Done in Portuguese and English. *Lond. 1736, 8°.* L.

4892 The Lords Protest in the last Session of Parliament, on the Bill for Indemnifying Persons who have been guilty of unlawful Importing Goods and Merchandize into this Kingdom, upon the Terms therein mentioned, and for inforcing the Laws against such Importation for the future. To which is added, The State of the National Debt, with an Estimate of the Navy Debt, as it stood December 1735. *Lond. 1736, F°.* O.

4893 TROWELL, SAMUEL. A Plan, for Preventing the Clandestine Running of Wool: Humbly offered to the Consideration of the Legislature. *n.p.* [*1736*], *F°.* L.

4894 [SMITH, SIMON]. The Golden Fleece: or the Trade, Interest, and Well-Being of Great Britain considered. With Remarks on the Rise, Progress, and present Decay of our Woollen Manufactures. Also an Estimate of this Valuable Trade, fairly and clearly stated, and the great Proportion given up Yearly to Foreigners, by Suffering (or Conniving at) the illegal Exportation of British and Irish Wool, and Woollen Goods throughly Manufactured in Ireland, to Foreign Parts. Likewise Heads for a Bill, to put an effectual stop to this matchless Evil....To which is added, a Scheme, or Proposal, for taking away many burthensome Duties on...Leather, Soap, Candles, Painted Silks, and Starch, by replacing the like sum...on a small Duty on Wool.... *n.p.* [*1736?*], *F°.* L.

For authorship see *Calendar of Treasury Books*, 1735–38, p. 512. Wrongly attributed to J. Munn in *A Short Essay on Trade*, 1741, p. 2. Another edn. 1736, 4°; 3rd edn. 1737, 8°; 4th edn. 1739, 8° (all L). A ms. version was circulated in 1731. See Smith's letter in LPRO, C.O. 388/94.

4895 A Letter from the Annual Committee of the Convention of Royal Boroughs, to the Several Boroughs of Scotland, by Order of the Last General Convention, for preventing the pernicious Practice of Smuggling.... *Edin. 1736, 4°.* E.

Reprinted in *Some Considerations on the Present State of Scotland*, 1744 (no. 5752).

4896 An Enquiry into the Misconduct and Frauds committed by Several of the Factors, Super-Cargoes, and Others, employed by the late and present Directors of the South-Sea Company. Shewing the Abuses and Breaches of Trust of the Company's Agents....With Copies of Original Letters sent to Sir J—— E——, when Sub-Governor of the South-Sea Company....By a considerable Stock-holder. *Lond. 1736, 8°.* L.

COLONIES

4897 A Letter from James Murray, in New-York in America; to the Reverend Mr. Baptist Boyd, Minister of the Gospel, in the Parish of Aughelow, and County of Tyrone; with his Description of the Country.... *Dublin, 1736, 8°.* DA.

4898 [Hutchinson, Thomas]. A Letter to a Member of the Honourable House of Representatives, on the present State of the Bills of Credit. *Boston, 1736, 8°.*

Reprinted in *Colonial Currency Reprints*, ed. by A. M. Davis, vol. 3 (1911), whence this entry is taken.

4899 The Melancholy State of this Province considered, in a Letter from a Gentleman in Boston to his Friend in the Country. [*Boston*], *1736. 8°.*

On the currency. Reprinted in *Colonial Currency Reprints*, ed. by A. M. Davis, vol. 3 (1911), whence this entry is taken.

4900 A Treaty of Friendship held with the Chiefs of the Six Nations at Philadelphia, in September and October, 1736. *Philadelphia, 1737, F°.* EU.

4901 Port of Charles-Town in South Carolina, November 1, 1736. An Account of sundry Goods Imported, and of sundry Goods of the Produce of this Province Exported, from the Year 1724, to the Year 1735. With the Number of Vessels entered and cleared each year. And a particular Account of the last Year. *Charles-Town, 1736, s. sh. obl. F°.* L.

FINANCE

4902 An Essay on the Sinking Fund. Wherein the Nature thereof is fully explained; and the Right of the Publick to that Fund asserted and maintained. *Lond. 1736, 8°.* LU.

2nd edn., corrected and much enlarged, 1737 (LU).

4903 A Dialogue between a Gentleman and Broker, concerning the Funds. To which is prefix'd, a Letter to Sir. R. Walpole. *Lond. 1736*, 8°. O.

Reprinted from *The Daily Journal*. The author's prefatory letter signed: J.S

4904 A Proposal humbly offer'd to the Consideration of the Members of the Legislature, for Raising a Certain Yearly Revenue to the Crown by a New Act of Parliament to be made for the better Regulating of Measure in Respect to Liquors; as Wine, Brandy, Rum, Cyder, Beer, Ale, Mum, &c. Such as are vended in Publick Houses, Cellars, Vaults; Or otherwise in Glass Bottles, Stone, or other Earthen Vessels.... *n.p.* [*1736?*], *F°*. L.

Signed A.M.

4905 A Collection of several Statutes and Clauses now in force, relating to the Duties upon Spirits, Malt, Candles, Sope, Callicoes, Starch, and Coffee, Tea, and Chocolate. With an Abridgment of the said Statutes and Clauses, and a Tables of the Rates upon several Commodities, shewing by what Acts they are Imposed. *Edin. 1736*, 8°. LU.

4906 The Case of the Dealers in Tea. *n.p.* [*1736*], *s. sh. F°*. LU.

For a duty ad valorem instead of the flat rate of 4/- a lb.

4907 A Scheme Humbly Offer'd to prevent the Clandestine Importation of Tea. *n.p.* [*1736*], *s. sh. F°*. LU.

For revising the duties.

4908 The Case of the Vagrant-Money, &c. *n.p.* [*1736?*], *s. sh. F°*. L.

Endorsed: The Case of the Vagrant-Money, &c. rais'd on the Inhabitants of the County Middlesex. Alleging misappropriation.

4909 A Bill for continuing the Duty of two Pennies Scots, or one sixth of a Penny Sterling, on each Pint of Ale and Beer, that shall be vended or sold, within the City of Glasgow and Villages of Garbells and Port-Glasgow, and Privileges thereof, for the Benefit of the said City and Villages. *n.p.* [*1736*], *F°*. LU.

4910 The Case of the Feuars, Land Owners, and other Inhabitants of the Village of Gorbells, with respect to the Bill for continuing the Duty of two Pennies Scots, or one Sixth of a Penny Sterling, on each Pint of Ale and Beer that shall be vended and sold within the City of Glasgow, and extending the same over the Villages of Gorbells and Port Glasgow, &c. *n.p.* [*1736*], *F°*. LLI.

4911 The Case of the Magistrates, and Town Council of the City of Glasgow. *n.p.* [*1736*], *F°*. LLI.

Against vesting the city's right to the product of the tax on ale in the Crown in order to compensate Daniel Campbell for damages sustained in the late riot.

4912 A Bill for laying a Duty of Two Pennies Scots, or one Sixth part of a Penny Sterling, upon every Scots Pint of Ale and Beer, brewed, or brought into, and sold, within the Town of Irvine and Liberties thereof: And for laying a Duty of One Penny Sterling upon every Tun, or Ten Horse-Loads of Coals, Carried to the Harbour of the said Town, and Shipped there for Transportation. *n.p.* [*1736*], *F°*. L.

4913 [Besse, Joseph]. A Brief Account of Many of the Prosecutions of the People call'd Quakers in the Exchequer, Ecclesiastical, and Other Courts, for Demands Recoverable by the Acts made in the 7th and 8th Years of the Reign of King William the Third, for the more Easie Recovery of Tithes, Church Rates, &c. Humbly submitted to the Consideration of the Members of both Houses of Parliament. *Lond. 1736*, *8°*. L.

For authorship see Joseph Smith, *A Descriptive Catalogue of Friends' Books*, 1867, I, 254.

4914 A Bill to enlarge, amend and render more effectual the Laws now in being for the more easy Recovery of Tythes, Church Rates and Oblations, and other Ecclesiastical Dues, from the People called Quakers. *n.p.* [*1736*], *F°*. LU.

Another edn., entitled: An Act for the more easy Recovery of Tythes...[1736], F°. (LU).

4915 The Case of the People called Quakers. *n.p.* [*1736?*], *s. sh. F°*. LU.

Against tithes.

4916 Papers relating to the Quakers Tythe Bill: viz. I. Extracts from the yearly Epistles of Meeting of Quakers....II. Remarks upon a Bill now depending in Parliament....III. The Country Parson's Plea against the Quakers Tythe Bill....IV. The Case of the People called Quakers. *Lond. 1736*, *8°*. O.

4917 Papers relating to the Quakers Tythe Bill: viz. I. The Case of the People Called Quakers. II. Extracts from the yearly Epistles of Meeting of Quakers, held in London relating to Tythes. III. A Supplemental Extract from the Quakers yearly Epistles relating to their Sufferings. IV. Remarks upon a Bill now depending in Parliament, to enlarge, amend, and render more effectual the Laws now in being for the more easy Recovering of Tythes, Church-rates, and Oblations, and other Ecclesiastical Dues from the People called Quakers: And also Remarks upon a printed Paper, intitled, The Case of the People called Quakers. V. The Country Parson's Plea against the Quakers Tythe Bill.... *Lond. 1736*, *8°*. L.

4th edn. 1736 (C). Another edn. Dublin, 1736, 'to which is added, An Answer to the Country Parson's Plea against the Quakers Tythe Bill, In a letter to the R.R. Author. By a Member of the House of Commons' (L). 6th edn. Dublin, 1737 (C).

4918 [Sherlock, Thomas]. The Country Parson's Plea, against the Quakers Bill for Tythes; humbly addressed to the Honourable the Commons of Great Britain in Parliament assembled. *Lond.* [*1736*], *F°*. LU.

For authorship see John Hervey, Baron Hervey, *Memoirs*, ed. by R. Sedgwick, 1931, II, 531.

4919 An Answer to the Country Parson's Plea against the Quakers Tythe-Bill. In a Letter to the R. R. Author. By a Member of the House of Commons. *Lond.* [*1736*], *8⁰*. O.

2nd edn. corrected 1736 (O); 3rd edn. 1736 (O); another edn. Dublin, 1736 (DNL). Attributed to 'Lord Harvey' in Joseph Smith's *Descriptive Catalogue of Friends Books*, II, 461, but Hervey states clearly (*Memoirs*, 1931, II, 531) that he wrote *The Quaker's Reply* and he is not likely to have written more than one pamphlet in this controversy.

4920 [HERVEY, JOHN, Baron Hervey]. The Quaker's Reply to the Country Parson's Plea, against the Quakers Bill for Tythes. *Lond.* [*1736*], *8⁰*. O.

For authorship see Hervey, *Memoirs*, 1931, II, 531.

4921 Extracts from the Yearly Epistles of Meeting of Quakers held in London, relating to Tythes. *n.p.* [*1736*], *F⁰*. LU.

4922 The Poor Vicar's Plea against the Quakers Bill as it stands at present Address'd to his Representatives in Parliament. *n.p.* [*1736*], *F⁰*. LSC.

Signed: A.B. Another edn. entitled: The Poor Vicar's Plea against the Quakers Bill, and for the present Benefit of Recovering his Small Tythes by the Help of the Ecclesiastical Court. Address'd to his Representatives in Parliament. n.p. [1736], 4⁰ (L).

4923 [GIBSON, EDMUND, Bishop of London]. Remarks upon a Bill now depending in Parliament, to enlarge, amend and render more effectual the Laws now in being, for the more easy Recovery of Tythes, Church-rates and Oblations, and other Ecclesiastical Dues from the People call'd Quakers: And also, Remarks upon a printed Paper, entitl'd, The Case of the People called Quakers. *n.p.* [*1736*], *F⁰*. LU.

For authorship see *D.N.B.* and Joseph Smith, *A Descriptive Catalogue of Friends' Books*, 1867, II, 460.

4924 SYNGE, EDWARD, Bishop of Ferns and Leighlin. Two Affidavits in relation to the demands of Tythe-Agistment in the Dioces of Leighlin; with an Introduction. *Dublin, 1736, 12⁰*. DA.

4925 Prescription Sacred: or, Reasons for Opposing the New Demand of Herbage in Ireland. [*Dublin*], *1736, 8⁰*. L.

DA copy has a ms. note: 'By Mr Nicholson of yᵉ Com—— of Meath [and in another hand] or by Mr Samuel Blackwood a Lawyer'. 2nd edn. 1736 (DA).

4926 [MACAULAY, ALEXANDER]. Property Inviolable: or, Some Remarks upon a Pamphlet entituled, Prescription Sacred. *Dublin, 1736, 8⁰*. L.

DA copy has a ms. note: 'Said to be written by Alexander McAuley'. See also L. Landa, *Swift and the Church of Ireland*, 1954, p. 140.

4927 The Report from the Committee appointed to take into Consideration the Petition of Samuel Low, and Others, (whose Names are thereunto Subscribed) in behalf of Themselves, and the Rest of the Gentlemen and Land-holders in this Kingdom. In relation to the New Demand of Tythe Agistment of Dry and Barren Cattle. Reported on the 18th Day of March, 1735. Published by Order of the House of Commons. *Dublin, 1735–6, F⁰*. LU.

4928 FOLKES, MARTIN. A Table of English Gold Coins, from the Eighteenth Year of King Edward III. when Gold was first coined in England. With their several Weights, and present intrinsic Values. *Lond. 1736, 4º.* LU.

Another edn. 1745, with silver coins and an appendix on Scottish coins; another edn. 1763 (both LU).

4929 To the Honourable the Knights, Citizens, and Burgesses of Great Britain, in Parliament assembled. Reasons for Rectifying an Error in the Standard of our Coins. By which Error, Great Britain, Ireland, and all His Majesty's Subjects, have lost an inconceivable Treasure, and many thousand Fair Traders become Bankrupts; to the Lessening the Publick Revenues, and great Increase of Taxes; the Discouragement of our Coinage, and the Distress and Hazard of all His Majesty's Subjects. As also, For bringing in a Bill effectually to encourage the Coinage of British Money of the True Standard, which will be a Loss to any Body to melt or export; and for making His Majesty's Mints the best Markets for Gold and Silver, as they ought always to be, though hitherto the worst. *n.p.* [*1736?*], *Fº*. L.

4930 An Answer to the Remonstrances of the People of Ireland against making any Alteration in the Coin. By their Friends in Great Britain, Containing Reasons for Regulating the Coin, with regard to the Trade between the two Kingdoms. *Lond. printed, Dublin reprinted, 1736, 12º*. L.

4931 A Letter from a Gentleman in the North of Ireland, to his Friend in Dublin, in Relation to the Regulation of the Coin. *Dublin, 1736, 8º*. DA.

4932 [SWIFT, JONATHAN]. A Letter from the Revd. J.S.D.S.P.D. to a Country Gentleman in the North of Ireland. *n.p. 1736, 8º*. L.

Signed: A. North. On coinage. A reprint of no. 19 of *The Intelligencer*.

4933 Reasons why we should not Lower the Coins now Current in this Kingdom. Occasion'd by a Paper, intitled, Remarks on the Coins Current in this Kingdom. *Dublin, 1736, 8º*. L.

Another edn. Dublin, n.d., 'To which is added, The Rev. Dean Swift's Opinion, delivered by him, in an Assembly of above One hundred and Fifty eminent Merchants who met at the Guild Hall, on Saturday the 24th of April, 1736, in order to draw up their Petition, and Present it to his Grace the Lord-Lieutenant against lowering said Coin' (L).

4934 Some Considerations on Lowering the Gold. *Dublin, 1736, Fº*. DA.

Signed: J——.

4935 Remarks upon a Paper Just Publish'd, intitled, Some Considerations on Lowering the Gold. *Dublin, 1736, 8º*. LU.

4936 Some Observations on the Present Currency, as well as the Intrinsick Value of the Several Coins in this Kingdom. In a Letter to A.S. Esq; *Dublin, 1736, 8º*. DA.

Signed: Mercator. Wagner (no. 164) considers that Sir John Browne was probably the author.

4937 A short Account of the Rise and present State of the Amicable Society for a Perpetual Assurance-Office. Together with the Manner, Terms and Advantages of their Insurances on Lives. *n.p.* [*1736*], *8o*. L.

Dated: May 27, 1736. Another edn. dated: July 9, 1742 (C).

4938 MAIR, JOHN. Book-keeping Methodiz'd; or, A Methodical Treatise of Merchant-Accompts, according to the Italian Form. Wherein the Theory of the Art is fully Explained, and reduced to Practice, by Variety of suitable Examples in all Branches of Trade.... *Edin. 1736*, *8o*. LICA.

Another edn. Dublin, 1737; 2nd edn. Edin. 1741; 3rd edn. Edin. 1749 (all LICA); many later editions.

TRANSPORT

4939 BADESLADE, THOMAS. The New Cut Canal, intended for improving the Navigation of the City of Chester, with the Low Lands adjacent to the River Dee, compared with the Welland, alias Spalding River, now Silted up, and Deeping-Fens adjacent, now Drowned....With a Defence of those Gentlemen who have been Undertakers to Drain Deeping-Fens, against the Reflections of Mr. Grundy.... *Chester*, [*1736*], *Fo*. L.

4940 GRUNDY, JOHN. An Examination and Refutation of Mr. Badeslade's New-cut Canal, &c. by Quotations from his own Words, as well as from Observations and Experiments made upon the River Welland, and the Country adjacent, in the Years 1731, 2, 3, 4, 5, and 6. Done for the Use of Drainers.... *Lond. 1736*, *4o*. O.

4941 A Bill to improve and make Navigable the River Ouze and Swale, from St. Mary's-Gate in the City of York, to Murton Bridge in the County of York; and to improve the Navigation of the River Dun, from Wilsick-house in the Parish of Barmby-Dun, to Sike-house-Ferry in the said County. *n.p.* [*1736*], *Fo*. L.

4942 A Bill to Explain and Amend an Act passed in the fourth and fifth Year of the Reign of her late Majesty Queen Anne, for making the River Stower navigable, from the Town of Manningtree in the County of Essex, to Sudbury in the County of Suffolk. *n.p.* [*1736*], *Fo*. L.

4943 Reasons for applying to Parliament, in order to explain and make more effectual the Act for amending the Strait Northern Road between Biggleswade and Alconbury White Post. *n.p.* [*1736?*], *Fo*. M (Cr).

4944 A Bill for Enlarging the Term and Powers granted by an Act passed in the Eleventh Year of the Reign of his late Majesty King George the First, intituled, An Act for repairing and amending the Road from Biggleswade in the County of Bedford to Bugden...and from the said Town of Bugden to the Town of Huntingdon.... *n.p.* [*1736*], *Fo*. L.

4945 A Bill for continuing the Term and Powers granted by an Act passed in the Fourth Year of the Reign of his late Majesty King George the First, Entitled, An Act for Repairing the Highways from Crown-Corner in the Town of Reading, (leading by and through the several Parishes of Shinfield and Heckfield...) to Basingstoke.... *n.p.* [*1736*], *F*o. L.

4946 A Bill for repairing the Highways from Sunning-Lane End next Twyford, to the Old Bear Inn in Reading in the County of Berks. *n.p.* [*1736*], *F*o. L.

4947 A Bill for Repairing and Widening the Road leading from the Water-side at Whitstable to St. Dunstan's Cross, near the City of Canterbury, in the County of Kent. *n.p.* [*1736*], *F*o. L.

4948 By the King, A Proclamation, For putting in Execution the Laws made to prevent tumults and riotous Assemblies, and for the more effectual punishing wicked and evil-disposed Persons going armed in disguise; and for punishing such Persons as shall wilfully and maliciously pull down or destroy Turnpikes for repairing Highways erected by Authority of Parliament; and for apprehending and bringing to Justice the Persons, who in September last were concerned in pulling down and destroying the Turnpikes so erected at Ledbury, in the County of Hereford.... *Lond. 1735* [*o.s.*], *s. sh. F*o. L.

Dated: 5 February 1735.

4949 A Bill for Enabling the Mayor, Bailiffs, and Burgesses of the Borough of New Windsor in the County of Berks, to repair and maintain their great Bridge over the River of Thames, leading from the said Borough of New Windsor to Eton in the County of Bucks. *n.p.* [*1736*], *F*o. L.

4950 A Bill for Building a Bridge cross the River Thames, from the New Palace Yard in the City of Westminster, to the opposite Side in the County of Surry. *n.p.* [*1736*], *F*o. L.

4951 An Abstract of the Act for building a Bridge cross the River Thames, from the New Palace Yard in the City of Westminster, to the opposite Shore in the County of Surrey. To which are added, the Terms of Insurances for the Benefit of the Adventurers, from (at least) one half of the Loss they must (otherwise) sustain by their Blanks, in the Lottery for Building a Bridge cross the said River as they are now finally settled and fixed.... *Lond. 1736, 8*o. O.

4952 Hawksmoor, Nicholas. A Short Historical Account of London-Bridge; with a Proposition for a New Stone-Bridge at Westminster. As also An Account of some Remarkable Stone-Bridges Abroad, and what the best Authors have said and directed concerning the Methods of Building them. Illustrated with proper Cuts.... *Lond. 1736, 4*o. LU.

4953 James, John. A Short Review of the several Pamphlets, and Schemes, that have been offered to the Publick, in relation to the Building of a Bridge at Westminster. With Remarks on the different Calculations made of the Rise and Fall of Water, which the Peers of a Stone-Bridge may occasion. To which are added, Some Hints and Computations that may be of Use for the better Understanding the Nature and Difficulty of such a Work. *Lond. 1736, 8o*. LG.

4954 Langley, Batty. A Design for the Bridge at New Palace yard, Westminster....With Observations on the several Designs published to this Time.... *Lond. 1736, 8o*. L.

4955 Conjectures as to the most proper Place, between Scotland-yard, and Vaux-hall, for Erecting a Bridge cross the River Thames, from Westminster to the opposite Surrey-shoar. Humbly submitted to the Consideration of the Honourable House of Commons. *n.p.* [*1736*], *s. sh. Fo*. L.

4956 Observations relating to the building of a Bridge. Most humbly submitted to both Houses of Parliament. *n.p.* [*1736*], *s. sh. Fo*. LU.

For a bridge over the Thames at the Horse Ferry rather than at Palace Yard.

4957 Reasons against Building a Bridge over the Thames at Westminster. *n.p.* [*1736*], *s. sh. Fo*. L.

4958 A Scheme for raising 60,000 l. without any Tax, upon the Inhabitants of the City of Westminster, for the building a Bridge cross the River of Thames, the Legs of Stone, and the Arches turn'd with Bricks (made on purpose, like those used in the Dome of St. Paul's which is 110 Foot wide) after the manner of the Brick-Bridge of Thoulouse, the greatest Arch of which is 100 Foot span; and to become a free Bridge in twenty-one Years, except a Small Duty to keep it in repair. By a Member of the Society, who have met in order to obtain a Bill. *n.p.* [*1736?*], *s. sh. Fo*. L.

4959 The Scheme delivered to the Members of the Honourable House of Commons, for raising 60000 l. to build a Bridge after the manner of that at Thoulouse: Examined in the Following Manner, By a Private Gentleman, who wishes Success to so laudable a Design. *n.p.* [*1736?*] *s. sh. Fo*. L.

4960 Some Considerations humbly offered to the Honourable Commissioners appointed by Act of Parliament for Building a Stone-Bridge over the River Thames, from the New Palace Yard, at Westminster to the opposite shore at Lambeth. Together with some Proposals relating to a Design Annexed, drawn for that Purpose. In a Letter to a Member of the Honourable House of Commons. The Second Edition. *Lond. 1736, 8o*. LG.

4961 Some Reasons for a small Lottery at this Time, for the Publick Uses herein after-mentioned. Humbly offered to the Consideration of both Houses of Parliament. *n.p.* [*1736*], *s. sh. Fo*. L.

For building a bridge at Westminster.

SOCIAL CONDITIONS

4962 A New Scheme for Reducing the Laws relating to the Poor into One Act of Parliament, and for the better providing the Impotent Poor with Necessaries, the Industrious with Work, and, for the Correction of the Idle Poor. *Lond. 1736, 8o*. LU.

2nd edn. 1737 (L).

4963 A Bill for the better Relief and Employment of the Poor, and for the more effectual punishing Rogues and Vagabonds; and for reducing the Laws relating to the Poor, and to Rogues and Vagabonds, into one Law. *n.p. [1736], Fo*. L.

4964 Izacke, Richard. An Alphabetical Register of divers Persons, who by their Last Wills...have given Tenements, Rents, Annuities, and Monies, towards the Relief of the Poor of the County of Devon, and City and County of Exon....By Richard Izacke....Faithfully printed from his original Manuscript....By Samuel Izacke. *Lond. 1736, 8o*. L.

4965 A Bill for the more equal Paying and better Collecting certain small Sums for Relief of Shipwrecked Mariners and Distressed Persons, His Majesty's Subjects, in the Ports of Cadiz and Port Saint Mary's in the Kingdom of Spain, or other Pious and Christian Uses, usually contributed to by the Merchants trading to the said Ports. *n.p. [1736], Fo*. L.

4966 [Gairdner, Andrew]. An Abstract of the Regulations and Statutes of the Charity-School, Orphan-Hospital and Work-House at Edinburgh. *Edin. 1736, 8o*. EP.

For authorship see H. & L. quoting New College Catalogue.

4967 A Further Account of the State of the Orphan-School, Hospital and Workhouse at Edinburgh. *Edin. 1736, 8o*. O.

4968 A Bill for the more easy and speedy Recovery of small Debts within the City of London, and the Liberties thereof. *n.p. [1736], Fo*. L.

4969 The Case of Peter Burton, James Mount, Edward Hasted, Henry Hatt, George Grew, Edmund Newton, Thomas Sheppard, and William Calvert, Clerk-Sitters of the Poultry and Woodstreet Compters, in the City of London, whose Freeholds will be greatly prejudiced, if not entirely destroyed in Case....A Bill for the more Easy and Speedy Recovery of small Debts within the City of London, should pass into a Law. *n.p. [1736], s. sh. Fo*. L.

4970 The Case of William Stewart and Samuel Wright, Clerks of the Papers of the Poultry and Woodstreet Compters in London; Whose Property will be greatly affected, if the Bill now depending in the Honourable House of Commons for the more easy and speedy Recovery of small Debts within the City of London, should pass into Law. *n.p. [1736?], s. sh. Fo*. LU.

4971 Reasons Against the Bill For the more easy and speedy Recovery of Small Debts, within the City of London and Liberties thereof; as the Same tends to erect a New Judicature, and humbly representing that the Extending the Jurisdiction of the present Court of Conscience, and preventing the Removal of Causes from the Mayors and Sheriffs Courts of the said City, will more effectually answer the Title of the said Bill. *n.p.* [*1736*], *s. sh. F°.* L.

4972 Reasons humbly offered in Favour of the Bill (now depending in Parliament) For the more easy and speedy Recovery of Small Debts within the City of London, and the Liberties thereof. *n.p.* [*1736*], *s. sh. F°.* MC.

4973 A Bill to enable the Justices of the Peace, acting for the Western Division of the County of Kent, to purchase a convenient Piece of Ground for building a Gaol for the said County, and for impowering the said Justices to apply part of the County Stock of the said Division towards the same. *n.p.* [*1736*], *F°.* L.

4974 [Jones, Erasmus]. Luxury, Pride, and Vanity, the Bane of the British Nation. *Lond.* [*1736*], *8°.* pp. 63. LU.

2nd edn., pp. 61, [1736] (LU); another edn. pp. 61, [1736] (LU). For authorship see *Notes and Queries*, vol. XI (1855), 419.

4975 A Collection of all the Pamphlets that were written pro and con on the British Distillery, whilst the Act for laying a Duty upon the Retailers of Spirituous Liquors, and for Licensing the Retailers thereof, was depending in Parliament. *n.p. 1736*, *8°.* MP.

An edition in one volume of nos. 4979, 4980, 4983–4, 4992–4.

4976 The Case of such of the Distillers as are the Younger Branch of the Trade. *n.p.* [*1736*], *F°.* pp. 3. LU.

4977 The Case of the Distillers Company, and Proposals for the better Regulating the Trade. *n.p.* [*1736?*], *F°.* LU.

4978 The Case of the Malt-Distillers, &c. *n.p.* [*1736*], *s. sh. F°.* LU.

4979 A Collection of Letters published in the Daily Papers relating to the British Distillery. *Lond. 1736*, *8°.* LU.

Signed: A Man of Kent.

4980 [Wilson, Thomas]. Distilled Spirituous Liquors the Bane of the Nation: being some Considerations humbly offer'd to the Hon. the House of Commons....To which is added, An Appendix containing the late Presentments of the Grand-Juries of London, Middlesex, and the Tower-Hamlets.... *Lond. 1736*, *8°.* LU.

2nd edn., 1736 (LU). For authorship see John Nichols, *Literary Anecdotes*, VIII (1814), 458.

4981 The Case of the Merchants, and Others, of the City of Bristol, Trading to the British Colonies in America. *n.p.* [*1736*], *s. sh. F°.* LU.

Against the duty on spirits.

4982 The Case of the Sugar-Trade, with Regard to the Duties intended to be laid on all Spirituous Liquors, Sold by Retail. *n.p.* [*1736*], *F*°. LU.

4983 An Impartial Enquiry into the Present State of the British Distillery; Plainly demonstrating the Evil Consequences of imposing any Additional Duties on British Spirits.... Wherein also the manifest Absurdities and gross Impositions on the Publick contained in a printed Pamphlet, entituled, Distilled Spirituous Liquors the Bane of the Nation. are fully Detected and Exposed. *Lond. 1736, 8*°. LU.

2nd edn. 1736 (O).

4984 A Supplement to the Impartial Enquiry into the Present State of the British Distillery. In Answer to the Second Edition of a Pamphlet, intituled, Spirituous Liquors the Bane of the Nation.... *Lond.* [*1736*], *8*°. LU.

4985 A Letter from a Member of Parliament to his Friend in the Country, containing, his Reasons for being against the late Act for preventing the Retail of Spirituous Liquors; in which the great Increase of the Civil List by this Act will be particularly considered. *Lond.* [*1736*], *8*°. L.

4986 The Life of Mother Gin; containing a true and faithful Relation of her Conduct and Politicks, in all the various and important Occurrences of State that she was engaged in during her Time.... *Lond. 1736, 8*°. L.

4987 Entry cancelled.

4988 Observations on the Case of the Working Coopers to the Distillers in and about the City of London. Humbly offered to the Considerations of the Honourable House of Commons. *n.p.* [*1736*], *s. sh. F*°. MP.

4989 Occasional Remarks upon the Act for laying a Duty upon the Retalers of Spirituous Liquors, &c. and for Licensing the Retalers thereof. *Lond. 1736, 8*°. LU.

4990 [Robe, Thomas]. A Proposal to Prevent the Common Tippling of Spirituous Liquors, in such manner as shall not any ways prejudice the Publick Revenue: as also, Means to Encourage the Exportation of Manufactur'd Spirits for foreign Markets.... *n.p.* [*1736*], *s. sh. F*°. LU.

Signed: Eboranos. For Robe's use of this pseudonym see *Ways and Means whereby his Majesty may Man his Navy*, 1734 (no. 4648).

4991 Reasons humbly Offer'd to the Honourable House of Commons, For the effectual Suppressing the excessive Drinking of the Liquor commonly called Gin, or Compound Spirits. *n.p.* [*1736?*], *s. sh. F*°. L.

4992 [Holden, Adam]. The Trial of the Spirits: or Some Considerations upon the Pernicious Consequences of the Gin-Trade to Great Britain.... By a Lover of Mankind. *Lond. 1736, 8*°. LU.

Signed: Philanthropos. 2nd edn. 1736 (LU). The Vindication of this, presumably by the same author, bears Holden's name.

4993 A Proper Reply to a Scandalous Libel, intituled, The Trial of the Spirits.... *Lond.* [*1736*], *8°*. L.

Signed: T.S. 2nd edn., with additions, [1736] (LU).

4994 HOLDEN, ADAM. A Vindication of a Pamphlet lately published, intituled The Tryal of the Spirits. Together with Some Observations relating to the West-India Trade, and the Encouragement of our Sugar Colonies abroad, and our useful Manufactures at home.... *Lond.* *1736*, *8°*. LU.

4995 RUDD, SAYER. To the Honourable the Commissioners of His Majesty's Excise. The Case of Dr Sayer Rudd, in Answer to An Information lodged against him, in the Excise Office, London, for retaling Spirituous Liquors. *n.p.* [*1736*], *s. sh. F°*. L.

Maintaining that he only sells 'a real Medicinal Cordial'.

4996 An Abstract of the Number of Protestant and Popish Families in the several Counties and Provinces of Ireland, taken from the Returns made by the Hearthmoney Collectors, to the Hearthmoney Office in Dublin, in the Years 1732 and 1733....With Observations. *Dublin*, *1736*, *8°*. L.

Wagner (no. 157) had seen a copy with a ms. attribution to David Bindon. He considered the attribution doubtful since he thought mistakenly that Bindon died in 1733.

4997 The Governours of the Bounty of Queen Anne for the Augmentation of the Maintenance of the Poor Clergy, made and established for that Purpose, are impowered to augment all Livings, not exceeding 50 l. per Annum; and the Number of Livings following have been certified to be capable of Augmentation. *n.p.* [*1736?*], *s. sh. F°*. LSC.

4998 The Return made by the Governors of the Bounty of Queen Anne, for the Augmentation of the Maintenance of the Poor Clergy, pursuant to an Order of the House of Lords of the 16th of April last: Together with an Account of what Sums of Money have been received by the said Governors for First Fruits and Tenths; and of what Sums of Money they have received, and from whom, for the Increase of the said Bounty in each Year since their Incorporation; what Part of those Sums have been laid out in each Year, and to what Uses, and what Part is now in their Hands, and where deposited.... *Lond.* *1736*, *F°*. O.

4999 A Bill, for the better Lighting the Streets of the City of London. *n.p.* [*1736*], *F°*. L.

5000 A Bill to Enable Thomas Smith, Esq. Lord of the Manor of Farlington, in the County of Southampton, to supply the Town of Portsmouth and Ports adjacent with Good and Wholesome Water, at his own proper Cost and Charges. *n.p.* [*1736*], *F°*. L.

1737

GENERAL

5001 Seasonable Observations on the present Fatal Declension of the General Commerce of England. In which the genuine Cause of the Decay of our Woollen Manufactures is particularly considered. And Plain and Parcticable [*sic*] Methods proposed for retrieving the National Trade, before it be past Recovery.... *Lond. 1737*, 8°. LU.

5002 A Brief Enquiry into the Nature and Use of Premiums, with respect to Trade. *Dublin, 1737*, 8°. DA.

5003 Plan by the Commissioners and Trustees for Improving Fisheries and Manufactures in Scotland, for the Application of the Funds under their Management for three Years, from Christmas 1736. [*Edin. 1737*], 8°. L.

Subsequently published triennially in 1740, 1743, 1746 and 1749 (all E).

5004 Act of the Town-Council of Edinburgh, touching the Admission of Unfreemen. [*Edin. 1737*], *s. sh. F°*. EU.

Dated: 9 February 1737.

5005 Act of the Town-council of Edinburgh, appointing the Apprentices and Servants of the Freemen of the said City, who have deserted their Service at, or since the 7th September 1736, to return thereto in a limited time. [*Edin. 1737*], *s. sh. F°*. EP.

Dated: 19 January 1737.

5006 Povey, Charles. The English Memorial to obtain Right and Property, as promised in His Majesty's Speech from the Throne: humbly presented to the King, Lords, and Commons, for the Restoration of an Estate and Fortune taken away by the Crown and Parliament, contrary to the Laws of Great-Britain.... *Lond. 1737*, *F°*. LU.

On the thwarting of his various schemes.

AGRICULTURE

5007 The best Mine above Ground; or, The most laudable and most certain Means of Enriching this Nation, by improving our Agriculture; and procuring the best Manure yet invented, at the most reasonable Expence.... *Lond. 1737*, 8°. L.

2nd edn. 1739 (LU); 3rd edn. Dublin 1742 (L), with introductory letters by Samuel Trowell and Philip Peck. Advocating the use of Thomas Liveings's patent salt compound.

5008 Dunbar, James. The Industrious Country-Man and Virtuous House-Wife's Companion. *Edin. 1737*, 8°. E.

Mostly hints on farming.

5009 [Macaulay, Alexander]. Some Thoughts on the Tillage of Ireland:

Humbly dedicated to the Parliament. To which is prefixed, A Letter to the Printer, from the Reverend Doctor Swift, Dean of St. Patricks', recommending the following Treatise. *Lond.* *1737*, *8°*. L.

Another edn. Dublin, 1738 (C); 3rd edn. Dublin, 1741 (DA). For authorship see ms. note in the C copy of the 1738 edition.

5010 A Bill for dividing and inclosing certain Open and Common Fields within the Lordship and Parish of Stallingborough, in the County of Lincoln. *n.p.* [*1737*], *F°*. L.

5011 An Act for Dividing and Inclosing certain Open and Common Fields, within the Lordship and Parish of Stallingborough, in the County of Lincoln. *n.p.* *1736–7*, *F°*. L.

5012 An Act for Inclosing and Dividing certain Common Pasture Grounds, called Purton Common and Purton Stoake Common, within the Parish of Purton, otherwise Puriton, in the County of Wilts. *n.p.* [*1737*], *F°*. L.

A bill.

5013 [Lee, Weyman]. An Essay to ascertain the Value of Leases and Annuities for Years and Lives, and to estimate the Chances of the Duration of Lives. Wherein are Many Observations on Bills of Mortality, on the State of the Coin, the Interest of Money, and the Price of Things, in different Ages: And Notice taken of several Writers on this Subject; and their Rules and Tables, particularly for the Valuation of Annuities for one or more Lives, are demonstrated to be erroneous. *Lond.* *1737*, *8°*. O.

The preface signed: W.L. Another edn., with author's name, 1738 (LU). John Richards in the preface to *Annuities on Lives*, 1739, thinks that Weyman Lee may, like Everard Fleetwood, be a pseudonym of Samuel Burroughs.

5014 A Proposal for the Satisfaction of the Demands of the Proprietors of the Water-works Bonds, and of all Persons claiming the said Bonds. *n.p.* [*1737?*], *s. sh. F°*. EU.

York Buildings Company.

5015 A Dialogue between an English-Man and a Dutch-Man, on the Subject of Trade, more especially the Fishing Trade....The Third Edition. *Lond.* *1737*, *8°*. LU.

5016 A Representation of the State of the English Oyster-Fisheries; and of the Hardships and Discouragements the Oyster-Dredgers of this Kingdom labour under, from the Duties upon Foreign Oysters imported being payable Ad Valorem on the Oaths of the Importers. With the Case and Observations stated on the Importers side. *Lond.* *1737*, *8°*. LU.

Includes nos. 5017–21.

5017 The Case of the Oyster-Dredgers, or Fisherman of the Oyster-Fisheries in Kent, Essex, Sussex and Southampton. With some Observations humbly addressed to the Honourable the House of Commons. *n.p.* [*1737*], *F°*. LU.

Endorsed: The Case of the English Oyster-Dredgers.

5018 The Case of the Essex Importers of French Oysters; Humbly submitted to the Consideration of the Honourable the House of Commons. *n.p.* [*1737*], *F°*. LU.

Endorsed: The Case of the Importers of Foreign Oysters.

5019 The Reply of the Oyster-Dredgers, or Fishermen of the Oyster-Fisheries in Kent, Essex, Sussex and Southampton; to the Case of the Essex Importers of French Oysters, humbly addressed to the Honourable the House of Commons. *n.p.* [*1737*], *F°*. LU.

Endorsed: A Reply to the Case of the Importers of French Oysters.

5020 Observations on the Reply of the Kentish, &c. Oyster-Dredgers to the Essex Importers Case. Humbly submitted to the Consideration of the Honourable the House of Commons. *n.p.* [*1737*], *s. sh. F°*. LU.

5021 Remarks on the Essex Importers Observations, &c. Humbly addressed to the Honourable the House of Commons. *n.p.* [*1737*], *s. sh. F°*. LU.

5022 A Friend in Need is a Friend in Deed: or, a Project, at this Critical Juncture, to gain the Nation a hundred thousand Pounds per Annum from the Dutch; by an Irish Whale Fishery. Inscrib'd to Arthur Dobbs Esq;.... *Dublin*, *1737*, *8°*. DG.

MANUFACTURES

5023 Hoppus, Edward. The Gentlemen's and Builder's Repository: or, Architecture Display'd.... *Lond.* *1737*, *4°*. LRIBA.

3rd edn. 1748 (L). The first edition, not seen, was published in 1728 under the title: Architectura Civilis.

5024 Salmon, William. The Country Builder's Estimator: or, the Architect's Companion. For Estimating of New Buildings, or Repairing of Old.... *Colchester*, [*1737?*], *12°*. LU.

Another issue, with an additional title-page bearing the imprint of James Hodges, Lond. n.d. (K); another issue, Lond. 1737 (K); 2nd edn., revised by E. Hoppus, Lond. 1737 (O); 3rd edn. 1746 (L); 4th edn. 1752 (L); and at least 5 later edns.

5025 [Tracy, John]. To the Right Honourable the Lord-Mayor and Court of Aldermen, assembled. A Proposal for preventing the Daily Abuses committed on the City Estates, and all other belonging to his Majesty's Subjects. *n.p.* [*1737?*], *s. sh. F°*. OUP.

Title taken from endorsement. Signed by author in ms. Proposing more stringent building regulations.

5026 The Case of the Paper-Makers. Humbly addressed to the Honourable the House of Commons. *n.p.* [*1737*], *F°*. LU.

Against the drawback of the duty on foreign paper granted to the university presses. Each copy has the name of the maker of the paper on which it is printed.

5027 The Case of the Stationers and Paper-Makers, and so forth, in the Kingdom of England. Humbly Addressed to the Honourable the House of Commons. *n.p.* [*1737 ?*], *s. sh. F°*. LU.

Against the drawback of the duty on foreign paper granted to the university presses.

5028 [Webb, Daniel]. The Sinking State of the Woollen Exportation-Trade and therein the Landed as well as Trading Interest in general: With the Cause thereof. Humbly represented by the British Woollen-Manufacturers, to the Honourable the Members of Parliament. With a Description of the Value of the real British and Irish Golden Fleece: or, An Estimate of the present Loss to this Trading Kingdom, by Exporting ours and the Irish Wool unmanufactur'd, and Woollen Goods also out of Ireland to Foreign Parts.... *Lond. 1737*, *F°*. LU.

For authorship see LPRO, C.O. 388/94.

5029 Some Considerations for Employing the Poor of this Kingdom and for Improving the Linnen and Woollen Manufactories; which is now in the greatest Decay, and loudly calls for the Aid of Parliament. By a Member of the House of Commons. *Lond. 1737*, *8°*. LU.

COMMERCE

5030 A Bill for the better Encouragement of Learning, by the more effectual Securing the Copies of Printed Books to the Authors or Purchasers of such Copies, during the Times, therein to be mentioned; and to repeal an Act passed in the Eighth Year of the Reign of her late Majesty Queen Anne, intituled, An Act for the Encouragement of Learning, by vesting the Copies of Printed Books in the Authors or Purchasers of such Copies...; and for the better Securing the Payment of the Drawback of the Duties for Paper used in Printing Books in the Latin, Greek, Oriental, and Northern Languages, within the two Universities of Oxford and Cambridge. *n.p.* [*1737*], *4°*. L.

5031 Considerations Humbly Offer'd to the Honourable Committee of the Whole House of Commons, to whom the Bill, For Encouragement of Learning is referr'd. *n.p.* [*1737 ?*], *s. sh. F°*. MC.

5032 [Robe, Thomas]. The History of the Ancient Office of Clerk of the Market of the King's Household; its Authority and Usefulness....To which is added, The Case of Thomas Robe and Charles Peter Esqrs; the present Clerk of the Market, who are but as one Officer. By Eboranos. *Lond. 1737*, *8°*. O.

Authorship deduced from internal evidence.

5033 Reasons for a War against Spain. In a Letter from a Merchant of London trading to America, to a Member of the House of Commons. With a Plan of Operations. *Lond. 1737*, *8°*. O.

Signed: L. D. 2nd edn. 1738 (L).

5034 The Case of Samuel Bonham, and the other Owners of the Anne Galley, Joseph Spackman, Master, bound from Guinea to the Island Jamaica, was taken by the Spaniards between Hispaniola and Jamaica, the 13th of June, 1728. *n.p.* [*1737*], *F°*. L.

5035 DOWNING, CLEMENT. A Compendious History of the Indian Wars; with an Account of the Rise, Progress, Strength and Forces of Angria the Pyrate. Also the Transactions of a Squadron of Men of War under Commodore Matthews, sent to the East-Indies to suppress the Pyrates.... With an Account of the Life and Actions of John Plantain, a notorious Pyrate in Madagascar.... *Lond. 1737, 12°*. L.

Another edn., ed. by Sir William Foster, Lond., 1924.

COLONIES

5036 A Proposal to supply the Trade with a Medium of Exchange, and to sink the Bills of the other Governments. *Boston, 1737, 8°*.

Reprinted in *Colonial Currency Reprints*, ed. by A. M. Davis, vol. 3 (1911), whence this entry is taken.

5037 BRICKELL, JOHN. The Natural History of North-Carolina. With an Account of the Trades, Manners, and Customs of the Christian and Indian Inhabitants.... *Dublin, 1737, 8°*. L.

Another edn. 1743 (L); another edn., ed. by J. B. Grimes, Raleigh, N.C., 1911. Almost wholly taken from J. Lawson's *New Voyage to Carolina*, 1709.

5038 An Account of sundry Goods Imported, and of sundry Goods of the Produce of this Province Exported, from the several Ports of Charles-Town, George-Town and Port-Royal in South-Carolina, from the First of November 1736, to the First of November 1737. With the Number of Vessels entered and cleared in each Port. *Charles-Town 1737, s. sh. obl. F°*. L.

5039 The Report of the Committee of the Commons House of Assembly of the Province of South-Carolina, on the State of the Paper Currency of the said Province. *Lond. 1737, 4°*. LPRO.

FINANCE

5040 [BARNARD, Sir JOHN]. A Proposal towards Lowering the Interest of all the Redeemable National Debts, to 3 per Cent per Annum. And thereby to Enable the Parliament to give immediate Ease to his Majesty's Subjects, by taking off some of the Taxes, which are most burthensome to the Poor, and especially to the Manufacturers. As likewise to give Ease to the People, by Lessening the Annual Taxes for the current Service of the Year. *n.p.* [*1737*], *s. sh. F°*. LU.

For authorship see *D.N.B.* and the authorities there cited.

5041 [BARNARD, Sir JOHN]. Reasons for the Representatives of the People of Great Britain to take Advantage of the Present Rate of Interest, for the more speedy Lessening the National Debt, and Taking off the most Burthensome of the Taxes. *n.p.* [*1737*], *F°*. L.

For authorship see ms. note by Adam Anderson in L. copy. Another edn. Lond. 1737, 8°, entitled: Reasons for the more speedy Lessening the National Debt, and Taking off the most Burthensome of the Taxes (LU). Also printed in *The Lords Protest on the Motion to Address His Majesty to settle 100,000 l. per Annum on the Prince of Wales...*, Lond. 1737, F°.

5042 Considerations occasioned by a Proposal for Reducing Interest to Three per Cent. With some general Thoughts upon Reductions. *Lond. 1737*, *8°*. LU.

5043 Considerations upon a Proposal for Lowering the Interest of all the Redeemable National Debts to Three per Cent. per Ann. And thereby Enabling the Parliament to give immediate Ease to His Majesty's Subjects, by redeeming such Taxes as are most burdensome to the Poor. *Lond. 1737*, *8°*. LU.

5044 A Letter to Sir —— on the Publication of a Paper, containing Reasons for the Representatives of the People of Great Britain to take Advantage of the present Rate of Interest, for the more speedy Lessening the National Debt, and taking off the most burthensome of the Taxes. *n.p.* [*1737*], *s. sh. F°*. O.

5045 Queries relating to the Reduction of the National Redeemable Debts, from Four to Three per Cent. per Ann..... *Lond. 1737*, *8°*. LU.

5046 Reasons against Lowering the Interest of the Redeemable National Debt, from 4 to 3 per Cent. Shewing this Scheme to be Detrimental to the Publick. In a Letter to a Member of Parliament. *Lond. 1737*, *8°*. LU.

5047 Remarks on the Observations on Publick Clamour, occasion'd by the Three per Cent. Bill, publish'd in the Daily Post on Saturday the 21st Instant. Addressed to Sir ——. *n.p.* [*1737*], *s. sh. F°*. MC.

5048 A Speech Without-Doors, addressed to the National Creditors for the Redeemables at 4 l. per Cent. *Lond. 1737*, *8°*. LU.

5049 A Proposal and Scheme for the Government's Raising by Subscription L.5,000,000 of Money; in order to pay off therewith the like Sum of the present 4 per Cent. South-Sea Annuities.... *n.p.* [*1737*], *s. sh. F°*. LU.

Dated: March 26, 1737.

5050 A Collection of all the Statutes now in Force, relating to the Excise upon Beer, Ale, and other Liquors: with An Abridgment of the said Statutes, and a Table of the Rates upon the Several Liquors, &c, shewing by what Acts they are Imposed. To which is added, A Table of Allowances for Common Brewers, &c. *Lond. 1737*, *8°*. O.

5051 CLELAND, CHARLES. Abstracts of the several Laws and Rules that are now in force, relating to the Importation and Exportation of Wines into and out of Great-Britain. With Complete Tables of the Net Duties, that are to be Paid on the Importing, and Repaid on the Exporting of the same.... *Lond. 1737*, 4°. LU.

5052 BACON, THOMAS. A Compleat System of the Revenue of Ireland, in it several Branches of Import, Export, and Inland Duties....Ordered to be Published by the Chief Commissioners and Governors of His Majesty's Revenue of Ireland. *Dublin, 1737*, 8°. LU.

5053 Instructions for Surveyors General, or Head Supervisors [of the Customs]. *Dublin*, [*c. 1737 ?*], 8°. DA.

5054 [PULTENEY, WILLIAM, Earl of Bath ?]. A Letter from a Member of Parliament to his Friend in the Country, upon the Motion to address his Majesty to settle 100,000 l. per Annum on His Royal Highness the Prince of Wales, &c. In which the antient and modern State of the Civil List, and the Allowances to the Heir apparent, or presumptive, of the Crown, are particularly consider'd. *Lond.* [*1737*], 8°. LU.

For authorship see H. & L., who quote no authority.

5055 [WHATLEY, ROBERT]. A Short History of a Ten Years Negociation, between a Prime Minister and a Private Gentleman. *Lond. 1737*, 8°. L.

On Whatley's claims to a sinecure and Walpole's refusal to give him one. Authorship obvious from internal evidence.

5056 Memorial for George Innes Collector of the City of Edinburgh's Duty on Ale. *n.p.* [*1737*], *F°*. E.

Dated: July 25, 1737. Signed: Ch. Areskine.

5057 Memorial for John Bell and William Bruce, Brewers in Edinburgh, Suspenders; against George Innes, Collector of the City of Edinburgh's Duty on Ale, Charger. *n.p.* [*1737*], *s. sh. F°*. E.

Dated: July 26, 1737. Signed: Ja. Graham.

5058 The Case of the Taxes and Assessments raised upon the County of Middlesex. *n.p.* [*1737*], *s. sh. F°*. O.

Reprinted in the following where it is shown to have been sponsored and probably written by Thomas Robe and Stephen Lebas.

5059 A Report from the Committee, to whom the Petition of the Churchwardens, Overseers of the Poor, and great Numbers of the Inhabitants of the several Parishes of St. Giles in the Fields, the Liberty of Saffron-hill, Hatton-garden, and Ely Rents in the Parish of St. Andrew Holbourn; St. Dunstan Stepney, St. Paul Shadwell, St. Anne in Middlesex, St. Sepulchres in Middlesex, St. Luke, Middlesex, and St. James Clerkenwell in the County of Middlesex, whose Names are thereunto subscribed on behalf of themselves, and the rest of the Parishes of the said County; and also the Petition of His Majesty's

Justices of the Peace for the County of Middlesex, in their General Sessions assembled, were Referred. *Lond. 1737*, *F°*. O.

The petition alleged oppressive taxation by the justices. Another issue, entitled: A Report, with the Appendix, from the Committee of the House of Commons...and the Proceedings of the said House thereupon. Lond., 1737, F° (O).

5060 OLLIVE, JOSEPH. A Plea on behalf of the people call'd Quakers, or an Answer to a Pamphlet intituled Papers relating to the Quakers Tithe-Bill; in which Answer, the Arguments in the Country Parson's Plea are considered, and the Clergy's pretended property in Tithes enquir'd into.... *Lond. 1737*, *8°*. L.

5061 An Account of the Proceedings and Debates on the Tithe Bill, which was brought into the House of Commons on a Petition delivered by the Quakers: To which is added, A List of those Peers who were for and against Committing the said Bill. *Lond. 1737*, *8°*. O.

5062 An Examination of a Book, lately printed by the Quakers; and by them distributed to the Members of both Houses of Parliament, intituled, A Brief Account of many of the Prosecutions of the People called Quakers, in the Exchequer, Ecclesiastical, and other Courts....So far as the Clergy of the Diocese of London are concerned in it. To which is added, The poor Vicar's Plea against the Quakers Bill; a Paper written while that Bill was depending the last Year. *Lond. 1737*, *8°*. L.

5063 A Defence of the Examination of a Book entituled, A Brief Account of many of the Prosecutions of the People call'd Quakers, &c. So far as the Clergy of the Diocese of London are concern'd in it: In Answer to a late Pamphlet published by the Quakers, by way of Vindication of that Part of their Brief Account. *Lond. 1737*, *8°*. O.

5064 [BESSE, JOSEPH]. A Vindication of a Book, intituled, A Brief Account of many of the Prosecutions of the People call'd Quakers, &c. lately presented to the Members of both Houses of Parliament; shewing the Fallacy and Injustice of the Calculations and Remarks in a late Book called An Examination, &c; the Evasions and Disingenuity of the Clergy of the Diocese of London in their Answers and Reflections; and the Falshood and Inconsistency of the Intelligences by Them published. To which are added, Remarks on the Poor Vicar's Plea.... *Lond. 1737*, *8°*. L.

For authorship see Joseph Smith, *A Descriptive Catalogue of Friends Books*, 1867, I, 254.

5065 Rees Griffith, Appellant. Thomas Lewis, Esq; Respondent. The Appellant's Case. *n.p.* [*1737*], *F°*. L.

Signed: Rob. Pauncefort. Jer. Griffith. Tithe dispute.

5066 Rees Griffith, Appellant, Thomas Lewis, Esq; Respondent. The Respondent's Case. *n.p.* [*1737*], *F°*. L.

Signed: J. Strange. R. Lloyd.

5067 Advice to the Industrious Tradesmen and Manufacturers of Ireland, upon the present Regulation of the Coin, with some Reasons for the present Reduction of the Gold. *n.p.* [*1737*], *s. sh. F°*. LU.

5068 A Citizen's Memorial to the P—— or, Ireland truly Jockied by the Absentees. Shewing it's not the desire of the Inhabitants to have their Coin Lower'd, as appears by the uproar of the Citizens in General, 1737. *n.p.* [*1737*], *s. sh. F°*. LU.

5069 An Excellent New Ballad, on the Modesty of the Bankers of Dublin, who are Content to loose Three Halfpence, and let the rest of the Kingdom loose no more than Two Shillings and Six Pence in every Four Pound Piece, by the late Reduction of the Coin.... [*Dublin*, *1737*], *s. sh. F°*. LU.

5070 The Hibernian Patriot: or, a Vindication of Dean Swift, in a Letter to Mr. G. F. in Dublin. *n.p.* [*1737*], *s. sh. F°*. DG.

On the reduction of gold.

5071 Ireland's Hue and Cry after the Gold Coins; in a Letter from Belfast to the Castle of Comfort. *Dublin*, *1737*, *s. sh. F°*. LU.

Signed: James Weaver, obviously a pseudonym.

5072 Ireland's Mourning Flagg....Some Queries occation'd by the Lowering of the Gold Coin. *Dublin*, *1737*, *s. sh. F°*. LU.

5073 A Letter concerning the Bankers of Dublin. *Dublin*, *1737*, *s. sh. F°*. LU.

5074 A Letter from a Gentleman in the Country to his Friend in Dublin; upon Account of the Present Regulation of the Coin. *n.p.* [*1737*], *s. sh. F°*. DA.

5075 A Letter from Obediah Grimstone Mare of Cork, to his Friend Nathan Loomstick in Dublin, Concerning the Lowering of the Gold Coin. *Dublin*, *1737*, *s. sh. F°*. DM.

5076 A Letter to a Member of Parliament, concerning the late Reduction of the Gold-Coin. *Dublin*, *1737*, *8°*. LU.

DA copy has a ms. attribution to Ed- Bruce.

5077 The Lord Knows What, By the Lord knows Who. [*Dublin*,] *1737*, *s. sh. F°*. Y.

Against the devaluation of gold.

5078 Queries concerning the Lowering of the Gold Coin. *Dublin* [*1737*], *s. sh. F°*. LU.

5079 [Berkeley, George, Bishop of Cloyne]. Queries relating to a National Bank, extracted from the Querist. Also the Letter containing a Plan or Sketch of such a Bank. Republished with Notes. *Dublin*, *1737*, *4°*. L.

5080 A Reply to the Principal Arguments for the Reduction of the Gold Coin, and some Considerations on the Consequences thereof. Dedicated to the truly Honourable Sir Richard Cox, Baronet. *Dublin*, *1737*, *8°*. DA.

5081 A Satyr on the Reduction of the Gold Coin. *n.p.* [*1737*], *s. sh. F°*. LU.

5082 [Robinson, Bryan]. A Short Essay on Coin. *Dublin*, *1737*, *8°*. LU.
Contains Newton's Mint Reports of 3 March and 23 June 1712 and 21 September 1717. Another edn., with author's name, entitled: An Essay on Coin, 1757 (L).

5083 [Robinson, Bryan]. An Appendix to a Short Essay on Coin. *Dublin*, *1737*, *8°*. DA.

5084 Short Reasons why our Gold-Money in Ireland should not be Lowered. *n.p.* [*1737*], *s. sh. F°*. LU.
Signed: J.R.

5085 A Short Answer to Short Reasons why our Gold-Money in Ireland should not be Lower'd. *Dublin*, *1737*, *8°*. DA.

5086 Some Reflections concerning the Reduction of Gold Coin in Ireland. Upon the Principles of the Dean of St. Patrick's and Mr. Lock: Humbly submitted to the Good People of Ireland. *Dublin*, *1737*, *8°*. LU.

5087 Some Reflections upon the Present Regulation of the Coin: Offered to the Consideration of the Poor of Ireland. [*Dublin*, *1737*], *s. sh. F°*. Y.

5088 To the most Worshipfull, and we hope Merciful, ye Judges, Juries, Officers, and Executioners of the Liberty. The Humble Address, by way of Petition of Stake Weagerer, Bacon Herd, and Strap Behind the Coach; in Behalf of Themselves, and the rest of their Condemn'd Brethren, who was Tryed and lawfully found Guilty, for the Massacrea of Hibernia Gold. *Dublin*, *1737*, *s. sh. F°*. LU.
On the verso is: The Lurgan Brown Nag's Feast.

5089 The Tryal and Conviction of those Worthy Patriots, who of late have Sold their Country as much as in them lay, viz. Stake Weagerer, Strap behind the Coach, Paver, Upstart, and Bacon Herd....For High Crimes and Misdemenor committed against our worthy and antient Friend Hibernia Gold.... [*Dublin*, *1737*], *s. sh. F°*. LU.

5090 Two and Two make Four: in a Letter to the Honest Traders of Ireland. *Dublin*, *1737*, *8°*. DA.
On the devaluation of gold.

5091 An Unprejudic'd Enquiry into the Nature and Consequences of the Reduction of our Gold. *Dublin: Printed in the Year*, *1737*, *8°*. DA.
Another edn., Dublin: Printed in the Year MDCCXXXVII (DA).

5092 The Wooden-Man in Essex-Street's Memorial, and Reasons against Lowering the Gold Coin. *Dublin*, *1737*, *s. sh. F°*. LU.

5093 By the Lords Justices and Council of Ireland, A Proclamation, Relating to the Half-pence and Farthings of Copper, Coined at His Majesty's Mint in His Tower of London, for the Service of this Kingdom, and for Continuing the Currency of the Copper-Money, Coined under the Patents of His Majesty's Royal Predecessors, and which is now

Current in this Kingdom, and for Prohibiting base Coin to be Used. *Dublin, 1737, s. sh. Fo.* C (Cr).

Dated: 6 May 1737.

5094 MACULLA, JAMES. Woods upon Woods; or a Brazen Trap Newly Laid, to Ensnare the People of Ireland. For Brass-Money is now Hibernia's Portion, instead of her Sterling Treasure. *Dublin, 1737, 8o.* DA.

5095 MACULLA, JAMES. The Parliament and Corporations of Ireland's Declaration, and Protest against Foreign Brass-Money. Set forth in a Supplement to Woods upon Woods; or, Hibernia in a Wood, about taking Britannia's Counterfeit Half-Pence and Farthings. *Dublin, 1737, 8o.* DA.

5096 Queries relating to the New Half-Pence and lowering the Coin. Addressed to all the good People of Ireland. *n.p. 1737, 4o.* L.

5097 A List of the Names of the Adventurers in the Bank of Scotland. February 3, 1737. *n.p. [1737], s. sh. Fo.* LU.

5098 Proposals by the Corporation of the London-Assurance, Established by His Majesty's Royal Charter, For Assuring Houses and other Buildings, Goods, Wares, and Merchandizes, from Loss or Damage by Fire. *n.p. 1737, s. sh. Fo.* LG.

5099 Proposals from the Sun Fire-Office, near the Royal Exchange, for Insuring Houses, and other Buildings, Goods, Wares and Merchandize, from Loss and Damage by Fire. *Lond. [1737], s. sh. 4o.* MC.

Dated: April 5, 1737.

5100 STEPHENS, HUSTCRAFT. Italian Book-keeping reduc'd into an Art: being an Entire, New and Compleat System of Accompts in General....To which is added, the greatest Variety of Merchants. *Lond. 1735, 4o.* L.

Another edn. Dublin, 1737, 8o; 2nd edn. ed. by J. Weir, Lond. [*c.* 1745], 4o; another edn. Dublin, 1754, 8o (all LICA).

TRANSPORT

5101 HULLS, JONATHAN. A Description and Draught of a new-invented Machine for carrying Vessels or Ships Out of, or Into any Harbour, Port, or River, against Wind and Tide, or in a Calm. For which, His Majesty has Granted Letters Patent, for the Sole Benefit of the Author, for the Space of Fourteen Years. *Lond. 1737, 8o.* L.

Another edn. 1855 (L); another edn. 1860 (L).

5102 The Case relating to the chusing a place for the Construction of a Harbour near the Downs, Truly, and Fairly Stated. *n.p. [1737], Fo.* LLI.

5103 The Case of the Undertakers of the River Dun consider'd and answer'd. *n.p. [1737?], s. sh. Fo.* O.

5104 Reasons for making the River Soare Navigable, from the Town of Leicester, to the River Trent in the County of Nottingham. *n.p. [1737], s. sh. Fo.* O.

5105 A Bill for making Navigable the River or Brook, called Worsley Brook, from Worsley Mills, in the County Palatine of Lancaster, to the River Irwell in the said County. *n.p.* [*1737*], *F*o. O.

5106 Reasons humbly offered for Passing the Bill for better Regulating the Company of Watermen, Wherrymen and Lightermen of the River Thames. *n.p.* [*1737 ?*], *s. sh. F*o. L.

5107 PHILLIPS, ROBERT. A Dissertation concerning the Present State of the High Roads of England, especially of those near London. Wherein in propos'd a New Method of Repairing and Maintaining them. Read before the Royal Society the Twenty-Seventh Day of January and the Third Day of February, 1736–7....Illustrated by Copper Plates. *Lond. 1737*, *8*o. LU.

5108 [A Collection of road acts.] *Lond. 1737*, *8*o. LU.

With a folding table of tolls to be paid at turnpikes in Surrey and Sussex. Includes: 4 Geo I. An Act for amending the Roads from the City of London to the Town of East Grinstead....
6 Geo I. An Act for enlarging the Term granted by....An Act for repairing the Highways leading from the Stones End in Kent-Street to the Lime-Kilns in East-Greenwich....
10 Geo I. An Act for amending the Road from the Stones End in Southwark to Highgate at the Entrance of Ashdown Forest.
4 Geo II. An Act for the more effectual repairing the Road leading from Godstone in the County of Surrey to Highgate at the Entrance into Ashdown Forrest.
10 Geo II. An Act for explaining, and amending, and making more effectual several Acts of Parliament made in the Fourth, Sixth and Tenth Years of the Reign of His late Majesty King George the First respectively, for repairing the several Roads, therein mentioned in the Counties of Surrey, Kent & Sussex...
1 Geo II. An Act for punishing such Persons as shall wilfully and maliciously pull down or destroy Turnpikes for repairing Highways, or Locks....

5109 The Case of the Parish of Stepney, in Respect to the Roads. *n.p.* [*1737 ?*], *F*o. LLI.

5110 A Bill for Enlarging the Term granted by an Act passed in the Twelfth Year of the Reign of his late Majesty King George the First, intituled, An Act for Repairing several Roads therein mentioned, leading into the City of Worcester; and for Repairing several other Roads lying contiguous to the same. *n.p.* [*1737*], *F*o. O.

5111 LANGLEY, BATTY. A Reply to Mr. John James's Review of the several Pamphlets and Schemes, that have been offered to the Publick, for the Building of a Bridge at Westminster; wherein his many Absurdities are detected.... *Lond. 1737*, *8*o. LU.

5112 Some useful Observations with Regard to the following First Scheme of a Lottery for Building the Bridge at Westminster; which Scheme, with proper Reasons for a Lottery at this Juncture, were humbly offered to the Consideration of both Houses of Parliament. *n.p.* [*1737 ?*], *F*o. LG.

SOCIAL CONDITIONS

5113 A Bill for the better Relief and Employment of the Poor. *n.p.* [*1737*], *F*°. pp. 19. LU.

5114 A Proposal for the Employment of the Poor, and the Amendment of their Morals. *n.p.* [*1737 ?*], *F*°. L.

5115 A Bill for the more Effectual Punishing Rogues and Vagabonds; and for the better Relief and Employment of such poor Persons, as are therein mentioned. *n.p.* [*1737 ?*], *F*°. LU.

5116 Clarke, Alured. A Sermon preached in the Cathedral Church of Winchester, before the Governors of the County-Hospital for Sick and Lame, &c. at the Opening of the said Hospital, on St. Luke's Day, October 18, 1736....To which are added, A Collection of Papers relating to the Hospital, in which are the Rules and Orders for the Management and Conduct of the House, &c. *Lond. 1737*, 4°. L.
2nd edn. 1737 (O).

5117 July 12. 1737. At a General Court of the Governors of the County-Hospital at Winchester. Some Alterations having been made in the Rule concerning the Admission of Patients, the Governors think it proper to acquaint the Subscribers.... *n.p.* [*1737*], *s. sh. F*°. LSC.
Followed by: A List of the Governors (and Others, who Subscribe one Pound or more, annually).

5118 An Account of the Establishment of the County-Hospital at Winchester, with the Proceedings of the Governors, &c. from the first Institution on St. Luke's Day, October 18, 1736, to Michaelmas, 1737. *n.p.* [*1737*], *F*°. L.
L has also: A View of the many peculiar advantages of Public Hospitals: With an Account of the County-Hospital at Winchester; and the Second Annual Report of the State of the Patients and the Accounts, at a General Court of Governors on St. Luke's Day, October 18, 1738. This was subsequently published annually. Nos. 6 and 7 (LSC) and no. 8 (O) bear the title: The State of the County Hospital at Winchester; with the Sixth (–Eighth) Public Report of the Patients, and Accounts from Lady-Day 1742 (–1744), to Lady-Day 1743 (–1745).

5119 A Vindication of the Managers of the Royal Infirmary of Edinburgh, from the Aspersions cast upon their Conduct in a late Pamphlet. *Edin. 1737*, 8°. O.

5120 Memorial concerning the Surgeons Hospital. [*Edin.*], *1737*, 4°. L.

5121 Swift, Jonathan. A Proposal for giving Badges to the Beggars in all the Parishes of Dublin. *Dublin, 1737*, *12*°. DA.
Another edn. Lond. 1737, 4° (L).

5122 Anno Regni Georgii II. Regis Magnae Britanniae, Franciae, & Hiberniae, Decimo. An Abridgement of an Act of Parliament made in a Session begun in Great-Britain, on the first Day of February, 1736. for the Relief of Insolvent Debtors. *Dublin, 1737*, 8°. DG.
With a note explaining that this had been printed at the instance of the insolvent debtors of Ireland who hope for similar legislation.

5123 An Act for Relief of Insolvent Debtors. *n.p.* [*1737*], *F*o. LU.
A bill.

5124 Clauses proposed to be added to the Insolvent Bill. *n.p.* [*1737*], *s. sh. F*o. LU.
Including among the beneficiaries sufferers in the South Sea bubble.

5125 The Case of Insolvent Debtors Confined in the several Goals in this Kingdom. *n.p.* [*1737?*], *F*o. L.
Endorsed: Some Reasons for an Act of Insolvency on Consideration of the Case of Prisoners confined for Debt in the several Goals of this Kingdom.

5126 The Case of Persons in Prison who are under Commissions of Bankruptcy. *n.p.* [*1737?*], *s. sh. F*o. LLI.

5127 A Scene of Corruption Discover'd: with Some Particulars of a Melancholy Place in a Letter to the Right Honourable Philip Lord Hardwick, Lord High Chancellor. By a Gentleman in Distress. *Lond.* [*1737*], *8*o. LU.
Signed: Philander. On debtors' prisons, particularly the King's Bench.

5128 The Worth of Liberty consider'd: in a Letter to a Member of the House of Commons upon the question, How far the late Act against the immoderate Use of Spirituous Liquors may affect the Properties of all the People. *Lond. 1737*, *8*o. L.

5129 Reasons humbly submitted against passing the Bill, For the more effectual preventing the unlawful playing of Interludes within the Precincts of the University of Cambridge, and the Places adjacent; and for explaining and amending so much of an Act passed in the last Session of Parliament, intituled, An Act for laying a Duty upon the Retailers of Spirituous Liquors, and for licensing the Retailers thereof, as may affect the Privilege of the University of Cambridge, with respect to licensing Taverns, and all other publick Houses, within the Precincts of the same. *n.p.* [*1737*], *s. sh. F*o. LLI.

5130 Rules and Orders for the Augmentation of the Maintenance of the Poor Clergy, &c. Ratified and Confirmed by His Majesty, under the Great Seal of Great-Britain, the 24th of May 1737. *n.p.* [*1737*], *s. sh. F*o. LSC.

5131 Some Considerations upon Pluralities, Non-Residence, and Salaries of Curates. *Lond. 1737*, *8*o. MP.

1738

GENERAL

5132 [ANDREWS, THOMAS]. An Enquiry into the Causes of the Encrease and Miseries of the Poor of England; which are shewn to be, I. Taxes, especially Excises and Customs. II. Luxury. III. Absence of our Great Men from their Countries. IV. Corruption at Elections. V. Inclosures of Commons. VI. Neglect of Apprenticing Poor Children. VII. Not Executing the Laws against Idle and Disorderly People. VIII. The great Number of Ale-Houses. Occasioned by the late Work-House Scheme; with some Objections to it.... By the Author of, The Dissuasive from Party and Religious Animosities. *Lond. 1738*, 8°. L.

For authorship see *Country Common-Sense*, (no. 5267), in which this is advertised as by the same author.

5133 MARKHAM, WILLIAM. A General Introduction to Trade and Business. Or, the Young Merchant's and Tradesman's Magazine.... *Lond. 1738*, 12°. LU.

2nd edn. 1739 (LU).

5134 The Master and Apprentice Instructed. Or Necessary Instructions to all Freemen of the City of London. And their Apprentices. By a Fellow-Citizen. *Lond. 1738*, 8°. LG.

5135 The Present State of Scotland. Enlarged, corrected, and amended [by Matthias Symson] from above One Thousand Errors in the former Editions. *Lond. 1738*, 8°. L.

A separate issue of pt. 2 of *The Present State of Great Britain, and Ireland... The Eighth edition*, originally compiled by Guy Miège. L copy has a ms. inscription by the editor.

5136 [MADDEN, SAMUEL]. Reflections and Resolutions proper for the Gentlemen of Ireland, as to their Conduct for the Service of their Country, as Landlords, as Masters of Families, as Protestants, as descended from British Ancestors, as Country Gentlemen and Farmers, as Justices of the Peace, as Merchants, as Members of Parliament. *Dublin, 1738*, 8°. LU.

Another edn., with author's name, 1816 (LU).

AGRICULTURE

5137 Agriculture the surest Means of National Wealth: and an Impartial Administration of Justice the best Encouragement to National Industry. Together with several Improvements in Agriculture recommended; but especially the Propagation of Saint Foin, and La Lucerne. *Dublin, 1738*, 12°. DNL.

Attributed to William Plunkett in Donald McDonald's *Agricultural Writers*, 1908, p. 209, without quoting authority.

5138 PLUNKETT, WILLIAM. A New Method of Farming. *Dublin, 1738, 8°.* DA.

5139 An Act for Inclosing and Dividing the Common Fields and Common Grounds in the Manors and Parishes of Binbrooke in the County of Lincoln. *n.p. 1738, F°.* L.

Catchword on p. 1: Wil-; another edn. [1738] (L). Catchword on p. 1; Compost; another edn. [1738] (L) Catchword on p. 1: of.

5140 An Act for Reducing the Stint of the Horse or Beast-Pastures, and Sheep-Commons, within the Manor, Town, and Parish of Castle Donnington, in the County of Leicester. *n.p. 1737–8, F°.* L.

5141 An Act for Inclosing and Dividing the Common Mead or Moor, called Speen Mead, or Speen Moor, in the County of Berks. *n.p. 1738, F°.* L.

5142. An Act for Inclosing and Dividing the Common Fields, Wastes, and Uninclosed Grounds, within the Manor, Township, or Hamlet of Ashenden, in the County of Bucks, and for making effectual certain Exchanges therein mentioned. *n.p. [1738], F°.* L.

5143 A Bill for the effectual Draining and Preservation of certain Fens called Cawdle Fen, Waterden and Redmoor. *n.p. [1738], F°.* O.

5144 A Bill to Enable the Adventurers, Owners and Proprietors of the Taxable Lands, and the Owners and Proprietors of the Free Lands in Deeping Fens, and other Fens in the County of Lincoln therein mentioned, to raise a competent Sum of Money for the effectual Draining and future Preservation of all the said Fens, according to their Agreement in that Behalf, and to carry the said Agreement into Execution, and for other the Purposes therein mentioned. *n.p. [1738], F°.* L.

5145 HUTCHINSON, FRANCIS, Bishop of Down and Connor. The State of the Case of Loughreagh and the Bann. *Dublin, 1738, 8°.* O.

On draining bogs.

5146 ELLIS, WILLIAM. The Timber-Tree improved; or, the Best Practical Methods of Improving different Lands with Proper Timber, and those Fruit-Trees whose Woods make the most profitable Returns to their Owners.... *Lond. 1738, 8°.* L.

2nd edn. 1741 (C); 3rd 1742 (O); 4th 1745 (OF). Pt. 2 1742 (no. 5611).

5147 A Bill for the more effectual Securing the Payment of Rents, and Preventing Frauds by Tenants. *n.p. [1738], F°.* L.

Another edn., with the blanks filled in, entitled: A Bill, intituled, An Act for the more effectual securing the Payment of Rents...(L).

5148 Reasons for a Law, to oblige Spiritual Persons and Bodies Politick, to renew their Leases for Customary and Reasonable Fines.... *Lond. [1738], 8°.* L.

5149 DOYLE, WILLIAM. Two Letters, wherein the Sovereignty of the British Seas, and that the sole Right of Fishing in them, appertaineth to the King of Great-Britain, &c. is Demonstratively Maintain'd and Asserted....With Remarks on the Dutch Fisheries on our Coasts and

Seas....With a New Map of the British Coasts and Seas.... *Lond.* *1738*, *8º*. LU.

2nd edn., containing a Third Letter and proposals for a Company for fishing the Nymph Bank, 1739 (E).

5150 KERVELL, EDWARD. The Golden Mine: or, the Benefits and Advantages arising from the Herring Fishery (Now in the Hands of the Dutch) humbly offer'd to the Consideration of the Merchants of London, &c. in order to the Revival of so Valuable a Branch of Commerce. *Lond.* [*1738*], *Fº*. LU.

Dated: Morgan's Lane, Southend, February 22, 1737.

MANUFACTURES

5151 The Laboratory, or School of Arts: In which are faithfully Exhibited and fully Explain'd, I. A Variety of curious and valuable Experiments in Refining, Calcining, Melting, Assaying, Casting, Allaying, and Toughening Gold; With several other Curiosities relating to Gold and Silver. II. Choice Secrets for Jewellers....III. Several uncommon Experiments for Casting in Silver, Copper, Brass, Tin, Steel and other Metals; likewise in Wax, Plaister of Paris, Wood, Horn, &c. With the Management of the respective Moulds. IV. The Art of making Glass....V. A Collection of very valuable Secrets for the Use of Cutlers, Pewterers, Brasiers, Joiners, Turners, Japanners, Book-binders, Distillers, Stone-Cutters, Limners, &c. VI. A Dissertation on the Nature and Growth of Saltpeter....Translated from the German. *Lond.* *1738*, *8º*. O.

The translator's dedication signed: G. Smith. 3rd edn. 'Compiled from German, and other foreign Authors....By G. Smith', 1750 (O). In this edition the dedication is signed: Godfrey Smith. In later editions George Smith is given.

5152 An Abstract of the several Acts of Parliament made for the Encouragement of the Manufacture of Buttons and Buttonholes wrought with the Needle, with some Observations. *n.p.* [*1738?*], *Fº*. LLI.

5153 The Case of the Manufacturers of Woven Buttons and Button Holes, and of the Throwsters, Twisters, Spinners, Winders, Dyers, and others employed in preparing Raw Silk, Mohair Yarn, and other Materials for manufacturing the same, in the Cities of London, Worcester and Coventry, and in the Towns of Nottingham, Birmingham, Nuneaton, and several other Places in this Kingdom. *n.p.* [*1738*], *Fº*. LLI.

5154 Some Remarks on the Present State of the Iron-Trade of Great Britain. *n.p.* [*1738?*], *s. sh. Fº*. LU.

For the prohibition of new or enlarged forges in the American colonies.

5155 The Arguments and Pretences made Use of by the Curriers, to support their Bill now depending in Parliament, Consider'd in a True and Impartial Light. *n.p.* [*1738?*], *Fº*. LLI.

5156 The Case of the Cordwainers in Behalf of Themselves, and other Manufacturers of Leather in this Kingdom. Humbly offered to the Honourable the House of Commons. *n.p.* [*1738*], *F°*. L.

Another edn. 'Humbly offered to the Right Honourable the House of Lords' (L).

5157 The Case of the Country Master-Cordwainers or Shoe-makers, humbly sets forth, to the Consideration of every impartial Reader.... *n.p.* [*1738*], *s. sh. F°*. LU.

5158 The Case of the Curriers and Others, Dealers in Leather: Humbly Address'd to the Honourable the House of Commons. *n.p.* [*1738 ?*], *s. sh. F°*. LU.

5159 The Case of the Master Shoemakers, in Relation to the Curriers and other Dealers in Leather Cutting and Selling Soles and Upper-Leathers to the Journeymen Shoemakers. *n.p.* [*1738 ?*], *s. sh. F°*. LLI.

5160 The Case of the Middling and Poorer Sort of Master Shoemakers; Humbly set forth to the Honourable the House of Commons. *n.p.* [*1738*], *s. sh. F°*. LU.

5161 Reasons for passing the Bill intitled an Act to obviate some Doubts which have arisen upon the Construction of an Act made in the First Year of the Reign of King William and Queen Mary, intitled, An Act for Explaining part of an Act made in the First Year of the Reign of King James I. concerning Tanned Leather, and for rendering more effectual a Clause in the said last mentioned Act, which obliges Curriers to curry Leather. *n.p.* [*1738 ?*], *s. sh. F°*. LG.

5162 The Proposal for taking off the Drawbacks allowed on Exportation of Foreign Linens, Threads, and Tapes, impartially considered. *n.p.* [*1738 ?*], *F°*. LU.

5163 [Bindon, David ?]. The Case of the British and Irish Manufacture of Linnen, Threads, and Tapes, fairly stated; in Answer to the Impartial Considerer. *n.p.* [*1738 ?*], *F°*. L.

A reply to the preceding. Presumably by the same author as the following.

5164 [Bindon, David ?]. A Letter from a Merchant who has left off Trade to a Member of Parliament. In which the Case of the British and Irish Manufacture of Linnen, Threads, and Tapes is fairly stated, and all the Objections against the Encouragement proposed to be given to that Manufacture fully answered. *Lond. 1738*, *8°*. L.

Another edn. n.p. 1738 (L); another edn. Belfast, 1738, 8° (D); another edn. 1753 (LU). For authorship see H. & L., who quote no authority.

5165 Reflections and Considerations occasioned by the Petition presented to the Honourable House óf Commons for taking off the Drawback on Foreign Linens, &c. *Lond. 1738*, *8°*. LU.

5166 [Maculla, James]. A Swift Warning to the People of Ireland, collected from the King and Parliament and Magistrates of this Kingdom's

Grants to prevent the Crown and Revenue, and Nation being wrong'd and losing a Hundred Thousand Pounds per Annum. *Dublin, 1738*, *8°*. DA.

On the manufacture of sub-standard pewter and brass ware. For authorship see Wagner 185.

5167 [MUNN, JOHN]. Observations on British Wool, and the Manufacturing of it in this Kingdom. With Remarks on the Wool, and Woollen Manufactories of France, Flanders and Holland, &c.... To which is annex'd, A Playcart or Proclamation, for Preserving the Woollen Manufactures in Flanders, publish'd in the Year 1731. Also a Scheme for preventing our Wool from being Owled Abroad for the future, if put into Practice. By a Manufacturer of Northamptonshire.... *Lond. 1738*, *4°*. LU.

2nd edn., with additions, 1739 (LU). For authorship see *Some Impartial Thoughts on the Woollen Manufacturies*, 1742 (no. 5634).

COMMERCE

5168 The Intelligencer: or, Merchants Assistant. Shewing, in an alphabetical manner, the Names and Places of Abode of all the Merchants and considerable Traders throughout the Cities of London and Westminster, and Borough of Southwark. With an exact Account of all the Stage-Coaches and Carriers in Great Britain, the Inns where they set up, and the Time of their Coming in, and Going out.... *Lond. 1738*, *16°*. EU.

5169 A List of the Subscribers, Officers, and Committee of the Society for the Encouragement of Learning. Together with the Rules of the said Society. 1738. *n.p.* [*1738*], *F°*. O.

The aim of the Society was to give authors better terms than publishers would.

5170 The Case of the Cheesemongers of the City of London, and Parts Adjacent, in Regard to the Bill now depending in The Honourable the House of Commons, for regulating the Cheese Trade in the several Counties of England and Wales. *n.p.* [*1738*], *F°*. LLI.

5171 LONDON. Barnard, Mayor. Tuesday the Thirty First Day of January, 1737. [*Lond. 1738*], *s. sh. F°*. LCRO.

An order suppressing a fair near Little-Tower-Hill for the buying and selling of old rags and cloths.

5172 EDINBURGH. Act of Council Regulating the Weighing of Coals and Metting of Victual at the Port of Leith. [*Edin. 1738*], *s. sh. F°*. EU.

Dated: 1 March 1738.

5173 Memorial for the Magistrates and Town-Council of Glasgow, Against the Bakers there. *n.p.* [*1738*], *F°*. E.

Dated: January 23, 1738. Signed: Will. Crosse. On the assize of bread.

5174 Memorial for Andrew Scott present Deacon and the haill other Members of the Incorporation of the Baxters of Glasgow, Against the Magistrates of Glasgow. *n.p.* [*1738*], *F*o. E.

Dated: 23rd January 1738. Signed: Ja. Fergusson. Followed by 'Observes as to some Mistakes in the Memorial for the Magistrates'.

5175 Petition for Andrew Scott Deacon, and the other Members of the Incorporation of Baxters in Glasgow, against the Magistrates of Glasgow. *n.p.* [*1738*], *F*o. E.

Dated: 6th February 1728. Signed: James Graham.

5176 A General Treatise of Naval Trade and Commerce, as founded on the Laws and Statutes of this Realm.... *Lond. 1738, 39, 8*o. 2 vols. O.

2nd edn. 1753 (Kress 5265).

5177 Francis Lynch, of Dublin, Merchant, Appellant. Martin Killikelly of Dublin, Merchant, Arthur Lynch and Company, of Bilbao, Merchants, Catharine Killikelly, Widow and Executrix of Luke Killikelly, late of Newfoundland, Merchant, deceased, and James and Thomas Lynch, Merchants in Cadiz, Respondents. The Appellant's Case. *n.p.* [*1738*], *F*o. L.

Signed: N. Fazakerley. Will. Hamilton. On the voyage of the *Matthew* galley in 1730–1 to Newfoundland, with bread, salt and brandy, and thence to Spain, with fish.

5178 Francis Lynch, Merchant, Appellant. Martin Killikelly, of Dublin, Merchant, and Arthur Lynch and Company, of Bilbao in Spain, Merchants, Respondents. The Case of the Respondents. *n.p.* [*1738*], *F*o. L.

Signed: J. Strange. W. Murray.

5179 Common Sense: its Nature and Use....Applied to the Spanish Affair. *Lond. 1738, 8*o. E.

5180 The Merchant's Complaint against Spain: containing I. Their Behaviour towards England in the peaceable Reign of King James I....II. A Letter from a Gentleman in the West-Indies to a Merchant in London, concerning Trade, the Pretensions of Spain to Georgia, the Depredations and Cruelties committed by their Guard Costa's on the English Merchants and Sailors.... *Lond. 1738, 8*o. LU.

5181 Strenuous Motives for an Immediate War against Spain....Inscribed to the Merchants of Great-Britain Trading to South America. *Lond. 1738, 8*o. LU.

5182 Moore, Francis. Travels into the Inland Parts of Africa: containing a Description of the Several Nations for the space of Six Hundred Miles up the River Gambia; their Trade, Habits, Customs...and Government....To which is added, Capt. Stibbs's Voyage up the Gambia in the Year 1723, to make Discoveries.... *Lond. 1738, 8*o. LU.

2nd edn. [1740] (L). Reprinted in *A New General Collection of Voyages and Travels*, vol. 2 (1745).

5183 A Faithful Narrative of the Capture of the Ship Derby, (belonging to the Honourable the East-India Company, Abraham Anselm Commander) by Angria the Pirate, on the Coast of Mallabar, December 26. 1735. With Several Affidavits, Letters, &c. relating to the Captain's Conduct, before, in, and after the Engagement. Also, A Particular Account of the Force of Angria, both by Land and Sea; and a List of the Gallies and Grabbs (belonging to the Company) at Bombay. The Whole Extracted from Memoirs under Captain Anselm's own Hand, and other Papers. *Lond. 1738, 8º*. L.

COLONIES

5184 KEITH, Sir WILLIAM. The History of the British Plantations in America. With a Chronological Account of the most remarkable Things which happen'd to the first Adventurers in their several Discoveries in that New World. Part I. Containing the History of Virginia; with Remarks on the Trade and Commerce of that Colony. *Lond. 1738, 4º*. L.

No more published.

5185 A Letter from John Ray of New York, to Peter Ennis of Colraine, Pedlar. *Dublin, 1738, 8º*. DA.

On emigration.

5186 [DOUGLASS, WILLIAM]. An Essay concerning Silver and Paper Currencies, more especially with Regard to the British Colonies in New-England. *Boston, [1738], 8º*.

Reprinted in *Colonial Currency Reprints*, ed. by A. M. Davis, vol. 3 (1911), whence this entry is taken.

5187 [VANS, HUGH]. Some Observations on the Scheme projected for emitting 60000 l. in Bills of a New Tenour, to be redeemed with Silver and Gold. Shewing the various Operations of these Bills, and their Tendency to hurt the Publick Interest. In a Letter from a Merchant in Boston, to his Friend in the Country. *Boston, 1738. 8º*.

Reprinted in *Colonial Currency Reprints*, ed. by A. M. Davis, vol. 3 (1911), whence this entry is taken.

5188 Port of Charles-Town in South-Carolina. An Account of sundry Goods Imported, and of sundry Goods of the Produce of this Province Exported from this Port, from the first of November 1737, to the first of November 1738. With the Number of Vessels entered inwards, and from whence arriv'd, cleared outwards, and where bound. [*Charleston, 1738*], *s. sh. obl. Fº*. L.

5189 BENNETT, JOHN. Two Letters and Several Calculations on the Sugar Colonies and Trade; addressed to Two Committees nominated by the West-India Merchants, &c. With an Appendix: containing, 1. Four Letters, concerning the flourishing Condition, large Extent, and prodigious Increase of the French Sugar Colonies; the Poverty, Weakness and Decay of the British Sugar Colonies; and their vast Importance to the Trade, Navigation, Wealth and Power of this Nation. 2. Some Proposals formerly presented to a Great Minister of State, for the Preservation and Advancement of the British Sugar Colonies, and Interests in the West-Indies: With an Addition of several Notes thereon. *Lond. 1738, 8°.* LU.

2nd edn. 1738 (LU).

5190 The Miserable Case of the British Sugar Planters; wherein is contained, Some Remarks on the Poverty, Distress, and other Difficulties, which they labour under; the Advantages of a Direct Exportation from the Sugar Islands to Foreign Markets; and the Consequences of losing or preserving our Sugar Colonies are considered; and Some Comparisons are made between the French and the English in Regard to the Sugar Trade. With a Proposal for Relief. By a Wellwisher to the Trade and Navigation of Great-Britain. *Lond. 1738, 4°.* LU.

FINANCE

5191 Some Thoughts on the Interest of Money in General, and Particularly in the Publick Funds. With Reasons for fixing the same at a lower Rate, in both Instances, with Regard especially to the Landholders. *Lond.* [*1738*], *8°.* LU.

2nd edn. [1743] (LU).

5192 For Opening Voluntary Subscriptions for Twenty Four Millions of Money: The Ladies Advocate, and General Reconciler. *n.p.* [*1738?*], *F°.* O.

A scheme to reduce the interest on the 4 per cent South Sea annuities. Followed by 'The New Lottery-Scheme for L. 6,000,000 of Money'.

5193 An Extract of such part of the Act of the 9th of Queen Anne, as relates to Secureing the Duty charged by that Act on Leather; whereby it will appear, That the Revenue cannot be liable to be defrauded by the Tanners cutting Tann'd Leather in small Pieces, any more than if Liberty were given to all or any other Persons to cut the same. *n.p.* [*1738?*], *s. sh. F°.* LLI.

5194 A Short View of the Inland Excise, and the Duties arising from Licences for selling Beer, Ale, Wines and Strong Waters by Retale in the Kingdom of Ireland. *n.p.* [*c. 1738?*], *F°.* DM.

The only copy seen is imperfect.

5195 Whatley, Robert. Letters and Applications relating to the Short History of a Ten Years Negotiation between a Prime Minister and a Private Gentleman, that passed from the Time of its being printed, (and in the Minister's Hands), in March 1737, to the publishing of it in March 1738. *Lond. 1738, 8°.* L.

5196 City Corruption and Mal-Administration Display'd; occasion'd by the Ill Management of the Publick Money in general: with some Remarks upon the Modest Enquiry into the Conduct of the Court of Aldermen, &c.... By a Citizen. *Lond. 1738*, *8°*. L.

2nd edn. 1738 (L); 3rd edn. 1739 (LG).

5197 An Apology for the Clergy of Ireland. In Respect of their Civil Rights, especially as to Agistment for dry and barren Cattle. *Dublin, 1737–8*, *8°*. L.

5198 Most Useful Tables, wherein is exactly calculated the total Sum of any Number of Pieces, from One to Fifty; of all the different Denominations of Gold Coin, now current in this Kingdom, as regulated by the late Proclamation. Wherein is also laid down, in different Columns, their Deficiencies, from 2d. to 8d. at 2d. per Grain. *Dublin, 1738*, *8°*. DA.

5199 An Abstract of the Original Charter of the Corporation of the Amicable Society for a Perpetual Assurance-Office, Dated 25 July, 5° Annae Reginae, An. Dom. 1706. *n.p.* [*1738?*], *8°*. OH.

The supplemental charter of 1729 and the By-Laws of the Corporation, dated 19 January 1737, are included.

5200 Proposals for Erecting an Office of Insurance from Loss or Damage by Fire in the City of Canterbury. *Canterbury, 1738*, *s. sh. F°*. O.

5201 CLARK, JOHN. Lectures on Accompts, or Book-keeping; after the Italian Manner, by Double Entry of Debtor and Creditor.... The Second Edition, Corrected and Amended. *Lond. 1738*, *4°*. LICA.

The first edition, not seen, was published in 1732.

TRANSPORT

5202 The Account of a Coal-Voyage in the Daily-Advertiser, Examin'd. With the proper Deductions for Nine Voyages. *n.p.* [*1738*], *s. sh. F°*. LU.

Endorsed: The Examination of the Masters Account of a Coal Voyage.... Dated 1729 in *University of London, Catalogue of the Collection of Broadsides*, 1930, no. 324 (1), and in T. S. Willan, *The English Coasting Trade*, where it is reprinted. But the *Daily Advertiser* was not founded until 1731, and see A. Boyer, *Pol. State of Great Britain*, May 1738.

5203 An Answer to the Lightermens Account of a Coal Voyage. *n.p.* [*1738*], *s. sh. F°*. LU.

5204 The State of a Coal Voyage to and from Newcastle. *n.p.* [*1738*], *s. sh. F°*. LU.

Dated 1729 in *University of London, Catalogue of the Collection of Broadsides*, 1930, no. 324 (3), and in T. S. Willan, *The English Coasting Trade*, where it is reprinted. But see A. Boyer, *Pol. State of Great Britain*, May 1738, where these and other figures are printed.

5205 A Bill for Inlarging the Time granted by an Act passed in the Third Year of the Reign of his late Majesty, entitled, An Act for Inlarging the Time granted by an Act passed in the Eighth Year of the Reign of her late Majesty Queen Anne, intitled, An Act for making a convenient Dock or Bason at Liverpool, for the Security of all Ships trading to and from the said Port of Liverpool, and for Inlarging the same, by making an additional Dock, and building a Pier in the open Harbour; and for Inlightening round the Dock, and the Streets of the said Town. *n.p.* [*1738*], *F°*. L.

5206 A Bill for ascertaining, preserving and improving the Navigation of the River Lee, from the Town of Hertford to the Town of Ware in the County of Hertford, and for preserving and improving the said River from the said Town of Ware to the City of London; and for enabling the Governor and Company of the New River, brought from Shadwell and Arnwell to London, the better to supply the Cities of London and Westminster, and the Suburbs and Liberties thereof, with good and wholesome Water, and for other the Purposes therein mentioned. *n.p.* [*1738*], *F°*. L.

5207 The Case of the Petitioners, Phillippa and John Walton, Gun-Powder-Makers; Owners and Occupiers of the Gun-Powder-Mills, situated at Waltham-Abbey. *n.p.* [*1738*], *F°*. LLI.

Endorsed: The Case of Phillippa and John Walton, Gun-Powder-Makers: humbly offered against the Bill, now depending, before the Honourable the House of Commons, for Ascertaining, Preserving, and Improving, the Navigation of the River Lee, &c.

5208 Reasons humbly offered to the consideration of the Honourable House of Commons, against Passing the Bill For Repairing the Road from the Stones-End in the Parish of St. Leonard Shoreditch in the County of Middlesex, through the Town of Hackney to Stanford Hill on the great Northern Road. *n.p.* [*1738*], *s. sh. F°*. LU.

5209 The Case of the Parish of St. Mary Magdalen, Bermondsey, in the County of Surry. *n.p.* [*1738*], *s. sh. F°*. L.

For an allowance for repairing the Kent road within the parish.

5210 A Short Narrative of the Proceedings of the Gentlemen, concerned in obtaining the Act, for building a Bridge at Westminster; and of the Steps, which the Honourable the Commissioners, appointed by that Act, have taken to carry it into Execution. In a Letter to a Member of Parliament in the Country; Together with his Answer. *Lond. 1738*, *8°*. L.

5211 Some Observations on the Scheme offered by Mess[rs.] Cotton and Lediard, for Opening the Streets and Passages to and from the Intended Bridge at Westminster. In a letter from one of the Commissioners for Building the said Bridge, to Mr. Lediard, and his Answer. With the Scheme and Plan prefix'd: To which is added, a Plan of the Lower

Parts of the Parishes of St. Margaret and St. John the Evangelist, from the Horse-Ferry to White-hall; Wherein several farther Improvements are delineated, and a Proposal for Establishing a Perpetual Fund, to defray the Expences of Paving, Watching, and Lighting the said Bridge, and keeping it in Repair. By Thomas Lediard. *Lond.* [*1738*], 4°. O.

The Scheme (not seen) was published in 1738.

5212 *Begin.* Westminster Bridge-Office, June 9th 1738. Whereas by an Act passed in the 9th Year of the Reign of his present Majesty.... [*Lond. 1738*], *s. sh. F°*. LG.

An order forbidding damage to the bridge.

5213 EDINBURGH. Act of Council regulating Hackney-Coaches. [*Edin. 1738*], *s. sh. F°*. EU.

Dated: 1 March 1738.

5214 EDINBURGH. Act of Council regulating Hackney Chairs. [*Edin. 1738*], *s. sh. F°*. ECA.

Dated: 1 March 1738.

5215 At Edinburgh, the Fourteenth Day of June, One thousand Seven Hundred and thirty eight Years. [*Edin. 1738*], *s. sh. F°*. ACC.

An Act of the Town Council establishing and regulating the Company of Porters.

5216 By the Lord Lieutenant and Council of Ireland, a Proclamation, Offering a Reward for the Apprehending and Convicting of the Persons Concerned in the Robbing of the Post-Boy, between Newry and Armagh. *Dublin, 1737* [*o.s.*], *s. sh. F°*. DPRO.

Dated: 3 February, 1737.

SOCIAL CONDITIONS

5217 LONDON. Barnard, Mayor. An Especial Court held on Shrove-Tuesday ...the Fourteenth Day of February, 1737 [o.s.]. [*Lond. 1738*], *s. sh. F°*. L.

Suggesting means to enforce the laws against rogues and vagabonds.

5218 LONDON. Barnard, Mayor. A Common-Council held in the Chamber of the City of London on Thursday the Second Day of March, 1737 [o.s.]. [*Lond. 1738*], *s. sh. F°*. LCRO.

A resolve to put into force the law against rogues and vagabonds.

5219 A Report from the Lords Committees, appointed to Enquire into the State of the Work-house of this City; and how the Several Acts of Parliament, Relating thereunto, have been Executed: Made, by the Lord Tullamoore, and Agreed to by the House, on Tuesday the 21st of March, 1737 [o.s.]. And the Resolutions of the House thereupon: Together with the Papers Refer'd to in the said Report. *Dublin, 1738*, 4°. D.

5220 A Summary View of the Rise, Constitution, and Present State of the Charitable Foundation of King Charles the Second, commonly called, The Scots Corporation in London. With an Alphabetical List of the Benefactors, taken from the Registers, and from the Tables hung up in their Hall. *Lond. 1738*, 4º. O.

5221 Some Reasons of One of the Trustees of the Publick Infirmary in James-street, Westminster, Against the altering the Time of the Weekly Board. *n.p.* [*c. 1738?*], *F*º. M (Cr).

5222 Some Reasons of a Member of the Committee, &c. of the Trustees of the Infirmary in James Street Westminster, near St. James's Park, for his dividing against the Admission of Venereal Patients. In a Letter to a Lady. *n.p.* [*1738*], *F*º. M (Cr).

Dated: December 7, 1738.

5223 A Letter from a Gentleman in Town, to his Friend in the Country, relating to the Royal Infirmary of Edinburgh. *n.p.* [*1738*], 4º. O.

Signed: Philanthropos. Dated: December 1, 1738.

5224 A Short View of the Rise and Progress of the Royal Infirmary now building in the City of Edinburgh. *n.p.* [*1738?*], *s. sh. F*º. L.

5225 To all Gentlemen, Owners, and Commanders of Ships and Vessels, and other Well-wishers to Trade and Navigation. *n.p.* [*1738?*], *s. sh. F*º. LU.

A proposal for raising a fund for the relief of old and needy mariners.

5226 To the Right Honourable Sir John Barnard, Knt. Lord Mayor, and to the Court of Aldermen of the City of London. The Humble Petition of great Numbers of the Officers, Seamen, and Seafaring Men in the Service of the Merchants, and of their Countrey, in behalf of Themselves and their Brethren, &c. *n.p.* [*1738*], *s. sh. F*º. LU.

On the verso is: A short Abstract of the Plan proposed in the Daily-Advertiser of the 17th of May 1738, for the Relief of the Poor, Aged, and otherwise Disabled Seamen in the Merchants Service.

5227 The Case of the Poor Widows of the Commission and Warrant Officers, of the Royal Navy. Most humbly offer'd to the compassionate Consideration of the Noble and Honourable Members of both Houses of Parliament. *n.p.* [*1738?*], *s. sh. F*º. LLI.

5228 LONDON. Barnard, Mayor. At a Meeting of the Right Honourable Sir John Barnard, Knight, Lord Mayor, and others His Majesty's Justices of the Peace for this City of London.... [*Lond. 1738*], *s. sh. F*º. LG.

An order to enforce the Act for laying a Duty upon Retailing of Spirituous Liquors, made 23 March 1738.

5229 The Speech of Nathaniel Blackerby, Esq; at a General Meeting of His Majesty's Justices of the Peace for the City and Liberty of Westminster...on Saturday, April 1. 1738....On Occasion of His Majesty's

Royal Proclamation.... For the more effectual putting in execution the Laws against retailing Spirituous Liquors, protecting the Officers of Justice, assisting the Magistrates, and suppressing all Combinations, Confederacies, &c. *Lond. 1738*, *4°*. LU.

5230 Sabourn, Reay. A Perfect View of the Gin Act, with its Unhappy Consequences; containing not only an Inquiry into, but also a full Account of the Power of the Justices of the Peace, as limited by that Law. The whole illustrated with Well-attested Cases of some unhappy Sufferers from the Villanies of Perfidious Informers. *Lond. 1738*, *8°*. L.

5231 A Short History of the Gin Act: or, an Impartial Account of the Conduct of Some of those who have been intrusted with the Execution of it. To which is annex'd, A Relation of the Hardships and Sufferings of Several Persons who have been convicted by the unjustifiable Artifices, as well as the Perjuries and Villanies of Informers. *Lond.* [*1738*], *8°*. L.

5232 Three Letters upon the Subject of the Gin Act, and Common Informers ... to which is added, A Letter in respect to the Lights in London, and the Present Darkness of Westminster. *Lond. 1738*, *8°*. LU.

1739

GENERAL

5233 [LYTTELTON, GEORGE, Baron Lyttelton]. Considerations upon the present State of our Affairs, at Home and Abroad. In a Letter to a Member of Parliament from a Friend in the Country. *Lond. 1739, 8°.* L.

2nd edn. 1739; another edn. Dublin, 1739, 12° (both L). Reprinted in his *Works*, 1774.

5234 [LYTTELTON, GEORGE. Baron Lyttelton]. Farther Considerations on the present State of Affairs, at Home and Abroad, as affected by the Late Convention, in a Letter to the Minister: with an Appendix; containing A true State of the South-Sea Company's Affairs in 1718. *Lond. 1739, 8°.* L.

2nd edn. 1739 (L). A sequel to *Considerations* and presumably by the same author although not included in the collected *Works*, 1774.

5235 [KEITH, Sir WILLIAM]. The Citizen: or, the Weekly Conversation of a Society of London Merchants on Trade, and other Publick Affairs. no. 1–25. 9 Feb.–27 July 1739. *Lond. 1739, F°.* L.

Reprinted in *A Collection of Papers....By Sir William Keith*, 1740.

5236 MURRAY, Sir ALEXANDER. A Letter and Remonstrance, &c. to the Right Honourable Philip Lord Hardwicke, Lord High Chancellor of Great Britain, Arthur Onslow, Esquire, Speaker of the House of Commons, and Mr. Attorney and Mr. Sollicitor General, from Sir Alexander Murray....In relation to a Petition and some Proposals, which he Addressed last Sessions to Both Houses of Parliament. Wherein the Miserable State of Scotland, from the Slavish Dependance of the People on a Few Families, and the Great Danger thence arising to Great Britain, are considered. With a New Method of Improving all the different Products of our Lands and Waters, and Paying off the National Debts. *Lond. 1739, F°.* LSC.

Subsequently included in *The True Interest of Great Britain, Ireland and our Plantations*, 1740 [1741].

5237 The Dublin Society's Weekly Observations. Vol. I. (No. 1, Jan. 4, 1736/7 to No. 52, Apr. 4, 1738.) *Dublin, 1739, 12°.* LU.

Originally published in *The Dublin Newsletter*, in *Pue's Occurrences* and in *The Dublin Journal*. Another edn., Lond. 1740, entitled: Essays and Observations on the following Subjects. VIZ. On Trade...Published by a Society of Gentlemen in Dublin' (C); another edn. Glasgow, 1756 (O); another edn. Dublin, 1763 (DS). Each paper is signed with initials. Those signed M are by William Maple; those signed P by Thomas Prior (Desmond Clarke, *Thomas Prior*, 1951, p. 33 (and errata).

5238 MADDEN, SAMUEL. A Letter to the Dublin-Society, on the Improving their Fund; and the Manufactures, Tillage, &c. in Ireland. *Dublin, 1739, 8°.* LU.

5239 Four Letters originally written in French, relating to the Kingdom of Ireland, accompanied with Remarks.... *Dublin, 1739, 12°.* LU.

The letters are dated 1735.

AGRICULTURE

5240 TROWELL, SAMUEL. A New Treatise of Husbandry, Gardening, and other Curious Matters relating to Country Affairs: containing a Plain and Practical Method of Improving all Sorts of Meadow, Pasture and Arable Land, &c.... To which are added, Several Letters to Mr. Thomas Liveings, concerning his Compound Manure for Land, with some Practical Observations thereon. *Lond. 1739, 8°.* L.

Almost wholly on Liveing's salt compound manure. Another edn. 1747, entitled: The Farmer's Instructor; or, the Husbandman and Gardener's Useful and Necessary Companion. Being a New Treatise of Husbandry, Gardening, and other curious Matters relating to Country Affairs.... First Begun by Samuel Trowell, Gent. and now compleated with a Supplement to every Chapter on Husbandry.... By Willam Ellis (O); 2nd edn. 1750 (R).

5241 The Farmer Restored: or the Landed Interest Preserved. Most humbly offered to the Consideration of the Right Honourable the House of Commons. *Lond. 1739, 4°.* L.

For compelling distillers to use malted corn only.

5242 An Act for making Divisions, Inclosures and Allotments of the open Corn Fields and common Pasture in the Lordship of Bewholm, otherwise Bewham, in the Parish of Nunkeeling in the County of York. *n.p.* [*1739*], *F°.* L.

A bill. Reintroduced and passed in 1740. L has both bill and act.

5243 An Act for confirming certain Articles of Agreement, between the Lord of the Manor of Hunmanby, and the Vicar and Freeholders of Hunmanby, in the County of York, for inclosing part of the Moor in Hunmanby aforesaid. *n.p.* [*1739*], *F°.* L.

5244 An Act for Inclosing Part of a Common or Waste-Grounds called Hill-Side, otherwise Lamden-Common in the Manor and Parish of Odiham, and County of Southampton. *n.p. 1738–9, F°.* L.

5245 An Act for inclosing Part of certain Common Fields in the Township of Pailton in the County of Warwick. *n.p. 1738–9, F°.* L.

5246 An Act for dividing and inclosing the Common Fields lying in the Manor of Shipton Moyne, within the Parish of Shipton Moyne and Dovel, in the County of Gloucester, commonly called the North and South Common Fields. *n.p.* [*1739*], *F°.* L.

5247 A Letter from a Gentleman in the Country, to a Member of Parliament. *Dublin, 1739, 8°.* DNL.

On developing the mineral wealth of Ireland.

5248 A Bill for the Publick Registring of all Deeds, Conveyances, Wills and other Incumbrances, that shall be made of, or that may affect any Honours, Manors, Lands, Tenements or Hereditaments, within that Part of Great Britain called England, wherein Publick Registers are not already appointed by Act of Parliament. *n.p.* [*1739*], *F°.* L.

Another edn. entitled: A Bill, intituled, An Act...(L)

5249 Entry cancelled.

5250 The Case of the Clerks of the Inrollment in Chancery, with Regard to so much of the Bill now depending in Parliament for publick registring of Deeds, &c. as relates to inrolling of Deeds at full Length. *n.p.* [*1739*], *s. sh. F°.* L.

5251 RICHARDS, JOHN. Annuities on Lives, and for Limited Terms of Years, considered: being Observations on what hath lately advanced by divers Authors, tending to depreciate the Value of Estates on those Tenures. To which is added, A Supplement to the Gentleman's Steward and Tenants of Manors Instructed. *Lond. 1739, 8°.* L.

5252 [COLBATCH, JOHN]. Reasons for altering the Method used at present in letting Church and College Leases, Address'd to a Member of Parliament. By a Senior Fellow of a College in Cambridge. *Cambridge, 1739, 8°.* L.

For authorship see ms. note in O copy.

5253 Some Considerations on the Laws which Incapacitate Papists from Purchasing Lands, from taking long or beneficial Leases, and from lending Money on real Securities. *Dublin, 1739, 8°.* LU.

Another edn. Lond. 1740 (O); 3rd edn. Dublin, 1741 (O).

5254 Information for His Grace the Duke of Northfolk, Sir Robert Sutton and Sir Robert Clifton...Sir Alexander Murray and Sir Archibald Grant ...The Honourable George Wade...Alexander Ouchterlony, Richard Graham and Peter Murdoch...Pursuers; against the Annuitants of the York-building Company, Defenders. *n.p.* [*1739*], *F°.* EU.

Dated: July 13, 1739. Signed: James Erskine.

5255 DOYLE, WILLIAM. A Letter to every Well-Wisher of Trade and Navigation. Containig [*sic*] a Relation of the Author's Discoveries on the Nymph-Fishing-Bank, near the South Coast of Ireland; with a curious Map, including the Nymph-Bank....Remarks on the Dutch and other Foreign Fisheries: and Means proposed for Rendering our Own successful.... *Dublin, 1739, 8°.* LU.

MANUFACTURES

5256 JONES, WILLIAM. The Gentlemen's or Builder's Companion. Containing Variety of usefull Designs for Doors, Gateways, Peers, Chimney-Pieces, Slab Tables, Pier Glasses, or Tabernacle Frames, Ceiling Pieces &c. Explained on Copper-Plates. *Lond. 1739, 4°.* LRIBA.

5257 Trade Reviv'd: or, the Ladies Undress'd, and Dress'd again. In a Dialogue between Mrs. Alamode, an Eminent London Milliner, and

Mrs. Edging, a Noted Buckinghamshire Lace-Woman. *Lond. 1739*, *4°*. MP.

Advocating the wearing of home-made lace.

5258 A Bill to obviate certain Doubts which have arisen upon the Construction of the Act of the First Year of the Reign of King William and Queen Mary, intitled, An Act for Explaining Part of an Act made in the First Year of the Reign of King James the First, concerning Tanned Leather. *n.p.* [*1739*], *F°*. LU.

5259 The Case of the Curriers of the City of London. *n.p.* [*1739*], *s. sh. F°*. LLI.

5260 The Case of the Leather-Sellers of the City of London, humbly submitted to the Consideration of the Honourable House of Commons. *n.p.* [*1739*], *s. sh. F°*. LG.

5261 The Case of the Sadlers, Humbly Address'd to the Hon.ble the House of Commons. *n.p.* [*1739 ?*], *s. sh. F°*. LU.

5262 The Case of the Sadlers, in behalf of the Bill now pending before the Right Honourable the House of Peers, to obviate some Doubts in an Act of the First Year of the Reign of King William and Queen Mary, relating to the buying and selling of Tanned Leather. *n.p.* [*1739*], *F°*. L.

5263 The Proposals of the Leather-Sellers of London for Amendments to the Curryers Bill. *n.p.* [*1739 ?*], *s. sh. F°*. LU.

5264 To the Right Honourable the Lords Spiritual and Temporal of Great-Britain, in Parliament Assembled. The Case of the Shoe-makers, and other Manufacturers of Leather in the Corporation of Ipswich. *n.p.* [*1739 ?*], *s. sh. F°*. LLI.

5265 A True Sketch humbly presented to the Right Honourable the House of Lords, shewing the Unreasonableness of the Curriers Bill passing into a Law. *n.p.* [*1739*], *s. sh. F°*. LG.

5266 [Temple, William]. The Case as it now stands, between the Clothiers, Weavers, and other Manufacturers with regard to the Late Riot, in the County of Wilts. Containing, Remarks on a Libel, entitled an Essay on Riots, printed in the Gloucester Journal, December 19, 1738; some Observations on the Prices of Labour, in the Woollen Manufacture and Husbandry; Considerations and Reflections on the Act for Maintaining the Poor.... Proofs of the Necessity of reducing the Price of Labour in our Manufactures, in order to keep and extend our Foreign Trade.... By Philalethes. *Lond. 1739*, *8°*. LU.

Some copies have a title-page reading 'The Case as it stands....By Philalethes, B.S.F.W.C.' For authorship see the ms. note in LU copy.

5267 [Andrews, Thomas]. Country Common-Sense....By a Gentleman of Wilts. *Gloucester*, [*1739*], *12°*. 3 pt. O.

Essays, mostly dealing with the woollen industry. The author's name is disclosed on p. 156. Pts. 2 and 3 were printed in London.

5268 [Andrews, Thomas]. The Miseries of the Miserable: or, an Essay towards laying the Decay of the Fine Woollen Trade, and the Unhappy Condition of the Poor Wiltshire Manufacturers. By a Gentleman of Wilts. *n.p. 1739, 12°.* LU.

For authorship see *Country Common-Sense* (no. 5267), where this is advertised as by the same author.

5269 Answers for Mr. Robert Freebairn His Majesty's Printer, to the Petition of Alexander Alison, Printer in Edinburgh. *n.p.* [*1739*], *F°.* E.

Dated: December 3. 1739. Signed: Alexr. Boswel.

5270 Unto the Right Honourable, The Lords of Council and Session. The Petition of Alexander Alison, Printer in Edinburgh. *n.p.* [*1739*], *F°.* E.

Dated: July 26, 1739. Signed: Hu. Forbes.

5271 Information for William Somervell Deacon of the Incorporation of Skinners of Edinburgh, and James Lees Deacon of the Incorporation of Furriers there, against Patrick Wilson and others. *n.p.* [*1739*], *F°.* E.

Dated: June 1. 1739. Signed: Will. Grant.

5272 Information for Peter Wilson, and others Skinners in the Burgh of Canongate, Pursuers; Against the Incorporation of Skinners in Edinburgh, Defenders. *n.p.* [*1739*], *F°.* E.

Dated: July 4, 1739. Signed: Ja. Fergusson.

5273 Ross, Robert. A Collection of Papers, relating to a Scheme, laid before the Trustees of the Linen Manufacture, for the more effectual Reformation of Lappers. *Dublin, 1739, 8°.* LU.

5274 Some Thoughts on the Importance of the Linnen-Manufacture to Ireland, and how to Lessen the Expence of it. *Dublin, 1739, 8°.* L.

COMMERCE

5275 A Bill, intituled, An Act for prohibiting the Importation of Books reprinted Abroad, and first composed or written, and printed in Great Britain; and for limiting the Prices of Books. *n.p.* [*1739*], *F°.* L.

5276 Andrew Scott, Deacon, and the other Members of the Incorporation of Bakers in Glasgow, Appellants. The Provost, Baillies, and Magistrates of Glasgow, Respondents. The Appellants Case. *n.p.* [*1739*], *F°.* L.

Signed: Ch. Areskine. W. Murray. The appeal was against the price fixed at the Assize of Bread. Included is an 'Account of the prime cost of six firlots (i.e. bushels) wheat, with the expence of manufacturing it'.

5277 Andrew Scot, Deacon, and the other Members of the Incorporation of Baxters in Glasgow, Appellants. The Magistrates and Town Council of Glasgow, Respondents. The Respondents Case. *n.p.* [*1739*], *F°.* L.

Signed: J. Erskine. J. Browning.

5278 [MELON, JEAN FRANCOIS]. A Political Essay upon Commerce. Written in French by Monsieur M*****. Translated, with some Annotations and Remarks, by David Bindon. *Dublin*, *1739*, *8°*. EU.

The notes are concerned with Irish affairs. The French edn. of 1754 bears the author's name.

5279 HALES, STEPHEN. Philosophical Experiments: containing Useful, and Necessary Instructions for such as undertake long Voyages at Sea. Shewing how Sea-Water may be made Fresh and Wholsome: and how Fresh-Water may be preserv'd Sweet. How Biscuit, Corn, &c. may be secured from the Weevel, Meggots, and other Insects. And Flesh preserv'd in hot Climates, by Salting Animals whole....Likewise a Proposal for cleansing away Mud, &c. out of Rivers, Harbours, and Reservoirs. Which were read before the Royal-Society.... *Lond. 1739*, *8°*. L.

5280 A Bill for taking off the Duties upon Woollen and Bay Yarn imported from Ireland to England, and for the Effectual Preventing the Exportation of Wool from Great Britain, and of Wool and Wool manufactured from Ireland, to Foreign Parts. *n.p.* [*1739*], *F°*. L.

Another edn., entitled: A Bill, intituled, An Act for taking off the Duties... [1739] (L).

5281 WEBBER, SAMUEL. A Short Account of the State of our Woollen Manufacturies, from the Peace of Ryswick to This Time. Shewing, their Former Flourishing, and their Present Ruinous Condition; and that they always flourished when France could not get our Wool, but declined in Proportion to the Quantities of Wool Exported to them. To which is added An Effectual Scheme to prevent the Exportation of our Wool, by an Universal Registry. *Lond. 1739*, *8°*. LU.

Another edn. Dublin, 1740 (DA); 2nd edn. Lond. 1741 (L).

5282 WEBBER, SAMUEL. The Woolen Manufacturers Scheme, Humbly Offered to the Commons of Great Britain, in Parliament assembled, which would put an Effectual Stop to exporting unmanufactured Wool, Worsted, or Yarn, to Foreigners, without taxing Sheep, Wool, or Goods, or making one Officer.... *n.p.* [*1739?*], *s. sh. F°*. MC.

5283 [BRIDGES, GEORGE]. A Letter writ by Segdirboeg, in answer to five written by Mr. Samuel Webber, upon the Decay of the Woollen Manufactories in Great Britain and Ireland: also to his Scheme to prevent that Iniquitous Traffick for the future, by an Universal Registry....Wherein is discovered the Design and Ambitious Views of the said Webber....To which is prefixed, An Abstract of the New Act made against the Illicite Exportation of Wool.... *Lond. 1739*, *8°*. L.

Segdirboeg is Geo. Bridges in reverse.

5284 [MUNN, JOHN]. Considerations relating to the Running of Wool. *n.p.* [*1739?*], *F°*. L.

Title taken from endorsement. Reprinted in the second edn. of the author's *Observations on British Wool*, 1739.

5285 [MUNN, JOHN]. Proposals, Humbly Offer'd to the Consideration of this Present Parliament, to put an Effectual Stop to that Pernicious and Ruinous Practice of Running Wool to Foreign Parts: And by laying a Farthing per Pound Duty on Wool to defray the necessary Expence thereof. *n.p.* [*1739?*], *F°*. LU.

Signed: the Northamptonshire Clothier, J.M. Authorship deduced from other works of Munn.

5286 Reasons to prove the Necessity of the Duty's being taken off Irish Yarn imported to England; and Securing Wool and Yarn from Foreigners. Humbly offered to the Consideration of Parliament, by the Traders in the Woollen Manufactures. *n.p.* [*1739*], *s. sh. F°*. LLI.

5287 BRIDGES, GEORGE. The Smuglers Defeated: or the Golden Fleece Reviv'd. In a familiar Method for the Restoration of Trade. By the Experience, Travels and Imprisonment of the Sufferer, by the Clandestine Exporters of Combed Wool, Raw Wool, and Woollen Yarn from Ireland to France. Together with Proposals for removing the Difficulties...to redress and relieve the Starving Conditions of Thousands of his Majesty's Subjects, the Poor Artificers depending on the Woollen Trade.... *n.p. 1739, 8°*. LU.

Signed: G.B. The author's full name is disclosed on p. 5.

5288 Some Thoughts on the Value of the British Woollen Exportation Trade; and on a general Register in each Kingdom of all Sheep and their Wool, &c. Humbly presented to the Consideration of their Honours the Members of both Houses of Parliament. By a British Woollen Manufacturer. *n.p.* [*1739?*], *s. sh. F°*. MP.

5289 JINKINS, Captain. Spanish Insolence corrected by English Bravery; being an Historical Account of the many Signal Naval Atchievements obtained by the English over the Spaniards from the year 1350 to the present Time. Collected by Original Papers communicated by the suffering Merchants, and the most authentick Histories.... *Lond. 1739, 8°*. L.

Captain Jinkins may be a pseudonym.

5290 [ROBINS, BENJAMIN]. An Address to the Electors and other free Subjects of Great Britain; occasion'd by the late Secession. In which is contain'd A Particular Account of all our Negociations with Spain, and their Treatment of us, for above Ten Years past. *Lond. 1739, 8°*. L.

3rd edn. 1739 (O). For authorship see *D.N.B.*

5291 An Address to the Merchants of Great-Britain: or, A Review of the Conduct of the Administration, with Regard to our Trade and Navigation: shewing how the Trading Interest have been impos'd upon by the Enemies of the Ministry: with a Justification of the Convention concluded between Great-Britain and Spain. By a Merchant retir'd. *Lond.* [*1739*], *8°*. L.

5292 [Gordon, Thomas]. An Appeal to the Unprejudiced, concerning the present Discontents occasioned by the late Convention with Spain. *Lond. 1739, 8o.* LU.

For authorship see H. & L. quoting J. Maidment as authority.

5293 The British Sailor's Discovery: or the Spanish Pretensions Confuted. Containing a short History of the Discoveries and Conquests of Spain in America, with a particular Account of the illegal and unchristian means they made Use of to establish their settlements there.... *Lond. 1739, 8o.* LU.

5294 The Case of Richard Copithorne, Sole Owner and Master of the Ship Betty Galley, Burthen 150 Tuns; relating to his being taken by the Spaniards, and the Losses sustained by himself and Freighters thereby. Humbly addressed to the Honourable the House of Commons. *n.p.* [*1739*], *s. sh. Fo.* LLI.

5295 The Convention between the Crowns of Great Britain and Spain, concluded at the Pardo on the 14th of January 1739, N.S....Published by Authority. *Lond. 1739, 4o.* LU.

5296 The Convention Vindicated from the Misrepresentations of the Enemies of our Peace. *Lond. 1739, 8o.* LU.

Another edn. Dublin, 1739 (D).

5297 Cotejo de la Conducta de S.M. con la de el Rey Britanico....His Catholick Majesty's Conduct compared with that of His Brittanick Majesty, as well with regard to what happened before the Convention of the 14th of January of this Year 1739 as to what has been done since.... *Lond.* [*1739*], *8o.* pp. 63. LU.

Spanish and English on opposite pages. Another edn. n.d., pp. 39 (L).

5298 [Cowley, J.]. A Description of the Windward Passage, and Gulf of Florida, with the Course of the British Trading-Ships to, and from the Island of Jamaica. Also an Account of the Trade Winds.... Illustrated with a Chart of the Coast of Florida, and the Islands of Bahama, Cuba, Hispaniola, Jamaica, and the adjacent smaller Islands. ...Whereby is demonstrated, the Precariousness of those Voyages to the West-India Merchants, and the Impossibility of their Homeward-bound Ships keeping clear of the Spanish Guarda Costa's....To which are added, some Proposals for the better securing of the British Trade and Navigation to and from the West-Indies.... *Lond. 1739, 4o.* L.

For authorship see the advertisement in Cowley's *A View of the British Trade to the Mediterranean*, 1744. 2nd edn. 1739 (EU).

5299 A Dissertation on the Present Conjucture; particularly with Regard to Trade. By a Merchant of Bristol. *Lond. 1739, 8o.* LU.

2nd edn. 1739 (O); another 2nd edn. Bristol, 1740 (LU).

5300 [Copithorne, Richard]. The English Cotejo: or the Cruelties, Depredations, and Illicit Trade charg'd upon the English in a Spanish Libel,

Lately Published, compared with the Murders, Robberies, Barbarities and clandestine Trade proved upon the Spaniards. By a Sufferer. *Lond.* [*1739*], *8°*. LU.

For authorship see H. & L., who quote no authority.

5301 An Exact List of All Those who voted for and against the late Convention in the House of Commons, the Names of the Places for which they serve, their several known Employments, their visible yearly Salaries, in distinct Columns; With an introduction proper to the Subject, and also certain Queries....To which is added, A List of all those who voted for and against the Excise, in the Year 1733.... *Lond. 1739*, *8°*. L.

Another edn. of the first part, n.d., F°, without title, the text beginning: The Publick having been imposed on (L).

5302 A List of the Members who voted For and Against the Convention, March 1738 [o.s.]. *n.p.* [*1739*], *s. sh. F°*. L.

5303 [WALPOLE, HORATIO, Baron Walpole]. The Grand Question, Whether War, or no War, with Spain impartially Consider'd: in Defence of the present Measures against those that delight in War. *Lond. 1739*, *8°*. LU.

For authorship see W. Coxe, *Memoirs of Horatio*, *Lord Walpole*, p. 466 n.

5304 The King of Spain's Protest, relating to the South-Sea Company, not printed with the Convention Treaty. *n.p.* [*1739*], *s. sh. 4°*. LU.

Dated: Pardo, Jan. 10. 1739.

5305 His Catholick Majesty's Manifesto, justifying his Conduct in relation to the late Convention. With his Reasons for not paying the Ninety-Five Thousand Pounds. (Manifeste de sa Majesté Catholique....) *Lond. 1739*, *8°*. LU.

English and French on opposite pages.

5306 An Examination of a Pamphlet, entitled His Catholic Majesty's Manifesto, &c. With Reasons for not Paying the 95000 l. *Lond. 1739*, *8°*. L.

5307 The King of Spain's Reasons for not paying the 95,000 l. stipulated in the Convention signed at the Pardo, 14 Jan. 1739, Examined. To which is added, The Convention and the Separate Articles.... *Lond. 1739*, *8°*. L.

5308 Observations upon the Manifesto of His Catholick Majesty; with an Answer to his Reasons for not paying the Ninety-Five Thousand Pounds. In Vindication of the Honour of Great Britain. *Lond. 1739*, *8°*. LU.

2nd edn. 1739 (LU).

5309 A Letter from a Merchant in London, to his Correspondent Abroad. In which the Present State of Affairs is impartially considered. *Lond. 1739*, *8°*. L.

Signed: M.C.

5310 [AMHURST, NICHOLAS ?]. A Letter to the Right Honourable Sir R—— W——, &c. upon the present Posture of Affairs, wherein, amongst other things, the Convention will be set in a clear Light....By Caleb Danvers, Esq; *Lond.* *1739*, *8°*. LU.

For attribution see H. & L., who quote no authority.

5311 Ministerial Prejudices in favour of the Convention, Examin'd and Answer'd. *Lond.* *1739*, *8°*. LU.

5312 The National Dispute; or, the History of the Convention Treaty, containing the full Substance of all the Proceedings, Debates, Pamphlets, Journals, Daily, and other Papers, published both for and against the late Convention. With necessary and proper Introductions thereto.... *Lond.* *1739*, *8°*. LU.

5313 Observations arising from the Declaration of War against Spain, with Considerations relating to the Future Management of it on the part of Great-Britain....By the Author of the Letter to Sir G—— C——, and The Conduct of the Livery, &c. *Lond.* *1739*, *8°*. L.

5314 [ROBINS, BENJAMIN]. Observations on the Present Convention with Spain. *Lond.* *1739*, *8°*. L.

Another edn. Dublin, 1739 (DA). For authorship see *D.N.B.*

5315 Peace and no Peace: or an Enquiry whether the late Convention with Spain will be more advantageous to Great Britain than the Treaty of Seville....Inscribed to the Merchants of Great-Britain. With a Postscript upon the King of Spain's Protest, which is not printed with the Convention. *Lond.* *1739*, *8°*. LU.

5316 Popular Prejudices against the Convention and Treaty with Spain, Examin'd and Answer'd. With Remarks on a Pamphlet, entitled, Considerations upon the Present State of our Affairs at Home and Abroad. *Lond.* *1739*, *8°*. LU.

Another edn. Dublin, 1739 (DA).

5317 A Reply to a Pamphlet intitled, Popular Prejudices against the Convention and Treaty with Spain, Examin'd and Answered. In a Letter to a Member of Parliament. *Lond.* *1739*, *8°*. LU.

2nd edn. 1739 (L).

5318 Some Remarks on a Pamphlet intitled Popular Prejudices against the Convention and Treaty with Spain. In a Letter to a Member of Parliament. *n.p.* [*1739*], *s. sh. F°*. L.

Title taken from endorsement.

5319 The Present State of Politicks in Europe. With some Observations on the present Posture of our own Affairs. *Lond.* *1739*, *8°*. L.

5320 A Proposal for Humbling Spain. Written in 1711. by a Person of Distinction. And now first printed from the Manuscript. To which are added, Some Considerations on the Means of Indemnifying Great Britain from the Expences of the Present War. *Lond.* [*1739*], *8°*. LU.

2nd edn. [1740] (LU).

5321 Reasons for giving Encouragement to the Sea-Faring People of Great-Britain, in Times of Peace or War, for the more effectually Destroying Enemies or Pirates at all Times. And for Distressing the Commerce of the Subjects of Spain at this Time. With some of the many remarkable Actions between the English and Spaniards at Sea. *Lond. 1739*, 8°. L.

5322 [PULTENEY, WILLIAM, Earl of Bath]. A Review of all that hath passed between the Courts of Great Britain and Spain, relating to our Trade and Navigation from the Year 1721, to the Present Convention; with some Particular Observations upon it. *Lond. 1739*, 8°. L.

For authorship see B.M. Catalogue.

5323 A Series of Wisdom and Policy: being a full Justification of all Our Measures, since the year 1721, inclusive; and especially of our late most Honourable Convention with Spain. *Lond. 1739*, 8°. LU.

5324 Several New, Pressing and Weighty Considerations for an Immediate War with Spain. With a reasonable Plan of making the whole Operations effectual, to the Reparation of our Merchants, the Securing the whole Effects of the South-Sea Company in America, the Reviving of our sinking Trade, the animating and uniting the Hearts of the Subjects, the Glory of His Majesty; and the promoting the Happiness of Great Britain, and all her Dominions at Home and Abroad. In a Letter to his Royal Highness the Prince of Wales, &c. By Mercator. *Lond. 1739*, F°. LSC.

5325 The Spanish Merchant's Address to all Candid and Impartial Englishmen: being a Short Enquiry into the general Conduct of the Administration, as it regards chiefly the Interests of Trade and Navigation, and the Money Affairs of the Nation.... *Lond. 1739*, 8°. L.

5326 [CAMPBELL, HUGH HUME, Earl of Marchmont]. A State of the Rise and Progress of our Disputes with Spain, and of the Conduct of our Ministers relating thereto. *Lond. MDCCXXIXX* [*1739*], 8°. LU.

For authorship see *An Historical View of the Principles, Characters, Persons, &c. of the Political Writers in Great Britain*, 1740, p. 47.

5327 A View of the Political Transactions of Great-Britain since the Convention was approv'd of by Parliament. In a Letter to an absenting Member. *Lond. 1739*, 8°. L.

5328 By the King, A Proclamation, For recalling and prohibiting Seamen from serving foreign Princes and States. *Lond. 1739*, *s. sh. F°*. LSC.

Dated: 15 June 1739.

5329 By the King, A Proclamation, For encouraging Seamen and Landmen to enter themselves on Board His Majesty's Ships of War. [*Lond. 1739*], *s. sh. F°*. LSC.

Dated: 15 June 1739.

5330 By the King, A Proclamation, For encouraging Seamen to enter themselves on Board His Majesty's Ships of War. *Lond. 1739, s. sh. F°.* C (Cr).

Dated: 27 September 1739.

5331 A Bill, intituled, An Act for the more effectual securing and encouraging the Trade of His Majesty's British Subjects to America, and for the Encouragement of Seamen to enter into His Majesty's Service. *n.p.* [*1739*], *F°.* L.

5332 A Bill intituled, An Act for Granting a Liberty to carry Sugars, of the Growth, Produce, or Manufacture of any of His Majesty's Sugar Colonies in America, from the said Colonies directly to Foreign Parts, in Ships built in Great Britain, and navigated according to Law. *n.p.* [*1739*], *F°.* L.

5333 [Hyam, Thomas]. Calculations, Shewing the Difference between bringing of Sugar from the English Plantations through Great Britain and from thence to the Dutch markets, and carrying them thither in the same Ship without Landing in Great Britain. *n.p.* [*1739*], *s. sh. F°.* L.

For authorship see ms. note on copy in B.M. Add. MS. 12431 f. 164.

5334 The Case of the British Sugar Colonies. *n.p.* [*1739*], *F°.* LLI.

Text begins: The Present Situation of the Trade of the Sugar Colonies. For direct exportation to the Mediterranean markets.

5335 The Sugar-Planters Reasons, for Desiring a direct Exportation from the British Colonies, to Foreign Parts, consider'd. *n.p.* [*1739*], *F°.* LLI.

5336 Consideration on the American Trade, before and since the establishment of the South-Sea Company. *Lond. 1739, 8°.* LU.

2nd edn., with additions, 1739 (L).

5337 Coope, Richard. A Letter to the Proprietors of the South-Sea Company. With a Dedication to George Heathcote, Esq;... *Lond. 1739, 8°.* LU.

Coope had been a Director of the Company from 1732.

5338 The Case of James Buchanan, Merchant in London, and Others, concerned and interested in the Ship Scipio, of which Alexander Mackpherson, was Master. *n.p.* [*1739*], *F°.* LLI.

The ship, carrying slaves, gold-dust & ivory, was seized by the French in the West Indies.

COLONIES

5339 A Bill, intituled, An Act for naturalizing such foreign Protestants, and others therein mentioned, as are settled, or shall settle in any of His Majesty's Colonies in America. *n.p.* [*1739*], *F°.* L.

5340 Fry, Richard. A Scheme for a Paper Currency. [*Boston, 1739*], *8°.*

Reprinted in *Colonial Currency Reprints*, ed. by A. M. Davis, vol. 3 (1911), whence this entry is taken.

5341 CALLENDER, JOHN. An Historical Discourse on the Civil and Religious Affairs of the Colony of Rhode-Island and Providence Plantations in New-England in America, from the first Settlement 1638, to the End of the first Century. *Boston, 1739, 8°.* L.

5342 South-Carolina. An Account of sundry Goods Imported and of sundry Goods of the produce of this province Exported, from the several Ports within the said province, from the First of November 1738, to the First of November 1739. With the Number of Vessels entered and cleared at each port. As also from whence arrived and where bound. *Charles-Town, 1739, s. sh. obl. F°.* L.

5343 [LESLIE, CHARLES]. A new and exact Account of Jamaica. Wherein the ancient and present state of that Colony, its importance to Great Britain, Laws, Trade, Manners and Religion, together with the most remarkable and curious animals, plants, trees, &c. are described.... *Edin. 1739, 12°.* JCB.

3rd edn., with author's name, Edin. 1740 (L). Another anon. edn., entitled: A New History of Jamaica, Lond. 1740 (L); 2nd edn. 1740 (O); another edn. Dublin, 1741 (L).

FINANCE

5344 Sir George Caswall, Knt. Jacob Sawbridge, Esq; Robinson Knight and Sir Henry Blunt, Bart. formerly Henry Blunt, Appellants, Thomas Houghton, Respondent. The Case of the Appellants. *n.p. [1739], F°.* L.

Signed: D. Ryder. J. Strange. South Sea stock bought in 1720.

5345 Sir George Caswall, Knight, Jacob Sawbridge, Esq; Robinson Knight, Esq; and Sir Henry Blunt, Baronet, Appellants. Thomas Houghton, Esq; Respondent. The Respondent's Case. *n.p. [1739], F°.* L.

Signed: J. Browne, W. Murray.

5346 To the Right Honourable the Lords Spiritual and Temporal in Parliament assembled. A State of the National-Debt, Provided or Unprovided for by Parliament, as it stood 31 Dec. 1737, and 31 Dec. 1738, together with an Account of the Produce of the Sinking Fund in that Year....Presented March 21, 1738–9.... *n.p. [1739], s. sh. F°.* MC.

5347 The Impartial Accomptant. To all Lovers of Great-Britain...is demonstratively made known how to Pay the National Debts, if 48 Millions, in Seven Years; and without a New Tax, or any Inconveniency to the People. *Lond. 1739, 8°.* LU.

Signed: Philo Britannicus. On the land tax and the window tax.

5348 Ambrose Farrell, Christian Dillon, Robert and Thomas Dillon, Executors of Theobald Dillon, Merchant, deceased, Appellants. Robert Jocelyn Esq; his Majesty's Attorney General of Ireland, in behalf of his Majesty, Respondent. The Appellants Case. *n.p. [1739], F°.* L.

Signed: W. Noel. Will. Hamilton. On duties on wine imported into Dublin in 1735 and 1736.

5349 Robert Dillon, Thomas Dillon, Ambrose Farrel, and Christian Dillon, Executors of the Last Will and Testament of Theobald Dillon, Merchant, deceased Appellants. Robert Jocelyn Esq; his Majesty's Attorney-General, on the Behalf of his Majesty Respondent. The Respondent's Case. *n.p.* [*1739*], *F°*. L.

Signed: D. Ryder. J. Strange.

5350 A Bill, intituled, An Act for the more easy assessing, collecting, and levying of County Rates. *n.p.* [*1739*], *F°*. L.

5351 Scurrility and Defamation Corrected; or A proper Answer to a late abusive Pamphlet, intituled, City Corruption and Mal-Administration Displayed. Being an Apology for the Conduct of the Gentleman of late Years, entrusted with the Management of the City's Affairs.... By a Lover of Truth. *Lond. 1739, 8°*. L.

5352 Phipps, Joseph. The Vestry laid Open; or, a Full and Plain Detection of the many Gross Abuses, Impositions, and Oppressions of Select-Vestries.... The third edition. *Lond. 1739, 8°*. LU.

5353 A Dissertation upon Tithes. With a Collection of Papers imperfectly published in the Gentleman's Magazine, in Answer to T.B. *Lond. 1739, 8°*. L.

Signed: J... H....

5354 An Examination of a Book, lately printed by the Quakers, and by them distributed to the Members of both Houses of Parliament; intituled, A Brief Account of many of the Prosecutions of the People called Quakers, in the Exchequer, Ecclesiastical, and other Courts; for Demands recoverable by the Acts made in the 7th and 8th Years of the Reign of King William III. for the more easy Recovery of Tythes, Church-rates, &c. So far as the Clergy of the Diocese of Lichfield and Coventry are concerned in it. *Lond. 1739, 8°*. L.

5355 [Besse, Joseph]. A Vindication of a Book intituled A brief Account of many of the Prosecutions of the People call'd Quakers, &c. presented to the Members of both Houses of Parliament, in Answer to a late Examination thereof, so far as the Clergy of the Diocese of Lichfield and Coventry are concerned in it: with an Appendix, in Reply to the Objections of Two Clergymen of the Diocese call'd St. David's. *Lond. 1739, 8°*. L.

For authorship see Joseph Smith, *A Descriptive Catalogue of Friends' Books*, 1867, I, 255.

5356 [Blacker, Samuel]. Property Vindicated: or, some Remarks upon a late Pamphlet, Intitled, Property Inviolable. *Dublin, 1739, 8°*. L.

Another issue, with the author's name on the title-page and with a dedication added, Dublin, 1739 (DNL). On tithe. A reply to no. 4926.

5357 Maculla, James. The Case of Ireland relating to the Scarcity of Copper Half-pence and Farthings, with the Remedies thereof. Humbly offered to the Consideration of the Parliament of Ireland. *Dublin, 1739, 8°*. C.

5358 On the Scarcity of Copper Coin. A Satyr. [*Edin.*], *1739*, *8°*. EU.
In verse.

5359 A Bill, intituled, An Act for explaining and making more effectual the several Laws therein mentioned for suppressing Lotteries denominated Sales, and other private Lotteries. *n.p.* [*1739*], *F°*. L.

5360 HAYES, RICHARD. Modern Book-keeping, or the Italian Method Improved. Containing Rules and Directions for Keeping Gentlemens and Merchants Accounts by Double Entry....The Second Edition. *Lond. 1739*, *8°*. L.
The first edition, not seen, was published in 1731.

TRANSPORT

5361 [NIXON, GEORGE]. An Enquiry into the Reasons of the Advance of the Price of Coals, within Seven Years past. In which are shewn, the great Impositions laid on the several Consumers by a Monopoly of that Commodity. And some Methods proposed for destroying the Present, and preventing all Future Monopolies and Combinations in the Coal Trade. *Lond. 1739*, *8°*. LU.
For authorship see E. Hughes, *North Country Life*, 1952, pp. 246–7.

5362 The Case of the Corporation of Hertford, and of the Inhabitants of the Town of Ware, and of several Farmers, Maltsters, Barge-Owners, and other Persons concerned in the Navigation on the River Lee, and of the New River Company, with relation to the Bill in Parliament concerning both the said Rivers. *n.p.* [*1739?*], *F°*. L.

5363 The Case of the Petitioners for the Bill, entituled, An Act for the ascertaining, preserving, and improving the Navigation of the River Lee, &c. now depending in the Right Honourable the House of Lords. *n.p.* [*1739*], *s. sh. F°*. LLI.
Almost identical with the preceding.

5364 Case of the Rev. John Lloyd, of Ryton in the County of Durham, a Petitioner against the Bill now depending in Parliament, intituled, An Act for Preserving, Ascertaining, and Improving the Navigation of the River Lee, &c. *n.p.* [*1739*], *F°*. LLI.

5365 Reasons humbly offered against passing the Bill, in the Form it now is, intituled, An Act, for ascertaining, preserving, and improving the Navigation of the River Lee.... *n.p.* [*1739?*], *F°*. LLI.

5366 *Begin.* Mansfield is a Town of considerable Trade in Malt.... *n.p.* [*1739*], *s. sh. F°*. LLI.
The case of Mansfield for safeguards in the turnpike bill for the Chesterfield to Worksop and the Chesterfield to Mansfield roads.

5367 A Bill for Inlarging the Term and Powers granted by an Act made in the Twelfth Year of the Reign of his late Majesty King George, intituled, An Act for Repairing the Roads in the Parishes of Kensington, Chelsea and Fulham, and other Parishes therein mentioned, in the County of

Middlesex; and for Repairing some other Roads in the Parish of Saint George Hanover-square, and the said Parishes of Kensington and Chelsea. *n.p.* [*1739*], *F°*. L.

5368 Labelye, Charles. A Short Account of the Methods made use of in Laying the Foundation of the Piers of Westminster-Bridge. With an Answer to the Chief Objections that have been made thereto.... *Lond. 1739*, *8°*. LU.

5369 A Bill to enlarge the Powers of the Commissioners for building a Bridge cross the River Thames, from the Woolstaple or thereabouts, in the Parish of Saint Margaret in the City of Westminster, to the opposite Shore in the County of Surrey; towards finishing the said Bridge under their Care, and to remove all Doubts and Difficulties concerning their purchasing and disposing of Houses and Ground, lying near to the Streets, Ways and Passages on each Side the River Thames, to and from the said Bridge; and also, to enable them to make Ways and Passages to and from both Houses of Parliament, and the Courts of Justice. *n.p.* [*1739*], *F°*. L.

5370 A Bill for building a Bridge cross the River Ribble, from the Township of Preston to the Township of Penwortham in the County Palatine of Lancaster. *n.d.* [*1739*], *F°*. L.
With a map.

5371 Reasons for Building a Bridge cross the River Ribble, betwixt the Townships of Preston and Penwortham in the County of Lancashire. *n.p.* [*1739*], *s. sh. F°*. LLI.

5372 The Case of the Inhabitants in the Suburbs of Bath, and of all Strangers that resort to that City, in Relation to the Hire of Chairs, Stated. In a Letter to a Member of Parliament. *n.p.* [*1739*], *F°*. LLI.

SOCIAL CONDITIONS

5373 Foley, Robert. Laws relating to the Poor, from the Forty-third of Queen Elizabeth to the Third of King George II. With Cases adjudged in the Court of King's Bench, upon the several Clauses of them. In a Method entirely New. *Lond. 1739*, *8°*. L.
2nd edn. 1743 (LU); 3rd edn. 1751 (L).

5374 A Bill, intituled, An Act for the more effectual punishing and suppressing of Rogues, Vagabonds, and other idle and disorderly Persons. *n.p.* [*1739*], *F°*. L.

5375 An Account of the Foundation and Government of the Hospital for Foundlings in Paris. Drawn up at the Command of her late Majesty Queen Caroline, and now published for the Information of those who may be concern'd in carrying on a like Design in this City. *Lond. 1739*, *8°*. O.

5376 A Copy of the Royal Charter, establishing an Hospital for the Maintenance and Education of Exposed and Deserted Young Children. *Lond.* *1739*, 8º. L.

Another edn., 1740, entitled: The Royal Charter, etc. (O).

5377 Proposals by the Magistrates and Town-Council of Aberdeen, for Erecting an Infirmary and Work-House in the City of Aberdeen. *n.p.* [*1739*], *F*º. LU.

5378 ABERDEEN. Act of Council anent the Infirmary and Work-House in Aberdeen. May 30th 1739. *n.p.* [*1739*], *s. sh. F*º. LU.

Title taken from endorsement.

5379 A Letter from a Gentleman in Town to his Friend in the Country, relating to the Royal Infirmary of Edinburgh. *Edin.* *1739*, 4º. O.

Signed: Philasthenes. Dated: November 30. 1739.

5380 A Bill, intituled, An Act for explaining and amending an Act passed in the Tenth Year of His present Majesty's Reign, intituled, An Act for Relief of Insolvent Debtors, and so much of an Act passed in the last Session of Parliament, as extends the Benefit of the said Act, for Relief of Insolvent Debtors, to Creditors whose Debtors were committed to Prison since the First Day of January, One thousand seven hundred and thirty, and were detained there upon the First Day of January, One thousand seven hundred and thirty six, and had chose to continue there. *n.p.* [*1739*], *F*º. L.

5381 The Case of Robert Martin, Thomas Glanfield, and Richard Chandler, Assignees of the Estate and Effects of Thomas Kerridge, Esq; under an Act passed in the Tenth Year of his present Majesty, intituled, An Act for Relief of Insolvent Debtors. With Observations on the same. *n.p.* [*1739*], *F*º. L.

5382 A Bill, intituled, An Act for the Amendment of the Law relating to the Administration of the Assets of Persons dying Insolvent, and for an equitable Division thereof amongst their Creditors. *n.p.* [*1739*], *F*º. L.

5383 Proposals from the City of Dublin, for Raising the Sum of Twenty five Thousand Pounds by Subscription for the Benefit of Widows of Clergy Men, and Others; by setling Jointures and Annuities at the Rate of Twenty five per Cent. With Directions for the Widow how to receive her Annuity, without any Delay, Charges, or Deductions. *Dublin,* *1739*, 8º. DA.

5384 A List of the Reduced Officers of His Majesty's Land Forces and Marines entitled to receive Half Pay in Great-Britain, with an Estimate of the Charge thereof for the Year 1739. Also, A List of the Reduced Officers of His Majesty's Land Forces and Marines entitled to receive Half Pay in Great-Britain, with an Estimate of the Charge thereof for the Year 1740. To which is added, Their Ages, Dates of their first Commissions, and the Time they were put upon Half Pay, and the Occasion thereof. *Lond.* *1739*, *F*º. O.

1740

GENERAL

5385 KEITH, Sir WILLIAM. A Collection of Papers and other Tracts, written occasionally on Various Subjects.... *Lond. 1740, 8°.* L.

Commerce, colonies. 2nd edn., 1749 (L).

5386 The Present State of the Revenues and Forces, by Sea and Land, of France and Spain. Compar'd with those of Great Britain. Being an Essay to demonstrate the Disadvantages under which France must enter into the present War, if the natural Force of Britain is vigorously exerted. To which is added, an Appendix: containing a View of those Countries of the Spanish West Indies that will probably be the Seat of the present War. *Lond. 1740, 8°.* LU.

Another edn. Dublin, 1740 (DA).

5387 The Universal Pocket-Book...containing amongst a great many other Particulars, I, A Map of the World....III. A Map of England, with an Account of the Number of Parishes, Market-Towns, Market-Days, Cities, Bishopricks, &c....VI. The Gardiner's Monthly Director in the Fruit, Flower and Kitchen Garden. VII. A Table of simple Interest at 5 per Cent. VIII. Rates of Watermen, Coachmen and Chairmen. IX. A Table ready cast up shewing the Value of any Quantity of Goods at any Price. X. Of the General and Penny Post.... XII. The Prices of the different Works, of Bricklayers, Masons, Joiners, Carpenters, Plumbers, Slaters, Painters, Plaisterers, Paviors, Smiths, Carvers, &c. XIII. Of Ancient and Modern Coins, Weights, Measures, &c. XIV. A New Plan of London, with a Description of whatever is remarkable. XV. An Account of all the Stage-Coaches, and Carriers in England and Scotland. XVI. A List of Places at Court, with their Salaries and in whose Gift.... *Lond. 1740, 12°.* O.

5388 A Compleat Guide to All Persons who have any Trade or Concern with the City of London and Parts adjacent; Containing I. The Names of All the Streets....II. The Names of the Churches...as also an Account of the City Companies, their Halls, &c. III. An Account of the Stage-Coaches and Carriers throughout England and Scotland; where they Inn, and when they Go out. IV. The Rates of Watermen, Hackney Coachmen, Chairmen, Carmen, and Porters; of the Penny Post Offices, where kept, and to what Places they send Letters. V. The Names and Places of Abode of the most Eminent Merchants and Traders in London, alphabetically digested. VI. Useful Tables, which shew the Value of any Quantity of Goods, from One Farthing to Twenty-seven Shillings.... *Lond. 1740, 12°.* L.

2nd edn. 1740; 3rd 1744; 4th 1749 (all L). Many later editions.

5389 The Distress'd State of Ireland Consider'd more particularly with Respect to the North. In a Letter to a Friend. *n.p. 1740, 12°.* DA.

5390 A List of Commodities Imported Yearly into Ireland, being such as may be either Raised or Manufactured therein, together with their Yearly Value, taken at a Medium for the Years, 1734, 1735, 1736. *Dublin*, [*1740*], *s. sh. F*o. L.

Dated: 25 March 1740. Issued by the Dublin Society, who give notice that they intend to encourage by premiums persons who are well skilled in such arts and manufactures.

5391 A Topographical and Chorographical Survey of the County of Down. Including some Part of the Natural and Civil History. Intended as an Essay towards a fuller Description of the Kingdom of Ireland, than has hitherto appeared. To which are annexed, Queries, recommended to the Curious, to enable them to make proper Enquiries in their respective Neighbourhoods. *Dublin*, *1740*, *8*o. L.

Another edn. London, 1740 (L).

AGRICULTURE

5392 The Rules to be observed by the Flax-Raisers appointed by the Trustees for the Manufactures, and by all others who apply to them for a Premium for raising Lint, &c. *n.p.* [*1740*], *8*o. E.

5393 Frugal Husbandry expressed in short Rules and Directions for the Growth and Improvement of Hops. *Dublin*, *1740*, *8*o. DA.

The preface signed: E.B.

5394 A Bill for making Divisions, Inclosures and Allotments of the open Corn Fields and Common Pasture in the Lordship of Bewholm, otherwise Bewham, in the Parish of Nunkeeling in the County of York, and for settling and establishing the Payment of a yearly Sum to the Impropriators of the Rectory of Nunkeeling aforesaid, and their Heirs, in lieu of Tythes arising within the said Lordship, pursuant to an Agreement between the said Impropriators and the Proprietors of the said Lands. *n.p.* [*1740*], *F*o. LHL.

5395 An Act for Confirming and Establishing an Exchange agreed upon between the Lord of the Manor and Rector of the Parish Church of Great Bircham, in the County of Norfolk; and for promoting and facilitating an Inclosure intended to be made of Divers Commons, Common Pasture, and Waste Grounds, lying in the said Parish of Great Bircham. *n.p.* [*1740*], *F*o. L.

The lord of the manor was Sir Robert Walpole; the rector Henry Bland.

5396 An Act for Confirming and Establishing Articles of Agreement and an Award for Dividing and Inclosing of a Common Down; and for Dividing and Inclosing and Exchanging of Lands, lying in the Tything of Charlton, in the Parish of Andover, in the County of Southampton. *n.p.* *1739–40*, *F*o. L.

5397 A Bill for dividing and inclosing several open Fields, Pastures, and Commons, in the Townships of Great Driffield, and Little Driffield, in the County of York; and for settling certain yearly Payments to the Prebendary of Driffield, for the Time being, in lieu of his Tythes, pursuant to an Award made for those Purposes. *n.p.* [*1740*], *F°*. LHL.

5398 An Act for Inclosing and Dividing the Common Fields, Common Pastures, and Waste Grounds, lying within the Manor and Township of Gunnerton, in the County of Northumberland. *n.p.* *1739–40*, *F°*. L.

5399 An Act for Confirming and Establishing certain Articles of Agreement made between Maurice Conyers, Esquire, Lord of the Manor of Rusthall, in the County of Kent, and the Right Honourable William Lord Abergavenny, and other the Freehold Tenants of the said Manor, relating to certain Buildings and Inclosures made and erected in and upon Part of the Wastes of the said Manor; and for making the said Agreement more effectual for the Purposes thereby intended. *n.p.* [*1740*], *F°*. LHL.

5400 An Act for Dividing and Inclosing the Common Fields in the Parish of Stivichall alias Stichall, in the County of the City of Coventry. *n.p.* [*1740*], *F°*. L.

5401 LEAFORD, JOHN. Some Observations made of the Frequent Drowned Condition of the South Level of the Fenns, and of the Works made for Draining the same; with a Scheme for Relieving that Level, by carrying those Works into Execution with some small Additions. *Lond.* *1740*, *4°*. O.

The dedication signed: John Leaford.

5402 A Bill for further and more effectually preventing the wilful and malicious Destruction of Collieries and Coal-works. *n.p.* [*1740*], *F°*. L.

5403 The Case of the Petitioner John Fletcher, and his Co-partners; against the Bill for further and more effectually preventing the wilful and malicious Destruction of Collieries and Coal-Works. *n.p.* [*1740*], *s. sh. F°*. L.

With a plan by Philip Hutchinson of several veins of coal in Derby and Nottingham.

5404 The Case of the Petitioners. *n.p.* [*1740*], *F°*. L.

Title from endorsement. For the bill to prevent the destruction of coalmines.

5405 O'CONNOR, MARTIN. A State of the Copper-Trade in Ireland, Humbly offered to the Consideration of the Honourable House of Commons. *n.p.* [*c. 1740 ?*], *F°*. DM.

5406 A Bill, intituled, An Act for the publick registring of Deeds, Conveyances, and Incumbrances, that shall be made of, or may affect Honors, Manors, Lands, Tenements, or Hereditaments, within that Part of

Great Britain called England, and the Dominion of Wales. *n.p.* [*1740*], *F°*. L.

Another edn. entitled: An Act for the Publick Registering of Deeds...[1740] (L).

5407 BROOKES, R. The Art of Angling, Rock and Sea-Fishing. With the Natural History of River, Pond, and Sea-Fish. Illustrated with 133 cutts. *Lond. 1740, 8°*. EU.

Contains 'A short Description of the Rise and Progress of all the noted Rivers in England' and 'An Account of the Navigation of the River Thames'.

MANUFACTURES

5408 LANGLEY, BATTY. The Builders Compleat Assistant, or a Library of Arts and Sciences, absolutely necessary to be understood by Builders and Workmen in general....The whole exemplified by 77 large quarto copper-plates. *Lond.* [*c. 1740, ?*], *8°*. L.

The plates are dated 1738. 3rd and 4th edns., both undated (L).

5409 LANGLEY, BATTY. The City and Country Builder's and Workman's Treasury of Designs: or, the Art of Drawing, and Working the Ornamental Parts of Architecture.... *Lond. 1740, 4°*. L.

Another edn. 1745, with 'By B.L.' on the title-page and the preface signed with the author's full name (O); 2nd edn. 1750 (L).

5410 To the Champion. *n.d.* [*c. 1740 ?*], *s. sh. F°*. MC.

On the linen manufacture.

5411 HAINES, HENRY. Treachery, Baseness, and Cruelty display'd to the full; in the Hardships and Sufferings of Mr. Henry Haines, late Printer of the Country Journal, or Craftsman; who now is, and for above Two Years has been, in close Imprisonment in the King's Bench, for a Fine of Two hundred Pounds, at the Suit of the Crown, for Printing and Publishing the Craftsman of July 2, 1737. *Lond. 1740, 8°*. L.

5412 Information for Mr. Robert Freebairn, His Majesty's Printer for Scotland, and Mr. John Baskett His Majesty's Printer for England his Partner, against the Representatives and Assignies of James Watson, Printer in Edinburgh, deceast. *n.p.* [*1740*], *4°*. E.

Dated: June 16, 1740. Signed: And. McDouall.

5413 Information for Richard Watkins Merchant in Edinburgh, against Mr. Robert Freebairn, John Basket and others. *n.p.* [*1740*], *4°*. E.

Dated: July 14th 1740. Signed: Ja. Graham.

5414 Brief Remarks on the past and present State of the Woollen Trade of England, relative to Ireland, and our Political Conduct in the Management of that Trade with Respect to our Neighbours on the Continent. Intermix'd with some few Observations on the low and neglected State of our Beneficial Fisheries....By a Lover of his Country. *Lond. 1740, 8°*. LU.

Signed: Mercator.

5415 A Copy of some Reasons Formerly Offered by the Gloucestershire Clothiers, to shew the True Cause of the Decay of the Worcester Trade. Proper to be perused at this present Time. *n.p.* [*c. 1740 ?*], *F*°. LU.

COMMERCE

5416 A Bill, intituled, An Act to prohibit, for a Time therein limited, the Exportation of Corn, Grain (Rice excepted) Meal, Malt, Flour, Bread, Biscuit, Starch, Beef, Pork, and Bacon. *n.p.* [*1740*], *F*°. L.

5417 [Cooley, William]. Considerations upon the Embargo on Provision of Victual. *Lond. 1741* [*1740*], *8*°. DA.

For authorship and date see C.J. xxiii, 545.

5418 Chandler, Edward, Bishop of Durham. A Charge delivered to the Grand-Jury, at the Quarter-Sessions held at Durham, on Wednesday, the 16th of July, 1740. concerning Engrossing of Corn and Grain, and the Riots that have been occasion'd Thereby....Published at the Unanimous Request of the Gentlemen of the Grand-Jury. *Durham,* [*1740*], *4*°. LU.

Another edn. Lond., 1756 (LU).

5419 Copy of the Minutes of the General Meeting of the Noblemen and Gentlemen of the County of Aberdeen, met at Aberdeen, the eighteenth Day of December, One Thousand seven hundred and forty Years, in Consequence of an Advertisement issued by Order of the Justices of Peace of the said County, conform to their Act, of the sixth of November last, and published through the County. *n.p.* [*1740*], *F*°. LU.

On the scarcity of victuals and the means to keep the county supplied.

5420 Edinburgh. Act of Council Regulating the Straw Market. [*Edin. 1740*], *s. sh. F*°. EU.

Dated: 29 August 1740.

5421 Edinburgh, October 29th, 1740. A Full and particular Account of the Proceedings of the Mob that happened in and about Edinburgh and Leith on Thursday the 23rd instant. *n.p.* [*1740*], *s. sh. F*°. C (Cr).

A meal mob.

5422 At Edinburgh, the Thirty first Day of October One thousand seven hundred and forty Years.... [*Edin., 1740*], *s. sh. F*°. ACC.

Fixing the price to be paid by the Town Council for oatmeal in the present scarcity.

5423 Act of the Town-Council of Edinburgh, for encouraging the Importation of Grain to the Port of Leith. [*Edin. 1740*], *s. sh. F*°. EU.

Dated: 19 December 1740.

5424 By the Lord Lieutenant and Council of Ireland, a Proclamation. *Dublin, 1739* [*o.s.*], *F*°. DPRO.

Dated: 19 January 1739. Against the export of corn.

5425 The Voice of the People. In an Apology for their late Insurrection against the Bakers and Forestallers in the City of Dublin.... *Dublin, 1740, 8°*. O.

5426 Britain's Mistakes in the Commencement and Conduct of the Present War. By a Merchant and Citizen of London. [*Lond.*], *1740, 8°*. L.
Another edn. Dublin, 1740 (O); 5th edn. Dublin, 1740 (DA).

5427 A Supplement to Britain's Mistakes in the Commencement and Conduct of the Present War. Wherein the late glorious Success of Admiral Vernon at Porto Bello is particularly considered. By a Merchant and Citizen of London. *Lond. 1740, 8°*. L.
Another edn. Dublin, 1740 (DA).

5428 An Essay on the Management of the Present War with Spain, as far as it has been hitherto Conducted on the Part of Great Britain. By an Impartial Hand. *Lond. 1740, 8°*. L.

5429 Great-Britain's Complaints against Spain Impartially Examin'd. And the Conduct of each Nation, from the Treaty of Utrecht to the late Declaration of War, compared. To which is added, An Abstract of the several Treaties which have been entred into between the Two Crowns, so far as they relate to the present National Disputes. *Lond. 1749, 8°*. L.

5430 Old England for Ever, or, Spanish Cruelty display'd; wherein the Spaniards Right to America is impartially examined and found defective....I. A Compleat History of America....II. Great Britain's Right to America prior to that of Spain....III. The Spaniards inveterate Hatred of the English....IV. A View of the Spanish Traffick to the West Indies....V. Spanish Tyranny....VI. Geographical Remarks on the Situation and Extent of America. *Lond. 1740, 8°*. L.

5431 [KEITH, Sir WILLIAM]. Some Useful Observations on the Consequences of the War with Spain. *Lond.* [*1740*], *8°*. L.
Reprinted in *A Collection of Papers....By Sir William Keith*, 1740 (no. 5385).

5432 A Bill, intituled, An Act for prohibiting Commerce with Spain. *n.p.* [*1740*], *F°*. L.

5433 The Advantages and Disadvantages which will attend the Prohibition of the Merchandizes of Spain, impartially examined, and humbly offered to the Consideration of the Parliament. By a Sussex Farmer. *Lond.* [*1740*], *8°*. L.

5434 The Case of several Merchants, trading to Spain, before the Act of Prohibition. *n.p.* [*1740*], *s. sh. F°*. LU.

5435 Considerations humbly offer'd against the Clause in the Bill now depending for the prohibiting Commerce with Spain, so far as it relates to the granting Time 'till Midsummer next, for the Importation of Spanish Wines. *n.p.* [*1740*], *s. sh. F°*. L.

5436 Considerations on the Bill for prohibiting the Importation of the Growth and Commodities of Spain, now depending in the House of Lords. *n.p.* [*1740*], *F*°. L.

5437 Reasons humbly offered by the Merchants of London, on Behalf of themselves, and the rest of his Majesty's Subjects trading to the Canary Islands, and in Behalf of John Crosse, Esq; his Majesty's Consul, and the British Factory there, against the Canary Islands being included in the Bill now depending in Parliament for prohibiting Commerce with Spain. *n.p.* [*1740*], *s. sh. F*°. L.

5438 BRIDGES, GEORGE. England's Last Shift: or the only Effectual Method to prevent the Clandestine Exportation of Wool, by which means alone, the Nation is to be preserved from inevitable Ruin....To which is annex'd, A Vindication of the Clothiers, &c. and the Fallacies and Calumnies of a late Author discovered and exposed. *Lond. 1740*, *8*°. CP.

5439 LONDON, JOHN. Some Considerations on the Importance of Woollen Manufactures, by which it will appear, the Necessity of immediately putting an effectual Stop to the carrying off our Wool unmanufactured to France. *Lond. 1740*, *8*°. LU.

5440 PLANK, STEPHEN. Proposals for the more effectual preventing the Exportation of Wooll, Wooll-Fells, Mortlings, Shorlings, Wooll-Flocks, or any Yarn made of Wooll, Fuller's Earth, or any Fulling-Clay, and for the Encouragement of the Woollen Manufactory. *n.p.* [*c. 1740?*]. *F*°. LLI.

5441 WEBBER, SAMUEL. Objections answered by the Woollen Manufacturers, Shewing the Deficiency of a Registry within 10 Miles of the Shoars (that's worse than doing nothing) any way short of a General Registry throughout Great-Britain and Ireland...more especially, as thereby we have projected an effectual Scheme, without making an Officer more in the Revenue, or putting his Majesty, or the Nation to any Charge; and can add farther to our Scheme, if in Case the French should ingage in an unjust War, how to secure our Wool, Yarn, &c. from their Privateers, setting the crafty Smugler at defiance (if our Scheme be made Law) how to get our Wool or Yarn from us. *n.p.* [*1740?*], *s. sh. F*°. LU.

5442 [WEBSTER, WILLIAM]. The Consequences of Trade, as to the Wealth and Strength of any Nation; of the Woollen Trade in particular, and the great Superiority of it over all other Branches of Trade. The present State of it in England and France, with an Account of our Loss, and their Gains. The Danger we are in of becoming a Province to France, unless an Effectual and Immediate Stop be put to the Exportation of our Wool. With a Narrative of the Steps taken by Mr. Webber, for getting an Act of Parliament to confirm a Charter granted him by his

Majesty, Nine Years ago, for an Universal Registry in Charter. By a Draper of London. *Lond. 1740, 8°.* LU.

2nd, 3rd and 4th edns. 1740 (all L); 5th edn. 1741 (LU). For authorship see *N. & Q.* ser. 1, vol. 12 (1855), p. 218.

5443 [WEBSTER, WILLIAM]. The Draper Confuted: or, A Candid and Impartial, but Full Answer to the Consequences of Trade....By a Friend to the Government (Andrew Freeport). *Lond. 1740, 8°.* LU.

For authorship see *N. & Q.* ser. 1, vol. 12 (1855), p. 218.

5444 Objections against the Importation of Irish Yarn Duty-Free, Impartially Considered. *n.p.* [*1740 ?*], *F°.* MP.

5445 [WEBB, DANIEL]. *Begin.* Sir, Trade, the greatest Jewel in the English Crown, having lost its Native Lustre, by the gradual Decay of the Woollen Manufacturies for Exportation.... *n.p.* [*c. 1740 ?*], *4°.* LPRO.

The only copy seen is enclosed in a letter of the author.

5446 Some General Observations on the Petitions now before the Honourable House of Commons of Great Britain, Praying a Remedy against the Running of Wool from Great Britain, and Wool and Woollen Goods from Ireland into Foreign Parts, and on a Scheme proposing a Method to prevent the same. Humbly offered to the Consideration of both Houses of Parliament, by many Considerable Traders concern'd in carrying on the Woollen Manufactory for Exportation, in and about the City of London. *n.p.* [*1740*], *F°.* L.

5447 That the Register for Kent and Sussex be extended round the Coast of England and Wales, with some Amendments, viz..... *n.p.* [*c. 1740 ?*], *s. sh. F°.* MC.

5448 Don John Further Display'd; being a Supplement to Considerations on the American Trade. *Lond. 1740, 8°.* MP.

5449 Reasons humbly offered for Reducing the Duty on China Silk. *n.p.* [*1740*], *s. sh. F°.* L.

5450 Observations on a Paper, intituled, Reasons humbly offered for Reducing the Duty on China Raw-Silk; and some Reasons against it. *n.p.* [*1740*], *s. sh. F°.* L.

Endorsed: Reasons against Reducing the Duty on China Raw-Silk.

5451 By the King, A Proclamation, For encouraging Seamen to enter themselves on board His Majesty's Ships of War. *Lond. 1739* [*o.s.*], *s. sh. F°.* LSC.

Dated: 31 January 1739.

5452 A Bill for Registering all Seamen, Watermen, Fishermen, Lightermen, Keelmen, Bargemen and Seafaringmen, capable of Service at Sea, throughout His Majesty's Dominions. *n.p.* [*1740*], *F°.* L.

5453 COWLEY, J. The Sailor's Companion, and Merchantman's Convoy. Shewing the Military Power of the Lord High-Admiral, and the Duty and Conduct of all Superior and Inferior Officers of the Royal Navy of Great Britain. Also, the Duty of Privateers.... *Lond. 1740, 12°.* L.

Another edn. Dublin, 1741 (DA).

5454 The Pay of the Officers and Men in the Royal Navy, together with the Number in each Rate, their Daily Allowance of Provisions, and the Number of Ships. *n.p.* [*1740 ?*], *s. sh. F°.* C (Cr).

COLONIES

5455 Ashley, John. Memoirs and Considerations concerning the Trade and Revenues of the British Colonies in America. With Proposals for rendering those Colonies more Beneficial to Great Britain. *Lond 1740, 8°.* LU.

A Second Part, 1743. Supplement, 1744 (both LU).

5456 Perrin, William. The Present State of the British and French Sugar Colonies, and our own Northern Colonies, Considered. Together with some Remarks on the Decay of Our Trade, and the Improvements made of late Years by the French in Theirs. *Lond. 1740, 8°.* LU.

5457 Proposals for the Relief and Encouragement of the British-Sugar-Islands. In a Letter to a Member of Parliament. *n.p.* [*c. 1740 ?*], *F°.* L.

Advocating concentration on coffee and cocoa.

5458 [Douglass, William]. A Discourse concerning the Currencies of the British Plantations in America: especially with Regard to their Paper Money: more particularly, in relation to the Province of the Massachusetts-Bay, in New England. *Boston, 1740, 8°.*

Davis notes that most of the copies he had seen had the attribution in ms. Postscript, 1740. Another edn., without postscript, Lond. [1741] (LU); another edn., with postscript, Lond. 1751 (L). The date of the first London edn, which has been attributed to 1739, is clearly fixed by the advertisements in the *Gentleman's Magazine* and the *London Magazine* for March 1741. Reprinted in McCulloch, *Currency*, 1857; by C. J. Bullock in 1897; and by A. M. Davis, in *Colonial Currency Reprints*, vol. 3 (1911), whence this entry is taken.

5459 [Douglass, William]. Postscript, to a Discourse concerning the Currencies of the British Plantations in America. [*Boston, 1740*], *8°.*

Reprinted in *Colonial Currency Reprints*, ed. by A. M. Davis, vol. 4 (1911), whence this entry is taken.

5460 [Vans, Hugh]. An Inquiry into the Nature and Uses of Money; more especially of the Bills of Publick Credit, Old Tenor. Together with a Proposal of some proper Relief in the present Exigence. To which is added, A Reply to the Essay on Silver and Paper Currences. *Boston, 1740, 8°.*

Reprinted in *Colonial Currency Reprints*, ed. by A. M. Davis, vol. 3 (1911), whence this entry is taken.

5461 A Letter from a Country Gentleman at Boston, to his Friends in the Country. [*Boston, 1740*], *8°*.

Reprinted in *Colonial Currency Reprints*, ed. by A. M. Davis, vol. 4 (1911), whence this entry is taken.

5462 A Letter relating to a Medium of Trade, in the Province of Massachusetts-Bay. *Boston, 1740, 12°*.

Signed: Philopolites. Reprinted in *Colonial Currency Reprints*, ed. by A. M. Davis, vol. 4 (1911), whence this entry is taken.

5463 [Smith, Wavell]. Two Letters to Mr. Wood, on the Coin and Currency in the Leeward Islands, &c. *Lond. 1740, 8°*. L.

For authorship see ms. note in L copy, 'said to be written by Wavell Smith. [Sr Joseph Banks]'.

5464 Baxter, Thomas. A Letter from a Gentleman at Barbadoes, to his Friend now in London, concerning the Administration of the late Gov. B——g. *n.p. 1740, 8°*. L.

Signed: Tho. Baxter.

FINANCE

5465 The Present State of the National Debt: with Remarks on the Nature of our Public Funds, and the Uses which a large National Debt may be of to a Sole M——r. *Lond. 1740, 8°*. LU.

5466 King, William. Reasons and Proposals for laying a Tax upon Dogs. Humbly addressed to the Honourable House of Commons. By a Lover of his Country. *Reading, 1740, 8°*. LU.

5467 Whatley, Robert. Judgment Signed in the Cause between the Right Honourable Sir Robert Walpole, and Mr. Whatley.... *Lond. 1740, 8°*. L.

On place-hunting.

5468 Parish Corruption in part display'd: or, a Narrative of some late Transactions in St. Luke's Parish, in the County of Middlesex: especially such as respect the Indicting for Forgery, and Out-lawing Mr. Thomas Sayers, the first Head-Church-Warden in that new Parish. *Lond. 1740, 8°*. L.

5469 Clarke, Stephen. A Short Vindication of the Clergy's Right to Tythes.... *York, 1740, 8°*. DA.

5470 A Defence of the Examination of a Book, entituled, A Brief Account of many of the Prosecutions of the People called Quakers, &c. So far as the Clergy of the Diocese of Lichfield and Coventry are concerned in it: In Answer to a late Pamphlet publish'd by the Quakers, by way of Vindication of that Part of their Brief Account. *Lond. 1740, 8°*. O.

5471 [Besse, Joseph]. Remarks on a late Pamphlet, called, A Defence of the Examination of a Book, entitiled, A Brief Account of many of the

Prosecutions of the People called Quakers, &c. So far as the Clergy of the Diocese of Lichfield and Coventry are concerned in it. *Lond.* *1740*, 8°. O.

For authorship see Joseph Smith, *A Descriptive Catalogue of Friends' Books*, 1867, I, 255.

5472 An Examination of a Book, lately printed by the Quakers; and by them distributed to the Members of both Houses of Parliament, entitled, A Brief Account of many of the Prosecutions of the People called Quakers, in the Exchequer, Ecclesiastical, and other Courts; for Demands recoverable by the Acts made in the 7th and 8th Years of the Reign of King William III. for the more easy Recovery of Tythes, Church-Rates, &c. So far as the Clergy of the Dioceses of Oxford, Glocester, and Chester, are concerned in it. *Lond.* *1740*, 8°. L.

5473 [BESSE, JOSEPH]. A Vindication of a Book intituled A Brief Account of many of the Prosecutions of the People called Quakers, &c. Presented to the Members of both Houses of Parliament. In Answer to a late Examination thereof, so far as the Clergy of the Dioceses of Oxford, Glocester, and Chester, are concerned in it. *Lond.* *1740*, 8°. O.

For authorship see Joseph Smith, *A Descriptive Catalogue of Friends' Books*, 1867, I, 255.

5474 [BESSE, JOSEPH]. Remarks on a late Pamphlet, called, A Defence of the Examination of a Book, entituled, A Brief Account of many of the Prosecutions of the People called Quakers, &c. So far as the Clergy of the Diocese of St. David's are concern'd in it. *Lond.* *1740*, 8°. O.

For authorship see Joseph Smith, *A Descriptive Catalogue of Friends' Books*, 1867, I, 255.

5475 Property Re-asserted, in Answer to the Arguments and Exceptions in a late Paper, Intituled, Property Vindicated. *Dublin*, *1740*, 8°. DA.

An answer to no. 5356.

5476 Ninian Brice, Ship-master in Glasgow, and others, Appellants. William Brice, Merchant in Glasgow, Respondent. The Appellants Case. *n.p.* [*1740*], F°. L.

Signed: W. Noel. Alex. Lockhart. A cargo of Wood's halfpence shipped to Boston, Mass.

5477 Ninian Bryce, John Orr of Barrowfield, Esq; and John Robertson, Writer in Glasgow Appellants. William Bryce, Merchant in Glasgow Respondent. The Respondent's Case. *n.p.* [*1740*], F°. L.

Signed: Ch. Areskine. W. Murray.

5478 HEWITT, JOHN. A Treatise upon Money, Coins, and Exchange, in regard both to Theory and Practice: giving a Full and Particular Account of the Nature and Origin of that most Useful and Intricate Part of Commerce. With Forms of Bills mostly in Use; and the Custom of Merchants relating thereto....As also Tables relating to the Conformity of different Weights and Measures. *Lond.* *1740*, 8°. LU.

Another edn. 1755 (L).

5479 The Case of John Hay, and the other separate Creditors of Samuel Burton, Esq; deceased. Humbly offered to the Consideration of the Creditors of the Bank lately kept by Samuel Burton and Daniel Falkiner, Esqrs. *Dublin, 1740, 8°*. L.

5480 The Case of Oswald Edwards, being an impartial and faithful Account of the Several and great Services he has done for the Creditors of the Bank lately kept by Samuel Burton and Daniel Falkiner, Esqrs. and of the ill-natur'd and ungenerous Treatment which he has had from Robert Roberts, Esq; *Dublin, 1740, 8°*. DA.

TRANSPORT

5481 The Case of the Glass-Makers, Sugar-Bakers, and other Consumers of Coals. *n.p.* [*1740*], *F°*. LLI.

Endorsed: The Case of the Consumers of Coals, with the Orders given for carrying on the Combination.

5482 A Bill to explain, amend, and render more Effectual an Act passed in the Thirty-ninth Year of the Reign of Queen Elizabeth, intituled, An Act for the better Maintenance and Well-keeping of Stains Bridge and Egham Causeway, being the Highway from London to the West Parts of England. *n.p.* [*1740*], *F°*. L.

5483 A Bill to give further Powers to the Commissioners for building a Bridge cross the River Thames from the City of Westminster to the opposite Shore in the County of Surrey; and to enable them raise a further Sum of Money towards finishing the said Bridge, and to perform the other Trusts reposed in them. *n.p.* [*1740*], *F°*. L.

5484 EDINBURGH. Act of Council regulating Hackney-Coaches. [*Edin. 1740*], *s. sh. F°*. EU.

Dated: 10 September 1740.

SOCIAL CONDITIONS

5485 A Bill for the better Relief and Employment of the Poor. *n.p.* [*1740*], *F°*. pp. 31. LU.

Another edn. with the blanks filled in, pp. 31, [1740] (L).

5486 A Bill to Explain and Amend an Act made in the Thirteenth Year of His Majesty's Reign, intituled, An Act for Amending and Inforcing the Laws relating to Rogues, Vagabonds, and other idle and disorderly Persons, and for reducing the same into One Act of Parliament; and also Amending the Laws for Erecting, Providing, and Regulating Houses of Correction. *n.p.* [*1740*], *F°*. L.

5487 A Bill, intituled, An Act for amending and enforcing the Laws relating to Rogues, Vagabonds, and other idle and disorderly Persons, and for reducing the same into one Act of Parliament; and also for amending the Laws for erecting, providing and regulating Houses of Correction. *n.p.* [*1740*], *F°*. L.

5488 Proposals towards raising a Supplemental Provision for the Poor; and for the Encouragement and Increase of Seamen within the Bills of Mortality; and at several Towns and Villages bordering on the Thames. Which may be carried into Execution, by Associations of the like Nature, in other Maritime Cities and Ports throughout Great-Britain and Ireland. *Lond.* *1740*, *8°*. LU.

On saving waste food for pig and cattle rearing.

5489 A Bill, intituled, An Act for the better and more easy collecting of Charity Money on Briefs. *n.p.* [*1740*], *F°*. L.

5490 Reasons in support of the Bill now depending before this Honourable House, for the better and more easy Collecting Charity-Money on Briefs. *n.p.* [*1740*], *s. sh. F°*. L.

5491 The Open Heart and Purse: or, British Liberality Display'd; being Memoirs of the Illustrious Bounties, Collections, Donations, and Charitable Contributions, in Great Britain and Ireland, for the Relief of Indigent Housekeepers, Families, and others, distressed by the Severity of the Frost, which commenc'd about London, in the Night of December 25, 1739; and began to abate on February 15, 17$\frac{39}{40}$... With an Alphabetical List of the Known Benefactors. *Lond.* *1740*, *8°*. LU.

5492 A Bill, intituled, An Act for confirming and enlarging the Powers granted by His Majesty to the Governors and Guardians of the Hospital, for the Maintenance and Education of exposed and deserted young Children, by His most Gracious Charter, bearing Date the Seventeenth Day of October, in this present Year, and to enable them to execute the good Purposes of the said Charter. *n.p.* [*1740*], *F°*. L.

5493 A List of the present Governors and Guardians of the Hospital for the Maintenance and Education of exposed and deserted young Children, incorporated by His Majesty's Royal Charter, bearing Date the 17th Day of October, 1739, and elected since to the 25th of June, 1740, inclusive. *n.p.* [*1740*], *8°*. O.

5494 Some Considerations on the Necessity and Usefulness of the Royal Charter, establishing an Hospital for the Maintenance and Education of Exposed and Deserted young Children. *Lond.* *1740*, *4°*. LU.

5495 A Sketch of the General Plan for executing the Purposes of the Royal Charter, establishing an Hospital for the Maintenance and Education of exposed and deserted Young Children; as reported by the Gentlemen desired to consider of a General Plan, for the executing the Charity, to the Committee for transacting the Affairs of the Hospital, on the 16th of July, 1740. *Lond.* *1740*, *8°*. O.

5496 The Report of the General Committee for directing, managing, and transacting the Business, Affairs, Estate, and Effects of the Corporation of the Governors and Guardians of the Hospital for the Maintenance and Education of exposed and deserted Young Children; relating to the General Plan for executing the Purposes of the Royal Charter, establishing this Hospital. *Lond. 1740, 8o*. LU.

5497 Proposals for raising an Infirmary, by Voluntary Subscription and Contribution, for the More Immediate Relieving the Sick and Diseased Poor. *n.p.* [*1740*], *Fo*. L.
London Hospital.

5498 The Statutes and Rules of George Watson's Hospital. *Edin. 1740, 8o*. E.

5499 An Enquiry into the Institution of the Hospitals of St. Bartholomew, Christ-Church, St. Thomas, Bridewell and Bethlem; with Some Observations on their Ancient and Present Government. *n.p.* [*1740?*], *Fo*. L.

5500 The Case of the Merchants of Great-Britain, residing at home, or in the British Factories in foreign Countries, with Respect to Persons obtaining Acts of Naturalization, without any Purpose of continuing in these Kingdoms. *n.p.* [*1740?*], *Fo*. LLI.

5501 Arnaud, Jasper. An Alarm to All Persons touching their Health and Lives: or, A Discovery of the most shocking, pernicious, and destructive Practices made use of by many in this Kingdom, who make and sell divers Kinds of Eatables and Drinkables; whereby Many languish in their Health, and lose their Lives; founded on Verity and Facts.... To which are added, Remarks on the Nature of the destructive Ingredients made use of in the aforesaid Practices in Relation to Health; Communicated to the Author by a Learned Physician. *Lond. 1740, 8o*. L.

5502 Edinburgh. Act of Council Relative to the Cleaning of the Streets. [*Edin. 1740*], *Fo*. EU.
Dated: 29 August 1740.

5503 A List of the Colonels, Lieutenant Colonels, Majors, Captains, Lieutenants, and Ensigns of His Majesty's Forces on the British Establishment. With the Dates of their several Commissions as such, and also the Dates of the first Commissions which such Colonels, Lieutenant Colonels, Majors, Captains, and Lieutenants had in the Army. Also, a List of the Colonels, Lieutenant Colonels, Majors, Captains, Lieutenants, and Ensigns of His Majesty's Forces on the Irish Establishment.... *Lond. 1740, Fo*. O.

1741

GENERAL

5504 The False Accusers accused; or the Undeceived Englishman: being an Impartial Enquiry into the general Conduct of the Administration.... By a Member of the House of Commons. *Lond. 1741*, 8°. LU.

3rd edn. 1741 (O).

5505 Minutes of several Resolutions of the Honourable House of Commons, in the Fifth, Sixth, and Seventh Sessions of the Eighth Parliament of Great Britain: being a Summary View of the most Remarkable Transactions of that August Assembly in the last Three Years. Illustrated with Explanatory Notes on the same. To which is annexed, An Abstract of the State of the National Debt, as it stood in the Years 1738, 1739, 1740. *Lond. 1741*, 8°. L.

Deals almost exclusively with economic affairs.

5506 The Universal Pocket Companion....Containing...I. A Geographical Description of the World....II. A Description and Map of England ...III. London describ'd....VII. The Names and Places of Abode of the Aldermen, Merchants, and principal Traders in London.... *London. 1741*, 8°. L.

Pt. 2 has a separate title-page reading 'The Trader's Pocket Companion: containing correct Tables...of universal use to merchants....By John Hewitt'.

5507 A Bill, intituled, An Act to supply some Defects in the Laws for repairing and rebuilding County Bridges, for repairing, enlarging, erecting and providing Houses of Correction, and for passing Rogues and Vagabonds. *n.p.* [*1741*], F°. L.

5508 MURRAY, Sir ALEXANDER. The True Interest of Great Britain, Ireland and our Plantations: or, a Proposal for making such an Union between Great Britain and Ireland, and all our Plantations, as that already made betwixt Scotland and England....And a New Method of Husbandry by Greater and Lesser Canals....With Proposals for Removing the Hurtful Parts of the Heretable Courts and Jurisdictions...in Scotland. *Lond. 1740* [*1741*], F°. LU.

5509 The Groans of Ireland. In a Letter to a Member of Parliament. *Dublin, 1741*, 8°. L.

A general economic survey.

AGRICULTURE

5510 ELLIS, WILLIAM. The Modern Husbandman: or the Practice of Farming: as it is now carried on by the most Accurate Farmers in several Counties of England. For the Month of May (–April). *Lond. 1741–44*, 8°. 12 pts. O.

After the part issue was completed, sets were issued in 4 volumes with collective title-pages dated 1744. In the Edin. Univ. Lib. and Congress copies the May issue is dated 1742. In the former set Jan. and Feb. are of the second edn. and are dated 1746. Another edn. Dublin, 1743, 44 (O).

5511 [BLACKWELL, ALEXANDER]. A New Method of improving Cold, Wet, and Barren Lands, particularly Clayey-Grounds. With the Manner of burning Clay, Turf, and Mole-Hills; as practised in North-Britain. To which is added, The Method of cultivating and raising Fruit Trees in such Soils. *Lond. 1741*, *8°*. L.

For authorship see *D.N.B.*

5512 An Act for Confirming and Establishing Articles of Agreement, and an Award for Dividing and Inclosing certain common Fields, and a Common called Chawton-Common, in the Parish of Chawton in the County of Southampton. *n.p. 1740–41*, *F°*. L.

5513 An Act for dividing and inclosing several open Fields, Pastures, and Commons, in the Townships of Great Driffield, and Little Driffield, in the County of York; and for settling certain yearly Payments to the Prebendary of Driffield, for the Time-being, in lieu of his Tythes, pursuant to an Agreement, and an Award made for those Purposes. *n.p.* [*1741*], *F°*. L.

5514 An Act for Inclosing and Dividing the common Fields, common Pastures, common Meadows and Waste-grounds in the Manor and Parish of Brincklowe, in the County of Warwick. *n.p.* [*1741*], *F°*. L.

5515 A Bill for dividing and inclosing the Common Fields lying in the Manor and Parish of Sherston Magna, in the County of Wilts. *n.p.* [*1741*], *F°*. L.

5516 An Act for Dividing and Inclosing the Common Fields, Lawnd, Wastes, and Uninclosed Grounds within the Manor and Parish of Wotton-Underwood in the County of Bucks; and for making effectual certain Exchanges therein mentioned. *n.p. 1741*, *F°*. L.

5517 A Bill for the Effectual Draining and Preservation of Waterbeach-Level, in the County of Cambridge, and to establish an Agreement between the Lord of the Manor of Waterbeach, cum Denny, and the Commoners within the said Manor. *n.p.* [*1741*], *F°*. L.

5518 PRIOR, THOMAS. A Proposal to prevent the Price of Corn from Rising too high, or Falling too low, by the means of Granaries. *n.p.* [*1741*], *8°*. L.

Another edn., anonymous, entitled: A Proposal for erecting Granaries in the City of Dublin and other Parts of the Kingdom, to prevent any scarcity of Corn for the future, Dublin, 1741, 8° (DA).

5519 A Dissertation on the Inlargement of Tillage, the Erecting of Public Granaries, and the Regulating, Employing, and Supporting the Poor in this Kingdom.... *Dublin*, *1741*, *8°*. L.

Signed: Publicola. Attributed to Thomas Dawson in the Lough Fea Library Catalogue (Wagner 199).

5520 A Letter from a Country Gentleman in the Province of Munster, to his Grace the Lord Primate of all Ireland. *n.p.* [*1741*], *8°*. DA.

Signed: Publicola. On the distressed state of agriculture.

5521 [Skelton, Philip]. The Necessity of Tillage and Granaries. In a Letter to a Member of Parliament Living in the County of ——. *Dublin, 1741*, 8°. DA.

Signed: Triptolemus. Reprinted in *The Complete Works of the late Reverend Philip Skelton*, 1824, v, 324–76.

5522 A Proposal for Lessening the Excessive Price of Bread Corn in Ireland. *Dublin, 1741*, 12°. LU.

3rd edn. 1757 (D). Suggesting improved farming methods and the provision of granaries.

5523 Cremer, Johann Andreas. Elements of the Art of Assaying Metals.... Translated from the Latin....To which are added, Several Notes and Observations not in the Original, particularly Useful to the English Reader. With an Appendix, containing a List of the chief Authors that have been published in English upon Minerals and Metals. *Lond. 1741*, 8°. LU.

5524 *Begin.* Mineral-Office, Finch-Lane, Nov. 21, 1741. *n.p.* [*1741*], *s. sh. F°.* L.

Notice from the Mineral and Battery Works Company that it has taken a lease of land near Ballycastle collieries in order to develop industries there and that a call is being made on shareholders to raise the necessary capital.

5525 London. Lambert, Mayor. *n.p.* [*1741*], *s. sh. F°.* LCRO.

An order prohibiting the taking of fish from the Thames smaller than here specified.

5526 Additional Orders Devised and agreed upon by the Right Honourable Daniel Lambert Esq. Lord Mayor of the City of London, Conservator of the River of Thames, Waters of Medway, and River Lee, for the Conservation and Preservation of the Spawn, Brood, and Fry of Fish therein as followeth. *n.p.* [*1741*], *s. sh. F°.* LCRO.

5527 An Essay on Ways and Means for Improving the Inland Navigation and Increasing the Number of Sailors in Great-Britain. Humbly offered to the Consideration of Parliament. *Lond. 1741*, 8°. LU.

On the herring fishery.

MANUFACTURES

5528 Unto the Right Honourable, The Lords of Council and Session, the Petition of James Edmond, Baker in Glasgow. *n.p.* [*1741*], *F°.* E.

Dated: December 22, 1741. Signed: Ja. Graham.

5529 The Charter and Grants of the Company of Stationers of the City of London, now in Force, containing a plain and rational Account of the Freemen's Rights and Privileges, fairly produced, and, where necessary, impartially explain'd. In order to ascertain the Authority annexed to the Office of Masters and Wardens, and to redress the Hardships and Miseries of the injured and oppressed Freemen.... *Lond. 1741*, 8°. LG.

5530 A Bill for the Improvement of the Manufacture of Woollen Broad Cloth, and to prevent Abuses in making of the same. *n.p.* [*1741*], *F°*. MP.

5531 Objections against the Bill for the Improvement of the Woollen Manufacture Answered. *n.p.* [*1741?*], *F°*. MP.

5532 A Letter to a Member of Parliament at London. Demonstrating, that to Encourage the Trade of Ireland, and particularly its Woollen Manufacture, is the real Interest of Great-Britain, and the surest Method to Curb the Exorbitant Power of France. *Dublin*, *1741*, *8°*. L.

Signed: Britannus.

COMMERCE

5533 [BLANCH, N.]. The Ax laid to the Root of the corrupt Tree: or, an Essay on the Hard Case of the Retale-Traders, Citizens, Shop-Keepers, &c. of the City of London. In regard to their Trade, as at present invaded by Hawkers and Pedlars....By a Liveryman. *Lond.* [*1741*], *8°*. L.

For authorship see *The Axe (Once more) Laid to the Root of the Tree*, 1743.

5534 LONDON. Lambert, Mayor. Tuesday the Second Day of June, 1741.... [*Lond. 1741*], *s. sh. F°*. LCRO.

An order suppressing a fair near Little-Tower-Hill for the buying and selling of old rags and cloths.

5535 LUCAS, CHARLES. Pharmacomastix: or, the Office, Use, and Abuse of Apothecaries explained; the present degenerate State of Pharmacy, with its manifold Corruptions and Adulterations, considered, and some Essays on reforming thereof: Humbly addressed to a Member of Parliament, with Intent to shew the necessity of amending and continuing a temporary Statute, for preventing Frauds and Abuses committed in the making and vending unsound, adulterate and bad Drugs and Medicines, now near expiring. By the Author of the Scheme on which the said Statute was founded. *Dublin*, *1741*, *8°*. O.

Signed: C. Lucas.

5536 A Bill for Securing to John Byrom, Master of Arts, the Sole Right of Publishing, and Teaching for Hire, by himself, or such as he shall Depute, for a certain Terms of Years, the Art and Method of Shorthand, invented by him. *n.p.* [*1741*], *F°*. L.

5537 Information for William Flockhart, for himself, and for the incorporated Trades of Dunfermline, Suspenders, against James Hog, Treasurer of the Guildry of Dunfermline, Charger. *n.p.* [*1741*], *F°*. E.

Dated: June 22, 1741. Signed: Hugh Murray-Kynnymound. On the right to sell wine and other foreign merchandise.

5538 The Profit and Loss of Great Britain in the present War with Spain. From July 1739 to July 1741. In a Letter to a Friend. *Lond.* *1741*, *8°*. L.

Signed: Honestus. Another edn. Dublin, 1741 (DA).

5539 A Bill to impower Joseph Porter, James Bourdieu, and Abraham Desmarette, to import a certain Quantity of Raw-silk, of the Growth of Spain, from Leghorn. *n.p.* [*1741*], *F*o. L.

Another edn., entitled: An Act to impower Joseph Porter...(O).

5540 LLOYD, EDWARD. Reasons for rendering Trade, to and from All Nations, Free to Export and Import every Commodity, Neat or Wrought, liable to no other Duty, but the Rate Ad Valorum [*sic*]. Proper to be considered by Mr. Webber, and others, that are for increasing and extending Restraints on the British and Irish Trade, by new Establishments, Registering and Excising Wool.... *n.p. 1741*, *8*o. LU.

5541 PLANK, STEPHEN. Proposals for the more effectual preventing the Exportation of Wool, &c. *n.p.* [*1741*], *s. sh. F*o. LPRO.

5542 SYMPSON, ANTHONY. A Short, Easy and Effectual Method to prevent the Running of Wool, &c. from Great-Britain and Ireland to Foreign Parts; Humbly submitted to the Consideration of Parliament. *Lond. 1741*, *8*o. LU.

5543 WEBBER, SAMUEL. An Account of a Scheme for preventing the Exportation of our Wool where the Particulars of it are set forth, and the Methods of putting it in Execution exemplified. To which is added, An Examination [by John London] of a Scheme offered by another Hand [S.M.], shewing the Defects and mischievous Consequences of it; as also Several material Extracts from Sir Walter Ralegh and Sir Francis Brewster, concerning the Consequences of the Woollen Trade, and the fatal Effects arising to this Nation from the Exportation of our Wool.... *Lond. 1740* [*o.s.*], *8*o. LU.

Another edn. 1741 (O).

5544 Considerations on Several Proposals for preventing the Exportation of Wool. With Heads of a Scheme for that Purpose: and also Some short Answers to Part of the Remarks on Mr. Webber's Scheme, and the Draper's Pamphlet. By a Member of the late Parliament. *Lond. 1741*, *8*o. LU.

5545 [WEBSTER, WILLIAM]. The Draper's Reply to Some Remarks on the Consequences of Trade, &c. To which is annex'd, An Essay on Mr. Webber's Scheme, Shewing, how inoffensive it will be if executed by Independent Patentees, and how destructive of our Liberties, if Excised. *Lond. 1741*, *8*o. L.

For authorship see *N. & Q.* ser. 1, vol. 12 (1855), p. 218.

5546 An Essay on the Improvement of the Woollen Manufacture, and of some other Branches of Trade depending thereon. Together with some Observations on the Danger of increasing M——l Power, by plausible Pretences to improve the Woollen Manufacture. By a Merchant. *Lond. 1741*, *8*o. LU.

Mostly on smuggling of wool.

5547 Remarks upon Mr. Webber's Scheme and the Draper's Pamphlet. *Lond. 1741*, 8º. LU.

5548 London, John. An Answer to the pretended Remarks on Mr. Webber's Scheme, and the Draper's Pamphlet; shewing, that the Remarker hath not made the least Objection to the Scheme which the Draper recommended, nor disprov'd the least Fact which he advanc'd: As also, that all that hath been alledged by the Gentleman's Magazine against it is groundless, and that the Truth of the Calculation is undoubted. To which is added, A Copy of the Letter which Mr. Webber received, concerning its being stipulated that France should have our Wool.... Also, A Petition, intended to have been presented to Parliament, praying, an Act to confirm the Charter which His Majesty granted Mr. Webber.... *Lond. 1741*, 8º. LU.

5549 [Cowper, Thomas]. A Short Essay upon Trade in general, but more Enlarged on that Branch relating to the Woollen Manufactures of Great Britain and Ireland; wherein is detected the scandalous Exaggerations and Calculations of Mess. Webber, London, and the Draper; and also a Method propos'd to prevent the Owling of unmanufactur'd Wool, by a Publick Registry, at such Expence, that the Crown may not suffer, or the Grower of Wool be oppress'd. Humbly address'd to the Lords Commissioners of Trade and Plantations. By a Lover of his Country, and the Constitution of Great-Britain. *Lond. 1741*, 8º. LU.
For authorship see C.J. xxiv, 158.

5550 [Cowper, Thomas]. To the Right Honourable the Lords Commissioners of Trade and Plantations: The following Supplement to my Essay on Trade is most humbly offered. *n.p.* [*1741*], 4º. LU.

5551 A Scheme for Keeping our Wool at Home; in order to Employ our Poor, and Recover the Foreign Markets for our Woolen Manufacture. With a Method for Raising a Fund of Two Millions for the more effectual accomplishing thereof.... *n.p.* [*1741*], *F*º. L.
Signed: S.M.

5552 [Newball, John]. A Scheme to prevent the Running of Wool from England to Foreign Parts. *n.p.* [*1741*], *s. sh. F*º. LPRO.
The copy seen is enclosed in a letter from the author. 5786 is a much expanded version, with author's name.

5553 Entry cancelled.

5554 A Bill for Opening a Trade to and from Persia through Russia. *n.p.* [*1741*], *F*º. O.

5555 A Letter to a Member of Parliament, relating to the Bill for the opening of a Trade, to and from Persia through Russia. *Lond. 1741*, 8º. LU.

5556 Reasons against the Repeal of that Clause of the Act of Navigation, which prohibits the Importation of Persia Raw Silk from any of the Dominions of Muscovy. *n.p.* [*1741*], *s. sh. F*º. LU.

5557 An Answer to the Reasons alledged against the Repealing a Clause in the Act of Navigation, in favour of the Russia Company: As also to a Pamphlet entitled, A Letter to a Member of Parliament, &c. *n.p.* [*1741*], *F°*. LU.

5558 A Reply to the Answer to the Reasons alledged against the Repealing a Clause in the Act of Navigation, in Favour of the Russia-Company, &c. *n.p.* [*1741*], *F°*. LU.

5559 [CAMPBELL, JOHN]. A Concise History of the Spanish America; containing a succinct Relation of the Discovery and Settlement of its several Colonies: a circumstantial Detail of their respective Situation, Extent, Commodities, Trade, &c. And a full and clear Account of the Commerce with Old Spain by the Galleons, Flota, &c. As also of the Contraband Trade with the English, Dutch, French, Danes, and Portugueze.... *Lond. 1741*, *8°*. LU.

Another edn. 1747, entitled: The Spanish Empire in America....By an English Merchant (LU). For authorship see *D.N.B.*

5560 A Bill, intituled, An Act for the Encouragement and Increase of Seamen, and for the better and speedier Manning His Majesty's Fleet. *n.p.* [*1741*], *F°*. L.

5561 Observations upon the Clause for Regulating the Wages of Seamen in the Merchants Service, in the Bill For the Encouragement of Seamen. *n.p.* [*1741*], *s. sh. F°*. L.

5562 By the King, A Proclamation, For encouraging Seamen to enter themselves on Board Our Ships of War. *Lond. 1740* [*o.s.*], *s. sh. F°*. L.

Dated: 19 March 1740.

COLONIES

5563 A List of Copies of Charters, from the Commissioners for Trade and Plantations, presented to the Honourable the House of Commons, in pursuance of their Address to His Majesty of the 25th of April, 1740. Viz. Maryland Charter...Connecticut Charter...Rhode-Island Charter...Pensylvania Charter...Massachusets Bay Charter...Georgia Charter.... *Lond. 1741*, *F°*. L.

5564 [SMITH, WAVELL]. Observations occasion'd by reading a Pamphlet, intitled, A Discourse concerning the Currencies of the British Plantations in America. In a Letter to *****. *Lond. 1741*, *8°*. L.

For authorship see ms. notes in JCB copy (Sabin 84538) and in L copy. Reprinted in *Colonial Currency Reprints*, ed. by A. M. Davis, vol. 4 (1911).

5565 [DOUGLASS, WILLIAM]. A Letter to —— —— Merchant in London, concerning a late Combination in the Province of the Massachusetts-Bay in New-England, to impose or force a Private-Currency called Land-Bank-Money. [*Boston*], *1741*, *8°*.

Reprinted in *Colonial Currency Reprints*, ed. by A. M. Davis, vol. 4 (1911), whence this entry is taken.

5566 A Letter to the Merchant in London, to whom is Directed a Printed Letter relating to the Manufactory Undertaking, dated New England, Boston February 21st 1740, 1. [*Boston*], *1741*, *8º*.

Reprinted in *Colonial Currency Reprints*, ed. by A. M. Davis, vol. 4 (1911), whence this entry is taken.

5567 [DOUGLASS, WILLIAM]. A Second Letter to —— —— Merchant in London, concerning a late Combination in the Massachusetts-Bay in New England, to impose or force a private Currency, called Land-Bank-Money. [*Boston*, *1741*], *8º*.

Reprinted in *Colonial Currency Reprints*, ed. by A. M. Davis, vol. 4 (1911), whence this entry is taken.

5568 [MARTYN, BENJAMIN]. An Account shewing the Progress of the Colony of Georgia in America from its First Establishment. *Lond. 1741*, *Fº*. L.

Published by the Trustees. For authorship see V. W. Crane, *The Promotion Literature of Georgia*, p. 295. Another edn. Annapolis, 1742; reprinted in P. Force, *Tracts and other Papers*, vol. 1 (1836), no. 5.

5569 [MARTYN, BENJAMIN]. An Impartial Enquiry into the State and Utility of the Province of Georgia. *Lond. 1741*, *8º*. LU.

For authorship see V. W. Crane, *The Promotion Literature of Georgia*, p. 294.

5570 TAILFER, PATRICK. A True and Historical Narrative of the Colony of Georgia, in America, from the First Settlement thereof until this present Period: Containing the most authentick Facts, Matters and Transactions therein. Together with His Majesty's Charter, Representations of the People, Letters, &c....By Pat. Tailfer, M.D. Hugh Anderson, M.A. Da. Douglas, and others, Land-holders in Georgia, at present in Charles-Town in South-Carolina. *Charles-Town*, *1741*, *8º*. pp. xxiv.176. JCB.

Sabin 94215. Another edn. Charles-Town, 1741, 8º, pp.xviii, 78, 87–118 (EU); another edn. Lond. 1741 (L). Reprinted in Force's *Tracts*, vol. 1 (1836), no. 4, and in *Georgia Hist. Soc. Collections*, vol. 2, 1842.

5571 WHITEFIELD, GEORGE. An Account of the Money Received and Disbursed for the Orphan-House in Georgia....To which is prefixed A Plan of the Building. *Lond. 1741*, *8º*. L.

5572 [KEIMER, SAMUEL]. Caribbeana. Containing Letters and Dissertations, together with Poetical Essays, on various Subjects and Occasions; chiefly wrote by several Hands in the West Indies, and some of them to Gentlemen residing there. Now collected together in Two Volumes. Wherein are also comprised, divers Papers relating to Trade, Government and Laws in general; but more especially, to those of the British Sugar-Colonies, and of Barbadoes in particular: as likewise the Characters of the most eminent Men that have died, of late Years, in that Island. To which are added in an Appendix, Some Pieces never before Published. *Lond. 1741*, *4º*. LU.

Extracts from the *Barbados Gazette*, 20 Nov. 1731–16 Dec. 1738. For authorship see *D.N.B.*

5573 Some Memoirs of the first Settlement of the Island of Barbados, and other Carribbee islands, with the succession of the Governours and Commanders-in-Chief of Barbados, to the year 1741. Extracted from antient records, papers, and accounts, taken from Mr. William Arnold, Mr. Samuel Bulkly, and Mr. John Summers, some of the first settlers, the last of whom was alive in 1688, aged 82. Also some remarks on the laws and constitution of Barbados. *Barbados, 1741, 8°.* L.

Another edn. 1743, entitled: Memoirs of the first Settlement...(L).

5574 The Importance of Jamaica to Great-Britain, consider'd. With some Account of that Island, from its Discovery in 1492 to this Time...An Account of their Fruits, Drugs, Timber and Dying-Woods...With an Account of their Trade and Produce; with the Advantages they are of to Great-Britain, Ireland, and the Colonies in North-America.... In a Letter to a Gentleman. In which is added, a Postscript, of the Benefits which may arise by keeping of Carthagena....With an Account of what Goods are used in the Spanish Trade.... *Lond.* [*1741*], *8°*. L.

FINANCE

5575 FLEMING, JAMES. A Collection of all the Irish and English Statutes now in force and use, relating to His Majesty's Revenue of Ireland, with Notes in the Margin....With a View of the Rates of Goods and Merchandizes Imported and Exported.... *Dublin, 1741, 4°.* LU.

5576 Proposals to raise Four Millions at 3 per Cent. or 570,000 Pounds a Year, to pay off the Money borrowed on the Pot-Act, Soap, Candles, &c. and for paying off the said Four Millions within Eight Years without any additional Tax. And for raising Twenty-thousand effective Men, that will serve His Majesty without Pay until Great-Britain shall be invaded by Foreigners. By an Officer of the Stamp-Duties. *Lond. 1741, 8°.* LU.

Proposes to reduce duties on spirits.

5577 A Proposal to raise 500,000 Pounds a Year, by Reducing the Duties, and Altering the Laws relating to the Retalers of Spirituous Liquors. *n.p.* [*1741?*], *s. sh. F°.* LU.

5578 Memorial in relation to the Duties of Excise, payable by the Common Brewers in Edinburgh. *Edin. 1741, 4°.* E.

Dated: 8th December 1741.

5579 Memorial for the Brewers of Edinburgh, in Relation to the Duties of Excise payable by them. *n.p.* [*1741*], *4°.* E.

Dated: Decem. 22, 1741.

5580 An Examination of a Book, lately printed by the Quakers; and by them distributed to the Members of both Houses of Parliament, intituled, A Brief Account of many of the Prosecutions of the People called

Quakers, in the Exchequer, Ecclesiastical, and other Courts; for Demands recoverable by the Acts made in the 7th and 8th Years of the Reign of King William III. for the more easy Recovery of Tythes, Church-Rates, &c. So far as the Clergy of the Diocese of Carlisle are concerned in it. *Lond. 1741, 8°.* O.

5581 [Besse, Joseph]. A Vindication of a Book, intituled, A Brief Account of many of the Prosecutions of the People called Quakers, &c. presented to the Members of both Houses of Parliament: in Answer to a late Examination thereof, so far as the Clergy of the Diocese of Carlisle are concerned in it. *Lond. 1741, 8°.* O.

For authorship see Joseph Smith, *A Descriptive Catalogue of Friends' Books*, 1867, I, 256.

5582 An Examination of the Quakers Brief Account: in Behalf of the Churchmen of the Diocese of Hereford. *Lond. 1741, 8°.* O.

5583 [Besse, Joseph]. A Vindication of a Book, intituled, A Brief Account of many of the Prosecutions of the People called Quakers, &c. presented to the Members of both Houses of Parliament: in Answer, to a late Examination thereof in Behalf of the Church-Men of the Diocese of Hereford. *Lond. 1741, 8°.* O.

For authorship see Joseph Smith, *A Descriptive Catalogue of Friends' Books*, 1867, I, 256.

5584 [Hayter, Thomas, Bishop of London]. An Examination of a Book, lately printed by the Quakers; and by them distributed to the Members of both Houses of Parliament, entitled, A Brief Account of many of the Prosecutions of the People called Quakers, in the Exchequer, Ecclesiastical, and other Courts; for Demands recoverable by the Acts made in the 7th and 8th Years of the Reign of King William III, for the more easy Recovery of Tythes, Church-Rates, &c. In Defence of the Clergy of the Diocese of York. *Lond. 1741, 8°.* O.

For authorship see *D.N.B.*

5585 [Besse, Joseph]. A Vindication of a Book, intituled, A Brief Account of many of the Prosecutions of the People called Quakers, &c. presented to the Members of both Houses of Parliament: in Answer to a late Examination thereof, in Defence of the Clergy of the Diocese of York. *Lond. 1741, 8°.* L.

For authorship see Joseph Smith, *A Descriptive Catalogue of Friends' Books*, 1867, I, 256.

5586 Scarcity of Bread no private Conspiracy or, Combination: or, the Draper inform'd of the True Cause. *Dublin, 1741, 8°.* DA.

Mostly on tithes.

5587 Innes, John. A Dissertation concerning the Arithmetick of Annuities: Wherein it is shewn, that this Branch of Arithmetick is hitherto deficient, with respect to true Rules....To which are subjoin'd Proposals for supplying this Defect. *Edinburgh, 1741, 4°.* LU.

5588 SIMPSON, THOMAS. The Doctrine of Annuities and Reversions, deduced from General and Evident Principles: with useful Tables, shewing the Values of Single and Joint Lives, &c. at different Rates of Interest.... *Lond. 1742* [*1741*], *8º*. DA.

5589 Peter Mackattie of London, Merchant, Appellant. John Frigg, Merchant in Findhorn, and James Fraser, Merchant in Inverness, in Company, Respondents. The Appellant's Case. *n.p.* [*1741*], *Fº*. L.

Signed: Fran. Chute. A Hume Campbel. On the insurance of *The Friendship* lost in the Bristol Channel in 1737.

5590 Peter Mackattie, Factor or Agent in London, Appellant. John Frigg of Findhorn, and James Fraser of Inverness in North-Britain, in Company, Merchants, Respondts. The Respondents Case. *n.p.* [*1741*], *Fº*. L.

Signed: W. Murray. C. Erskine.

5591 HAYES, RICHARD. The Gentleman's Complete Book-keeper.... *Lond. 1741*, *8º*. L.

TRANSPORT

5592 An Act for Incorporating the Undertakers of the Navigation of the River Dee. *n.p.* [*1741*], *Fº*. L.

5593 A Bill for the better Preservation of the Publick Roads of that Part of Great-Britain called England. *n.p.* [*1741*], *Fº*. L.

5594 A Bill for Repairing and Inlarging the Roads from the Town of Selby, in the West-Riding of the County of York, to the Town of Leeds; and from thence (in Two several Branches, One through Bradford and Horton, and the Other through Bowling and Wibsey) to the Town of Halifax, in the same Riding. *n.p.* [*1741*], *Fº*. L.

5595 Information for Walter Scot, John Balfour, Merchants, and others, Proprietors of the Stage-coach betwixt Edinburgh and Leith; against James Reid Burgess in Edinburgh. *n.p.* [*1741*], *Fº*. E.

Dated: November 3. 1741. Signed: Ja. Graham.

5596 Information for James Reid, Burgess and Guild-brother of Edinburgh, against John Balfour Merchant in Edinburgh, and others. *n.p.* [*1741*], *4º*. E.

Dated: November 2. 1741. Signed: And. Macdoual.

5597 Information for Walter Scot, John Balfour, and others, Proprietors of the Stage-coach plying betwixt Edinburgh and Leith, against James Reid Burgess of Edinburgh. *n.d.* [*1741*], *Fº*. E.

Dated: December 2. 1741. Signed: And. Macdoual.

5598 Unto the Right Honourable the Lords of Council and Session, The Petition of Walter Scot, John Balfour, and John Clarkson, Proprietors of the Stage-coach plying betwixt Edinburgh and Leith. *n.p.* [*1741*], *s. sh. Fº*. E.

Dated: December 9. 1741. Signed: Hu. Forbes.

SOCIAL CONDITIONS

5599 Some Regulations with regard to the Begging Poor; and a Scheme for providing Employment for Labourers of all kinds; in a Letter to the Author of the Scots Magazine.... *Edin. 1741*, 8º. LU.

Signed: A Lover of Mankind.

5600 JONES, GRIFFITH. An Address to the Charitable and Well-Disposed; in behalf of the Poor in the Principality of Wales. *Lond. 1741*, 8º. O.

5601 The Statutes and By-Laws of the Corporation of the Governor and Directors of the Hospital for Poor French Protestants, and their Descendants, residing in Great-Britain. *Lond. 1741*, 4º. LU.

French and English on opposite pages.

5602 The Acts relating to the Work-House of the City of Dublin. *Dublin, 1741*, 8º. DA.

5603 The Ladies Advocate; or an Apology for Matrimony. In Answer to the Batchelor's Monitor. *Lond. 1741*, *s. sh. F*º. L.

Cost of living estimates. *The Batchelor's Monitor* was first published in 1729 under the title of *The Batchelor's Estimate* (no. 4031).

5604 The Case of the Poor Widows of the Commission and Warrant Officers of the Royal Navy, on the Establishment of 1732. Most humbly offered to the compassionate Consideration of the Noble and Honourable Members of Both Houses of Parliament. *n.p.* [*1741*], *s. sh. F*º. L.

5605 Valor Beneficiorum Ecclesiasticorum in Hibernia: or the First-Fruits of all the Ecclesiastical Benefices in the Kingdom of Ireland, as taxed in the King's Books: with an Account shewing how this Royal Fund vested in Trustees hath hitherto been disposed of. *Dublin, 1741*, 8º. O.

1742

GENERAL

5606 [ILIVE, JACOB]. A New and Compleat Survey of London.... By a Citizen, and Native of London. *Lond. 1742, 8°.* O.

The dedication signed: The Author, and dated 7 March 1742. Another issue with the dedication signed: J. Ilive, and dated 1 Nov. 1742 (L).

5607 SMART, JOHN. A Short Account of the several Wards, Precincts, Parishes, &c. in London. *n.p.* [*1742*], *8°.* O.

The title is taken from p. 3. Preceding this is a leaf containing an address by the author 'To the Deputies and Common Council Men of the several Wards in the City of London'. Dated 27 Feb. 1741 [o.s.].

AGRICULTURE

5608 An Act for Dividing and Inclosing, Setting out and Allotting, certain Common Fields and Inclosures within the Manor and Parish of Aston Cantlow, in the County of Warwick. *n.p.* [*1742*], *F°.* L.

5609 An Act for Confirming and Establishing certain Articles of Agreement, and an Indenture, between the Right Honourable Francis Earl Godolphin, and the Dean and Chapter of Ely, for making a Partition and Division of a certain Heath or Heath-ground, in the County of Cambridge, and for rendering the same Agreement and Indenture more effectual for the Purposes therein mentioned. *n.p.* [*1742*], *F°.* LHL.

5610 A Bill for Confirming and Establishing an Exchange agreed to be made of certain Lands in the Parish of Sutton, in the County of Bedford, between Sir Roger Burgoyne, Baronet, Lord of the Manor, and Doctor Crane, Rector of the Church of Sutton, in order to promote and facilitate the Inclosure of the Common Fields and Common Grounds in the said Parish; and for securing to the said Rector an Equivalent for his Tythes arising in the said Parish of Sutton. *n.p.* [*1742*], *F°.* LHL.

5611 ELLIS, WILLIAM. The Second Part of the Timber-Tree Improved.... *Lond. 1742, 8°.* O.

The *Timber-Tree improved* was published in 1738 (no. 5146).

5612 HAMILTON, JAMES, Schoolmaster in East-Calder. Virgil's Pastorals Translated into English Prose; as also His Georgicks.... To which is added, an Appendix, shewing Scotland's chief and principal worldly Interest. *Edin. 1742, 12°.* LU.

The appendix is concerned with improvements in Scottish agriculture.

MANUFACTURES

5613 ROBERTS, HUGH. An Imitation of a Model for Water-Works, contrived after the nearest Manner to save Friction, and likewise be made capable of draining the deepest Mine and greatest Quantity of Water that was ever done by any other Engine. *n.p.* [*1742*], *s. sh. F°*. L.

'Dated this 25th of May 1742.'

5614 An Act to prevent the Counterfeiting of Gold and Silver Lace; and for Settling and Adjusting the Proportions of Fine Silver and Silk; and for the better Making of Gold and Silver Thread. *n.p.* [*1742*], *F°*. O.

A bill.

5615 A Bill for Granting a Bounty upon certain Species of British and Irish Linens exported; and taking off the Duties on Foreign Raw or Brown Linen Yarns imported. *n.p.* [*1742?*], *F°*. O.

5616 A Bill to enable George Warren, Esq; his Heirs and Assigns, to make a Sluice or Tunnel through Part of the Glebe belonging to the Rectory of Stockport, in the County of Chester; and to use and enjoy the same for conveying Water to Stockport Mills. *n.p.* [*1742*], *F°*. L.

Corn mills.

5617 An Act to enable George Warren, Esquire, his Heirs and Assigns, to make a Sluice or Tunnel through part of the Glebe belonging to the Rectory of Stockport, in the County of Chester; and to use and enjoy the same for conveying Water to Stockport Mills. *n.p.* [*1742*], *F°*. L.

5618 The State of the Case of the Clothing Trade, as it regards a Bill proposed to be brought into the House of Commons, to Explain, Amend and Enforce a Clause contained in an Act made in the 4th and 5th of Philip and Mary, Chap. 5. Sect. 33. as also several Clauses of an Act made in the 5th of Queen Elizabeth, Chap 4. Humbly offered to the Consideration of the Honourable Members of that House. *n.p.* [*1742?*], *s. sh. F°*. MP.

For enforcing apprenticeships.

5619 A Bill for the more effectual Preventing any Cloth, or Woolen Goods, remaining upon the Rack or Tenters, or any Wool left out to dry, from being stolen or taken away in the Night-time. *n.p.* [*1742*], *F°*. L.

COMMERCE

5620 Information for James Hog, late Treasurer of the Gildry of Dunfermline, Charger; against William Buntine, Baxter, and William Flockhart, Wright, in Dunfermline, Suspenders. *n.p.* [*1742*], *F°*. E.

Dated: November 1. 1742. Signed: Rob. Craigie. On the right to sell wine.

5621 A list of merchant-ships taken by the Spaniards.... *n.p.* [*1742*]. *39×25 cm*. Kress S. 1886.

5622 Hireling Artifice Detected: or, the Profit and Loss of Great-Britain, in the present War with Spain, set in its True Light; by laying before the Publick, as Full, Compleat, and Regular a List as can be had, of the British Ships taken since the Beginning of the War; with proper Remarks upon the List, and upon our Conduct both at Home and Abroad. *Lond. 1742, 8o.* O.

5623 The Profit and Loss of Great-Britain and Spain, from the Commencement of the Present War, to this Time, Impartially Stated; by laying before the Publick, as Perfect and Regular a List, as can be had, of all the Ships taken from either Nation, since the Beginning of the War, to this Time; with proper Remarks upon the List of British Ships, in a Pamphlet intitled, Hireling Artifice Detected. In a Letter to the Author. *Lond. 1742, 8o.* LU.

Signed: Philalethes.

5624 A Short Account of the late Application to Parliament made by the Merchants of London upon the Neglect of their Trade: with the Substance of the Evidence thereupon; as sum'd up by Mr. Glover. *Lond. 1742, 8o.* LU.

2nd and 3rd edns. 1742 (both LU); 4th edn. Dublin, 1742 (DA); 5th edn. Lond. 1751 (L); 6th edn. Lond. 1774 (LU). On the failure to protect them against Spanish attacks.

5625 A Bill for the better Protecting and Securing of the Trade and Navigation of this Kingdom in Times of War. *n.p. [1742], Fo.* LU.

Ensuring that a sufficient part of the Fleet shall always be engaged in protecting merchant ships.

5626 An Abstract of several Clauses in an Act of Parliament passed in the Twelfth Year of King George the Second, intituled, An Act for taking off the Duties upon Woollen and Bay Yarn imported from Ireland to England...so far as the same relate to the Exportation of Wooll, Woollen or Bay Yarn, Wooll-fells, Shortlings, Mortlings, Wooll-flocks, Worsted Yarn, from Great Britain to foreign Parts, and of the said Goods, as also Cloth, Serge, Bays, Kerseys, Says, Frizes, Druggets, Cloth-serges, Shalloons, Stuffs, and other Draperies, and Woollen Manufactures, or mixed with Wooll, or Wooll-flocks, from Ireland to foreign Parts (except certain Parts in England.) *Lond. 1742, s. sh. Fo.* OUP.

5627 Report from the Commissioners for Trade and Plantations; in pursuance of the Address of the Honourable House of Commons to his Majesty, of the Fifth of March last, to direct the said Commissioners, during the Recess of Parliament, to prepare a Scheme for the Registring the Wool of Great Britain and Ireland, to be laid before the House the next Session of Parliament. *n.p. 1741 [o.s.], Fo.* L.

5628 Bridges, George. A Whip for the Smugglers: or, a Curb to France. Shewing the only Way to Prevent Wool-Smuggling; wherein their

Methods are clearly discover'd. With an Appeal to Both Houses of Parliament, drawn up as the Heads of a Bill, and most humbly submitted to the Consideration of the Legislative Body of Great Britain and Ireland. *Lond. 1742*, *8°*. L.

5629 GEE, J. An Impartial Enquiry into the Importance and Present State of the Woollen Manufactories of Great-Britain: as likewise of the Improvements they are capable of Receiving. In Several Letters to a Member of Parliament.... *Lincoln, 1742*, *8°*. LU.

5630 LAYBOURNE, HENRY. A Scheme to prevent the Exportation of Wool Unmanufactur'd. Most Humbly Submitted to the Right Honourable the Two Houses of Parliament. *Stamford*, [*1742*], *8°*. LU.

5631 STRONGCASTLE, CORNELIUS. An Essay to Prevent the Exportation of Wool, and Retrieve the Woollen Manufacture of England.... *Lond. 1741–2*, *8°*. LU.

5632 [SMITH, JOHN]. The Grasiers Advocate: or, Free Thoughts of Wool, and the Woollen Trade. Occasioned chiefly by reading and comparing two late Pieces upon the Subject, viz. The Consequences of Trade, &c. by a Draper of London, and An impartial Enquiry into the Importance and present State of the Woollen Manufactories of Great Britain, by J. Gee. *Lond.* [*1742*], *8°*. LU.

For authorship see Smith's *Chronicon Rusticum-Commerciale*, 1747, II, 374.

5633 A Letter to a Right Honourable Member of Parliament, demonstrating the absolute Necessity of Great Britain's assisting the House of Austria....As also the Safest and most Practicable Methods to put a Stop to the Exportation of our Wooll. By an Impartial Hand. *Lond. 1742*, *8°*. LU.

Signed: Britannicus.

5634 Some Impartial Thoughts on the Woollen Manufacturies, wherein the Merits of the several pieces wrote on this subject within these few years are occasionally considered. With Remarks upon Mr. Webber's Scheme, and other Schemes for preventing the exportation of British and Irish Wooll. By George-Andrew-Patrick-Briton. *Lond. 1742*, *8°*. L.

5635 SPILMAN, JAMES. A Journey through Russia into Persia; by two English Gentlemen, who went in the Year 1739, from Petersburg, in order to make a Discovery how the Trade from Great Britain might be carried on from Astracan over the Caspian. To which is annex'd, A summary Account of the Rise of the famous Kouli Kan, and his Successes, till he seated himself on the Persian Throne. *Lond. 1742*, *8°*. LU.

5636 [HOUSTOUN, JAMES]. A True and Impartial Account of the Rise and Progress of the South Sea Company; wherein the Assiento Contract is particularly considered....With Observations on a late Pamphlet, intituled, Considerations on the American Trade, before and since the

Establishment of the South Sea Company....Humbly addressed to Admiral Vernon. By a Gentleman now resident in Jamaica. *Lond. 1743* [*1742*], 8°. LU.

For authorship see Sabin no. 97095.

COLONIES

5637 The Royal Charter for establishing a Civil Government at Gibraltar, to which is prefixed a Prefatory Discourse recapitulating the Benefits which have been proposed therefrom. *Lond. 1742*, 8°. O.

5638 [Blenman, Jonathan]. Remarks on several Acts of Parliament relating more especially to the Colonies abroad; as also on diverse Acts of Assemblies there: together with a Comparison of the Practice of the Courts of Law in some of the Plantations with those of Westminster-Hall; and a modest Apology for the former, so far as they materially differ from the latter. Wherein is likewise contain'd, a Discourse concerning the 4½ per cent Duty paid in Barbados, and the Leeward Islands. *Lond. 1742*, 8°. L.

For authorship see Adam Anderson's ms. note in L copy.

5639 [Stephens, William]. A State of the Province of Georgia, attested upon Oath in the Court of Savannah, November 10, 1740. *Lond. 1742*, 8°. L.

For authorship see *Colonial Records of the State of Georgia*, v, 406. Reprinted in P. Force, *Tracts and other Papers*, I, (1836) no. 3.

5640 Stephens, William. A Journal of the Proceedings in Georgia, beginning October 20, 1737....To which is added, A State of that Province, as attested upon Oath in the Court of Savannah, November 10, 1740. *Lond. 1742*, 8°. 3 vols. L.

Reprinted in *Colonial Records of the State of Georgia*, vol. 4 and suppl., 1906, 1908.

5641 The Resolutions of the Trustees for Establishing the Colony of Georgia in America, in Common-Council assembled, this eighth Day of March in the Year of our Lord One thousand seven hundred and forty-one, relating to the Grants and Tenure of Lands within the said Colony. *n.p.* [*1742*], F°. De Renne.

5642 An Account shewing what Money has been received by the Trustees for the Use of the Colony of Georgia, and how they discharge themselves thereof, with Observations thereon. *n.p.* [*1742*], *s. sh.* F°. De Renne.

5643 Stephens, Thomas. The Hard Case of the Distressed People of Georgia. *n.p.* [*1742*], F°. LSC.

Dated: April 26th 1742.

5644 Whitefield, George. A Continuation of the Account of the Orphan-House in Georgia, from January, 174$\frac{0}{1}$ to June 1742.... *Edin. 1742*, 8°. L.

A later edn. continues the account to January 1742–3 (JCB. Sabin 103496).

FINANCE

5645 [MORRIS, CORBYN]. A Letter from a By-stander to a Member of Parliament: wherein is examined what Necessity there is for the Maintenance of a Large Regular Land-Force in this Island; what Proportions the Revenues of the Crown have born to those of the People, at different Periods from the Restoration to His present Majesty's Accession.... *Lond. 1741* [*o.s.*], *8*°. L.

Dated 26 February, 174$\frac{1}{2}$. 2nd edn. 1742 (L); 3rd edn. 1743 (O). Authorship acknowledged in his *An Essay towards illustrating the Science of Insurance*, 1747.

5646 A Proper Answer to the By-stander. Wherein is shewn I. That there is no Necessity for, but infallible Ruin in the Maintenance of a large regular (or mercenary Land Force in this Island....III. That Publick Credit is now upon a more stable Foundation than ever it was before the Year 1734, and can be ruined by nothing but bad Oeconomy, Temporary Expedients, and Loss of Trade.... *Lond. 1742*, *8*°. L.

Attributed to Pulteney, according to *D.N.B.* article on Corbyn Morris.

5647 [CARTE, THOMAS]. A Full Answer to the Letter from a By-stander, &c. Wherein his false Calculations, and Misrepresentations of Facts in the Time of King Charles II. are refuted; and an Historical Account is given of all the Parliamentary Aids in that Reign....By R—— H——, Esq; *Lond. 1742*, *8*°. L.

For authorship see no. 5717 and *D.N.B.*

5648 A Bill, intituled, An Act for Indemnifying such Persons as shall, upon Examination make Discoveries touching the Disposition of Publick Money, or concerning the Disposition of Offices, or any Payments or Agreements in respect thereof; or concerning other Matters relating to the Conduct of Robert Earl of Orford. *n.p.* [*1742*], *F*°. L.

5649 Some Observations on a Bill entituled, An Act for Indemnifying such Persons as shall upon Examination make Discoveries touching the Disposition of Publick Money, or concerning the Disposition of Offices, or any Payments or Agreements in Respect thereof; or concerning other Matters relating to the Conduct of Robert Earl of Orford. *Lond. 1742*, *8*°. LU.

5650 The Thoughts of a Private Gentleman on the Late Indemnifying Bill. In a Letter to his Friend in the Country. *Lond. 1742*, *8*°. LU.

5651 A Report from the Committee of Secrecy, Appointed to Enquire into the Conduct of Robert Earl of Orford, during the last Ten Years of his being First Commissioner of the Treasury, and Chancellor and Under-Treasurer of His Majesty's Exchequer.... *Lond. 1742*, *F*°. LU.

5652 A Further Report from the Committee of Secresy, appointed to enquire into the Conduct of Robert Earl of Orford, during the last Ten Years of his being First Commissioner of the Treasury, and Chancellor and Under-Treasurer of His Majesty's Exchequer. With the Appendix. *Lond. 1742*, *F°*. pp. 20. 44. L.

Another edn., 'Published from an Examined Copy', Lond., 1742, F°, pp. 83 (O); another edn. Lond., 1742, 8°, pp. 132 (O); another edn. Dublin, 1742, 8° (DA); another edn., 'To which is Prefixed, The First Report', Lond. 1742, 8°, pp. 52 (O).

5653 An Account of what was done by a Great Man [Walpole] from the Beginning of the Year, 1720. to the End of the Year, 1721. relating to the Undoing of the South-Sea Directors. *Lond. 1742*, *8°*. L.

Written in 1722.

5654 Manley, William. A Collection of the Laws of the Customs now in Force, to prevent Frauds and Abuses in the Revenue, and the illegal Importation and Exportation of prohibited and uncustomed Goods.... Together with a List of the several Head and Member Ports and Creeks thereto belonging, in England and Wales; and the Names, Descriptions, and Dimensions of the lawful Keys, Wharfs, &c..... *Lond. 1742*, *8°*. LU.

5655 An Exact Abridgement of all the Acts of Parliament relating to the Excise. Part I. On Beer, Ale, Brandy, Vinegar, and other Liquors. *Cambridge*, *1742*, *8°*. L.

5656 Memorial for the Brewers of Glasgow, in Relation to the Duties of Excise payable by them. *n.p.* [*1742*], *4°*. E.

Dated: June 24. 1742. Signed: Henry Home.

5657 Information for Mr. John Blackstock Collector of Excise, Pursuer before the Justices of the Peace for the Shire of Lanerk, for His Majesty and himself, against Mr. Robert Luke, Common Brewer in Glasgow. *n.p.* [*1742*], *4°*. E.

Dated: 12th July, 1742. Signed: Pat. Halden. Peter Wedderburn.

5658 To the Right Honourable the Lord Mayor, Aldermen, and Commons of the City of London in Common-Council assembled. *n.p.* [*1742*], *F°*. L.

The report of the committee appointed to enquire into the state of the city's finances from 1730 to 1740, dated 10 Feb. 1741 [o.s.].

5659 The Report of the Committee, to whom the Petition of the Principal Inhabitants of the Several Parishes of St. Martin in the Fields, St. Anne, St. James, St. George Hanover-Square, and St. Margaret, within the Liberty of Westminster...against their Select Vestry was referred, made to the Honourable the House of Commons by the Right Honourable John Lord Percival, Chairman of the said Committee, on Tuesday the 25th Day of May, 1742. The whole shewing the Nature and Management of the said Select Vestry, for several Years past, with the Committee's Remarks thereupon. *Lond. 1742*, *F°*. L.

5660 A Scheme for Utterly Abolishing the present Heavy and Vexatious Tax of Tithe. In a Letter to a Member of Parliament. *Dublin, 1742, 8°.* DA.

Signed: A.E.I.O.U. 2nd edn. 1763 (L).

5661 An Examination of a Book, lately printed by the Quakers; and by them distributed to the Members of both Houses of Parliament, intitled, A Brief Account of many of the Prosecutions of the People called Quakers ... So far as the Clergy of the Diocese of Canterbury are concern'd in it. *Lond. 1742, 8°.* L.

5662 [Besse, Joseph]. A Vindication of a Book, intituled, A Brief Account of many of the Prosecutions of the People called Quakers, &c. presented to the Members of both Houses of Parliament: in Answer to a late Examination thereof, so far as the Clergy of the Diocese of Canterbury are concerned in it. With an Appendix, Demonstrating that Tithes are an Oppression to the Husbandman, a Burden too Heavy for Him to bear, and undoeth many. *Lond. 1742, 8°.* LF.

For authorship see Joseph Smith, *A Descriptive Catalogue of Friends' Books*, 1867, I, 256.

5663 Vallavine, Peter. Observations on the Present Condition of the Current Coin of this Kingdom. With some Account of the several Ways of Diminishing the Coin, which have hitherto been discover'd, and the Methods made use of to prevent those Evils. Particularly, the late evil Practice of Filing Guineas....Also some farther Remarks upon the Inconveniences the Publick suffer by the Deficiency and Scarcity of the Silver Coin, and the Currency of Foreign Money.... *Lond. 1742, 8°.* L.

5664 An Appeal to the People of England, the Publick Companies and Monied Interest, on the Renewal of the Charter of the Bank. *Lond. 1742, 8°.* L.

5665 Some Considerations relating to the intended Bank New Contract. *Lond. 1742, F°.* L.

TRANSPORT

5666 Elstobb, William. Some Thoughts on Mr. Rosewell's, and Other Schemes, now propos'd for Amending Lynn Channel and Harbour, In a Letter to the Merchants, Owners, and Masters of Ships, belonging to the said Place. *n.p. 1742, 4°.* L.

Another edn. Norwich, 1742, 4° (O). The only copy seen of the Norwich edition is imperfect at the end; Elstobb's name does not appear on the title-page.

5667 Grundy, John. A Scheme for Making that Branch of Trent running by Newark Town Side Navigable by Locks, without being any ways hurtful to the Navigation of the Main Trent above or below the Island, or to that of the Kelham-Branch. *n.p. [1742], F°.* M (Cr).

5668 A Bill for making the Branch or Channel of the River Trent Navigable, which runs close under the Town and Castle of Newark, from a place called the Upper Wear in the Parish of Aversham, in the County of Nottingham, to a Place called The Crankleys, in the Parish of South-Muscam in the same County. *n.p.* [*1742*], *F°*. L.

With a map.

5669 A Survey of the two Branches of ye Trent from their deviding at the place called ye Upper Ware to their joining again at the Crankley's. taken Jan.^{r} 1740. *n.p.* [*1742*], *s. sh. F°*. O.

The letterpress is the case of the Borough of Newark for the Trent Navigation Bill.

5670 Objections to the Bill for making the Branch of the Trent running by Newark, Navigable. (The Observations of Mr. Grundy, Junior, the Surveyor.) *n.p.* [*1742*], *F°*. L.

With a map.

5671 The Laws and Constitutions of the Company of Watermen and Lightermen, Rowing on the River Thames, betwixt Gravesend in the County of Kent, and Windsor in the County of Bucks. *n.p.* *1742*, *8°*. LG.

5672 EDINBURGH. Act of Council regulating Hackney Coaches. [*Edin.* *1742*], *s. sh. F°*. AU.

Dated: 25 August 1742.

5673 By the Lords Justices and Council of Ireland, a Proclamation, Offering a Reward for the Apprehending and Convicting of the Persons concerned in the Robbing the Post-Bag and Post-Mail, in the Road coming from Cashel to the Town of Clonmel, in the County of Tipperary. *Dublin*, *1742*, *s. sh. F°*. DPRO.

Dated: 25 October 1742.

SOCIAL CONDITIONS

5674 A Bill for Remedying some Defects in the Act made in the Forty-third Year of the Reign of Queen Elizabeth, intituled, An Act for the Relief of the Poor. *n.p.* [*1742 ?*], *F°*. L.

5675 Observations upon the Vagrant Laws; proving that the Statutes in Queen Elizabeth's Time are the most proper Foundation for a Law of that Nature: and that all Alterations that have been made since, have been for the worse. *Lond.* *1742*, *4°*. LU.

5676 An Account of the Rise, Progress, and State of the London Infirmary, supported by Charitable and Voluntary Subscription, for the relief of Sick and Diseased Manufacturers, Seamen in Merchant Service, and their Wives and Children, from the first Institution on the 3d of November, 1740, to the 12th of May, 1742, inclusive. *Lond.* *1742*, *4°*. O.

Subsequently published annually. L has copies of all the reports to 1750 either in the separate folio form or, appended to the annual sermon in quarto.

5677 Bath, March the Fourth, MDCCXLI. The Hospital in this City being nearly finished.... *Bath*, [*1742*], *s. sh. F*o. O.

Regulations for the admission of patients.

5678 WARBURTON, WILLIAM. A Sermon preached at the Abbey-Church at Bath, for Promoting the Charity and Subscription towards the General Hospital or Infirmary of that City; on Sunday, October 24. 1742.... To which is added, A short Account of the Nature, Rise, and Progress, of the General Infirmary at Bath. *Lond. 1742*, *8*o. O.

5679 Letters Patent in favours of the Orphan Hospital. [*Edin. 1742*], *4*o. L.

5680 A Bill for the more easy Recovery of small Debts. *n.p.* [*1742?*], *F*o. L.

5681 A List of the Widows, relieved by the Governors of the Charity, for the Relief of poor Widows and Children of Clergymen, in the Year 1741. *n.p.* [*1742?*], *4*o. O.

5682 A Scheme for Providing an Yearly Annuity to Widows of Ministers of the Established Church of Scotland. *n.p.* [*1742?*], *4*o. O.

1743

GENERAL

5683 BICKHAM, GEORGE. The British Monarchy: or, a New Chorographical Description of all the Dominions subject to the King of Great Britain. Comprehending the British Isles, the American Colonies, the Electoral States, the African & Indian Settlem^{ts}. and enlarging more particularly on the respective Counties of England and Wales.... *Lond. 1743, Fo.* L.

Other edns. 1748 and 1749 (both L).

5684 The History and Present State of the British Islands: describing their respective Situations, Buildings, Customs, Arts and Sciences, Manufactures, Husbandry, Plants, Animals, Minerals, Forests, Rivers, Fisheries, &c. And more particularly of the County of Middlesex, and City of London; shewing the Antient as well as present State of that Metropolis, and Remarks on the several great trading Companies, and on their foreign Trade to all Parts of the World.... *Lond. 1743, 8o.* 2 vols. LG.

Apparently an anonymous reissue of vols. 14 and 15 of an edition of Thomas Salmon's *Modern History*.

5685 An Enquiry into the Melancholy Circumstances of Great Britain: more particularly in regard to the Œconomy of Private Families and Persons, Gentlemen, Clergy, Farmers, Merchants, Tradesmen, Mechanicks, &c. With Observations on the New Methods of Living and Diversions in both City and Country, with some Remedies to prevent the Ruin of private Families; and Remarks upon our Trade in general, and especially of such Commodities as are imported for Luxury, or injurious to our Manufactures. Also some Hints to prevent the growing Poverty of these Nations. *Lond.* [*1743*], *8o.* LU.

5686 [RALPH, JAMES]. A Critical History of the Administration of Sr Robert Walpole, now Earl of Orford. Collected chiefly from the Debates in Parliament, and the Political Writings on both Sides....To the Whole are Prefix'd, Some Particulars of Mr. Walpole's Public Life, before the Year 1721. By a Gentleman of the Middle-Temple. *Lond. 1743, 8o.* LU.

For authorship see *D.N.B.*

5687 BURRINGTON, GEORGE. Seasonable Considerations on the Expediency of a War with France; arising from a faithful Review of the State of both Kingdoms. To which are added...A short Comparison, between the British and French Dominions; and a State of the French Revenues, and Forces in the Year, 1701. *Lond. 1743, 8o.* LU.

5688 Britons Awake, and Look about you; or, Ruin the Inevitable Consequence of a Land-War, whether Successful, or Not....By a Lover of his Country. *Lond. 1743, 8o.* O.

5689 A Short History of the Highland Regiment; interspersed with Some Occasional Observations as to the Present State of the Country, Inhabitants and Government of Scotland. *Lond. 1743, 8°.* E.

Another edn. 1747, entitled: Remarks on the People and Government of Scotland (E).

AGRICULTURE

5690 The Rational Farmer, and Practical Husbandman. Containing, Remarks on the Principles of Vegetation, viz. Salts of all kinds, Sulphurs, Earth, Water, Air, Heat, and celestial Influences; with the Reasons and Manner of their promoting Fertility in different Soils, apply'd to Practise in the various Branches of Husbandry and Gardening....To which is added, The British Herbal.... *Lond. 1743, 4°.* SU.

Published in numbers. Only about half the projected *Rational Farmer* is included in the only copy seen, to judge by the scheme given in the first number. The last leaf of *The Rational Farmer* bears on the recto the words 'The End of the First Part' and on the verso an announcement that Part the Second will be published in a few weeks. This announcement has been pasted over and perhaps pt. 2 was never published.

5691 Select Transactions of the Honourable the Society of Improvers in the Knowledge of Agriculture in Scotland. Directing the Husbandry the different Soils for the most profitable Purposes, and containing other Directions, Receipts and Descriptions. Together with an Account of the Society's Endeavours to promote our Manufactures. Prepared for the Press by Robert Maxwell of Arkland...and revised by the Preses and a Committee appointed for that End. *Edin. 1743, 8°.* L.

5692 An Act for Confirming, and Rendering more effectual, certain Articles of Agreement, and an Award, for Inclosing and Dividing certain Common Fields, and Common Downs, within the Manor and Parish of Aston Tirrold, in the County of Berks. *n.p.* [*1743*], *F°.* L.

5693 An Act for the Inclosing and Dividing the Common Fields and Waste Grounds lying within the Manor of Dummer, in the Parish of Dummer, in the County of Southampton. *n.p. 1742–3, F°.* L.

5694 An Act for Confirming, Establishing, and making Effectual, certain Articles of Agreement made and entered into for inclosing and dividing the several Common Fields lying in the Township or Hamlet of Earley, in the Parish of Sonning, in the County of Berks; and for Exchanging several antient Inclosures within the said Township or Hamlet of Earley aforesaid. *n.p.* [*1743*], *F°.* L.

5695 A Bill for Inclosing and Dividing the Common, or Moor, called Elvington-Moor, within the Manor and Parish of Elvington, in the County of York. *n.p.* [*1743*], *F°.* L.

5696 An Act for Inclosing and Dividing the Common, or Moor, called Elvington-Moor, within the Manor and Parish of Elvington, in the County of York. *n.p.* [*1743*], *F*°. L.

5697 An Act for Dividing and Inclosing certain Common Fields within the Parish of Great Brington, in the County of Northampton. *n.p.* [*1743*], *F*°. L.

5698 Unto the Right Honourable, The Lords of Council and Session, the Petition of the Governor and Company for raising of Thames Waters in York-buildings. *n.p.* [*1743*], *4*°. EU.

On the lease of mines by Sir Alexander Murray. Signed: Ch. Areskine. Dated: February 24th, 1743.

5699 Answers for Edward Duke of Norfolk, Sir Robert Clifton, Sir Robert Sutton, Sir Archibald Grant, General George Wade, William Neilson, Richard Graham and Peter Murdoch, all principal Leasees of Sir Alexander Murray's Mines in the Shires of Argyle and Peebles, and Alexander Ouchterlony, and others their Assignies; to the Petition of the Governor and Company of Undertakers, for raising the Thames Water in York-buildings. *n.p.* [*1743*], *s. sh. F*°. EU.

Signed: Ro. Craigie. Dated: June 16th, 1743.

5700 Unto the Right Honourable, the Lords of Council and Session, the Petition of the Governor and Company for raising Thames Waters in York-buildings. *n.p.* [*1743*], *s. sh. F*°. EU.

Signed: Ja. Fergusson. Dated: November 30th, 1743.

MANUFACTURES

5701 [Plumer, Fr.]. Reasons against the Bill now depending in Parliament, for restraining the Use of Gold and Silver-Lace, Embroidery, &c. In a Letter from a Citizen to a Member of Parliament. *Lond. 1743*, *12*°. LU.

Signed: A Manufacturer. For authorship see H. & L. quoting B.M. Catalogue.

5702 Charter and By-Laws of the Loriners Company, London. *n.p. 1743*, *8*°. O.

5703 An Act for Vesting in John Elwick, Esquire, the sole Property of an Engine for making Stone Pipes, and to enlarge the Term granted by Letters Patent for that Purpose. *n.p.* [*1743*], *F*°. L.

The original grant was to John Tuite.

COMMERCE

5704 Mackenzie, Murdoch. Proposals for Surveying and Navigating, by Subscription, the Orkney Islands. *n.p.* [*1743*], *F*°. O.

5705 Act of the Magistrates and Council of the City of Edinburgh, Regulating the Assize and Weight of Bread within the City of Edinburgh and Suburbs thereof. [*Edin. 1743*], *s. sh. F°*. ACC.

5706 Act of Sederunt of the Lords of Council and Session, Relative to the Act of the Magistrates and Council of the City of Edinburgh regulating the Assize and Weight of Bread. [*Edin. 1743*], *s. sh. F°*. ACC.

Dated: 25 February 1743.

5707 By the Lords Justices, A Proclamation, Requiring Quarantine to be performed by Ships coming from the Island of Sicily, or any other of the Ports in the Mediterranean. *Lond. 1743, s. sh. F°*. LSC.

Dated: 12 July 1743.

5708 By the Lords Justices and Council of Ireland, a Proclamation Requiring Quarantine to be performed by Ships coming from any Port or Place in the Kingdom of Sicily, or from the Mediterranean. *Dublin, 1743, F°*. DPRO.

Dated: 18 July 1743.

5709 By the Lords Justices and Council of Ireland, a Proclamation, Requiring Quarantine to be performed by all Ships and Vessels coming from the Island of Sicily, or from or through the Mediterranean. *Dublin, 1743, F°*. DPRO.

Dated: 8 August 1743.

5710 MIDDLETON, CHRISTOPHER. A Vindication of the Conduct of Captain Christopher Middleton, in a Late Voyage on Board His Majesty's Ship the Furnace, for Discovering a North-west Passage to the Western American Ocean. In Answer to certain Objections and Aspersions of Arthur Dobbs, Esq;.... *Lond. 1743, 8°*. L.

Another edn. Dublin, 1744 (DA).

5711 By the Lords Justices and Council of Ireland, a Proclamation. *Dublin, 1743, s. sh. F°*. DPRO.

Dated: 6 June 1743. Against James Mahony and other smugglers of brandy.

5712 An Enquiry how far it might be expedient, and, at this Time more particularly, seasonable, to permit the Importation of Irish Cattle, upon Conditions of Advantage and Security to the Woollen Trade of Great Britain. The several Judgments of Sir W. Temple and Mr. Locke in reference thereto. With Remarks on certain Passages in a late Piece, entitled, The Groans of Ireland. Also an Examination of some Opinions, which have been advanced, for making a Law (to prevent absolutely the illicit Exportation of Wool) effectual and salutary. To which is added, a Postscript, to Mr. Laybourne's Scheme, &c. *Lond. 1743, 8°*. LU.

5713 [SMITH, JOHN]. The State of our Wool and Woollen Trade Review'd. Wherein some Objections to The Grasiers Advocate, &c. are consider'd;

and the Heads of a new Scheme of Universal Registry offer'd to publick Examination.... *Lond.* 1743, 8°. MP.

For authorship see Smith's petition to the House of Commons, *Journals*, XXIV, 542.

5714 A New General Collection of Voyages and Travels: consisting of the most Esteemed Relations, which have been hitherto published in any Language. *Lond.* 1745–47 [1743–47], 4°. L.

Published by Thomas Astley in weekly parts. Probably edited by John Green. See G. R. Crone and R. A. Skelton, 'English Collections of Voyages and Travels, 1625–1846', in *Richard Hakluyt and his Successors*, 1946, pp. 98–100.

COLONIES

5715 An Enquiry into the State of the Bills of Credit of the Province of the Massachusetts-Bay in New-England: in a Letter from a Gentleman in Boston to a Merchant in London. *n.p.* 1743, 8°.

Reprinted in *Colonial Currency Reprints*, ed. by A. M. Davis, vol. 4 (1911), whence this entry is taken.

5716 [STEPHENS, THOMAS]. A Brief Account of the Causes that have retarded the Progress of the Colony of Georgia, in America; attested upon Oath. Being a proper Contrast to A State of the Province of Georgia. Attested upon Oath; and some other Misrepresentations on the same Subject. *Lond.* 1743, 8°. L.

For authorship see ms. note in John Carter Brown Library copy.

FINANCE

5717 [MORRIS, CORBYN]. A Letter to the Reverend Mr. Thomas Carte, Author of the Full Answer to the Letter from a Bystander. By a Gentleman of Cambridge. *Lond.* 1743, 8°. C.

2nd edn. 1744 (C). For authorship see the following entry and *D.N.B.*

5718 [CARTE, THOMAS]. A Full and Clear Vindication of the Full Answer to a Letter from a By-Stander. In which all the Cambridge Gentleman's Cavils and Misrepresentations of that Book, in his Letter to Mr. Thomas Carte, are exposed and refuted. By the Author of the Full Answer. *Lond.* 1743, 8°. L.

For authorship see *D.N.B.*

5719 A State of the Expence of the Late War. *Lond.* 1743, *s. sh. obl. F°.* O.

An engraved chart of expenses, 1702–13.

5720 The Ruin of Thousands, the Triumph of One: or, England's Great V——. A Dialogue between Robin the Cashier, and Robin the Premier. Concluding with the Groans of the South-Sea Sufferers. *Lond.* 1743, 8°. LU.

5721 [Blanch, N.]. The Axe (Once more) Laid to the Root of the Tree.... Published for the universal Benefit of Mankind. And Dedicated to the Land-Holders of the British Dominions. By a Friend to Truth and the Christian Religion. *Lond. 1743*, 8°. LU.

The LU copy, which consists of the preface only, is signed with the author's name in ms. Urging reduction of the rate of interest.

5722 [Decker, Sir Matthew]. Serious Considerations on the several High Duties which the Nation in General (as well as it's Trade in Particular) labours under: with a Proposal for Preventing the Running of Goods, Discharging the Trader from any Search, and Raising all the Publick Supplies by One Single Tax. By a Well-Wisher to the Good People of Great-Britain. *Lond. 1743*, 8°. pp. 32. LU.

Another edn. 1743, pp. 30 (L); 2nd, 3rd, 4th and 5th edns. 1744 (all LU); 6th edn. 1748 (O); 7th edn., with author's name, 1756 (LU). Also printed as the second part of the 1751 Dublin edn. of the same author's *Essay on the Causes of the Decline of the Foreign Trade* (LU).

5723 [Waller, William]. A Free and Impartial Enquiry into the Extraordinary and Advantagious Bargain, (lately under the Consideration of Parliament) for remitting Money for the Pay of the Forces Abroad, for the Year 1743. Being a Faithful Specimen of the Œconomy and Management of the Present Administration in Domestic Affairs. *Lond. MDCXLIII [1743]*, 8°. LU.

For authorship see H. & L. quoting Cambridge University Library Catalogue.

5724 An Examination of the Conduct of several Comptrollers of the City of London, in relation to the City's Estate, call'd Conduit-Mead, now New Bond-Street, &c. Wherein the Reasoning of those Officers to induce the City to let new Leases thereof now, being upwards of twenty Years before the Expiration of the present Lease, is refuted, and the true Design of the whole disclosed. By a Person acquainted with the Estate and Proceedings. *Lond. 1743*, 8°. LG.

Another edn. 1744, entitled: The City-Secret; or Corruption at all Ends of the Town; Containing a Succinct History of an 100,000 l. Jobb, &c....(LG).

5725 A Bill to Oblige Overseers of the Poor to produce Poors Rates. *n.p. [1743]*, F°. L.

5726 A General Rate for the County of Norfolk. *Norwich, 1743*, 4°. O.

5727 By the Lords Justices and Council of Ireland, a Proclamation, offering a Reward for Apprehending and Convicting several Persons concerned in Coining and Uttering false Money. *Dublin, 1742, s. sh.* F°. DPRO.

Dated: 7 March 1742 [O.S].

TRANSPORT

5728 Boyd, Hugh. An Account of the Progress of Ballycastle Harbour, together with a Representation of the Present State of the Works. *Dublin, 1743*, 4°. C.

5729 A Bill for Enlarging the Term and Powers granted by an Act, passed in the Third Year of the Reign of his present Majesty, for repairing and widening the Road from that Part of Chatham, which lies next to the City of Rochester, to Saint Dunstan's Cross, near the City of Canterbury, in the County of Kent. *n.p.* [*1743*], *F°*. LU.

5730 [LABELYE, CHARLES]. The Present State of Westminster Bridge. Containing a Description of the said Bridge, as it has been ordered into Execution by the Right Honourable, &c. the Commissioners appointed by Parliament, and is now carrying on. With a True Account of the Time already Employed in the Building, and of the Works which are now done.... *Lond. 1743, 8°*. L.

2nd edn. corrected, 1743 (L). Authorship deduced from internal evidence.

SOCIAL CONDITIONS

5731 A Bill for Amending, and making more Effectual, the Laws relating to Rogues, Vagabonds, and other idle and disorderly Persons; and also the Laws for Erecting and Providing Houses of Correction. *n.p.* [*1743*], *F°*. L.

5732 A Bill to Amend and make more Effectual the Laws relating to Rogues, Vagabonds, and other idle and disorderly Persons, and to Houses of Correction. *n.p.* [*1743*], *F°*. LU.

Another edn., entitled: A Bill, intituled, An Act to amend and make more effectual the Laws relating to Rogues...[1743] (L).

5733 Edinburgh, 26th October 1743. [*Edin. 1743*], *s. sh. F°*. EU.

Act of the Town Council ordering the seizure of beggars.

5734 The Laws of the London Infirmary. *Lond. 1743, 4°*. L.

5735 Statutes, Rules, and Orders, for the Government of the County Hospital, for Sick and Lame Poor, establish'd in the Town of Northampton. *Northampton, 1743, 8°*. O.

5736 An Account of the Publick Hospital for the Diseased Poor in the County of York. *York, 1743, 8°*. O.

5737 Proposed Regulations for the Charity Work-house or Hospital of Edinburgh. [*Edin. 1743*], *4°*. ACC.

Dated: June 13, 1743.

5738 Regulations for the Charity Work-house or Hospital of Edinburgh. *Edin. 1743, 12°*. O.

Another edn. 1750 (O).

5739 The Relative Duty of Creditors and Debtors considered. Shewing, the indispensable Obligation Debtors are under to make the utmost Restitution to their Creditors; and proposing some Arguments and Reasons for the Gentleness and Compassion of Creditors towards insolvent Debtors. With some Objections answered, and Cases relating to this Subject stated and cleared, in a Sermon preached in the Chappel of the Fleet Prison, Jan. 23, 1742–3. *Lond. 1743, 8°*. LU.

5740 The Law for and against Bankrupts: containing All the Statutes, Cases at Large, Arguments, Resolutions, Judgments and Decrees, under the Head of Bankruptcy, down to the Present Time....By a late Commissioner of Bankrupts. [*Lond.*] *1743*, *8°*. O.

5741 A Letter to a Friend in the Country, in relation to the New Law concerning Spirituous Liquors. *Lond. 1743*, *8°*. LU.

Dated: Channel Row, March 7, 1743.

5742 HALES, STEPHEN. A Description of Ventilators: whereby Great Quantities of Fresh Air may with ease be conveyed into Mines, Goals, Hospitals, Work-Houses and Ships, in exchange for their Noxious Air. An Account also of their Great Usefulness in many other Respects: as in Preserving all Sorts of Grain....As also in drying Corn, Malt, Hops, Gun-Powder, &c....Which was read before the Royal Society in May 1741. *Lond. 1743*, *8°*. LU.

5743 William Weir of Waygateshaw, Esq; Appellant. Arthur Nasmyth, John Syme, Charles Hamilton, William Cullen, James Hamilton, William Allan, and others, Respondents. The Appellant's Case. *n.p.* [*1743*], *F°*. LHL.

Signed: Rob. Craigie. W. Murray. On the damage to his granary by the inhabitants of Hamilton during the famine of 1740.

5744 William Weir of Waygateshaw, Esq; Appellant. William Cullen and Charles Hamilton, Magistrates of the Burgh of Hamilton [and others the counsellors of the Burgh]...Respondents. The Case of the Respondents William Cullen, Charles Hamilton, John Sym, and Arthur Naismith only. *n.p.* [*1743*], *F°*. LHL.

Signed: W. Noel. Will. Hamilton.

5745 A Scheme, for Providing an Annuity to Ministers Widows, and a Stock to their Children; humbly offered to the Consideration of the Ministers of the Established Church of Scotland, by a Committee of the Commission of the late General Assembly, appointed to Draw up the Same, and Transmit it to the several Presbyteries. *Edinburgh*, *1743*, *4°*. O.

Dated: 3 January 1743.

5746 Representation and Scheme for providing an Annuity to Ministers Widows, and a Stock to their Children; humbly offered to the Consideration of the Venerable Assembly of the Church of Scotland, to meet at Edinburgh the 12th of May 1743, by a Committee of the Commission of the late General Assembly.... *Edin. 1743*, *4°*. E.

5747 Scheme for providing an Annuity to Ministers Widows, and a Stock to their Children; past and resolved by the General Assembly of the Church of Scotland, met at Edinburgh the 12th May, 1743. In order to a humble Application to the Legislature, for an Act of Parliament, to render the same effectual. *Edin. 1743*, *4°*. LSC.

Another edition of the preceding.

5748 Memorial concerning the Scheme for providing an Annuity to Ministers Widows, and a Stock to their Children, past and resolved by the late General Assembly of the Church of Scotland, met at Edinburgh the 12th Day of May 1743, in order to a humble Application to the Legislature, for an Act of Parliament to make the same effectual. *n.p.* [*1743*], *F*°. L.

1744

GENERAL

5749 A Supplement to Dr. Harris's Dictionary of Arts and Sciences....By a Society of Gentlemen. *Lond. 1744, F°.* L.

John Harris's *Lexicon Technicum* was first published in 1704.

5750 [WEBB, DANIEL ?]. An Essay presented; or a Method humbly proposed, to the Consideration of the Honourable the Members of both Houses of Parliament: by an English Woolen Manufacturer, to Pay the National Debts, without a new Tax, to inlarge Trade in general, by Reviving and Securing for Time to come, the British Woolen Exportation Trade, and preventing the Running of Brandy, Tea, &c. in; and to improve all waste Uncultivated Lands, within his Majesty's British Dominions. *Lond. 1744, 8°.* LU.

For attribution see ms. note in O copy. Mainly suggesting that the title to all waste lands should be vested in the Crown and that they should then be sold for development.

5751 [BLANCH, N.]. A New, Easy, and Infallible Method for Improving Estates Thirty per Cent. per Annum, without Toil, Trouble, or Charge...To which are added, Two very Curious Letters, wrote to the Honourable House of Commons, the first Sessions of this Parliament, on two of the most important Subjects in the World, Trade, and Interest of Money....By Philanthropos. *Lond. 1744, 8°.* LU.

Attribution based on similarity to Blanch's previous writings. Against tithes; for workhouses; and for the reduction of the rate of interest.

5752 [FORBES, DUNCAN]. Some Considerations on the Present State of Scotland: in a Letter to the Commissioners and Trustees for improving Fisheries and Manufactures. To which is subjoined, A Letter from the Annual Committee of the Convention of Royal Boroughs, to the several Boroughs of Scotland, by Order of the General Convention, for preventing the pernicious Practice of Smuggling. *Edin. 1744, 8°.* LU.

For authorship see H. & L. quoting Advocates' Library Catalogue and W. R. Scott, *Scottish Economic Literature*, no. 436. The second Letter is dated 3 Sept. 1736 and was published separately in that year (no. 4895). 3rd edn. of the two 1744 (E).

5753 [HARRIS, WALTER]. The Antient and Present State of the County of Down. Containing a Chorographical Description, with the Natural and Civil History of the same....With a Survey of the New Canal; as also, a New and Correct Map of the County. *Dublin, 1744, 8°.* L.

For authorship see *D.N.B.*

AGRICULTURE

5754 Adam's Luxury, and Eve's Cookery; or, the Kitchen-Garden display'd. In Two Parts. I. Shewing the best and most approved Methods of raising and bringing to the greatest Perfection, all the Products of the Kitchen-Garden....II. Containing a large Collection of Receipts for dressing all Sorts of Kitchen-Stuff....To which is added, The Physical Virtues of every Herb and Root.... *Lond. 1744*, 8º. L.

5755 Directions for the raising of Flax after the Flanders method. [*Edin. 1744*], 8º. MP.

Followed by 'By the Commissioners and Trustees for improving Fisheries and Manufactures in Scotland, The Conditions upon which those who undertake to raise Flax, are to have the Encouragement of 15 s. per Acre for the Years 1744 and 1745'.

5756 [GOULD, WILLIAM]. A Letter to the Commoners in Rockingham Forrest. Wherein is briefly and plainly shewn, the Right of Common they are intitled to in the Forrest; and a Method propos'd, by which they may preserve their Rights at a very easy Expence, if they will unanimously pursue it. By a Commoner. *Stamford, 1744*, 8º. L.

For authorship see William Upcott, *A Bibliographical Account*, 1818, p. 1024.

5757 An Act for inclosing the Common and Waste Ground, called Bassledon Heath, in the County of Berks. *n.p.* [*1744*], Fº. L.

5758 A Bill for Inclosing and Dividing the Common Fields called Flecknoe, in the Parish of Wolfhampcoat, in the County of Warwick. *n.p.* [*1744*], Fº. LU.

5759 An Act for Inclosing and Dividing the Common Fields called Flecknoe, in the County of Warwick, into just Allotments and Proportions. *n.p. 1743–4*, Fº. L.

5760 An Act for confirming an Agreement made to exchange certain Rights of Common in the Parishes, Townships, or Hamlets, of East Langton, West Langton, Church Langton, and Thorpe Langton, in the County of Leicester; and for settling an Yearly Sum, to be paid to the Rector of West Langton, and his Successors, in Lieu of Tithes. *n.p.* [*1744*], Fº. L.

5761 An Act for Inclosing and Dividing the Common, called The Severals, and The Moor, lying in the Manor and Parish of Mareham Le Fen, in the County of Lincoln. *n.p. 1743–4*, Fº. L.

5762 An Act for confirming Agreements made for inclosing and dividing Part of North-Stoneham Common, in the County of Southampton. *n.p.* $174\frac{3}{4}$, Fº. L.

5763 An Act for extinguishing a Right of Common claimed by and belonging to the Owners and Proprietors of antient Burgages and Tenements in

Ripon, Littlethorpe, and Bondgate, in the County of York, and for settling and providing an Equivalent for the said Common Right. *n.p. 1743–4, F°.* L.

5764 An Act for Dividing and Inclosing certain Common Fields in the Hamlet of Shipton, in the Parish of Winslow, in the County of Bucks. *n.p. 1743–4, F°.* L.

5765 An Act for Dividing and Inclosing the Common Fields, called the North-Field and South-Field, in the Parish of Westonbirt, in the County of Gloucester. *n.p. 1743–4, F°.* L.

5766 Unto the Right Honourable the Lords of Council and Session, the Petition of James Stirling, Esq; Agent for the Scots Mine Company at Leadhills. *n.p. [1744], 4°.* E.
Dated: February 23. 1744. Signed: James Ferguson.

5767 Answers for Edward Sommers and Leonard Pratt, Workmen at Leadhills; to the Petition of James Stirling, Agent for the Scots-Mine Company at Leadhills. *n.p. [1744], 4°.* E.
Dated: June 8th, 1744. Signed: William Grant.

5768 Unto the Right Honourable the Lords of Council and Session, the Petition of the Governor and Company for working Mines, Minerals, &c. in Scotland, and James Stirling, Esq; their Agent. *n.p. [1744], 4°.* E.
Dated: June 25, 1744. Signed: Ch. Areskine.

5769 Dutch Policy: or, The only Means of Growing High and Mighty, both by Sea and Land, without any Regard to the Ballance of Power in Europe. Containing the particular Methods by which that Politic Nation have from Time to Time encreased their Fishing Trade, which they call their Golden-Mine, and the Advantages they have gained over the English thereby. *Lond. 1744, 8°.* LU.

MANUFACTURES

5770 An Act for preventing Draymen, Brewers Servants, and others, from selling, pawning, and making away with Barrels, Casks, Butts, and other Vessels intrusted with them respectively, without the Consent of the Owners and Proprietors thereof. *n.p. [1744], F°.* L.
A bill.

5771 Reasons humbly offered in Behalf of the Bill, intituled, An Act for preventing Draymen, Brewers Servants, and others, from selling, pawning and making away with Barrels, Casks, Butts, and other Vessels, intrusted with them respectively, without the Consent of the Owners and Proprietors thereof. *n.p. [1744], s. sh. F°.* LLI.

5772 Some Observations in relation to the Linen Manufactures of Great Britain and Ireland. *n.p. [1744?], F°.* L.

5773 Remarks on the observations in relation to the linen manufactures of Great-Britain and Ireland. *n.p. [1744?], 31½ cm.* Kress 4730.

COMMERCE

5774 The Frauds and Abuses of the Coal-Dealers Detected and Exposed; in a Letter to an Alderman of London. *Lond. 1743–4, 8°.* L.

2nd edn. 1745; 3rd edn. 1747 (both L).

5775 Information for Daniel Midwinter, William Innes, John Knapton, Paul Knapton, Andrew Millar, and others, all of London, Book-sellers, and their Attorney or Factor, Pursuers; against Gavin Hamilton, Andrew Stalker, and others, Booksellers in Edinburgh and Glasgow, Defenders. *n.p.* [*1744*], *4°*. E.

Dated: November 30, 1744. Signed: Will. Grant. On infringement of copyright.

5776 Information for Mess. Hamilton and Balfour Booksellers in Edinburgh, Andrew Stalker Bookseller in Glasgow, and other Booksellers in these Cities, Defenders; against Andrew Millar, and others, Booksellers in London, Pursuers. *n.p.* [*1744*], *4°*. E.

Dated: December 3, 1740. Signed: Henry Home.

5777 Additional Information for Mess. Hamilton and Balfour, Andrew Stalker, and others, Booksellers in Edinburgh and Glasgow, Defenders; against Andrew Millar, and others, Booksellers, Pursuers. *n.p.* [*1744*], *4°*. E.

Dated: December 13. 1744. Signed: Ja. Graham junior.

5778 A Letter from an Old Citizen of London, to the Wine-Merchants and Coopers thereof. *Lond. 1744, F°.* LG.

Signed: Old Cives. On wines seized in merchants' cellars as prohibited imports from Spain.

5779 By Order of the Honourable Magistrates of the City of Edinburgh, A Table of the Weight and Prices of Bread to be sold and bought within the City and Liberties thereof.... [*Edin. 1744*], *s. sh. 4°*. ACC.

Dated: November 19. 1744.

5780 [Decker, Sir Matthew]. An Essay on the Causes of the Decline of the Foreign Trade, consequently of the Value of the Lands of Britain, and on the Means to Restore Both. Begun in the Year 1739. *Lond. 1744, 4°.* L.

2nd edn., with author's name, Dublin, 1749, 12° (L); another 2nd edn., anonymous, Lond. 1750, 12° (L); 4th edn., with author's name and with *Serious Considerations on the several High Duties* added, Dublin, 1751 (LU); another edn. anon., Edin. 1756 (L). Reprinted in *A Select Collection of Scarce and Valuable Tracts on Commerce*, ed. by J. R. McCulloch, 1859, as by Mr. Richardson, quoting Francis Fauquier as authority. The authorship is discussed in Palgrave's *Dictionary of Political Economy* under the heading Decker.

5781 The Case of several Merchants of London, who trade to Portugal, Spain, and Italy, and who suffer'd by having their Ships and Effects seized in Ports, and taken at Sea by the Spaniards in the Year 1718, and since. *n.p.* [*1744?*], *F°.* LU.

5782 Horsley, William. A Treatise on Maritime Affairs: or a Comparison between the Commerce and Naval Power of England and France.... *Lond. 1744, 8°.* LU.

5783 Cowley, J. A View of the British Trade to the Mediterranean: shewing, its Importance to us, its Precarious Situation at present, and that a total Loss of it must ensue, unless the Views of France and Spain are vigorously opposed. To which is prefix d, A Chart of the Mediterranean Sea.... *Lond. 1744, 4°.* L.

5784 Bridges, George. Plain Dealing: or the whole Method of Wool-Smuggling Clearly Discover'd, and the Weakness of the Laws in Force, put in a clear Light; with Methods proposed, and humbly submitted to both Houses of Parliament, by Way of Amendments to the Wool Act, that may effectually prevent Wool Smuggling for the future, without Expences to the Government. *Lond. 1744, 8°.* L.

5785 Laybourne, Henry. Tracts upon our Wool, and Woollen Trade. Wherein are consider'd the Irish Produce and Disposal of it; Advantages by preventing the Running of Wool....With Considerations on Mr. Gee's Impartial Enquiry....And a Reply to his Letter. *Stamford, 1744, 8°.* LU.

5786 Newball, John. A Scheme to prevent the Running of Wool Unmanufactur'd. Re-printed with several Additions. Together with Notes upon Trade and Industry, Idleness and Extravagance. And also a Scheme to prevent the Smuggling of Brandy, Tea, &c. into England: to encourage the Fair Trader, and encrease His Majesty's Revenues. *Stamford, [1744], 8°.* LU.

2nd edn., with additions, [1745] (LU). First printed [1741] (no. 5512).

5787 [Smith, John]. A Supplement to the State of our Wool and Woollen Trade reviewed, &c. Being a further Defence (chiefly historical) of a Scheme (which has been humbly presented to Parliament) for preventing the clandestine Exportation of Wool from Great Britain and Ireland both.... *Lond. 1744, 8°.* DA.

5788 A Bill for Enlarging and Regulating the Trade to the Levant Seas. *n.p. [1744], F°.* L.

Another edn., entitled: A Bill intituled, An Act for enlarging and regulating the Trade to the Levant Seas (L).

5789 The Case of the Governor and Company of Merchants of England, trading to the Levant Seas. *n.p. [1744], F°.* L.

5790 A Proof of the Decay of the Turkey Trade, as appears by the Custom-house Accompts for the last Five Years, compared with the Five foregoing. *n.p. [1744], F°.* L.

5791 Reasons against the Bill now depending in Parliament, intituled, A Bill for Inlarging and Regulating the Trade to the Levant Seas. *n.p. [1744], F°.* LU.

5792 Reasons for Passing the Bill, intituled, An Act for Inlarging and Regulating the Trade to the Levant Seas, now depending before the House of Lords; Humbly offered to the Consideration of their Lordships. *n.p.* [*1744*], *F*o. L.

5793 Short Reasons in Behalf of the Levant Company. *n.p.* [*1744*], *s. sh. F*o. LU.

5794 Short Remarks on the Turkey Trade, now under the Consideration of the Right Honourable the House of Lords. *n.p.* [*1744*], *s. sh. F*o. L.

5795 SMITH, WILLIAM. A New Voyage to Guinea: describing the Customs, Manners, Soil, Climate, Habits, Buildings, Education, Manual Arts, Agriculture, Trade, Employments...and whatever else is memorable among the Inhabitants. Likewise, An Account of their Animals, Minerals, &c..... *Lond. 1744*, *8*o. L.

Smith was sent in 1726 to survey the settlements of the Royal African Company.

5796 The Case of the Royal African Company of England, on Behalf of Themselves, and all Others His Majesty's Subjects trading to Africa and the British Colonies and Plantations in America. *n.p.* [*1744*], *s. sh. F*o. LU.

5797 The Importance of Effectually Supporting the Royal African Company of England Impartially Consider'd; Shewing, that a Free and Open Trade to Africa, and the Support and Preservation of the British Colonies and Plantations in America, depend upon maintaining the Forts and Settlements, Rights and Privileges belonging to that Corporation, against the Encroachments of the French, and all other Foreign Rivals in that Trade. With a Map, shewing the Situation of the several European Forts and Settlements in that Country. In a Letter to a Member of the House of Commons. *Lond. 1744*, *4*o. L.

Another edn. 1745 (O). A ms. note by Francis Hargrave in L copy attributes the work to Charles Hayes, the Secretary of the Company. Malachy Postlethwayt, however, claims the authorship in his *The Importance of the African Expedition considered*, 1758, p. xviii.

5798 DOBBS, ARTHUR. An Account of the Countries adjoining to Hudson's Bay, in the North-west Part of America: containing A Description of their Lakes and Rivers, the Nature of the Soil and Climates, and their Methods of Commerce, &c. Shewing the Benefit to be made by settling Colonies, and opening a Trade in these Parts; whereby the French will be deprived in a great Measure of their Traffick in Furs, and the Communication between Canada and Mississippi be cut off. With An Abstract of Captain Middleton's Journal, and Observations upon his Behaviour during his Voyage, and since his Return....The whole intended to shew the great Probability of a North-west Passage.... *Lond. 1744*, *4*o. L.

5799 MIDDLETON, CHRISTOPHER. A Reply to the Remarks of Arthur Dobbs, Esq; on Captain Middleton's Vindication of his Conduct on board his

Majesty's Ship the Furnace, when sent in Search of a North-west Passage, by Hudson's-Bay, to the Western American Ocean.... *Lond.* *1744*, *8°*. L.

5800 DOBBS, ARTHUR. Remarks upon Capt. Middleton's Defence: wherein his Conduct during his late Voyage for discovering a Passage from Hudson's-Bay to the South-Sea is impartially Examined.... *Lond.* *1744*, *8°*. L.

5801 His Majesty's most Gracious Declaration, For the Encouragement of His Ships of War and Privateers. *Lond.* *1744*, *s. sh. F°*. L.

Dated: 29 March 1744.

5802 By the King, A Proclamation. *Lond.* *1744*, *s. sh. F°*. C (Cr).

Dated: 14 June 1744. On the distribution of prize money.

5803 By the King, A Proclamation, Appointing the Distribution of the Bounty for taking or destroying Ships of War or Privateers of the Enemy. *Lond.* *1744*, *s. sh. F°*. C (Cr).

Dated: 7 November 1744.

5804 Adm. V——n's Opinion upon the Present State of the British Navy: in a Letter to a Certain Board. To which is annex'd by way of Illustration, his Letter to the Secretary of the same Board. *Lond.* *1744*, *8°*. L.

5805 A Bill, intituled, An Act for the better securing of the Trade of this Kingdom by Cruizers and Convoys. *n.p.* [*1744*], *F°*. L.

5806 The Bill (with the Amendments) for the more Speedy and Effectual Manning of His Majesty's Fleet. *n.p.* [*1744*], *F°*. L.

5807 A Bill for the more speedy and effectual Manning of His Majesty's Fleet, as it was Engross'd, and order'd for a Third Reading. *n.p.* *1744*, *8°*. O.

COLONIES

5808 A Bill to prevent the Issuing of Paper Bills of Credit in the British Colonies and Plantations in America, to be Legal Tenders in Payments for Money. *n.p.* [*1744*], *F°*. L.

5809 An Account of the Rise, Progress and Consequences of the two late Schemes commonly call'd the Land-Bank or Manufactory Scheme and the Silver Scheme, in the Province of the Massachusetts-Bay.... *n.p.* *1744*, *8°*.

Reprinted in *Colonial Currency Reprints*, ed. by A. M. Davis, vol. 4 (1911), whence this entry is taken.

5810 A Letter from a Gentleman in Boston, to his Friend in Connecticut. [*Boston*, *1744*], *8°*.

Reprinted in *Colonial Currency Reprints*, ed. by A. M. Davis, vol. 4 (1911), whence this entry is taken.

5811 Moore, Francis. A Voyage to Georgia. Begun in the Year 1735. Containing, an Account of the Settling the Town of Frederica, in the Southern Part of the Province; and a Description of the Soil, Air, Birds, Beasts, Trees, Rivers, Islands, &c. With the Rules and Orders made by the Honourable the Trustees for that Settlement; including the Allowances of Provisions, Cloathing, and other Necessaries to the Families and Servants which went thither. Also, a Description of the Town and County of Savannah, in the Northern Part of the Province; the Manner of dividing and granting the lands, and the Improvements there.... *Lond. 1744*, 8°. L.

Reprinted in the *Georgia Historical Society Collections*, vol. 1, 1840

FINANCE

5812 The State of the National Debt, as it stood Dec. 31, 1742, and on Dec. 31, 1743.... *Lond. 1744*, 8°. L.

Attested by John Dawson.

5813 Publick Funds for Publick Service, by raising Three Millions of Money, or a Million and a Half, with Ease and Ability, without Charge of Collecting, or affecting Land or Trade, or burdening Tax upon Tax. With Reasons for the same.... *Lond. 1744*, 8°. L.

Proposes a tax on holders of government stock.

5814 Proposals to raise Ten Millions and Five Hundred Thousand Pounds a Year, to which is added, a Proposal publish'd in the Year 1740 to raise Four Millions, at 3 per Cent. or Five hundred and seventy thousand Pounds a Year, to pay off the Money borrowed on the Pot-Act, Soap, Candles, &c. without any Additional Tax. By an Officer of the Stamp-Duties. *Lond. 1744*, 4°. L.

5815 A Serious Address to the Proprietors of the Publick Funds, occasion'd by Several Late Schemes for Reducing their Interest, or Subjecting them to Taxes: in which the Rights of Publick Creditors are explained and asserted....And concluded by a Rational Proposal for strengthening their Security, and for the better Support of Publick Credit.... *Lond. 1744*, 8°. L.

5816 Horsley, William. Serious Considerations on the High Duties Examin'd: Address'd to Sir Matthew Decker. *Lond. 1744*, 8°. LU.

5817 An Account shewing that Sugars will hardly do more than pay the Charges that attend the making thereof, and sending to England, if an additional Duty of 2s. 6d. per hund. be laid on the same, and they sell but for 24s. per hund. *n.p.* [*1744*], *s. sh. F°*. LU.

5818 The Case of the Refiners of Sugar in England. *n.p.* [*1744*], *s. sh. F°*. LU.

Endorsed: The Sugar Refiners Case.

5819 Considerations against laying any New Duty upon Sugar; wherein is particularly shewn, That a New Imposition will be ruinous to the Sugar Colonies, insufficient for the Purposes intended, and greatly conducive to the Aggrandizement of France. *Lond. 1744, 8°.* LU.

2nd edn. 1746, entitled: Considerations relating to a New Duty upon Sugar (Sabin 102826). Tentatively attributed to C. A. Heath in H. & L. without quoting authority.

5820 Reasons against laying an Additional Duty on Muscovada Sugar, and more particularly against levying it by an Excise on Refined Sugar. *n.p. [1744], s. sh. F°.* LU.

A printed note on the endorsement reads: The first Reasons being published in Haste, it has been thought proper to republish them, with some Amendments and Additions.

5821 Reasons against laying any further Duty upon Sugar. *n.p. [1744], s. sh. F°.* LU.

Last line: of this Kingdom. Another edn. [1744]. Last line: February 13th (LU).

5822 [ASHLEY, JOHN]. A Supplement. On Taxes in general on British Sugar. *n.p. [1744], 8°.* L.

The only copy seen is without title-page. For authorship see the following entry.

5823 ASHLEY, JOHN. A Supplement to the Second Part of the Memoirs of John Ashley, Esq; concerning the Trade and Revenues of the British Colonies in America, on Taxes upon Sugar. The Second Edition. *Lond. 1744, 8°.* O.

2nd edn. of the preceding.

5824 Considerations on the Duties upon Tea, and the Hardships suffer'd by the Dealers in that Commodity. Together with a Proposal for their Relief. Collected from the Champion, and publish'd at the Request of the Tea-Dealers. *Lond. 1744, 8°.* LU.

Included is a letter from a correspondent signed: J. M. who identifies himself in a ms. note in LU copy as John Mackmath of Prince's Street, Rotherhith.

5825 LONDON. Committee of City Lands. Journal 24, Fol. 145, A. (Wednesday, 13 Sept. 1732.) *n.p. [1744?], F°.* L.

Printed in connection with the Conduit Meads investigation.

5826 A Short View of the Frauds, Abuses, and Impositions of Parish Officers, with some Considerations on the Laws relating to the Poor; shewing how the Deficiencies therein might be remedied, by fixing a Qualification for the Choice of Churchwardens and Overseers, by limiting the Sums to be raised by their Rates, and by bringing them to Account properly for the Monies that come into their Hands. *Lond. 1744, 4°.* LU.

Another edn. Edin. 1749 (EP).

5827 A True State of the Case in respect to the late Disputes in the Parish of St. Leonard's Shoreditch, concerning the Poor's Rates, with a Narrative of the Proceedings both in the King's-Bench and at Hicks's-Hall, &c. With some Observations thereon. By a Parishioner. *Lond. 1744, 8°.* L.

5828 [Webster, William]. An Appeal to the Common Sense Common Honesty and Common Piety of the Laity, in respect to the Payment of Tythe, &c. *Lond. 1744, 8°.* LU.

In the preface the author mentions his *Clergy's Right of Maintenance* which was published under his name.

5829 A Bill more effectually to Prevent the Receiving of Stolen Goods, by the Regulating of Pawn-brokers. *n.p.* [*1744*], *F°.* L.

5830 An Apology for the Business of Pawn-Broking. By a Pawn-Broker. *Lond. 1744, 8°.* LU.

Without publisher's name. Another issue, printed for J. Collyer (LU); 2nd edn. 1744 (LU). One of the LU copies has a ms. note of authorship now illegible. Foxwell recorded it as by Thomas Wise, with a query. Reprinted in *A Select Collection of Scarce and Valuable Economical Tracts*, ed. by J. R. McCulloch, 1859.

5831 The Gentleman's and Lady's Accomptant: or, An Essay toward rendering the most approved Method of keeping Accompts very Plain, Pleasing and Useful to the Nobility and Gentry.... *Lond. 1744, 4°.* LICA.

TRANSPORT

5832 Unto the Right Honourable, The General Convention of the Royal Boroughs, The Petition of the Magistrates, Town-Council, and whole Inhabitants of the Burgh of Kinghorn. *n.p.* [*1744*], *s. sh. F°.* ACC.

Dated: July 4. 1744. For aid in rebuilding the harbour.

5833 The Case of the Constables, Churchwardens, Overseers of Poor, and other Inhabitants of the Town of Wakefield, in the West Riding of the County of York. *n.p.* [*1744*], *s. sh. F°.* LU.

Endorsed: The Case on the Wakefield Petition. For power to increase the assessment for rates of the undertakers for making the Aire and Calder navigable.

5834 A Bill for Explaining and Amending an Act passed in the Sixth Year of his present Majesty's Reign, intituled, An Act to Recover and Preserve the Navigation of the River Dee...and another Act passed in the Fourteenth Year of his present Majesty's Reign, intituled, An Act for Incorporating the Undertakers of the Navigation of the River Dee; and for Repealing the Tonage-Rates payable to the said Undertakers; and for granting to them other Tonage or Keelage-Rates in lieu thereof.... *n.p.* [*1744*], *F°.* LU.

5835 GRUNDY, JOHN, sen. and JOHN, jun. A Scheme for the restoring and making perfect the Navigation of the River Witham from Boston to Lincoln, and also for draining the Low-Lands and Fenns contiguous thereto. *n.p. 1744, 8º*. L.

5836 A Bill (with the Amendments) to Amend and render more Effectual the Laws in Being for the Preservation of the publick Roads. *n.p.* [*1744*], *Fº*. L.

5837 A Bill for Repairing the Road from the Town of Buckingham, in the County of Bucks, to Warmington, in the County of Warwick. *n.p.* [*1744*], *Fº*. LU.

5838 A Bill for Repairing the Road leading from a Place called the Bound Stone, in the Parish of Cann, in the County of Dorset, through the Town of Shaftesbury to Bow Bridge, in the Road to Sherborn in the said County. *n.p.* [*1744*], *Fº*. L.

5839 A Bill for Enlarging the Term and Powers granted by an Act passed in the Fourth Year of the Reign of his present Majesty, for Repairing the Road leading from Chappel on the Heath, in the County of Oxon, to the Quarry above Bourton on the Hill, in the County of Gloucester. *n.p.* [*1744*], *Fº*. LU.

5840 A Bill for making more effectual the several Acts of Parliament passed for Repairing the Road from Cherill through Calne to Studley-Bridge, in the County of Wilts. *n.p.* [*1744*], *Fº*. LU.

5841 A Bill for continuing and enlarging the Term and Powers, granted by an Act of Parliament, passed in the Thirteenth Year of the Reign of his late Majesty King George the First, for repairing the Road from Cranford-bridge, in the County of Middlesex, to that End of Maidenhead-bridge which lies in the County of Bucks. *n.p.* [*1744*], *Fº*. LU.

5842 A Bill for Enlarging the Term and Powers granted by an Act passed in the Third Year of the Reign of his present Majesty, for Repairing the Road leading from Galley-corner, adjoining to Enfield Chase, in the Parish of South Mims, in the County of Middlesex, to Lemsford Mill, in the County of Hertford. *n.p.* [*1744*], *Fº*. LU.

5843 A Bill for continuing the Term and Powers granted by an Act passed in the First Year of his present Majesty's Reign, intituled, An Act for Repairing and Amending several Roads leading to and from the Borough of Evesham, in the County of Worcester; and for making the same more Effectual. *n.p.* [*1744*], *Fº*. LU.

5844 A Bill for Repairing and Widening the Road, leading from a Place called Harlow Bush Common, in the Parish of Harlow, in the County of Essex, to a Place called Stump Cross, in or near the furthermost Part of the Parish of Great Chesterford, in the said County. *n.p.* [*1744*], *Fº*. LU.

5845 A Bill for Continuing, and making more Effectual, an Act passed in the Second Year of the Reign of his present Majesty, intituled, An Act for Repairing the Road leading from Cannals Gate to the City of Lichfield, and from the said City to Stone, and from thence to the End of the County of Stafford in the Post Road towards Chester; and also from the Town of Burton upon Trent to the said City of Lichfield...and also from the said City of Lichfield to High Bridges.... *n.p.* [*1744*], *F°*. LU.

5846 A Bill for further Continuing and making more Effectual an Act made in the Eleventh Year of his present Majesty's Reign, intituled, An Act for repairing the Roads from the Town of Loughborough...to the Town of Derby...and from the said Town of Derby to the Town of Brassington...and from the said Town of Derby to Hurdloe-house in the Parish of Hartington.... *n.p.* [*1744*], *F°*. LU.

5847 A Bill for rectifying Mistakes, and supplying Defects, in an Act passed the last Session of Parliament, for Continuing an Act made in the Thirteenth Year of the Reign of his late Majesty King George the First, for amending and repairing the Roads from Luton in the County of Bedford, to Westwood Gate in the said County; and for repairing the Roads from Luton to Saint Alban in the County of Hertford; and for making the said Acts more effectual. *n.p.* [*1744*], *F°*. LU.

5848 A Bill for Repairing the Road leading from the End of Midleton Tyas-lane over Gatherly-Moor to Greetabridge, and from thence to Bowes, in the North Riding of the County of York. *n.p.* [*1744*], *F°*. LU.

5849 A Bill for Inlarging the Term and Powers granted by an Act passed in the Third Year of the Reign of his present Majesty, intituled, An Act for Repairing the Roads leading from a Gate, called Shipston Toll-Gate, at Bridgetown, in the Parish of Old Stratford, in the County of Warwick, through Alderminster and Shipston upon Stower, to the Top of Long Compton Hill, in the said County; and to make the same more Effectual. *n.p.* [*1744*], *F°*. LU.

5850 A Bill for making more effectual several Acts passed for repairing the Road leading from the Stones End, in the Parish of Saint Leonard, Shoreditch, in the County of Middlesex, to the furthermost Part of the Northern Road, in the Parish of Enfield, in the same County, next to the Parish of Cheshunt, in the County of Hertford, and for amending the Road from the Watch-house in Edmonton, to the Market-Place in Enfield. *n.p.* [*1744*] *F°*. LU.

5851 A Bill for Continuing an Act passed in the Thirteenth Year of the Reign of his late Majesty King George the First, so far as the same relates to the Repairing the Road from Studley-bridge to Chippenham in the County of Wilts, and for Amending the Road from Chippenham to Pickwick in the said County. *n.p.* [*1744*], *F°*. L.

5852 A Bill to Explain and Amend Two Acts of Parliament made in the Twelfth and Thirteenth Years of the Reign of his present Majesty (For giving further Powers to the Commissioners for Building a Bridge cross the River Thames, from the City of Westminster, to the opposite Shore in the County of Surrey) and for making the said Acts more effectual. *n.p.* [*1744*], *F°*. LU.

SOCIAL CONDITIONS

5853 The Annual Account of the Bristol Infirmary for the Year, ending December 21, 1744. With a short Account of that Charity from the Beginning to this Time. *n.p. 1744, 4°*. LU.

5854 GREY, RICHARD. The Encouragement to Works of Charity and Mercy, from Christ's Acceptance of them as done to Himself. A Sermon preached...before the President and Governors of the County Infirmary for Sick and Lame Poor, on Thursday, March 29, 1744.... To which are added, The Statutes of the said Infirmary. *Northampton, 1744, 8°*. O.

5855 Verses occasioned by seeing Proposals for Founding an Hospital for Incurables in the City of Dublin. Humbly inscribed to Her Grace the Dutchess Dowager of Marlborough. *Dublin, 1744, 8°*. DG.

5856 DAVIES, THOMAS. The Laws relating to Bankrupts, brought Home to the present Time.... [*Lond.*] *1744, F°*. LU.

5857 A Bill for Raising and Establishing a Fund for a Provision for the Widows and Children of the Ministers of the Church of Scotland, and of the Heads, Principals, and Masters, of the Universities of Saint Andrews, Glasgow, and Edinburgh. *n.p.* [*1744*], *F°*. L.

5858 A Bill to Explain and Amend an Act passed in the Ninth Year of the Reign of His present Majesty, intituled, An Act for the better Enlightning of the Streets of the City of London. *n.p.* [*1744*], *F°*. LU.

5859 Colonel Charles Straton in old Montrose, Appellant. The Magistrates and Town Council of Montrose Respondents. The Appellant's Case. *n.p.* [*1744*], *F°*. L.

Signed: W. Murray. Al. Lockhart. On damage to the appellant's granary during the famine of 1741.

5860 Colonel Charles Straton, Appellant. David Skinner, Merchant, and Provost of the Burgh of Montrose [and others, the magistrates and town council of the Burgh]...Respondents. The Case of the Respondents. *n.p.* [*1744*], *F°*. L.

Signed: R. Craigie. C. Erskine.

1745

GENERAL

5861 The Present Ruinous Land-War, proved to be a H——r War, by the Facts as well as Arguments; or the Opposition fully Vindicated: By a Lover of his Country. *Lond.* *1745*, *8°*. L.

5862 The Present State of Scotland Consider'd: and its declining and sinking Condition charged upon the Conduct of the landed Gentlemen, &c. Shewing that they have involved themselves, and their Country, in Poverty. That the only Mean of relieving their Estates, of suppressing destructive Trades, and saving Scotland from impending Ruin, is by their joining together to promote Home Manufacture, the landed Interest being chiefly concerned in this important Attempt. *Edin.* *1745*, *8°*. LU.

5863 A View of the Grievances of Ireland. By a True Patriot. *Dublin*, *1745*, *8°*. L.

2nd edn. 1745 (DA).

5864 Proposals for collecting Materials for publishing the Antient and Present State of the several Counties of Ireland in Descriptions Natural, Civil, Ecclesiastical, Historical, Chorographical, &c. With a Table of Queries annexed. *n.p.* [*1745*], *8°*. DA.

5865 An Account of the Rise of the Physico-Historical Society. [*Dublin*, *1745*], *8°*. DA.

AGRICULTURE

5866 ELLIS, WILLIAM. Agriculture Improv'd: or, the Practice of Husbandry Display'd. Chiefly shewn by Facts, Perform'd in all Sorts of Land, according to the Old Plain, and the New Drill, Way of Farming.... *Lond.* *1746* [*1745*], *8°*. 2 vols. O.

5867 Report from the Committee to whom the Petition of Several Yeomen, Farmers and Grasiers in the Counties of Middlesex, Surrey, and Kent...in Behalf of Themselves and many Others concerned in the Growth of Corn, and the Breeding and Fatting of Cattle was Referred.... *Lond.* *1745*, *F°*. LU.

5868 A short view of the advantages which probably may arise from the scheme for encouraging flax-husbandry in Ireland. *Dublin*, *1745*, *8°*. Kress 4748.

5869 An Account of the present Epidemical Distemper amongst the Black Cattle: together with a Method of Cure.... By a Member of the College of Physicians. *Lond.* *1745*, *8°*. L.

5870 An Act for Inclosing and Dividing the Common Fields in Faxton, within the Parish of Lamport in the County of Northampton, and for giving a Recompence to the Rector of the said Parish, in Lieu of his Tythes of the said Common Fields. *n.p.* *1744–5*, *F°*. L.

5871 ELSTOBB, WILLIAM. The Pernicious Consequences of Replacing Denver-Dam and Sluices, &c. consider'd; in a Letter to Mr. John Leaford. Wherein his Arguments contained in a Pamphlet entitled, Observations, &c. are fairly and candidly examined. *Cambridge*, *1745*, *8°*. O.

5872 LABELYE, CHARLES. The Result of a View of the Great Level of the Fens, taken at the desire of His Grace the Duke of Bedford, &c. Governor, and the Gentlemen of the Corporation of the Fens, in July 1745. *Lond.* *1745*, *4°*. L.

5873 Unto the Right Honourable the Lords of Council and Session, the Petition of Sir Archibald Grant of Monnymusk Baronet. *n.p.* [*1745*], *s. sh. F°*. EU.

On the lease of Sir A. Murray's mines. Signed: And. Macdouall. Dated: February 7th, 1745.

5874 Unto the Right Honoureble, The Lords of Council and Session, the Petition of Sir Archibald Grant of Monnimusk, Baronet. *n.p.* [*1745*], *s. sh. F°*. EU.

Signed: And. Macdoual. Dated: February 13. 1745. Includes 'Proposals by Luke Walker...for working a Part of the Mines...at Strontein'.

5875 Unto the Right Honourable the Lords of Council and Session, the Petition of John Pringle Writer to the Signet, Factor appointed by your Lordships upon the Estate of Charles Murray of Stanhope. *n.p.* [*1745*], *s. sh. F°*. EU.

Signed: Alex. Lockhart. Dated: February 14. 1745.

5876 Depositions of the Witnesses in the Cause, James Stirling Esquire, Agent for the Scots Mine Company; against Leonard Pratt and Edward Sommers. *n.p.* [*1745*], *F°*. E.

Dated: Januray [*sic*] 15th, 1745.

5877 Memorial for the Governor and Company for working Mines, Minerals, &c. in Scotland, and James Stirling, Esq; their Agent. *n.p.* [*1745*], *4°*. E.

Dated: January 18. 1745. Signed: Ro. Dundas.

5878 Memorial for Edward Sommers and the Representatives of Leonard Pratt, Workmen at Leadhills, Defenders; with respect to the Proof led in the Action of Damages, pursued at the Instance of James Stirling, Agent for the Scots Mine Company at Leadhills, against them. *n.p.* [*1745*], *F°*. E.

Dated: January 21st 1745.

5879 O'CONNOR, MARTIN. An Account of the Nature and Conditions of a Charter, to be granted for the working and manufacturing Mines and

Minerals in Ireland; Together with some general Heads relating to the Advantages that must necessarily result from that laudable Establishment. In a Letter to the Right Honourable Thomas Lord Southwell. *Lond. 1745*, *8º*. O.

5880 COSIN, JOHN. The Names of the Roman Catholics, Nonjurors, and others, who refus'd to take the Oaths to his late Majesty King George. Together with their Titles, Additions, and Places of Abode; the Parishes and Townships where their Lands lay; the Names of the then Tenants and the Annual Valuation of them. Transmitted to the late Commissioners for the Forfeited Estates of England and Wales...in the Year 1715. *Lond. 1745*, *8º*. L.

The dedication is signed: James Cosin (son of the compiler). 2nd edn. 1746, published by Charles Cosin (O). Another edn. 1862.

5881 Answers for James Peachey and other Trustees for the Annuitants on the York-buildings Company's Estates, and their Factor; to the Petition of Edward Duke of Norfolk, and others, pretended Creditors of the said York-buildings Company. *n.p.* [*1745*], *s. sh. Fº*. EU.

Signed: Ja. Graham. Dated: January 3d, 1745.

5882 Observes for His Grace the Duke of Norfolk and Partners, upon the State of the Tacks and Management of the Estates of the York-building Company. *n.p.* [*1745*], *s. sh. Fº*. EU.

Dated 12th February 1745.

5883 Minutes. His Grace the Duke of Norfolk and Partners; against the Annuitants of the York-building Company. *n.p.* [*1745*], *s. sh. Fº*. EU.

Dated: 16th February 1745.

5884 Considerations on the State of the British Fisheries in America, and their Consequence to Great Britain. With Proposals for their Security, by the Reduction of Cape-Breton, &c. which were humbly offer'd, by a Gentleman of a Large Trade of the City of London, to His Majesty's Ministers, in January 1744–5. *Lond. 1745*, *Fº*. L.

MANUFACTURES

5885 SALMON, WILLIAM. The London and Country Builder's Vade Mecum: or, The Compleat and Universal Architect's Assistant. Comprehending the London and Country Prices of the different Works of Bricklayers, Masons, Carpenters, Joyners, Glasiers, Plumbers, Slaters, Plaisterers, Painters, Paviours, Carvers, Smiths, &c.... *Lond. 1745*, *8º*. LU.

2nd edn. 1748 (K); and at least 3 later edns.

5886 SWAN, ABRAHAM. The British Architect: or, The Builder's Treasury of Stair-Cases.... *Lond. 1745*, *Fº*. LRIBA.

2nd edn. 1750 (LRIBA); and later edns.

5887 Report from the Committee to whom the Petition of the Merchants, and Others, of Great Britain and Ireland, Dealers in, and Manufacturers of, Linens, Threads, and Tapes, made in Great Britain and Ireland...was Referred. *n.p. 1744* [*o.s.*], *F°*. LU.

5888 A Bill, intituled, An Act for more effectually preventing the Stealing of Linen, Fustian, and Cotton Goods and Wares, in Buildings, Fields, Grounds, and other Places used for Printing, Whitening, Bleaching, or Drying the same. *n.p.* [*1745*], *F°*. L.

5889 Memorial for the linen-manufacturers of Scotland.... *n.p.* [*174⁴⁄₅*], *19.5 cm.* Kress S. 1914.

5890 Remarks on the Present State of the Linnen-Manufacture of this Kingdom. And Queries relating to the Further Improvement thereof.... *Dublin, 1745, 8°*. O.

5891 The Case of the Master-Linen-Weavers, Manufacturers, and Dealers in the Linen Trade of the City of Dublin, most humbly submitted to the Consideration of the Honourable the Knights, Citizens, and Burgesses, in Parliament assembled. *n.p.* [*c. 1745?*], *F°*. DNL.
Against the conspiracy of journeymen to raise wages.

5892 A Letter to a Member of Parliament, on the Importance of Liberty; towards Enjoying the National Benefit of any useful Branch of Manufactures, &c. *Lond. 1745, 8°*. LU.
The case of the journeymen tailors.

COMMERCE

5893 Robe, Thomas. Ways and Means for the Suppression of Knavery, and to raise Great Sums of Money for the Government's Use, without any New Taxation; and save, to all His Majesty's Honest Subjects, near Half a Million of Money Annually, by Selling Weight and Measure in due Proportion.... *Lond. 1745, 8°*. LU.
For enforcing the fees of clerks of the market.

5894 London. Hoare, Mayor. Tuesday the 10th Day of December, 1745.... *n.p.* [*1745*], *s. sh. F°*. L.
An order that coal-meters, corn-meters, salt-meters and fruit-meters are not to measure or allow to be carried away any goods without warrant from the Lord Mayor or his deputy.

5895 By Order of the Honourable Magistrates of the City of Edinburgh, A Table of the Weight and Prices of Bread to be sold and bought within the City and Liberties thereof.... [*Edin. 1745*], *s. sh. 4°*. ACC.
Dated: March 13. 1745.

5896 Sutton Samuel An Historical Account of a New Method for extracting the foul Air out of Ships, &c. With the Description and Draught of the Machines, by which it is performed: and the Relation given thereof by Dr Mead, to the Royal Society. *Lond. 1745*, 8°. L.

2nd edn. 1749; 3rd edn. 1757 (both L).

5897 [Lowndes, Thomas]. A State of the Coal-Trade to Foreign Parts, by way of a Memorial to a supposed very great Assembly. *Lond. 1744–5*, F°. L.

For authorship see *Journal of the Commissioners for Trade and Plantations*, 1742–1749, p. 149, 5 Feb. 1744/5.

5898 The Case of Several Persons, convicted (for divers Penalties, or now under Prosecution for the same) for clandestine Importing and Running Prohibited and Unaccustomed Goods. *n.p.* [*1745*], F°. LLI.

5899 Bonell, George. Proposals for Preventing the Infamous and Clandestine Exportation of our Wool and Woollen Yarn from Great Britain and Ireland....Together with easy and effectual Ways and Means to pay the Interest, now wanted, of 12,000,000 l. for the Service of the Government. *n.p.* [*1745?*], F°. LU.

5900 [Lowndes, Thomas]. A Method to prevent, without a Register, the Running of Wool from Ireland to France, and to other Foreign Parts; in order to re-establish the Woolen Manufacture of England. Shewing at the same Time, how to Raise a Fund, wherewith to Erect and Maintain such a Number of English Protestant Schools in Ireland as the Legislature shall think proper; and also greatly to Encourage and Extend the Linen Manufacture of Ireland. *n.p. 1745*, F°. LU.

The author's name is disclosed on p. 16. Another edn. [Lond.], 1745, 8° (O).

5901 [Bradshaw,]. A Scheme to prevent the Running of Irish Wools to France, and Irish Woollen Goods to Foreign Countries; by prohibiting the Importation of Spanish Wools into Ireland, and permitting the People of Ireland to send their woollen Goods to England, (not for Consumption, but Re-exportation) under a Duty at Importation, to be drawn back on Exportation from England to Foreign Countries. Humbly offer'd to the Consideration of Parliament. By a Merchant of London. *Lond.* [*1745*], 8°. L.

Another edn. Dublin, 1745 (L); another edn., with author's name, Lond. 1754 (L).

5902 A Short and Easy Method of Preventing the Clandestine Exportation of Wool: to the mutual Advantage of Britain and Ireland: together with a Proposal for obliging all Foreign Nations to contribute to the Support of the British Navy, by a Duty upon the Provisions of Ireland, without the least Disadvantage to that Kingdom, and to the great Advantage of the British Commerce. *Lond. 1745*, 8°. LU.

Another edn. Dublin, 1745 (L).

5903 [Postlethwayt, Malachy ?]. The African Trade, the great Pillar and Support of the British Plantation Trade in America: shewing, That our Loss, by being beat out of all the Foreign Markets for Sugar and

Indigo by the French, has been owing to the Neglect of our African Trade; which only, can supply our Colonies with Negroes, for the making of Sugars, and all other Plantation Produce: That the Support and Security of the Negroe-Trade depends wholly on the due and effectual Support of the Royal African Company of England, which has hitherto preserved this invaluable Trade to these Kingdoms.... *Lond. 1745*, 4°. L.

Signed: A British Merchant. Attribution based on a ms. note in L copy.

5904 The Present State of the British and French Trade to Africa and America Consider'd and Compar'd: with some Propositions in Favour of the Trade of Great Britain. *Lond. 1745*, 8°. L.

5905 MIDDLETON, CHRISTOPHER. Forgery Detected. By which is evinced how groundless are all the Calumnies cast upon the Editor, in a Pamphlet published under the Name of Arthur Dobbs, Esq; *Lond. 1745*, 8°. L.

A criticism of *Remarks upon Captain Middleton's Defence*, 1744. On the North-West Passage.

5906 DOBBS, ARTHUR. A Reply to Capt. Middleton's Answer to the Remarks on his Vindication of his Conduct, in a late Voyage made by him in the Furnace Sloop, by Orders of the Lords Commissioners of the Admiralty, to find out a Passage from the North-west of Hudson's Bay, to the Western and Southern Ocean of America....To which is added, A Full Answer to a late Pamphlet published by Capt. Middleton, called Forgery Detected. *Lond. 1745*, 8°. L.

5907 MIDDLETON, CHRISTOPHER. A Rejoinder to Mr. Dobbs's Reply to Captain Middleton.... *Lond. 1745*, 8°. L.

5908 MIDDLETON, CHRISTOPHER. A Reply to Mr. Dobbs's Answer to a Pamphlet, entitled, Forgery Detected. *Lond. 1745*, 8°. L.

5909 Articles of Agreement, for carrying on an Expedition, by Hudson's Streights, for the Discovery of a North-West Passage to the Western and Southern Ocean of America. Dated March 30, 1745. *Lond. 1745*, 8°. L.

Another edn. Dublin, 1745 (DA).

5910 Report relating to the finding a North-West Passage. *n.p.* [*1745*], *s. sh. F°*. L.

By a committee of the House of Commons.

5911 THOMAS, PASCOE. A True and Impartial Account of a Voyage to the South-Seas, and round the Globe, in His Majesty's Ship the Centurion, under the command of Commodore George Anson.... *Lond. 1745*, 8°. L.

5912 A Collection of Voyages and Travels....From the curious and valuable Library of the late Earl of Oxford. Interspersed and illustrated with Notes.... *Lond. 1745*, *F°*. 2 vols. L.

Reissued in 1747 as vols. 7, 8 of the *Collection of Voyages and Travels* originally published by Awnsham and John Churchill in 1704.

5913 An Infallible Project for the more effectual speedy and easy Manning of the Navy of England, without that intollerable and unparallel'd Practice of Pressing, plainly Demonstrated. With Observations on our Marine Affairs in general, and some Thoughts on Trade. Likewise an Account of the Excellent Management of the Marine in France, well worthy of our Imitation. Humbly inscribed to the Consideration of the Legislature. By a Seaman. *Lond. 1745*, 8°. LU.

5914 Observations and Proposals concerning the Navy: with an Enquiry into its present Condition; shewing its Insufficiency to defend us from a sudden Attack of the French.... *Lond. 1745*, 8°. L.

COLONIES

5915 Auchmuty, Robert. The Importance of Cape Breton to the British Nation.... *Lond. 1745*, *F°*. L.

5916 Durell, Philip. A Particular Account of the taking Cape Breton from the French, by Admiral Warren, and Sir William Pepperell, the 17th of June, 1745. With a Description of the Place and Fortifications; the Loss it will be to the French Trade.... *Lond. 1745*, *F°*. L.

5917 A Letter to a Member of Parliament, concerning the Importance of our Sugar-Colonies to Great Britain. By a Gentleman, who resided many Years in the Island of Jamaica. *Lond. 1745*, 8°. L.

L copy has a ms. attribution to Samuel Dicker.

5918 Smith, William, Rector of St. John's, Nevis. A Natural History of Nevis, and the rest of the English Leeward Charibee Islands in America. With many other Observations on Nature and Art.... *Cambridge, 1745*, 8°. L.

FINANCE

5919 A Survey of the National Debts, the Sinking Fund, the Civil List, and the Annual Supplies: giving a clear and impartial Account of our Present State with regard to Publick Money. With Tables of the National Debts for 1716 and the five last Years.... *Lond. 1745*, 8°. LU.

5920 A Scheme for improving Small Sums of Money, by which, Great Part of the Nation's Specie, which now lies dead and unimproved, may be employed to the most important Uses of the Government, of Trade, and of private Persons. Exhibiting, at One View, the certain Reward of virtuous Servants, and the yearly Profit which will arise from thus imploying their Wages, or any Small Sum, from five to twenty Pounds.... *Lond. 1745*, 4°. L.

Fund to enable the small investor to lend to the government.

5921 An Enquiry how far the Commissioners of His Majesty's Land-Tax, have Power to Alter the Quota's Assessed within the several Hundreds or Divisions, throughout Great Britain; conformable to an Act 4th of K. William and Q. Mary, for Granting to Their Majesties an Aid of Four Shillings in the Pound, for one Year, for carrying on a Vigorous War against France. In a Letter to the Right Honourable the L**D C**P***R....By a Commissioner of one of the Aggrieved Parishes in the City and Liberty of Westminster. *Lond.* *1745*, *8°*. LU.

5922 The Law concerning Pawn-Brokers and Usurers: containing all the Statutes and Cases in Law and Equity extant, which relate to Pawns and Usury, disposed under proper Heads.... *Lond.* *1745*, *12°*. LU.

5923 A Bill, intituled, An Act for the more effectually preventing the Receiving of Stolen Goods, by the Regulating of Pawnbrokers. *n.p.* [*1745*], *F°*. L.

5924 A Letter from a Discounter in Bishopgate-Street, to a Pawnbroker in Long-Acre. *Lond.* *1745*, *8°*. LU.

Signed: Abraham Ben Little Wright.

5925 A Plain Answer to a late Pamphlet, intitled, The Business of Pawnbroking stated and defended. Shewing the false Reasoning, and Mis-stating of several Facts contained in that Pamphlet. And also discovering and displaying some of the many Secrets in that Business, practised by the Initiated Pawnbrokers. With some Hints humbly proposed for their Better Regulation. By an Impartial Hand. *Lond.* *1745*, *8°*. LU.

5926 [De Veil, Sir Thomas]. Reasons against Licensing Pawnbrokers: humbly offer'd to the Consideration of the Legislature, occasion'd by a Bill for that Purpose depending in the House of Commons. Wherein the Pamphlet, intitl'd, An Apology for the Business of Pawnbroking, is Examined and Confuted; and the Practice of Pawnbrokers in general prov'd to be injurious to Trade, an Encouragement to Rogues, and destructive to Society: Demonstrated by Variety of Examples. *Lond.* *1745*, *8°*. LU.

For authorship see ms. note in LU copy.

5927 The Charitable Corporation Vindicated, as well when in the Heighth of Trade, as in its present Situation: together with Some Reasons why it deserves the Protection and Assistance of the Legislature; and the Concurrence of every Individual, who wishes well to the Publick. By Mr. Innes, Solicitor to the Corporation. *Lond.* *1745*, *8°*. LU.

TRANSPORT

5928 Report, and Estimate Subjoined, relating to the Harbour proposed to be made from Sandwich into the Downs, near Sandown Castle, Anno 1744. *n.p.* [*1745*], *F*o. L.

Signed by W. Whorwood, John Redman, John Major, Tho. Slade, Ch. Labelye, R. Charles; dated 24 Jan. 1744–5; and addressed to the Lords of the Admiralty.

5929 State of the Harbour of Peterhead. *n.p.* [*c. 1745?*], *8*o. LU.

5930 Reasons for Encouraging the making of a Safety for Ships at Ballycastle Colliery, at the Risque of private Undertakers. *n.p.* [*1745?*], *8*o. L.

5931 GRUNDY, JOHN. A Further Illustration of Messrs. Grundy's Scheme for Restoring and making Perfect, the Navigation of the River Witham, from Boston to Lincoln; and also for Draining the Low Lands and Fens contiguous thereto. Mr. Coppin's Scheme is here answer'd, by such stated Facts, as demonstrate the said Scheme to be drawn from false Data, and wrong Principles.... *Stamford, 1745, 8*o. C.

Coppin's Scheme (not seen) was published in 1745.

SOCIAL CONDITIONS

5932 An Act for rendering more Effectual the several Acts passed for the Erecting of Hospitals and Workhouses within the City of Bristol, for the better employing and of maintaining the Poor thereof. *n.p. 1744–5, F*o. L.

5933 Rules and Orders of the London Infirmary. *Lond. 1745, 8*o. O.

5934 Statutes and Constitutions for the Government of an Infirmary or Hospital, to be established at Lincoln, for the Sick and Lame Poor in that County and City. *Lincoln, 1745, 8*o. O.

5935 Regulations or By-Laws of the Corporation of the Orphan-Hospital and Work-house at Edinburgh: Approven of by a general Meeting of the Corporation on Monday the 21st of November 1743. With a Preface, shewing the Rise and Progress of the same. *Edin. 1745, 8*o. E.

5936 A Draught of the Heads of a Bill to Prevent Frauds committed by Bankrupts, &c. prepared by the Merchants and Traders of the City of Dublin, and by Them, intended to be laid before the Legislative Power of this Kingdom, the next Session of Parliament. *Dublin, 1745, 8*o. DA.

5937 A Letter to a Member of Parliament, concerning a Bankruptcy Bill. *Dublin, 1745, 8*o. D.

5938 PAGET, W. The Humours of the Fleet. A poem...With a Preface, containing a Sketch of the Author's Life. *Birmingham,* [*1745?*], *8*o. L.

Another edn., anonymous, Lond. 1749 (L).

5939 A Scheme for raising a Fund for a Provision for the Widows and Orphans of Excisemen in Scotland: promised in a late Letter from a Gentleman in Edinburgh, to his Friend, an Officer of Excise, in the Country. With the Reasons why the said Scheme has not been sooner published. *Edin. 1745*, *8°*. O.

5940 The Clergyman's Intelligencer: or, a compleat Alphabetical List of all the Patrons in England and Wales, with the Dignities, Livings, and Benefices in their Gift; and their Valuation annex'd. To which is added, An Alphabetical Index of all the Benefices.... *Lond. 1745*, *8°*. L.

5941 A Bill intituled, An Act for making the Surgeons of London and the Barbers of London Two Separate and Distinct Corporations. *n.p.* [*1745*], *F°*. L.

5942 The Case of the Barbers of London. *n.p.* [*1745*], *F°*. L.

5943 EDINBURGH. Act of Council for keeping clean the Streets of the City of Edinburgh, and Suburbs thereof. [*Edin. 1745*], *s. sh. F°*. EU.
Dated: 14 August 1745.

1746

GENERAL

5944 NEWBALL, JOHN. A Concern for Trade, and the various Consequences; relating to the Encrease and Decrease, and the equal and unequal Circulation of Trade. Also Remarks on the Bill, intitl'd, A Bill to amend and render more effectual the Laws in Being for the Preservation of the publick Roads. Shewing, the many Inconveniences which must attend Inland Traders, &c. should the said Bill pass into a Law. ...(Re-printed with Additions.) Also a Postscript, pointing out the Cause of our present Troubles, Means to extinguish them, and a Caution to prevent the future Rise of them. *Stamford*, [*1746 ?*], *8o*. L.

5945 An Appeal to Caesar, on the Nature and Situation of our Public Affairs. *Lond. 1746*, *8o*. LU.

Signed: An Englishman. On taxation, smuggling, etc.

5946 The Criterion: or, some Propositions fairly stated. I. Distillation Dissected....II. Preventing Knavery under the Cloak of Honesty.... III. Means to take off the Payment of the Poors Rate within the Bills of Mortality, and the Poor better provided in every Respect. IV. To make Rogues honest, and become useful Members of the Community. ...By Justitia. *Lond. 1746*, *8o*. LU.

II. is 'A Proposal for the more effectual regulating of Weight and Measure'

5947 An Enquiry into the Causes of the late Rebellion, and the proper Methods for preventing the like Misfortune for the future. *Lond. 1746*, *8o*. L.

5948 Entry cancelled

5949 *Begin:* Right Honourable and very loving Friends and Neighbours. [*Edin. 1746*], *Fo*. ACC.

The agenda of the Convention of Royal Burghs, July 1746

5950 [CHETWOOD, WILLIAM RUFUS ?]. A Tour through Ireland. In several Entertaining Letters. Wherein the present State of that Kingdom is considered; and the most noted Cities, Towns, Seats, Rivers, Buildings, &c. are described....Part I.... *Dublin, 1746*, *8o*. LU.

The editor's advertisement signed: W.R.C. 2nd edn. Dublin, 1748 (DA); another edn. Lond. 1748 (O). This edition is without the editor's advertisement and is said to be 'By Two English Gentlemen'. For authorship see H. & L., who attribute the work to Chetwood without quoting any authority.

5951 SMITH, CHARLES [and HARRIS, WALTER]. The Ancient and Present State of the County and City of Waterford: Being a Natural, Civil, Ecclesiastical, Historical and Topographical Description thereof.... Together with new and correct maps.... *Dublin, 1746*, *8o*. L.

2nd edn. 1774 (O). For Harris's part in the work see *Analacta Hibernica*. no. 6, 1934, p. 249.

AGRICULTURE

5952 Agriculture Anatomiz'd: or, a New Treatise of Husbandry, containing a Plain and Practical Method of Improving all Sorts of Meadow, Pasture and Arable Land, &c.... With an Account continued through the Work, how the Tillage of Ireland may be improved by a cheap Manure, easily convey'd to any Part of the Kingdom, by which the Hazard of a future Scarcity may be prevented.... *Dublin, 1746, 8º*. DA.
Advocating the use of Liveings's manure.

5953 An Order of His Majesty in Council, containing Rules, Orders, and Regulations, for the more effectual preventing the spreading of the Distemper which now rages amongst the Horned Cattle in this Kingdom. *Lond. 1745 [o.s.], Fº*. LCRO.
Dated: 12 March 1745.

5954 BROCKLESBY, RICHARD. An Essay concerning the Mortality, now prevailing among the Horned Cattle, in several Parts of Europe, and chiefly about London. Wherein a plain and successful Method is laid down to treat the diseased Cattle, and to prevent, in good Measure, the rapid Progress of this fatal Disorder. *Lond. 1746, 8º*. O.

5955 A Bill for Dividing and Inclosing several Common Fields, and Common Grounds, in the Parish of Upway, and County of Dorset. *n.p. [1746], Fº*. L.

5956 An Act for Confirming and Establishing Articles of Agreement, and an Award for Inclosing and Dividing certain Common Fields within the Parish of Inkpen in the County of Berks. *n.p. [1746], Fº*. L.

5957 An Act for Establishing and Confirming an Inclosure and Division of the Common Fields, Wastes, and Common Grounds, in the Manor of Kelfield in the County of York: And for Impowering the Lord of the said Manor to raise Money to finish and compleat the said Inclosure. *n.p. [1746], Fº*. L.

5958 An Act for giving further Time to the Commissioners therein named, to execute the Powers and Authorities remaining unexecuted of a former Act of Parliament, made in the Seventeenth Year of his present Majesty, intituled, An Act for Extinguishing a Right of Common claimed by and belonging to the Owners and Proprietors of antient Burgages and Tenements in Ripon, Littlethorpe, and Bondgate, in the County of York; and for settling and providing an Equivalent for the said Common Right. *n.p. 1745–6, Fº*. L.

MANUFACTURES

5959 LOWNDES, THOMAS. Brine-Salt Improved: or, the method of making Salt from Brine, that shall be as good or better than French Bay-Salt. In a Letter to the Right Honourable the Lords Commissioners of the Admiralty. Dated 8 July, 1746. *Lond. 1746, 4º*. LU.

5960 Charter of the British Linen Company. *Edin. 1746*, 4°. L.

Dated: 5 July 1746. With 'The Rules and By-laws of the British Linen Company...September 17th 1746'.

5961 Scheme concerted by Several Noblemen and Gentleman of Scotland, with the Shop-keepers in Edinburgh, for promoting the Woollen Manufacture, especially Broad Cloth made of Scots Wool. *n.p. 1746*, F°. AU.

Endorsed: A Scheme for Promoting the Woollen Manufacture in Scotland.

5962 The Case of the Bakers of the City of Dublin, and the Liberties thereof. Humbly submitted to the Consideration of both Houses of Parliament. *n.p.* [*1746*], F°. DNL.

COMMERCE

5963 *Begin:* Sir, The present Embargo on Cheese and Butter prevents the same from being exported to any of His Majesty's Dominions Abroad, as likewise to Holland and Hambro.... *n.p.* [*1746*], *s. sh.* F°. LSC.

Dated: 24 Feb. 1745–6. For the removal of the embargo.

5964 Unto the Right Honourable the Lords of Council and Session, the Petition of the Booksellers of London; against the Booksellers of Edinburgh and Glasgow. *n.p.* [*1746*], 4°. E.

Dated: July 15. 1746. Signed: Alex. Lockhart.

5965 Answers for the Book-sellers of Edinburgh and Glasgow, to the Petition of Daniel Midwinter, and other Book-sellers in London. *n.p.* [*1746*], 4°. E.

Dated: December 21. 1746. Signed: Henry Home.

5966 A Bill more Effectually to prevent the Frauds and Abuses committed on the Admeasurement of Coals within the City and Liberty of Westminster, and that Part of the Duchy of Lancaster adjoining thereto, and the several Parishes of Saint Giles in the Fields, Saint Mary le Bon, and such Part of the Parish of Saint Andrew Holborn, as lies in the County of Middlesex. *n.p.* [*1746*], F°. L.

Another edn., entitled: A Bill, intituled, An Act more effectually to prevent the Frauds...(L).

5967 Reasons humbly proposed by several Inhabitants of the City and Liberty of Westminster, against the Coal-jobb Bill. *n.p.* [*1746?*], F°. L.

This is almost certainly the paper drawn up by Samuel Johns at the instance of Thomas Allen which was censured by the House of Commons. See *C.J.* xxv, 148. The bill was to prevent frauds in the admeasurement of coals in Westminster.

5968 The Natural Interest of Great-Britain, Demonstrated. In a Discourse in two Parts . . . Part I. *Lond. 1746*, 8°. MP.

Signed: T.W. A reissue of pt. 1, entitled *The Present Condition of Great-Britain . . . With a true State of the Case between Us and the Dutch . . .*, 1746 (L). Kress copy of this issue misdated 1736. *The Nutural Interest of Great Britain, in its Present Circumstances, Demonstrated . . . Part II* bears date 1748 (L). A new edition of both parts, entitled *The British Sleepers*, 1748 (L). Mainly on salt.

5969 The Important Question Discussed; or, a Serious and Impartial Enquiry into the True Interest of England with respect to the Continent. *Lond. 1746, 8°.* LU.

Another edn. Dublin, 1746 (C). Tentatively attributed to Samuel Squire, Bishop of St. David's, in L catalogue.

5970 A Detection of the Views of those who would, in the present Crisis, engage an Incumber'd, Trading Nation, as Principals, in a ruinous expensive Land-War; in Answer to a Pamphlet lately published, entitled, The Important Question discuss'd, &c. *Lond. 1746, 8°.* LU.

5971 A Bill for Preventing the Infamous Practice of Smuggling. *n.p.* [*1746*], *F°.* L.

5972 [Newball, John]. The Contrast: also Further Considerations on the Concern for Trade. With Proposals how to amend and render more effectual the Laws in being for the Preservation of the Publick Roads, and to preserve Trade....By Phil' Anglus. *Lond.* [*1746*], *8°.* L.

A sequel to *A Concern for Trade* (no. 5944), which bore the author's name.

5973 [Smith, Simon]. The Danger of Great Britain and Ireland becoming Provinces of France: or, A short View of the British Products compared with those of France; by which it will most evidently appear, that the Fleets and Armies of France, are at this Time maintained out of the Bowels of Great Britain and Ireland, by the infamous Practice of Smuggling....By the author of the Golden Fleece. *Lond. 1745–6, 8°.* L.

For authorship see no. 4894. On saving the woollen industry by a scheme to prevent the exportation of wool.

5974 The Schemers Scrutiny. Containing I. Serious Considerations on the several High Duties, &c. seriously considered. II. The Merchant of London's Scheme to prevent the Running of Irish Wools to France, examined. III. An Undermine to Mr. Thomas Lowndes's intended Countermine. IV. A short State of the Case of the Smuggling of our Wool to France. To which are added, Reasons why the Publick should not believe the Terms of the present Loan to be the Scheme of Sir John Barnard, Knt. *Lond. 1746, 8°.* O.

5975 Seasonable Considerations relating to the Smugglers. *Lond. 1746, 4°.* LU.

5976 Lockman, John. To the long-conceal'd First Promoter of the Cambrick and Tea-Bills: An Epistle. Writ at the Close of last Session of Parliament. *Lond. 1746, 4°.* L.

A poem on smuggling. Addressed to Stephen Theodore Janssen according to the ms. note on L copy.

5977 Some Important Frauds committed in Trade, and the Revenue in Ireland Laid Open: with an Account of the Scheme that was formed for a general Detection thereof; and of the Proceedings of the Managers for the Crown, in the Prosecution of the Seizure made at Wexford. With other Particulars relating thereto. *Lond. 1746, 8o*. LU.

On the smuggling of spirits.

5978 [POSTLETHWAYT, MALACHY]. The National and Private Advantages of the African Trade Considered: being an Enquiry, how far it concerns the Trading Interest of Great Britain, effectually to Support and Maintain the Forts and Settlements in Africa; belonging to the Royal African Company of England: shewing also what Support and Encouragement the Dutch and the French give to their respective African Companies....With a new and correct Map of the Coast of Africa, and all the European Settlements.... *Lond. 1746, 8o*. LU.

2nd edn., with author's name, 1772.

5979 Unto the Right Honourable, the Lords of Council and Session, the Petition of John Jamieson Merchant in Glasgow. *n.p.* [*1746*], *Fo*. O.

Dated: December 8. 1746. Signed: Hen. Home. Trade to Virginia.

5980 A Description of the Coasts, Tides, and Currents, in Button's Bay, and in the Welcome: being the North-West Coast of Hudson's Bay... taken from Scrog's, Crow's, Napier's, and Smith's Journals, made in the Years 1722, 1737, 1740, 1742, 1743, and 1744. Also, from the Discoveries made in 1742, in the Voyage in the Furnace Bomb, and Discovery Pink, commanded by Captain Middleton and Captain Moor; shewing from these Journals, a Probability, that there is a Passage from thence to the Western Ocean of America. *Lond.* [*1746*], *8o*. L.

Another edn. Dublin, 1746 (DA).

5981 The Laws, Ordinances, and Institutions of the Admiralty of Great Britain, Civil and Military....In Two Volumes. *Lond. 1746, 8o*. LU.

5982 A Bill for the better Protecting and Securing the Trade and Navigation of This Kingdom, in Times of War. *n.p.* [*1746?*], *Fo*. L.

5983 A Bill for Explaining and Amending an Act of the Thirteenth Year of his present Majesty's Reign, intituled, An Act for the more effectual Securing and Encouraging the Trade of his Majesty's British Subjects to America; and for the Encouragement of Seamen to enter into his Majesty's Service; and of another Act of the Seventeenth Year of his present Majesty's Reign, intituled, An Act for the better Encouragement of Seamen in his Majesty's Service, and Privateers to annoy the Enemy; and also of another Act of the Eighteenth Year of his present Majesty's Reign, intituled, An Act for the more effectual Recovering and Collecting of certain Duties granted towards the Support of the Royal Hospital at Greenwich; and to oblige Agents for Prizes to register their Letters of Attorney; and for Enlarging certain Powers in the said several Acts; and making the same more effectual. *n.p.* [*1746*], *Fo*. L.

COLONIES

5984 Pepperell, Sir William. An Accurate Journal and Account of the Proceedings of the New-England Land-Forces, during the late Expedition against the French Settlement on Cape Breton, to the Time of the Surrender of Louisbourg.... With a Computation of the French Fishery on the Bank of Newfoundland, Acadia, Cape Breton, and the neighbouring Shores, Gulphs, Harbours, &c. as it was carried on before the present War.... *Exon, 1746, 8°.* L.

5985 The Great Importance of Cape Breton, Demonstrated and Exemplified, by Extracts from the best Writers, French and English, who have treated of that Colony.... With the Reasons that induced the People of New-England to subdue this formidable and dangerous Rival, and that should determine the British Nation never to part with it again, on any Consideration whatever.... *Lond. 1746, 8°.* O.

5986 [Bollan, William]. The Importance and Advantage of Cape Breton, Truly Stated, and Impartially Considered. With Proper Maps. *Lond. 1746, 8°.* L.

For authorship see Sabin 6215.

5987 The Importance of Cape Breton Consider'd; in a Letter to a Member of Parliament, from an Inhabitant of New-England. *Lond. 1746, 8°.* O.

Signed: Massachusettensis. Attributed to Robert Auchmuty in the Kress Catalogue (S.1916).

5988 Two Letters concerning some farther Advantages and improvements that may seem necessary to be made on the taking and keeping of Cape Breton. Humbly offered to public Consideration. *Lond. 1746, 12°.* JCB.

5989 By the Council of Proprietors of the Eastern Division of New-Jersey, met at Perth-Amboy, the 25th Day of March, 1746, in Behalf of themselves, and the rest of the General Proprietors of the Eastern Division of New-Jersey, whom they represent. *n.p. [1746], F°.* LPRO.

A statement on their rights and on the late land riots at Newark. Reprinted in *Archives of the State of New Jersey*, ser. 1, vol. 6, pp. 297–323.

5990 A Brief Vindication of the Purchassors against the Propritors in a Christian Manner. *New-York, 1745–6, 8°.* LPRO.

Reprinted in *Archives of the State of New Jersey*, ser. 1, vol. 6, pp. 266–92.

5991 Borden, William. An Address to the Inhabitants of North-Carolina; occasioned by the difficult Circumstances the Government seems to labour under, for want of a Medium, or something to answer in lieu of Money; for the Encouragement of the People, in regard to Business: To which is added, A Proposition for a Paper-Currency.... *Williamsburg, 1746, 4°.* Kress 4797.

L has a photostat made in 1936 by the Mass. Hist. Soc. from the copy in the possession of the Society.

5992 [CROKATT, JAMES]. Observations concerning Indigo and Cochineal.... *Lond.* *1746*, *12º*. NYP.

Sabin 87904. Dedicated to the Planters of South-Carolina. For authorship see Sabin.

5993 An Essay concerning Slavery, and the Danger Jamaica is expos'd to from the too great Number of Slaves, and the two little Care that is taken to manage Them. And a Proposal to prevent the further Importation of Negroes into that Island. *Lond.* [*1746*], *8º*. LU.

Attributed to Edward Trelawney, Governor of Jamaica, in H. & L. without quoting authority.

5994 A Letter from a Friend at J[amaica], to a Friend in London: giving an Impartial Account of the Violent Proceedings of the Faction in that Island. *Lond.* [*1746*], *8º*. LU.

FINANCE

5995 [BARNARD, Sir JOHN]. A Proposal for raising Three Millions for the Service of the Government. *n.p.* [*1746*], *s. sh. Fº*. Kress 4827.

For authorship see Barnard's *A Defence of several Proposals*, 1746, where this is reprinted.

5996 [BARNARD, Sir JOHN]. A Second Proposal for Raising Three Millions for the Service of the Government. *n.p.* [*1746*], *Fº*.

For authorship see Barnard's *A Defence of several Proposals*, where this is reprinted, and whence this entry is taken.

5997 A Letter to Sir John Barnard, upon his Proposals for raising three Millions of Money for the Service of the Year 1746. From a Member of the House of Commons. *Lond.* [*1746*], *8º*. LU.

2nd and 3rd edns. [1746] (both LU).

5998 Remarks on a Letter to Sir John Barnard: in which the Proposals of that worthy Patriot are vindicated, and a late Important Transaction set in a true Light. By an Enemy to Jobbs. *Lond.* *1746*, *8º*. LU.

2nd edn. 1746 (LU).

5999 A Second Letter to Sir John Barnard, upon his Proposals for raising three Millions of Money for the Service of the Year 1746. From a Member of the House of Commons. *Lond.* *1746*, *8º*. LU.

6000 [A Third Letter to Sir John Barnard]. [*Lond.* *1746*], *8º*. LU.

The title is conjectural, for the only copy seen lacks title-page. The text begins: Having if I mistake not, convinced you in my last.

6001 BARNARD, Sir JOHN. A Defence of several Proposals for Raising of Three Millions of Money for the Service of the Government, for the Year 1746. With a Postscript, containing some Notions relating to Publick Credit. *Lond.* *1746*, *8º*. LU.

6002 A Letter to a Member of Parliament, occasioned by the Rejecting Sir John Barnard's Scheme. *Lond. 1746, 8o.* LU.

Attributed to Barnard himself by E. H. Tedder in Palgrave's *Dictionary of Political Economy.*

6003 An Essay on the Inequality of our Present Taxes, particularly the Land-Tax; and on the Means to raise, by an Equal, Easy Taxation, the Necessary Supplies within the Year. *Lond. 1746, 8o.* LU.

6004 A Letter to all who propose to be Adventurers in the Present Lottery. In which is shewn incontestibly, that it is in their own Power to save many Thousand Pounds in the Purchase of their Tickets: also the vast Disadvantage of buying Shares of the Office-keepers, who rate a Ticket so shared at Twelve Pounds, and have besides a large Discount on all that are Prizes. Together with Instructions how to save both these Excesses.... *Lond. 1746, 8o.* L.

6005 A Bill, intituled, An Act for the farther Punishment of Persons going armed or disguised, in Defiance of the Laws of Customs or Excise; and for Indemnifying Offenders against those Laws, upon the Terms in this Act mentioned; and for Relief of Officers of the Customs in Informations upon Seizures. *n.p.* [*1746*], *Fo.* L.

6006 National Oeconomy recommended, as the only means of retrieving our Trade and securing our Liberties; occasioned by the Perusal of the late Report of a Committee of the House of Commons relating to the Army; by which, many gross and important Abuses appear to have been committed in that Article of the Publick Expence, for many Years past, as proved by Abstracts of the said Report. In a Letter to a Member of the said Committee. *Lond. 1746, 8o.* L.

6007 Reasons most humbly proposed for encouraging the British Coinage, and preventing the Melting and Exporting that which is, and shall be coined for the Service of the British Dominions and Plantations: That our Money, Credit, Trade and Honour may be most justly and happily increased...against the secret and open Attempts of the Enemies of our Holy Religion, and Protestant King and Country. *n.p.* [*1746*], *s. sh. Fo.* L.

Signed: Theophilus Regis & Patriae, B.

6008 The Art of Stock-jobbing: a Poem, in Imitation of Horace's Art of Poetry. By a Gideonite. *Lond. 1746, 8o.* O.

6009 A Bill more effectually to prevent the infamous Practice of Stockjobbing. *n.p.* [*1746*], *Fo.* L.

6010 The Case of the Charitable Corporation. *n.p.* [*1746*], *s. sh. Fo.* L.

For power to make a call on the shareholders.

6011 A Bill to Regulate Insurance on Ships belonging to the Subjects of Great Britain, and on Merchandizes or Effects laden therein. *n.p.* [*1746*], *Fo.* L.

Another edn. entitled: A Bill, intituled, An Act to regulate Insurance...(L).

TRANSPORT

6012 GRIFFITHS, ROGER. An Essay to prove that the Jurisdiction and Conservancy of the River Thames, &c. is committed to the Lord Mayor and City of London...by Prescription, Charters, Acts...&c. To which is added a Brief Description of those Fish...caught in the Thames, or sold in London....And, also of the Water-Carriage on the River Thames...with a List of the Keys, Wharfs, and Docks. *Lond. 1746, 8º.* LU.

6013 The Great Importance of the Shannon Navigation to the Whole Kingdom of Ireland; humbly submitted to the serious Consideration of the Commissioners of the Tillage and Inland Navigation Act. *Dublin, 1746, 8º.* DA.

6014 A Bill to Impower Lora Pitt, Widow, to erect a Bridge or Bridges over the River Froome; and to make a Road or Causeway to the East-End of the Town of Dorchester, over Lands in the Manor of Forthington in the County of Dorset, belonging to his Royal Highness the Prince of Wales, as Parcel of his Duchy of Cornwall. *n.p.* [*1746*], *Fº.* L.

6015 An Abstract of the Orders to be Observed by the Carr-men of the City of London, and Liberties thereof, Published by the Worshipful the Governors of Christ's-Hospital.... [*Lond.*] *1746, s. sh. Fº.* L.

SOCIAL CONDITIONS

6016 A Bill, intituled, An Act to obviate certain Difficulties in the Laws now in being relating to the Poor; and for allowing some Warrants of Justices of the Peace granted in one County or Place, to be executed in other Counties or Places. *n.p.* [*1746*], *Fº.* L.

6017 STEPHENS, DAVID. Thoughts of Present Concernment, for the Relief of the Poor in a Scarcity of Corn. Shewing some experienced Methods new and old, whereby a poor Man is enabled, on poor Ground, to Garden, and thereby with small Expence of either Time, Labour or Money, make a comfortable and speedy Provision for his Family in either a scarce or plentiful Year. Designed at first as Part of the Employment, and for raising Part of the Subsistence of Boys educated in Charter-Schools...and now published for the Benefit of the Poor in general. By a Member of the Incorporated Society. *Dublin, 1746, 8º.* C.

6018 The Royal Charter, establishing an Hospital for the Maintenance and Education of exposed and deserted Young Children. With the Act of Parliament establishing the same. Together with the By-Laws of the said Corporation, and the Regulations for Managing the said Hospital.

...Together with the Accounts of the said Hospital from its Commencement, till 25 March, 1745, and a List of the Governors on the said 25 March. *Lond. 1746, 8º.* L.

6019 A Bill, intituled, An Act for better securing the Payment of such Shares of Prizes taken from the Enemy, as are granted to the Royal Hospital at Greenwich; and for granting to the said Hospital the Shares of Run-men in all Prizes taken from the Spaniards, and for the Coinage of Prize Gold and Silver. *n.p.* [*1746*], *Fº.* L.

6020 The Middlesex County Hospital, for the Small-Pox and Inoculation; situated in Windmill-Street, Tottenham-Court-Road, instituted July 2, 1746.... *n.p.* [*1746?*], *Fº.* L.

Reasons for founding and encouraging the hospital, with rules for its governance.

6021 An Account of the Proceedings of the Society for Establishing a Public Infirmary at Salop with a List of Subscribers and Benefactors October 1st. 1746. (No. 1.) *n.p.* [*1746*], *Fº.* O.

6022 Rules and Orders for the Government of the Salop Infirmary. *n.p. 1746, 8º.* O.

6023 The Charter of His Majesty King George II. for Erecting and Endowing St. Patrick's Hospital. Founded by the Last Will of the Reverend Doctor Jonathan Swift...for the Reception of Ideots, Lunaticks, and Incurables. Printed by Order of the Trustees. *Dublin, 1746, 8º.* O.

6024 Reasons humbly offered, to shew, that an Act for Relief of Insolvent Prisoners and Fugitives for Debt is, at this Juncture, expedient, upon further Motives than have induced the Legislature to pass former Acts of that Kind. *n.p.* [*1746?*], *s. sh. Fº.* LLI.

6025 A Bill for Amending the Laws relating to Bankrupts. *n.p.* [*1746*], *Fº.* L.

Another edn. entitled: A Bill, intituled, An Act for amending the Laws relating to Bankrupts (L).

6026 The Cases of divers Persons, Prisoners within the Walls of His Majesty's Prison of the Fleet, whose Names are hereafter mentioned, reciting Grievances imposed upon them, by John Eyles, Esq; the present Warden of the said Prison, humbly submitted to the Consideration of the Legislature. *n.p.* [*1746*], *s. sh. Fº.* LLI.

Endorsed: The Cases of Prisoners Grievances....

6027 GRIFFIN, JOHN. Proposals for the Relief and Support of Maimed, Aged, and Disabled Seamen, in the Merchants Service of Great Britain.... *Lond. 1746, 8º.* LU.

6028 [SMITH, SAMUEL]. An Account of the Veteran Scheme. *n.p.* [*1746*], *Fº.* DA.

The scheme was to provide comforts for the soldiers engaged in suppressing the '45. DA copy has a dedication in ms. signed: Samuel Smith.

1747

GENERAL

6029 CAMPBELL, R. The London Tradesman. Being a Compendious View of all the Trades, Professions, Arts, both Liberal and Mechanic, now practised in the Cities of London and Westminster. Calculated for the Information of Parents, and Instruction of Youth in their Choice of Business.... *Lond. 1747*, 8°. L.

3rd edn. 1757 (L).

6030 A General Description of all Trades, digested in Alphabetical Order: by which Parents, Guardians, and Trustees, may, with greater Ease and Certainty, make choice of Trades agreeable to the Capacity, Education, Inclination, Strength, and Fortune of the Youth under their Care.... *Lond. 1747, 12°*. LU.

6031 [COADE, GEORGE]. A Letter to the Honourable the Lords Commissioners of Trade and Plantations. Wherein the Grand Concern of Trade is asserted and maintained. With an Attempt to prove, that our Nobility, Gentry, and Clergy, are more nearly concernd in Trade, in its Success and Consequences, than even the Merchant or Trader himself....By an Impartial Hand. *Lond. 1747*, 8°. LU.

2nd edn., with author's name, 1748 (LU).

6032 [CARTERET, JOHN, Earl Granville ?]. The State of the Nation, for the Year 1747, and Respecting 1748. Inscribed to a Member of the present Parliament. *Lond. 1747*, 8°. L.

2nd edn. 1747 (O); 3rd edn. 1748 (L); another edn. Dublin, 1748, 12° (DA). For authorship see H. & L. quoting Gladstone Library Catalogue.

6033 The State of the Nation Consider'd, in a Letter to a Member of Parliament. *Lond.* [*1747*], 8°. L.

4th ed. [1747 ?] (MP).

6034 A Scheme, I. To raise immediately Fifty or Sixty Thousand Men, without any Expence to the Government, any Detriment to Trade, or the Liberty of the Subject. II. To raise, by easy Methods, a large Sum likewise immediately, in order to augment our Sea-Forces. III. To suppress at once the Smugglers, so as to afford a great Advantage to the Fair Dealer, and increase the Custom-House Revenues. In a Letter to a Member of Parliament. By Nicholas Machiavelli, Esq; *Lond. 1747*, 8°. O.

I. proposes that each parish should support a number of soldiers. II. is for a tax on the clergy and on civil servants.

6035 [RAY, JAMES]. A Journey through Part of England and Scotland along with the Army...Wherein the Proceedings of the Army, and of the Happy Suppression of the Rebellion in the Year 1746. are particularly described. As also the Natural History and Antiquities of the several Places passed through. Together with the Manners and Customs of the different People, especially of the Highlanders. By a Volunteer.... *Lond.* *1747*, *8°*. E.

Another edn. Lond. [1747?], 4°, not 'by a Volunteer' (E). For authorship see ms. note in E copy. Certainly much of the material in this book is to be found in Ray's *Compleat History of the Rebellion*, 1749.

AGRICULTURE

6036 ROGERSON, JOHN. The Hop-Planter's Assistant; containing, an Accurate and Exact Collection of useful Tables, shewing the Price of any Quantity of Hops, &c....To which is added, An Useful Table, for those that deal in Clover-Seed.... *Lond.* *1747*, *12°*. L.

6037 Conditions upon which the Premium of 15s. per Acre for raising Flax is to be allowed. And Rules and Directions for raising Flax, to be followed by such as intend to claim the said Premium. Published by Order of the Commissioners and Trustees for improving Fisheries and Manufactures in Scotland. [*Edin.* *1747*], *8°*. L.

6038 MAXWELL, ROBERT. The Practical Bee-Master: or, a Treatise, wherein the Management of Bees, both in common Hives, and in the Colony Way, without killing them for their Honey, is, Step by Step and on all probable Occurrences, better and more particularly directed, than in any Book hitherto published. *Edin.* *1747*, *8°*. L.

2nd edn. 1750 (R). Reissued as part of J. Reid's *The Scots Gardiner*, 1756 (O).

6039 A Bill for impowering Henry Earl of Uxbridge to inclose Part of the Wast Lands of the Manor of Iver in the County of Bucks, pursuant to an Agreement between him and the Tenants of the said Manor. *n.p.* [*1747*], *F°*. L.

6040 An Act to impower Mary Stillington, Widow, to execute a Power vested in Joseph Stillington, Esquire, her late Husband, deceased, for raising Money to complete the Inclosure of the Common Fields and Common Grounds in the Manor of Kelfield in the County of York. *n.p.* [*1747*], *F°*. LHL.

6041 Some Alterations, which, it is conceived, may be very usefully made in the Laws relating to Butter and Butter-Casks in Ireland. Offered to the Consideration of the Publick. *Dublin*, *1747*, *8°*. DA.

6042 HOOSON, WILLIAM. The Miners Dictionary. Explaining not only the Terms used by Miners, but also containing the Theory and Practice of that most useful Art of Mineing, more especially of Lead-Mines.... Being Observations made by the author, from more than forty years practice and experience, at the Mines in the High and Low Peak in Derbyshire, Shropshire, South and North-Wales, and the North of England. *n.p.* *1747*, *8°*. L.

6043 LINDEN, DIEDERICK WESSEL. A Letter to William Hooson, A Derbyshire miner. Shewing the Mistakes, and Errors, committed in his lately publish'd Miners Dictionary. With a Preface setting forth the Reasons for making the said publick. *Chester*, *1747*, *8°*. L.

L copy has copious ms. notes by Lewis Morris.

6044 A Bill, intituled, An Act for taking away and abolishing the Heretable Jurisdictions in that Part of Great Britain called Scotland.... *n.p.* [*1747*], *8°*. MP.

Another edn. entitled: A Bill for Taking away and Abolishing the Heretable Jurisdictions in that Part of Great Britain called Scotland.... n.p. [1747], 8° (MP).

6045 TURNBULL, P. A Cursory View, of the Ancient and Present State of the Fieffs, or Tenures, in both Parts of the United Kingdom. *Lond.* [*1747*], *8°*. LU.

6046 An Ample Disquisition into the Nature of Regalities and other Heretable Jurisdictions, in that part of Great Britain called Scotland, as now under the Consideration of Parliament....By an English gentleman. *Lond. 1747*, *8°*. EU.

6047 [MACDOUALL, ANDREW, Lord Bankton]. An Essay upon Feudal Holdings, Superiorities, and Hereditary Jurisdictions, in Scotland. Shewing, I. The Nature of Feudal Holdings....II. The Errors and gross Misrepresentations, touching the same, in a late Pamphlet, entituled, Superiorities display'd, or Scotland's Grievance on account of Holdings and Hereditary Jurisdictions, &c. III. That these Holdings, Superiorities and Jurisdictions have not been any of the Causes of the Rebellions, 1715, or 1745. IV. That the infringing the same may be dangerous to our happy Constitution. *Lond. 1747*, *8°*. LU.

For authorship see H. & L. quoting the Cambridge University Library copy.

6048 Observations upon a Bill, entituled, An Act for taking away, and abolishing the heritable Jurisdictions in that Part of Great Britain called Scotland.... *Edin. 1747*, *8°*. L.

6049 Roll or List of the Claims, entered in the Court of Session in Scotland, in Pursuance of an Act of Parliament, past in the 20th Year of the Reign of His present Majesty, entituled, Act for Abolishing Heretable Jurisdictions, &c. *n.p.* [*1747*], *F°*. E.

6050 Two Orders of the Right Honourable the Lords Spiritual and Temporal in Parliament assembled, made the Fifth of August last, requiring the Lords of the Session in Scotland to lay before their Lordships, at the Beginning of this Session of Parliament, Matters relating to Heretable Jurisdictions and Heretable Sheriffships, in that Part of Great Britain called Scotland. Together with the Returns made by the said Lords of Session, pursuant to the said Two Orders. *Edin. 1747*, *8°*. E.

MANUFACTURES

6051 LANGLEY, BATTY. The Builder's Director, or Bench-Mate: being a Pocket-Treasury of the Grecian, Roman, and Gothic Orders of Architecture, made easy to the meanest Capacity by near 500 Examples. ...Engraved on 184 Copper Plates....Written for the Use of Gentlemen delighting in True Architecture; and for Masters and Workmen to Draw from and Work after. *Lond. 1747, 12°*. L.

Another issue, entitled: The Builder's Bench-Mate, 1747 (O); another edn., with original title, 1751 (L); another edn. 1767 (L).

6052 LANGLEY, BATTY. Exaction Detected: or, the Prices of Bricklayers Matarials [*sic*] and Works, Prime Cost and Retail, justly ascertained, in all Parts of the Kingdom.... *Lond. 1747, 8°*. LU.

Reissued in 1748 and 1749 as: The London Prices of Bricklayers Materials and Works, both of New Buildings and Repairs, Justly Ascertained, etc. (both L); 2nd edn., with this title, 1750 (LU).

6053 GARRET, DANIEL. Designs, and Estimates, of Farm Houses, &c. for the County of York, Northumberland, Cumberland, Westmorland, and Bishoprick of Durham. *Lond. 1747, F°*. O.

6054 POSTLETHWAYT, MALACHY. Considerations on the Making of Bar Iron with Pitt, or Sea Coal Fire; and thereby to save the Nation above Two Hundred Thousand Pounds per Annum we at present pay for Foreign Bar Iron.... *Lond. 1747, 8°*. LU.

6055 The Interest of Great Britain, in Supplying Herself with Iron: Impartially Consider'd. *n.p.* [*c. 1747?*], *8°*. L.

With 'A List of the Forges in England and Wales: With an Account of the Quantity of Iron they have Annually made and do now make'.

6056 SMITH, JOHN, LL.B. Chronicon Rusticum-Commerciale; or, Memoirs of Wool, &c. Being a Collection of History and Argument, concerning the Woolen Manufacture and Woolen Trade in general.... *Lond. 1747, 8°*. L.

2nd edn., 1757, 56, entitled: Memoirs, of Wool, Woolen Manufacture, and Trade...(L).

6057 An Appeal to the Common Sense of Scotsmen, especially those of the Landed Interest, and more especially Freeholders, if their own Conduct be not the Source of their Misery? And, if their own vigorous Efforts be not the only Mean of their Relief? Together with a Proposal of the last Importance for saving the Country from Ruin, and preventing future Insurrections and other dismal Consequences of extreme Poverty and Want; in answer to the Groans of its wretched Inhabitants. *Edin. 1747, 8°*. LU.

On woollen manufacture.

6058 By the Lord Lieutenant and Council of Ireland, a Proclamation. *Dublin, 1747, F°*. DPRO.

Dated: 4 November 1747. Against the combination of the journeymen broad-weavers.

COMMERCE

6059 [WARBURTON, WILLIAM]. A Letter from an Author, to a Member of Parliament, concerning Literary Property. *Lond. 1747*, *8°*. LU.

Reprinted in his *Works*, 1788, vol. VII.

6060 Unto the Right Honourable the Lords of Council and Session, the Petition of Gavin Hamilton & John Balfour, and others, Booksellers in Edinburgh, Andrew Stalker and others, Booksellers in Glasgow, Defenders, against Andrew Millar and others, Booksellers in London, Pursuers. *n.p.* [*1747*], *4°*. E.

Dated: January 15. 1747. Signed: Ja. Graham.

6061 Answers for Daniel Midwinter, William Innes, John Knapton, Andrew Millar, and others, all of London, Booksellers, and their Attorney or Factor, Pursuers; to the Petition of Gavin Hamilton and John Balfour, and others, Booksellers in Edinburgh, Andrew Stalker and others, Booksellers in Glasgow, Defenders. *n.p.* [*1747*], *F°*. E.

Dated: Feb. 27th, 1747. Signed: William Grant.

6062 Memorial for Gavin Hamilton, and others, Booksellers in Edinburgh, Andrew Stalker, and others, Booksellers in Glasgow, Defenders; by way of Supplement to their Petition presently depending, and a Reply to the Pursuers Answers. *n.p.* [*1747*], *F°*. E.

Dated: May 29, 1747.

6063 Memorial and Condescendence for Messieurs Hamilton and Balfour and others Booksellers in Edinburgh, and Andrew Stalker and others Booksellers in Glasgow. *n.p.* [*1747*], *4°*. E.

Dated: June 29. 1747. Signed: Henry Home. John Grant.

6064 Unto the Right Honourable The Lords of Council and Session, the Petition of Daniel Midwinter, William Innes, Aaron Ward, and others, all of London, Booksellers, and William Elliot Writer in Edinburgh their Attorney or Factor, Pursuers. *n.p.* [*1747*], *4°*. E.

Dated: Decemb. 9. 1747. Signed: W. Grant. On infringement by Scottish booksellers of their copyright in E. Chambers's *Cyclopaedia*.

6065 Memorial for the Booksellers of Edinburgh and Glasgow, relating to the Process against them by some of the London Booksellers; which depended before the Court of Session, and is now under Appeal. *n.p.* [*1747 ?*], *4°*. O.

6066 Some Reasons humbly offered, for Supporting and Continuing the Dublin Market for Linen-Yarn, as it is now settled and established in the Yarn-Hall, lately erected near the Linen-Hall. *Dublin, 1747*, *8°*. DA.

6067 HOUSTOUN, JAMES. Dr. Houstoun's Memoirs of his Own Life-time. Containing, among other Curious Particulars, during upwards of Thirty Years Travels, An Account of I. The Scotch Settlement at

Darien. II. The great Advantages accruing to Great Britain from an Incorporated Union of the Whole Island. III. The Rise and Progress of the Royal African and Assiento Companies. IV. The Rise and Fall of the grand South Sea Bubble, &c. in 1720. V. The Conduct of the Spaniards, and Manner of their Trade in the West Indies. VI. The secret Expedition thither in 1740. VII. Some Anecdotes of the Government of Jamaica, with the Characteristicks of its Inhabitants. VIII. The Importance of Cape Breton to the British Nation. IX. An Essay on Genius and Education. Collected from the Author's Original Manuscripts, and Publish'd by Jacob Bickerstaff, M.A. *Lond. 1747*, *8º*. L.

Reissued in 1747, as: Memoirs of the Life and Travels of James Houstoun.... Collected and Written by his Own Hand, and again in 1753 as: The Works of James Houstoun (both L). Jacob Bickerstaff is, of course, a fictitious character.

6068 Seasonable Reflections on the late Convention, concluded the 3d of May last, between the Courts of Vienna and Turin, for Partitioning between them the Territories belonging to the Republic of Genoa; especially shewing the injurious Consequences to the British Trade, should Savona and Final be annexed, in Virtue of any future General Peace, to the Dominions of the House of Savoy. In a Letter from an English Merchant residing at Leghorn, to his Correspondent at London. *Lond.* [*1747*], *8º*. LU.

6069 Considerations humbly offer'd in favour of the Bill now depending in Parliament to repeal an Act made in the Thirteenth Year of his present Majesty's Reign, intitled, An Act for prohibiting Commerce with Spain, &c. *n.p.* [*1747*], *Fº*. L.

6070 Answers for Robert Rae of Little-Govan, to the Petition of John Jamieson Merchant in Glasgow. *n.p.* [*1747*], *Fº*. O.

Dated: January 27. 1747. Signed: Will. Grant. Further papers in this case are of legal rather than economic interest, but Andrew Chalmers gave his opinion on 11 January 1748 that the books of this Virginia venture were 'either unintelligible to me or expressly contradictory to themselves'.

6071 By the King, A Proclamation. *Lond. 1746*, *s. sh. Fº*. C (Cr).

Dated: 12 February 1746 [o.s.]. Pilots to be eligible for prize-money.

6072 [MONCREIFF, JOHN]. Galba. A Dialogue on the Navy. *Lond. 1748* [*1747*], *8º*. L.

Reprinted, with author's name, in *Three Dialogues on the Navy*, 1759.

6073 A Scheme for Equipping and Maintaining Sixteen Men of War, of twenty Guns each; for securing our Trade from the Insults of the French and Spaniards, &c. without the least expence to the Nation.... By a Veteran. *Lond. 1747*, *8º*. O.

COLONIES

6074 Douglass, William. A Summary, Historical and Political, of the first Planting, progressive Improvements, and present State of the British Settlements in North-America; with some transient Accounts of the Bordering French and Spanish Settlements. By W.D. M.D. *Boston, 1747–1753, 8°.* L.

Issued in parts, of which the later numbers have the author's full name. Reissued in Boston, 2 vols., 1749, [52]; and [1758] (both WLC). Another edn. Lond. 1755; another edn. Lond. 1760 (both L).

6075 By the Council of Proprietors of the Eastern Division of New-Jersey, met at Perth-Amboy the 25th Day of March, 1747, in Behalf of themselves and the rest of the General Proprietors of the Eastern Division of New-Jersey, whom they Represent. *n.p.* [*1747*], *F°.* LPRO.

6076 [Crokatt, James]. Further Observations Intended for Improving the Culture and Curing of Indigo, &c. in South Carolina. *Lond. 1747, 12°.* L.

For authorship see Sabin 87849. Letters to the author in the book are addressed to Mr. J.C.

6077 Between Mary Carver...Jane, Frances, and Anne Thompson [and others]...Appellants. Against a Decree made by the Court of Exchequer on the 6th of December 1745. David Polhill, Esq; and Others on Behalf of Themselves and Others, Proprietors of Shares in the Gold and Silver Mines in Jamaica. Respondents. The Appellants Case. *n.p.* [*1747*], *F°.* L.

Signed: D. Ryder. K. Evans. The gold and silver mines were imaginary.

6078 William Wood, Appellant. David Polhill, Esq; and others, on Behalf of themselves, and other the Proprietors of Gold and Silver Mines in Jamaica, Respondents. The Appellant's Case. *n.p.* [*1747*], *F°.* L.

Signed: Tho. Clarke, Cha. Yorke.

6079 Mary Carver...Jane, Frances, and Anne Thompson [and others]... Appellants...David Polhill, Esq; Charles Polhill, Esq; [and others]... for and on Behalf of themselves, and several others, Proprietors of Eighty-eight Shares in a Project for working Gold and Silver Mines in Jamaica, Respondents. William Wood, Gentleman Appellant. The said David Polhill, Esq; and Others, Respondents. The Case of the Respondents to both these Appeals. *n.p.* [*1747*], *F°.* L.

Signed: W. Murray. J. Browne.

FINANCE

6080 Henriques, Jacob. A Proposal a Second Time further and more fully explain'd, for discharging the National Debts.... *Lond. 1747, F°.* LLI.

6081 LANE, Sir RICHARD. To the Honourable the Commons of Great-Britain in Parliament Assembled. *n.p.* [*1747*], *F°*. L.

A scheme to pay off the national debt by the issue of exchequer-bills.

6082 A Scheme to secure and extend the Credit and Strength of the British Nation. *Lond. 1747*, *4°*. L.

Endorsed: A Scheme to secure and extend the Credit of the British Nation. By proportioning Taxes to Property. To which are added, Remarks and Computations on Insurance and Convoys.

6083 Between Joseph Chitty, Esq; Appellant. And His Majesty's Attorney-General, on Behalf of His Majesty, Respondent. The Appellant's Case. *n.p.* [*1747*], *F°*. L.

Signed: T. Bootle. A. Hume-Campbell. On the duties to be paid on raisins.

6084 In the Exchequer. The Attorney-General, on behalf of his Majesty, Informant. Against Joseph Chitty, of London, Merchant, Defendant. The said Joseph Chitty, Appellant. The Attorney-General, on behalf of his Majesty, Respondent. Upon an English Information for the Duty of Malaga or Great Raisins, which pay a Duty of 10s. 2d.$\frac{7}{40}$ ths per Hundred Weight, and which were entred by the Defendant as Lexia Raisins, for which he paid Duty only 6s. 4d. $\frac{29}{40}$ ths per Hundred. The Respondent's Case. *n.p.* [*1747*], *F°*. LHL.

Signed: D. Ryder. W. Murray.

6085 Considerations relating to the laying any Additional Duty on Sugar from the British Plantations. Wherein is shewn, that such Duty will be injurious to the Commerce and Navigation of this Kingdom, ruinous to our Sugar Colonies, beneficial to those of France, and insufficient for the Purposes intended. *Lond. 1747*, *8°*. LU.

6086 The State of the Sugar-Trade; shewing the Dangerous Consequences that must attend any additional Duty thereon. *Lond. 1747*, *4°*. L.

6087 The Annual Committee of the Royal Burrows having advised Lawyers, in relation to the Act of Parliament, granting to his Majesty certain Rates and Duties upon Windows and Lights. They were of Opinion.... *n.p.* [*1747*], *s. sh. F°*. AU.

Dated: Edinburgh, 25th March 1747.

6088 The Secret History and Memoirs of the Barracks of Ireland. *Lond. 1747*, *8°*. L.

Suggesting wholesale mismanagement and peculation. 2nd edn. 1747; 3rd edn. 1747 (both L).

6089 A Short Account of some of the Grievances the People in the North of Ireland groan under, by means of the Exorbitant Demands and Illegal Exactions of the Clergy. In a Letter to a Member of Parliament. By a Linnen-Draper. *n.p. 1747*, *8°*. DA.

6090 MILLAN, JOHN. Coins, Weights & Measures, Ancient & Modern, of all Nations. Reduced into English on above 100 Tables, Collected &

methodiz'd from Newton, Folkes, Arbuthnot, Fleetwood, &c..... *Lond. 1747, 8o*. L.

6th edn. 1749 (L).

6091 No. 37. A preamble to the books for taking a subscription for eighteen hundred thousand pounds for support of the credit of the Bank of England, and for circulating Exchequer bills. Dated the 1st October 1747. *n.p.* [*1747*], *Fo*. Kress 4869.

6092 HODGSON, JAMES. The Valuation of Annuities upon Lives; deduced from the London Bills of Mortality. *Lond. 1747, 4o*. LU.

6093 A Bill to Prohibit Insurance on Ships belonging to France, and on Merchandizes or Effects laden thereon, during the present War with France. *n.p.* [*1747*], *Fo*. L.

6094 MORRIS, CORBYN. An Essay towards illustrating the Science of Insurance. Wherein it is attempted to fix, by precise Calculation, several important Maxims upon this Subject; to solve various Problems, and Cases of Contest; and particularly to balance, whether it be nationally advantageous to insure the Ships of our Foreign Enemies....By the Author of A Letter from a Bystander. *Lond. 1747, 8o*. LU.

Dedication signed: Corbyn Morris.

6095 MORRIS, CORBYN. An Essay towards deciding the Important Question, whether it be a National Advantage to Britain to Insure the Ships of her Enemies?...By the Author of a Letter from a Bystander. *Lond.* [*1747*], *8o*. LU.

Dedication signed: Corbyn Morris. 2nd edn. 1758 (L).

6096 An essay to prove that all insurance on ships and goods at sea, beyond the interest of the assured, ought to be prohibited. By a merchant. *London, 1748, 20 cm*. Kress S. 1929.

6097 The Case of the Annuitants, Subscribers, and Bond-Creditors of the Mercers Company. *n.p.* [*1747*], *Fo*. L.

On the annuities issued by the Company.

6098 The Universal Library of Trade and Commerce; or, a General Magazine for Gentlemen, Ladies, Merchants, Tradesmen...&c. &c. Containing I. The Art of Penmanship....II. A compleat System of Arithmetic. ...III. Directions for Mercantile Business....IV. An easy System of Accounts on a new Plan....V. A Series of Merchants Accounts; or, the Italian Method of Book-keeping made plain and easy. By the most Celebrated Masters.... *Lond. 1747, 4o*. L.

Part I is The Complete Penman....By William Richards.

TRANSPORT

6099 A Bill for Building a Bridge cross the River of Thames, from the Parish of Walton upon Thames in the County of Surry, to the opposite Shore in the Parish of Shepperton in the County of Middlesex. *n.p.* [*1747*], *Fo*. L.

SOCIAL CONDITIONS

6100 London. At a General Quarter Sessions of the Peace.... *n.p.* [*1747*], *s. sh. F*o. L.

An order to raise £100 by a rate in order to put into force the Act to amend and make more effectual the laws relating to rogues.

6101 [Canning, Richard]. An Account of the Gifts and Legacies that have been given and bequeathed to Charitable Uses in the Town of Ipswich; with some Account of the present State and Management, and some Proposals for the future Regulation of them. *Ipswich, 1747, 8*o. O.

For authorship see John Nichols, *Illustrations*, vi, 541.

6102 Middlesex County Hospital, for the Small-Pox and Inoculation.... *n.p.* [*1747*], *F*o. MC.

An appeal for funds. Signed: R. Poole.

6103 The Middlesex County-Hospital, for the Reception of Small-Pox Patients, and also of such who are freely disposed to be inoculated for the same....A List of the Subscribers and Benefactors to the Hospital above-mentioned. *n.d.* [*1747*], *s. sh. F*o. MC.

6104 A List of Subscribers and Benefactors to the Middlesex County Hospital for the Small-Pox.... *n.p.* [*1747*], *s. sh. F*o. O.

Later than the preceding.

6105 Middlesex County Hospital for the Small-Pox, at the Bottom of Windmill-Street, Tottenham-Court-Road, instituted July 2, 1746, for the Relief of poor House-keepers, Servants and Strangers.... *n.p.* [*1747*], *s. sh. F*o. O.

A general appeal followed by 'The State of the Middlesex County Hospital, for the Small-Pox, from its first Institution, to April 29, 1747'. Reports were subsequently published annually. L has the 1750 one.

6106 The Groans of the Oppressed; or, Reasons for Reviving, Extending and Perpetuating the late Law for preventing Frivolous and Vexatious Arrests, &c..... *Lond. 1748* [*1747*], *8*o. LU.

6107 To the King's most excellent Majesty, the Right Honourable the Lords Spiritual and Temporal, and Commons in Parliament assembled. The humble Petition of the Prisoners, confin'd for Debt in his Majesty's Prison of the Fleet, on behalf of themselves and all other Prisoners for Debt, within the several other Goals of this Kingdom. *n.p.* [*1747?*], *s. sh. F*o. LLI.

6108 Considerations concerning the Expediency of a General Naturalization of Foreign Protestants, and Others. *Lond. 1747, 8*o. LU.

6109 A Letter to Sir John Phillips Bart. occasion'd by a Bill brought into Parliament to Naturalize Foreign Protestants. *Lond. 1747, 8*o. LU.

Signed: Anglo-Nativus.

6110 A Bill for the Relief and Support of maimed and disabled Seamen, and the Widows and Children of such as shall be killed, slain, or drowned in the Merchants Service. *n.p.* [*1747*], *F*o. L.

6111 The Case of the Masters of Ships, and other Officers and Seamen, in the Merchants Service: humbly offer'd to the Consideration of the Honourable House of Commons. *n.p.* [*1747*], *s. sh. F°*. L.

For the erection of a hospital for merchant seamen.

6112 Reasons for Erecting and Endowing for ever, a plain, neat, cheap, convenient and strong Hospital, with a Surgery, Infirmary, School, Chapel and Chest, near London, for the Relief and Support of such Officers and Seamen, as shall be (by Old Age, Loss of Limbs, Sight, Hearing, or by Sickness or other Misfortunes in the Merchants Service) rendered unable to get their Livings by Sea or Land, or to make any Provision for their aged and helpless Widows and Children. *n.p.* [*1747?*], *s. sh. F°*. L.

6113 A Bill, intituled, An Act for the better adjusting and more easy Recovery of the Wages of certain Servants; and for the better Regulation of such Servants. *n.p.* [*1747*], *F°*. L.

1748

GENERAL

6114 The Case Re-stated; or an Examine of a late Pamphlet, intitled, The State of the Nation for the Year 1747, &c. Wherein the Disingenuity, and secret Views of the Author are exposed, and the Conduct of the present Administration explained and justified. In a Letter to a Friend. *Lond.* [*1748*], *8°*. L.

Another edn. Dublin, 1748 (DNL).

6115 The Groans and Miseries of Great Britain, modestly stated: or, An Appeal from the People to their Representatives. Being a faithful Remonstrance of Grievances.... By the Author of the Dialogue in the Gardens of Luxemburg, between an Old Whig and a Nonjuror, &c. *Edin. 1748, 12°*. L.

Mostly concerned with the national debt and smuggling.

6116 The State of the Nation, with a General Balance of the Publick Accounts. *Lond. 1748, 8°*. LU.

2nd edn. 1748 (C). Another edn. Dublin, 1749 (C).

6117 A Supplement to the State of the Nation; being Free-Thoughts on the Present Critical Conjuncture. *Lond. 1748, 8°*. L.

6118 A Collection of Tracts on several useful and interesting Subjects, relating to publick affairs....I. A Proposal to prevent such Dreadful Conflagrations, as have lately happened in London....II. Reasons for altering the Method of our Land-Carriage....III. A Scheme to prevent Robberies....IV. A Scheme proposed for preserving Sailors from that inveterate Scurvy....V. A Method for the Preservation of our River and Pond Fisheries....VI. A Proposal for increasing our National Wealth, by a moderate Restraint and Limitation of Exportation of our Tin and Lead unwrought. *Lond. 1748, 8°*. L.

AGRICULTURE

6119 Ellis, William. A Compleat System of Experienced Improvements, made on Sheep, Grass-Lambs, and House-Lambs: or, the Country Gentleman's, the Grasier's, the Sheep-Dealer's, and the Shepherd's Sure Guide.... *Lond. 1749* [*1748*], *8°*. L.

Another edn. Dublin, 1749 (DNL).

6120 [Davis, John]. An Essay concerning Pestilential Contagion: occasion'd by the Distemper now Raging among the Cattle. With a Method proposed to prevent its Progress. By Iater. *Lond. 1748, 8°*. O.

For authorship see H. & L. quoting E. Green's *Bibliotheca Somersetensis.*

6121 An Essay, occasion'd by the Contagious Distemper still raging among the Cattle in many Parts of this Kingdom. With a Note of what has been publish'd concerning the supposed Efficacy of Jesuit's Bark in that Case, both by Way of Cure and Prevention. *Lond. 1748*, 8°. L.

6122 An Act to Confirm and Establish an Agreement for Inclosing and Dividing certain Common Fields in the Hamlet of Badbury in the County of Wilts. *n.p.* [*1748*], *F°*. L.

6123 An Act for the Inclosing, Dividing, and Exchanging the Common Fields, Common Pastures, Common Meadows, and other Grounds, in the Manor and Township of Faceby in Cleveland, in the North Riding of the County of York; and for providing certain Recompences to the Impropriators and Vicar of Faceby, in lieu of their Tythes. *n.p.* [*1748*], *F°*. L.

6124 A Bill for Confirming and Establishing Agreements, for Inclosing and Exchanging Lands in Holton, in the County of Lincoln; and for rendering the same more effectual for the Purposes thereby intended. *n.p.* [*1748*], *F°*. O.

6125 An Act for Confirming and Establishing Agreements, for Inclosing and Exchanging Lands in Holton, in the County of Lincoln; and for rendering the same more effectual for the Purposes thereby intended. *n.p.* [*1748*], *F°*. L.

6126 An Act for Inclosing certain Common Pasture-Grounds within the Manors and Parishes of Langwith and Pleasley, and the Hamlets of Stony Houghton and Shirbrook, in the said Parishes, in the County of Derby. *n.p.* [*1748*], *F°*. L.

6127 An Act for Confirming Articles of Agreement, and an Award, for Inclosing and Dividing the Heaths, Wastes, Fields, and Common-grounds, in the Township of Norton juxta Twicross, in the County of Leicester. *n.p.* [*1748*], *F°*. L.

6128 An Act to Confirm and Establish an Agreement for Inclosing and Dividing a large open Common Pasture-Ground, called Somergangs, otherwise Somergams, in the Parish of Drypool, in the County of York. *n.p.* [*1748*], *F°*. L.

6129 Labeyle, Charles. The Result of a Particular View of the North Level of the Fens. Taken in August, 1745. *Lond. 1748*, 8°. O.

6130 Neale, Thomas. The Ruinous State of the Parish of Manea in the Isle of Ely, with the Causes and Remedy of it, humbly represented in a Letter to Matt. Robinson Morris, Esq; Lord of the Manor of Coveney with Manea. *n.p. 1748*, 8°. O.

On drainage.

6131 An Act for Draining and Preserving certain Fen Lands in the several Parishes of Maney, Upwell, Welney, Downham, Witcham, and in a certain extra-parochial Place in Byal-Fen, within the Isle of Ely and County of Cambridge. *n.p.* [*1748*], *F°*. O.

6132 HARDY, WILLIAM. The Miner's Guide: or, Compleat Miner. Containing, I. A succinct Account of a Vein in the Earth.... II. The Customs, Laws and Articles of the High and Low-Peak.... III. An Account of the Load-Stone.... IV. Several curious and useful Tables, in most Branches in Mining.... V. A brief Account of the Assaying the two Metals Lead and Copper.... *Sheffield*, *1748*, *8°*. LU.

2nd edn. Birmingham, 1762 (L); another edn. Wirksworth, 1810 (L).

6133 Copy of the Report and Certificate of the Lords of Council and Session in Scotland, made to His Majesty in his Privy Council, pursuant to the Act of Parliament passed in the Twentieth Year of His Majesty's Reign, For taking away and abolishing the Heretable Jurisdictions, in that Part of Great Britain called Scotland; and for making Satisfaction to the Proprietors thereof, &c. *n.p.* *1748*, *F°*. L.

6134 A Genuine List of the Jurisdictions entered in the Court of Sessions in Scotland, in pursuance of a Late Act of Parliament; with the Sums claimed by the Proprietors as their Value. To which is annexed, An Alphabetical Index, referring to the Names of the several Claimants and the Principal Jurisdictions mentioned in the List. The Whole being carefully collected with the Records of Court, by James Budge. *Lond.* *1748*, *8°*. E.

6135 Information for Archibald Duke of Douglas, William Earl of Sutherland, and others, Claimants of Regalities and heritable Sheriffships, &c. Against His Majesty's Advocate, on behalf of his Majesty. *n.p.* [*1748*], *4°*. MP.

Dated: January 6. 1748.

6136 Information for His Majesty's Advocate, Respondent, to the Claims of his Grace the Duke of Douglas, William Earl of Sutherland, Sir Andrew Agnew of Lochnaw, Baronet, and others, Lords and Gentlemen, Claimers of heretable Jurisdictions of Sheriffships, Regalities, &c. *n.p.* [*1748*], *4°*. MP.

Dated: January 5. 1748.

MANUFACTURES

6137 BROWNRIGG, WILLIAM. The Art of making Common Salt, as now Practised in Most Parts of the World; with several Improvements Proposed in that Art, for the Use of the British Dominions. *Lond.* *1748*, *8°*. LU.

6138 Extract of a Letter from Mr. Thomas Lowndes, to the Honourable the Commissioners for Victualling His Majesty's Navy, dated 18 April, 1748. *n.p.* [*1748*], *s. sh. F°*. L.

On the unfair trial of his brine salt in Newfoundland.

6139 Lowndes, Thomas. A Seasonable Hint for our Pilchard and Coast Fishery: or, a Letter of Advice to the Brine-Salt Proprietors of Great-Britain and Ireland. Dated 23 April, 1748. *Lond. 1748*, 4°. L.

COMMERCE

6140 Letters on Trade. Letter I. To the Farmer. *Dublin, 1748*, 8°. DNL.

Signed: A Merchant. Attributed to James Digges La Touche by Wagner (no. 214).

6141 A Second Letter on Trade. To the Farmer. *Dublin, 1748*, 8°. Y.

Signed: A Merchant. Attributed to James Digges La Touche by Wagner (no. 214).

6142 Two Letters on Trade. *Dublin Printed: London Reprinted, 1748*, 8°. D.

Signed: A Merchant. A reprint of the two preceding.

6143 The Case of the Fair-Trader. *n.p.* [*1748?*], *F°*. L.

Against hawkers, pedlars and petty chapmen, and against auction sales

6144 A Bill, intituled, An Act to revive and amend an Act made in the Tenth Year of the Reign of King George the First, intituled, An Act for the better viewing, searching, and examining all Drugs, Medicines, Waters, Oils, Compositions, used or to be used for Medicines, in all Places where the same shall be exposed to Sale, or kept for that Purpose, within the City of London and Suburbs thereof, or within Seven Miles Circuit of the said City. *n.p.* [*1748*], *F°*. L.

6145 Some Observations upon the Bill entituled An Act, to revive and amend the Act, for the better Examination of Drugs, and Medecines, within London, and seven Miles. *n.p.* [*1748*], *F°*. L.

6146 The Case of the Apothecaries. *n.p.* [*1748*], *F°*. L.

6147 The Apothecary Display'd: or, an Answer to the Apothecary's Pamphlet, called Frauds detected in Drugs. Wherein his Profession and Important Character is Truly Considered. *Lond. 1748*, 8°. L.

6148 Reasons for Regulating the Trade of Apothecaries. *n.p.* [*1748?*], *s. sh. F°*. LG.

6149 Penkethman, John. A Collection of several Authentick Accounts of the History and Price of Wheat, Bread, Malt, &c. from the coming in of William the Conqueror to Michaelmas 1745. With some occasional Remarks. *Lond. 1748*, 4°. L.

1st edn. 1638. The advertisement at the end of the L copy announces ten appendices but only one appears to have been published. This is 'An Account of the true Market-price of Wheat, and Malt, at Windsor, for 100 Years. Began & publish'd by W.m Fleetwood B.p of Ely from 1646. to 1706. And since continued in the same Manner', which is also found separately. Another edn. 1765 (L).

6150 The Assize of Bread made of Wheat, by Order of the Right Honourable the Lord-Mayor of the City of Dublin, to commence on Monday Morning next [3 Oct. 1748]. *Dublin, 1748, s. sh. F°.* DA.

6151 By the Lord Lieutenant and Council of Ireland, a Proclamation. *Dublin, 1747* [o.s.], *s. sh. F°.* DPRO.

Dated: 23 February 1747. Against the export of grain and other provisions to France.

6152 Impartial Remarks on the Present Posture of Publick Affairs. Addressed to His Grace the Duke of Bedford....Proving that it is the Interest of Great-Britain not to conclude a Peace at present with France. Also setting forth the Ill Consequences of Supplying the French with Corn Clandestinely or Otherwise, at this Critical Juncture. *Lond. 1748, 8°.* L.

The address to Bedford signed: Hibernicus.

6153 National Prejudice, opposed to National Interest, Candidly Considered in the Detention or Yielding up Gibraltar and Cape-Breton by the Ensuing Treaty of Peace: With some Observations on the Natural Jealousy of the Spanish Nation, and how far it may Operate to the Prejudice of the British Commerce if not removed at this Crisis. In a Letter to Sir John Barnard, Knight. *Lond. 1748, 8°.* L.

6154 The Preliminaries productive of a Premunire: or, Old England caught in a Trap....With some particular Remarks on the 10th and 20th Articles, concerning the Assiento Treaty, and the Loan on Silesia, worthy to be considered in the present Juncture by all Merchants, or others, that have any interest in Commerce, or Share in the publick Funds. *Lond.* [*1748*], *8°.* LU.

6155 The Pr–t–st of the M–ch–ts of G——t B——n, against the Pr–l–m–ry A–t–s for a Peace, lately signed at A–x-la-Ch–pp–le. *Lond. 1748, 8°.* L.

6156 Andrew Wight [and others]...Appellants. Rachel Stewart...Respondent. The Case of the Appellants. *n.p.* [*1748*], *F°.* L.

Signed: William Grant. C. Erskine. [And in ms. W. Hamilton.] On the *Catharine* of Leith sent to France with a cargo of coal in 1715.

6157 Andrew Wight [and others]...Appellants. Rachel Stewart...Respondent. The Respondent's Case. *n.p.* [*1748*], *F°.* L.

Signed: W. Murray. A. Hume-Campbell.

6158 Information for Thomas and Adam Fairholmes Merchants in Edinburgh; against Robert Chrystie and Company, Merchants in Glasgow. *n.p.* [*1748*], *F°.* O.

Dated: June 16. 1748. Signed: Tho. Hay. Tobacco to be exported to Holland.

6159 Information for Robert Christie and Company, Merchants in Glasgow, Pursuers, against Thomas and Adam Fairholms, Merchants in Edinburgh, and others, Creditors of George Anderson Merchant in Alloa. *n.p.* [*1748*], *F°.* O.

Dated: June 13. 1748. Signed: Alex Lockhart.

6160 NEWBALL, JOHN. Inland Traders Vindicated: or, Some Remarks on the Reverend Mr. Smith's Scheme, intitled, Memoirs of Wool: shewing the dangerous Consequences which must ensue, should the Government give a Sanction to the said Scheme.... *Stamford, 1748, 8°*. LU.

6161 The Case of the Creditors of the Royal African Company. *n.p.* [*1748*], *s. sh. F°*. L.

6162 The Case of the Royal African Company of England and their Creditors. *Lond. 1748, 4°*. LU.

6163 Answers to the Objections against the Proposals of the Royal African Company for settling the Trade to Africa. In a Second Letter to a Member of Parliament. *n.p. 1748, F°*. L.

Signed: Philopatris.

6164 Seasonable Observations on the Trade to Africa. In a Letter to a Member of Parliament. *Lond. 1748, 4°*. LU.

6165 Reasons for laying a Duty on French and Spanish Indico, and granting a Bounty on what is made in the British Plantations. *n.p.* [*1748*], *F°*. LPRO.

The only copy seen has a ms. note: 'Received from Mr. Crokatt'.

6166 Ill-judged Bounties tend to Beggary on both Sides: or, Observations on a Paper, intituled, Reasons for laying a Duty on French and Spanish Indico, and granting a Bounty on what is made in the British Plantations. *Lond. 1748, 8°*. CP.

6167 Considerations on the Advantages of yielding up to Spain the un-expired Term of the Assiento Contract for an Equivalent. Shewing that at all Times, the Execution of it had been injurious to the general Trade of England, but particularly to that with Spain and our Colonies; and more especially to the Stock-Proprietors of the South-Sea Company, that had fatally experienced the vesting their Directors with any Power over their Property....By a Proprietor of the Trading Stock. *Lond.* [*1748*], *8°*. L.

6168 [SWAINE, CHARLES]. An Account of a Voyage for the Discovery of a North-West Passage by Hudson's Streights, to the Western and Southern Ocean of America. Performed in the year 1746 and 1747, in the Ship California, Capt. Francis Smith, Commander. By the Clerk of the California. Adorned with Cuts and Maps. *Lond. 1748, 8°*. L.

For authorship, cf. B. Solis-Cohen in *Papers of the Bib. Soc. of America*, vol. 37 (1943), p. 308.

6169 ELLIS, HENRY. A Voyage to Hudson's-Bay, by the Dobbs Galley and California, in the Years 1746 and 1747, for discovering a North West Passage; with an accurate Survey of the Coast, and a short Natural History of the Country. Together with a fair View of the Facts and Arguments from which the future finding of such a Passage is rendered probable.... *Lond. 1748, 8°*. L.

Another edn. Dublin, 1749, 8° (DA).

6170 [MONCREIFF, JOHN]. Camillus. A Dialogue on the Navy. Proposing a Plan to render that Wooden Wall, by Means which will both ease and extend our Commerce, the firm and perpetual Bulwark of Great Britain. By the Author of Galba. *Lond. 1748, 8°.* L.

Reprinted, with author's name, in *Three Dialogues on the Navy*, 1759.

COLONIES

6171 LITTLE, OTIS. The State of Trade in the Northern Colonies Considered; with an Account of their Produce, and a particular Description of Nova Scotia. *Lond. 1748, 8°.* LU.

The preface signed: Otis Little. Another edn., Boston 1749 (Sabin 41523).

6172 A Word in Season to all True Lovers of their Liberty and their Country; both of which are now in the utmost Danger of being forever lost. By Mylo Freeman, &. *Boston 1748, 8°,*

Reprinted in *Colonial Currency Reprints*, ed. by A. M. Davis, vol. 4 (1911), whence this entry is taken.

6173 WHITEFIELD, GEORGE. A Brief Account of the Rise, Progress, and present Situation, of the Orphan-House in Georgia. In a Letter to a Friend. *Edin. 1748, 8°.* E.

FINANCE

6174 An Enquiry into the Nature, Foundation, and Present State of Publick Credit. Wherein the National Wealth is justly calculated; the Present Inequality of our Publick Taxes demonstrated; and the Consequences that may naturally be expected from a Dishonourable Peace, or the Continuance of an Unsuccessful War, plainly pointed out. By a Friend to Trade and Liberty. *Lond.* [*1748*], *8°.* L.

6175 An Essay upon Publick Credit, in a Letter to a Friend. Occasioned by the Fall of Stocks. *Lond. 1748, 8°.* L.

2nd and 3rd edns. 1748 (both L).

6176 HENRIQUES, JACOB. An Advertisement, creditable and profitable to the General, as never better was offered to any Nation. *n.p.* [*1748*], *s. sh. F°.* L.

Two lottery schemes.

6177 HENRIQUES, JACOB. A short Abstract of the most material Matters from the large Proposal lately deliver'd; and most humbly submitted to the honourable Parliament, for discharging the National Debts. *Lond. 1747–8, s. sh. F°.* LLI.

6178 A proposal for a tax for the supplies of the war, that will be useful and easy, not affect trade, and will have a tendency to increase the political strength of the nation. *Lond. 1748, 19½ cm.* Kress 4923.

Increased land tax on the unmarried.

6179 Proposals for raising an Annual Sum of Money for the Service of His Majesty. *n.p.* [*c. 1748?*], *s. sh. F°*. LU.

Proposing that coal-heavers be registered and pay fees for registration.

6180 Ways and Means; or an Easy Method to Raise the Supplies, in a Letter to an High-Constable. By G. Rusticus. *Lond. 1748*, *8°*. LU.

6181 English Liberty in some cases worse than French Slavery: exemplified by Animadversions upon the Tyrannical and Anti-constitutional Power of the Justices of the Peace, Commissioners of Excise, Customs, and Land-Tax, &c. Containing a particular Relation of the barbarous and oppressive Methods made Use of in Raising the Land-Tax of this Kingdom.... *Lond. 1748*, *8°*. LU.

Signed: Philalethes.

6182 Reasons grounded on Facts. Shewing, I. That a new Duty on Sugar must fall on the Planter. II. That the Liberty of a direct Exportation to Foreign Markets will not help him in this Case. III. That a new Duty will not certainly increase the Revenue. And, IV. That it will probably occasion the Desertion of our Sugar Islands. *Lond. 1748*, *8°*. LU.

2nd edn., with additions, 1748 (L).

6183 *Begin.* The present Duty upon Tobacco for Home Comsumption is 4⅞d per lb. *n.p.* [*1748*], *s. sh. 4°*. L.

Against any increase. According to a ms. note by Adam Anderson in L copy, distributed at the door of the House of Commons 7 Jan. 1747/8.

6184 A Winter Evening's Conversation in a Club of Jews, Dutchmen, French Refugees, and English Stock-Jobbers, at a noted Coffee-House in Change-Alley. By which the whole Secret of the Late Subscription is laid open, the Character of a worthy Magistrate vindicated, and the true Cause of our agreeing so precipitately to the Preliminaries, detected. *Lond. 1748*, *8°*. LG.

6185 A List of the Inhabitants of the Ward of Farringdon-Within, with the several Sums of Money charged on them for the Orphan's Tax for the Year 1747, by the Aldermen and Common Council of the said Ward. *n.p.* [*1748?*], *s. sh. F°*. LG.

Anomalies are pointed out in a letter signed: Randle Wicksted, one of the Collectors.

6186 A Short View of the Prejudice arising both to the Country and Revenue, from the Imposition on Ale and Beer granted to the City of Edinburgh and other Boroughs in Scotland.... *Edin. 1748*, *4°*. EP.

6187 A List of the Brokers of the City of London, at M[ichaelmas], 1748. *n.p.* [*1748*], *s. sh. F°*. LG.

6188 The Case of the Mercers Company, humbly submitted to the Consideration of Parliament. *n.p.* [*1748*], *F°*. L.

With regard to the annuities issued by them.

6189 The Names of the Worshipful the Master, Wardens, Assistants, and Generality of the Worshipful Company of Mercers, London, 1748. *n.p.* [*1748*], *s. sh. Fo.* LG.

6190 A Bill for Relief of the Annuitants and Creditors of the Mercers Company. *n.p.* [*1748*], *Fo.* LU.

6191 A Bill for better Regulating of Assurances on Ships, and Goods laden thereon, and for preventing Frauds therein. *n.p.* [*1748*], *Fo.* L.

TRANSPORT

6192 MORRIS, LEWIS. Plans of Harbours, Bars, Bays and Roads in St. George's-Channel....With an Appendix Concerning the Improvements that might be made in the several Harbours, &c. for the better securing the Navigation in those Parts. Together with a Short Account of the Trade and Manufactures on that Coast. [*Lond.*], *1748*, *obl. 4o.* O.

New edn., edited by William Morris, 1801 (O).

6193 An Abstract of Mr. Charles Labelye's Reports relating to the Improvement of the River Wear, and Port of Sunderland, made in July 1748. *Newcastle upon Tyne* [*1748 ?*], *4o.* L.

6194 A Bill for Repairing the High Road from Piersbridge to Kirkmerrington in the County of Durham; and from thence to the Turnpike Road near Sunderland Bridge in the same County. *n.p.* [*1748*], *Fo.* L.

6195 LANGLEY, BATTY. A Survey of Westminster Bridge, as 'tis now Sinking into Ruin. Wherein the Cause of the Foundation giving way under the Sinking Pier, and its dislocated Arches, is not only accounted for; but also that the whole Structure is likewise subject to the same immediate (if not unavoidable) Ruin. With Remarks on the Piratical Method used for Building the Piers.... *Lond. 1748*, *8o.* LU.

6196 EDINBURGH. Act of Council regulating Hackney-Coaches. [*Edin. 1748*], *s. sh. Fo.* ECA.

Dated: 14 Dec. 1748.

SOCIAL CONDITIONS

6197 An Account of the Donations to the Parish of Newark upon Trent, in the County of Nottingham. By a Parishioner. *Lond. 1748*, *4o.* O.

6198 A Proposal for Relief and Punishment of Vagrants, particularly such as frequent the Streets and Publick Places of Resort, within this Kingdom. *Lond. 1748*, *8o.* LU.

6199 LONDON. Ladbroke, Mayor. An Especial Court held on...Tuesday the Second Day of February, 1747.... *n.p.* [*1748*], *s. sh. Fo.* LG.

An order enforcing the Act to amend and make more effectual the laws relating to rogues.

6200 A Bill for the further Relief of the Orphans and other Creditors of the City of London. *n.p.* [*1748*], *F*°. LU.

6201 A Bill for the Relief of Insolvent Debtors. *n.p.* [*1748*], *F*°. L.

6202 [Salmon, Thomas]. Considerations on the Bill for a General Naturalization, as it may conduce to the Improvement of our Manufactures and Traffic, and to the strengthening or endangering the Constitution.... *Lond. 1748*, *8*°. LU.

For authorship see *D.N.B.*

6203 Seasonable Observations on the Naturalization Bill, now depending in Parliament; and also a clear Computation of the City of London's Remonstrance to the House against it, shewing the Advantages that will accrue to Great-Britain by a Naturalization. *Lond. 1748*, *4*°. LU.

6204 The Report from the Committee of the Guild-Hall Subscription towards the Relief Support and Encouragement of the Soldiers employed in suppressing the Rebellion in MDCCXLV. *Lond. 1747* [*o.s.*], *F*°. L.

6205 Smith, Samuel. A List of the Subscribers to the Veteran Scheme. Begun at Sir Joseph and Sir Thomas Hankey's, and James Colebrook's, Esq; and afterwards carried on at Guild-Hall, for the Relief, Support and Encouragement of his Majesty's Forces, employed in suppressing the late Rebellion, together, with the Distribution of the Necessaries to the Army, and the Application of the Money subscribed. *Lond. 1748*, *F*°. L.

6206 Copy of His Majesty's Warrant for a Patent to be passed per saltum, under the Great Seal appointed by the Treaty of Union to be kept and made use of in place of the Great Seal of Scotland, authorizing the Officers of His Majesty's Revenue of Excise there, to raise a Fund by a Contribution among themselves, for the better Support of their Widows and Orphans; and for erecting the Contributers into a Corporation for that charitable Purpose. *n.p.* [*1748?*], *8*°. LU.

6207 Reasons for applying to the King and Parliament for an Augmentation of the Stipends of the Ministers of the Church of Scotland. With Objections against such an Application, and Answers to them. *Edinburgh, 1748*, *8*°. E.

Reprinted in *A Collection of all the Papers published in relation to the Scheme for Augmenting the Stipends of the Established Clergy in Scotland*, 1751.

6208 The Reasons for applying to the King and Parliament for an Augmentation of Stipend to the Ministers of the Church of Scotland, Examined. In a Letter to a Friend. *Edin. 1748*, *8*°. ENC.

2nd edn. 1748 (M (Cr)). Reprinted in *A Collection of all the Papers published in relation to the Scheme for Augmenting the Stipends of the Established Clergy in Scotland*, 1751.

6209 The Reasons for augmenting Ministers Stipends in Scotland, illustrated and inforced. With Remarks on a pamphlet, intitled, The Reasons for applying to the King and Parliament examined; in a Letter to a Friend. By a sincere wellwisher to our happy constitution in Church and State. *Edin. 1748, 8°.* ENC.

Reprinted in *A Collection of all the Papers published in relation to the Scheme for Augmenting the Stipends of the Established Clergy in Scotland*, 1751.

6210 [WEBSTER, ALEXANDER]. Calculations, with the Principles and Data on which they are instituted: relative to a late Act of Parliament, intituled, An Act for raising and establishing a Fund for a Provision for the Widows and Children of the Ministers of the Church, and of the Heads, Principals, and Masters of the Universities of Scotland. Shewing the Rise and Progress of the Fund. Published by Order of the Trustees nominated in the said Act of Parliament. *Edin. 1748, F°.* EU.

For authorship see Hew Scott, *Fasti Ecclesiae Scotianae*, 1915, I, 120.

6211 The Memorial of the Trustees appointed in a late Act of Parliament, intituled, An Act for establishing a Fund for a Provision to Ministers Widows, &c. *n.p.* [*1748*], *4°.* EU.

6212 The Representation of the Trustees appointed in a late Act of Parliament, entituled, An Act for establishing a Fund for a Provision to Ministers Widows, &c. to the General Assembly of the Church of Scotland. *n.p.* [*1748*], *4°.* EU.

6213 LONDON. Ladbroke, Mayor. Tuesday the 19th Day of April 1748.... [*Lond. 1748*], *s. sh. F°.* LCRO.

An order to reprint a clause relating to servants in the Act for the better preventing mischiefs that may happen by fire, with the clause.

6214 A General Registry of Births, kept at the Heralds Office on St. Bennet's Hill near St. Paul's, London. *n.p.* [*1748 ?*], *s. sh. F°.* OUP.

An account of its establishment.

6215 The State preferable to the Church; or, Reasons for making Sale of the whole present Property of the Church, in England and Ireland, for the use of the State; and for rendering the Clergy more equal among themselves, less vexatious and onerous to the Laity, and more dependent on their Head, by subjecting them to the Exchequer for their Stipends, as practised in Holland. With a view of the Self-denying Conduct of the Popish Clergy, in Exegencies of the State and particularly of our own, under Philip and Mary....In a Letter from a Country Gentleman to the Representative of his County in Parliament. *Lond. 1748, 8°.* LU.

1749

GENERAL

6216 [POSTLETHWAYT, MALACHY]. A Dissertation on the Plan, Use, and Importance, of The Universal Dictionary of Trade and Commerce; Translated from the French of the late Celebrated Mons. Savary, Inspector-General of the Manufactures of the Custom-House of Paris: with such considerable Additions and Improvements, as will appear at large throughout this Dissertation; and which will more particularly accommodate the same to the Trade and Navigation of the British Empire.... *Lond. 1749*, *4°*. O.

The *Dictionary*, 1751–5, was translated and edited by Postlethwayt.

6217 Miscellaneous Reflections upon the Peace, and its Consequences. More especially on a just, as well as real and national Oeconomy, the Regard due to Subjects, who have served in Quality of Soldiers, Seamen, or Marines, the Necessity of providing for the Security of our Frontiers, and of rendering the Peace solid and lasting.... *Lond. 1749*, *8°*. L.

Advocates emigration to America.

6218 A Bill to Continue several Laws for preventing Exactions of the Occupiers of Locks and Wears upon the River of Thames Westward, and for Ascertaining the Rates of Water-Carriage upon the said River; And for Continuing, Explaining, and Amending, the several Laws for the better Regulation of Attornies and Sollicitors; And for Regulating the Price and Assize of Bread; And for Preventing the Spreading of the Distemper amongst the Horned Cattle. *n.p.* [*1749*], *F°*. L.

6219 RAY, JAMES. A Compleat History of the Rebellion....Likewise the natural History and Antiquities of the several Towns thro' which the Author pass'd with his Majesty's Army; together with the Manners and Customs of the different People, particularly the Highlanders.... *York*, *1749*, *12°*. O.

6220 [HENRY, WILLIAM ?]. An Appeal to the People of Ireland. Occasioned by the Insinuations and Misrepresentations of the Author of a Weekly Paper, entitled, The Censor. Proving that the Principles laid down in that Paper, and the Author's Reflections upon England are unjust, ungrateful, and in their Consequences, highly injurious to the Linen Manufacture, to the Charter Schools, and to the whole Protestant Interest of Ireland. By a Member of the Incorporated Society for promoting English Protestant Schools in Ireland. *Dublin*, *1749*, *8°*. C.

Signed: W. Britanno-Hibernus. 2nd edn. 1749 (DA); 3rd edn. 1749 (O). For authorship see H. & L., who quote no authority.

6221 Hints relating to some Laws that may be for the Interest of Ireland to have Enacted. In a Letter to a Member of Parliament. *Dublin*, *1749*, *8°*. LU

AGRICULTURE

6222 The case of killing infected beasts, briefly considered. *Manchester* [*1749*], *8o*. Kress 4949.

6223 Considerations concerning the Distemper which still spreads itself among the Horned Cattle in this Kingdom.... By a Physician. *Lond. 1749*, *8o*. EU.

6224 An Act for Confirming and Establishing certain Articles of Agreement for inclosing and dividing the Common Fields and Common Grounds in the Tything of Broad-Blunsdon in the County of Wilts; and making the same more effectual for the Purposes therein mentioned. *n.p.* [*1749*], *Fo*. L.

6225 An Act for Inclosing and Dividing Eastwoodhey Down, and the open and common Fields of Eastwoodhey and Hollington, in the County of Southampton, pursuant to an Agreement entered into for that Purpose. *n.p.* [*1749*], *Fo*. L.

6226 An Act for Confirming and Establishing an Agreement for dividing and inclosing certain open Fields and Lands in the Manors of Wakerley and Wittering, in the County of Northampton. *n.p.* [*1749*], *Fo*. L.

6227 An Act for Inclosing and Dividing certain Commons and Wastes within the Manor and Parish of Watlington in the County of Norfolk. *n.p.* [*1749*], *Fo*. L.

6228 A Bill for Draining and Improving certain Fen-lands lying in Denver, Upwell, Outwell, and Welney.... *n.p.* [*1749*], *Fo*. L.

6229 A Bill for Draining and Preserving certain Fen-lands and low Grounds in the several Parishes of Sutton, Mepall, Whicham, Chatteris, Doddington, and a Place called Byal-Fen in the Isle of Ely, and County of Cambridge; and also in the Parishes of Somersham, and Pidley with Fenton, in the County of Huntingdon. *n.p.* [*1749*], *Fo*. L.

6230 An Act for Draining and Preserving certain Fen-lands and low Grounds in the several Parishes of Sutton, Mepall, Witcham, Chatteris, Doddington, and a Place called Byal-Fen in the Isle of Ely, and County of Cambridge; and also in the Parishes of Somersham, and Pidley with Fenton, in the County of Huntingdon. *n.p.* [*1749*], *Fo*. L.

6231 A Bill for the more effectual Draining and Preserving of several Fen-lands and Field-lands, in the Bounds and Precincts of Whittlesey, in the Isle of Ely, in the County of Cambridge. *n.p.* [*1749*], *Fo*. L.

6232 [Jackson, Alderman]. The Wealth of Great Britain in the Ocean, exemplified from materials laid before the Committee of the House of Commons, appointed last Sessions of Parliament, to examine into the

State of the British Fisheries. And from the Public Records, and other authentic Evidences. *Lond. 1749, 8°.* LU.

A copy advertised in Peter Murray Hill's Catalogue 51 no. 108 has the attribution in ms.

6233 [VERNON, Admiral EDWARD]. Considerations upon the White Herring and Cod Fisheries: in which the Design of carrying on and improving them, in the Manner proposed by a Society trading with a Joint Stock, is fully explained, and freed from all Objections. *Lond. 1749, 8°.* pp. 58. LU.

Another edn. 1749, pp. 52 (LU). For authorship see H. & L. quoting H. B. Wheatley as authority.

6234 [GRANT, FRANCIS]. A Letter to a Member of Parliament, concerning the Free British Fisheries; with Draughts of a Herring-Buss and Nets, and the Harbour and Town of Peterhead. *Lond. 1750 [1749], 8°.* LU.

On p. 10 is printed a letter from Swift to the author, which is reprinted as addressed to Grant in *The Works of Jonathan Swift*, ed. by J. Nichols, XIII (1801), p. 120.

6235 Contract of Copartnery of the Edinburgh Whale-Fishing Company. [*Edin. 1749*], *8°.* LU.

Both copies seen (LU and MP) are imperfect.

MANUFACTURES

6236 A Bill to Amend and render more Effectual an Act made in the Thirteenth Year of his present Majesty's Reign (intituled, An Act to Explain and Amend an Act made in the First Year of the Reign of her late Majesty Queen Anne (intituled, An Act for the more effectual Preventing the Abuses and Frauds of Persons employed in the working up the Woolen, Linen, Fustian, Cotton, and Iron Manufactures of this Kingdom) and for extending the said Act to the Manufactures of Leather); and to extend the same to the Manufactures of Silk; and also to extend a Clause in an Act made in the Twelfth Year of the Reign of his late Majesty King George the First (for preventing unlawful Combinations of Workmen employed in the Woolen Manufactures) to Journeymen Dyers, and Journeymen Hot-pressers, and all other Persons employed in the said Woolen Manufactures. *n.p.* [*1749*], *F°.* L.

6237 HALFPENNY, WILLIAM. A New and Compleat System of Architecture Delineated, in a variety of Plans and Elevations of Designs for Convenient and Decorated Houses. Together with Offices and Out-Buildings proportioned thereto.... *Lond. 1749, obl. F°.* L.

6238 For the obviating of all future Misunderstandings, or Pretence of Misunderstandings, the Antient Rules are particularized as follow: [*Lond. 1749?*], *s. sh. F°.* OUP.

Samuel Richardson's regulations for the compositors in his printing shop, with his wage scale. Reprinted in I. G. Philip, *Sir William Blackstone and the Reform of the Oxford University Press*, 1957, pp. 124–6.

6239 Unto the Right Honourable the Lords of Council and Session, the Petition of the Magistrates and Town-Council of Aberdeen, and of William Davidson Merchant and Bailie there, and others, Proprietors of Houses in the Street called the Nether-Kirkgate of Aberdeen. *n.p.* [*1749*], *F*o. E.

Dated: January 9. 1749. Signed: Alex. Lockhart. Against the erection of a soap works.

6240 Answers for Walter Leith and George Leslie Merchants in Aberdeen, to the Petition presented in Name of the Magistrates and Town-Council of Aberdeen, William Davidson Merchant and one of the present Baillies there, and others. *n.p.* [*1749*], *4*o. E.

Dated: January 16. 1749. Signed: Geo. Brown.

6241 Answers for Walter Leith and George Leslie Merchants in Aberdeen, to the Petition presented in Name of the Magistrates and Town Council of Aberdeen, William Davidson Merchant, and one of the present Baillies there and others. *n.p.* [*1749*], *F*o. E.

Dated: February 9. 1749. Signed: Francis Garden.

6242 COX, Sir RICHARD. A Letter from Sir Richard Cox, Bart. to Thomas Prior, Esq; shewing, from experience, a sure Method to establish the Linen-Manufacture; and the Beneficial Effects, it will immediately produce. *Dublin*, *1749*, *8*o. LU.

Another edn. Lond. 1749 (L); another edn. Boston, Mass., 1750 (Kress S. 1979); 3rd edn. Dublin, 1752 (DA).

6243 PRIOR, THOMAS. An Essay to Encourage and Extend the Linen-Manufacture in Ireland, by Præmiums and other Means. *Dublin*, *1749*, *8*o. L.

2nd edn. 1749 (L).

6244 To the Right Honourable and Honourable the Knights, Citizens and Burgesses in Parliament assembled. The humble Petition of Joseph Sexton of the City of Limerick Merchant. *n.p.* [*1749*], *F*o. DM.

For encouragement for his paper mill.

6245 The Case of the Silk and Worsted Weavers. In a Letter to a Member of Parliament. *Dublin*, *1749*, *8*o. DA.

6246 The Journeymen Hoziers Reply to the Censor. *Dublin*, *1749*, *s. sh. F*o. C.

Dated Oct. 2, 1749. No. 16 of *The Censor* had attacked the journeymen's associations in the woollen trade.

6247 A Vindication of the Broad Cloth Weavers. Being the Journeymens Answer to Mr. Textor's Letter in the Sixteenth Censor. Number II. *Dublin*, *1749*, *8*o. DA.

COMMERCE

6248 An Essay on the Increase and Decline of Trade, in London and the Out-Ports; wherein is shewn, That Monopolies have been the Ruin of the London Commerce; That Luxury and high Living have, in all Ages, been the Bane of Trade....That the Inhabitants of London are now richer, and daily gain greater Wealth than in any Time past....That no People in the Kingdom have so little Reason to complain of the Burden of Taxes as the Inhabitants of London....That all Merchants in the Out-Ports are not clandestine Dealers, and licensed Smugglers, as hath in too general Terms been asserted; And that it is the Interest of London to have the Out-Ports share with it in some Branches of Commerce.... *Lond.* *1749*, *8°*. LU.

6249 Considerations on the Coal Trade. More particularly as it concerns the Consumers within the City and Liberty of Westminster, and Parts adjacent: To which are added some Observations concerning the Office appointed for the Regulation of the same. *n.p.* [*1749?*], *s. sh.* *F°*. L.

On the need to enforce the regulations concerning measuring.

6250 A Bill for making a Free Market for the Sale of Fish in the City of Westminster; and for preventing the Forestalling and Monopolizing of Fish. *n.p.* [*1749*], *F°*. L.

6251 A Bill to prevent the Mischiefs which may happen by keeping too great Quantities of Gunpowder in any one Place, or carrying too great Quantities of Gunpowder together from one Place to another. *n.p.* [*1749*], *F°*. L.

6252 The Case of the Free Scriveners of London: set forth in a Report from a Committee of the Court of Assistants of the Company of Scriveners, London: to the Master, Wardens and Assistants of the Company. At their Court holden the 23d Day of June 1748. *Lond.* *1749*, *4°*. O.

Against interloping scriveners 'who are neither free of the Company, nor of the City'.

6253 James Arbuthnot, Esq;...Appellant. Walter McFarlane of McFarlane, Esq; Respondent. The Appellant's Case. *n.p.* [*1749*], *F°*. L.

Signed: Wm. Murray. A. Hume-Campbell. On the sale of cattle by drovers in Dumbarton and Argyll in 1739.

6254 James Arbuthnot, Esq; Appellant. Walter McFarlane, of McFarlane, Esq; Respondent. The Respondent's Case. *n.p.* [*1749*], *F°*. L.

Signed: Al. Forrester. C. Erskine.

6255 The Advantages of the Definitive Treaty, to the People of Great-Britain, Demonstrated. *Lond.* *1749*, *8°*. DA.

6256 [TUCKER, JOSIAH]. A Brief Essay on the Advantages and Disadvantages, which respectively attend France and Great Britain, with regard to Trade. With some Proposals for removing the Principal Disadvantages of Great Britain. In a new and concise Method. *Lond.* *1749*, *8°*. C.

2nd edn. 1750 (O); 3rd edn., with author's name, 1753 (L). Reprinted in *A Select Collection of Scarce and Valuable Tracts on Commerce*, ed. by J. R. McCulloch, 1859, p. 309.

6257 A Defence of the Dutch, against the Imputations of Fraud, Cruelty, and Perfidiousness. Shewing how Dutch Industry may become profitable to Great Britain in the Herring Fishery; and this Kingdom restored to a prosperous Condition, by Good Oeconomy, and A more spirited Policy; particularly with regard to the Encroachments of France, and the Untractableness of Spain. To which is added, A Supplement, relating to the Settlement of Nova Scotia. *Lond. 1749*, *8º*. C.

6258 The Staple Contract, betwixt the Royal Burrows of Scotland, and the City of Campvere in Zealand. With the Several Amplifications, Prolongations, and Ratifications thereof. Published by Order of the General Convention of Royal Burrows, in July 1749. To which is prefixed, An historical Account of the Staple, by a Private Gentleman [Charles Stewart]. *Edin. 1749*, *8º*. LU.

Another edn. 1776 (E). Reprinted in William Maitland's *History of Edinburgh*, 1753. For Stewart's authorship of the preliminary essay see William Steven, *The History of the Scottish Church*, *Rotterdam*, 1833, p. 288 n. The same authority is quoted in H. & L. for the attribution of the whole compilation to James Yair, but the wording of the note does not seem to me to bear out the attribution.

6259 By the Lords Justices and Council of Ireland, a Proclamation. *Dublin*, *1749*, *Fº*. DPRO.

Dated: 10 July 1749. Continuing the quarantine on ships coming from West Barbary.

6260 A Free Apology in Behalf of the Smugglers, so far as their Case affects the Constitution. By an Enemy to all Oppression, whether by Tyranny, or Law. *Lond. 1749*, *8º*. L.

6261 A Bill for Extending and Improving the Trade to Africa. *n.p.* [*1749*], *Fº*. pp. 9. L.

6262 O'Connor, M. Considerations on the Trade to Africa. Together with a Proposal for securing the Benefits thereof to this Nation. For Fixing and Ascertaining the Capital Stock of the Royal African Company of England. For Uniting the Creditors and Proprietors thereof in One Joint, or Common Interest. For raising the Sum of Two Hundred Thousand Pounds to be employed in the Trade and Service of that Corporation. And (by Means of a Parliamentary Allowance) for Establishing their Affairs...upon a solid and lasting Foundation.... *Lond. 1749*, *8º*. L.

6263 The Case of the Creditors of the Royal African Company of England. *n.p.* [*1749?*], *Fº*. L.

6264 A Detection of the Proceedings and Practices of the Directors of the Royal African Company of England, from their first Establishment by Charter in the Year 1672, to the present Year 1748. With Remarks on the Use and Importance of the British Forts and Settlements on the Coast of Guiney, and the Necessity of speedily putting them upon a proper Establishment. *Lond. 1749*, *8º*. LU.

6265 An Antidote to Expel the Poison contained in an Anonymous Pamphlet, lately published, entitled, A Detection of the Proceedings and Practices of the Directors of the Royal African Company of England, &c. Being intended not only as a full Answer to this Pamphlet, but to all others of the like Nature, that may come out hereafter. *Lond. 1749, 8º*. LU.

6266 A Letter to a Member of Parliament, concerning the African Trade. *n.p.* [*1749?*], *F*º. L.
Signed: A.Z.

6267 Proposals for Settling and Preserving the British Trade to Africa. And for Purchasing from the present Royal African Company all their Forts, Castles, Lands, Territories, and Property there, in order thereto. *n.p.* [*1749?*], *F*º. L.

6268 The Royal African: or Memoirs of the Young Prince of Annamaboe. Comprehending a distinct Account of his Country and Family...his Condition while a Slave in Barbadoes; the true Cause of his being redeemed; his Voyage from thence; and his Reception here in England. Interspers'd throughout with several Historical Remarks on the Commerce of the European Nations, whose Subjects frequent the Coast of Guinea.... *Lond.* [*1749*], *8º*. L.
2nd edn. [1749?] (L).

6269 A Short Narrative and Justification of the Proceedings of the Committee appointed by the Adventurers, to prosecute the Discovery of the Passage to the Western Ocean of America; and to Open and extend the Trade, and Settle the Countries beyond Hudson's Bay. With an Apology for their postponing at present their intended Application to Parliament.... *Lond. 1749, 8º*. EU.

6270 Reasons to shew, that there is a great Probability of a Navigable Passage to the Western American Ocean, through Hudson's Streights, and Chesterfield Inlet, from the Observations made on board the Ships sent upon the late Discovery; supported by Affidavits, which coincides with several Former Accounts. Humbly offered to the Consideration of the Lords and Commons assembled in Parliament. *Lond. 1749, 8º*. L.

6271 Papers presented to the Committee appointed to inquire into the State and Condition of the Countries adjoining to Hudson's Bay, and of the Trade carried on there. *Lond. 1749, F*º. L.

6272 Report from the Committee appointed to Inquire into the State and Condition of the Countries adjoining to Hudson's Bay, and of the Trade carried on there. [*Lond.*], *1749, F*º. L.

6273 The Case of the Hudson's-Bay Company. *n.p.* [*1749*], *F*º. L.

6274 A short View of the Countries and Trade carried on by the Company in Hudson's-Bay; shewing the Prejudice of that exclusive Trade, and Benefit which will accrue to Great-Britain, by opening and extending that Trade, and settling those Countries. *n.p.* [*1749*], *F*º. L.

6275 A Short State of the Countries and Trade of North America. Claimed by the Hudson's Bay Company, under Pretence of a Charter for Ever, of Lands without Bounds or Limits, and an exclusive Trade to those unbounded Seas and Countries; shewing the Illegality of the said Grant, and the Abuse they have made of it.... *Lond. 1749, 8°.* EU.

6276 POSTLETHWAYT, MALACHY. Considerations on the Revival of the Royal-British-Assiento; between His Catholick-Majesty, and the Honourable the South-Sea Company. With an humble Attempt to unite the African-Trade to that of the South-Sea Company, by Act of Parliament. *Lond. 1749, 8°.* L.

6277 Three Letters to the Proprietors of Stock in the East-India Company, relative to the Question to be Ballotted for on Wednesday, January 3d, 1749 [o.s.]. By a Director. *Lond. 1749, 8°.* LU.

6278 The Bill for Amending, Explaining, and Reducing into One Act of Parliament, the Laws relating to the Government of His Majesty's Ships, Vessels, and Forces by Sea. *n.p.* [*1749*], *F°.* L.

Another edn., entitled: The Bill, with the Amendments, for Amending .... [1749] (L).

6279 Considerations on the Bill for the Better Government of the Navy. By a Sea Officer. *Lond. 1749, 8°.* O.

6280 An Examination and Refutation of a late Pamphlet, intitled, Considerations on the Navy Bill....By a Real Sea Officer. *Lond. 1749, 8°.* L.

6281 Remarks on a Pamphlet, called, Considerations on the Bill for the better Government of the Navy....By a Sea-Officer. *Lond. 1749, 8°.* L.

6282 Objections to the Thirty-Fourth Article of the Navy Bill. *Lond. 1749, 8°.* L.

On the position of half-pay officers.

6283 A Narrative in Justification of Injured Innocence. Wherein Cowardice, Fraud, Tyranny, and Oppression are detected and exposed. Together with some of the principal Causes of that extreme Aversion which Seamen commonly shew to the Royal Navy and the Service of their Country....Written by a Country Gentleman. *Lond. 1749, 8°.* M.

COLONIES

6284 Reasons for giving up Gibraltar. Illustrated with accurate Plans....And a Summary of its State, Situation, and Government. With an Appendix. Containing Extracts of the Addresses to the Throne from the City of London, and other Cities, Counties and Boroughs, &c. In the Years 1726 and 1727, regarding the Importance of Gibraltar.... *Lond. 1749, 8°.* LU.

6285 A Geographical History of Nova Scotia. Containing an Account of the Situation, Extent and Limits thereof. As also of the various Struggles between the Two Crowns of England and France for the Possession of that Province. Wherein is shewn, the Importance of it, as well with Regard to our Trade, as to the securing of our other Settlements in North America. To which is added, An Accurate Description of the Bays, Harbours, Lakes, and Rivers, the Nature of the Soil, and the Produce of the Country. Together with the Manners and Customs of the Indian Inhabitants. *Lond. 1749, 8°.* L.

6286 A Bill to Regulate and Restrain Paper Bills of Credit in the British Colonies and Plantations in America, and to prevent the same being legal Tenders in Payments for Money; and for the better enforcing his Majesty's Orders and Instructions throughout the said Colonies and Plantations. *n.p. [1749], F°.* L.

6287 A Brief Account of the Rise, Progress, and Present State of the Paper Currency of New-England. And of the Measures taken by the Massachusetts Province, for establishing a Silver Currency for the Future. Together with some Proposals for rendering those Measures more effectual. *Boston, 1749, 8°.*

Reprinted in *Colonial Currency Reprints*, ed. by A. M. Davis, vol. 4 (1911), whence this entry is taken.

6288 The Case of the Inhabitants in Pensilvania. *n.p. [1748], F°.* L.

Against the colonial currency bill.

6289 Report from the Committee of Conference, Appointed to take into Consideration that Part of His Excellency the Governor's Speech, which relates to the State of the Paper Currency in the Province of South-Carolina. *n.p. [1749], s. sh. F°.* LPRO.

6290 The Case of the Deputies of the Moravian Brethren. *n.p. [1749], s. sh. F°.* L.

For exemption from taking oaths and carrying arms in order to encourage them further to settle in America.

6291 Report from the Committee to whom the Petition of the Deputies of the United Moravian Churches in behalf of themselves and their United Brethren, was referred: Together with some Extracts of the Most Material Vouchers and Papers contained in the Appendix to the said Report. *Lond. 1749, F°.* L.

6292 A Bill for Encouraging the People known by the Name of Unitas Fratrum, or United Brethren, to settle in his Majesty's Colonies in America. *n.p. [1749], F°.* L.

6293 The Alarm-Bell: or, Considerations on the Present Dangerous State of the Sugar Colonies; with a Memorial, and Observations concerning the Islands of St. Lucia, Dominico, St. Vincent, and Tabago. To which are added, Queries and Answers relating to the African Trade. *Lond. 1749, 4°.* L.

6294 Tabago: or, a Geographical Description, Natural and Civil History, together with a full Representation of the Produce, and other Advantages arising from the Fertility, excellent Harbours, and happy Situation of that famous Island.... *Lond.* [*1749*], *8*°. LU.

2nd edn. [1749?] (EU).

FINANCE

6295 The Petition and Proposal of Jacob Henriques to the Honourable House of Commons, for paying the National Debt, &c. [*Lond. 1749*], *4*°. L.

6296 Machiavel's Letter to the Lords and Commons of G****-B******, proposing infallible Methods to pay the National Debt, likewise proving the Necessity of repealing the Test Act.... *Lond.* [*1749*], *8*°. LU.

6297 A List of the Names of the several Nominees (with their Ages) subscribed upon an Act passed in the 4th Year of the Reign of King William and Queen Mary, commonly called The Million Act, as they were delivered in to the Exchequer...at Midsummer last, for Payment of the Dividend then due upon the Benefit of Survivorship. *n.p. 1749*, *F*°. L.

6298 The Ladies Advocate. Or, Option for Option. *n.p.* [*c. 1749?*], *F*°. LG.

On lowering the rate of interest on government stocks from 4 per cent to 3 per cent.

6299 A New Proposal and Scheme for the Government's Raising by Subscription L.6,000,000 of Money; in order to pay off therewith the like Sum of the present 4 per Cent South-Sea Annuities: And convert, with the Consent of the Proprietors, the like Sum also into Annuities of 3 per Cent per Annum, not redeemable till after 14 or 7 Years, &c. *n.p.* [*c. 1749?*], *obl. F*°. LG.

Endorsed: Some Special Reasons....Shewing, That the Reduction of all the 4 per Cent Funds to 3 per Cent Annuities at once, cannot be for the General Good and Benefit....

6300 The Present Taxes compared to the Payments made to the Publick within the Memory of Man. With some Thoughts on the possible Consequences that may ensue from the National Debts. In a Letter to a Member of Parliament, from a Country Farmer. *Lond. 1749*, *8*°. L.

6301 Some Considerations upon Taxes, and upon the Debts of the Nation. By the Author of a Scheme for Establishing a Militia of 17000 Volunteers, &c. *Eton* [*1749*], *4*°. L.

6302 [Nugent, Robert Craggs, Earl Nugent]. Considerations upon a Reduction of the Land-Tax. *Lond. 1749*, *8*°. L.

For authorship see ms. note in L copy.

6303 Great Britain's Deplorable State, and the Hardship of the Tax on Houses and Lands; shewed from her past Conduct, present Debts, and great Taxes. In which what is offer'd in a Pamphlet, intitled, Considerations upon a Reduction of the Land-Tax, as far as it would still load Houses and Lands, is fully examin'd and disprov'd....By a Country Gentleman. Part I. *Lond.* [*1749*], *8°*. LU.

6304 A Compleat Alphabetical List of the Stamp-Duties. Whereby may be found, what Stamps are required on all Sorts of Deeds, Writings, and Agreements, &c. of What Nature or Kind soever. The Second Edition. *Lond. 1749*, *8°*. LU.

The first edn. (not seen) was published in 1745 (*C.B.E.L.* II, 691).

6305 Unto the Right Honourable the Lords of Council and Session the Petition of Alexander Alison Deputy-Cashier of Excise. *n.p.* [*1749*], *F°*. O.

Dated: 16th November 1749. Signed: Alex. Lockhart. Salt duties and debentures.

6306 Answers for Agnes Seton, Relict of Alexander Williamson, some time Provost of Kirkcaldy, deceast, and John Ross, eldest Son of the deceast Patrick Ross of Innernethie Advocate, and his Tutors, Defenders; to the Petition of Alexander Alison, Deputy-Cashier of Excise, Pursuer. *n.p.* [*1749*], *F°*. O.

Dated: December 12. 1749. Signed: Rob. Craigie.

6307 KIRKPATRICK, MARTIN. A Proposal for the better preventing Frauds in the Collection of the Customs of the City of Dublin. Offered in the Year 1742....With a Preface. *Dublin, 1749*, *8°*. L.

6308 A List of the Reduced Officers of His Majesty's Land-Forces and Marines, intitled to receive Half-Pay in Great Britain. With an Estimate of the Charge thereof, for the year 1749.... *n.p. 1749*, *F°*. L.

6309 The Case of Charles Moore, late Master Cooper of the Victualling Office. Humbly offered to the Serious Consideration of the C——mm——rs for V——ll——g His Majesty's N——y. *Lond. 1749*, *8°*. O.

Signed: Charles Moore. Alleging mismanagement and fraud in the Office.

6310 Unto the Right Honourable the Lords of Council and Session, The Petition of William Gray and John Clark, Tacksmen of the common Mills of Perth, and of the Magistrates and Town-Council of Perth, for their Interest. *n.p.* [*1749*], *F°*. O.

Dated: February 2. 1749. Signed: R. Dundas. Maintaining their right to levy a duty on all flour brought into the burgh.

6311 Answers for James Rait Merchant in Dundee, Allan Clark, George Maxton and Laurence Millar, Baxters in Perth, to the Petition of William Gray and John Clark, Tacksmen of the Mills of Perth. *n.p.* [*1749*], *4°*. O.

Dated: February 14. 1749. Signed: Gilb. Elliot.

6312 MASSY, CHARLES, Dean of Limerick. A Collection of Resolutions, Queries, &c. wrote on occasion of the present Dispute in the City of Limerick. *Limerick, 1749*, *8°*. O.

On the misgovernment of the city.

6313 Canterbury, 27th October, 1749. Sir, The Hop-Planters in this City and Country round about, have always been accustomed to pay a Composition of ten shillings an Acre for the Tythe of their Hops.... *n.p.* [*1749*], *s. sh. F*° L.

A circular announcing a scheme to petition Parliament to ascertain the tithe of hops.

6314 SIMON, JAMES. An Essay towards an Historical Account of Irish Coins, and of the Currency of Foregin [*sic*] Monies in Ireland. With an Appendix: containing Several Statutes, Proclamations, Patents, Acts of State, and Letters relating to the Same. *Dublin*, *1749*, *4*°. LU.

6315 A List of the Names of all such Proprietors of the Bank of England, who are Qualified to Vote at the Ensuing Election....March 25th, 1749. *Lond*. *1749*, *F*°. LU.

6316 The Right Honourable Mary, Countess of Kildare, and Others, Appellants. Robert Burton, Esq; Charles Burton, Merchant...and Francis Burton [and others]...Respondents. The Appellants Case. *n.p.* [*1749*], *F*°. L.

Signed: D. Ryder. John Browne. On the affairs of Burton's Bank, Dublin.

6317 The Right Honourable Mary Countess of Kildare [and others]... Appellants. Robert Burton [and others]...Respondents. The Case of the Respondents, Robert Burton, Charles Burton, and Francis Burton. *n.p.* [*1749*], *F*°. L.

Signed: W. Murray. P. Jodrell.

6318 The Right Honourable Mary, Countess of Kildare [and others]... Appellants. Robert Burton [and others]...Respondents. The Case of the Respondents Benjamin Burton, Francis Bindon, and John Hardy. *n.p.* [*1749*], *F*°. L.

Signed: A. Hume-Campbell. C. Yorke.

6319 The Right Honourable Mary Countess of Kildare, and Other. Appellants. Robert Burton [and others]...Respondents. The Case of the Respondents the Trustees. *n.p.* [*1749*], *F*°. L.

Signed: Tho. Clarke. Cha. Waller.

6320 The Right Honourable Mary Countess of Kildare, and Others, Appellants. Robert Burton, Esq; Daniel Falkiner, Esq; and Others, Respondents. The Respondent Daniel Falkiner's Case. *n.p.* [*1749*], *F*°. L.

Signed: Wm. Noel.

6321 Faction against the Charitable Corporation Detected. With Remarks on a Speech for withholding Relief from that Company. Shewing to Demonstration, its vast Utility, and the Gross Absurdity of its most virulent Opposers.... *Lond*. [*1749*], *8*°. LG.

6322 Reasons for reviving the Charitable Corporation, in a Letter to a Member of Parliament. *Lond*. *1749*, *8*°. O.

Signed: A Citizen.

6323 Memorial for Sir James Dalrymple of Haills, Baronet, called as a Defender, in the Process at the Instance of the Directors of the Society for Insurance of Houses in Edinburgh from Fire, against the Royal Bank of Scotland, now before the Lords by Information. *n.p.* [*1749*], *s. sh. F°*. LU.

Signed: Dav. Dalrymple, Junr.

6324 Terms, Methods and Advantages of Insuring Lives, in the Office of the Amicable Society for a Perpetual Assurance, kept in Serjeant's-Inn, Fleet-street. *Lond. 1749, s. sh. F°*. LG.

6325 CROSBY, THOMAS. The Book-Keeper's Guide. Wherein the Theory of that Art is clearly explain'd, and the Practice render'd easy and familiar.... *Lond. 1749, 8°*. L.

6326 DODSON, JAMES. The Accountant, or, the Method of Book-Keeping, deduced from Clear Principles, and illustrated by a variety of examples. *Lond. 1750* [*1749*], *4°*. L.

TRANSPORT

6327 A Bill for Amending, Enlarging, and Preserving, the Harbour of Ellenfoot, in the County of Cumberland. *n.p.* [*1749*], *F°*. L.

6328 The Case relating to an Harbour for Ships detained by Contrary Winds in the Downs, which is an open Road, where Ships are exposed to the Danger of being Wrecked in Stormy Weather. *n.p.* [*1749*], *F°*. L.

With a map.

6329 Remarks on the Case delivered in Support of the Petition for Making an Harbour at Ramsgate. *n.p.* [*1749*], *F°*. L.

6330 A Bill for Enlarging and Maintaining the Harbour of Ramsgate, and for Cleansing, Amending, and Preserving the Haven of Sandwich. *n.p.* [*1749*], *F°*. L.

6331 A Bill for the better ascertaining, recovering, and collecting, certain Duties commonly called Wharfage-duties, payable upon the Importation and Exportation of Goods and Merchandizes into, or out of, the Harbour of the Borough and Town of Waymouth and Melcombe Regis...and for the better repairing, and keeping in Repair, the said Harbour, and the Wharfs.... *n.p.* [*1749*], *F°*. L.

6332 A Bill for making more Effectual an Act passed in the Eleventh and Twelfth Years of the Reign of King William the Third, for the better Preserving the Navigation of the Rivers Avon and Froome; and for Cleansing, Paveing, and Enlightning the Streets of the City of Bristol ...and for Regulating Hackney-Coachmen, Halliers, Draymen, and Carters, within the said City, and Liberties thereof. *n.p.* [*1749*], *F°*. L.

6333 EDWARDS, RICHARD. Observations on the Decay of the Outfalls or Loss of the Channels of divers weak Rivers, particularly of the River Neen, otherwise Wisbeach River, and Shire-Drain, humbly offered to the Consideration of the honourable Corporation of Adventurers, and of all Gentlemen, Merchants, and others interested in the preserving the Navigation of the said River, and in draining the Lands thereto adjacent, in the great Level of the Fens called Bedford Great Level. With a Scheme to recover the said Navigation, and drain the said Lands Effectually. To which is added, the Form of a Reservoir lately invented for the scouring the Sands out of the Mouths of any weak Rivers. *Lond. 1749, 8º.* O.

6334 A Bill for preserving and improving the Navigation of the River Ouze in the County of Norfolk, by impowering the Lightermen and Bargemen navigating thereon, to hale with Horses on the Banks of the said River; and for providing a reasonable Satisfaction to the Owners of the said Banks. *n.p.* [*1749*], *Fº.* L.

6335 The Case of the Land-Owners interested in the Banks on each Side of the River Owze, in the County of Norfolk, between Stowbridge and the Port of Lynn. *n.p.* [*1749*], *Fº.* L.

Endorsed: Some Considerations on the Haling Bill on the River Owze.

6336 SHAPLEIGH, JOHN. Highways: a Treatise, shewing the Hardships, and Inconveniences of Presenting, or Indicting Parishes, Towns, &c. for not repairing the Highways. And offering several material Additions, and Amendments to the Laws now in Being, for the better, and more effectual Repairing of the same. *Lond. 1749, 8º.* LU.

2nd edn. 1750 (MP).

6337 A Bill for enlarging the Term and Powers granted by an Act passed in the Eighteenth Year of the Reign of His present Majesty, for Repairing the High Road, leading from Borough-Bridge, in the County of York, through North-Allerton, in the same County, to Croft-Bridge on the River Tees; and from thence through Darlington, in the County of Durham, to the City of Durham, and for making the same more effectual. *n.p.* [*1749*], *Fº.* L.

6338 A Bill for Continuing Two Acts of Parliament, the one passed in the Thirteenth Year of the Reign of his late Majesty King George the First, for amending the several Roads leading from the City of Bristol; and the other passed in the Fourth Year of the Reign of his present Majesty, to explain and amend the same Act; and for making the said Acts more effectual; and also for Repairing other Roads herein-mentioned. *n.p.* [*1749*], *Fº.* L.

6339 A Bill for Repairing and Widening the Road leading from the Well at the North-West End of the Town or Village of Farnborough in the County of Kent, to a Place called Riverhill, in the Parish of Sevenoakes, in the said County. *n.p.* [*1749*], *Fº.* L.

6340 A Bill for Inlarging the Term and Powers granted by an Act passed in the Third Year of the Reign of his present Majesty, for repairing the several Roads leading into the City of Hereford. *n.p.* [*1749*], *F*o. L.

6341 A Bill for Continuing, and making more Effectual, Two Acts of Parliament, one passed in the Tenth Year of the Reign of Her late Majesty Queen Anne, and the other in the Eighth Year of the Reign of His late Majesty King George the First, for Repairing the Highway between a certain Place called Kilburn Bridge in the County of Middlesex, and Sparrows Herne in the County of Hertford. *n.p.* [*1749*], *F*o. L.

6342 A Bill for Repairing and Widening the Road leading from the Town of Kingston upon Thames in the County of Surry, to a Place called Sheetbridge, near Petersfield in the County of Southampton; and also the Road from Hindhead Heath, where the Chichester Road breaks out of the Portsmouth Road, through Fernhurst Lane and Midhurst, to the City of Chichester in the County of Sussex. *n.p.* [*1749*], *F*o. L.

6343 A Bill for Repairing the Road from the West Cowgate near the Town of Newcastle upon Tyne, by or through Kenton, Pont-Eland, Higham-dykes, Newham-Edge, Belsay-Mill, and South Middleton, to the North Side of the River Wanspeck, in the County of Northumberland. *n.p.* [*1749*], *F*o. L.

6344 A Bill for repairing the Road from North-Shields in the County of Northumberland, to the Town of Newcastle upon Tyne. *n.p.* [*1749*], *F*o. L.

6345 A Bill to Continue Two Acts of Parliament, One of the First and the other of the Ninth Year of the Reign of his present Majesty, for Repairing and Enlarging the Road leading from the House called The Bells, in the Parish of Saint Margaret's, in Rochester, to Maidstone in the County of Kent; and for Repairing and Enlarging other Roads therein mentioned. *n.p.* [*1749*], *F*o. L.

6346 A Bill for Continuing and making more Effectual Two Acts of Parliament, the one passed in the Eleventh Year of the Reign of his late Majesty King George the First, and the other in the Third Year of the Reign of his present Majesty, for repairing the Roads leading from Sherbrooke-Hill near Buxton and Chapel in the Frith...through the Town of Stockport...to Manchester.... *n.p.* [*1749*], *F*o. L.

6347 A Bill for the better Repairing the Highways, and Cleansing the Streets within the Parish of Saint Leonard Shoreditch, in the County of Middlesex; and for the better Enlightening the open Places, Streets, Lanes, Passages, and Courts there; and Regulating the nightly Watch, and Bedels, within the said Parish. *n.p.* [*1749*], *F*o. L.

6348 A Bill for Opening and Making a New Road from the East End of New-Street in the Parish of Saint John, Southwark, along a Street called Saint Saviour's Dock-head...to Millpond-Bridge.... *n.p.* [*1749*], *F*o. L.

6349 A Bill for enlarging the Term and Powers granted by an Act passed in the Twentieth Year of the Reign of his present Majesty, For Repairing the High-Road leading from the Town of Stockton upon Tees, to Darlington, and from thence through Winston to Barnard-Castle in the same County, and for the effectual amending of the same. *n.p.* [*1749*], *F°*. L.

6350 A Bill for Repairing the Road leading from Wansford-Bridge in the County of Northampton, to the Town and Borough of Stamford in the County of Lincoln. *n.p.* [*1749*], *F°*. L.

6351 A Bill for inlarging the Term and Powers granted by an Act made in the Third Year of the Reign of his present Majesty, intituled, An Act for making a new Road, and for repairing and amending the antient Road, between the Towns of Wisbech and March, in the Isle of Ely, and County of Cambridge. *n.p.* [*1749*], *F°*. L.

6352 MARQUAND, CHARLES. Remarks on the Different Constructions of Bridges, and Improvements to secure their Foundations on the different Soils where they are intended to be Built.... *Lond. 1749*, *4°*. L.

6353 Observations on a Pamphlet lately published, entitled, Remarks on the different Constructions of Bridges, and Improvements to secure their Foundations, &c. by Charles Marquand. In which the Puerility of that Performance is Considered. *Lond. 1749*, *8°*. L.

6354 The Case of the Deputy Post-Masters. *n.p.* [*1749*], *F°*. L.

6355 The Case of the Innkeepers, and Keepers of Livery Stables; and also of the several Owners and Proprietors of Inns, and Livery Stables, and of Lands lett therewith. *n.p.* [*1749*], *F°*. L.
For the relaxation of the law concerning post chaises.

SOCIAL CONDITIONS

6356 WATTS, JOHN. A Black Scene open'd: being the True State of Mr. John Kendrick's Gift to the Town of Reading; and of the Decree which was made by the Barons of the Exchequer, in the Fourteenth Year of King Charles the First, in favour of the Poor of the said Town. And also of the Misapplication of the Lands and Rents ever since. *n.p. 1749*, *8°*. O.

6357 State of the Present Funds of the Charity Work-House of the City of Edinburgh; and Proposals for applying to the Legislature for an Act of Parliament, for establishing a more equal and certain Fund for the Maintenance and Support of the Begging Poor, and Out-Pensioners of the said City. *n.p.* [*1749?*], *F°*. L.

6358 Memorial for the Magistrates and Council of the City of Edinburgh, containing a short Account of the Erection of the Charity Work-house, the Reasons for applying to the Legislature, in order to procure the Establishment of a certain and equal Fund for the Maintenance and

Employment of the Poor belonging to this City and Royalty: with Answers to the Objections, against applying to Parliament for a Poors Rate. *n.p.* [*1749*], *4°*. L.

6359 Observations by the Committees of the Writers to the Signet, and of the Heritors and Housholders of Edinburgh, upon a Memorial for the Magistrates and Council, concerning the Affair of the Poors-Rate, &c. [*Edin. 1749*], *4°*. EP.

6360 Remarks for the Magistrates and Council of the City of Edinburgh, upon a Pamphlet, signed by Ten Gentlemen, entituled, Observations by the Committees of the Writers to the Signet, and of the Heretors and Householders of Edinburgh, upon a Memorial for the Magistrates and Council, concerning the Affair of the Poors Rate, &c. [*Edin. 1749*], *4°*. EP.

Signed: Jos. Williamson.

6361 Alarm to the Housholders and Heritors of the City of Edinburgh: in Copies of Proposals sent off by some in the City, for procuring an Act of Parliament, to impose a Poors-Rate thereon, and of a Letter sent by one of the said Housholders and Heritors, to a Friend at London, containing Observations upon, and Objections against, said Proposals. *Edin. 1749*, *8°*. LU.

6362 A Letter from a Gentleman in Edinburgh to a Friend at London; in relation to the Proposals for establishing by Law an equal and certain Fund, for Maintenance and Support of the Begging Poor, and Out-Pensioners of the City of Edinburgh. *n.p.* [*1749*], *F°*. L.

Another edn. [1749], 4° (L).

6363 Letter from a Gentleman in Edinburgh, to a Member of Parliament, concerning the Scheme for establishing a Poors-Rate in Edinburgh. *n.p.* [*1749*], *4°*. EP.

EP copy has a ms. attribution to William Budge.

6364 Copy of a Letter to a Member of the Town-council of Edinburgh. [*Edin. 1749*], *s. sh. F°*. EP.

A reply to the preceding.

6365 Memorial containing the Reasons for opposing (by all lawful Means) the Imposition, at this Time, of a Poors-Rate on the City of Edinburgh, by Authority of Parliament.... By a Committee of Heritors, appointed by a very numerous Meeting, held in Mary's-Chappel the 14th instant. [*Edin. 1749*], *4°*. LU.

Dated: February 20. 1749.

6366 The Mite. An Essay upon the Office of Church-Deacons, and the Duty of Charity, calculated for discovering, that the late Application by the Town-Council of Edinburgh, for a Law imposing, upon House-Holders there, a Tax (instead of the Publick Collections on the Lord's Day, &c.) for maintaining their Charity Work-House, is destructive to the said Office and Duty, &c....By a Lover of Peace and Truth. *Edin. 1749, 8°.* EP.

6367 Resolutions of his Majesty's most excellent Blue-Gowns, anent the Poor's Tax. [*Edin. 1749*], *s. sh. F°.* EP.

6368 To the K——'s most excellent M——y, and to the L—— S—— and T——, and C——, in this present P—— assembled, The most humble Petition and Address of his Majesty's most excellent Band of Pensioners, commonly called, the Blue-gowns of Scotland. [*Edin. 1749*], *F°.* EP.

Against the poors-rate.

6369 To the Trades, Heritors and Housholders of Edinburgh. [*Edin. 1749*], *s. sh. F°.* EP.

On the establishment of the workhouse.

6370 Account by A.C., Writer in Edinburgh, of his conduct in a certain Particular, concerning the Poors-Rate, – – – – occasion'd by a Letter in the Edinburgh Evening Courant. [*Edin. 1749*], *4°.* EP.

EP copy has a ms. attribution to Alexander Cunningham.

6713 A True Narrative of certain Circumstances relating to Zachariah Williams, an aged and very infirm poor Brother Pensioner, in Sutton's Royal Hospital, the Charter-House; declaring some few of the many ill Treatments, and great Sufferings, he endured; and the great Wrongs done to him, in order to his Expulsion out of the said House; and for a Pretext to deprive him of his just and appointed Rights therein.... *Lond. 1749, 8°.* L.

6372 An Account of the Hospital for the Maintenance and Education of Exposed and Deserted Young Children. In which is the Charter, Act of Parliament, By-Laws and Regulations of the said Corporation. By Order of the Governors of the said Hospital. *Lond. 1749, 8°.* L.

6373 [Stedman, John]. The History and Statutes of the Royal Infirmary of Edinburgh. *Edin. 1749, 12°.* O.

Another edn. 1778, 4°. For authorship see Edinburgh University Library Catalogue.

6374 A Bill for the more easy and speedy Recovery of small Debts, within the Town and Borough of Southwark.... *n.p.* [*1749*], *F°.* L.

6375 The Report of the Trustees, appointed by Act of Parliament, for managing the Fund raised and established for a Provision for the Widows and Children of the Ministers of the Church of Scotland, &c. to the General Assembly of the said Church.... *n.p.* [*1749*], *4°.* EU.

6376 Account of the Proceedings of the Committee of the late General Assembly, for considering what relates to the Augmentation of Ministers Stipends, at their stated Meeting the 7th of November 1749, and some subsequent Diets. *n.p.* [*1749*], *s. sh. F°.* E.

Includes 'Calculation shewing, at a Medium, the necessary annual Expence of a Minister's Family on the South-side of Forth'.

6377 The Substance of a Speech, delivered by a Right Honourable Member of the Venerable Assembly of the Church of Scotland, in the Debate upon an Application to Parliament for an Augmentation of Ministers Stipends. *n.p.* [*1749*], 4°. AU.

Reprinted in *A Collection of all the Papers published in relation to the Scheme for augmenting the Stipends of the Established Clergy in Scotland*, 1751.

6378 Information for the Visitor and Collector of the Maltmen-Calling in Glasgow, Pursuers and Respondents, against John Luke Distiller in Glasgow, Defender and Appellant. *n.p.* [*1749*], *F°*. E.

Dated: July 24. 1749. Signed: Henry Home. On Luke's refusal to contribute to the poor-box.

6379 EDINBURGH. Act of Council regulating the Time for emptying and laying down Ashes, foul Water and other Nastiness. [*Edin. 1749*], *s. sh. F°*. EU.

Dated: 12 July 1749.

6380 An Inquiry into the Right of Free Subjects; in which the Cases of the British Sailors and Common Soldiers are distinctly Consider'd and Compar'd.... *Lond. 1749*, 8°. L.

6381 To the Good People of Great Britain and Ireland. The humble Address of Daniel Dettingen, late of Gen. Sir John Ligonier's Regiment of Horse. In behalf of himself and the rest of the disbanded Soldiers and cashiered Sailors of these Kingdoms. *Dublin, 1749*, 8°. L.

6382 An Account of the Late Proceedings in Parliament, relating to the Money granted for the Relief of the City of Glasgow. With the Substance of most of the Speeches made upon that Occasion. *Lond. 1749*, 8°. E.

Glasgow had suffered in the '45, by forced loans, and in other ways.

1750

GENERAL

6383 HEATH, ROBERT. A Natural and Historical Account of the Islands of Scilly; describing their Situation, Number, Extent, Soil, Culture, Produce, Rarities, Towns, Fortifications, Trade, Manufacture, Inhabitants.... And, lastly, A general Account of Cornwall. *Lond.* *1750*, *8º*. L.

6384 The Laird and Farmer. A Dialogue upon Farming, Trade, Cookery, and their Method of Living in Scotland, balanc'd with that of England. In sixteen chapters. By a Native of the Country: who has had a high Connection with Masters and Tenants, and knows the Manner and Method of their Common People's Living, &c. *Lond.* *1750*, *8º*. L.

Another issue (C), 'by the Author of the Familiar Catechism', has the date on the title-page misprinted 1740 for 1750.

6385 MACKENZIE, MURDOCH. Orcades: or a Geographic and Hydrographic Survey of the Orkney and Lewis Islands, in Eight Maps....Also an Account of the Orknney Islands.... *Lond.* *1750*, *Fº*. EU.

6386 [MACKENZIE, JAMES]. The General Grievances and Oppression of the Isles of Orkney and Shetland.... *Edin.* *1750*, *8º*. E.

Another edition, with author's name, 1836.

6387 POEKRICH, RICHARD. A Letter to a Member of Parliament, complaining of some Public Grievances, relating to the Kingdom in general, and this City in Particular. With Proper Schemes for redressing them. By a Lover of his Country. *Dublin*, *1750*, *8º*. DA.

Signed: Richard Poekrich.

6388 [PERCEVAL, JOHN, 2nd Earl of Egmont ?]. A Representation of the State of the Trade of Ireland, laid before the House of Lords of England, on Tuesday the 10th of April, 1750, on Occasion of a Bill before that House, for laying a Duty on Irish Sail Cloth imported into Great-Britain. *Dublin*, *1750*, *8º*. DA.

2nd edn. 1750 (C); 3rd edn. 1755 (C). One copy in DA has a ms. note 'said to be written by Lord Egmont'. A copy in C has this same attribution in a modern hand.

6389 A Copy of His Majesty's Royal Charter for Incorporating the Dublin-Society. Dated the Second Day of April, 1750. *Dublin*, *1750*, *8º*. DA.

6390 A List of the Members of the Dublin-Society Named in the Charter. Also of the Members Elected since the opening of the Charter. *Dublin*, *1750*, *8º*. C.

6391 SMITH, CHARLES. The Antient and Present State of the County and City of Cork...To which are added, Curious Notes and Observations, relating to the erecting and improvement of several Arts and Manufactures, either neglected or ill prosecuted in this County. Embellished with new and correct Maps.... *Dublin*, *1750*, *8º*. L.

New edn. Cork, 1893, 94, ed. by R. Day and W. A. Copinger.

AGRICULTURE

6392 ELLIS, WILLIAM. The Modern Husbandman, complete in eight volumes. Containing I. The Practice of Farming...for every Month in the Year. II. The Timber and Fruit-Tree improved....III. Agriculture improved, or, the Practice of Husbandry displayed....IV. Chiltern and Vale Farming explained.... *Lond.* *1750*, *8o*. L.

6393 TEMPLE, WILLIAM. A Refutation of one of the Principal Arguments in the Rev. Mr Smith's Memoirs of Wool; both from Matters of Fact, and his own Assertions. *Lond.* *1750*, *8o*. O.

On the comparative price and quality of English and foreign wool.

6394 SMITH, JOHN. The Case of the English Farmer, and his Landlord. In Answer to Mr. Temple's (pretended) Refutation of one of the principal Arguments in Memoirs of Wool. By the Author of those Memoirs. *Lincoln*, [*1750*], *8o*. L.

The dedication signed: John Smith. Defending his account of the comparative prices of English and foreign wool.

6395 ELLIS, WILLIAM. The Country Housewife's Family-Companion: or Profitable Directions for whatever relates to the Management and good Œconomy of the Domestick Concerns of a Country Life, according to the Present Practice, of the Country Gentleman's, the Yeoman's, the Farmer's, &c. Wives, in the Counties of Hertford, Bucks, and other Parts of England.... *Lond.* *1750*, *8o*. O.

6396 Rules and Directions for raising Flax and Hemp in Scotland, after the Flanders and other approved Methods. [*Edin.* *1750*], *8o*. L.

Published by the Commissioners and Trustees for improving Fisheries and Manufactures in Scotland.

6397 PULLEIN, SAMUEL, Some Hints intended to Promote the Culture of Silk-worms in Ireland. Addressed to the Dublin Society. *Dublin*, *1750*, *8o*. DA.

6398 Observations on the Regulations which have been made for Preventing the Spreading of the Distemper among the Cattle. *n.p.* [*1750?*], *Fo*. LU.

6399 Thoughts on the Present Laws for Preserving the Game. And some Methods proposed for making a Game Law, both Useful and Effectual. *Lond.* *1750*, *8o*. O.

6400 An Act for Confirming Articles of Agreement for Inclosing and Dividing the Commons, and Waste Grounds, within the Manor of Culcheth, in the County of Lancaster. *n.p.* [*1750*], *Fo*. L.

6401 An Act for Inclosing and Dividing certain Common Fields and Common Grounds called Nether Heyford Common Fields, lying and being in the Parishes of Nether Heyford, Stow with Nine Churches, and Bugbrooke, in the County of Northampton; and for Extinguishing all

Right of Common in certain Meadows, Pastures, and Inclosed Grounds in the said Parishes; and providing a Recompence to the Rectors of the said Parishes in lieu of Tythes. *n.p.* [*1750*], *F°*. L.

6402 A Bill for Better Securing the Property of the Owners of Mines from Theft and Robbery. *n.p.* [*1750*], *F°*. L.

6403 LINDEN, DIEDERICK WESSEL. Three Letters on Mining and Smelting; in which a Method is laid down, whereby these useful Sciences may be greatly Improved. To which is added, a Fourth Letter; setting forth, a Discovery of an easy Method to secure Ships Bottoms from Worms.... *Lond. 1750, 8°*. L.

6404 A Proposal, for Raising a Fund of 150,000 l. to encourage the Tinners in Cornwall and Devonshire, and for the better Carrying on, and Improving the Tin Trade in General. *n.p.* [*1750*], *s. sh. F°*. O.

6405 A Bill for the Encouragement of the British White Herring and Cod Fisheries. *n.p.* [*1750*], *F°*. L.

Another edn., n.d. 8°, entitled A Bill intituled An Act for the Encouragement of the British White Herring Fishery (LU).

6406 COLE, THOMAS. A Short Narrative of the Proceedings, of the Society appointed to Manage the British White Herring Fishery, established by Act of Parliament. Shewing the Names of the Managers; the Course of the several Shoals of Herrings; the prime Cost; the Method of Catching, Curing, and Packing; what the same sell for at foreign Markets; the Bulk and Dimensions of the Herring Busses and Yaugers, &c. With Seasonable Hints for improving and extending the British White Herring Fishery, on the Coast of Wales.... *Lond. 1750, 8°*. LU.

6407 The best and most approved Method of curing White-Herrings, and all Kinds of White-Fish....By a Trader in Fish. *Lond. 1750, 8°*. L.

6408 England's Path to Wealth and Honour; in a Dialogue between an Englishmand and a Dutchman. To which is added, Articles relating to the Dutch Herring-Fishery. *Lond. 1750, 8°*. L.

6409 [CAMPBELL, JOHN]. An Exact and Authentic Account of the Greatest White-Herring-Fishery in Scotland, carried on yearly in the Island of Zetland, by the Dutch only....And a Method laid down, whereby we may easily engross that Trade into our own Hands....By a Gentleman who resided Five Years on the Island. *Lond. 1750, 8°*. L.

Another edn., with author's name, Edin. 1885 (L).

6410 The Fisheries Revived: or, Britain's Hidden Treasure Discovered. Proving, that not only our future Wealth, but Security, will depend upon that inestimable Trade.... *Lond. 1750, 8°*. LU.

6411 His Majesty's Royal Charter, granted on the Eleventh Day of October, 1750...for incorporating the Society of the Free British Fishery, with

Power to make By-Laws, &c. for the Improvement of the British White Herring Fisheries, and better Regulation of the Trade thereof; and for preventing Frauds and Impositions in the Management of the same. *Lond. 1750*, *8°*. LU.

6412 Plans and Proposals transmitted to the Committee on the British Fishery. By Several Hands. *Lond. 1750*, *8°*. LU.

6413 Reasons in support of the Act for the Encouragement of the British White Herring Fishery. *n.p.* [*1750?*], *s. sh. F°*. LLI.

6414 Some Considerations on the British Fisheries. With a Proposal for establishing a General Fishery, on the Coasts of Ireland, Addressed to the Rt. Honourable the Lord ——. *Dublin, 1750*, *8°*. L.

6415 [Lockman, John]. The Vast Importance of the Herring Fishery, &c. to these Kingdoms: as respecting the National Wealth, our Naval Strength, and the Highlanders. In Three Letters, addressed to a Member of Parliament. *Lond.* [*1750*], *8°*. LU.

2nd edn., with dedication signed with author's name, 1750 (LU).

MANUFACTURES

6416 London. The Report of the Committee appointed to Examine the Petitions of the Masters and Journeymen Freemen. To the Right Honourable the Lord Mayor Aldermen, and Commons, of the City of London, in Common-Council assembled. *n.p.* [*1750*], *F°*. LCRO.

On the employment of non-freemen. Dated: 20 May 1750.

6417 The Privileges of the Free-Artificers of the City of London, defended; in an Appeal to the Committee appointed to receive the Complaints of the Masters of the several Manufactures in this City, against their Journeymen. *Lond.* [*1750*], *8°*. O.

6418 Morris, Robert. Rural Architecture: consisting of Regular Designs of Plans and Elevations for the Buildings in the Country.... *Lond. 1750*, *4°*. L.

6419 Langley, Batty. The Workman's Golden Rule for Drawing and Working the Five Orders in Architecture.... *Lond. 1750*, *16°*. L.

6420 Jeffries, David. A Treatise on Diamonds and Pearls. In which their Importance is considered: and Plain Rules are exhibited for ascertaining the Value of both: and the True Method of manufacturing Diamonds. *Lond. 1750*, *8°*. LU.

6421 An Act for securing the sole Property, Benefit, and Advantage, of an Engine invented by Israel Pownoll, Deceased, for raising Ballast, Sullage, and Sand; and for removing Banks, Shelves, and Shoals, in Rivers and Harbours; to the Children of the said Israel Pownoll, for a certain Term of Years. *n.p.* [*1750*], *F°*. L.

6422 The Iron-Trade of Great-Britain Impartially Considered. *n.p.* [*c. 1750 ?*], *F°*. MP.

6423 The State of the Trade and Manufactory of Iron in Great-Britain considered. *n.p. 1750*, *8°*. L.

An abridgement of *The Interest of Great Britain, in Supplying Herself with Iron*, [*c.* 1747] (no. 6055).

6424 The Case of the British Linen-Manufacturers. *n.p.* [*1750 ?*], *F°*. L.

6425 A complete collection of the acts of Parliament, allowing, and relating to the bounties payable on the exportation of british and irish linens: with an abstract, shewing...the species of linen intitled to bounty, & the bounty payable thereon. *Edin. 1750*, *8°*. Kress 5021.

6426 State of facts relating to the linen-manufacture of Great Britain and Ireland. *n.p.* [*1750 ?*], *35½ cm*. Kress 5082.

6427 Observations on a Paper called The State of Facts relating to the Linen Manufacture of Great Britain and Ireland. *n.p.* [*1750 ?*], *F°*. L.

6428 RAMSAY, DAVID. The Weaver and Housewife's Pocket-book; containing Rules for the right Making of Linen Cloth.... *Edin. 1750*, *8°*. LU.

6429 The Case of the Linen Manufacture of Ireland, relative to the Bleaching and the Whitening of the same. Humbly offered and submitted, to the Wisdom and Consideration of the Right Honourable, and Honourable the Trustees thereof. *n.p.* [*c. 1750*], *F°*. DM.

Endorsed: A State of the Case in Relation to the Rolling Boards made use of in the Linen Manufacture of Ireland.

6430 Premiums given by the Linen Board of Ireland for the Encouragement of that Manufactory. *n.p.* [*1750 ?*], *F°*. L.

Title from endorsement.

6431 State of the mutual Processes betwixt John Bird late of London, Potter, and Robert Dinwiddie Merchant in London, Laurence Dinwiddie and Patrick Nisbet Merchants in Glasgow, and Robert Finlay Tanner there. *n.p.* [*1750*], *4°*. E.

Dated: November 1. 1750. Signed: Pat. Boyle. On the Glasgow earthenware factory, with comparisons with English factories.

6432 YAPP, B. The Shoemaker's Case, with their Appeal unto Caesar, and both Houses of Parliament, for an Act to prevent the Exportation of Unwrought Leather; and to take of the Drawback. Together, with a Letter to Sir John Strange, Knt., Master of the Rolls. *Lond. 1750*, *8°*. CP.

6433 Henry Cottingham, Mercer, to the Silk-Weavers of the City of Dublin. *n.p.* [*c. 1750 ?*], *F°*. C.

He only imports pieces from Lyons to obtain the patterns.

COMMERCE

6434 [Perry, William]. A Treatise on Trade: or, the Antiquity and Honour of Commerce. Shewing how Trade was esteemed by the Egyptians, Jews, Greeks and Romans, and on what Footing of Worship it stands with us. Addressed to the Country-Gentlemen of England. *Lond. 1750, 8°.* LU.

For authorship see H. & L. quoting H. B. Wheatley as authority.

6435 A Letter from Hugh Boyd, Esq; of Ballycastle, to a Member of Parliament, on the late Scarcity of Coals in the City of Dublin. *Dublin, 1749–50, 8°.* L.

On the lack of storage facilities and the difficulties of transport from England and Scotland.

6436 Reynardson, Samuel. A State of the English Weights and Measures of Capacity, as well antient as modern; with some Considerations thereon: being an Attempt to prove, that the present Avoirdepois Weight is the legal and ancient Standard for the Weights and Measures of this Kingdom. *Lond. 1750, 4°.* LU.

6437 Case of British Merchants, Owners of Ships, and others, relative to the Employment and Increase of British Shipping, and British Navigators. *n.p. [1750], F°.* L.

Endorsed: A Case for the Employment and Increase of British Shipping, and British Navigators. Contains 'An Account of all the Foreign Shipping which have Enter'd in at the several Ports of England...for two several Years ending at Christmas 1743 and 1747, and one Year ending Lady-day 1749'. Wants to limit the exportation of drawback and bounty goods to British shipping only.

6438 An Answer to the Remarks published in the Daily Advertiser, on a Case for the Employment and Increase of British Shipping, and British Navigators. *n.p. [1750], s. sh. F°.* L.

With the text of the *Remarks*, 'Taken from the General Advertiser, February 5, 1749–50.'

6439 Postlethwayt, Malachy. The Merchants' Public Counting-House: or New Mercantile Institution: wherein is shewn, the Necessity of young Merchants being bred to Trade with greater Advantages than they usually are. With a practicable Plan for that Purpose.... *Lond. 1750, 4°.* L.

2nd edn., with a supplement, 1751 (LU).

6440 Translation of the King of Sardinia's Edict, of Grants, Favours, and Privileges, for a Free Port in the Roads of Nizza, and Saint Ospizio, and the Port of Villa Franca. The 12th of March, 1749. *Lond. 1750, F°.* E.

6441 The Case of the Russia Merchants. *n.p. [1750], s. sh. F°.* L.

For a bill to permit them to import Persian silk via Russia.

6442 A Bill, intituled, An Act for permitting Raw Silk of the Growth or Produce of Persia, purchased in Russia, to be imported into this

Kingdom from any Port or Place belonging to the Empire of Russia. *n.p.* [*1750*], *F°*. L.

6443 Reasons humbly offered against Passing the Bill, intituled, An Act for permitting Raw-Silk of the Growth or Produce of Persia, purchased in Russia, to be imported into this Kingdom from any Port or Place belonging to the Empire of Russia. *n.p.* [*1750*], *F°*. L.

6444 Reasons humbly offered by the Silk Manufacturers of Great Britain, in favour of the Bill for Importing Persia Raw-Silk from Russia. *n.p.* [*1750*], *F°*. L.

6445 Observations on the Silk Manufacturers Reasons in Favour of the Russia Bill. Humbly Offered. *n.p.* [*1750*], *F°*. L.

6446 Proposals for Preserving, Extending and Protecting, the British Trade in Africa. *n.p.* [*1750 ?*], *F°*. L.

6447 Reasons in Support of the Proposals for Preserving, Extending, and Protecting, the British Trade in Africa. *n.p.* [*1750 ?*], *F°*. L.

6448 A Bill for Extending and Improving the Trade to Africa. *n.p.* [*1750*], *F°*. pp. 15. L.

6449 Papers laid before the Honourable House of Commons by the Commissioners for Trade and Plantations, pursuant to an Address of the House of Lords to his Majesty, the 8th of June 1749. For the better Securing, Improving, and Extending, the Trade to Africa. *Lond.* *1750*, *F°*. L.

6450 An Account of the several Forts and Settlements on the Gold Coast, and at Whydah, in Africa; shewing to whom they belong, and their Differences from each other; with Observations and Queries concerning a proposed Regulated Company. *n.p.* [*1750 ?*], *F°*. L.

6451 Remarks on a Paper, intituled, Reasons why the City of London should nominate a Majority of the Committee of Direction for the Trade to Africa. *n.p.* [*1750 ?*], *s. sh. F°*. LLI.

6452 A Short View of the Dispute between the Merchants of London, Bristol, and Leverpool and the Advocates of a New Joint-Stock Company, concerning the Regulation of the African Trade. *Lond.* *1750*, *4°*. LU.

6453 Remarks on a Pamphlet, intituled, A Short View of a Dispute between the Merchants of London, Bristol, and Liverpool, and the Advocates of a Joint-Stock Company, concerning the Regulation of the African Trade. In a Letter to a Member of Parliament. *Lond.* *1750*, *4°*. M.

6454 A Bill, intituled, An Act to encourage the Importation of Pig and Bar Iron from His Majesty's Colonies in America; and to prevent the Erection of any Mill or other Engine for Slitting or Rolling of Iron; or any Plating Forge to work with a Tilt Hammer; or any Furnace for making Steel in any of the said Colonies. *n.p.* [*1750*], *F°*. L.

6455 Considerations on the Bill now depending before the Honourable House of Commons, for Encouraging the Importation of Pig and Bar Iron from America, &c. *n.p.* [*1750*], *F°*. L.

Endorsed: The Case of the English, American, and Swedish Iron, considered

6456 National Considerations upon Importing Iron in Bars from America, &c. *n.p.* [*1750?*], *s. sh. F°*. L.

6457 Reasons for the present Application to Parliament for Liberty to import Salt from any Part of Europe directly into his Majesty's Colonies in America. *n.p.* [*1750*], *F°*. L.

6458 ELLIS, HENRY. Considerations on the Great Advantages that would arise from the Discovery of the North West Passage, and a clear Account of the most Practicable Method for Attempting that Discovery. *London, 1750, 4°*. T.

6459 Journal or Narrative of the Boscawen's Voyage to Bombay in the East-Indies, Benjamin Braund, Commander....Anno 1749. By a Young Gentleman, Passenger on Board....To which are added, Two Letters sign'd Philalethes, address'd to, and return'd from the Remembrancer. ...Also Some Occasional Thoughts on Freedom in Trade, High Duties, Smuggling, Shipwrecks, &c. as spoken to a Society for Free Enquiry, November 1747. By Philalethes, a Member thereof. *Lond 1750, 8°*. L.

The letters of Philalethes are about the East India Company. 2nd edn. 1751 (O).

6460 A Letter to a Proprietor of the East-India Company. *Lond. 1750, 8°*. LU.

6461 [DRAPER,]. A Speech intended to have been made at a General Court of the Proprietors of East-India Stock, held at their House in Leadenhall-street, on Wednesday, the 21st Day of March, 1750. By a Proprietor. *Lond.* [*1750*], *8°*. LU.

The advertisement signed: Orient. LU copy has a ms. note on the last page which mentions 'Orient alias Mr. Draper'.

COLONIES

6462 A Short View of the Encroachments of France in America; and of the British Commerce with Spain. *Lond. 1750, 8°*. L.

6463 Massachusetts in Agony: or, Important Hints to the Inhabitants of the Province: calling aloud for Justice to be done to the Oppressed; and to avert the Impending Wrath over the Oppressors. By Vincent Centinel. *Boston, 1750, 8°*.

Reprinted in *Colonial Currency Reprints*, ed. by A. M. Davis, vol. 4 (1911), whence this entry is taken.

6464 Some Observations relating to the Present Circumstances of the Province of the Massachusetts-Bay; humbly offered to the Consideration of the General Assembly. *Boston, 1750, 4°*. L.

Reprinted in *Colonial Currency Reprints* ed. by A. M. Davis, vol. 4 (1911).

6465 A Genuine Account of Nova Scotia: containing, a Description of its Situation, Air, Climate, Soil and its Produce; also Rivers, Bays, Harbours, and Fish, with which they abound in very great Plenty. To which is added, His Majesty's Proposals, as an Encouragement to those who are willing to settle there. *Lond. printed, Dublin reprinted, 1750*, *8°*. L.

6466 [MARTIN, SAMUEL]. An Essay upon Plantership, humbly inscribed to all the Planters of the British Sugar-Colonies in America. The second edition, corrected and enlarged. By an Old Planter. *Antigua, 1750*, *8°*. L.

The dedication signed: Agricola Antegonianus; 4th edn., with author's name, 1765 (L); 5th 1773 (L); 7th 1785 (L).

6467 HUGHES, GRIFFITH. The Natural History of Barbadoes. In ten books. *Lond. 1750*, *F°*. L.

FINANCE

6468 HOOKE, ANDREW. An Essay on the National Debt, and National Capital: or, The Accompt truly stated, Debitor and Creditor. Wherein is shewn, that the Former is but a diminutive Part of the Latter; and a practicable Scheme exhibited, whereby the whole may, with great Facility, be paid off, at once, exclusive of the Aid of the Sinking Fund, and without any Diminution of the present Revenues of the Crown, or annual Expences of the People. *Lond. 1750*, *8°*. L.

2nd edn. 1751 (L).

6469 [MASSIE, JOSEPH]. An Essay on the Governing Causes of the Natural Rate of Interest; wherein the Sentiments of Sir William Petty and Mr. Locke, on that Head, are considered. *Lond. 1750*, *8°*. LU.

Another edn., with author's name, ed. by J. H. Hollander, Baltimore, 1912.

6470 [BARNARD, Sir JOHN]. Considerations on the Proposal for Reducing the Interest on the National Debt. *Lond. 1750*, *8°*. L.

2nd edn. 1750 (M (Cr)). Both the L and O copies have manuscript attributions of authorship.

6471 Annotations on a Late Pamphlet intituled, Considerations on the Proposal for reducing the Interest on the National Debt. *Lond. 1750*, *8°*. L.

6472 Considerations on the Proposal for the Reduction of Interest, so far as it relates to the East-India Company, and on the Question to be Ballotted for, at the East-India House, on Wednesday next, the 3rd of January [1750]: with some Remarks on what past at the two General-Courts on the Subject.... *Lond.* [*1750?*], *8°*. LU.

Dated: December 30, 1749.

6473 A Copy of a Letter wrote to a Member of Parliament, after the Proposals for reducing the Publick Debt were rejected at the last General Court of the Bank of England; wherein is inserted, A Copy of the Preamble to the Act of the 9th of Queen Anne, for Reducing the Interest of Money from 6 to 5 per Cent. Very proper to be consider'd by all Landed Gentlemen, Merchants and Traders, especially such as are Members of the House of Commons. *Lond. 1750*, 8°. LU.

6474 The Necessity of Lowering Interest and Continuing Taxes, demonstrated. In a letter to G.B. *Lond. 1750*, 8°. L.

6475 The Case of the Officers and Seamen of the Prince Frederick and Duke Private Ships of War, who took the Two Rich French Prizes called the Lewis Erasmus and Marquis d'Antin. *n.p.* [*1750?*], *F*°. L.

For prize money.

6476 Ductor Mercatorius: or, the Young Merchant's Instructor with respect to the Customs: being a minute and particular Detail of the Regular Method of Proceeding at Out-Port Custom-Houses in the several Branches of Marine Commerce....By the late Deputy-Comptroller of the Customs at Sunderland. *Newcastle upon Tyne, 1750*, 8°. LU.

6477 The Placeman's Estimate: In a Letter from a Member of Parliament to his Brother. To which is added, His Brother's Answer. *London printed, Dublin, re-printed, 1750*, 8°. O.

6478 A Conversation between a Blacksmith and a Merchant, upon the Subject of passing Guineas by Weight only. *Dublin, 1750*, 8°. L.

6479 A List of the Names of all such Proprietors of the Bank of England, who are Qualified to Vote at the Ensuing Election...March 25th, 1750. *Lond. 1750*, *F*°. LU.

6480 Proposals from the Sun Fire-Office, near the Royal Exchange, for Insuring Houses, and other Buildings, Goods, Wares and Merchandize, from Loss and Damage by Fire. *Lond.* [*1750*], *s. sh. F*°. OUP.

Dated: May 25, 1750.

TRANSPORT

6481 At Edinburgh, the 6th Day of June, One thousand seven hundred and fifty Years. [*Edin. 1750*], *s. sh. F*°. ECA.

An Act of Council prohibiting carters from carrying off and selling as ballast the stones on the shore at Leith which served as breakwaters.

6482 Reasons for passing the Bill for the more effectual Repairing and Preserving the Piers and Harbour of Whitby in the County of York. *n.p.* [*1750*], *F*°. L.

6483 [Newball, John]. Proposals to preserve the Publick Roads, without Prejudice to Trade, Excess of Tolls or Turnpikes. Also a brief Discourse, shewing that Inland Trade is the chief Support of Societies, consequently the Support of the Nation; that the present Run of

Post-Chaises tends greatly to the Ruin of Both; and that unequal Taxes, and unequal Privileges, are oft attended with pernicious Consequences....By Phil' Anglus. *Lond. 1750, 8°.* O.

Title-page advertises other books issued under Newball's name. Table of contents of the O tract volume in which this occurs gives Newball as author.

6484 A Bill for Repairing the Road leading from Westwood-Gate in the Parish of Knotting in the County of Bedford over Ditchford-Bridge, through the Towns of Kettering and Rothwell in the County of Northampton, to the Town of Market-Harborough in the County of Leicester. *n.p.* [*1750*], *F°*. L.

SOCIAL CONDITIONS

6485 Sessions Cases adjudged in the Court of King's Bench, chiefly touching Settlements, from the latter End of Queen Ann's Reign to the present Time.... *In the Savoy, 1750, 8°*. L.

6486 The Present State, of the Charitable Infirmary of Corke for the Year 1750. *Corke, 1750, 4°*. DNL.

6487 A Dissertation on Credit. *n.p.* [*c. 1750?*], *F°*. L.

On imprisonment for debt.

6488 The Junior's Precedence: illustrated in a New Impression of Two Acts of Parliament made in Ireland, for the Recovery of Small Debts, and in an Abstract of divers Acts, appointing a Public Register in Dublin, for Deeds, Wills, &c. affecting Lands and Tenements, in that Kingdom. To which is added, An Explanation of the Utility and Practice thereof; Wherein the Necessity of extending the like Benefit to South-Britain, is considered. With an Appendix; shewing the Necessity of Courts of Conscience.... *Lond. 1750, 8°*. O.

6489 London. A Bill to explain and amend two several Acts of Common-Council, the one passed the fifteenth Day of April, One thousand six hundred and six, and the other the Fourth Day of July One thousand seven hundred and twelve, concerning Foreigners. *n.p.* [*1750?*], *F°*. L.

6490 London. Cokayne, Mayor. A Common-Council holden in the Chamber of the Guildhall of the City of London, on Thursday the 22d Day of November 1750....An Act to explain and amend two several Acts of Common-Council, the one passed the Fifteenth Day of April, One thousand six hundred and six, and the other the Fourth Day of July One thousand seven hundred and twelve, concerning Foreigners. [*Lond.*] *1750, F°*. LG.

6491 The State and Case of the Native Servants. Most Humbly offered to the Consideration of the Publick. *Dublin, 1750, s. sh. F°*. L.

For a tax on foreign servants.

6492 A Brief History of the Protestant Episcopal Church, known by the Name of Unitas Fratrum, or United Brethren. Together with the Reasons for and against the Privileges granted them in the British Dominions in the Year 1749; so as they are inserted in the Months of April and May of the Universal Magazine. *Dublin*, *1750*, *8°*. L.

6493 To the Venerable Assembly of the Church of Scotland, to meet at Edinburgh the 10th Day of May 1750, the Report of the Committee appointed by the last General Assembly to have under Consideration what concerns the Augmentation of Ministers Stipends. *n.p.* [*1750*], *8°*. O.

6494 STEEL, WILLIAM. Memorial shewing the Reasonableness and Necessity of an immediate Application to the King and Parliament for augmenting the small Stipends in Scotland. *Edin.* *1750*, *8°*. O.

2nd edn., revised and enlarged, 1750 (EU). Reprinted in *A Collection of all the Papers published in relation to the Scheme for Augmenting the Stipends of the Established Clergy of Scotland*, 1751.

6495 A Letter to a Clergyman, concerning the Augmentation of Stipends. *Edin.* *1750*, *8°*. E.

Reprinted in *A Collection of all the Papers published in relation to the Scheme for Augmenting the Stipends of the Established Clergy in Scotland*, 1751.

6496 SHORT, THOMAS. New Observations, Natural, Moral, Civil, Political, and Medical, on City, Town, and Country Bills of Mortality. To which are added, Large and Clear Abstracts of the best Authors who have wrote on that Subject. With an Appendix on the Weather and Meteors. *Lond.* *1750*, *8°*. L.

6497 A Letter from a Gentleman in Town to his Friend in the Country, recommending the Necessity of Frugality. *Lond.* *1750*, *8°*. LU.

ADDENDA

A1 Mièɢᴇ, Gᴜʏ. The New State of England, under Our Present Monarch K. William III. In Three Parts. Containing, I. A General Account of England.... II. Of the Original, Temper, Genius, Language, Trade, Religion and Government of the English.... III. A Description of the High Court of Parliament, Privy Council, and all Courts of Judicature. And a more Exact List of the present Officers, in Church and State. The Fourth Edition, with great Improvements. Lond. 1701, 8°. LU.

A reissue 'with a supplement of the New Establishment, 1702; 5th edn. 1703; 6th edn. 1707 (all O). Continued as: *The Present State of Great Britain*, 1707; 2nd edn., entitled *The Present state of Great Britain and Ireland*, 1711; 3rd edn. 1715; 4th 1718; 5th 1723 (all O); 6th 1728 (LIHR); 7th 1731 (L); 8th 1738 (O); 9th 1742 (LIHR); 10th, revised by S. Bolton, 1745; 11th MDCCLIVIII [1748] (both O).

A2 The Case of the Manufacturers of, and Dealers in Silk Goods, under the New Projected Duty. *n.p.* [*1712*], *s sh. F°*. O.

A3 By the King, A Proclamation, For Allowing the Importation of Swedish Iron from all Places other than from the Dominions of the King of Sweden. *Lond. 1717*, *s sh. F°*. L.

Dated: 13 February 1717 [o.s.].

A4 The Case of the Guardians for and on the Behalf of Mrs. Arabella Pershall, an Infant . . . against a Bill, brought into the Right Honourable the House of Lords, this present Session, For the Inclosing of a Common, called Gratwood-Heath . . . *n.p.* [*1720*], *s. sh. F°*. O.

Endorsed: The Case of Mrs. Arabella Pershall, (by her Guardians,) against the Bill, For Inclosing Gratwood-Heath. To be Heard on Saturday the 16th of January, 1719 [o.s.].

A5 Considerations on the Unhappy Accidents that attended the last Undertaker in his Works at Dagenham Breach. With Remarks on the Excuses made Use of to screen the Deficiency of the Workmanship, in a Treatise, entitled, An Account of the Stopping Dagenham Breach, &c. And also, Reasons to prove, that the proper Rules for stopping Breaches, or performing any the like Works, contain'd therein, and the Proposal for rendering the Port of Dublin more commodious, are not the only and the best in the World... By a Gentleman who was concern'd. *Lond.*, *1723*, *8°*. O.

An Account is no. 3112.

A6 Sept. 6. 1729. Assisa Panis. [*Cambridge*, *1729*], *s. sh. obl. 8°*. CUA.

A7 Reasons Humbly Offered to the Consideration of the Honourable House of Commons, for Encouraging the Distilling of British Spirits. *n.p.* [*1733?*], *s. sh. F°*. O.

ADDENDA

A8 A Bill for making effectual such Agreement as shall be made between the Charitable Corporation for Relief of industrious Poor, by assisting them with small Sums upon Pledges at legal Interest, and their Creditors. *n.p.* [*1733*], *F°*. O.

A9 Reasons humbly offer'd for Relief of the Charitable Corporation, &c. *n.p.* [*1733?*], *F°*. O.

Title in 5 lines. Another edn. with title in 2 lines, and without 'Remarks upon several foreign Lotteries', [1733 ?], *s. sh. F°* (O).

A10 A Bill for erecting Piers in, and for Repairing and keeping in Repair, the Harbour of Little-Hampton, called Arundell-Port, in the County of Sussex. *n.p.* [*1733*], *F°*. O.

A11 A Bill for the better Regulation of Lastage and Ballastage in the River Thames. *n.p.* [*1733*], *F°*. O.

A12 Reasons humbly offered by the Merchants and Traders of the City of London, in favour of a Bill Intitled, An Act to prevent the removing of Suits out of the Courts of Record, of any City or Town-Corporate within that part of Great-Britain, called England, where the Matters in demand do not exceed a Sum to be limited in the Bill, so far as it relates to the Courts of Record within the said City of London. *n.p.* [*1733*], *s. sh. F°*. O.

A13 BROOKS, RICHARD. Observations on Milling Broad and Narrow Cloth, &c. Shewing I. The many destructive Errors that attend the common Method of Milling, and Reading or Tighting of Cloth, durings its Milling. And, II. The many Advantages that accrue, instead thereof, from the Use of a new Instrument, called a Regulator. To which is annexed, A Certificate signed by several of the most eminent Clothiers in the Superfine Trade. *Lond. 1743*, *8°*. O.

A14 The Assize of Bread. Set April 19. 1737. [*Cambridge, 1737*], *s. sh. obl. 8°*. CUA.

A15 LEADBETTER, CHARLES. The Royal Gauger; or, Gauging made Easy, as it is actually practised by the Officers of his Majesty's Revenue of Excise. In Two Parts. Part I. Containing the practical Methods of finding the Area's and Contents of such Superficies and Solids, as are the Foundation of Gauging. . . . Part II. Shewing the necessary Steps to be taken for obtaining Employment in the Excise . . . Together with such Directions for the Officer's Conduct as are necessary for ascertaining and securing the respective Duties, to which the following Professions are liable. 1. Victuallers, 2. By-Brewers, 3. Common-Brewers, 4. Maltsters, 5. Malt Compounders, 6. Dealers in Cyder, 7. Wine Importers, 8. Distillers, 9. Tanners, 10. Tawers, 11. Oil Dressers, 12. Sope-makers, 13. Chandlers, 14. Starch-makers, 15. Paper-makers, 16. Hop-Planters. . . . *Lond. 1739*, *8°*. L.

A16 The Case of John Gibson, Late of London, Coal-Factor. *n.p.* [*1750*]. *F°*. L.

Arrested for money owed for customs duties.

INDEX OF TITLES

An asterisk indicates that there is an entry at this point in the Addenda to the Indexes on p. 978.

INDEX OF TITLES

INDEX OF TITLES

INDEX OF TITLES

INDEX OF TITLES

INDEX OF TITLES

INDEX OF TITLES

INDEX OF TITLES

INDEX OF TITLES

INDEX OF TITLES

INDEX OF TITLES

INDEX OF TITLES

INDEX OF TITLES

INDEX OF TITLES

INDEX OF TITLES

INDEX OF TITLES

INDEX OF TITLES

INDEX OF TITLES

INDEX OF TITLES

INDEX OF TITLES

INDEX OF TITLES

INDEX OF TITLES

INDEX OF TITLES

INDEX OF TITLES

INDEX OF TITLES

INDEX OF TITLES

INDEX OF TITLES

INDEX OF TITLES

INDEX OF TITLES

INDEX OF TITLES

INDEX OF TITLES

INDEX OF TITLES

INDEX OF TITLES

INDEX OF TITLES

INDEX OF TITLES

INDEX OF TITLES

INDEX OF TITLES

INDEX OF TITLES

INDEX OF TITLES

INDEX OF TITLES

INDEX OF TITLES

INDEX OF TITLES

INDEX OF TITLES

INDEX OF TITLES

INDEX OF TITLES

INDEX OF TITLES

INDEX OF TITLES

INDEX OF TITLES

INDEX OF TITLES

INDEX OF TITLES

INDEX OF TITLES

INDEX OF TITLES

INDEX OF TITLES

INDEX OF TITLES

INDEX OF TITLES

INDEX OF TITLES

INDEX OF TITLES

INDEX OF TITLES

INDEX OF TITLES

INDEX OF TITLES

INDEX OF TITLES

INDEX OF TITLES

INDEX OF TITLES

INDEX OF TITLES

INDEX OF TITLES

INDEX OF TITLES

INDEX OF TITLES

INDEX OF TITLES

INDEX OF TITLES

INDEX OF TITLES

INDEX OF TITLES

INDEX OF TITLES

INDEX OF TITLES

INDEX OF TITLES

INDEX OF TITLES

INDEX OF TITLES

INDEX OF TITLES

INDEX OF TITLES

INDEX OF TITLES

INDEX OF TITLES

INDEX OF TITLES

INDEX OF TITLES

INDEX OF TITLES

INDEX OF TITLES

INDEX OF TITLES

INDEX OF TITLES

INDEX OF TITLES

INDEX OF TITLES

INDEX OF TITLES

INDEX OF TITLES

INDEX OF TITLES

INDEX OF TITLES

INDEX OF TITLES

INDEX OF TITLES

INDEX OF TITLES

INDEX OF TITLES

INDEX OF TITLES

INDEX OF TITLES

INDEX OF TITLES

INDEX OF TITLES

INDEX OF TITLES

INDEX OF TITLES

INDEX OF TITLES

INDEX OF TITLES

INDEX OF TITLES

INDEX OF TITLES

INDEX OF TITLES

INDEX OF TITLES

INDEX OF TITLES

INDEX OF TITLES

INDEX OF TITLES

INDEX OF TITLES

GENERAL INDEX

GENERAL INDEX

GENERAL INDEX

GENERAL INDEX

GENERAL INDEX

GENERAL INDEX

GENERAL INDEX

GENERAL INDEX

GENERAL INDEX

ADDENDA TO INDEXES

(1) INDEX OF TITLES

(2) GENERAL INDEX

For EU product safety concerns, contact us at Calle de José Abascal, 56–1°, 28003 Madrid, Spain or eugpsr@cambridge.org.

www.ingramcontent.com/pod-product-compliance
Lightning Source LLC
LaVergne TN
LVHW090252210926
848480LV00001B/2
* 9 7 8 0 5 2 1 1 8 9 5 9 0 *